Presented to

Kingwood Branch Library
By

**Donated by the National Charity
League – Kingwood Chapter**

Harris County
Public Library

your pathway to knowledge

Gale Contextual Encyclopedia of American Literature

Gale Contextual Encyclopedia of American Literature

VOLUME 2

F–K

GALE
CENGAGE Learning

Detroit • New York • San Francisco • New Haven, Conn • Waterville, Maine • London

**Gale Contextual Encyclopedia
of American Literature**

Project Editors: Anne Marie Hacht and Dwayne
D. Hayes

Editorial: Ira Mark Milne

Rights Acquisition and Management: Kelly Quin,
Robyn Young, and Tracie Richardson

Composition: Evi Abou-El-Seoud

Manufacturing: Wendy Blurton

Imaging: John Watkins

Product Design: Jennifer Wahi and Pam Galbreath

For product information and technology assistance, contact us at
Gale Customer Support, 1-800-877-4253.
For permission to use material from this text or product,
submit all requests online at **www.cengage.com/permissions.**
Further permissions questions can be emailed to
permissionrequest@cengage.com

Cover photographs reproduced by permission. Steinbeck, John, photograph. The
Library of Congress; Angelou, Maya, photograph. AP Images; Fitzgerald, F. Scott,
photograph. The Library of Congress; Twain, Mark, photograph. The Library of Congress;
Poe, Edgar Allan, public domain; London, Jack, photograph. The Library of Congress;
Hughes, Langston, 1943, photo by Gordon Parks. The Library of Congress; Dickinson, Emily.
The Library of Congress; Hemingway, Ernest, photograph. AP Images; Hemingway, Ernest,
photograph. AP Images; Lee, Harper, photograph. AP Images; Tan, Amy, 1993, photograph.
AP Images; Walker, Alice, photograph. AP Images.

While every effort has been made to ensure the reliability of the information presented
in this publication, Gale, a part of Cengage Learning, does not guarantee the accuracy of the
data contained herein. Gale accepts no payment for listing; and inclusion in the publication
of any organization, agency, institution, publication, service, or individual does not imply
endorsement of the editors or publisher. Errors brought to the attention of the publisher
and verified to the satisfaction of the publisher will be corrected in future editions.

Editorial Data Privacy Policy. Does this publication contain information about you as
an individual? If so, for more information about our editorial data privacy policies,
please see our Privacy Statement at www.gale.com.

Library of Congress Cataloging-in-Publication Data

Gale contextual encyclopedia of American literature / editorial, Anne Marie
Hacht, Dwayne D. Hayes.
　　p. cm.
　Includes bibliographical references and index.
　　ISBN 978-1-4144-3130-7 (set) -- ISBN 978-1-4144-3131-4 (v. 1) --
　ISBN 978-1-4144-3132-1 (v. 2) -- ISBN 978-1-4144-3133-8 (v. 3) --
　ISBN 978-1-4144-3134-5 (v. 4) -- ISBN 978-1-4144-3139-0 (e-book)
　　1. American literature--Encyclopedias. 2. American literature--Bio-bibliography.
　3. Authors, American--Biography--Dictionaries. 4. American literature--History and
　criticism--Encyclopedias. I. Hacht, Anne Marie. II. Hayes, Dwayne D.

　PS21.G36 2009
　810'.9--dc22   2008051753

978-1-4144-3130-7 (set)　　　　　　1-4144-3130-9 (set)
978-1-4144-3131-4 (vol. 1)　　　　　1-4144-3131-7 (vol. 1)
978-1-4144-3132-1 (vol. 2)　　　　　1-4144-3132-5 (vol. 2)
978-1-4144-3133-8 (vol. 3)　　　　　1-4144-3133-3 (vol. 3)
978-1-4144-3134-5 (vol. 4)　　　　　1-4144-3134-1 (vol. 4)

This title is also available as an e-book.
ISBN-13: 978-1-4144-3139-0 ISBN-10: 1-4144-3139-2
Contact your Gale, a part of Cengage Learning sales representative for ordering information.

Printed in the United States of America
1 2 3 4 5 6 7 13 12 11 10 09

Contents

C

VOLUME 2

F-G

H

VOLUME 3

L

N-Q

VOLUME 4

R

S

Introduction

How to Use This Book

The *Gale Contextual Encyclopedia of American Literature* is a resource for students who seek information beyond the simple biographical details of an author's life or a brief overview of the author's major works. This book is designed to offer a comprehensive view of how an author's work fits within the context of the author's life, historical events, and the literary world. This allows for a greater understanding of both the author's work and the cultural and historical environment in which it was created.

The *Gale Contextual Encyclopedia of American Literature* is divided into entries, each focused on a particular writer who has made significant contributions to literature. In some cases, these individuals may be known primarily for actions and contributions outside the realm of literature. John F. Kennedy and Martin Luther King Jr., for example, are two figures famous for their political activism; Rachel Carson is known primarily as a biologist and ecologist; Cotton Mather is remembered for his connection to the infamous Salem Witch Trials. However, all of these figures have, aside from their other accomplishments and activities, created significant works of literature that have stood the test of time and affected readers beyond the borders of their own cultures.

This book is best used not just to locate the facts of a writer's life and work, but as a way to understand the social, literary, and historical environment in which the writer lived and created. By understanding the context of the writer's work, you are more likely to recognize key themes and stylistic traits as elements of larger trends in the literary world, as well as understand the impact of historical events from a new and unique perspective.

Sections Found within Each Entry in This Book

Each entry in this book is divided into three main parts: Works in Biographical and Historical Context; Works in Literary Context; and Works in Critical Context. These sections are discussed below.

In addition, each entry includes: a Key Facts section, containing birth/death date information as well as a list of major works; a Responses to Literature section, containing discussion and writing activities related to the author in question; a

Further Reading section that includes bibliographic citations as well as reputable sources of additional material about the author in the form of books, periodicals, or Web sites; a Literary and Historical Contemporaries sidebar, listing several famous contemporaries of the author; and a Common Human Experience sidebar, offering examples of other literary or artistic works that share themes or techniques with those of the subject of the entry.

Works in Biographical and Historical Context In this section, you will find information about how events and concerns in the author's life helped to shape the author's work. For example, Kurt Vonnegut's experiences in a German prison camp in Dresden during the Allied bombing of that city in 1945 led him to write *Slaughterhouse-Five* (1969), while events surrounding Watergate (the political scandal that brought about the resignation of President Richard Nixon) led him to write *Jailbird* (1979). This section also includes information on historical events or trends that had an effect on the author. For example, the scientific and technological advancements of the late twentieth century greatly influenced the subject matter of the popular fiction of Michael Crichton, which often centered on the theme of modern technology run amok.

Works in Literary Context In this section, you will find information about how the author's work fits within the context of literature in general. This may include a description of a stylistic trait exhibited in the author's writing; for example, Mark Twain is known for his brilliant use of colloquial speech, and information on this technique—as well as examples of how the author used it—can be found in his entry. This section may also include a discussion of the writer's work as it exists within a specific genre, such as Southern Gothic fiction or modernist poetry. Finally, the Works in Literary Context section may contain discussion of specific themes commonly found in the author's work. The writings of James Baldwin, for example, frequently address the theme of race relations.

Works in Critical Context In this section, you will find a survey of critical and popular opinion related to the author and the author's most important works. The emphasis is on contemporary opinions, or those formed by readers and critics at the time the author's work was first published. In some cases, critical or popular opinion from the time of publication may not be available; this may be due simply to the passage of time, or due to the writer's lack of fame during his or her own lifetime. This section also includes information on how critical or popular opinion of an author has changed over time. Herman Melville's masterwork *Moby-Dick* (1851) met with a tepid reception upon publication, but is now considered one of the finest achievements in American literature. Kate Chopin's novella *The Awakening* (1899) earned her critical scorn and ruined her career, but the work is now considered a breakthrough in women's literature. Conversely, some works that enjoyed widespread acclaim initially are less well regarded or even forgotten today. Joel Chandler Harris's *Uncle Remus* books (published between 1880 and 1905) based on African American folk tales were popular with white and black readers in the North and South at the time; today, many critics accuse Harris (a white journalist) of misappropriating elements of African American culture, and his work has fallen out of favor. Likewise, James Branch Cabell was one of the most celebrated writers of the 1920s, made internationally famous because of the scandal stirred up by the obscenity charges attached to his 1919 novel *Jurgen*; today, his work is rarely read.

Other Information Contained in This Book

In addition to the entries for individual authors, this book also contains a chronology that indicates some major historical events related to the development of American literature. At the end of the book, you will find a glossary of terms—primarily literary and historical in nature—that are used in various entries throughout the book, along with a brief explanation of each term, a general index, and a nationality/ethnicity index.

Advisory Board

Alicia Baker Elley
taught undergraduate and high school literature, composition, and technical writing classes for over ten years. She is currently district librarian for the Harmony Independent School District in Texas.

Maureen Reed
has taught literature, history, and American Studies courses at Minnesota State University Moorhead, Lewis and Clark College, and Portland State University. She earned a Ph.D. in American Studies from the University of Texas at Austin and held a Fulbright Lectureship in American Studies at the University of Regensburg in Germany.

Roger K. Smith
has been a teacher of English, writing, and other humanities courses at such institutions as Ithaca College, Rutgers University, and Edward R. Murrow High School (Brooklyn). He holds a BA from Swarthmore College and an MA from New York University.

Patrick Walsh
holds a Ph.D. in history from the University of Texas at Austin. He has taught English and Multidisciplinary Studies at Concordia College and Minnesota State University, in Moorhead, Minnesota. A Fulbright Lecturer in American Studies at the University of Passau in Germany, he now teaches at the Catlin Gabel School in Portland, Oregon.

Chronology

This chronology contains a brief overview of some of the major events in the history of American literature. This includes the development of technologies and tools that advanced the writing and publishing process, as well as some significant historical events that had an impact on the development of literature.

1500–1700

1576   English explorers begin searching for the Northwest Passage, a hoped-for water route around North America to Asia.

1607   Jamestown settlement established in Virginia.

1620   The Pilgrims traveling from England aboard *The Mayflower* reach Cape Cod and form a settlement at Plymouth, Massachusetts.

1624   The Dutch establish a city called New Amsterdam on the island of Manhattan. The city later became known as New York City, a major center of American commerce and publishing.

1630   Massachusetts Bay Colony Governor John Winthrop begins keeping his journal of life in New England. William Bradford, governor of Plymouth, begins his own book, later titled *History of Plymouth Plantation*.

1650   Anne Bradstreet publishes her first volume of poetry.

1689   Enlightenment thinker John Locke anonymously publishes *Two Treatises of Government*, a work that attacks the idea of the "divine right" of kings and argues for a government that operates with the consent of the governed. The work exerts a strong influence over eighteenth-century French philosophers and America's founding fathers.

1692–1693

The Salem Witch Trials are conducted. One hundred fifty people are arrested and accused of witchcraft, twenty-nine are convicted, and eighteen are executed.

1700–1800

1702   Cotton Mather publishes *Magnalia Christi Americana*, described as an ecclesiastical history of New England. It is one of the first works that attempts to define the American experience.

1718   The city of New Orleans, Louisiana, is founded by French and Canadian settlers.

1732   Benjamin Franklin begins writing *Poor Richard's Almanac*.

1740   Religious leader Jonathan Edwards begins writing his *Personal Narrative*.

1754–1763

The French and Indian War is fought between France and Great Britain and their respective Native American allies. The conflict is part of a broader power struggle between France and Great Britain that is waged in Europe (the Seven Years War).

1762   Jean-Jacques Rousseau publishes *The Social Contract*, a landmark work of political philosophy.

1767   Daniel Boone explores territory west of the Appalachian Mountains.

1770   British soldiers fire into a crowd of rowdy, protesting colonists in Boston, killing five. The event, which helps spark the American Revolution, becomes known as the Boston Massacre.

1773   The British Parliament enacts the Tea Act; in protest, a group of men dressed as Native Americans dump a shipment of tea from Great Britain into Boston Harbor, an event called the Boston Tea Party.

1774   The British Parliament passes measures collectively known as the Intolerable Acts in an effort to punish Massachusetts for the Boston Tea Party.

1775   Patrick Henry gives his famous "Give me liberty, or give me death" speech; Paul Revere goes on his "midnight ride" to warn colonists to take arms against approaching British soldiers; Minutemen fight the British in Lexington and Concord, the first battles of the American Revolution.

1776   Thomas Paine publishes *Common Sense*; Thomas Jefferson writes, and Congress adopts, the Declaration of Independence.

1781   British general Charles Cornwallis surrenders to American General George Washington at Yorktown, ending the American Revolution.

1789   A mob storms the Bastille prison in Paris, France, setting off the French Revolution.

1794   Thomas Paine publishes *The Age of Reason*.

1800–1900

1800   John Chapman, also known as "Johnny Appleseed," travels through the Ohio Valley region giving settlers apple seeds.

1803   President Thomas Jefferson negotiates with France to purchase the Louisiana Territory for $15 million; Jefferson sets Meriwether Lewis and William Clark off on an expedition of the newly acquired territory and the lands west of it for the purpose of determining whether a water route existed between the Missouri River and the Pacific Ocean.

1812–1815   Great Britain and the United States fight the War of 1812.

1819   Washington Irving publishes *The Sketch Book* containing such well-known short stories as "The Legend of Sleepy Hollow" and "Rip Van Winkle."

1820   Congress passes the Missouri Compromise, by which slavery is prohibited in the northern Louisiana territory, Maine is admitted to the Union as a free state, and Missouri is admitted as a slave state. The delicate balance between the interests of slave and free states is preserved for the next three decades.

1821   Sequoyah develops a Native American alphabet and uses it to help Cherokees read and write their own language.

1831   Nat Turner leads a slave rebellion in Virginia in which fifty-five white people are killed; Turner is captured and executed; several eastern Native American tribes are removed from their homelands and forced to march to Oklahoma Territory, a harsh, deadly journey dubbed "the trail of tears."

1832   Samuel Morse invents the telegraph.

1836   Texas declares its independence after revolting against Mexico; Ralph Waldo Emerson publishes *Nature*.

1841   Brook Farm, a utopian cooperative, is established in West Roxbury, Massachusetts, by Unitarian minister George Ripley.

1845   The United States annexes Texas.

1846–1847   Mexican-American War waged; the United States wins the short war, and gains much of what is now the western United States, including present-day California, Arizona, Nevada, Utah, New Mexico, Colorado, and Wyoming.

1848   Women's Rights Convention held in Seneca Falls, New York.

1849   After gold is discovered in California in 1848, a rush of prospectors—known as forty-niners—flood into California in hopes of striking it rich.

1850   Nathaniel Hawthorne publishes *The Scarlet Letter*; after much bitter debate, Congress passes the Compromise of 1850, which includes multiple provisions designed to maintain a balance between the relative power of slave and free states in Congress.

1851   Herman Melville publishes *Moby-Dick*.

1852   Harriet Beecher Stowe publishes *Uncle Tom's Cabin*.

1854 Henry David Thoreau publishes *Walden.*

1855 Walt Whitman publishes his first version of the poetry collection *Leaves of Grass.*

1859 Abolitionist John Brown attacks the U.S. arsenal at Harper's Ferry, West Virginia, in an attempt to gain weapons to start a slave insurrection; he is captured, tried, and hanged.

1861–1865

United States Civil War fought between the Union and the pro-slavery Confederate States of America. The war is effectively ended with the surrender of Confederate general Robert E. Lee to Union general Ulysses S. Grant, in Appomattox, Virginia, in 1865; President Abraham Lincoln is assassinated in 1865.

1869 The Fifteenth Amendment to the Constitution grants African Americans the right to vote.

1876 Alexander Graham Bell invents the telephone.

1879 Thomas Edison invents the electric light bulb.

1884 Mark Twain publishes *Adventures of Huckleberry Finn.*

1890 *The Poems of Emily Dickinson* is published posthumously, by the poet's sister.

1895 Stephen Crane publishes *The Red Badge of Courage.*

1898 The United States and Spain fight the Spanish-American War. The United States quickly wins the war, and gains Puerto Rico, Guam, and the Philippines. The war establishes the United States as a major world power.

1900–Now

1901 A major oil strike is made at Spindletop, Texas.

1903 Orville and Wilbur Wright launch the first successful manned airplane flight in Kitty Hawk, North Carolina; Henry Ford founds the Ford Motor Company.

1909 The National Association for the Advancement of Colored People (NAACP) is formed.

1914 World War I begins in Europe.

1917 The United States enters World War I on the side of the Entente Powers.

1918 Germany and its allies are defeated, and World War I ends.

1920 The Nineteenth Amendment to the Constitution grants women the right to vote.

1925 F. Scott Fitzgerald publishes *The Great Gatsby.*

1926 Ernest Hemingway publishes *The Sun Also Rises*; the Radio Corporation of America (RCA) organizes the National Broadcasting Company (NBC): the first radio network set up for public entertainment and information.

1927 American pilot Charles Lindbergh flies solo across the Atlantic Ocean from New York to France.

1929 The U.S. stock market crashes, causing financial panic; William Faulkner publishes *The Sound and the Fury.*

1929–1939

The Great Depression, a global economic downturn, causes widespread unemployment and deflation.

1932 Amelia Earhart becomes first woman to fly solo across the Atlantic Ocean.

1936 Eugene O'Neill wins Nobel Prize in Literature.

1938 Thorton Wilder publishes the play *Our Town*; Pearl S. Buck wins Nobel Prize in Literature.

1939 World War II begins in Europe with the German invasion of Poland.

1940 Richard Wright publishes *Native Son*; Carson McCullers publishes *The Heart Is a Lonely Hunter.*

1941 Japanese fighter pilots attack the United States naval base at Pearl Harbor, Hawaii. The United States declares war on Japan and, subsequently, on Japanese ally Germany, effecting U.S. entry into World War II; the U.S. begins the Manhattan Project, a secret program to develop an atomic bomb.

1942 President Franklin Roosevelt signs an executive order authorizing the forced relocation of Japanese Americans to internment camps for the duration of the war.

1945 The United States drops atomic bombs on the Japanese cities of Hiroshima and Nagasaki, killing more than 100,000 people. Japan surrenders. Germany surrenders.

1947 Jackie Robinson becomes the first African American major-league baseball player; Tennessee Williams publishes the play *A Streetcar Named Desire.*

1948   Congress approves the Marshall Plan for the reconstruction and assistance of Europe; Jewish state of Israel proclaimed; first television broadcast of *Texaco Star Theater*, hosted by Milton Berle—the first major television program in America.

1949   William Faulkner wins Nobel Prize in Literature.

1950   Senator Joseph McCarthy claims that the United States State Department has been infiltrated by communists; President Harry Truman sends U.S. troops to Korea after communist North Korea invades pro-Western South Korea; Isaac Asimov publishes *I, Robot*.

1951   J. D. Salinger publishes *The Catcher in the Rye*.

1953   Senator Joseph McCarthy becomes chairman of the Senate Committee on Government Operations and launches his notorious investigations into purported communist activity in the United States.

1954   The Supreme Court case *Brown v. the Board of Education of Topeka* declares segregation in public schools unconstitutional; Ernest Hemingway wins Nobel Prize in Literature.

1955   Dr. Martin Luther King Jr. leads the Montgomery Bus Boycott.

1957   Jack Kerouac publishes *On the Road*; Theodore Seuss Geisel (Dr. Seuss) publishes *The Cat in the Hat*; the Soviet Union launches *Sputnik 1*, sparking the U.S./Soviet space race.

1959   Lorraine Hansberry publishes the play *A Raisin in the Sun*.

1960   Harper Lee publishes *To Kill a Mockingbird*; birth control pills are made available to the public.

1962   Cuban Missile Crisis occurs: a tense standoff between nuclear superpowers the United States and the Soviet Union; John Steinbeck wins Nobel Prize in Literature.

1963   President John F. Kennedy assassinated in Dallas, Texas.

1964   Congress passes the Civil Rights Act, prohibiting racial discrimination in public places.

1965   President Lyndon Johnson escalates hostilities against North Vietnam, ordering bombing raids; Dr. Martin Luther King Jr. leads a civil rights march from Selma to Montgomery, Alabama; African American rights activist Malcolm X assassinated; Voting Rights Act passed by Congress.

1968   Martin Luther King Jr. assassinated; presidential candidate Robert Kennedy assassinated.

1969   Kurt Vonnegut publishes *Slaughterhouse-Five*; astronaut Neil Armstrong becomes first human to set foot on the moon.

1974   President Richard Nixon resigns in the wake of the Watergate scandal.

1975   Vietnam War ends.

1976   Saul Bellow wins Nobel Prize in Literature.

1978   Isaac Bashevis Singer wins Nobel Prize in Literature.

1979   Radical Islamists storm the American embassy in Iran and take fifty-two hostages, most of whom are held for 444 days.

1981   The IBM personal computer first becomes available.

1984   Sandra Cisneros publishes *The House on Mango Street*.

1986   Cormac McCarthy publishes *Blood Meridian*.

1989   The Berlin Wall is torn down.

1990   First commercial dial-up access to the Internet becomes available; the Soviet Union collapses, and independent nations are formed of its former territory.

1993   Toni Morrison wins Nobel Prize in Literature.

1998   President Bill Clinton impeached by the U.S. House of Representatives.

2001   In a coordinated suicide mission, radical Islamists associated with terrorist organization al-Qaeda hijack commercial airliners and crash them into the World Trade Center in New York City and the Pentagon building in Virginia, killing nearly 3,000 people; Jonathan Franzen publishes *The Corrections*.

2003   The United States invades Iraq and topples the regime of Saddam Hussein.

2009   Barack Obama sworn in as president of the United States, the first African American ever elected to that office.

F-G

William Faulkner

BORN: *1897, New Albany, Mississippi*

DIED: *1962, Byhalia, Mississippi*

NATIONALITY: *American*

GENRE: *Fiction*

MAJOR WORKS:

The Sound and the Fury (1929)

As I Lay Dying (1930)

Light in August (1932)

Absalom! Absalom! (1936)

Go Down, Moses (1942)

Overview

A preeminent figure in twentieth-century literature, William Faulkner created a profound and complex body of work in which he explored social decay in the American South. He set many of his novels and short stories in Yoknapatawpha County, a fictional landscape reflecting the geographic and cultural background of his native Mississippi. Faulkner's works reflect the tumultuous history of the South while perceptively exploring the human character. The fundamental theme of his fiction, Faulkner said in his Nobel Prize acceptance speech in 1950, is "the human heart in conflict with itself." He utilized a variety of striking narrative techniques to convey this struggle.

Works in Biographical and Historical Context

Mississippi Heritage William Cuthbert Falkner was born in New Albany, Mississippi, on September 25, 1897. (He added the letter u to his name in 1918.) He grew up in the nearby town of Oxford, where his family moved when he was four. His upbringing was genteel and gave him a profound sense of his Southern heritage. His father worked for his family's railroad businesses,

later becoming the business manager of the University of Mississippi.

William Faulkner had an adventurous youth as the oldest of four boys, learning how to handle guns and to hunt. An indifferent student, he went to high school in Oxford, Mississippi, but dropped out in 1915, then worked for a time as a clerk in his grandfather's bank. He had, however, been reading poetry with an older friend, Phil Stone, who contributed significantly to Faulkner's literary education.

During World War I, Faulkner tried to enlist in the U.S. Army, but was rejected because of his small stature. With Stone's help, Faulkner hatched a scheme to talk his way into the Royal Canadian Air Force by affecting a British accent and forging letters of recommendation. The war ended before he experienced combat duty, however, so he returned to his hometown, attending the University of Mississippi for a little over a year.

From Poetry to Prose Faulkner was already writing in earnest, primarily poetry. He published his first poem in the *New Republic* on August 6, 1919. After dropping out of Ole Miss, he went to New York City and was briefly employed as a bookstore clerk at the Doubleday store on Fifth Avenue. Returning to Oxford in late 1921, he was hired as postmaster at the university and held that position for nearly three years. He resigned, however, when the postal inspector noticed that Faulkner often brought his writing to the post office and became so immersed in what he was doing that he ignored patrons.

His postal career aborted, Faulkner called on his former employer at Doubleday Books, Elizabeth Prall, who now lived in New Orleans and was married to novelist Sherwood Anderson. For the first half of 1925, Faulkner lived with the Andersons. Although his verse had been published in his first full-length book, *The Marble Faun* (1924), he realized that his prose was more accomplished, and he was encouraged by Anderson to write fiction. His first novel, *Soldier's Pay* (1926), tells a story typical of its time, the aftermath of World War I. It centers on a

William Faulkner   *William Faulkner, 1955, photograph. Pictorial Press Ltd. / Alamy.*

physically and emotionally scarred veteran who finds only further disillusionment when he returns home to the South. Faulkner followed that up with *Mosquitoes* (1927), a mildly satirical study of the New Orleans literary scene. Neither of these novels received much critical notice.

Faulkner traveled to Europe for several months in 1925, lingered a while longer in New Orleans, then returned to Oxford, where he finally settled down. In 1927 and 1928 he worked on many short stories, developing a clearer understanding of the material he would use for his fiction: his region of Mississippi, which he called his "postage stamp of native soil." His next full-length work, originally titled *Flags in the Dust*, is the first of his novels set in Yoknapatawpha County. Published as *Sartoris* (1929), it is his first storytelling novel in which legends, tall tales, and gossip are interwoven with a story based on his family's history. After several publishers rejected the manuscript, Faulkner became disgusted with the publishing industry. Abruptly, he decided to stop worrying about whether others liked his work and to write only for himself.

The Sound and the Fury

Writing with no thought of publication, Faulkner achieved mastery of both his material and his technique. *The Sound and the Fury* (1929) is a boldly experimental work, with a complex structure incorporating multiple narrative viewpoints, long and convoluted sentences, and a thorough intermingling of past and present. The book chronicles the disintegration of one family, the Compsons, and through their perspective, it reflects the deterioration of community and traditional values in the modern South.

The title refers to the famous soliloquy in Shakespeare's *Macbeth*, in which Macbeth laments that life is "a tale / Told by an idiot, full of sound and fury, / Signifying nothing." These words have a literal significance in Faulkner's novel, for its first section is narrated by the mentally retarded Benjy Compson, whose comprehension of time is fuzzy. Next comes the viewpoint of Benjy's brother Quentin, who is quite intelligent but whose severe depression undoes him. Here the writing throws grammar and punctuation to the wind to follow the stream of Quentin's consciousness as he approaches suicide. Both Benjy and Quentin are obsessed with their sister Caddy; though none of the four sections of the book presents her point of view, the novel documents her tragic journey through life.

The Sound and the Fury received enthusiastic reviews, but sold only a few copies on its first printing. Meanwhile, Faulkner's first love, Estelle Oldham, divorced her husband, took custody of their two children, and married Faulkner in June of 1929. The need to make money prompted Faulkner to take a night job at a power plant. He had earlier written a sordid potboiler he hoped would sell well. Before *Sanctuary* hit the shelves in 1931, Faulkner did a major rewrite to tone it down somewhat. It became his best-selling novel, although critics disparaged the work for its sensationalistic violence.

As I Lay Dying and Today We Live

While working at the powerhouse, Faulkner quickly wrote *As I Lay Dying* (1930), which he referred to immodestly as a "tour de force." Again Faulkner surprised his readers with a tale of almost epic stature about poor rural people. The novel consists of fifty-nine interior monologues providing constantly shifting points of view. Fifteen different narrators portray the odyssey of the Bundren family from the backwoods of Yoknapatawpha to the city of Jefferson with the dead body of Addie, the family matriarch. The dying Addie had asked to be buried there with her kin, so responsibility and obligation lie behind the macabre journey. The tale is told with passion and sympathy, but also a touch of irony and mockery, so readers have difficulty deciding whether the book is comic or tragic.

Faulkner also wrote an impressive number of high-quality short stories during this period. He sold many of them to national magazines such as *Saturday Evening Post* in order to boost his income. Many of these stories cover, in concentrated form, material later developed in novels. Faulkner's first short-story collection, *These 13* (1931), received more laudatory reviews than had any of his novels.

Financial hardship pressed on Faulkner throughout the 1930s. He was supporting a wife, two children, and his mother, after his father died in 1932. He lost a brother in a plane crash in 1935, and supported his widow and child as well. The Great Depression of the 1930s caused book sales to plummet, and Faulkner's pessimistic novels were unpopular and out of keeping with the public mood. In 1932, he traveled to the one place where a writer could make a decent living: Hollywood. He returned to work there often during the next decades, even though he strongly disliked the place, and formed a good relationship with top director Howard Hawks. He was able to transform one of his own stories, "Turn About" (1932) into a screenplay, produced by Hawks as *Today We Live* (1933). He worked on several other films, but fled from the movie capital as soon as he had enough money to pay his bills.

Peak of Productivity   Faulkner continued producing novels of supreme literary merit, such as *Light in August* (1932), which examines the origins of personal identity and the roots of racial conflicts. The novel introduces many characters, centering on Joe Christmas, an orphan who is trying to uncover his true identity, including his racial ancestry, by piecing together bits of hearsay information. The narrative works through numerous flashbacks, frequently shifting from character to character. Many critics felt the novel suffered from faulty structure, though it was later recognized as a masterpiece.

Faulkner's next major novel, *Absalom! Absalom!* (1936), is considered by many to be his finest. It focuses on Thomas Sutpen, a tragic character with a passion for creating and controlling a self-contained world. Many of the "facts" regarding Sutpen and the other characters are based on unreliable information, or different versions of the same story, and the novel thus questions the human capacity to know the truth about anything.

Yoknapatawpha Stories   A short story called "Barn Burning," published in *Harper's* in 1939, introduced the Snopes family into the life of Yoknapatawpha County. Faulkner stretched the Snopes's history into a trilogy of novels, starting with *The Hamlet* (1940). Unlike the Compson and Sartoris families, the shrewd businessman Flem Snopes has little connection to or pride in the Southern heritage; his interest is sheer self-advancement. The second and third books in the trilogy, *The Town* (1957) and *The Mansion* (1959), portray Flem Snopes a bit more sympathetically, but his avaricious nature is unchanged. The Snopes family represent a stage in the decline of the South in which commerce and material gain wipe out human considerations and traditions.

Some critics believe that *The Hamlet* was the last publication of Faulkner's peak period. In the dozen years since the composition of *The Sound and the Fury*, he had accomplished what many other writers would be satisfied to call a life's work. But he was hardly finished. He stitched several previously published short stories together into a novel, *Go Down, Moses* (1942), that chronicles a century in the history of Yoknapatawpha County. Through episodes in the life of Isaac McCaslin, Faulkner delves into issues of race and slavery, stewardship and exploitation of land, and the disappearing wilderness.

LITERARY AND HISTORICAL CONTEMPORARIES

William Faulkner's famous contemporaries include:

John Dos Passos (1896–1970): American novelist who used stream of consciousness and other experimental expressive techniques.

Ernest Hemingway (1899–1961): American novelist and short-story writer extremely influential for his economy of prose; Nobel Prize winner, 1954.

Thomas Wolfe (1900–1938): American novelist called the best writer of his generation by William Faulkner.

John Steinbeck (1902–1968): American novelist, author of *The Grapes of Wrath* (1939); Nobel Prize winner, 1962.

Langston Hughes (1902–1967): American poet and short-story writer, a leading figure of the Harlem Renaissance.

Public Recognition   Despite his prolific rate of publication, Faulkner remained strapped financially, so he returned to Hollywood in the 1940s. He had a hand in writing two of Howard Hawks's best pictures, *To Have and Have Not* (1944) and *The Big Sleep* (1946), both starring Humphrey Bogart and Lauren Bacall. At this point, most of his books had gone out of print. A compilation called *The Portable Faulkner* (1946), edited by Malcolm Cowley, changed this situation considerably, and with the many soldiers returning from World War II who now went to colleges and universities, Faulkner's books were suddenly in demand.

In November 1950 it was announced that Faulkner had won the 1949 Nobel Prize in Literature. He traveled to Oslo and gave a memorable speech—rapidly, and in a low voice. Following the prize, his books sold more than ever before and were translated into many languages. Faulkner had heretofore voiced opinions about social and political matters only through his books, but now podiums and lecterns were offered from everywhere, and he took seriously his obligations as a public figure. He spoke out against segregation in Mississippi in the mid-1950s; however, he also opposed involvement by the federal government to enforce integration. This moderate position won him few friends.

Faulkner won the Pulitzer Prize and the National Book Award for *A Fable* (1954), an allegorical story of a Jesus figure who causes a temporary cease-fire during World War I. After completing the Snopes trilogy, Faulkner wrote his final novel, *The Reivers* (1962), a last nostalgic glance at Yoknapatawpha County which was published shortly before his death, and earned him, posthumously, his second Pulitzer Prize.

Works in Literary Context

William Faulkner revealed a talent for poetry, as well as drawing, from an early age. As a teenager he wrote romantic poetry in the model of the eighteenth century Scottish poet Robert Burns and the Victorian poet Algernon Swinburne. His friend, Phil Stone, introduced him to the writings of the French novelist Honoré de Balzac and the French Symbolist poets. A major influence on the direction of his work was Sherwood Anderson, who had already written his celebrated story collection *Winesburg, Ohio* (1919) when Faulkner met him. It was Anderson who steered Faulkner from poetry to prose, and who suggested that he write about the region where he came from. Other literary influences on Faulkner include Mark Twain, who brought vernacular storytelling and regional humor into American literature, and Irish writer James Joyce, who advanced stream-of-consciousness narration.

A County of the Mind Fifteen of Faulkner's novels and dozens of his short stories are set in Yoknapatawpha County, his fictional representation of his northern Mississippi region. Its county seat, Jefferson, is modeled after Oxford. Depicted in both the past and the present, Yoknapatawpha is populated with a vast spectrum of people—the Indians who originally inhabited the land, the landed gentry, yeoman farmers, poor whites, blacks, carpetbaggers, and bushwhackers. Faulkner was justifiably proud of the kingdom he had erected in his imagination. Although there are some inconsistencies in the Yoknapatawpha novels, the saga as a whole offers a microcosm of the Deep South in its history and culture. The greatness of Faulkner's design led critics to recognize that he was not just a provincial author, but that his regional stories had universal appeal.

The Past in Faulkner One of Faulkner's chief thematic preoccupations is the past, and this theme is also reflected in the form of his fictions. In a famous analogy, French philosopher and literary critic Jean-Paul Sartre compared the Faulknerian character's point of view to that "of a passenger looking backward from a speeding car, who sees, flowing away from him, the landscape he is traversing. For him the future is not in view, the present is too blurred to make out, and he can see clearly only the past as it streams away before his obsessed and backward-looking gaze." Faulkner's pages are filled with characters who are fettered to the past, from Quentin Compson in *The Sound and the Fury* to the Reverend Gail Hightower in *Light in August*, who endlessly relives the glory of his grandfather's cavalry charge. Over and above the personal obsessions of individual characters, Faulkner perceived the pull of history and nostalgia as an affliction affecting the South as a whole. As he famously wrote in *Requiem for a Nun* (1951), "The past is never dead. It's not even past."

Modernistic Style Faulkner's writing style is keyed to his themes. The stylistic methods most closely associated with his treatment of the past are his use of long sentences, flashbacks, and multiple viewpoints. Complicated sentence structures can hold a moment aloft indefinitely for the author, or a character, to dwell upon. Flashbacks are even more clearly related to Faulkner's interest in the past. Narration in which the time reference is ambiguous, such as Benjy Compson's section of *The Sound and the Fury*, demonstrates still more forcefully the enmeshment of past and present. By telling a story from several points of view, Faulkner adds a further dimension to his concept of time; the past is subject to continual reevaluation and open to conflicting interpretations. Other characteristic points of Faulkner's modernistic style include the flagrant reiteration of certain words, seemingly excessive strings of adjectives, and deliberately vague pronoun references, as well as Joycean stream of consciousness, sometimes without punctuation.

An American Original By any measure, William Faulkner is one of the most highly esteemed authors in all of American literature. That a high school dropout from the poorest region of the United States, working in relative isolation and under intense financial pressure, could produce so many top-flight works of fiction in a compressed period of time is a remarkable achievement. Some of his writing is rather difficult to understand, and some difficult to stomach; a great deal of it is dazzling in its originality. Faulkner elevated the stature of regional or local-color fiction and was largely responsible for the revival of Southern literature in the mid-twentieth century. His influence on the genre sometimes called "Southern gothic" is seen in authors such as Truman Capote, Flannery O'Connor, and Cormac McCarthy. As one of the most frequently studied American authors, he has reached a rarefied stature among intellectuals and a permanent place in the American literary pantheon. He also won a devoted following in the European literary scene; intellectuals such as Jean-Paul Sartre and Albert Camus championed his writing.

Works in Critical Context

Faulkner is now recognized as a giant, but he labored in obscurity for much of his career. Books now considered classics made no discernible impact when first published. Critics and readers alike were unappreciative and reluctant to accept the challenge his experimental and modernistic texts presented. The most commercially successful of his early works, *Sanctuary*, had an undue and unfavorable influence on his reputation. For years, he was dismissed as a purveyor of the grotesque; more charitable critics perceived him as merely a regional writer. Only later did a critical consensus emerge that while Faulkner's material was regionally focused, his concerns were universal.

Postwar Resurgence Between 1939 and 1942, several important examinations of Faulkner appeared in literary journals. Although hardly noticed by the public, Faulkner was esteemed by many of his fellow writers. His work had also attracted a substantial following in France. Despite this stature, in the 1940s each of his books dropped out of print, partly because of lack of popular interest, partly due to the war effort. The publication of *The Portable Faulkner* in 1946 created a resurgence of interest. Editor Malcolm Cowley's introduction, stressing the Southern legend that Faulkner had created in his works, served as a springboard for future critics. "Faulkner performed a labor of imagination that has not been equaled in our time, and a double labor," Cowley asserted. "First, to invent a Mississippi county that was like a mythical kingdom, but was complete and living in all its details; second, to make his story of Yoknapatawpha County stand as a parable or legend of all the Deep South."

The turning point for Faulkner's reputation came when he won the Nobel Prize. Up until then, many readers remained wary of him, and even the *New York Times* expressed the fear that the rest of the world might consider Yoknapatawpha County an accurate depiction of life in America. Faulkner's reply was contained in his acceptance speech. He explained that it is the writer's duty and privilege "to help man endure by lifting his heart, by reminding him of the courage and honor and hope and pride and compassion and pity and sacrifice which have been the glory of his past." The stirring speech caused many to change their opinion of him overnight.

Grist for the Academic Mill   For sixty years since the Nobel Prize, Faulkner has been a cornerstone of American literary scholarship. Early critics and readers sought correspondences between Faulkner's life and his fiction, an unrewarding line of inquiry since there are few direct parallels between Faulkner as a person and his characters. Cleanth Brooks, a prominent practitioner of the New Criticism, produced two of the most meticulous studies of Faulkner's work, in 1963 and 1978. Since then, academics of all stripes have written thousands of articles and monographs on Faulkner, including psychoanalytic, linguistic, feminist, postmodern, political, and genre-based criticism. Scholars have probed his views on history, slavery, identity, community, and morality. They have concluded that his genius lies in the ability to portray all types of characters, and in the use of a variety of narrative voices. A recent volume edited by Linda Wagner-Martin, entitled *William Faulkner: Six Decades of Criticism* (2002) provides a useful overview of Faulkner studies.

Responses to Literature

1. What insights does Faulkner shed on issues of race in Southern society in *Light in August, Absalom, Absalom!* or *Go Down, Moses*?

2. Write about how Faulkner's innovative writing techniques—for example, the use of stream of consciousness narration in *The Sound and the Fury*—supports, or distracts from, the themes in his work.

3. In 1956, Faulkner said, "I discovered that my own little postage stamp of native soil was worth writing

---

COMMON HUMAN EXPERIENCE

William Faulkner's use of bizarre and macabre imagery to depict the decadence of Southern society helped create a literary genre called Southern Gothic. Many subsequent works of fiction, such as the following distinguished titles, have employed these literary elements in service of social critique.

A Streetcar Named Desire (1947), by Tennessee Williams. A landmark of the American theatre, made famous by Marlon Brando's feverish portrayal of the brutal Stanley Kowalski.

Other Voices, Other Rooms (1948), by Truman Capote. A teenage boy encounters his paralytic father, and grows to accept his homosexuality, in Truman Capote's sensationalistic debut novel.

Wise Blood (1952), Flannery O'Connor. This novel presents a satire of religion, such as the "Holy Church of Christ Without Christ," but is also a serious portrait of a spiritual crisis.

To Kill a Mockingbird (1960), by Harper Lee. Lee's only published novel is one of the most widely read books dealing with Southern racism.

No Country for Old Men (2005), by Cormac McCarthy. A botched drug deal puts a hunter, a hitman, and a sheriff into each other's sights, in this thriller later made into an Oscar-winning film.

---

about and that I would never live long enough to exhaust it." In what specific ways do his stories from Yoknapatapha County transform local material into something of universal interest?

4. Write an essay about how Faulkner portrays sibling relationships in *The Sound and the Fury* and/or *As I Lay Dying*.

BIBLIOGRAPHY

Books

Adams, Richard P. *Faulkner: Myth and Motion.* Princeton, N.J.: Princeton University Press, 1968.

Backman, Melvin. *Faulkner, The Major Years: A Critical Study.* Bloomington: Indiana University Press, 1966.

Blotner, Joseph L. *Faulkner: A Biography.* 2 vols. New York: Random House, 1974.

Bockting, Ineke. *Character and Personality in the Novels of William Faulkner: A Study in Psychostylistics.* Lanham, MD: University Press of America, 1995.

Brooks, Cleanth. *William Faulkner: Toward Yoknapatawpha and Beyond.* New Haven and London: Yale University Press, 1978.

Carothers, James B. *William Faulkner's Short Stories.* Ann Arbor, Mich.: UMI Research Press, 1985.

Clarke, Deborah. *Robbing the Mother: Women in Faulkner*. Jackson: University Press of Mississippi, 1994.

Davis, Thadious M. *Faulkner's "Negro": Art and the Southern Context*. Baton Rouge: Louisiana State University Press, 1983.

Gray, Richard J. *The Life of William Faulkner: A Critical Biography*. Oxford: Blackwell, 1994.

Howe, Irving. *William Faulkner: A Critical Study*. Chicago: University of Chicago Press, 1975.

Matthews, John. *The Play of Faulkner's Language*. Ithaca, N.Y.: Cornell University Press, 1982.

Minter, David. *William Faulkner: His Life and Work*. Baltimore: Johns Hopkins University Press, 1980.

Volpe, Edmond L. *A Reader's Guide to William Faulkner*. New York: Farrar, Straus and Giroux, 1964.

Wagner-Martin, Linda, ed. *William Faulkner: Six Decades of Criticism*. East Lansing: Michigan State University Press, 2002.

Welty, Eudora. *On William Faulkner*. Jackson: University Press of Mississippi, 2003.

Williamson, Joel. *William Faulkner and Southern History*. New York: Oxford University Press, 1993.

✺ Lawrence Ferlinghetti

BORN: *1919, Yonkers, New York*

NATIONALITY: *American*

GENRE: *Poetry, drama, nonfiction*

MAJOR WORKS:

A Coney Island of the Mind (1958)

Her (1960)

Endless Life (1984)

Lawrence Ferlinghetti   *Ferlinghetti, Lawrence, photograph. AP Images.*

Overview

As poet, playwright, publisher, and spokesman, Lawrence Ferlinghetti helped to spark the San Francisco literary renaissance of the 1950s and the subsequent Beat movement in American literature. Ferlinghetti was one of a group of writers, later labeled the "Beat Generation," who felt strongly that art should be accessible to all people, not just a handful of the highly educated. His lively poetry is imbued with American idiom and the influence of modern jazz. Ferlinghetti's most important contribution to American literature may have been the bookstore he founded, City Lights Books, which continues to publish counterculture writers.

Works in Biographical and Historical Context

Fortune Amid Tragedy Lawrence Monsanto Ferling was born in Yonkers, New York, on March 24, 1919. His father, an Italian immigrant, had shortened the family name upon arrival in America. Only in his adulthood did Ferlinghetti discover the lengthier name and restore it as his own.

He began his life in the midst of crisis and loss. His father died suddenly before he was born, and when he was two, his mother suffered a nervous breakdown and was institutionalized. It was his mother's aunt Emily Mendes-Monsanto who rescued him from this tragic situation and whisked him off to France for several years. When Emily returned to her estranged husband in New York, Lawrence suffered a second loss. Breaking with her husband for the final time, she was forced to put the child into an orphanage for seven months until she found a position as governess to a wealthy family in Bronxville, New York. When his aunt disappeared suddenly, Lawrence was allowed to stay with the family and was sent to elite private schools, first in the Bronx and then in Massachusetts.

Ferlinghetti enrolled at the University of North Carolina in 1937 and graduated with a degree in journalism four years later. He then joined the navy. During World War II he was stationed in France, participating as a lieutenant commander during the Normandy invasion in 1944. After his discharge, he took advantage of the G.I. Bill to continue his education. He completed a master's degree in literature from Columbia University before returning to France to study at the Sorbonne, where he achieved his doctorate with a dissertation on the city as a symbol in poetry.

City Lights and the Pocket Poets Ferlinghetti returned from Paris in 1951 and moved to San Francisco. For a short time he supported himself by teaching languages and by doing freelance writing for art journals and the *San Francisco Chronicle*. Attending literary soirées at Kenneth Rexroth's apartment, he became attuned to the city's offbeat character. In 1953 he joined with Peter D. Martin to publish a magazine, *City Lights*, named after a 1931 Charlie Chaplin film. In order to subsidize the magazine, the two men opened the City Lights bookstore on the edge of Chinatown—where it flourishes still.

City Lights was the country's first all-paperback bookstore, and before long it was a popular gathering place for San Francisco's avant-garde writers and artists. Ferlinghetti began publishing his Pocket Poets series in 1955, leading off with the first book of his own poems, *Pictures of the Gone World*. The left-wing political sentiments in these verses met an appreciative response among young people agonizing over the nuclear arms race and cold war politics of the time, as the United States and the Soviet Union each sought to build up arsenals of weaponry with which to potentially destroy the other. San Francisco became a hub of artistic experimentation and left-wing social activism during the 1950s, with the Beats leading the charge. By the late 1960s, San Francisco was the center of the counterculture movement in America.

The Howl Trial Ferlinghetti was now at the center of a literary and cultural groundswell. Among his friends were writers such as Rexroth, Kenneth Patchen, and Jack Kerouac. In 1955, a young Allen Ginsberg walked into the bookshop and introduced himself to its proprietor with a collection of poems. It was Ferlinghetti who drove the poets to the historic Six Gallery reading at which Ginsberg unveiled his poem "Howl." Immediately recognizing it as a classic work of art, Ferlinghetti offered to publish the work. The Pocket Poets edition of *Howl and Other Poems* appeared in 1956 and sold out quickly. A second shipment was ordered from the British printer, but U.S. authorities seized it on the grounds of alleged obscenity. Thus began a landmark censorship trial that helped spark a new literary movement.

Under arrest for printing and selling indecent material, Ferlinghetti engaged the American Civil Liberties Union for his defense and welcomed his court case as a test of the limits of free speech. Not only did he win the suit on October 3, 1957, but the case established a legal precedent in the United States that allowed for the publication of D. H. Lawrence's *Lady Chatterly's Lover* (1928) and Henry Miller's *Tropic of Cancer* (1934) in the next decade. Through the attention the trial generated, Ferlinghetti and Ginsberg became national and

LITERARY AND HISTORICAL CONTEMPORARIES

Lawrence Ferlinghetti's famous contemporaries include:

Saul Bellow (1915–2005): American novelist and Nobel Prize winner best known for works such as *The Adventures of Augie March* (1953) and *Humboldt's Gift* (1975).

Primo Levi (1919–1987): Italian author whose memoir *If This Is a Man* (1947) chronicles his experiences in a Nazi concentration camp.

Jack Kerouac (1922–1969): Charismatic American author of the Beat Generation, known for the novel *On the Road* (1957).

Norman Mailer (1923–2007): American novelist, essayist, and political activist who won two Pulitzer Prizes for his books *Armies of the Night* (1968) and *The Executioner's Song* (1979).

John F. Kennedy (1917–1963): President of the United States, 1961–1963; author of the Pulitzer Prize–winning *Profiles in Courage* (1955).

international public figures, leading a revolution in thinking as well as writing.

Jazz Poet In another arena Ferlinghetti became a public figure during the late 1950s. He and Kenneth Rexroth had taken to experimenting with a combination of brother arts, poetry and jazz. They performed nightly in clubs and theaters. Ferlinghetti's motives were explicit: he sought to expand the audience for poetry by redeeming it from the ivory towers of academia and offering it as a shared experience with ordinary people. His efforts revived an almost forgotten oral tradition of poetic improvisation.

In 1958, New Directions Press published Ferlinghetti's second book, *A Coney Island of the Mind*. It is a broad collection including his open-form work from *Pictures of the Gone World*, seven poems that came out of the poetry-and-jazz work as "Oral Messages," and the lyric and surrealistic writing of the "Coney Island" poems. This collection became a key work of the Beat period and one of the most popular books of contemporary American poetry, rivaled only by Ginsberg's *Howl and Other Poems*.

Ferlinghetti's novel *Her* was published in 1960. It is an autobiographical work, absurdist and expressionistic in vision and form, that focuses on the narrator's pursuit of a woman. Like all Ferlinghetti's work, *Her* is forcefully driven toward expanded consciousness. The 1960s also witnessed Ferlinghetti's work with experimental theater. In two collections of short plays, he employed the gamut of theatrical devices—clowning, mime, verbal nonsense, dream and fantasy scenes, and black comedy—in a spectacle of assault on

COMMON HUMAN EXPERIENCE

Lawrence Ferlinghetti lent his poetic voice to many antiestablishment causes. These other celebrated poems take on similar causes:

"To Roosevelt" (1905), by Ruben Dario. The great Nicaraguan poet declares a dignified resistance to Yankee imperialism.

"Dulce et Decorum Est" (1918), by Wilfred Owen. A poetic protest against "the old lie" of nationalism and the glory of war.

"September 1, 1939" (1939), by W. H. Auden. The poet later came to regret the stirring tone of this famous response to Adolf Hitler's invasion of Poland; in later versions of the poem, Auden changed the line "We must love one another or die" to "We must love one another and die."

"Howl" (1956), by Allen Ginsberg. The fundamental text of the Beat Generation is Ginsberg's long-line rant about outcasts in a nightmarish America he calls "Moloch."

"Somebody Blew Up America" (2001), by Amiri Baraka. The sardonic perspective of this poem about the September 11 attacks garnered its fair share of controversy.

the audience. The basic goal, intrinsic to the Beat movement, was a head-on confrontation with existence.

Public Engagement Throughout his career, Ferlinghetti has consistently asserted that a poet's life and work must remain engaged with current social and political issues. This sentiment divided the Beat movement in the 1960s, between the "engaged" and the "disengaged," the aloof "cool" of the Beat hipster and the heated protest of the activist spokesman whose social consciousness burned to transform the world. Ferlinghetti's social and political commitments were overt, but he also sought to maintain his credibility and his "cool." Two books of his poetry from the 1960s, *Starting from San Francisco* (1961) and *The Secret Meaning of Things* (1969), reflect the poet's expanded consciousness as he journeyed outward and inward through Europe, Zen Buddhism, drugs, and social issues. Ferlinghetti published most of the poems from these two collections as broadsides, in the tradition of printing political and lyric poems on sheets to be posted for the public. This pattern of broadside publishing has since become a main feature of small-press publication. For Ferlinghetti, it was a way of allowing his personal confrontations with the world to become a public matter.

Lawrence Ferlinghetti has remained a literary fixture for decades, through his bookstore and publishing ventures as well as his own writing. Two later collections of his poetry, *Endless Life* (1984) and *These Are My Rivers*

(1993), provide insight into the development of his style and thematic concerns, not only with political matters but with the nature of beauty and the poetic imagination. In 1998, Ferlinghetti was named poet laureate of San Francisco—a position he used, characteristically, as a soapbox to advocate for several progressive causes.

Works in Literary Context

Early in his life, Ferlinghetti was inspired by two American writers from two different centuries, both associated with the romantic movement: Henry David Thoreau and Thomas Wolfe. A third American master, Walt Whitman, helped him find the free, open form and the public, bardic voice that he would refine into his own style. Ferlinghetti's literary identity took shape in San Francisco among the contemporaries who became the core of the Beat movement. Breaking the dam of cultural convention, the Beats recognized as their predecessors other innovators and rebels, writers like William Blake, Arthur Rimbaud, Whitman, Guillaume Apollinaire, and Ezra Pound.

The Beats Ferlinghetti often claimed that he was actually a bohemian, not a Beat. Nevertheless, he performed numerous functions essential to the development of the Beat movement, through his bookstore and City Lights Press, as well as his role in the *Howl* obscenity case. At the same time, his own body of work contributed to the signature Beat style. The Beats created a poetics akin to the practices of abstract expressionist art, or of jazz. The Beat writer, like the jazz musician, was measured by the authenticity, spontaneity, and intensity of his response to the world. Ferlinghetti developed his own spontaneous form in the "Oral Messages" poems of *A Coney Island of the Mind*. Employing the language of the streets, Ferlinghetti and his fellow Beats expanded the boundaries of acceptable literary language and subject matter. They wrote about sex, drugs, and other vices with defiant nonconformity.

The Oral Tradition One of Ferlinghetti's most lasting contributions to literary culture is the oral poetry he fashioned, which in fact re-created an oral tradition in contemporary poetry. Using colloquial bluntness, mocking alliteration and wordplay, internal and multiple rhyme, and other lively techniques, he created a highly accessible vehicle for satire and social commentary. He made creative use of everyday American idioms, alluding to sports and entertainment as easily as to literary precursors. Biographer Larry Smith observes that Ferlinghetti became "the contemporary man of the streets speaking out the truths of common experience, often to the reflective beat of the jazz musician. As much as any poet today he . . . sought to make poetry an engaging oral art." The contemporary genres of performance poetry, such as poetry slams, owe a debt to Ferlinghetti, as well as to Ginsberg.

Works in Critical Context

Ferlinghetti's writing has brought him notable popular success. *A Coney Island of the Mind* ranks along with Ginsberg's *Howl* as one of the most widely known volumes of American poetry published after 1950. However, Ferlinghetti's work has met with a lukewarm critical reception. Some critics have remarked that his verse is undisciplined, sentimental, and lacking in stylistic variation. Others praise what they see as his honest energy and the spontaneous, oral quality of his work. General critical assessment of Ferlinghetti's writing seems to be that it contributed to the open, vibrant sensibility of the Beat movement, but that unlike the work of Ginsberg or Kerouac, it was not particularly innovative. The retrospective collection *Endless Life: Selected Poems* (1984) prompted some critics to reappraise the importance of his work to contemporary poetry.

If certain academics grumbled about Ferlinghetti's work, it is worth recalling that he spent his career railing against the kind of poetry geared to the educated elite. Other critics respected his engagement in current events. John Trimbur, writing in the journal *Western American Literature*, defends Ferlinghetti from the charge of being "the literary entrepreneur of the Beat generation," and applauds him for writing "public poetry to challenge the guardians of the political and social status quo for the souls of his fellow citizens."

Responses to Literature

1. Compare Ferlinghetti's *A Coney Island of the Mind* to Allen Ginsberg's *Howl and Other Poems*. In what ways do they seem to represent a common artistic movement? In what ways are the two works different?

2. Lawrence Ferlinghetti wrote very politically motivated poetry. What is the difference between political art and political propaganda? Explore some of Ferlinghetti's work to help you define the distinction as you perceive it.

3. The Beat poets believed in expression of emotion over realistic description of the physical world. Compare the Beat aesthetic to the philosophies of the Romantic poets such as Samuel Taylor Coleridge and William Wordsworth. How are they similar? How are they different?

4. Some of Ferlinghetti's poems, such as the "Oral Messages" in *A Coney Island of the Mind*, were intended to be read aloud with musical accompaniment, especially modern jazz. What does a musical background add to the meaning and experience of a poem? Is there a fundamental difference between spoken poetry with musical accompaniment, and songs?

BIBLIOGRAPHY

Books

Cherkovski, Neeli. *Ferlinghetti: A Biography*. Garden City, N.J.: Doubleday, 1979.

Ehrlich, J. W. *Howl of the Censor*. San Carlos, Calif.: Nourse Books, 1961.

Rexroth, Kenneth. *American Poetry in the Twentieth Century*. New York: Herder & Herder, 1971.

Silesky, Barry. *Ferlinghetti, The Artist in His Time*. New York: Warner Books, 1990.

Skau, Michael Walter. *Constantly Risking Absurdity: The Writings of Lawrence Ferlinghetti*. Troy, N.Y.: Whitston, 1989.

Smith, Larry. *Lawrence Ferlinghetti: Poet-at-Large*. Carbondale and Edwardsville: Southern Illinois University Press, 1983.

Periodicals

Hopkins, Crale D. "The Poetry of Lawrence Ferlinghetti: A Reconsideration." *Italian Americana* (1974): 59–76.

Ianni, L. A. "Lawrence Ferlinghetti's Fourth Person Singular and the Theory of Relativity." *Wisconsin Studies in Contemporary Literature* 8 (Summer 1967): 392–406.

Trimbur, John. Review of *Endless Life: Selected Poems*. *Western American Literature* 17 (Spring 1982).

✸ Harvey Fierstein

BORN: *1954, Brooklyn, New York*

NATIONALITY: *American*

GENRE: *Drama, fiction*

MAJOR WORKS:

Torch Song Trilogy (1981)

La Cage Aux Folles (1983)

Tidy Endings (1988)

The Sissy Duckling (2005)

A Catered Affair (2007)

Overview

A well-known actor who became prominent as a gay rights and AIDS activist beginning in the 1980s, Harvey Fierstein also is highly regarded as an author of such popular plays as *Torch Song Trilogy* (1981) and *La Cage Aux Folles* (1983). Such award-winning plays helped open up American theater audiences to homosexual themes. His plays focus on the joys and griefs of gay life and often address problems of love, relationships, and commitment. Fierstein often draws on his own life and experiences as a gay man to write his plays and film scripts.

Works in Biographical and Historical Context

Coming Out as Homosexual Fierstein was born on June 6, 1954, in Brooklyn, New York, the son of Irving

Harvey Fierstein   *Fierstein, Harvey, photograph. AP Images.*

professional acting career, and he knew that his future lay in the theater, he chose to earn a fine arts degree in art from the Pratt Institute in Brooklyn, graduating in 1973.

While Fierstein's acting career was taking off after he completed his degree, he also began writing plays. His early plays, such as *In Search of the Cobra Jewels* (1973) and *Freaky Pussy* (1975), were primarily campy vehicles for his exploration of homosexuality's raunchy aesthetic dimension and were generally ignored outside of Greenwich Village, New York City. Such plays were not indicative of his talent as a writer, which did not fully bloom until after his first relationship ended when his partner of two years left him for a woman he later married. While seeing a therapist, Fierstein was advised to channel his emotions into words.

Torch Song Trilogy This advice led to Fierstein's breakthrough work, *Torch Song Trilogy*, composed of three one-act plays he began writing in 1976 with *International Stud*. Drawing from his own life, the play, as a whole, focuses on a young man as he comes out as a homosexual, his relationship to his mother, and his search for love and a family. In the long-running original productions, which moved from Off-Off-Broadway to Broadway, Fierstein played the primary character, Arnold Beckoff, and became a star. He won numerous awards, including Tony Awards for both the play and his performance. Fierstein later wrote the screenplay for the popular 1988 film version.

Fierstein's next major work was the book for the musical *La Cage Aux Folles* (1983), another gay-themed Broadway smash that won him a Tony Award. Adapted from Jean Poiret's play of the same name, the musical is the story of a middle-aged homosexual couple who must deal with one of the men's son's forthcoming marriage to a fiancée from a highly conservative family. This gay love story emphasized the commonality of the characters with their predominantly straight audience.

Becoming AIDS Activist Not all of Fierstein's plays found a wide audience or were critically embraced. *Spookhouse* (1983) depicted a troubled family that owned and lived above a Coney Island spookhouse. His 1987 play *Safe Sex*—made up of three one-acts about homosexuals learning to live in the era of AIDS, two of which he starred in, essentially playing himself—was not a success and closed after only a week on Broadway. By this time, AIDS was greatly affecting gay life. The disease that became known as AIDS was first diagnosed in 1980. The blood-transmitted disease spread rapidly among promiscuous gay men at first, though they were not the only group affected. Still, for many years, AIDS was considered a gay men's disease, leading to controversy over funding-related medical research, treatment, and the many people who suffered from it.

After writing the book for another notorious musical flop, *Legs Diamond* (1988), Fierstein generally moved away from stage acting and writing to focus on roles in film and television. One acclaimed project was adapting

and Jacqueline Harriet (Gilbert) Fierstein, who were Jewish immigrants from Eastern Europe. His father worked as a handkerchief manufacturer, while his mother was employed as a school librarian. Raised in Brooklyn, Fierstein and his brother were encouraged by their parents to take in the many cultural offerings in New York, including opera and Broadway. By the time he was thirteen years old, Fierstein realized he was gay and "came out" to his family, who were supportive of him.

As a teenager, Fierstein began appearing on stage in gay clubs as a drag queen, often performing the songs of such bygone stars as Ethel Merman. During this time period, gay clubs were common but not always accepted and often the focus of police raids. While several such clubs were raided and closed in June 1969, a raid on the Stonewall Inn that month that ended in the building being engulfed in fire. This incident sparked the gay rights movement in the United States.

Launched Professional Acting Career The popularity of Fierstein's drag performances caught the attention of pop art icon Andy Warhol, who cast the seventeen-year-old Fierstein as the lead character in Warhol's 1971 stage revue *Pork*. While this production launched Fierstein's

Tidy Endings, the last play in *Safe Sex*, into an award-winning drama for HBO. Fierstein also starred in the project. He also narrated a number of television shows on AIDS awareness and appeared on television sitcoms. Within a few years, Fierstein was garnering as much attention for his acting as his plays. He had supporting roles in two blockbuster films, *Mrs. Doubtfire* (1993) and *Independence Day* (1996), for example.

Triumphant Return to Broadway   In the early 2000s, Fierstein returned to the stage, first as an actor, then as a writer. He was highly acclaimed and won another Tony Award for his role in drag as Edna Turnblad, the mother of the teenage heroine in the 2002 hit Broadway musical *Hairspray*, then played a well-received Tevye in the Broadway revival of *Fiddler on the Roof* in 2004. In 2002, he published a book for children, *The Sissy Duckling*, and five years later, he wrote *A Catered Affair* (2007), the book for his first new Broadway production in years. Based on previous television and film versions of the story, the musical focuses on the broken Hurley family, which has been trying to cope with loss by moving forward. As of 2008, Fierstein is still a committed AIDS activist, and he continues to live and work in New York.

Works in Literary Context

Together with such dramatists as Larry Kramer and Tony Kushner, Fierstein is one of the major gay playwrights in the late twentieth century. In his writings, especially his plays, Fierstein draws on his background as a gay man and writes about the homosexual experience in the United States in ways that appeal to a heterosexual audience. Coming of age in a pre-AIDS world, he embraces conventional values and often depicts gay men dealing with family situations, both their families of origin and the families they create for themselves. Along the same lines, the theme of searching for love and relationships also is a major concern for Fierstein. As an author, Fierstein was influenced by Warhol, who cast him in his one and only play, *Pork* (1971); the twentieth-century English playwright Noël Coward; and Restoration dramatist William Wycherley (c.1640–1715), as well as his own life experiences.

Importance of Family   In many of Fierstein's plays, he explores familial relationships, deeming them important but often complicated and conflicted. He is frequently concerned with and depicts an allegiance to family values, though never without difficulties. *Widows and Children First!*, the last one-act play that makes up *Torch Song Trilogy*, features a number of struggling familial relationships. Arnold Beckoff must deal with the rebuking, and often disrespectful, nature of his mother, Mrs. Beckoff, who has problems accepting his homosexuality. Arnold also is a single father to a gay teenage son, David, whom he adopted. *Spookhouse* focuses on a more conventional, yet still problematic, family. The straight but dysfunctional Janiks family features a sociopathic son whom his mother wants imprisoned for his own good and the good

of the family. At the heart of *La Cage Aux Folles* is a stable gay couple, Albin and Georges, who have raised a son, Jean-Michele, to adulthood. Jean-Michele poorly repays Albin's mothering by banishing him from the family flat when his fiancé and her right-wing parents visit to meet the in-laws. Fierstein emphasizes the long-term commitment between Albin and George and stresses the importance of respecting oneself and others, especially parents.

Romantic and Sexual Relationships   A number of plays by Fierstein feature characters who are looking for, trying to maintain, or dealing with the effects of romantic and sexual relationships. As a result of this quest, the characters often face challenges, personal sacrifice, and pain. Each play in *Torch Song Trilogy* explores the complex love relationship between Arnold and Ed. Arnold cannot be impersonal about sex, longing for romance, commitment, monogamy, and children to mother. The three one-act plays in the *Safe Sex* trilogy examine the effects of AIDS on gay men's lives, particularly their love lives. Fear is the predominant emotion as Fierstein depicts relationships out of balance from scares about AIDS, fears of letting a lover get close, and of the potential loss of both lover and life. The character Manny, who used to live for sex, paralyzes himself with worry over infecting more men, even while praying for the renewal of the romantic possibilities he regards as now blighted by his HIV status.

Works in Critical Context

Critics have responded more positively to Fierstein's hit plays, such as *Torch Song Trilogy* and *La Cage Aux Folles*, than his failures, such as *Safe Sex* and *Legs Diamond*. While

COMMON HUMAN EXPERIENCE

In *Safe Sex*, Fierstein explores the lives of gay men in the age of AIDS. Here are some other plays yhat deal with AIDS and its effect on people's lives:

As Is (1985), a play by William Hoffman. This was the first Broadway play to deal with the topic of AIDS. It focuses on the relationship between two men, one of whom has the disease.

The Normal Heart (1985), a play by Larry Kramer. Produced Off-Broadway, this play explodes with the playwright's anger over AIDS as a destructive disease in both the homosexual and heterosexual communities.

Jerker (1986), a play by Robert Chesley. In this play, Chesley explores a relationship between two men that ends when one of them dies from AIDS.

Zero Positive (1988), a play by Harry Kondoleon. In this comedy, two characters test positive for the AIDS virus, compelling one to launch into an artistic frenzy.

the playwright has some detractors who point to his appeal to straight audiences as a negative, other critics laud his ability to depict the lives of gay men in a way that straight audiences can relate to. Critics generally agree that Fierstein's writings—whether they address AIDS, sexuality, or family conflicts—touch all groups of people.

Torch Song Trilogy When the three plays that form *Torch Song Trilogy* premiered separately at various Off-Off-Broadway clubs between 1976 and 1981, they were, at first, modestly received. With support from the Glines, a cultural organization devoted to homosexual issues, the plays opened together as *Torch Song Trilogy* at an Off-Off-Broadway theater in 1981. The show was about to close during its first year when it began receiving enthusiastic reviews from mainstream critics, such as Mel Gussow of the *New York Times*. The play then moved to Broadway and ran for several more years. Gussow commented that the three separate pieces were skillfully integrated into a single cohesive play, "giv[ing] us a progressively dramatic and illuminating portrait of a man who laughs, to keep from collapsing. ... The cumulative effort is one to be experienced and savored." Further explaining the success of the play, Michiko Kakutani of the *New York Times* wrote "It is not concerned with homosexuality or minority-group rights but with more universal matters such as the relationship between mothers and sons and flowering of narcissism into love and familial bonds."

La Cage Aux Folles During the original Broadway run of *La Cage Aux Folles*, critics derided Fierstein's book for not taking chances. Despite being the first Broadway musical to feature a homosexual couple, the play was

"hardly the great gay breakthrough that advance reports had touted," according to Richard Christiansen of the *Chicago Tribune*. Other reviewers agreed that the potentially controversial musical was much less daring than expected, but they still lauded the show as highly entertaining and enjoyable. Christiansen wrote that the show was "definitely a hit and a show that gets the new Broadway season off to a smashing start." *New York Times* theater critic Frank Rich agreed, describing *La Cage Aux Folles* as "the schmalziest, most old-fashioned major musical Broadway has seen since *Annie*."

Responses to Literature

1. Read *Spookhouse* and the Tennessee Williams play *The Glass Menagerie* (1944). Write an essay in which you compare and contrast the mother figures in both plays.

2. Research the definition of and background information about torch songs. Create a presentation in which you explain how torch songs relate to the ideas and themes of the plays that make up *Torch Song Trilogy*.

3. In a small group, discuss Fierstein's depiction of unspoken tensions between homosexuals and heterosexuals in several of his plays.

4. Read the play *Torch Song Trilogy*, then watch the film version. In a paper, compare and contrast the power of the two versions. Do you think Fierstein diluted the play's more controversial elements for the film, as critics have suggested?

BIBLIOGRAPHY

Periodicals

Christiansen, Richard. Review of *La Cage Aux Folles*. *Chicago Tribune* (August 23, 1983).

Gussow, Mel. "Fierstein's *Torch Song*." *New York Times* (November 1, 1981): 81.

Kakautani, Michiko. "Fierstein and *Torch Song*: A Daring Climb From Obscurity." *New York Times* (July 14, 1982): C17.

Rich, Frank. Review of *La Cage Aux Folles*. *New York Times* (August 22, 1983).

❂ Jack Finney

BORN: *1911, Milwaukee, Wisconsin*

DIED: *1995, Greenbrae, California*

NATIONALITY: *American*

GENRE: *Fiction, nonfiction, drama*

MAJOR WORKS:

The Body Snatchers (1954)

The Third Level (1957)

Time and Again (1970)

From Time to Time (1995)

Jack Finney   *Kim Komenich / Time Life Pictures / Getty Images*

Overview

Author Jack Finney is best known for his classic science fiction novels *The Body Snatchers* (1954) and *Time and Again* (1970). His books are considered well written, often ingenious, and emotionally effective, whether thrilling or nostalgic in nature. In all of his works, but especially those focused on time travel, Finney offers a sense of precise detail and atmospheric power. His "pod people" from *The Body Snatchers* have become cultural icons, open to many possible interpretations.

Works in Biographical and Historical Context

Growing up in Chicago   Jack Finney was born Walter Braden Finney on October 2, 1911, in Milwaukee, Wisconsin. Because Finney was an intensely private man, little is known of his personal life. His father died when he was two years old, and he and his mother then moved to Chicago to live with his grandparents. His mother, a homemaker, who was skilled in sewing and woodworking, was remarried to a railroad and telephone worker named Frank Berry. Finney, therefore, grew up in the Chicago of the 1910s and 1920s, a time when gangsters, such as Al Capone, attained notoriety, and the expanding, thriving city also became known as a center for jazz.

Finney received his education at Knox College in Galesburg, Illinois. At some point after graduating, he moved to New York City, where, in the 1940s, he worked for an advertising agency as a copywriter. Whether he served in the Armed Forces in World War II is unknown.

Begins Writing Suspense Stories   In 1946, after the war ended, Finney began writing suspense short stories. One of these stories, "The Widow's Walk" (c. 1946), won an award from *Ellery Queen's Mystery Magazine*. Finney continued to write and publish short stories that had elements of fantasy and science fiction, though he placed them in leading slick magazines like *Collier's*, the *Saturday Evening Post*, and *McCall's* instead of pulp magazines like *Amazing Science-Fiction Stories*, which specialized in such genres.

Until the end of the 1940s, there was little science fiction published in book form. Novels were usually serialized in the pulps, cheap magazines named for the rough, cheap, pulpy newsprint on which they were printed. The pulps were the major forum for adventure stories of the mystery, detective, Wild West, or sea adventure types. Most mystery and science fiction writers wrote for pulps in a distinctive style, and by the 1940s, pulps were where the leading science fiction writers published. Slick magazines were considered more mainstream, and their stories of this time period were stylistically and thematically superior.

Moves to California   Around 1950, Finney married Marguerite Guest, with whom he had two children, Margie and Kenneth. By 1954, the family was living in Mill Valley, California, where Finney would spend the rest of his life, making his living as a writer working from home. In 1954, he published his first novel, *Five Against the House*, a story of enterprising college students who plan to rob a Reno, Nevada-based casino. The novel was adapted for a film in 1955.

Publishes The Body Snatchers   Also in 1954, Finney published his next novel, *The Body Snatchers*. Perhaps his best-known work, the novel was originally serialized in *Collier's*. Inspired by the scientific idea that life may have originated in outer space, Finney told the story of alien invaders who emerge from pods and physically duplicate "Earthlings"—residents of a small town in the United States (later revealed to be his own Mill Valley), who are then destroyed. The novel was published in the early days of the cold war between the United States and the communist Soviet Union, and some readers saw an anti-communist message in it. The conformity and consumerism of American society in the 1950s was also seen by some as having relevance for the novel. The novel was adapted for the screen in 1956, 1978, and 1993 as *Invasion of the Body Snatchers*. Finney collaborated on the screenplay for the first version, which is generally considered the best.

LITERARY AND HISTORICAL CONTEMPORARIES

Finney's famous contemporaries include:

Don Siegel (1912–1991): This American film director helmed *Invasion of the Body Snatchers*, the 1956 version of *The Body Snatchers*. He also directed *The Beguiled* (1970) and *Dirty Harry* (1971).

Jack Lemmon (1925–2001): This American actor starred in the film version of Finney's novel *Good Neighbor Sam* (1963).

Albert Einstein (1879–1955): This German-born American physicist devised many theories, including his famous theories of relativity. After World War II, he campaigned against nuclear weapons.

Rod Serling (1924–1975): This American television personality and television writer hosted and wrote for his classic science fiction anthology *The Twilight Zone* (1959–1964).

Richard Matheson (1926–): This American novelist, screenwriter, and television writer often wrote in the science fiction genre. His science fiction books include *The Shrinking Man* (1956), and he also wrote scripts for *The Twilight Zone*.

However, none of the film versions features the happy ending found in the novel, and Finney himself only earned a total of $15,000 from the films.

Finney continued to produce works regularly in the 1950s and 1960s. He published a play, *Telephone Roulette* (1956), then a collection of short stories, *The Third Level* (1957), which focused on the theme of time travel. Returning to novels, he wrote *Assault on a Queen* (1959), a thriller about a plot to burglarize the luxury ship *Queen Mary*. Drawing on his own days in advertising, Finney published *Good Neighbor Sam* in 1963. Both novels were adapted for film in the 1960s.

Time Travel Novels For Finney's next two novels, he again returned to the theme of time travel. The protagonist of *The Woodrow Wilson Dime* (1968) goes to an alternate, parallel world through the use of one of its coins and achieves success there by bringing such things as zippers and musicals. In 1970, Finney published another of his better-known novels, *Time and Again*. This story focused on a New York City–based advertising illustrator, Simon Morley, who goes back to the 1880s while collaborating on a secret project involving time travel. There, he finds romance.

Finney continued to publish books intermittently through the 1970s and 1980s. Still focused on science fiction themes, *Marion's Wall* (1973) details the misadventures that ensue when the ghost of a silent film actress inhabits the body of an introverted woman to probe the likelihood of a revived film career for her. After the unsettling *Night People* (1977), about two couples performing increasingly risky pranks, Finney published a nonfiction book, *Forgotten News: The Crime of the Century, and Other Lost Stories* (1983), which recounted long-forgotten events that once drew considerable attention in the nineteenth century. Using old newspapers, Finney found reports on the development of the helicopter, the abandoning of a sinking ship, and the gruesome murder of a doctor.

Writes Sequel to Time and Again Shortly before his death, Finney published his last original book. Because *Time and Again* had proved so popular, his agent convinced him to write a sequel, *From Time to Time* (1995), that focused on Simon Morley traveling through time to try to prevent World War I by saving a diplomat who otherwise would die on the ill-fated voyage of the *Titanic*. However, *From Time to Time* was less successful than the original and met with only mixed reviews.

Finney died of pneumonia on November 14, 1995, in Greenbrae, California, at the age of eighty-four.

Works in Literary Context

A writer who focused primarily on science fiction and thriller themes, Finney often looked at the present with a critical eye. A number of his best-known works used time travel—a literal escape from the present—to explore the idea of alienation from his current time and a return to the past or alternate time. While not all his novels and short stories showed nostalgia for the past, the lure of change, as in reincarnation, for example, was also present in some of his books. Even in his crime and suspense fiction, such as *Assault on a Queen* and *The Night People*, there is a touch of the sentimentalized past or a jaundiced view of the present that helps to fuel the engine of the plot. As a writer, Finney was influenced by his work in advertising as well as the social and political tensions of post–World War II America. *The Body Snatchers*, for example, can be interpreted in light of the fear of communism that swept through the United States in the 1950s, the idea being that people could be mysteriously and insidiously taken over by an alien mode of thinking.

Time Travel Finney believed that in his theme of time travel he showed the past as flawed, though overall, it is presented as offering a cleaner, gentler way to live. For Finney, the breaking apart of time was usually an experience to be treasured. The past was, for him, another country that afforded a more casual pace of life, a time when faces carried less anxiety, more cheerful optimism. For example, Simon Morley in *Time and Again* returns to the 1880s and finds love. All the short stories in *The Third Level* feature time travel. In the title tale, a commuter discovers a train that regularly travels from New York City to the more simple year of 1894. However, not all of Finney's time travel stories moved from the present into the past to find a sense of peace. In

"Such Interesting Neighbors," a couple moves from the future to present-day California to escape the ominous prevalence of nuclear weapons. In this story, the present is a safer place to live than a seemingly horrible future.

Looking for a Thrill   In a number of Finney's non–time travel novels, the protagonists are trying to escape the present and add something to their lives by performing a thrilling act. In *Five Against the House*, for example, the college students at the center of the story are looking for excitement to enhance their dull academic lives. To do so, they create an elaborate plan to rob a casino. Adults take a similar tactic in *The Night People*. In this novel, two bored couples in San Francisco practice increasingly risky pranks that bedevil the police and amaze fellow Californians. Finney took this idea of a challenging thrill to a new level in *Assault on a Queen*. This time the protagonists are older thieves and professional adventurers who take on a bigger target: the *Queen Mary* steamship. To rob this passenger liner, they plan to re-float a sunken World War I U-boat. By taking on such challenges, Finney's characters emphasize the problematic nature of the present as well.

Works in Critical Context

Finney and his works were never fully embraced by critics. For example, a number of critics found Finney's time travel fiction to be escapist, too nostalgic, and sentimental. However, many reviewers praised *Time and Again* in particular. While its sequel, *From Time to Time* was not as well received, Finney's classic science fiction novel *The Body Snatchers* has been lauded and examined since publication as an example of Cold War American literature and an allegory of 1950s life.

Time and Again   Critics and readers alike found *Time and Again* to be well written. Especially lauded were the exceptional historical details, including photographs, that Finney put in the book. In a *New York Times* review of the novel, the critic called it "an inviting and highly readable piece of entertainment," adding that Finney "has created a piece of nostalgic suspense that is not without its special poignancy." Similarly, W.G. Rogers wrote in the *New York Times Book Review* that with *Time and Again*, Finney had concocted "a most ingenious confection of time now and time then." Rogers concluded that, through the novel, "you go back to a wonderful world and have a wonderful time doing it."

From Time to Time   The sequel to *Time and Again*, *From Time to Time*, focused on Simon Morley's efforts to prevent World War I by traveling to the past, met with only mixed reviews from critics. Reviewing the book in the *Los Angeles Times Book Review*, Charles Champlin commented, "Finney is ingenious in his manipulations of the What Ifs, building to a last ironic comment on the consequences of attempting to rewrite history. But it is the way Finney recaptures the past that gives these novels their uncommon appeal." However, in the *New York Times*, Michiko Kaku-

---

COMMON HUMAN EXPERIENCE

In *The Body Snatchers*, Finney describes an alien invasion of Earth that results in humans being compromised. Here are some other works that focus on the replacement of humans by aliens:

The Puppet Masters (1951), a novel by Robert Heinlein. In this novel, aliens are taking over the bodies of humans via a parasite. A government official tries to prevent them from taking over the Earth.

"The Father-Thing" (1954), a short story by Philip K. Dick. In this science fiction horror short story, a child realizes that his father has been replaced by an alien-grown version of him and that he and his mother are next.

It Came from Outer Space (1953), a film directed by Jack Arnold. In a small Arizona town, aliens take on the form of local humans to repair their spacecraft.

The Nightmare People (1990), a novel by Lawrence Watt-Evans. In this novel, Edward Smith awakens to find all the inhabitants of his apartment complex missing. They later reappear, strangely altered, and Smith joins others in fighting the mysterious invaders to stop them from taking over the world.

---

tani found the novel less impressive. Kakutani wrote, "the formulaic nature of *From Time to Time* makes the readers aware of the novel's flaws: its labored setup ... its deliberately meandering storyline ... its need to ridiculously simplify hugely complex events like a world war and its causes."

Responses to Literature

1. Read the novel *Five Against the House* and watch the film version, which starred Kim Novak and was released in 1955. Compare and contrast the novel with the film version in a paper. Finney allegedly disliked the film version. In your paper, offer your suggestions about why he was not happy with the film version.

2. In a small group, discuss *The Body Snatchers*, focusing on interpretation. Interpretations offered about the book include reading it as an allegory on the perils of communism, of McCarthy-style anticommunism, of consumer conformity, and of fringe-cult obedience. While Finney denied all these interpretations, offer your opinions on these interpretations or devise one of your own.

3. Create a presentation based on a forgotten event you find in Finney's nonfiction book about technological advances in the nineteenth century, *Forgotten News*. Do your own research on the topic as well, and link the event to an aspect of a novel or short story by Finney.

4. Watch one of the film versions of *The Body Snatchers* after reading the novel. How does the film version you chose reflect Finney's themes as well as the era in which it was filmed?

BIBLIOGRAPHY

Books

Seabrook, Jack. *Stealing Through Time; On the Writings of Jack Finney.* Jefferson, NC: McFarland & Co., 2006

Periodicals

Champlin, Charles. Review of *From Time to Time. Los Angeles Times Book Review* (March 26, 1995): 11.

Kakutani, Michiko. Review of *From Time to Time. New York Times* (February 3, 1995): C28.

Review of *Time and Again. New York Times* (August 2, 1970).

Rogers, W. G. Review of *Time and Again. New York Times Book Review* (July 25, 1970): 24.

✵ F. Scott Fitzgerald

BORN: *1896, St. Paul, Minnesota*

DIED: *1940, Hollywood, California*

NATIONALITY: *American*

GENRE: *Fiction*

MAJOR WORKS:
This Side of Paradise (1920)
The Beautiful and the Damned (1922)
The Great Gatsby (1925)
Tender Is the Night (1934)

F. Scott Fitzgerald   Fitzgerald, F. Scott, photograph. The Library of Congress.

Overview

One of the most prominent novelists and short-story writers of the Roaring Twenties, F. Scott Fitzgerald was known as the "spokesman of the Jazz Age." In his works, he examines a generation's search for the elusive American dream of wealth, success, and happiness. Much like his personal experience, Fitzgerald's works mirror the headiness, ambition, despair, and disillusionment of America in his lifetime. His best-known novel, *The Great Gatsby* (1925), is considered one of the most penetrating descriptions of American life in the 1920s.

Works in Biographical and Historical Context

Class Division in Family Francis Scott Key Fitzgerald was born on September 24, 1896, in St. Paul, Minnesota. He was the son of Edward and Mollie (McQuillan) Fitzgerald. His mother was a rich heiress from a wealthy local family. His father was employed first as a furniture manufacturer, then by Procter & Gamble after his business failed. Over the course of Fitzgerald's

childhood, Edward Fitzgerald's job took his family from St. Paul to Buffalo and Syracuse, New York. After his father lost his job with Procter & Gamble, the family returned to St. Paul to live on Fitzgerald's mother's inheritance and the support of her family.

Over time, the young Fitzgerald developed an inferiority complex as a result of the class divisions within his family. Fitzgerald's mother's family had gained their wealth through the hard work of his Irish immigrant grandfather's wholesale grocery business. His father's family, on the other hand, was well bred and prestigious—in fact, Fitzgerald was named for his great-great uncle Francis Scott Key, who wrote "The Star-Spangled Banner." Out of this divergent background arose his ability to experience a wealthy lifestyle, yet he always felt somewhat like an outsider, never fully part of this class. Thus as a young man, he both emulated and loathed the rich, powerful, and beautiful, a social group with whom he maintained a lifelong love-hate relationship.

Published at Princeton Fitzgerald was interested in writing poetry and dramas, and he aspired to become a great writer even as a youth. Privately educated early on, he wrote original plays for amateur productions while attending St. Paul Academy. He continued to write such plays while attending the Newman Academy, a prep school located in Hackensack, New Jersey. In 1913 Fitzgerald entered Princeton University, where he composed lyrics and wrote sketches for productions of the Triangle Club. Fitzgerald also appeared in Triangle Club productions as an actor. His first stories were published in Princeton's literary magazine *Nassau Lit.*

Fitzgerald's education at Princeton was interrupted by World War I. This conflict began in Europe in 1914 after the assassination of Archduke Franz Ferdinand, the heir to the Austro-Hungarian throne. Because of political tensions and entangled alliances, nearly the whole of Europe soon became involved in the conflict. The United States joined the war on the side of Great Britain and France in 1917 after Germany's naval fleet began sinking American merchant ships in British waters. Ultimately, 10 million soldiers died and twenty million were wounded during the course of the "Great War."

Serving His Country   Fitzgerald volunteered for the army in 1917 and went to training camp in Alabama. On the weekends, Fitzgerald worked on the earliest drafts of his first novel, *This Side of Paradise* (1920). He served in the army until 1919, without seeing action in the conflict or serving overseas. After leaving the service, Fitzgerald briefly lived in New York City and worked at an advertising agency, Barron Collier. He eventually returned to St. Paul and finished *This Side of Paradise*. The book was published to much acclaim, as it was the first American novel to deal with college undergraduate life in the World War I era.

The success and money Fitzgerald earned from *This Side of Paradise* allowed him to marry Zelda Sayre, a socially prominent daughter of an Alabama Supreme Court judge whom he met while at training camp. During the 1920s, Zelda Fitzgerald significantly affected her husband's life and career. She was his personal literary consultant and editor, and she matched Fitzgerald's extravagant tastes and passion for living in the moment. For some time, the couple lived a decadent lifestyle on Long Island, which inspired his novel *The Great Gatsby.*

Writing from Abroad   In the early days of their marriage, Fitzgerald produced several volumes of short stories, including *Flappers and Philosophers* (1920) and *Tales of the Jazz Age* (1922). He also wrote several unsuccessful plays, including *The Vegetable; or, From President to Postman* (1923) and *How to Live on $36,000 a Year* (1924). His second novel, *The Beautiful and the Damned* (1922), was also produced during this period. It was a lively but shallow book that was originally published serially in *Metropolitan Magazine* from 1921 to 1922.

Fitzgerald next turned his attentions to *The Great Gatsby,* completing the novel while living in Europe from 1924 to 1926. When the novel was published in 1925, it was recognized as a great leap forward for Fitzgerald's craft and career. He published a third collection of short stories, *All the Sad Young Men,* in 1926 to favorable reviews.

A Great Depression   After completing *The Great Gatsby,* he began his fourth novel, which he worked on for nine interrupted years. Fitzgerald was distracted on several fronts. The alcoholism he had developed in his earlier years worsened, and his wife became increasingly mentally unstable. Furthermore, Fitzgerald was falling further into debt. These and other factors led Fitzgerald and his wife to return to the United States in December 1926. In 1927 Fitzgerald went to Hollywood for two months to work on a film treatment for a silent film, *Lipstick,* that was never made. He was able to make money by regularly writing and publishing short stories in periodicals in the late 1920s, but he soon faced new challenges.

His wife's fragile state culminated in a mental breakdown, and she was ultimately diagnosed with and hospitalized for schizophrenia in 1930. Fitzgerald himself became depressed as well. In addition to sadness over his wife's condition, he was feeling the economic effects of the stock market crash of 1929. The stock market crashed after an investment boom in 1924, which was fueled by investors buying stocks with purely speculative money. The stocks themselves were also wildly overvalued, and their worth plummeted as the economy took a downturn. The failure of the stock market sent the country spiraling into the Great Depression, which left the United States and then the world in a dramatic and sustained depression throughout the 1930s.

Decline in Output   As Fitzgerald struggled with these problems, his alcoholism worsened. The quality and amount of his writing declined as a result, and he nearly stopped writing in the mid-1930s. Yet over time, he labored over what some considered his most psychologically complex and aesthetically ambitious novel, *Tender Is the Night* (1934). Like Fitzgerald's previous novels, it focuses on the spiritual emptiness of rich young Americans. He then published his last collection of short stories, *Taps at Reveille* (1935), which received little critical attention.

In the late 1930s, Fitzgerald continued to write short stories and essays for periodicals, and he also tried to start his life anew by moving to California to become a motion picture screenwriter. Employed first by Metro-Goldwyn-Mayer and later as a freelancer, Fitzgerald contributed to fourteen films, including *Gone with the Wind* (1939), but he received a credit on only one of them. While in Hollywood, Fitzgerald became romantically involved with Sheilah Graham, a local gossip columnist, while his wife remained hospitalized.

Also during this time, Fitzgerald wrote, but did not finish, his last novel, *The Last Tycoon,* about the motion picture industry. His work was fatally interrupted when Fitzgerald died suddenly of a heart attack in Hollywood on December 21, 1940, at the age of forty-four. His heart attack was believed to be induced by his long addiction to alcohol. *The Last Tycoon* was published in its unfinished form in 1941, after his death.

LITERARY AND HISTORICAL CONTEMPORARIES

F. Scott Fitzgerald's famous contemporaries include:

William Faulkner (1897–1962): This American novelist wrote acclaimed books about the South in the 1920s. *The Sound and the Fury* (1929) is considered to be his masterpiece.

Louis Armstrong (1901–1971): This African American trumpeter created recordings in the 1920s that are considered to be milestone performances in the history of modern jazz.

Herbert Hoover (1874–1964): This American president served from 1929 to 1933. He was criticized by contemporaries for having caused the Great Depression and for worsening it with his poor leadership.

Charles Lindbergh (1902–1974): This American aviator became a hero of the Jazz Age by becoming the first person to fly across the Atlantic Ocean.

Gertrude Stein (1874–1946): This American writer was an expatriate who moved to France in 1903 and remained there until her death. An experimental writer, her works include *Three Lives* (1909). She, like Fitzgerald, is considered a member of the "Lost Generation."

Works in Literary Context

Fitzgerald is generally regarded as the most gifted and insightful literary chronicler of the Roaring Twenties. The glamour and indifference of the youthful, affluent characters portrayed in his novels were derived from Fitzgerald's own life and that of his wife and friends. Fitzgerald was further inspired by the events and values of American society in the 1920s and 1930s, especially the Jazz Age generation.

Autobiographical Elements In *This Side of Paradise* and *The Beautiful and the Damned*, Fitzgerald examined the lives of young characters who much resembled Fitzgerald and his friends. Hedonistic and acquisitive yet also jaded and rebellious, these affluent East Coast youths helped secure the popular image of a "lost generation" both entranced and repelled by American materialism. *The Great Gatsby* called upon his experiences living among wealthy New Yorkers. Indeed, Fitzgerald and his wife attended many lavish Long Island parties similar to those that Gatsby hosts in the book. The colorful variety of characters in the novel, from flappers to gangsters to intellectuals, no doubt reflected the spectrum of his own acquaintances.

Fitzgerald took a different tone in *Tender Is the Night*, which was set against the backdrop of expatriate life in Europe in the 1920s. The story focuses on a brilliant young psychiatrist, Dr. Richard Diver, and his schizophrenic wife, Nicole. The story closely parallels Fitzgerald's own life during this period, reflecting the disillusionment and strain he felt from both the Great Depression and his wife Zelda's development of schizophrenia and eventual breakdown.

Reflection of American Society In addition to reflecting the circumstances of his own life, many of Fitzgerald's best-known works also reflected American society in the post–World War I era. His second and third novels, as well as his short-story collections published between novels, showed a growing awareness of the shallowness and brutal insensitivity that have been accoutrements of American society. This was most famously accomplished in *The Great Gatsby*, where Fitzgerald portrayed the decay of traditional American values in a suddenly prosperous society. He scrutinized the consequences of the Jazz Age generation's adherence to false values by drawing a contrast between the immortality and shallowness of the East and the innocence and virtue of the West, highlighting the persistence of illusions and dreams in the face of sordid reality.

In the novel, Fitzgerald employs a first-person narrator, Nick Carraway, to tell the story of Jay Gatsby, a farmer's son-turned-racketeer, whose ill-gotten wealth is acquired solely to gain acceptance into the sophisticated, moneyed world of the woman he loves, Daisy Fay Buchanan. Gatsby's romantic illusions about the power of money to buy respectability and Daisy's love were skillfully and ironically interwoven with episodes that depicted what Fitzgerald viewed as the callousness and moral irresponsibility of the affluent American society. Set amid the glamour and the raucousness of the 1920s, Gatsby's tragic quest and violent end foretold the collapse of an era and the onset of disillusionment with the American dream.

Works in Critical Context

Although Fitzgerald is now regarded as a major twentieth-century writer, only a few of his novels and short stories were greatly acclaimed during his lifetime. *This Side of Paradise* was well received when it was first published, but novels like *The Great Gatsby* and *Tender Is the Night* were initially commercial disappointments, despite critical appreciation for them. By the time of his death, Fitzgerald was virtually forgotten and unread, a relic of a decade seemingly long in the past. In the 1950s, however, Fitzgerald's work was rediscovered, and a critical revival led to the publication of numerous volumes of stories, letters, and notebooks. Since that time, critics have universally praised Fitzgerald's mastery of style and technique that renders even his most trivial efforts entertaining and well executed. He is regarded as a profound and sensitive artist, and he lives on as the unparalleled voice of the Jazz Age.

The Great Gatsby Although it eventually gained the respect of many prominent American writers and is now considered a classic, when it was published, *The Great Gatsby* was popular only with critics. Fanny Butcher, writing in the *Chicago Daily Tribune* noted that "*The Great Gatsby* proves that Scott Fitzgerald is going to be a writer, not just a man of one book." In *Dial*, critic Gilbert Seldes went further by writing, "Fitzgerald has more than matured; he has mastered his talents and gone soaring in a beautiful flight, leaving behind him everything dubious and tricky in his earlier work, and leaving even farther behind all the men of his own generation and most of his elders."

Despite such positive reviews, *The Great Gatsby* marked the beginning of the author's decline in popularity. Only twenty-four thousand copies of the novel were initially printed, and the book was not reprinted during his lifetime. After Fitzgerald's resurgence in popularity in the second half of the twentieth century, though, *Gatsby* became respected by critics, scholars, and readers alike for its intriguing motifs and symbols and its scathing social commentary.

Tender Is the Night When first published, *Tender Is the Night* received decidedly mixed reviews. Some critics deemed it a masterpiece. Gilbert Seldes took this opinion in the *New York Evening Journal*, declaring emphatically that Fitzgerald had "written the great novel." Yet the novel drew criticism from many others for being chronologically confusing and thematically unfocused. For example, critic James Gray in the *St. Paul Dispatch* deemed *Tender Is the Night* a "big, sprawling, undisciplined, badly coordinated book." In *The Nation*, William Troy contended that Fitzgerald was merely repeating his early work. Troy claimed, "Dick Diver [the main character] turns out to be Jay Gatsby all over again. ... And the repetition of the pattern turns out to be merely depressing." After Fitzgerald's death, however, the novel was accepted as exhibiting far more depth and narrative canniness than early critics perceived. In fact, later examinations of *Tender Is the Night* conclude that the circle of wealthy expatriates that Fitzgerald so knowledgeably depicted expertly symbolizes the Western world in decline.

Responses to Literature

1. In a group, discuss how characters like Nick Carraway, Jay Gatsby, Daisy Buchanan, and Myrtle Wilson embody different aspects of life in the 1920s. Consider how they fit in with both the specific world around them as well as wider American society in the 1920s.

2. Pick a novel or short story by Fitzgerald and write an essay in which you create an overview of the 1920s as depicted by his work. How did people dress? What luxury items did they enjoy? What did they do for fun? Reference passages from Fitzgerald's work in your answers.

3. F. Scott Fitzgerald was one of several American artists part of what was dubbed the "Lost Generation." Research the characteristics of this group and

---

COMMON HUMAN EXPERIENCE

Fitzgerald's novels, especially *The Great Gatsby*, epitomize aspects of American life in the post–World War I to Great Depression period. Here are some other works that reflect American society during this time:

The Sun Also Rises (1926), a novel by Ernest Hemingway. This novel explores the lives of American expatriates whose experiences in World War I left them passing time aimlessly in Parisian cafés. As a result, they were dubbed "The Lost Generation."

The Jazz Singer (1927), a film featuring Al Jolson. The star of Broadway musicals in the 1920s, Jolson's role in this feature-length film helped revolutionize the moving picture industry by being the first to showcase musical numbers and a talking sequence.

Babbitt (1922), a novel by Sinclair Lewis. This satirical novel features a critical look at middle-class life in the United States through the character of George Babbitt, a middle-aged realtor.

The Weary Blues (1926), a poetry collection by Langston Hughes. These poems are stark and brutal visions of the poverty and anger felt by African Americans in the Jazz Age by a leading figure in the Harlem Renaissance.

---

write an essay that discusses why you think Fitzgerald was part of it. Include at least three other authors who are also identified with this group, and what they have in common with Fitzgerald.

BIBLIOGRAPHY

Books

Berman, Ronald. *The Great Gatsby and Fitzgerald's World of Ideas.* Tuscaloosa: University of Alabama Press, 1997.

De Koster, Katie, ed. *Readings on the F. Scott Fitzgerald.* Westport, Conn.: Greenwood Press, 1997.

Prigozy, Ruth. *F. Scott Fitzgerald.* Woodstock, N.Y.: Overlook Press, 2001.

Periodicals

Butcher, Fanny. Review of *The Great Gatsby. Chicago Daily Tribune*, April 18, 1925.

Gray, James. Review of *Tender Is the Night. St. Paul Dispatch*, April 12, 1934.

Seldes, Gilbert. Review of *The Great Gatsby. Dial* (August 1925).

———. Review of *Tender Is the Night. New York Evening Journal* (April 12, 1934).

Troy, William. Review of *Tender Is the Night. Nation* (May 9, 1934).

✸ Fannie Flagg

BORN: *1941, Birmingham, Alabama*

NATIONALITY: *American*

GENRE: *Fiction, drama*

MAJOR WORKS:

Coming Attractions (1981)

Fried Green Tomatoes at the Whistle Stop Café
(1987)

Welcome to the World, Baby Girl! (1998)

A Redbird Christmas (2004)

Overview

Fannie Flagg began her career as a television and film personality, but it was her novels and screenplays that earned her acclaim in the 1980s. Through such novels as *Coming Attractions* (1981) and *Fried Green Tomatoes at the Whistle Stop Café* (1987), Flagg explores the South of the past—most often, the 1950s—through casts of primarily female characters and splashes of homespun humor. She depicts the hardships and delights of small-town life through the eyes of female residents. The characters in Flagg's fiction live out their creator's belief in optimism, hard work, and following one's dreams.

Works in Biographical and Historical Context

An Early Love of Film Flagg was born Patricia Neal on September 21, 1941, in Birmingham, Alabama, the daughter of William H. and Marion Leona (LeGore) Neal. Her father was a small business owner and a movie theater projectionist who tried to get rich in many moneymaking schemes. From an early age, Flagg was a fan of popular movies and aspired to join that world. To that end, she joined a theater group in Birmingham when she was fourteen years old and entered beauty pageants from the ages of sixteen to twenty-two to gain exposure. She also changed her name to Fannie Flagg when she was seventeen. Flagg also wanted to write stories, but she suffered from dyslexia and found it very difficult to write. In fact, she received poor grades in creative writing because she had trouble spelling.

In the South of Flagg's childhood, racial and class tensions ran high. The South had been racially segregated for generations, and while the end of the Civil War saw African American slaves freed, the rights they gained were often compromised by various state laws and other legal means. By the mid-1950s, civil rights issues involving African Americans were being tested in court. For example, in the 1954 case *Brown v. Board of Education*, the Supreme Court ruled that legal segregation violated the Fourteenth Amendment. The civil rights movement would continue to challenge legal and cultural bias against African Americans for decades to come. It was against this backdrop that Flagg

was competing in beauty pageants in Alabama and developing her creative side. The racial tensions of her childhood would later be regularly featured in her writing.

The Silver Screen After high school, Flagg studied acting at the Pittsburgh Playhouse in 1962. By the mid-1960s, Flagg had found a job as a television talk show host and producer on Birmingham's *Morning Show* on WBRC-TV. In 1965 Flagg appeared at a New York City comedy club. This appearance caught the attention of Allen Funt, the creator of *Candid Camera*, who approached Flagg about working on the show. She began her career as a writer on the hidden camera television series, but Funt soon moved her into a regular role in front of the camera. She remained on the show until 1967 and rejoined it when it was revived from 1974 to 1980. Flagg then recorded two comedy albums, *Rally 'Round the Flagg* (1967) and *My Husband Doesn't Know I'm Making This Phone Call* (1971).

Flagg appeared regularly on television in the 1970s. She took roles on *The New Dick Van Dyke Show* from 1971 to 1973 and in the television movie *The New, Original Wonder Woman* (1975). In addition, Flagg was a regular guest on the game show *Match Game* throughout the decade.

Flagg's career continued to grow on screen and stage throughout the 1970s. She began acting regularly in films, appearing in *Five Easy Pieces* (1970) and *Grease* (1978). Flagg moved to Broadway in 1979 with a role in *The Best Little Whorehouse in Texas*, in which she eventually played the featured role, Miss Mona. Flagg returned to television with a two-year run on the series *Harper Valley* from 1981 to 1982.

Published First Novel Despite her exposure, Flagg became unhappy with her acting career—what she really wanted to do was write. So in 1981, she published her first novel, *Coming Attractions*. The humorous story revolves around the 1952 diary entries of eleven-year-old Daisy Fay Harper and chronicles her growth and development over the next six years. Harper is the daughter of a ladylike mother and an alcoholic projectionist father who is always looking for a get-rich-quick scheme. Through her journal entries, Flagg draws Daisy as a magnet for mishaps, trouble, and zany coming-of-age stories. *Coming Attractions* became a best seller and reflected a popular trend of looking back at the 1950s with a sense of nostalgia. Flagg continued to have a nostalgic bent in her subsequent works.

Flagg's writing career reached new heights with *Fried Green Tomatoes at the Whistle Stop Café* (1987). The book takes place in Alabama in both the past and the present. The present tale chronicles the growing friendship between Ninny, a nursing home resident, and Evelyn, a middle-aged woman unsure of what to do with the rest of her life. The past, set during the Depression era, focuses on Ninny's sister-in-law Idgie Threadgoode, a tomboy who defends blacks and rescues her friend, Ruth Jamison, from an abusive husband. The pair build a life together and open a café in Whistle Stop, Alabama. The novel was a best seller when it was published in 1987, but it reached a bigger audience a few years later with the release of the popular film version in 1991. Flagg cowrote the screenplay (with Carol Sobieski) and was nominated for an Academy Award. She also published a related cookbook *Fannie Flagg's Original Whistle Stop Café Cookbook* (1993).

The Simple Life After the success of *Fried Green Tomatoes*, Flagg published several novels in the 1990s, including *Daisy Fay and the Miracle Man* (1992), which was merely a republished version of *Coming Attractions* with a new title. After a multiyear hiatus from writing, Flagg published a new novel, *Welcome to the World, Baby Girl!* (1998). This book was a sequel of sorts to *Coming Attractions* and focuses on Dena Nordstrom, a girl from the Midwest who moves to New York City and becomes a successful television interviewer. She later grows homesick for her grandmother's home.

In the early 2000s, Flagg published several more novels, including *Standing in the Rainbow* (2002), a portrait of the small town of Elmwood Springs, Missouri. This was followed with *A Red Bird Christmas* (2004), a Christmas story set in the South. It focuses on the relationship between a terminally ill man, an orphaned girl, a pet cardinal, and the residents of a small Alabama community. Flagg again used Elmwood Springs as the setting for *Can't Wait to Get to Heaven* (2006). Flagg continues to live and write in Santa Barbara, California.

Works in Literary Context

Inspired by her own childhood in the South in the 1950s, Flagg's novels are usually set in midcentury, small-town America. Although her writing career is generally separated from her acting career, some of her acting roles affected the style of her fiction. For example, her use of bittersweet humor in some of her novels resembled the stage work necessary for her role in *The Best Little Whorehouse in Texas*. Flagg's interest in Southern settings placed her in the tradition of Tennessee Williams's play, *Cat on a Hot Tin Roof*, in which she also acted. In addition, she emphasized the importance of, and humor within, interpersonal relationships, particularly between women. Flagg was influenced by such authors as Williams, Eudora Welty, and Flannery O'Connor.

The Importance of Relationships At the core of many of Flagg's novels is an emphasis on the relationships between people, primarily females, but also within families. For example, in *Coming Attractions*, the touching and humorous relationship between Daisy and her father is a recurring motif of the novel. Flagg shows their sweet and funny bond as she depicts Daisy helping her father run the projector at the town theater and taking part in some of his get-rich-quick schemes. In *A Redbird Christmas*, a terminally ill man named Oswald T. Campbell and an orphaned girl named Patsy Casey find healing in the bond they form as well as the great community of Lost

LITERARY AND HISTORICAL CONTEMPORARIES

Fannie Flagg's famous contemporaries include:

Erma Bombeck (1927–1996): This American humor writer drew on her own experiences as a wife and mother to satirize and celebrate the American family. Her books include *If Life Is a Bowl of Cherries, What Am I Doing in the Pits?* (1978).

Dwight D. Eisenhower (1890–1996): This American president served two terms that covered much of the 1950s. During his time in office, he became involved with the burgeoning civil rights movement, signing the Civil Rights Act of 1957 into law.

Diane Sawyer (1945–): This American television journalist commanded a multimillion-dollar salary while exercising considerable influence over program format and content. In the 1980s, she was the first female correspondent for *60 Minutes* and later joined ABC.

Goldie Hawn (1945–): This American actress and comedienne appeared on the comedy series *Rowan and Martin's Laugh-In* from 1968 to 1970. She then launched a successful film career with roles in such movies as *Private Benjamin* (1980).

Tennessee Williams (1911–1983): This American playwright is acknowledged as one of the greatest dramatists of the post–World War II era. His plays include *The Glass Menagerie* (1944).

River, Alabama. In *Standing in the Rainbow*, the Smith family of Elmwood Springs, Missouri, illustrates similar themes of closeness and caring.

But it is the friendships among women that particularly shine in Flagg's fiction. *Fried Green Tomatoes*, for example, depicts several meaningful female relationships. One is between Ninny Threadgoode, an eighty-year-old woman in a nursing home, and Evelyn Couch, a younger woman who visits her mother-in-law at the home. Ninny tells Evelyn stories of two other close women, Ruth and Idgie, a relationship of the past that is implied to be an intimate love affair. The stories of Idgie and Ruth inspire Evelyn to change her life and is Flagg's way of illustrating the transformative power of female relationships.

A Funny Streak Flagg has a flair for the funny, and she depicts these and other relationships with a sense of humor. In *Coming Attractions*, subtle ironic twists and amusing episodes permeate the novel. Indeed, Daisy's many adventures have a zany, hilarious edge to them. One of the funnier episodes involves a bizarre mortgage scam in which her father holds a fake séance for a group of people. To his great surprise, his audience suddenly starts speaking in tongues—one lady throws off her hearing aid

COMMON HUMAN EXPERIENCE

Several of Flagg's novels are set in the South in the mid-twentieth century. As a result, they reflect a nostalgia for a simpler past, yet one tainted with racial tension. Here are some other novels that are also set in the South during this time period:

"A Good Man Is Hard to Find" (1955), a short story by Flannery O'Connor. This story focuses on a trip to Florida in which a family travels through several Southern states, gets into a car accident, and lose their lives. The story tacitly suggests that Americans have lost their spiritual direction.

Intruder in the Dust (1948), a novel by William Faulkner. In this book, an eccentric old African American named Lucas Beauchamp is saved from a false-murder charge through the efforts of fair-minded whites.

To Kill a Mockingbird (1961), a novel by Harper Lee. In this novel, lawyer Atticus Finch defends an innocent black man accused of raping a white woman.

Ludie's Son (1988), a novel by Dirlie Herlihy. Set in the South in the 1950s, a young girl named Marty becomes aware that she has grown up surrounded by discrimination through her friendship with Ludie, an African American. White boys accuse Marty of having a relationship with Ludie's brother and threaten to lynch him.

and claims that she can suddenly hear. While *Fried Green Tomatoes* was not as outwardly humorous as *Coming Attractions*, Flagg includes many small moments of humor, especially through the character of Dot Weem, who writes a column in *Weems Weekly*. In another funny moment, Ninny tells Evelyn of a time when she threw a broom at a cat in a tree. Because the broom stuck, she could not sweep the floors. Similarly, the bad luck of the unskilled town beautician named Tot Whooten adds laughs to *Standing in the Rainbow*, while eccentric community members like Mildred in *A Redbird Christmas*, who keeps dying her hair outlandish colors every few days, gives the novel an oddball, relatable edge. Such humorous touches add depth, wit, and humanity to Flagg's stories and characters.

Works in Critical Context

Critical reception to Flagg's works has been as positive as the author's message. Although occasionally faulted for certain overwritten passages, her novels have been praised for their heartwarming nostalgia and realistic sense of time and place. Critics have also commented on Flagg's talent for entertaining storytelling and her well-researched attention to detail. The humor that Flagg weaves through the day-to-day lives of her characters has been appreciated by reviewers, who generally think the mixture of laughter and the power of friendship is one of the strengths of her fiction.

Coming Attractions   Flagg's first novel *Coming Attractions* impressed both critics and readers alike with its humorous yet sensitive portrayal of adolescence in the 1950s South. Critics praised the skill with which Flagg balanced the adventures of Daisy with the harsh realities of adolescence. As Gerald Einhaus of the *National Review* commented, "Miss Flagg has accurately pegged the emotions and expressions of a teenaged girl, as Daisy Fay … comments on a life that is wild and improbable by any standard." In *Publishers Weekly*, Barbara A. Bannon wrote that Flagg "has put together a rollicking, funny, bubbling novel." Similarly, *New York Times* writer Laura Cunningham concluded that "A lot of people are going to enjoy Daisy Fay Harper 'cause she's just as sweet as her favorite movie-munchin' candy, Bit-O-Honey."

Fried Green Tomatoes at the Whistle Stop Café   Like *Coming Attractions*, *Fried Green Tomatoes* was lauded from its initial publication, even by fellow authors such as Harper Lee, Erma Bombeck, and Eudora Welty. Critics were especially impressed by Flagg's depiction of the relationship between the two main characters in the flashbacks. In the *New York Times Book Review*, Jack Butler thought that novel had minor flaws such as presenting too many details concerning insignificant events. But Butler found much to like, noting that "[t]he core of the story is the unusual love affair between Idgie and Ruth, rendered with exactitude and delicacy, and with just the balance of clarity and reticence that would have made it acceptable in that time and place." In his review, Butler also praised Flagg's portrayal of the time period, pointing out that she "evokes, in fine detail, Hoovervilles, the Klan, a 'hunting camp' that is more nearly a juke joint, a hot jazz spot in the black section of Birmingham and many other settings." A *Publishers Weekly* contributor concluded that "the book's best character, perhaps, is the town of Whistle Stop itself. Too bad the trains don't stop there anymore."

Responses to Literature

1. Research the Great Depression in the South. Create a presentation in which you link the setting of the flashbacks in *Fried Green Tomatoes* to historical events and trends of the time.

2. Write your own short story or poem based on what you know about Elmwood Springs through Flagg's novels set in that fictional Missouri town.

3. Compare and contrast the film version of *Fried Green Tomatoes* with the novel. How do the versions differ? How are they similar? Which do you like better, and why?

4. Read *Coming Attractions*, which tells a story using the journal entries of Daisy Fay Harper. Then, write your own short story using the diary form employed by Flagg.

BIBLIOGRAPHY

Periodicals

Bannon, Barbara J. Review of *Coming Attractions*. *Publishers Weekly* (April 10, 1981): 58.

Butler, Jack. "Love with Reticence and Recipes." *New York Times Book Review* (October 18, 1987): 14.

Cunningham, Laura. "Lovers and Movies." *New York Times Book Review* (August 2, 1981): 15.

Eisenhuas, Gerald. Review of *Coming Attractions*. *National Review* (August 20, 1982): 1038.

Review of *Fried Green Tomatoes at the Whistle Stop Café*. *Publishers Weekly* (August 28, 1987): 64–65.

Rockler, Naomi R. "A Wall on the Lesbian Community: Polysemy and Fried Green Tomatoes." *Women's Studies in Communication* (Spring 2001): 90–106.

Web sites

Hillard, Gloria. *"High hurdles didn't stop Fannie Flag."* Retrieved November 20, 2008, from http://www.cnn.com/books/news/9901/12/flagg/ Last updated on January 12, 1999.

✸ Jonathan Safran Foer

BORN: *1977, Washington, D.C.*

NATIONALITY: *American*

GENRE: *Fiction, short stories*

MAJOR WORKS:

Everything Is Illuminated (2002)

Extremely Loud and Incredibly Close (2005)

Jonathan Safran Foer   *David Levenson / Getty Images*

Overview

Considered one of the best young authors in the United States in the early twenty-first century, Jonathan Safran Foer writes about difficult subjects like the Holocaust and the September 11, 2001, terrorist attacks on the United States in unusual, challenging ways. Both of his novels—*Everything Is Illuminated* (2002) and *Extremely Loud and Incredibly Close* (2005)—feature sojourning protagonists trying to understand what happened to an important family member. Foer also weaves in visual elements, primarily in the latter work, to underscore his themes and characters.

Works in Biographical and Historical Context

A Born Performer   Born February 21, 1977, in Washington, D.C., Foer is the son of Albert Foer and Esther (Safran) Foer. His father was a jeweler who later founded the American Antitrust Institute, while his mother is a Polish émigré and president of a public relations firm. Foer is the middle of three sons, all of whom pursued media careers, and he was raised in a middle-class household.

As a child, Foer was a natural performer and colorful character. However, he was traumatized by an incident that affected his later writing. He was eight years old when he was one of the victims of a chemical explosion that occurred while he was attending a summer program at an elementary school. The event had a profound impact on him.

Embraced Writing Career   Foer attended Georgetown Day School, a private prep school. A popular high school student, he decided he wanted to be a brain surgeon and was the valedictorian of his class. When Foer entered Princeton University, he studied philosophy and literature instead of medicine. He was awarded the Writing Thesis Prize from his freshman to senior years. One of his teachers and mentors was the novelist Joyce Carol Oates, who boosted his interest in writing and helped him become a professional writer.

During his college years, Foer had an experience that led to his first novel. In 1997, Foer traveled to the Ukraine to increase his knowledge of his family's history. Specifically, he wanted to delve into the life of his grandfather during World War II and find the woman who saved his grandfather from the Holocaust. Even before

LITERARY AND HISTORICAL CONTEMPORARIES

Jonathan Safran Foer's famous contemporaries include:

Elijah Wood (1981–): This American actor has appeared in films since childhood. He played the character of Foer in the 2005 film adaptation of *Everything Is Illuminated*.

Dale Peck (1967–): This American novelist is best known for his debut *Martin and John: A Novel* (1993).

Nicole Krauss (1974–): This American novelist is married to Foer. Her first novel, *Man Walks Into a Room* (2002), was shortlisted for the *Los Angeles Times* Book Award.

Chelsea Clinton (1980–): This American consultant and hedge fund employee is the daughter of former president Bill Clinton and his wife, Secretary of State Hillary Rodham Clinton.

Zadie Smith (1975–): This British novelist is considered a leading young writer. Her novels include *White Teeth* (2000) and *On Beauty* (2005).

Nazi Germany launched what became a globe-encompassing war in 1939, leader Adolf Hitler regarded Jews as an inferior people. After depriving them of their rights in the late 1930s, he implemented a plan to murder all the Jews in Europe. The Holocaust was the result, a program of extermination intended to kill all Jews. Though Hitler did not fully succeed, millions of Jews died as a result. World War II itself was the most destructive war in world history. After his journey to the Ukraine, Foer began writing *Everything Is Illuminated* while still a student.

Early Publications Foer earned his BA in philosophy from Princeton, then held a variety of jobs as he worked on what became his first novel. Among his posts were morgue assistant, receptionist at a public relations firm, math tutor, ghostwriter, jewelry seller, farm sitter, and assistant archivist. While working at these jobs, Foer was publishing short fiction, receiving the 2000 Zoetrope: All Story Fiction Prize. In 2001, he served as the editor of *Convergence of Birds: Original Fiction and Poetry Inspired by Joseph Cornell.*

That same year, Foer published an excerpt of what would become his first novel in the *New Yorker*. Titled "The Very Rigid Search," the excerpt built interest in his forthcoming publication. Before the novel was put in print, Foer published another significant short story, "A Primer for the Punctuation of Heart Disease," in a 2002 edition of the *New Yorker*. Foer would also publish short stories in such magazines as the *Paris Review, Conjunctions,* and the *New York Times.*

Published Novels Foer's impressive first novel, *Everything Is Illuminated*, was finally published in 2002. The title comes from a line in the novel by Milan Kundera, *The Unbearable Lightness of Being* (1984). The novel is a fictionalized account of Foer's 1997 journey to the Ukraine with the fictional Foer as the main character. Praised by many major publications, *Everything Is Illuminated* won the National Jewish Book Award and the *Guardian* First Book Award in 2002 and the William Saroyan International Prize for Writing in 2003. The novel was turned into a film in 2005, then a stage play in 2006.

Foer published his second novel, *Extremely Loud and Incredibly Close*, in 2005. Again dealing with difficult subject matter, the story focuses on the reaction of nine-year-old Oskar Schell to the death of his father during the 9/11 terrorist attacks. On September 11, 2001, al-Qaeda terrorists hijacked a number of commercial airliners and crashed them into the World Trade Center in New York City and the Pentagon in Washington, D.C. Thousands of people lost their lives in the attacks, and American society has been unsettled in the years following the event. Over the course of the novel, Oskar, an overeducated, oversensitive, and possibly autistic son of one of 9/11's casualties, discovers a key to the meaning of the 9/11 tragedy. Like *Everything Is Illuminated*, the novel was well received, translated into several languages, and is being adapted for film.

In 2005, Foer also wrote an opera libretto, *Seven Attempted Escapes from Silence*. He continues to write while living in Brooklyn, New York, with his novelist wife Nicole Krauss, whom he married in 2004, and their son, Sasha.

Works in Literary Context

Foer's two novels emphasize the importance of searching in the past to understand one's self and, perhaps, the present. He uses innovative literary techniques as well as visual art to underscore and enhance his stories. Foer also employs historical events like the Holocaust, the bombing of Dresden, and the September 11 attacks as a part of the motivation for his characters' journeys. While his themes are socially relevant—the desire to understand what happened to members of their family predominates—Foer includes elements of empathy and humor as well. As a writer, Foer has been influenced by his own family's history, his knowledge of Judaism and New York, contemporary events like the 9/11 terrorist attacks, and the visual arts. He also cites the influence of such authors as Isaac Bashevis Singer, James Joyce, Franz Kafka, Orhan Pamuk, and Bruno Schulz.

Journey of Discovery In both of Foer's novels, the main characters go on journeys of discovery. The journey is a time-tested narrative device in fiction, going back to the *Odyssey* by Homer. Some of the greatest American novels, such as *The Adventures of Huckleberry Finn* by Mark Twain, follow their protagonists into unknown lands and situations. In *Everything Is Illuminated*, Foer offers a fictional account of his 1997 journey to learn more about his family history in the Ukraine. He goes to the country only with the knowledge that his grandfather had escaped from the Holocaust with the help of a woman in his Ukrainian hometown, the shtetl (small Jewish village) of Trachimbrod. The fictional Foer is helped by Alex Perchov, an entrepreneurial young Ukrainian translator whose family owns a travel business catering to Jews seeking their roots. Oskar's journey in *Extremely Loud and Incredibly Close* also involves family. His father, Thomas, was killed in the September 11, 2001, attacks on the World Trade Center in New York City. While looking through his father's possessions, he finds a key labeled "Black." This key compels Oskar to find all New Yorkers bearing this last name in hopes of gaining information about the attacks and his father. In addition, *Extremely Loud and Incredibly Close* includes information about Oskar's grandparents' journey of discovery: their lives.

Lack of Knowledge   While Foer's characters go on a journey of discovery, they do not always gain the knowledge they desire. Foer's fictional visit at the center of *Everything Is Illuminated*, like his real one, provides little illumination about his grandfather's past. For example, the only trace of Trachimbrod is a memorial plaque, so the character Foer begins writing a novel about imagined history of the town from its founding in 1791 to its destruction during World War II. He shares excerpts with Perchov in the letters that form the core of the novel. In *Extremely Loud and Incredibly Close*, Oskar also does not gain the knowledge he seeks about his father's death, though he does meet a range of New Yorkers during his quest. Both Oskar and the people he interacts with learn something about themselves and each other. However, both novels emphasize the importance of the journey over whatever knowledge the protagonists acquire.

Works in Critical Context

Foer's novels are praised by critics for their sincerity and power. His strong writing style and humor are often lauded, as is his ability to elicit an emotional response from readers. Many critics also note Foer's strong characterizations, interesting characters, and distinctive voice. While some detractors find the author's work gimmicky at times—especially in the presentation of parts of *Extremely Loud and Incredibly Close*—Foer is generally highly regarded as a leading voice in the new generation of American literature.

Everything Is Illuminated   *Everything Is Illuminated* was praised by many critics for offering a distinct voice and vision. Marie Arana, writing in the *Washington Post Book World*, argues that Foer lived up to the high expectations created by the *New Yorker* excerpt. She writes, "Rarely does a writer as young ... display such virtuosity and wisdom. His prose is clever, challenging, willfully constructed to make you read it again and again." The *New York Times*' Janet Maslin concurred, stating that the novel

---

COMMON HUMAN EXPERIENCE

In both of Foer's novels, the Holocaust plays at least a minor role in affecting the primary characters. Here are some other works in which the characters are affected by the Holocaust:

"The Tumblers" in *For the Release of Unbearable Urges* (1999), a short story by Nathan Englander. In this story, a group of Jews are destined for the concentration camps, but they board the wrong train and find themselves with a group of entertainers. They devise an acrobatic act to save themselves and avoid a gruesome end.

The Amazing Adventures of Kavalier & Clay (2000), a novel by Michael Chabon. This novel is set in the 1930s and 1940s in the United States and focuses on two Jewish cousins who create a successful comic book series. One of the cousins, Josef Kavalier, is a Czech who has fled the Nazis and feels guilt and grief over the loss of his family.

The Diary of Anne Frank (1947), a nonfiction book by Anne Frank. This classic work of literature is the diary of a Jewish girl who, with her family, was successfully hiding from the Nazis. After two years, the family was discovered and sent to concentration camps, where only Frank's father, Otto, survived.

Jacob's Rescue (1947), a young adult novel by Malka Drucker and Michael Halperin. Set during World War II, this fictionalized account of a true event describes two young Jewish boys being hidden by Gentiles in Poland until the war ends.

"is a complex, ambitious undertaking. ... [T]he payoff is extraordinary: a fearless, acrobatic, ultimately haunting effort to combine inspired mischief with a grasp of the unthinkable."

In reviews of *Everything Is Illuminated*, critics also commented on the novel's mix of comedy and tragedy. In the *Chicago Tribune* "Books" section, Molly McQuade writes, "The author offers sympathy and irony without shrinking from their contrasts. Although the novel seeks to resurrect the memory of a community of Jews massacred by the Germans, Foer doesn't shy away from applying warm mockery to the wiles of their forebears."

Extremely Loud and Incredibly Close   Like *Everything Is Illuminated*, *Extremely Loud and Incredibly Close* was well received by critics when it was published in 2005. In *Commentary*, Sam Munson observes that Foer demonstrates "a natural gift for choosing subjects of great import and then pitching his distinctive voice sharply enough to be heard above their historical din." Other reviewers praised the depth of the novel. Matthew L. Moffett of the *School Library Journal* comments that the novel's "humor works as a deceptive, glitzy cover for a fairly serious tale about loss and recovery." Moffett also notes that Foer leads the story to "a powerful conclusion that will make even the most jaded hearts fall." *Entertainment Weekly* contributor Jennifer Reese finds enjoyment in Oskar's "wonderfully unquiet brain and his sweet soul, his ageless questions, silly school jokes, uncanny observations, and raw misery, all of which bring home a little more of the specific human pain of 9/11."

Responses to Literature

1. Read both *Extremely Loud and Incredibly Close* and Kurt Vonnegut's *Breakfast of Champions* (1973). Write a paper in which you compare and contrast the authors' use of photographs, illustrations, and experiments in typography.

2. Watch the film *The Tin Drum* (1979) or read Günter Grass's 1959 novel of the same name on which the film was based. In a group, discuss whether you believe, as some critics contend, that Oskar in *Extremely Loud and Incredibly Close* is based on the protagonist of the *The Tin Drum*.

3. In an essay, compare and contrast the novel and film versions of *Everything Is Illuminated*. Which version do you believe is more effective?

4. Research the historical events discussed in one of Foer's books. In an essay, discuss how the events add to or affect the story. Can you imagine creating a similar story with other historical events?

BIBLIOGRAPHY

Periodicals

Arana, Marie. "Dream Time." *Washington Post Book World* (April 21, 2002): 5.

Codde, Philippe. "Philomela Revisited: Traumatic Irony in Jonathan Safran Foer's *Extremely Loud and Incredibly Close*." *Studies in American Fiction* (Autumn 2007): 241.

Kohn, Robert E. "Foer's *Everything Is Illuminated*." *Explicator* (Summer 2007): 245.

Maslin, Janet. "Searching for Grandfather and a Mysterious Shtetl." *New York Times*, April 22, 2002.

McQuade, Molly. "Novel's Joint Narrative Creates an Enchanting World." *Chicago Tribune*, "Books," May 19, 2002.

Moffett, Matthew L. Review of *Extremely Loud and Incredibly Close*. *School Library Journal* (July 2005): 131.

Munson, Sam. "In the Aftermath." *Commentary* (May 2005): 80.

Reese, Jennifer. "Mourning Glory: In Jonathan Safran Foer's *Extremely Loud and Incredibly Close*, 9/11 Haunts a Young Prodigy." *Entertainment Weekly*, March 25, 2005, p. 75.

Solomon, Deborah. "The Rescue Artist." *New York Times Magazine* (February 27, 2005): 40.

✸ Horton Foote

BORN: *1916, Wharton, Texas*

DIED: *2009, Hartford, Connecticut*

NATIONALITY: *American*

GENRE: *Drama, screenplays, teleplays*

MAJOR WORKS:
The Trip to Bountiful (1953)
The Chase (1956)
Tender Mercies (1983)
The Young Man from Atlanta (1995)

Overview

Prolific author Horton Foote has produced significant works for the stage, screen, and television that have earned him many honors, including Academy Awards and a Pulitzer Prize. In his usually minimalist works, he primarily focuses on the experiences of characters living in rural Southern milieus. Often incorporating autobiographical elements, Foote's dramas are distinguished by emotional and narrative restraint and generally emphasize character development while examining themes related to social and individual change.

Horton Foote   *Foote, Horton, photograph. AP Images.*

Works in Biographical and Historical Context

Raised in Small-Town Texas Albert Horton Foote Jr. was born on March 16, 1916, in Wharton, Texas, a small town that subsequently became the model for the fictional town of Harrison in many of his works. Foote's parents were Albert Foote, Sr., a merchant and cotton farmer, and his wife, Hallie, who helped run their store. Raised in a middle-class setting, Foote was a precocious reader from an early age. Having spent the whole of his childhood in Wharton, he graduated from Wharton High School in 1932.

Determined to become an actor, Foote studied the craft in California at the Pasadena Playhouse School of Theatre from 1933 to 1935, and in New York at the Tamara Darkarhovna School of Theatre from 1937 to 1939. At the time, the United States, as well as much of the world, was mired in the Great Depression. After the stock market crash of October 1929, millions of Americans lost their savings, could not find jobs, and were hard-pressed to survive. The Great Depression lasted throughout the 1930s, though conditions for some improved because of President Roosevelt's New Deal programs that, among other things, provided temporary jobs for millions in public-works programs.

Launched Acting Career Living in New York City by the end of the 1930s, Foote was cast in a number of productions between 1937 and 1942. While working as an actor, he discovered his talent as a dramatist and began writing plays. In 1942, his first play, *Texas Town*, was produced in New York. It was followed by *Out of My House* (1942) and *Only the Heart* (1944). These early plays are emotionally restrained dramas which emphasized character development and are set within the social context of small-town Texas in the early twentieth century.

At the beginning of his writing career, Foote also worked in Washington, D.C., first as a workshop director at the King Smith School of Creative Arts in 1944, and then as a manager of Productions, Inc., from 1945 to 1948. In addition, he married Lillian Vallish in June 1945; the couple eventually had two sons and two daughters. While remaining active in the theater in the 1950s with such plays as the Western drama *The Chase* (1952), Foote began writing for the new popular medium of television. While the basic technology behind television was developed in the late 1920s and 1930s, it was not until the early 1950s that televisions (black and white only) were readily available and affordable on the mass market, or that networks developed programming for the new medium. Many popular early shows on these networks were plays and dramatic works, and it was there that Foote found his niche.

Acclaimed Writing for Television During this decade, Foote produced a number of highly regarded television dramas—both original scripts and adaptations from his stage plays—for such shows as *Kraft Playhouse* and *Playhouse 90*. One popular original script was *The Trip to Bountiful* (1953), which Foote originally wrote for television, later adapted for Broadway, and eventually reworked into an acclaimed screenplay. The story of *Bountiful* focuses on an elderly woman who escapes the cramped Houston apartment that she shares with her contentious daughter-in-law and unsupportive son. She then journeys to her hometown, hoping to relive her peaceful past. Though she finds Bountiful deserted, she enjoys several blissful reveries before being retrieved by her son and his wife. Foote occasionally adapted the work of other Southern writers for television as well, including a highly regarded adaptation of William Faulkner's *Old Man* in 1959.

During the 1950s, Foote also wrote his only novel, *The Chase* (1956). It was based on his 1952 play. He also began writing screenplays. His first script was an adaptation of a minor Southern novel, Clinton Seeley's *Storm Fear* (1956). This film was indifferently received by both the critics and the public. However, his next screenplay, *To Kill a Mockingbird* (1962), was greeted enthusiastically by both critics and moviegoers. Foote won an Academy Award for his adaptation of Harper Lee's Pulitzer Prize-winning novel. Following the success of *Mockingbird*, Foote wrote such screenplays as *Baby, the Rain Must Fall* (1964), *Hurry Sundown* (1967), and *Tomorrow* (1972).

Semi-Retirement, then Academy Award After *Tomorrow*, Foote did not write another screenplay for over a decade. He withdrew into semi-retirement and lived on a farm in New Hampshire with his family during the 1970s. Foote did turn his attention to television again for a time. Among his notable projects in this period were two plays for public television, including adaptations of a story by Flannery O'Connor, *The Displaced Person* (1977) and a story by Faulkner, *Barn Burning* (1980).

Foote then won his second Academy Award for his original screenplay *Tender Mercies* (1983). The story focuses on a famous country singer who succumbs to alcoholism and loses his career and marriage. Eventually, he finds solace with a young widow and her son in a Texas roadside motel. Foote wrote the script at the request of actor Robert Duvall, who had starred in *Tomorrow*. Foote was also nominated for an Academy Award for an adaptation of his teleplay *The Trip to Bountiful*, released in 1985.

A Dramatic Cycle Even before his successful return to the screen, Foote had begun work on a nine-part dramatic cycle called *The Orphan's Home*, which was based on the life of his parents and their families in the early twentieth century. The cycle, which includes the televised productions *1918* (1984), *On Valentine's Day* (1985), and *Convicts* (1991), follows several generations of the Robedeaux family. It depicts their hardships amidst the decline of the plantation aristocracy in southern Texas. Foote also reworked material from *The Orphan's Home* into the television miniseries *Story of a Marriage* (1987).

LITERARY AND HISTORICAL CONTEMPORARIES

Horton Foote's famous contemporaries include:

Carson McCullers (1917–1967): This American writer is identified with the Southern literary tradition. Among her best-known works are the novel *The Heart Is a Lonely Hunter* (1940) and the novella *The Ballad of the Sad Café* (1943).

Tennessee Williams (1911–1983): This American playwright is considered one of the greatest dramatists of the second half of the twentieth century. His plays include *The Glass Menagerie* (1944).

Margaret Mitchell (1900–1949): This American writer only published one novel, *Gone with the Wind* (1936). Set in the Civil War-era South, it won the Pulitzer Prize in 1937 and was later adapted into a popular film.

Robert Duvall (1931–): This American actor has appeared in hundreds of television and film roles. Among his memorable roles was the lead in Foote's *Tender Mercies* and Colonel Kilgore in *Apocalypse Now* (1979).

George H. W. Bush (1924–): This American businessman and politician worked in the oil business in Texas before being elected vice president in 1980 and president in 1988. He is also the father of President George W. Bush, elected president in 2000 and 2004.

Additionally in this time period, he wrote two dramas, *The Road to the Graveyard* (1985) and *Blind Date* (1986), both of which focused on the outmoded sexual conventions of two rural Texas communities. His *Dividing the Estate* (1989) is set in Harrison in 1987, and focuses on a relatively wealthy, aging matriarch and the family members who want her money. As reflected in the play, Americans of the late 1980s were dealing with an economic collapse in which such Texas industries as farming and oil struggled to survive. Businesses in Houston went bankrupt on a regular basis, and banks failed in numbers not seen since the Great Depression.

Continued to Write Late in Life Foote continued to write a number of original plays in the 1990s and early 2000s. These plays were sometimes directed by his daughter Daisy. He was the playwright-in-residence for New York's Signature Theatre Company for a time beginning in the mid-1990s. In 1995, his play *The Young Man from Atlanta* won the Pulitzer Prize for drama. Set in the 1950s, it follows the struggles of Will and Lily Dale Kidder as they seek to reconcile themselves with their son's death, a possible suicide. Foote followed *Atlanta* with *The Last of the Thortons* (2000). It is set in a nursing home where the residents and their visitors are from the same small town in Texas. They review their lives both past and present with varying degrees of resignation. Other plays of this time period include *The Last of the Thortons* (2000) and *The Day Emily Married* (2004).

Foote also wrote two autobiographies, *Farewell: A Memoir of a Texas Childhood* (1999) and *Beginnings: A Memoir* (2001). Awarded the National Medal of the Arts in 2000, Foote died in March 2009.

Works in Literary Context

In much of his works, Foote focuses on dramas that feature small town or rural settings and stories written in a lean style. He stresses the subtle and the intimate in his characters and plotting. His rural Texas dramas in particular reveal the fundamentals and universals of the human condition. While Foote may be better known for his screenplays, including *To Kill a Mockingbird* and *Tender Mercies*, it is on the stage where his artistry most frequently and most clearly manifests itself. Foote has become known for works that pierce to the core of human relationships from the cradle to the nursing home. In his writing, Foote has been influenced greatly by his hometown of Wharton, Texas, and its residents.

Realism Much of Foote's drama treats the common man and woman realistically in disturbing but strangely comforting stories. The pathos that ordinary people undergo, the nobility of the neglected and the forgotten, the profound humor in unsuspected houses and families, the suffering around every corner, the substantiality of what is taken for granted, the high stakes wagered in backstairs games: these constitute his subjects. Foote's realism pertains to the times and places he has both lived in and imagined, and his ear for speech is true and his characters recognizable and individualized. For example, the plays that make up the *Orphans' Home* cycle offer readers aspects of life itself. Similarly, the elderly widow at the center of *The Trip to Bountiful* lives a life and undergoes a journey that is entirely realistic, from her difficult relationship with her son and daughter-in-law to finding her hometown abandoned. *The Trip to Bountiful* reveals the elusiveness of the past while it reflects realistically on time, memory, death, and rebirth.

Focus on Middle Class For Foote, common, middle-class life is full of quiet terror and mystery. His works sometimes seem bland to some critics and readers because he has chosen to work within what amounts to formal constraints. He confines his dialogue to the probable iterations of small-town Southerners. Yet, as Foote has repeatedly demonstrated, these ordinary lives contain much passion. For example, *1918* is set in Harrison during the waning days of World War I and in the midst of a deadly influenza epidemic. Most of Foote's characters believe the war is the more compelling crisis, while one neighbor after another dies from the flu. Gradually, it becomes obvious that the war, despite its global significance, serves Harrison as a mere diversion from the much deadlier, more inexplicable crisis moving silently through town. Among the points the play makes is that extremes of experience—including horror, tragedy, courage, and redemptive love—can be found in middle-class homes and middle-class lives. Similarly, *The Young Man from Atlanta* concerns the lives of ordinary Texans living in Harrison in the 1950s who must deal with their son's death, probably by suicide, as well as his implied homosexuality.

Works in Critical Context

Although some critics fault Foote for unoriginal thematic concerns and antiquated dramatic techniques, many applaud his deliberate avoidance of melodrama and recognize the intelligence, compassion, and humor in his writing. Both his early plays and television work were treated kindly by critics who found them both artful and realistic. With the exception of *Hurry Sundown* (1966), which received scathing reviews, Foote has been lauded for his screenplays as well, especially his adaptation of *To Kill a Mockingbird* and his original script for *Tender Mercies*. Overall, critics have found Foote's ability to convey much about his characters and their lives and languages in a minimalist style highly appealing.

Tender Mercies Critics and audiences alike lauded Foote's script for this Academy Award–winning film. True to Foote's enduring, subtle style, "the excitement of *Tender Mercies* lies below the surface," wrote David Sterritt in the *Saturday Evening Post*. "It's not the quick change of fast action, the flashy performances or the eye-zapping cuts. Rather it's something much more rare—the thrill of watching characters grow, personalities deepen, relationships ripen and mature." Vincent Canby of the *New York Times* commented that "Foote's screenplay ... doesn't overexplain or overanalyze. It has a rare appreciation for understatement, which is the style of its characters if not of the actual narratives." Canby called Foote's *Tender Mercies* "the best thing he's ever done for films."

The Orphans' Home Critical response to Foote's ambitious series was divided between opponents and proponents of Foote's typically subdued style. Writing in the *National Review*, Chilton Williamson, Jr., thought Foote "trivializes life into a banal serenity," while Canby argued that Foote's characters, "being so resolutely ordinary, become particular." In the *New York Times*, Canby called *1918* a "writer's movie.... One that, for better or worse, pays no attention to the demands for pacing and narrative emphasis that any commercially oriented Hollywood producer would have insisted on." Canby contended that "The very flatness of its dramatic line is its dramatic point." Author Reynolds Price is quoted in *Christian Century* as saying that the *The Orphans' Home* cycle "will take its rightful place near the center of our largest American dramatic treatments."

Responses to Literature

1. Read the novella *Old Man* (1939) by William Faulkner, then the television script of Foote's adap-

COMMON HUMAN EXPERIENCE

Many of Foote's works are set in various communities in Texas. Here are some other works that are set in and reveal an aspect of the Lone Star state:

Terms of Endearment (1975), a novel by Larry McMurtry. This novel is set in Houston, Texas, and focuses on the life of Aurora Greenway and her relationship with her daughter, Emma Horton.

Hud (1963), a film directed by Martin Ritt. Based on a novel by McMurtry, this film stars Paul Newman as the charming but selfish and destructive son of a cattle rancher in Texas.

Red River (1948), a film directed by Howard Hawks. This complex western stars John Wayne and Montgomery Clift and focuses on a difficult cattle drive through Texas in the mid-nineteenth century.

The Diezmo (2005), a novel by Rick Bass. This novel is loosely based on the Mier Expedition, chronicling the experiences of teenager James Alexander, who joined the militia ordered by Sam Houston to patrol the border with Mexico in 1842.

tation. In an essay, compare and contrast the original with the adaptation.

2. In a small group, watch the film version of *To Kill a Mockingbird*, then discuss why you believe the adaptation was a success. Do you think Harper Lee's novel had more power than the film or vice versa? What elements of a film are beyond the writer's control?

3. Create a presentation involving Foote's original plays that feature Harrison, Texas, as a setting. How does the setting work across these plays? How does Harrison and its citizens relate to Foote's home of Wharton, Texas, and the people in his life?

4. Research the author Katherine Anne Porter and read several of her works. Some critics have suggested that Foote's writings have much in common stylistically with Porter's. In an essay, present an argument in which you either agree or disagree with this assessment, using examples from the authors' work to support your argument.

BIBLIOGRAPHY

Books

Briley, Rebecca Luttrell. *You Can Go Home Again: The Focus on the Family in the Works of Horton Foote*. New York: Peter Lang, 1993.

Porter, Laurin. *Orphans' Home: The Voice and Vision of Horton Foote*. Baton Rouge: Louisiana State University Press, 2003.

Watson, Charles S. *Horton Foote: A Literary Biography*. Austin: University of Texas Press, 2003.

Periodicals

Canby, Vincent. "The Screen: Texas, Vintage *1918*, directed by Ken Harrison." *New York Times* (April 26, 1985).

———. "Film View: *Tender Mercies* Stands Out in a Fine Off-Season Crop." *New York Times* (March 13, 1983): sec. 2, p. 21.

Sterritt, David. Review of *Tender Mercies*. *Saturday Evening Post* (October 1983).

Wall, James M. "Home, Family, Religion." *Christian Century* (February 19, 1997): 179.

Williamson, Chilton Jr. *National Review* (June 14, 1985; June 6, 1986).

✸ Shelby Foote

Shelby Foote   *Frederick M. Brown / Getty Images*

BORN: *1916, Greenville, Mississippi*

DIED: *2005, Memphis, Tennessee*

NATIONALITY: *American*

GENRE: *Fiction, nonfiction*

MAJOR WORKS:

Follow Me Down (1950)

Shiloh (1952)

The Civil War: A Narrative (1958–1973)

September, September (1978)

Overview

Historian and fiction writer Shelby Foote is highly regarded for both his expansive, three-volume historical work *The Civil War: A Narrative* (1958–1973) and for his novels and short stories concerning the heritage of the American South. Although frequently considered a regional writer whose works evoke the traditions and the consciousness of the American South, Foote has been praised for the universality of his vivid settings and characterizations.

Works in Biographical and Historical Context

Childhood Shaped by Loss and the Civil War   Born in Greenville, Mississippi, on November 17, 1916, Foote was the son of Shelby Dade and Lillian (Rosenstock) Foote. His father was a business executive with Armour and Company, and his father's family had been distinguished citizens of Mississippi for generations. As a young boy, Foote moved frequently throughout the region with his parents because of his father's job. After his father died suddenly of septicemia in the early 1920s, Foote

returned with his mother to live in Greenville, where she worked as a legal secretary.

During his childhood, Foote met the writer William Alexander Percy, and became close friends with Walker Percy, his nephew and ward. He learned much about books and learning from William Percy, and became fascinated with the American Civil War early in life. Indeed, Greenville, like the rest of the South, continued to be shaped in the present by the war. The South's lost-cause myth had memorialized war into a romantic way of life.

Beginning a Career   Foote spent his teenage years and early adulthood living through the Great Depression. After the stock market crash of October 1929, millions of Americans lost their savings, could not find jobs, and were hard pressed to survive. The Great Depression lasted for the whole of the 1930s, though conditions for some improved because of President Franklin Roosevelt's New Deal programs that, for example, provided temporary jobs for millions through public works programs.

Foote was the editor of his high school newspaper during the early 1930s, but he dedicated his time to making his principal's life difficult. Foote later claimed the principal retaliated by urging the University of North Carolina to reject his application. However, the Great Depression was in full force and there were fewer students able to afford a college education, so the school ultimately relented.

In 1935, Foote entered the University of North Carolina, where he wrote his first stories for the school's literary journal, *Carolina Magazine*. He spent most of his time at Carolina focusing on English and history courses, but he ignored classes, such as mathematics, that bored him. Foote dropped out of college in 1937 to write his first novel. While he completed the book, it was rejected by publishers, in part for being too derivative of James Joyce.

Military Service in World War II Foote joined the Mississippi National Guard in 1939. When his unit was mobilized the following year, he became a sergeant in the U.S. Army and was sent to Northern Ireland. He remained in the service for much of World War II.

After leaving his military base without permission to meet his Irish girlfriend in Belfast, Foote was court-martialed and discharged from the army in 1944. That year, he married that girlfriend, Tess Lavery. This was the first of his several marriages. Upon his discharge, Foote went back to the United States and worked briefly as a reporter for the Associated Press in New York City. In 1945, he enlisted in the Marine Corps. Foote served in the Marines only a few months as World War II reached its conclusion. Following his release from the service later in 1945, he returned to the South where he continued to write while holding such jobs as radio station copy writer, construction worker, and reporter for the *Delta-Times Democrat*. In 1946, Foote published his first short story in a professional publication. Drawing upon the draft of his unpublished novel, "Flood Burial" appeared in the *Saturday Evening Post*.

Published First Novels The sale of the story compelled Foote to work on his novel, and he soon found success. His first three novels—*Tournament* (1949), *Follow Me Down* (1951), and *Love in a Dry Season* (1951)—were linked to portray a small area of Mississippi, the fictional Jordan County and its fictional community of Bristol, which was modeled on Foote's hometown. *Tournament* was created out of portions of his unfinished first novel, and focused on the transformation of Hugh Bart from successful landowner to destitute gambler following the sale of his plantation—a situation that mirrored the experiences of Foote's own grandfather. *Follow Me Down* was based on an actual murder trial and is often considered his best novel. *Love in a Dry Season* was set in the 1920s to World War II-era South, and focused on the area's changing fortunes in that time period.

Recognized as a rising young novelist, Foote then turned to historical fiction with *Shiloh* (1952). This novel focuses on a major and especially bloody Civil War battle, and was his first popular success. The battle was recreated through monologues of six soldiers from both of the contending armies. Foote's next work, *Jordan County: A Landscape in Narrative* (1954) presents the same fictional area of Mississippi as his first three novels in seven connected short stories and novellas. That same year, he was asked to write a brief history of the Civil War, a task that

LITERARY AND HISTORICAL CONTEMPORARIES

Foote's famous contemporaries include:

James Joyce (1882–1941): This Irish author was a leading figure in modernist literature. His novels include *The Portrait of the Artist as a Young Man* (1916).

Franklin Delano Roosevelt (1882–1945): The thirty-second president of the United States, Roosevelt was elected to four terms in office and led the country through the Great Depression and most of World War II.

Ken Burns (1953–): This American documentarian has produced numerous documentaries, primarily for PBS, including *Baseball* (1994) and *Unforgivable Blackness* (2005).

Thomas Wolfe (1900–1938): This American author wrote highly autobiographical novels noted for their energy, emotion and rhetorical language. Among his best-known works is *Look Homeward, Angel* (1929).

Harper Lee (1926–): This American author was raised in the South and explored racial tensions in her Pulitzer Prize–winning novel, *To Kill a Mockingbird* (1960).

ultimately resulted in his best-known work. By this time, Foote had left Greenville to live in Memphis, Tennessee.

Decades Spent on The Civil War: A Narrative In the late 1950s, Foote began writing *The Civil War: A Narrative*, the work that earned him the most amount of critical praise. A nonfiction history of the Civil War, the three volumes that form *The Civil War: A Narrative* include: *Fort Sumpter to Perryville* (1958), *Fredericksburg to Meridian* (1963), and *Red River to Appomattox* (1973). While many critics have considered the series a masterpiece, some academics criticized the books for their lack of footnotes and other scholarly conventions.

To produce the first two volumes, Foote wrote eight hours a day, seven days a week. Following the publication of the first two volumes, he accepted a series of temporary appointments at various foundations, colleges, and universities. For example, he was a Ford Foundation fellow in 1963 and 1964, and was a lecturer at the University of Virginia in 1963. At the same time, Foote was the playwright in residence at the Arena Theater in Washington, D.C., where he adapted his novel *Jordan County* for the stage. It was produced in 1964. From 1966 to 1967, he was writer-in-residence at the University of Memphis, then held the same position at Hollins College in 1968.

Affected by the Civil Rights Movement Despite the critical acclaim and professional recognition he received, Foote found the 1960s challenging. The civil rights movement reached its apex as African Americans fought for

COMMON HUMAN EXPERIENCE

In *September, September*, Foote touches on the black experience in the United States. Here are other novels that tackle this perspective:

Go Tell It on the Mountain (1953), a novel by James Baldwin. This book traces the life of John Grimes from the age of fourteen, including his hatred of white people and his becoming a Baptist.

1959: A Novel (1992), a novel by Thulani Davis. This book explores the impact of the civil rights movement through the eyes of a twelve-year-old girl living in Virginia.

Invisible Man (1952), a novel by Ralph Ellison. This classic work of literature details the story of a black man growing up in the white world of the 1940s.

A Lesson Before Dying (1993), a novel by Ernest J. Gaines. Set in Louisiana in the 1940s, Jefferson, a poor, young African American, is at the wrong place at the wrong time and is charged with murder after a robbery in which a white man is killed.

their basic rights and against segregation, especially in the South. While Foote supported the display of Confederate symbols, which brought charges of his advocacy of white supremacy, his views on race relations were progressive as he supported full racial integration. Yet he dismissed many advocates of civil rights, especially northern white activists and agitators who came to the South to affect change but knew nothing of Southern history or the intricate balance of Southern race relations. While the race tumult of the 1960s intensified, Foote toiled to complete the last volume of *The Civil War*, which took longer to complete than the other two volumes combined.

Returning to fiction in the late 1970s, Foote published the novel *September, September* (1978), about a kidnapping and ransom of an African American boy, the grandson of a wealthy black man, by three white men in Memphis. Using such historical events as the racial-integration crisis in Little Rock, Arkansas, and the launching of Sputnik in 1957 as a backdrop for his story, Foote relates factual events of the period to his characters' racial attitudes, creating a microcosm of American society in the 1950s. In 1981, Foote published another nonfiction work, *The Novelist's View of History*.

Greater Fame   While Foote was somewhat well known by the late 1980s, he gained a much wider audience when he appeared as a narrator and commentator in Ken Burns's lauded eleven-hour television documentary, *The Civil War* (1990), which aired on PBS. Over 40 million people saw Foote act as one of the conducting spirits and guides of each episode, making him a public speaker

much in demand. In the 1990s, Foote also produced new nonfiction works, including another Civil War book, *Stars in Their Courses: The Gettysburg Campaign* (1994), which provided an in-depth analysis of that dramatic battle. In addition, Foote wrote two novels, *Child by Fever* (1995) and *Ride Out* (1996). He also wrote introductions to several collections of short stories by Anton Chekhov, and edited one, Chekhov's *Longer Stories from the Last Decade* (1999). The recipient of numerous accolades in the last years of his life, Foote died on June 27, 2005, in Memphis, Tennessee, at the age of eighty-eight.

Works in Literary Context

While Foote is primarily known for his *The Civil War: A Narrative* trilogy, his interest in novel writing informed and drove his nonfiction works. Foote characterized himself as a novelist, and his ability as a storyteller enabled him to write compelling history. Though his depiction of the conflict in *The Civil War* is generally considered balanced, his novels are often concerned with Southern themes, including racial tensions and the various effects of the war on Southerners. To fully explore the South, Foote incorporated various literary techniques, including multiple points of view and the creation of a fictional region within the South in which a number of his stories were placed. As a writer, Foote was greatly influenced by such authors as his childhood mentor William Alexander Percy, as well as Tacitus, Stendhal, Leo Tolstoy, and Marcel Proust.

Multiple Points of View   In several of Foote's novels, he incorporates multiple points of view to tell his story. Such a technique adds depth to the plot and greater understanding of the characters and their motivations. The first novel by Foote to incorporate this technique was *Follow Me Down*. The novel focuses on the story of a fanatically religious Mississippi farmer who murders a teenage girl for whom he has abandoned his wife and family. The use of multiple points of view allows eight characters—including the protagonist and minor characters—to comment in a limited first-person viewpoint on their reactions to the murder. A work of historical fiction, *Shiloh* recreates the well-known Civil War battle through the eyes of six soldiers from both sides. These narrators describe different aspects of the three-day confrontation. By adroit maneuvering, Foote brings the respective narratives into contact with each other.

Fictional Locales   Many of Foote's novels as well as his collection *Jordan County: A Landscape in Narrative* are focused around a fictional locale. This microcosm is centered on the delta country in Lake Jordan. This fictive area includes two counties (Issawamba, Jordan), the Solitaire Plantation, and the town of Bristol on the Mississippi River. Through cross reference, Foote links the episodes from one novel and story to another. For example, the novella *Pillar of Fire* in *Jordan County* relates the story of

Isaac Jameson, the founder of the Solitaire Plantation and a patriarch of the delta. *Tournament* then supplies information about the man, Hugh Bart, who brought Solitaire back from devastation by war and reconstruction. Similar ties can be found in all the books centered around this area.

Works in Critical Context

Foote's nonfiction *The Civil War: A Narrative* has been lauded by many critics as one of the most impressive studies of the conflict ever written, While some detractors have questioned the intellectual merit of the work, other commentators have focused on the comprehensiveness of his chronicle. While not as frequently studied by American critics as his historical work, Foote's fiction is nevertheless praised as an impressive analysis of the American South. French critics in particular have written numerous studies of his fiction, and have compared the interlocking settings and characters in his fictional world of Jordan County to those of William Faulkner's Yoknapatawpha County.

The Civil War: A Narrative Generally, *The Civil War* is noted for its balanced treatment of all fronts of the American Civil War: northern, southern, eastern, and western. For critics, Foote's mastery of such features as character, plot, setting, and narrative voice—traits of fiction not traditionally integrated into historical writing—distinguish *The Civil War* as a narrative history. Some detractors have derided *The Civil War* for ignoring important political, social, and economic factors. In the *New York Times Book Review*, Nash K. Burger praised *The Civil War* as "a remarkable achievement, prodigiously researched, vigorous, detailed, absorbing." Similarly, M. E. Bradford of the *National Review* noted, "There is, of course, a majesty inherent in the subject." Later in the review, Bradford wrote that "the credit for recovering such majesty to the attention of our skeptical and unheroic age will hereafter ... belong to Mr. Foote."

Shiloh Critics consider *Shiloh* a complex depiction of the multitudinous aspects of the Civil War. Commentators have also recognized Foote's ability to create memorable characterizations of both fictional and historical figures of the battle. Of this book, published on the ninetieth anniversary of the battle, Thomas H. Landess wrote in the *Mississippi Quarterly* that the novel "is unique as a twentieth century chronicle of war," and one that "pushes the action of the novel towards the level of pure epic."

Responses to Literature

1. Read both Foote's *Shiloh* and Stephen Crane's *The Red Badge of Courage* (1895). Both books are graphic fictional treatments of modern warfare. In a small group, discuss how the books treat the topic. Is one book more effective than the other?

2. Read at least one volume of *The Civil War: A Narrative* and either Homer's *Iliad* (c. eighth century B.C.E.) or part of Marcel Proust's *Remembrance of Things Past* (1913–1927). Foote patterned his work on both of these books, hoping to match their epic significance. In a paper, explain several ways in which Foote achieved this goal.

3. Watch several episodes of *The Civil War* (1990), the documentary by Ken Burns. In an essay, explore how Foote's appearances in the documentary relate to or illustrate themes in his own historical trilogy of the war.

4. Foote admitted that the structure of *Follow Me Down* owes much to the Robert Browning epic narrative poem *The Ring and the Book* (1868–1869). Create a presentation in which you demonstrate how you believe Browning's poetic structure affected Foote's structural choices in the novel.

BIBLIOGRAPHY

Books

Chapman, C. Stuart. *Shelby Foote: A Writer's Life.* Jackson, Miss.: University Press of Mississippi, 2003.

Phillips, Robert L., Jr. *Shelby Foote: Novelist and Historian.* Jackson: University Press of Mississippi, 1992.

Tolson, Jay. *The Correspondence of Shelby Foote and Walker Percy.* Jackson, Miss.: Center for Documentary Studies, 1997.

Periodicals

Bradford, M. E. Review of *The Civil War. National Review* (February 14, 1975).

Burger, Nash K. Review of *The Civil War. New York Times Book Review* (March 6, 1975).

Landess, Thomas H. "Southern History and Manhood: Major Themes in the Works of Shelby Foote." *Mississippi Quarterly* (Fall 1971): 321–347.

Richard Ford

BORN: *1944, in Jackson, Mississippi*

NATIONALITY: *American*

GENRE: *Fiction*

MAJOR WORKS:
The Sportswriter (1986)
Rock Springs (1987)
Independence Day (1995)

Overview

Considered one of the finest fiction writers of his generation, Richard Ford is best known for his novel *The Sportswriter* (1986) and its sequel *Independence Day* (1995). He is often celebrated for his portrayal of everyday

Richard Ford   *Ford, Richard, photograph. © Jerry Bauer. Reproduced by permission.*

contemporary American life. While troubled and deeply flawed, Ford's characters are ultimately both sympathetic and optimistic. Ford has been compared to Ernest Hemingway for his laconic, masculine prose, to Walker Percy as a Southern writer, and to Raymond Carver for his minimalism and style of "dirty realism."

Works in Biographical and Historical Context

Itinerant Childhood Born February 16, 1944, in Jackson, Mississippi, he was the son of Parker Carrol and Edna (Aiken) Ford. As Ford grew up, he lived directly across the street from celebrated Southern writer Eudora Welty. His father was a traveling salesman, and Ford and his mother accompanied his father on many road trips. When not taken on these trips with his parents, Ford often stayed with his maternal grandparents at a hotel they owned in Little Rock, Arkansas. This sense of itinerancy influenced Ford's fiction in the creation of characters who are psychologically and culturally, as well as geographically, rootless.

When Ford was sixteen years old, his father died of a heart attack. This crisis compelled Ford to develop a strong sense of personal responsibility for his life. This sense of importance of accepting accountability for one's

life choices also became a central theme of Ford's fiction. After completing high school, Ford entered Michigan State University where he earned a B.A. in literature in 1966. Ford then briefly enrolled in law school at Washington University in St. Louis, Missouri, but decided to pursue a writing career instead. In 1968, Ford married Kristina Hensley, a research professor, whom he credited as a major influence on his development as a writer. By this time, Ford was studying creative writing at the University of California at Irvine, earning an M.F.A. in 1970. There, he studied with writers such as E. L. Doctorow and Oakley Hall.

The United States was involved in armed conflict in Vietnam, later known as the Vietnam War, beginning in 1964. The United States supported the more democratic South Vietnamese government, and fought against the Communist party of North Vietnam. By the early 1970s, it was clear the United States could not win the war, and pulled out of the country in the mid-1970s. Ford remained in college during much of the conflict, and unlike hundreds of thousands of other American men, did not serve in Vietnam. However, he later touched on the effects of the war and those who fought it in *The Ultimate Good Luck* (1981), whose main character was a Vietnam veteran.

Published First Novel After completing his M.F.A., Ford produced a number of early stories, many of which were rejected by literary magazines. He also spent six years working on what became his first novel. In addition, Ford was employed at various universities in the 1970s. From 1974 to 1976, Ford was a lecturer in creative writing at the University of Michigan. In 1976, Ford finally published his first novel, *A Piece of My Heart*, which concerned two very different men who cross paths during one week of an annual turkey-hunting season on an island in the Mississippi Delta. The novel was praised for its evocation of the South and the people who lived there. At the time the book was published, there was nationwide interest in the South as Democrat Jimmy Carter, a peanut farmer, who had served one term as Georgia's governor, was elected president in 1976. He was elected partly because he was regarded as an outsider at a time when voter discontent with Washington and politics was quite high.

In the late 1970s, Ford returned to academia as an assistant professor of English at Williams College from 1978 to 1979, then taught creative writing at Princeton from 1979 to 1980. Ford published his second novel in 1981, the crime thriller *The Ultimate Good Luck*. In the novel, he explores the life of an American living in Mexico, Vietnam War veteran Harry Quinn. Quinn becomes drawn reluctantly into violence and murder as he tries to get his ex-lover's drug-trafficking brother out of jail. *The Ultimate Good Luck* was poorly received by critics, and Ford took a break from fiction writing for a time. He began contributing articles to a sports magazine, *Inside Sports*. After the magazine folded, his wife suggested that he write a novel about a man who is happy. These experiences led to his best-received work.

Creating Frank Bascombe *The Sportswriter* (1986) focuses on Frank Bascombe, an alienated, middle-aged sportswriter reflecting on his life over an Easter weekend after his nine-year-old son has died and his marriage has collapsed. The first-person narrative shows Frank reflecting on why he gave up after writing fiction for a secure living writing about sports, and clearly reflects many of Ford's own life experiences. Lauded by many critics when it was published, the novel was named one of the five best books of 1986 by *Time* magazine. Firmly established as a critically acclaimed, best-selling author, Ford focused primarily on writing and publishing fiction.

In 1987, Ford published his first book of short stories, *Rock Springs*. The stories focus on lonely, damaged people, and are primarily set in Montana. Ford's next novel, the brief *Wildlife* (1990), features forty-six-year-old Joe Brison looking back to three days in his life when he was sixteen years old. Living in rural Montana in 1960, he is witness to the breakup and end of his parents' marriage. Working in a different genre, Ford wrote a screenplay, *Bright Angel*, in 1991. It was based on two of his short stories, "Children" and "Great Falls."

A Pulitzer Prize After serving as an instructor at Harvard University in 1994, Ford returned to the character of Frank Bascombe in his next novel *Independence Day* (1995). Set in 1988, the protagonist has lost his job and his wife has moved with their two surviving children to Connecticut with her new husband, but he tries to find a new life working in real estate sales. A Fourth of July weekend spent trying to reconnect with his surviving, but troubled, son at various sport halls of fame forces him to take stock of life and the nature of independence in people's lives. *Independence Day* marked the first time an author received both the Pulitzer Prize and the PEN/Faulkner Award for the same novel.

Next, Ford published a collection of novellas, *Women with Men: Three Stories* (1997). In the late 1990s, he also edited several collections of other people's writing, including *Essential Tales of Chekhov* (1998). In addition, Ford taught at Northwestern University for a year from 1997 to 1998.

Returning to Frank In 2001, Ford published another collection of his own fiction, *A Multitude of Sins*, which evoked a mixed reaction from critics. Many of the stories focus on characters engaged in extramarital affairs. In 2006, Ford published his third novel featuring Frank Bascombe, *The Lay of the Land*. Set in 2000, the novel is set between the presidential election and the final decision by the U.S. Supreme Court which resulted in George W. Bush's winning the presidency. The presidential election between Bush and his opponent, Al Gore, was so close in November 2000 that there was no clear-cut winner for five weeks. The main controversy was centered on Florida where the state's electoral votes were in dispute and the winner would be given the presidency. Though the ballots

started to be recounted there, the Supreme Court ended attempts by Gore to have the Florida votes recounted by people and not machines. Bush was given the presidency.

The Lay of the Land was intended to be the final installment of the saga. Frank is fifty-five years old, still selling real estate, suffering from a prostate tumor, being cared for by daughter Clarissa, and dealing with the loss of his second wife, Sally, who discovered her previous husband is not dead as originally believed. Set over a Thanksgiving Day weekend, Frank deals with family matters by inviting his first wife and son for dinner. Critics were somewhat disappointed by the book, as comedy had been replaced by tragedy, but many appreciated the consistent voice Ford gave Frank over the three books. Ford continues to write from his home in East Boothbay, Maine, where he lives with his wife.

Works in Literary Context

In Ford's fiction, he focuses on characters who never evade the realities that were attendant upon their own choices and their own successes and failures. He creates many characters who wander and wonder widely, seeking some connection with others but often experiencing their most vivid moments of awareness in utter solitude. In

---

LITERARY AND HISTORICAL CONTEMPORARIES

Richard Ford's famous contemporaries include:

George W. Bush (1946–): The forty-third president of the United States, Bush was in office during the September 11, 2001, terrorist attacks on New York City and Washington.

Tom Brokaw (1940–): A highly respected American television journalist, Brokaw was the longtime host of the *NBC Nightly News*. He is also an author, writing such books as *The Greatest Generation* (1998).

Carson McCullers (1917–1967): This American writer is a leading author in the Southern literary tradition. Her works include the novels *Reflections in a Golden Eye* (1941) and *The Member of the Wedding* (1946).

Rick Reilly (1958–): This well-respected American sportswriter won at least ten National Sportswriter of the Year awards. He spent much of his career with *Sports Illustrated*, and wrote such sports-related books as *Who's Your Caddy?*; *Lopping for the Great, Near Great, and Reprobates of Golf* (2003).

Mitch Albom (1958–): A distinguished American sports journalist, Albom has been an award-winning writer for the *Detroit Free Press* for several decades. He also wrote such popular novels as *The Five People You Meet in Heaven* (2003).

COMMON HUMAN EXPERIENCE

Ford's novels featuring Frank Bascombe focus on fractured relationships with his family, other people, and indeed, the greater world. Here are some other books that have a similar topic:

The Wonders of the Invisible World: Stories (1999), a short story collection by David Gates. These ten stories focus on people with broken relationships, including the Jewish woman at the heart of "Beating" who has had enough of her leftist husband.

The Death of the Heart (1938), a novel by Elizabeth Bowen. After a lifetime of isolation, a young woman struggles to find herself in society. Along the way, she finds love and confronts betrayal and suffering caused by relationships.

Marry Me: A Romance (1976), a novel by John Updike. In this novel, a couple is in love but they are already married to other people. Jerry wants his freedom, but does not want to give up his wife, while Sally is tormented with guilt over destroying Jerry's family and her own.

The Way People Run (1999), a short story collection by Christopher Tilghman. In this collection, the author explores the suffocation and emotional suppression of family life, including the deep emotional connections and disconnections in his characters' existence, including their inner lives.

settings as diverse as Mississippi, Montana, and Paris, Ford situates characters who struggle to come to terms with their pasts, presents, and futures. Ford's central thematic concerns include loneliness, alienation, male-female relationships, family life, yearning for human connection, and a sense of disappointment in the American dream. As an author, Ford was influenced by John Keats, his mentors at the University of California at Irvine, E. L. Doctorow and Oakley Hall, as well his experiences growing up as the son of a traveling salesman and living in the South. While some critics believe that Ford's writings display the influence of Faulkner and the Southern literary tradition, the author often rejects these ideas.

Lives in Transition In a number of Ford's short stories and novels, he focuses on settings and circumstances to explore people, and sometimes families, whose lives are in transition, often unexpectedly, as they experience profound changes. Ford shows how these changes take place and affect those involved during such times. In *Wildlife*, for example, Joe Brison describes what he witnessed at home when he was sixteen years old. In one weekend, he sees the dissolution of his family when his mother has an affair while his father is gone. The stories in *Rock Springs* mostly focus on characters in transit, moving from one town to another or one way of life to another. Several stories in *Women with Men* focus on the moment of change, including "Great Falls." In this story, a young man recounts watching his father put the barrel of a revolver under the chin of a man he has caught in bed with his wife. When the boy meets his mother the next day, he knows that his father will never let her come back and realizes that his life has turned suddenly. He also knows that he is left with puzzling questions to which he will never find answers.

Compact Time Ford often sets his novels over short, well-defined periods of time, allowing a full exploration of the effect of specific events on his characters. He focuses specifically on the moment when change and ruin begin. Sometimes this time is spent in contemplation, or it is merely a moment of change. *Wildlife*, for example, takes place over only three days when the marriage of Joe Brison's parents falls apart. Similarly Ford's best known novels *The Sportswriter* and its sequels *Independence Day* and *The Lay of the Land* each focus on a different holiday weekend in which Frank Bascombe reflects on his life and reveals much about his relationships with others, including his family. For example, *The Sportswriter* takes place over an Easter weekend during which Frank engages in contemplative reveries about marriage, sports, life in suburban New Jersey, and the art of storytelling.

Works in Critical Context

Ford has garnered widespread critical acclaim for his portraits of middle-class American life, especially in the way he has portrayed modern lives characterized by loneliness, alienation, and the yearning for connection. Reviewers have admired Ford's well-crafted prose, rich with descriptive detail and a strong sense of place. He has also been commended for a fresh perspective, skillful storytelling, effective use of a first-person narrative, and accurate rendering of American vernacular speech. A number of reviewers have criticized his portrayal of women, claiming that his perspective is essentially masculinist. Other critics have defended his representation of female characters, arguing that the women in his fictions are usually stronger and more self-assured than the men.

Wildlife Critics were divided over Ford's fourth novel, *Wildlife*. Jonathan Yardley, in the *Washington Post*, was not pleased with the way the characters smoothed "each other's passage through life with pearls of pop-psychological wisdom" or with the abundance of metaphors in the narrative. "Like a puppy with a slipper, Ford sinks his teeth into those metaphors, shakes them all over the place and refuses to let them go," Yardley also noted. Writing in the London *Times*, Victoria Glendinning commented that "there is something obsessional and over-tidy in the jigsaw neatness of his writing, his interlocking themes and images, his modest conclusions," but she allowed that the story is "beautifully made" and noted that Ford "has far more to teach Europeans about ordinary American life and the American psyche than have the flashier East Coast novelists." Toronto *Globe & Mail* critic Trevor Ferguson called it "a superb novel" and concluded, "[The novel] is also, like its characters and its vision of America, strangely contradictory—at once affirmative and self-limiting. Applaud or berate him ... Ford and his stylistic decisions deserve heated debate."

Independence Day In reviews of *Independence Day*, critics have praised Ford's ability to evoke sympathy among readers for a protagonist as common, unremarkable, and unheroic as Frank Bascombe. While some reviewers have dismissed the plot of *Independence Day* as sketchy and uninteresting, others have found in its plainness a metaphor for the quiet desperation of everyday life. Critics have also praised Ford as masterful in his use of descriptive detail in *Independence Day*, particularly in his depiction of the book's setting and his understanding of the real estate business. "With *Independence Day*," Michiko Kakutani observed, "Mr. Ford has written a worthy sequel to *The Sportswriter* and galvanized his reputation as one of his generation's most eloquent voices."

Responses to Literature

1. In reviews of *The Lay of the Land*, critics have compared Frank Bascombe to John Updike's recurring character Rabbit Angstrom, though Ford disagrees. In an essay, compare and contrast these characters and offer your opinion about what they mean for the authors.

2. The three novels featuring Frank Bascombe are each set over a holiday weekend in which intense emotional conflicts surface. Write your own short story set around such an event—be it holiday, birthday, or wedding—in which people often have expectations that are unmet.

3. In his writing, how does Ford depict the effects of the end of a marriage, an extramarital affair, or a divorce on the children involved? Pick a story in which Ford explores this topic, and describe how he handles this theme.

4. In a group, discuss how the concept of happiness plays out in the three novels featuring Frank Bascombe.

BIBLIOGRAPHY

Books

Guagliardo, Huey, ed. *Perspectives on Richard Ford*. Jackson: University Press of Mississippi, 2000.

Walker, Elinor Ann. *Richard Ford*. New York: Twayne, 2000.

Periodicals

Ferguson, Trevor. Review of *Wildlife*. *Globe & Mail* (July 7, 1990).

Glendinning, Victoria. Review of *Wildlife*. *London Times* (August 9, 1990).

Kakutani, Michiko. Review of *Independence Day*. *New York Times* (June 13, 1995): C17.

Yardley, Jonathan. Review of *Wildlife*. *Washington Post* (June 20, 1990).

⊛ Hannah Webster Foster

BORN: *1758, Salisbury, Massachusetts*

DIED: *1840, Montreal, Canada*

NATIONALITY: *American*

GENRE: *Fiction*

MAJOR WORKS:

The Coquette; or The History of Eliza Wharton (1797)

The Boarding School; Or Lessons of a Preceptress to her Pupils (1798)

Overview

One of the earliest American novelists, Hannah Webster Foster wrote two books of note. Her epistolary novel, *The Coquette; or The History of Eliza Wharton* (1797), was one of the first of its kind in America, and is considered perhaps the finest sentimental novel of the early national period. Foster's other novel, *The Boarding School; Or Lessons of a Preceptress to her Pupils* (1798), was one of the first fictional accounts of education in the United States. By the twentieth century, Foster was considered a major spokesperson for greater female liberty in early American writing because of the content and spirit of her two works.

Works in Biographical and Historical Context

Raised in Massachusetts Foster was born Hannah Webster on September 10, 1758, in Salisbury, Massachusetts. She was the daughter of Grant Webster, a merchant in Boston of some social standing, and his wife, Hannah Wainwright Webster. There is little of substance known about her childhood and education. Her mother died in 1762, and Foster was sent to a boarding school to receive her education. Also, as a girl and young woman, she was locally known for her cleverness and beauty.

By the early 1770s, Webster was living in Boston, and in the 1780s, she began publishing short political pieces in local newspapers. These articles attracted the attention of Reverend John Foster, a popular minister who was a graduate of Dartmouth College, lived in Brighton, Massachusetts, and was the pastor of the First Church there. The couple married in April 1785, and she moved into his

LITERARY AND HISTORICAL CONTEMPORARIES

Hannah Webster Foster's famous contemporaries include:

Susanna H. Rowson (1762–1824): This American novelist wrote the first best seller in the United States, *Charlotte Temple: A Tale of Truth* (1791).

Aaron Burr (1756–1836): This American lawyer, politician, and soldier served as the vice president of the United States under Thomas Jefferson.

Joel Barlow (1754–1812): This American poet and diplomat wrote the antimonarchical tract *The Conspiracy of Kings* (1792). He was a friend of Elizabeth Whitman and also believed to be a possible seducer of Whitman.

Mercy Otis Warren (1728–1814): This American author was the first significant woman historian. She wrote an eyewitness account of the American Revolution, *History of the Rise, Progress, and Termination of the American Revolution* (1805).

William Hill Brown (1765–1793): This American author wrote the first American novel, *The Power of Sympathy, or the Triumph of Nature Founded in Truth* (1789). It was published anonymously, and was a story of the seduction and ruin of a young woman.

parish. There, Foster became a leader in social and literary activities, and had six children with her husband between 1786 and 1796. Soon after her marriage and the birth of her first child, Foster also became an author.

The Coquette   In 1797, Foster published *The Coquette; or The History of Eliza Wharton*, one of the earliest epistolary novels—in which the story is told through a series of letters—in the United States. An immediate success and best seller, it was based on a well-known story of the time period about Elizabeth Whitman. This well-educated thirty-seven-year-old unmarried woman from a prominent Connecticut family died in childbirth at an inn in 1789. In the novel, Wharton had become pregnant by Sanford (based on Pierrepont Edwards), her lover and perhaps husband, if they did secretly marry as the novel hinted. John Foster was distantly related by marriage to Whitmans' father, and it is believed that Foster probably knew most of the facts and rumors about the Whitman case.

Foster offered a sympathetic take on Whitman's story, emphasizing how American society of the time period circumscribed women's lives. She also claimed that the novel's worth arose from its didactic or educational value—a popular justification for novels in the early republic—but it was also read for its details of seduction and betrayal. Some critics derided Foster for using her imagination and not adhering to the facts of the story,

including identifying Whitman's unknown seducer. Like other novels published in the new United States, *The Coquette* raised important questions about the nature of the new country, including the role of women and if their freedoms should be restricted. The American Revolution, which saw the United States form its own country after breaking away as colonies of Great Britain, and the nation-making that followed opened up avenues for women as they participated in debates over the shape of the new nation and women's role within it.

Question of Authorship   Because Foster's name was not on *The Coquette*, there was also some question of the author's true identity during her lifetime and in the decades after. It was merely signed "A Lady of Massachusetts" during its original printings as well as during its peak of popularity, from 1824 to 1828. Indeed, Foster's name did not appear on the novel until the 1866 edition. *The Coquette* remained popular throughout the nineteenth century.

Educating About Education   In 1798, Foster published her only other novel, *The Boarding School; Or Lessons of a Preceptress to her Pupils*. Also published anonymously, the work takes the form of a series of lectures to students from a preceptress (a female teacher), while presenting ideas about female education. The teacher, Mrs. Williams, educates at a very select boarding school where only seven students are admitted at a time. She lectures on such subjects as temper and manners, dress, politeness, reading, and filial and fraternal affection.

Foster counsels against reading novels—except those which teach moral improvement—and discourages romantic ideas about love and marriage. *The Boarding School* was not popular at the time, though the topic was. Many early American novels emphasized better education for young women as a way to empower them to make decisions that would lead them away from damnation and toward morality. Plot lines of novels in the time period often emphasized the idea that if women received adequate education, they would be able to guard themselves against the advances of immoral men.

Contributed to a Journal   While Foster primarily focused on her family after the publication of *The Boarding School* and did not write any other published novels, she did contribute anonymously to *The Monthly Anthology or Magazine of Polite Literature*, a Federalist journal. After Foster's husband died, she moved to Montreal, Canada, where two of her daughters—Elizabeth Lanesford Cushing and Harriet Vaughan Cheney—lived and wrote essays and magazine articles. She died on April 17, 1840, in Montreal, in the home of Elizabeth Cushing, the wife of Dr. Frederick Cushing. Foster was eighty-one years old.

Works in Literary Context

While both of her novels were considered sentimental, Foster was addressing common themes, including the plight of young women living in a conservative American society. She chronicled the changing values of the new country in *The Coquette* and *The Boarding School*, including those related to young women, their marriage prospects, and their sexuality. Foster also addressed some of the fundamental gender and political issues of the 1790s, especially in *The Coquette*. In addition, both novels were written not primarily as straightforward narratives but at least partially as epistolary novels.

Social Change   In both of her novels, Foster includes ideas about social changes that she believed would benefit women of all ages. *The Coquette* focuses on social change through the character of Eliza Wharton. Though the novel was considered sentimental fiction, Wharton is not a fainting, stereotypical sentimental heroine, but a rebel. She tries to define herself against the limitations society imposed upon late-eighteenth-century women, as she tried to remain true to her heart while remaining a respected member of the established social order. Forced to choose between two suitors—Sanford and Reverend Boyer—she essentially wants neither, and is later rejected by both. Her relationship with the married Sanford, when she is in her late thirties and a spinster, is an act of calculated self-destruction rather than coquetry. In *The Boarding School*, Foster advocates better female education. The novel also castigates the double sexual standard, insisting that a girl once seduced is not necessarily a "bad" woman and should not be ostracized by her society. Foster also insists that men be held much more accountable for their sexual behavior and transgressions and be made to share equally the burden of their illicit actions.

Epistolary Novels   Both of Foster's works can be considered examples of epistolary novels. An epistolary novel is told through the medium of letters written by one or more of the characters. In *The Coquette*, Foster uses the epistolary mode, a powerful means of characterization, creating personal levels of diction that vary among the characters who seem to be writing from their souls. Eliza Wharton's letters, for example, are especially revealing of her changes in mood and temper. Because the letters are written by multiple characters, her multiple-point-of-view technique allows the main correspondents to describe and comment on a single event from two or even three different angles. These partly overlapping accounts together form a double- or even triple-layered story. *The Boarding School* is a cross between an epistolary novel and a conduct book. It essentially lacks plot, but is a series of thinly disguised lectures on female conduct and virtue, followed by a series of letters gleaned from the correspondence between Mrs. Williams, the teacher, and some of her former students. The lectures are a series of moral vignettes on conventional conduct-book topics, while the letters attempt to create a narrative for the novel.

Works in Critical Context

While *The Boarding School* was not embraced when it was originally published, *The Coquette* was popular from

COMMON HUMAN EXPERIENCE

The Coquette is often considered an excellent example of an early epistolary novel. Here are some other significant epistolary novels of the eighteenth century:

> *Pamela* (1740), a novel by Samuel Richardson. This book is considered the original epistolary novel. It focuses on a the story of a servant girl's struggle against her master's attempts to seduce her.
> *Clarissa: Or the History of a Young Lady* (1747–1748), a novel by Samuel Richardson. Perhaps Richardson's best-known and most classic work, it chronicles the life of the titular character, a young woman who divorces herself from her family to avoid a marriage, but who ultimately dies after taking up with a man who rapes her.
> *The Expedition of Humphrey Clinker* (1771), a novel by Tobias Smollett. This novel is both a comedy and social commentary, which focuses on Matthew Bramble's journey around England seeking better health.
> *Evelina; or, A Young Lady's Entrance into the World* (1778), a novel by Fanny Burney. This novel of manners is presented by the letters of seventeen-year-old Evelina Anville primarily to her guardian, Rev. Arthur Villars, as she reaches maturity and enters society.

its initial printing and has remained in print into the twenty-first century. Modern critics have lauded both books for revealing much about late-eighteenth-century attitudes towards women as well as Foster's own beliefs about how society unduly restricted, if not failed, them. In both works, reviewers have noted, the author proves herself to be an important spokeswoman for changing social values.

The Coquette; or The History of Eliza Wharton
Critics consider *The Coquette* one of the best examples of the sentimental novel published in the early United States. Psychologically astute, well plotted, and carefully written, reviewers have noted that the novel sensitively portrays the life and death of Whitman. In its depiction of an intelligent and strong-willed heroine, the novel is believed to transcend many of the conventions of its time and place. Originally read as a seduction novel in the vein of the novels of Samuel Richardson, it is now considered one of the key texts of early American literature. It is particularly appreciated for the intelligent and artistically convincing ways in which it reexamines familiar dichotomies such as personal integrity versus social responsibility, personal versus universal freedom, and passion versus reason.

Modern critics also laud Foster's handling of epistolary style in the novel, noting how she employs letters to present multiple points of view, and how she uses written versus spoken language to distinguish between levels of intimacy and formality in the communication between characters in the novel. In *Essays in Literature*, Dorothy Z. Baker noted:

> *The Coquette* is considered a tragic novel in that it depicts the seduction and fall of a young woman, and the reader can track the tragic disintegration of Eliza Wharton against her flagging commitment to precision and clarity in her language, her mode of self-expression. However, Foster's emphasis on the value of language alerts the reader to another movement in the novel ... the voice of her society is awakened to its compromised public voice regarding virtue, honor, and friendship.

The Boarding School; Or Lessons of a Preceptress to her Pupils While critics have lavished praise on *The Coquette* since it was put in print, *The Boarding School* was not the best seller or popular success that its predecessor was. Early reviewers and readers were not impressed by Foster's plain and pragmatic critique of conventional domestic gender relations. Writing in 1801, a reviewer in *The American Review and Literary Journal* reproached Foster for having failed to at least provide a good model for letter writing and argued that her moral lessons were not original. The reviewer concluded:

> In these days, when so many books of questionable utility are published, it may be thought some commendation to say of the present volume, that if it is not calculated to do much good, it will do little harm, unless to the bookseller.

Modern critics have noted that *The Boarding School* was didactic and prosaic, lacking in art and ingenuity. They also point out that the letters in the novel lack the narrative unity and epistolary dynamics that Foster successfully employed in *The Coquette*. Despite the lack of critical kudos for the novel, modern critics have lauded Foster for advocating changes to social values to benefit young women. Some such critics have noted that if the novel is read not as novel but as a guide to society life for middle-class women, *The Boarding School* offers the contemporary reader fascinating sociological insight into the daily life of the average American woman at the end of the eighteenth century.

Responses to Literature

1. A number of critics believe that *The Coquette* shows the influence of eighteenth-century author Samuel Richardson. Research Richardson and his works, and write an essay comparing Foster's work to Richardson's. Aside from the obvious epistolary style, how are they similar? How do the two authors portray women differently?

2. With the advent of the Internet and cell phones, the art of letter writing has lost its luster. How would you write a novel like *The Coquette* today? Write a short story in which you use a modern equivalent of letters—for example, text-messaging.

3. Research how women were educated in the late eighteenth century. Using *The Boarding School* as a point of comparison, create a presentation on the subject.

4. One subject touched upon in both of Foster's novels is the idea that novel reading negatively affected young female readers and their moral development. In a group, discuss these ideas in terms of the books. Also debate modern equivalents for novel reading—such as television—as poor influences. How do they compare with the past?

BIBLIOGRAPHY

Books

Richards, Jeffrey H. "The Politics of Seduction: Theater, Sexuality, and National Virtue in the Novels of Hannah Foster." In *Essays in Performance and History*, edited by Della Pollock. Chapel Hill: University of North Carolina Press, 1998, pp. 238–257.

Periodicals

Baker, Dorothy Z. "'Detested be the epithet!': Definition, Maxim, and the Language of the Social Dicta in Hannah Webster Foster's *The Coquette*." *Essays in Literature* (September 1996): 58.

Bontatibus, Donna. "Foster's *The Coquette*." *The Explicator* (Summer 2000): 188.

Brown, Gillian. "Consent, Coquetry, and Consequences." *American Literary History* (1997): 625–652.

Korobkin, Laura H. "'Can Your Volatile Daughter Ever Acquire Your Wisdom?' Luxury and False Ideals in *The Coquette*." *Early American Literature* (Winter 2006): 79.

Review of *The Boarding School; Or Lessons of a Preceptress to her Pupils. The American Review and Literature Journal* (1801).

✺ Benjamin Franklin

BORN: *1706, Boston, Massachusetts*

DIED: *1790, Philadelphia, Pennsylvania*

NATIONALITY: *American*

GENRE: *Nonfiction, essays, autobiography*

MAJOR WORKS:

A Dissertation on Liberty and Necessity, Pleasure and Pain (1725)

Poor Richard's Almanack (1732–1757)

Experiments and Observations on Electricity (1751)

Autobiography of Benjamin Franklin (1868)

Benjamin Franklin   *Franklin, Benjamin, photograph. The Library of Congress.*

Overview

A leader in the American Revolution, Benjamin Franklin was one of the founders of the American political tradition and a distinguished scientist, diplomat, and humanist. He was also one of the best-known and most-admired men of letters in the world during the mid-1700s, and is considered an epitome of the American Enlightenment. His most renowned literary efforts include the annual *Poor Richard's Almanack* (1732–1757) and his posthumously published *Autobiography* (1868).

Works in Biographical and Historical Context

Self-Educated   Born January 17, 1706, in Boston, Massachusetts, Franklin was one of thirteen children of Josiah Franklin, a candlemaker, and his wife, Abiah Folger Franklin. His parents were devout Puritans. Puritans were a religious group who stood against the practices of the Church of England. Like many other Puritans, Franklin's family had left England and moved to the colonies in New England in search of religious freedom.

Franklin received little formal schooling as his family was poor, but learned to read at an early age and his family encouraged intellectual discussions. By the age of eleven, he was working in his father's shop making candles and

soap, though he was soon unhappy doing this trade. The following year, Franklin left his father's trade to work for his brother, James, a printer of a Boston newspaper. While learning the printing business, Franklin became a voracious reader of every word that came into the shop.

Silence and Enlightenment   James Franklin founded his own paper, *New England Courant*, in 1721. Franklin soon began writing clever essays of his own criticizing the Boston establishment, and publishing them in the paper. Some of the essays were written under the name Silence Dogood, a fictional parson's widow. He used irony and satire in the pieces written under her name, which were later collected in *The Dogood Papers* (1722). When authorities imprisoned James Franklin for his own critical articles, Franklin continued the paper on his own for a time.

In 1723, the seventeen-year-old Franklin left home and moved to Philadelphia, Pennsylvania, to work as a printer with Samuel Keimer. By this time, Franklin had begun to embrace the ideas of such Enlightenment thinkers as physicist Sir Isaac Newton and philosopher John Locke. The Enlightenment, which began in the sixteenth century and lasted until the late seventeenth century, was a movement that promoted the use of reason to learn truth. During this time period, many important scientific advances and discoveries were made through the use of observation and experimentation.

Poor Richard   Franklin went to England in 1724, where he quickly became a master printer and lived among the writers of London. There, he also published a deistical pamphlet, *A Dissertation on Liberty and Necessity, Pleasure and Pain* (1725), which stressed the necessity of frugality to achieving success. He returned to Philadelphia a few years later and started his own press. Franklin began publishing a newspaper, the *Philadelphia Gazette*, and later a publication called *Poor Richard's Almanack*. He began publishing the former in 1729 and soon turned it into one of the leading papers in the colonies. The latter was put in print beginning in 1732, and Franklin continued to release new editions until 1757.

Poor Richard's Almanack brought Franklin great success in the colonies, then abroad, selling ten thousand copies annually. Intended to improve himself and others, his almanacs included weather predictions, short sayings adapted from folk and European sources, a history of European kings and dates of courts, tides, fairs, recipes, a meetings calendar, and the movement of planets and eclipses. Through the almanac's fictional character, his persona of Richard Saunders under which Franklin published the almanac, the book is filled with maxims Franklin gathered from many sources which he then adapted to the circumstances of the impoverished Richard.

Political and Scientific Endeavors   In Philadelphia in the late 1720s, Franklin took on such governmental posts as clerk of the Pennsylvania Assembly and postmaster of

Philadelphia. He became the official printer of Pennsylvania in 1730. Franklin also began a new focus in promoting organizations that benefited society. For example, in 1727, he formed Junto, a society of tradesmen who shared business information and were involved in activities that benefited society.

These years also marked the beginning of his scientific endeavors. Franklin invented the Franklin stove (a metal stove used for heating a room), then became fascinated with electricity. His invention in 1750 of the lightning rod (a metal rod that is set on top of a building to protect it from being damaged if it is struck by lightning) added to his reputation. In his well-known experiment, Franklin used a kite to prove that lightning is a form of electricity. Franklin's letters to England concerning his discoveries and theories about electricity brought him fame as did his book on the subject *Experiments and Observations on Electricity* (1751).

In 1751, Franklin was elected to the Pennsylvania Assembly, beginning a period of public service that would last until nearly the end of his life. A leader in the dominant Quaker political party, Franklin created lawmaking strategies and wrote powerful statements defending the right of the people's elected representatives to regulate the government of Pennsylvania. As a representative to the Assembly, Franklin was initially loyal to the British Empire, including during the French and Indian War.

This war, which lasted from 1754 to 1763, was fought between France and Great Britain in North America. At its end, the British gained control of land east of the Mississippi River. To defend the British Empire, Franklin persuaded the Assembly to pass Pennsylvania's first militia law, allotted money for defense, and appointed government representatives to carry on a war. While Franklin considered Britain the benevolent head of the American colonies, he was occasionally alarmed by British indifference toward the colonists.

Working Abroad for American Interests Franklin lived in England from 1757 to 1762, seeking aid to restrain the power of the Penn family in Pennsylvania. (The Penn family founded the colony.) Returning to America, he traveled throughout the colonies for nearly two years as the deputy postmaster general for North America. He would hold this post for nearly twenty years, and during that time greatly improved the postal service. Franklin also continued his aid to poorer members of his family and to the family of his common-law wife, Deborah, with whom he became involved in 1730. They had two children, Frankie, who died as a small child, and daughter Sarah. Deborah Franklin also raised her husband's illegitimate son, William.

In 1764, Franklin lost his seat in the Pennsylvania Assembly. However, he returned to England as Pennsylvania's agent, with a special assignment to request that Pennsylvania be taken over as a royal colony. Franklin decided not to make the request because the royal government seemed dangerous at the time. Remaining in England for nine years, he became the foremost American spokesman in Britain.

The Beginnings of the American Revolution Franklin played a central role in the great crises that led to the Declaration of Independence in 1776. For example, the 1765 Stamp Act placed a tax on all business and law papers and printed materials in the American colonies. Many colonists opposed the tax as taxation without representation. After learning of the violent protest against the Stamp Act, Franklin stiffened his own stand against the measure. In a dramatic appearance before Parliament in 1766, Franklin outlined American insistence on self-government. When the tax was removed, Franklin again expressed his faith in American prospects within the British Empire.

In 1774, Franklin's tenure in England came to an unhappy end. Against his instructions, his friends in Massachusetts published letters by Massachusetts governor Thomas Hutchinson that Franklin had obtained confidentially. Exposed as a dishonest schemer, Franklin was reprimanded by the British in 1774 and removed from his position as postmaster general. Franklin left England in March 1775, and the American Revolution began the following month.

Gaining French Support The American Revolution was a war in which the American colonies fought for independence from Great Britain. During the first months of the revolution, Franklin enjoyed the surge for independence and was soon a confirmed revolutionary. In 1776, he helped draft the Declaration of Independence and was among those who signed it. Franklin used his skills as a diplomat when he was appointed as a representative to France. There, he negotiated an alliance with King Louis XVI which led to the French lending their armies and navies to America. Much of the gunpowder used by American revolutionaries was actually obtained from France, a longtime rival of Great Britain. Franklin also secured other outside aid.

Franklin was still in France when the British surrendered after the Battle of Yorktown in 1781. The following year, he set the main terms of the final peace agreement between England and the colonies as other peace commissioners, including John Adams and John Jay, made their way to the Paris-based peace talks. Franklin, Jay, and Adams made a peace treaty of genuine national independence in 1783.

Constitution and Autobiography Returning to Philadelphia from France in 1785, Franklin spent three years as the president of the Supreme Council of Pennsylvania. Though ill, he continued to work on his *Autobiography* which remained unfinished at his death and was first published posthumously as *Autobiography of Benjamin Franklin* in 1868. (It was not published in its complete form until 1874.) Covering only the years from 1731 to 1757 and originally begun in 1771, the *Autobiography* was written to provide guidance to his son William.

In the summer of 1787, Franklin attended the Constitutional Convention and urged that the resulting Constitution be ratified. He also approved the inauguration of the new government under President George Washington. A month after writing a major essay against slavery, Franklin died peacefully in Philadelphia on April 17, 1790, at the age of eighty-four.

Works in Literary Context

Considered one of America's greatest writers, Franklin brought to his writing a broad humanism and selflessness, employed a sense of grace and wit, and promoted ideas of the Enlightenment. Possessed of an infinitely curious mind fixed on understanding and improving the world around him, he sought a better life for people of all classes and situations through his actions and his writings. He gave an American flavor to the epistolary and essay forms, mastered the use of persona in creating the first memorable American comic character, and retained a homespun sense of humor that resonated for generations. In his over twenty thousand different works, he was stylistically focused on clarity, precision, and propriety. His major literary influences included Joseph Addison, John Locke, Jonathan Swift, John Bunyan, and Daniel Defoe. Franklin often focused on scientific and rational thought; he also firmly believed in God and his spiritual beliefs shaped the world view that emerged in his works.

Humor Franklin's reputation as a humorist derives from his *Autobiography*, *Poor Richard's Almanacks*, and a number of his published essays. In Franklin's *Autobiography*, he renders his rags-to-riches story with exaggeration and a sly sense of humor. Writing under the pseudonym Richard Saunders in his almanacs, Franklin portrays Richard as a figure of satire in the earliest editions. Richard is a brow-beaten farmer who considers himself an accomplished astrologer. The humor in the annual publications is also found in his poems and in his maxims or sayings, many of which have remained popular to this day. The essays included in *The Dogood Papers* also employ a satiric sense of humor. Written by a sixteen-year-old Franklin, the epistolary essays take on the narrative voice of the fictional young widow who addresses with humor such topics as alcoholism, religious fanatics, and fashion. For example, in "Dogood XII," she argues against abstinence from alcohol, maintaining that some people's outlooks and personalities improve after they have consumed alcoholic beverages.

Highest Good In nearly all of his writings, Franklin aims for the highest good of humankind. Franklin's work appeals to human reason and strives to socially and morally better people. Through his publications, he also hoped to improve greater society as well. His almanacs are educational, if not moralizing, and he used them to instruct common people by conveying to them the compressed knowledge and wit of his many proverbs, along with innumerable charts, lists, and facts ranging from agricultural to cosmological. Franklin's satires and essays

LITERARY AND HISTORICAL CONTEMPORARIES

Benjamin Franklin's famous contemporaries include:

Thomas Jefferson (1743–1826): This American lawyer and statesman wrote the Declaration of Independence. After serving as governor of Virginia from 1779 to 1782, Jefferson served as the secretary of state during the administration of George Washington and was elected president himself in 1800.

John Jay (1745–1829): This diplomat and statesman co-authored *The Federalist Papers* (1787–1788). He also helped negotiate the peace treaty with Great Britain recognizing American independence. Jay was also the first chief justice of the U.S. Supreme Court.

George Washington (1732–1799): The first president of the United States, Washington also was the military commander of colonial troops during the American Revolution.

King George III (1738–1820): The British monarch during the American Revolution, George III was conservative in his views and stood for traditional values. He oversaw many changes in the British Empire, including the loss of the American colonies and the formation of the United Kingdom of Great Britain and Ireland in 1801.

John Adams (1735–1826): This American lawyer and statesman represented Massachusetts in both Continental Congresses and helped negotiate the peace treaty that ended the Revolutionary War. Adams later served as an ambassador to Great Britain and vice president before being elected president himself in 1796.

were usually written with a particular political or social end in mind. Even his writings on religion and science, such *Experiments and Observations on Electricity*, underscore the importance of his utilitarian worldview.

While his *Autobiography* was originally written as an instructional guide for his son William, Franklin also hoped others would be influenced by and imitate the path he took in life. By explaining how he rose from obscurity to influential public person, Franklin wanted others to learn from their mistakes and achieve their highest good in whatever form that might take. Similarly, the essays written as Dogood in the *The Dogood Papers* are satiric, but also intended to highlight and correct what the fictional widow perceives as the important moral concerns of the Boston society in the 1720s. Though humorous, the essays show that even at sixteen, Franklin was already concerned with underscoring the highest good for people.

Works in Critical Context

Critics have praised Franklin's works—primarily his *Autobiography* and his many *Poor Richard Almanacks*—for

COMMON HUMAN EXPERIENCE

Franklin's *Poor Richard's Almanack* was a popular seventeenth-century source of information. Here are some other almanacs from colonial America:

Tulley's Almanac (1687), by John Tulley. Printed in Saybrook, Connecticut, Tulley compiled what is believed to be the first humorous almanac.

An Almanacke for New-England for the Year 1639 (1639), by William Peirce. This almanac was printed by Stephen Daye in Cambridge, Massachusetts. It was probably the first almanac put out in America, and was one of the first English-language publications to be issued from the press in British North America.

Astronomical Diary and Almanack (1726–1764), by Nathaniel Ames. This series of almanacs had a massive following and outsold all other almanacs produced in the colonies. It is considered the forerunner of Franklin's *Poor Richard's Almanack.*

The Rhode Island Almanack (1728), by James Franklin. Written by Franklin's half-brother, it was the first almanac written in the Franklin family. The almanac was written by "Poor Robin," and was influenced by the humorous British almanacs also entitled Poor Robin.

creating for himself an identity as one of the first true American citizens. The vast majority of criticism has focused on his legitimacy as an artist, especially in relation to his *Autobiography*. Some critics have argued that Franklin's works lack artistic merit. Others have objected to that characterization, praising the simplicity and lucidity of his style. Scholars have acknowledged, however, that the vast majority of Franklin's writings were designed for utilitarian rather than literary purposes.

Poor Richard's Almanack   When the first issue of *Poor Richard's Almanack* was published in 1732, it was an immediate hit with readers and sold second only to the Bible over the course of its run. Critics believe that Franklin's almanac was the most popular nonreligious publication of its day because of the range of information it included and the humor and wit included therein. Historians believed that the single greatest reason for the success of *Poor Richard's* was Franklin's ability to spice the prosaic matter of the ordinary almanac with the more engaging commentary than his competitors could write. Over the years, scholars have focused their attention on such issues as the source of Richard's name and the source of his proverbs. Critics lauded his Franklin's ability to rewrite proverbs derived from other sources in order to incorporate American elements or make them shorter. Calling the almanacs "an institution," Carl Van Doren in his *Benja-*

min Franklin noted that "Franklin as Poor Richard was merely insisting that the first thing to build in their [the colonists'] house was the plain foundation. But with how much wit and charm he insisted!"

Autobiography of Benjamin Franklin   Franklin's *Autobiography of Benjamin Franklin* was the most popular autobiography in U.S. history and considered by critics to be his most stylistically developed literary achievement. It is still considered one of the finest examples of the genre. Critics and scholars have noted that the *Autobiography* communicates wit, morality, candor, and integrity in a light, self-deprecating style that fluctuates widely on topics related to Franklin's diverse interests. Although considered inaccurate in some details, critics consider *Autobiography* a major document in the history of the American Republic. Some critics, however, have observed that Franklin's attention to the virtues of industry, prudence, and frugality led to an unflattering caricature of him as a smug, priggish pedant.

Most early reviews of the *Autobiography* were overwhelmingly positive. Early twentieth-century authors such as D. H. Lawrence and William Carlos Williams faulted Franklin for his apparent complacency. Later reviewers questioned the accuracy of this portrait, claiming that Franklin was adopting the pose of a naïve narrator in order to create a universally accessible image of a fallible but self-made man. As Jennifer Jordan Baker writes in *Early American Literature*:

As both a tale of his own rise to wealth and social prominence as well as more speculative archetype of the success *other* Americans might achieve, the *Autobiography* ultimately operates as a financial instrument ... that attests to the economic promise of America.

Responses to Literature

1. In a group, discuss the proverbs and maxims found in *Poor Richard's Almanack*. Do you believe they still have relevance today?

2. Research the American Enlightenment and Franklin's role within it. In an essay, link your findings to one of his many works.

3. Create a presentation about Franklin's use of humor and satire. How does humor add to one of his works?

4. Read *The Dogood Papers*. Write an essay in a similar style and voice on a moral or social issue of today.

BIBLIOGRAPHY

Books

Bowen, Catherine Drinker. *The Most Dangerous Man in America: Scenes from the Life of Benjamin Franklin.* Boston: Little, Brown, 1974.

Clark, Ronald W. *Benjamin Franklin: A Biography.* New York: Random House, 1983.

Hawke, David Freeman. *Franklin.* New York: Harper & Row, 1976.

Isaacson, Walter. *Benjamin Franklin: An American Life.* New York: Simon & Schuster, 2003.

Lopez, Claude-Anne and Eugenia W. Herbert. *The Private Franklin: The Man and His Family.* New York: Norton, 1975.

Middlekauf, Robert. *Benjamin Franklin and His Enemies.* Berkeley, Calif.: University of California Press, 1996.

Morgan, Edmund S. *Benjamin Franklin.* New Haven, Conn.: Yale University Press, 2002.

Schiff, Stacy. *A Great Improvisation: Franklin, France, and the Birth of America.* New York: Holt, 2005.

Schoenbrun, David. *Triumph in Paris: The Exploits of Benjamin Franklin.* New York: Harper & Row, 1976.

Van Doren, Carl. *Benjamin Franklin.* New York: Viking Press, 1938.

Wright, Esmond. *Franklin of Philadelphia.* Cambridge, Mass.: Belknap Press of Harvard University Press, 1986.

Periodicals

Baker, Jennifer Jordan. "Benjamin Franklin's *Autobiography* and the Credibility of Personality." *Early American Literature* vol. 35, no. 3 (2000): 274–293.

Jonathan Franzen

BORN: *1959, Western Springs, Illinois*

NATIONALITY: *American*

GENRE: *Fiction, essays*

MAJOR WORKS:
The Corrections (2001)
How To Be Alone: Essays (2002)

Overview

Regarded as one of the best emerging novelists of the twenty-first century, Jonathan Franzen is also a strong believer in both the power and necessity of literature. His award-winning novel *The Corrections* (2001) is often deemed one of the best works of literature written in the last twenty years. While Franzen's work is commonly held in high esteem, the author has managed to garner significant controversy for his resolute convictions about publishing, writing, and the direction of American tastes. In addition to his fictional works, Franzen has also published several highly regarded essay collections, including *The Discomfort Zone: A Personal History* (2006).

Works in Biographical and Historical Context

Midwestern Childhood Franzen was born on August 17, 1959, in Western Springs, Illinois, to Earl T. and Irene (Super) Franzen. His father was a railroad company exec-

Jonathan Franzen   *AP Images*

utive; his mother, a homemaker. His family moved to the St. Louis suburb of Webster Groves, Missouri, where he grew up. Webster Groves later became the setting for at least two of his novels. As a child, Franzen was quite timid and he focused most of his energies on reading and academic achievement.

Franzen majored in German at Swarthmore College, and earned his BA in 1981. While at Swarthmore, he also penned a column for the student newspaper. The following year, he was awarded a Fulbright Fellowship, which he used to spend the year at the Freiet Universität (Free University) in Berlin, which was still divided by the superpowers into western and eastern sectors. When Franzen returned to the United States, he married writer Valerie Cornell. Then, from 1983 to 1987, he worked at Harvard University as a research assistant in earth and planetary sciences.

Focus on Literature During this time period, Franzen and Cornell dedicated themselves to the creation and enjoyment of literature while living in Somerville, a relatively inexpensive part of Boston. Though their financial situation was difficult, Franzen describes these years as idyllic. In 1987, he submitted an eleven-hundred-page manuscript that eventually became his first novel. The edited version of this work became *The Twenty-Seventh City* (1988), which focused on the political maneuvering of Susan Jammu, as she leads the police force of a futuristic St. Louis, Missouri, and tries to turn the city around. *The Twenty-Seventh City* won the Whiting Writers' Award. Hailed by critics as a writer of great promise, Franzen emerged as a literary celebrity despite his young age and lack of credentials.

Even with the success that came with *The Twenty-Seventh City*, Franzen and Cornell's marriage began to suffer. Using royalties from the book, the couple traveled through Europe and hoped to mend their relationship. While in Europe, Franzen began working on what became his second novel, *Strong Motion* (1992). Set in Boston, the novel presents a complex series of events, including a number of earthquakes and illicit dumping of toxins into wells below the city, which cause the city's underlying bedrock to become unstable. The story centers on Louis Holland, a radio enthusiast who becomes involved in the mystery behind these events. The book sold poorly. Franzen suffered personal losses at this time as well: both of his parents died and his marriage ended. For a time, Franzen considered quitting writing entirely.

Turn to Journalism Ultimately rejecting this idea, Franzen approached *The New Yorker* about writing his piece of journalism. The magazine accepted his idea and he eventually became a contributing writer for the periodical. While writing for *The New Yorker*, he also contributed pieces to other magazines, including *Harper's*.

In 1996, the year Franzen received a Guggenheim Foundation fellowship and published the essay "Perchance to Dream: In an Age of Images, a Reason to Write Novels" in *Harper's*. The essay focused on the reasons authors write. He also lamented the power that certain media and entertainment outlets—particularly the Internet and television—have over the minds of the American public, as well as the seeming inability of a literary novel to engage the masses. Reaction to the article was relatively mild, but it earned Franzen a reputation among critics as a high-minded if pretentious writer.

The Corrections While he continued his association with *The New Yorker*, Franzen also continued to work on his fiction. While working on minor characters, he wrote a scene about an elderly couple on a cruise ship—a piece that he considered perhaps the finest writing of his career. In near seclusion, Franzen focused exclusively on these characters, ultimately creating the Lambert family, who form of the core of his novel, *The Corrections* (2001). A 568-page opus, the book relates the disintegration of the family at the end of the twentieth century and the beginning of the twenty-first.

A seriocomic tale, the book details the desire of family matriarch, Enid Lambert, to gather her three children—Gary, Chip, and Denise—for a final visit before their father is lost to Parkinson's disease. *The Corrections* charts the reluctance of the Lambert children to return to their childhood home. It also touches on contemporary events in the United States, including the Internet stock bubble of 1997–1998, and the subsequent "market correction" of 2000.

Written over six years, *The Corrections* was somewhat autobiographical. Franzen believed he had written a work of "high art" that would engage the masses. Despite his own missteps—including his publicly stated discomfort with *The Corrections* being selected by Oprah Winfrey for her highly rated television show's book club, and his implied assertion that the book might be beyond the comprehension of a typical reader—the book became a best seller. The novel won the National Book Award for Fiction in 2001.

Success as an Essayist After *The Corrections*, Franzen published a collection of thirteen essays that originally appeared in *The New Yorker* and other periodicals. Most of the pieces in the well-received *How To Be Alone: Essays* (2002) comment in some fashion on the modern world, and on the effects a media-saturated culture brings to bear on both writers and their readers. Other topics include a description of his father's demise due to Alzheimer's Disease. Critics noted that the essays show the continued development of Franzen's writing and thought.

Franzen followed *How to Be Alone* with another collection of essays, *The Discomfort Zone: A Personal History* (2006), which form a memoir. The six essays therein cover Franzen's life from childhood to adulthood, and delineate his journey of self-discovery. Critics praised the collection for both its wit and its revelations of a complex and conflicted author. In 2007, Franzen published his translation of the 1891 play *Spring Awakening* by Frank Wedekind and provided an extensive introduction. Franzen lives and works in New York City.

Works in Literary Context

In his novels, Franzen attempts to tackle what he perceives as significant social ills in contemporary American culture. In particular, he focuses on the excessive level of control businesses exert over American thought. Corporate America and the ruthlessness of the New Economy—which he paints as working against improving the world in order to achieve potentially disastrous and shortsighted goals—are frequent targets of Franzen's writings. He also rails against modern American consumerism, ennui, and corruption, and describes how individuals and families in the United States are affected by these situations. In Franzen's first three novels, events that could be corrected with relative ease if acted upon promptly instead spin out of their participants' control. As an author, Franzen was greatly influenced by writers such as Don DeLillo and William Gaddis.

Cities Suffering from Corruption In Franzen's first two novels, a primary focus is on major American cities, already in a state of disarray, that become further corrupted by mankind. Both *The Twenty-Seventh City* and *Strong Motion* also feature people who seek to save their cities. *The Twenty-Seventh City*, for example, is based on the premise that St. Louis, once the fourth largest city in the United States, later fell to twenty-seventh. Hoping to revitalize St. Louis, city leaders hire Susan Jammu, an American-born cousin of Indian leader Indira Gandhi, to head the police force. Many Indian families move to the city, changing its demographic makeup. Jammu comes to the job with her own plans, and she pushes through a proposal to reinvent the city center. She is not afraid to use underhanded means to reach her goals. In contrast, *Strange Motion* is set in Boston and focuses on Renee Seitchek, a Harvard seismologist, and Louis Holland, a young employee at a failing radio station. The pair become embroiled in a mystery involving a series of earthquakes that rock Boston and the chemical company responsible for causing them. The company, it is revealed, has been disposing of waste products by injecting them into abandoned wells beneath the city.

Family and Personal Struggles   In both his fiction and nonfiction, Franzen touches on ideas about families—and individuals therein—in conflict within themselves and each other. Franzen admitted that the family of Louis Holland in *Strange Motion* was partially based on his childhood observations of his parents' friends. Family conflict takes center stage in his best known work, *The Corrections*. Alfred and Enid Lambert are a long-married couple reaching their twilight years when Alfred develops Parkinson's Disease and other medical problems. Enid is forced to take charge of their lives, and decides to invite their three children home for one final Christmas before Alfred dies. Sections of the book focus on the separate lives of the Lambert siblings and their parents in states of personal, professional, and emotional crisis. While Franzen admits that *The Corrections* has autobiographical elements, he offers more personal examples of the struggles of himself and his family in *The Discomfort Zone: A Personal History*.

Works in Critical Context

While they acknowledge the flaws of his early novels, reviewers have consistently recognized Franzen as a master of the story form. Many critics regard him as the standard-bearer of the "Great American Novel"—a work employing compelling ideas and intense, precise language to inspire thought and debate about the course of American culture. In this regard, critics favorably compare Franzen to Thomas Pynchon and Don DeLillo. Franzen is also often commended for his shrewd sense of humor. While critical reaction to Franzen's novels has been generally positive, some reviewers have expressed dissatisfaction with his style and manner, especially his wordiness. These commentators maintain that he frequently loses control of the central focus of his novels, veering through an unnecessarily labyrinthine passage of complicated plot twists and unrelated elements.

The Twenty-Seventh City   Critics were divided over Franzen's first novel, *The Twenty-Seventh City*. While Richard Eder of the *Los Angeles Times Book Review* noted that the book's plot was obscure and complex, he praised the young novelist's imagination and foresight. He wrote that Franzen's view of America is "startlingly exact." Calling *The Twenty-Seventh City* "unsettling and visionary," Michele Slung declared in the *Washington Post Book World* that it "is not a novel that can be quickly dismissed or easily forgotten: it has elements of both 'Great' and 'American.'" Desmond Christy, writing in the Manchester *Guardian* commented, "Novelists are expected to understand their characters; few bring a city to life so vividly as Franzen."

The Corrections   Better received than his first two novels, *The Corrections* was praised by reviewers as a complex, movingly honest portrayal of family dynamics. Critics also asserted that he fulfilled much of the early promise he demonstrated with his first two works of fiction. In the *New York Times*, Michiko Kakutani called the novel "a remarkably poised performance, the narrative held together by a myriad of meticulously observed details and tiny leitmotifs that create a mosaiclike picture of America in the waning years of the twentieth century." *Entertainment Weekly* reviewer Benjamin Svetkey also reviewed the book favorably. Svetkey remarked:

COMMON HUMAN EXPERIENCE

In *The Twenty-Seventh City*, Franzen offers a fictional and futuristic look at St. Louis. Here are some other works that offer glimpses of future societies:

Infinite Jest (1996), a novel by David Foster Wallace. This novel is set in the not-so-distant future of the United States when corporate sponsors have taken over the calendar. The United States is now part of a new political entity, and New England has been sold to Canada for use as a toxic waste dump.

1984 (1948), a novel by George Orwell. This science-fiction classic portrays life in Oceania, a totalitarian state controlled by a mysterious Inner Party that demands blind devotion to its leader, Big Brother.

Soylent Green (1973), a film directed by Richard Fleischer. Set in the twenty-first century, it depicts a dark and desperate world where people's principal food—the titular soylent green—is discovered to be made of deceased citizens.

Surveillance (2007), a novel by Jonathan Raban. Set in the near future, the Department of Homeland Security has expanded its surveillance programs and even private citizens spy on each other.

It's a big, ambitious, unwieldy hybrid of a book, a literary novel and a social document, an intimate family portrait and a sprawling cultural landscape, a floor wax and a dessert topping—but Franzen somehow manages to glue it all together with surprising warmth and wit.

Responses to Literature

1. Based on your reading of *The Twenty-Seventh City*, write a futuristic short story about your own home town. How will it be different twenty years from now?

2. In a small group, discuss the family conflicts in *The Corrections*. Do you think the conflicts are effectively resolved in the end?

3. Research the possibility of earthquakes really happening in Boston. Write an essay in which you link your findings to the events of *Strong Motion*. Based on your findings, is the book's premise plausible or not?

4. Read Franzen's essay "Perchance to Dream: In an Age of Images, a Reason to Write Novels," which originally appeared in *Harper's*. With a partner, stage a debate over the ideas Franzen expresses. Do you agree with the author? Why or why not?

BIBLIOGRAPHY

Books

Dempsey, Peter. *Jonathan Franzen's The Corrections: A Reader's Guide*. New York: Continuum, 2005.

Periodicals

Christy, Desmond. Review of *The Twenty-Seventh City*. *Guardian* (January 29, 1988): 17.

Eder, Richard. Review of *The Twenty-Seventh City*. *Los Angeles Times Book Review* (September 4, 1988).

Kakutani, Michiko. "A Family Portrait as Metaphor for the '90s." *New York Times* (September 4, 2001): E1.

Slung, Michele. Review of *The Twenty-Seventh City*. *Washington Post Book Review* (September 4, 1988).

Svetkey, Benjamin. "Domestic Drama: Jonathan Franzen's Carefully Crafted *The Corrections* Finds One Family on the Edge of a Nervous Breakdown." *Entertainment Weekly* (September 14, 2001): 85.

✹ Charles Frazier

BORN: *1950, Asheville, North Carolina*

NATIONALITY: *American*

GENRE: *Fiction*

MAJOR WORKS:

Cold Mountain (1997)

Overview

Dubbed a natural-born storyteller, Charles Frazier is best known for his award-winning debut novel *Cold Mountain* (1997). Praised for his ability to fully capture the language and landscape of the American Civil War era, he became an overnight literary sensation with the publication of his best-selling book.

Works in Biographical and Historical Context

Raised in North Carolina   Charles Robinson Frazier was born on November 4, 1950, in Asheville, North Carolina. He is the son of Charles O. Frazier and his wife Betty. Raised in the mountainous part of western North Carolina, he lived in the towns of Andrews and Franklin. His father was a high school principal in Franklin; his mother worked as a school librarian and administrator. While Frazier was growing up, the civil rights movement was gaining strength, especially in the South. It protested the persistent racism and segregation in many areas of life for African Americans, especially those living below the Mason-Dixon Line. One result of this struggle was the desegregation of public schools—the admittance of black students into schools formerly meant only for whites.

Charles Frazier   *Frazier, Charles, photograph. AP Images.*

After completing high school in 1969, Frazier entered the University of North Carolina at Chapel Hill. He earned his BA in 1973, then began graduate work at Appalachian State University. There he met his future wife, Katherine, whom he married in 1976. Frazier continued to work on his PhD in English at the University of South Carolina. While completing his degree, Frazier taught early American literature courses at the University of Colorado. His experiences as an avid traveler in South America led to his first writing project. Frazier coauthored a nonfiction guide, *Adventuring in the Andes: The Sierra Guide to Peru, Bolivia, the Amazon Basin, and the Galapagos* (1985).

Novel Inspiration   In 1986, Frazier earned his PhD with his dissertation *Geography and Possibility: Man and the Landscape in Recent Western Fiction*, his daughter Annie was born, and he and his wife returned to North Carolina. He then taught at North Carolina State on a part-time basis and raised show ponies on his property outside of Raleigh. Frazier occasionally published a short story, but learning aspects of his family history inspired a much larger project. While researching the family's ancestry, Frazier's father came across a reference to a great-great-grandfather who had served in the Confederate

army during the Civil War, was injured, and deserted a military hospital to make his way back to Cold Mountain in western North Carolina. Though Frazier could find no more about his ancestor's story, he began researching local and state archives for old journals and letters from the Civil War era.

In 1989, urged by his wife to quit teaching and write full-time, Frazier focused all his energy on his Civil War project. Using such sources as the journals of Frederick Law Olmsted (who traveled in the Great Smoky Mountains) and the writings of naturalist William Bartram, Frazier spent the next eight years producing what would become *Cold Mountain* (1997). This novel follows Inman, a Confederate soldier wounded in battle. He deserts before his injury heals enough to force him back to war, and he works his way back to his love, Ada Monroe, while evading the "Home Guard," a posse that seeks out deserters and carries out summary executions. While Inman is making his journey, Ada runs the family farm with the help of a rough-mannered local girl.

Even before its publication in 1997, *Cold Mountain* received positive word of mouth. It became a best seller within a month of its June 1997 release and won the National Book Award later that year. Frazier then spent the next few years doing publicity for the novel while continuing to raise show ponies.

Publishes Thirteen Moons   In 2002, Frazier signed a deal worth $8.25 million for his second novel that was based on his submitting a one-page outline. While it had been several years since *Cold Mountain* was completed, his idea came from research he had conducted while writing that novel. That research revealed that in or about 1900 the patients of a North Carolina state psychiatric hospital included a one-hundred-year-old man, William Holland Thomas, who sometimes refused to speak any language but Cherokee. He was not a Native American, but he was an orphan who had grown up among the Cherokee in North Carolina. He ultimately became the chief of a Cherokee clan and for a time represented that clan in Washington, D.C. In his novel *Thirteen Moons*, Frazier drew on Thomas's long life and experiences with the Cherokee people, with the politics of that era, and with the Civil War. Frazier spent the next four years writing the book, which was published in 2006. While reviews were mixed, a number of critics embraced both the story of Will Cooper, as Thomas was called in the novel, and Frazier's depiction of the Cherokee community in which Cooper lived.

After completing *Thirteen Moons*, Frazier took time off from writing. He continues to live with his wife and daughter on his North Carolina farm, where he still breeds horses.

Works in Literary Context

Frazier's type of literary and historical fiction is rich with authentic details that reflect the period in which the

LITERARY AND HISTORICAL CONTEMPORARIES

Frazier's famous contemporaries include:

Kaye Gibbons (1960–): Gibbons, a novelist who is a native North Carolinan, helped get Frazier's *Cold Mountain* published. Her works include *Charms for the Easy Life* (1993).

Bill Clinton (1946–): This American president served two consecutive terms in office in the 1990s. He is also a best-selling author who received a $10 million advance for his memoir, *My Life* (2004).

Anthony Minghella (1954–2008): This British screenwriter and director oversaw the film adaptation of *Cold Mountain* (2003). He also directed and wrote the screenplay of the 1996 film *The English Patient*, for which he won a best-director Academy Award in 1997.

Don DeLillo (1936–): DeLillo wrote the novel *Underworld* (1997), which was a contender for the National Book Award the year *Cold Mountain* won.

Shelby Foote (1916–2005): This American historian was a Civil War expert. He wrote a three-volume history of the war, *The Civil War: A Narrative* (1958–74).

COMMON HUMAN EXPERIENCE

In *Cold Mountain*, Frazier offers a Civil War solider's story—that of a wounded Confederate deserting to make his way home. Here are some novels about the Civil War that offer other perspectives:

The Red Badge of Courage (1895), a novel by Stephen Crane. In this novel, Crane offers a view of the Civil War from the perspective of a young soldier who experiences cowardice, guilt, fear, and ultimately triumph.

The Killer Angels (1974), a novel by Michael Shaara. This novel describes the climactic struggle at Gettysburg from multiple perspectives of the key participants on both sides.

Andersonville (1954), a novel by MacKinlay Kantor. This novel tells the story of the Union soldiers who were prisoners of war in the infamous Andersonville prison. The novel won the Pulitzer Prize for fiction in 1956.

"An Occurrence at Owl Creek Bridge" (1890), a short story by Ambrose Bierce. Bierce's famous story tells the tale of a Confederate sympathizer hanged by Union troops.

novels were set. The history of the South, primarily in the nineteenth century, is the author's main focus. While *Cold Mountain* takes place during and shortly after the Civil War, *Thirteen Moons* encompasses a century of American history and includes information about Cherokee culture. In each of his novels, Frazier also sends his characters on a journey that transforms their lives. Frazier was influenced by early American literature and nineteenth-century sources, such as journals that he uncovered in the course of his extensive research for both books. *Cold Mountain* also shares many features with the *Odyssey* (c. 700 B.C.E.), an epic poem by the ancient Greek poet Homer.

An Authentic Vernacular In *Cold Mountain*, Frazier drew on many sources to come up with the period detail and vocabulary that gave the novel its historical accuracy and appeal to readers. Frazier was able to re-create and describe the landscape of a rural, genuinely rustic American South just after the Civil War, using the vocabulary of that time period. He employs the names of tools, like maul and froe, no longer used, as well as older terms for local plants, animals, and crops. Frazier's penchant for authentic language also extends to the characters's nuances of dialect and phrasing. *Thirteen Moons* was similarly authentic in its span of a hundred years of American culture, and it included accurate depictions of the Civil War, notable historical figures, Cherokee culture, and the Trail of Tears (the forcible removal of Cherokee from their homes in states like North Carolina to Oklahoma, causing the deaths of thousands).

Transformational Journey Both of Frazier's novels feature characters who experience a life-transforming journey. In *Thirteen Moons*, the journey is one of a whole life. Frazier outlines Cooper's life from the time he is an orphan, to his adoption into a Cherokee clan, and his becoming a Cherokee chief. Cooper's journey also includes experiences like fighting for the Confederacy during the Civil War, serving in the state legislature, and meeting such figures as Andrew Jackson. His journey ends with his death at a psychiatric hospital in North Carolina. *Cold Mountain* also has a Civil War and North Carolina focus. Inman embarks on a trip home that is fraught with difficulties, as he must avoid the Home Guard, recover from his injuries, and keep himself alive amid foul weather and attacks from wild animals and other refugees. In contrast, Ada's adventure takes place only on her farm, but her father's death forces her to evolve from a genteel woman to an independent and capable farmer. Her own journey of self-discovery and survival is aided by the self-reliant Ruby, a local farm girl who teaches Ada how to run her farm.

Works in Critical Context

Frazier's works have been generally praised by critics for their historical detail and authenticity. Reviewers note that his extensive research for both *Cold Mountain* and *Thirteen Moons* lend the novels an air of realism. While *Cold Mountain* was greatly praised, however, many critics found *Thirteen Moons* less powerful, more wordy, and not as gripping as Frazier's debut.

Cold Mountain From its initial publication, *Cold Mountain* received nearly unanimous positive reviews from critics. Reviewers specifically praised Frazier's skill with antiquated language, as well as his ability to capture the natural world of the era. As Mel Gussow in the *New York Times* notes, the novel "is filled with flavorful details: language (tools like maul and froe, spurtle, fleam, and snath), crops, food, books and Cherokee legends." Gussow added, "Mr. Frazier is a stickler for authenticity." *Cold Mountain* also won praise for giving the ideological underpinnings of the Civil War rather short shrift in comparison to others of its genre. Writing in the *Library Journal*, David A. Berona proclaims it a "monumental novel" and "a remarkable effort that opens up with a historical past that will enrich readers."

Thirteen Moons Unlike *Cold Mountain*, *Thirteen Moons* received mixed reviews from critics. Many reviewers made issue of the $8.25 million advance Frazier received for the book, with a number of them noting that this worked out to twenty thousand dollars per page and declaring that the novel did not live up to these standards. For example, while Louis Menand in the *New Yorker* praises Frazier's "gift for violence" and his "Darwinian" nature, Menand also notes, "There is too much lapidary sententiousness, too much moral reverb, in the prose. . . . We could take the characters more seriously if the author took them less seriously." In *Entertainment Weekly* Jennifer Reese compared Frazier's two novels, with *Thirteen Moons* coming out the worse. Reese writes, "Will's tale is, by turns, amusing, bawdy, bloody, and poignant, but finishing one baggy character never leaves you panting for the next." As William Brett concludes in the *Spectator*, "*Thirteen Moons* is sound in its historical fiction. But as a novel it's disappointing."

Responses to Literature

1. Some critics have noted the parallels between *Cold Mountain* and Homer's *Odyssey*. In an essay, outline what you believe are the similarities and differences between these works.

2. *Cold Mountain* is sometimes grouped with two other literary novels published in the early and mid-1990s: David Guterson's *Snow Falling on Cedars* (1994) and Cormac McCarthy's *All the Pretty Horses* (1992). In a small group, discuss what these books have in common. How do they represent a literary tradition? Which book do you connect with most, and why?

3. Research the conditions in psychiatric hospitals in the early 1900s. In a presentation, compare your findings to Frazier's depiction in *Thirteen Moons*.

4. In a paper, compare and contrast *Cold Mountain* with the film version, directed by Anthony Minghella and released in 2003. Which version do you think best represents the story?

BIBLIOGRAPHY

Periodicals

Berona, David A. Review of *Cold Mountain*. *Library Journal* (May 15, 1997): 100.

Brett, William. "Back to the Appalachians." *Spectator* (November 18, 2006).

Gifford, Terry. "Terrian, Character and Text: Is *Cold Mountain* by Charles Frazier a Post-Pastoral Novel?" *Mississippi Quarterly: The Journal of Southern Culture* (Winter 2001–2002): 87–96.

Gussow, Mel. Review of *Cold Mountain*. *New York Times* (August 15, 1997): B1, B7.

Heddendorf, David. "Closing the Distance to *Cold Mountain*." *Southern Review* (Winter 2000): 188–195.

Menand, Louis. "Dispossession." *New Yorker* (October 2, 2006): 92.

Reese, Jennifer. "Half-Full *Moons*." *Entertainment Weekly* (October 6, 2006): 72.

⚙ Russell Freedman

BORN: *1929, San Francisco, California*

NATIONALITY: *American*

GENRE: *Nonfiction, fiction*

MAJOR WORKS:

Lincoln: A Photobiography (1987)

Kids at Work: Lewis Hine and the Crusade Against Child Labor (1994)

Babe Didrickson Zaharis: The Making of a Champion (1999)

Freedom Walkers: The Story of the Montgomery Bus Boycott (2006)

Overview

Best known as the writer of a wide array of nonfiction books for younger writers that includes extensive visuals, Russell Freedman is an innovator who introduced historical revisionism to children's literature. Instead of sanitized, myth-filled histories often targeted at children, Freedman's "information books" are as readable as fiction books but with complex information presented in an understandable and entertaining fashion with photographs to complement and supplement the text. Among his best-known works is *Lincoln: A Photobiography* (1987), which won the 1988 Newbery Medal.

Russell Freedman   *Freedman, Russell, photograph by Carlo Ontal. Reproduced by permission of Russell Freedman.*

Works in Biographical and Historical Context

Literary Upbringing   Born on October 11, 1929, in San Francisco, California, Russell Bruce Freedman is the son of Louis Nathan and Irene (Gordon) Freedman. Russell's father was a publishing representative for Macmillan and filled their home with books. In this way Freedman was exposed to literature from an early age, became an avid reader, and, thanks to his father's professional contacts, was able to meet some of the leading authors of the twentieth century, including John Steinbeck.

As a youth, Freedman's two favorite books were Robert Louis Stevenson's novel *Treasure Island* (1883) and Ernest Thompson Seton's natural history book *Wild Animals I Have Known* (1898). Freedman did not distinguish between nonfiction and fiction at the time, but as he grew older, he realized that a nonfiction book like Seton's could entertain him as thoroughly as a fictional tale. *Wild Animals I Have Known* became a starting point in his interest for nonfiction reading—an interest that contributed to his decision to become a professional writer.

Served in Korea   Freedman attended San Jose College from 1947 to 1949, then earned his BA from the University of California at Berkeley in 1951. After graduation, he served in the army for two years as a member of the U.S. Army's Counterintelligence Corps. Freedman spent part of his time in the army serving in Korea during the Korean War. After World War II, Korea was artificially divided between a communist north, influenced by the Soviets, and a democratic south, influenced by the United States. In 1950, North Korean armed forces struck across the demarcation line and into South Korea, launching the war. The United States sent troops in support of South Korea. The seesaw struggle lasted for three years, saw the United States alone suffer 140,000 casualties, and the borders essentially remain the same at the end of the conflict as they were at the beginning.

When he was released from the service, Freedman held a variety of writing positions in which, he later admitted, he learned to write. He took a job as a reporter and editor for the Associated Press in San Francisco from 1953 to 1956. In 1956, Freedman moved to New York City to work in the television-publicity department as a writer for J. Walter Thompson, an advertising agency. Freedman left Thompson in 1960, and joined the Columbia University Press in 1961. There he worked as an associate staff member of the *Columbia Encyclopedia*.

Inspired by Teens   Freedman published his first book, *Teenagers Who Made History* in 1961. The book was inspired by a *New York Times* article about a blind sixteen-year-old who invented a Braille typewriter. Researching further, Freedman learned that Louis Braille had also been sixteen when he invented the Braille alphabet, a system that allows blind people to read with their hands. This information compelled Freedman to wonder what other significant achievements had been made by young people. Based on further research, *Teenagers Who Made History* offers a collection of biographies of influential young people.

Freedman followed *Teenagers* with a history of space travel, *Two Thousand Years of Space Travel* (1965) and the biographies *Thomas Alva Edison* (1966) and *Jules Verne: Portrait of a Prophet* (1968). While his writing career was taking off, Freedman held other posts. He was an editor for the Crowell-Collier Educational Corporation from 1964 to 1965. A few years later, in 1969, Freedman joined the faculty of the New School for Social Research. He remained a writing-workshop instructor with the New School until 1986.

Animal Books   In the late 1960s, Freedman began writing the works that make up the bulk of his early career: animal books. He wrote more than twenty such books, sometimes in collaboration with James E. Morriss, which sought to explain, in simple language, some of the scientific concepts of the animal kingdom. These books include *How Animals Learn* (1969), *Animal Instincts* (1971), and *The Brains of Animals and Man* (1972). The titles were well-received by the educational community.

Freedman followed these books with further explorations of the animal kingdom, including *The First Days of Life* (1974) and *How Birds Fly* (1977). Some of these works feature detailed drawings that illustrated Freedman's words. By the end of the 1970s, Freedman switched to photographs to enhance the text and make his books stronger and clearer. *Hanging On: How Animals Carry Their Young* (1977) was one his first books to utilize photographs.

Focus on History   In 1980, Freedman took a break from chronicling wildlife to write about human beings. While attending a photographic exhibit at the New York Historical Society, Freedman was struck by the photographs of children in the nineteenth and early twentieth century. Freedman decided to tell the story behind these photographs, attempting to convey a sense of what life was like at that time. The resulting book was *Immigrant Kids* (1980). Freedman continued to produce books on animals, but from this point forward he focused more and more of his writings on people. Books like the award-winning *Children of the Wild West* (1983) and *Cowboys of the Wild West* (1985) were praised for their accurate portrayal of life in the Old West.

Continuing to separate fact from fiction, Freedman next turned to an intriguing president. In 1987, Freedman published one of his most lauded works, *Lincoln: A Photobiography*. Including many photographs, the work examines the man behind the myth and shows Lincoln to be a highly complex and paradoxical figure who is vastly more interesting than the Lincoln of legend and history textbooks. Freedman won the Newbery Medal for the work, one of the few nonfiction titles to be so honored in the history of the award.

Award-Winning "Photobiographies"   Following the success of *Lincoln*, Freedman continued to write about historical figures in "photobiographies" or "information books" from the late 1980s to the early 2000s. These works won him numerous awards. These include *Franklin Delano Roosevelt* (1990), *Kids at Work: Lewis Hine and the Crusade Against Child Labor* (1994), and *The Voice That Challenged a Nation: Marion Anderson and the Struggle for Equal Rights* (2005). Many titles were linked to social and historical issues. For example, *Kids at Work* illustrated the plight of children forced to work in the early 1900s, as revealed by investigative reporter Lewis Hine. Working for the National Child Labor Committee from 1908 to 1918, Hine toured the United States recording visual proof of children doing backbreaking, grueling, and often dangerous work.

Freedman has continued to publish such challenging historical works as *The Adventures of Marco Polo* (2006) and *Who Was First? Discovering the Americas* (2007). In 2007, Freedman received a National Humanities medal. He continues to live and work in New York City.

Works in Literary Context

In many of his books, Freedman heightens the interest of his subject by including photographs and other illustrations to accompany the text. Through painstaking research, Freedman finds the most appropriate images available to lend a sense of immediacy to his words. Freedman also

employs a consistently evenhanded, objective approach to subjects that have been distorted and romanticized. He focuses on historical truths rather than myth building. As an author, Freedman was greatly influenced by several books he read in his youth, including *Treasure Island*, *Wild Animals I Have Known*, and Hendrik Willem Van Loon's *The Story of Mankind* (1921).

Historical Truths   In many of Freedman's biographies and history books, the author's primary goal is to set the record straight. For example, in his first biography, *Lincoln: A Photobiography*, Freedman offered a realistic, complex view of the legendary president, instead of including the usual myths that were often included in books, especially those for younger readers, about Lincoln. Similarly, his *Franklin Delano Roosevelt* reveals the subject in all his complexity. Without sentiment or pathos, Freedman looks honestly and directly at the man and his times. Freedman does not overload the facts, but offers a keen sense of balance and form in the composition and arrangement of information. In *The Adventures of Marco Polo*, Freedman offers an evenhanded examination of this fourteenth-century adventurer who traveled to the Middle East, India, and China. Freedman includes questions about the truths of some of Polo's alleged escapades. In his book *Freedom Walkers: The Story of the Montgomery Bus Boycott* (2006), Freedman uses actual recorded words and

COMMON HUMAN EXPERIENCE

Some of Freedman's books, like *Freedom Walkers: The Story of the Montgomery Bus Boycott*, offer a perspective on the civil rights movement for young readers. Here are some other books for children about the civil rights movement:

> *Freedom Riders: John Lewis and Jim Zwerg on the Front Lines of the Civil Rights Movement* (2006), a nonfiction book by Ann Bausum. In this book, the author highlights two young participants in the 1961 freedom ride to Montgomery, Alabama, to promote equal rights for African Americans.
>
> *Rosa* (2005), a nonfiction book by Nikki Giovanni. This biography of Rosa Parks tells about the life of the seamstress who refused to give up her seat on a Montgomery, Alabama, bus in 1955. Her act helped launch the Montgomery bus boycott and contributed to the greater civil rights movement.
>
> *A Picture Book of Martin Luther King, Jr.* (1989), a nonfiction book by David Adler and Robert Casilla. This illustrated biography of the Baptist minister and civil rights leader emphasizes his philosophy and practice of nonviolent civil disobedience.
>
> *Through My Eyes* (1999), a memoir by Ruby Bridges and Margo Lundell. In this autobiography, Bridges recounts how she, as a six-year-old, became the first African American to integrate the William Frantz Elementary School in New Orleans.

deeds from participants in the civil rights movement to show everyday truths about the persons involved.

Illustrations   Another characteristic of many of Freedman's books is the use of photographs and other visuals. The use of pictures adds depth to his story and brings home the reality of many historical situations. While *Lincoln: A Photobiography* includes only five photographs, they show the ravages of the presidency on the embattled Lincoln during his four years in office. Archival photographs show the extent of Marian Anderson's life and influence as a singer and civil rights activist in *The Voice That Challenged a Nation: Marian Anderson and the Struggle for Equal Rights*. Farm Security Administration photographs, including some by well-known photographers Dorothea Lange and Walker Evans, document life during the Great Depression in *Children of the Great Depression* (2005). Not all the pictures are about the harshness of life during this difficult time; Freedman includes references to music and films as diversions. Sometimes Freedman uses paintings and drawings for illustrations if he believes the art would be more effective. For example, in *Buffalo Hunt* (1988), Freedman employs paintings of artist adventurers who traveled West

in the 1800s, when Indians depended on the American bison to fulfill material and spiritual needs, to illustrate his premise. *The Adventures of Marco Polo* includes maps, illustrations, and photographs to tell a well-rounded story.

Works in Critical Context

Critics have praised Freedman's compelling and dynamic yet straightforward approach to nonfiction as well as his ability to explain technical subjects in a clear, interesting way. Nearly all of Freedman's historical works are reviewed positively by critics for their approach to history and their readability. His animal books also receive critical attention for being thorough and engaging studies of animals. Freedman has perhaps been most lauded for his biographies of important figures in American history. Overall, his books are considered informative, well-written, and entertaining.

Kids at Work: Lewis Hine and the Crusade Against Child Labor   *Kids at Work: Lewis Hine and the Crusade Against Child Labor* was Freedman's chronicle of child laborers in the late nineteenth and early twentieth centuries. Reviewing the book for the *New York Times Book Review*, Iris Tillman Hill writes that Freedman "has an unerring instinct for the right quotation from the photographer's own writing. He captures the spirit of Lewis Hine in his vivid text and provides an insightful look at an important era in American labor history." Critics also laud the way *Kids at Work* came together. Roger Sutton observes in the *Bulletin of the Center for Children's Books* that Freedman's "fluent text" delineates the harshness of the photographic material as well as the decency of Lewis Hine himself. Sutton adds, "Spaciously designed, the book moves easily between words and pictures."

Babe Didrickson Zaharis: The Making of a Champion   In *Babe Didrickson Zaharis: The Making of a Champion* (1999), Freedman tells the story of the remarkable career of Didrickson, who broke records in golf, track and field, and other sports, and all at a time when opportunities for females in athletics were very limited. "Freedman is on top of his game with this engaging profile of one of this century's most remarkable athletes and larger-than-life personalities," writes Luann Toth in a *School Library Journal* review. Toth concludes, "Befitting a champion, this superbly crafted, impeccably documented biography ranks head and shoulders above its peers." A reviewer in *Horn Book* believes "Freedman's measured yet lively style captures the spirit of the great athlete," and that the plentiful black-and-white photographs "capture Babe's spirit and dashing good looks." A contributor for *Publishers Weekly* calls Freedman's biography "exemplary" and concludes that this "celebratory work gives readers a chance to cheer Zaharias's legendary life."

Responses to Literature

1. Using photographs you have taken yourself or to which you have access, write a photobiography of

someone you know. Integrate the photos thoroughly into your text.

2. Read both previously written books for young readers on President Abraham Lincoln and as Freedman's book on Lincoln. In an essay, explain how Freedman's text and story differ from the books you have chosen. Is Freedman's superior? Why or why not?

3. Create a presentation about Freedman's animal behavior books. How did the books evolve as the series continued? Did the addition of illustrations enhance the effectiveness of these books?

4. In a small group, debate the arguments Freedman sets forth in *Who Was First?: Discovering the Americas* (2007). In your opinion, who really discovered America first? Support your statement with details from Freedman's book.

BIBLIOGRAPHY

Periodicals

Hill, Iris Tillman. Review of *Kids at Work: Lewis Hine and the Crusade Against Child Labor*. *New York Times Book Review* (November 13, 1994): 23.

Review of *Babe Didrickson Zaharis: The Making of a Champion*. *Horn Book* (September–October 1999): 623.

Review of *Babe Didrickson Zaharis: The Making of a Champion*. *Publishers Weekly* (July 19, 1999): 196.

Sutton, Roger. Review of *Kids at Work: Lewis Hine and the Crusade Against Child Labor*. *Bulletin of the Center for Children's Books* (1994): 44–45.

Toth, Luann. Review of *Babe Didrickson Zaharis: The Making of a Champion*. *School Library Journal* (July 1999): 106.

✲ Betty Friedan

BORN: *1921, in Peoria, Illinois*

DIED: *2006, in Washington, D.C.*

NATIONALITY: *American*

GENRE: *Nonfiction*

MAJOR WORKS:

The Feminine Mystique (1963)

The Second Stage (1981)

Beyond Gender: The New Politics of Work and Family (1997)

Overview

A renowned figure in the women's movement, Betty Friedan gained prominence in the early 1960s for her nonfiction work, *The Feminine Mystique* (1963). A bestseller, her book has been credited with revitalizing interest in the women's movement and she herself co-founded the National Organization of Women (NOW). In addi-

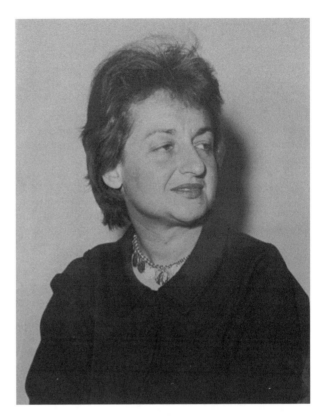

Betty Friedan   *Friedan, Betty, photograph. The Library of Congress.*

tion to women's rights, Friedan was also interested in labor rights, minority rights, and the problem of discrimination against the aged.

Works in Biographical and Historical Context

Encouraged to Write Betty Friedan was born Betty Naomi Goldstein in Peoria, Illinois, on February 4, 1921, one year after women in the United States won the right to vote. She was the daughter of Harry and Miram (Horowitz) Goldstein. Her father was a Russian Jewish immigrant and a jeweler, while her mother had been a journalist until her marriage. The eldest of three children, Friedan was raised in comfort for much of her childhood and encouraged to strive for excellence in all she did.

When the Great Depression hit, her parents struggled to support the family. Her parents fought more, with her mother lashing out at her father. Friedan then became determined to find the fulfillment for herself that her mother never did achieve.

Gifted Student Encouraged by her mother to become a journalist, Friedan began writing for her school newspaper in junior high school. She continued to write in high school, where she also started a campus magazine with a male classmate. Graduating from high school at the age of seventeen, she went to Smith College, where she proved to be a gifted student.

There, Friedan studied psychology and served as the editor of the school's newspaper. After her graduation with a psychology degree summa cum laude in 1942, Friedan entered graduate school at the University of California at Berkeley. After one year of study, she won a research fellowship to complete her PhD. However, faced with the necessity of sacrificing marriage and motherhood in pursuit of an academic career, as well as her boyfriend's threat to break up with her if she took it, she turned down the fellowship.

Reporter, then Domestic Life After breaking up with the boyfriend, Friedan left California and moved to New York City. There, she found employment at a Greenwich Village workers' newspaper as a reporter. Covering strikes and labor disputes, Friedan learned about discrimination in the workplace—not only by employers against male workers but also by employers and unions against women. She also became politically active in New York City.

Within a few years, Friedan met and married Carl Friedan. The couple soon had their first child, Daniel, and she took a year's maternity leave from her newspaper job. Friedan returned to her post a little reluctantly, but she was fired from this position after requesting a second maternity leave after the birth of her son Jonathan. Friedan's employers felt she could not be a good mother and work all day. During this period in time, it was common practice for employers to fire women when they became pregnant.

Freelance Writer Leaving New York, the couple found a home in the suburbs, and Friedan prepared to settle into a full-time career as a mother. She also gave birth to a third child, Emily. Before long, though, she began to feel frustrated about her role. Friedan then became a freelance writer for women's magazines, such as *Cosmopolitan* and *Parents*. Her early articles were frequently about women as wives and mothers. When she tried to sell stories about women who were living outside of traditional roles, she was told that such profiles were not really what American women wanted to read.

Noticing that editors frequently eliminated references to her subjects' careers from her articles as well, Friedan began interviewing housewives about their lives. She was also influenced by learning that many of her talented former classmates from Smith College were extremely frustrated by their restrictive roles as mothers and wives in the mid-1950s. Friedan wrote an article on the subject for *McCall's*, but because of its pessimistic tone, the magazine decided not to run it. Other women's magazines turned it down or would only run it with substantial revisions, so she decided to expand it into a book.

The Feminine Mystique This research formed the basis of what would become her best-known work, *The Feminine Mystique* (1963). In the book, she argues that the "feminine mystique"—the belief that women gained

fulfillment only from marriage and motherhood—was responsible for the boredom, fatigue, and dissatisfaction that has pervaded the lives of many American women. Although women gained the right to vote in 1920, they were still largely discriminated against over forty years later, finding their abilities to contribute to society limited by chauvinism in the home and the workplace. The book sold over three million copies by 1966 and sparked the feminist movement.

Recognized as a leader by women, Friedan began lecturing throughout the country, explaining her ideas for change and dispelling the myth that women should be totally satisfied with just being wives and mothers. Also continuing to work as a journalist, Friedan was covering the Third National Conference of Commissions on the Status of Women when she discussed with other women the idea of an organization like the NAACP (National Association for the Advancement of Colored People) to protect women's rights.

NOW and Political Activism In 1966, Friedan co-founded the National Organization of Women (NOW) and served as its president until 1970. Under her guidance, NOW lobbied for the legalization of abortion, the passage of the Equal Rights Amendment, and the equal treatment of women in the workplace. Friedan, however, came into frequent conflict with radical feminists over the issue of lesbianism as a political stance, which she opposed on the grounds that it alienated mainstream women and men sympathetic to the movement. During this time period, Friedan's personal life also changed. She moved to New York City without her husband in 1966, and the couple divorced in 1969.

After resigning the presidency of NOW in 1970, Friedan turned her attention to women who were not fully in agreement with the women's movement. She wanted to include even the doubtful homemakers in the struggle for equality. Calling it a "human" rights movement, Friedan reached out to men and women through her popular column in *McCall's*.

Political infighting between Friedan and such prominent activists as Gloria Steinem and Bella Abzug disrupted the 1973 National Women's Political Caucus. Friedan later indirectly accused them of manipulating the balloting to prevent the participation of her supporters. Friedan discussed this controversy and chronicled her early involvement with the women's movement in *It Changed My Life* (1976), a collection of her speeches and previously published writings interspersed with retrospective commentary.

Throughout the 1970s, 1980s, and 1990s, Friedan taught at various universities including Temple University, Yale University, Queens College, and the New School for Social Research. She also campaigned for the Equal Rights Amendment, which had been repeatedly defeated. In addition, Friedan continued to publish books on rights-related topics. In *The Second Stage* (1981), she discussed the emergence of the dangerous Superwoman myth—the unrealistic image of the woman who effortlessly juggles her career, marriage, and children.

Published Late in Life   Over a decade later, Friedan published *The Fountain of Age* (1993) which focused on discrimination against older workers by businesses as well as general rights of the elderly and aged, and *Beyond Gender: The New Politics of Work and Family* (1997), which also focused on discrimination. In 2000, Friedan published her autobiography *Life So Far: A Memoir*. She died on February 4, 2006, in Washington, D.C., of congestive heart failure.

Works in Literary Context

Friedan's writings exemplify her commitment to social equality and social justice, irrespective of gender or age. Through such works as *The Feminine Mystique*, she helped create a social revolution that changed the way Americans viewed women and women viewed themselves. In such later books as *The Fountain of Age*, Friedan tried to effect social change related to age discrimination, especially in the workplace. As an author, Friedan was influenced by her psychology studies and journalism background, historical and social changes that occurred in her lifetime, and the stories of many women's lives that were shared with her over the years.

Women's Issues   Most of Friedan's best-known books, including *The Feminine Mystique* and *The Second Stage*, focus on issues related to women, their place in society, and the challenges they face. In *The Feminine Mystique*, for example, Friedan argues the post–World War II boom of suburban homes and labor-saving devices thrust women into unfulfilling domestic routines. This lack of fulfillment, she believes, resulted in widespread boredom, depression, and anxiety, as well as an increase in the number of women addicted to tranquilizers and alcohol. To combat these problems, Friedan advocated increased educational and career opportunities as well as creativity and courage for women. While *The Feminine Mystique* drew supporters to the feminist movement, *The Second Stage* offered Friedan's critique of a result of the feminist movement while acknowledging that women had made great strides. Dubbing the woman who could do it all—career, marriage, and children—as the Superwoman, she believed that such a figure was as far removed from reality as the perfect housewives depicted in magazines in the 1960s and could have lasting negative effects on the women's movement. Describing this phenomenon as the "feminist mystique," Friedan suggested that women should begin to rely on support networks and that men and women should join together to create true equality.

Discrimination   In both *The Feminine Mystique* and *The Second Stage* as well as her other books, Friedan acknowledges the negative effect discrimination has on people's lives, the feminist movement, and greater society. *The Feminine Mystique* highlights the role the media

LITERARY AND HISTORICAL CONTEMPORARIES

Friedan's famous contemporaries include:

Gloria Steinem (1934–): This American activist was a leader of the women's movement in the late twentieth century, and was often in conflict with Friedan. Steinem was also a founder of *Ms.* magazine.

Bella Abzug (1920–1998): This American women's rights and civil rights activist also worked as a labor lawyer. She served two terms in the U.S. House of Representatives, and wrote *Gender Gap: Abzug's Guide to Political Power for Women* (1984).

Erica Jong (1942–): This American novelist was known for her frank, satirical treatment of sexuality. Her works, including *Fear of Flying* (1973), have been interpreted as pioneering efforts toward an authentic and free expression of female sexuality.

Vance Packard (1941–1996): This American social journalist wrote *The Hidden Persuaders* (1957), a book about hidden messages in advertising. The work started out as an article that he could not get published. Packard's work inspired Friedan to turn her unwanted magazine article into *The Feminine Mystique*.

Florence Rosenfeld Howe (1929–): This American author and historian was a leader of the contemporary feminist movement and helped found The Feminist Press in 1970. Her books include *Traditions and the Talents of Women* (1991).

and advertising played in creating an image of an ideal housewife, creating a situation where women face discrimination if they try to break free of this role. Men also face a similar type of discrimination as they have to play a certain type of masculine role in order to be accepted by society. In her collection *It Changed My Life*, Friedan reiterates the need for feminists not to discriminate themselves. She emphasizes that they should not exclude men from the movement nor to chastise those women who wish to be attractive by wearing cosmetics. While *The Fountain of Age* is personal as Friedan considers the prospects she personally faced in growing old, she also emphasizes that there is widespread ageism in the workplace and society. Yet, Friedan argues that the aging process is not necessarily the time of decline that the media and other forces would depict. She argues that such a heightened involvement with the process of living has allowed women to remain vigorous and able to fight against continued discrimination.

Works in Critical Context

Critics have acknowledged Friedan's role in the launching of the contemporary women's movement, and that her

COMMON HUMAN EXPERIENCE

In *Life So Far*, Friedan offers her autobiography as a feminist. Here are some other biographies and autobiographies of famous women activists:

Susan B. Anthony: A Biography of a Singular Feminist (1988), a biography by Kathleen Berry. This biography offers the life story of a leading nineteenth-century figure in the fight for women's rights.

Sojourner Truth and the Struggle for Freedom (1987), a biography by Edward Claflin and Jada Rowland. This biography emphasizes how Truth spoke out courageously for freedom and equality for slaves and women.

Five Sisters: The Langhorne Sisters of Virginia (2000), a biography by James Fox. This biography includes information about Nancy Langhorne, who married Lord Waldorf Astor. As Lady Astor, she became the first female member of Parliament and was a strong advocate for women's rights.

Living My Life (1930), an autobiography by Emma Goldman. This autobiography details the author's life as an anarchist who immigrated to the United States from Russia in 1886. While working in a sweatshop, she began speaking out about women's rights.

works, especially *The Feminine Mystique*, had an important place in the movement. While initial reaction to the book was mixed, it has become regarded as a classic work of early feminist literature. It remains regarded as an influential work that served as the impetus for change in many women's lives. Friedan's other books received less critical attention, but such works as *The Fountain of Age* were regarded as representative of her shift to related issues like age-related discrimination. Overall, many reviewers were divided over the content of Friedan's books and the effectiveness of her writing.

The Feminine Mystique   Reaction to *The Feminine Mystique* was diverse for both critics and its target audience. Friedan and her book were not warmly received by some feminists, who viewed her as somewhat reactionary and bourgeois. Other critics praised her for exploding the myth of woman as content homemaker who would defer her own interests to take care of her family. Sylvia Fleis Fava, writing in the *American Sociological Review*, notes that "Friedan tends to set up a counter-mystique; that all women must have creative interests outside the home to realize themselves. This can be just as confining and tension-producing as any other mold." More recent critics believe that *The Feminine Mystique* still has relevance, with Stacey Kauder of *Herizons* noting, "It remains a feminist classic today."

It Changed My Life: Writings on the Women's Movement   Friedan's collection of writings from the 1960s and 1970s, *It Changed My Life: Writings on the Women's Movement*, was somewhat well-received as a book in which she sorts out the healthy, productive elements of the women's movement from the petty, divisive ones in an attempt to gain a new focus. Writing in the *Village Voice*, Eliot Fremont-Smith notes, "She wants us to *Get Together* in a cause that is right and good for all of us, women, men, children, grandparents, single people, everybody." However, some critics took issue with her depiction of the politicking behind such events as the National Women's Political Caucus. Stephanie Harrington of the *New York Times Book Review* questions Friedan's "half-light between innuendo and substantial accusation, juxtaposing names and her version of events with and letting the implications fall where they may" approach. Furthermore, critics like Sara Sanborn in the *Saturday Review* faulted Friedan for her maternal attitude toward her accomplishments. Sanborn described it as "a self-justifying, even self-regarding tone ... as though Friedan was afraid that we might forget our debt to her."

Responses to Literature

1. In an essay, examine the ideas Friedan brought up in *The Feminine Mystique* through the eyes of someone living in the early twenty-first century. Do you think the problems she brings up still exist today?

2. Create a presentation about the National Organization of Women, including Friedan's role in founding the organization. How do you think NOW has affected American society since its inception?

3. In a small group, discuss the *The Feminine Mystique* and *The Second Stage*, focusing on the evolution of Friedan's thoughts. Do you see a link between the books? Is *The Second Stage* a true sequel to *The Feminine Mystique*? Why or why not?

4. Research age discrimination and related legislation in the early twenty-first century. Write a paper in which you link *The Fountain of Age* to current ageism issues. Do you think ageism exists? How does it affect you when an elderly person suffers from discrimination?

BIBLIOGRAPHY

Books

Henry, Sondra and Emily Taitz. *Betty Friedan: Fighter for Women's Rights*. Springfield, N.J.: Enslow, 1990.

Hennessee, Judith Adler. *Betty Friedan: Her Life*. New York: Random House, 1999.

Horowitz, Daniel. *Betty Friedan and the Making of The Feminine Mystique: The American Left, the Cold War, and Modern Feminism*. Amherst: The University of Massachusetts Press, 1998.

Periodicals

Fava, Sylvia Fleis. Review of *The Feminine Mystique*. *American Sociological Review* (December 1963): 1053–1054.

Fremont-Smith, Eliot. Review of *It Changed My Life: Writings on the Women's Movement*. *Village Voice* (June 28, 1976): 43–44.

Harrington, Stephanie. Review of *It Changed My Life: Writings on the Women's Movement*. *New York Times Book Review* (July 4, 1976): 7–8.

Kauder, Stacey. Review of *The Feminine Mystique*. *Herizons* (Summer 2006): 42.

Sanborn, Sara. Review of *It Changed My Life: Writings on the Women's Movement*. *Saturday Review* (July 24, 1976).

❀ Robert Frost

BORN: *1874, San Francisco, California*

DIED: *1963, Boston, Massachusetts*

NATIONALITY: *American*

GENRE: *Poetry*

MAJOR WORKS:

"The Road Not Taken" (1916)

"Stopping by Woods on a Snowy Evening" (1923)

A Further Range (1936)

In the Clearing (1962)

Overview

The winner of four Pulitzer Prizes for poetry, Robert Frost holds a unique and almost isolated position in American letters. He stands at the crossroads of nineteenth-century American poetry and modernism, for in his verse may be found the culmination of many nineteenth-century tendencies and traditions as well as parallels to the works of his twentieth-century contemporaries. Taking his symbols from the public domain, Frost developed an original, modern idiom and sense of directness and economy that reflect the imagism of Ezra Pound and Amy Lowell. Frost favored New England idioms, characters, and settings in his poetry.

Works in Biographical and Historical Context

Childhood in San Francisco Born Robert Lee Frost on March 26, 1874, in San Francisco, California, he was the son of William Prescott Frost Jr. and his wife Isabelle (Moodie). His father was from New England, and worked variously as a teacher, editor, and politician, while his mother was a native of Scotland who also was employed as a teacher. Frost spent the first decade of his life in San Francisco, until his father's death from tuberculosis in 1884.

Robert Frost   *Frost, Robert, photograph. The Library of Congress.*

Because William Frost wanted to be buried in New England, Robert, his mother, and younger sister Jeanie went east for the funeral. The family could not afford to return to California, and settled in Salem, Massachusetts, where Robert's grandfather had offered them a home. Isabelle Frost eventually found a teaching job at a school to support her family.

Inspired by Literature As a young boy, Frost greatly enjoyed hearing his mother read to him. She introduced him to a large variety of literature and inspired him to become an excellent reader. He soon decided that he wanted to be a poet as well. Though Frost lacked enthusiasm for school during his elementary years, he later became a serious student and was co-valedictorian of his class at Lawrence High School with Elinor White. Frost was also the class poet.

After graduating from high school in 1892, Frost entered Dartmouth College, but soon dropped out. He had become engaged to his high school classmate, White, who was still attending college. Frost then held a series of jobs, including mill worker, newspaper reporter, and teacher, and wrote poetry all the while.

Published First Poem In 1894, Frost sold his first poem, "My Butterfly," to the New York *Independent*. Because his fiancée did not react enthusiastically to a specially printed copy he gave her, Frost suffered an emotional crisis and believed their engagement over. Frost wandered south to Virginia and North Carolina, and even contemplated suicide.

The crisis was smoothed over, and Frost married White in 1895. He then tried to make a career of teaching. Frost helped his mother run a small private school in Lawrence, where his first son was born. He also tried to continue his own education, by attending Harvard for two years. However, undergraduate study proved difficult while he was raising a family, and he became physically and mentally exhausted. Frost also continued to write poetry, and published thirteen poems between 1894 and 1902.

Personal Problems   Frost and his wife added a daughter to their still-growing brood. Robert decided to try chicken farming on a Methuen, Massachusetts, farm purchased by his grandfather. In 1900, when Frost's nervousness was diagnosed as a sign that he might possibly contract tuberculosis, he moved his expanding family and poultry business to Derry, New Hampshire.

There, Frost's eldest child died, and, in 1906, Frost himself was stricken with pneumonia and almost died. A year later, his fourth daughter died. The accumulated grief and suffering, as well as lesser frustrations in his personal and business life, compelled Frost to turn to writing more poetry. Once again, Frost also tried teaching, first in Derry, then in Plymouth, New Hampshire.

Focus on Poetry in England   In 1912, Frost was nearly forty and had only published a few poems, but he nevertheless decided to focus exclusively on his art. He sold his farm and used an allowance from his grandfather to go to England and write. The family settled on a farm in Buckinghamshire, and Frost began writing prolifically as he attempted to perfect his distinct poetic voice. New acquaintances like American poet Ezra Pound helped Frost get published in magazines, though Frost later resented Pound's excessive management. Frost also began meeting people in literature who inspired and expand his knowledge of poetry.

Frost soon published his first major volumes of poetry, *A Boy's Will* (1913) and *North of Boston* (1914). Both of these volumes were well-received, featuring excellent examples of his lyric and narrative poems. These poems also immediately established his reputation as a nature poet of New England, for he addressed not only its loveliness but the isolation, harshness, and pain its residents must endure.

Sudden Fame   Frost and his family returned to the United States in 1915 primarily because of the outbreak of World War I. This conflict began in Europe in 1914 after the assassination of Archduke Franz Ferdinand, the heir to the Austro-Hungarian throne. Because of political tensions and entangling alliances, nearly the whole of Europe soon became involved in the conflict. The United States joined the war on the side of Great Britain and France in 1917 after Germany's naval fleet began sinking American merchant ships in British waters. Ultimately, ten million soldiers died and 20 million were wounded during the course of the "Great War."

When the Frosts returned to the United States in 1915, after the outbreak of World War I, *North of Boston* was a best seller and Frost was famous. Sudden fame embarrassed Frost, who had always avoided crowds. He withdrew to a small farm in Franconia, New Hampshire, but financial need saw him responding to demands for readings and lectures. In 1915 and 1916, for example, he was a Phi Beta Kappa poet at Tufts College and Harvard University. Frost soon conquered his shyness, and developed a brief and simple speaking manner that made him one of the most popular performers in America and abroad.

Built on Fame   In 1916, Frost published another lauded collection, *Mountain Interval*. The following year, Frost became one of the first poets-in-residence on an American college campus: He taught at Amherst from 1917 to 1920. In 1919, Frost moved his farming to South Saftsbury, Vermont. The following year, he co-founded the Bread Loaf School of English at Middlebury College, serving there each summer as a lecturer and consultant. From 1921 to 1923, Frost served as a poet-in-residence at the University of Michigan.

Near the end of his stay in Michigan, Frost published a new volume of poetry, *New Hampshire* (1923). Frost received the first of four Pulitzer Prizes in 1924 for the collection. After moving back and forth between Amherst and the University of Michigan in the mid-1920s and before taking a longer-term job at Amherst in 1926, Frost published *West Running Brook* (1928), which continued his experiments in tonal variations and the mingling of lyrics and narratives.

Continued Success Amid Tragedy   In the 1930s, Frost suffered the painful death of another daughter, but returned to Harvard in 1936 and published another collection, *A Further Range*, that year. At the same time, the United States was facing an economic crisis. In 1929, the American stock market crashed, which launched the Great Depression. The failure of the stock market caused the economy—first in the United States then around the world—to fall into a dramatic and sustained depression that lasted through the 1930s.

Because of Frost's weak lungs, his doctors ordered him south in 1936, and thereafter he spent his winters in Florida. Frost was a member of Harvard's staff for two years. After his wife died of a heart attack in 1938, Frost resigned his post at Amherst and sold his house. That same year, Frost was elected to the Board of Overseers at Harvard, and he began a three-year stay there in 1939.

Controversial Later Works   As World War II began, Frost continued to produce challenging poetry. World War II began in Europe when Nazi Germany invaded Poland in September 1939 and overran the country. The

United States entered the war in 1941, after Japan bombed an American naval base in Hawaii. The war was fought in a number of theaters in Europe, Asia, Africa, and the South Pacific, involving sixty-one countries and leaving 55 million people dead.

After two more collections of lyric poetry, *A Witness Tree* (1942) and *Steeple Bush* (1945), Frost's style became more experimental. In 1945, he wrote *A Masque of Reason*, an updated version of the biblical story of Job. *A Masque of Mercy* (1947) was a companion verse-drama based on the biblical story of the prophet Jonah. In 1949, Frost put out his *Complete Poems.*

Late Honors and Last Collection   While Frost published a few original works in the 1950s and early 1960s, he also received many awards and honors. In addition to being twice honored by the U.S. Senate, he also received honorary doctorates from Oxford and Cambridge. In 1961, Frost read a poem, "The Gift Outright," at the presidential inauguration of John F. Kennedy.

Frost published his last collection of original poetry, *In the Clearing*, in 1962. He died on January 29, 1963, in Boston, Massachusetts, of complications following an operation. By the time of his death, Frost was considered the unofficial poet laureate of the United States.

Works in Literary Context

In his poetry, Frost described natural scenes with vivid imagery, celebrated ordinary rural activities, and mused upon the mysteries of existence. In doing so, he subtly developed dramatic tension he frequently left unresolved, ambiguous, and open to interpretation. He strove for the sense of sound, for the colloquial, for a tension between the natural rhythm of speech and the basic iambic meter of English verse. Frost felt that the emotion that began a poem should generate a form through likenesses and dissimilarities and lead to a clarification of experience. For Frost, this was a way to spontaneity and surprise. His work led back to aspects of Thomas Hardy, Emily Dickinson, Ralph Waldo Emerson, Oliver Wendell Holmes, James Russell Lowell, and John Greenleaf Whittier. Frost's poems also recall William Wordsworth, eighteenth-century landscape poets, John Donne, and the Latin idylls and eclogues of Theocritus and Virgil. But Frost's irony and ambiguity, his concreteness and colloquial tone, his skepticism and honesty, all ensure his poetry is also unmistakably modern.

Nature   Frost often favored nature imagery in his poems, both to make moral observations and explore deeper emotions. What he finds in nature is sensuous pleasure. In his work Frost is also sensitive to the earth's fertility and to man's relationship to the soil. Yet he is aware of the distinction, the ultimate separateness, of nature and man. In addition, Frost's poetry illustrates the ways in which the decaying effects of nature are held at bay by the forms into which readers mold their understanding of their environment. Frost's complex use of nature imagery plays out in

LITERARY AND HISTORICAL CONTEMPORARIES

Robert Frost's famous contemporaries include:

Edna St. Vincent Millay (1892–1950): Millay was a lyric poet widely viewed as representative of the modern woman liberated from Victorian traditions. A political radical and feminist, her works include *Renascence* (1917).

Charles Lindbergh (1902–1974): This American aviator was the first person to fly across the Atlantic Ocean. This accomplishment caught the imagination of the world and made him a popular hero in the early twentieth century.

Charlie Chaplin (1889–1977): This British-born silent film comedian created the character of the Little Tramp and was a founding partner in United Artists. His films include *The Gold Rush* (1925) and *City Lights* (1931).

Willa Cather (1873–1947): Cather wrote about America's agrarian past with a mixture of nostalgia and realism. Her works included *O Pioneers!* (1913).

T. S. Eliot (1888–1965): This American poet found his lyrical voice while living in England and became recognized as the most influential poet writing in English after the publication of *The Waste Land* (1922).

various ways in his poetry. In *A Boy's Will*, the poem "Storm Fear" presents a man awed and subdued by sublime natural forces. The same collection also features "Into My Own," the speaker yearns to enter a dark forest, which metaphorically represents the mysteries of self and life.

Frost's use of nature imagery also evolved and matured over the course of his career. The poem "Birches" from *Mountain Interval* features a speaker who wonders whether a bent birch branch was caused by a child at play or by natural elements and metaphorically links tree-climbing with aspirations toward heaven. Midcareer poems like "Spring Pools" and "Tree at My Window" show this theme maturing. The latter features a speaker who links his emotional fluctuations with the varying kinds of weather endured by a tree outside the speaker's room. Frost continued to explore the nature imagery and themes even into his last collection. In "In Winter in the Woods," Frost's final poem in *In the Clearing*, the speaker is once again contemplating a relationship between nature and self.

Speech Patterns and New England Vernacular   Frost enriched his style by setting traditional meters against the natural rhythms of speech. Drawing his language primarily from the vernacular, he avoided artificial poetic diction by employing the accent of a soft-spoken New Englander. Frost did not merely imitate the New England

COMMON HUMAN EXPERIENCE

Frost's poems, especially the poetry found in his early volumes, are considered excellent but challenging examples of lyric poetry. Here are some other thought-provoking collections of lyric poetry published during Frost's lifetime:

> *Lyrics of a Lowly Life* (1895), a poetry collection by Paul Laurence Dunbar. This collection of lyric poems by the first major black literary professional in the United States features poems that insert black dialect into traditional English verse forms.
>
> *War Is Kind* (1899), a poetry collection by Stephen Crane. This volume of lyric poetry employs abstract language to symbolize the clash of spiritual aspiration with the absurdity of actual experience.
>
> *The Children of the Night* (1897), a poetry collection by Edwin Arlington Robinson. This poetry collection features the well-known lyric portrait "Richard Cory." Through such lyric poems, Robinson illuminates the troubled interior experiences of individuals, families, and communities.
>
> *Lustra* (1916), a poetry collection by Ezra Pound. This collection expands the possibility of English lyric poetry by incorporating Chinese, Greek, and Provençal models.

farmer idiom, but achieved something more complex in his poetry. He felt that the poet's ear must be sensitive to the voice in order to capture with the written word the significance of sound in the spoken word in something he called "sentence sounds" or "the sounds of sense." "The Death of the Hired Man," for example, consists almost entirely of a dialogue between Mary and Warren, her farmer husband. In the poem, Frost takes the prosaic patterns of their speech and makes them lyrical. Other poems in *North of Boston*—including "Mending Wall," "Home Burial," and "The Housekeeper"—are intensely psychological word portraits in the everyday rural dialect of his New England characters.

Works in Critical Context

Warmly embraced by critics from his first collection of poems, Frost's critical reputation waned during the latter part of his career. Most critics acknowledge that Frost's poetry in the 1940s and 1950s grew more and more abstract, cryptic, and even sententious. His political conservatism and religious faith, hitherto informed by skepticism and local color, became more and more the guiding principles of his work. His final three collections received less enthusiastic reviews yet contain several pieces later acknowledged as among his greatest achievements, including "The Gift Outright." Although Frost is

still generally recognized as a major American poet, many critics express reservations about his artistry. These commentators usually cite such shortcomings as simplistic philosophy, expression of stock sentiments, failure to delve deeply into thematic concerns, and inability to universalize distinct concerns of rural New England.

A Boy's Will Frost's first major collection, *A Boy's Will*, captured the critical imagination of even leading American poets. Reviewing the British edition of the book, Pound writes in *Poetry: A Magazine of Verse* that the collection "has the tang of the New Hampshire woods, and it has just this utter sincerity. ... This man has the good sense to speak naturally and to paint the thing, the thing as he sees it." Other critics also praised the poems in *A Boy's Will*, with *The Dial*'s William Morton Payne, finding part of "Flower-Gathering" laudable by noting, "The desire for the solitary soul for companionship has rarely found such beautiful expression. ..." Payne concludes, "In their simple phrasing and patent sincerity, his songs give us the sort of pleasure that we have in those of *Shropshire Lad* of Mr. [A. E.] Housman."

A Witness Tree Like many of his later collections, the Pulitzer Prize–winning *A Witness Tree* received mixed reviews from critics. Reviewing the collection in *Books*, Wilbert Snow notes a few poems "which have a right to stand with the best things he has written." For Snow, these poems include "Come In," "The Silken Tent," and "Carpe Diem," especially. Yet Snow went on: "Some of the poems here are little more than rhymed fancies; others lack the bullet-like unity of structure to be found in *North of Boston*." On the other hand, Stephen Vincent Benét in the *Saturday Review of Literature* writes that Frost had "never written any better poems than some of those in this book." Benet concludes that "This is a beautiful book, serene, observing, and passionate."

Responses to Literature

1. Read the poem "The Gift Outright" and research the presidency of John F. Kennedy as well as the era in which he was elected. In an essay, link the themes and imagery of the poem to the findings of your research.

2. Read some of Frost's poems written in New England vernacular, perhaps those in *North of Boston*. Write a few poems of your own in which you mimic the vernacular you hear in your everyday life, but inspired by the poetic devices Frost employs.

3. Frost's later poetic collections were sometimes derided by critics, though they contain some of his best-known poems. In a small group, discuss why you think this is so. Do you like his later poems better than his earlier poems? How do they reflect the era in which he lived?

4. Create a presentation about Frost's verse dramas, *A Masque of Reason* and *A Masque of Mercy*. How do

these works relate to his other poems? Where do they fit into his career? What are their strengths and weaknesses?

BIBLIOGRAPHY

Books

Cramer, Jeffrey S. *Robert Frost Among His Poems: A Literary Companion to the Poet's Own Biographical Contexts and Associations.* Jefferson, N.C.: McFarland, 1996.

Parini, Jay. *Robert Frost: A Life.* New York: Henry Holt, 1999.

Pritchard, William H. *Frost: A Literary Life Reconsidered.* New York: Oxford University Press, 1984.

Periodicals

Benét, Stephen Vincent. Review of *A Witness Tree.* *Saturday Review of Literature* (April 25, 1942).

Payne, William Morton. Review of *A Boy's Will. The Dial* (September 16, 1913): 211–12.

Pound, Ezra. Review of *A Boy's Will. Poetry: A Magazine of Verse* (May 1913): 72–74.

Snow, Wilbert. Review of *A Witness Tree. Books* (May 10, 1942).

 # Robert Fulghum

BORN: *1937, Waco, Texas*

NATIONALITY: *American*

GENRE: *Essays, nonfiction, fiction*

MAJOR WORKS:

All I Really Need to Know I Learned in Kindergarten: Uncommon Thoughts on Common Things (1988)

It Was on Fire When I Lay Down on It (1989)

Maybe (Maybe Not): Second Thoughts on a Secret Life (1993)

Overview

Best known for his thought-provoking books *All I Really Need to Know I Learned in Kindergarten: Uncommon Thoughts on Common Things* (1988) and *It Was on Fire When I Lay Down on It* (1989), Robert Fulghum's inspirational works are popular best sellers. Critics have suggested that the themes explored in the author's essays touch readers with their simplicity, humor, insight, and universal nature. While Fulghum, a former minister, injects a spiritual component into his books, his essays also emphasize the importance of little joys found in everyday life. He touches on the importance of the mundane and highlights the fragile connections that keep people attached to their loved ones and the human community at large.

Robert Fulghum   *Fulghum, Robert, photograph. AP Images.*

Works in Biographical and Historical Context

Strict Upbringing Born June 4, 1937, in Waco, Texas, Fulghum was the only child of Lee and Eula (Howard) Fulghum. His alcoholic father was an executive with Sears, Roebuck and Company, and Fulghum was raised in a strict Southern Baptist home on a ranch in Waco. His mother expected him to become a minister. Fulghum's relationship with his parents, especially his mother, was strained. Feeling rebellious after high school graduation, he embarked on a journey to discover himself and the world around him.

Fulghum first briefly attended the University of Colorado. During the summers, he helped support himself with odd jobs, including stints as a singing cowboy at dude ranches in the American West and as an amateur rodeo performer. He returned home when his father became ill and his parents suffered from financial difficulties. Fulghum then began attending Baylor University. He graduated from Baylor with a degree in history and philosophy in 1957. That same year, he married his college sweetheart, Marcia McClellan, with whom he had three children.

Attended Unitarian Seminary After a brief stint in IBM's management training program, in which he realized corporate culture was not for him, Fulghum moved to California. There he attended the Starr King School for the Ministry, a Unitarian seminary, in Berkeley. At the time, Beat poetry and the counterculture revolution were taking hold in California and soon spread

LITERARY AND HISTORICAL CONTEMPORARIES

Robert Fulghum's famous contemporaries include:

Rick Warren (1954–): A pastor and author, Warren is the founder of the largest church in the Southern Baptist Convention, the Saddleback Church in California. He wrote the inspirational best seller *The Purpose Driven Life: What on Earth Am I Here For?* (2003).

Paul Harvey (1918–2009): Harvey is a radio broadcaster famous for his long-running syndicated radio show, which blends hard news and homespun witticisms.

Andy Rooney (1919–): This American writer, newspaper columnist, and television personality has had a regular humor segment on the CBS newsmagazine series *60 Minutes* since 1978. His books include *A Few Minutes with Andy Rooney* (1981).

Jack Kerouac (1922–1969): This American author is often considered one of the leading lights of the Beat movement. His novels include *On the Road* (1957).

Oprah Winfrey (1954–): Winfrey is a world-famous television personality and actress best known for her long-running syndicated talk show *The Oprah Winfrey Show*. On her show, she emphasizes inspirational stories.

to the rest of the country. Both phenomena were subcultures that were disillusioned with mainstream morality and defied it by establishing new aesthetic standards in literary and lifestyle choices.

While a seminary student, Fulghum embraced the look and activities of counterculture. He also supported himself and his wife by working as a bartender, psychiatric-patient counselor, prison counselor, and painter. Fulghum earned a degree in divinity from Starr King and was ordained to the ministry of the Unitarian Church in 1961.

Life as a Minister Fulghum then became a part-time minister in Bellingham, Washington, where he and his wife began their family. In 1966, Fulghum moved to another part-time ministry at Edmonds Unitarian Church in Seattle, Washington. While working there, he participated in other activities and held other jobs. For example, he went to Birmingham, Alabama, for a civil rights march to oppose segregation and support basic civil rights for African Americans. By 1971, Fulghum also became an art instructor at the Lakeside School in Seattle, Washington.

While Fulghum's life was full, there were problems. He and his wife had grown apart, and he considered suicide. Continuing his adventurous streak, Fulghum went to Japan in 1972 to study at a Zen Buddhist monastery. There, he met the woman who would become his second wife, Lynn Edwards. Fulghum divorced his first wife in 1973, then married Edwards in 1975. The couple

lived on a houseboat on Seattle's Lake Union and spent their summers traveling the world.

From Minister to Best-Selling Author In 1985, Fulghum retired from ministry at Edmonds Unitarian Church and became a minister emeritus there. Three years later, he also left his art instructor position at Lakeside School. Soon, however, he had a new career as an author. During his ministry of more than two decades, Fulghum had jotted down daily insights for use in sermons and church newsletter-articles, essays, and columns.

One of these works in particular had struck a chord. The piece, which focused on the valuable life lessons learned in kindergarten, first sparked interest within the Unitarian community. After being copied and passed around, Fulghum's work made it beyond the Unitarian circuit and into the mainstream. It was read into the Congressional Record, featured on various radio shows, and reprinted in several major newspapers and magazines. A literary agent came across the essay, and, impressed by the writing, contacted Fulghum. The result was Fulghum's first book.

Fulghum published *All I Really Need to Know I Learned in Kindergarten: Uncommon Thoughts on Common Things* in 1988, and it was an immediate smash best seller. Though critics were underwhelmed, the book won immediate public acclaim and appeared on several best-seller charts.

In 1989, Fulghum published his second best seller, *It Was on Fire When I Lay Down on It*. Like *All I Really Need to Know*, *It Was on Fire When I Lay Down on It* is a collection of thought-provoking compositions that appealed more to general readers than to critics.

Continued Literary Success Fulghum continued to produce books on similar themes through the late 1990s. In 1991, he published *Uh-Oh: Some Observations from Both Sides of the Refrigerator Door*, which offers advice on how to overcome problematic situations that begin with one party uttering the phrase "uh oh." While *Maybe (Maybe Not): Second Thoughts from a Secret Life* (1993) is in the same vein as *All I Really Need to Know*, *From Beginning to End: The Rituals of Our Lives* (1995) is more narrowly focused.

In *From Beginning to End*, Fulghum examines the ways in which human beings create meaning and give structure to their lives through public rituals. He looks at public events such as weddings, funerals, school reunions, and church services. Fulghum includes more information from his own life, and writes about his reunion with the daughter he gave up for adoption in 1958.

Break from Publishing Fulghum published two books in 1997—*True Love: Real Life Stories* and *Words I Wish I Wrote*—then took a decade-long break from writing. In that time, he traveled the world and pursued such new interests as learning how to dance the tango. Fulghum returned to publishing in 2007 with a new collection of essays, *What On Earth Have I Done?: Stories, Observations, and Affirmations*. As with his previous works, this collection finds meaning in ordinary life and often offers moral lessons. Fulghum continues to live and write in Seattle, but also spends time on the Greek island of Crete.

Works in Literary Context

In his successful collections of vignettes and homilies of everyday life, Fulghum carved out a niche among popular nonfiction writers, emphasizing the beauty and wonder in the ordinary and offering a positive vision of modern existence. Featuring a simple style and much repetition, Fulghum gives readers hopeful messages meant to counter the difficult aspects of the modern world. He also points out reasonable alternatives to the ways people react to life. Fulghum points out the importance of basic human values and commonplace rituals that reveal people's inherently good natures. Fulghum was influenced in his writings by his varied life experiences, especially the years he spent as a Unitarian minister and related training.

Appreciating and Improving Everyday Life   In his essay collections, Fulghum emphasizes certain basic principles of everyday life. Wanting his readers to enjoy and appreciate their lives, he often invokes simple pleasures as the means of a better way to live. His first book, for example, urges people to approach their everyday existence by living a life as balanced as a day in kindergarten. Other essays in the collection feature Fulghum's discussion of the real joys associated with transportation and the simple pleasures derived from using crayons. The essays in subsequent books share this overall theme. *It Was on Fire When I Lay Down on It* and *Maybe (Maybe Not)* look at such subjects as parenting, traveling, joy, sorrow, ironing a shirt, and selling chocolate in similar fashion. Even *What on Earth Have I Done?* includes such vignettes as a sock-buying trip to a department store to show how to find depth in common tasks.

Humor   While Fulghum uses his essays and their stories to help his readers, he employs humor to enhance their appeal and to underscore the lessons he offers. In *All I Really Need to Know*, for example, his stories include a bride who vomits on her wedding guests during the ceremony and his observation of a neighbor who walks straight into a spider web and runs away screaming. Fulghum retells the latter experience from the point of view of the small creature that built the web. Another humorous anecdote involves woodsmen who fell trees by yelling at them. The title essay in *It Was On Fire When I Lay Down on It* focuses on a man in a small town rescued from his smoldering bed by an emergency squad; his response when asked how it happened gives the book its title. Fulghum's use of humor extended through his later books, including *What On Earth Have I Done?* In this collection, his humorous anecdotes include dressing like a rabbit while trick-or-treating with his grandchildren and befriending someone who does not speak the same language.

COMMON HUMAN EXPERIENCE

Most of Fulghum's essays collections, including *All I Really Need to Know I learned in Kindergarten: Uncommon Thoughts on Common Things*, feature humorous insight into the human condition often with a dose of personal faith. Here are some other works that share this theme:

Chicken Soup for the College Soul: Inspiring and Humorous Stories About College (1999), a story collection by Jack Canfield and Kimberly Kirberger. This collection provides guidance, support, and inspiration for college students through inspirational, often humorous short stories.

It's Not Easy Being Green: And Other Things to Consider (2005), a nonfiction and fiction collection by Jim Henson. This posthumous collection of letters, personal notebooks, stories, and songs illuminates both Henson's artistic talent and positive philosophy of life.

Traveling Mercies: Some Thoughts on Faith (1999), autobiographical essays by Anne Lamott. In this collection, Lamott traces the development of her faith through both troubled times and good ones with humor and poignant anecdotes.

The Gospel According to Peanuts (1965), nonfiction by Robert L. Short. In this book, theologian Short examines the values and symbolism found in the often humorous, extremely popular *Peanuts* comic strip by Charles Schulz.

Works in Critical Context

Despite the popularity of Fulghum's books, they have received little serious critical attention. While some acknowledge the attraction of his simple philosophy, others characterize it as feel-good prose of little real substance. For example, *It Was on Fire When I Lay Down on It* was deemed by some reviewers as slightly sugarcoated and mundane, while others praised the author's witty stories, remarking on Fulghum's valuable insights. Though few would argue his books have real literary merit, they nevertheless have struck a chord with the reading public who have made them classics of modern popular culture.

All I Really Need to Know I Learned in Kindergarten: Uncommon Thoughts on Common Things   Although the public received the volume with considerable enthusiasm, critics generally reviewed the book with skepticism. Commentators labeled the essays variously as homespun wisdom, inspired observations, and "philosophical tofu"— a reference to the soybean food product that is trendy, bland, and fairly insubstantial. In a review for the *New York Times*, Patricia Leigh Brown acknowledges Fulghum's unabashed sentimentality, noting that "Robert Fulghum at times can be like drinking five-cent lemonade;

it is only after you've downed the Dixie Cup that you realize how much sugar is at the bottom." Ruth Bayard Smith of the *New York Times Book Review* acknowledges some value in Fulghum's words. Smith writes, "To be sure, some of this reads like a cross between Erma Bombeck and Andy Rooney. ... Moreover, he makes no claim to intellectual depth; he knows that the appeal of his message lies in its simplicity." In contrast, Jeff Danziger, writing in the *Christian Science Monitor*, calls the essays "extremely well written with a friendly and economical prose." He concludes, "Several of the essays will give you the ever-popular lump in the throat."

Uh-Oh: Some Observations from Both Sides of the Refrigerator Door In common with *All I Really Need to Know*, *Uh-Oh: Some Observations from Both Sides of the Refrigerator Door* received a mixed response from critics. A perceived repetition of style and substance drew a negative response from critics like Andrea Cooper, who wrote in the *New York Times Book Review*, "A better editor would have changed that embarrassing title, smoothed the fragmented, ad-copy writing style and encouraged Mr. Fulghum to experiment beyond his predictable format with longer, more substantive reflections." Martin Brady of *Booklist* adds, "Not all of [his message] is pithy ... sometimes Fulghum comes across as Andy Rooney crossed with Richard Bach." Other reviewers found his loosely connected essays refreshing. "He's sincere, and his message feels good," writes *People*'s Louisa Ermelino. "Sure, Fulghum is overbearing, oversimplified and saccharine. But he's also touching, practical, and wise."

Responses to Literature

1. After reading one of Fulghum's books, write your own inspirational personal essay about an anecdote in your life. Make sure that your story has appeal to other readers.

2. Research the Unitarian Church and its beliefs and values. In a presentation, relate the values of the church to Fulghum's philosophies as demonstrated in one or more of his books.

3. Read one or more books by humorist Erma Bombeck. Critics sometimes compare Fulghum and his books to Bombeck. In an essay, explore this comparison further. Do you believe the writers are more alike or different? In what ways?

4. In a small group, discuss Fulghum's psychological and spiritual appeal. Why do you think his books are so popular?

BIBLIOGRAPHY

Periodicals

Brady, Martin. Review of *Uh-Oh: Some Observations from Both Sides of the Refrigerator Door*. *Booklist* (July 1991): 2009.

Brown, Patricia Leigh. Review of *All I Really Need to Know I Learned in Kindergarten: Uncommon*

Thoughts on Common Things. *New York Times* (December 21, 1988).

Cooper, Andrea. Review of *Uh-Oh: Some Observations from Both Sides of the Refrigerator Door*. *New York Times Book Review* (September 15, 1991): 26.

Danziger, Jeff. Review of *All I Really Need to Know I Learned in Kindergarten: Uncommon Thoughts on Common Things*. *Christian Science Monitor* (October 24, 1988): 22.

Ermelino, Louisa. "From Beginning to End." *People* (July 24, 1995): 24.

Smith, Ruth Bayard. Review of *All I Really Need to Know I Learned in Kindergarten: Uncommon Thoughts on Common Things*. *New York Times Book Review* (March 19, 1989): 23.

❀ Margaret Fuller

BORN: *1810, Cambridgeport, Massachusetts*

DIED: *1850, New York City*

NATIONALITY: *American*

GENRE: *Nonfiction*

MAJOR WORKS:

Summer on the Lakes, in 1843 (1844)
Woman in the Nineteenth Century (1845)
Papers on Literature and Art (1846)

Overview

Considered one of the most intellectually gifted American women of the nineteenth century, Margaret Fuller was a journalist, early feminist writer, and a central figure with the transcendentalists. She is perhaps best known as the first editor of the transcendentalist journal *The Dial* and the author of the feminist treaty *Woman in the Nineteenth Century* (1845). The radical nature of Fuller's work and her failure to conform to conventional standards of femininity made her a self-proclaimed outsider in nineteenth-century culture. Many critics today praise Fuller as a pioneer feminist whose writings, in some cases, anticipate the work of scholars today.

Works in Biographical and Historical Context

Early Intellectual Education Born Sarah Margaret Fuller in Cambridgeport, Massachusetts, on May 23, 1810, she was the daughter of Timothy Fuller and his wife, Margaret (Crane). Her father was a lawyer and politician who once served in both the Massachusetts legislature as well as the U.S. House of Representatives. Fuller showed her intellectual nature from an early age, compelling her father to insist that she receive a classical education equivalent to a boy's. With his personal guidance, she was tutored in Latin, Greek, French, Italian, German, history, mathematics, and grammar. By the

Margaret Fuller   *Hulton Archive / Getty Images*

age of six, Fuller was translating the works of the ancient Roman poet, Virgil. Yet, her father's strict educational program took its toll on her health as a child, causing Fuller to later regret not having a more normal childhood.

In 1821, recognizing that their daughter had little social interaction with other children outside the family, the Fullers sent her to Dr. John Park's school in Boston, which she attended for little more than a year. Her only other formal schooling was at Susan Prescott's school in Groton, which she attended from 1824 to 1826. Fuller was a student at this female seminary to learn the social graces appropriate to a young lady but was not challenged by the educational aspect of the school. Though Fuller mingled with Harvard students and acquired a reputation for being a sharp and intelligent conversationalist by the late 1820s, she always regretted that, as a woman, she was denied a formal Harvard education. Indeed, it would be several decades before women would receive an equivalent education at Radcliffe—a partner college of Harvard—and even longer before women would be admitted directly to Harvard itself.

Transcendentalism   When her father moved the family to a farm in Groton, Massachusetts, in 1831, she resented the move and missed city life. She spent her free time teaching her younger siblings and studying German litera-

ture and criticism. While living in Groton, she became acquainted with the intellectuals and ministers who made up the Transcendentalist Club. The transcendentalist movement was a philosophic school that emphasized intuition and direct experience over rationalism and traditional authority. This uniquely American strain of Romanticism placed an emphasis on nature as a mirror of self.

Fuller's interest in self-improvement and new German criticism, as well as her ambivalence towards institutional religion, made her an integral figure in the transcendentalist movement. Because she lacked the educational and professional opportunities of the men in the group, Fuller was also aware of being both an insider and outsider. Yet, her relationships with Ralph Waldo Emerson and other male transcendentalists pushed her to redefine the nature of friendship, going beyond traditional gender expectations to call for men as well as women to behave with empathy and love toward their friends.

Teaching and Promoting Women's Education   When Fuller's father died unexpectedly from cholera in 1835, Fuller took up teaching to help support her family. By 1836, Fuller was employed as a teacher in the Temple School, run by Bronson Alcott. There, she taught Latin and French. From 1837 to 1838, she taught at the Greene Street School in Providence. As a teacher, Fuller experimented with interactive dialogues as a teaching method. She also began writing criticism and translating German literature. By 1839, her family's financial situation had improved and Fuller joined her mother in Boston, where she resumed her friendships with the leading figures of the transcendentalist movement.

Fuller's teaching and her experiences with the transcendentalists contributed to her successful Conversation Clubs. In 1839 in Boston, Fuller began hosting "conversations" for educated women, which continued until she left New England in 1844. Fuller's series of conversations, which drew many of the wives, fiancées, daughters, and sisters of the all-male Transcendentalist Club, encouraged women to view themselves as intellectual beings rather than weak-minded females. Other contemporary issues were also covered. These seminars lasted for thirteen weeks annually, and grew in reputation and drew larger audiences each time.

The *Dial* and the *Tribune*

In 1840, Fuller became the first editor of the *Dial*, the magazine of the transcendentalists. Though Fuller resigned the editorship in 1842, she was the most prolific contributor to the periodical during its initial five-year run. She published many essays and critical reviews, using her unique perspective: Objecting to the normal critical practice of measuring literary works against external standards, Fuller believed the reviewer had to enter into the spirit of a given work and understand its central vision. Only then, with that understanding, could she analyze and judge the text at hand.

LITERARY AND HISTORICAL CONTEMPORARIES

Fuller's famous contemporaries include:

Ralph Waldo Emerson (1803–1882): This American poet, essayist, and minister was a leading figure in the transcendentalist movement. In such essays as "Self Reliance" (1844), he outlined the transcendentalist philosophy.

Henry David Thoreau (1817–1862): This American writer and naturalist was also a scientist and biologist. A major transcendental writer, he is best known for his book *Walden* (1854), which discussed simple, self-reliant living.

Elizabeth Palmer Peabody (1804–1894): This American author and education reformer was the country's foremost advocate of kindergarten education. Between 1873 and 1875, she published the magazine *Kindergarten Messenger*.

Harriet Martineau (1804–1894): This English teacher and author wrote everything from children's books to essays and histories to novels. One of her best-known works is her candid posthumous *Autobiography* (1877), which detailed her difficult life.

Robert Browning (1812–1889): This British poet and playwright is considered one of the major poets of the Victorian age. His works include *Paracelsus* (1835). Fuller met Browning while living in Italy.

Fuller published her first book in 1844, *Summer on the Lakes, in 1843*. This collection of travel essays was written after her 1843 tour of the Great Lakes with her friend Sarah Clarke. The book landed her a job in New York City with Horace Greeley's progressive newspaper, the *New York Tribune*. She worked as a journalist, literary critic, and editor for the paper and was paid a salary equivalent to what a man in her position would have earned. Fuller was the first woman on an American newspaper's editorial staff, and her column appeared regularly on the *Tribune*'s front page.

Through the *Tribune*, Fuller used her influence to promote then-unknown American authors—such as Edgar Allan Poe, Herman Melville, and Nathaniel Hawthorne—and suggested that Henry Wadsworth Longfellow's poetry was overrated. She praised the works of Lydia Sigourney, Caroline Kirkland, and Anna Mowatt, and championed George Sand, the radical French novelist whose behavior shocked most American readers.

During her two-year stint with the *Tribune*, Fuller published *Woman in the Nineteenth Century* (1845). A shorter version had originally been published as a long essay entitled "The Great Lawsuit: Man *versus* Men; Women *versus* Women" in 1843. In the work, Fuller laid out her feminist vision, challenging the gender roles demanded by American society.

Challenging Female Stereotypes At this time, Americans believed in the "doctrine of separate spheres." God and biology dictated that women should remain in the home, rear children, and exert their moral influence. A woman's smaller brain and predisposition to excitability were said to render her unfit for positions of authority in social and political life. Men, with greater strength and larger brains, were to occupy the sphere of public life. In her book, Fuller dismissed the cultural stereotypes of women, especially when that image led to a subservient role in marriage. On a broader level, Fuller argued for an essentially androgynous understanding of the intellect and emotions that would acknowledge both the feminine and masculine in men's and women's minds. *Woman in the Nineteenth Century* marked her as a leading theorist in the cause of American feminism and helped launch the women's rights movement, but was highly controversial in its time.

In 1846, Fuller published a collection of criticism previously published in various periodicals, *Papers on Literature and Art*. That same year, she went to Europe, in part to serve as a foreign correspondent for the *Tribune*. She was one of America's first foreign correspondents. Fuller became an ardent supporter of the Italian movement for unification and independence and sent the *Tribune* reports of the 1848 Italian revolution, which eventually achieved the goal of a united Italy.

Part of War in Italy In Italy, Fuller also took a lover, Marquis Giovanni Angelo Ossoli, a Roman nobleman who had turned Roman Republican. They had a child, Angelo, in 1848, and may have secretly married in 1849 or 1850. With the failure of the Roman revolution, Fuller returned to the United States with her husband and son in 1850. Their ship ran aground and sank off Fire Island near New York. All three died in the wreck on July 19, 1850, and Fuller's body was never recovered. Fuller had in her possession manuscripts for what would have been a history of the Italian revolution, which were also lost at sea.

Works in Literary Context

As a strong advocate of a woman's right and need to fulfill her potential, Fuller's published writings contributed to the development of American feminism and emphasized greater ideas about equality. She also played a significant role in the spread of the ideals of transcendentalists through her work as founding editor and chief contributor to the *Dial*. As well as providing transcendentalism a vehicle for expression, Fuller's work for the *Dial* established her, along with Edgar Allan Poe, as one of the most important literary critics in nineteenth-century America. As an author, Fuller was greatly influenced by the writers and theories she learned during her formidable education, members of the transcendentalist circle (especially Ralph Waldo Emerson), and such diverse authors as Adam Smith, Sir Walter Scott, Lord Byron, Jean-Jacques Rousseau, Johann Wolfgang von Goethe, Friedrich Schiller, and George Sand.

Transcendentalism Throughout her work—as well as her life—Fuller was greatly influenced by, and expressed the ideals of, the transcendentalists. Their philosophy centered around social reform, self-truth, self-reliance, and personal excellence. Fuller hoped to instill in women an intellectual self-reliance and a sense of inner worth through her Conversation Club, and each of her books—as well as her many essays and works of criticism—took on a similar tone. Her work on the *Dial* also promoted the transcendental philosophy and ideas, as did the pieces she published in the *New York Tribune*. In these works, Fuller advocated a comprehensive criticism that balanced an emphasis on what she terms "genius," in a move to educate her fellow readers. Fuller also showed the influence by transcendental ideas about self-reliance in her best-known work, *Woman in the Nineteenth Century*.

Equality In many of her works, Fuller also highlighted the ways in which various groups in American society were oppressed and exploited. As a social reformer, she was sympathetic to women abandoned by society, such as prostitutes, as well as other oppressed groups, including Indians, blacks, the poor, and the physically and mentally disabled. She often appealed for a change in status for such people. In *Woman in the Nineteenth Century*, for example, Fuller called for complete equality between males and females, and compared the struggle for women's rights with the abolition movement. She insisted that all professions be open to women and contended that women should not be forced to submit to the men in their lives—husbands, fathers, or brothers. Even in the travel essays which make up *Summer on the Lake*, Fuller highlighted such concerns. The book called attention to the exploitation of Native Americans, abuse of the environment, and mistreatment of pioneer women. Fuller also touched upon these issues in her criticism. In the *New York Tribune*, Fuller lauded *The Narrative of the Life of Frederick Douglass: An American Slave* (1845), expressing hope that readers of the book would truly understand how slavery affected the enslaved.

Works in Critical Context

Aside from the controversial nature of Fuller's feminist theories, early criticism of her writings focused on her literary style, which was modeled on the classics, but was considered far too ornate and lengthy. Contemporary assessments of her work were also colored by resistance to Fuller's strong personality. In addition, the heavy-handed editing of her papers and diaries after her death—by such famous contemporaries as William Henry Channing, James Freeman Clark, and Ralph Waldo Emerson—suppressed some of the more controversial aspects of her life and work.

COMMON HUMAN EXPERIENCE

Fuller's *Woman in the Nineteenth Century* is considered an example of an early feminist text. Here are some other influential early feminist books:

A Vindication of the Rights of Women (1792), nonfiction by Mary Wollstonecraft. This early example of feminist philosophy features the author's argument for women's education.

The Awakening (1899), a novel by Kate Chopin. Through the story of Edna Pontellier, Chopin illustrates the independent nature that women began recognizing in themselves in the nineteenth century.

History of Woman Suffrage (1881), nonfiction by Elizabeth Cady Stanton and Susan B. Anthony. This collection of writings covers much about the struggles of the American women's rights movement in the nineteenth century.

Woman, Church, and State (1893), nonfiction by Matilda Joslyn Gage. This nonfiction work explores the role of the church in women's oppression throughout history.

As a result, succeeding generations of critics have underestimated her contributions to the nineteenth-century struggle for women's equality. While *Woman in the Nineteenth Century* was considered the inspiration for the 1848 women's rights convention in Seneca Falls, for example, the work virtually disappeared after the publication of a second edition in 1855. Since the 1970s, Fuller's work has been reexamined and her critical reputations restored primarily through the efforts of feminist scholars. She is now considered a pivotal figure in the development of American feminism in the nineteenth century.

Woman in the Nineteenth Century Fuller's best-known work, *Woman in the Nineteenth Century* was highly controversial in its time. Some critics believed Fuller's notions would destroy the stability and sanctity of the home. Some objections were lodged on religious grounds as her ideas were considered contrary to the divine order. In a contemporary review published in the *Christian Examiner and Religious Miscellany*, a sympathetic critic concludes, "She has discussed a delicate topic delicately and fearlessly; without prudish folly, without timidity, as a true woman should. . . . What she has said needed to be said. . . ." While many feminist critics embraced Fuller's book by the late twentieth century, a critical divide remained. As Fritz Fleischmann wrote in *Women's Studies and Literature*:

> *Woman in the Nineteenth Century* (1845) is one of the most fascinating, but also one of the most frustrating texts in the literature of feminist thought, as generation after generation of critics

has demonstrated. The reasons for this frustration are not clear. Is it the lack of feminist bravado or moral uplift? ... Is it Fuller's intellectuality, her erudition, that readers have found forbidding?

Summer on the Lakes, in 1843 Like *Woman*, Fuller's first book *Summer on the Lakes, in 1843* also received many mixed, if not negative, reviews from contemporary critics. Orestes A. Brownson in *Brownson's Quarterly Review* admits that her "writings we do not like. We dislike them exceedingly." Yet, he concludes, "It is marked by flashes of a rare genius, by uncommon and versatile powers, by sentiments at times almost devout; but after all it is a sad book, and one which we dare not commend." More positively, Caleb Stetson in the *Christian Examiner and Religious Miscellany* comments, "Knowing the extraordinary endowments of its author, we looked for an uncommon book, and we were not disappointed. It is indeed an uncommon book, not at all like an ordinary journal of travel." Today, many critics consider *Summer* one of the finest American examples of the literary excursion. Other critics have seen mostly disorder in Fuller's combination of descriptive sketches, literary extracts, dramatic dialogues, fiction, and poetry. Still others find the work a center of dramatic interest in the narrator's struggle with the various cultural scripts of nineteenth-century America.

Responses to Literature

1. Read *Woman in the Nineteenth Century*, then research the first women's rights convention in Seneca Falls, New York. Many historians see a link between Fuller's book and the start of the women's rights movement in the nineteenth century. In an essay, outline your observations about the link between the two events.

2. Create a presentation in which you describe the 1848 revolution which created a unified Italy. In your presentation, tie in Fuller's experiences in the country with social and political events.

3. Have members of a small group read several issues of the *Dial*, then discuss how the pieces you have read relate to the transcendentalist movement. Do you find the topics relevant to current daily life in America?

4. Write a research paper on women's education in the nineteenth century and the general role of women in society during this time period. Include information abut Fuller's education, and other women who had similarly demanding schooling. Also compare her role in society to that of a typical woman of the time.

BIBLIOGRAPHY

Books

Allen, Margaret Vanderhaar. *The Achievement of Margaret Fuller*. University Park, Penn.: Penn State Press, 1979.

Deiss, Joseph Jay. *The Roman Years of Margaret Fuller*. New York: Thomas Y. Cromwell, 1969.

Fleischmann, Fritz. "Margaret Fuller, the Eternal Feminine, and the 'Liberties of the Republic'." In *Women's Studies and Literature*, edited by Fritz Fleischmann and Deborah Lucas Schneider. Eralangen, Germany: Palm & Enke, 1987, pp. 39–57.

Von Mehren, Laurie. *Minerva and the Muse: A Life of Margaret Fuller*. Amherst: University of Massachusetts Press, 1994.

Watson, David. *Margaret Fuller: An American Romantic*. New York: St. Martin's Press, 1988.

Periodicals

Brownson, Orestes A. A review of *Summer on the Lakes, in 1843. Brownson's Quarterly Review* (October 1844): 546–547.

A review of *Woman in the Nineteenth Century. The Christian Examiner and Religious Miscellany* (May 1845): 416–417.

Stetson, Caleb. A review of *Summer on the Lakes, in 1843. The Christian Examiner and Religious Miscellany* (September 1844): 274–276.

✸ Ernest J. Gaines

BORN: *1933, Pointe Coupee Parish, Louisiana*

NATIONALITY: *American*

GENRE: *Fiction, nonfiction*

MAJOR WORKS:
The Autobiography of Miss Jane Pittman (1971)
In My Father's House (1978)
A Gathering of Old Men (1983)
A Lesson Before Dying (1993)

Overview

Considered one of the most significant Southern writers of the second half of the twentieth century, Ernest J. Gaines has consistently based his fictional work on the African American cultural and storytelling traditions of rural southern Louisiana. Best known as the author of the critically acclaimed novels *The Autobiography of Miss Jane Pittman* (1971) and *A Lesson Before Dying* (1993), he brought new awareness of African American contributions to the history and culture of the American South. Many critics have observed the originality of Gaines's prose, noting the distance of his aesthetic philosophies from such contemporary literary trends. Commentators have often compared Gaines's fictional treatment of his native Louisiana parish to that of William Faulkner's Yoknapatawpha County and James Joyce's Dublin.

Ernest Gaines   *Gaines, Ernest, photograph. AP Images.*

Works in Biographical and Historical Context

Raised in Rural South   Gaines was born on January 13, 1933, in the bayous of Pointe Coupee Parish near Oscar, Louisiana, to Manuel and Adrienne J. (Colar) Gaines. Both of his parents were sharecroppers who worked the local River Lake Plantation. As a youth, Gaines also worked in the fields, digging potatoes for fifty cents a day from the time he was nine years old until the age of fifteen. While his parents worked, Gaines and his twelve younger siblings were essentially raised by Augusteen Jefferson, a paraplegic aunt who served as the model for the recurrent aunt figure in Gaines's writings. Though bright, Gaines received limited schooling; the cycle was five to six months between the time of harvesting and the time of planting. Jefferson continued to act as Gaines's guardian after his parents separated in 1941, and he grew up listening to the discussions of his aunt's friends. Subsequently, Gaines lost touch with his father, who served in World II before returning to New Orleans.

Educated in California   In 1948, Gaines joined his mother and merchant marine stepfather in Vallejo, California, where the couple had moved several years earlier, so he could become better educated. There, Gaines attended high school for the first time and soon developed a passion for reading, especially the novels of Leo Tolstoy, Nikolai

Gogol, and Ivan Turgenev. Gaines later became a student at Vallejo Junior College before he enlisted in the U.S. Army in 1953. He served at the end of the Korean War, a conflict that lasted from 1950 to 1953. The United States sided with the democratic South Koreans as they sought to repel the aggression of Communist-controlled North Korea into their territory. The war ended with a stalemate and essentially the same borders as before the conflict began.

When his tour ended in 1955, Gaines enrolled at San Francisco State College. In 1956, he published his first short story about the rural South, "Turtles," in the first issue of the school's literary magazine, *Transfer.* One year later, Gaines earned his bachelor's degree. In 1958, he received a Wallace Stegner fellowship and entered the graduate creative writing program at Stanford University. Gaines withdrew the following year after winning the Joseph Henry Jackson award for his short story "Comeback" and dedicated himself to writing full-time.

Published First Novel   Gaines published his first major novel *Catherine Carmier* in 1964. Set during the onset of the American civil rights movement, the novel chronicles the love affair between Jackson Bradley, a young African American man recently returned to Bayonne after completing his education, and the title character, a daughter of a bigoted Creole sharecropper who forbids his family members from associating with anyone with darker skin than their own. Gaines followed *Catherine Carmier* with a well-received novel about adultery and miscegenation, or the intermarrying of races, called *Of Love and Dust* (1967) and a collection of previously published short stories, *Bloodline* (1968). Among the most acclaimed was "The Sky Is Gray."

In the early 1970s, Gaines had a major breakthrough as a writer with his novel *The Autobiography of Miss Jane Pittman* (1971). Widely recognized as Gaines's masterpiece and an immediate success, the novel chronicles a folk history of African American experience in the United States from the Civil War and Reconstruction through segregation and the civil rights era, as narrated from the perspective of the 108-year-old title character. The same year that the novel was published, 1971, Gaines published his only children's book, *A Long Day in November*, and became a writer-in-residence at Denison University for a year.

Branching Out   Gaines's next novel, *In My Father's House* (1978), was considered by many critics to be the author's most pessimistic work. Principally set in urban Baton Rouge, the novel concerns the relationship between Philip Martin, a prominent civil rights leader at the height of his career, and Robert X, a troubled young man who is one of Martin's three illegitimate children from an affair decades earlier. Gaines's literary reputation continued to grow, however, with another major novel *A Gathering of Old Men* (1983). Styled as a detective story, the novel depicts a group of seventeen elderly black men who collectively make a defiant stand against past injustices by

LITERARY AND HISTORICAL CONTEMPORARIES

Gaines's famous contemporaries include:

Dwight D. Eisenhower (1890–1996): This American president served two terms that covered much of the 1950s. During his time in office, he was forced to become involved with the burgeoning civil rights movement, signing the Civil Rights Act of 1957 into law.

Harper Lee (1926–): This American author was raised in the South and explored racial tensions in her only book, *To Kill a Mockingbird* (1960).

Oprah Winfrey (1953–): This television talk show host is one of the highest paid entertainers in the world. Her series, *The Oprah Winfrey Show*, has been atop of the ratings since its inception in the mid-1980s.

Carson McCullers (1917–1967): This American writer is a leading author in the Southern literary tradition. Her works include the novels *Reflections in a Golden Eye* (1941) and *The Member of the Wedding* (1946).

Alice Walker (1944–): This African American novelist, short-story writer, and poet is a native of the South. She is best known for her Pulitzer Prize–winning novel *The Color Purple* (1982), which is set in the South during the 1930s.

separately claiming responsibility for the murder of a hostile member of a violent Cajun clan.

In 1983, Gaines joined the faculty of the English department at the University of Southern Louisiana as a writer-in-residence. He then taught part of each year at the university as a professor of English and spent his summers in San Francisco. While focusing on teaching, Gaines did not produce another novel for a decade.

A MacArthur Genius In 1993, Gaines published, *A Lesson Before Dying*, which earned him a National Book Critics Circle Award for the best American book of fiction. Set both in a jail and on a plantation in Bayonne during a six-month span in 1948, the novel focuses on the friendship between Jefferson, a barely literate young man sentenced to death, and Grant Wiggins, a rural schoolteacher disillusioned and displaced by his work. The interaction between the men eventually transforms the pair as they recognize the meaning of human dignity. That same year, Gaines received a MacArthur Foundation "genius" grant in recognition of his literary accomplishments.

Gaines continued to be lauded in the late 1990s and early 2000s. In 1996, he received the Chevalier de l'Ordre Arts et des Lettres, Paris. In 2004, Gaines was nominated for a Nobel Prize in Literature in recognition of his body of work. In 2005, Gaines was named the writer-in-residence emeritus at the University of South-

western Louisiana. That same year, he published *Mozart and Leadbelly: Stories and Essays*. In these pieces, Gaines discusses why he became a writer, his early life in Louisiana, the inspirations behind his books, and his portrayal of the black experience. By 2006, Gaines was working on a new novel. He continues to live and work in Lafayette, Louisiana, and San Francisco.

Works in Literary Context

Gaines's major works offer an uncommon African American perspective on the rural Deep South, recalling and re-creating the places and people who inhabit the region. Primarily set in the imaginary locale of fictional Bayonne, Louisiana, Gaines's fiction depicts the complexities of a culturally diverse community that includes blacks, whites, Creoles, and Cajuns. With authentic dialects and convincing characterizations, Gaines has typically written first-person narratives that chronicle the struggles and sufferings of humble black protagonists who possess a strong attachment to the land. Although racial themes often inform the principal themes of his writing, Gaines also displays universal human ideals through particular characters that inhabit a particular place. In addition, he consistently displays the inherent dignity of characters that range from pitiable to contemptible. While Gaines was influenced by such authors as William Faulkner, Ernest Hemingway, Gertrude Stein, Leo Tolstoy, Ivan Turgenev, Anton Chekhov, Gustave Flaubert, and Guy de Maupassant, his early childhood experiences of working in the fields, fishing in local swamps, and listening to the discussions of his aunt's friends, provided core material for his writings.

Authentic Southern Setting and Characters As depicted and drawn by Gaines, South Louisiana, the region of his youth and literary imagination, is beautiful and distinctive with unique cultural, linguistic, and social patterns. His stories and novels depict his fascination with the interplay of caste and class among the ethnic groups of the area: blacks, mixed-race Creoles, Cajuns, white Creoles, and Anglo whites. Also key to Gaines's fiction is that blacks and mixed-race Creoles, who were once fairly stable as subsistence farmers, have been dispossessed of the best land or displaced altogether by Cajuns, who are favored by the plantation lords because they are white and use mechanized agricultural methods. Under such socioeconomic conditions, young blacks leave, though they often find themselves drawn back to Louisiana. Such is the case with *Catherine Carmier*. In this novel, the protagonist is the educated and alienated Jackson Bradley, who returns to his native parish to claim the love of the title character. Racial prejudices and tensions, as well as related violence found in the South, are at the center of *A Gathering of Old Men*. Historical reflections and the racial inequalities of the Southern justice system are also found in *A Lesson Before Dying*.

Alienation Between Fathers and Their Children
In varying degrees throughout his fiction, Gaines employs the theme of alienation between fathers and sons. In some cases, fathers and sons are searching for each other. Sometimes, the father is not even in the story, but his absence has an effect on the children in the story. This is the primary theme of *In My Father's House*, which focuses on the alienation between prominent civil rights leader the Reverend Phillip Martin and one of the three children he abandoned years ago. At the peak of Martin's career, he is confronted by his troubled young son, known as Robert X. Robert finds Martin to confront and kill the father whose neglect he sees as responsible for the family's disintegration. Martin ultimately confronts pasts and learns about the effect his actions have had on his first family. Similarly, in "Bloodline," the central character, Cooper Laurent, must come to terms with his father's role in his painful past in order to claim his manhood. Alienation between fathers and children can also be found in several familial relationships in *Catherine Carmier* and *A Gathering of Old Men*.

Works in Critical Context

Since his first novels, Gaines has been recognized as an integral interpreter of Southern history and culture. He has been noted for voicing the stories of contemporary Southern African American men—a perspective many scholars feel has seldom been represented in the past half-century as prominently as in Gaines's fiction. The author has drawn wide praise for his ability to capture the character and speech of ordinary black people of the South, whom he portrays with strength and compassion. While reviewers have charted a shift in his use of black folk materials and storytelling traditions that has accompanied the evolution of his literary vision, other commentators have focused on his thematic recurrence of the African American male's rite of passage to manhood, the cultural definition of black masculinity, and the relationships between fathers and sons. Many reviewers have also commended Gaines's fiction for realizing typical human motivations and emotions concerning such topics as American racial relations, human rights, and personal responsibility.

The Autobiography of Miss Jane Pittman   Critics generally found Gaines's novel *The Autobiography of Miss Jane Pittman* to be at the epitome of his fictional power. "To travel with Miss Pittman from adolescence to old age is to embark upon a historic journey, one staked out in the format of the novel," writes Addison Gayle Jr., in *The Way of the World: The Black Novel in America*. "Never mind that Miss Jane Pittman is fictitious, and that her 'autbiography,' offered up in the form of taped reminiscences is artifice," adds Josh Greenfield in *Life*, "the effect is stunning." Many critics believe that Gaines's gift for drawing convincing characters is clearly demonstrated in *The Autobiography of Miss Jane Pittman*. "His is not ... an 'art' narrative, but an authentic narrative by an authentic ex-slave, authentic even though both are Gain-

es's inventions," Jerry H. Bryant comments in the *Iowa Review*. "So successful is he in *becoming* Miss Jane Pittman, that when we talk about her story, we do not think of Gaines as her creator, but as her recording editor."

A Lesson Before Dying   Similarly, critics lauded *A Lesson Before Dying* as a gripping exploration of racial tension and the perseverance of the victims of injustice. Sandra D. Gaines of the *Detroit Free Press* notes that Gaines "creates a compelling, intense story about heroes and the human spirit" and that "education encompasses more than the lessons taught in school." *Commonweal* critic Madeline Marget likens the ordeal of Jefferson, a young man sentenced to death for a crime he did not fully understand, to the crucifixion of Jesus Christ. Marget writes, "*A Lesson Before Dying* is Gaines's retelling of the Passion—a layered and sensual story of a suffering man and his life-changing struggle," one that Gaines explores "through a narrative of tremendous velocity."

Responses to Literature

1. Research the legal system during the time and place in which *A Lesson Before Dying* is set. In an essay, discuss how the novel reflects the realities of justice in this time period.

COMMON HUMAN EXPERIENCE

Gaines's fictional works are powerful representations of aspects of the South, often fraught with racial tensions. Here are some other works that take a similar point of view:

I Know Why the Caged Bird Sings (1970), an autobiography by Maya Angelou. This volume covers the early years of Angelou's life, from living in segregated Stamps, Arkansas, to being sexually abused in St. Louis. Angelou eventually overcomes such abuse and prejudice to succeed.

Song of Solomon (1977), a novel by Toni Morrison. This novel follows Milkman Dead from Michigan to various settings in the South as he searches for himself and his black heritage.

The Piano Lesson (1987), a play by August Wilson. This play focuses on a brother and sister who quarrel over a piano that has been in the family for generations. Boy Willie, a sharecropper who lives in the South, wants to sell the piano to buy the land on which their ancestors were slaves, but his sister Berenice wants to keep the piano because of the family history carved on it.

A Soldier's Play (1987), a play by Charles Fuller. This play centers on the murder investigation of Technical Sergeant Vernon Waters, a martinet in charge of a unit of black soldiers stationed in Louisiana during World War II.

---

2. Read *The Autobiography of Miss Jane Pittman*, then watch the Emmy Award–winning 1974 television adaptation. How does the adaptation compare with the novel? Which version best illustrates the story Gaines is trying to tell?

3. Create a presentation about plantation culture in the South in the early to mid-twentieth century. Include examples from Gaines's novels and short fiction to describe the environment and conditions.

4. Read Gaines's short story "The Sky Is Gray" (in *Bloodline*) and Eudora Welty's short story "A Worn Path" (1940). Gaines has said his short story has been patterned after Welty's. In a small group, debate this idea, using specific examples from the stories. How do you interpret the relationship between the stories?

BIBLIOGRAPHY

Books

Doyle, Mary Ellen. *Voices from the Quarters: The Fiction of Ernest J. Gaines.* Baton Rouge: Louisiana State University Press, 2002.

Estes, David C. *Critical Reflections on the Fiction of Ernest J. Gaines.* Athens: University of Georgia Press, 1994.

Gayle, Addison, Jr. *The Way of the New World: The Black Novel in America.* New York: Doubleday, 1975.

Periodicals

Bryant, Jerry H. "From Death to Life: The Fiction of Ernest J. Gaines." *Iowa Review* (Winter 1972): 206–210.

Davis, Sandra D. Review of *A Lesson Before Dying.* *Detroit Free Press* (June 6, 1993): 7J.

Greenfield, Josh. Review of *The Autobiography of Miss Jane Pittman.* *Life* (April 30, 1971).

Marget, Madeline. Review of *A Lesson Before Dying.* *Commonweal* (June 6, 2000): 23.

✸ Tess Gallagher

BORN: *1943, Port Angeles, Washington*

NATIONALITY: *American*

GENRE: *Poetry, fiction*

MAJOR WORKS:

Instructions to the Double (1976)

The Lover of Horses and Other Stories (1986)

Moon Crossing Bridge (1992)

Overview

Tess Gallagher is noted for verse considered both philosophically and emotionally profound. While the publication of her early poems coincided with the emergence of a new feminist literature in the United States, Gallagher's

Tess Gallagher   *Gallagher, Tess, photograph. © Jerry Bauer. Reproduced by permission.*

poems transcend gender in their exploration of what it means to be human, inviting readers to observe the dynamics of human experience. In addition to illuminating relations between family members, Gallagher's lyrics explore the contrasts between childhood and adulthood, along with dreams and reality.

Works in Biographical and Historical Context

Finding Poetry in Childhood   The oldest of five children, Gallagher was born on July 21, 1943, in Port Angeles, Washington, into a family of timber loggers. As a child, she helped her father—a hard-working, hard-drinking man—with logging and later did farm work on the small ranch her family owned, and she spent her free time playing among the giant trees in the Olympic forest. As a result, references to the natural beauty of Washington State and to childhood memories, such as salmon fishing with her father, appear consistently throughout her poetry. According to Gallagher, the highlight of her adolescence was receiving a horse from her uncle. Naming the filly Angel Foot, Gallagher felt as if she had found a kindred spirit. Unsurprisingly, richly symbolic horses abound in Gallagher's writings, figures embodying a harmony of intellect and instinct, gentleness and strength.

Writing with Roethke At the age of sixteen, Gallagher began working as a reporter for the *Port Angeles Daily News*. With plans to become a journalist, she entered the University of Washington after graduating from high school. Finding journalism classes dull compared to actual newspaper work, Gallagher enrolled in a creative writing class taught by Pulitzer Prize–winning poet Theodore Roethke in 1963. Her first poems for Roethke's class concern her father and explore her origins. Although she knew she had found her calling, Gallagher neither completed her bachelor's degree nor pursued writing for several years because of a series of personal upheavals during the 1960s. Following Roethke's death in August 1963, Gallagher's fifteen-year-old brother was killed in an auto accident, and in 1964, she married Lawrence Gallagher, who soon joined the U.S. Marine Corps. When her husband left on a tour in Southeast Asia during the Vietnam War, Gallagher stayed home and earned a BA in English from the University of Washington in 1967.

From Iowa to Ireland After her marriage ended in 1968, Gallagher entered graduate school at the University of Washington, studying under Mark Strand, who would later become an American poet laureate. Gallagher completed her MA in 1971. The next year, she did advanced work in poetry, cinema theory, and moviemaking as a teaching fellow at the Iowa Writers' Workshop, where she met poet Michael Burkard, whom she married in 1973. Gallagher's first book, the poetry chapbook *Stepping Outside*, was published in 1974, the same year she received her MFA degree from the University of Iowa. Gallagher and Burkard shared teaching posts during the mid-1970s until marital tensions prompted her travel to Ireland. Living there near the Ballindoon graveyard, Gallagher wrote poems in which she sought to reconcile conflicting forces in her life and art: loyalty and independence, domesticity and restlessness, narrative lucidity and lyric intensity. In 1977, she returned to the United States, and she and Burkard were divorced that summer.

Love and Collaboration In November 1977, Gallagher met Raymond Carver, a short-story writer who became her collaborator, critic, and soul mate. While *Instructions to the Double* (1976) and *Under Stars* (1978) had won Gallagher recognition as a promising young poet, Carver held equal stature in short fiction, thanks to his debut collection *Will You Please Be Quiet, Please?* (1976). During the 1980s, even as each writer gained stature in his and her primary genre, the two helped reshape each other's art. Gallagher, for example, published *The Lover of Horses* (1986), a collection of short stories based on themes well established in her poetry: the unruly interplay of self and family, individual and community, male and female, word and deed.

Finding Life in Death Gallagher's collaboration with Carver was cut short when he was diagnosed with lung cancer. The couple married in June 1988, two months before Carver died at the age of fifty. During Carver's illness, Gallagher encouraged him to write, and the result

was *A New Path to the Waterfall* (1989), a collection of poems that bears Carver's name but is clearly a joint work. Consumed with memorializing Carver, Gallagher spent several years ensuring that his remaining works were published, that his books were translated into other languages, that documentaries about him were filmed, and that friends committed their memories of him to paper. Gallagher's deep mourning permeates her next book of poetry, *Moon Crossing Bridge* (1992). In the poems of this collection, Gallagher accompanies the spirit of a loved one into death and then returns to life. In the closing poems, she finds that, far from reducing her capacity to love, her husband's death has taught her to love without reservation and fear.

Continued Collaborations Artistically, culturally, and spiritually, Gallagher's horizons continue to expand. Teaching appointments and fellowships have taken her from Whitman College in Washington to Japan. Collaborating with author Hiromi Hashimoto, Gallagher has translated her own short stories into Japanese. With Liliana Ursu and Adam Sorkin, she has worked on translating Ursu's poems from Romanian to English. In 2007, Gallagher and Josie Gray, an Irish painter and storyteller, published *Barnacle Soup: And Other Stories from the West of Ireland*.

Works in Literary Context

Living with an alcoholic father, studying under Theodore Roethke, traveling alone in Ireland—Gallagher's writing

COMMON HUMAN EXPERIENCE

With the confessional poets of the 1950s and 1960s emerged a genre of writing that forever changed American poetry. Spurred by the publication of Robert Lowell's *Life Studies* (1959), the confessional poetry movement has impacted generations of writers. Listed below are other examples of confessional poetry that explore personal details about a writer's life with neither modesty nor discretion:

"Daddy" (1966), a poem by Sylvia Plath. In "Daddy," Plath directly addresses her father, using images of the Holocaust to express the hostility she feels toward him.
What the Living Do (1999), a collection of poetry by Marie Howe. Dramatic without being hysterical, these poems, a memorial to Howe's brother, unflinchingly reveal a childhood of abuse.
Heart's Needle (1959), a volume of poetry by W. D. Snodgrass. This collection of highly personal poems about a father's love for his daughter has led many academics to deem Snodgrass a founder of the confessional poetry movement.

has always been influenced by events and people in her life. Without a doubt, Gallagher's life and art were most profoundly inspired by her relationship with Raymond Carver. However, scholars also recognize the importance of her place in the emergence of a new kind of feminist literature. In an interview with Daniel Bourne, Gallagher says, "I began in that generation of women writers who stepped forth out of the feminist revolution. That was very, very, formative. Sylvia Plath and Anne Sexton were extremely important ... to the forming of my mind." Indeed, much like the works of Sexton and Plath, the central subject of most of Gallagher's books is selfhood, a female writer's quest for personal and artistic independence. To achieve it, she must cast off the stereotypes—siren, servant, victim—forced on her by a patriarchal culture, or a society in which primarily men hold positions of power. By the end of her odyssey, she has found the antidote to insecurity: self-discovery and, ultimately, self-reliance.

Confessional Poetry Popularized in the 1950s and 1960s by writers including Anne Sexton and John Berryman, confessional poetry delves into subject matter that had never before been openly discussed in American poetry. Speaking in the first person, confessional poetry often shocks readers as it addresses such private experiences as trauma, depression, death, and relationships, usually from an autobiographical perspective. Much of Gallagher's verse, especially her earlier works, belongs to the genre of confessional poetry.

Two notable poems from *Instructions to the Double* derived from the confessional school include "Breasts" and "Black Money." Using her breasts as a vehicle for self-reflection in the former poem, Gallagher recounts her discovery of womanhood, her disillusionment with that role, and, finally, her acceptance of herself as a woman. As Gallagher moves from the physical to the emotional in "Black Money" she draws on her childhood in Washington to investigate the complex relationship between father and daughter. Autobiographical in presentation, both "Breasts" and "Black Money" explore memories from childhood to early adulthood that mark crucial moments of transition in Gallagher's development.

Works in Critical Context

While some reviewers have found her persona inappropriately intrusive in pieces ostensibly about others, most have praised Gallagher's sensitive and insightful exploration of personal issues and familial relationships. Recognizing Gallagher's gift for disguising universal truths without negating their impact, Jim Elledge writes:

> On the surface, Tess Gallagher's poems seem little more than observations on ordinary events which she has witnessed or, more often, in which she has participated. ... However, an intense emotional conflict lies submerged beneath the calm images and metaphors ... which raises otherwise mundane subjects to art of a high caliber.

Critics have particularly commended the rhythmic qualities of Gallagher's verse, observing that her use of colloquial cadences lends her poems the natural flow of conversation. Writer Joyce Carol Oates, for instance, has observed that "it is impossible to read Tess Gallagher's poems without being drawn into their mesmerizing rhythms and convinced of the rightness of her intense yet unforced images."

Moon Crossing Bridge In 1997, Gallagher published *Moon Crossing Bridge*, a series of sixty poems centering on the theme of loss and grieving prompted by the death of her husband in 1988. Scholar Marilyn Kallet praises *Moon Crossing Bridge* as "a rare document of loss, faith, and returns—return to the site of loving and to the gradual last breath, return to life's immediate summonings." In regard to the obvious difficulty of undertaking such painful personal material, critic Margaret Holley determines: "The elegiac danger of self-indulgence is routed here by a poetic spirit that is genuine, generous, good-humored, open, and uncommonly sure and mysterious in its touch." Impressed by Gallagher's raw honesty in her poems, Judith Kitchen writes, "Whatever such material may ultimately mean to her private life, it has left her a more powerful, confident, and convincing poet."

Other critics, however, find several of the poems in *Moon Crossing Bridge* to be overly sentimental. Academic Mark Jarman, for example, eschews those poems in the collection that have a tendency toward excessive emotion.

"Gallagher has always been best in the short, spare, basically narrative lyric," he writes, "and that is how she is best in this book of grief." Suzanne Shane agrees, declaring, "The reader becomes aware of the poet's discrepancies in translating her emotional fabric into language: pieces of many poems blur into vagueness and problematic ambiguities, approaching sense and implying contingencies that fall away." What moves many readers of *Moon Crossing Bridge*—sentiment—is what others consider the volume's weakness.

Responses to Literature

1. The main focus in *Moon Crossing Bridge* is Gallagher's loss of her husband. In what ways does Gallagher use metaphor and imagery to express loss in these poems? Find examples from at least three different poems.

2. Some critics condemn many of the poems in *Moon Crossing Bridge* for being overly sentimental. In your opinion, what does this mean? How does this relate to the idea that authors must bare their souls in order to create lasting works of art?

3. Choose a story from Gallagher's collection *The Lover of Horses* and compare it to a short story by Raymond Carver. Can you identify similarities in style or subject between the two stories?

4. Explain the following lines from Gallagher's poem "Instructions to the Double:" "It's a dangerous mission. You / could die out there. You / could go on forever." Why do such dualities appear in so much of Gallagher's poetry?

BIBLIOGRAPHY

Books

Gallagher, Tess. *Instructions to the Double*. St. Paul, Minn.: Graywolf Press, 1975.

Periodicals

Bourne, Daniel. "A Conversation with Tess Gallagher." *Artful Dodge* 38/39 (Spring 2001): 4–21.

Elledge, Jim. "*Willingly* by Tess Gallagher." *Poetry Magazine* 146 (August 1985): 293.

Henry, Patrick. "Introduction: Raymond Carver and Tess Gallagher." *Philosophy and Literature* 22 (October 1998): 413–416.

Holley, Margaret. "Myth in Our Midst: the Multiple Worlds of the Lyric." *Michigan Quarterly Review* vol. XXXII, no. 1 (Winter 1993): 150–164.

Jarman, Mark. "Journals of the Soul: TessGallagher's *Moon Bridge Crossing*." *The Hudson Review* vol. XLVI, no. 2 (Summer 1993): 415.

Kallet, Marilyn. "The Real Work of Grieving—Tess Gallagher's Poetry." *American Book Review* (August 1993): 18.

Karp, Vicki. "Two Poets: Several Worlds Apart." *Parnassus* 12/13 (1985): 415–421.

Oates, Joyce Carol. "The Authority of Timelessness: 'Under the Stars.'" *The Ontario Review* 12 (Spring, Summer 1980): 103–104.

Shane, Suzanne. "Tess Gallagher's *Moon Crossing Bridge*." *Western American Literature* vol. 28, no. 1 (Spring 1993): 86.

❂ Diana Garcia

BORN: *1960, San Joaquin Valley, California*

NATIONALITY: *American*

GENRE: *Fiction, poetry*

MAJOR WORKS:

Love Lessons (1999)

Help Wanted (2000)

When Living Was a Labor Camp (2000)

Overview

Diana Garcia began her career as a minor romance novelist whose works feature Hispanic heroines. Since making the transition to poetry, she has contributed to a vital body of contemporary Hispanic American literature.

Works in Biographical and Historical Context

California to Arizona Born in a migrant-labor camp in California's San Joaquin Valley in 1960, Garcia's family moved to Tucson, Arizona, soon after her birth. As a result, Garcia considered herself an "almost-native" of Tucson for many years. For Garcia and her family, the mountains surrounding Tucson offered not only a beautiful view, but also opportunities for camping and hiking with her three sisters and their children. Along with the mountains, Tucson's rich Hispanic heritage plays a significant role in Garcia's works.

The Romance Novels Before the publication of *Love Lessons*, Garcia worked for many years as a systems analyst for an international computer company. She found the job both interesting and challenging. A devotee of romance novels by authors like Jude Deveraux, Garcia found herself drawn to writing in that genre. In an interview with Cathy Sova, she says, "The lovely thing about romance is that it includes every kind of book you can think of—history, mystery, suspense, humor—and you're guaranteed a happy ending … a happy ending is very important to me."

A casual writer for many years, Garcia believes that writing is the greatest possible escape from the demands of life because the worlds she creates in her works are all hers. After discovering online writers' groups, Garcia was introduced to the Romance Writers of America, a group that matched her with a partner who critiqued one of her

LITERARY AND HISTORICAL CONTEMPORARIES

Garcia's famous contemporaries include:

Sandra Cisneros (1954–): Cisneros is one of the first Hispanic American authors to achieve commercial success. Cisneros is praised for her contribution of a Hispanic American perspective to feminist literature. One of her best-known novels is *The House on Mango Street* (1984).

Laura Esquivel (1950–): Esquivel is a Mexican author whose novel *Like Water for Chocolate* (1989) became a huge best seller. Part novel and cookbook, it discusses the relationships between men and women in Mexico.

Nicholas Sparks (1965–): Sparks is a best-selling American author. With the publication of *The Notebook* (1996), Sparks became one of only two contemporary authors to have a novel remain for over a year on the *New York Times* hardcover and paperback book bestseller lists.

Wendy Coakley-Thompson (1966–): Coakley-Thompson is an African American novelist. In her fiction, Coakley-Thompson addresses issues concerning racial identity and interracial relationships.

Naomi Shihab Nye (1952–): Nye is an American poet of Palestinian descent. Nye's poetry explores the similarities and differences between cultures.

Leila Abouzeid (1950–): Abouzeid's novel, *In the Year of the Elephant: A Moroccan Woman's Journey Toward Independence* (1989), is one of the first works by a Moroccan woman to be translated from Arabic into English.

manuscripts. Though her helper's assessment was harsh, she was driven to get better. While most romance writers enter contests with the hope of being discovered, Garcia chose not to follow that path. She explains:

> Personally, I know that I am the harshest critic of my writing. By the time I'm happy with a story, someone else's subjective opinion means very little to me. Since the contest judge is probably not going to buy my manuscripts, I just keep writing and getting my subjective opinions where it counts—from the editor's desk.

Garcia's first romance novel, *Love Lessons* (*Lecciones amorosas*), was published in 1999, and it was followed by *Help Wanted* (*Aviso oportuno*) in 2000. Both of these works feature Hispanic American heroines who are single mothers, none of whom is looking for love when it strikes. In 2001, Garcia published her third romance novel, *Stardust*, which tells the story of a doctor who meets a rugged, reclusive man who offers her hospitality

when she lands her private plane in a remote area. All three of Garcia's romance novels were met with lukewarm reviews.

From Migrant Worker to Professor   Between publishing romance novels, Garcia debuted her first collection of poetry, *When Living Was a Labor Camp,* in 2000. In this collection, which is a tribute to the Chicano workers of California, Garcia explores the joys and heartaches of living and working in a migrant-labor camp. Migrant workers are people who travel from place to place for temporary employment, usually on a seasonal basis. Early in the twentieth century, the numbers of Hispanics rapidly increased with the growth of the agricultural and cotton industries. Each spring, these workers would travel from Mexico or towns on the Mexican border to the Pacific Coast states and return home at the end of the season. Born in a migrant-labor camp herself, Garcia offers an insider's look at the sorrows and joys of camp life. The book won the Before Columbus Foundation's American Book Award.

Garcia's poetry has also appeared in *The Kenyon Review* and in several anthologies. In addition, she has read from *When Living Was a Labor Camp* at various universities, including the University of Arizona, where she was featured in the poetry center's visiting poets and writers reading series. Currently, she is a professor in the Division of Humanities and Communication at California State University, Monterey Bay.

Works in Literary Context

Garcia has said that her love of romance novels made writing her own a natural choice. Her influences in this genre include Jude Deveraux, whose "writing is so perfect yet unpretentious" that Garcia remains "truly in awe of her craft." She also cites Karen Robards, Theresa Medeiro, and Susan Elizabeth Phillips as inspirations to her romance writing. In regard to her poetry, Garcia's heritage provides a rich background for her character portrayals.

Selecting the Perfect Setting   Selecting an appropriate setting for her books did not come easily for Garcia. For her first stab at writing, she chose to set her plot in India, a location virtually unknown to her. As a result, she says, "it was just awful." After that attempt, she began writing long historical romances set in the seventeenth century. However, researching the specifics of that time period—the language, dress, food, transportation, and other details—proved daunting. Determined to refine her writing skills, Garcia decided to "pull ... [her] characters back home." Consequently, the heroine from *Love Lessons* is from Phoenix and *Help Wanted* is set in Tucson. By trading the foreign settings of her earliest novels— places she had never been—for familiar territory, Garcia was able to focus on developing her characters more fully and realistically. With *When Living Was a Labor Camp,* Garcia returns to her roots for the setting: California's

San Joaquin Valley. By doing so, she allows the setting itself to give voice to its people.

Works in Critical Context

Because of the vast difference between the genres of Garcia's work, criticism has naturally varied greatly. Overall, Garcia's romance novels have received lukewarm reviews, the general consensus being that they are quick, light reads. Garcia's collection of poetry, however, has received critical evaluation from an academic standpoint not afforded to her romance novels.

Love Lessons   *Love Lessons*, Garcia's first published novel, tells the story of Susanna Diaz, a single mother who is also an aerospace engineer, and photographer Daniel Stephens, whose daughter joins Susanna's in trying to fix their parents up with each other. Despite its many lines of dialogue written in Spanish, *Love Lessons*, says critic Kristen Ramsdell, reads at a "fast pace." Reviewer Cathy Sova, however, points out that "it will take more than some Spanish sentences and a reference to a quinceanera to bring a Latino flavor to [publisher] Encanto romances."

While Ramsdell praises the novel's "likable characters" and Sova says the novel "offers creditable characterizations," critic Monica Schwarze deems the characters to be "repulsive people." She calls Susanna a "too-stupid-to-live heroine" and Daniel a "testosterone-driven hero." Even the daughters, says Schwarze, "who had the potential of being the most interesting characters, never rose above the level of mediocrity." On the other hand, Sova finds that "the two girls are as strong as the hero and heroine, and natural-sounding in their interactions." Though Schwarze concludes that *Love Lessons* is unrealistic and trite, Sova is more forgiving, citing restrictions by Garcia's publisher as a possible reason why the plot is "forced and predictable."

When Living Was a Labor Camp   The poetry collection *When Living Was a Labor Camp* has been highly praised not only for its poignant depiction of the lives of California's migrant workers, but also for its vivid sensory details. Noting the power of Garcia's experience, writer Leroy V. Quintana observes, "There is no doubt she knew 'the sweet-salt toil of harvesting the fields.'" The result, he continues, "is a volume of poetry that examines and instructs about life on the margin where, toiling in the vineyard, you continually find yourself in a row 'as far from the beginning as the end.'" Some of Garcia's poems impart a sense of deep-rooted anger, while others exalt life's small victories. No matter their tone, however, all of the poems are pointed, lyrical, and exacting.

According to scholar Tey Diana Rebolledo, *When Living Was a Labor Camp* is more than a poetic account of the world of the migrant-labor camp. Indeed, it exemplifies the "Chicano movement and its effect on migrant workers, the difficulties of Chicanos who were trying to get an education ... the Vietnam War, the difficult relationships Chicanas have with Chicano men, and the

---

COMMON HUMAN EXPERIENCE

Garcia's *When Living Was a Labor Camp* is written in the tradition of the works of the Chicano Renaissance, an explosion of literary activity by Hispanic Americans during the 1960s and early 1970s. Inspired in part by the civil rights movement, Chicano writers sought to give their people a sense of identity in works that emphasized the need for educational, economic, political, and social equality. Here are some other works that exemplify the Chicano Renaissance:

Bless Me, Ultima (1972), a novel by Rudolfo Anaya. This classic piece of Hispanic American literature reveals a young man's questions about life and death, good and evil, and destiny.

Chicano: 25 Pieces of a Chicano Mind (1969), a collection of poetry by Abelardo Delgado. Drawing on the oral traditions of the Hispanic American culture, these poems reflect the struggles and hopes of Chicanos.

Chicano Renaissance: Contemporary Cultural Trends (1971), a nonfiction book edited by David R. Maciel, Isidro D. Ortiz, and María Herrera-Sobek. This academic work traces the history of the Chicano Renaissance, providing an informative reference for Hispanic American literature today.

And the Earth Did Not Part (1971), a collection of short stories by Tomá Rivera. Through a year in the life of a young boy, this book exposes the abuses faced by migrant workers in the United States during the 1940s and 1950s.

Sketches of the Valley and Other Works (1973), a novel by Rolando Hinojosa-Smith. Examining the lives of Anglo and Hispanic American residents of a fictitious border town in Texas, this four-part novel is composed of loosely connected narratives, monologues, dialogues, and sketches.

---

friendships between women." All of this, critics agree, is done with humor, beauty, irony, and, perhaps most importantly, with hope. Rebolledo concludes that what can be learned from the collection is that "we have a tradition and we have a history; we each need to take responsibility to remember them and to pass them on, and we can do so with creativity and with pleasure."

Responses to Literature

1. Investigate the history of the romance-novel genre. What are its origins? Create a timeline showing the publication dates of at least five major romance novels per decade from the 1950s to the present day. Why do you think romantic fiction is such a popular genre?

2. Adopt the persona of an individual living in a migrant-labor camp and write a poem that could be included in Garcia's *When Living Was a Labor Camp*.

3. Research the Chicano Renaissance. Who were its primary leaders? What was the purpose of this movement? How does it differ from the African-American Harlem Renaissance?

BIBLIOGRAPHY

Books

Rebolledo, Tey Diana. *The Chronicles of Panchita Villa and Other Guerrilleras: Essays on Chicana/Latina Literature and Criticism*. Austin: University of Texas at Austin, 2005.

Periodicals

Ramsdell, Kristin. "Review of *Love Lessons*/Lecciones amorosas," *Library Journal* (August 1999): 70.

Web sites

Galloway, Teresa. *Review of Help Wanted*. Retrieved December 1, 2008, from http://www.likesbooks.com/cgi-bin/bookReview.pl?BookReviewId=4672.

Quintana, Leroy V. *Diana Garcia*.. Retrieved December 10, 2008, from http://www.tucsonweekly.com/gbase/CityWek/Content?oid=45069.

Schwarze, Monica. *Review of Love Lessons*. Retrieved November 30, 2008, from http://www.likesbooks.com/cgi-bin/bookReview.pl?BookReviewId=4673.

Sova, Cathy. *New Faces 48: Diana Garcia*. Retrieved November 30, 2008, from http://www.theromancereader.com/nf-garcia.html.

◉ John Gardner

BORN: *1933, Batavia, New York*

DIED: *1982, Susquehanna, Pennsylvania*

NATIONALITY: *American*

GENRE: *Fiction, nonfiction*

MAJOR WORKS:

The Sunlight Dialogues (1972)

Grendel (1971)

On Moral Fiction (1978)

Overview

Known for his unique writing style and opinionated literary views, John Champlin Gardner was a philosophical novelist, a medieval scholar, a university professor, and a controversial critic. He worked in a multitude of genres, including children's fiction, opera libretti, translations, and scholarly criticism, and his writings reflected the rich legacy

John Gardner   *Gardner, John, 1973, photograph. AP Images.*

of Western culture. Believing that an artist is morally obligated to create works that offer hope for mankind, Gardner criticized many of his contemporaries for being more concerned with technique than truth, while he himself addressed such timeless questions as the nature of good and evil and the power of guilt and redemption in people's lives.

Works in Biographical and Historical Context

Music and Literature   Gardner was born in Batavia, New York, on July 21, 1933. With a mother who taught high school English and a father who was well versed in the Bible and Shakespeare, Gardner was surrounded by literature throughout his childhood. A frequent listener to Metropolitan Opera radio broadcasts, Gardner cultivated a taste for serious music and proved to be a talented musician himself by playing the French horn and singing in various choirs. As an adult, he remained a loyal devotee to opera, and among his many literary productions are libretti for three operas composed by Joseph Baber.

A Haunting Tragedy   As a boy, Gardner worked on his father's dairy farm. When Gardner was eleven, he was driving a tractor that was towing a one-ton cultipacker, a machine used for flattening fields before planting. When the tractor suddenly stalled, his younger brother, who had been riding on the tractor's tow-bar, was thrown under the cultipacker and crushed. Blaming himself for his brother's death, Gardner was haunted by nightmares and flashbacks of the tragedy throughout his life, and much of his work reflects his struggles with questions of guilt, responsibility, and redemption.

University Experiences Drawn to its liberal arts and music programs, Gardner attended DePauw University from 1951 to 1953. After marrying Joan Louise Patterson in 1953, Gardner transferred to Washington University in St. Louis, graduating in 1955, and then began his graduate work at the University of Iowa, where he studied medieval literature and creative writing. In 1956, he received his master's degree in English from the University of Iowa, and a PhD two years later. Although his doctoral dissertation was a novel, Gardner did not begin his career as a novelist. Initially, he taught medieval literature and creative writing at Oberlin College in Ohio. Because of his controversial literary ideas and teaching methods, however, he moved from one university to another throughout his teaching career. Nevertheless, he became a prominent creative writing professor.

Success in the Fiction Genre During the early 1960s, Gardner's writing consisted primarily of scholarly articles. When his first novel, *The Resurrection*, was published in 1966, Gardner received little notice. His second novel, *The Wreckage of Agathon* (1970), gained more critical attention, but he was still not established as a writer of major importance.

As a professor of English specializing in medieval literature, Gardner had been teaching the Anglo-Saxon epic *Beowulf* (c. 1000) for several years. In 1969, Gardner received a grant to work on a retelling of *Beowulf* from the monster's point of view. Published in 1971, *Grendel* was the first of Gardner's novels to bring him critical acclaim as well as popular success. The work was praised as a literary tour de force and named a book of the year by both *Time* and *Newsweek* magazines in 1971.

The overwhelming success of *Grendel* established Gardner's reputation in the literary world, and his publisher agreed to print *The Sunlight Dialogues*, a novel that had previously been rejected for publication. Again, Gardner's work was met with praise, and the book remained on the *New York Times* best-seller list for sixteen weeks. Additionally, Gardner was awarded the National Education Award, followed by the prestigious Guggenheim Fellowship for 1973–1974. This grant allowed Gardner to give up teaching to focus on his writing. The result was the award-winning novel *October Light* (1976).

Writing Criticism In addition to novels, Gardner wrote a number of thought-provoking works on the purpose and craft of fiction. His criticism was hailed, as were his novels, as unsettling. *On Moral Fiction*, written in part before his novels were published, contains many pointed statements that negatively assess the works of other major

novelists. Many of Gardner's peers were insulted, and some offended critics evaluated Gardner's subsequent works from a fighting stance.

Children's Literature In addition to novels, Gardner wrote children's books based on such stories as *Sir Gawain and the Green Knight* (c. 1375). Drawing on his knowledge of medieval literature, Gardner's children's books are fairy tales retold with original twists, modernized stories in which recognizable characters speak in today's clichés, or unlikely contemporary characters are revived by the magic of the past. The result is a collection of books that has been instrumental in familiarizing children with sophisticated classic literature.

Life Changes Commissioned to translate the *Epic of Gilgamesh* (c. 2000 B.C.E.) into a work that would be accessible to modern readers, Gardner studied the Mesopotamian story, one of the oldest major epics in literature, from 1974 to 1976. Around the same time, he was diagnosed with colon cancer and underwent two operations that left him weak and unable to devote all of his time to writing. Nonetheless, he taught classes at the State University of New York at Binghamton, where he met fellow professor Liz Rosenberg. Recently divorced from his first wife, Gardner became involved with Rosenberg, and the two married in 1980, only to divorce two years later when he fell in love with Susan Shreve, a writer.

On September 14, 1982, a few months after the publication of the novel *Mickelson's Ghosts*, Gardner was

COMMON HUMAN EXPERIENCE

With its twist on the *Beowulf* epic by narrating the story from the monster's point of view, *Grendel* is an example of metafiction, which is fiction about fiction. General characteristics of metafiction can include: history that becomes fiction, arbitrary language, an author who appears to have no power, or reality that becomes no longer understandable. Other examples of metafiction include the following:

Pale Fire (1962), a novel by Vladimir Nabokov. This work is presented as a poem entitled "Pale Fire" by John Shade, a fictional author, complete with an introduction and commentary by a fictional friend of his.

Forrest Gump (1994), a film directed by Robert Zemeckis. Though the title character in this film meets historical figures, influences pop culture, and plays a part in historic events of the twentieth century, he is oblivious to their significance.

Slaughterhouse-Five (1969), a novel by Kurt Vonnegut. Devoting the first chapter to an author's preface in which he apologizes for the story to come, Vonnegut manipulates fiction and reality throughout the work.

Midnight's Children (1981), a novel by Salman Rushdie. By combining the novel form with various non-Western texts such as Sanskrit epics, Rushdie depicts an entire society through the story of one person.

killed in a motorcycle accident in Susquehanna, Pennsylvania. Twelve years after his death, a volume of Gardner's literary reviews and essays appeared as *On Writers and Writing* (1994). The collection includes Gardner's critical response to the fiction of John Steinbeck, John Cheever, and Bernard Malamud, among others, as well as an autobiographical essay.

Works in Literary Context

Gardner's earliest influences came from his family, as his parents' appreciation of literature and music were a guiding force in his development as a writer and critic. Specifically, he cited the work of Geoffrey Chaucer as his greatest writing inspiration from childhood. Thematically, the unfortunate personal tragedy Gardner experienced early in his life—his role in the death of his brother—motivated him to explore repeatedly the question of human responsibility versus chance, as well as issues of guilt and redemption in his works.

The Purpose of Literature In *On Moral Fiction*, Gardner presents what he believes is the purpose of literature: to promote moral values, to be life-affirming, and to tell a story. Gardner attempts to follow William Faulkner's lead toward some kind of credible, meaningful con-

firmation of life, something beyond the mere fantasies of wish fulfillment he saw in many of his contemporaries. Artists, Gardner contends, are responsible for creating inspirational works that celebrate life—not give voice to despair—as they address timeless philosophical questions. Several of his novels, in fact, feature protagonists who are professional or amateur philosophers, characters allowing Gardner to discuss such issues as the nature of chaos, good and evil, and mortality.

Gardner's works also demonstrate the power of art and its role in Western culture, most notably in *Grendel*, in which Gardner explicitly asserts the significance of art and the artist as a means of affirming the moral meaning of life. In *Beowulf*, Grendel is a terrible beast that terrorizes a kingdom; however, Gardner transforms the monster into a lonely, intelligent outsider with a weakness for poetry. Juxtaposing Grendel with his mother, Gardner emphasizes, through her inarticulateness, the importance of language in the development of civilization. Fittingly, Gardner names the poet in *Grendel* "the Shaper," and Grendel, haunted by the Shaper's words, comes to realize that the poet is the guiding force in society, for he is the one who inspires hope in the hearts of his listeners. Such is the power of art, Gardner shows, that even a monster can be moved by it.

Works in Critical Context

Gardner's novels provoked a wide range of critical responses and, unlike many academic fictions, were appreciated by a large audience, as evidenced by his three best sellers. "Very few writers … are alchemist enough to capture the respect of the intellectual community *and* the imagination of others who lately prefer [Jacqueline] Susann and [Judith] Krantz," observed reviewer Craig Riley. He continues, "Based on critical acclaim, and sales volume, it would seem that this man accomplished both." Although Gardner is unquestionably one of academic literature's most commercially successful authors, many critics consider his novels unwieldy and overly philosophical, in particular *The Resurrection* and *Mickelson's Ghosts*.

Critics have often made negative use of *On Moral Fiction* in interpreting Gardner's later works, reading Gardner's complex, philosophically provocative novels from an uncompromising moral perspective. *On Moral Fiction* itself was judged as arrogant, self-serving, and wrongheaded, and many critics disputed Gardner's contention that art can radically change people's lives. Nevertheless, his work is widely respected for its innovative approach to addressing questions of universal human concern.

The Wreckage of Agathon Attracting more attention than its predecessor, Gardner's second published novel, *The Wreckage of Agathon*, was met with harsh criticism by those detractors who felt the book was little more than boring melodrama. Other critics, however, declared that *The Wreckage of Agathon* proved Gardner's skill as an antiquarian, as a writer who could weave elements from ancient history into "a novel transcending history and effectively embracing all of it, a philosophical drama that accurately describes the wreckage of the twentieth century as well as of Agathon, and a highly original work of imagination," as reviewer Christopher Lehmann-Haupt put it. Composed mostly of dialogue, the novel exposes Gardner's "manic glee in disputation," or "delight in forensic and rhetorical flashiness for its own sake," scholar David Cowart observed. With themes including the relation between individuals and the social orders they encounter, *The Wreckage of Agathon*, said academic Paul West:

> delineates the mental motion of the individual as sacred, whether he's a seer or not ... and it exuberantly calls into question society's categorical insistences—the things brought into being at our own expense to protect us against ourselves, other people, and, putatively, other societies.

Responses to Literature

1. At the time Gardner was writing *Grendel*, the United States was involved in the Vietnam War. Investigate the antiwar movement during this time. How does the struggle between good and evil in *Grendel* compare to the struggle between Vietnam War supporters and protestors?

2. Read selections from *On Moral Fiction*. According to Gardner, what is the role of fiction in the world? How do Gardner's stories fulfill his ideas of what fiction should be? In what ways do his stories fall short?

3. Gardner's work is often classified as postmodernist. Do you agree with this assessment? Do you think any one of his books is more postmodern than the rest?

4. Describe Gardner's philosophy regarding art and morality. Do you believe that an artist is morally responsible for creating inspirational works that address the timeless questions of humanity? How does entertainment factor into Gardner's artistic philosophy? Are his novels entertaining?

BIBLIOGRAPHY

Books

Cowart, David. *Arches and Light: The Fiction of John Gardner*. Carbondale, Ill.: Southern Illinois University Press, 1983.

Henderson, Jeff. *John Gardner: A Study of the Short Fiction*. Boston: Twayne, 1990.

Howell, John M. *Understanding John Gardner*. Columbia, S.C.: University of South Carolina Press, 1993.

McWilliams, Dean. *John Gardner*. Boston: Twayne, 2004.

Periodicals

Lehmann-Haupt, Christopher. "Looking for the Novelist." *New York Times* (September 24, 1970): 45.

Locke, Richard. "Grendel is a Beauty of a Beast." *New York Times* (September 4, 1971): 19.

Maddocks, Melvin. "Making Ends Meet." *Time* (December 20, 1976): 74.

Riley, Craig. "John Gardner." *Best Sellers* (April 1984): 267–269.

West, Paul. "Black Comedy in Ancient Sparta: *The Wreckage of Agathon*." *New York Times Book Review* (November 15, 1970): BR3.

Web sites

Murray, Kim. *Gardner, John Champlin, Jr.*. Retrieved December 5, 2008, from http://www.pabook.libraries.psu.edu/palitmap/bios/Gardner__John.html.

✺ Rick Geary

BORN: *1946, Kansas City, Missouri*

NATIONALITY: *American*

GENRE: *Nonfiction, fiction*

MAJOR WORKS:

Jack the Ripper: A Journal of the Whitechapel Murders, 1888–1889 (1995)

Spider-Man: Ghosts, Ghouls, and the Hobgoblin (1996)

The Fatal Bullet: The Assassination of President James A. Garfield (2001)

The Lindbergh Child: America's Hero and the Crime of the Century (2008)

Overview

Rick Geary is a prominent cartoonist whose illustrations have appeared in the *New York Times* and the *Los Angeles Times*, as well as *National Lampoon* and *MAD* magazines long admired for their comics. In addition to numerous illustrations and comic books, he is also known for his contributions to the graphic novel genre, notably his work for the *Treasury of Victorian Murder* series. Among Geary's most widely circulated illustration is his logo for the audiobook publisher Recorded Books.

Works in Biographical and Historical Context

Mad About Art Geary was born on February 25, 1946, in Kansas City, Missouri, and grew up in Wichita, Kansas. As a child, he was not an avid reader or collector of comics. However, when he discovered *MAD Magazine* at the age of thirteen, Geary was intrigued by the idea of humorous illustration. Although he grew up

LITERARY AND HISTORICAL CONTEMPORARIES

Geary's famous contemporaries include:

Sergio Aragonés (1937–): This Spanish-born cartoonist has won nearly every award in his field for his comic book series *Groo the Wanderer* and his contributions to *Mad Magazine*.

Kim Deitch (1944–): Deitch uses a drawing style suggestive of 1930s cartoons to explore states of reality, pop culture, and the power of art.

Robert Crumb (1943–): Recognized for his satirical view of the American mainstream as much as his distinctive style of illustration, Crumb has avoided the mainstream comic book publishing industry while still earning accolades from the industry.

Mark Evanier (1952–): In addition to writing comic books for Disney, Evanier is noted for his animation work on the television series *Garfield and Friends*.

Chevy Chase (1943–): Chase is an Emmy Award–winning actor, comedian, and writer who has appeared in several National Lampoon movies.

wanting to be an artist of some sort, he never particularly planned to draw comics.

In 1968, Geary graduated with a bachelor's degree in art and film from the University of Kansas in Lawrence, where his first cartoons were published in the *University Daily Kansan*. After earning his master's degree in 1971, Geary worked as a staff artist for two weekly papers in Wichita, the *Prairie Journal* and the *Wichita Independent*. For both publications, he drew political cartoons, caricatures, illustrations for articles and ads, lettering and headlines, and ad layout. When the *Independent* went out of business in 1975, Geary moved to San Diego, California.

Geary began his work as a freelance cartoonist and illustrator two years later. Beginning in 1979, he began drawing portraits of famous people—from authors to public figures—for postcards and rubber stamps. After his agent went to New York in 1979 and showed Geary's work to the new "Funny Pages" editor of *National Lampoon*, Geary started to contribute regularly to the publication, a relationship that lasted until the magazine's last issue in 1992. His work also began appearing on a regular basis in *Heavy Metal* and *Dark Horse Comics*. Showcasing his deadpan wit, much of his early comic work has been collected in *Housebound with Rick Geary* (1991).

Publications Across the Country

In January 1987, Geary married Deborah Lee Chester, a teacher, and the couple lived in New York City from 1988 to 1992. During these years, Geary regularly provided illustrations for *The New York Times Book Review*. Additionally, his illustrations appeared in *MAD*, *Spy*, *Rolling Stone*, and the *Los Angeles Times*. Geary then returned to San Diego, where he has done illustration work intermittently for dozens of West Coast publications.

Comics and Graphic Novels

Geary has written and illustrated an assortment of comic books and graphic novels for a number of publishers, including three adaptations for the brief revival of the *Classics Illustrated* series (1990–1991). In 1994, Geary received the Book and Magazine Illustration Award from the National Cartoonists Society. He has also written and illustrated two Spider-Man children's books for Marvel Comics, and his children's comic "Society of Horrors" ran in *Disney Adventures* magazine from 1999 to 2006.

Geary's most extensive project to date has been the *Treasury of Victorian Murder*, an ongoing nonfiction graphic novel series that focuses on unsolved nineteenth-century crimes, including those involving Jack the Ripper and Lizzie Borden. In 2007, after living more than thirty years in San Diego, Geary and his wife moved to Carrizozo, New Mexico, where he continues to write graphic novels for the *Treasury of Victorian Murder* series. Most recently, Geary launched the *Treasury of XXth Century Murder* series, which debuted *The Lindbergh Child: America's Hero and the Crime of the Century* (2008).

Works in Literary Context

In an interview with Susan Magliaro, Geary said that "there are several cartoonists and illustrators (too numerous to list) whom I've admired over the years, though their work may bear little resemblance to my own." He names his principal overall influence to be illustrator Edward Gorey, whose work is characterized by simple, dense black lines against a white background lacking any kind of shading. Gorey, declares Geary, has "affected me since I first saw his mini-books in the early seventies."

Victorian Elements

Inspired by what he calls Gorey's "twisted and playful Victorian-Edwardian sensibility," Geary often employs literary styles that are typical of popular nineteenth-century works in his *Treasury of Victorian Murder* books. According to Bradford W. Wright, Geary exhibits "a true talent for capturing the images, mood and even language of Victorian society. His approach is so effective that this work looks and reads as if it could have been produced in the 1840s." *Jack the Ripper* (1995) and *The Borden Tragedy* (1997), for instance, depend on excerpts from journals for the stories' narration, while *The Fatal Bullet: The Assassination of President James A. Garfield* (2001) compares the morality of President James Garfield with that of his assassin. With artwork reflecting what he calls "a certain deadpan humor," Geary creates haunting stories that not only document famous murders, but also point out the hypocrisies of Victorian society.

Police Procedural In addition to adding a Victorian literary perspective to his *Treasury of Victorian Murder* graphic novels, Geary details the murders in the style of a police procedural, a sub-genre of the crime novel which realistically describes the actions and procedures of criminal investigators. In *Jack the Ripper*, Geary's characters sift through evidence that includes coroners' reports, witnesses' accounts, and actual clues police gathered during their investigations of the infamous murders. The police procedural method is apparent as well in *The Borden Tragedy*. Here, Geary presents not only the murders of Abby and Andrew Borden, but also the trial and acquittal of their daughter, Lizzy.

Works in Critical Context

Geary's work is consistently greeted with enthusiasm by both critics and readers. His art and writing are recognized as superlative, and he is widely considered one of the best comic illustrators and writers in the business. As the graphic novel has risen in popularity, Geary's works have received more and more recognition in the field, with various titles earning awards such as Publishers Weekly Best Book of 2008 and YALSA (Youth Librarians) Great Graphic Novel for Teens (2007 and 2008).

The Treasury of Victorian Murder Series Reviewers have commended Geary's meticulous research for his works in the *Treasury of Victorian Murder* graphic novel series. Geary does not attempt to solve the crime; instead, he presents all the evidence he has collected in his research, introducing a variety of possible suspects and outcomes without sacrificing factual accuracy and clarity. In his interview with Magliaro, Geary commented on his personal theories about the murders he chronicles: "I'm quite satisfied with the mystery remaining a mystery. In fact, I think that what draws me to these classic unsolved crimes like Jack and Lizzie and Mary Rogers is their essential unknowability."

Adding to the historical authenticity of the stories are Geary's intriguing illustrations, which are drawn from unusual points of view that not only provide intricate details, but also enhance the tone of the story. For example, in *The Borden Tragedy*, "It's Geary's artfully precise reconstruction of turn-of-the-century Fall River that makes this work so haunting, and such a delight," writes reviewer Ray Olson. Olson similarly praises the power of Geary's illustrations in *The Fatal Bullet: The Assassination of President James A. Garfield*. Remarking that Geary "surpasses his own bravura" with this work, Olson cites the "subtly expressive facial drawing, and skillful juxtaposition of frames" as particular strengths. He continues: "The comics medium arguably communicates the facts more forcefully and memorably than any of the many other works about the crimes."

Critics have also noted the educational value of Geary's *Victorian Murder* works. In reference to *The Mystery of Mary Rogers* (2001), reviewer Christine C. Menefee concludes that "with its commendable historical accuracy, [it] would also enliven studies of U.S. history."

COMMON HUMAN EXPERIENCE

Combining fact with striking illustrations, Geary's graphic novels in the *Treasury of Victorian Murder* series fall into the mystery story subgenre of police procedurals. Other police procedural works include the following:

The Last Dance (2000), a novel by Ed McBain. In this novel, one of fifty in McBain's 87th Precinct series, Steve Carella and his fellow detectives from the 87th Precinct investigate a number of crimes in Isola, a fictional city based on Manhattan.

Blood Count (1986), fiction by Dell Shannon. The cases Detective Luis Mendoza and his Los Angeles colleagues are investigating in this novel include the murder of a newborn, a string of hit-and-run accidents involving the same vehicle, and the assault of a twelve-year-old girl.

V as in Victim (1955), fiction by Lawrence Treat. Generally recognized as the first police procedural, this novel features police officer Mitch Taylor as he teams up with other officers to solve a hit-and-run crime using methods employed by real policemen.

Furthermore, Geary's *Victorian Murder* books have been applauded for their enormous appeal to reluctant readers. In 1996, *Jack the Ripper* was selected for the Quick Picks for Reluctant Young Adult Readers List by the American Library Association's Young Adult Services Division.

Responses to Literature

1. Many classics in literature have been rewritten as graphic novels. Do you believe that graphic novels can be regarded as literature? Do you see any benefit in reworking classic literature into the graphic novel form?

2. Select a United States president and create two pages of a graphic novel in which you depict that person's early life. You may do your drawings by hand, or you may use photos or other artists' renderings to illustrate your frames. (If you do, be sure to give credit to the originator of the image.)

3. Read several different historical accounts of the assassination of James A. Garfield. Then read Geary's *The Fatal Bullet*. How does Geary's version compare to what is documented as history?

4. Though his writing has not received as much attention as his illustrations, Geary carefully adapts his writing style to the subject matter of each of his works. Choose one title from either of his *Treasury of Murder* works, and explain how the writing style reflects the story, time, and culture in which the book is set.

BIBLIOGRAPHY

Periodicals

Ching, Edith. "Review of *Harry Houdini: Escape Artist*." *School Library Journal* (December 2002): 124.

Goldsmith, Francisca. "Review of *The Borden Tragedy*." *School Library Journal* (March 1998): 249.

Marantz, Sylvia S. "Review of *Inside the Airport*." *School Library Journal* (September 1990): 215.

Menefee, Christine C. "Review of *The Mystery of Mary Rogers*." *School Library Journal* (August 2001): 213.

Olson, Ray. "Review of *The Fatal Bullet: A True Account of the Assassination, Lingering Pain, Death, and Burial of James A. Garfield, Twentieth President of the United States: Also Including the Inglorious Life and Career of the Despised Assassin Guiteau*." *Booklist* (July 1999): 1919.

Olson, Ray. "Review of *The Borden Tragedy*." *Publisher's Weekly* (January 19, 1998): 364.

Web sites

Hooper, Terry. *Rick Geary—The Man Who Draws Gumby*. Retrieved October 31, 2008, from http://www.comicsbulletin.com/features/115479220239661.htm. Last updated in 2008.

Lizzie Andrew Borden Virtual Museum and Library. *Rick Geary, Artist and Author of The Borden Tragedy*. Retrieved November 3, 2008, from http://www.lizzieandrewborden.com/Writers Corner/Interviews/InterviewRickGeary.htm. Last updated in 2008.

NBM Comics. *Rick Geary*. Retrieved October 31, 2008, from http://www.nbmpub.com/mystery/geary.html. Last updated in 2008.

Rick Geary: Cartoonist-Illustrator. *Biography*. Retrieved October 31, 2008, from http://www.rickgeary.com. Last updated in 2008.

■ Theodor Geisel

S*ee* *Dr. Seuss*

✹ Kaye Gibbons

BORN: *1960, Nash County, North Carolina*

NATIONALITY: *American*

GENRE: *Fiction*

MAJOR WORKS:

Ellen Foster (1987)

A Virtuous Woman (1989)

Sights Unseen (1995)

The Life All Around Me by Ellen Foster (2005)

Kaye Gibbons *Gibbons, Kaye, photograph. © Jerry Bauer. Reproduced by permission.*

Overview

Best known for fictional works about self-reliant Southern women who transcend the difficult circumstances of their lives, Kaye Gibbons entered the American literary scene with the publication of *Ellen Foster* (1987), a Southern coming-of-age novel. Set predominantly in rural Southern communities, Gibbons's novels are told in plain, direct regional language through first-person narrators. From the matriarchal folk healer to the uncompromising eleven-year-old, her powerful protagonists are guided by an innate wisdom and a steely determination not to succumb to self-pity.

Works in Biographical and Historical Context

Marked by Mental Illness Kaye Gibbons was born on May 5, 1960, in a small rural community in Nash County, North Carolina. Gibbons's father was a poor tobacco farmer who struggled with alcoholism and was often abusive. Her mother suffered from bipolar disorder, which causes a person to experience extreme swings from periods of depression to periods of mania, a state that includes intense activity and sleeplessness. She committed suicide when Gibbons was ten years old, and Gibbons's father died only a few years later from complications associated with alcoholism. Afterwards, Gibbons was passed around from relative to relative, a lifestyle that provided her much of the material that evolved into *Ellen Foster*. By the time she was twenty, Gibbons had also been diagnosed with bipolar disorder.

From Poetry to Prose After graduating from high school, Gibbons attended North Carolina State University on a scholarship, majoring in English with the intent of becoming a teacher; however, her interest in writing led her to enroll at the University of North Carolina at Chapel Hill. There, Gibbons became familiar with the works of James Weldon Johnson, an African American poet whose use of common speech patterns and idioms in his writing greatly influenced Gibbons's prose style. Already a wife and mother of two by this time, Gibbons enrolled in a literature class taught by Louis Rubin, a renowned teacher and noted scholar of Southern literature, as well as the founder of the Algonquin Press. After Gibbons showed him a poem she had written from the viewpoint of an African American girl, the character who later became Ellen Foster's friend Starletta, Rubin encouraged Gibbons to develop the poem into a novel. Two months later, she presented him with a manuscript that she had written during a six-week manic episode.

Accolades and Oprah *Ellen Foster* won Gibbons the Sue Kaufman Prize for First Fiction from the American Academy and Institute of Arts and Letters. Encouraged by her initial success, Gibbons again turned to the rural south for her second novel, *A Virtuous Woman*, published in 1989 to wide praise in the United States and abroad. That same year, Gibbons received a grant from the National Endowment for the Arts to write her next novel, *A Cure for Dreams* (1991), which also won several major writing awards.

During the early 1990s, the overwhelming success of Gibbons's literary career was accompanied by stressful personal events. She went through a divorce, relocated to New York City, returned to North Carolina, changed publishers, and remarried. Nevertheless, such tumultuous changes did not hinder Gibbons's literary accomplishments, as she continued to produce works welcomed by both critics and the general reading public. A major boost to Gibbons's career came in 1997, when *Ellen Foster* and *A Virtuous Woman* were chosen as selections for the Oprah Book Club and promoted nationally on *The Oprah Winfrey Show*. Because of this publicity, *Ellen Foster* alone sold nearly 800,000 additional paperback copies ten years after its initial publication.

Opening Up to the Public Since the appearance of *Sights Unseen* (1995), Gibbons has been open about her own battle with bipolar disorder, and her efforts to share her condition with others led to the autobiographical work *Frost and Flower: My Life with Manic Depression So Far* (1995). Currently, Gibbons lives in Raleigh with

her husband and their five children. Aside from her work as a writer, Gibbons is active in the Raleigh community, serving on the Board of Directors for the Friends of the Library of North Carolina State, and volunteering for the Books for Children Project.

Works in Literary Context

Despite the challenges of her young life—or more likely because of them—Gibbons has developed into a writer with a distinctive voice. Many of her works focus on an individual's alienation from society and the ways in which class status serves to limit the choices available to individuals. Certainly this issue of alienation is one that Gibbons was well acquainted with as a child, given her family's poverty and her mother's suicide. The influence of her past is especially evident in her novels. Another aspect of Gibbons's life that has had a profound impact on her writing is her bipolar disorder. Although this condition has become more treatable, Gibbons is careful, for she does not want to sacrifice the creativity that has allowed her to become an award-winning novelist.

Strong Southern Females Gibbons's novels focus on the lives of strong Southern females who boldly face adversity and, in doing so, inspire those around them. In contrast, most of the male characters appearing in Gibbons's works are unsympathetic figures, who, says reviewer Stephen McCauley, are "3D;" that is, the men in a Gibbons novel can usually be counted on to "disappoint, disappear, and die." With extraordinary courage, her women persevere, daring to challenge what some people might call fate. In the novels featuring young narrators, *Ellen Foster* and *Sights Unseen*, for example, Gibbons's trademark heroine is, as reviewer Kathryn Harrison notes, "a girl who, having lost her mother—having lost all comfort and safety—attacks the chaos of her life with heartbreaking bravery." No matter her age, the typical Gibbons protagonist proves to be a resilient female survivor, one who faces hardship

COMMON HUMAN EXPERIENCE

Gibbons is best known for *Ellen Foster*, a novel about a self-reliant Southern girl whose search for family and a sense of belonging have universal appeal. Listed below are other works whose main characters seek the security and love of a familial relationship:

> *Bastard Out of Carolina* (1992), a novel by Dorothy Allison. A finalist for the 1992 National Book Award, Allison's novel is controversial for its graphic depiction of Southern poverty, illegitimacy, and the sexual abuse of a child, who eventually goes to live with relatives.
>
> *Tell Me That You Love Me, Junie Moon* (1968), a novel by Marjorie Kellogg. Kellogg drew from personal experience to write this novel about three emotionally and physically damaged young characters who attempt to become a family and make a home for themselves.
>
> *Wuthering Heights* (1847), a novel by Emily Brontë. In this novel, an orphan brought to live at Wuthering Heights becomes abused and treated like a servant once his benefactor dies.

with intelligence and a strong will while waging quiet wars against abuse, against sexist inequality, even against life's everyday burdens. Whether escaping an abusive father, as does Ellen Foster, or preparing her family for life without her, as does the dying Ruby Stokes in *A Virtuous Woman*, Gibbons's protagonists demonstrate a self-assured approach to the trials of life.

Works in Critical Context

Critical reaction to Gibbons's novels has been mostly favorable. Many critics applaud her realistic portrayal of contemporary Southern life and her use of dialogue, contending that it avoids the contrivances of Southern colloquialisms and skillfully arranges the cadence of words to give characters their Southern flavor. Some critics note that Gibbons's protagonists display traditional social and moral values as they face the challenges of life. As scholar Julian Mason has observed, Gibbons is a writer who has "taken the perseverance of the human spirit ... for her continuing literary domain."

The negative criticism Gibbons has received is based on the unflagging perfection of her protagonists, leading commentators to determine that their pluck and perseverance sometimes border on caricature. While some reviewers have condemned the predictability of some of Gibbons's plots, they also concede that her stories are engaging and realistically told and often reveal, as Ralph C. Wood observes, a "deep truth [which] is narrative and

practical, not abstract and theoretical." Without a doubt, her firmly grounded sense of place, combined with believable and often heartrending characterizations, has won Gibbons a significant readership.

Ellen Foster   In large part because of Gibbons's adept handling of sensitive themes, critics have been lavish in their admiration of *Ellen Foster*. A reviewer for *Kirkus Reviews* calls the book a "child's-eye tale of evil giving way to goodness—and happily far more spunky than sweet." An unnamed reviewer for *Publishers Weekly* notes that the book resembles "a Victorian tearjerker, transplanted to the South," and offers a cautious recommendation: "Some readers will find the recital of Ellen's woes mawkishly sentimental, but for others it may be a perfect summer read." Fellow writer Alice Hoffman describes *Ellen Foster* as "filled with lively humor, compassion and integrity," suggesting that Ellen Foster is possibly "the most trustworthy character in recent fiction."

In regard to Gibbons's ability to control Ellen's point of view, critic Pearl K. Bell commends Gibbons for giving narrative authority to a child. Bell writes:

> Ellen has a rare capacity for seeing through phonies and figuring things out, but Gibbons never allows us to feel the slightest doubt that she is only 11. ... The voice of this resourceful child is mesmerizing because we are right inside her head. The words are always flawlessly right. ... Ellen is an original who remains sweet and loving through the worst of times. Thus does Gibbons persuade us, as few writers can, that even a terrible childhood can be a state of grace.

If not for Ellen's narrative voice, the terrible events of her young life could easily result in melodrama. According to reviewer Brad Hooper, however, Gibbons controls her narrative with such skill that *Ellen Foster* is "never weepy or grim, despite the subject matter." Additionally, reviewer Linda Taylor confirms that Ellen is believable "because although she has a dark tale to tell, she will not engineer sympathy for her effects." Though some consider Ellen's narrative voice to be a correct portrayal of the world from a child's viewpoint, other critics question her believability as a narrator, arguing that her perspective is often too mature and knowing to be that of a child. While Ellen's instinctual wisdom might not be realistic for that of an eleven-year-old girl, even the novel's strongest detractors can agree that Gibbons has created a clear voice to be reckoned with.

Responses to Literature

1. In *Ellen Foster*, says scholar Veronica Makowsky, Gibbons has attempted "to rewrite the saga of the American hero by changing 'him' to 'her' and to rewrite the Southern female bildungsroman by changing its privileged, sheltered, upper-class heroine to a poor, abused outcast." Explain what Makowsky means by this statement, using your

library or the Internet for research if necessary. Do you support her assessment?

2. Why is *Ellen Foster* often taught along with *The Adventures of Huckleberry Finn* (1884) by Mark Twain, *The Catcher in the Rye* by J. D. Salinger (1951), and *To Kill a Mockingbird* (1960) by Harper Lee? What characteristics does Gibbons's novel share with these other works? How is her work different?

3. How does Ellen Foster define home at the beginning of *Ellen Foster*? How does her conception of home change during the novel? What is your definition of home and family? Do you believe that Gibbons's message in the novel is that family members are unreliable and that people cannot rely on anyone other than themselves?

4. Research the effects of foster homes on American children. Make sure your investigation includes autobiographical accounts as well as research studies about life in the foster care system. How does living in a foster home impact a child's ability to build relationships with others?

BIBLIOGRAPHY

Books

"Kaye Gibbons (1960–)." *Contemporary Literary Criticism*. Edited by Sharon K. Hall. Vol. 50. Detroit: Gale Research, 1988, pp. 46–50.

Mason, Julian. *Contemporary Writers of the South*. Edited by Joseph M. Flora and Robert Bain. Westport, Conn.: Greenwood Press, 1993, pp. 156–168.

Periodicals

Bell, Pearl K. "Southern Discomfort." *New Republic* (February 29, 1988): 38–41.

Harrison, Kathryn. "Tara It Ain't." *New York Times Book Review* (July 19, 1988): 12.

Hoffman, Alice. "Shopping for a New Family." *New York Times Book Review* (May 31, 1987): 13.

Hooper, Brad. "Review of *Ellen Foster*." *Booklist* (September 1, 1987): 27.

Makowsky, Veronica. "The Only Hard Part Was the Food: Recipes for Self-Nurture in Kaye Gibbons's Novels." *Southern Quarterly* (Winter–Spring 1992): 103–112.

McCauley, Stephen. "He's Gone, Go Start the Coffee." *New York Times Book Review* (April 11, 1993): 9–10.

Taylor, Linda. "A Kind of Primitive Charm." *Sunday Times* (May 8, 1988): G6.

Wood, Ralph C. "Gumption and Grace in the Novels of Kaye Gibbons." *The Christian Century* vol. 109, no. 27 (September 23–30, 1992): 842–846.

✶ Charlotte Perkins Gilman

BORN: *1860, Hartford, Connecticut*

DIED: *1935, Pasadena, California*

NATIONALITY: *American*

GENRE: *Nonfiction, fiction*

MAJOR WORKS:

"The Yellow Wallpaper" (1892)

Women and Economics: A Study of the Economic Relation Between Men and Women as a Factor in Social Evolution (1898)

Herland (1915)

Overview

Charlotte Perkins Gilman was one of the most prominent feminists and social activists in the period from the 1890s to the 1930s. Her *Women and Economics* (1898), an examination of women's roles in the world of capitalism, earned her wide recognition, and for several decades she was considered the leading intellectual of the women's movement. While her nonfiction promotes her social theories, her fiction depicts the realization of her feminist ideals with a humor and satire that had been, for the most part, unseen

Charlotte Perkins Gilman *Gilman, Charlotte Anna Perkins, 1920, photograph.* © *Bettmann / Corbis.*

in feminist literature up to that time. Ironically, Gilman is best known today for her least characteristic work, "The Yellow Wallpaper" (1892), a short story based on her own experience, detailing with dramatic intensity and authenticity a young woman's mental breakdown.

Works in Biographical and Historical Context

Great Aunts Gilman was born on July 3, 1860, in Hartford, Connecticut, to Frederick Beecher Perkins, a noted librarian and magazine editor, and Mary Fritch Perkins. Although Gilman's father frequently abandoned the family for long periods of time and eventually divorced his wife in 1869, he directed Gilman's early education, and emphasized her study of history and the sciences. This was unusual for the time, because women were generally educated only in domestic matters and were expected to remain the keepers of the household; they were still nearly fifty years from earning the right to vote in the United States, and farther still from other forms of equality with men.

Because of her father's absence, Gilman frequently stayed with relatives, including her renowned reform-minded great-aunts: Harriet Beecher Stowe, the abolitionist and author of *Uncle Tom's Cabin* (1852), as well as the famous feminist activists Catherine Beecher and Isabella Beecher Hooker. Such influential women were instrumental in developing Gilman's feminist convictions and her desire to effect social reform.

The Rest "Cure" In her early adulthood, Gilman supported herself as a teacher and commercial artist and, at the age of twenty-four, married Charles Walter Stetson, also an artist. Following the birth of their daughter in 1884, Gilman suffered from severe depression, leading her to consult the noted neurologist S. Weir Mitchell, who prescribed his rest cure. This treatment, prescribed almost exclusively to women, consisted of committing the patient to bed rest for months, during which time the patient was deprived of all mental, physical, and social activities—reading, writing, and painting were explicitly prohibited. For Gilman, the rest cure itself almost drove her insane, and she eventually removed herself from Mitchell's care. Soon after, convinced that her emotional problems were in part the result of the confines of marriage, she left her husband.

Activist Actions In 1888, Gilman moved to California, where she helped edit feminist publications, assisted in the planning of the California Women's Congresses of 1894 and 1895, and was instrumental in founding the Women's Peace Party. After spending several months at Hull House in Chicago at the invitation of social reformer Jane Addams, Gilman toured the United States and England, lecturing about women's rights and labor reform. During the 1890s, Gilman, who had been producing verse and journal entries for years, became increasingly active as a writer and in 1892 published her most famous work,

"The Yellow Wallpaper," followed by *In this Our World* (1893), a collection of poems noted not only for their concern with feminist issues, but also for their humor.

A Forerunner in Feminism In 1898, Gilman published *Women in Economics*, a feminist manifesto that has its origin in Charles Darwin's theory of natural selection. In the book, Gilman argues that women's secondary status in society, and especially their economic dependence on men, is the result of a male-oriented capitalist society, not a result of biological inferiority. In 1900 Gilman married George Houghton Gilman, a man who was supportive of her ardent involvement in social reform. Throughout the next several years, Gilman devoted her writing efforts to activism. She wrote essays, including *Concerning Children* (1900) and *Human Work* (1904), both of which asserted her view that women should work outside of the home for equal pay, fully using their abilities for the benefit of society and for their own satisfaction.

From 1909 through 1916, Gilman published *The Forerunner*, a monthly journal; at the end of each issue, she told her readers that the magazine was not a women's magazine because it was designed to offer practical solutions for human existence. As a vehicle for advancing social awareness, *The Forerunner* is widely known as her single greatest achievement; however, Gilman could never make it financially profitable. During these years, Gilman also wrote fiction and poetry. In her fiction, Gilman portrays women struggling to achieve self-sufficiency or adapting to newfound independence. Her short stories frequently show women how to change their lives or redesign society, while her last three books of fiction, *Moving and Mountain* (1911), *Herland* (1915), and *With Her in Ourland* (1916), are utopian novels depicting societies in which attitudes toward women and their abilities have radically changed.

The Simplest of Human Rights After Gilman left *The Forerunner* in 1916, her productivity as a writer decreased considerably. Her next book was not published until 1923, and twelve more years passed before her autobiography appeared. That same year, after learning that she suffered from inoperable cancer, Gilman took her own life by inhaling a large dose of chloroform. She wrote in a final note that "when one is assured of unavoidable and imminent death, it is the simplest of human rights to choose a quick and easy death in place of a slow and horrible one." She died on August 17, 1935, in Pasadena, California, at the age of seventy-five.

Works in Literary Context

Besides her famous activist great-aunts, Gilman was influenced by John Stuart Mill's *On the Subjection of Women* (1869), which proposes, among other progressive ideas, that the nature of women cannot be defined so long as women are denied access to intellectual pursuits and all social institutions. As women's roles have continued to evolve, Gilman's suggestions for the improvement of society through the power of women continue to be significant. Many modern feminist nonfiction works reflect the influence of Gilman's ideas, and readers continue to discover in her thoughts much that is relevant to contemporary problems.

Limitations Placed on Women   Whether fiction or nonfiction, Gilman's works exemplify the major themes supporting her lifelong conviction that women have rights, women have knowledge, and women have talents that should be respected. "The Yellow Wallpaper," for example, conveys a general concern with the role of women in nineteenth-century society, especially within the realms of marriage, maternity, and domesticity. The narrator's confinement to her home and her feelings of being dominated by her husband are indications of the many domestic limitations that society imposes on women, and the yellow wallpaper symbolizes this oppression of a woman who feels trapped by society's expectations of her as a wife and mother.

Women and Economics expands this idea of a woman being controlled by a male-dominated world. In this essay, Gilman offers what was in her era a radical theory: the position of women in society is directly related to economic factors controlled by men, and because of these factors, women are dependent on men for their existence. She maintains that women need work of value in the marketplace and that their domestic responsibilities should be assigned value as well.

Gilman's works also express her disapproval of the ways in which society discourages women's creativity and self-expression. In *Women and Economics*, she points to women authors of the past such as Harriet Martineau, who had to hide her writing under her sewing whenever visitors came because sewing was an acceptable feminine activity, while writing was for men. Gilman fictionalizes this idea of subversive writing in "The Yellow Wallpaper." In the story, the narrator's urge to express herself through writing is prohibited by her rest cure. Nevertheless, her creative impulse is so strong that she assumes the risk of secretly writing in a diary, which she hides from her husband. Ultimately, Gilman's writings emphasize the fact that women have the same intellectual and creative capabilities as men, only women have not been permitted to exercise them as men have.

Works in Critical Context

In the years since Gilman's death, her literary reputation has rested primarily on "The Yellow Wallpaper," which remains a classic both for its feminist perspective and its disconcerting depiction of madness. Her activist publications are less read today, but this is not because they are regarded as insubstantial; rather, it is because much of what Gilman advocates in terms of social equality has become more readily acknowledged as belonging to an ideal society. Additionally, her economic theories have appeared less radical in the years since her death.

LITERARY AND HISTORICAL CONTEMPORARIES

Charlotte Perkins Gilman's famous contemporaries include:

Margaret Sanger (1879–1966): Believing that birth control gave a woman control over her health, Sanger founded the American Birth Control League, later known as Planned Parenthood, in 1914.

Emma Goldman (1869–1940): A Lithuanian immigrant to the United States, Goldman was a writer and orator famous for her political activism as an anarchist.

Henry Clay Frick (1849–1919): Frick was a controversial businessman involved in the Homestead Works steel mill strike, one of the bitterest labor disputes in American history.

Olive Schreiner (1855–1920): The fiction of this South African writer and political pacifist addresses the treatment of women.

Károly Laufenauer (1848–1901): This Hungarian scientist was an innovator in the treatment of neuropathologies, particularly disorders affecting women.

"The Yellow Wallpaper"   Praised by Elaine Hedges as "one of the rare pieces of literature we have by a nineteenth-century woman who directly confronts the sexual politics of the male-female, husband-wife relationship," "The Yellow Wallpaper," considered Gilman's best work of fiction, is also her least typical. Rather than an optimistic vision of what women can achieve, the story is a first-person account of a young mother's mental deterioration, a tale "wrenched out of Gilman's own life ... and unique in the canon of her works," Hedges says. Even though "the real purpose of the story was to reach Dr. S. Weir Mitchell," Gilman writes in her autobiography, "and convince him of the error of his ways," her contemporary readers were more frightened by the story's narrative than inspired to change the treatment of depression. In fact, the work was reprinted as a horror story in William Dean Howell's *The Great Modern American Stories* in 1920.

Although early reviewers interpreted "The Yellow Wallpaper" as either a horror story or a case study in psychosis, most modern critics see it as a feminist indictment of society's subjugation of women. Ann D. Wood, for instance, declares that "The Yellow Wallpaper" reflects Gilman's "nightmare vision of sick women dependent on male doctors who use their professional superiority as a method to prolong their patients' sickness and, consequently, the supremacy of their own sex." Contemporary critics have discussed "The Yellow Wallpaper" from a broad range of perspectives: biographical, historical, psychological, feminist, semiotic, and socio-cultural. Furthermore, the work has sparked an ongoing critical debate over the symbolic meaning of the wallpaper and the implications of the story's ending.

COMMON HUMAN EXPERIENCE

Writers have turned to utopias throughout history as veiled criticisms of society. Gilman is no exception. For example, in *Herland*, Gilman creates a utopian society made up entirely of women with a culture, political system, and familial arrangement that has grown out of the society of women, rather than simply the absence of men. Listed below are other utopian works:

Utopia (1516), fiction by Sir Thomas More. With this work describing a fictional island with a seemingly perfect political, legal, and social arrangement, More coined the word "utopia."

News from Nowhere (1890), a novel by William Morris. The main character in this novel awakens to find himself in a utopian socialist society in which private property, a monetary system, and class divisions are nonexistent.

The Utopia Reader (1999), an anthology edited by Gregory Claeys and Lyman Sargent. From Plato to modern-day thinkers, this collection demonstrates mankind's need to envision an ideal society.

Responses to Literature

1. Investigate writings, both fiction and nonfiction, published at the end of the 1800s about hysteria and other "women's problems." Also, research the various "medical" treatments for such conditions, including Mitchell's rest cure. Why do you think depression and other mental illnesses in women were approached differently than they were in the cases of men? Do you think Gilman's prescribed treatment would have been the same had her doctor been a woman? What if a male patient exhibited the same symptoms?

2. For many years, the inequality of pay between men and women for the same work has been a topic of debate. After researching the history of this issue, create a timeline showing major events in this ongoing debate, from its origins to today. Can you think of certain jobs that do not warrant equal pay for men and women?

3. Read Emily Dickinson's "Much madness is divinest sense" and "She rose to his requirement." Explain how these two poems relate to "The Yellow Wallpaper."

4. "The Yellow Wallpaper" is narrated in the form of a journal by an unnamed woman. What effect does this method of narration have on the meaning of the story? How does it affect the reader? How would "The Yellow Wallpaper" be different had Gilman told the story in a traditional first-person narrative? What about if the story were told from an objective third-person point of view?

BIBLIOGRAPHY

Books

Allen, Polly Wynn. *Building Domestic Liberty: Charlotte Perkins Gilman's Architectural Feminism.* Amherst: University of Massachusetts Press, 1988.

Beer, Jane. *Kate Chopin, Edith Wharton, and Charlotte Perkins Gilman: Studies in Short Fiction.* New York: St. Martin's Press, 1997.

Dock, Julie Bates, ed. *Charlotte Perkins Gilman's "The Yellow Wall-Paper" and the History of Its Publication and Reception.* University Park: Pennsylvania State University Press, 1998.

Gilman, Charlotte Perkins. *The Living of Charlotte Perkins Gilman: An Autobiography.* New York: Appleton-Century, 1935.

———. *The Yellow Wallpaper.* Afterword by Elaine Hedges. New York: The Feminist Press, 1973.

Hill, Mary A. *Charlotte Perkins Gilman: The Making of a Radical Feminist, 1860–1896.* Philadelphia: Temple University Press, 1980.

Kessler, Carol Farley. *Charlotte Perkins Gilman: Her Progress Toward Utopia.* Syracuse, N.Y.: Syracuse University Press, 1995.

Knight, Denise D. *Charlotte Perkins Gilman: A Study of the Short Fiction.* New York: Twayne, 1997.

Lane, Ann J. *To Herland and Beyond: The Life and Work of Charlotte Perkins Gilman.* New York: Meridian, 1991.

Scharnhorst, Gary. *Charlotte Perkins Gilman.* New York: Twayne, 1985.

✺ Allen Ginsberg

BORN: *1926, Newark, New Jersey*

DIED: *1997, New York, New York*

NATIONALITY: *American*

GENRE: *Poetry*

MAJOR WORKS:

Howl and Other Poems (1956)

Kaddish and Other Poems (1961)

Overview

Allen Ginsberg enjoyed a long career as a leading figure in twentieth-century poetry and culture, in part because of his literary works, but also because of his social and political activities. A longtime spokesperson for the country's disaffected youth, Ginsberg was a prominent figure in the counterculture and antiwar movements of the 1960s, as well as a leading member of the Beat Generation, a group of American writers and artists whose creative efforts and

Allen Ginsberg *Ginsberg, Allen, photograph. © Jerry Bauer. Reproduced by permission.*

lifestyles represented a vehement rejection of middle-class values. With the publication of "Howl" (1956), Ginsberg stunned critics and readers alike with his innovative and, according to some, obscene verse.

Works in Biographical and Historical Context

A Difficult Childhood Born on June 3, 1926, in Newark, New Jersey, Ginsberg endured an emotionally troubled childhood that is reflected in many of his poems. His mother, a Russian-born Jew and member of the Communist Party in the United States, suffered from various mental illnesses and was periodically institutionalized during Ginsberg's adolescence. His father, also of a Jewish, Russian-immigrant background, was a high school teacher and poet whose work frequently appeared in the literary journals of the day. Ginsberg's home life was marked by his mother's mental breakdowns, his father's strict discipline, and his own adolescent confusion and isolation as he became increasingly aware of his homosexuality, which he concealed from both his peers and his parents until he was in his twenties.

Surrounded by Writers First introduced to poetry by his father, the young Ginsberg read Metaphysical and Romantic poetry extensively. His interest in poetry was furthered by talks with his mentor, the poet William Carlos Williams, who lived in nearby Paterson, where Ginsberg attended high school. After graduation, Ginsberg attended Columbia University. Although he enjoyed the classes he had with instructors Lionel Trilling and Mark Van Doren, both well-known writers and critics, Ginsberg considered the intellectual interaction he had with experimental author and friend William S. Burroughs to be of utmost importance to his development as a writer. In addition to familiarizing Ginsberg with books by significant French authors, Burroughs introduced Ginsberg to Jack Kerouac and Neal Cassady. These men, along with several West Coast writers, would later form the heart of the Beat movement, a group of writers who characteristically wrote in the language of the street, about supposedly unrespectable and unliterary topics.

Mystic Pursuits In the summer of 1948, Ginsberg had a profound mystical vision while reading the works of William Blake. Ginsberg felt that this experience had allowed him to penetrate the mysteries of the universe. In later years, Ginsberg tried to recapture the experience in writing, seeking to attain higher states of visionary awareness. This desire for a mystical state of being prompted him, along with his Beat friends, to experiment with an assortment of drugs. When their indulgences resulted in Ginsberg's being arrested as an accomplice to theft, Ginsberg entered a plea of insanity and subsequently spent eight months in a mental institution. There, he met Carl Solomon, who both challenged Ginsberg's academic theories about poetry and strengthened his understanding of contemporary poetry's potential for expressing political resistance.

Howl Is Heard After graduating from Columbia in 1949, Ginsberg remained in New York City and worked various jobs. In 1954, he moved to San Francisco, where the Beat movement was developing through the activities of poets Kenneth Rexroth and Lawrence Ferlinghetti. Ginsberg first came to public attention with the publication of *Howl and Other Poems*, a reflexive lamentation on the moral and social ills of the post–World War II era. His public reading of "Howl" to a spellbound audience in San Francisco demonstrated the power of his work as an oral medium and set standards for poetry readings throughout the United States.

In 1957, *Howl* became the subject of a landmark obscenity trial. Because of its graphic sexual language, the San Francisco Police Department arrested Ferlinghetti, the publisher, for distributing obscene material. The ensuing trial attracted national attention as such distinguished literary figures as Walter Van Tilberg Clark and Mark Schorer spoke in defense of *Howl*. Schorer testified that Ginsberg's use of crude language is not gratuitous, but

LITERARY AND HISTORICAL CONTEMPORARIES

Allen Ginsberg's famous contemporaries include:

Jack Kerouac (1922–1969): With the book *On the Road* (1957), Kerouac became a cult hero who epitomized the Beat movement in America.

Frank O'Hara (1926–1966): O'Hara's poetry attempts to capture with words the effects such painters as Jackson Pollock had created on canvas.

Larry Rivers (1923–2002): Attracted to abstract expressionism, Rivers was a painter who also admired realism, and he attempted to combine those two movements in his works.

Robert Duncan (1919–1988): In addition to poetry, Duncan wrote "The Homosexual in Society," an essay comparing the troubles of homosexuals in America to those of African Americans and Jews.

Marie-Claire Blais (1939–): Early works by this French Canadian author use experiments with language to depict the hostilities of society.

necessary to capture the rhythms of ordinary speech. The testimony eventually persuaded Judge Clayton W. Horn to rule that *Howl* was not obscene, and Ferlinghetti was acquitted. The qualities cited in its defense helped make *Howl* the manifesto of the Beat movement.

Political Attention Ginsberg followed *Howl* with *Kaddish and Other Poems* (1961). "Kaddish," a poem similar in style and form to "Howl," is based on the traditional Hebrew prayer for the dead and tells the life story of Ginsberg's mother. During the 1960s, however, Ginsberg attracted more attention for his political activism than for his poetry. He helped organize antiwar demonstrations and advocated "flower power," a strategy in which protestors would promote such positive values as peace and love in opposition to the death and destruction caused by the Vietnam War. Ginsberg was arrested at a protest in New York City in 1967 and was subdued with tear gas at the 1968 Democratic National Convention in Chicago. He was again arrested in 1972 for demonstrating against President Richard Nixon at the Republican National Convention in Miami. These experiences inform much of Ginsberg's work of the 1960s and early 1970s, including *Planet News* (1968), a collection of poems that are considered impressionistic collages of that era.

Buddhist Interests In 1970, Ginsberg's interest in Eastern religions eventually led him away from drugs to the teachings of Chogyam Trungpa Rinpoche, a Buddhist abbot from Tibet. In addition to taking courses at Trungpa's Naropa Institute in Boulder, Colorado, Gins-

berg taught poetry classes there. As his works increasingly revealed the influence of Eastern philosophy, meditation, and yoga, Ginsberg formally committed to the Buddhist faith in 1972. Two years later, Ginsberg and fellow poet Anne Waldman cofounded the Jack Kerouac School of Disembodied Poetics as a branch of Trungpa's Naropa Institute.

Keeping the Beat Throughout the 1980s, Ginsberg kept the Beat flame burning by giving readings to enthusiastic audiences across the United States. In the 1990s, he explored the unification of words and music and composed several poems that he often performed as songs. In addition to showing Ginsberg's ongoing desire and capacity for experimentation, his songs complement a lifetime of active involvement with opening up the self to the world through a radical redefining of the language of poetry.

Posthumous Publications Already suffering from diabetes and chronic hepatitis, Ginsberg was diagnosed with liver cancer early in the spring of 1997. Soon after hearing this news, Ginsberg wrote twelve short poems, finishing them only one day before he had a stroke and lapsed into a coma. He died on April 5, 1997, in New York City. Ginsberg's posthumous publications include *Death and Fame: Poems, 1993–1997*, which contains those last twelve brief poems, and *Deliberate Prose: Selected Essays, 1952–1995*, a collection of over 150 essays.

Works in Literary Context

Despite Ginsberg's unconventional beliefs and unconventional literary style, he was immeasurably influenced by such established poets as Walt Whitman, William Carlos Williams, and William Blake. Like that of Whitman, Ginsberg's verse is characterized by the raw, spontaneous language of experience. While much of Ginsberg's work is reminiscent of Williams in that both focus on the commonplace details of everyday life, Ginsberg's lyric improvisations are the result of his experiences with hallucinogenic drugs, the teachings of Zen Buddhism, and visions—the notion of which was inspired by religious visionary poet Blake. When *Howl* was published, Ginsberg drew attention not only as a literary sensation, but also as an icon for the counterculture of his generation, especially with the publicity of the *Howl* obscenity trial.

Politics and Protest A major theme in Ginsberg's poetry—indeed, his life—was politics. Echoing his libertarian political convictions, Ginsberg's poetry reflects his belief in individual expression over traditional structure. Scholar Kenneth Rexroth calls this aspect of Ginsberg's work "an almost perfect fulfillment of the long, Whitman, Populist, social revolutionary tradition in American poetry." In a number of poems, Ginsberg refers to the union struggles of the 1930s, popular radical figures, the McCarthy Communist hunts, and other leftist elements of the American political scene. In "Wichita Vortex Sutra," Ginsberg attempts to end the Vietnam War through a kind of magical, poetic evocation. Similarly, he endeavors to eradicate the dangers of nuclear power through the magic of a poet's breath in "Plutonian Ode." Other poems, including "Howl," although not expressly political in nature, nonetheless carry strains of strong social criticism.

Works in Critical Context

Critical evaluation of Ginsberg's work has varied considerably. According to some critics, Ginsberg is one of the most influential poets of his generation and occupies a prominent position in American literature. Says scholar James Campbell: "No one has made his poetry speak for the whole man, without inhibition of any kind, more than Ginsberg." While some critics have praised Ginsberg's unstructured form and his exploration of controversial subject matter, others have considered his skill overrated, arguing that Ginsberg became famous not so much because of his work, but because of his political protests, advocacy of drug use and homosexuality, poetry readings, and collaboration with rock bands. Critic Bruce Bawer, for example, calls Ginsberg "the father of a generation of Americans to whom 'culture' is a word most often used immediately following the word 'drug.'" No matter the diverse opinions about his poetry and his notorious reputation, most critics acknowledge Ginsberg's contribution in introducing and legitimizing experimental poetry to a wider audience.

"Howl" "Howl," a long-line poem in the tradition of Walt Whitman, is an outcry of rage and despair against a destructive, abusive society. Reviewer Kevin O'Sullivan declares the poem "an angry, sexually explicit poem . . . considered by many to be a revolutionary event in American poetry." The poem's raw, honest language and its "Hebraic-Melvillian bardic breath," as Ginsberg calls it, stunned many traditional critics when it was first published. Poet James Dickey, for instance, refers to "Howl" as "a whipped-up state of excitement" and concludes that "it takes more than this to make poetry. It just does." Critic Walter Sutton deems "Howl" "a tirade revealing an animus directed outward against those who do not share the poet's social and sexual orientation."

Other critics have responded to "Howl" more positively. Poet Richard Eberhart, for example, calls "Howl" "a powerful work . . . [that is] a howl against everything in our mechanistic civilization which kills the spirit. . . . Its positive force and energy come from a redemptive quality of love." Academic Paul Carroll judges it "one of the milestones of the generation." Appraising the impact of "Howl," critic Paul Zweig notes that it "almost singlehandedly dislocated the traditionalist poetry of the 1950's," while reviewer Reed Whittemore recognizes that "Howl" is one of "a small number of earth-moving angry poems of this century, poems that poets (and people) who come after have been unable to ignore."

COMMON HUMAN EXPERIENCE

Throughout *Howl*, Ginsberg explores themes of identity, nationality, and transcendence. He passionately condemns the material values that threaten what he considers one's birthright to achieve self-realization and evade the alienating forces of social control. Other works that celebrate mankind and his place in society include the following:

Song of Myself (1855), a poem by Walt Whitman. Fusing the universal with the particular, this poem, almost two thousand lines long, reveals the equality and splendor of all people and things.

Smoke and Steel (1920), a poetry collection by Carl Sandburg. Attempting to find beauty in an industrialized society, these free verse poems helped establish Sandburg as a poet of the common man in America.

Canto General (1950), an epic poem by Pablo Neruda. Neruda, whose life was filled with both poetic and political activity, composed this poem as a portrait of the South American continent and its people.

Responses to Literature

1. Pretend you are the judge in the trial of Lawrence Ferlinghetti, who was arrested on charges of obscenity for publishing *Howl*. Provide a written document containing arguments on both sides of the issue, as well as a detailed justification of your final ruling.

2. In what way are Ginsberg's vision and his poetic techniques similar to those of Walt Whitman? How does his work differ from Whitman's?

3. Many of Ginsberg's contemporaries viewed him as a publicity hound rather than a poet. Do you agree with this perspective? Is it fair to judge a poet by activities beyond his or her writing, much like other celebrities? Why or why not?

4. Read Ginsberg's "A Supermarket in California." Why do you think this piece is considered a poem? What poetic devices does it use? Would it make more sense to classify "A Supermarket in California" as prose instead of poetry?

BIBLIOGRAPHY

Books

Bawer, Bruce. *Prophets & Professors: Essays on the Lives and Works of Modern Poets.* Ashland, Ore.: Story Line Press, 1995.

Campbell, James. *Syncopations: Beat, New Yorkers, and Writers in the Dark.* Berkeley, Calif.: University of California Press, 2008.

Carroll, Paul. *The Poem in Its Skin*. Chicago: Follett, 1968.

O'Sullivan, Kevin. *Newsmakers 1997 Cumulation: The People behind Today's Headlines*. Edited by Sean R. Pollock. Farmington Hills, Mich.: Gale, 1997, pp. 493–495.

Rexroth, Kenneth. *American Poetry in the Twentieth Century*. Freiburg im Breisgau, Germany: Herder, 1971.

Sutton, Walter. *American Free Verse*. New York: New Directions Publishing, 1973.

Periodicals

Dickey, James. "Confession Is Not Enough." *New York Times* (July 9, 1961): C15.

Eberhart, Richard. "West Coast Rhythms." *New York Times Book Review* (September 2, 1956): 7–18.

Whittemore, Reed. "From 'Howl' to 'Om.'" *New Republic* 163 (July 25, 1970): 17–18.

Zewig, Paul. "A Music of Angels." *Nation*, vol. 208, no. 10 (March 10, 1969): 311–313.

✺ Nikki Giovanni

BORN: *1943, Knoxville, Tennessee*

NATIONALITY: *American*

GENRE: *Poetry, nonfiction*

MAJOR WORKS:

Black Feeling, Black Talk (1968)

The Collected Poetry of Nikki Giovanni: 1968–1998 (2003)

Nikki Giovanni   *AP Images*

Overview

Poet Nikki Giovanni gained widespread popularity for being a fierce promoter of African American rights during the Second Black Renaissance, a period of rapid cultural change and literary development for blacks in the 1960s. Since that time, she has evolved from an aggressive, explosive revolutionary to a quieter voice of universal sensitivity and artistic beauty. Though many early admirers have faulted her in later years for taking a less confrontational stance toward societal change, Giovanni contends that as the world has changed, so have her ideas. As a result of her best-selling recordings and her speaking tours, Giovanni has made her poems accessible to multigenerational and international audiences.

Works in Biographical and Historical Context

A Heritage Rich in Language   Giovanni was born on June 7, 1943, in Knoxville, Tennessee, but her family soon moved to a predominantly black community in Wyoming, Ohio, a suburb of Cincinnati. Spending her sophomore and junior years of high school in Tennessee with her grandparents, Giovanni was greatly influenced by her outspoken grandmother, who instilled in the girl an intense appreciation for her African American heritage. Both grandparents, as well as Giovanni's mother, were gifted storytellers, and this early exposure to the power of spoken language would influence Giovanni's career as a poet, particularly her penchant for colloquialisms, or informal words and phrases associated with common speech.

Encouraged by several teachers, Giovanni enrolled at Fisk University, a prestigious all-black college in Nashville, Tennessee. Her independent spirit, however, led to her being asked to leave by the school's Dean of Women. After a new dean assumed leadership, Giovanni was invited back, and she returned to Fisk in 1964 determined to be an ideal student. Active and highly respected at the university, she became a leader in political and literary activities on campus during what would prove to be an important era in African American history.

Revolution, Renaissance, and Reform   At the time Giovanni returned to Fisk, the United States was in a state of tumult caused by both the civil rights movement and the Vietnam War. Elijah Muhammad, Malcolm X, and the

Nation of Islam encouraged blacks to pursue radical self-assertion and revolutionary change. The National Association for the Advancement of Colored People (NAACP), the Southern Christian Leadership Conference (SCLC), the Student Non-Violent Coordinating Committee (SNCC), and the Congress of Racial Equality (CORE) were among the groups that were in full action, fighting for the liberation and equality of African Americans. Antiwar demonstrations and other protests erupted on college campuses throughout the country as students demanded social and political change.

While Giovanni was at Fisk, the Second Black Renaissance emerged as black writers and other artists looked for new ways to express their distinctive culture to an increasingly interested public. Once a supporter of 1964 Republican presidential candidate Barry Goldwater, Giovanni rejected her conservative views in favor of the radicalism she encountered in fellow classmates. In addition to participating in the Fisk Writers Workshop taught by novelist John Oliver Killens and editing *Elan*, the campus literary magazine, Giovanni organized a campus chapter of the SNCC. At that time, the organization was promoting the idea of "black power" to effect social and economic reform.

A Voice of Power   After graduating in 1967 with a degree in history, Giovanni continued her studies at the University of Pennsylvania before taking classes at Columbia University's School of Fine Arts, a time saddened by the death of her beloved grandmother. Responding to the assassinations of civil rights leaders and the urgent need to raise awareness of African American rights, Giovanni published *Black Feeling, Black Talk* (1968) and *Black Judgement* (1968), her first two books of poetry. From a militant African American perspective, Giovanni reflects the anger and enthusiasm of the writers and activists she became involved with during the 1960s. These early volumes quickly established Giovanni as a prominent new voice in black literature. Dubbed the "Princess of Black Poetry," she was in great demand as a speaker at colleges throughout the United States.

Effects of Motherhood   During the summer of 1969, Giovanni gave birth to a son. Although she was criticized for having a child out of wedlock, Giovanni stood by the decision she had made as a young girl: she would never marry because the institution of marriage was inhospitable to women. After Giovanni became a mother, her work shifted in focus, reflecting a change in her priorities. The tone of her poetry became warmer, concerned less with revolution and more with such themes as family love and the nature of poetry itself. She formed her own publishing cooperative in 1970 and the following year published the first of her children's books, *Spin a Soft Black Song* (1971), a collection of poems written for her son.

Reaching Her Public   Giovanni, who felt she had a personal mission to talk directly to African Americans in

LITERARY AND HISTORICAL CONTEMPORARIES

Nikki Giovanni's famous contemporaries include:

Jesse Jackson (1941–): This American civil rights activist was a candidate for the Democratic presidential nomination in 1984 and 1988.

Ruby Bridges (1954–): Bridges was the first black child to attend an all-white school in the South.

Amiri Baraka (1934–): Baraka, a poet, revolutionary political activist, and lecturer, founded the Black Arts Movement in Harlem in the 1960s.

H. Rap Brown (1943–): Brown gained prominence in the 1960s as chairman of the Student Nonviolent Coordinating Committee and the Justice Minister of the Black Panther Party.

John Sinclair (1941–): Sinclair, a poet, was the leader of the White Panther Party, a militantly antiracist group that assisted the Black Panthers during the civil rights movement.

her poetry, discovered a way to achieve this goal when she began recording her poems against a background of gospel music. Her first album, *Truth Is on Its Way* (1971), was a success with the older generation as well as with the young; she later explained that she had wanted the work to be something that her grandmother would have enjoyed. Encouraged by the success of her recording, Giovanni turned to a variety of media to reach as wide an audience as possible. In addition to publishing more books, she appeared on television talk shows, and she made several audio- and videotapes in which she discusses poetry and African American issues with other poets.

A dynamic speaker and prolific writer, Giovanni's popularity as a lecturer has increased along with her success as a poet and children's author. Throughout the years, her works have included a wide range of topics: African American political leaders, national holidays, equal rights, hip-hop music, and even termites. She has received numerous awards, including the first Rosa L. Parks Woman of Courage Award. Since 1989, Giovanni has been an English professor at Virginia Tech in Blacksburg, Virginia.

Works in Literary Context

While the turbulent 1960s and the Second Black Renaissance gave direction to Giovanni's voice, the seeds of activism were sown during the time she spent with her grandmother. A woman of powerful character, Giovanni's grandmother inspired the young girl to speak out about things that were important to her. Her grandmother's proud sense of race was also a strong influence, teaching Giovanni to value her place in black culture and to

COMMON HUMAN EXPERIENCE

Considered the Second Black Renaissance, the 1960s were significant for African Americans seeking freedom and recognition for the achievements of their race. As a result, writers during this decade addressed such themes as black pride, self-actualization, race relations, and justice. Listed below are works written during the Second Black Renaissance that represent the emergence of new African American literature in America:

This Child's Gonna Live (1969), a novel by Sarah E. Wright. Weaving Bible verses with obscenities, this book is about an impoverished black family struggling to improve its situation in Maryland during the 1930s.

The Soul Brothers and Sister Lou (1968), fiction by Kristin Hunter. In this story, a lonely teenager learns to be proud of such strengths of African American life as family, spirituality, and a rich cultural heritage.

I Want a Black Doll (1968), fiction by Frank Hercules. A novel about the interracial marriage of a white woman and a black man, this work depicts the trials the couple must overcome when they move to New York during a time of great racial tension.

recognize her responsibility to fellow African Americans. Without a doubt, Giovanni's power has reached thousands of individuals of all ethnic backgrounds.

Musical Diction Conscious of the importance of diction—a writer's choice and control of words—Giovanni's emphasis on the sound of language in her poetry has earned her considerable attention. As in the collection *Re: Creation* (1970), she oftentimes manipulates language to conform to song-like rhythms, creating musical word arrangements that reflect jazz and blues songs. In fact, the poem "Ego Tripping" ends in a sudden shift to the words of a popular blues song: "I am so perfect so divine so ethereal so surreal / I cannot be comprehended / except by my permission / I mean ... I ... can fly / like a bird in the sky." Because of Giovanni's skill with language, the meaning of her poetry is enhanced by the cadences of individual lines. *Blues: For All the Changes—New Poems* (1999) is a collection that pays homage to jazz and the blues, specifically the blues singer Alberta Hunter. In *Blues*, says reviewer Calvin Reid, "jazz riffs mingle with memories of going to the ballpark with her father to see the Cincinnati Reds."

Spirituals In *On My Journey Now: Looking at African American History through the Spirituals* (2007), Giovanni examines the various human needs that have been served by the words and music of old-time spiritual songs. Complete with lyrics, the book discusses the place of spirituals

in the lives of the black community. In addition to expressing their religious devotion and boosting their spirits as they suffered the brutalities of slavery, spirituals provided a means for slaves to communicate with each other without being discovered, especially when sharing information about the activities of the Underground Railroad. The influences of this rich oral history can be seen throughout Giovanni's work, most notably in the recordings she has made in which she recites her poetry against a background of gospel music.

Works in Critical Context

Critics praised Giovanni's early work for its raw emotion, energy, and commitment to black issues. However, later works have led formerly enthusiastic readers to question her shift from political issues to personal experiences, and Giovanni has been accused of abandoning the African American movement. One such opponent is Paula Giddings, who writes, "Giovanni has evolved to be that creature which often finds itself estranged from the history which created it." In contrast, Giovanni's supporters contend that she appeals to an audience who feels disconnected from radical and violent protest poetry and that her work still reflects the African American experience, though from a more personal slant. Recognizing the strength and consistency of Giovanni's voice, William J. Harris argues: "On the whole what is most striking about Giovanni's poetry is that she has created the charming persona of 'Nikki Giovanni' [who] is honest, searching, complex, lusty, and, above all, individualistic and charmingly egotistical."

Blues: For All the Changes—New Poems The publication of *Blues* in 1999 marks Giovanni's movement into the twenty-first century with poetry that is, says reviewer Donna Seaman, "socially conscious, outspoken, and roguishly funny." She continues: "Giovanni makes supple use of the irony inherent in the blues, writing tough, sly, and penetrating monologues that both hammer away at racism and praise the good things in life." Her first volume of poetry in five years, *Blues* was published after Giovanni's battle with lung cancer. Writes Denolynn Carroll, the volume "offers thoughts on her battle with illness, on nature, and on the everyday—all laced with doses of harsh reality, a mix of socio-political viewpoints, and personal memories of loss."

Responses to Literature

1. Giovanni has been called a forerunner in the world of rap music. Explain why she has earned this reputation. What specific elements of Giovanni's works show her influence on rap?

2. In her autobiography, Giovanni writes, "It is un-American not to fight." Do you believe this is true? How does this idea apply to the United States as a country as well as to individuals?

3. Giovanni often makes references to ancient and American history in such poems as "The Great Pax Whitie," "Ego Tripping," and "Poem of Angela Yvonne Davis." What effect does the use of historic facts and figures have on the emotional impact of these poems? Are the poems less accessible because of Giovanni's references?

4. Much of Giovanni's early work deals with the African American revolution of the late 1960s. Are these poems still relevant today? Do you consider Nikki Giovanni a "political" poet? How do her poems about social issues compare with her love poems or her reflections on childhood?

BIBLIOGRAPHY

Books

Fowler, Virginia. *Nikki Giovanni*. Boston: Twayne, 1992.
Giovanni, Nikki. *The Collected Poetry of Nikki Giovanni: 1968–1998*. New York: William Morrow, 2003.
———. *Cotton Candy on a Rainy Day*. Introduction by Paula Giddings. New York: William Morrow, 1978.
———. *Ego-Tripping and Other Poems for Young People*. Foreword by Virginia Hamilton. Chicago: Lawrence Hill Books, 1993.
Harris, William J. "Sweet Soft Essence of Possibility: The Poetry of Nikki Giovanni," in *Black Women Writers (1950–1980): A Critical Evaluation*. Edited by Mari Evans. New York: Doubleday, 1984, pp. 218–228.
Josephson, Judith P. *Nikki Giovanni: Poet of the People*. Berkeley Heights, N.J.: Enslow Publishers, 2003.
Lee, Don L. *Dynamite Voices I: Black Poets of the 1960s*. Detroit: Broadside Press, 1971.

Periodicals

Carroll, Denolynn. "Review of *Blues: For All the Changes—New Poems*." *American Visions* (October 1999): 34.
Reid, Calvin. "Nikki Giovanni: Three Decades on the Edge." *Publishers Weekly* (June 28, 1999): 46.
Seaman, Donna. "Review of *The Collected Poetry of Nikki Giovanni*." *Booklist* (December 15, 2003): 721.

✶ Ellen Glasgow

BORN: *1873, Richmond, Virginia*

DIED: *1945, Richmond, Virginia*

NATIONALITY: *American*

GENRE: *Fiction, nonfiction*

MAJOR WORKS:
Virginia (1913)
Barren Ground (1925)
Vein of Iron (1935)
In This Our Life (1941)

Ellen Glasgow   *Glasgow, Ellen, photograph. The Library of Congress.*

Overview

Ellen Glasgow's work is often credited as being the first of the powerful new Southern literature that dominated the American literary scene during the early twentieth century. A realist with a tragic view of human potential, Glasgow began her career at a time when most Southern fiction works were romanticized portraits of the ideals and institutions lost after the Civil War. She rebelled against this unrealistic tradition, depicting the South's social and moral code as restrictive and false, along with satirizing its idealization of the past.

Works in Biographical and Historical Context

A Quiet World of Isolation Born in Richmond, Virginia, on April 22, 1873, Ellen Glasgow was the eighth of ten children of Francis Thomas Glasgow, a manager of an iron works company, and Anne Jane Gholson, a descendant of one of the oldest families in Tidewater, Virginia. Receiving little formal education, Glasgow was privately tutored and read science and history books, as well as fiction and poetry, from her father's expansive library. Despite her siblings, Glasgow often felt isolated from everyone, and her deafness at the age of sixteen certainly contributed to her loneliness. When her mother, a delicate woman whose mental and physical health deteriorated

LITERARY AND HISTORICAL CONTEMPORARIES

Glasgow's famous contemporaries include:

Harry F. Byrd (1887–1966): Byrd was a Virginia newspaper publisher and prominent politician, who was a member of one of Virginia's most respected families. He served in the United States Senate from 1933 to 1965 and was a dominant figure in the Virginia Democratic Party.

Charlotte Perkins Gilman (1860–1935): Gilman was an American novelist, lecturer, and social activist. Best known for her novella "The Yellow Wallpaper", Gilman was often criticized for her unconventional personal life.

Ring Lardner (1885–1933): An American humorist and short-story writer, Lardner is known for satirical sketches of American life in the early 1900s.

James Branch Cabell (1879–1958): Widely recognized as one of the first contemporary writers from the South, Cabell, a native of Richmond, Virginia, and Glasgow's close friend, wrote novels that satirized what he saw as the South's contradictions.

Susan Glaspell (1882–1948): An American playwright, Glaspell wrote dramas that satirize psychoanalysis and defend women's rights.

Katherine Mansfield (1888–1923): The penetrating, yet sensitive characterization in this New Zealand–born author's short stories typically centers around women and children.

quickly after she had a nervous breakdown, died in 1893, Glasgow felt even more alienated from her family.

Because writing was not considered an appropriate pursuit for a young Southern woman in the late nineteenth century, Glasgow secretly wrote her first novel, *Sharp Realities* (1890), but destroyed the manuscript after a literary agent told her to go home and have babies. Nevertheless, her determination to be a writer triumphed. Still, Glasgow's first distributed novel, *The Descendant* (1897), was published anonymously. With a storyline involving an educated liberal trying to overcome the stigma of his illegitimate birth and an aspiring painter whose self-sacrifice for her lover results in her own destruction, the work created a mild uproar for its daring social commentary. When the book was attributed to Harold Frederic, a popular writer of the day, Glasgow was pleased, for she believed that being assumed to be a male writer was a high compliment.

Love Affairs and Social Histories During the years from 1899 to 1905, Glasgow was involved in a devastating love affair with a married man whom she later referred to in her writing as Gerald B. Despite the emotional pain caused by this relationship, Glasgow was artistically pro-

ductive. Turning to Virginia's social history in Civil War times, Glasgow's next three works, *The Voice of the People* (1900), *The Battle-Ground* (1902), and *The Deliverance* (1904), blend tragedy and comedy in depicting characters from various social classes in the South. In 1918 Glasgow attempted suicide when another relationship ended, and her subsequent work for several years reflects a halfhearted approach to her writing.

Feminine Creations By the 1920s, Glasgow was creating women characters who chose to live independently and to have careers rather than marry unsuitable men. The culmination of this theme came with *Barren Ground* (1925), the novel many consider to be her masterpiece. Glasgow's tendency to criticize male characters while praising her feminine creations continued in the three satiric novels that followed: *The Romantic Comedians* (1926), *They Stooped to Folly* (1929), and *The Sheltered Life* (1932). In addition to writing at the top of her ability during the 1920s and 1930s, Glasgow had also begun to be recognized as an important novelist, not simply as a writer of best sellers for women readers.

More Than a Southern Woman Late in her life, Glasgow became especially sensitive about being described as merely a "Southern writer" or, worse, a "maiden lady." She viewed herself as both a distinguished writer, not limited to local-color excellence, and a well-traveled woman, rich in experience and scholarship. By the time of her death from heart disease in 1945, Glasgow had received a number of awards in the literary world, including a Pulitzer Prize in 1942 for her last completed novel, *In This Our Life* (1941), though critical consensus contends that the award was given for Glasgow's whole body of work rather than for only this novel. As Glasgow had instructed, her literary executors published her memoirs under the title *The Woman Within* (1954) after her death.

Works in Literary Context

That Glasgow succeeded as a writer can be partly attributed to her unwillingness to be conventional in any role. Unapologetic for her literary ambition, she was content to be judged by the literary standards that had traditionally been established for male writers, as such evaluation equated her with the masters who had so influenced her as a writer. In her late teens, her sister's fiancé, Walter McCormack, introduced her to Charles Darwin, John Stuart Mill, and other thinkers who helped shape her views of humankind and society. With his philosophy of fate and social determinism, novelist Thomas Hardy also had a profound impact on much of her work. By the end of her career, Glasgow's work was similar in scope to those panoramic Russian novels she so admired—covering a wide span of time, many characters, many experiences, and with themes that carry import to any reader, regardless of generation.

Southern Literary Renaissance Many scholars of Southern literature regard Glasgow, along with Kate

Chopin, author of *The Awakening* (1899), as a precursor to the literary movement known as the Southern Literary Renaissance that emerged in the 1920s. Generally not sharing philosophical principles to the regional movement, the Southern Literary Renaissance, according to literary academic Anne E. Rowe, similarly emphasized the importance of southern heritage and environment in people's lives. Following the path Glasgow helped pave, most of the writers of the Southern Literary Renaissance, including William Faulkner, Robert Penn Warren, and Thomas Wolfe, view individual lives through setting and tradition in works that nevertheless are universal in their implications. Glasgow was, says scholar C. Hugh Holman, "the first writer to apply the principles of critical realism and a detached and ironic point of view to the people, the region, and the problems of the American South."

Like no other writer of her time, Glasgow attempted to relate the South to the rest of the world, thus laying the foundation for the Southern Literary Renaissance. Her fiction is an account of the old plantation civilization invaded by industrialization and a rising middle class; of a society dying under outmoded manners, opinions, and methods; and of a woman's place in such an environment. Her novels vary in range and tone from the comic to the tragic, the two opposing realms bridged by her ironic sense of the disparities in human existence. In *Barren Ground* and *Vein of Iron* (1935), Glasgow creates fiction of epic and, occasionally, tragic depth. These novels are notable for their lifelike characters, controlled language, and the infusion of what Glasgow called "blood and irony," a phrase she coined for the realistic, critical focus of her narration. Most importantly, these are the primary novels that led to the Southern Literary Renaissance.

Works in Critical Context

At the time she was writing, Glasgow was discussed alongside contemporaries Willa Cather and Edith Wharton, other writers praised for capturing the social aura of a transitory period in American history. Contemporary critic Henry Seidel Canby deemed Glasgow "a major historian of our times, who, almost single-handedly, rescued southern fiction from the glamorous sentimentality of the Lost Cause." Even so, in later years, Glasgow's work slipped into critical disregard and popular neglect. Glasgow herself had predicted that in time she would be considered little more than a regional writer or a minor novelist of manners, an insight that has unfortunately proven correct, despite her being one of the most important Southern writers of her day and the winner of the 1942 Pulitzer Prize.

Early in Glasgow's career, critical opinion of her work varied according to its origin: in the South, she was severely criticized for her negative portrayals; in the North, she was lauded as the South's first realist and as a master of satire. With the passage of time, however, Glasgow's realism was interpreted as something more akin to idealization; her

---

COMMON HUMAN EXPERIENCE

In many of Glasgow's novels, female characters lead unhappy lives as they search for self-identity in a society dominated by conventional male attitudes. Here are other works that examine women's roles in society:

The Dry Heart (1947), a novel by Natalia Ginzburg. With an unassuming conversational style, this Italian novel focuses on the unhappiness endured by women through penetrating dialogue.

"The Yellow Wallpaper" (1892), a short story by Charlotte Perkins Gilman. Offering a sharp critique of marriage and motherhood, this story is the creative result of Gilman's struggle with postpartum depression.

A Room of One's Own (1929), nonfiction by Virginia Woolf. Based on a series of lectures, this essay discusses the status of women and the difficulties of being a female artist.

The Awakening (1899), a novel by Kate Chopin. In this controversial novel, a young Creole wife finds herself smothered by marriage and motherhood and seeks escape through an adultery and art.

---

plots were often felt to be unreal, and the uncommon success of her heroines led many critics to believe that she refused to accept the world as it was. Though many have praised her knowledge of Virginia social life and manners, her ability to interpret the complexities of Southern history, and her insight into the intricacies of human nature, other critics have attacked Glasgow for her failure to pay closer attention to the structure and form of her novels.

Barren Ground Although Glasgow received recognition for *Virginia* (1913), she did not gain wide critical acclaim until the publication of *Barren Ground* in 1925. Other than a few reviewers who thought the plot of the novel too slow and boring, the critical reception of *Barren Ground* was overwhelmingly positive. Many reviewers praised the novel as a distinguished epic masterpiece. In *Ellen Glasgow: The Contemporary Reviews*, Dorothy McInnis Scura quotes critic Archibald Henderson, who compares Glasgow to Thomas Hardy and Emile Zola and says, "Surely *Barren Ground* is a great novel—great in austerity, great in art, great in humanity." Perhaps the highest compliment of all came from *New York Herald Tribune Books* editor Stuart P. Sherman: "She treats provincial life from a rational point of view; that is, without sentimentality, without prejudice, with sympathy, understanding, passion, and poetic insight, yet critically and with a surgical use of satire." Despite what reviewers at the time wrote, however, *Barren Ground* was not a commercially popular book, most likely because of its solemn tone.

Recent feminist criticism of *Barren Ground* has heightened interest in Glasgow by emphasizing her concern with the roles of women in society and with the values of patriarchal culture, in which males are the dominating force. Many critics consider *Barren Ground* to be Glasgow's greatest achievement, the one novel in which she most poignantly expresses the feminist struggle for freedom and individuality in a hostile environment. Glasgow's characterization of Dorinda Oakley embodies the complexity of the female mind and heart. Often compared to Glasgow herself, Dorinda is the author's concept of the model woman who refuses to feel guilt or repentance over an illegitimate child; instead, she utilizes her talents and reaps success from the supposedly barren land.

Responses to Literature

1. Although the burden on a woman to live up to a man's ideal is a theme throughout Glasgow's work, many readers find Glasgow herself old-fashioned in her preoccupation with romantic love and with the beauty and goodness of her female characters. How would you explain this apparent contradiction?

2. Scholar C. Hugh Holman defines a novel of manners as "a work in which the outer forms of a relatively closed society are stable, so that a character may be tested against them as against a fairly inflexible yardstick of conduct and belief." With this definition in mind, would you consider Glasgow a novelist of manners? Why or why not?

3. Compare Glasgow's observation of the South to that of agrarian poet and critic John Crowe Ransom. What factors do you think contributed to their different beliefs about the same geographical region? Formulate your own definition of regionalism based on both writers' depictions of the South. How did their viewpoints evolve during the course of their careers?

4. Glasgow considered herself a feminist. How is the feminism of her period reflected in her work? How does her work hold up to scrutiny from feminist scholars today? In her fictional versions of society, what kinds of power, if any, do women have?

BIBLIOGRAPHY

Books

Auchincloss, Louis. *Ellen Glasgow*. Minneapolis: University of Minnesota Press, 1964.

Goodman, Susan. *Ellen Glasgow: A Biography*. Baltimore, Md.: Johns Hopkins University Press, 1998.

Holman, C. Hugh. *Three Modes of Southern Fiction*. Athens: University of Georgia Press, 1966.

Raper, Julius Rowan. *From the Sunken Garden: The Fiction of Ellen Glasgow, 1916–1945*. Baton Rouge: Louisiana State University Press, 1980.

Rouse, Blair. *Ellen Glasgow*. Boston: Twayne, 1962.

Scura, Dorothy McInnis. *Ellen Glasgow: The Contemporary Reviews*. Cambridge, Mass.: Cambridge University Press, 1992.

Periodicals

Canby, Henry Seidel. "Ellen Glasgow: Ironic Tragedian: *The Virginia Edition of the Works of Ellen Glasgow*." *Saturday Review of Literature* 18 (September 10, 1938): 3–4.

Sherman, Stuart P. "The Fighting Edge of Romance: *Barren Ground*." *New York Herald Tribune Books* (April 9, 1925): 22.

Steele, Oliver. "Ellen Glasgow's Virginia: Preliminary Notes." *Studies in Bibliography* (1974): 265–289.

Web sites

Rowe, Anne E. *Library of Southern Literature*. Retrieved September 29, 2008, from http://docsouth.unc.edu/southlit/regionalism.html. Last updated on September 29, 2008.

⊛ Susan Glaspell

BORN: *1876, Davenport, Iowa*

DIED: *1948, Provincetown, Massachusetts*

NATIONALITY: *American*

GENRE: *Drama, fiction*

MAJOR WORKS:

Trifles (1916)

"A Jury of Her Peers" (1917)

The Verge (1921)

Alison's House (1930)

Overview

Susan Glaspell was a prominent fiction writer and playwright and one of the original contributors to the "little theater movement" of the 1910s and 1920s. Thematically, much of her work explores the repercussions of women's physical and psychological oppression in the patriarchal culture of early twentieth century America. Glaspell is also known for confronting American idealism and offering a new perspective of what being "American" means.

Biographical and Historical Context

Youth and Journalism in the Midwest Susan Glaspell was born on July 1, 1876, in Davenport, Iowa, the second of three children. Glaspell's pioneer heritage would inspire material for her later plays and fiction.

Glaspell was educated in public schools, then worked as a reporter for the *Davenport Morning Republican*. While attending Drake University from 1895 to 1899, she served as literary editor and writer for the college newspaper. During her college days, she also acted as society editor for another newspaper, the *Davenport Weekly Outlook*, in which

Susan Glaspell   *Glaspell, Susan, photograph. AP Images.*

she published her first short story, "Tom and Towser" (1896). After graduation, she worked as a statehouse and legislative reporter for the *Des Moines Daily News*. Though Glaspell was successful as a newspaper writer, she ventured into freelance fiction writing, publishing short pieces in popular magazines and journals.

George Cram Cook   Glaspell attended the University of Chicago in 1903, but she decided to return to her hometown, where she joined a socialist group and met the man who would greatly influence her life: George Cram Cook. Cook was engaged, but he and Glaspell became involved. After a few years, Cook and his wife divorced, and Glaspell lived with him in New York City. They married in April 1913.

Success in Early Writing   Glaspell was a prolific writer during her relationship with Cook. Her first novel, *The Glory of the Conquered: The Story of a Great Love*, was a best-seller in 1909. Her second, *The Visioning* (1911), was more realistic in style and did not make as much of a splash with the critics. Glaspell also experimented during this time with the short-story genre, combining sentimental realism and moral themes with political critique,

as illustrated by a collection of her best short works published in 1912.

Drama and "The Little Theater Movement"
Cook encouraged Glaspell to branch out from fiction to drama. Glaspell shared his interest in American theater, a passion cultivated by their involvement in various liberal and socialist groups in New York as well as in the emergent "little theater movement," a movement in which small theater companies staged experimental works dismissed by the commercial theater. Cook and Glaspell collaborated on the one-act *Suppressed Desires* (1915), a satire about the emerging popularity of Freudian psychoanalysis. The play was not staged at that time due to its topic, but it was performed by one of the "little theater" companies after Glaspell became famous.

Provincetown   In Provincetown, Massachusetts, Glaspell, Cook, and a group of friends produced an "informal" production of *Suppressed Desires* along with Neith Boyce's *Constancy* (1915), a one-act play that focused on the way men and women defined fidelity. During this time, Glaspell published her third novel, *Fidelity* (1915), which was not well received because it portrayed an "emancipated" woman involved in an adulterous relationship.

Trifles and "A Jury of Her Peers"   Glaspell relied on her journalism experience to write *Trifles* (1916), often considered her best-known work. A one-act play, *Trifles* follows the investigation of the murder of a farmer, John Wright. His wife Minnie, who never appears onstage, has been charged with the crime. Two of Minnie's female acquaintances track down the reasons Minnie behaved as she did. The play became a standard repertory piece for many little theater companies. In 1917, Glaspell adapted the play into a short story, "A Jury of Her Peers," which became a canonical text for many introductory English literature courses.

Provincetown Players, Eugene O'Neill, and Other Famous Playwrights   Cook decided to move the Provincetown theater company to New York City and formally incorporated the group as the Provincetown Players in September 1916. Years later, the Provincetown theaters would offer some of the most innovative drama to be staged in New York. Glaspell was active in the company, taking acting roles, directing, and helping to oversee the daily operations of the Players' home, the Playwright's Theatre. She also developed a close relationship with playwright Eugene O'Neill. Glaspell and O'Neill became critically acclaimed playwrights, along with other members of the group, which included famous women writers Edna St. Vincent Millay, Djuna Barnes, and Edna Ferber.

Dramatic Years   Over the next few years, Glaspell wrote several more one-act plays, including *The People* (1917), *Close the Book* (1917), *The Outside* (1917), and *Woman's Honor* (1918). In 1919, Cook and Glaspell took a "sabbatical" year and returned to Davenport where they devoted themselves to writing. When they came back to New York in 1920, Glaspell produced *Inheritors* (1921) and *The Verge* (1921). *Inheritors* repeats themes found in her previous plays: the right of free speech, the public university as defender of democratic ideals, and the sociopolitical evils of racial prejudice.

The Death of Cook, and Becoming "Mrs. Norman Matson" Cook died suddenly in 1924 from a rare disease. Glaspell devoted herself to finishing Cook's remaining projects and looking after his two children. Glaspell also wrote a biography of Cook. She also soon became involved with novelist and playwright Norman Matson, and although they never formally married, biographical materials published after 1924 sometimes acknowledge her as Mrs. Norman Matson. Glaspell and Matson collaborated on *The Comic Artist* (1927), a drama that successfully played in London but was not a critical success on Broadway at its debut in 1933.

Alison's House and Glaspell's Later Projects *Alison's House* earned Glaspell the 1931 Pulitzer Prize. Inspired by Genevieve Taggard's 1930 biography of Emily Dickinson, Glaspell had intended to write an adaptation of this biographical piece, but she built the story of *Alison's House* around the fictional poet Alison Stanhope of Iowa after the Dickinson estate refused Glaspell the right to use Dickinson's name or poems. From 1936 to 1938, Glaspell also served as the director of the Midwest Play Bureau of the Federal Theater Project and wrote one

more play, *Springs Eternal* (1945). Her major works in the latter part of her life were novels: *The Morning Is Near Us* (1940), *Norma Ashe* (1942), and Judd Rankin's *Daughter* (1945). Glaspell died, in Provincetown, of pulmonary embolism and viral pneumonia in July 1948.

Works in Literary Context

Glaspell's work lays bare the desires of women, particularly for self-expression and fulfillment. She often used abstract dramatic experiments in both narrative and form to illustrate her themes, a creative strategy that frequently turned away critics. Though at times audiences did not understand her symbolism, Glaspell forced them to confront a new interpretation of gender, the American spirit, and the legacy of democratic idealism.

Women's Autonomy In 1912, thirteen of Glaspell's short stories were published as the collection *Lifted Masks*, and although they provide good examples of "local-color" fiction, thematically they address a woman's struggle for autonomy in a patriarchal culture. Glaspell's plays also resonate with the same theme. For example, in *The Verge*, the female protagonist is actually driven insane in her quest for her own freedom. Glaspell also addresses similar themes in her novels, as exemplified by *Fidelity* (1915). In that work, a woman refuses to marry the man with whom she runs away and instead moves to New York to join the feminist movement.

The Symbolism of Expressionism Expressionism, a literary movement that took hold in the early twentieth century, uses symbolism to convey inner human experience. Glaspell participated in this movement, as shown in her play, *The Verge*. In this drama, certain stage elements are exaggerated to represent the female protagonist's personal development and experiences. When the woman feels trapped in her situation, Glaspell cues the audience with such unusual visual elements as framing the woman behind a "bulging window" that demonstrates the character's emotional isolation as well as her imprisonment. Glaspell provides another symbol in the strong shaft of light that beams from a trap door to illuminate a "Breath of Life" plant. In the spotlight, the plant then represents a bright spot in this dark world.

Works in Critical Context

Scholars have long gravitated toward Glaspell's feminist themes; however, despite winning a Pulitzer Prize, Glaspell was not included in the canon until the 1970s. Still, a thorough analysis of Glaspell's main fiction and drama was virtually ignored until the 1980s. Now, Glaspell is studied as a key part of the development of American drama.

Trifles Because there have not been many performances of *Trifles* in mainstream theatrical venues, production reviews are few. Most critical commentary focuses on the short story version of the play, "A Jury of Her Peers," and its contributions to feminist ideals in literature. Contemporary playwright Megan Terry praises the play: "I admire the control, the precision and the power of *Trifles*. It never tires. It seems to be a perfect play and accomplishes all the playwright's intentions. It is a model of subtlety and understatement." Other critics echo the positive sentiment. For example, Linda Ben-Zvi suggests: "Glaspell does not actually present the victimization of women or the violent acts such treatment may engender. Instead, she stages the potential for female action and the usurpation of power."

The Verge   Recently, Glaspell's *The Verge* has inspired a resurgence in scholarly study. Although *The Verge* received mixed reviews for its first production in 1921, the majority of the comments were negative and called the play too abstract and confusing. Some also could not identify with Claire and characterized her as unpleasant and annoying. The title of Percy Hammond's review for the *New York Herald* at the time of the play's publication sums up his opinion: "What *The Verge* Is About, Who Can Tell." Yet, as Barbara Ozieblo notes, some members of The Heterodoxy, a radical woman's club in the early twentieth century, classified Glaspell as "a playwright who dared to show how society takes its revenge on a woman rebel." The members of the group championed Glaspell's message and defended its difficult stylistic elements. Now, feminist theorists categorize the drama as an important, overlooked work. In 1991, the play was staged at a conference at Brigham Young University.

Responses to Literature

1. With a group of your classmates, discuss the role of women in today's society. Do you think American culture can still be considered "patriarchal"? In what ways are men and women equal and unequal?

2. "A Jury of Her Peers" is an adaptation of Glaspell's one-act play *Trifles*. In a short essay, evaluate the main differences between telling a story through narration and telling it through drama. How does each form change character development, plot development, thematic development?

3. With a classmate, use the Internet to research the women's suffrage movement in America. Write a report for the class on the leaders of this movement, their arguments for giving women the right to vote. Then discuss how some of these political figures, arguments, and issues show up in certain selections of Glaspell's work.

4. In *Alison's House*, Alison Stanhope is modeled after New England poet Emily Dickinson. With a classmate, research Emily Dickinson, then create a report for the class that describes the similarities and differences between Dickinson and the fictional Stanhope. As part of your report, offer your opinion about

---

COMMON HUMAN EXPERIENCE

Glaspells's short stories, plays, and novels confront issues of women's identity, oppression, and agency. Other texts that focus on this same theme are:

A Man's World (1915), a stageplay by Rachel Crothers. This novel focuses on Frank Ware, a female writer raising a friend's illegitimate son in a bohemian neighborhood of New York City, and on the conflict that ensues when she discovers the boy's father is her fiancé.

Steaming (1905), a drama by Nell Dunn. This British drama takes place during the "women-only" days at a Turkish bath where various women go to escape the pressures of everyday life in a patriarchal society at the turn of the century.

The Vagina Monologues (1894), a stageplay by Eve Ensler. This groundbreaking, episodic play features a series of monologues, read by different women, all of whom provide their individual perspectives on the vagina.

A Stage of Their Own: Feminist Playwrights of the Suffrage Era (1992), a critical anthology by Sheila Stowell. This book recovers selections of previously lost feminist drama and analyzes the feminist debate generated inside these plays. Featured authors include Elizabeth Robins, Elizabeth Baker, and Cicely Hamilton.

---

whether you think *Alison's House* is an accurate portrayal of the Dickinson family.

BIBLIOGRAPHY

Books

"*Alison's House*." *Drama for Students*. Edited by Ira Milne and Jennifer Greve. Detroit: Gale, 2007. 1–21.

Cambridge Guide to Women's Writings in English. Edited by Lorna Sage, Germaine Greer, and Elaine Showalter. Cambridge, U. K.: Cambridge University Press, 1999. 275–76.

Carpentier, Martha C. *The Major Novels of Susan Glaspell*. Gainesville: University Press of Florida, 2001.

Cotsell, Michael. *The Theater of Trauma: American Modernist Drama and the Psychological Struggle for the American Mind, 1900–1930*. New York: Peter Lang, 2005.

"A Jury of Her Peers." *Short Stories for Students*, Vol. 3. Edited by Kathleen Wilson. Detroit: Thomson Gale, 1998, 154–76.

Makowsy, Veronica. *Susan Glaspell's Century of American Women: A Critical Interpretation of Her Work*. New York: Oxford University Press, 1993.

Ozieblo, Barbara. *Susan Glaspell: A Critical Biography*. Chapel Hill: University of North Carolina Press, 2000.

Papke, Mary E. *Susan Glaspell: A Research and
    Production Sourcebook.* Westport, Conn.:
    Greenwood, 1993.
"*Trifles.*" *Drama for Students.* Edited by David Galens.
    Detroit: Thomson Gale, 2000, 216–233.

Periodicals

Dymkowski, Christine. "On the Edge: The Plays of
    Susan Glaspell." *Modern Drama* 31 (1998):
    91–105.
Friedman, Sharon. "Feminism as Theme in
    Twentieth-Century American Women's Drama."
    American Studies 24 (1994): 69–89.

✸ Louise Glück

BORN: *1943, New York, New York*

NATIONALITY: *American*

GENRE: *Poetry*

MAJOR WORKS:
Firstborn (1968)
Descending Figure (1980)
Triumph of Achilles (1985)
Ararat (1990)
Wild Iris (1992)

Louise Glück   *AP Images.*

Overview

The verse of Louise Glück has been described as technically precise, grim, and insightful. She often uses myth to
explore the universally and emotionally painful experiences involving family, relationships, and death. She has
been awarded fellowships from the Guggenheim and
Rockefeller foundations, as well as from the National
Endowment for the Arts. She was the U.S. poet laureate
from 2003 to 2004 and won the Pulitzer Prize for her
collection *Wild Iris.* In recent years, she has taught poetry
at prestigious universities across the United States and is
currently on the faculty at Yale University.

Biographical and Historical Context

Young Influences On April 22, 1943, Glück was
born to a Wellesley-educated mother and a father who
was a first-generation Hungarian American businessman.
Her parents' first daughter died before Glück's birth, and
this tragic fact inspired Glück to explore themes of death,
grief, and loss throughout her future work, particularly in
her inaugural collection of poetry, *Firstborn.* Her struggle
with anorexia as a teenager also influenced the stark
imagery and personal themes in her poetry. Glück left
her last year of high school to engage in a seven-year
program of psychoanalysis. Glück has frequently said that
going through that the intense internal exploration
taught her to think and to analyze her own voice. Glück

began writing poetry at an early age, and in an essay
called, "Education of the Poet," she noted:

> From the time, at four or five or six, I first started
> reading poems, first thought of the poets I read as
> my companions, my predecessors—from the begin-
> ning I preferred the simplest vocabulary. What fas-
> cinated me were the possibilities of context.

After finishing her cycle of psychoanalysis, Glück
enrolled in a poetry workshop at Columbia University,
taught by Leonie Adams, a poet known for her metaphysical, devotional style. After two years, Glück met and
studied with distinguished poet Stanley Kunitz, a relationship that would shape her work as a poet. In 1967, Glück
was honored with the Academy of American Poets Prize,
and a year later, her collection *Firstborn* was published.

Firstborn *Firstborn* comprised lyrics Glück had previously published in various journals. Critical reception was
favorable, and she was hailed a poet of great promise.
Though the subject matter of the collection is for the
most part apolitical, the personal, confessional, and often
angry tone of the book reflects the mood of the United
States during that year, as the nation became further
engaged in the Vietnam War and reeled from a string of
political assassinations and societal changes.

Mythological and Historical Tradition in the 1980s and 1990s With her award-winning collections *Descending Figure* and *The Triumph of Achilles*, Glück used mythology to contextualize the limited scope of ordinary, human experiences. Similarly, in *Ararat*, Glück unified a series of lyrics into an archetypal, yet decidedly personal narrative about the death of a father, bereavement, and the surviving family. For that collection, Glück was honored with the Library of Congress's Rebekah Johnson Bobbitt National Prize for Poetry. Two years later, in 1992, Gluck won the Pulitzer Prize, as well as the Poetry Society of America's William Carlos Williams Award for her collection, *Wild Iris*. In 1996, she published the collection, *Meadowlands*, which employs the epic Greek tale of the *Odyssey* to show the disintegration of a marriage. In 1999, Glück won the coveted $50,000 Böllingen Prize from Yale University for her collection *Vita Nova* (1999). In an interview with Glück for the *Harvard Advocate*, Brian Phillips observed:

> Something … that struck me about *Vita Nova* as a title was the irony of its historical reference. Obviously, in the late middle ages in Italy the phrase 'vita nuova' was used by Dante and others to indicate a new commitment of a romantic ideal of love. But you [Glück] seem to sort of update that phrase to mean life after the disintegration of the romantic relationship.

Honored Titles and Teaching Because of her poetic prowess, Glück has held a number of prestigious titles and honored positions. For example, in 1999, she was elected a chancellor of the Academy of American Poets, and in the fall of 2003, replaced Billy Collins as the Library of Congress's twelfth Poet Laureate Consultant in poetry. In 2003, she became the new judge of the Yale Series of Younger Poets, a position she held until 2007. Glück has also taught poetry at many schools including Columbia, University of Iowa, University of California at Berkeley, and Harvard. Glück is currently an adjunct professor and the Rosencranz Writer-in-Residence at Yale University.

Works in Literary Context

Glück's poetry resonates with the influences of other famous poets. Critics often comment on how shades of mentor Stanley Kunitz are apparent in her work, as well as on the "confessional" style Glück borrows from Robert Lowell, Sylvia Plath, and Anne Sexton. Glück often revises poetic, historic, and mythic traditions to provide her own twist on common subjects.

Glück's poetry has few themes and few moods. Whether she is writing autobiographically or assuming a persona, at the center of every poem is an "I" who is isolated from family, or bitter from rejected love, or disappointed with what life has to offer. Her world is bleak; however, it is depicted with a lyrical grace, and her poems are attractive if disturbing. One reason reviewers cite for

---

LITERARY AND HISTORICAL CONTEMPORARIES

Louise Glück's famous contemporaries include:

Billy Collins (1941–): An American poet who served two terms as U.S. poet laureate (2001–2003), Collins was selected by New York to be their State Poet in 2004. In recent years, he has been known for his poem "Names," written in honor of the victims of the September 11, 2001, terrorist attacks in New York and Washington, D.C.

Stanley Kunitz (1905–2006): Kunitz was a mentor to Glück who served two years (1974–1976) as the Library of Congress consultant in poetry and one term as U.S. poet laureate in 2000.

Adrienne Rich (1929–): An American poet, essayist, and feminist whose well-known works include *Diving into the Wreck* (1973).

Audre Lorde (1934–1992): Lorde is an American activist known for her poetry and theoretical work dealing with lesbian and gay rights, racial issues, and feminism.

Eavan Boland (1944–): An Irish feminist poet whose work criticizes racial and gender discrimination and celebrates the "ordinariness" of women's experiences.

Glück's seemingly unfailing ability to capture her reader's attention is her expertise at creating poetry that many people can understand, relate to, and experience intensely and completely. Her poetic voice is uniquely distinctive and her language is deceptively straightforward. She also has the ability to create poetry with a dreamlike quality that at the same time deals with the realities of passionate and emotional subjects.

Family Most of Glück's work is about family; the relationships are generally selfish if not hostile. Whether the personae are apparently based on Glück's own family (grandmother, mother, father, husband, sister, cousin) or part of an imaginary family of misfits (hunchback, cripple, whore), they are united, not by love, but by the heated blood of anger or the cold blood of their shared ambivalence. All seem to have inherited a basic pessimism and resignation to the letdowns of life. Instead of finding solace in the company of one another, they find conflict. What should be love between a man and a woman is the most disappointing of all relationships, In some poems there is sexual desire but there is no sense of tenderness or affection associated with sex, only an animal brutality.

Poetic Myth Myth is a common theme in much of Glück's work. In entitling her 1990 collection *Ararat*, Glück uses the reference to the biblical myth—Ararat, a mountain in present-day Turkey, was the biblical site of

COMMON HUMAN EXPERIENCE

Glück's poetry uses myth to explore experiences, emotions, and issues common throughout time and shared by all humanity. Other texts that use myth in this way are:

Autobiography of Red: A Novel in Verse (1998), a "novel in verse" by Anne Carson. This experimental poetic "novel" uses the myth of Geryon and Herakles—a giant who battles with a son of Zeus—to reflect the emotions involved in a love affair, issues of gender and sexuality, and the world of appearances.

Eurydice (1905), a poem by H. D. (Hilda Dolittle). This verse relies on the Greek myth of Eurydice's romance with Orpheus to reflect H. D.'s personal experience with an unfaithful husband and her stand against the patriarchal oppression of the early twentieth century.

Outside History (1990), a poetry collection by Eavan Boland. This collection includes "Daphne with her Thighs in Bark," a poem that uses the Greek myth of Daphne, who was turned into a laurel tree to escape the adulation of Apollo, to explore issues of female identity.

Gods and Mortals: Modern Poems on Classical Myths (2001), a poetic anthology by Nina Kossman. The collection offers more than three hundred twentieth-century poems, all which offer retellings of myth and legend. Authors include Rainer Maria Rilke, Robert Graves, and D. H. Lawrence.

Noah's landing of the ark—to connect to universal themes and subjects. These poems address how a father's death results in his widow's personal crisis, and conflict between sisters. In her third collection, *Meadowlands* (1996), Glück used the epic story of King Odysseus, his wife Penelope, and their son Telemachus to illustrate the ordinary theme of a marriage coming apart.

Works in Critical Context

From her first collection, *Firstborn*, Glück has been a critically acclaimed poet recognized for her ability to hone in on a universal experience with intimacy and communality. Helen Vendler, a reviewer in *New Republic*, summed up Glück's appeal for the reader:

> Glück's cryptic narratives invite our participation: we must, according to the case, fill out the story, substitute ourselves for the fictive personages, invent a scenario from which the speaker can utter her lines, decode the import, 'solve' the allegory. Or such is our first impulse. Later, I think ... we read the poem, instead, as a truth complete within its own terms, reflecting some one of the innumerable configurations into which experience falls.

Wrote Anna Wooten in the *American Poetry Review*, "Glück has a gift for getting the reader to imagine with her, drawing on the power of her audience to be amazed. She engages a 'spectator' in a way that few other poets can do." However, some critics have not embraced Glück's work as passionately and have critiqued her negative portrayals of women, particularly the way in which artistic expression and female sexuality, at times, seem like opposing forces.

The Triumph of Achilles Critics praised Glück's *The Triumph of Achilles* not only for its exploration of love through the metaphor found in classical myths and the Bible, but for Glück's direct style. Wendy Lesser noted in the *Washington Post Book World*:

> 'Direct' is the operative word here: Glück's language is staunchly straightforward, remarkably close to the diction of ordinary speech. Yet her careful selection for rhythm and repetition, and the specificity of even her idiomatically vague phrases, give her poems a weight that is far from colloquial.

In their biographical and critical study of Glück, James K. Robinson and Martha Sutro commented on Gluck's innovations and poetic risks, writing: "In *The Triumph of Achilles*, Glück sticks with her perennial subject, that of human loss, but she experiments with new types of poems, from narratives and extended, mixed sequences to songs and orientalist attempts at capturing the immediate."

The House on the Marshland Critics lauded Glück's lyrical ability with the publication of her second collection, *The House on the Marshland* (1975). Helen Vendler commented on Glück's poetic development in her review of the collection for the *New Republic*: "The leap in style from Glück's relatively unformed first book to *The House on Marshland* suggests that Glück is her own best critic." Glück's mentor Stanley Kunitz wrote: "Those of us who have waited impatiently for Louise Glück's second book can rejoice that it confirms and augments the impression of a rare and high imagination."

Wild Iris Glück's Pulitzer Prize–winning collection, *Wild Iris* (1992), adapts the meditative, hymnal lyric and garden metaphor of nineteenth-century poet Emily Dickinson and seventeenth-century poet George Herbert to investigate questions of faith and the role of human beings in the larger, natural world. Judith Kitchen from the *Georgia Review* also connected Glück's style in this collection to the natural world of poet Robert Frost:

> Like Frost, Glück looks for the moment she will see *beyond* and *through*. The poems are simultaneously passionate and remote, as though written with the white heat of a distant star. Their visionary mode may even provide an entry into the snowy fields.

In a positive review in the *Times Literary Supplement*, Stephen Burt compared the volume to the poetry of Sylvia Plath. He commented, "Glück's skeletal lines, with their unexpected stops, make her poems all gaps and essentials, full of what art books call 'negative space.'" Burt noted that this was the first of Glück's books to be pubished in England, and he concluded: "Like those spare, demanding poets, Dickenson, Housman and Plath, Glück's can appeal to many people who don't read much modern poetry; those who do had better not miss out."

Responses to Literature

1. Much of Glück's work uses myth as a metaphor to discuss personal issues and painful circumstances. Choose one of Glück's poems and write an essay in which you discuss how her use of the mythical turns the ordinary into epic. How do you think this connection helps the reader identify with her poetry on a deeper level?

2. Write an allegorical poem in which you cast yourself as a mythical figure and turn a small, ordinary incident in your life into an epic journey. Use one of Glück's poems as inspiration, and afterward, write a paragraph about how your original work was influenced by hers.

3. With another classmate, compare a selection of poems from Glück's *The Triumph of Achilles* with a selection from Anne Carson's *The Autobiography of Red*. Discuss tone, style, and use of myth. Present your analysis to the class.

4. Anna Wooten wrote: Glück "engages a 'spectator' in a way that few other poets can do." Choose one of Glück's poems and write an essay describing how Glück "engages a spectator." In the beginning of your essay, you may want to note how you define "spectator," in order to build on your point.

BIBLIOGRAPHY

Books

Contemporary Women Poets. Detroit, Mich.: St. James Press,1997.

"Glück, Louise (Elisabeth)." *Major Twenty-first-Century Writers.* Vol. 2. Edited by Tracey Matthews. Detroit: Gale,2005.

"Glück, Louise." *Modern American Literature.* Edited by Joann Cerrito and Laurie DiMauro. Detroit: St. James Press,1999. 435–37.

Robinson, James K. and Martha Sutro. "Glück, Louise (Elisabeth)." *Contemporary Poets.* Edited by Thomas Riggs. Detroit.: St. James Press, 2001. 428–430.

Vendler, Helen. *The Music of What Happens: Poems, Poets, Critics.* Cambridge, Mass.: Harvard University Press, 1988.

Periodicals

Baker, David. "Kinds of Knowing." *Kenyon Review.* 15 (Winter 1993): 184–92.

Burt, Stephen. "The Nervous Rose." *Times Literary Supplement.* No. 4911 (May 16, 1997): 25.

Hart, Henry. "Story-tellers, Myth-makers, Truth-sayers." *Georgia New England Review.* 15:4 (Fall 1993): 192–206.

Kitchen, Judith. "The Woods Around It." *Georgia Review.* (Spring 1993): 145–159.

Web sites

Philips, Brian. "A Conversation with Louise Glück." *Harvard Advocate.* Summer 1999. Accessed December 9, 2008, from http:// www.thehar vardadvocate.com/.

⊛ Rodolfo "Corky" Gonzales

BORN: *1928, Denver, Colorado*

DIED: *2005, Denver, Colorado*

NATIONALITY: *American*

GENRE: *Poetry*

MAJOR WORKS:

I Am Joaquín/Yo Soy Joaquín: An Epic Poem (1967)

Overview

Rodolfo "Corky" Gonzales was an activist and spokesperson for the Chicano movement in the United States. Because of its social impact, his only published work, the epic poem *I Am Joaquín/Yo Soy Joaquín* (1967), is often considered more of a social commentary than a literary work of art.

Works in Biographical and Historical Context

Childhood in Denver and the Depression Gonzales was born on June 18, 1928, in Denver, Colorado, to a family of migrant workers. He was the youngest of five brothers and three sisters. Gonzales's mother died when he was two, and his father never remarried. The children grew up in a barrio of Denver during the Great Depression. By the age of ten, Gonzales was working in the sugar-beet fields in the spring and summer. Because of his job, he attended a number of schools inside and outside of Colorado, and graduated from Manual High School at the age of sixteen in 1944. In his youth, Gonzales had a quick temper, which sparked his uncle to describe him as "always popping off like a cork." This behavior earned him the nickname "Corky," which remained throughout his life.

Boxing as a Teenager With the money he got working in the sugar-beet fields, Gonzales saved enough money to attend college. He enrolled in the University of Denver, but his education cost more than he had saved, so he was forced to drop out. However, as a teenager, Gonzales had cultivated a passion for boxing, and in 1947 he began his professional boxing career. He became the third-rank contender in the World Featherweight category of the

Rodolfo "Corky" Gonzales speaking at the Colorado State Penitentiary   © *Bettmann / Corbis*

National Boxing Association and was considered one of the best featherweight fighters in the world. Gonzales's success in boxing earned him a spot in the Colorado Sports Hall of Fame and earned him the public recognition that he would later use during his political career.

Civil Rights Leader   In 1955, Gonzales left boxing to get involved in business and politics and Chicano civil rights. His father had emigrated from Mexico to Colorado and often told him about the Mexican Revolution, Mexico's history, and the pride of the Mexican people. These stories inspired Gonzales to become active in his community. In 1960, on behalf of John F. Kennedy, he organized the Viva Kennedy presidential campaign in Colorado, which was intended to appeal to Latino voters. He was also appointed chairman of the Denver National Youth Corps, an antipoverty program. In 1963, he founded "Los Voluntarios" (The Volunteers), a grassroots organization dedicated to Chicano youth. "Los Voluntarios" was also the forerunner of the organization Crusade for Justice, an urban civil rights and cultural movement, also founded by Gonzales. The Crusade for Justice raised political awareness through political action and education. In 1966, Gonzales became the chairman of another organization, The War on Poverty. However, he soon resigned

from his leadership positions in these organizations to focus his attention on championing solely Chicano causes. To rally the community behind Chicano nationalism, Gonzales organized public demonstrations, from high-school walkouts to protests against police brutality.

I Am Joaquín   It was around this time that Gonzales published *I Am Joaquín/Yo Soy Joaquín*. The epic poem reflects Gonzales's passionate efforts to promote Chicano nationalism. Gonzales has said of the work:

> Writing *I Am Joaquín* was a journey back through history, a painful self-evaluation, a wandering search for my peoples, and most of all, for my own identity. The totality of all social inequities and injustices had to come to the surface. All the while, the truth about our own flaws—the villains and the heroes had to ride together—in order to draw an honest, clear conclusion of who we were, who we are, and where we are going.

In the poem, Gonzales shares his vision of the "Chicano," who is neither Indian nor European, neither Mexican nor American, but rather a blend of conflicting identities.

Efforts in Activism   A year later, Gonzales led a Chicano contingent in the Poor People's March on Washington, D.C., a march that began in Mississippi and ended in the nation's capital. It was intended to stress the need for economic aid to the poorest communities of the United States. It was during this event where Gonzales issued his "Plan of the Barrio." The plan outlined ways to improve housing and education in poor Chicano communities, as well as to encourage the support, growth, and success of barrio-owned businesses. It also called for the restitution of Pueblo lands. Gonzales suggested forming a Congress of Aztlán to successfully achieve these goals.

To generate unity and support among Chicano youth, in 1969 Gonzales organized the first Annual Chicano Youth Liberation Conference. This conference attracted Chicano youth from across the United States, as it was an event to address historical injustice toward Mexican-Americans and to strategize for a better future for them in society. Through these and other sociopolitical activities, Chicano youth were encouraged to vocalize their opinions about their unequal position in American society and to publicly show how Mexican-Americans contributed to the American experience. During this time, Gonzales sought alternatives to what he saw as "gringo" (white) social institutions and founded a private school exclusively for Chicano students that was intended to build their self-esteem and cultural pride. The school was named after Tlatelolco, an area of Mexico City that was once an autonomous city-state under the Aztec empire. Tlatelolco became the site for student activism, and today, the school symbolizes the complicated history of identity and social progress for indigenous and Mestizo people.

Withdrawing from Public Life In 1973, Gonzales's career trajectory was drastically changed when a man was arrested for jaywalking in front of the Crusade for Justice headquarters. Public protests against the persecution led to confrontations between demonstrators and police. A gun battle ensued, and a bomb exploded in the Downing Terrace apartments, which were owned by the Crusade. One man was killed and seventeen were injured, including twelve police officers. Gonzales blamed the Denver police department for the bombing and suggested they used grenades on the building. However, a detective reported the scene of the explosion was a "veritable arsenal." Though Gonzales's involvement in the incident was eventually disproven, his connection to the organizations on trial forced him to retreat from the public eye. He remained active in the Chicano movement, but kept a much lower profile.

Tragedy In 1987, Gonzales was in a car accident that left him in significantly poor health. In 1995, he was hospitalized with acute liver disease. A decade later, he experienced renal and coronary distress. Despite his condition, he checked out of the hospital and proclaimed to his doctors, "I'm indigenous. I'm going to die at home among my family." Gonzales died in Denver in 2005, and was survived by his wife, Geraldine Romero Gonzales, and their six daughters and two sons.

LITERARY AND HISTORICAL CONTEMPORARIES

Gonzales's famous contemporaries include:

Martin Luther King Jr. (1929–1968): King was an African American human rights icon known for the 1963 march on Washington D.C., his "I Have a Dream" speech, and the 1955 Montgomery Bus Boycott.

Ruben Salazar (1928–1970): Salazar was a Mexican American journalist killed by police during the National Chicano Moratorium March against the Vietnam War in 1970 in East Los Angeles. The incident became a symbol of the unfair treatment of Latinos by law enforcement.

Alurista (1947–): Alurista is a Chicano activist and poet, born Alberto Baltazar Urista Heredia. Alurista is credited with popularizing the Chicano movement–era concept of "Aztlán," a rightful, historical home for Chicanos.

César Chávez (1927–1993): Chavez was a Mexican American farmworker, labor leader, and human rights activist whose work led to many improvements for union laborers.

José Montoya (1932–): Montoya is an influential Chicano bilingual poet. Montoya is currently the poet laureate of Sacramento, California.

Works in Literary Context

Though Gonzales did write a few unpublished plays, he is best known for his epic poem, *I Am Joaquín/Yo Soy Joaquín*. The poem was hugely popular within the Chicano movement, which used it as a touchstone for the cause. It was transformed from poem to stage play, and eventually to a film produced by the Teatro Campesino.

The Social and Spiritual Context of I Am Joaquín/Yo Soy Joaquín Gonzales framed the contemporary realities of Chicano identity and conflict of *I Am Joaquín/Yo Soy Joaquín* in metaphysical and spiritual dimensions. The protagonist, Joaquín, travels to the past to personify famous figures of the Aztec world, the Spanish colonial period, the Mexican independence movement, nineteenth-century Mexico, and the Mexican revolution in 1910. The poem also turns to Our Lady of Guadalupe, the patron saint of Mexico, and Tonantzin, her pre-Mexican counterpart, to explore the role of women throughout the times. In the end, the poem arrives back in the present and addresses the negative situation of the contemporary Chicano before leaving an optimistic note about the future for the reader.

Epic Heroes as Role Models *I Am Joaquín/Yo Soy Joaquín* brings to life the epic heroes of Mexican and Chicano history to generate a cultural pride and grow a collective sense of self-determination among these peoples.

COMMON HUMAN EXPERIENCE

Gonzales's *I Am Joaquín/Yo Soy Joaquín* serves as both a social statement and a literary representative of the Chicano cause. Here are some other works that adopt this same theme:

The Man Who Could Fly and Other Stories (2006), a short-story collection by Rudolfo Anaya. In this collection, which spans thirty years of work, the founder of Chicano literature uses the Southwestern landscape to reflect the internal conflicts of his characters.

The Last Generation: Prose and Poetry (1999), a multi-genre collection by Cherríe Moraga. In this work, Moraga, a Chicana lesbian, resists assimilation and calls for the formation of a "Queer Aztlán," an inclusive Chicano tribe in which cooperation is rewarded over competition.

We Happy Few (2006), a novel by Rolando Hinojosa. This dramedy goes inside the social and cultural politics of a university campus set in a town on the Texas-Mexico border. Racism raises the stakes in the conflict over who has the power at this university and this community.

Rebellion is the Circle of a Lover's Hands (1990), a poetry collection by Martin Espada. The thirty-four poems in this collection comment on the victimization of alienated Hispanics, and use that victimization to reflect the plight of all oppressed minorities.

The protagonist personifies each cultural hero during important historical moments that illustrate personal acts of sacrifice for Mexican-Chicano freedoms and identity. For example, the poem's first major event is marked by Aztec ruler Cuauhtémoc's final rebellion against the Spaniards in Tenochtitlan, followed by an incident in the Mexican-American War (1846–1848) in which "niõos héroes/(young heroes)"—Mexican military cadets—choose to die rather than surrender to American forces invading Mexico City. Gonzales has his protagonist move on from there to World War II and finally to Vietnam. These and other events chronicled in the poem reflect Gonzales's interest and belief in Chicano history, freedom, identity, and self-pride.

Works in Critical Context

At the time of its publication, *I Am Joaquin/Yo Soy Joaquín* was a mimeographed leaflet, widely circulated in order to be read during various protest activities organized by the Chicano movement. The poem can also be seen as the inspiration for the Chicano Literary Renaissance, from the late 1960s to the mid-1970s. Although the word Chicano was a vulgar, class-based term used in Mexico to classify people of dubious character, *I Am Joaquín/Yo Soy Joaquín* inspired a new, positive use of the term.

I am Joaquín/Yo Soy Joaquín Since the publication of Gonzales's epic poem, critics have commented on the work's marriage of social activist intent and artistic merit. Catharine Wall wrote that

> Gonzales combines the poetic sensibilities of Walt Whitman's "Song of Myself" (1855) and Allen Ginsberg's "Howl" (1956) as Joaquín, a Chicano Everyman, explores himself and the history of the Chicano people—from the pre-Columbian and colonial periods, through independence and revolution up to the present day.

David Conde also remarked on the social and literary impact of the poem:

> There is little doubt that *I Am Joaquín* was written as a social document that sought to instill Chicano pride and identity as well as encourage community activism. . . . The literary merit of the work comes from the manner in which the poem is constructed and how theme and structure come together to produce a superior artistic experience. Its epic quality comes from the depiction of a dual journey into the postclassic world of pre-Columbian meso-America as well as into the contradictions of the Chicano heritage.

Responses to Literature

1. With a partner, research the Chicano movement. Create a report for your class in which you define the movement and describe its important players. Include parts of poems, speeches, or other texts to illustrate the language and imagery of the movement.

2. Choose one historical event fictionalized in *I am Joaquín/Yo Soy Joaquín* and write an essay about how that event represents a personal act of sacrifice in the achievement of Chicano freedoms and identity.

3. The terms "Chicano," "Hispanic," "Latino," and "Mexican American" share complicated boundaries and histories. Research each term and write a report about their definitions, origins, and what each commonly refers to today.

BIBLIOGRAPHY

Books

Acuña, Rodolfo. *Occupied America: A History of Chicanos.* New York: Harper and Row, 1988.

Conde, David. *Dictionary of Literary Biography, Volume 122: Chicano Writers, Second Series.* Edited by Francisco A. Lomeli. Detroit: Gale Group, 1992, pp. 111–114.

Marin, Christine. *A Spokesman of the Mexican American Movement: Rodolfo "Corky" Gonzales and the Fight for Chicano Liberation, 1966–1972.* San Francisco: R. and E. Research Associates, 1977.

Muñoz, Carlos. *Youth, Identity, Power: The Chicano Movement.* New York: Verso, 1989.

Wall, Catharine. "Latino Poetry." *Notable Latino Writers.* Pasadena, Calif.: Salem Press, 2006, pp. 800–815.

Periodicals

Bruce-Novoa, Juan. "The Space of Chicano Literature." *Colores.* 1:4 (October 1975): 30–33.

Websites

"Rodolfo Gonzales." *Biographicon.* 10 Nov. 2008 http://http://75.125.242.10/view/gqhh7.

Hartley, George. "I am Joaquín: Rodolfo 'Corky' Gonzales and the Retroactive Construction of Chicanismo." Ohio University. 10 Nov. 2008 http:// http://epc.buffalo.edu/authors/hartley/pubs/corky.html.

✱ Frances Goodrich

BORN: *1890, Belleville, New Jersey*

DIED: *1984, New York, New York*

NATIONALITY: *American*

GENRE: *Drama*

MAJOR WORKS:

The Thin Man (1934)

It's a Wonderful Life (1946)

Father of the Bride (1950)

Seven Brides for Seven Brothers (1955)

The Diary of Anne Frank (1959)

Frances Goodrich   *AP Images*

Overview

Frances Goodrich, along with her husband Albert Hackett, wrote prolifically for the Hollywood screen and created wildly popular comedies, successful musicals, and the Pulitzer Prize–winning drama *The Diary of Anne Frank.* Goodrich and Hackett's wide range of talent, combined with their tireless work ethic, made them one of Hollywood's most successful and sought-after husband-and-wife writing team ever. Their screenplays easily translated into films that were more often than not met with wide popular appeal. Their success spanned three decades, and the films based on their screenplays are still watched today and are the subjects of modern remakes.

Works in Biographical and Historical Context

A Privileged Life   Frances Goodrich was born in 1890 in Belleville, New Jersey, a small bucolic town surrounded by woods and wildflowers. Goodrich was born into a family with social status and wealth. Her father, Henry Goodrich, was a New York City lawyer. Her mother, Madeleine Christy Lloyd, came from a family of intellectuals, artists, and writers. Goodrich's uncle Henry Lloyd, her mother's brother, was a lawyer, journalist, editor, and author. As a child Goodrich visited her Uncle Henry, whom she held in high regard, at his forty-bedroom home. Henry often entertained his friends, who included writers Robert Louis Stevenson, the famous Scottish author of *Treasure Island*, and the prominent African American writer Booker T. Washington. Goodrich was exposed to alternative ideas and progressive thinking in her privileged early years.

Goodrich attended Vassar College for women, one of the nation's most prestigious all-female schools. At Vassar she was bitten by the theater bug and spent much of her time directing plays. David L. Goodrich, in his biography of Goodrich and Hackett, *The Real Nick and Nora* (2001), states that in Goodrich's Vassar yearbook her personal quotation read "Silence there, please! We're rehearsing." Goodrich graduated from Vassar in 1912 and went to New York City to study social work at her father's request. She soon found her way into acting and in 1916 made her Broadway debut in the production *Come Out of the Kitchen.*

LITERARY AND HISTORICAL CONTEMPORARIES

Goodrich's famous contemporaries include:

Ernest Hemingway (1899–1961): An American novelist and short-story writer, Ernest Hemingway is notable for his simple, straightforward style and realistic dialogues, which often depict the atrocities of war. His novel, *To Have and Have Not*, was adapted for film in 1944. He won the Nobel Prize in Literature in 1954.

Harper Lee (1926–): Harper Lee is a Southern writer famous for her novel *To Kill a Mockingbird* (1960). Her novel was translated into an Academy Award–winning screenplay in 1962.

Adolf Hitler (1889–1945): Chancellor of Germany from 1933 to 1945, Hitler led the German nation into World War II. The Germans conquered much of Europe and committed extensive genocide.

Greta Garbo (1905–1990): This Swedish-born actress triumphed in Hollywood during the silent film era and the Golden Age.

Cecil B. DeMille (1881–1959): An American film director, Cecil B. DeMille was renowned for his spectacular films, including *Samson and Delilah* (1949) and *The Ten Commandments* (1956).

The Third Time is the Charm for Romance Goodrich was moderately successful on the stage, finding steady acting work but never given major roles. However, she wasn't as fortunate in her romantic life. While working on the show *Come Out of the Kitchen* Goodrich met and fell in love with the actor Robert Ames. They married in 1917, and although it was rocky from the start because of his drinking, they remained married for six years. In 1927 Goodrich, now divorced from Ames, married the Newbery Award–winning author Hendrik Willem Van Loom, but their marriage was brief. In fact, it was in the same year of her marriage to Van Loom that Goodrich met Albert Hackett, a young actor nine years her junior, who would later become her partner for life, in work and in love. Goodrich and Hackett married in 1931 and stayed together until she died in 1984.

Hollywood's Golden Years Both Goodrich and Hackett wanted to get out of the acting business. They put their heads together and began writing the comedy play *Up Pops the Devil*. After a short run on the stage, *Up Pops the Devil* was adapted for film, and in 1931 the writing duo headed for Hollywood. In the thirties, Hollywood confronted the ugliness of the Great Depression with glamour and glitz. Alluring actresses like Greta Garbo and Jean Harlow flooded the silver screen in long, jeweled gowns. And although there were fewer moviegoers, 60 to 75 million people continued to seek escape from the grim reality of poverty and unemployment, through a few hours of glamour and humor on the big screen. The film industry was rapidly evolving from black-and-white silent films to talking films, and in 1932 the era of Technicolor began.

Five major studios, MGM, Twentieth Century Fox, Paramount, Warner Bros, and RKO, dominated Hollywood during this time. Goodrich and Hackett wrote under contract for MGM from 1933 to 1939, and in this period they wrote thirteen films, the most famous being *The Thin Man* series. In 1954 the team moved to RKO studios to collaborate on a new film that would prove to be a departure from their previous comedy. Working with director Frank Capra, Goodrich and Hackett wrote the screenplay for *It's a Wonderful Life* a movie about a man who considers his life a failure. He contemplates suicide, but his guardian angel appears and shows him he is wrong. The film was considered a screenplay triumph by critics, but it did not receive box-office success. However, it seems to have touched a sentimental streak among movie audiences. This has led to its sustained popularity over the decades; it is one of today's winter-holiday classics.

A More Serious Project After completing *It's a Wonderful Life* MGM contracted Goodrich and Hackett to adapt to the silver screen the recently published *Anne Frank: The Diary of a Young Girl*, the story of a Jewish girl and her family forced to hide for two years in an attic during the Nazi occupation of Holland. The project, however, was later cancelled by the studio. The topic was deemed too somber and sad to have wide public appeal. Unable to set the project aside, Goodrich and Hackett continued to write the screenplay themselves. They worked for two years on the adaptation and went to great lengths to capture the truth and feelings revealed in the diary. Goodrich and Hackett met with Otto Frank, Anne's father. They even traveled to the Netherlands and visited the attic where the Franks were concealed. This research helped them capture the claustrophobic atmosphere and convey the tension of the Franks' life in hiding. *The Diary of Anne Frank* opened on stage in 1955 and became the apex of the writing duo's career. It won them a Pulitzer Prize for drama, a Tony Award, as well as critical acclaim, international popular success, and recognition from their peers.

Going Back Home Goodrich and Hackett wrote their final film, *Five Finger Exercise*, in 1962. It proved to be unsuccessful. Seventy-two years old and ready to retire, Goodrich gave up her writing and left California to return to the East Coast with her husband. The successful couple lived a lavish life in New York City until Goodrich died of cancer in 1984. Partners in the fullest sense of the word, the couple had been together for fifty-three years. Their screenplays continue to attract large audiences; they have also become popular subjects for remakes, including the 1991 version of *Father of the Bride*, starring Steve Martin.

Works in Literary Context

Goodrich's screenplays run the gamut from mysteries, comedies, musicals, to serious drama. Her works contribute to the advancement of American film and literature during the Golden Age of Hollywood with artful dialogue and dramatic timing. While many of the films coming out of Hollywood relied on big name stars and glamour to attract audiences, America flocked to Goodrich's films for the entertaining exchanges between the well-rendered characters and to glimpse the depths of humanity.

Masterful Dialogue Sophisticated dialogues are what best characterize Goodrich's films. Although many of her characters exude style and glamour, it is through their witty conversations and quips that the essence of their relationships are revealed. With her film *The Thin Man* Goodrich uses subtle humor to skillfully portray the intimate and comedic relationship between the husband and wife detective team. The plots of the *The Thin Man* series were often superficial and almost impossible to follow, but the sophistication of the dialogue was fresh and original. Goodrich's ability to communicate delicate matters was finely honed, to avoid violation of the Hays Production Code, which was a set of morality guidelines that began to be enforced in 1934.

Adapting Literature to Film Most of Goodrich's work was based on previously published works. Adapting literature to film is complicated, and in some film and literary circles, not advisable. Her first great success, *The Thin Man* series, was based on Dashiell Hammett's popular detective books. Goodrich and Hackett developed Nick and Nora Charles, the main characters, beyond the descriptions given in the novel, and although the Charleses were conceived by Hammett, the details—the camaraderie and equality within the marriage, the playful gestures that give the marriage its sense of fun—were fleshed out by Goodrich and Hackett. Goodrich's adaptations constructed wonderfully dramatic and yet funny scenes. Still, the highpoint of Goodrich's career was her subsequent adaptation of *Anne Frank: The Diary of Young Girl*, in which she was able to reinterpret the material with a theatrical theme and develop moving stage characters.

Works in Critical Context

Goodrich's work was widely praised both during her career and later as her screenplays continued to provide material for fresh versions. Some critics claimed that her earlier comedic work lacked depth, and that they could not be considered serious works. However, Goodrich provided great emotional depth in her later works *It's a Wonderful Life* and *The Diary of Anne Frank*, showing that she did not lack depth in her writing ability.

The Thin Man

In the comedic murder mystery *The Thin Man* plot and action take the backseat to character and dialogue. Good-

COMMON HUMAN EXPERIENCE

Many of Goodrich's screenplays were based on previously published literature that was translated to the screen. Here are some other literary works that have been adapted to film.

Beloved (1987), a novel by Toni Morrison narrates the brutality of slavery and the family love needed to overcome tragedy and trials. *Beloved* won the Pulitzer Prize in 1987 and was adapted into a film in 1998.

Gone With the Wind (1936), is a saga by Margaret Mitchell that reveals the struggles of one family in the South before, during, and after the Civil War. It was adapted into an Academy Award-winning film in 1939.

Forrest Gump (1986), a novel by Winston Groom that describes the improbable and amazing life of one man over many decades. The 1994 film version starred Tom Hanks.

rich's lyrical dialogue and comedic flashes were considered bold and brilliant for her time. Although the screenplay does provide clues to the murder mystery, it is more like an elegant dance of dialogue. Roger Ebert says of the film, "It is about personal style. About living life as a kind of artwork."

The Diary of Anne Frank After a long and respected career in Hollywood and on Broadway, the Goodrich-Hackett writing team finally received special public recognition for a project that was one of their last efforts. *The Diary of Anne Frank*, which opened on Broadway in 1955, was the high point of their careers. The play received the New York Drama Critics Circle Award, the Tony Award, and the Pulitzer Prize in 1956. Adapted from the diary that Anne Frank kept while she and her family hid from the Nazis, the play occupied most of Goodrich and Hackett's time and attention from 1953 to 1955. The subject was a departure for them, and they researched the material scrupulously. As a result, they produced a play the critics praised for its fidelity to the spirit of the girl's diary. Film critic Brooks Atkinson wrote in the *New York Times* in 1955 "From any practical point of view the job of making a play out of the diary of Anne Frank is impossible. Perhaps that is why Mr. and Mrs. Hackett have succeeded so well. They have not contrived anything; they have left the tool-kit outside the door of their workroom. They have absorbed the story out of the diary and related it simply."

Responses to Literature

1. Goodrich started her career during the Golden Age in Hollywood. Using your library and the Internet,

find out more about Hollywood's Golden Age. What were the most common themes in film in the 1930s? From a historical perspective, why do you suppose audiences and film studios were attracted to these themes?

2. In 1934, the film industry enforced the Hays Production Code, a form of moral censorship. Using your library and the Internet find out more about the Hays Production Code. What happened to the Production Code? How are films regulated today? Do you agree or disagree that art should be censored for the good of the public?

3. Many of Goodrich's works were adapted from literary works. While reading Goodrich's screenplays, determine how her works are different from the literature that inspired them. In her screenplays, how does she reveal the characters' inner thoughts to the audience? Why do you think many literary adaptations fail at the box office, or are not as good as the book? Why do you think Goodrich's screenplays succeeded in translating literature to the screen?

4. In *The Diary of Anne Frank* Goodrich and Hackett masterfully capture the claustrophic situation of the Franks living in an attic. What techniques are employed to capture this feeling? How do the scenes change as the reader spends more and more time with the Franks in the attic?

BIBLIOGRAPHY

Books

Ehrlich, Evelyn. "Frances Goodrich and Albert Hacket." *Dictionary of Literary Biography*, Vol. 26: *American Screenwriters*, Detroit: Gale Research, 1984.

Goodrich, David L. *The Real Nick and Nora: Frances Goodrich and Albert Hackett, Writers of Stage and Screen Classics.* Carbondale: Southern Illinois University Press, 2004.

Periodicals

Atkinson, Brooks. "Theatre: The Diary of Anne Frank." *New York Times* (October 6, 1955)

Evans, Greg. "The Diary of Anne Frank." *Variety* (December 1997): vol. 369, no. 5.

Web sites

Anne Frank. Retrieved November 19, 2008, from http://www.annefrank.com.

Film History of the 1930s. Retrieved November 19, 2008 from http://www.filmsite.org/30sintro.html.

Frances Goodrich Biography (1890–1984). Retrieved November 19, 2008 from http://www.film reference.com/film/93/Frances-Goodrich.html,

The Motion Picture Production Code of 1930. Retrieved November 19, 2008 from http://www.artsrefor mation.com/a001/hays-code.html.

Publicity About Anne Frank and Her Diary. Retrieved November 19, 2008 from http://www.annefrank. org/content.asp?PID=406&LID=2.

Roger Ebert Reviews The Thin Man. Retrieved November 19, 2008 from http://rogerebert.suntimes.com/ apps/pbcs.dll/article?AID=/20021222/REVIEW S08/40802010/1023.

⊛ Sue Grafton

BORN: *1940, Louisville, Kentucky*

NATIONALITY: *American*

GENRE: *Fiction*

MAJOR WORKS:
The Lolly Madonna War (1969)
"A" Is for Alibi (1982)
"B" Is for Burglar (1985)
"O" Is for Outlaw (1998)
"T" Is for Trespass (2007)

Overview

Sue Grafton is often credited with introducing the hard-boiled woman detective. Her popular female detective, Kinsey Millhone, appeared initially in 1982 in *"A" Is for Alibi*, the beginning of a highly successful mystery series in which each new book is titled alphabetically. With copies of her books available in twenty-six different languages, and each new book reaching the best-seller list after initial publication, Grafton clearly holds a secure place as a monumental writer and renovator of the mystery genre.

Works in Biographical and Historical Context

Growing Up Fast Sue Taylor Grafton was born in Louisville, Kentucky, April 24, 1940, to Cornelius Warren Grafton and Vivian Harnsberger Grafton. She was the second of two children, three years younger than her

Sue Grafton *Grafton, Sue, 2002, photograph. AP Images.*

sister, Ann. Her father was a successful municipal-bond attorney, and her mother was a former high school chemistry teacher. Both parents were devoted lovers of literature, and the house was full of a wide variety of books, which the girls were encouraged to read. From her parents she learned a love of the written word and the pleasure of exploring ideas.

From her parents, however, Grafton also learned more painful lessons about human nature and personal relationships. Both parents were alcoholics. From the time that Sue was five years old, until her mother died fifteen years later, her mother lived in a nonfunctioning state of alcoholic stupor, with only periodic bouts of recovery. Her father drank a couple of jiggers of whiskey in the morning and headed out to work, leaving his daughters to fend for themselves and for their mother. Without adult guidance, Grafton did pretty much whatever she wanted to, which she credits as the perfect training for her writing career. Grafton began to write, both as a way to understand her daily life and as a way to escape from it. Writing became a way for her to ground herself.

Love, Marriage, and Tragedy

With dreams of becoming a writer, Grafton attended the University of Louisville where she majored in English. In 1959 Grafton transferred to Western Kentucky State Teachers College where she met and married her first husband, James L. Flood. She was only eighteen years old when they were wed. Their first child, Leslie, was born in January 1960, but the marriage was already beginning to break apart. Less than four months after Leslie's birth, Grafton's mother, stricken with cancer, committed suicide on Grafton's twentieth birthday. Grafton's second child, Jay, was born in 1961. Grafton went on to finish her studies at the University of Louisville. Soon afterward, when her son was only four months old, she and James Flood divorced.

Making Ends Meet

Grafton began graduate studies in English in 1961 at the University of Cincinnati. However, she did not like graduate school. She despised the intense analysis that she considered to be leaching the lifeblood out of literature. She left the program, more determined than ever to become a writer and to do it her own way. In the years that followed, Grafton worked a variety of jobs to pay the bills while she wrote short stories and novels at night. Ready for a relationship again, she married Al Schmidt in 1962. Her third child, Jamie, was born in 1966. At home with her children during the day, and working nights and weekends, Grafton continued to write. She wrote seven novels during the 1960s. She managed to publish her fourth and fifth works, *Keziah Dane* in 1967 and *The Lolly Madonna War* in 1969. In 1972 MGM studios bought the movie rights to *The Lolly Madonna War* for $25,000, the largest single amount Grafton had yet received for her writing, enough to suggest that she could make a living as a writer.

Success and Stability

Grafton's personal life wasn't going well, as her second marriage was crumbling. Selling the movie rights to *The Lolly Madonna War* gave her enough financial security to leave her second husband in 1972. She and Schmidt went through a bitter divorce. In fact, twelve years later when she published her first mystery novel she claimed that the specific impetus for the plot came out of her frustrations and anger over the custody fights she was still engaged in with Schmidt. Through the 1970s, Grafton continued to get work writing for television and movies. In 1974 she met Steven Humphrey and realized they were a good match. In 1975 Humphrey went to Ohio State University to begin the doctoral program in philosophy, and the following year Grafton joined him there, continuing to write screenplays and teleplays while living in Columbus. They were married in 1978 and have had a supportive, strong, and secure relationship for more than twenty years.

In this same period of growing personal stability in the late 1970s, Grafton also came to some major decisions about her writing career. She was comfortably successful as a screenwriter and thought she could continue to earn money in this way, but, again, she needed to be able to write her own way. Around 1977 she decided to focus on her solo writing. After her husband received his degree in 1981, they moved to Santa Barbara, where Grafton completed the first novel in the mystery series, *"A" Is for Alibi*, in 1982. For readers and reviewers alike the major appeal of the novel lies in the irrepressible central character, detective Kinsey Millhone. Kinsey Millhone is a professional private investigator who narrates the novels. She is a tough loner with few possessions, and a wisecracking cynic who plays along the edges of legality in her investigations. She willingly picks locks, steals mail, and tells lies. Yet, there is a core of morality unique to the detective for which she will unhesitatingly risk bodily harm. Millhone's dry wit, her combination of bravery and vulnerability, and her gritty determination to solve the case engaged audiences around the world.

An Alphabet of Millhone

Grafton took three years to produce the second novel in the series. *"B" Is for Burglar* appeared in 1985, after which a Millhone novel appeared annually through *"M" Is for Malice*, published in 1996. Beginning with *"N" Is for Noose* (1998), Grafton began to slow the pace to every eighteen months in order to ensure that she could maintain the quality of the work. Each novel had a larger first-edition print run than the previous one. Grafton continues to work her way through the alphabet and has declared that the last one will be titled *"Z" Is for Zero*. She claims that each book is the most difficult she has ever written. However, she has been able to sustain her series by continuing to find new situations for Millhone, new questions about human behavior for her to explore, and by letting Millhone evolve as a character. Grafton shares time between her homes in Montecito, California, and Louisville, Kentucky, where she gives classes and continues to write. After she published *"T" Is for Trespass* in 2007, only six letters in the alphabet remained for the completion of the alphabet series.

LITERARY AND HISTORICAL CONTEMPORARIES

Grafton's famous contemporaries include:

John Le Carré (1931–): English author of espionage thrillers, David John Moore Cornwell, spent several years working in the British Foreign Service as a secret agent, which forced him to write under the pseudonym John Le Carré.

Lawrence Block (1938–): Prolific American crime novelist known primarily for his series featuring the alcoholic New York detective Matt Scudder.

Stephen King (1947–): An American novelist and short-story writer specializing in the horror genre, perennial best-seller King has been successful in translating his books to film and is recognized as a pop culture icon.

Marcia Muller (1944–): Marcia Muller helped create the tough female detective genre with her books featuring detective Sharon McCone. She has written over twenty Sharon McCone novels.

Mikhail Gorbachev (1931–): Leader of the Soviet Union from 1985 to 1991, Gorbachev presided over the nation during the collapse of the Soviet empire, including the demolition of the Berlin Wall.

Works in Literary Context

Grafton writes in the tradition of hard-boiled detective fiction, popularized by writers such as Raymond Chandler and Dashiell Hammett, but she expands and revises the genre through a rich exploration of the psychology that lies behind the detective's actions, as well as the actions of other figures in her novels. She cares deeply about the private life and thoughts of her protagonist Kinsey Millhone. This psychological exploration may be explained through Grafton's own psychological journeys and the realization that Kinsey Millhone is Grafton's alter ego.

A New Style of Hard-Boiled Mystery Around 1977, when Grafton decided to concentrate on writing novels, she relished the idea of creating a female version of Dashiell Hammett's hard-boiled private eye Sam Spade, the type of private eye who relies on grit and brawn more than wits and intellect. After years of writing, however, Grafton has moved from considering the hard-boiled genre a form of escapist literature, with an emphasis on the tough persona of the detective as a figure of fantasy, to a belief that the detective novel allows for an examination of social issues. Her novels repeatedly explore issues of class divisions, corruption in the systems intended to permit society to function (such as the judiciary or health care systems), and divisive attitudes, such as ageism and homophobia. One theme receiving the most consistent and biting attention in her novels is a study in the many ways families can fail their members. The predominance of Grafton's theme of family pain and her abiding interest in the dark side of human motivations are not unexpected if one considers the author's own life, especially her troubled childhood.

The Alter Ego Grafton is unusual among writers in that she openly calls her central character her alter ego. She writes in *Kinsey and Me* (1992) that she sees Kinsey as "a stripped-down version of my 'self' ... a celebration of my own freedom, independence and courage." In one of the many parallels that can be drawn between Grafton's experience and that of her protagonist, a major family shift occurred when Grafton was five years old and her father returned from World War II, and her mother began to drink heavily. This is the same age at which Kinsey's parents died in a car accident. Grafton felt abandoned when her father left most of his estate to her stepmother. So it is no surprise that Kinsey Millhone fears abandonment above all else in life. Grafton's mapping of her own experience onto Kinsey's psyche is obvious, not only in the fear of abandonment but also in having Kinsey's parents' deaths close to her birthday, just as her own mother took her life on Grafton's birthday.

Works in Critical Context

Kinsey Millhone first appeared in 1982 in *"A" Is for Alibi*, beginning the highly successful series that continued with alphabetical titles. More than halfway through the alphabet and with more than 42 million copies of "A" through "T" sold in the United States alone, Grafton can be considered a successful innovator of the hard-boiled mystery genre.

"A" Is for Alibi Grafton published *"A" Is for Alibi* with a first-edition run of six thousand copies. She dedicated the novel to her father, who died just prior to its publication. It won the second Mysterious Stranger Award from the Cloak and Clue Society in Milwaukee, an award in the shape of a witch, which still perches on her computer as she writes. It was considered a well-crafted mainstream novel, rich in sensory details and complex characters. The plot twists are fast-paced and satisfying, and the dialogue has both realism and snap. The conclusion of the novel, however, came in for some negative commentary from reviewers. Stung by a few of the reviews, Grafton took three years to produce the second novel in the series.

"O" Is for Outlaw Kinsey becomes highly introspective in the novel *"O" Is for Outlaw* (1998). In one of the biggest surprises in the series, Grafton forces Kinsey to reevaluate leaving Mickey, her husband: She had walked out in 1972 when he asked her to give him an alibi for a night when he was accused of beating a suspect to death. By denying this, Kinsey later discovers that she may have contributed to Mickey's demise as he quit the police, drank too much, and lived and worked in shabby circumstances.

Admirably, Kinsey's persistent drive to balance the scales includes herself. If she was wrong about Mickey, she must seek his forgiveness and try to make it right. Emily Melton, in her review, welcomed *"O" Is for Outlaw* as a reversal of the leveling off she saw in Grafton's earlier novels. She says it is "a novel of depth and substance that is, in every way," the best of the series.

Responses to Literature

1. Grafton writes in the genre of hard-boiled detective fiction. Using your library and the Internet, find out more about the hard-boiled genre. What qualities make detective fiction hard-boiled? What are some of the challenges that might arise when creating a hard-boiled female detective?

2. Grafton's protagonist, Kinsey Millhone, is often considered a hard-boiled feminist. Using your library and the Internet, find out more about the feminist movement in the 1970s. What character traits would a feminist detective most likely have? Are there obstacles that a female detective would have to overcome that a male detective would not?

3. As Grafton has aged and matured, so, too, has her character Kinsey Millhone, growing ever more introspective and thoughtful with each novel. While reading Grafton's early novels, look for moments in which Kinsey is reacting impulsively. How do you think an older, more mature Kinsey would react? In Grafton's later works, look for moments when Kinsey is thoughtful, and consider how a younger Kinsey might have been portrayed in the earlier novels.

4. Kinsey Millhone is Sue Grafton's alter ego on paper. An alter ego's thoughts, ideas, and speech mirror those of the author's internal ideas. What elements of Kinsey's life and character do you think most likely represent Sue Grafton? What can a fictional alter ego accomplish that a true-life person might not be able to? Considering this, how might Kinsey and Sue be different?

BIBLIOGRAPHY

Books

Christianson, Scott. *Feminism in Women's Detective Fiction.* Toronto: University of Toronto Press, 1995.

Hevener Kaufman, Natalie, and Carol McGinnis Kay. *"G" Is for Grafton: The World of Kinsey Millhone.* New York: Henry Holt and Co., 1997.

Hoyser, Elizabeth. *Great Women Mystery Writers: Classic to Contemporary.* Westport, Conn.: Greenwood Press, 1994.

Irons, Glenwood. *Gender, Language, and Myth: Essays on Popular Narrative.* Toronto: University of Toronto Press, 1992.

Klein, Kathleen Gregory. *The Woman Detective: Gender and Genre.* Urbana: University of Illinois Press, 1988.

COMMON HUMAN EXPERIENCE

Grafton's popular crime novels feature the female private eye Kinsey Millhone. Here are some of Kinsey's female predecessors in the detective genre:

The Thin Man (1934), a novel by Dashiell Hammett. The husband-wife team of Nick and Nora Charles solves crimes in high style in this comic whodunit, made into a classic film starring William Powell and Myrna Loy.

Harriet the Spy (1964), a novel by Louis Fitzhugh. An eleven-year-old girl writes her stealthy observations and secret thoughts in a notebook in this charming children's novel.

Charlie's Angels (1976), a television show produced by Aaron Spelling. Three attractive women work as detectives for the mysterious Charlie in this titillating TV show, a hit for the ABC network.

Indemnity Only (1982), a novel by Sara Paretsky. This novel introduces V. I. Warshawski, a tough working-class Chicago private eye who tackles corporate wrongdoing. Paretsky's novels rival Grafton's in popularity.

Periodicals

Franklin, Barbara H., "'W' Is for Writer." *University of Louisville Alumni Magazine*, Fall 1995.

Schaffer, Rachel. "Grafton's Black Humor." *Armchair Detective* (Summer 1997).

Web sites

"Sue Grafton: Author of the Kinsey Millhone Mysteries." Retrieved November 23, 2008, from http://www.suegrafton.com/.

Collins, R. D. "The Hard Boiled School of Detective Fiction: A Brief History." Retrieved November 20, 2008, from http://www.classiccrimefiction.com/hardboiled.htm.

✹ Zane Grey

BORN: *1872, Zanesville, Ohio*

DIED: *1939, Altadena, California*

NATIONALITY: *American*

GENRE: *Fiction*

MAJOR WORKS:

The Last of the Plainsmen (1908)

The Heritage of the Desert (1910)

Riders of the Purple Sage (1912)

The U.P. Trail (1918)

The Vanishing American (1925)

Zane Grey   *Grey, Zane, photograph. AP Images.*

Overview

Zane Grey, often called the "father of the Western," holds an important place in American popular culture. A pioneer of the Western novel, Grey played a major role in creating the myth of the American cowboy. This myth promotes the independent, virile male in a rugged, demanding environment, praising the virtues of the primitive West over the cultivated East. Though they have been criticized as formulaic, Grey's works won him immense popularity. More than almost any modern American novelist, Zane Grey caught the imaginations of several generations of readers. From 1910 until 1925, his books appeared regularly on best-seller lists, and even today, in both hardcover and paperback, his fiction remains popular. His novels have been translated into so many languages and published in so many editions that exact sales figures are virtually impossible to ascertain, although estimates suggest that well over 130 million copies of his books have been sold during the past seventy-five years.

Works in Biographical and Historical Context

A Dentist with a Dream   Born in Zanesville, Ohio, on January 31, 1872, Pearl Zane Grey's boyhood was spent fishing and playing baseball, reading classics and dime novels, and scribbling his own short stories. At the University of Pennsylvania he played baseball and halfheartedly studied dentistry while he dreamed of a career as a writer. Graduating in 1896, he started a dental practice in New York City. From 1898 to 1904 he struggled to establish his practice, and it was during this period that he began writing articles on outdoor life for popular magazines, such as *Field and Stream*.

Tales of his Ancestors   His first attempt at realizing his dream was *Betty Zane* (1903), a fictional account of Grey's own Ohio ancestors. *Betty Zane*, and Grey's two subsequent efforts, were historical romances. Grey couldn't find a publisher, so he published the works at his own expense. Meanwhile, he had found his own romance with Lina Elise Roth, who unreservedly believed in his talent. With Lina's support, Grey closed his dental practice in 1904 to devote his time to writing.

A Trip to the Wild West   Grey received little encouragement for his writing, save from his wife, and he continued to gather rejection slips. Just as it seemed he would have to return to dentistry, he met "Buffalo" Jones, who suggested that Grey accompany him back to his Arizona ranch to observe the West firsthand and to write about Jones's efforts to crossbreed cattle with buffalo. Enthusiastically, Grey agreed, and he became entranced with Western life. He crossed the desert on horseback to the Grand Canyon, and along the way he participated in such unfamiliar activities as chasing buffalo, capturing wild horses, killing mountain lions, and exploring Indian ruins. He penned and published a nonfiction account of that 1907 visit called *The Last of the Plainsmen*.

The Romantic West   Grey had found his subject in the American West as a result of his visit to Arizona. He then recast his Western adventures in fictional form. Grey's own taste in literature was for the romantic, and he realized that the West was still close enough to frontier conditions for him to use it as a splendid testing ground of a man's worth. His first proper novel of the West, *The Heritage of the Desert* (1910), met only moderate sales. It tells the story of the rise to manhood of an Eastern misfit, John Hare. Hare's encounters with sandstorms and stampedes, and his battles with rustlers and gunmen, educate him in the ways of the West. He learns the Darwinian lesson that only the fittest survive, that he must kill or be killed, and thus he assimilates what Grey calls "the heritage of the desert." The novel ends peacefully with a vision of future happiness with the woman he loves. Grey had found in this work the elements of adventure, suspense, and history that he would continue to use to make himself the most popular writer of his time.

The Formula Works   This simple initiation formula, in which an Easterner grows from innocence to experience and to ultimate success in the West, is repeated variously in all of Grey's novels. Perhaps his most popular version of this formula can be found in *Riders of the Purple Sage* (1912), when Lassiter, a prototypical gunman with a mysterious past, rides into the life of Jane Withersteen, a woman beset by troubles. A series of violent confrontations with forces of evil teach Jane that she must fight, while Lassiter learns from her the influence of love. Although the crucial initiation is Jane's, for she absorbs the Darwinian lesson so important in Grey's thinking, the softening of Lassiter exemplifies the romantic side of Zane Grey's version of the West. *Riders of the Purple Sage* ensured that Grey's struggles to establish himself as a writer were at an end. From then on he easily outdistanced other American writers in sales and popular, although not critical, appreciation.

The West through New Eyes For the next decade, while he continued relying on his standard formula for inspiration, Grey infused his writing with creative energy and vigor. Each best seller tells a story that follows a similar pattern of initiation, but with modifications, transformations, and through fresh eyes. For example, the protagonist who matures after encountering the masculine West is a wealthy Eastern woman in *The Light of Western Stars* (1914). Grey's pages swarm with character types and themes in American life that writers had previously ignored and in some cases have yet to receive adequate literary attention. He told stories about Mormons, Mexicans, buffalo hunters, forest rangers, fishermen, the railroad, the telegraph, labor radicalism, and the list could be extended even further.

In his Western novels, Grey broke free from the nineteenth-century dime novel approach to adventure stories, making several important innovations. Grey created the figure of the mysterious outlaw or gunfighter enlisted to fight on the side of good. He wrote Western stories, particularly *The Light of Western Stars*, from a woman's point of view. He examined the love between an Indian chief and a white girl in *The Vanishing American* (1925). Finally, he established the motif of the Western environment as a test of character.

Grey's later novels began to lose their popular appeal. Hastily conceived and mechanically written, the plots grew more repetitive and the characters shallower. Nonetheless, his works continued to sell. Even after his death in 1939, his publishers kept bringing out his unfinished manuscripts, and today Grey still ranks among the bestselling popular novelists of all time.

Works in Literary Context

Despite flagrant excesses of style and awkward language, Grey gave people what they wanted. Opening one of his 63 novels, or attending one of the 105 feature films based on his stories, his enthusiasts approached an imaginative frontier. There they could find an affirmation of traditional values. They could share in a successful initiation

---

LITERARY AND HISTORICAL CONTEMPORARIES

Grey's famous contemporaries include:

William S. Hart (1870–1946): American actor of the silent screen who became the most well-known star of Westerns.

Jack London (1876–1916): American author of adventure stories such as *The Call of the Wild* (1903).

Charles Chaplin (1889–1977): An English comedy actor whose silent film role as the "Tramp" made him the first major worldwide movie star.

Agatha Christie (1890–1976): This English novelist published mysteries and plays starting in the 1920s. She is one of the most renowned authors worldwide.

F. Scott Fitzgerald (1896–1940): A novelist of the Jazz Age, Fitzgerald illuminated the Eastern bourgeois lifestyle in his novels and short stories.

Georgia O'Keeffe (1887–1986): O'Keeffe, an American painter who was inspired by the American Southwest and desert life, was famous for her bright colors and larger-than-life flowers.

Woodrow Wilson (1856–1924): President of the United States from 1913 to 1921, Wilson guided the nation through the First World War.

---

process. They could escape from the pressures of the twentieth century. Rather than teach his readers about modern life, Grey tantalized them with the possibilities of romance, providing along the way some of the finest descriptions of nature in Western writing.

Western Fiction Grey embellished with his own richly pictorial imagination an adaptation of the "easterner goes West to learn about life" pattern of Owen Wister's bestselling *The Virginian* (1902). Grey used vivid descriptions of Western landscapes and popular, formulaic plots to establish the "Western" as a distinct literary genre. Critics agree that Grey's depiction of the Western landscape was one of the strongest elements of his writing. "He portrays it as an acid test of those elemental traits of character which he admires," writes T. K. Whipple in *Study Out the Land: Essays*. "It kills off the weaklings, and among the strong it makes the bad worse and the good better. Nature to him is somewhat as God is to a Calvinist—ruthlessly favoring the elect and damning the damned."

Romanticism Critics now believe that Grey should be read as a romantic rather than a realistic writer. He gained his knowledge of the West through firsthand experience, making many trips there, and performed extensive research on historical background, especially for *The U.P. Trail* (1918), his history of the transcontinental railroad. However, he was more interested in portraying heroic figures

COMMON HUMAN EXPERIENCE

Grey's novels relate the experience of the protagonist's growth through trial and hardship to determine true inner strength. Here are some other literary works that delve into the rite of passage from different angles.

The Red Badge of Courage (1895), a novel by Stephen Crane. This novel tells the story of a young man growing up surrounded by the death and destruction of the Civil War.

Adventures of Huckleberry Finn (1884), a novel by Mark Twain. In this American classic, a young boy learns who his friends truly are during an adventurous raft trip down the Mississippi River.

The General (1927), a film written and directed by Clyde Bruckman and Buster Keaton. A young engineer, turned away when he tries to enlist in the Confederate Army, proves his mettle in a locomotive chase in this silent comedy acclaimed as one of the cinema's finest achievements.

The Curious Incident of the Dog in the Night-Time (2003), a novel by Mark Haddon. This novel details the confusion in the life of a young autistic boy dealing with the implosion of his parents' relationship.

pitted against forces of evil or nature to triumph or perish, rather than fully dimensional characters.

There are many romantic elements in Grey's works. The grand scale of scenery and action in Grey's stories can be considered the first of these. The action, too, is appropriately intense yet extravagant and vividly portrayed. Another typically romantic characteristic of Grey's books is his nostalgia for an earlier, simpler, and morally more vital time, which grows out of a disenchantment with modern middle-class culture. Grey's heroes are more than merely doers of mighty deeds that rebuke the weaklings of the present. There is a more highly developed philosophical discontent behind their actions. Grey's Eastern characters represent the decadence and failure of bourgeois cultural aspirations that can only be cured by a return to a more natural moral system. These inclinations in his work link him to the tradition of the English romantic poets, as well as romantic modernists, such as D. H. Lawrence.

Works in Critical Context

Grey never received the critical acclaim his popular audience felt he deserved. Many critics attacked the lack of realism in his novels, pointing out that his stories were melodramatic and nostalgic, that he fumbled love scenes to an embarrassing degree, that his plots were often unbe-

lievable, and that his characters were never complete. Other critics, apologizing for his faults, attempted to illustrate his literary attributes and contributions. Recently, critics have become receptive to the works of Zane Grey, suggesting that he excelled as a writer of romance, a peculiar literary genre outside the rules and criteria of realism.

The Heritage of the Desert Grey's first Western romance, *The Heritage of the Desert*, introduced the thematic pattern that he used repeatedly throughout his career, the "rite of passage." This pattern focused on the innocent initiated into a new world, the outsider who must face conflict and emerge as a hero or heroine with a new understanding of life. For Grey, the West, with its distinctive moral and symbolic landscape, offered a unique setting for the development of this theme. The harsh realities of the country and the violence of a lawless society provided a field of action wherein his protagonists, usually high-bred Easterners, would learn to confront their environment and discover their basic human values. Despite the critical debates as to his place in the literary world, there is no doubt that Zane Grey was a first-rate storyteller. His novels have reached an estimated fifty-one million readers, and many movies have been adapted from his works. Through his colorful descriptions and romantic images, Grey brought the Old West to life for millions of readers. Danney Goble states in the *Journal of Arizona History*: "Within a few years the plots and characters would become standard. But Grey's combination of brutal violence and saccharine romance—a heady mixture all but unknown to his predecessors in the writing of frontier fiction—established his claim to a gold mine which he exploited time and again."

Riders of the Purple Sage Many critics believe *Riders of the Purple Sage* is Grey's best novel, mainly because he loosened the restraints of his formula and allowed the story to grow at its own pace. Grey affirmed the idealistic principle behind his writing when he acknowledged that his fiction spoke to "the spirit, not the letter, of life." Certainly this is true of *Riders of the Purple Sage*, where one finds violence mixed with romantic interludes and panoramic scenery. Designed for readers who sought the pleasures of escaping into romance rather than for those who wanted to read about the realities of Western life, *Riders of the Purple Sage* presents a fictional frontier where might finally is synonymous with right and where idyllic dreams do come true.

Responses to Literature

1. Grey's novels tell the story of Eastern men discovering their true spirit in the West. Use your library and the Internet to find out more about "the roaring twenties" of the East Coast Jazz Age. Why would readers consider an Easterner as inferior in the Western environment? How were the East Coast and the West different in the 1920s?

2. During the 1920s the automobile was gaining popularity, conflicting directly with the industries that depended on horses. Using your library and the Internet, research the societal conflicts that were debated during the popularization of the automobile. Why do you think horses remained as the principal form of transportation in the West so much longer than they did in the East?

3. Grey's works have been reexamined in a new romantic light. Choose a scene from Grey's works that best exemplifies the major romantic elements in his fiction. How does the narrator describe the environment? What elements of the action could be considered romantic?

4. The rugged Western environment often acted as an antagonist as much as any of the characters in Grey's fiction. Citing one or more of Grey's works, describe how the environment is a character in the book. How does the protagonist have to deal with the environment? Does the environment influence his journey in a positive or a negative way?

BIBLIOGRAPHY

Books

Cawelti, Jahon G. *The Six-Gun Mystique*. Bowling Green, Ohio: Bowling Green University Popular Press, 1971.

Farley, G. M. *Zane Grey, a Documented Portrait: The Man, the Bibliography, the Filmography*. New Orleans: Portals Press, 1985.

Gay, Carol. *Zane Grey, Story-Teller*. Columbus: State Library of Ohio, 1979.

Gruber, Frank. *Zane Grey: A Biography*. Tulsa: World Publishing, 1970.

Kant, Candace C. *Zane Grey's Arizona*. Flagstaff, Ariz.: Northland Press, 1984.

Kimball, Arthur G. *Ace of Hearts: The Westerns of Zane Grey*. Fort Worth: Texas Christian University Press, 1993.

May, Stephen J. *Zane Grey: Romancing the West*. Athens: Ohio University Press, 1997.

Ronald, Ann. *Zane Grey*. Boise: Boise State University, 1975.

Warren, Don. *A Bibliographical Checklist of the Writings of Zane Grey*. Collinsville, Conn.: Country Lane Books, 1986.

✹ John Grisham

BORN: *1955, Jonesboro, Arkansas*

NATIONALITY: *American*

GENRE: *Fiction*

MAJOR WORKS:

A Time to Kill (1989)

The Firm (1991)

The Pelican Brief (1992)

The Chamber (1996)

The Appeal (2008)

John Grisham *Grisham, John, 1992, photograph. Frank Capri / Hulton Archive / Getty Images.*

Overview

The immensely popular author of thrillers in which the major characters are lawyers confronting dangerous situations, John Grisham is best known for his novel *The Firm* (1991), which centers around a recent Harvard Law School graduate who, after learning that his firm is heavily involved in organized crime, risks his life to help the Federal Bureau of Investigation (FBI) indict his associates and their Mob bosses. It is no understatement that John Grisham has achieved the status of a genuine pop-culture icon. His works perennially spend months on the best-seller lists, have numbered more than 60 million in print across the world, and have been translated into thirty-one languages. Dubbed "grab-it-at-the-airport" novels, they have also made their author a multimillionaire.

Works in Biographical and Historical Context

Moving Around John Grisham was born in Jonesboro, Arkansas, on February 8, 1955. During his childhood he and his family moved frequently so his father, an itinerant construction worker, could find employment. As a boy, Grisham didn't dream of becoming a writer but rather a professional baseball player. However, he was an avid reader. Each time the family took up residence in a new town, Grisham would immediately go to the public library to get a library card. In 1967, when Grisham was twelve years old, the family moved to a more permanent home in Southaven, Mississippi. There Grisham enjoyed greater success in high school athletics than he did in English composition, a subject in which he earned a D grade.

Learning Law   After graduating from high school, Grisham attended Mississippi State University where he earned a degree in accounting. He went on to earn his law degree at the University of Mississippi, anticipating a career as a tax attorney, but quickly changed to criminal defense, which he found more interesting. Shortly after graduating from law school, Grisham married Renee Jones and returned to Southaven where he set up a small practice as a defense attorney.

Although his practice was successful, Grisham was not happy and grew restless. He switched to the more lucrative field of civil law and won many cases, but a sense of personal dissatisfaction remained. Hoping to somehow make a difference in the world, he entered politics with the aim of reforming the educational system in Mississippi, historically one of the nation's poorest states. Running as a Democrat, he won a post in the state legislature in 1984. Four years later, he was reelected. After a total of six years in public office, Grisham, convinced that he would never be able to cut through the red tape of government bureaucracy in his effort to improve Mississippi's educational system, resigned his post in 1990.

"What If…"   While practicing law, Grisham heard the gripping testimony of a young girl who was raped and left for dead. Unable to stop thinking about the case, Grisham began to wonder what would have happened if the victim's father had killed the rapist and were put on trial. This "what if …" situation became the impetus for his first novel. Set in fictional Clanton, Mississippi, *A Time to Kill* (1989) centers around the trial of a black Vietnam veteran who murders two white men after they brutally rape his ten-year-old daughter. The novel relates attorney Jake Brigance's defense of the grieving father before an all-white jury as well as the numerous attempts made on Brigance's life by the Ku Klux Klan. Writing his first novel, let alone publishing it, was no easy task for Grisham. Already working seventy hours a week in his law practice, Grisham had to work on his manuscript at five in the morning for three years.

Finishing the manuscript in 1987, Grisham next had to look for an agent. He was turned down by several before finally receiving a positive response. Agent and author encountered a similarly difficult time trying to find a publisher. Wynwood Press finally agreed to publish five thousand copies of the book, and Grisham received a check for $15,000. He purchased a thousand copies of the book himself, peddling them at meetings and libraries and giving many of them away to family and friends.

Already Writing the Next One   Despite the limited initial success of *A Time to Kill*, Grisham was not discouraged from trying his hand at another novel. In fact he had already started work on his second novel, the day after he finished *A Time to Kill*. The second time around, he decided to follow guidelines set forth in a *Writer's Digest* article for plotting a suspense novel. The result was *The Firm* (1991), the story of a corrupt Memphis-based law firm established by organized crime for purposes of shielding and falsifying earnings. Recruited to the practice is Mitchell McDeere, a promising Harvard law graduate who is overwhelmed by the company's apparent extravagance. When he runs afoul of the good guys, McDeere finds himself in seemingly endless danger.

Grisham was not as motivated when writing *The Firm* as he had been when composing *A Time to Kill*, but with his wife's encouragement he finished the book. Before he even began trying to sell the manuscript, he learned that someone had acquired a bootlegged copy of it and was willing to give him $600,000 to turn it into a movie script. Within two weeks, Doubleday, one of the many publishers that had previously rejected *A Time to Kill*, offered Grisham a contract. The novel was listed on the *New York Times* best-seller list for nearly a year and sold approximately ten times as many copies as its predecessor. By the time the film version was released, there were more than 7 million copies of *The Firm* in print. This amazing success gave Grisham the means to build his dream house, quit his law practice, and devote himself entirely to writing.

Formula-Driven Success   In a mere hundred days, Grisham wrote his follow-up to *The Firm*. Another legal thriller, *The Pelican Brief* (1992) tells the story of a brilliant, beautiful female law student named Darby Shaw. When two Supreme Court justices are murdered, Shaw hypothesizes as to why the crimes were committed. Soon she is running for her life, while bravely continuing to investigate the conspiracy. In reviewing *The Pelican Brief*, some critics complained that Grisham had followed the premise of *The Firm* far too closely. Despite such criticism, Grisham was also praised for creating another exciting story. Made into a film starring Denzel Washington and Julia Roberts, *The Pelican Brief* enjoyed success comparable to *The Firm*, selling millions of copies.

Six months later, Grisham put together another best-seller, titled *The Client* (1993). This legal thriller focuses on a young boy who, after learning a sinister secret, turns to a motherly lawyer for protection from both the Mob and the FBI. Like *The Firm* and *The Pelican Brief*, the book drew lukewarm reviews but became a best seller and a major motion picture. For a time in the spring of 1993, after *The Client* came out and *A Time to Kill* was republished, Grisham was in the rare and enviable position of having a book at the top of the hardcover best-seller list and books in the first, second, and third spots on the paperback best-seller list. Grisham has acknowledged that his second, third, and fourth books were formula-driven. He also admitted to rushing through the writing of *The Pelican Brief* and *The Client*, which resulted in lower-quality books. Yet, he also complained that the critical community treats popular writers harshly.

A Novel a Year With his fifth novel, Grisham departed from his proven formula and proceeded at a more leisurely pace. He took a full nine months to write *The Chamber* (1994), a book in which the "good guys" and "bad guys" are not as clearly defined as in his previous efforts. The novel tells the tale of Ku Klux Klansman Sam Cayhall, who is on death row for the murder of two young sons of a Jewish civil rights attorney. After languishing in prison for years, Cayhall is surprised by the arrival of his estranged grandson, Adam Hall. Hall, an attorney, sets out to reverse his grandfather's death sentence, even though he considers Sam to be the family demon. The novel is a careful study of a family's history, an examination of the relationship between lawyer and client, and a description of life on death row.

Grisham has continued writing a novel a year. He has realized greater success than most writers will enjoy in a lifetime. When not writing, Grisham spends time with his daughter Shea and son Ty. Grisham lives with his family, sharing time between one home in Mississippi and another in Charlottesville, Virginia. He also spends time devoted to philanthropic causes. In 2005 he and his wife started the Rebuild the Coast Fund organization to help Hurricane Katrina victims after the devastating hurricane destroyed much of the southern coast. He still loves baseball and is an avid fan of his son Ty's team. Grisham serves as the local Little League commissioner and has built several ball fields on his property where kids can play.

Works in Literary Context

When Grisham began writing his first novel, he never dreamed that he would become one of America's best-selling novelists and help create the new genre of "legal thriller." Yet, the appeal of books such as *The Firm, The Pelican Brief*, and *The Client* has been so great that the reading public regularly buys millions of copies of his books, and nearly all of his novels have been turned into major motion pictures.

Legal Thrillers Grisham, along with lawyer-turned-writer Scott Turow, is credited with developing the legal thriller, a sub-genre of crime fiction. In legal thrillers, the action is narrated from the point of view of the lawyer, just as most crime fiction is narrated from the perspective of the police or detective. Differing from other crime fiction is the fact that the protagonist is a regular person, not a crime fighter equipped to face dangerous situations. However, upon uncovering truth and justice through intellectual investigation, the protagonist finds himself in peril, and in order to save himself or his clients, he must perform heroic deeds.

LITERARY AND HISTORICAL CONTEMPORARIES

Grisham's famous contemporaries include:

Tom Clancy (1947–): An American author specializing in high-tech espionage novels that have been successfully turned into movies.

Scott Turow (1949–): An American author of popular thrillers such as *Presumed Innocent* (1987) and a practicing lawyer in Chicago.

Bill Clinton (1946–): Served as president of the United States from 1993 to 2001. He presided over the economic boom period fueled by the Internet revolution.

Bill Gates (1955–): Gates founded Microsoft software company in 1976, which became the dominant software developer for PC computers in the 1990s, making Gates among the world's wealthiest men.

Stephen King (1947–): An American novelist and short story writer specializing in the horror genre. King has been successful in translating his books to film and is recognized as a pop culture icon.

Amy Tan (1952–): Tan is an American writer whose works focus on the cultural and generational gaps between successive generations of Chinese Americans.

Southern Literature Many of Grisham's works take place in the South. His first book, *A Time to Kill*, is set in a fictional Mississippi town. *The Firm* narrates the story of a lawyer in a high-powered Memphis law firm. And his novel *The Chamber* (1994) chronicles the family saga of a Mississippi family whose patriarch is awaiting execution on death row. Grisham's work has traits of Southern Gothic literature with its wide cast of seedy, loathsome characters. Following in the footsteps of fellow Mississippian William Faulkner, Grisham reveals the sordid underbelly of Southern social issues such as racism and prejudice in the legal system through his literature.

Works in Critical Context

Although his novels are sometimes characterized as simplistic, lacking plausible plots and developed characters, Grisham is often praised for highly suspenseful, compelling narratives that display his extensive legal knowledge. Some critics have argued that Grisham displays considerable talent as a writer, maintaining that his characterizations are accurate and well developed and his dialogue arresting and realistic. Like a composer, he brings all his themes together at the crucial moment for a gripping, and logical, finale.

A Time to Kill Upon its initial publication in 1989, *A Time to Kill* received very little critical attention, but the overwhelming success of *The Firm* sparked interest in Grisham's first novel, which was then praised by critics as

COMMON HUMAN EXPERIENCE

In Grisham's novels, ordinary people are called upon to perform extraordinary, heroic feats in order to save themselves and to right injustices. Here are some other literary works that delve into the theme of ordinary man turned hero:

To Kill a Mockingbird (1960), a novel by Harper Lee. An Alabama lawyer named Atticus Finch bravely defends a black man accused of raping a white woman.

Presumed Innocent (1987), a novel by Scott Turow. A prosecutor who must prove his innocence when accused of the murder of one of his colleagues. In order to do so, he must solve the crime.

The Kite Runner (2003), a novel by Khaled Hosseini. A successful writer returns to Afghanistan to rescue the son of his best friend, whom he abandoned in wartime.

In the Time of the Butterflies (1994), a novel by Julia Alvarez. The Mirabal sisters struggle for freedom during the Trujillo dictatorship in the Dominican Republic.

forceful, dramatic, and thought-provoking. Commentators cited Grisham's legal expertise as well as his authentic portrayal of customs and values in the American South as some of the strengths of *A Time to Kill*. It has been praised for its compelling plot, use of complex legal details, and commentary on such controversial topics as racism and vigilantism. *A Time to Kill* is now considered by some as the finest of Grisham's novels.

The Firm Upon *The Firm*'s publication, several reviewers argued that Grisham had not attained a high art form, although it was generally conceded that he had put together a compelling and thrilling narrative. *Los Angeles Times Book Review* critic Charles Champlin wrote that the "character penetration is not deep, but the accelerating tempo of paranoia-driven events is wonderful." The *Library Journal* noted that Grisham "set a daringly high standard, one that his readers will hope he can reach again and again." Grisham is clearly able to captivate the reader with his blend of intriguing legal predicaments, high tension, and unexpected plot twists.

Responses to Literature

1. Grisham's novels often tell the story of a person who has been unjustly accused of a crime. Using your library and the Internet, find out more about false convictions in the United States. What changes occurred regarding the death penalty in the United States in the 1990s? What types of evidence are commonly used to overturn false convictions? Why would the topic of a false conviction make an appealing thriller?

2. Grisham's novel *The Chamber* tells the story of a Ku Klux Klan (KKK) member and his family. Using your library and the Internet, research the history of the KKK. Is the KKK still active in the South or elsewhere in the United States? Should an organization based on hate and violence enjoy all the liberties guaranteed by the U.S. Constitution?

3. Grisham's works are characterized by compelling action and fast-moving dialogue. Choose a scene from Grisham's works that best exemplifies these two elements. Describe how the narrator keeps the action moving. How does the dialogue contribute to the action?

4. Grisham has been credited with taking complex legal issues and translating them to the reader in simple, yet complete explanations. Examine the language of a legal explanation in Grisham's works. How is Grisham's legal language different from the rest of the language in the book?

BIBLIOGRAPHY

Books

Best, Nancy. *Readings on John Grisham*. San Diego: Greenhaven Press, 2003.

Conley-Weaver, Robyn. *John Grisham*. San Diego: Lucent Books, 1999.

Guest, David. *Sentenced to Death: The American Novel and Capital Punishment*. Jackson: University Press of Mississippi, 1997.

Lanier, Nace Y. *Theology of John Grisham*. Dallas: Dallas Theological Seminary, 2000.

Pringle, Mary Beth. *John Grisham: A Critical Companion*. Westport, Conn.: Greenwood Press, 1997.

Schaller, Barry R. *A Vision of American Law: Judging Law, Literature, and the Stories We Tell*. Westport, Conn.: Praeger, 1997.

Periodicals

Diggs, Terry K. "Through a Glass Darkly: John Grisham and Scott Turow Lay Down the Law for Millions of Americans. Just What Is It They're Trying to Tell Us?" *ABA Journal* (October 1996).

Web sites

John Grisham: The Official Site. Retrieved December 1, 2008, from http://www.randomhouse.com/features/grisham/main.php.

The Mississippi Writer's Page: John Grisham. Retrieved December 1, 2008, from http://www.olemiss.edu/depts/english/ms-writers/dir/grisham_john.

✺ Judith Guest

BORN: *1936, Detroit, Michigan*

NATIONALITY: *American*

GENRE: *Fiction*

MAJOR WORKS:
Ordinary People (1976)
Second Heaven (1982)
Killing Time in St. Cloud (1988)
Errands (1997)
The Tarnished Eye (2004)

Overview

Judith Guest is a best-selling author, known primarily for her first two novels, *Ordinary People* and *Second Heaven*. Both books are set in contemporary middle-class suburbia, both have a troubled adolescent male as a central figure, and both portray characters grappling with such problems as suicide, depression, divorce, and child abuse. Guest illuminates common problems that many families struggle through, with a storytelling skill that makes the reader feel that no problem is truly ordinary.

Works in Biographical and Historical Context

A Transient Childhood Judith Guest was born on March 29, 1936, in Detroit, Michigan. She was the oldest of four siblings. In her childhood, her family moved around while her father, an aspiring businessman, tried different jobs. When she was eight the family moved to Oscoda, Michigan, so that her father could try his luck at another business. Guest's mother did not like living in the country, and as a result the family soon moved back to Detroit, where they lived with Guest's grandparents before settling into an apartment and into the city again. Guest attended many grade schools during this time. However, the family owned a small cabin on Lake Huron where they would always spend their summers, and this fact lent a sense of stability to her early years. The family still owns the cabin today.

Raising a Family Guest began writing when she was twelve, but she never shared any of her work with her family. After graduating from high school she attended the University of Michigan and began studying English and psychology. Intimidated by the creative writing classes, she chose a career as a teacher rather than a writer and graduated with a degree in education in 1958. That same year Guest married Larry Lavercombe, a business executive. She became pregnant with her first son, and took a job teaching first grade. With the birth of two more boys, her family and work life consumed her days. Guest put aside her writing to raise her three boys, Larry, John, and Richard.

Judith Guest   *Guest, Judith, 1976, photograph. AP Images.*

The Decision to Write During the 1970s Guest and her family were living in Palatine, Illinois, a Chicago suburb. As her boys entered school, Guest was once again able to look at a career of writing. For a short time she worked for various newspapers, and tried her hand at journalistic writing. She did not like the constraints and deadlines of journalism and soon took up fiction again. In 1970 she wrote a short story and sent it to a contest, where it placed sixtieth out of one hundred entrants.

The war in Vietnam was at its height and American society was becoming more fragmented. After taking a writing seminar, Guest was inspired to translate the nuances of this fractured contemporary suburban life onto the pages of fiction. In 1975 she decided to dedicate herself completely to writing her first novel. She worked for three years on *Ordinary People*. Guest states that her decision to concentrate on finishing her project was the most important decision she has made about her writing.

The Publishing Game After Guest finished *Ordinary People* she sent the manuscript to two publishers who both sent her biting rejection letters. The second publisher stated that the writing was not capable of sustaining a reader's interest. Undeterred, Guest sent the manuscript to Viking Press. When submitting a manuscript, writers usually send a cover letter with a book summary and the first two or three chapters to a potential publisher. An interested publisher will contact the writer and solicit the rest of the manuscript. Guest however, had

LITERARY AND HISTORICAL CONTEMPORARIES

Judith Guest's famous contemporaries include:

Jimmy Carter (1924–): The thirty-ninth president of the United States, from 1977 to 1980, Carter presided over the nation during hard economic times, with record inflation and high interest rates.

Colleen McCullough (1937–): McCullough is an Australian novelist whose book *The Thorn Birds* was a best seller in 1977.

Toni Morrison (1931–): An American Nobel Prize–winning novelist, Morrison details the lives of black Americans through their many struggles and emotional trials.

Jack Nicholson (1937–): This American actor won an Academy Award for best actor for his portrayal of a man in an insane asylum in the film *One Flew over the Cuckoo's Nest* in 1975. He often portrays dark and disturbed characters.

sent her entire manuscript, which Viking Press held for eight months before replying that they were indeed interested in publishing the work. This made *Ordinary People* the first unsolicited manuscript accepted by Viking Press in twenty-six years.

Success and Hollywood *Ordinary People*, the story of a family torn apart by the untimely death of a child, was an instant success. The novel was selected by four book clubs, serialized in *Redbook*, and had paperback rights sold to Ballantine for $635,000. In 1980, Robert Redford made his directorial debut and won an Oscar when he adapted *Ordinary People* for the screen. Guest herself approved of the ending, which was more inconclusive than the ending of the book. She also commended the acting, particularly Mary Tyler Moore's portrayal of Beth, the mother. The film adaptation created an even bigger audience for Guest's work.

Guest has written other novels, including *Second Heaven*, which appeared in 1982, *Killing Time in St. Cloud*, a work written with Rebecca Hill, and *Errands*. As with her first novel, these works present ordinary people dealing with extraordinary circumstances, struggling to maintain connections with others in the midst of loss and grief.

Still Writing Today Guest lives in Edina, Minnesota, with her husband, her three sons, and seven grandchildren. She continues to write, and is working on a sequel to her mystery novel *The Tarnished Eye* (2004).

Works in Literary Context

Guest's works describe the decline of traditional society and the family. The content of her stories was inspired by her childhood. Guest has said that her interest in cold and emotionally distant characters originates in experiences with her own relatives. Her father did not share his feelings openly. For example, he never told his daughter about the pain he must have felt when he was ten years old and his own father died. Guest translated these experiences into the pages of her suburban novels in a believable and realistic manner.

The Suburban Novel After the Second World War, baby boomers left the cities and moved into nicely manicured suburbs. There, everything from the lawn to the picket fence was maintained in a neat and orderly fashion. However, Guest's books capture the pain and suffering that occurs behind the closed doors of the apparent suburban bliss. In Guest's works the forms of civility between the characters are maintained through a cold, self-controlled lack of emotional expression. The orderliness of the characters' lives contrasts sharply with the agony that they are feeling, despite the superficial gloss that they show the world. Emotions are expressed through subtle body language or changes in routine behaviors. For example, stress is perceived when a character puts too many ice cubes in the evening martini. Guest shows the reader, in this new type of suburban novel, that there is real tension behind the manicured lawns, although it just might be covered up with a quick spray of perfume.

Realism Guest's works have been credited for their realism in portraying the complexities and sensitivities of family relationships. Although her characters are appealing and intelligent, they are depicted as they appear in everyday life. Guest's characters are not glamorized, but rather portrayed realistically. This allows the reader to see the ugly, sordid side of their inner thoughts. Guest's dialogue also reveals true teen angst and reasoning. The anxiety of adolescence is revealed in the smooth and realistic dialogue.

Works in Critical Context

While *Ordinary People* was an instant popular success, many critics considered it too plain in tone, with an unrealistic conclusion. However, the underlying irony of the work was praised by others, as well as the sensitive and realistic depiction of teen angst. *Second Heaven* also received critical recognition for realistically portraying the complications of contemporary adolescent life. In both novels, Guest describes with sympathy those who, for the most part, live or aspire to live on that middle ground where good and evil struggle, where happiness is not expected to come easily, and where love has more to do with giving than with taking.

Ordinary People Guest's *Ordinary People*, was judged a rather bland and far from ironic novel, yet its title hints at a complicated irony. On the one hand, the book suggests, there are no ordinary people, but rather that all people are extraordinary in their pain and suffering. And on the other hand, ordinary people are what the characters' hope to become, if they can conquer their fears. Regarding *Ordinary People*, the critic Lee L. Lemon said in his article "First Novel," "It tours through the stereotypes of much contemporary fiction so precisely and so humanely that the reader cares."

For reviewer Melvin Maddocks in *Time*, "The author writes almost too unerringly clever dialogue. Everything is buried in the ubiquitous wisecrack—the ironic putdowns and self-putdowns by which Americans play tag with their terror of failure." But Maddocks also acknowledged the success of the book. Guest "has written a truly haunted story in which agony gives gloss a run for the money. The Furies in her suburb are real, even if she seems to banish them with a spray of Airwick." The reviewer for *Kirkus Reviews* took a similarly positive view, commenting that the book succeeded in "communicating a sense of life both felt and experienced without ever trespassing beyond actuality. *Ordinary People* is an exceptionally real book."

Second Heaven It took Guest seven years to write *Second Heaven*. Her acute perceptions of how most people feel and think makes her second novel especially significant. She avoids the sensational, knowing that restrained reporting of the unpleasant is more effective. The main characters are a trio of two adults and an adolescent, whose lives resemble three lines narrowing until they meet, rather than three points of a triangle destined always to be separate. Critic Judith Chettle reflects, "In describing the journey of these three people to a satisfactory equilibrium, she has given us a book that is neither pop schlock nor great literature but a work of humanity and good sense to which we can respond with pleasure." Jonathan Yardley, in the *Washington Post Book World*, thought the novel a worthy successor to *Ordinary People*. He wrote that "Guest is an extraordinarily perceptive observer of the minutiae of domestic life, and she writes about them with humor and affection."

Responses to Literature

1. In *Ordinary People* Guest examines the effects of grief and depression on a family. Using your library and the Internet, research modern mental-health treatment and the history of mental-health treatment. How were those suffering from depression and other psychological afflictions dealt with fifty years ago? A hundred years ago? How have both the mental-health field and societal perceptions of mental illness changed since the book was written?

2. Guest takes a look at one family's reaction and grief over the loss of a loved one. Using your library and the Internet, find out how other cultures deal with death. Pick two cultures from two different continents and research funeral traditions. In what ways are the grieving processes from these cultures different or similar to those in the United States? How are

> # COMMON HUMAN EXPERIENCE
>
> Guests's books detail the ironic trivialities of modern life in the face of tragedy. Here are some other literary works that examine the banality of life during stressful moments.
>
> *Catch-22* (1961), a novel by Joseph Heller. This work chronicles the bureaucratic operation at the end of World War II, painting with humor the requirements that soldiers have to complete in the face of battle, death, and despair.
>
> *The Accidental Tourist* (1985), a novel by Anne Tyler. This narrative is the story of Macon Leary, whose family begins to disintegrate after the loss of his son in a senseless killing.
>
> *The Sun Also Rises* (1926), a novel by Ernest Hemingway. The author here explores the complications of relationships through the everyday rabble-rousing of a group of American friends living in Europe.

they similar or different from the action in *Ordinary People*?

3. Guest was credited with portraying adolescent speech very realistically. While reading Guest's early novels analyze one scene of teen dialogue. Does it seem realistic to you? How has youth-culture language changed since the publication? Rewrite the scene to express the same ideas using contemporary teen language.

4. Many of Guest's characters are emotionally cold and do not allow themselves to express their emotions with words. While reading Guest's works, look for the subtle ways in which one character reveals his or her emotions without words. Make a list of the character's actions and how each action reveals the character's emotions and what that emotion is.

BIBLIOGRAPHY

Periodicals

Braginsky, Dorothea. "Review of *Ordinary People*." *Psychology Today* (August, 1976).

Chettle, Judith. "Fine Novel of Ordinary Lives." *Christian Science Monitor* (November 7, 1982).

Chettle, Judith. "Dazed by School." *Chicago Tribune* (November 20, 1988).

Dickstein, Lore. Review of *Ordinary People*. *New York Times Book Review* (July 18, 1976).

Lemon, Lee L. "First Novel." *Prairie Schooner* (Winter 1976/1977).

Maddocks, Melvin. "Suburban Furies." *Time* (July 19, 1976): 68, 70.

Review of *Ordinary People. Kirkus Reviews* (March 1, 1976): 271.

Thorburn, David. Review of *Ordinary People. The Yale Review* (Summer 1977).

Wood, Michael. "Crying for Attention." *New York Review of Books* (June 10, 1976).

Yardley, Jonathan. "Earth and Heaven: Judith Guest's Encore to *Ordinary People.*" *Washington Post Book World* (September 22, 1982): B1, B15.

Web sites

Judith Guest: The Official Site. Retrieved December 6, 2008, from http://www.judithguest.com.

❊ John Gunther

BORN: *1901, Chicago, Illinois*

DIED: *1970, New York, New York*

NATIONALITY: *American*

GENRE: *Nonfiction, fiction*

MAJOR WORKS:

Bright Nemesis (1932)

Inside Europe (1936)

The High Cost of Hitler (1939)

Death Be Not Proud: A Memoir (1949)

Eisenhower, the Man and the Symbol (1952)

John Gunther   *Gunther, John, photograph. AP Images.*

Overview

John Gunther rocketed to fame and fortune with the publication of his nonfiction book *Inside Europe*, and this gave him access to world leaders and world perspectives. Although Gunther enjoyed the jet-set life that his journalistic career fostered, he also suffered great personal tragedy, with the deaths of his two children. He wrote about the death of his seventeen-year-old son in his book *Death Be Not Proud: A Memoir*. As a journalist, novelist, and biographer Gunther offered his readers a fresh new insight to the world in which they lived.

Works in Biographical and Historical Context

An Inquisitive Fact Finder   John Gunther was born in Chicago to Eugene and Lisette Gunther. His father was a traveling businessman and his mother a school teacher. With his father often away, it was his mother who primarily raised John and his sister. As a boy, John showed a great interest in fact-finding and collecting. When he was only eleven years old he set out with the ambitious goal of writing an encyclopedia. Somewhat introverted, he had a less than remarkable academic record at Lake View High School, from which he graduated in 1918.

Making a Career in Journalism   Although his father had other plans for him, Gunther enrolled at the University of Chicago and began studying chemistry. However, he proved less than dedicated to that science, and in his second year he switched to English, a move that affected the rest of his life. Soon Gunther experienced, for the first time in his life, social popularity through his position as the editor of the student newspaper, the *Daily Maroon*. After graduating from the university in 1922, Gunther traveled around Europe for a short time. When he returned to the United States he was determined to make a career in journalism. He worked for two years, learning the ropes as a cub reporter for the *Chicago Daily News*.

Front Row Seats in Europe   Gunther quit his job for the *Chicago Daily News* in 1924 and moved to Europe. He worked as a freelance journalist in London picking up odd jobs until he was again hired by the Chicago newspaper as its roving "swing man," traveling around Europe to fill correspondent positions that were currently vacant. Between 1926 and 1929 he worked in every country in Europe except Portugal. In 1927, Gunther married Frances Fineman, a fellow journalist working in Europe. He had first met her in Chicago in 1921. Fineman traveled and worked all over Europe with Gunther. In 1929 they had a daughter, Judy, who died suddenly before she was able to celebrate her first birthday. In 1930, their son John Jr. was born.

The paper gave him his own news bureau in Vienna in 1930, and he remained there until 1935. This gave him the opportunity to closely observe the rise of fascism in Germany and Austria. Before World War II, Gunther wrote some of the first articles about the ascendancy of Adolf Hitler and the dangers of his philosophic outlook. This gave the German police, the Gestapo, reason enough to place Gunther on their death list.

Triumph as a World Chronicler During his time as a journalist, Gunther managed to write four novels, including *Bright Nemesis*. None of his fiction met with success and reviewers considered his work in this form stale and ordinary. At his wife's prompting, Gunther decided to write about what he had learned during his many years reporting as a correspondent and traveling around Europe. He took only seven months to complete the manuscript for *Inside Europe*, even after being moved from Vienna to London, where he took on even greater responsibilities. The book was published in 1936 to great success. Gunther had managed to casually write about each country in Europe, just as the continent was facing the crisis of fascism and the rise of Hitler in Germany and Benito Mussolini in Italy. The book introduced the general public to these political leaders, who would later become household names as they terrorized the world. With *Inside Europe* the common reader could satisfy his curiosity without feeling too bogged down in details.

Gunther continued to revise *Inside Europe* during World War II. He published several other editions of the book that led him to fame and fortune. However, he also went on to create other "Inside" works. From 1937 to 1939 Gunther and his family traveled throughout Asia, and in 1939 he published *Inside Asia*, followed by *Inside Latin America* just two years later. With his newfound fame and fortune Gunther was able to meet with politicians and statesmen all over the world and to get them to speak candidly during his interviews.

A Study of the United States In 1944 Gunther's marriage to Frances Fineman ended in divorce. Gunther returned to the United States and embarked on a new mission: to use the same technique he had used in his analysis of other continents, to produce an overview of the American nation. During the next thirteen months he traveled to every state, interviewed ten to twenty people each day, and wrote over a million words of notes. He spent another fourteen months putting together his manuscript. In 1946 he published the result, *Inside U.S.A.*, which was a huge success. It sold half a million copies in three months.

Personal Tragedy Shared Just as Gunther was finishing work on *Inside U.S.A.*, his life plummeted into despair with the diagnosis of his son Johnny's brain cancer. One month after the publication of the book, Johnny died. During the battle that the family waged to keep Johnny alive, Gunther chronicled his pain in a personal

LITERARY AND HISTORICAL CONTEMPORARIES

John Gunther's famous contemporaries include:

Dwight D. Eisenhower (1890–1969): Eisenhower was the thirty-fourth president of the United States, from 1953 to 1961. As a U.S. Army general he served as supreme commander of the Allied Forces in Europe during World War II.

John Steinbeck (1902–1968): This American novelist was awarded the Pulitzer Prize in 1940 and the Nobel Prize in Literature in 1962 for his compassionate portrayals of the poor, especially itinerant farm laborers, during the Great Depression and the Dust Bowl years of the 1930s.

Ernest Hemingway (1899–1961): An American Nobel Prize–winning novelist, Hemingway worked in Europe through World War I and the Spanish Civil War, and wrote fiction with journalistic clarity.

Edward R. Murrow (1908–1965): A television broadcast journalist who achieved fame during World War II, Murrow was recognized for gritty and honest reporting.

memoir to help with the grieving process. Gunther never intended to publish the work. However, he was prompted to offer the memoir as a book in order to help other grieving parents deal with similar tragedies, and in 1949 *Death Be Not Proud* was published. This is the work by which Gunther is most remembered today. It was filmed as a television movie in 1975, starring Robby Benson.

Living Big and Writing Big In 1948 Gunther married Jane Perry Vandercook; the couple adopted a son, Nicholas. With the help of his new wife, Gunther continued to write "Inside" books and other sociopolitical nonfiction, including his memoir of General Dwight D. Eisenhower *Eisenhower, the Man and the Symbol*, written before the famous military leader was elected president. Gunther entertained often in his New York home and lived a lavish lifestyle as a celebrity journalist until his own death from cancer in 1970.

Works in Literary Context

Gunther's early works document the political and cultural landscape on a world scale, and they analyze the major continents region by region. His writing was thorough and yet simplistic and entertaining. It attracted common readers, not university PhDs, and it satisfied the public's curiosity about the world abroad. In doing so, he created a new, dynamic style of reporting called "inside" reporting. Gunther is most remembered for his sensitive treatment of death and grieving in his skillful memoir *Death Be Not Proud*, a chronicle of his seventeen-year-old son's struggle for life.

COMMON HUMAN EXPERIENCE

Gunther's book *Death Be Not Proud* develops the theme of accepting death in the face of life. Here are some other literary works that examine the process of trying to make sense out of death.

> *Cures for Heartbreak* (2007), a novel by Margo Rabb. The author delivers a poignant account of family members struggling to communicate with each other after the loss of their mother.
>
> *Ordinary People* (1976), a novel by Judith Guest. In this tale, a suicidal teen grapples to understand why he still lives after his brother has died in a drowning accident.
>
> *In Memoriam* (1850), a poetry collection by Alfred Lord Tennyson. It took this famed British poet seventeen years to write this verse, which seeks to understand the early and sudden death of his best friend.

"Inside" Journalism   In the late nineteen century, William Randolph Hearst and Joseph Pulitzer, owners of the nation's largest newspapers, declared that journalists had a mission to defend the public interest. In response, journalists searched for sensationalist news and their stories touted shocking headlines to attract readers. This sensationalist journalism eventually led to more investigative journalism, in which reporters took risks to get to the bottom of stories and scandals. Eventually, with the use of the first wireless radio transmitter in 1901, broadcasting journalism and transatlantic wire communications became widespread. Gunther traveled Europe at the zenith of American foreign correspondence, when Americans were excited by and eager for instant news. With the publication of *Inside Europe*, Gunther used an investigative, journalistic approach to uncover the political climate in Europe, as the war and political upheaval loomed.

The Memoir   Although often seen as interchangeable, a memoir is different from an autobiography, in that it is a reflection of one section of the writer's life that is not meant as an entire life history. Gunther's memoir of his son's struggle for life, *Death Be Not Proud*, has maintained a place in the literary world because his approach to the subject remains as valid today as it was when the book was written. It is a story of love between a boy and his family, and it searches for answers to the unfairness of the boy's plight.

Works in Critical Context

Although *Inside Europe* was criticized for lacking in journalistic objectivity, it won public approval and had remarkable sales for a book of nonfiction. This was also true of Gunther's memoir, *Death Be Not Proud*, which received critical recognition for its honest and sensitive treatment of death. It continues to be read and studied in literature classes today.

Inside Europe   Gunther's *Inside Europe* was an instant success in the United States and was quickly translated and distributed abroad. In Europe critics felt that Gunther had helped educate the world about their precarious situation. Harold Nicolson commended the book, saying it was "a serious contribution to contemporary knowledge." J. H. Freeman, writing for the *Times Literary Supplement*, called the book "a dramatic, entertaining and informative record of the Europe of the moment." The reviewer also commented that the "character-readings of the dictators and would-be dictators are illuminating but not always respectful. Mr. Gunther describes Herr Hitler as given to insomnia and emotionalism; the German people are the chief emotional reality of his life." In the United States some critics felt that Gunther had allowed himself to distort the truth by inserting his own views and had made the book too personal. In his 1936 review Malcolm Cowley said that the book "distorts the author's picture and often weakens his judgment of events."

Death Be Not Proud   In *Death Be Not Proud* Gunther's elegant prose exposes the pain of death and loss without becoming overly sentimental and dramatic. He uses his memoir to illuminate what is important in life, and to reflect on what "good" truly is. It is Gunther's son's embracing of life and his own fearlessness in the face of death that eventually allows the author to accept the inevitable without despair.

Responses to Literature

1. Gunther lived in Vienna, Austria, just prior to World War II. Using your library and the Internet. research the rise of fascism in Austria and Germany. Who were the fascist leaders in Europe prior to World War II? What alliances did they make with each other? What led Germany to democratically choose a fascist leader?

2. Gunther chronicles his son's cancer and experimental treatments in *Death Be Not Proud*. Using your library and the Internet, research the history of cancer and its treatment. How have survival rates changed since Gunther's son's cancer was detected? How has the treatment changed?

3. Gunther was credited and criticized for introducing the general public to the complexities of pre–World War II Europe in a captivating, yet perhaps overly simplified prose. While reading Gunther's early geopolitical works, think about how the language differs from academic writing. How does Gunther keep the material interesting? Should the narrative be less personal and more objective? Why or why not?

4. Gunther's memoir *Death Be Not Proud* narrates the story both from an adult's and a child's point of view, using his son's journals. While reading this work, reflect on the different levels of emotional maturity in the two narratives. How do the two points of view differ? How are they similar?

BIBLIOGRAPHY

Books

Cuthbertson, Ken. *Inside: The Biography of John Gunther*. Chicago: Bonus Books, 1992.
Gunther, John. *A Fragment of Autobiography*. New York: Harper, 1962.
Pridmore, Jay. *John Gunther: Inside Journalism*. Chicago: University of Chicago Library, 1990.

Periodicals

Cowley, Malcolm. "The Personal Element." *New Republic* (February 12, 1936).
Freeman, J. H. "Dictators & Others: An American Looks at Europe." *Times Literary Supplement*, no. 1776 (February 15, 1936): 124.
Rovere, Richard H. "Inside." *New Yorker* (August 23, 1947).
Schlesinger, Arthur. "A Man From Mars." *Atlantic Monthly* (April 1997).
"John Gunther: An Obituary." *New York Times* (May 30, 1970).

Web sites

"John Gunther. Abbreviated profile from *World Authors 1900–1950*." Retrieved December 6, 2008, from http://www.hwwilson.com/print/14gunther.html.
"Personal Information for Frances Fineman Gunther." Retrieved December 6, 2008, from http://jwa.org/archive/jsp/perInfo.jsp?personID=518.
"*Death Be Not Proud*: TV Movie." Retrieved December 6, 2008, from http://www.imdb.com/title/tt0072854/.
"John Gunther." Retrieved December 6, 2008, from http://www.nndb.com/people/875/000048731/.

✺ David Guterson

BORN: *1956, Seattle, Washington*

NATIONALITY: *American*

GENRE: *Fiction*

MAJOR WORKS:
Snow Falling on Cedars (1994)

Overview

In 1995, David Guterson won the PEN/Faulkner Award for his novel *Snow Falling on Cedars* (1994), a story about how the mysterious death of a local fisherman in

David Guterson *Guterson, David, photograph by Jill Sabella. Reproduced by permission of Jill Sabella.*

1954 affects a Japanese American family. *Snow Falling on Cedars* was an international success, selling more than 2 million copies in the United States alone, was translated into more than twenty-one languages, and was adapted into a critically acclaimed film of the same title. Guterson's more recent novels, *East of the Mountains* (1999) and *Our Lady of the Forest* (2003), have been noted for their attention to detail and their universal moral themes.

Biographical and Historical Context

Northwest Inspiration Guterson, the son of an attorney and a homemaker, grew up with two brothers and two sisters in Seattle, Washington. Guterson and his siblings spent much time in the lush landscape surrounding Seattle, an environment that obviously inspired the settings of his novels. The family frequently spent holidays at Soap Lake, east of the city, and this locale, along with the Columbia River Basin (a favorite getaway for Guterson in his twenties), was the basis for the hunting trip of the fictional Ben Givens in Guterson's *East of the Mountains* (1999). Guterson enjoyed books as a child, but did not begin seriously writing until his junior year of college when a teacher of short fiction awoke Guterson to the enjoyment of creating stories and playing with

LITERARY AND HISTORICAL CONTEMPORARIES

David Guterson's famous contemporaries include:

Patricia Cornwell (1956–) Cornwell, an American crime writer, is known for her series of novels featuring medical examiner Dr. Kay Scarpetta.

Carl Hiaasen (1953–): Hiaasen began writing as a journalist, but turned to writing satiric "environmental thrillers" against a rich Florida backdrop.

Mitch Albom (1958–): Albom, an author, sports journalist, and broadcaster, is known for his inspirational novels like the best-selling *Tuesdays with Morrie* (1997).

Tim Burton (1958–): Burton, a film director and screenwriter, is known for his Gothic filmmaking style, as well as for the dark atmosphere and detail of the stories he tells.

words. Guterson often had sat in on his father's trials and had imagined himself following in his father's footsteps. But the creative writing bug took hold.

Diverse Interests Before attending the University of Washington in 1974, Guterson was an average student. Once at the university, however, Guterson engaged in a multitude of subjects, from human anatomy and botany to Asian American history. These diverse interests would provide ample fodder for his early short stories and later long fiction, as did the summers he spent clearing brush and fighting fires for the U.S. Forest Service.

Marriage, Teaching, and Raising Kids In 1978, Guterson graduated with a BA in English from the University of Washington and, one year later, married Robin Ann Radwick, whom he had known since high school. Still passionate about writing, Guterson enrolled in the Master's program in Creative Writing at Brown University. Not connecting stylistically with the program at Brown, Guterson left. He later returned to the University of Washington, where he joined their creative writing program and worked with prominent writers, including Charles Johnson.

In 1982, after Guterson finished his degree at the University of Washington, he and his wife took their newborn son, Taylor, on a tour across Europe in a Volkswagen van. The family returned to Seattle four months later, bankrupt. Two years later, in 1984, their second child, Travis, was born, and the family moved to Bainbridge Island, thirty-five minutes west of Seattle by ferry. Guterson joined Bainbridge High School as an English teacher (a position he would hold for a decade). Guterson and his wife had a third son, Henry, in 1986, and a daughter, Angelica, in 1993.

Published at Last Several of Guterson's early stories had found their way to journals, including *The Iowa Review* and *Prairie Schooner*. In 1989, Guterson published a collection of these stories under the title *The Country Ahead of Us, The Country Behind*. This collection of ten stories was a bildungsroman of sorts, a group of coming-of-age stories about young men or boys at defining moments in their lives. Guterson, in a 1999 interview with *Publishers Weekly*, suggests these stories reveal a young writer still searching for his own voice.

A Lucrative Career in Nonfiction While Guterson began writing his first novel, he launched into another genre: nonfiction. He wrote articles on a myriad of topics like the environment and travel, and his work appeared in popular periodicals, including *Esquire* and the *New York Times*. At this time, he also acted as a contributing editor for *Harper's*. While at *Harper's*, Guterson's writing on homeschooling caught the eye of a book editor. Guterson published *Family Matters: Why Homeschooling Makes Sense* (1992).

Snow Falling on Cedars For more than five years, Guterson researched the setting and history that would serve as the foundation for *Snow Falling on Cedars*. The details of the novel emerged from his intense study of the Japanese internment during World War II, gillnetting (or fishing by means of a net placed vertically in the water), salmon fishing, and small island communities in Washington. Set in the 1950s, the novel tells the story of a Japanese-American man accused of murdering a respected fisherman on the fictional San Piedro Island. The novel hit number one on the *New York Times* best-seller list and received positive reviews from critics. Guterson was also honored with such literary prizes as the PEN/Faulkner Award (1995), the American Booksellers Book of the Year Award (1995), and the Pacific Northwest Booksellers Award (1995). At the turn of the twenty-first century, the novel became the most successful paperback that Vintage ever published. Success for Guterson continued as Universal Pictures adapted the book for film in 1999, the same year that the author published his second novel, *East of the Mountains*.

Casting a Wide Fictional Net For *East of the Mountains*, Guterson also conducted extensive research; in order to tell the story of a retired heart surgeon with cancer who has lost his desire to live, Guterson visited both Italy and the desert in Eastern Washington, learned about apple farming, and interviewed migrant workers from Mexico. The learning experiences inspired Guterson to create vivid characters like the illegal immigrant fruit-picker as well as flashbacks to World War II and the Italian countryside where the protagonist was once stationed. *East of the Mountains* disappointed some critics after the acclaim of *Snow Falling on Cedars*. Guterson's third novel,

Our Lady of the Forest, moved away from the moral themes in Guterson's previous novels to blend the mystical with humor and cynicism. The story focuses on a town falling apart with the loss of their logging industry and a teenager who sees the Virgin Mary. The novel received mixed reviews.

The Other Guterson returns to the Washington forest in *The Other* (2008). The novel's protagonist, John William, is a recluse as well as the sole heir to a banking and timber fortune, a man who shuns society. But the book tells the story of his longtime friendship with another man, Neil Countryman, a boy he met in high school. Guterson still lives in Washington, on an island in Puget Sound, where he continues to write novels.

Works in Literary Context

In Guterson's work, the setting plays an important role in the story, particularly in shaping lives and actions of the characters. Guterson primarily leans on the woods of the Pacific Northwest for inspiration and, in an interview, once said, "The cycle of decay is so overwhelmingly present here. Everything human disappears in this landscape."

Relationship with the Land The plot of the novel *Snow Falling on Cedars* is anchored by a murder caused by an old family feud over land. Years before the book begins, the father of the would-be victim agrees to sell a plot of land to the father of the would-be accused, a Japanese immigrant. Because a law prohibits Japanese immigrants from owning property, the men put the land in the name of the accused, who is American born. However, years later, when the Japanese American family becomes interned, the original landowner dies and his wife sells the farm to someone else. The characters in the novel are inextricably tied to the land, and their strong sense of place is the basis for the novel's ethos. This connection between a community and its environment is a running theme throughout much of Guterson's work. As he told *Book*: "I think that people don't have enough of a sense of place these days. That's why we have so much environmental devastation: People don't live in the landscape; they just live temporarily on it."

Heroes of the Common People Guterson once told *Book*, "Stories will always matter—stories that present human beings in crisis, deciding how to confront their struggles, how to be fully human. Stories deliver us the heroes of the common people." Each one of Guterson's novels addresses this theme of human triumph, particularly over personal adversity. In *East of the Mountains*, the protagonist heads to the desert of Washington State to end his life, but instead meets various strangers who make him reevaluate his choices and gain new perspective on his future. In *Our Lady of the Forest*, a teenager's vision of the Virgin Mary riles up her small town as well

COMMON HUMAN EXPERIENCE

Guterson is known for his strong plots, but Guterson's rich settings also are a trademark. Other novels that emphasize the connection between people and places include:

Absalom, Absalom! (1936), a novel by William Faulkner. In this tale set in fictional Yoknapatawpha County, an ambitious West Virginian moves to Mississippi to start a plantation and a family dynasty.

Texas (1985), a novel by James Michener. This epic tale of the Lone Star State spans from the time of the earliest European explorers through the modern age, and includes both historical and fictional characters as participants.

The Highest Tide (2008), a novel by Jim Lynch. Newspaper journalist Lynch's first novel is a bildungsroman about a teenager and his relationship with the Puget Sound, a relationship that changes both his life and his role within his community.

as the world around it, ultimately offering an unusual "fable" of both greed and hope. *Snow Falling on Cedars* uses murder and a family history to make its characters revisit their ideas of right and wrong, of morality, and of justice.

Works in Critical Context

Although critics greeted *Snow Falling on Cedars* with vast praise, they viewed Guterson's later novels with mixed opinions. Guterson's deft use of setting detail and texture in *Snow Falling on Cedars* seemed to fall flat in his later work according to some critics, often overpowering his characterization and plot.

Snow Falling on Cedars *Snow Falling on Cedars* was lauded for its characterization, courtroom drama, and lyrical language. Pico Iyer of *Time* complimented the "beautifully assured and full-bodied story," while Tom Deignan of the *World and I* noted the novel's "long-winded" style, but was quick to suggest the story has "a lush, rugged landscape and good old courtroom drama to serve as the book's sturdy spine." *Booklist* reviewer Dennis Dodge saw the book as "compellingly suspenseful on each of its several levels."

Our Lady of the Forest Critical expectations were high for Guterson's third novel, and reviews were, on the whole, positive. *Publishers Weekly* thought the "gloominess of this uncompromising novel" might alienate or depress some readers, yet Pico Iyer of *Time* liked the dark elements, suggesting the tone of the novel offered "an unflinching picture of [Nathaniel] Hawthorne's descendants in the wake of [rock star] Kurt Cobain." In other words, Iyer viewed the book as a contemporary attempt at revisiting traditional stories with edgy, moral messages.

Responses to Literature

1. Critics praise Guterson for his attention to detail, particularly with regard to his settings. Choose a familiar place, and write a one-page essay that evokes the mood and feel of that setting through rich sensory details.

2. *Our Lady of the Forest* depicts a young girl who thinks she saw the Virgin Mary. Write a one-page essay describing what you would do if you had a similar "vision." What would it mean to you? Who would you tell?

3. Using resources at your library and the Internet, research the American internment of Japanese people during World War II. How do the facts of this historical event lend themselves to the themes Guterson emphasizes, such as the connection between people and the land?

BIBLIOGRAPHY

Books

Contemporary Novelists. 7th ed. Detroit: St. James Press, 2001.

Periodicals

Blades, John. "David Guterson: Stoic of the Pacific Northwest." *Publishers Weekly* (April 5, 1999).

Deignan, Tom. "A Farewell." *World and I* (September 1999).

Donahue, Bill. "Living in His Landscape, the Northwesterner Looks East of the Mountains with His New Novel." *Book* (November 2000).

Goldstein, Patrick. "*Snow Falling on Cedars* Was No Simple Screenplay." *Los Angeles Times* (December 12, 1999).

Iyer, Pico. Review of *Snow Falling on Cedars. Time* (September 26, 1994).

Levi, Jonathan. Review of *East of the Mountains. Los Angeles Times* (May 9, 1999).

Review of *Snow Falling on Cedars. Publishers Weekly* (August 1, 1994).

Riley, Sheila. Review of *Snow Falling on Cedars. Library Journal* (August 1994).

Stuhr, Rebecca. Review of *Our Lady of the Forest. Library Journal* (June 2003).

H

✪ Albert Hackett

BORN: *1900, New York, New York*

DIED: *1995, New York, New York*

NATIONALITY: *American*

GENRE: *Screenplays, drama*

MAJOR WORKS:

The Thin Man (1934)

Father of the Bride (1950)

The Diary of Anne Frank (1955)

Overview

Albert Hackett was a dramatist and screenwriter whose career in Hollywood spanned several decades. From *The Secret of Madame Blanche* (1933) to *Five Finger Exercise* (1962), Hackett's films exemplify both professionalism and popular appeal—hallmarks of Hollywood screenwriting at its best. While he received little recognition from the press over the years, Hackett wrote screenplays that appealed to varied audiences, some of which are renowned as American classics.

Works in Biographical and Historical Context

Actor and Screenwriter Hackett began his career as an actor. Born in New York City to an acting couple, Hackett made his New York stage debut at the age of six and performed in silent films and on stage. In 1927, while acting in Denver, Hackett met fellow actress Frances Goodrich. The two turned their attention to writing and so began a long career of collaborative screen and playwriting projects. Their earliest efforts were unsuccessful, but in 1930, their play, *Up Pops the Devil*, opened in New York. A comedy set in a writer's milieu in Greenwich Village, it dealt with the marital complications arising from a two-career family. Hackett and Goodrich were married on February 7, 1931, the same year in which *Up Pops the Devil* was filmed.

During the 1930s, America would succumb financially and emotionally to the Great Depression. The average American income plummeted by forty percent during this time. American farmers in the Great Plains and Midwest were substantially impacted by the devastating Dust Bowl. America's political and economic structure was in a state of upheaval. Major Hollywood studios, such as M-G-M, understood that money was a scarce commodity; they also understood that film could serve as an escape for citizens who were devastated by monetary woes. From 1933–1939, M-G-M hired Hackett and Goodrich to write thirteen films, many of which were box-office successes, that provided the public with humor, thrills, and music—escapes during a tumultuous time in American life.

Hackett and Goodrich's first assignment with M-G-M was to adapt Martin Brown's 1923 Broadway melodrama, *The Lady*; the film was released in 1933 as *The Secret of Madame Blanche*. It was followed by two story adaptations, *Penthouse* (1933), a gangster tale set in high society, and *Fugitive Lovers* (1934), a gangster melodrama. Although these films are nearly forgotten today, when first released they were praised by critics for their amusing dialogue and excellent performances.

The Thin Man and Beyond *The Thin Man* (1934) is acclaimed as Hackett and Goodrich's first major popular and critical success. Based on the novel by Dashiell Hammett and directed by W. S. Van Dyke, *The Thin Man* typifies the best of Hollywood in the 1930s. Nick and Nora Charles (William Powell and Myrna Loy) are a wealthy, happy-go-lucky couple who stumble into a murder mystery that keeps them pleasantly engaged while offering little real anger. The film's success resulted from a happy combination of talents, including those of the director, screenwriters, actors, and technicians. By working together, they succeeded in capturing a vision of America as it would have liked to be in 1934. *The Thin Man* was an immediate success and won Hackett and Goodrich an Academy Award nomination. M-G-M, foreseeing the box-office potential of a Thin Man series, engaged all the principals for two sequels.

Albert Hackett   *Nancy R. Schiff / Hulton Archive / Getty Images*

Between the Thin Man films, M-G-M assigned Hackett and Goodrich to a variety of projects ranging from the melodramatic *Chained* (1934), for which they received no credit, to the lavish spectacles of the Jeanette MacDonald-Nelson Eddy operettas. Hackett and Goodrich's first musical assignment was the first pairing of MacDonald and Eddy in the highly successful *Naughty Marietta* (1935). More musical assignments followed, limited to standard operettas such as *Rose Marie* (1936) and *The Firefly* (1937). Hackett and Goodrich's job was to take well-known, but exceedingly old-fashioned stories and rewrite them in a modern idiom. In at least one case, their updating may have given them the opportunity to editorialize: some critics suggested that the new plot and dialogue for *The Firefly*, with its story of a Spanish dancer during the Napoleonic wars, provided a parallel to the Spanish Civil War. As a rule, however, these assignments rarely gave the screenwriters an opportunity to do more than a perfunctory linking of songs.

Hackett and Goodrich's other M-G-M projects during this period included an ordinary comedy, *Small Town Girl* (1936), and a remake of their own screenplay for *Penthouse*, retitled *Society Lawyer* (1939). With an increasing lack of enthusiasm for Hollywood, Hackett and Goodrich returned to Broadway, where Hackett resumed his acting career in the long-running play, *Mr. and Mrs. North* (1941). In 1942, their own play, *The Great Big Doorstep*, opened on Broadway but closed after twenty-eight performances.

Back to Film   Hackett and Goodrich returned to Hollywood, this time to work for Paramount, and were assigned to one of that studio's biggest and most prestigious projects. They began work on adapting *Lady in the Dark*, the 1941 Broadway musical hit.

World War II would dominate American life during the 1940s—Hitler, the holocaust, and the bombing of Pearl Harbor impacted the American public, as well as Hollywood, during this time. Despite the studio's reputation for sophisticated comedy, Paramount assigned Hackett and Goodrich to *The Hitler Gang* (1944), a semi-documentary on Hitler's rise to power, incorporating German footage. This project, however, was little suited for Hackett and Goodrich. The two left Paramount in 1946 for more rewarding assignments; one of these was *It's a Wonderful Life* (1946), a film by Frank Capra about a man (James Stewart) who considers his life a failure until his guardian angel appears and shows him he is wrong.

As the war ended, a revival in the arts, as well as domestic job growth, would flourish in America. During this time, Hackett and Goodrich returned to M-G-M, where they reestablished their reputation as writers of trenchant comedy dialogue. Their first assignment was *The Pirate* (1948), an adaptation of S. N. Behrman's 1942 play. Since *The Pirate* had not been a musical play, Hackett and Goodrich had the responsibility of integrating the new Cole Porter score with the film's dialogue.

Despite the commercial and critical failure of the film, producer Arthur Freed immediately assigned Hackett and Goodrich to another musical project, *Easter Parade* (1948). The film was enormously successful at the box office, and the screenplay won Hackett and Goodrich a Writers Guild award.

Perfecting Several Genres   The Hacketts followed *Easter Parade* with another hit musical, *In the Good Old Summertime* (1949), and two more films which perfectly suited their talents and are among their finest work: *Father of the Bride* (1950) and *Father's Little Dividend* (1951). *Father of the Bride*, a comedy based on the novel by Edward Streeter and directed by Vincente Minnelli, was greeted with delight by both the public and critics. It was nominated for Academy Awards for best picture, best screenplay, and best actor (Spencer Tracy), and was seventh on *Variety*'s list of top-grossing films of 1950. *Father's Little Dividend* nearly equaled the popularity of its predecessor. Hackett and Goodrich wrote both the original story and the screenplay for this film.

These two films presented Hackett and Goodrich with their last opportunity to write sophisticated domestic comedy for the screen. Routine assignments followed these successes and included such projects as *Too Young to Kiss* (1951) and *Give a Girl a Break* (1954). Hackett and Goodrich worked on the big-budget musical *Seven Brides for Seven Brothers* in 1954; it was a box-office success and earned the screenwriters another Academy Award nomination. But neither it nor *The Long, Long*

Trailer (1954) provided characters or situations that allowed for the witty dialogue exchanges, or the acting tours de force, that had been the basis of Hackett and Goodrich's best comedies.

After a long and respected career in Hollywood and on Broadway, the writing team finally received public recognition for a project that was one of their last efforts. *The Diary of Anne Frank* opened on Broadway in 1955. Adapted from the diary that a young Jewish girl kept while she and her family hid from the Nazis in Amsterdam during World War II, the play occupied most of Hackett and Goodrich's time and attention from 1953 to 1955. The play won the Pulitzer Prize for Drama in 1956, while the filmed adaptation won a Writers Guild award and three Academy Awards in 1959.

Their last film for M-G-M was *Gaby* (1956) with Leslie Caron. This wartime melodrama was followed by a drama about marriage for 20th Century-Fox, *A Certain Smile* (1958). *Five Finger Exercise* (1962) would receive less than stellar reviews, ultimately persuading Hackett and Goodrich to leave Hollywood and return to New York. The two remained in New York until their passing: January 29, 1984 and March 16, 1995, respectively.

Works in Literary Context

Adapted Screenplays A screenplay based on another source, such as a novel, play, or even another film, is not always met with critical or popular success. However, some of Hackett and Goodrich's most renowned films were adapted from other sources, such as books and short stories. *The Thin Man* (1934), which is arguably their most acclaimed achievement, is based on an early detective novel by Dashiell Hammett. Hackett and Goodrich's screenplay for *It's a Wonderful Life* (1946) is loosely based on a short story by Philip Van Doren Stern titled "The Greatest Gift." Other Hackett and Goodrich screenplays based on other sources include *The Diary of Anne Frank* (1955), *The Secret of Madame Blanche* (1933), *Penthouse* (1933), and *Fugitive Lovers* (1934).

The Screwball Comedy Filmed in just two weeks and released during the Great Depression, *The Thin Man* includes elements of murder and mystery, missing persons and suspense. Yet fans of this award-winning film, written by Hackett and Goodrich, soon notice that any sort of suspenseful plot is secondary to its whimsical antics. Because it combines slapstick with farcical situations, *The Thin Man* is considered part of the screwball comedy genre. Famous film critic Roger Ebert points out that *The Thin Man* is essentially a "drawing room" comedy. "One of the movie's charms," notes Ebert, "is the playfulness with which [the characters] treat each other, and life." It is thought that the screwball comedy, among other genres, allowed for an escape from angst during the tumultuous Depression. *The Thin Man*, and other comedies of the time, such as *It*

Happened One Night (1934), eased troubled spirits and helped bring comedy to the forefront of cinema.

Works in Critical Context

While Hackett and Goodrich are often remembered for writing witty and uproarious comedies during the 1930s, their interests during the 1950s would eventually turn to drama. No matter the genre or subject matter, many critics assert that the writing duo had a knack for cultivating witty dialogue that enabled both stage and screen actors alike to shine.

The Thin Man

Hackett and Goodrich received critical praise for writing the witty repartee of *The Thin Man*. The film's script, most notably the comical dialogue between the leading actors, earned Hackett and Goodrich an Academy Award nomination for Best Writing. Film critic Welford Beaton compares *The Thin Man* to the highly acclaimed film, *My Man Godfrey*. He notes that both films offer interesting characters assembled in a sophisticated comedy, but makes a point of elevating the *The Thin Man* one step further. According to Beaton, the writing of *The Thin Man* is timed in such a way that it allows its audience to absorb the film's dialogue, enabling viewers to "finish [their] laughs before anything else is said . . . a privilege that few films accord us." As film critic Mordaunt Hunt asserts, *The Thin Man* is "an excellent combination of comedy and excitement."

COMMON HUMAN EXPERIENCE

Examples of farce run rampant in Hackett and Goodrich's screenplays. Other works with similar styles include:

The Importance of Being Earnest (1895), a play by Oscar Wilde. This play is still enjoyed by audiences for its lighthearted observations of social relations in the Victorian era.

You Can't Take It With You (1938), a film by Frank Capra. Capra adapted this comic love-story from a Pulitzer Prize-winning play by George S. Kaufman and Moss Hart. The film was nominated for seven Academy Awards, including Best Picture.

The Philadelphia Story (1940), a film by George Cukor. This comic gem stars Katharine Hepburn, Cary Grant, and James Stewart in a tale of marriage, divorce, and re-marriage.

A Confederacy of Dunces (1980), a novel by John Kennedy Toole. This Pulitzer Prize-winning work chronicles the life of a dismal man in his thirties who meets a number of quirky characters on his quest for employment.

Will & Grace (1998), a television series by David Kohan and Max Mutchnick. Highly regarded by critics and audiences, *Will & Grace* is renowned for its lively characters and laugh-out-loud dialogue.

The Father of the Bride

Critics note that very few films have captured premarital angst as brilliantly as *The Father of the Bride* (1950). Among the best films of 1950, according to *The New York Times*, film critic Bosley Crowther notes how Hackett and Goodrich helped to create a film filled with "all the satire of [a] modern tribal matrimonial rite . . . possessing warmth and poignancy." Crowther notes that M-G-M released a "honey of a picture of American family life."

Responses to Literature

1. Look up reviews and plot summaries for *Father of the Bride* (1950) as well as the newer version of the film released in 1991 that stars Steve Martin. Describe scenes from both films. How do these storylines compare? Are the issues that the characters face the same in both films, or have times changed dramatically?

2. Using the Internet, research the American economy in the 1930s and the Great Depression. Next, research films that were written by Hackett and Goodrich during this period. How did their films reflect the state of the country at the time they were made? Explain and provide examples.

3. Do you think Hackett and Goodrich's experience as actors enabled them to write better scripts? Explain how their experiences reading and performing scripts might have influenced their writing.

BIBLIOGRAPHY

Books

Goodrich, David L. *The Real Nick and Nora: Frances Goodrich and Albert Hackett, Writers of Stage and Screen Classics.* Carbondale, Ill.: Southern Illinois University Press, 2007.

Nichols, Bill, ed. *Movies and Methods.* Los Angeles: University of California Press, 1976.

Knopf, Robert, ed. *Theater and Film.* New Haven, Conn.: Yale University Press, 2005.

Ferguson, Russell, ed. *Art and Film Since 1945: Hall of Mirrors.* New York: The Monacelli Press, 1996.

Frank, Anne, Albert Hackett, and Frances Goodrich. *The Diary of Anne Frank; Play and Related Readings.* Boston: Houghton Mifflin College Division, 1996.

Rosenbaum, Jonathan. *Essential Cinema.* Baltimore, Md.: The John Hopkins University Press, 2004.

Periodicals

McCaffrey, Donald W. "Goodrich, Frances, and Albert Hackett." *International Dictionary of Film and Filmmakers* (December 2008).

Web sites

Albert Hackett Biography (1900–1995). Accessed December 8, 2008, from http://www.filmreference.com/film/82/Albert-Hackett.html.

Frances Goodrich Biography (1890–1984). Accessed December 8, 2008, from http://www.filmreference.com/film/93/Frances-Goodrich.html.

The History of Film; Film History of the 1930s. Accessed December 8, 2008, from http://www.filmsite.org/30sintro.html.

✸ Alex Haley

BORN: *1921, Ithaca, New York*

DIED: *1992, Seattle, Washington*

NATIONALITY: *American*

GENRE: *Historical fiction, biography*

MAJOR WORKS:

The Autobiography of Malcolm X (co-author) (1965)

Roots: The Saga of an American Family (1976)

Overview

Best known for his acclaimed historical novel, *Roots: The Saga of an American Family* (1976), Alex Haley inspired the nation to take an interest in black history and the

Alex Haley   *CBS / Landov*

study of African American genealogy. Haley's book, which traces his Afro-American ancestry back to a tiny village in Gambia, West Africa, spawned one of the most ambitious television productions ever undertaken.

Works in Biographical and Historical Context

Stories About Africa   Alex Murray Palmer Haley was born August 11, 1921, in Ithaca, New York. He was the oldest of three sons born to Simon Alexander Haley, a college professor, and Bertha George Palmer, a teacher. When he was young, they took Alex to Henning, Tennessee, where he grew up with his extended family. He remembers listening for hours as his family reminisced about their ancestors. One story in particular, told by his grandmother, piqued Haley's interest. An African ancestor refused to respond to the slave name "Toby," declaring instead that his name was "Kintay." These initial stories would serve as the basis from which the *Roots* saga grew.

Adventures on the Seas Leads to Writing   Not a stellar student in high school, Haley graduated with a C average at the age of fifteen. He then entered college preparing for a career in education. In 1939, Haley opted for a different path and enlisted in the U.S. Coast Guard

as a messboy. To alleviate the boredom while cruising in the southwestern Pacific, he began writing. His first venture included writing love letters for his shipmates. He expanded his range with maritime adventure stories that he submitted to several American magazines. A series of rejection slips followed before his first work was accepted for publication by *This Week*, a syndicated Sunday newspaper supplement. The Coast Guard, pleased with the positive publicity, created a position for Haley—chief journalist.

A Starving Freelance Writer   In 1959, Haley retired from the Coast Guard and decided to become a full-time writer. Determined to make a living at writing, Haley moved into a basement apartment in New York City's Greenwich Village. He was in debt and saw no brightness in his immediate future. Finally, Haley received a check for an article he had written. The payment fell short of the recognition he desired, but it did herald the beginning of assignments from more and more magazines, one of which was *Reader's Digest*.

Eventually, Haley's commitment to writing paid off when he received an assignment from *Playboy* to interview jazz trumpeter Miles Davis, creating the interview feature for the magazine. Soon afterward, he was asked to write a feature about Black Muslim leader Malcolm X. Malcolm asked Haley to assist him with his autobiography. The book, *The Autobiography of Malcolm X* (1965), was published just weeks before Malcolm X was assassinated.

A Career Launched   *The Autobiography of Malcolm X* sold over five million copies and launched Haley's writing career. Published at the height of the Civil Rights Act, the Voting Rights Act of 1965 (which eliminated various barriers to voting registration), and the Black Power movement, the autobiography became required reading for many courses in colleges. It was not uncommon to find young black men on street corners, in subways, or walking along the streets with copies of the book in their hands.

With his reputation established as a writer, Haley began research on his next project, a book about civil rights. However, he became sidetracked when he wandered into the National Archives Building in Washington, D.C., and began researching his own genealogy. At the time, Haley did not know that this search would eventually lead him to "50 or more archives, libraries and research repositories on three continents," before his curiosity would be satisfied, and that his efforts would culminate with the writing of *Roots*, published twelve years later.

Researching the Family Tree   For the next eleven years, Haley traced his family tree and recorded his findings, his research funded by a publishing house as well as *Reader's Digest*. Haley relied on his grandmother's oral history and traveled to Gambia where he met a griot, or oral historian. Haley learned the story of Kunta Kinte, a young man from the small village of Juffure, Gambia in

LITERARY AND HISTORICAL CONTEMPORARIES

Alex Haley's famous contemporaries include:

Malcolm X (1925–1965): This African American leader rose to prominence in the mid-1950s as the outspoken national minister of the Nation of Islam under Elijah Muhammad. He opposed the mainstream civil rights movement, publicly calling for black separatism and rejecting nonviolence and integration as effective means of combating racism.

Lyndon Baines Johnson (1908–1973): The thirty-sixth president of the United States, Johnson created new programs in health, education, and human rights, and pushed major tax and civil rights laws through Congress. His term is marked by the Great Society Program and the War on Poverty.

Cesar Chavez (1927–1993): This American labor leader was instrumental in organizing the Mexican-American migrant farm labor force to improve their rights. He founded the United Farm Workers of America, a labor union for which he served as president.

Norman Mailer (1923–2007): Best known for his controversial style established in *The Naked and the Dead* (1948), Mailer is also famous for his nonfiction narratives, written in the style of New Journalism, in which he relates factual events from his own perspective.

Muhammad Ali (1942–): A three-time world heavyweight boxing champion. Born as Cassius Clay, he won the light-heavyweight gold medal in the 1960 Olympics in Rome. When he joined the Nation of Islam, he changed his name to Ali and refused to serve in Vietnam. Ali, known for his lyrical charm and boasts, is often called the "greatest fighter in the twentieth century."

John Amos (1939–): This American actor played the older Kunta Kinte on the television mini-series *Roots*.

West Africa, who was captured into slavery and sent to America.

In Haley's book, he chronicles the life of Kunta Kinte, a proud African forced to endure the middle passage—the brutal shipment of Africans to be sold in the Americas—and made a slave on the Waller plantation in the United States. The narrative is based on factual events, whereas the dialogue, thoughts, and emotions of the characters are fictionalized. Although it took Haley twelve years to research and write *Roots*, it did not take nearly that long for it to reach the pinnacle of success.

Roots *Becomes a Phenomenon* *Roots: The Saga of an American Family* was published in 1976, the same year the United States celebrated its bicentennial. The work reminded Americans about the country's past, both shameful and honorable. Though the book became a bestseller, much

of the success of *Roots* can be attributed to the airing of the television mini-series in early 1977, which dramatically portrayed the saga outlined in the book.

The television show attracted one hundred and thirty million American viewers. Many critics felt that racial tension in America would be aggravated by *Roots*. While *Time* did report several incidents of racial violence following the telecast, it commented that

> most observers thought that in the long term, *Roots* would improve race relations, particularly because of the televised version's profound impact on whites.... A broad consensus seemed to be emerging that *Roots* would spur black identity, and hence black pride, and eventually pay important dividends.

Two years following its publication, the book had won two hundred seventy-one awards, including a citation from the judges of the 1977 National Book Awards, as well as the Pulitzer Prize. Within this short time, over eight million copies of the book had been printed in twenty-six languages. The television adaptation was nominated for thirty-seven Emmys. During this time, Haley signed at least five hundred copies of the book daily, spoke to an average of six thousand people a day, and traveled round trip coast-to-coast at least once a week.

Controversy and Lawsuits In addition to fame and fortune, *Roots* also brought Haley controversy. In 1977, two published authors, Margaret Walker and Harold Courlander, alleged separately that Haley plagiarized their work. Charges brought by Walker were later dropped, but Haley admitted that he unknowingly lifted three paragraphs from Courlander's *The African* (1968). A settlement was reached whereby Haley paid Courlander $500,000.

***Life After* Roots** The *Roots* phenomenon turned Haley into an entrepreneur. He formed the Kinte Corporation in California, a foundation for the study of black American genealogy. Haley's success was marked by relentless hours of autographing tours and press interviews on radio and television, as well as in newspapers. Nevertheless, he found time to write a novella, *A Different Kind of Christmas* (1988), a book about slave escapes during the 1850s, and begin another epic novel, *Queen: The Story of an American Family* (1993), a book that traces three generations of the paternal side of Haley's family. The work was completed by David Stevens. In 1992, while traveling to a speaking engagement in Seattle, Washington, Haley suffered a heart attack. He was buried in his hometown in Henning, Tennessee.

Works in Literary Context

Historical Fiction and African Heritage Alex Haley's reputation in the literary world rests upon *Roots*; however, critics seemed unsure whether to treat the work as a novel or as a historical account. Upon its release, it was classified as nonfiction. Historians criticized the work, claiming it contained numerous errors. Haley, however, never claimed the book was factual, calling it "faction," a mixture of fact and fiction. Despite the controversy, the public image of *Roots* appears not to have suffered. It is still widely read in schools, and many college and university history and literature programs consider it an essential part of their curriculum. According to Haley himself, *Roots* is important not for its names and dates but as a reflection of human nature: "*Roots* is all of our stories . . . . It's just a matter of filling in the blanks . . . ; when you start talking about family, about lineage and ancestry, you are talking about every person on earth."

Haley attempted to authenticate as much of the material in *Roots* as possible. With over ten years of extensive research and meticulous attention to detail, Haley emerged as the first black American to trace his ancestry back to Africa. He is credited by many for helping to foster better race relations. Hence, his mark on history will not only be as a creative writer but as a civil rights advocate. Haley bridged a part of the gap between the historical liaisons of Africans and Afro-Americans, and his name has become synonymous with the desire to know about heritage and roots.

Works in Critical Context

Haley's literary fame rests on two books: *The Autobiography of Malcolm X* and *Roots: The Saga of an American Family*. It is *Roots* that has brought him international recognition. The book itself has been judged to be "an epic work destined to become a classic of American literature."

Roots: The Saga of an American Family Not only is *Roots* a story about Haley's ancestors, it is also a story about American history and slavery. The book and television series penetrated domestic, foreign, societal, cultural, geographical, racial, gender, age, and socioeconomic barriers with a laser effect. Of that effect, Paul Zimmerman of *Newsweek* wrote that "Haley has written a blockbuster in the best sense—a book that is bold in concept and ardent in execution, one that will reach millions of people and alter the way we see ourselves." In regard to the televised version, Vernon Jordan, former director of the National Urban League, remarked in a *Time* article that *Roots* was "the single most spectacular educational experience in race relations in America."

Not all critics were impressed with Haley's work. Some noted the wording was clunky, and the characters nothing more than stereotypes. They found fault with his portrayal of the slave trade and criticized his fictionalization of history. Regardless of the flaws, *Roots* provided a black perspective to America about its black heritage. It provided a view of history that was previously untold. In the thirtieth year edition of *Roots*, Michael Eric Dyson writes in the introduction,

> Haley's monumental achievement helped convince the nation that the black story is the American story.

COMMON HUMAN EXPERIENCE

Other authors have researched facts to create historical fiction, stories set in a specific period that focus on a significant event or person. Some of these stories span several generations, as does Haley's *Roots*.

War and Peace (1869), a novel by Leo Tolstoy. This epic novel is centered on Napoleon Bonaparte's invasion of Russia in 1812. Sometimes cited as the greatest novel ever written, the story features more than five hundred characters and chronicles the interrelated histories of several families over the course of a generation.

Centennial (1974), a novel by James Michener. This work fictionalizes the history of Colorado from prehistoric times up to 1974—covering 136 million years. Michener highlights the story of those who developed the American West: Native Americans, pioneers, cowboys, trappers and hunters, traders, gold seekers, and ranchers.

Shogun (1975), a novel by James Clavell. This novel concerns William Blackthorne, a character loosely based on Will Adams. Blackthorne, an Englishman serving as a pilot on a Dutch ship, arrives in Japan in the 1600s to break up the Portuguese monopoly on Japanese trade.

Death Comes for the Archbishop (1927), a novel by Willa Cather. In this historical fiction, Bishop Latour is sent to New Mexico in 1831 to minister to the people of his diocese and restore their neglected faith. Cather based her character, Bishop Latour, on Bishop Jean Baptiste L'Amy, who came to America as a French missionary priest.

He also made it clear that black humanity is a shining beacon that miraculously endured slavery's brutal horrors . . . . [it] sparked curiosity among ordinary citizens by making the intricate relations between race, politics and culture eminently accessible.

Responses to Literature

1. Haley used library sources, historical records, and oral records to trace his family lineage. Using similar techniques, research your family tree, reaching as far back as possible. What new information did you learn?

2. Americans were not the first people to enslave Africans. Using your library and the Internet, research the slave trade of Africa and create a timeline documenting your results.

3. Discuss how Haley's book *Roots* changed how Americans viewed slavery in a historical context. What impact do you think his work had on American awareness of history?

4. Watch the film *Gone With the Wind* and the mini-series *Roots*. How do the films differ in their portrayals of enslaved Africans? Why do you think the portrayals are so different?

BIBLIOGRAPHY

Books

The Black Press U.S.A. Iowa State University Press, 1990.

Gonzales, Doreen. *Alex Haley: Author of Roots.* Berkeley Heights, N.J.: Enslow Publishers, 1994.

Shirley, David. *Alex Haley.* New York: Chelsea House, 1994.

Williams, Sylvia B. *Alex Haley.* Edina, Minn.: Abdo & Daughters, 1996.

Periodicals

Ames, Katrine and Ronald Henkoff. "Uprooted." *Newsweek* 93 (January 22, 1979): 10.

Boyd, H. "Plagiarism and the Roots Suits." *First World* 2, no. 3 (1979): 31–33.

Elliot, Jeffrey. "Alex Haley Talks to Jeffrey Elliot," *Negro History Bulletin* 41 (January 1978): 782–785.

Forbes, Cheryl. "From These Roots: The Real Significance of Haley's Phenomenon." *Christianity Today* 21 (May 6, 1977): 19–22.

Granfield, M. "Uncle Tom's Roots." *Newsweek* 89 (February 4, 1977): 100.

Web sites

The Kunta Kinte-Alex Haley Foundation, Inc. Retrieved September 25, 2008, from http://www.kintehaley.org/. Last updated 2003.

✸ Donald Hall

BORN: *1928, New Haven, Connecticut*

NATIONALITY: *American*

GENRE: *Poetry, prose, essay*

MAJOR WORKS:

Exiles and Marriages (1955)

Kicking the Leaves (1979)

The Happy Man (1986)

The One Day (1988)

Overview

A respected writer, educator, poet, and editor, Donald Hall is best known for his poetry about nature. His work explores the juncture of nature, culture, and local and natural history. Hall has also published books on baseball and writing, as well as children's books.

Donald Hall   *AP Images*

Works in Biographical and Historical Context

Early Literary Influences Donald Andrew Hall was born on September 20, 1928, in New Haven, Connecticut, the son of Donald Andrew Hall Sr., a businessman, and Lucy Wells Hall. Hall divided his time growing up between Connecticut and his grandparents' New Hampshire farm. In an essay in the *New York Times Book Review*, Hall claims that his childhood influenced his choice on his writing career: his mother read poems to him often and his grandfather not only recited poetry all day, he was also an interesting storyteller.

By the age of twelve, Hall began writing, influenced by his reading of Edgar Allan Poe. At age sixteen, he met Robert Frost at the Bread Loaf Writers' Conference and published his first work that same year.

Hall was educated at Harvard, receiving a BA in 1951. He then studied at Oxford, receiving another degree in 1953. After returning to the United States, Hall spent three years as a junior fellow in Harvard's Society of Fellows while working on *Exiles and Marriages* (1955). This collection, which garnered critical acclaim, was written in a tightly structured style that featured formal rhyme and meter.

Returning Home to Write In 1957, Hall took a teaching position at the University of Michigan, where he taught until 1975. During this time, Hall wrote poems that were driven by image rather than narrative, attempting to create an emotional effect without telling a specific tale. When his grandmother passed away, Hall left Ann Arbor and the University of Michigan in order to write full-time. He returned to his family's farm, Eagle Pond Farm, in New Hampshire with his second wife, poet Jane Kenyon. The house was significant to Hall; it is where his grandmother and mother had been born and where he had spent his summers while growing up. Eagle Pond Farm became even more central to Hall's work as evidenced by his poems in *Kicking the Leaves* (1979). The poems explore and celebrate the continuity between generations, as the speaker reminisces about the past and anticipates the future.

More Success and Awards Hall's next book of poetry, *The Happy Man* (1986), won the Lenore Marshal Poetry Prize. The book examines Hall's life on the farm and the significance it had on his youth. *The One Day* (1988), his next collection, was nominated for the Pulitzer Prize. The work is one long poem divided into three sections. Hall uses two narrative voices, one of a female sculptor and the other a male, to interpret the meaning of life and examine middle age.

Cancer, Death, and Grief Hall was able to support his family by writing poetry and essays. In 1989, while worrying about his mother's gastrointestinal examination, he learned that he had colon cancer. By 1992 the cancer had metastasized to his liver. After surgery and chemotherapy, the cancer went into remission, though his chances of surviving the next five years were slim. Then in 1994, while still on guard against a return of the cancer and concerned for his wife's future, he discovered that Kenyon had leukemia.

Hall worked on his next book of poems, *The Old Life* (1996). The poems read as a verse autobiography, a summation of Hall's life that treats the familiar themes of life on his grandparents' farm, family, and writing. Only at its end does its chronology reflect instead the impending deaths of first his mother and then his wife. Kenyon died in 1995 at age forty-seven, after a bone marrow transplant failed to reverse the course of her leukemia. Fittingly, the last poem in *The Old Life* is "Without," a poem that details explicit grief over Kenyon's death, and that is, as its speaker points out, devoid of punctuation.

Poet Laureate Hall continues to live on his New Hampshire farm and to write. In addition to his poetry, Hall is a prolific author of biography, criticism, anthologies, essays, memoir, and children's literature. In 2005 Hall published a memoir about his wife, *The Best Day the Worst Day: Life with Jane Kenyon*. In 2006 Donald Hall was appointed the U.S. poet laureate.

LITERARY AND HISTORICAL CONTEMPORARIES

Hall's famous contemporaries include:

Robert Bly (1926–): This American poet is one of the most prominent and influential figures in contemporary American poetry. Noted for his imagistic verse and unadorned language, Bly's poems focus on the immediate, emotional concerns of daily life.

Ralph Nader (1935–): American lawyer and people's advocate who rose to fame by exposing dangerous flaws in industrial wastes and products, such as automobiles and packaged meat. Running on the Green Party ticket, Nader has saught the presidency of the United States several times since 1996.

Jane Kenyon (1947–1995): American poet and translator who wrote about the inner psyche and her battle with depression.

James Dickey (1923–1997): Dickey was regarded as a major American poet who wrote with clarity about the American experience. Though he was an accomplished poet, he is best known for his novel *Deliverance*, which later became an acclaimed motion picture.

Adrienne Rich (1929–): American poet praised for lyrical and highly crafted poems in which she explores a variety of socially relevant subjects, including feminism and civil rights.

Works in Literary Context

Nature Poetry Hall has a reputation as a nature poet, writing about New Hampshire, nature, and the cycle of life and death. Billy Collins of the *Washington Post* calls Hall a "plainspoken rural poet."

From the beginning, Hall's poetry has focused on the relationship between human beings and their environment. For example, in the poem "New Animals," Hall describes a dream in which his grandparents return to the farm with exotic animals—zebras, giraffes, and ostriches—to replace its hens and cattle. In *Here at Eagle Pond* (1990), Hall takes this dream to mean that his grandfather approves of his decision "to raise poems on this farm instead of stock," a sanction that is vital to his sense of connection and place. Hall has disclaimed regionalism, but his sense of belonging and attachment to Eagle Pond Farm and the greater world of rural New England remains vital to his work.

Free Verse Hall's earliest poems were metrically formal, but *The Alligator Bride* (1969) shows Hall was willing to experiment with free verse. Hall developed a more expressive and imaginative range, paying particular attention to sound. He values a poem's aural quality as much as its appearance on the page. He favors simple, direct language

COMMON HUMAN EXPERIENCE

A recurring theme in Hall's poetry concerns the role of death in the life cycle. These works also explore the role of death in life:

The Odyssey (c. 720 BCE), an epic poem by Homer. This Greek epic recounts the travels of Odysseus and his crew as they sail home to Ithaca after the Trojan War. As Odysseus makes his "life journey," he learns that though his death is inevitable, he must embrace and accept all aspects of his life.

"Nothing Gold Can Stay" (1923), a poem by Robert Frost. This poem describes the fleeting nature of beauty, emphasizing that change is inevitable. People, like objects in nature, grow, change, and die.

"Ode to the West Wind" (1820), a poem by Percy Bysshe Shelley. This poem examines opposing forces in nature. Shelley portrays the west wind as a destructive yet beneficial force that is also a power of change. The wind is part of nature's cycle. The speaker compares nature's seasons to human development and ponders permanent death.

"Lapis Lazuli" (1939), a poem by William Butler Yeats. In this poem, Yeats argues that society often rebuilds itself even though it crumbles due to its own destructive devices. The speaker claims that rejuvenation of life is dependent upon the artist. The cycle of both creation and destruction preserves our existence.

combined with surrealistic imagery. Hall has identified as crucial to his conception of poetry a force he calls "the vatic voice," which provides the inspiration for his poems. According to the poet, the vatic voice is something that all people possess internally, although there is no means of controlling when and where it will surface. Poets merely cultivate their ability to listen to the voice when it speaks.

Works in Critical Context

Critical response to Hall's work has generally been favorable. His carefully crafted poetry and thoughtful prose are widely praised for their clarity and integrity, and his selection as United States poet laureate—a position held by only thirteen people before him—indicates his standing among his contemporaries.

Kicking the Leaves As a volume, *Kicking the Leaves* welcomes the narrator back to a house built by his great-grandfather, Benjamin C. Keneston, a home in which many generations lived and died, linked by stories and everyday objects. In *Poet and Critic*, Brent Spencer describes the collection as "mostly poems about memory, yet not mere

reminiscence. The effort in these poems is to look for that part of the past that lives on into the present."

The One Day *The One Day* represents a gathering of material that Hall had been working on since 1971 and even earlier. Hall developed the 110 ten-line stanzas and worked with them for about four more years before he thought of structuring the long narrative poem into three parts. The poem takes the form of tightly wrought ten-line stanzas: building blocks, as Hall calls them, for the "house of dying." Critics have seen the work variously as the portrait of a midlife crisis and an excoriation of modern spiritual corruption. Frederick Pollack writes that the poem as a whole "may be the last masterpiece of American Modernism. Any poet who seeks to surpass this genre should study it; any reader who has lost interest in contemporary poetry should read it."

Liam Rector, reviewer for the *Los Angeles Times Book Review*, claimed that "with *The One Day* he moves out into a different terrain from his recent mature books, *Kicking the Leaves* and *The Happy Man*." Daniel Mark Epstein from *America* labeled *The One Day* as Hall's midlife crisis poem, "a painful time for men and women alike." Epstein added that Hall "uses mid-life [in the poem] as a metaphor that works on several levels—personal, historical and mythic." In the *Washington Post Book World*, David Lehman praised the book as "loud, sweeping, multitudinous, an act of the imperial imagination" and declared that

high on Hall's thematic agenda are age and aging, rage and raging against the dying of the light, but his powerful rhetorical gestures and dazzling juxtapositions communicate a pleasure even beyond the skillful treatment of such themes.

Responses to Literature

1. Hall is noted for giving interviews. Using your library and the Internet, locate at least three of Hall's interviews. Write a short report describing his views on writing and poetry.

2. Read several of Hall's poems from *Kicking the Leaves*. Choose one poem and write a brief analysis of the poem's theme and use of rhythm and sound. Point out evidence of gifts from the past.

3. After Kenyon's death, Hall wrote several pointed poems about love and death. Read some of his poems from the collection *Without*. What do you learn about Hall from these poems? What do you learn about his relationship with his wife? What do these poems teach the reader about dying?

4. Read the *Ox-Cart Man* (1979), a children's book by Hall. How does Hall present his theme about the cycle of life? Discuss whether you find this story comforting or sad. Explain your reasons, using the text to support your position.

BIBLIOGRAPHY

Books

Hornback, Bert G., ed. *"Bright Unequivocal Eye:" Poems, Papers and Remembrances from the First Jane Kenyon Conference.* New York: Peter Lang, 1998.

Rector, Liam, ed. *The Day I Was Older: On the Poetry of Donald Hall.* Santa Cruz, Calif.: Story Line Press, 1989.

Periodicals

Chisolm, Scott. "An Interview with Donald Hall." *Tennessee Poetry Journal* 2 (Winter 1971): 26–48.

Cramer, Jeffrey S. "With Jane and Without: An Interview with Donald Hall." *Massachusetts Review* 39, no. 4 (1998–1999): 493–510.

Mills, Ralph J., Jr. "Donald Hall's Poetry." *Iowa Review* 2 (Winter 1971): 82–123.

McNair, Wesley. "Taking the World for Granite: Four Poets in New Hampshire." *Sewanee Review* 104, no. 1 (1996): 70–81.

Myers, George, Jr. "An Interview with Donald Hall about *The One Day.*" *Ploughshares* 17 no. 1 (1991): 71–75.

Pollack, Frederick. "Donald Hall's *The One Day.*" *Salmagundi* (Winter 1990): 344–350.

Scharf, Michael. "Donald Hall: Elegies from Eagle Pond." *Publishers Weekly* 245, no. 12 (1998): 72–73.

Walsh, Chris. "'Building the House of the Dying': Donald Hall's Claim for Poetry." *Agni* 47 (1998): 175–183.

Web sites

"Donald Hall: Online Resources." Retrieved September 28, 2008, from http://www.loc.gov/rr/program/bib/hall/hall.html#bio. Last updated on September 10, 2008.

✺ Jane Hamilton

BORN: *1957, Oak Park, Illinois*

NATIONALITY: *American*

GENRE: *Fiction*

MAJOR WORKS:
The Book of Ruth (1988)
A Map of the World (1994)
Disobedience (2000)
When Madeline Was Young (2006)

Overview

Jane Hamilton attracted critical attention after her work *The Book of Ruth* (1988) was awarded the PEN/Hemingway Foundation Award for best first novel. Her reputation as a significant contemporary novelist grew considerably when two of her books, *The Book of Ruth* and *A Map of the World* (1994) were selected by the Oprah Book Club, extending her readership to include mainstream audiences.

Jane Hamilton   *Dave Schlabowske / Time Life Pictures / Getty Images*

Works in Biographical and Historical Context

Growing Up in Chicago A member of the "baby boomer" generation, Jane Hamilton was born on July 15, 1957, in Oak Park, Illinois, a suburb of Chicago. She was the youngest of five children born to Allen and Ruth (Hubert) Hamilton, and she displayed an early interest in reading and writing. Her artistic efforts were encouraged by several women in her family, including her mother, who worked as a theater critic for the *Chicago Daily News* and published a poem "A Song for a Fifth Child" in the *Ladies Home Journal*, and her grandmother, who was a former journalist. A lifelong resident of the Midwest, Hamilton typically chooses small towns in states like Illinois and Wisconsin for the settings of her novels.

The Publishing Field and the Apple Orchard Hamilton majored in English at Carleton College in Northfield, Minnesota, where she graduated with a Bachelor of Arts in 1979. While in school, Hamilton displayed promise as a young writer, earning the Class of 1885 Prose Award in both 1977 and 1979. Despite her success as an undergraduate, she was refused admission from graduate programs in creative writing. In the face of this disappointment, Hamilton decided to move to New York to work as an editor with a publishing company. However, she aborted her plan after visiting a friend at an

LITERARY AND HISTORICAL CONTEMPORARIES

Hamilton's famous contemporaries include:

Jane Smiley (1949–): American author and recipient of the 1992 Pulitzer Prize for fiction, to whom Jane Hamilton is often compared.

Alice McDermott (1953–): American author whose novel *Charming Billy* (1998) was awarded the National Book Award.

Ann Patchett (1963–): American author best known for her novel *Bel Canto* (2001), which was awarded the PEN/Faulkner Award and the Orange Prize for Fiction in 2002.

Michael Cunningham (1952–): American author whose novel *The Hours* (1998) was awarded the Pulitzer Prize for fiction and the PEN/Faulkner award in 1999.

Jamaica Kincaid (1949–): A native author of the West Indies, Kincaid is known for the personal style and honesty that characterizes both her fiction and nonfiction writing.

COMMON HUMAN EXPERIENCE

Resilience in the face of tragedy is a common theme throughout Hamilton's fiction. Other works that explore this theme include the following:

The *Odyssey* (c. 720 B.C.E.), an epic poem by Homer. Known for his wit and resilience, Odysseus faces many challenges on his journey back to his home in Ithaca after the Trojan War.

The Island of Doctor Moreau (1896), a novel by H. G. Wells. A man is shipwrecked and survives a year on an island filled with strange creatures and mysterious science experiments.

Man's Search for Meaning (1946), a memoir by Viktor Frankl. In this work the author describes his experiences in a Nazi concentration camp and how he managed to find a reason to live in spite of the horrific circumstances he endured.

The Diary of a Young Girl (1947), a memoir by Anne Frank. Written while the Jewish author and her family hid in an attic during the Nazi occupation of the Netherlands, this work chronicles Anne Frank's emotional battle against despair as she lives in fear of capture and death.

Farm Life in Wisconsin As an up-and-coming fiction writer, Hamilton found that farm life suited her and helped cultivate her confidence. As quoted by scholar Marcia Noe in the *Dictionary of Midwestern Literature*, Hamilton speaks to the advantages of her new environment: "It was good to be in a place that was off the beaten path in terms of writing. I was not as self-conscious as I would have been had I lived in New York." Shortly after her arrival in Wisconsin, her first short story, "My Own Earth" (1983), was published in *Harper's* magazine. By the end of that year the magazine had published a second story, "Aunt Marji's Happy Ending," which was later included in *The Best American Short Stories, 1984*.

Success as a Novelist Throughout the 1980s and 1990s, Hamilton split her time between her family—she gave birth to two children, a son and a daughter—and her fiction writing. Her first novel, *The Book of Ruth*, was an immediate success and was later awarded the PEN/Hemingway Award, the 1989 Banta Award, and the Great Lakes College Association New Writers Award. These accolades helped her secure a grant from the National Endowment for the Arts in 1993 for a second novel, *A Map of the World*. Both books were chosen by the American television talk-show host Oprah Winfrey for her book club, which began in 1997. After their selection, both novels gained an international readership and became best sellers. *A Map of the World* was adapted for film and released in 1999.

Hamilton has published more novels since *A Map of the World*: *A Short History of a Prince: A Novel* (1998), *Disobedience* (2000), and *When Madeline Was Young* (2006). Hamilton continues to live and write from her orchard farmhouse in Wisconsin.

Works in Literary Context

Hamilton's novels focus on themes including suffering, redemption, and resilience within American families living in the Midwestern United States. Her work is influenced by the books she read as a teenager, including *Jane Eyre* (1847), by Charlotte Brontë; *The Diary of a Young Girl* (1947), by Anne Frank; and the works of Herman Hesse and J. D. Salinger. She has listed Lorrie Moore, Carol Shields, Kevin Canty, Carol Anshaw, and Michael Cunningham among the authors she has read and admired as an adult.

Suffering, Redemption, and Resilience Hamilton's novels are typically set in the rural or suburban areas of the American Midwest, in oppressive social environments that close in on their protagonists, threatening their spirits. Within this setting, Hamilton insightfully explores the interplay of family members caught in dysfunctional and tragic situations that require resilience and strength of character. The internal lives of her characters is a central focus of Hamilton's fiction, with her protagonists sharing their introspection and psychological insights through first-person narration.

apple orchard in Rochester, Wisconsin, which was owned by the friend's cousin, Robert Willard. In 1982 Hamilton married Willard and began a new life in Wisconsin.

Works in Critical Context

While all of her novels have received considerable praise for their psychological realism and thematic content, a number of reviewers have criticized Hamilton for constructing plots that are too melodramatic, like television soap operas. In particular, some have argued that the plot of *A Map of the World* is predictable and uninteresting. By contrast, Hamilton supporters often point to her characterization and sensitive portrayal of life in the American Midwest. Most agree that Hamilton's work is marked by a distinctive authorial voice, precise language, and nuanced characterizations. In particular, she is known for her treatment of the experiences of women, although she has also been commended for the believable male point of view she constructs in *The Short History of a Prince* and *Disobedience*.

A Map of the World   Writing for *People*, Joanna Kaufman acknowledges the emotional strength of Hamilton's writing: "Like a lot of books singled out for praise, *A Map of the World* can be described as a page turner. But in this case, the pages are turned with trembling hands." Also speaking to the work's ability to affect its readers, John Skow, writing for *Time*, labels the novel "a mischievous and unsettling marital melodrama" and goes on to add that it "would be soap opera if the author were not unusually good at transforming acute, intuitive perceptions into sentences." Likewise, Viva Hardigg in *U. S. News & World Report* praises Hamilton's craft: "Hamilton's special genius lies in blending the quotidian and the mythic. Ordinary details become luminous under her pen as she describes human pain with a rare, limpid force—unshackled by melodrama." *Publisher's Weekly* declared, "Booksellers should send up three cheers of greeting for this haunting second novella."

Critical studies of Hamilton's work are currently limited to relatively short publications in academic periodicals and popular magazines. However, she is treated by the literary community as a serious contemporary author with a distinct voice and secure place in American letters.

Responses to Literature

1. Discuss the Macivers's motivations for taking care of Madeline in *When Madeline Was Young*. To what extent are Aaron and Julia's actions self-serving? Explain your view using examples from the text.

2. Why does Hamilton choose *Disobedience* as the title for her book about an extramarital affair? What does her choice imply about familial roles in modern society?

3. What role does storytelling play in *Disobedience*? What does Hamilton seem to be communicating about the importance of storytelling in the human experience? Explain your opinion citing evidence from the novel.

4. The climax of *The Book of Ruth* comes as no surprise to most readers. How does the author foreshadow the book's climax? Does this technique enhance or detract from the climactic power of the events?

BIBLIOGRAPHY

Books

Greasley, Philip A. *Dictionary of Midwestern Literature.* Bloomington: Indiana University Press, 2001.

Periodicals

Brownrigg, S. "*Disobedience* by Jane Hamilton." *New York Times Book Review* (November 19, 2000): 9.

Bush, Trudy. "Jane Hamilton, *A Map of the World.*" *Christian Century* 112 (May 24, 1995): 567.

Hardigg, Viva. "Jane Hamilton, *A Map of the World.*" *U.S. News & World Report* 116 (June 13, 1994): 82.

Kaufman, Joanne. Review of *A Map of the World. People* 41, May 30, 1994, p. 30.

Review of *A Map of the World. Publishers Weekly* 241, April 4, 1994, p. 57.

Skow, John. Review of *A Map of the World. Time* 143, June 27, 1994, p. 75.

Web sites

Jane Hamilton. Retrieved November 26, 2008, from http://www.randomhouse.com/features/janehamilton/index.html.

Hertzberg, Mark. "First she threw one away—Jane Hamilton discarded a book before completing her latest novel." *Journal Times.* Retrieved November 26, 2008, from http://www.journaltimes.com.

Virginia Hamilton

BORN: *1936, Yellow Springs, Ohio*

DIED: *2002, Dayton, Ohio*

NATIONALITY: *American*

GENRE: *Fiction, biography, folktales*

MAJOR WORKS:

Zeely (1967)

The House of Dies Drear (1968)

M. C. Higgins the Great (1974)

Paul Robeson: The Life and Times of a Free Black Man (1974)

The People Could Fly (1986)

Overview

Virginia Hamilton established herself as one of the most prolific and influential writers for children and young adults. She was a productive writer, having produced a new book almost every year since 1967. Hamilton experiments with techniques and theme, primarily depicting contemporary African American life and its historical and cultural heritage.

Works in Biographical and Historical Context

The Gift of Storytellers Virginia Hamilton was born on March 12, 1936, in Yellow Springs, Ohio, home of Antioch College. Her grandfather, Levi Perry, escaped from slavery and made his way north to Yellow Springs where he settled on land that remains in the Perry family today. She is the youngest of the five children of musician Kenneth James Hamilton and Etta Belle (Perry) Hamilton. Her parents, avid readers and great storytellers, inspired Hamilton to write.

Hamilton began writing stories at an early age. She was a good student, finishing at the top of her high school class. The aspiring writer attended Antioch College on a full scholarship, where she was one of very few African American students. She studied creative writing, earning a degree in 1955, and later attended Ohio State University, still writing short stories all the while. She moved to New York to attend the New School for Social Research, hoping to improve her craft, and supported herself as a part-time cost accountant.

New York and Africa While in New York City, Hamilton became more satisfied with her writing. One of her favorite models at this time was Carson McCullers. Hamilton felt she learned from McCullers's writing "what a good sentence was." During this period Hamilton also met Arnold Adoff, a poet, whom she married in 1960. She and her husband traveled to Spain and to Africa. Going to Africa had been an enduring dream of Hamilton's; it made "a tremendous impression" on her, she said, even though her stay was brief.

A Successful First Book In 1967, Hamilton published her first book, *Zeely*, a story based on a short story she wrote in Ohio. The book is about a young girl called Geeder who spends a summer on her uncle's farm. She develops a childish infatuation for Zeely Taber, a six and one-half foot tall young black woman. Geeder imagines the young woman is a Watusi queen. Through her imagination and fascination with Zeely, Geeder discovers a lot about herself. *Zeely* was chosen as an American Library Association Notable Book for 1967 and was also awarded the Nancy Block Memorial Award for promoting racial understanding. It was one of the few children's books about African Americans and one that provided a positive view.

Family Ties and the Underground After the success of *Zeely*, Hamilton and her family returned to Yellow Springs where she began research on her next book, *The House of Dies Drear* (1968). Hamilton researched the Underground Railroad and gathered stories from relatives who used the Railroad in order to secure their freedom. This book received the Ohioan Book Award and the Edgar Allan Poe Award for best juvenile mystery.

Writing Biographies and More Awards Between 1968 and 1974 Hamilton wrote seven more books, among them a biography of W. E. B. Du Bois. This book was dedicated to her father, who had a longtime admiration for the black intellectual and his battles against discrimination and second-rate citizenship. Like all of her books, the Du Bois biography is a record of black survival against unfair odds. Implicit in the portrayal of this black man of dignity is the dignity of the black race.

A second nonfiction work was published in 1974, her biography *Paul Robeson: The Life and Times of a Free Black Man*. The year 1974 also saw the publication of *M. C. Higgins the Great*, her sixth novel and winner of the Newbery Medal, the National Book Award, and the Boston Globe Award.

Fantasy and the Environment Between 1978 and 1981, Hamilton produced the Justice trilogy: *Justice and Her Brothers* (1978), *Dustland* (1980), and *The Gathering* (1981). These books deal with an eleven-year-old girl, Justice, and her thirteen-year-old identical twin brothers who live in a town very much like Yellow Springs, where Hamilton grew up. While the characters are contemporary and realistically drawn, the stories are futuristic and contain elements of extrasensory power. In this series, Hamilton was able to reveal her interest in ecology and genetics.

A True Legacy Over the years, Hamilton wrote over thirty-five books, from folktales to fantasies, realistic novels to biographies; books read by children and adults. Her work has won extensive critical praise as well as numerous awards. In 2002, Virginia Hamilton passed away due to breast cancer.

Works in Literary Context

Multicultural Children's Books The goal of multicultural literature is to celebrate all cultures in American society. Many multicultural writers of children's books tend to focus on folktales and historical novels. Thanks to Virginia Hamilton, there exists a more assorted collection of literature available to children about African American ethnicity. Writing primarily for children, she seems largely concerned with delineating black characters that foster feelings of self-worth and understanding in her young readers. The characters in her books take pride in themselves, regardless of what outsiders think. While African American characters are featured in all of her books, she is primarily a writer focused on characterization, setting, and plot.

Stories of Survival Survival is an important ingredient in Hamilton's books. Her husband even refers to her books as "survival primers." Being a black woman in a white-male-dominated society taught Hamilton a great deal about survival, an essential element in the story of the black experience in America. She recounts the survival story of slaves risking their lives for freedom in *The House of Dies Drear*. In *The Gathering*, survival is related to changes in the environment.

Family Unity   Family unity and her portrayal of supportive family relations is a strong theme in Hamilton's work. Aunts, uncles, and cousins are portrayed realistically, with their various jealousies and rivalries surfacing, as well as love. Some families are traditional while others are more contemporary—children living with a single parent, interracial families, and families based on bonds rather than blood. Though the members are distinctive, there is always love.

Language and Dialect   Hamilton's books are praised for her use of language, natural dialogue, and dialect. She varies the speech patterns, using the language suited for a particular era or location. In *The People Could Fly: American Black Folktales* (1985) Hamilton uses creative dialect to retell black folktales; in *Junius Over Far* (1985) she uses a Caribbean dialect. She captures the musical sound of language, which makes her books appealing to children. Hamilton was a skillful experimenter with language who was not afraid to take chances by challenging her readers. She used a rich, imaginative, and unique prose style that varied in each of her later books, suiting the language to subject.

Works in Critical Context

Hamilton's folktales, contemporary fables, biographies, realistic novels, and fantasy stories have all been well received, evidenced by her winning every major award in her field. As Ethel L. Heins wrote in *Horn Book*: "Few writers of fiction for young people are as daring, inventive, and challenging to read—or to review—as Virginia Hamilton. Frankly making demands on her readers, she nevertheless expresses herself in a style essentially simple and concise." And Betsy Hearne in *Bookbird* claims

> Virginia Hamilton has heightened the standards of children's literature as few others have. She does not address children or the state of children so much as she explores with them, sometimes ahead of them, the full possibilities of boundless imagination.

Zeely   Hamilton's first book is about a young girl (Geeder) who views Zeely, a neighbor, as a queen, though in truth, Zeely tends to hogs. Some reviewers said that Geeder's character was not fully realized and that the encounter scene between Zeely and Geeder was anticlimactic. But most praised Hamilton's use of language, her ability to create a mood piece that has a special appeal to young girls. In *Written for Children*, John Rowe Townsend states *Zeely* is "a book without bitterness or paranoia . . . it is deeply concerned with black dignity: the splendor of Zeely in contrast with her humble occupation, the association of night traveling with escape from slavery."

LITERARY AND HISTORICAL CONTEMPORARIES

Virginia Hamilton's famous contemporaries include:

Octavia Butler (1947–2006): This American writer was one of the few African Americans in the science fiction field. Her works, such as *Parable of the Sower* (1995), focus on genetic engineering, advanced alien beings, and the nature and proper use of power.

Eloise Greenfield (1929–): This American award-winning author of poetry, fiction, and biography often writes from a youngster's point of view. She focuses on youths who are comfortable with themselves and who are able to express their feelings.

Shel Silverstein (1930–1999): American writer, illustrator and cartoonist. Silverstein's best known works include *A Light in the Attic* (1981) and *The Giving Tree* (1964).

Hillary Rodham Clinton (1947–): Hillary Clinton has served as the nation's First Lady, a New York Senator, a U.S. presidential candidate, and as Secretary of State. Her 1996 book, *It Takes a Village and Other Lessons Children Teach Us*, was a bestseller.

Roald Dahl (1916–1990): British writer of both children's fiction and short stories for adults, Dahl is best known as the author of *Charlie and the Chocolate Factory* (1964).

The House of Dies Drear   In 1968 Hamilton's second book, *The House of Dies Drear*, was published. It is the story of a thirteen-year-old black boy who moves from his home in North Carolina to Ohio and into the house of Dies Drear, an abolitionist operating an Underground Railroad station in his house. The house has a past of ghosts and murders, and the sliding panels and secret tunnels all help to create an atmosphere of mystery. Reviewers praised her writing skills, her use of language handled with poetic precision, sentences of high polish, and imaginative characters. Zena Sutherland in *Saturday Review* calls it "memorable literature that gives dignity to black heritage." Dorothy Sterling in *The New York Times Book Review* writes, "*The House of Dies Drear* is written with poetic precision. Miss Hamilton polishes her sentences with care, develops her characters with imagination and love."

Responses to Literature

1. Using the library and the Internet, research the history of the Underground Railroad and its impact on slavery. How does Hamilton's book, *The House of Dies Drear*, support the information you found? What new or different information do you learn from Hamilton's book?

COMMON HUMAN EXPERIENCE

Many of Hamilton's themes concern self-discovery and taking pride in oneself—an important lesson for children. Here are other works that focus on pride, in both self and culture:

A Separate Peace (1960), a novel by John Knowles. This novel chronicles the coming of age of two prep-school friends, Finny and Gene. Set in a prep school for boys during World War II, the story focuses on the bonds of friendship and self-discovery.

When Legends Die (1968), a novel by Hal Borland. The story recounts a Ute Indian boy's search for his identity as he holds on to the old ways and rejects white civilization.

The Ransom of Mercy Carter (2001), a novel by Caroline B. Cooney. Based on actual events, this novel describes the difficult journey Mercy must make when she is made a prisoner by Mohawk Indians. The young girl struggles with her emotions as she is torn between her family traditions and a growing respect for the Indian way of life.

Sounder (1972), a film directed by Martin Ritt. Adapted from the Newbery Award-winning novel by William Armstrong, *Sounder* is a story about an African American sharecropping family, family bonds, and their dog Sounder.

2. Read *Justice and Her Brothers* and write a review about Hamilton's use of characterization, setting, and plot. Do you find the book believable? Why or why not?

3. Read one of Hamilton's folktales. Discuss how the use of dialect enhances the authenticity of the story. Do you think the dialect distracts the reader or entertains the reader? Explain your position.

BIBLIOGRAPHY

Books

Apseloff, Marilyn. *Virginia Hamilton/Ohio Explorer in the World of Imagination.* Columbus, Ohio: The State Library of Ohio, 1979.

MacCann, Donnarae and Gloria Woodard, eds. *The Black American in Books for Children: Readings in Racism.* Metuchen, N.J.: Scarecrow Press, 1972.

Mikkelsen, Nina. *Virginia Hamilton.* New York: Twayne, 1994.

Wheller, Jill C. *Virginia Hamilton.* Minneapolis, Minn: ABDO & Daughters, 1997.

Periodicals

Heins, Paul. "Virginia Hamilton." *Horn Book* 51 (August 1975): 344–348.

Hopkins, Lee Bennett. "Virginia Hamilton." *Horn Book* 48 (December 1972): 563–569.

———. "Virginia Hamilton." *More Books by More People* 51 (1974): 199–207.

Langton, Jane. "Virginia Hamilton, the Great." *Horn Book* 50 (December 1974): 671–673.

Web sites

Virginia Hamilton Online. Retrieved October 1, 2008, from http://www.virginiahamilton.com/home.htm. Last updated in 2001.

Dashiell Hammett

BORN: *1894, St. Mary, Maryland*

DIED: *1961, New York City*

NATIONALITY: *American*

GENRE: *Fiction*

MAJOR WORKS:

Red Harvest (1929)

The Dain Curse (1929)

The Maltese Falcon (1930)

The Glass Key (1931)

The Thin Man (1934)

Overview

A celebrated author of American crime fiction, Dashiell Hammett is widely considered the originator of the "hard-boiled" detective story. He is the creator of some of the most enduring characters in mystery fiction, including detective Sam Spade and married sleuths Nick and Nora Charles.

Works in Biographical and Historical Context

Early Career as a Detective Hammett was born on May 27, 1894, on his grandfather's farm near Baltimore, Maryland, to Richard and Annie Bond Hammett. His education was limited: in 1908 he left the Baltimore Polytechnic Institute after being enrolled in the high school for less than a semester. Hammett contributed to the family's failing finances with a series of office jobs. In 1915, he began working for the Baltimore office of the Pinkerton's National Detective Agency, an organization that provided a variety of services from insurance investigations to strike-breaking. He traveled throughout the western United States on assignment for the agency for two years, and his experiences as a Pinkerton operative provided much of the material for his subsequent career as a writer.

Service during World War I Beginning with his induction in June 1918, Hammett served during World War I with the U.S. Army Motor Ambulance Corps at Camp Mead, Maryland. He contracted Spanish influenza, which later progressed to tuberculosis, and received a medical discharge from the army in May 1919. The next year, having relocated to the West Coast and briefly

Dashiell Hammett   *Hammett, Samuel D., photograph. The Library of Congress.*

returned to work for Pinkerton, he was admitted to Cushman Hospital in Tacoma, Washington. Hammett was hospitalized at Cushman and another Public Health Service hospital in San Diego from November 1920 until May 1921. During that time he commenced a relationship with one of his nurses at Cushman, Josephine Dolan, whom he married in July 1921 when she was six months pregnant with their first child. The Hammetts eventually had two daughters, Mary, born in 1921, and Josephine, born in 1926.

Hammett continued to work as a Pinkerton operative for as long as his health permitted. In 1921, he participated in two of the most famous criminal investigations of the day, involving the murder charge against movie comedian Fatty Arbuckle and the theft of $125,000 in gold specie from the ocean freighter *Sonoma*. In 1922, he entered Munson's Business College with the intention of training to be a journalist. Hammett supported his family primarily with a disability stipend from the military.

Writing Career Begins   Hammett turned his attention to writing and published his first story, "The Parthian Shot" (1922), in the magazine *The Smart Set*. Over the

next several years he wrote prodigiously, publishing in a variety of genres from light verse and comic sketches to articles for professional journals, but he had his most promising success when he utilized his experience as a detective. In one of his earliest published works, "From the Memoirs of a Private Detective" (1923), which also appeared in *The Smart Set*, Hammett offers twenty-nine brief—some only a sentence long—anecdotes and insights from his Pinkerton years.

Hammett found his greatest success in *Black Mask*, a pulp magazine devoted to stories of crime and adventure. In October 1923, he published "Arson Plus," his first *Black Mask* story featuring a nameless operative for the Continental Detective Agency. *Black Mask* readers took to the character immediately, and Hammett published almost exclusively in the magazine for the next three years, featuring the Continental Op, as he is conventionally known, in twenty-six stories.

Brief Hiatus from Writing   Hammett took a hiatus of nearly a year from writing fiction beginning in 1926, spurred by a conflict with the *Black Mask* management over payment, as well as by the necessity to find more secure employment after the birth of his second daughter. In March 1926, he began writing advertising copy for the Albert S. Samuels Jewelry Company. Hammett later dedicated *The Dain Curse* (1929) to Samuels, and named several of its characters after his Samuels Jewelry coworkers.

Hammett's chronic health problems worsened, necessitating that he give up working full time for Samuels and live essentially separately from his family after July 1926. Despite his condition, he drank heavily and pursued a series of sexual affairs. Hammett's *The Glass Key* (1931) is dedicated to one of his lovers, Nell Martin, who dedicated her novel *Lovers Should Marry* (1933) to him. He also returned to writing fiction, at the invitation of former infantry captain Joseph T. Shaw, the new editor of *Black Mask*, who considered Hammett the exemplar of the direction in which he intended to take the magazine. In January 1927, the same month that *Black Mask* announced his return, Hammett began a stint of nearly three years reviewing mystery novels for *The Saturday Review of Literature*, a position he probably gained with Shaw's help.

Career as a Novelist   Hammett's first novel, *Red Harvest* (1929), was published by Knopf. It originally appeared in *Black Mask* from November 1927 to February 1928 as four interrelated stories. Although *Red Harvest* is not explicitly a political novel, it is informed by the labor unrest Hammett had witnessed during his years as a Pinkerton op.

Hammett began his second novel, *The Dain Curse* (1929), immediately upon completing *Red Harvest*. It also first appeared serially in *Black Mask*, from November 1928 to February 1929. With its generational curse, incest, drug use and brainwashing, religious cultism, and diabolical mastermind for a villain, the plot of *The Dain Curse* is

Hammett's most exotic. *The Dain Curse* received positive reviews when it was published as a novel.

Hs next novel, *The Maltese Falcon* (1930), was an immediate critical and popular success, reprinted seven times in its first year. The novel was widely proclaimed to have reinvented the mystery genre. The protagonist, Sam Spade, particularly seemed unprecedented to the reviewers. The novel has been adapted for the screen three times, most notably in a 1940 Warner Bros. production directed by John Huston and starring Humphrey Bogart as Spade.

Affair with Lillian Hellman

Hammett went to Hollywood in the summer of 1930; the motion-picture industry, which had recently made the transition to sound, welcomed writers of good dialogue. With his wit and style, he immediately fell in with a coterie of writers who had their initial success in New York, including Ben Hecht, S. J. Perelman, and Nunnally Johnson. Hammett's first screenplay, for the Paramount movie *City Streets* (1931), was a success at the time. Perhaps most significantly, Hammett was introduced to Lillian Hellman, a script reader for M-G-M, in November 1930. She was significantly younger than Hammett and, like him, married, but the two began an affair.

Hammett had already completed his fourth novel, *The Glass Key* (1931), before *The Maltese Falcon* was published. Considered by many—including the author himself—to be his best novel, *The Glass Key* is Hammett's further attempt to break with the conventions of detective fiction. The protagonist of the novel, Ned Beaumont, is not a detective—he is, in fact, a criminal. *The Glass Key* garnered Hammett's usual positive reviews, although perhaps inevitably it was judged to miss the high standard established by *The Maltese Falcon*.

After writing four novels in less than three years, Hammett took another three years to complete his fifth and last novel, *The Thin Man* (1934). *The Thin Man* rivaled *The Maltese Falcon* as Hammett's greatest popular success, although it has subsequently been judged his weakest novel by most critics. At the time of the publication of *The Thin Man* Hammett was at the height of his fame; however, his literary output ended with that novel because of a variety of factors, including his alcoholism and ill health and to some extent his stormy relationship with Hellman.

Chronic Writer's Block Ends Literary Career

Hammett's literary career effectively ended with the publication of *The Thin Man*. In March 1934 he published his last original story, "This Little Pig," in *Collier's* magazine. He was for the rest of his life plagued by a profound sense of writer's block. Over the years of their relationship, as Hammett's celebrity waned and Hellman became more prominent, Hammett served as an editor and writing mentor to her, a role he approached with generosity and conscientiousness.

In 1934, he collaborated briefly on a comic strip for the Hearst newspaper syndicate, *Secret Agent X-9*, with *Flash Gordon* creator Alex Raymond. He also found more work in Hollywood, planning sequels for *The Thin Man* and adapting his story "On the Make" for the Universal movie *Mister Dynamite* (1935). Hammett made a lot of money in Hollywood during the first half of the decade, ultimately selling the rights to his *Thin Man* characters to M-G-M for $40,000 in 1937. His ability to spend outstripped his capacity to earn, however, and by the latter half of the decade his career as a screenwriter had been fatally undermined by his reputation for unreliability.

Political Involvement

During his time in Hollywood, Hammett was involved in the activities of the Screen Writers Guild, which, since its formation in 1933, had been engaged in rancorous labor negotiations with studio executives, and became a member of the Communist Party in 1936 or 1937. In 1938, he was elected chairman of the Motion Picture Artists Committee. In the turbulent political climate of the early 1940s, Hammett was a vocal antifascist and opponent of the war in Europe, serving as president of the League of American Writers beginning in 1941. During this period, he adapted Hellman's antifascist play *Watch on the Rhine* (1940) for the screen and taught writing courses in propaganda techniques. In September 1942, Hammett was accepted into the army at the age of forty-seven, and served first in New Jersey and later in Alaska's Aleutian Islands.

Discharged as a sergeant in September 1945, Hammett returned uneasily to civilian life. He was still a literary celebrity, with paperback editions of his magazine fiction introducing his stories to a new readership, although Hammett was receiving little money from them. He resumed drinking heavily, but after being told by doctors he was drinking himself to death, Hammett was finally able to give up alcohol for good by the end of 1948. He rededicated himself to his political commitments. Hammett's activities, along with those of many others, came under government scrutiny for being "Communist" and "un-American." In March 1953, he testified before the Senate Committee on Government Operations, chaired by Senator Joseph McCarthy, concerning the purchase by the State Department of books by known Communists. Hammett's books were pulled from State Department libraries around the world, although President Dwight Eisenhower had them replaced when he learned of the action.

Financial Problems and Deteriorating Health

In the latter part of the 1950s, Hammett was plagued by health and financial problems. His books were out of print; the royalties from his creations had long run out; and from 1951 until his death he was subject to a federal judgment for tax evasion. He did work on an autobiographical novel during this period, "Tulip," which he abandoned sometime around 1953; the extant fragment of it was published in *The Big Knockover* (1966), edited by Hellman. Hammett died of lung cancer on January 10, 1961. As a veteran of two wars, Hammett was buried in Arlington National Cemetery, over the objections of commentators in the press who recalled his Communist activities.

Works in Literary Context

Writing in a terse prose style frequently compared to that of Ernest Hemingway, Hammett focused on the investigations of callous, cynical private detectives who became the archetype for scores of protagonists in American television, popular literature, and film. Hammett's writing was heavily influenced by his experiences working as a private detective.

Realism and Hardboiled Crime Fiction   Prior to Hammett, detective fiction was primarily based on a formula established by the short stories of Edgar Allan Poe. The success of Hammett's fiction popularized hardboiled crime fiction, a style first adopted by Carroll John Daly earlier in the 1920s. Although Hammett retained elements of the traditional English mystery, he abandoned the genre's genteel, idealized characters and exotic settings, favoring a more realistic approach to the seedy world of urban crime. In Hammett's fiction, gangland criminals, corrupt officials, police, and even detectives share a degree of guilt. Critics have praised Hammett's colorful characterizations, his accurate reproduction of vernacular or common speech, and his use of realistic detail. Hammett's artistic legacy is a vision of a violent, morally rudderless society in which his characters try to navigate with only their own ethical codes to guide them. His prose—brutal, ironic, and slangy—quickly and permanently came to be considered the epitome of the hard-boiled style.

Works in Critical Context

Hammett gained a readership when he began publishing his crime fiction in *Black Mask*, but he did not achieve widespread popular success until the publication of *The Maltese Falcon*, the novel which many claim changed the face of crime fiction. While most of his fiction was met with praise, his reputation as a writer was overshadowed by his political affiliations at the time of his death.

By the end of the twentieth century, Hammett's literary reputation seemed secure. New printings of his works continued to appear, and in 1999 the Library of America edition of his complete novels was published. His lean, ironic prose and understated, sometimes mean, sometimes romantic view of human nature has continued to exert an influence, particularly on detective fiction, but also on literature and popular culture more generally, including motion pictures and television.

Red Harvest   Response to Hammett's first novel, *Red Harvest*, was enthusiastic, with most reviewers seemingly thrilled by its sensational aspects. The French novelist André Gide, writing in the *New Republic*, praises Hammett's dialogue, "in which every character is trying to deceive all the others and in which the truth slowly becomes visible through a fog of deception." Herbert Asbury, writing in *Bookman*, calls it "the liveliest detective story that has been published in a decade" and refers to the murder of Dinah

---

LITERARY AND HISTORICAL CONTEMPORARIES

Hammett's famous contemporaries include:

Raymond Chandler (1886–1959): Along with Hammett, Chandler elevated the genre known as the hardboiled detective story into an American art form with works such as *The Big Sleep* (1939) and *The Long Goodbye* (1953).

Robert Graves (1895–1985): Graves was an English author considered one of the most distinctive and lyrical voices in twentieth-century English poetry; he is also widely respected for his prose works, including the novel *I, Claudius* (1934), winner of the Hawthornden Prize and the James Tait Black Memorial Prize.

Lillian Hellman (1905–1984): One of the most successful and respected American playwrights of the 1930s and 1940s, Hellman is best known as the author of *The Children's Hour* (1934) and *The Little Foxes* (1939).

Chester Himes (1909–1984): Himes was an American author best known for the serial detective novels he wrote towards the end of his career.

Kenneth Millar (1915–1983): An American author and major figure in the American detective genre, Millar is credited with providing detective fiction with a psychological depth that emphasizes individual motivation.

Brand as an "excellent crime" and "one of the high points" of the novel. Asbury compared Hammett favorably to Ernest Hemingway, a subject to which reviewers and scholars have often returned. The stylistic similarities between the two authors are readily apparent: both favor unadorned—at times opaque—descriptions and characterization. Less superficially, critics recognized that Hammett had imbued the crime genre with a world-weariness and existential anxiety similar to Hemingway's modernism. It is a quality Gide refers to in his journals as Hammett's "implacable cynicism."

Responses to Literature

1. Discuss Sam Spade's relationship with power and authority in *The Maltese Falcon*. How does his distrust influence his actions?

2. To what extent is Sam Spade an antihero? Use examples from *The Maltese Falcon* to support your views.

3. Hammett's writing style is famously described as "hardboiled." Find several examples of this style in one of his works, and explain how this style enhances the mood and tone of the work.

4. Compare and contrast the Continental Op from *Red Harvest* with Sam Spade from *The Maltese Falcon*. How are the characters similar, and how are they different?

COMMON HUMAN EXPERIENCE

Many of Hammett's stories concern the world of urban crime and unsolved murders. Other works that explore these themes include the following:

The Long Goodbye (1953), a novel by Raymond Chandler. This story follows detective Philip Marlowe as he is first arrested for a murder he did not commit and then becomes the primary investigator in the case.

The Lady in the Morgue (1936), a novel by Jonathan Latimer. Private detective William Crane tries to uncover the true identity of a woman whose body is stolen from the morgue before it is identified.

I, the Jury (1947), a novel by Mickey Spillane. Half detective thriller and half murder mystery, this work follows detective Mike Hammer and his commitment to avoiding the inadequacies of the U.S. judicial system by finding the murderer of his friend and killing him himself.

BIBLIOGRAPHY

Books

Dooley, Dennis. *Dashiell Hammett.* New York: Ungar, 1984.

Edenbaum, Robert I. "The Poetics of the Private Eye: The Novels of Dashiell Hammett." *Tough Guy Writers of the Thirties,* edited by David Madden. Carbondale, Ill.: Southern Illinois University Press, 1968, pp. 80–103.

Gregory, Sinda. *Private Investigations: The Novels of Dashiell Hammett.* Carbondale, Ill.: Southern Illinois University Press, 1985.

Hellman, Lillian. Introduction to *The Big Knockover and Other Stories* by Dashiell Hammett. New York: Random House, 1966.

Johnson, Diane. *Dashiell Hammett: A Life.* New York: Random House, 1983.

Layman, Richard. *Dashiell Hammett: A Descriptive Bibliography.* Pittsburgh, Pa.: University of Pittsburgh Press, 1979.

Margolies, Edward. *Which Way Did He Go?: The Private Eye in Dashiell Hammett, Raymond Chandler, Chester Himes, and Ross Macdonald.* New York: Holmes & Meier, 1982, pp. 17–31.

Metress, Christopher. *The Critical Response to Dashiell Hammett.* Westport, Conn.: Greenwood Press, 1994.

Nolan, William F. *Dashiell Hammett: A Casebook.* Santa Barbara, Calif.: McNally & Loftin, 1969.

Symons, Julian. *Dashiell Hammett.* San Diego, Calif.: Harcourt Brace Jovanovich, 1985.

Wolfe, Peter. *Beams Falling: The Art of Dashiell Hammett.* Bowling Green, Ohio: Bowling Green University Popular Press, 1980.

Periodicals

Alvarez, A. "The Thin Man." *Spectator* (February 11, 1966): 1969–1970.

Balzelon, Donald T. "Dashiell Hammett's Private Eye: No Loyalty Beyond the Job." *Commentary* 7 (1949): 467–472.

Chandler, Raymond. "The Simple Art of Murder." *Atlantic Monthly.* (December 1944): 53–59.

Gardner, Frederick. "The Return of the Continental Op." *Nation* (October 31, 1966): 454–456.

Metress, Christopher. "Dashiell Hammett and the Challenge of New Individualism: Rereading *Red Harvest* and *The Maltese Falcon.*" *Essays in Literature* 17 (1990): 242–260.

Schulman, Robert. "Dashiell Hammett's Social Vision." *Centennial Review* 29 (Fall 1985): 400–419.

Whitley, John S. "Stirring Things Up: Dashiell Hammett's Continental Op." *Journal of American Studies* 14 (1980): 443–455.

✸ Lorraine Hansberry

BORN: *1935, Chicago, Illinois*

DIED: *1965, New York City*

NATIONALITY: *American*

GENRE: *Drama*

MAJOR WORKS:

A Raisin in the Sun (1959)

Overview

Lorraine Hansberry gained historical importance as the first black woman to have a play on Broadway, the first black and youngest American to win the New York Drama Critics Circle Award, and a trailblazer whose success enabled other blacks to get their plays produced. Her first play, *A Raisin in the Sun* (1959), remains her most enduring work.

Works in Biographical and Historical Context

Growing Up amongst Strong Leaders Hansberry was born in 1930 in Chicago, Illinois, to Carl A. Hansberry and Nanny Perry Hansberry. She was the youngest of four children. Throughout her childhood, thanks to her family's deep involvement in the black community, she was surrounded by black politics, culture, and economics. Her father, a real estate agent, was very active in the NAACP and Urban League and donated large amounts of money to various causes. In addition, he served as a U.S. Marshal and ran for Congress. Her mother, a former schoolteacher, was a ward committeewoman and was also dedicated to striving for social and political change. Her uncle, William Leo Hansberry, a professor at Howard University, was so noted a scholar of African history that a college was named in his honor at the University of Nigeria. Also into Hansberry's

Lorraine V. Hansberry   *Hansberry, Lorraine V., photograph. The Library of Congress.*

Chicago home came such important and representative figures of the black community as Paul Robeson, Duke Ellington, Walter White, Joe Louis, and Jesse Owens. Partly because of her parents' attitudes and partly because of these visitors, Hansberry never felt in awe of the famous and, while in high school, wrote letters to congressmen, senators, and even the president concerning civic issues of importance to her.

Hansberry vs. Lee   In 1938 Hansberry's father, risking jail, challenged Chicago's real estate covenants, which legally upheld housing discrimination, by moving his own family into a white neighborhood. While her father was in court, a mob gathered in front of the house and began shouting and throwing bricks. A bodyguard ended the conflict by showing a loaded gun, but not before a large concrete slab was thrown just past the eight-year-old Hansberry's head. In spite of this reception, she and her family remained in the house until a lower court ordered them to leave. With the help of the NAACP, her father fought the case all the way to the United States Supreme Court, which struck down the restrictive covenants in the famous *Hansberry vs. Lee* decision in 1940. Unfortunately, the practice of restrictive covenants continued in Chicago, even though the law no longer supported them. The idea of a black family moving into a predominantly white neighborhood—and receiving a less-than-friendly welcome—would later be the central focus of Hansberry's play *A Raisin in the Sun.*

In addition to his disillusionment over the outcome of this legal battle, Carl Hansberry was soon disturbed by the segregation of blacks in the U.S. Army during World War II. One of his sons, Carl, Jr., served in a segregated unit and the other, Perry, contested his draft because he refused to serve in an army that discriminated against blacks. Carl Hansberry's embitterment over continuing American racial injustice eventually led him to purchase a house in Mexico City, where he planned to permanently relocate his family. However, he died on March 17, 1946, before he could complete preparations for the move, and the family remained in Chicago.

Desire to Write   In 1948, violating a family tradition of attending Howard University, Hansberry chose to go to the University of Wisconsin. There she saw a production of Sean O'Casey's *Juno and the Paycock* (1924), which eventually sparked in her the desire to write "the melody as I knew it—in a different key," a desire that she fulfilled in *A Raisin in the Sun* (1959). Unhappy with many of her courses, Hansberry left the university in 1950 "to seek an education of a different kind" in New York. As part of this new education, she started to work writing articles for Paul Robeson's radical black newspaper, *Freedom.* She also reviewed books and dramas by blacks, and, in 1952, she became an associate editor.

Social Justice Activism   Hansberry became involved in peace and freedom movements—marching on picket lines, speaking on Harlem street corners, and taking part in delegations to try to save persons whom she considered to be unjustly convicted of crimes. Moreover, when Paul Robeson was unable to travel to the Intercontinental Peace Congress in Montevideo, Uruguay, in 1952 because the State Department denied him a passport, she went as his representative. This trip gave her the invaluable opportunity to meet a large number of women from other countries and to compare notes on the circumstances of their lives. She later commented on what she learned from these women in her unpublished essay "Simone de Beauvoir and *The Second Sex*: An American Commentary, 1957."

Marriage & Family Life   In 1953, she married Robert Nemiroff, an aspiring writer and graduate student in English and history at New York University. Given her interests, it was appropriate that she became acquainted with him in a picket line protesting discrimination. Hansberry resigned from full-time work at *Freedom* in 1953 to concentrate on her creative efforts. From 1953 to 1956, she had three plays in progress while holding down a series of jobs—as a "tag-putter-inner-and-outer" in the garment fur industry, a typist, a production assistant in a theatrical firm, a staff member of *Sing Out* magazine, and recreation leader at the Federation for the Handicapped. In 1956, her husband and Burt D'Lugoff wrote the hit song "Cindy, Oh Cindy," and shortly afterwards he went to work running a

LITERARY AND HISTORICAL CONTEMPORARIES

Hansberry's famous contemporaries include:

James Baldwin (1924–1987): Baldwin was an African American author recognized as one of the most important writers in post–World War II American literature. In his works, he exposed racial and sexual polarization in American society, and challenged readers to confront and resolve these differences.

Malcolm X (1925–1965): A dynamic and influential twentieth-century African American leader, Malcolm X rose to prominence in the mid-1950s as the outspoken national minister of the Nation of Islam under Elijah Muhammad.

Martin Luther King, Jr. (1929–1968): Nobel Peace Prize winner King was a minister, activist, and author recognized as one of the driving forces of the civil rights movement in the United States during the 1960s.

Maya Angelou (1928–): Angelou is an African American author best known for *I Know Why the Caged Bird Sings* (1970), the first of her series of autobiographical novels.

Ralph Ellison (1914–1994): Ellison was an American author best known for his novel *Invisible Man* (1952), which was awarded the National Book Award in 1953.

music publishing firm for their friend, Philip Rose. As a result, the couple's financial situation improved enough that Hansberry could concentrate full-time on her writing.

Success as a Playwright   For a while, Hansberry worked simultaneously on a novel, several plays, and an opera, but she turned increasingly to one play that she eventually chose to title *A Raisin in the Sun* from a line in Langston Hughes's poem "Harlem," which wondered if a dream deferred might "dry up / like a raisin in the sun"—or if it might eventually explode. This title points up the bitterness of the social conditions that forcibly and continuously defer the aspirations of the black family in the play. Hansberry completed the play in 1957 and, after an enthusiastic response from her husband, read it to their friends Burt D'Lugoff and Philip Rose. To her astonishment, Rose announced the next morning that he would like to produce it on Broadway. When *A Raisin in the Sun* finally opened at the Ethel Barrymore Theatre on March 11, 1959, Hansberry's drama drew favorable reviews from all seven of the crucially influential New York newspaper critics and began a highly successful run of 538 performances.

Her play's success made Hansberry an overnight sensation. She sold the movie rights to *A Raisin in the Sun* to Columbia Pictures in 1959, and the resulting film earned a nomination for Best Screenplay of the Year from the Screenwriters Guild and a special award at the Cannes Film Festival, both in 1961.

In 1960 producer-director Dore Schary commissioned Hansberry to write a drama on slavery for NBC to commemorate the centennial of the Civil War. However, the program was eventually canceled amid a battery of questions about Hansberry's "attitude" toward the material. Hansberry completed the play, which she called *The Drinking Gourd* (1972), and it was published after her death.

In 1961 she and her husband moved from their Greenwich Village apartment, where they had been living since their marriage, to a house in a tranquil, wooded area in Croton-on-Hudson, New York. From this peaceful and secluded place, she maintained the necessary balance between her public and private commitments. In 1962, Hansberry mobilized support for the Student Non-Violent Coordinating Committee (SNCC) in its struggle against Southern segregation.

Battle against Cancer   In 1963, Hansberry was hospitalized for tests, with the results suggesting cancer. Nevertheless, she persisted in her various commitments. On May 24, at the request of James Baldwin, she joined a meeting of several prominent blacks and a few whites with Attorney General Robert Kennedy to discuss the racial crisis. On June 19, she chaired a meeting in Croton-on-Hudson to raise money for SNCC. Only five days later, she underwent an unsuccessful operation in New York. She would continue to spend time in and out of the hospital until her death from cancer a year and a half later.

In 1964 Hansberry's marriage ended in divorce, but her creative collaboration with Nemiroff continued, and the two of them continued to see each other daily until her death. In early October, Hansberry moved to the Hotel Victoria in New York to be near rehearsals of her play *The Sign in Sidney Brustein's Window* (1964), which was being produced by Nemiroff and Burton D'Lugoff. The play received mixed reviews. Hansberry died on January 12, 1965.

During the last year and a half of her life, Hansberry spent considerable time working on her African play, *Les Blancs* (1970). The basic plotting, characterization, thematic development, and the majority of the speeches were Hansberry's, with Nemiroff completing the rest of the play. *Les Blancs* opened at the Longacre Theatre on November 15, 1970, and, having received mixed reviews, closed after forty-seven performances.

Works in Literary Context

Although her life was brutally curtailed by cancer at only thirty-four, Hansberry's contribution to Afro-American culture was of considerable significance. As dramatist, film and television scriptwriter, novelist, poet, and essayist, she was among the greatest celebrators of the black spirit, as well as one of the sharpest intellects and keenest observers of her time. Her writing was strongly influenced by the presence of strong role models both in her family and in the community in which she grew up.

The Black Experience Clearly, Hansberry's emphasis on black social conditions, black strength, black struggle, and Pan-Africanism make *A Raisin in the Sun* a drama first and foremost about the black experience. This does not rule out universal dimensions to the play, however. Hansberry's masterful orchestration of a variety of complex themes, her skillful portrayal of black American—and African—lifestyles and patterns of speech, her wit, wisdom, and powerful dramatic flair all help to place *A Raisin in the Sun* among the finest dramas of the twentieth century and make it the cornerstone of the black theater movement.

Perhaps the best indication of the contemporary significance of Hanberry's meaning for blacks came in 1975 when Woodie King, Jr., began to prepare a documentary on the black theater. He decided to call his film "The Black Theater Movement: *A Raisin in the Sun* to the Present" because he found that of the more than sixty people he interviewed "over forty... said that, at one time or another, they had been influenced or aided, or both, by Lorraine Hansberry and her work."

Universal Concerns In addition to being an accomplished playwright, Hansberry was also a master prose stylist and finished a wealth of published and unpublished essays on black history, black art, black feminism, the Cuban missile crisis, the House Un-American Activities Committee, existentialism, the civil rights movement, world literature, her own work, and the many other topics that interested her. While her drama frequently dealt with the black experience, a wide range of universal concerns were her focus. Her last published play, *What Use Are Flowers?* (1972), revealed the range of her awareness, dealing with the meaning of civilization in the context of its capacity for self-destruction through nuclear warfare. This range was further demonstrated by the two versions of *To Be Young, Gifted and Black*, the play (produced in 1969), and the much more extensive informal biography (published in 1969) her former husband and literary executor, Robert Nemiroff, put together after her death from segments of her plays, essays, speeches, and poems.

Works in Critical Context

Hansberry was highly regarded in her day for the artistic merit of her most famous work, *A Raisin in the Sun*, and its enormous success on Broadway. Many critics appreciated Hansberry's ability to appeal to issues that included, but also extended beyond, race. However, her short career—as well as some skepticism over the true significance of her work—has left her literary legacy perhaps less secure than other African American writers of the same period.

A Raisin in the Sun The critical success of *A Raisin in the Sun* was confirmed when the New York Drama

COMMON HUMAN EXPERIENCE

While much of her work focuses on the experiences of African Americans, Hansberry extends upon the theme of racial inequality to the more general theme of humanity's capacity for self-destruction. Other works that explore this theme include the following:

Cat's Cradle (1963), a novel by Kurt Vonnegut. In this work, the author satirizes science and religion as he tells the story of ice-nine, a substance designed by scientists which ends up destroying virtually all living things on Earth in only a matter of days.

Oryx and Crake (2003), a novel by Margaret Atwood. In this story, the collapse of human civilization is driven by a society which values extreme commodification of everything, including human lives.

An Inconvenient Truth (2006), a film documentary directed by Davis Guggenheim. This work, based on a popular presentation developed by Al Gore, presents evidence that human activities have created a global warming effect that is making Earth increasingly uninhabitable for many forms of life, including people.

Critics Circle voted it Best Play of the Year over Tennessee Williams's *Sweet Bird of Youth* (1959), Archibald MacLeish's *JB* (1958), and Eugene O'Neill's *A Touch of the Poet* (1958). However, not all critics, then or now, agreed with the generally positive assessment. Tom F. Driver of the *New Republic* argues in his review that *A Raisin in the Sun* "is old-fashioned," adhering to the "over-worked formulas... of the 'domestic play.'" He also contends that "much of its success is due to our sentimentality over the 'Negro question'" and that "it may have been Miss Hansberry's objective to show that the stage stereotypes will fit Negroes as well as white people." The novelist, Nelson Algren, claims that "*Raisin* does not assert the hardbought values the Negro has won," and dismisses the significance of the play: "Dramatically, *Raisin* does for the Negro people what hair straightener and skin-lightener have done for the Negro cosmetics trade." Social critic Harold Cruse termed it "the most cleverly written piece of glorified soap opera I, personally, have ever seen on a stage."

Responses to Literature

1. In what ways does *A Raisin in the Sun* reflect the societal changes that led to the civil rights movement? Support your views using examples from the play.

2. Read Langston Hughes's poem "Harlem" (sometimes referred to as "A Dream Deferred") and discuss what happens when dreams are deferred. How does this relate to the concept of the American Dream and to Hansberry's play *A Raisin in the Sun*?

3. What similarities and differences do you notice between characters of different generations in *A Raisin in the Sun*? How can you account for such differences?

4. In *A Raisin in the Sun*, to what extent do the Youngers believe in stereotypes? How would their lives be different if stereotypes and prejudice did not exist?

BIBLIOGRAPHY

Books

Abramson, Doris E. *Negro Playwrights in the American Theatre: 1925–1959.* New York: Columbia University Press, 1969.

Bigsby, C. W. E. *Confrontation and Commitment: A Study of Contemporary American Drama, 1959–1966.* Columbia, Mo.: University of Missouri Press, 1968.

Cruse, Harold. *The Crisis of the Negro Intellectual.* New York: William Morrow, 1967.

Isaacs, Harold R. *The New World of Negro Americans.* New York: John Day, 1963.

Scheader, Catherine. *They Found a Way: Lorraine Hansberry.* Chicago: Children's Press, 1978.

Periodicals

Brown, Lloyd W. "Lorraine Hansberry as Ironist." *Journal of Black Studies* 4 (March 1974): 237–247.

Carter, Steven R. "Commitment Amid Complexity: Lorraine Hansberry's Life-in-Action." *MELUS* 7 (Fall 1980): 39–53.

Hairston, Loyle. "Lorraine Hansberry: Portrait of an Angry Young Writer." *Crisis* 86 (April 1979): 123–124, 126, 128.

Kaiser, Ernest and Robert Nemiroff. "A Lorraine Hansberry Bibliography." *Freedomways* 19 (Fourth Quarter 1979): 285–304.

Ness, David E. "*The Sign in Sidney Brustein's Window:* A Black Playwright Looks at White America." *Freedomways* 11 (Fourth Quarter 1971): 359–366.

Terkel, Studs. "An Interview with Lorraine Hansberry." *WFMT Chicago Five Arts Guide* 10 (April 1961): 8–14.

✿ Joy Harjo

BORN: *1951, Tulsa, Oklahoma*

NATIONALITY: *American*

GENRE: *Poetry, drama*

MAJOR WORKS:

What Moon Drove Me to This? (1980)

She Had Some Horses (1983)

Secrets from the Center of the World (1989)

In Mad Love and War (1990)

The Woman Who Fell from the Sky (1994)

Joy Harjo   *Harjo, Joy, photograph by Abdoo Studios, Inc. Reproduced by permission of the photographer.*

Overview

Joy Harjo is a poet, scriptwriter, and musician. Strongly influenced by her Muskogee Creek heritage, feminist ideology, and background in the arts, Harjo frequently incorporates Native American myths, symbols, and values into her writing. Her poetry additionally emphasizes the Southwest landscape and the need for remembrance and transcendence.

Works in Biographical and Historical Context

A Rural Oklahoma Beginning Joy Harjo was born on May 9, 1951, in Tulsa, Oklahoma, to Allen W. and Wynema Baker Foster. She is of French, Irish, and Cherokee descent on her mother's side, and Muscogee (Creek) on her father's. Harjo, who is a registered member of her father's tribe, the Muscogee Creeks, credits her great-aunt, Lois Harjo Ball, with teaching her about her Indian identity.

Harjo's interest in writing reflects the influence of both of her parents. Her mother composed unpublished country songs, while her father came from a long line of tribal speakers and leaders. In "Writing with the Sun," an autobiographical essay, Harjo says that her interest in poetry was stirred when her mother gave her a Louis Untermeyer anthology as an eighth birthday present. She also credits her interest in poetry to predawn walks outdoors around her family home, explaining that she sang with the dawn chorus of birds and insects to guide the sunrise. "That combination of voices," she says, "was poetry, and therein was my first understanding of poetry."

A Painter Becomes a Poet   Harjo knew from an early age that she wanted to be involved in the arts. Initially, however, she wanted to follow in the steps of her grandmother and great-aunt and become a painter. Painting, rather than poetry, was her first artistic love.

At age sixteen, Harjo attended boarding school at the Institute of American Indian Arts in Santa Fe, New Mexico. Here, her talents as an artist were encouraged. A year later, Harjo had a son, Phil Dayn. After graduation, the young mother moved back to Oklahoma, joined a Native American dance troupe, and worked a series of odd jobs before pursuing a college education.

It was when she was in her early twenties that Harjo first began to consider herself a writer. She was enrolled as an undergraduate student at the University of New Mexico and raising two small children. (Her daughter, Rainy Dawn, was born in 1973). Upon hearing American poet Galway Kinnell and Native American writers Simon Ortiz and Leslie Marmon Silko read from their works, Harjo was inspired to change her major from painting to poetry.

Inspired by the Southwest   As an undergraduate, Harjo completed her first poetry collection, a nine-poem chapbook titled *The Last Song* (1975). Most of the poems are set in either Oklahoma or New Mexico and are often linked to the landscape and to the idea of survival. Though the poems have a definite modern feel, their roots in the red-dirt country of Oklahoma are obvious. The poems reflect her strong connection to the landscape, history, and native people of the Southwest.

In 1976, Harjo completed her degree in English at the University of New Mexico, and two years later she earned a master of fine arts in creative writing from the University of Iowa. In 1978 she also won the first of two grants from the National Endowment for the Arts. In her introduction to *How We Became Human*, Harjo says that during these years she read the work of many American and international poets, including Richard Hugo, Audre Lorde, Okot p'Bitek, and Pablo Neruda. She attended multicultural poetry readings in New York City and in Amsterdam, expanding her awareness and knowledge of world poetry.

Travel and Other Ventures   The late 1970s and early 1980s was a busy time for Harjo. She published her first full-length book of poetry, *What Moon Drove Me to This?* in 1979. She also served on the editorial staff of several literary magazines, among them *Contact II* and *High Plains Literary Review*. Furthermore, she branched out into a new form of writing: scriptwriting. She wrote scripts for television shows and a movie called *Origin of Apache Crown Dance*

LITERARY AND HISTORICAL CONTEMPORARIES

Joy Harjo's famous contemporaries include:

Leslie Marmon Silko (1948–): Leslie Silko is one of the foremost authors to emerge from the Native American literary renaissance of the 1970s. Her novels and poems blend Western literary forms with the oral traditions of her Laguna Pueblo heritage to communicate Native American concepts concerning time, nature, and spirituality and their relevance in the contemporary world.

Simon Ortiz (1941–): A noted Native American poet and writer, Ortiz writes stories with a message. He encourages his people to always be aware of their native traditions and the beauty of nature and the environment.

N. Scott Momaday (1934–): This Native American author is known for his novels and poetry collections that communicate the oral legends of his Kiowa heritage. In 1969 he became the first American Indian to win the Pulitzer Prize in fiction for his novel *House Made of Dawn* (1968), which had a tremendous impact on the development of Native American literature in the United States.

Branford Marsalis (1960–): This American saxophonist is considered one of the giants in jazz, though he also gives classical performances. He is a three-time Grammy winner.

Roberta Hill Whiteman (1947–): A poet of Wisconsin Oneida heritage, Whiteman is known for her work in *Star Quilt*, (1984) a collection of poetry that connects daily experience from her culture to respect for self and nature.

(1985). In addition to her writing projects, Harjo traveled abroad and met other indigenous poets.

In 1989 Harjo collaborated with Stephen Strom on the critically acclaimed *Secrets from the Center of the World*. In this volume, Strom's striking photographs of Navajo country in the Four Corners area are accompanied by Harjo's prose poetry. A year later, Harjo published *In Mad Love and War* (1990), which won many accolades and prizes, including the American Book Award, the William Carlos Williams Award, and the Delmore Schwartz Memorial Award, all in 1991. The book's success solidified her position as a major Native American poet and as an important figure in American poetry.

More Art, More Praise   Harjo continued to receive critical recognition with her next collection, *The Woman Who Fell from the Sky* (1994). The poems in this collection focus on music, storytelling, the land, and human spirit.

During this time, Harjo's involvement with the arts expanded into new areas. An avid saxophone player, Harjo experimented with setting her poems to music. She eventually formed her own band, Joy Harjo and Poetic Justice, in which she plays saxophone and also recites and sings versions

COMMON HUMAN EXPERIENCE

Harjo's poems reveal the interconnectedness of all things. For example, she places humans in a subordinate position to land and views the land with an awareness of its own history. Here are other works that explore the sense of continuity and interconnectedness:

The Force That through the Green Fuse Drives the Flower (1934), a poem by Dylan Thomas. This poem is viewed as an expression of the unity of life. Using symbols and confusing imagery, Thomas makes the point that the forces of life and death are one and the same.

Walden; or, Life in the Woods (1854), nonfiction prose by David Henry Thoreau. In this autobiographical essay, Thoreau advocates a simple, self-sufficient way of life free from self-imposed social and financial obligations. He suggests through his work that a more intimate relationship between human beings and nature is an antidote to consumerism.

Ceremony (1977), a novel by Leslie Marmon Silko. In this work, Silko incorporates Laguna myths and historical incidents to reflect the Pueblo's connection to the natural world. Interweaving free verse poetry and narrative prose, the novel presents a philosophy about the nature of land and how ritual is connected to the earth and the universe.

Song of Myself (1855), a poem by Walt Whitman. From Whitman's *Leaves of Grass*, this long poem explores the connection between all people. It offers a glimpse of Whitman's mystic vision of equality, the universal self, the divinity of nature, and spiritual knowledge.

of her poems. With Poetic Justice, Harjo's poems are set into a mixture of traditional Native American drumming and jazz saxophone that Harjo has called "tribal-jazz-reggae."

By 1998, Harjo's many artistic accomplishments had earned her the Lifetime Achievement Award from the Native Writers' Circle of the Americas. Sponsored by a 1998 grant from the Lila Wallace-Reader's Digest Fund, Harjo worked with Atlatl, a nonprofit organization dedicated to increasing access to literature in Native American communities.

Harjo eventually traveled to Hawaii where she currently resides. She maintains a faculty appointment at the University of California, Los Angeles, where she is currently listed as a professor in the English department. Harjo continues to write poetry, travel with her two bands, Poetic Justice and Real Revolution, and present her poetry around the world.

Works in Literary Context

Harjo's work is largely autobiographical, informed by her love of the natural world and preoccupation with tran-

scendence, survival, and the limitations of language. The search for freedom, self-actualization, and nature are central to her poetry.

Imagery and Symbolism Harjo's work is replete with symbolic images, especially animals such as horses and crows. The collection *She Had Some Horses* (1983) is filled with horses: prehistoric horses, black horses, blue horses, running horses, drowning horses, and ice horses. These different kinds of horses represent types of people, from those who willingly serve others to those who are aloof and self-centered. Harjo has said the horses represent "different aspects of probably any person." In her poems, horses also serve as mediators between external and internal forces, since, in the words of Harjo, "they make swift connections between wind and blood."

Another Native American symbol Harjo incorporates in her work is the crow. Harjo says in her notes in *How We Became Human* that she considers crows to be "the chorus, outlining and commenting on the unfolding drama of this world." In "Watching Crow, Looking South Toward the Manzano Mountains," for example, the crow is an ambiguous, open figure, revealing edges while at the same time expanding the reader's perspective. Crows appear throughout "There Was a Dance, Sweetheart," mostly as watchful, interested, yet uninvolved presences. In some of Harjo's work, crows may be seen as an influence responsible for shaping the relationship between two characters.

Works in Critical Context

Harjo has been consistently praised for the thematic concerns of her writing, and her poetry has been included in several anthologies of Native American poetry. Southwestern imagery is dominant in her work, and she uses it to emphasize the plight of the individual and to communicate Creek values, myths, and beliefs. Though her focus is on Native Americans, critics have said that overall, her work has universal relevance. As poet Dan Bellm has put it, "Harjo's work draws from the river of Native tradition, but it also swims freely in the currents of Anglo-American verse—feminist poetry of personal/political resistance, deep-image poetry of the unconscious, 'new-narrative' explorations of story and rhythm in prose-poem form." While some critics have chided Harjo for being too political and for carrying a banner for too many causes at once—Harjo writes of war, peace, native concerns, economics, crime, poverty, love, hate, revolution, and death—readers have expressed fondness for her consideration of some of the most important issues of our time. Harjo's fans also enjoy her powerful voice and clear vision, and they appreciate that she does not tell her reader how to feel but simply shares the truth as she sees it.

What Moon Drove Me to This? *What Moon Drove Me to This?* includes poems filled with imagery that paints women as earth, people as horses, and wind as mother. The poems also demonstrate Harjo's ongoing interest in

Navajo horse songs. Critics praised this collection, saying it shows Harjo's continued ability to find and voice the deep spiritual truths underlying everyday experiences, especially for Native Americans. The poems are also praised for capturing the search for freedom and self-actualization. In the poem, "Looking Back," for example, the full moon acts as a spirit or guide, a beacon to higher meaning and experience. Or, as critic Jim Ruppert calls it, an entrance into "mythic space."

In Mad Love and War The poems in this multi-award-winning collection are rich and varied, drawing on many different areas. Harjo's Native American voice is very present and is expressed through images of deer, laughing birds, lizards, storms, crows, and rabbits. But Harjo moves beyond these symbols and traditions to detail the lives and deaths of dreamers who failed because of circumstances or violence. The result is a collection of poetry that is appreciated by readers and critics for its passion and overt concern with politics, tradition, remembrance, and the transformational aspects of poetry.

In *World Literature Today*, John Scarry writes "Harjo's range of emotion and imagery in this volume is truly remarkable. She achieves intimacy and power in ways that send a reader to every part of the poetic spectrum for comparisons and for some frame of reference." For example, in the poem "Autobiography," a mother describes how God created humans to inhabit the earth. Reviewer Leslie Ullman from the *Kenyon Review* writes of this poem, "Like a magician, Harjo draws power from overwhelming circumstance and emotion by submitting to them, celebrating them, letting her voice and vision move in harmony with the ultimate laws of paradox and continual change." Commenting on the poem "Javelina," Ullman added that Harjo's

> stance is not so much that of a representative of a culture as it is the more generative one of a storyteller whose stories resurrect memory, myth, and private struggles that have been overlooked, and who thus restores vitality to the culture at large.

More praise for the volume is found in the *Prairie Schooner*, where reviewer Kathleen West writes, "*In Mad Love and War* has the power of beauty and prophecy and all the hope of love poised at its passionate beginning. It allows us to enter the place 'we haven't imagined' and allows us to imagine what we will do when we are there."

Responses to Literature

1. Read at least three of Harjo's poems from *She Had Some Horses*. Write a short paper in which you discuss the symbolism of the horses. In your opinion, what is Harjo's overriding message in these poems? What role do horses play in delivering this message?

2. Discuss the social and political implications of *In Mad Love and War*. What criticisms does Harjo

make of society and culture, and what devices does she use to do this?

3. Using the Internet or your library, find recordings of the music Harjo has set to her poetry. Write a review of her performance. What do you think about setting poetry to music? Does it change anything about a poem? Does it add to or subtract from a poem? Explain your position using examples from the poems you have read and the music you have listened to.

4. After reading at least five of Harjo's poems, discuss what you gleaned about Harjo and her culture. What attitude does Harjo have toward white people? Using her poems as evidence, state if you think her work has universal appeal or if it is favored primarily by Native Americans.

BIBLIOGRAPHY

Books

Allen, Paula Gunn. *The Sacred Hoop: Recovering the Feminine in American Indian Traditions.* Boston: Beacon Press, 1986.

Bloom, Harold. *Native American Women Writers.* Philadelphia: Chelsea House, 1998.

Bruchac, Joseph, ed. *Survival This Way: Interviews with American Indian Poet.* Tucson: University of Arizona Press, 1987.

Swann, Brian, and Arnold Kurpat, eds. *I Tell You Now: Autobiographical Essays by Native American Writers.* Lincoln: University of Nebraska Press, 1987.

Wilson, Norma C. *The Nature of Native American Poetry.* Albuquerque: University of New Mexico Press, 2001.

Periodicals

Byson, J. Scott. "Finding the Way Back: Place and Space in the Poetry of Joy Harjo." *MELUS* 27 (Fall 2002): 169–196.

Lang, Nancy. "Twin Gods Bending Over: Joy Harjo and Poetic Memory." *MELUS* 18 (Fall 1993): 41–49.

Leen, Mary. "An Art of Saving: Joy Harjo's Poetry and the Survival of Storytelling." *American Indian Quarterly* 19 (Winter 1995): 1–16.

Web sites

"Joy Harjo." Retrieved October 8, 2008, from http://www.miracosta.cc.ca.us/home/gfloren/harjo.htm. Last updated on October 20, 2007.

"Joy Harjo." Retrieved October 8, 2008, from http://www.joyharjo.com/JoyHarjoHome.html. Last updated October 2008.

"Joy Harjo." *Voices from the Gaps: Women Writers of Color.* University of Minnesota. Retrieved from http://voices.cla.umn.edu/vg/Bios/entries/harjo_joy.html. Last updated on May 17, 2007.

✺ Frances Ellen Watkins Harper

BORN: *1825, Baltimore, Maryland*

DIED: *1911, Philadelphia, Pennsylvania*

NATIONALITY: *American*

GENRE: *Fiction, poetry, nonfiction*

MAJOR WORKS:

Moses: A Story of the Nile (1869)
Sketches of Southern Life (1872)
Iola Leroy (1892)

Overview

Frances Ellen Watkins Harper, a celebrated orator and social activist, was one of the most popular black poets of the nineteenth century. Today, she is considered a minor poet of the abolitionist era whose works possess historic rather than artistic significance.

Works in Biographical and Historical Context

An Early Propensity for Literature According to her longtime friend and fellow activist William Still, Harper was born on September 24, 1825, to free parents in Baltimore, Maryland, then a slave state. Within three years she was orphaned and living with relatives, most

Frances E. W. Harper   *Harper, Frances E. W., photograph.*

likely in the home of her uncle, William Watkins. A dedicated abolitionist and defender of civil rights, Watkins ran a school for free black youths that was well known for its classical academic orientation and strict standards of behavior. Harper attended the school until she was thirteen years old, the age at which she was expected to begin earning a living. She excelled in her uncle's unusually sophisticated course of study. In particular, she learned both literary and oratorical skills and a sense of responsibility to moral, political, and religious concerns. She took her first job working in the home of the Armstrong family, where her responsibilities included caring for the children, sewing, and keeping house. Noticing young Frances's propensity for literature, her employers allowed her access to the wealth of their family-run bookstore during her spare time.

Teaching Career At the age of twenty, Harper published her first book of poems, *Forest Leaves* (c. 1845), of which no known copies exist. The publication of this volume ushered Harper into a small group of African American writers able to print literature. Around 1850, Harper left Baltimore, moving to Ohio to become the first female teacher at Union Seminary, a school founded by the African Methodist Episcopal Church. William Watkins had left for Canada, after being forced to sell his house and his school in the hostile environment following the passage of the Compromise of 1850 and its new provisions for remanding fugitives from slavery. The Fugitive Slave Act, a part of the Compromise of 1850, meant that free blacks could be taken into custody as an escaped slave based solely on the sworn claim of a white person, and that anyone harboring an alleged runaway slave could be fined and imprisoned. After working for some time in Ohio, Harper discovered she was not suited to teaching, though she had great respect for that profession. In her later fiction she always pays homage to those who choose teaching as a profession, often giving her heroes, regardless of gender, the task of educating the newly emancipated population.

Commitment to the Antislavery Cause During the early 1850s, Maryland passed a new law that made it illegal for free blacks to enter the state on punishment of enslavement. This law made Harper a further outcast in a country that already discriminated against anyone identified as of African heritage. Punctuating her exile was the fate of a young man who had entered Maryland only to be captured and returned to slavery. He managed to escape but was soon recaptured and died from exposure. From this horrific story, so real a possibility for her had she attempted to return home, was born her ardent commitment to antislavery. She wrote, "Upon that grave I pledged myself to the Anti-Slavery cause."

Harper then moved briefly to Philadelphia. She began publishing her poems in various abolitionist papers, including the *Liberator, Frederick Douglass' Paper*, and the *Provincial Freeman*. After delivering her first lectures in

Boston, she was invited to a position as lecturer for the Maine Anti-Slavery Society, becoming the only black person and one of few women on the circuit. Her first extant volume, *Poems on Miscellaneous Subjects* (1854), was published in Philadelphia. The great popularity of this work brought Harper to the attention of a wider audience and facilitated her way into abolitionist circles. The book was reprinted several times, selling more than twelve thousand copies within five years.

Harper's long career as a fiction writer began with the publication of "The Two Offers" (1859), the earliest known short story by an African American writer. The story appeared in the *Anglo-African Magazine*, one of the first literary journals entirely devoted to the written efforts of African Americans. The story is significant both in its own right and also for what it reveals about many of the issues that concerned Harper throughout her life.

Marriage and Family Life   Harper chose not to marry until 1860, when she was thirty-five years old. She married a widower, Fenton Harper, and moved to a farm in Ohio, purchased largely with her own savings. A few years later, she gave birth to a daughter, Mary, who joined Fenton's three children from a previous marriage. Although Harper contributed to the household economy by making and selling butter, she continued to be active in public life.

Disaster struck Harper when Fenton Harper died on May 23, 1864, leaving her with four small children to feed, and his creditors descended to claim everything they had jointly owned to pay debts she did not know he had. Though she had always been sensitive to women's concerns, this experience brought Harper new appreciation for women's powerlessness under the law. This experience reconfirmed Harper's stated belief that women should not be solely dependent on men. She rededicated herself to the causes of abolition and equal rights for all. Within months of her husband's death, Harper had moved to New England with her daughter, and she was again giving public lectures. Meanwhile, the Civil War raged on, with Americans of all color in both the Northern Union and Southern Confederacy anxiously awaiting the outcome.

Reconstruction in the South   After the Civil War, Harper devoted her energies to the newly freed black population and the work of reconstructing the war-battered South. She concluded her first tour of the South in 1867 and returned to Philadelphia, but went back less than a year later, traveling to all but two southern states between 1868 and 1871. During this busy time, Harper also published a serialized novel and three additional books of poetry. *Poems* (1871) collected poems that mostly had previously been published separately. Some critics consider *Moses, A Story of the Nile* (1869), a book-length poem in blank verse on the Old Testament patriarch, to be the height of Harper's poetic endeavors. *Sketches of Southern Life* (1872), a series of poems based on Harper's travels, received critical acclaim for its experimentation with black dialect and its focus on folk char-

acters. Harper also experimented with dialect in *Minnie's Sacrifice, Sowing and Reaping: A Temperance Story* (1869), her first novel, which was serialized in the *Christian Recorder*. She went even further in her exploration of dialect and folk wisdom in *Iola Leroy; or, Shadows Uplifted* (1892), her last and most famous novel. Both of these novels focus on the Civil War and Reconstruction. Similarly, *Trial and Triumph* (1888–1889) confronts the parallel themes of racial and gender inequality.

Minnie's Sacrifice was published while Union troops still occupied Southern territory; the subsequent three novels were published after Union troops had withdrawn and efforts at Reconstruction had failed. Racial violence and other forms of racial oppression were facts of everyday life in the South. Harper decided not to devote her energies to depicting this violence but instead to focus on strategies for building black communities from within. Harper continued to be active in organizations for progressive political and social change until the end of her life. In 1896 she helped to found the National Association of Colored Women, becoming its vice president the following year. This organization brought together such notable women activists as Harriet Tubman, Mary Church Terrel,

COMMON HUMAN EXPERIENCE

Much of Harper's written work concerns slavery. Other works that focus on this theme include the following:

Uncle Tom's Cabin; or, Life among the Lowly (1852), a novel by Harriet Beecher Stowe. One of the best-selling books of the nineteenth century, this work intensified tensions in the sectional conflict that ultimately led to the Civil War by portraying the cruelty of slavery.

Narrative of the Life of Frederick Douglass, an American Slave, Written by Himself (1845), a memoir by Frederick Douglass. One of the most read pieces of abolitionist literature, this work tells the story of the author's experiences as a slave and well-known orator.

Incidents in the Life of a Slave Girl (1861), a memoir by Harriet Jacobs. In this work the author details the horrors of slavery, particularly with regard to the abuse inflicted upon young girls and women.

and Ida Wells-Barnett in addressing on a national scale the struggle for civil rights for blacks and women.

Harper also was active in the Universal Peace Union from at least 1893 until her death in 1911. *The Peacemaker*, the official organ of the organization, often carried notices of Harper's speeches to the assembly and copies of her poems, one published as late as 1909. Harper's health declined after 1901. Though offered assistance by several convalescent homes, some of which she had helped establish, she refused, citing her desire for independence and love of liberty. Her daughter, Mary, who apparently lived with her throughout her life, died a short time before she did. Harper died on February 22, 1911.

Works in Literary Context

Harper captivated audiences with dramatic recitations of her antislavery and social reform verse. A social lecturer whose long life was devoted to abolition, freedmen's rights, Christian temperance, and women's suffrage, Harper used prose and poetry to enhance her message and stir audience emotions. While she wrote against slavery, she also broke away from the purely propagandistic mode of the antislavery poet and became one of the first black writers to focus on national and universal issues.

Antislavery and Social Reform Imitative of the works of Henry Wadsworth Longfellow and John Greenleaf Whittier, the poems in *Poems on Miscellaneous Subjects* are primarily anti-slavery narratives. Although Harper believed that black writers "must write less of issues that are particular and more of feelings that are general," most of her poetry is about the issue of slavery. For example, *Sketches of Southern*

Life, a collection of poems considered one of her best works, is narrated by ex-slaves Aunt Chloe and Uncle Jacob. With wit and charm, they provide a commentary on the concerns of Southern blacks: family, education, religion, slavery, and Reconstruction. Harper extends upon her treatment of these themes in her fiction works.

Women's Suffrage and Temperance Harper consistently supported women's suffrage—or right to vote—in her writings. In *Minnie's Sacrifice, Sketches of Southern Life*, and *Sowing and Reaping*, for example, she includes debates about the appropriateness of women voting. The discussion in *Minnie's Sacrifice* entered into the suffrage debate just after the Fifteenth Amendment to the U.S. Constitution was adopted by Congress and was being ratified by the states. The debate over the wording of the amendment, which excluded race but retained gender as criteria for suffrage, was still fresh in the memories of activists who, earlier allied in their opposition to slavery, had divided themselves into camps supporting black male or white female suffrage. Harper supported suffrage for all women, not just white women, as was sometimes proposed. A decade later, Harper linked the question of woman suffrage to temperance, or the avoidance of alcohol; this coincided with her involvement with the Women's Christian Temperance Union.

Harper's activist and writing career was truly remarkable for its length and consistency, as well as for its depth and breadth. Recently, she has begun to be recognized as, in the words of Frances Smith Foster, not only "the most popular African-American writer of the nineteenth century, but also one of the most important women in United States history."

Works in Critical Context

Harper was among the most popular black writers of her day, and her work was read in abolitionist papers and other publications devoted to improving social justice for African Americans in the nineteenth century. Her work was highly regarded for its criticism of racial inequality and patriarchy, as well as for the hope Harper conveyed in her rhetorical style.

Harper sparked renewed interest among twentieth-century scholars, who recognized her as a figure of more historic than artistic importance. Described variously as an early feminist, one of the first African American protest poets, and—in the words of Patricia Liggins Hill—"a major healer and race-builder of nineteenth-century America," Harper nonetheless made aesthetic contributions of pioneer significance.

Moses: A Story of the Nile *Moses: A Story of the Nile* is considered, by some critics, to be Harper's best poetic work. For example, when discussing the poem's artistic merits, Joan R. Sherman writes, "Mrs. Harper maintains the pace of her long narrative and its tone of reverent admiration with scarcely a pause for moralizing. *Moses* is Mrs. Harper's most original poem and one of considerable power." Indeed, some scholars judge *Moses: A Story of the Nile* to be exceptional in its quality when compared to the rest of Harper's work. Patricia Hill writes, "With the exception of *Moses: A Story of the Nile*... and *Sketches of Southern Life*..., Harper's poetry varies little in form, language, and poetic technique." Similarly, Maryemma Graham notes that "Watkins's remarkable power and dramatic appeal as a poet come from her strong, rhetorical, oral style."

Responses to Literature

1. What value does Harper place on self-reliance for women? Discuss her perspective on marriage in the context of her fiction, providing examples from her work to illustrate your statements.

2. What do Maria and Robert's birthmarks symbolize in *Iola Leroy*? What other symbols did you notice in the novel?

3. Who was Harper's original audience? Why do you think her work remained largely dismissed by the literary community until recently?

4. What role does biracial identity play in *Minnie's Sacrifice*?

BIBLIOGRAPHY

Books

Boyd, Melba Joyce. *Discarded Legacy: Politics and Poetics in the Life of Frances E. W. Harper*. Detroit, Mich.: Wayne State University Press, 1994.

Carby, Hazel. *Reconstructing Womanhood: The Emergence of the Afro-American Woman Novelist*. New York: Oxford University Press, 1987.

Christian, Barbara. *Black Women Novelists: The Development of a Tradition, 1892–1976*. Westport, Conn.: Greenwood Press, 1980.

Foster, Frances Smith, ed. *A Brighter Coming Day: A Frances Ellen Watkins Reader*. New York: Feminist Press, 1990.

Still, William. *The Underground Railroad*. Chicago: Johnson, 1970.

Tate, Claudia. *Domestic Allegories of Political Desire: The Black Heroine's Text at the Turn of the Century*. New York: Oxford University Press, 1992.

Washington, Mary Helen. *Invented Lives: Narratives of Black Women, 1860–1960*. New York: Doubleday/Anchor, 1988.

Periodicals

Ammons, Elizabeth. "Legacy Profile: Frances Ellen Watkins Harper (1825–1911)." *LEGACY* 2 (Fall 1985): 61–66.

Bacon, Margaret Hope. "'One Great Bundle of Humanity': Frances Ellen Watkins Harper (1825–1911)." *Pennsylvania Magazine of History and Biography* 113 (January 1989): 21–43.

Ernest, John. "From Mysteries to Histories: Cultural Pedagogy in Frances E. W. Harper's *Iola Leroy*." *American Literature* 64 (September 1992): 497–518.

Love, Alfred. "Memorial Tribute to Mrs. Frances E. W. Harper." *The Peacemaker* 30 (1911): 118–119.

McDowell, Deborah E. "'The Changing Same': Generational Connections and Black Women Novelists." *New Literary History* 18 (Winter 1987): 281–302.

Young, Elizabeth. "Warring Fictions: Iola Leroy and the Color of Gender." *American Literature* 64 (June 1992).

✸ Joel Chandler Harris

BORN: *1848, Eatonton, Georgia*

DIED: *1908, Atlanta, Georgia*

NATIONALITY: *American*

GENRE: *Fiction*

MAJOR WORKS:
Uncle Remus, His Songs and His Sayings: Folklore of the Old Plantation (1880)
Uncle Remus and His Friends (1892)
The Tar-Baby and Other Rhymes of Uncle Remus (1904)

Overview

Joel Chandler Harris was a successful journalist who gained national attention when he published a series of plantation stories told by the fictional slave Uncle Remus about the trickster Br'er Rabbit.

Works in Biographical and Historical Context

Growing up in Poverty Joel Chandler Harris was born December 9, 1848, near Eatonton, Georgia. The illegitimate son of an Irish day-laborer, Harris was perpetually embarrassed by his family situation and his appearance (he was a shocking redhead), twin insecurities that eventually resulted in chronic shyness. Several of Harris's biographers note that he developed his particular sense of humor in the attempt to overcome this shyness.

First Job as a Typesetter's Apprentice At age thirteen Harris went to work as a typesetter's apprentice to Joseph Addison Turner, editor and publisher of the weekly *Countryman*. Harris soon discovered that he and Turner shared a common sense of humor. As he took on greater responsibility with the *Countryman*, Harris was given the opportunity to write for print.

In 1864, near the close of the American Civil War, a detachment of General William Tecumseh Sherman's Federal troops ransacked Turnwold. Turner's finances shrank significantly as a result of the war, and in 1866 the publication of the *Countryman* was halted. Harris moved to Macon to take a job as a typesetter with the *Telegraph*.

Joel Chandler Harris   *Harris, Joel Chandler, photograph. The Library of Congress.*

tation slaves. The sketches were immediately hailed as the most accurate and entertaining tales of their type.

It was not until 1879 that these sketches featured Uncle Remus, the character who propelled Harris to literary fame. With Uncle Remus as his mouthpiece, Harris recounted all the slave legends and folktales he had absorbed as a young man. Harris's admirers found a compelling air of authenticity in the narrative voice of Uncle Remus; to many, he was a portrait of life before the war. The first collection of Uncle Remus stories, *Uncle Remus, His Songs and His Sayings: Folklore of the Old Plantation* (1880) consisted mostly of animal tales focused on the crafty, nearly sinister deeds of Br'er Rabbit. It was immensely popular and gained the attention of folklorists and philologists.

Success of the Remus Stories   Following his first book in 1880, Harris published four more in the next ten years, including his second collection of Remus stories, *Nights With Uncle Remus: Myths and Legends of the Old Plantation* (1883). By this time he had read deeply on the literature of folklore and introduced this volume with a thirty-one-page discussion of the origin of his stories.

By 1890 Harris was acclaimed as America's most accomplished dialect writer, and his literary popularity was assured. Throughout the decade of the 1890s he maintained a prolific pace that resulted in twelve more volumes, including one Uncle Remus collection, *Uncle Remus and His Friends: Old Plantation Stories, Songs, and Ballads with Sketches of Negro Character* (1892). During this period Harris also produced adult fiction, an autobiography, juvenile fiction, and regional tales. Near the end of the decade Harris introduced a female counterpart to Remus in *The Chronicles of Aunt Minervy Ann* (1899).

Retirement from the Atlanta Constitution   In 1900, Harris retired from the *Atlanta Constitution* and signed a new publishing contract that allowed him to devote his full energies to his stories and his large family. In that year he published *On the Wing of Occasions* (1900), his first collection of "Billy Sanders" stories. Sanders, a young middle-class Georgian with a good deal of homespun philosophy, first appeared as a Confederate Army private in a *Saturday Evening Post* serial. Three more Billy Sanders volumes appeared in the next decade. The Billy Sanders stories did not receive the acclaim the Remus yarns had achieved, but they were generally popular and kept Harris's name before the public.

A Difficulty in Writing Novels   From as early as 1878, when he had serialized "The Romance of Rockville" in the weekly edition of the *Constitution*, Harris had been frustrated with his efforts to write a novel. In 1896 he produced *Sister Jane: Her Friends and Acquaintances* but recognized deficiencies in the book. *Sister Jane* offered interesting and accurate glimpses of small-town life in Middle Georgia, but as a novel it was plodding and improbable, as critics were not hesitant to point

Along with his newly developed maturity, Harris took away memories of plantation life that provided the foundation for his career as a journalist and author.

Harris worked variously as a typesetter and book reviewer in Georgia and Louisiana until 1867, when he accepted an editorial position with the *Monroe Advertiser* in Forsyth, Georgia. Harris spent three satisfying years as a staff writer with the paper, then took an associate editor's position with the Savannah *Morning News*.

Uncle Remus is Born   Harris had a daily column in Savannah—"Affairs in Georgia"—which provided readers with a dose of pointed observation, local color, and humor. Harris quickly gained a regular following. He was, in fact, second only to his contemporary Mark Twain in reputation as a Southern humorist. Following a local outbreak of yellow fever in 1876, Harris left Savannah for Atlanta, where he took a position with the *Constitution*, where he would remain for ten years. At the request of his editor- in-chief, Evan P. Howell, Harris published a series of sketches done in African-American dialect, a homespun interpretation of the speech of plan-out. Now, near the end of his career, he tried again with *Gabriel Tolliver: A Story of Reconstruction* (1902). Criticism was mixed, but the book does provide a characterization of the lives of both whites and blacks in the Reconstruction period.

A Little Union Scout (1904) was published following serialization in the February and March issues of the *Saturday Evening Post*. Some critics considered the short novel chronicling the adventures of two young Confederates and an African American slave as one of Harris's most imaginative works, and popular reaction was enthusiastic. Then, after a hiatus of twelve years, there followed three new Uncle Remus volumes: *The Tar-Baby and Other Rhymes of Uncle Remus* (1904), *Told by Uncle Remus: New Stories of the Old Plantation* (1905), and *Uncle Remus and Br'er Rabbit* (1907). The new stories suggest Harris was unhappy with the direction the New South was taking, and public reaction to these volumes was less than enthusiastic.

By 1905, Harris was at the height of his literary reputation. In May of that year he was named a charter member—one among twenty—of the American Academy of Arts and Letters, joining such luminaries as Mark Twain, Henry Adams, and Henry James. In October, President Theodore Roosevelt visited Atlanta and publicly acclaimed the author as one of Georgia's foremost citizens.

Uncle Remus's Magazine   At age fifty-seven, Harris embarked on a new literary venture. On June 1907, after more than a year of preparation, *Uncle Remus's Magazine* made its debut, with Harris as its editor. The publication preached a cheerful philosophy and practiced tolerance in all matters. Its motto—"Typical of the South–National in Scope"—suggested it offered to the whole nation those Southern qualities of sentiment and affection in which Harris took such pride. At the end of the magazine's first year Harris wrote that it "has had a success far beyond the hopes of those engaged in producing it."

In May 1908 *Uncle Remus's Magazine* absorbed the *Home Magazine*, published by Bobbs-Merrill in Indianapolis. Combined circulation was said to be 200,000. Harris was overtaxed by the responsibilities of editing the magazine; he wrote much of its content and received a never-ending flow of visitors, and his health began to fail early in 1908. Doctors described his illness as acute nephritis and cirrhosis of the liver. In June he was confined to his bed, where he died on July 3, 1908.

Works in Literary Context

In his own day, Harris was one of America's most popular authors, known throughout the world for his humorous folktales about African American life told through the dialect of kindly old Uncle Remus. His writing was influenced by his experiences living and working on the Turnwold plantation.

LITERARY AND HISTORICAL CONTEMPORARIES

Joel Chandler Harris's famous contemporaries include:

Mark Twain (1835–1910): Considered the father of modern American literature, Twain is known in particular for his classic novel *The Adventures of Huckleberry Finn* (1884).

Henry James (1845–1916): An American literary critic and master of fiction who, in his later years, came to prefer Europe to the United States first in letters and later in politics.

W. E. B. Du Bois (1868–1963): Widely remembered for his dispute with Booker T. Washington over the role to be played by African-Americans in American society, Du Bois treated this issue at length in his famous *The Souls of Black Folk* (1903).

Henry Adams (1838–1918): The American author regarded less for his contribution to literature and more for his contribution to the history of ideas; in his best-known work, *The Education of Henry Adams: A Study in Twentieth-Century Multiplicity* (1907), Adams presents his view of the world as less stable and coherent than it once was and predicts this trend will continue unabated.

Theodore Roosevelt (1858–1919): The twenty-sixth President of the United States, Roosevelt promoted the Progressive movement and believed the United States needed to play a greater role in international affairs.

Plantation Life in the Antebellum South   The modern reader may have difficulty appreciating the Uncle Remus tales. The dialect requires concentration and the humor is less than obvious to residents of a different era. At the turn of the century, however, as a nation only recently at war with itself tried to turn its back on sectional differences, Harris's romance of the old plantation, his fiction of kind masters and appreciative slaves, and his apparent affirmation of African American simplicity and white superiority (which on a close second look was no affirmation at all) were all balms for still-festering wounds.

Harris arranged the tales as follows: Uncle Remus is bound in service to a young white boy, to whom he relates all the fictions, myths, and legends he absorbed as a slave. Br'er Rabbit is the protagonist of the majority of these tales. Faced with seemingly insurmountable odds, Br'er Rabbit unfailingly resorts to wit, and in several cases homicide, to overcome his antagonists.

Modern Appeal   More than a hundred years after the publication of the first Uncle Remus tales, the stories are still widely read and enjoyed. Some critics argue that, despite his social and political agenda, Harris provided the African-American community an invaluable service by recording tales that may have otherwise been lost to

COMMON HUMAN EXPERIENCE

An idealized version of race relations in the antebellum South features prominently in Harris's fiction. Works that offer other perspectives on this theme include the following:

Uncle Tom's Cabin (1852), a novel by Harriet Beecher Stowe. In this best-selling work the author portrays the cruelty of slavery in a manner that exacerbated existing sectional tensions leading up to the Civil War.

Incidents in the Life of a Slave Girl (1861), a memoir by Harriet Jacobs. This story focuses on the abuse female slaves endured at the hands of white slave owners.

Beloved (1987), a novel by Toni Morrison. This haunting novel, dealing with the deep psychological legacy of slavery, was declared in a *New York Times* survey the finest work of American fiction published between 1980 and 2005.

The Wind Done Gone (2001), a novel by Alice Randall. Reacting against the idealized version of the antebellum South presented in Margaret Mitchell's *Gone with the Wind* (1936), this work tells its story from the perspective of a mulatto slave instead of the rich white Scarlett O'Hara.

history. Recent African-American authors, however, have reclaimed this body of folklore and presented it without the dialect treatment or mediation of Uncle Remus.

Works in Critical Context

As a journalist and author of fiction, Harris enjoyed immense success and popularity during his lifetime. In fact, many critics ranked him second only to Mark Twain as the best Southern humorist. Among his published works, his tales of Uncle Remus drew the most critical acclaim.

Popularity of Uncle Remus *Uncle Remus: His Songs and His Sayings* was an immediate success; ten thousand copies were sold in the first four months and critical reviews were overwhelmingly favorable. "Mr. Harris's book is altogether excellent of its kind," a *New York Times* (December 1, 1880) reviewer wrote, "and in preserving certain quaint legends and giving us exactly the sounds of the negro dialect, he has established on a firm basis the first real book of American folk lore." Harris's contemporary, the critic William Malone Baskervill, quoting an unspecified source in his *Southern Writers: Biographical and Critical Studies* (1896), noted that "'Uncle Remus'... belong[s] to the class of [literature] which 'has nothing but pleasant memories of slavery, and which has all the prejudices of caste and pride of family that were the natural results of the system.'"

Contemporary Perspectives on Uncle Remus Many critics concur that the latent racism of the Uncle Remus tales continues to bedevil Harris's work. In fact, the merit of Uncle Remus as children's literature has been called into question on several occasions because of its racist assumptions. Harris himself believed that slavery had been beneficial to African-Americans, and had helped to lift them from a state of savagery toward Christianity and American citizenship.

Responses to Literature

1. Why do you think Uncle Remus tells his stories to a white boy? Support your opinion with examples from the Uncle Remus stories.

2. Compare and contrast the view of slavery presented in Harris's Uncle Remus stories with that of Charles W. Chesnutt's Uncle Julius stories.

3. Why do you think Harris's stories held appeal for African-Americans as well as for white audiences?

4. How would you describe Harris's view of race relations in the South before the Civil War? Use examples from his fiction to support your opinion.

BIBLIOGRAPHY

Books

Bickley, Jr., R. Bruce, ed. *Critical Essays on Joel Chandler Harris*. Boston: G. K. Hall, 1981.

Bone, Robert. *Down Home: A History of Afro-American Short Fiction from Its Beginnings to the End of the Harlem Renaissance*. New York: Putnam's, 1975.

Brash, Walter. *Br'er Rabbit, Uncle Remus, and the "Cornfield Journalist": The Tale of Joel Chandler Harris*. Macon, Ga.: Mercer University Press, 2000.

Brookes, Stella Brewer. *Joel Chandler Harris—Folklorist*. Athens, Ga.: University of Georgia Press, 1950.

Cousins, Paul M. *Joel Chandler Harris: A Biography*. Baton Rouge, La.: Louisiana State University Press, 1968.

Harlow, Alvin P. *Joel Chandler Harris: Plantation Storyteller*. New York: Messner, 1941.

Harris, Julia Collier. *The Life and Letters of Joel Chandler Harris*. Boston & New York: Houghton, Mifflin, 1918.

Lee, Walter Wideman. *Joel Chandler Harris*. New York: The Century Company, 1909.

Wiggins, Robert Lemuel. *The Life of Joel Chandler Harris, from Obscurity in Boyhood to Fame in Early Manhood*. Nashville, Tenn.: Publishing House Methodist Episcopal Church, South, 1918.

Periodicals

Cochran, R. "Black Father: The Subversive Achievement of Joel Chandler Harris." *African American Review* 38 (2004): 21–34.

Strickland, William Bradley. "A Check List of the Periodical Contributions of Joel Chandler Harris (1848–1908)." *American Literary Realism* 9 (Summer 1976): 207–209.

Jim Harrison

BORN: *1937, Grayling, Michigan*

NATIONALITY: *American*

GENRE: *Fiction, nonfiction, poetry*

MAJOR WORKS:

Legends of the Fall (1979)

Dalva (1988)

The Woman Lit by Fireflies (1990)

Off to the Side (2002)

Returning to Earth (2007)

Overview

Jim Harrison is a contemporary American author whose literary reputation rests on his mastery of the novella—a mastery that became widely recognized after the publication of his trilogy *Legends of the Fall*. In addition to fiction, Harrison has made significant contributions to poetry, nonfiction, children's literature, and screenwriting.

Works in Biographical and Historical Context

Growing up in Michigan James "Jim" Harrison was born in Grayling, Michigan, on December 11, 1937, to Winfield Sprague Harrison, a country agricultural agent, and Norma Olivia Wahlgren Harrison. He was the second of five children born to the Harrisons. When he was three, Harrison's family moved to the small town of Reed City, Michigan. In 1945, a playmate accidentally injured the young Harrison with a broken glass laboratory beaker, leaving him blind in one eye. The injury would later influence Harrison's writing. As a child, Harrison spent a lot of time hunting, fishing, and hiking in the Michigan wilderness and eventually learned to find solace in nature. Four years after his injury, the Harrisons moved again, this time to Haslett, Michigan, so that they would be within commuting distance from Michigan State University.

Eclectic Experiences as a Teenager During his teenage years, Harrison had an eclectic range of experiences that critics often note as being among the greatest influences on his writing. In 1951, at the age of fourteen, Harrison experienced a religious conversion at a Baptist revival and became active as a preacher at fundamentalist youth fellowships. Contrasting his conversion were his experiences hitchhiking around the United States to investigate the bohemian life. With only ninety dollars and the typewriter he was given for his seventeenth birthday, Harrison began his journey after his father gave him a ride to the highway.

Jim Harrison *Ulf Andersen / Getty Images*

Jim Harrison

It was during this time that he worked as a busboy at the Stanley Hotel in Estes Park, Colorado, and later visited New York City's Greenwich Village.

Education in Comparative Literature In 1956, Harrison enrolled at Michigan State University in East Lansing, only to drop out a year later. After a brief hiatus—which he spent living in New York, Boston, and San Francisco—he returned to M.S.U. in 1959. Harrison then married Linda May King on October 10 of that same year. He graduated with his bachelor's degree in 1960 and enrolled in a master's program, where he met and formed strong relationships with other writers, including Dan Gerber, Tom McGuane, and Robert Dattila. Also in 1960, the first of two daughters, Jamie Louise, was born.

Harrison's education was interrupted a second time, in 1962, when his father and younger sister Jamie, both died in a car accident. He left Michigan to live with his brother in Boston and work as a book salesman. In 1965, he returned to Kingsley, Michigan, where he worked as a laborer and published three poems in *Nation* and five in *Poetry*. Aided by author Denise Levertov, Harrison was then able to publish his first poetry collection, *Plain Song* (1965). He finished his master's thesis, "The Natural History of Some Poem" in 1965, completing his master's in comparative literature in 1966.

Teaching in New York After finishing his graduate work, Harrison became an assistant to Herbert Weisinger, who served as his mentor, He also accepted a position as an associate professor of English at the State University of New York in Stony Brook. While there, he published a limited-edition chapbook, *Walking* (1967), and the poetry collection *Locations* (1968). In addition, he organized a world poetry conference.

Return to Michigan In 1969, Harrison and his family returned to Michigan and bought a farm. He then collaborated with Dan Gerber on a film about the timber wolf, and on a literary magazine entitled *Sumac*, which ceased publication several years later. Harrison received a Guggenheim fellowship that enabled him to continue publishing poetry after sustaining a severe back injury while hunting. During his recovery, Harrison wrote his first novel *Wolf* (1971). Shortly after its publication, Harrison and Gerber traveled to Moscow and Leningrad (now St. Petersburg) on a literary pilgrimage. His second daughter, Anna Severin, was born in 1971.

Experience Screenwriting Builds Important Relationships In 1975, Harrison wrote the screenplay *A Good Day to Die* and met Jack Nicholson on the set of *Missouri Breaks*. Nicholson financed Harrison's writing during 1978, the year he wrote *Legends of the Fall*, one of Harrison's most famous works and one that was eventually adapted for film in 1994. Harrison continued to work as a successful screenwriter until 1997.

Trilogy Establishes Harrison's Literary Reputation The success of *Legends of the Fall* established Harrison's reputation as a significant figure in contemporary literature. Throughout the 1980s and 1990s he expanded his roster of published works to include more fiction, screenplays, and collections of his nonfiction journalism. It was during this period that E. P. Dutton published *Dalva*, which many critics argue is his best work of fiction. In 1990, the same year he published another successful work of fiction, *The Woman Lit by Fireflies*, Harrison was awarded the Mark Twain Award for distinguished contribution to Midwestern literature.

After producing many publications during the 1980s and 1990s, Harrison decided to write a memoir, *Off to the Side*. This, however, did not mark the end of Harrison's career as a fiction writer. Since the publication of his memoir, Harrison has published novels, poetry, and various nonfiction collections at a rate that matches his earlier production.

In 2005, The Meijer Foundation purchased Harrison's collected papers as a donation to the Grand Valley State University Special Collections, where they are now housed and updated annually. Harrison and his wife currently live in Arizona and Montana. In 2007, he published the popular novel *Returning to Earth* and was elected as a member of the Academy of Arts and Letters. His most recent publication is *The English Major* (2008), a novel.

Works in Literary Context

Harrison has written in a variety of genres throughout his literary career, including poetry, fiction, nonfiction, and children's literature. In addition, he has collaborated with his daughter Jamie on Hollywood screenplays. Contributing most significantly to Harrison's literary reputation is his mastery of the novella, which was widely recognized after the publication of trilogy *Legends of the Fall*. Influences on Harrison's work include his childhood blinding in one eye, his experiences in the woods of north-central Michigan, his religious conversion as a teenager, and the time he spent hitchhiking to various American cities during the 1960s.

The Natural World: A Regional Perspective Much of Harrison's fiction depicts life in remote areas of the Northern United States—Michigan's Upper Peninsula, the mountains of Montana, and Nebraska's sand hills. For example, like much of his work, *Return to Earth* is set in Michigan where the terrain is rugged and the climate extreme. In it, the characters are inextricably linked to their environment. In other works, Harrison becomes involved with regional Native American history. In the title piece of *Legends of the Fall*, for example, Harrison emphasizes soul history, which indicates that the transgressions of American settlers and the U.S. government against Native American populations are still felt in the present day. Interwoven with his other themes are the complexities of human relationships and the author's perspective on food, wine, and sex in the human experience.

Works in Critical Context

Harrison is seen by many as a regional writer and is often compared to other regionalist authors. In the words of Heller McAlpin of the *The San Francisco Chronicle*, "His writing bears earthy whiffs of wild morels and morals and of booze and botany, as well as hints of William Faulkner, Louise Erdrich, Herman Melville and Norman Maclean." Harrison has also been compared to Ernest Hemmingway for his "tales of strong men living an embittered life." Such comparisons formed the basis of some harsh reviews of his first three novels, with some critics dismissing him as a writer fixated on the myth of the macho male. However, after the success of *Legends of the Fall*, many of Harrison's works have enjoyed a positive reception with critics, with many praising the honesty of his prose and ability to explore the needs of the human soul. Will Blythe, in the *New York Times Book Review*, comments: "[Harrison's] books . . . are as grounded as Thoreau's in the particulars of American place—its rivers and thickets, its highways and taverns." "Harrison's language seems to come straight from America's center of gravity, the core of the country where people still live by a code and think for themselves. . . . After 25 books Harrison is . . . closing in on the status of a national treasure," writes Anthony Brandt of *National Geographic Adventure*.

Dalva   *Dalva* has been widely regarded as Harrison's best novel. Jonathan Yardley, in an appreciative review in *Washington Post Book World*, commented that the novel was "moving, interesting and satisfying. It is his his most ambitious work to date; he fulfills this ambition to a degree that, if there is any such thing as literary justice, should bring him a substantial and appreciative readership." Harrison's fellow novelist Louise Erdrich expressed a similarly positive response to the novel in her *Chicago Tribune* review. She described *Dalva* as "big-hearted, an unabashedly romantic love story, a grim chronicle of changing time, an elegantly crafted set of imaginary diaries, a work of humor and a unified lament." Erdrich also expressed her admiration for the language and characterization in the novel, as well as the fact that it is full of interesting information, "advice on wine, horses, and observations on desert flora and fauna, birds, and the work of Edward Curtis." In the *Times Literary Supplement*, John Clute had a less enthusiastic response to the novel, but found it nonetheless worth reading. He acknowledged that *Dalva* was an attempt by Morrison to widen his subject-matter, and commented that although it "might not seem a markedly convincing attempt to broaden this palette . . . there are moments of insight and pleasure throughout its considerable length which make the effort worthwhile."

The English Major   Alan Cheuse of the *Chicago Tribune* describes *The English Major* as "a bawdy and engaging

---

LITERARY AND HISTORICAL CONTEMPORARIES

Jim Harrison's famous contemporaries include:

Gary Snyder (1930–): An American author, Snyder's stature as both a counterculture figure and an innovative and important mainstream poet places him in an uncommon position in contemporary literature; he is the recipient of several literary honors and awards, including a Pulitzer Prize for his poetry collection *Turtle Island* (1974).

Denise Levertov (1923–1997): A British-born American poet, Levertov corresponded with famous poets, including T. S. Eliot, from a young age and whose work is noted for its political, feminist, and religious themes.

Ted Kooser (1939–): Kooser is an American author and U.S. Poet Laureate Consultant to the Library of Congress from 2004 to 2006.

Peter Matthiessen (1927–): An American novelist and naturalist, Matthiessen writes with compassion and conviction about vanishing cultures, oppressed peoples, and exotic wildlife and locales.

Louise Erdrich (1954–): In her fiction and poetry Erdrich draws on her Ojibwa heritage to examine complex familial and sexual relationships among full- and mixed-blood Native Americans as they struggle with questions of identity in white Euro-American culture.

Russell Chatham (1939–): An American landscape artist, Chatham has sold works to numerous authors, including Kurt Vonnegut, Eudora Welty, and Hunter S. Thompson.

Dan Gerber (1940–): Gerber is a Michigan-born poet who coedited the literary magazine *Sumac* with Harrison from 1968 to 1972

---

new novel" and pitches it to nearly everyone: "Wives, daughters of America, for your reading Papa, this ribald, questing, utterly charming and Zen-serious novel about being male, 60 and (well, almost) alone, is the book of the year." Similarly, Tim McNulty of *The Seattle Times* offers high praise for one of Harrison's latest bestsellers, "After a long and idiosyncratic literary career, Harrison the storyteller is still at the top of his game." Carol Schneck of Schuler Books and Music found the climax of the novel "both exhilarating and terrifying" and the book "charming from start to finish!"

Responses to Literature

1. Discuss the theme of revenge in *Legends of the Fall*. What, if anything, do you think the author is trying to communicate about the use of revenge in human relationships?

2. Harrison makes numerous references to Greek mythology in *True North* (2004). Why do you think

---

COMMON HUMAN EXPERIENCE

Life for people living in remote regions of the northern United States features prominently in Harrison's fiction. Other works that explore this theme include:

A River Runs Through It (1976), a collection of novellas by Norman Maclean. In the wilderness of Montana and Idaho, the characters in these stories experience an intimate connection with nature by fly-fishing, logging, and living in the rugged terrain.

Love Medicine (1984), a novel by Louise Erdrich. Through a collection of narrators, one for each chapter, the author draws from Chippewa myths to cover sixty years of story-telling on a fictional Chippewa reservation in North Dakota.

Ten Little Indians (2003), a collection of short stories by Sherman Alexie. With this work the author offers nine stories after lives of Native Americans who live life at a cultural crossroads.

Peace Like a River (2001), a novel by Leif Engler. This story follows Reuben Land, age eleven, who leaves his Minnesota home in search of his brother who has been charged with murder.

he does this? To what extent is the novel structured like a Greek or Shakespearean tragedy?

3. Explain the meaning of the following statement from *Returning to Earth*, citing evidence from the text: "We've been so inept and careless about death in America and have paid big for the consequences." To what extent do you agree with this opinion?

4. How does the setting of *Returning to Earth* shape the character's lives on a physical, emotional, and spiritual level? Explain your answer using examples from the novel.

BIBLIOGRAPHY

Books

McDemott, Robert J. *Conversations with Jim Harrison.* Jackson, Miss.: University Press of Mississippi, 2002.

Reilly, Edward C. *Jim Harrison.* New York: Twayne, 1996.

Smith, Patrick A. *The True Bones of My Life: Essays on the Fiction of Jim Harrison.* East Lansing, Mich.: Michigan State University Press, 2002.

Periodicals

Burger, Frederick. "Macho Writer: He Despises the Term, the Man They Call the New Hemingway." *Philadelphia Inquirer* (July 23, 1980).

Clute, John. "Elegiac Heirs." *Times Literary Supplement.* No. 4486 (March 24, 1990): 299.

Davis, Todd F., and Kenneth Womak. "Embracing the Fall: Wilderness as Spiritual Transformation in the Novels of Jim Harrison." *Western American Literature* (Summer 2003).

Erdrich, Louise. Review of *Dalva. Chicago Tribune—Books* (March 20, 1988): 1.

Golden, Michael. "The Next Great American Writer." *Smoke Signals* (White Line Issue, 1981).

Jones, Allen M. "Six Short Essays About Jim Harrison." *A Profile in Poetry* (July 16, 2006).

Love, Keith. "Literary Voice in the Wilderness." *Los Angeles Times* (April 12, 1988).

McGrath, Charles. "Pleasures of a Hard-Worn Life." *New York Times* (July 25, 2007).

Roberson, William. "'Macho Mistake': The Misrepresentation of Jim Harrison's Fiction." *Critique* (Summer 1988).

Roelofs, Ted. "A Stranger in His Own Land." *Grand Rapids Press* (October 11, 1998).

Rohrkemper, John. "Natty Bumpo Wants Tobacco: Jim Harrison's Wildness." *The Great Lakes Review* (1983).

Siegal, Eric. "A New Voice from the North Country: A Portrait of a Prodigal Poet Who Came Home to Michigan." *Detroit Free Press* (April 16, 1972).

Yardley, Jonathan. "A Lonely Heart in the Heartland." *Washington Post Book World* (March 6, 1988): 3.

✸ Bret Harte

BORN: *1836, Albany, New York*

DIED: *1902, Camberley, Surrey, England*

NATIONALITY: *American*

GENRE: *Fiction, poetry, drama*

MAJOR WORKS:

The Luck of Roaring Camp and Other Sketches (1870)

Overview

At the height of his career, Bret Harte was one of the best-known American writers of the nineteenth century. In such classic short stories as "The Luck of Roaring Camp," "The Outcasts of Poker Flat," and "Tennessee's Partner," he nostalgically portrayed the mining camps and ethnic groups of California during the gold rush of 1849. Although Harte's fiction received less recognition later in his career, elements of his work—especially its regional flavor and his creation of such stock characters as the seedy prospector, the cynical gambler, and the frontier prostitute—greatly influenced his contemporaries and later writers of popular Westerns.

Works in Biographical and Historical Context

Growing Up on the East Coast Harte was born by the name Francis Brett Hart on August 25, 1836, in Albany, New York, to a schoolteacher and his wife. An

Bret Harte   *Harte, Bret, photograph. AP Images.*

unhealthy child, he was tutored at home, where he read such authors as Charles Dickens, Edgar Allan Poe, and Washington Irving. When Harte was nine years old his father died, and his family moved to New York City. When Harte was eighteen, his mother remarried, and the family moved to San Francisco. Shortly thereafter Harte left home. Over the next decade he held several jobs, most significantly that of apprentice printer for the journal *Northern Californian*, where he was eventually given editorial responsibilities.

Editorial Influence
After his marriage in 1862, Harte supplemented his journalist's income by serving as a government clerk at the San Francisco Mint. In 1865, Harte became editor of the *Californian*, where he commissioned Mark Twain, who was then a relatively unknown author, to write a weekly story for the journal. Regarding Harte's editorial influence, Twain later remarked that it was Harte who "trimmed and schooled me patiently until he changed me from an awkward utterer of coarse grotesqueness to a writer of paragraphs and chapters." Harte became editor of the *Overland Monthly* in 1868, and during his tenure with the journal his poem "Plain Language from Truthful James" (1870, also called "Heathen Chinee"), as well as such stories as "The Luck of Roaring Camp," (1868) appeared in its pages and inspired what his biographer George Stewart termed a "literary epidemic" of imitations.

Life on the Western Frontier
Harte drew upon his observations of the California gold rush for some of his most famous fiction. In 1848, gold was discovered in California, and it attracted a rush of settlers, called forty-niners, who hoped to make their fortune out west. Although few became rich, many people stayed, and eventually turned what had been tiny towns like San Francisco into large, metropolitan hubs. Other industries like agriculture were developed alongside mining efforts, as were new methods of transportation, most especially transcontinental rail lines, accompanying the rush out west. The expansion of the rail lines involved the importation of "Coolie labor"—large numbers of Chinese workers. While settlers were pushing their way west, many Native Americans were forced off of their land, usually violently. Shortly after the beginning of the rush, in 1850, California was admitted as a state to the United States.

Monetary Success and Financial Mismanagement
After the success of the *Overland*, Harte received offers of editorial positions from across the country. In 1871 he signed a one-year contract for the unheard-of sum of $10,000 with the *Atlantic Monthly*, which gave the magazine exclusive rights to a minimum of twelve stories and poems and made Harte the highest-paid American writer of the time. However, he was careless about fulfilling his contract, and it was not renewed. In need of a new source of income, he went on a lecture tour from 1872 to 1875, but the proceeds barely covered his expenses and the demands of creditors became an increasing problem. He had fallen steeply from the heights of literary fortune.

Revived Popularity Late in His Career
In a further attempt to recover his financial solvency, Harte collaborated with Twain on a stage adaptation of "Heathen Chinee," entitled *Ah Sin*. Performed in 1877, the drama was a failure. Later that year, Harte called on contacts in political circles that helped him obtain a consulate in Crefeld, Germany, and, two years later, in Glasgow, Scotland. He remained a prolific writer for the last twenty-two years of his life, publishing a volume of short stories almost yearly. Supported by a wealthy patron named Mrs. Van de Velde, Harte moved to London in 1885 and became a favorite in literary and social circles.

Harte died of throat cancer at Madame Van de Velde's home in Surrey on May 5, 1902.

Works in Literary Context

As founding editor of the *Overland Monthly* in 1868, Harte was instrumental in promoting the careers of an entire generation of Western writers. A pioneering Western local-colorist, he burst upon the national scene with the publication of a series of popular tales and poems set in the California mining camps and boomtowns of the Gold Rush that crystallized his reputation as a rising literary star. Lured east by offers of wealth and prestige, he signed in 1871 what was then the most lucrative

LITERARY AND HISTORICAL CONTEMPORARIES

Bret Harte's famous contemporaries include:

Horatio Alger (1832–1899): An American author whose uplifting fiction, published in dime novels, helped give shape to the "American dream."

Kate Chopin (1851–1904): Considered among the most important women in nineteenth-century American fiction, Chopin is best known for her novel *The Awakening* (1899), a once-scandalous account of one woman's growing sexuality in the American South during the Victorian era.

Ambrose Bierce (1842–1914): Bierce was a noted American author whose literary reputation is based primarily on his short stories about the Civil War and the supernatural.

Mark Twain (1835–1910): The famous American author best-known for his classic novel *The Adventures of Huckleberry Finn* (1884).

Joaquin Miller (1837–1913): Miller was an American author who enjoyed temporary fame as "The Kit Carson of poetry" in London.

Joel Chandler Harris (1848–1908): The popular American author known for his folktales of plantation life told by the fictional Uncle Remus, a kindly African-American slave.

contract in the history of American letters. A prototype of the man of letters as a man of business, he was able to make a successful living through his writing. Although he never fully realized the promise of his early *Overland Monthly* tales, he was for the rest of his life a steady writer of Western fiction that enjoyed wider popularity in England and Europe than in the United States.

Stories of Frontier Life: An Appeal to Sentiment
In his stories Harte offered a sentimental depiction of the gold-rush era of 1849, and he found favor with the reading public through sensationalistic fiction that featured grotesque or idealized characters and a strong appeal to sentiment. These qualities earned him the title of the "Dickens among the pines." Just as Charles Dickens had created larger-than-life characters who became standard representations of English personalities, Harte invented such frontier types as the seedy prospector Kentuck, the hard-bitten gambler Jack Hamlin, and the dance-hall girl. These characters' outward churlishness is essential to Harte's most familiar plot formula: to expose the "heart of gold" beneath a coarse or depraved exterior. Thus, the callous miners in "The Luck of Roaring Camp" become the sensitive and self-sacrificing guardians of a child born to a prostitute, and the cynical Jack Hamlin reveals a

concern for others in "An Heiress of Red Dog" (1879) and "Mr. Jack Hamlin's Meditation" (1899). Reversing the formula, Harte portrayed corruption disguised as innocence in *M'liss* (1873), a novella in which a pubescent schoolgirl becomes a seductress, and juxtaposed outward respectability with underlying viciousness in "Heathen Chinee," a ballad relating how two Anglo-Saxon Americans scheme to cheat, but are instead outwitted by, a Chinese immigrant.

Perhaps the most outstanding example of the typical Harte story is "Tennessee's Partner" (1869). Presenting an idealized view of friendship between two miners, the story contrasts the uncouth and untutored appearance of Tennessee's partner with his extremely virtuous magnanimity toward Tennessee. Not only does the partner forgive Tennessee for seducing his wife, but he also tries to save Tennessee from execution during a trial for robbery. Loyalty is further celebrated by the story's sentimental ending, in which the two men are pictured embracing after death as they meet at heaven's gate. Although Harte occasionally experimented with different characters and settings, his stories of American frontier life in the mid-nineteenth century are considered his most typical and important works.

Fading Popularity Though the *Spectator* averred in its obituary that he had "probably exerted a greater influence on English literature than any other American author," the succeeding years have not been kind to Harte's reputation. At best, Harte is now regarded as a preeminent satirist, an astute critic of sham sentiment, and an elegant stylist. His gradual disappearance from American literature anthologies may be attributed to the shifting winds of literary fashion rather than the intrinsic qualities of his best writing.

Works in Critical Context

Early in his career, Harte received virtually undisputed acclaim as a short story writer, with critics offering similar praise for his skill as a humorist. After 1880, however, reviewers began to criticize Harte's fiction for its reliance on coincidence and melodramatic prose. Mark Twain, whose talent Harte had discovered and fostered, was one of the earliest and most outspoken detractors of Harte's fiction. Applying the criteria of realism, with its demand for a faithful rendering of details, Twain noted grave flaws in Harte's work, including inaccurate representations of frontier vernacular, faulty observation, and subservience of fact to sentiment. Other critics concurred with Twain's judgments, emphasizing the maudlin emotional responses Harte solicited in even his best stories. In spite of the decline of his critical standing in the United States, Harte continued to please audiences abroad and became especially popular in England, where his fiction was favorably compared with that of Charles Dickens. Nevertheless by 1943, when the prominent critics Cleanth Brooks and

Robert Penn Warren wrote a derisive appraisal of "Tennessee's Partner," the view of Harte as a Victorian sentimentalist was widely held.

East Coast Praises "The Luck of Roaring Camp"

Although "The Luck of Roaring Camp" was hardly mentioned in the local press, the story was hailed in the East. The September 30, 1868 *Springfield Republican* declared it "the best magazine story of the year," and James T. Fields invited the author to contribute similar tales to the pages of the *Atlantic*. Author Kate Chopin later wrote in the December 9, 1900 *St. Louis Republic* that the story "reached across the continent and startled the academics on the Atlantic Coast." The story helped attract a national audience to the *Overland Monthly*. In July 1870 the magazine sold as many copies in the East as in the states of California, Nevada, and Oregon, and according to Bayard Taylor in the August 5, 1870 *New York Tribune*, it was "more extensively and appreciatively noticed" in the eastern press than in California.

Recent Reassessments of Harte

In recent decades, some critics have begun to reassess the strengths and modernity of Harte's fiction. J. R. Boggan, for instance, contends that the sentimentality of the narrator of "The Luck of Roaring Camp" is intended to be ironic rather than sincere. Others note that Harte's influence as a preeminent regionalist writer and creator of standard American character types helped further the evolution of an American literature independent of European tradition. In describing Harte's influence, Granville Hicks wrote: "Harte, though he may not have been in any strict sense the founder of American regionalism, was the first writer to gain popularity after the Civil War by the exploitation of sectional peculiarities, and there is little doubt that his example directly inspired many of the writers of the seventies, eighties, and nineties." For this achievement Harte remains an important figure in the development of American literature.

Responses to Literature

1. From your reading of "Plain Language of Truthful James," what is your impression of the author's attitude toward the culture of frontier life in the West? Support your opinions with examples from the poem.

2. Compare and contrast Uncle Billy with the other outcasts in "The Outcasts of Poker Flat." Are any of the characters in this story heroic? Why or why not?

3. In some ways, Bret Harte served as a mentor for his contemporary Mark Twain. What similarities and differences do you notice between their work?

4. How does Harte's fiction construct stereotypes about people on the frontier? Are these stereotypes still relevant today?

COMMON HUMAN EXPERIENCE

Throughout Harte's fiction, life on the frontier of the United States during the gold rush era is a central focus. Other works that explore this theme include the following:

Roughing It (1872), by Mark Twain. Twain's second published book, which humorously recounts his failed attempts at panning for gold, helped secure his place as America's leading humorist.

A Frontier Lady (1932), a memoir by Sarah Royce. In this work the author tells of her family's journey out West and their subsequent life in early California.

Roaring Camp: the Social World of the California Gold Rush (2001), a nonfiction work by Susan Lee Johnson. Providing contrast to the stereotypes of the Old West, this work of social history paints a compelling view of life on the frontier.

John Sutter: A Life on the North American Frontier (2006), a biography by Albert L. Hurtado. The story of a Swiss expatriate who founded a settlement in California's Sacramento Valley but failed to realize his dreams of prosperity.

BIBLIOGRAPHY

Books

Barnett, Linda Diz. *Bret Harte: A Reference Guide*. Boston: G. K. Hall, 1980.

Duckett, Margaret. *Mark Twain and Bret Harte*. Norman, Okla.: University of Oklahoma Press, 1964.

Merwin, Henry Childs. *The Life of Bret Harte*. Boston & New York: Houghton Mifflin, 1911.

Morrow, Patrick D. *Bret Harte: Literary Critic*. Bowling Green, Ohio: Bowling Green University Popular Press, 1979.

Pemberton, T. Edgar. *The Life of Bret Harte*. London: Pearson, 1903.

Stewart Jr., George R. *Bret Harte: Argonaut and Exile*. Boston: Houghton Mifflin, 1931.

Periodicals

Boggan, J. R. "The Regeneration of Roaring Camp." *Nineteenth Century Fiction* 22 (December 1967): 271–280.

Conner, William F. "The Euchring of Tennessee: A Reexamination of Bret Harte's 'Tennessee's Partner.'" *Studies in Short Fiction* 17 (Spring 1980): 113–120.

Dam, Henry J. W. "A Morning with Bret Harte." *McClure's* 4 (December 1894): 38–50.

Duckett, Margaret. "Plain Language from Bret Harte." *Nineteenth Century Fiction* 11 (March 1957): 241–260.

May, Ernest R. "Bret Harte and the *Overland Monthly*." *American Literature* 22 (November 1950): 260–271.

Morrow, Patrick D. "The Predicament of Bret Harte."
   American Literary Realism 5 (Summer 1972): 181–188.
Scherting, Jack. "Bret Harte's Civil War Poems: Voice of
   the Majority." *Western American Literature* 8 (Fall
   1973): 133–142.
Thomas, Jeffrey F. "Bret Harte and the Power of Sex."
   Western American Literature 8 (Fall 1973): 91–109.
Timpe, Eugene F. "Bret Harte's German Public."
   Jahrbuch fur Amerikastudien 10 (1965): 215–220.

✸ Robert Hass

BORN: *1941, San Francisco, California*

NATIONALITY: *American*

GENRE: *Poetry*

MAJOR WORKS:

Field Guide (1973)

Praise (1979)

Twentieth Century Pleasures: Prose on Poetry (1984)

Sun Under Wood: New Poems (1996)

Time and Materials: Poems 1997–2005 (2007)

Robert Hass   *Hass, Prof. Robert, photograph. AP Images.*

Overview

Despite Robert Hass's success as a translator and critic, it is for his own musical, descriptive, meditative poetry that he is primarily recognized: Hass has served two terms as U.S. poet laureate. Following the example of former laureate Rita Dove, Hass took the opportunity afforded by the position to play an active role in raising awareness of the importance of literacy. As a result, one critic observes, "He has shaped [the poet laureate position] to become more like a missionary drummer in the provinces of commerce than as a performing bard in celebrity coffeehouses." Because of these efforts, "Robert Hass is the most active Poet Laureate of the United States we've ever had," believes Los Angeles Times Book Review contributor Frances Mayes, "and he sets a standard for those who follow."

Works in Biographical and Historical Context

Growing Up with the Beat Generation   Born in San Francisco on March 1, 1941, Hass grew up in the suburbs of San Rafael, California, and attended private Catholic school. He came to identify at a young age with the literary culture of the West Coast, with its affinities for the local landscape, radical politics, alternative religions, Asian influences, and experimentalism. Widely recognized for his attachment to the northern California coastal region, he is, as Alan Williamson observed in *American Poetry Review*, the poet "who has made California landscape most memorably symbolic." His immediate family comprised his father, Fred Hass, a businessman; his mother, Helen Dahling Hass, whose alcoholism is a major subject in *Sun Under Wood: New Poems* (1996); an older brother, who encouraged him to become a writer; and a sister.

From an early age Hass embraced poetry as a vocation. He grew up in the San Francisco Bay area at a time when the poetry community there was the focus of national attention: the Beat Generation, led by such writers and poets as Jack Kerouac and Allen Ginsberg, and centered around the legendary bookstore City Lights. Growing up in the 1950s in San Francisco, a young writer could get the sense that poetry was relevant to the lives people actually lead. Consequently, Hass's poems have an intimacy that is grounded in lived experience and the natural world, with frequent references to art, literature, politics, and history.

Hass earned his undergraduate degree at Saint Mary's College of California in 1963. While a student, he married his first wife, Earlene Leif. Hass went on to earn a Masters and PhD at Stanford. His three children with Earlene—Leif, Kristin, and Luke—were born while both parents attended graduate school. At Stanford, Hass studied with the poet and critic Yvor Winters, a proponent of New Criticism, a school of thought influential from the 1920s through the 1960s that held that, in analyzing literature, nothing but the words on the page mattered, not the author's life, nor the circumstances under which the work was created. Other poets with whom he associated included John Matthias, James McMichael, John Peck, and Robert Pinsky.

While working on his PhD, Hass took a teaching position at the State University of New York, Buffalo. When he graduated, in 1971, he returned to California to teach at his alma mater, St. Mary's. In 1989, he was offered a position at the University of California, Berkeley, where he still teaches. The same year, he and Earlene divorced. Hass married fellow poet Brenda Hillman in 1995.

Becoming a Poet Hass's first volume of poetry, *Field Guide*, was the winning collection in the 1973 Yale Series of Younger Poets competition. Metrically regular and thematically unified throughout most of the collection, the poems convey a striking sense of place and Hass's deep imaginative connections to place: the book is divided into three sections, with each section arranged as a kind of map or guide to natural and historical landscapes. His sharp perceptions and penetrating descriptions of the natural and the artificial reveal an attachment to this world that is both sensuous and spiritual.

Hass confirmed his ability with *Praise* (1979), his second volume of poems, which won the William Carlos Williams Award. The twenty-four poems question the possibility of mapping raised in *Field Guide*, as Hass's intense scrutiny of the act of writing imaginatively makes his relationship to his material more complicated. Throughout *Praise*, Hass takes up the problems of poetic representation and pushes on the pressure points of the imagination, revealing its limitations, which seem, in the end, to be its true source of power. Hass's next volume of poetry, *Human Wishes* (1989), sees the poet taking a meditative turn, focusing on earthly pleasure, catalogues of the everyday, and the social reality that surrounds people. In a departure from his previous work, *Human Wishes* contains a section of short prose pieces in addition to the more formal poetry.

Even while garnering accolades for his poetry, Hass had not abandoned his training as a critic. In 1984, he came out with *Twentieth Century Pleasures: Prose on Poetry*, a collection of previously published essays and reviews. In the volume, the author examines American writers (including Robert Lowell and James Wright) as well as European and Japanese poets. The essays are often conversational, blending personal response with critical insight. Hass's essays and reviews attempt more than objective analysis: they explore his own relationship as a poet to the poetry he analyzes. Many of Hass's fellow literary critics appreciated the book, honoring it with the 1984 National Book Critics Circle award, among others.

Wearing the Crown of Laurels From 1995 to 1997, Hass set aside his personal role as poet to take up the mantle of the nation's poet, serving as U.S. poet laureate and poetry consultant to the Library of Congress. Long a largely ceremonial position, the poet laureate has recently become far

more of a public advocate for poets and their work, a potentially thankless task. But, Hass exerted great energy as a political activist, using his position as national poetry advocate to launch discussions on general literacy, education spending, and environmental protection. Prior to becoming poet laureate, Hass had frequently cited and identified with Oscar Wilde's line about politics taking up too many of one's evenings, but during his two years in the position, Hass regularly forfeited the time he normally devoted to his own work. He traveled extensively, giving speeches to business and community groups around the country.

Sun Under Wood (1996) won for Hass his second National Book Critics Circle Award, this time for poetry. Much of the work in *Sun Under Wood* was completed before Hass became poet laureate, and it is possible to sense in this collection a building ambivalence about the place of poetry in a world desperately in need of the kind of purposeful political and social action Hass would take on during his laureateship. Hass's poetic work since then has been collected in *Time and Materials: Poems 1997–2005* (2007).

Works in Literary Context

Connecting Poetry to the Natural and Personal World
Hass's first inspiration as a young writer was the Beat Generation. In a *Publishers Weekly* interview in 1996, Hass

COMMON HUMAN EXPERIENCE

Hass's first collection of poems, *Field Guide*, focuses intensely on a sense of place. Here are some other works that have become famous for their evocation of place:

Swann's Way (1913), the first volume of Marcel Proust's novel *Remembrance of Things Past*. In *Swann's Way*, the novel's narrator goes to great lengths to evoke the scenes of his childhood; the result is that the reader can almost feel and even smell the surroundings.

Sunshine State (2002), a film written and directed by John Sayles. This film is made up of the intertwining tales of several citizens of a small coastal town in Florida, a place on the verge of economic expansion that could threaten its identity.

Arabian Sands (1959), a travel narrative by Wilfred Thesiger. In *Arabian Sands*, Wilfred Thesiger recounts his journeys through the arid deserts of Saudi Arabia, which he comes to understand as living, breathing thing, just before the coming of the automobile, when men still traveled solely on the backs of camels.

Alaska (1988), a historical novel by James Michener. Beginning with the geological creation of North America and continuing into modern times, this sweeping novel uses both historical figures and invented characters to paint a detailed picture of America's forty-ninth state.

explained to Michael Coffey, "I started out imagining myself as a novelist or essayist, but then Gary Snyder and Allen Ginsberg came along; and poetry, imbued with the whole lifestyle of the Beats, was much more exciting." The free, jazzy, musical style of the Beat poets eventually made way for a more technical, controlled style, influenced by the theories of literature Hass was exposed to in graduate school. Ivor Winters's New Critical influence is evident, particularly in Hass's early work, which tends toward a less spontaneous, more concentrated formal artistry; embedded in Hass's work are subtle traces of his deliberate and extensive poetic preparation. In "Some Notes on the San Francisco Bay Area As a Culture Region: A Memoir," collected in his *Twentieth Century Pleasures: Prose on Poetry* (1984), Hass acknowledges the early influence of Kenneth Rexroth, who was, he explains, "the first one to teach me that there could be an active connection between poetry and my own world." The work of Snyder is also evident in Hass's affinity for haiku and his propensity for locating and naming the natural world in his poems. Hass has cited William Wordsworth and Ezra Pound as favorite poets, but the subtlest influence on his poetry may well be Wallace Stevens, whose later poems in particular seem to inform Hass's meditative disposition.

Works in Critical Context

Field Guide and Praise Even among the limited audience for poetry in twentieth-century America, Hass was a hit from day one. "He is a fine poet," Michael Waters relates in *Southwest Review* regarding *Field Guide*, "and his book is one of the very best to appear in a long time." Waters also notes that the primary focus of the book is "naming things, of establishing an identity through one's surroundings, of translating the natural world into one's private history. This is a lot to accomplish, yet Robert Hass manages it with clarity and compassion." In the *Ontario Review*, Linda W. Wagner agrees that "*Field Guide* is an impressive first collection.... Hass's view of knowledge is convincing.... One can be reminded only of the best of Hemingway." According to William Scammell in the *Times Literary Supplement*, the poems in *Praise*, Hass's second book, "unite freshness and wonder with a tough, inventive imagination." Writing in the *Chicago Review*, Ira Sadoff remarks that *Praise* "might even be the strongest collection of poems to come out in the late seventies." Sadoff also notes that *Field Guide* "was intelligent and well-crafted; it tapped Hass's power of observation carefully and engagingly." Nevertheless, the reviewer had "reservations" about *Field Guide* that "stemmed from some sense of chilliness that seemed to pervade a number of poems, as if the poems were wrought by an intellect distant from its subject matter." Sadoff continued: "I have no such problems with *Praise*.... [It] marks Hass's arrival as an important, even pivotal, young poet."

Responses to Literature

1. Hass's *Twentieth Century Pleasures: Prose on Poetry* (1984) is a collection of essays on poetry, some of them personal. Pick an essay from the book on a poet you are interested in, and read it alongside some poems by that poet. Start a discussion about Hass's take on the poet. How does he respond? What are the kinds of things he notices? Are they the same things you notice?

2. Hass famously used his position as poet laureate to advance the cause of literacy. How have some other U.S. poets laureate capitalized on the position? Research another U.S. poet laureate, focusing on his or her time in office. What were his or her goals? What did he or she accomplish? Write a report based on your results.

3. Hass has cited the poet Kenneth Rexroth as one of his major influences. Read some of Rexroth's poems alongside some of Hass's earlier work, and see if you can trace any similarities. Pay attention to aspects of poetry such as meter, imagery, and form.

BIBLIOGRAPHY

Books

Altieri, Charles. *Self and Sensibility in Contemporary American Poetry.* Cambridge, Mass.: Cambridge University Press, 1984.

Periodicals

Clines, Francis X. "A Poet's Road Trip Along Main Street, U.S.A." *The New York Times* (December 9, 1996).

Coffey, Michael. Interview with Robert Hass. *Publishers Weekly* (October 28, 1996).

Cavalieri, Grace. "Robert Hass: An Interview." *American Poetry Review* (January/February 1994): 35–39.

Mayes, Frances. Review of *Sun Under Wood. Los Angeles Times Book Review*, April 13, 1997.

Pollock, Sarah. "Robert Hass." *Mother Jones* (March/April 1997): 18–20.

Sadoff, Ira. Review of *Praise. Chicago Review* (Winter 1980).

Scammell, William. Review of *Praise. Times Literary Supplement* (May 28, 1982).

Wagner, Linda. Review of *Field Guide. Ontario Review* (Fall 1974).

Waters, Michael. Review of *Field Guide. Southwest Review* (June 1975).

Nathaniel Hawthorne   *Hawthorne, Nathaniel, photograph. Source unknown.*

Nathaniel Hawthorne

BORN: *1804, Salem, Massachusetts*

DIED: *1864, Plymouth, New Hampshire*

NATIONALITY: *American*

GENRE: *Fiction*

MAJOR WORKS:

Twice-Told Tales (1837)

The Scarlet Letter, a Romance (1850)

The House of the Seven Gables (1851)

The Marble Faun; or, The Romance of Monte Beni (1860)

Overview

Although Nathaniel Hawthorne called himself "the obscurest man in American letters," his achievements in fiction, both as short-story writer and novelist, are too great to ignore. Even though fame was slow to come and the financial rewards remained relatively thin throughout his career, Hawthorne claimed a central place in American letters, becoming, in time, an influential force in the artistic development of such writers as Herman Melville, Henry James, William Dean Howells, William Faulkner, and Flannery O'Connor.

Works in Biographical and Historical Context

Early Literary Experiences Born July 4, 1804, in Salem, Massachusetts, Nathaniel Hawthorne (who added a "W" to the family name) was the middle child of Nathaniel and Elizabeth Manning Hathorne, descendants of Puritan settlers in the Salem area. His father, captain of a ship, died in 1808 in Surinam (Dutch Guiana), and his mother raised the family with the help of relatives. Nathaniel's early education was at home, owing to a leg injury from playing ball. This injury helped to fashion his personality: he became an assiduous reader of such authors as John Bunyan and William Shakespeare, and acquired, as he later lamented, his "cursed habits of solitude." While preparing for college he launched a newspaper, *The Spectator*, imitating the famous British journal of the same name written by Richard Steele and Joseph Addison and served as writer, editor, printer, and publisher. This short-lived (1711–1712) project had to be produced in his spare time because he served as both secretary and bookkeeper in his uncle's stagecoach office and pressed forward with his preparatory studies. This experience in the workaday world revealed something important to him, as he told his sister Ebe: "No man can be a Poet and a Book Keeper at the same time."

In 1821, Hawthorne enrolled in Bowdoin College, in Maine, where his friends included the poet Henry Wadsworth Longfellow. Knowing that he would have to take up some profession, Hawthorne rejected the church as a calling but seriously considered becoming a writer, producing some short stories and the beginnings of a romance novel,

Fanshawe, during this period. He returned to his family in Salem in 1825 and completed the romance begun at Bowdoin. He offered *Fanshawe* to publishers, but finding no one interested, he printed it at his own expense in 1828. Later, Hawthorne came to be so ashamed of the book that he tried to round up and destroy every copy; he was so closemouthed about its appearance that not even his wife knew he had published the work.

His failed novel behind him, Hawthorne now attempted to make his mark as a writer of tales and sketches that would epitomize New England. After attempts at bundling his stories into books to sell to publishers turned up nothing, he began publishing them individually in the *Salem Gazette* and other publications. These tales, such as "Young Goodman Brown," which appeared first in *The New-England Magazine* in 1835, stake out Hawthorne's fictional territory: his consuming interest in the nation's history, particularly the Puritan past; his exploration of the psychological and emotional factors underlying human behavior; his eagerness to understand the power and politics of sexuality; his probing of sin, concealment, guilt, penance, and redemption; and his willingness to entertain and dramatize different points of view on social, political, cultural, and religious questions.

"Young Goodman Brown" grapples with the past of Hawthorne's hometown, Salem, the site of the infamous witch trials of 1692. Set in the period just preceding the trials, the tale centers around a young bridegroom who determines to investigate rumors of occult activity in his community and winds up witnessing, or believing he has witnessed, his pastor, his wife, Faith, and his fellow churchmen about to take part in a witches' Sabbath. The discovery shakes his faith and his senses loose from their foundations; though he recovers from the incident, his confidence in his community is permanently broken. The psychological ambiguity of the story—did he see, or only believe he saw?—illuminates the tragic inevitability of the real-life Salem witch hunt, during which the participants' sense of reality became, under social pressure, easily distorted and resulted in the deaths by hanging of fourteen of the accused.

The Writing Life

Hawthorne spent the ten years after college writing, submitting, receiving rejection notices, and, in moments of frustration, burning manuscripts. A temporary break in his routine came in January 1836, when he became editor of *The American Magazine of Useful and Entertaining Knowledge*, located in Boston. He and his sister Elizabeth wrote most of the copy. By June, the publisher had gone bankrupt, and Hawthorne returned to Salem. He wrote to his friend and fellow writer Longfellow, "I have secluded myself from society; and yet I never meant any such thing.... I have made a captive of myself and put me in a dungeon; and now I cannot find the key to let myself out." He wanted his tales "to open an intercourse with the world," as he suggested in his preface to the 1851 re-publication of *Twice-Told*

Tales, and they did: the original publication of *Twice-Told Tales* in 1837 caught the attention of his neighbor, the publisher and bookseller Elizabeth Palmer Peabody, who reviewed the book enthusiastically and promoted it with such friends as Ralph Waldo Emerson. In absorbing Hawthorne into her social circle, Peabody brought him together with her sister Sophia, his future wife.

Hawthorne's association with the Peabodys introduced rapid change. He began publishing a series of history books for children, published by Peabody, and then won a political appointment in the Boston Customs House, which he hoped would afford him the income to marry Sophia but proved to be dusty, stifling work that did little to advance his goal. In 1841, he set his sights on a utopian experiment in communal living at nearby Brook Farm in West Roxbury; he invested in the project, but stayed only half a year, his creativity at a low thanks to the hog-tending and stable-mucking that were his regular chores. Instead, he married Sophia in July 1842 and moved with her to Concord, Massachusetts, where they occupied the Old Manse, the home of Emerson's grandfather. He was able to write and she to paint, and their social world was populated with such literary figures as Henry David Thoreau, Emerson, Bronson Alcott (father of Louisa May Alcott), and Margaret Fuller. This was Hawthorne's most productive period; in the three years he lived at the Old Manse, he wrote twenty sketches and tales, including "The Birth-Mark" (1843) and "Rappaccini's Daughter" (1844). The Hawthornes also welcomed a daughter, Una, in 1844.

Unable to make ends meet in Concord, Hawthorne returned to Salem, where his son Julian was born shortly after. He took another political appointment at the Salem Custom House, which occupied his mornings but left him some free time to write. The 1848 election of President Zachary Taylor, a member of the Whig party, meant that Democratic appointees could simply be replaced; though Hawthorne's literary and political friends argued for his continued support, he was dismissed after Taylor took office in 1849.

Revisiting Romance, this Time with Success

Rocked by the death of his beloved mother soon afterward, and living on savings, Hawthorne turned with force and intensity to his most famous work: *The Scarlet Letter* (1852), a return to the Puritan past that had so absorbed him in the earliest stages of his writing career. *The Scarlet Letter* chronicles the social and emotional experience of two lovers who have produced a child out of wedlock: forced to wear a large red "A" on her breast, signifying "Adulterer," Hester Prynne is publicly punished by her community with a mean-spirited, intolerant rigor, while the father of her child, whose identity she refuses to reveal, suffers the internal torment of intense guilt and the secret manipulations of Hester's husband, who suspects the truth. The competing yet also complementary powers of concealment and revelation drive the story and give shape to the characters in their suffering. *The Scarlet Letter* won instant praise but failed to bring in funds sufficient for the Hawthornes to remain in Salem. They found more economical quarters in the Berkshires, at Stockbridge, celebrated for its summer colony of intellectuals and writers.

Once the family settled in, Hawthorne enjoyed another extremely productive period, writing *The House of the Seven Gables* (1851) and adding a preface to a new edition of *Twice-Told Tales* (1851), among other projects. This flurry of creativity enabled him, for the first time, to meet the family's expenses. Although his move to Stockbridge would be a permanent farewell to a town he had grown to dislike, his mind was drawn back to Salem, the setting of *The House of the Seven Gables*, whose villain, Judge Pyncheon, was based on the enemy who had him dismissed from the Custom House, Charles Wentworth Upham. The novel is something of a lament over the burden of inheritance and family history but unlike *The Scarlet Letter* it ends happily.

It was while composing *The House of the Seven Gables* that Hawthorne met Herman Melville; their relationship was to have an important effect on literary history. It was Hawthorne who inspired Melville, a greatly underappreciated writer in his lifetime, to rewrite *Moby-Dick; or, The Whale* (1851). He dedicated the novel to Hawthorne.

Though the family's time in Stockbridge was relatively happy and productive—and included the birth of another daughter, Rose—the Hawthornes longed to return to Concord, and by 1852 had bought the home of their friend Bronson Alcott. In this period of transition, Hawthorne began *The Blithedale Romance* (1852), based on his experiences with communal living at Brook Farm before his marriage. Though he dubbed the story a "romance," the work could easily pass as a novel of ideas or social criticism. It is anchored in the troubles of a rapidly industrializing America and weighs the day's issues, particularly the women's rights question that had risen to national prominence in the 1840s, led by such figures as Elizabeth Cady Stanton and Susan B. Anthony.

Getting Involved with Politics In 1852, politics reentered Hawthorne's life. His friend Franklin Pierce won the Democratic presidential nomination, and Hawthorne rushed to write a biography that was to be used in the campaign. He was paid only $300 for the project and received no royalties, considering the book a favor for a friend. The gesture was to be turned to Hawthorne's advantage: he requested, and was granted, an appointment as Consul in Liverpool, England. This would allow him the income to repair his home in Concord and take his wife on a long-promised Italian tour. He continued to write and publish while plans for his appointment were finalized, and the family set sail on July 6, 1853. While literature fell into the background during his time in England, Hawthorne actively kept a journal, recording his impressions of English life and English people, which he later mined for his articles and stories. In 1858, the

Hawthorne family embarked on their tour of Italy, visiting galleries, spending time with communities of expatriate Americans, and observing the wonders of the art world. This experience inspired *The Marble Faun* (1860), about three artists and their faun-like aristocratic Italian friend; the past and present of Italy, where the novel is set, is woven into the narrative, which Hawthorne completed upon returning to England.

After nearly seven years away, the Hawthornes returned to Concord in 1860. Though he continued to write, Hawthorne never published another novel during his life. (His children brought out a number of his works, culled from journals, in the years and decades after his death.) The American Civil War (1861–1865) sparked a new energy, however, and in 1862, Hawthorne spent a month in Washington, D.C., visiting his friends in government. These visits led to a long piece in *The Atlantic Monthly* titled "Chiefly About War Matters," in which he is at times critical of Abraham Lincoln and the actions of the North. This and other essays were collected in the volume *Our Old Home* (1863), which Hawthorne

COMMON HUMAN EXPERIENCE

In *The Scarlet Letter*, Hawthorne examines the toll that Dimmesdale's guilty secret takes on his well-being. Here are some other works that explore the interrelation of secrets and guilt:

Who's Afraid of Virginia Woolf? (1962), a play by Edward Albee. Over the course of a long night of drinking and recriminations, the secrets of two couples come out. For George and Martha, the emotional center of the play, it is the imaginary son whom they have used to both comfort and torture each other over the course of their long, childless marriage.

Crime and Punishment (1866), a novel by Fyodor Dostoyevsky. The hero of this classic Russian novel, young Raskolnikov, carefully plans the murder of an old woman almost as a philosophical test. He is unprepared, however, for the psychological torments which follow his experiment.

Atonement (2001), a novel by Ian McEwan. The atonement of the novel's title describes the narrator's attempt to right a grave wrong she commits in adolescence when she half-knowingly accuses her sister's lover of a rape he did not commit. The events of history sweep the lovers apart, and the narrator's lie proves to be an act for which she can never atone.

Mad Men (2007–), a television series created by Matthew Weiner. The central character of *Mad Men*, Don Draper, is a successful Madison Avenue advertising executive whose life is based upon a lie: the appropriated identity of a fallen comrade in the Korean War. Though he abandons his true past, of which he is ashamed, it relentlessly haunts his present.

dedicated to his old friend Franklin Pierce, now considered a traitor to the North's cause. Hawthorne's circle of acquaintance was largely offended and even outraged by the gesture.

Unbeknownst to him, Hawthorne was suffering from stomach cancer when in 1864 he embarked on a trip south, hoping the warmer climates might do him good. He made it only as far south as Philadelphia when his traveling companion, his publisher William D. Ticknor, took sick and died. Hawthorne returned to Boston to spend some time with Franklin Pierce. The two men traveled on to New Hampshire, where Hawthorne's condition worsened. Sometime in the early morning hours of May 19, 1864, Hawthorne died in his sleep.

Works in Literary Context

The American Renaissance
The decades before the Civil War saw a flowering of literary activity in America. Such works as Walt Whitman's poetry collection *Leaves of Grass* (1855), Herman Melville's novel *Moby-Dick; or, The Whale* (1851), the short stories of Edgar Allan Poe, and the philosophical works of Ralph Waldo Emerson and Henry David Thoreau along with Hawthorne's stories and novels represent the best of this movement, referred to as the American Renaissance and sometimes as American Romanticism (not to be confused with British Romanticism, which peaked a generation earlier). While some of Hawthorne's early work took some inspiration from the Scottish novelist Sir Walter Scott (1771–1832), his allegiance was really to the uniquely American focus on the individual which was being celebrated by the other writers of the American Renaissance. Until this period, the literary culture of America looked mostly to Europe as the source of its culture and its traditions. The American themes that were to be taken up in the mid-nineteenth century—nature, the pioneer spirit, the striving of the individual—required a reorientation of literary identity. The writers of this movement began looking to America's past and to the details of its culture and its landscape for their inspiration, seeing America as a rich source of characters and themes.

Works in Critical Context

The Scarlet Letter Reviewers were prepared to take any work of Hawthorne's seriously and often to pass from the book being reviewed into an assessment of his total work. Two aspects of *The Scarlet Letter* drew special comment: the personal and political elements in "The Custom House," the essay that opens the novel, and the moral question some reviewers saw in the introduction of Hester as a character and the failure to provide for her the punishment normally to be expected. Those who did not wish to plead the cause of Salem against the author, as a rule, found "The Custom House" a delightful sketch. Even those who attacked the romance on moral or theological grounds, as did Orestes Brownson, were ready to grant Hawthorne's power and artistry. While Hawthorne's contemporaries undoubtedly found the novel powerful, it is in more recent years that the book has mounted the heights of critical attention. Today's critics reading the novel see layers of social and psychological complexity, with critic Olivia Gatti Taylor, for instance, fascinated with Hawthorne's exploration of the "effects of sin upon the human consciousness."

The Blithedale Romance Though *The Scarlet Letter* has made the largest impact of all of Hawthorne's works, his novel *The Blithedale Romance* (1852) garnered more critical attention in Hawthorne's day. Critic Edwin Percy Whipple, to whom Hawthorne had sent a draft asking for advice about the work, praised it highly, stating that it

seems to us the most perfect in execution of any of Hawthorne's works, and as a work of art, hardly equaled by anything this country has produced....
The romance, also, has more thought than any of its predecessors; it is literally crammed with the results

of the most delicate and searching observation of life, manners and character, and of the most piercing imaginative analysis of motives and tendencies; yet nothing seems labored.

A generation later, novelist Henry James wrote, "The finest thing in *The Blithedale Romance* is the character of Zenobia, which I have said elsewhere strikes me as the nearest approach that Hawthorne has made to the complete creation of a person."

Responses to Literature

1. Herman Melville was so inspired by Hawthorne's work—and by meeting the author—that he rewrote what was to become his most famous novel, *Moby-Dick; or, The Whale* (1851). Read Melville's novel, and then write a short essay comparing his style to Hawthorne's. Are there similarities in use of language, imagery, symbolism, or mythology? Where do you think the two writers found common ground?

2. Most of Hawthorne's work came out during his lifetime, but a good number of works, including his journals, were brought into print by his wife and children after his death. Read some of this posthumously published work, such as *Passages from the American Note-Books of Nathaniel Hawthorne* (1868) or *Septimius: A Romance* (1872), and start a discussion about the issues surrounding posthumous publication. Is it what the author would have wanted? Do you think the author's wishes should matter? What do you think were the motivations of Hawthorne's family in publishing these materials? Is the world ultimately the better for having these works in circulation?

3. The American Renaissance was one of those rare spontaneous movements in literary history to concentrate a mass of creativity into a very short period of time. Research the lives of the movement's main authors—Poe, Emerson, Thoreau, Whitman, Melville, and Hawthorne—being sure to read some samples of each of their work. What do you think is responsible for this burst of creativity by writers working in such diverse genres? To help answer the question, read some critical articles on the movement, and think about what was going on historically in mid-nineteenth century America that might have determined the writers' choices.

BIBLIOGRAPHY

Books

Bell, Michael Davitt. *Hawthorne and the Historical Romance of New England*. Princeton, N.J.: Princeton University Press, 1971.

Bell, Millicent. *Hawthorne's View of the Artist*. Albany: State University of New York Press, 1962.

Hawthorne, Julian. *Hawthorne and His Circle*. New York: Harpers, 1903.

Matthiessen, F. O. *American Renaissance: Art and Expression in the Age of Emerson and Whitman*. New York: Oxford University Press, 1941.

Ponder, Idol and Melinda, eds. *Hawthorne and Women: Engendering and Expanding the Hawthorne Tradition*. Amherst: University of Massachusetts Press, 1999.

Waggoner, Hyatt H. *Hawthorne: A Critical Study*. Cambridge, Mass.: Harvard University Press, 1955.

Turner, Arlin. *Nathaniel Hawthorne in His Times*. New York: Oxford University Press, 1980.

Periodicals

Adams, Richard P. "Hawthorne's Provincial Tales." *New England Quarterly* 30 (March 1957): 39–57.

Cox, James M. "The Scarlet Letter: Through the Old Manse and the Custom House." *Virginia Quarterly Review* 51 (1975): 432–447.

Gatti Taylor, Olivia. "Cultural Confessions: Penance and Penitence in Nathaniel Hawthorne's *The Scarlet Letter* and *The Marble Faun*." *Renascence: Essays on Values in Literature*, Winter 2005.

✹ Robert Hayden

BORN: *1913, Detroit, Michigan*

DIED: *1980, Ann Arbor, Michigan*

NATIONALITY: *American*

GENRE: *Poetry*

MAJOR WORKS:
Heart-Shape in the Dust (1940)
The Lion and the Archer (1948)
Selected Poems (1966)
Words in the Mourning Time (1970)
The Night-Blooming Cereus (1972)

Overview

The African American poet Robert Hayden faced the classic dilemma of the twentieth-century minority artist: the desire to be known primarily by his professional appellation, rather than his racial one. Instead of ignoring the problem, Hayden attacked it head-on, mastering traditional poetic forms while embracing black history and black experience among his themes, and always refusing to subordinate art to race.

Works in Biographical and Historical Context

An Education in Books, Love, and Poverty Robert Hayden—whose given name was Asa Bundy Sheffey—was born in Detroit, Michigan, on August 4, 1913. When his parents separated, he became the foster son of neighbors and was rechristened. The Haydens never legally adopted Robert, but they provided him with a home and

Robert Hayden *Hayden, Robert, photograph. Fisk University Library. Reproduced by permission.*

an education. He did not become reacquainted with his birth mother until his teens, when she returned to Detroit. The young Hayden often found himself in the midst of an emotional tug-of-war: between his two mother figures and between the women and his difficult foster father.

Hayden had vision problems as a child but became an avid reader nonetheless, thanks to the books his birth mother sent him throughout his childhood. The Haydens were uneducated people, but neither this nor their poverty prevented them from encouraging Robert's pursuit of an education. He entered Wayne State University on a scholarship in 1932 and majored in Spanish and minored in English, with aspirations to become a teacher. Acting in a play by the Harlem Renaissance poet Langston Hughes brought him into contact with the first of the many major poets he was to encounter. He showed Hughes some of his poetry, only to be told that his work was not original. In a 1977 interview he agreed with Hughes, but at the time, he said, he was crestfallen.

Delving into History After graduation Hayden worked with the Federal Writers' Project (FWP) from 1936 to 1938. This Detroit-based project was started in 1935 under the New Deal program's Works Progress Administration at the height of the Great Depression. It was meant to put writers to work producing texts, mostly nonfiction, that would be of significance to American

culture. For the FWP Hayden researched local black folklore and history. His next project involved compiling information on the Underground Railroad in Michigan while working part-time as a theater, movie, and music critic for the *Michigan Chronicle*, a black weekly paper.

In 1940 Hayden married Erma Morris, a concert pianist and aspiring composer. After a summer in New York, where Hayden pursued his historical research and Erma studied at Juilliard, the couple returned to Detroit, where Robert found himself unemployed thanks to the dismantling of the Works Progress Administration. Hayden then decided to go back to school for his master's degree, enrolling at the University of Michigan in Ann Arbor in 1941. His only child, Maia, was born the following year. At Michigan he was afforded the opportunity to study poetry with W. H. Auden, then a visiting professor. Auden gave him personal advice as well as valuable criticism of his poems, which Hayden credited with helping him to develop his own individual style. Twice, Hayden won the university's Hopwood Award for poetry by a student. After completing his master's degree in 1944, Hayden remained at Michigan for two years as a teaching fellow and had the distinction of being the first black member of the English department's teaching staff. When a position as assistant professor of English opened at Nashville's black Fisk University in 1946, Hayden and his family made the move to the segregated South.

Growing as a Poet Hayden's style continued to evolve during the 1940s. His output in this decade was slender—*The Lion and the Archer* (1948) contained only six poems—thanks to the demands of a full teaching schedule and active mentorship of his students. Though a short collection, the poems in *The Lion and the Archer* show a much more condensed and sophisticated use of language than his earlier work.

Hayden's best-known black history poem was written and repeatedly revised during this period. "Middle Passage" is famous for the way it blends lyric, dramatic, and narrative techniques. It is composed of three sections that offer different slants on the slave trade. It contains the thoughts of slave ship officers, a retired slave trader's recollections about Africa, and the story of the slave rebellion aboard the Cuban vessel *Amistad* and the blacks' eventual return to Africa, thanks to U.S. justice. Particularly striking is the poem's use of many forms of discourse: ship names, logs, diaries, prayers, hymns, legal depositions, parodies, and orations are all featured. All of these are joined together by lyric commentary that tries to come to terms with this "voyage through death / to life upon these shores."

The 1940s also saw the introduction of a new influence in Hayden's life: religion. Raised a Southern Baptist, Hayden was seeking a new direction in 1943 when he found Baha'i, a religious faith that follows the teachings of the Persian prophet Baha'u'llah (1817–1892). Baha'i emphasizes the unity of all religions and the brotherhood of humankind. Hayden found the Baha'i emphasis on social ethics and world peace ideal for the twentieth century. The Baha'i outlook appears in Hayden's poem "In Light half nightmare, half vision," where human suffering in Germany, South Africa, Korea, and America are related to the suffering of Baha'u'llah.

Engaging with History   The 1960s began the most significant phase of Hayden's literary career, bringing the middle-aged poet both unanticipated recognition and rejection. The temper of the times, especially the civil rights movement, seemed to give the poet fresh creative drive. *A Ballad of Remembrance* (1962) brought Hayden international recognition when it won the Grand Prize for Poetry at the First World Festival of Negro Arts at Dakar, Senegal, in 1966. An American version of *A Ballad of Remembrance* was published as *Selected Poems* in 1966 and included an assortment of other poems, with themes including black history, the quest for the meaning of human existence, Mexico (where Hayden had spent a year in the 1950s on a Ford Foundation fellowship), racism, and autobiography. The volume represents the finished artist, a view Hayden himself shared.

The civil rights era brought Hayden both overdue praise and unexpected enmity. African American writing was now being judged on merit rather than ethnicity by the white establishment, but at the same time a new racial emphasis dominated the critical judgment of some blacks. These mostly young critics rejected the idea that the black writer should speak for or to anyone outside his own race. This school of thought focused on the search for a black aesthetic, a notion with political overtones, based on the idea that blacks and whites are fundamentally different. Such a philosophy was anathema to Hayden, both as a Baha'i and an artist: in his view, poetry was poetry, no matter who wrote it. At the first Black Writers' Conference, held at Fisk in 1966, Hayden was accused of coming dangerously close to being antiblack for his refusal to be categorized as a "black poet." It was four years before Hayden could deal artistically with these attacks, which he did in *Words in the Mourning Time* (1970). The most significant poem in *Words in the Mourning Time* is "El–Hajj Malik El–Shabazz," a summation of the life of Malcolm X. It is significant that Hayden chose Malcolm X as his subject, as Malcolm X was the quintessential embodiment of black rage, but he was also quintessentially American. In the poem, Hayden addresses his feelings about being a black artist in America through Malcolm X's life.

As the 1960s drew to a close, many predominantly white universities began actively recruiting black students and faculty, and in 1969 Hayden returned to his alma mater, the University of Michigan, as professor of English. With his next work, *The Night-Blooming Cereus*, Hayden broke away from the black historical themes of his earlier work and moved toward more private symbolism. Although Hayden was criticized for this move, some argued that all along he had used the features of black

LITERARY AND HISTORICAL CONTEMPORARIES

Robert Hayden's famous contemporaries include:

Rosa Parks (1913–2005): American civil rights activist Parks helped launch the modern civil rights movement in 1955 by refusing to give up her seat on a Montgomery, Alabama, bus. Parks worked as a seamstress and a secretary for most of her life, but her actions in 1955 made her an icon of the civil rights movement.

Jesse Owens (1913–1980): American track and field athlete Owens stunned the world at the 1936 Summer Olympics in Berlin, where he won four gold medals. Hitler sought to use the Berlin Olympics to showcase "Aryan supremacy," but Owens stole the show. In later years, Owens criticized the U.S. government for not honoring his Olympic achievements.

Robert Lowell (1917–1977): American poet. Often referred to as a "confessional" poet, Lowell often spoke frankly about his own life in his poems. Lowell's poetry, however, is also steeped in history, and Lowell himself was often engaged with many of important moments in U.S. history, including the civil rights movement and the Vietnam War.

Randall Jarrell (1914–1965): American poet. Like Hayden, Jarrell was greatly influenced by W. H. Auden early in his career. Later, Jarrell wrote extensively about his time in the army and helped revive the fortunes of many of his fellow poets as a popular critic in magazines such as the *New Republic*.

Baha'u'llah (1817–1892): founder of the Baha'i faith who preached that humanity is all part of one single race that must find unification in a global society. Followers of Baha'i view him as a prophet the way Muslims view Muhammad.

history and the black experience as universal human symbols, to which anyone could relate.

The 1970s were a happier period for Hayden: he won the Russell Loines Award in 1970 and was elected to the American Academy of Poets in 1975. He published *Angle of Ascent: New and Selected Poems* in 1975 and in 1976 was appointed the first black consultant in poetry to the Library of Congress (the American equivalent to England's poet laureate). His appointment was renewed the following year. He was at work on a collection of new and selected poems (published as a revised version of *American Journal* in 1982) when he was hospitalized in Ann Arbor, Michigan, with a heart ailment. He died on February 25, 1980.

Works in Literary Context

Echoes of the Harlem Renaissance   Hayden's early work, which he viewed as apprentice efforts, derives much

COMMON HUMAN EXPERIENCE

Robert Hayden's poem "Middle Passage" is a hodge-podge of literary and nonliterary styles, suggesting that there are many ways to tell a powerful story, and they all count. Here are some other works that use a collage of styles to tell their stories:

Moby Dick: Or, the Whale (1851), a novel by Herman Melville. To tell the story of one man's obsession with a single white whale, Melville often departs from traditional narration to include long descriptions of various aspects of whales and the whaling industry, bringing history and context to Captain Ahab's quest.

American Splendor (2003), a film written and directed by Shari Springer Berman and Robert Pulcini. Based on the autobiographical comic books of Harvey Pekar, the film combines documentary storytelling and animation with traditional fictional film to tell the story of Pekar's personal life and the creation of his much-revered comic book series, the ironically titled *American Splendor* (1976).

Ulysses (1922), a novel by James Joyce. Though the novel takes place in the course of just one day in the life of Leopold Bloom, parts of *Ulysses* range over all of literary history, as the narrator imitates one author or writing style after another. The massive novel also incorporates newspaper reports, advertising copy, and street dialogue as it illuminates Bloom's world.

Infinite Jest (1996), a novel by David Foster Wallace. Wallace's 1100-page novel takes place at an elite tennis academy and a halfway house for recovering addicts. The details of the worlds Wallace describes are provided by many unexpected forms of discourse, including lists of the results of tennis matches and long, rambling radio broadcasts.

of its style and substance from the Harlem Renaissance, the great flowering of literary activity that began among the African American writers of New York in the 1920s and spread across the country and abroad. The young writers whose creativity sparked the renaissance were the first generation of African Americans to grow up unfettered by slavery, and the wide variety of literary genres they embraced—from poetry to drama to journalism to philosophy—reflects the realization of African American culture. Hayden's early poetry shows his indebtedness to his literary predecessors. For example, his poem "The Negro to America" recalls Langston Hughes's poems "I, Too, Sing America" and "Let America be America Again" in its assertion that until democracy applies to the least of Americans, no American can truly claim to be free. Similarly, Hayden's "Poem for a Negro Dancer" is indebted to Countee Cullen's "Heritage" and Claude McKay's "Harlem Dancer." Hayden joins Cullen in advocating the value of a heritage that should not be corrupted by

contact with the West, and joins McKay in emphasizing that, like the dancer who performs for the lurid eyes of customers in a Harlem cabaret, black people must hold some part of themselves free from the degrading implications that compensation for their art can sometimes bring. In other words, Hayden, like some of his colleagues, believed that art produced from the souls of black people cannot be bought and sold.

Works in Critical Context

Selected Poems   For most of his career, Hayden's work received little critical response on its own merits. It wasn't until 1966, with the publication of *Selected Poems*, that Hayden first enjoyed widespread attention from the nation's literary critics. As the *Choice* critic remarked at the time, *Selected Poems* showed Hayden to be "the surest poetic talent of any Negro poet in America; more importantly, it demonstrated a major talent and poetic coming-of-age without regard to race or creed." With each succeeding volume of poems his reputation was further enhanced. By appointment as consultant in poetry to the Library of Congress in 1976, Hayden was generally recognized as one of the country's leading black poets.

Critics often point to Hayden's unique ability to combine the historical and the personal when speaking of his own life and the lives of his people. Writing in *Obsidian: Black Literature in Review*, Gary Zebrun argued that

the voice of the speaker in Hayden's best work twists and squirms its way out of anguish in order to tell, or sing, stories of American history—in particular the courageous and plaintive record of Afro-American history—and to chart the thoughts and feelings of the poet's own private space.... Hayden is ceaselessly trying to achieve ... transcendence, which must not be an escape from the horror of history or from the loneliness of individual mortality, but an ascent that somehow transforms the horror and creates a blessed permanence.

Responses to Literature

1. Robert Hayden, who spent so much of his career writing about African American history, got his start in Detroit with the Federal Writers' Project, part of the Works Progress Administration. Learn more about the project's activities in Detroit by reading Elizabeth Clemens's *The Works Progress Administration in Detroit* (2008), which includes archival photographs alongside the text.

2. Hayden's poem "Middle Passage" weaves together three perspectives on the slave trade, illuminating the conditions onboard the slave ships during their trips across the ocean. Research the realities of these conditions and write an essay describing and evaluating Hayden's representation of history. How do the various perspectives in the poem work together? What techniques does the poet use to get you emotionally involved?

How does the poetic treatment differ from the more straightforward accounts you will find in history books?

3. Hayden wanted to be considered a poet, not a black poet. Start a discussion on the importance of the writer's identity to the formation of the work, as well as to a reader's ability to interpret it. Should we consider "who" a writer is when discussing his or her work? Expand your discussion to include other writers who are minorities, immigrants, women, or another group that struggles with similar "labeling" issues.

BIBLIOGRAPHY

Books

Davis, Arthur P. "Robert Hayden." In *From the Dark Tower: Afro-American Writers 1900–1960.* Washington, D.C.: Howard University Press, 1974.

Davis, Charles T. "Robert Hayden's Use of History." In *Modern Black Poets.* Englewood Cliffs, N.J.: Prentice Hall, 1973.

Hatcher, John. *From the Auroral Darkness: The Life and Poetry of Robert Hayden.* Oxford: George Ronald, 1984.

O'Brien, John. *Interviews with Black Writers.* New York: Liveright, 1973.

Periodicals

Faulkner, Howard. "'Transformed by Steeps of Flight': The Poetry of Robert Hayden." *CLA Journal* (June 1978).

Oehlschlaeger, Fritz. "Robert Hayden's Meditation on Art: The Final Sequence of *Words in the Mourning Time.*" *Black American Literature* (Fall 1985).

Parks, Gerald. "The Baha'i Muse: Religion in Robert Hayden's Poetry." *World Order* (Fall 1981).

Review of *Selected Poems. Choice* (May 1967).

Williams, Pontheolla T. "Robert Hayden: A Life Upon These Shores." *World Order* (Fall 1981).

Zebrun, Gary. Review of *Selected Poems. Obsidian: Black Literature in Review* (Spring 1981).

■ H.D.

SEE *Hilda Doolittle*

✹ William Least Heat-Moon

BORN: *1939, Kansas City, Missouri*

NATIONALITY: *American*

GENRE: *Nonfiction*

MAJOR WORKS:

Blue Highways: A Journey into America (1982)

PrairyErth (A Deep Map) (1991)

River-Horse: A Voyage Across America (1999)

Roads to Quoz: An American Mosey (2008)

Overview

William Least Heat-Moon is as much a traveler as he is an author. He traverses the country, exploring the rural nooks and crannies of America's lesser-known roads in both words and pictures. As a photographer, Heat-Moon's work is both expansive and ethereal. As a writer, he is intimate and warm, humorous and poetic, and always ready for a new cross-country adventure. Heat-Moon's excursions are detailed in his books *Blue Highways: A Journey into America* (1982), *PrairyErth (A Deep Map)* (1991), and his most recent work, *Roads to Quoz: An American Mosey* (2008).

Works in Biographical and Historical Context

Sowing the Seeds of Wanderlust William Least Heat-Moon was born William Lewis Trogdon on August 27, 1939. He grew up in Kansas City, Missouri, with his father Ralph, an attorney, his mother Maurine, a homemaker, and his older brother. The name he currently uses professionally was given to him by his father, whose ancestry is partially Osage Indian. The name "Heat Moon" derives from Sioux Indian lore. Ralph would affectionately call his older son "Little Heat Moon" and the younger William "Least Heat Moon." Although the family never used these names publicly, his pride in his Native American heritage inspired William Trogdon to use his adopted name when he became a writer as an adult.

As a boy, Heat-Moon dreamed of becoming a writer or photojournalist when he grew up. However, he remained close to home even after he reached college age. At the University of Missouri at Columbia, Heat-Moon earned an impressive array of four degrees—two baccalaureates, a Master of Arts, and a doctorate—over the span of about twenty years. However, it was during his time in the U.S. Navy (1964–1965) that Heat-Moon had his most profoundly life-altering experience. While enduring an unhappy stint serving aboard U.S.S. *Lake Champlain*, he began reading John Steinbeck's recently published travelogue *Travels with Charley: In Search of America* (1962). The account of Steinbeck's whimsical yet spiritually engaged trip watered the seeds of wanderlust already planted in Heat-Moon's mind. As he told *Publishers Weekly*:

> I liked the traveling—but when we were locked in the ship, I did not like that, and this book, when I had a moment to read it here and there, gave me a great escape. I said to myself, "One of these days I want to take a trip around the country."

Despite this revelation, Heat-Moon remained in Missouri for more than a decade after he left the Navy in 1965. He first took an intermittent teaching position in Columbia, Missouri, at Stephens College. Heat-Moon worked at the college from 1965 to 1968 and then returned twice in the 1970s. Heat-Moon found himself at a crossroads after losing his job at the college and being on the verge of losing Lezlie, his wife of ten years. With

William Least Heat-Moon   *Keith Philpott / Time Life Pictures / Getty Images*

his personal life in a state of flux, Heat-Moon finally resolved to take the trip he first dreamed of while reading *Travels with Charley.*

Adrift on "Blue Highways"

On March 20, 1978, with only $450 to spare, the thirty-eight-year-old Heat-Moon boarded his well-equipped van (which he fancifully christened "Ghost Dancer" as a reference to a Native American resurrection ceremony) and hit the road. He decided to limit his trip to only the smallest, most off-the-beaten-path roads he could find, roads he nicknamed "Blue Highways." The three-month journey was both an escape from his troubled home life and a quest for himself. As he trekked across the country, his thoughts continually traveled back to his childhood. He recalled his boyhood dream of becoming a writer and photographer. Having unlashed the domestic and career ties that previously bound him, Heat-Moon concluded that he would indeed follow this dream.

Heat-Moon started collecting stories and shooting photographs as he bounced from one odd small town to the next. He had conversations with a colorful assortment of individuals: runaways and hitchhikers, medical students and prostitutes, country store owners and barkeeps. All the while he kept a journal of these encounters. By the end of the trip, he had enough delightful anecdotes, folksy insights, and harrowing tales to fill a book. Thir-

teen thousand miles later, Heat-Moon returned to Missouri and started working on his first book. During the four years it took him to finish it, he worked as a clerk in a local courthouse. When the time came to sell the book, he quit his clerking position to take a night job at a newspaper, so he could spend his mornings and afternoons hunting for an interested publisher. In 1982 *Blue Highways: A Journey into America* was published by Fawcett Crest. Although the book was greeted with mixed reactions from the critical press, it became a major favorite with readers and found a place on the *New York Times* bestseller list for an impressive forty-two weeks.

Explorations Small and Great

While Heat-Moon spent the mid-1980s lecturing at the University of Missouri School of Journalism, the massive success of *Blue Highways* gave Heat-Moon the opportunity to continue writing and traveling. The result of his next venture, and of eight years of research, was *PrairyErth (A Deep Map)*, published in 1991. This time out, Heat-Moon limited himself to a single area, Chase County, Kansas, but the scope of the book was, in its own way, broader than that of *Blue Highways.* Along with recording conversations with the locals, such as a Kaw Indian whose tribe had been uprooted by settlers, he examined, in untold hours spent in libraries and court houses, the history of this grassland region. Heat-Moon collected the wealth of data and stories into an unusual and seemingly randomly structured book that the author compared to Native American storytelling. He also avoided the sort of judgmental remarks that caused some critics to dismiss *Blue Highways*. Consequently, Heat-Moon had another bestseller on his hands.

Heat-Moon's next trek found him riding the waves rather than the roads, in an attempt to retrace the legendary voyage of Lewis and Clark, the first explorers to successfully mount an expedition from the East Coast to the Pacific and back. Aboard a twenty-two-foot motorboat, he sailed 5,222 miles, starting in New York harbor, in one hundred days. The harrowing journey is documented in the semifictional *River-Horse: A Voyage Across America* (1999). Heat-Moon reserves plenty of moments to observe the beauty of the rolling waters that surround him, to share folktales, historical nuggets, human encounters, and inject his unique humor into the story. Significantly, the book is also concerned with environmental and ecological issues. Following the book's publication, Heat-Moon told Powells.com, "I wanted *River-Horse* to be a kind of service book to help along some of these environmental causes that have so much to do with the quality of life we're going to face in the next century."

In Search of the Extraordinary   Most recently, Heat-Moon published *Roads to Quoz: An American Mosey* (2008), which found him accompanied by his wife Q for his latest venture. The couple search for the head of the Ouachita River in Arkansas, as they reenact an expedition quite a bit less well-known than the one accomplished by Lewis and Clark. The Dunbar-Hunter Expedition (1804) was one of four treks commissioned by President Thomas Jefferson into the 800,000 square miles of land the U.S. bought from France known as the Louisiana Purchase. The book's mysterious title is a reference to an eighteenth century term for "anything out of the ordinary." As usual, the heart of the story can be found in Heat-Moon's encounters with various Americans, but its greatest drama lies in an attempt to find the truth behind the murder of his great-grandfather.

Although ambitious, the trip documented in *Roads to Quoz* was hardly as demanding or dangerous as the ones he described in *Blue Highways* or *River-Horse*, hence his description of it as a "mosey." "The great enemy on the 'Blue Highways' trip, being on the road those three months, was desolation," he told SF Gate.com. "It was a threat every single day of the trip, as I remember it now. But with this one, with a fellow traveler, and a good one, as Q is, desolation was never a problem." When he is not exploring or moseying across America, Heat-Moon continues to make a home in Columbia, Missouri, where he owns a tobacco farm.

Works in Literary Context

Travel Literature   A broad genre, travel literature (also known as the "travelogue" format) is essentially defined as

---

LITERARY AND HISTORICAL CONTEMPORARIES

Heat-Moon's famous contemporaries include:

William Faulkner (1897–1962): The Nobel Prize–winning American author William Faulkner is regarded as one of the most important and influential writers of the twentieth century. Heat-Moon has said he is heavily influenced by Faulkner, who died the same year Heat-Moon earned his masters degree.

Richard M. Nixon (1913–1994): Nixon was the thirty-seventh president of the United States. In 1972, Nixon signed the Clean Water Act, of which Heat-Moon writes in *River-Horse: A Voyage Across America*.

N. Scott Momaday (1934–): The Pulitzer Prize—winning writer Momaday brought the nation's attention to Native American literature upon the publication of his novel **House Made of Dawn** (1968).

Larry McMurtry (1936–): American writer McMurtry is best known for writing the Pulitzer Prize-winning western *Lonesome Dove* (1985) and the coming-of-age novel *The Last Picture Show* (1966), which he later adapted into an Oscar-winning film for director Peter Bogdanovich.

Michael Dorris (1945–1997): Dorris wrote such significant works of Native American literature as the novel *A Yellow Raft in Blue Water* (1987) and the nonfictional *The Broken Cord: Fetal Alcohol Syndrome and the Loss of the Future* (1989).

---

a writer's account of her/his journey to unfamiliar places, in which he documents the topography, history, culture, and/or locals of the place. Travel literature stands in contrast to travel journalism by way of its consistent narrative structure and the writer's personal perspective, which is often expressed in terms contrasting the writer's own home environment. The history of travel writing is a decidedly long one. One of the first examples of the genre, Pausanias's *Description of Greece*, dates back to the second century. Throughout the years, the genre has persisted and grown and been tackled by writers Charles Dickens (*Pictures from Italy*, 1846), Herman Melville (*Typee: A Peep at Polynesian Life*, 1846), and Robert Louis Stevenson (*Travels with a Donkey in the Cévennes*, 1879). Other writers, including Paul Theroux and Heat-Moon himself, have specifically devoted themselves to the genre.

Ecology   As a theme in literary works, ecology is a relatively recent one. In fact, when Rachel Carson's *Silent Spring* (1962) was published, she was actually criticized for conveying her scientific exposé of the detrimental effects of pollution and pesticides on the environment with fluid, literary prose. However, Carson's book proved to be both a seminal one and one with some precedent.

COMMON HUMAN EXPERIENCE

In his book *Blue Highways: A Journey into America*, Heat-Moon describes his many colorful encounters during a road trip throughout the United States. Other literary works about road trips include:

On the Road (1957), a novel by Jack Kerouac. Kerouac's novel, considered one of the definitive books of the Beat Generation, is a partly autobiographical account of a series of spur-of-the-moment road trips he and a cast of friends took throughout America during the late 1940s.

Travels with Charley (1962), a nonfiction book by John Steinbeck. Steinbeck's beloved travelogue is a document of a cross-country trek he took with his pet poodle Charley. Steinbeck's famed travels took him from Long Island, New York, across the country to the Salinas Valley in California.

Wild at Heart (1990), a novel by Barry Gifford. Gifford's darkly comic crime novel follows the incorrigible romantics Sailor and Lula as they take a road trip fraught with violent encounters.

Driving Mr. Albert: A Trip Across America with Einstein's Brain (2001), a nonfiction book by Michael Paterniti. This is the humorous true story of Paterniti and eighty-four-year-old doctor Thomas Harvey's journey from New Jersey to California to deliver the brain of the world's most famous scientist to his granddaughter Evelyn.

Narrative classics such as Ernest Hemingway's *The Old Man and the Sea* (1952), William Faulkner's *Big Woods: The Hunting Stories* (1955), and Jack London's *The Call of the Wild* (1903) are just a few literary works that examine themes of ecology and conservation. Contemporary works that combine literary narrative with ecological concerns include Steven Zaillian's *A Civil Action* (1995) and Heat-Moon's *River-Horse* (1999).

Works in Critical Context

Heat-Moon has enjoyed consistent favor from readers, his books often ending up on bestseller lists, but his relationship with critics is less consistent. He has been called out for not only his self-conscious writing style but also his arguably biased treatment of those he writes about. Still, few writers of travel literature have ever achieved the steady popularity of Heat-Moon.

Blue Highways: A Journey into America Heat-Moon's first work, *Blue Highways: A Journey into America*, was criticized for its sometimes unflattering portrayals of the small-town Americans he encountered during his travels. A review in the *Hudson Review* complains, "Heat Moon's sometimes defective sensibility manifests itself in snap judgments he makes of the people he meets along the way. If they are laid back, helpful, chatty, he is bound to wax poetic and philosophical about the mysterious bonds between us. If, however, they are truculent, grinding axes that are not sympathetic with Heat Moon's own, then they are haughtily dismissed as drones of the evil moneyed class." However, other critics were far more complimentary, such as Anatole Broyard of the *The New York Times*, who deems the book "wonderful" and that it might give the reader "a little flush of national pride."

River-Horse: A Voyage Across America Like so much of his work, Heat-Moon's *River-Horse: A Voyage Across America* had its fans and detractors in the critical world. A review in *Newsweek* chided the book for its "contrived" premise and "fussy writing" and concluded, "It would be a very tolerant reader who wouldn't want to jump ship before Heat-Moon hits Ohio." However, negative reviews did not affect the book's considerable popularity with readers and certain critics. A reviewer for *Booklist* found the book's stories to possess "a timeless quality . . . all remarkably spellbinding and enchanting," and summed the work up as an "excellent book."

Responses to Literature

1. Environmental issues are among the many subjects Heat-Moon addresses in his book *River-Horse: A Voyage Across America*. Read the book and explain what you learned about environmental issues in an essay. Be sure to support your response with details from the book.

2. Heat-Moon has said that the structure of his book *PrairyErth (A Deep Map)* was influenced by Native American storytelling, which is distinguished by its wandering style. Read *PrairyErth (A Deep Map)* and explain how the author uses unconventional narrative techniques to convey his ideas.

3. Heat-Moon has often said that John Steinbeck's book *Travels with Charley* was a major influence on his debut book *Blue Highways: A Journey into America*. Read both books, and then write an essay explaining how you think Steinbeck's book influenced Heat-Moon's. Support your conclusions with details from both books.

BIBLIOGRAPHY

Books

Oppliger, Aaron J., ed. *Newsmakers*. Detroit, Mich.: Gale Group, 2000.

Periodicals

Broyard, Anatole. "Book of the Times." *The New York Times* (January 13, 1983).

Leventhal, Ted. "River Horse: A Voyage Across America (review)." *Booklist* (August 1999): 1980.

Jones, Malcolm. "Reflections on the Water." *Newsweek* (November 15, 1999).

McDowell, Robert. "In Pursuit of Life Itself." *Hudson Review* (Summer 1983).

Plummer, William. "William Least Heat-Moon Interview." *People Magazine* (February 28, 1983): 72.

Web sites

Hank Nuwer.com. *William Least Heat-Moon: Interview with Hank Nuwer; "The Road To Serendipity."* Accessed November 22, 2008, from http://www. hanknuwer.com/William%20Least%20Heat%20 Moon%20(Trogdon).html.

Paula Gordon.com. *Connect.* Accessed November 23, 2008, from http://www.paulagordon.com/shows/ heatmoon.

On Point Radio.org *William Least Heat-Moon.* Posted November 11, 2008, from http://www.onpointradio. org/shows/2008/11/william-least-heat-moon.

Weich, Dave. *William Least Heat-Moon: Participatory Armchair Rivering.* Accessed December 6, 2008, from http://www.powells.com/authors/ leastheatmoon.html.

Publishers Weekly.com. *William Least Heat-Moon: Navigating America.* Accessed December 6, 2008, from http://www.publishersweekly.com/article/ CA167308.html.

SF Gate.com. *Interview with William Least Heat-Moon.* Accessed December 6, 2008, from http://www. sfgate.com/cgi-bin/article.cgi?f=/c/a/2008/11/ 14/RVPC143Q7J.DTL.

Artful Dodge. *A Conversation with William Least Heat-Moon.* Accessed November 23, 2008, from http://www.wooster.edu/ArtfulDodge/interviews/ heat-moon.htm.

✹ Robert Heinlein

BORN: *1907, Butler, Missouri*

DIED: *1988, Carmel, California*

NATIONALITY: *American*

GENRE: *Fiction*

MAJOR WORKS:

The Man Who Sold the Moon (1950)

Starship Troopers (1959)

Stranger in a Strange Land (1961)

The Moon Is a Harsh Mistress (1966)

Overview

Robert Heinlein, novelist and short-story writer of far-reaching and incisive science fiction, was the "one author who has raised science fiction from the gutter of pulp space opera . . . to the altitude of original and breathtaking

Robert Heinlein © *Ed Kashi / Corbis*

concepts," as Alfred Bester maintained in *Publishers Weekly.* Some critics have even compared Heinlein's influence on the genre to that of the legendary H. G. Wells. Heinlein brought a military and engineering background and a gift for constructing a story to a genre that long struggled to be considered literature.

Works in Biographical and Historical Context

A Circuitous Path to Writing Robert Anson Heinlein was born in small-town Butler, Missouri, on July 7, 1907, but was raised along with his six brothers and sisters in Kansas City. He spent a year at the University of Missouri before accepting an appointment to the U.S. Naval Academy at Annapolis. After graduating in 1929, ranked twentieth in a class of 243, he spent five years as a gunnery officer on aircraft carriers. He was forced to retire from the Navy on permanent disability after developing tuberculosis in 1934. He then briefly attended the University of California, Los Angeles, studying physics and mathematics, but his continuing ill health forced him to move to Colorado to recuperate. In the next few years he tried a variety of ventures, including mining for silver in

Colorado, selling real estate, and running (unsuccessfully) for public office, back in California.

In 1938, while casting about for a way to raise money to make a mortgage payment on his home, he chanced upon an editorial in *Astounding Science-Fiction*, which suggested that readers try their hands at writing and submit a story for publication and a cash prize. Heinlein, who had been reading science fiction almost as long as he had known how to read, worked on his submission for four days, and he liked it enough to send it first to a higher paying market (*Collier's*), where it did not sell. Then, eventually, he sent it to *Astounding Science-Fiction*, where it did. "Life-Line," which later appeared in the story collection *The Man Who Sold the Moon* (1950), appeared in the August 1939 issue, and Heinlein's career as a science-fiction writer had begun. In the next three years Heinlein published twenty-eight stories of varying lengths, under a variety of pseudonyms. All but four of these stories appeared in *Astounding Science-Fiction* or *Unknown Worlds*. They radically changed the face of science fiction.

War and Other Industries For a time during World War II, Heinlein stopped writing science fiction. Instead, he lent his expertise in aeronautical engineering to the Philadelphia naval yards. When Heinlein returned to writing in 1947, he set his sights on better-paying markets, moving from the cheaper pulp magazines to such prestigious mainstream glossies as the *Saturday Evening Post*, *Argosy*, and *Bluebook*. Heinlein was the first major science fiction writer to break out of category and reach the larger general fiction market. In the process, he broke down the walls that had isolated science fiction for so long. His work also began to be published in hardcover. After some revision he reprinted such *Astounding Science-Fiction* stories as "Beyond This Horizon" (1948) and "Sixth Column" (1949), and he began a new series of original juvenile fiction, the first being his earliest hardcover book, *Rocketship Galileo* (1947).

In the 1950s Heinlein moved away from magazines and even the short-story form, concentrating on his young adult fiction and the occasional adult novel. During the 1950s he also branched out into television, working on the "Tom Corbett: Space Cadet" series (based largely on his own youth-market novel *Space Cadet* (1948)), and into the movies with *Destination Moon* (1950) and *Project Moonbase* (1953).

A New Sense of Purpose In 1957 Heinlein participated in a lecture series at the University of Chicago, arguing that the real ideas in literature—about society, humanity, and the future—were to be found in science fiction rather than what is "now being palmed off on us as 'serious literature.'" The opinion reflected in the other three lectures in the series, however, can be summed up by one of their titles, "The Failure of the Science Fiction Novel as Social Criticism." Heinlein seems to have taken the criticism of his genre to heart, for the next few years saw the publication of novels that grapple concretely with issues concerning human society.

The first was *Starship Troopers* (1959), which postulates a world run by military veterans. It was the first of Heinlein's books to speculate not on future scientific changes, but on societal changes. The novel was attacked by some critics for its supposed fascist and militaristic tendencies, and it earned Heinlein a reputation as a right-winger. Although, according to fellow science fiction writer Isaac Asimov, Heinlein had described himself as a "flaming liberal" in the 1930s and 1940s, he shifted to the right in the ensuing decades. Heinlein would defend the anti-communist witch hunt led by Senator Joseph McCarthy in the early 1950s, which was spurred by Cold War fears of the spread of communism and ruined the careers of many Washington and Hollywood figures. He would also support arch-conservative Barry Goldwater in his presidential run against Lyndon Johnson in 1964. Despite the controversy over Heinlein's politics, *Starship Troopers* is still one of Heinlein's most popular novels. It won a Hugo Award in 1960 and was still popular enough three decades later to be loosely adapted into a Hollywood blockbuster by Paul Verhoeven in 1997.

Heinlein followed *Starship Troopers* with another controversial novel that met with strong opposition. This work featured quite different speculations about the future. *Stranger in a Strange Land* (1961), perhaps Heinlein's best-known work, tells the story of a Martian with psychic powers who establishes a religious movement on Earth; members of his Church of All Worlds engage in unorthodox sexual practices and live in small communes. The novel has sold more than three million copies, garnered Heinlein another Hugo Award, created an intense cult following, and even inspired a real-life Church of All Worlds, founded by some devoted readers of the book.

The Last Decades In subsequent novels Heinlein continued to speculate on social changes of the future, dealing with such controversial subjects as group marriage and incest. In *The Moon Is a Harsh Mistress* (1966), lunar colonists practice a variety of marriage forms owing to a shortage of women on the moon. In *I Will Fear No Evil* (1971), an elderly, dying businessman has his brain transplanted into the body of a young woman, who he then impregnates with his own previously stored sperm. *Time Enough for Love: The Lives of Lazarus Long* (1973) explores varieties of incest that might become possible due to future scientific developments such as cloning, time travel, and immortality. In these novels of the 1960s and 1970s, Diane Parkin-Speer writes in *Extrapolation*, "a defense of unconventional sexual love is [Heinlein's] central theme.... The ideal sexual love relationship, first presented in *Stranger in a Strange Land*, is heterosexual, nonmonogamous, and patriarchal, with an emphasis on procreation. The protagonists of the novels and their various sexual partners express unorthodox sexual views and have no inhibitions or guilt."

In the mid-1960s Heinlein moved to California from Colorado, where he had been living with his third wife, Virginia, since the late 1940s. He continued to produce novels throughout the 1970s and 1980s, despite varying degrees of ill health. A lifelong smoker, Heinlein died of emphysema-related heart failure on May 8, 1988.

Works in Literary Context

Science Fiction Before Heinlein came along to change the face of science fiction, the genre's two major types were represented primarily by H. G. Wells (1866–1946) and Edgar Rice Burroughs (1875–1950). For Wells, science fiction was a set of literary devices for discussing the present. *The Time Machine* (1895), for example, uses the journey into the future as a device for attacking Victorian attitudes on scientific progress, biological evolution, and class relationships. For Burroughs, on the other hand, science fiction was action-adventure escape literature. Readers are invited to forget their daily problems and journey to Mars for a series of fabulous and successful adventures. Wells used the future to offer insights into his own present; Burroughs used the future as a refuge from the present, as a setting for exciting daydreams. But Heinlein and his first editor at *Astounding Science-Fiction*, John W. Campbell, Jr., had an entirely different notion as to what science fiction should be and do. They wished to make the future believable, plausible, possible. Heinlein's stories convinced a whole generation that man will really be able to do things they could only imagine now—and that generation grew up and sent Apollo missions to the Moon in 1969. Heinlein's speculative science fiction showed that the future need not be either a symbolic representation of the present or a refuge from real-life problems. It is also something to be shaped by people today. As Heinlein wrote in 1952, "Youths who build hot-rods are not dismayed by spaceships; in their adult years they will build such ships. In the meantime they will read stories of interplanetary travel." Heinlein wrote many such stories for exactly that audience.

Works in Critical Context

Heinlein is widely considered the "dean" of science-fiction writers. Although some critics find fault with some of the conclusions he draws from his rigid logic, almost all agree that his bold exploration of social themes actively challenges prevailing views of society, and has helped elevate science fiction from escapist entertainment to literature of the first order. His works, especially *Stranger in a Strange Land*, have maintained a cult-like popularity, and his later works were greeted with anticipation, hitting numerous best-seller lists. Heinlein won four Hugo Awards for his novels and the first Nebula Grandmaster Award for overall achievement in the science fiction genre.

LITERARY AND HISTORICAL CONTEMPORARIES

Robert Heinlein's famous contemporaries include:

Barry Goldwater (1909–1998): American politician. A five-time U.S. Senator from Arizona, Goldwater was a major force behind the birth of modern-day conservatism. As the Republican nominee for president in 1964, Goldwater campaigned hard against the perceived intrusion of the federal government in the lives of its citizens. Goldwater's liberal views on social issues, however, distanced him from the religious right in the 1980s.

Ian Fleming (1908–1964): British writer. Best known as the creator of the fictional spy James Bond, Fleming wrote novels that many critics dismissed as "genre fiction." Like Heinlein, though, Fleming had serious ideas that he tried to communicate in his entertaining and imaginative novels, such as *Casino Royale* (1953), *Diamonds Are Forever* (1956), and *Dr. No* (1958).

Lillian Hellman (1905–1984): American playwright and activist. Hellman was among the most high-profile victims of Joe McCarthy's anti-communist Congressional hearings in the early 1950s. Called before the committee to "name names" of communists, Hellman refused to implicate her partner, the writer Dashiell Hammett, and was subsequently blacklisted. Hellman's most famous play, *The Children's Hour* (1934) deals with the ruinous effects of rumors at a boarding school.

Elia Kazan (1909–2003): Greek-American director, producer, and writer. Kazan directed some of the most memorable films and plays in American history, including *Death of a Salesman* (1949) for the stage and *A Streetcar Named Desire* (1951) and *On the Waterfront* (1954) for the screen. Kazan's career, however, was mired in controversy due to his cooperation with Joe McCarthy's House Un-American Activities Committee. In his testimony to HUAC, Kazan named names of suspected communists in Hollywood, thereby destroying their careers.

Stranger in a Strange Land Because of its weighty themes, Heinlein's novels have always generated a strong response from critics. *Stranger in a Strange Land* was, as David N. Samuelson wrote in *Critical Encounters: Writers and Themes in Science Fiction*, "in some ways emblematic of the Sixties.... It fit the iconoclastic mood of the time, attacking human folly under several guises, especially in the person or persons of the Establishment: government, the military, organized religion." Robert Scholes and Eric S. Rabkin wrote in *Science Fiction: History, Science, Vision* that "the values of the sixties could hardly have found a more congenial expression." Heinlein explained to R. A. Jelliffe in the *Chicago Tribune* that, in *Stranger in a Strange Land*, he intended to "examine every major

COMMON HUMAN EXPERIENCE

Starship Troopers imagines a world entirely dominated by the military. Here are some other works that explore the consequences of military control:

Star Wars (1977), a film by George Lucas. George Lucas's original installment of the *Star Wars* franchise (which includes three movies in the original trilogy and a prequel trilogy produced two decades later) is set in a fictional galaxy populated by commingling societies of humans, aliens, and robots, and ruled by an evil Empire intent on quashing any signs of rebellion.

1984 (1949), a novel by George Orwell. In George Orwell's famous nightmare vision, a militaristic totalitarian government—headed by a ubiquitous yet shadowy figure known as Big Brother—controls every aspect of society, from family life to social life to language through constant surveillance. The protagonist's brave but desperate attempt to live as he chooses proves just how pervasive government control really is.

Children of Men (2006), a film directed by Alfonso Cuaron, adapted from the 1992 novel of the same name by P. D. James. *Children of Men* imagines a near future in which there is worldwide infertility. With no more babies being born and the population aging, the fabric of society begins to come apart while the government's power over its citizens keeps increasing.

"The Secret Miracle," a short story by Jorge Luis Borges from the collection *Ficciones* (1944). Set during the Nazi occupation of Prague during World War II, "The Secret Miracle" mourns the silencing of art by Fascism. In the story, a Czech playwright sentenced to death by firing squad begs for a year to complete his final play; though his request is denied, time stops while, in his mind, he spends a year completing the play. The moment it is finished, time resumes and he is executed.

axiom of the Western culture, to question each axiom, throw doubt on it—and, if possible, to make the antithesis of each axiom appear a possible and perhaps desirable thing—rather than unthinkable." This ambitious attack caused a major upheaval in science fiction.

Responses to Literature

1. The experimental communities described in Robert Heinlein's fiction have had many real-life counterparts, from John Humphrey Noyes's Oneida community to Jim Jones's Jonestown to David Koresh's Branch Davidians. Using the Internet and your library, research a real-life experimental commune. What made it work? Why did it eventually fail? What conclusions can you draw about the nature of experiments in communal living?

2. Heinlein wrote about space travel long before it was achieved, but many of his visions have yet to come true. Read one or two of Heinlein's stories from the 1940s, 1950s, or 1960s and think critically about the visions of the future they present. Have any elements of the stories come to pass? Write an essay in which you outline what you see as Heinlein's vision of the future, and assess that vision in light of our current reality.

3. Much of Heinlein's fiction, including *Stranger in a Strange Land*, uses such adult themes as sexuality as a window into human society. Read the novel, and then start a discussion on the function of sexuality in the story, and in our society in general. How far is Heinlein's vision from reality? Can sexuality be read as a metaphor? What do our rules about sexuality say about our society?

BIBLIOGRAPHY

Books

Asimov, Isaac. *I, Asimov: A Memoir.* New York: Doubleday, 1994.

Franklin, Howard Bruce. *Robert A. Heinlein: America as Science Fiction.* New York: Oxford University Press, 1980.

Moskowitz, Sam. *Seekers of Tomorrow: Masters of Modern Science Fiction.* New York: Ballantine, 1967.

Samuelson, David N. "The Frontier Worlds of Robert A. Heinlein." In Clareson, Thomas D., ed. *Voices for the Future*, volume 1. Bowling Green, Ohio: Bowling Green University Popular Press, 1976.

Scholes, Robert and Eric S. Rabkin. *Science Fiction: History, Science, Vision.* New York: Oxford University Press, 1977.

Slusser, George Edgar. *The Classic Years of Robert A. Heinlein.* San Bernardino, Calif.: Borgo Press, 1977.

Wollheim, Donald A. *The Universe Makers: Science Fiction Today.* New York: Harper & Row, 1971.

Periodicals

Bester, Alfred. "Robert Heinlein." *Publishers Weekly* (July 2, 1973).

Jelliffe, R. A. "Alice in Wonderland Tale for Space Age Grownups." *Chicago Tribune* (August 6, 1961).

Parkin-Speer, Diane. "Robert A. Heinlein: The Novelist as Preacher." *Extrapolation* (Fall 1979).

❀ W. C. Heinz

BORN: *1915, Mount Vernon, New York*

DIED: *2008, Bennington, Vermont*

NATIONALITY: *American*

GENRE: *Journalism, fiction*

MAJOR WORKS:

The Professional (1958)

W. C. Heinz   *AP Images*

Run to Daylight! (1963)

M.A.S.H. (1968), co-authored with H. Richard Hornberger under the shared pseudonym of Richard Hooker

Once They Heard the Cheers (1979)

American Mirror (1982)

Overview

W. C. Heinz wore many hats as a writer: he was a war correspondent, a medical reporter, a novelist, and, most notably, a sportswriter, where his writing on boxing earned him a place in sports-writing history. He was also an early proponent of the New Journalism, plumbing the depths of his own experience in order to capture the essence of his subjects.

Works in Biographical and Historical Context

Finding a Voice Through Journalism   Wilfred Charles "Bill" Heinz was born on January 11, 1915, in Mount Vernon, New York, his parents' only child. He studied

political science at Middlebury College in Vermont while serving as sports editor of the college's paper and yearbook. He graduated in 1937 and the same year landed a job as a messenger boy at the *New York Sun*. Having advanced to copyboy within two years, Heinz impressed Keats Speed, the city editor, by writing a piece on cleaning women who trudged to work in Manhattan in the early mornings from Mount Vernon and the Bronx. As a result, he was placed on staff as a city reporter. Within another two years he was married to Elizabeth B. Bailey; they eventually had two daughters.

As a city reporter, rewrite man, and feature writer, Heinz reported on various New York stories until the fall of 1943, when he answered the call of duty in World War II and became a *Sun* war correspondent. He spent seven weeks aboard a U.S. Navy aircraft carrier in the Atlantic Ocean on patrol for submarines, and then a month in Brazilian waters with the Fourth Fleet. In April 1944, he arrived in London to report on Allied preparations for the invasion of Normandy, and at the end of May he departed on his D-Day assignment aboard the battleship USS *Nevada*, covering the bombardment of Normandy in support of Allied troop landings. In August, when the Germans captured the *Sun*'s chief European war correspondent, Heinz replaced him and remained with the First Army through the final days of the war in Europe.

Heinz has said that it was his World War II experiences that taught him to write. In a 1961 *Newsweek* interview he describes the war as "a patsy for learning writers . . . the perfect foil, the perfect sparring partner. It was so dramatic, you couldn't write it badly." His most important piece of wartime reporting—a stark, gripping account of the execution of three captured German spies in U.S. Army uniforms and with an American jeep behind American lines—could not appear for censorship reasons until December 1949, when *True* magazine published it as "The Morning They Shot the Spies."

Finding a Home as a Sportswriter   Shortly after V-E (Victory in Europe) Day Heinz returned to the United States, where the *Sun* gave him a three-month vacation, a $1,000 bonus, and a promotion. He was then assigned to the newspaper's Washington, D.C., bureau as a feature writer, focusing, at his own request, on sports. His early days as a sportswriter, chronicled much later in his life in *Once They Heard the Cheers* (1979), were spent writing features, sketches of athletes in training and teams in preparation, wrap-ups of earlier contests, and general assignments. One of his first sports-writing bylines was an atmospheric piece about things heard and seen as he left Yankee Stadium. Heinz also became a habitué of Stillman's Gym in Manhattan, then the most famous boxing gymnasium, where he soaked up the language and mystique of the fight.

In 1949 he began his own sports column, "The Sport Scene," which appeared five times a week. He wrote about the people in the sports world as well as sporting events as

LITERARY AND HISTORICAL CONTEMPORARIES

W. C. Heinz's famous contemporaries include:

Norman Mailer (1941–2007): An American novelist and journalist, Mailer shared Heinz's enthusiasm for boxing and, like Heinz, helped shape the style of writing that became known as the New Journalism.

Rocky Graziano (1919–1990): An American street fighter who later became one of boxing's greatest knockout artists, Graziano was a favorite subject of Heinz's writing.

Ring Lardner, Jr. (1915–2000): American screenwriter and journalist who wrote many screenplays, including the film adaptation of *M.A.S.H.* (1970).

Joe Louis (1914–1981): American boxer who was considered a national hero during World War II for his earlier, 1938 victory over German heavyweight champion Max Schmeling.

Vince Lombardi (1913–1970): Born in an Italian neighborhood in Brooklyn, Lombardi's success as a head coach of the Green Bay Packers brought him to the attention of Heinz. Lombardi only lost one post-season game during his nine years as a head coach in the NFL.

Walter Cronkite (1916–): Cronkite was an American journalist who, for nineteen years, was the anchor of the *CBS Evening News*. He was often referred to as "the most trusted man in America" during the 1970s.

John F. Kennedy (1917–1963): Kennedy served during World War II, was elected as a senator for Massachusetts in 1953, wrote a Pulitzer Prize-winning book titled *Profiles in Courage* (1955), and became the youngest person elected president of the United States in 1960.

Professional is the story of middleweight boxing contender Eddie Brown, preparing for his first title fight, as seen through the eyes of sportswriter Frank Hughes, working on a magazine article on the fighter. Widely praised for its authenticity, honest dialogue, and deep understanding of the fight game and its denizens, *The Professional* served as a vehicle for several of the writer's essential beliefs about boxing, which he saw as highly scientific, and at the same time as an art form.

In 1963 Heinz brought out *Run to Daylight!*, an account of a season spent with legendary Green Bay Packers football coach Vince Lombardi. *Run to Daylight!*, which represented a new kind of sports writing, detailed the workings of a coach's mind and was narrated in first-person from Lombardi's point of view. It was, according to Robert Lipsyte of *The New York Times*, perhaps the first among contemporary sports books to reach a larger audience, and it was a critical hit as well, with *Esquire* columnist George Frazier praising the "poetry in W. C. Heinz's prose."

In the late 1960s Heinz collaborated with Dr. H. Richard Hornberger who, as Richard Hooker, was credited with sole authorship of the 1968 novel *M.A.S.H.* This fast-paced, episodic account of three surgeons of the 4077th Mobile Army Surgical Hospital during the Korean War was the basis for the popular 1970 film and the even more popular television series (1972–1983).

Having left fiction behind, Heinz spent several years in the late 1970s revisiting the athletic heroes he most admired. His interviews would form the basis of *Once They Heard the Cheers*, a then-and-now selection of portraits of individuals he first wrote about in their heydays. Heinz prefaced his portraits with autobiographical recollections of his boyhood, wartime reporting experiences, and tentative start as a sports reporter for the *Sun*. At the age of eighty-nine he was inducted into the International Boxing Hall of Fame. He died in Bennington, Vermont, on February 27, 2008.

Works in Literary Context

The New Journalism Beginning in the 1960s, many journalists began experimenting with viewpoints and storytelling techniques deemed unconventional by the mainstream press. Writers of "New Journalism"—as it would later be labeled—often wrote in the first person, and included their own opinions and experiences in their reporting instead of maintaining an objective tone and viewpoint. Norman Mailer, Hunter S. Thompson, and Truman Capote were early pioneers of the genre. Jack Newfield, writing in *Dutton Review* in 1970, cited Heinz as one of the few forerunners of the New Journalism to come from the world of sports writing. Heinz's innovative approach to sports writing—often breaking traditional molds through new approaches in language, structure, and subject—was designed to get to the essence of reality. Heinz never sought to propagate a new genre, however, instead keeping his focus on the humanity of his subjects.

diverse as baseball, boxing, and horse races. He also continued to publish magazine articles, which he had been doing since the early 1940s. Some of his stories, like "The Fighter's Wife" (1950), explore the private lives that run parallel to sporting events as well as the games themselves. Thirteen of his freelance magazine pieces from the 1940s through the 1960s were later collected in *American Mirror* (1982).

Shortly after the demise of the *Sun* in 1950, Heinz wrote his first piece for *Life*, a straightforward account of the newspaper's final day ("Last Day") that underscored the staff's professionalism even in the newspaper's final hours of existence. That summer he wrote a sports column for the *New York Daily News*, and spent the rest of the 1950s as a freelance writer, contributing articles to many of the day's major publications, including *Collier's*, *Look*, the *Saturday Evening Post*, and *Esquire*.

Expanding into New Forms Heinz's main achievement of the 1950s was his novel *The Professional* (1958). The

Works in Critical Context

The Professional   Contemporary reviewers found much to praise in *The Professional*. Robert Cromie in *Booklist* described the novel as "a strong, expressive story free of stereotypes and melodrama." An unnamed reviewer for *The New Yorker* referred to it as "precise, poignant and absolutely honest . . . its climax, if devastating, is not in the least pitiless." Herbert Kupferberg, writing in the *New York Herald Tribune*, called Heinz "a stylist among sports writers," alluding to Hemingway's work by praising the "affection, insight and lyricism one usually finds in novels about bullfighting." Not all reviews were uniformly positive, however. Although praising the novel's sincerity and citing several particular scenes, Robert Daley in *The New York Times* was critical of the use of the noncombatant narrator and found the emotion of the leading character obscure and the driving narrative force lacking. Charles Fenton, writing in the *Saturday Review*, lauded the author's skill and perception but ultimately felt the novel's characterization was too one-sided and that the author was unsuccessful in his "insistence that a skilled professional athlete is in the last analysis something remarkable among human beings." One acerbic *Time* critic found fault with Heinz for using the historical present and for addressing the reader as "you." The critic, although noting that Heinz had crafted a "reasonably effective story" with some "wonderful examples of tough prose," concluded, "*The Professional*, in short, is a classic example of the Hemingwayward conviction that small words must be used to denote big things," finding the book lacking in "the quality of thought." As for Hemingway himself, he seems to have liked the book: in his introduction to the paperback reprint, George Plimpton cited a 1958 visit to Havana with Hemingway, who praised the book as the only good boxing novel he had ever read. A. J. Liebling, a penetrating boxing observer in his own right, wrote Heinz personally to praise him for *The Professional*.

Responses to Literature

1. Heinz wrote both fiction and nonfiction on the subject of boxing. Compare the descriptions of the fighter in *The Professional* to those in the boxing essays collected in *What A Time It Was: The Best Of W. C. Heinz On Sports* (2001). In what ways do the two types of writing differ in style?

2. *M.A.S.H.* was written about army medics in the Korean War (1950–1953) but was turned into a successful film and an even more successful television series in the 1970s, when an entirely different war was being waged. Do some research into the Vietnam War and then watch the film version of *M.A.S.H.* (1970). How might the film be seen as commentary on what was going on in Vietnam?

COMMON HUMAN EXPERIENCE

W. C. Heinz spent much of his career writing about boxing. Here are some other works that see poetry in the drama of the fight:

The Sweet Science (1956), a collection of essays by A. J. Liebling. A collection of his essays on boxing from the 1930s, 1940s, and 1950s published in *The New Yorker*, *The Sweet Science* explores the human experience as well as the nitty-gritty of the heyday of boxing, when Sugar Ray Robinson and Joe Louis ruled the ring.

On Boxing (1987), essays by Joyce Carol Oates. An expansion of a *New York Times Magazine* article, Joyce Carol Oates's *On Boxing* laments the commercial and media circus that has sprung up around boxing while exploring the sport's roots in history and human drama.

Million Dollar Baby (2004), a film directed by Clint Eastwood. Winner of the Academy Award for Best Picture, *Million Dollar Baby* pairs an obscure boxing trainer with a young female hopeful whose ambition to become a professional fighter enables his thwarted fatherly love to find an outlet. Clint Eastwood stars alongside Hilary Swank, who also won an Oscar for her performance.

Write a paper in which you analyze the film's commentary on Vietnam, or on war in general.

3. In addition to W. C. Heinz, some of the greatest writers of the twentieth century, from Hemingway to DeLillo, have devoted their energies to writing about professional sports. Such artistic homage might seem at odds with certain images associated with modern sports, such as tailgate parties, rioting soccer fans, and scantily clad cheerleaders. Start a discussion about the cultural and artistic value of sports in our society. What do professional sports have to teach us about our culture?

BIBLIOGRAPHY

Books

Cosell, Howard. *Cosell on Cosell*. Chicago: Playboy Press, 1973.

Halberstam, David, ed. *The Best American Sportswriting 1991*. Boston: Houghton Mifflin, 1991.

Periodicals

Daley, Robert. "Before the Title Go; *The Professional* By W. C. Heinz." *The New York Times Book Review* (January 5, 1958).

Kupferberg, Herbert. Review of *The Professional*. *New York Herald Tribune Book Review* (January 5, 1958).

Liebling, A. J. "The Scribes of Destiny." *The New Yorker* (September 28, 1946).

Lipsyte, Robert. Review of *Run to Daylight! The New York Times Book Review* (October 27, 1963).

Newfield, Jack. "Journalism: Old, New and Corporate." *Dutton Review* 1 (1970).

"Out of the Ring." *Newsweek* (October 9, 1961).

Walters, Harry F. and George Hackett. "Real Hawkeye Pierce." *Newsweek* (February 28, 1983).

✹ Joseph Heller

BORN: *1923, Brooklyn, New York*

DIED: *1999, East Hampton, New York*

NATIONALITY: *American*

GENRE: *Fiction*

MAJOR WORKS:

Catch-22: A Novel (1961)

Overview

Joseph Heller established himself as a major satirist in the field of twentieth-century American fiction. A new phrase was added to the American lexicon from the title of his first novel *Catch-22* (1961). The term "catch-22" has become accepted in *Webster's New World Dictionary* and the *Oxford English Dictionary* and denotes a bureaucratic paradox, having the effect of entrapping the subject. Throughout his almost forty years as a novelist, Heller used humor and satire to give expression to the horrors of war and to a distrust of bureaucracy and government that reached its peak during the Vietnam War. His fiction radically altered a whole generation of readers' perceptions of America.

Works in Biographical and Historical Context

To War and Back Joseph Heller was born in Brooklyn, New York, to Russian-Jewish immigrants on May 1,

Joseph Heller *Heller, Joseph, photograph. AP Images.*

1923. He had a secular upbringing, his mother being more concerned with social issues than religious observance. His father died when Heller was five. He grew up in Coney Island, a neighborhood whose beach boardwalk and carnival atmosphere were to reappear in much of his later work. At the age of thirteen, he briefly held a job as a Western Union messenger boy, an experience he drew on for his 1962 story "World Full of Great Cities." In his teens he tried his hand at writing short stories while holding brief jobs as a file clerk in a casualty insurance company, a blacksmith's helper in a naval yard, and a shipping file clerk.

In 1942, at the height of World War II, Heller joined the U.S. Army Air Corps and from May 1944 to mid-1945 was stationed on Corsica, a large Mediterranean island located off the southern coast of France. He flew about sixty combat missions as a bombardier, earning the Air Medal and rising to the rank of lieutenant. The thirty-seventh mission over Avignon, which he flew, proved to be one of the most dangerous of the war and was later written into *Catch-22* in the descriptions of Snowden's death.

On his discharge from the Air Corps Heller married Shirley Held, enrolled at the University of Southern California under the G.I. Bill, and subsequently transferred to New York University. New York remained Heller's preferred location, partly because of the brisk tempo of life and partly because—as he wisecracked at a press conference—the people are so unfriendly. Heller's first published work was "I Don't Love You Any More," an account of a returned soldier, which came out in the servicemen's issue of *Story* in 1945. He graduated Phi Beta Kappa in 1948 and the next year earned an MA degree at Columbia University, where his professors included Lionel Trilling. In 1949 he received a Fulbright scholarship to St. Catherine's College, Oxford, a university to which he would return much later in life, in 1991, as a Christensen Visiting Fellow.

On his return to the United States from Oxford, Heller accepted a post as an instructor in English at Pennsylvania State University. Finding the place and the teaching uncongenial, Heller left in 1952 to write advertising copy for *Time*. In 1956 he moved on to *Look* magazine before serving as promotion manager at *McCall's* from 1958 to 1961. All of this commercial experience would eventually feed directly into his second novel, *Something Happened* (1974), a tale of a corporate man and his inability to find happiness despite his success.

Writing an Anti-War Masterpiece The opening chapter of *Catch-18*, as Heller's classic was originally called, was published in *New World Writing* in 1955. The chapter was then extensively revised and shortened, and Heller worked at the novel through the rest of the decade. Built upon the hearty mistrust of authority engendered by his own war experiences, the novel centers on the character of John Yossarian and his encounters with the terror, heartbreak, bureaucracy, and especially the absurdity of war. Its title, which has become one of twentieth-century America's most deeply-rooted figures of speech, refers to a (fictional) bureaucratic trick to keep pilots flying dangerous war missions. One cannot fly missions if one is insane, so the "catch" goes, but not wanting to fly missions is itself proof of sanity. With this deft piece of circular logic, Heller sets the tone for the absurdity—and poignant hopelessness—of the story to follow.

Despite its current status as a classic, and despite an elaborate promotional campaign, *Catch-22* was slow to sell at first. Some reviewers were openly hostile. For example, Whitney Balliett in *The New Yorker* complained that the book gives the impression of having been "shouted onto paper." One of the problems faced by Heller was the reviewers' lack of preparedness for the unorthodox experimentalism of the work. Heller attacks not only the institutionalized authority of the military but also the conventions of novelistic realism.

The commercial success of *Catch-22* had enabled Heller to leave his job at *McCall's*, and, having always been interested in the theater, Heller embarked on his first stage production in 1966. On a visit to Yale, Heller mentioned the idea of a dramatic adaptation of the ideas in *Catch-22* to Robert Brustein, dean of the Yale Drama School. Brustein was enthusiastic and helped secure Heller a temporary appointment at Yale. In doing so, Brustein had transformed the drama school into an important location for the theater of protest against the Vietnam War.

Heller's play *We Bombed in New Haven* (1967) was first produced at Yale and is a work that constantly disrupts the theatrical illusion with, for example, the curtain half-rising as if in error to reveal the actors still getting ready for the production. In the play Heller achieves the dislocation of language from reality by having a character declare, "There is no war taking place," only to have his words interrupted by an explosion. *We Bombed in New Haven* includes many allusions to other wars, but the common consciousness of the Vietnam War was paramount in 1967. Heller's anti–Vietnam War stance came out in more direct ways as well. In interviews he gave in the late 1960s Heller repeatedly expressed his conviction that the Cold War had induced the beliefs that communism must be stopped and that American youth would have to die in a war long after any rationale for such beliefs had disappeared. When he contributed to a 1967 collection of statements, *Authors Take Sides on Vietnam*, he was absolutely forthright in his condemnation: "I am against the military intervention of the US in Vietnam. It was a ghastly choice, and thousands die each month because of it."

Branching Out as a Novelist

Heller's second novel, *Something Happened* (1974), was originally planned to have a much stronger continuity with *Catch-22* than the finished novel displayed. The novel, about business exec-

LITERARY AND HISTORICAL CONTEMPORARIES

Joseph Heller's famous contemporaries include:

Norman Mailer (1923–2007): American novelist and journalist. Mailer, like Heller, embodied a new counter-cultural style that emerged in the U.S. after World War II. Mailer helped shape the style of writing that became known as the New Journalism.

Lenny Bruce (1925–1966): Bruce was the first American comedian to overtly challenge obscenity standards, Bruce was known for his pointed social commentaries in his stand-up routine.

Kurt Vonnegut (1922–2007): Best known for his novel *Slaughterhouse-Five* (1969), Vonnegut's absurdist, satirical style has much in common with Heller's. Like Heller, Vonnegut was also active in various anti-war movements.

Rod Serling (1924–1975): American television writer. Best known as the creator of the science fiction program *The Twilight Zone* (1959–1964), Serling pushed the boundaries of his medium with surreal stories that often revealed a strong social or political message.

Robert Altman (1925–2006): American filmmaker. Like Heller, Altman was often drawn to dark, satirical comedy. His movie *M.A.S.H.* (1970), for instance, is a comedic take on army doctors during the Korean War.

utive Bob Slocum in the doldrums of a midlife crisis, was originally flavored by the protagonist's wartime memories. Instead the novel focuses on corporate culture, which is depicted as largely benign, unlike the military culture portrayed in *Catch-22*. Whereas Yossarian in *Catch-22* resisted authoritarian culture, Slocum's insecurity attracts him to the structure corporate culture provides.

In his next novel, *Good as Gold* (1979), Heller returns to the Coney Island of his childhood, and the Jewish-American culture that characterized it. Heller set out to produce a tongue-in-cheek account of the "Jewish Experience in America" and paints a comic but unflattering portrait of the antagonisms running through the Gold family. Heller's fourth novel, *God Knows* (1984), is based on the biblical story of David. Although the book immediately became a bestseller, many of the reviews were hostile, drawing comparisons with the comic monologue "The Two Thousand-Year-Old Man," by Heller's longtime friend, Mel Brooks. Despite its departure from Heller's usual preference for contemporary subjects, this novel bears a close thematic relevance to his other works through the related issues of authority and justice, as played out in the father-son relationship. One of the central problems in *God Knows*—a problem explored in

COMMON HUMAN EXPERIENCE

Much of Heller's writing hinges on troubled father-son relationships. Here are some classic works that explore the bond between fathers and sons:

Fathers and Sons (1862), a novel by Ivan Turgenev. Turgenev's novel casts the clash between generations, politically and culturally, as essentially the classic family drama of sons rejecting their fathers' values, and defining themselves in opposition to them. Turgenev's masterpiece became a large influence on many of the Russian greats such as Tolstoy and Dostoyevsky.

Death of a Salesman (1949), a play by Arthur Miller. The salesman of the title is Willy Loman, whose delusions about his failed career have done irreversible damage to his sons: one son has accepted Willy's definition of success, and so condemns himself to failure; the other son lives a lie in a futile attempt to please his father.

Hamlet (c. 1600), a play by William Shakespeare. After a visit from the ghost of his dead father, whom Hamlet rightfully suspects was murdered by his uncle in a bid for power, Hamlet's psyche is twisted into knots over how best to avenge the death and do justice to his father's memory and legacy.

"Letter to His Father" (1919), an essay in letter form by Franz Kafka. Kafka's letter to his father was written with the intention of actually delivering it, though his father never read it. Intended to bring father and son closer together, the letter is instead a harsh characterization of a relationship dominated by fear and impossible expectations.

Catch-22 as well as *Good as Gold*—lies in David's relation to his two symbolic fathers, Saul and God. The position of fathers in the Jewish tradition, no matter what the era, is absolutely central and bound up with questions of religion and assimilation.

A Brush with Death In December 1981, while in the middle of writing *God Knows*, Heller was suddenly afflicted with a serious disease that attacks the nervous system, Guillain-Barré Syndrome, which for a time paralyzed him completely. He later published an account of his ordeal in *No Laughing Matter* (1986), describing the worst stage of his illness as a figurative descent into hell. Cowritten by his friend Speed Vogel, *No Laughing Matter* has three supporting storylines: the comedy of Mel Brooks's interference with the hospital authorities, the drawn-out legal wrangling of Heller's divorce, which was going on at the time, and the growing love between himself and his nurse, Valerie Humphries, whom he married a year after the book was published.

After his recovery Heller experienced a surge in productivity. He finished *God Knows*, wrote his portions of *No Laughing Matter*, and started his next novel, *Picture This* (1988), a story steeped in history and art. Using Rembrandt's painting *Aristotle Contemplating a Bust of Homer* as a focal point, the novel is set in two time periods: the painter's Netherlands of the seventeenth century CE, and the ancient philosopher's Athens of the fifth century BCE. By using contemporary terms like "gulag" out of context, Heller encourages the reader to compare historical periods to twentieth-century history, especially Nazism and the Cold War.

Heller's last novel, *Closing Time* (1994), was publicized as the long-awaited sequel to *Catch-22* and focuses on the characters' childhood New York memories. In this sense *Closing Time* becomes partly autobiographical; there is even a minor character called Joey Heller. His last book was *Now and Then: From Coney Island to Here* (1998), a memoir. Heller died of a heart attack at his home in New York on December 12, 1999, at the age of seventy-six.

Works in Literary Context

War Stories On all levels *Catch-22* questions the conventions of the American war novel. By incorporating elements from the twentieth century's classic war stories, but with a twist, the novel upends the genre while carving out a place for itself. It includes a farcical reprise of the lake journey to freedom in Ernest Hemingway's *A Farewell To Arms* (1929), when Orr rows to Sweden. James Jones, author of *From Here to Eternity* (1951), used the army to represent the stratifications of American society, while Heller uses it to demonstrate the paranoia of the McCarthy era. Norman Mailer's *The Naked and the Dead* (1948) includes a diverse group of men, from the Irishman to the homosexual to the man with a PhD; *Catch-22* includes a similarly diverse mix of characters, but satirizes it. With the character of Milo, who is engaged in mysterious international trade, Heller anticipated the treatment of World War II in later novels like Thomas Pynchon's *Gravity's Rainbow* (1973), where warfare is presented as a screen erected to conceal the real commercial processes taking place.

Works in Critical Context

As is the case with many novelists whose first efforts are hugely successful, *Catch-22* was both a blessing and a curse. It ensured that everything Heller wrote from then on would be taken seriously, but also that his later novels would be compared, perhaps unfairly, to his blockbuster. Critics wrote thoughtfully—and generally favorably—about all of his subsequent novels, but none of the later novels came close to capturing the imagination of the public the way *Catch-22* did.

Catch-22 At the time of its publication in 1961, Heller's antiwar novel met with modest sales and lukewarm reviews. But by the middle of its first decade it became a favored text of the counterculture. *Catch-22* "came when we still cherished nice notions about WW II," Eliot Fremont-Smith recalled in the *Village Voice*. "Demolishing these, it released an irreverence that had, until then, dared not speak its name." With more than ten million copies in print at the end of the twentieth century, *Catch-22* has become generally regarded as one of the most important novels of the postwar era. The title itself has become part of the language, and its hero Yossarian, according to Jack Schnedler of the *Newark Star-Ledger*, "has become the fictional talisman to an entire generation."

Reviewers also noted the relevance of the World War II novel for the Vietnam generation. "There seems no denying that though Heller's macabre farce was written about a rarefied part of the raging war of the forties during the silent fifties," Josh Greenfeld wrote in a *New York Times Book Review* article, "it has all but become the chapbook of the sixties." Joseph Epstein likewise summarized in *The Washington Post Book World*: *Catch-22* "was a well-aimed bomb."

Responses to Literature

1. Joseph Heller is one of those novelists whose body of work is forever overshadowed by one novel, in his case *Catch-22*. Why is this? Read *Catch-22* and another of Heller's novels, and write an essay in which you speculate on the justice or injustice of this reputation. Do his other works deserve to be part of the literary canon as well?

2. Much of Heller's writing—both fiction and nonfiction—is suffused with the spirit of Coney Island, the Brooklyn neighborhood where he grew up. What does the neighborhood seem to represent to Heller? Provide examples from Heller's own writing to support your analysis.

3. It is generally accepted that *Catch-22* is an antiwar novel, though it never explicitly states, "War is bad." How does Heller get this point across? Write a paper in which you explore Heller's techniques. Consider his use of satire, absurdity, and irony, as well as his portrayal of authority figures.

BIBLIOGRAPHY

Books

Keegan, Brenda M. *Joseph Heller: A Reference Guide.* Boston: G. K. Hall, 1978.

Potts, Stephen W. *From Here to Absurdity: The Moral Battlefields of Joseph Heller.* 2nd ed. San Bernardino, Calif.: Borgo Press, 1995.

Ruderman, Judith. *Joseph Heller.* New York: Continuum, 1991.

Seed, David. *The Fictions of Joseph Heller: Against the Grain.* New York: St. Martin's Press, 1989.

Sorkin, Adam J., ed. *Conversations with Joseph Heller.* Jackson, Miss.: University Press of Mississippi, 1993.

Woolf, Cecil and John Bagguley, eds. *Authors Take Sides on Vietnam: Two Questions on the War in Vietnam Answered by the Authors of Several Nations.* New York: Simon and Schuster, 1967.

Periodicals

Epstein, Joseph. "Joseph Heller's Milk Train: Nothing More to Express." *The Washington Post* (October 6, 1974).

Fremont-Smith, Eliot. "Kvetch-22." *The Village Voice* (March 5, 1979).

Schnedler, Jack. *The Newark Star-Ledger* (October 6, 1974).

Reilly, Charlie. "An Interview with Joseph Heller." *Contemporary Literature* (Winter 1998).

✸ Lillian Hellman

BORN: *1905, New Orleans, Louisiana*

DIED: *1984, Martha's Vineyard, Massachusetts*

NATIONALITY: *American*

GENRE: *Drama*

MAJOR WORKS:
The Children's Hour (1934)
The Little Foxes (1939)
Pentimento: A Book of Portraits (1973)

Overview

Lillian Hellman has been called one of the most influential female playwrights of the twentieth century, the voice of social consciousness in American letters, and the theater's intellectual standard-bearer. Her work and her life were deeply steeped in politics, American history, and scandal, and at the time of her death in 1984, Hellman could claim more long-running Broadway dramas—five—than could any other American playwright, including Tennessee Williams, Edward Albee, and Thornton Wilder.

Works in Biographical and Historical Context

An Eccentric Childhood Lillian Florence Hellman, the only child of German Jewish parents, was born in New Orleans, Louisiana, on June 20, 1905. Her childhood was spent moving back and forth between New York City, where her mother's family had relocated, and New Orleans. The two worlds could not have been more different. When in New York, Hellman lived with her mother's wealthy relatives on West 95th Street; when in New Orleans, she lived in a boardinghouse full of eccentric roomers and run by her beloved aunts, her father's

Lillian Hellman   *Hellman, Lillian, 1966, photograph. AP Images.*

enced the writing of two plays: *Watch on the Rhine* (1941) and *The Searching Wind* (1944).

In 1930, Hellman and Kober moved to Hollywood, where Kober had been offered a scriptwriter position with Paramount. Through Kober's connections, Hellman got a job writing synopses of potential material for MGM, a position she lost thanks to her militant support for the nascent Screen Writers' Guild, a union formed to fight back against wage reductions instituted by studios. Her marriage also ended, on amicable terms, in 1932. By this time Hellman had begun a relationship with Dashiell Hammett, the former Pinkerton agent and best-selling writer of detective stories, that was to last until his death in 1961. Biographer William Wright wrote that Hammett's "collaboration" with Hellman was not as much in the development of her plays as it was in the development of Hellman herself.

In the early 1930s, Hellman returned to New York and made her first forays into playwriting. Hammett was finishing up work on his last novel, *The Thin Man* (1934), whose witty and madcap female heroine, Nora, was purportedly modeled on Hellman and suggested an idea for a play based on a British court case he had read about. The true story of two women who ran a boarding school for girls in Scotland and were ruined after a student falsely accused them of a lesbian relationship appealed to Hellman. Hammett supervised the writing and extensive rewriting of the resulting play, *The Children's Hour* (1934). At 691 performances, it became Hellman's longest-running production and one of her most popular plays.

On to Broadway   The success of *The Children's Hour* helped land Hellman a job as a Hollywood screenwriter at MGM, earning a hefty salary. Her next play, *Days To Come* (1936), was a flop and prompted something of a hiatus from the theater. She traveled through Europe, met Ernest Hemingway, and returned to the United States ready to write her most successful play, *Little Foxes* (1939), which involved prodigious amounts of research filling several notebooks. An excoriating look at the rivalries and disloyalty among a turn-of-the-century Southern family, the play explores how the wealthy Hubbard clan of New Orleans schemes to keep itself rich and powerful, at the expense of both outsiders and each other.

In 1939, now an established playwright, Hellman bought Hardscrabble Farm, a 130-acre property in New York, which remained her primary residence until she was forced to sell it to pay legal bills and taxes thirteen years later. Hellman's next play, *Watch on the Rhine* (1941), was a direct response to the political climate of the times. Set in 1940, when the United States had yet to get involved in World War II, the play entered the ongoing debate on American neutrality. By placing an antifascist message within a domestic situation, she implicated all Americans through the idea that those who chose to ignore the international crisis were helping to perpetuate it. The play ran for 378 performances, won the Drama

unmarried sisters. The rooming house would reappear in Hellman's 1951 play *The Autumn Garden*, and the situation of two sisters devoted to their married brother appeared, albeit with violence and intrigue unknown to the Hellman sisters, in *Toys in the Attic* (1960). The one constant in her life was her black nurse, Sophronia Mason, whom Hellman describes in her memoirs as "the first and most certain love of my life." She is the only person from Hellman's childhood who escaped criticism in her writings.

Into the Literary Life   After short tenures at two universities—New York University and Columbia University—Hellman left college at the age of nineteen. Her first job was as a manuscript reader for Horace Liveright, owner of the prestigious publishing firm of Boni and Liveright, which, during its heyday, published some of the great American authors of the twentieth century. In December 1925, Hellman married press agent, screenwriter, and playwright Arthur Kober, and in 1926, she moved with him to Paris so he could edit the *Paris Comet*, a new English-language literary periodical. In 1929, four years before Adolf Hitler's rise to power, Hellman decided to go back to school and enrolled at the university in Bonn, Germany. She was recruited by a Nazi student group and briefly considered joining, mistakenly thinking it was a socialist organization. When the reality hit her, she promptly left Germany, recalling in her memoirs that "for the first time in my life I thought about being a Jew." This experience later influ-

Critics' Circle Award, and the movie version, for which Hammett wrote the screenplay, was cited as one of the best movies of 1943. *The Searching Wind* (1944), Hellman's next play, continues in the same vein of political activism, with its plot ranging through the cradles of fascism, Mussolini's Italy, and Hitler's Germany. Like *Watch on the Rhine*, *The Searching Wind* condemns inaction in the face of injustice.

The Pitfalls of Politics   By the late 1940s, Hellman's political involvement began to cause her professional trouble. With the onset of the Cold War immediately after the end of World War II, paranoia about the spread of communism took hold on many levels of society; congressional hearings led by Senator Joseph McCarthy, intending to root out secret communists in a variety of industries, including the arts, caused the ruin of many a career. By 1949, at the height of McCarthyism, Hellman had learned that she was blacklisted in Hollywood for supposed communist involvement; she remained blacklisted, unofficially, until the early 1960s. But, Hellman did not abandon her political efforts. Instead, she seemed to become more publicly involved in political activities. She was active in Henry Wallace's presidential campaign in 1948, working on some of the Progressive Party committees and assisting in the formation of the party platform, all the while denying that communists controlled the party. That same year she accepted an assignment from the *New York Star* to travel to communist Yugoslavia to interview Marshal Tito; the trip resulted in a series of six articles praising his accomplishments.

Artistic Departure   In the midst of her political troubles, Hellman brought out *The Autumn Garden* (1950), a thematic and stylistic departure. Its subject matter has nothing to do with politics, and its style shows the influence of the Russian playwright Anton Chekhov, whom Hellman had been reading. Rather than cast her characters in situations they cannot escape, as she had always done, here Hellman's characters are trapped in their own lives.

Her next project, *The Lark* (1955), about the life of Joan of Arc, saw the inauguration of her professional relationship with the composer and conductor Leonard Bernstein, whom she would go on to work with on a musical version of Voltaire's 1759 novel *Candide*, produced in 1956. Hellman's work on the play received generally bad reviews and brought on a case of writer's block. When she finally returned to the theater, with 1960's *Toys in the Attic*, she turned to her own childhood for inspiration. It was to be her last original play, and she won her second New York Drama Critics' Circle Award. Revolving around the lives of two unmarried sisters and their married brother, *Toys in the Attic* develops themes of the consequences of self-deception, the folly of clinging to dreams, Southern depravity, and repressed sexuality.

Memoir and Scandal   After the failure of her next play, an adaptation, Hellman turned to the autobiographical *An*

LITERARY AND HISTORICAL CONTEMPORARIES

Hellman's famous contemporaries include:

Tennessee Williams (1911–1983): American playwright. The author of some of the best-known plays of twentieth-century American theater, including *A Streetcar Named Desire* (1948), Williams also struggled with substance abuse throughout his life.

Joseph McCarthy (1908–1957): American politician. A two-term Senator from Wisconsin, McCarthy rose to fame in 1950 by announcing that he had discovered a communist conspiracy within the U.S. government. The following period of anti-communism greatly damaged the lives of left-leaning writers including Hellman.

Edmund Wilson (1895–1972): American literary critic. Writing for such eminent publications as *The New Yorker* and *The New Republic*, Wilson was considered the most important literary critic of his generation.

Mary McCarthy (1912–1989): American author McCarthy was known for her incisive wit as a critic and her unconventional political positions. An ideological feud with Hellman led to a lawsuit that only ended with Hellman's death.

Simone de Beauvoir (1908–1986): French writer and philosopher de Beauvoir, along with her lifelong partner Jean-Paul Sartre, was a central figure in twentieth-century intellectual life. Among her many works is *The Second Sex* (1949), a foundational text of modern feminism.

Frida Kahlo (1907–1954): Kahlo was a Mexican painter who, like Hellman, was often overshadowed during her lifetime by her partner, the Mexican painter Diego Rivera. Also like Hellman, Kahlo was an iconoclast whose radical politics were inseparable from her art.

Unfinished Woman (1969), winner of the National Book Award, which takes the reader from Hellman's childhood, through her trips to Europe and encounters with Hemingway and F. Scott Fitzgerald, and into her significant adult friendships and relationships. The second volume of her memoirs, *Pentimento: A Book of Portraits*, was published in 1973. One of its chapters, "Julia," brought Hellman a lot of attention, not all of it good. It tells the story of Hellman's involvement with anti-Nazi resistance, by helping a friend smuggle a large sum of cash across international borders. The story was made into a popular film starring Jane Fonda, but the truth of Hellman's account—and even her involvement at all—were called sharply into question. Hellman's last volume of memoirs, *Scoundrel Time*, was published in 1976, and it too was attacked for being a self-serving, inaccurate account of her experience as an unwilling witness before HUAC.

Throughout the 1960s and 1970s, Hellman was much in demand as a visiting lecturer at some of the most

COMMON HUMAN EXPERIENCE

In both her personal life and her work, Hellman grappled with the power of accusations to ruin lives. Here are some other works which explore similar themes:

The Crucible (1953), a play by Arthur Miller. Set during the Salem witch trials of 1692, Arthur Miller's play is a commentary on the modern-day witch hunt led by Senator Joseph McCarthy and the House Un-American Activities Committee. In both real-life events, lives and careers were ruined by little more than a pointed finger.

A Passage to India (1924), a novel by E. M. Forster. Set in India in the days of British rule, *A Passage to India* explores the complex interactions of race, colonialism, and gender when a young, confused Englishwoman accuses an Indian doctor of attempted rape.

The Front (1976), a film written by Walter Bernstein and directed by Martin Ritt. Starring Woody Allen as a bookie who agrees to serve as a front for blacklisted television writers during the McCarthy era, *The Front* shows the lighter side of the career-ruining effects of McCarthyism.

Atonement (2001), a novel by Ian McEwan. At thirteen, the narrator of *Atonement* half-knowingly accuses her sister's lover of a rape he did not commit. The events of history sweep the lovers apart, and the narrator's lie proves to be an act for which she can never atone. The novel was made into an Academy Award-nominated film in 2007.

prestigious universities in America and received a number of honorary degrees. Along with the adulation, however, came renewed attacks on Hellman's word in her memoirs. Perhaps the most notorious was the writer Mary McCarthy's pronouncement on *The Dick Cavett Show* in 1980 that "every word she writes is a lie, including 'and' and 'the.'" Hellman immediately filed a libel suit for more than two million dollars against McCarthy, Cavett, and the television station. The suit was still in litigation at the time of Hellman's death; it was later dismissed, but not before McCarthy had gone bankrupt in the process.

Hellman's career wound down with the publication of a semi-autobiographical novel and a book about cooking. She died on Martha's Vineyard on June 30, 1984, after many years of enduring emphysema and poor eyesight. At her death, her estate was valued at $4 million, making her one of the most successful writers of her generation.

Works in Literary Context

Southern Gothic A child of the South, Hellman produced some of her best work when she turned her energies toward representing her roots. In doing so, she

added to a rich stock of twentieth century American writing, including work by William Faulkner, Tennessee Williams, Flannery O'Connor, and Carson McCullers, which explored the grotesqueness and pathos inherent in human nature through the themes of the American South. The best of the genre, loosely dubbed Southern Gothic, blends negative tropes, such as racism or ignorance, with positive ones, such as generosity or family loyalty to convey not just the essence of the South, but contemporary society as well. The traits of Southern Gothic are most obvious in Hellman's *The Little Foxes*, with its tale of the scheming members of the Hubbard clan, and in *Toys in the Attic*, set in New Orleans.

Political Theater The stage has long been a platform for political commentary, favored by the ancient Greek playwrights and William Shakespeare as well as the dramaturges of modern times. The German playwright and director Bertolt Brecht (1898–1956) used the stage as a forum for his Marxist philosophy, and produced plays in response to the political climate of his day. While Hellman's political plays were neither as avant-garde as Brecht's and the other proponents of twentieth-century political theater, nor as ideological, they were strongly worded commentaries on the responsibilities we all bear for world events. In *Watch on the Rhine*, for example, she offers an image of the dangers of Nazism to American audiences who were largely opposed to entering the war at the time.

Works in Critical Context

Pentimento: A Book of Portraits Hellman's second installment of her memoirs garnered much critical notice, most notably for its sophisticated writing style. *New York* critic Eliot Fremont-Smith praised *Pentimento: A Book of Portraits* for its "extraordinary richness and candor and self-perception, and triumph considering the courage such a book requires, a courage that lies, [the author] shows by example, far deeper than one is usually inclined to accept." Muriel Haynes, in a *Ms.* review, calls *Pentimento* "a triumphant vindication of the stories the author threw away in her twenties because they were 'no good.' These complex, controlled narratives...have an emotional purity her plays have generally lacked."

Less impressed was *London Magazine* reviewer Julian Symons, who states that the memoir "is not, as American reviewers have unwisely said, a marvel and a masterpiece and a book full of perceptions about human character. It is, rather, a collection of sketches of a fairly familiar kind," also noting that the characters "may be real or partly fictionalized." By far the best known section of the book is "Julia," the story of Hellman's friendship during the 1930s with a rich young American woman working in the European underground against the Nazis. In *Pentimento*, as in her other books, Hellman was occasionally criticized by the press for presenting her facts unreliably, bending the truth to support her views. Paul Johnson, writing for the British journal *Spectator*, cited an article casting doubt whether "Julia" actually existed. "What [Boston University's Samuel McCracken] demonstrates, by dint of checking Thirties railway timetables, steamship passenger lists, and many other obscure sources, is that most of the facts Hellman provides about 'Julia's' movement and actions, and indeed her own, are not true." Johnson further suggested that what Hellman had been presenting all along is a left-wing apologia for World War II and the McCarthy era that followed.

Responses to Literature

1. Hellman was just one of many Hollywood luminaries whose careers and reputations were compromised by McCarthyism. Using your library and the Internet, research another creative figure to be blacklisted. Write a paper in which you explore the effects of the accusations on your subject's life and career. Was there an element of truth? How did your subject respond? Was he or she ever able to bounce back?

2. Two film versions were made of *The Children's Hour*. In the first, released in 1936 and called *These Three*, a heterosexual triangle substitutes for the homosexuality in the play; the second version, which came out in 1961, restored the original scenario. Watch both films, and compare them in a short essay. Does the story lose anything when the nature of the accusation changes? In which version is Hellman's message about slander more apparent? Which film is more effective?

3. Hellman was accused of stretching the truth in her memoirs, especially *Pentimento* and *Scoundrel Time*. Read one or both of these memoirs, and start a discussion about the ethics of mixing fact and fiction. Is it ever justified? Why might an author of a memoir want to embellish his or her story? Is there literary value to doing so? Think also about recent scandals surrounding falsified memoirs. Why do they rouse such indignation?

BIBLIOGRAPHY

Books

Dick, Bernard F. *Hellman in Hollywood*. Rutherford, N.J.: Fairleigh Dickinson University Press, 1982.

Estrin, Mark, ed. *Critical Essays on Lillian Hellman*. Boston: G. K. Hall, 1989.

Mellen, Joan. *Hellman and Hammett: The Legendary Passion of Lillian Hellman and Dashiell Hammett*. New York: HarperCollins, 1986.

Rollyson, Carl. *Lillian Hellman: Her Legend and Her Legacy*. New York: St. Martin's Press, 1988.

Wright, William. *Lillian Hellman: The Image, The Woman*. New York: Simon & Schuster, 1986.

Periodicals

Fremont-Smith, Eliot. Review of *Pentimento: A Book of Portraits*. *New York* (September 17, 1973).

Haynes, Muriel. Review of *Pentimento: A Book of Portraits*. *Ms.* (January 1974).

Johnson, Paul. "Nil Nisi Bunkum." *Spectator* (July 14, 1984).

Norman, Marsha. "Articles of Faith: A Conversation with Lillian Hellman." *American Theatre* (May 1984).

Symons, Julian. Review of *Pentimento: A Book of Portraits*. *London Magazine* (August/September 1974).

⊛ Mark Helprin

BORN: *1947, New York, New York*

NATIONALITY: *American*

GENRE: *Fiction, nonfiction*

MAJOR WORKS:

Ellis Island and Other Stories (1981)
Winter's Tale (1983)
A Soldier of the Great War (1991)
Memoir from Antproof Case (1995)
Freddy and Fredericka (2005)

Overview

Mark Helprin is a contemporary author whose fiction is often seen as an assault on realism. His tales are filled with fantastic adventures and a dreamlike quality, and according to Helprin, can be seen as devotional literature. Helprin's novels have been criticized for vagueness of their morality and the lack of a strong narrative structure. However, Helprin has won many awards for his fiction, and even when critics take exception with him, they are quick to point out that he is a writer with great imagination and talent.

Works in Biographical and Historical Context

Growing Up in New York City Mark Helprin was born in New York City on June 28, 1947. His mother, Eleanor Lynn, was a leading lady on Broadway during the late 1930s; his father, Morris, worked as a reporter, movie critic, and editor for the *New York Times* before he went to work as a publicity manager for movie studios and eventually became the president of Alexander Korda's London Films. The details of Helprin's youth are unclear; he has admitted that as a storyteller he tends to exaggerate anecdotes about his life. However, as reported by Jean W. Ross in the *Dictionary of Literary Biography Yearbook 1985*, "he has described himself as Jewish by birth and by faith, although not in the orthodox tradition. He has also remarked on his determined pursuit of exceptional experiences in life; he is, for example, a skilled mountain climber." These aspects of Helprin's life are reflected in his

Mark Helprin *Courtesy MarkHelprin.com*

fiction. For example, he uses the Holocaust as the back-drop for his short story "Perfection" (2004).

A Writing Career Begins with Short Stories After Helprin graduated from secondary school, he attended Harvard University and earned his BA degree in 1969. While at Harvard, he began writing short stories. In 1969, two of these were accepted by *The New Yorker* and later included in his collection *A Dove of the East* (1975).

Military Service in Israel After graduating from Harvard, Helprin entered the doctoral program in English at Stanford, but he left after a short time to move to Israel. He returned to Harvard in 1970, where he obtained a master's degree in Middle Eastern studies in 1972. Back in Israel again, he was drafted into that nation's army and became a dual citizen of Israel and the United States. He served in the military from 1972 to 1973. This experience later helped him with the detailed descriptions of warfare in his novel *A Soldier of the Great War*.

First Novel is Favorably Received After his military service, Helprin spent a short time at Princeton and a postgraduate year at Magdalen College, Oxford, England. Helprin's first novel was *Refiner's Fire: The Life and Adventures of Marshall Pearl, a Foundling* (1977), which received a mostly favorable critical response. He

married Lisa Kennedy, a tax attorney and banker, on June 28, 1980. They have two daughters, Alexandra Morris and Olivia Kennedy.

Literary Career Helprin's next work, *Ellis Island and Other Stories,* had the rare distinction for a collection of short stories of winning a PEN/Faulkner Award, the National Jewish Book Award, and an American Book Award nomination. In fact, it has received the most enthusiastic critical reception of all his works. In 1982 he also received the Prix de Rome from the American Academy and Institute of Arts and Letters. Helprin's second novel, *Winter's Tale*, was on the *New York Times* best-seller list for four months, but it met with mixed reviews from critics. In 1984, Helprin was awarded a Guggenheim fellowship. Helprin then worked with illustrator Chris Van Allsburg on a well-received version of *Swan Lake* (1989) and wrote his novel *A Soldier of the Great War*, which was followed four years later by *Memoir from Antproof Case*. His most recent work is *Freddy and Fredericka.* In addition to the three volumes of short stories and five novels Helprin has published to date, he has also authored three books for children, all illustrated by Chris Van Allsburg, and numerous nonfiction commentaries that address themes including politics, aesthetics, and culture.

Works in Literary Context

Mark Helprin explained in a *Paris Review* interview with James Linville in 1993 that his models for writing were William Shakespeare, Dante Alighieri, John Milton, Anton Chekhov, and William Butler Yeats, because they held other jobs. It is perhaps not surprising then that critics argue the key to Helprin's almost legendary reputation lies in his diversity, especially in the forms and genres he employs, sometimes intermixing them in highly imaginative ways. Helprin is an unapologetically Romantic writer, and his work lies in a direct line with the visionary works of William Wordsworth, Ralph Waldo Emerson, William Blake, and Walt Whitman.

Romanticism and Spiritual Transcendence The human desire for spiritual transcendence is the thematic focus of much of Helprin's fiction. His tales usually involve a survivor who has experienced a profound loss and needs to heal his or her spirit to overcome despair. For Helprin, nature and art are essential in this process of regeneration. Helprin's first collection, *A Dove of the East* has several stories that exhibit this power. In the title story, the protagonist's wife and parents are killed during World War II. In caring for a hurt dove, he is able to balance his grief with the wonder of nature. In "The Silver Bracelet," a young girl is orphaned and she creates beautiful music out of her pain. The power of these two forces is derived from their continuity and the hints they provide about the divine. Helprin's works always have moral implications, the most important of these being a sense of justice that Helprin brings to apocalyptic proportions in *Winter's Tale*, the plot of which is the destruction of New York City and its rebirth as a city of absolute justice.

Magic Realism: Dreams and Nostalgia Less consistently found, but still important to understanding Helprin's work, is the use of dreams. Dreams are important in the Helprin narrative to show the continuity of time and to help blur the line between fantasy and reality. He does this in a short story from *Ellis Island*, "The Schreuderspitze," where the main character encounters the healing power of nature through his dreams about mountain climbing. Part of the fantasy prevalent in Helprin's work comes from his nostalgia for things past. There are two stories in *Ellis Island* that are reminiscent of the past, the historical past in "Martin Bayer" and personal past in "A Vermont Tale." *Winter's Tale* combines the nostalgia and dream imagery of *Ellis Island* with the romance of *Refiner's Fire*. The descriptions of nineteenth-century New York City from *Winter's Tale* celebrate the past, too unrealistically according to some reviewers. *Winter's Tale*, perhaps Helprin's most romantic work, is also filled with imagery that seems to derive as much from literature and folklore as it does from the author's imagination. In Helprin's novel *A Soldier of the Great War* he takes his major themes and places them in the realistic and grim context of World War I. Helprin uses his personal knowledge of military life to create vivid descriptions of the violence, the cruelty, and sometimes the glory, of war.

LITERARY AND HISTORICAL CONTEMPORARIES

Mark Helprin's famous contemporaries include:

James Patterson (1947–): A popular American author, Patterson is best known for his *Alex Cross* series (fourteen books published between 1992 and 2008) and *Women's Murder Club* mystery thriller series (seven books published between 2001 and 2008).

George W. Bush (1946–): Bush, a Republican politician, served as the forty-sixth governor of Texas and the forty-third President of the United States.

Paul Auster (1947–): A provocative experimental novelist whose work represents an amalgam of several genres, Auster is best known for his *New York Trilogy*, which consists of *City of Glass* (1985), *Ghosts* (1986), and *The Locked Room* (1986).

J. K. Rowling (1965–): A British author of novels for young readers, Rowling caused an overnight sensation with her first book, *Harry Potter and the Philosopher's Stone* (1997).

Ann Beattie (1947–): Beattie is an American author whose fiction concerns members of the post–World War II, "baby boom" generation, whose passivity and inability to comprehend themselves or others trap them in unsatisfactory life situations.

Works in Critical Context

From the beginning critics have agreed that Helprin is a talented writer who provides his readers with a wide range of settings and a graceful prose. Helprin's work is often described as sprawling, expansive, and inventive, and most critics agree that there is a depth to his prose. *Ellis Island and Other Stories* is the work that made Helprin a favorite of the critics. He won numerous awards for the work, and the success of his writing within the context of these stories is the reason that many critics believe Helprin's style works best in the short story form. His dreamlike fantasy novels are praised for their imagination, but they are often criticized for being vague. *Winter's Tale* in particular suffered from this criticism. Critics complain that this, Helprin's most controversial work, lacks the precision of *Ellis Island*, that the story is forced, and that there is a lack of a strong narrative. *Winter's Tale* has been called unconvincing because it is almost too romantic, and projects idealism at the expense of reality. Others were impressed with the affirmative nature of the tale and found it a great source of comfort and hope to modern man. With *A Soldier of the Great War*, Helprin seemed to have overcome some of the complaints about his earlier work. He was praised for his simple language and for the choice of his themes.

Ellis Island and Other Stories This collection of stories produced a chorus of critical praise. Rhoda Koenig

COMMON HUMAN EXPERIENCE

The human desire for spiritual transcendence is central to Helprin's fiction. Other works that explore this theme include the following:

Bhagavad Gita is a Hindu religious text written between the fifth and second centuries B.C.E. It has been translated into English many times, notably by Christopher Isherwood and Swami Prabhavananda in 1944. In this sacred scripture, the god Krishna explains the different paths to realize Brahman (the divine essence) through the practice of yoga.

Phenomenology of Spirit (1807), a philosophical treatise by Georg Wilhelm Friedrich Hegel. In this work, Hegel lays out an idealist philosophy that defines freedom as transcendence of the self.

Siddhartha (1922), a novel by Herman Hesse. A wealthy man leaves his family to go in search of the meaning of life and eventually reaches his goal of spiritual transcendence, enlightenment, and compassion.

Island (1962), a novel by Aldous Huxley. On the island of Pala, people live in paradise—a utopian society where the goal of life is a type of spiritual transcendence.

in *New York* magazine selected the title story as the best in the collection. Some of the other stories, she wrote, "long on mood and short on plot, seem like watercolor sketches for more finished work, but the majority of them shimmer with the bright and lavish metaphors of this most accomplished artist." Reynolds Price in the *New York Times Book Review* noted the wide range of settings in the collection, both in time and place, commenting that "Such an ambitious reach is almost unheard of in our short fiction since Poe." Price went on to state that the author's purpose "seems to be the rapid deduction and communication of a personal metaphysics.... His technical confidence and his admirable concern for texture... go far toward compelling a reader's cooperation in the aim." For A.V. Kish, writing in *Best Sellers*, "Each story is true to itself, created by a writer whose language is a thing of beauty and a joy to read."

Winter's Tale *Winter's Tale*, Helprin's second novel, held a place on the *New York Times* best-seller list for four months. Seymour Krim, writing for *Washington Post Book World*, described the allegorical novel as "the most ambitious work [Helprin] has yet attempted, a huge cyclorama" with a theme "no less than the resurrection of New York from a city of the damned to a place of universal justice and hope." In his view, however, which was one of several negative critical responses to the book, it turned out to be "a self-willed fairy tale that even on its own terms refuses to convince." In the *Chicago Tribune Book World*, Jonathan Brent called the book "a pastiche of cliches thinly disguised as fiction, a maddening welter of earnest platitudes excruciatingly dressed up as a search for the miraculous." In the opinion of *Newsweek*'s Peter S. Prescott, "Helprin fell into the fundamental error of assuming that fantasy can be vaguer than realistic fiction." In the view of Benjamin De Mott of the *New York Times Book Review*, however, not through the unique and compelling characters or "merely by studying the touchstone passages in which description and narrative soar highest" can the reader "possess the work": "No, the heart of this book resides unquestionably in its moral energy, in the thousand original gestures, ruminations...writing feats that summon its audience beyond the narrow limits of conventional vision, commanding us to see our time and place afresh." *Detroit News* reviewer Beaufort Cranford found that the book "fairly glows with poetry. Helprin's forte is a deft touch with description, and he has as distinct and spectacular a gift for words an anyone writing today." Further, Cranford noted, "Helprin's fearlessly understated humor shows his comfort with a narrative that in a less adroit grasp might seem too much like a fairy tale." *Openers* editor Ann Cunniff, who also caught the humor in *Winter's Tale*, wrote about "the beautiful, dreamlike quality" of some of Helprin's passages and "frequent references to dreams in the book." "All my life," Helprin explained to Cunniff, "I've allowed what I dream to influence me. My dreams are usually very intense and extremely detailed and always in the most beautiful colors.... Frequently, I will dream, and simply retrace that dream the day after when I write. It's just like planning ahead, only I do it when I'm unconscious."

Responses to Literature

1. Explain the significance of the love that develops between the title characters in the novel *Freddy and Fredericka*.

2. Using examples from the text, explain the importance of truth in the story "Perfection" from Helprin's collection *The Pacific and Other Stories* (2004). In this context, also explain the meaning of the story's title.

3. Compare and contrast Helprin's *Winter's Tale* with Shakespeare's play by the same name. Why do you think Helprin chose to model some aspects of his novel after this particular work?

4. A number of critics have argued that *Winter's Tale* is too vague and clichéd. Others find the author's style magical and poetic. To what extent do you agree with these assessments of the novel? Explain what you like or don't like about the way it is written, using examples from the book.

BIBLIOGRAPHY

Books

Bodine, Paul. "Mark Helprin." *Operative Words, Essays and Reviews on Literature and Culture.* San Jose, Calif.: Writers Club Press, 2002, 154–56.

Periodicals

Broyard, Anatole. Review of *Winter's Tale. New York Times* (September 2, 1983): C20.

Field, Leslie. "Mark Helprin and the Postmodern Jewish-American Fiction and Fantasy." *Yiddish* 7, no. 1 (1987): 57–65.

Koenig, Rhoda. "The Invisible Helping Hand: *Ellis Island and Other Stories.*" *New York* Vol. 14, no. 5 (February 2, 1981): 52–53.

Johnson, Mark. "A Conversation with Mark Helprin." *Image: A Journal of the Arts and Religion* 17 (Fall 1997): 48–59.

Kish, A. V. "Fiction: *Ellis Island and Other Stories.*" *Best Sellers* Vol. 41, no. 1 (April 1981): 6.

Lytal, Benjamin. "Helprin, Mark. *Freddy and Fredericka.*" *New York Sun* Arts & Letters Section (July 13, 2005).

Neumeyer, Peter. Review of *Swan Lake. New York Times Book Review* Vol. 94 (November 12, 1989): 28.

O'Grady, Selina. "Land of the Free and the Home of the Vulgar." *San Francisco Chronicle* (July 10, 2008): E3.

Prescott, Peter S. "Worst of Times." *Newsweek* Vol. CII, No. 12 (September 19, 1983): 78, 81.

Price, Reynolds. "The Art of American Short Stories." *New York Times Book Review* (March 1, 1981): 1, 20.

Royal, Derek Parker. "Unfinalized Moment in Jewish American Narrative." *Shofar: An Interdisciplinary Journal of Jewish Studies* 22, no. 3 (2004): 1–11.

Towers, Robert. "Assaulting Realism." *Atlantic Monthly* Vol. 252, No. 3 (September 1983): 122–23.

Web sites

Mark Helprin. Accessed December 6, 2008, from http://www.markhelprin.com.

⊛ Ernest Hemingway

BORN: *1899, Oak Park, Illinois*

DIED: *1961, Ketchum, Idaho*

NATIONALITY: *American*

GENRE: *Fiction*

MAJOR WORKS:
The Sun Also Rises (1926)
A Farewell to Arms (1929)
To Have and Have Not (1937)
For Whom the Bell Tolls (1940)
The Old Man and the Sea (1952)

Ernest Hemingway   *Hemingway, Ernest, photograph. AP Images.*

Overview

Novelist and short story writer Ernest Hemingway was known as much for his masculine behaviors—hunting, fishing, his obsession with the bullfight, his numerous marriages—as for his finely honed prose style, whose spare directness seemed to speak the truth with an unmistakable intensity. Winner of the Nobel Prize in Literature, Hemingway did not just mingle with the literary lights of his generation; his work and his style influenced generations of writers to come.

Works in Biographical and Historical Context

Early Formative Experience Hemingway was born in Oak Park, Illinois, an affluent and conservative suburb of Chicago, on July 21, 1899. He was the second of six children and the first son of Clarence Edmunds Hemingway, a physician, and Grace Hall Hemingway. In childhood and adolescence Hemingway spent summers with his family at Windemere, their house at Lake Walloon in northern Michigan. His hunting and fishing adventures and his contact with the Ojibway Indians, as well as his observations of the troubled relationship between his parents, became the material for many of his stories, including "Indian Camp" (1925), "The Doctor and the Doctor's Wife" (1924), and "Fathers and Sons" (1933), all featuring Nick Adams, a recurrent autobiographical protagonist.

The village of Oak Park had a good library and a high school that provided Hemingway with a sound education, especially in composition, language, literature, and history. There he read the great English writers and made his first forays into writing, contributing to the school newspaper and its literary magazine. Hemingway's competitive spirit also drove him to box, play football, and run track, though he was never an outstanding athlete.

Lessons in Journalism   As a student reporter Hemingway was prolific but unexceptional. His experience working for the school paper helped prepare him for his first job, however, as a cub reporter with the *Kansas City Star*, then considered one of the best newspapers in America. In addition to having the advice of first-rate journalistic professionals, Hemingway had to make his writing comply with the one hundred and ten rules of the *Kansas City Star* style sheet, requiring him to avoid adjectives and to use short sentences, brief paragraphs, vigorous English, and fresh phrases. Later, Hemingway remarked that these rules, which influenced his style as a fiction writer, were the best he had ever learned.

World War I had been raging in Europe since 1914, but the United States, which had tried to maintain its neutrality, did not get involved until 1917. Determined to go to Europe and participate in the war effort, Hemingway left the *Kansas City Star* at the end of April 1918 and joined an American Red Cross ambulance unit that assisted the Italian Army, one of America's allies. That July, at Fossalta, he was hit by shrapnel and suffered severe leg wounds; he was sent to an American Red Cross hospital in Milan to recover. His experiences in Italy would later form the basis for his novel *A Farewell to Arms* (1929).

When Hemingway arrived home in January 1919, he attempted a career as a fiction writer, but his work was widely rejected by mass-market magazines. In 1920 he left again, this time for Toronto, to reestablish himself as a journalist by freelancing for the *Toronto Star*. He returned to Chicago in May of that year and worked for *The Cooperative Commonwealth*, a monthly magazine. He met and became engaged to twenty-eight-year-old Hadley Richardson, whom he married in September of 1921. In Chicago he also met Sherwood Anderson, whose *Winesburg, Ohio* (1919) had gained wide acclaim. Anderson befriended Hemingway, encouraged his writing efforts, and convinced him that Paris was the place for a serious writer.

European Horizons   Supported by Hadley Hemingway's trust fund, Hemingway and his wife left for Paris at the end of the year. He carried letters of introduction from Anderson to Sylvia Beach (publisher and owner of the bookstore Shakespeare and Company) and the Modernist writers Gertrude Stein and Ezra Pound. Hemingway met Pound in February of 1922, and the friendship proved to be an invaluable one for Hemingway's development as a writer. Pound helped him hone his style, get his early work published, and also oversaw his literary education, exposing him to the work of poet T. S. Eliot and novelist James Joyce, whose groundbreaking *Ulysses* (1922) had just been published by Beach. In March of 1922, Hemingway met Gertrude Stein, whose experimental poetry and prose was inspired by the work of the painters with whom she socialized, including Henri Matisse and Pablo Picasso. At her Paris apartment Hemingway studied these artists and especially admired the work of Paul Cézanne; in the original ending to the short story "Big Two-Hearted River" (1925), Hemingway's alter-ego Nick Adams says that he wants to write the way Cézanne painted.

Continuing to work as a stringer for the *Toronto Star*, Hemingway went to Lausanne, Switzerland, in November 1922 to cover a peace conference on a territorial dispute between Greece and Turkey. On the way his wife's suitcase was stolen, and with it Hemingway lost almost all of his unpublished work. The papers were never recovered. In June 1923 Hemingway made his first trip to Spain, where he immersed himself in the culture of bullfighting, which became a perennial favorite subject. He returned again a month later for his first Fiesta of San Fermín in Pamplona, known for its famous running of the bulls.

Becoming Literary   Hemingway's first book, *Three Stories & Ten Poems*, was published in 1923. Although the poems in the volume merited little acclaim, the stories were praised. The Hemingways then left Paris for Toronto, where Hemingway was put on salary as a full-time reporter with the *Toronto Star*. After the birth of their first son, John Hadley Nicanor (Bumby) Hemingway, in October, Hemingway resigned his post and returned to Paris to work on a new journal devoted to experimental fiction, the *Transatlantic Review*.

By April 1924 Hemingway's *In Our Time*, a thirty-two-page volume consisting of eighteen vignettes, was on sale in Paris at Shakespeare and Company. It was limited to one hundred and seventy copies and covered themes that would appear repeatedly in Hemingway's later work, including bullfighting and war scenes. Hemingway also began publishing his stories in literary journals (known as "little magazines"). The next year, he signed a contract with Boni and Liveright, a major publisher, to bring out an expanded version of *In Our Time*; reviewers praised it, but the volume did not sell well. Around the same time, Hemingway met the novelist F. Scott Fitzgerald; their friendship would become one of the most important in Hemingway's life.

In July 1925 Hemingway returned to Pamplona for his second Fiesta of San Fermín with his wife and a diverse group of friends. The excitement of the Fiesta and the tensions among the group formed the basis of

Hemingway's first novel, *The Sun Also Rises* (1926), which Hemingway began writing immediately after the adventure ended.

Life's Complications

In 1926 Hemingway and Hadley separated, after it became clear he was involved with Pauline Pfeiffer, a wealthy American who worked for French *Vogue*. They divorced in 1927. Soon afterward, Hemingway and Pfeiffer were married. Hemingway had wanted to return to the United States for several years, and he and Pauline, who was pregnant, sailed for Key West from France in the spring of 1928. (Their son Patrick was born in June.) In December Hemingway learned, via telegram, that his father had shot himself, having suffered depression for many years. After the funeral, Hemingway finished *A Farewell to Arms* and in the spring brought his family back to France.

A Farewell to Arms, published in September 1929, was praised from the outset, and the first printing sold out so quickly as to require three more printings before the end of the year. By February 1930 Hemingway had earned more than $30,000 in royalties. In *The Sun Also Rises* Hemingway had shown the effects of World War I upon the generation whose lives it touched, the so-called "Lost Generation." In his second novel he focused upon the war itself, tracing the events that took a toll on the young people who participated in it.

In November of 1931 Pauline Hemingway gave birth to their son Gregory, and the following month Hemingway finished *Death in the Afternoon* (1932), the novel about bullfighting he had long wanted to write. Although the book revealed Hemingway's considerable research and knowledge about bullfighting, as well as his most extensive public presentation of his writing philosophy, *Death in the Afternoon* was not embraced by Americans.

Hemingway's writing life involved more than just novel writing during this period. He was at work on the story collection that would contain perhaps his most famous story, "A Clean, Well-Lighted Place" (1933), and began contributing articles on hunting and fishing to the brand-new magazine *Esquire*. In 1933 the Hemingways embarked on a two-month African safari, which inspired his next book, *Green Hills of Africa* (1935).

World Events Again Intervene

While work was underway on his next novel, *To Have and Have Not*, Hemingway again heard the call of Spain. The year 1936 saw the beginning of the Spanish Civil War, in which a military uprising led to a three-year-long war between a fascistic military and the left-leaning democratic government of Spain. The efforts of writers like Hemingway and George Orwell, who not only traveled to Spain to fight the Fascists but sent home reports on the war, brought international attention to the crisis.

Martha Gellhorn, a young writer whom Hemingway knew in Key West, also went to Spain to report on the war; she and Hemingway soon began an affair. When in 1939 Hemingway moved to Cuba to write his novel about the Spanish Civil War, *For Whom the Bell Tolls* (1940), Gellhorn followed him there, and Pauline filed for divorce. *For Whom the Bell Tolls*, dedicated to Gellhorn, received positive reviews in major American newspapers and in leading magazines. The novel sold 491,000 copies within six months of its publication, and Hemingway's critical reputation, which had declined throughout the 1930s, was once again restored, and his fame and fortune had never been greater. As soon as his divorce from Pauline was final, he and Gellhorn were married at Sun Valley, Idaho, in November of 1940.

After the publication of *For Whom the Bell Tolls*, Hemingway's literary productivity waned. At the end of 1940, at the onset of World War II, he bought the Finca Vigia, his home near Havana, and he and Gellhorn left at the beginning of the new year to cover the war in China—Gellhorn for *Collier's* and Hemingway for *PM*, a liberal New York tabloid. In his dispatches for *PM* he often appeared prophetic, predicting correctly that the United States would be forced into war when Japan attacked American bases in the Pacific. He produced just eight articles during his Far East assignment, "only enough," he said, "to keep from being sent home."

With an influx of Nazi agents into Cuba and U-boats steadily sinking ships in the Caribbean, Hemingway proposed to officials at the American Embassy and to the U.S. ambassador to Cuba that he set up a private counterintelligence agency. The Cuban prime minister granted him permission, and Hemingway organized a group he called the Crook Factory, outfitting his fishing boat for U-boat surveillance. During this time Hemingway's drinking increased, and his marriage deteriorated as Gellhorn spent more time away from Cuba on journalistic assignments.

Into the Theater of War

At the end of October 1943 Gellhorn left Cuba again to cover the war in Europe for *Collier's*. Early in 1944 Hemingway usurped her position with the magazine, agreeing to go to Europe for *Collier's* as their front-line correspondent, a role women were not permitted to fill. In this capacity he took part in some of the more iconic moments of the war, the first being the landing of Allied soldiers on Omaha Beach, Normandy, on June 6, 1944, otherwise known as D-Day. Hemingway was posted on a landing craft taking soldiers ashore. He chose to reboard the soldiers' main transport ship rather than try to land with the soldiers, perhaps missing an opportunity but perhaps saving his life: ten other landing craft were destroyed attempting to land. Reporting on the confusion, fear, death, and destruction, Hemingway observed, "Real war is never like paper war, nor do accounts of it read much the way it looks."

Hemingway was also stationed briefly with General George Patton's Third Army and then participated in the liberation of Paris on August 25, 1944. Recalling his feelings about Paris as he looked down on the city with American forces of liberation, he wrote,

LITERARY AND HISTORICAL CONTEMPORARIES

Hemingway's famous contemporaries include:

Jean-Paul Sartre (1905–1980): A French philosopher and writer best known for his contributions to existentialist philosophy, Sartre was a central figure in twentieth-century intellectual life who was often at odds with the political and social status quo.

F. Scott Fitzgerald (1896–1940): American novelist Fitzgerald was Hemingway's friend, mentor and rival. Hemingway expressed admiration for Fitzgerald's 1925 novel, *The Great Gatsby*, while also hoping that he might some day surpass his friend. Fitzgerald's alcoholism contributed to his early demise.

Francisco Franco (1892–1975): Spanish general and politician who led an uprising of the military against Spain's left-leaning Popular Front government, an event which galvanized intellectuals around the world to support Spain's fledgling democracy against Franco's forces from 1936 to 1939.

George Orwell (1903–1950): English writer who, like Hemingway, was profoundly marked by the Spanish Civil War, a war that contributed to Orwell's famous mistrust of totalitarian government and euphemistic language as shown in his novel *Nineteen Eighty-Four* (1949).

Humphrey Bogart (1899–1957): Bogart was an American actor who often played characters that could have been invented by Hemingway: brash, virile, but often quietly sensitive. Bogart, with his cigarette and fedora, is an icon of mid-century Hollywood.

John Dos Passos (1896–1970): American writer Dos Passos was at the forefront of literary and artistic modernism in the 1920s. A radical leftist who eventually drifted to the right, Dos Passos often feuded with Hemingway and fell from critical favor.

I couldn't say anything more then, because I had a funny choke in my throat and I had to clean my glasses because there now, below us, gray and always beautiful, was spread the city I love best in all the world.

While in Europe Hemingway had begun an affair with Mary Welsh, an American journalist working in London. After the war ended, Hemingway returned to Cuba; Welsh followed him, and after their respective divorces were finalized, they were married, in Havana, in March 1946.

The Last, Erratic Decade Having published no fiction at all in the 1940s, Hemingway returned to novel-writing, tentatively; the work he produced in the mid-1940s was not published until many years after his death. After a 1948 trip to Italy, Hemingway was finally able to bring a novel to completion; the result was *Across the River and Into the Trees* (1950), which received poor—and at times even hostile—reviews. *The Old Man and the Sea* (1952), which Hemingway turned to next, proved to be something of a parable of his life in recent years: an old fisherman, having gone eighty-four days without catching a fish, takes his boat far out to sea, spends three days wrestling with an enormous marlin, and then has to battle the sharks to keep his catch. Like the old man, Hemingway suffered a dispiriting dry stretch, but caught his giant marlin with *The Old Man and the Sea*. The story ran in its entirety in five million copies of *Life*, and the 50,000 copies printed in book form sold out in ten days.

The rest of the 1950s brought Hemingway a series of extreme highs and lows. At the end of their 1953–1954 African safari, the Hemingways survived a near-fatal plane crash, only to have their rescue plane crash the very next day. Though they survived the second crash as well, newspapers around the world carried obituaries, many of them riddled with other inaccuracies. Later that year Hemingway was awarded the Nobel Prize in Literature, something which for years he had watched go to writers he believed were undeserving. But, by the end of 1955 Hemingway was laid low again, this time by illness. He bounced back by the end of 1956, well enough to make another trip to Europe and returned to renewed productivity. Back in Cuba, despite his poor health and constant interruptions, Hemingway returned to his work: *True at First Light* (1999), *The Garden of Eden* (1986), and *A Moveable Feast* (1964), a memoir about Paris in the 1920s.

As revolutionary activity increased in Cuba, Hemingway feared he would be a target during the overthrow of the Batista government, and he and his wife left Cuba for Ketchum, Idaho. Their move proved to be in the nick of time: Fidel Castro overthrew the government and took control of Cuba on January 1, 1959. The Hemingways departed for Spain in 1959 after Hemingway agreed to write about the bullfight season for *Life* magazine.

During the 1959 Spanish trip—and another in 1960, to gather more material—Hemingway displayed highly erratic behavior. His depression and insomnia growing, his paranoia more obvious, and his nerves uncontrollable, he checked into the Mayo Clinic in Rochester, Minnesota, at the end of November and underwent a series of electroshock therapy treatments. He was released in January of 1961. By March, Hemingway's depression had returned, and he had to be restrained because of suicide attempts. He returned to the Mayo Clinic for additional electroshock therapy in April and was released in June, his psychiatrist confident of Hemingway's improvement. But, back in Idaho, in the early morning of July 2, 1961, Hemingway at last succeeded in killing himself.

Works in Literary Context

Modernist Prose One of Hemingway's greatest contributions to literature was his distinctive prose style, one that seems stripped down of all superfluous words but nevertheless seems to pulse with emotion. He did not develop this style in a vacuum, however; some of it came from his no-frills journalistic training, and some of it came from the influence of his Modernist peers, particularly his friends Ezra Pound and Gertrude Stein. Malcolm Cowley, assessing the importance of Stein and Pound to his literary development, wrote,

> One thing he took partly from [Stein] was a colloquial—in appearance—American style, full of repeated words, prepositional phrases, and present participles, the style in which he wrote his early published stories. One thing he took from Pound—in return for trying vainly to teach him to box—was the doctrine of the accurate image . . . ; but Hemingway also learned from him to bluepencil most of his adjectives.

Hemingway was one of a new generation of writers to break away from the wordy, lengthy prose that characterized much of popular literature leading up to World War I.

The Literature of War From Homer's *Iliad* (c. 8th century BCE) to Leo Tolstoy's *War and Peace* (1869), war, particularly men's heroic actions in battle, was a fertile subject for literature. But, the mass death in World War I, occasioned by new types of warfare, called for a new literary response to war, one which recognized how very inglorious violence, suffering, and loss can be. Thanks to Hemingway's experience with war, he joined the ranks of those men, dubbed the "Lost Generation" by Gertrude Stein, who were so deeply affected by World War I that it affected their worldview and, in turn, their contributions to literature.

Works in Critical Context

The Sun Also Rises With *The Sun Also Rises*, Hemingway made something of a critical splash. The reviewer for *The New York Times* thought *The Sun Also Rises* fulfilled the promise of Hemingway's earlier work and that the novel was "unquestionably one of the events of an unusually rich year in literature." Conrad Aiken states in the *New York Herald Tribune Books* that "in many respects" Hemingway was "the most exciting of contemporary writers of fiction." The novel's influence extended to real life, as well: in his *Exile's Return* (1951) Malcolm Cowley observed Hemingway's influence upon young men and women who were acting out roles suggested by the novel's characters Jake Barnes and Brett Ashley. Looking back at *The Sun Also Rises* in 1953, biographer/critic Carlos Baker underscored qualities noted by contemporary reviewers of the novel that caused it to endure and contribute to Hemingway's literary reputation. Baker cited the purity of Hemingway's language and denotative power of dialogue; his devotion to fact and personal knowledge; his skill in evoking and controlling emotional states; and his use of symbolic landscape.

A Farewell to Arms *A Farewell to Arms* was widely reviewed, and critical response was predominantly favorable, affirming that Hemingway had become a major writer who exerted strong influence upon American literature. Henry

Hazlitt of *The New York Sun* thought the novel Hemingway's "finest," calling him "the young master," and observing that it was Hemingway whom young and older writers were imitating. There was evolving not only a "Hemingway school" but also a "Hemingway cult," strengthened by convincing dialogue and a distinctive style. In *The Nation* Clifton Fadiman acknowledges Hemingway as "one of the best craftsmen alive" and concludes, "There seems no reason why *A Farewell to Arms* should not secure the Pulitzer Prize." Although the book did not win a Pulitzer, the high regard for Hemingway's work was so commonplace that Henry Seidel Canby states in *The Saturday Review of Literature* that among things "not permitted in contemporary criticism" was "to attack Ernest Hemingway."

Responses to Literature

1. Hemingway was drawn to Paris in the 1920s, where he found a vibrant, groundbreaking community of artists. It turned out that what they were doing was creating a new movement now known as Modernism. Using your library and the Internet, research literary Modernism. What was new about this movement? What were these writers doing that had not been done before?

2. Hemingway found the Fiesta of San Fermín, in Pamplona, Spain, incredibly inspiring, incorporating

---

COMMON HUMAN EXPERIENCE

Much of Hemingway's fiction revolves around the lives and experiences of Americans living abroad. Here are some other works which explore the expatriate experience:

Tender Is the Night (1934), a novel by F. Scott Fitzgerald. Fitzgerald's last completed novel, *Tender Is the Night* weaves the intrigue that develops among a group of American friends into the sun-baked atmosphere of the South of France in the 1920s.

The Portrait of a Lady (1881), a novel by Henry James. *The Portrait of a Lady*, considered by many to be James's masterpiece, focuses on the experiences of American heiress Isabel Archer as she makes her way through Europe, fending off marriage proposals in an effort to remain autonomous. Her mistakes—as well as what she learns from them—are often a commentary on the friction between the old world and the new.

Cabaret (1972), a film directed by Bob Fosse. Based on the Broadway musical of the same name, *Cabaret* is set in Berlin in 1931, at the dawn of Hitler's rise to power. It centers around Sally Bowles, an aspiring American cabaret performer, whose hapless innocence serves as a prism for the trouble then building in Germany.

---

his experiences at bullfights and with the running of
the bulls into much of his fiction and journalism.
Read *The Sun Also Rises*, and then research the
present-day Fiesta of San Fermín. What has changed
about the festival? What has remained the same?
Does it still have the same potential to inspire? Why
or why not? Write up your findings in a short paper.

3. Hemingway's distinctive writing style is much imi-
tated, much beloved, and much parodied by other
writers. Contests have even been held for the worst
imitations of Hemingway. Study Hemingway's style
closely, reading it out loud to get a feel for the way it
sounds and how it works, and the write your own
entry for the "bad Hemingway" contest. Check out
*The Best of Bad Hemingway: Choice Entries from the
Harry's Bar & American Grill Imitation Hemingway Competition* (1989) for inspiration.

BIBLIOGRAPHY

Books

Baker, Carlos. *Ernest Hemingway: A Life Story.*
    New York: Scribners, 1969.
Bruccoli, Matthew J., ed. *Conversations with Ernest
    Hemingway.* Jackson, Miss.: University Press of
    Mississippi, 1986.
Cowley, Malcolm. *Exile's Return: A Literary Odyssey of the
    1920s.* Harmondsworth, England: Penguin, 1979.
Mellow, James R. *Hemingway: A Life without
    Consequences.* Boston: Houghton Mifflin, 1992.
Wagner, Linda Welshimer. *Ernest Hemingway: A
    Reference Guide.* Boston: G. K. Hall, 1977.

Periodicals

Aiken, Conrad. Review of *The Sun Also Rises. The New
    York Herald Tribune Books* (October 31, 1926).
Canby, Henry Seidel. Review of *A Farewell to Arms. The
    Saturday Review of Literature* (October 12, 1929).
Fadiman, Clifton. Review of *A Farewell to Arms. The
    Nation* (October 30, 1929).
Hazlitt, Henry. Review of *A Farewell to Arms. The New
    York Sun* (September 28, 1929).
"Marital Tragedy: *The Sun Also Rises* by Ernest Hemingway."
    The New York Times (October 31, 1926).

✵ Beth Henley

BORN: *1952, Jackson, Mississippi*

NATIONALITY: *American*

GENRE: *Drama*

MAJOR WORKS:
Am I Blue (1973)
Crimes of the Heart (1979)
The Miss Firecracker Contest (1980)

Beth Henley   *Henley, Beth, photograph. AP Images.*

Overview

Beth Henley is a member of the new breed of American
playwrights dedicated to preserving regional voices on
the stage. Henley's Mississippi upbringing provides the
background for a host of Southern-accented plays, one of
which, the black comedy *Crimes of the Heart* (1979),
won her a Pulitzer Prize when she was twenty-nine.

Works in Biographical and Historical Context

A Southern Upbringing   Elizabeth Becker Henley
was born on May 8, 1952, in Jackson, Mississippi, to
Charles Boyle Henley, an attorney, and Elizabeth Josephine Becker Henley, an actress. Her Southern upbringing had a great influence on her writing. As she explains,
"In my house, people were more inclined to sit around
the kitchen table and talk than to watch TV." In addition, the South was experiencing a tense time in the
1950s and 1960s due to the civil rights movement, and
the public debate inspired by this unrest surely worked its
way into Henley's dialogue. Though acting was Henley's
original career interest, she had written her first play and
had it produced before receiving her BFA in 1974 from
Southern Methodist University. *Am I Blue*, a one-act
play, was staged in the fall of 1973 and was just the
beginning of a varied writing career.

After undergraduate school, Henley undertook a year of graduate work and teaching at the University of Illinois at Champaign, in addition to participating in summer stock at New Salem State Park. Nevertheless, lacking confidence in her acting abilities and unsure as to whether she possessed the necessary qualities to be a writer, in 1976 Henley moved to Los Angeles to be with director-actor Stephen Tobolowsky, with whom she still lives. Encouraged, however, by her S.M.U. friends, especially Tobolowsky and director Frederick Bailey, Henley soon turned again to writing.

Her first full-length attempt, *Crimes of the Heart*, was submitted by Bailey in the Great American Play Contest sponsored by the Actors Theatre of Louisville. It won the contest and was produced there in 1979, before moving to Broadway in 1981. The work eventually won Henley a Pulitzer Prize, marking the first time in twenty-three years that a woman had won the prize for drama. Further recognition for the play included a New York Drama Critics Circle Award, a Guggenheim Award, and a Tony nomination.

A Life of Quiet Recognition   Following her first success, Henley continued to write. Four additional plays have been produced, though none has received the acclaim of *Crimes of the Heart*. Published in *The Ten Best Plays of 1983–1984*, *The Miss Firecracker Contest* (1980) had been staged in regional theaters before moving to the Manhattan Theatre Club and enjoying an extended run Off-Broadway. Several more plays have followed.

From Stage to Screen   Henley's talent is not limited to play writing. For instance, she teamed up with Budge Threlkeld in 1985 to write the pilot of *Survival Guides* for PBS. The half-hour episode was directed by Jonathan Demme. Henley explained to Beverly Walker in *American Film*, "It was my first collaboration. Budge wanted to help me out of a depression I'd lapsed into after my play [*The Wake of Jamey Foster*] had bombed on Broadway." Appearing in this segment were David Byrne, front-man of the band Talking Heads, and Rosanna Arquette, both of whom Henley would work with again.

She helped write the screenplay for *True Stories* (1986), along with Tobolowsky and musician David Byrne, which depicts the day-to-day occurrences of Virgil, Texas. Byrne, the movie's director and narrator, says that much of the script was inspired by articles found in grocery-store tabloids—accounts of incredible, yet supposedly "true," stories. Henley actually claims to have done very little, for as she explained in the Walker interview, "I am very honored to have a credit, but all I really did was help David organize his ideas."

In 1986 Henley worked on *Crimes of the Heart*, a film adaptation of her play. Starring Diane Keaton as Lenny, Jessica Lange as Meg, and Sissy Spacek as Babe, the movie was directed by Bruce Beresford. The cast—also including Tess Harper as Chick and Sam Shepard as Doc—strengthened the film and gave spark to the script.

LITERARY AND HISTORICAL CONTEMPORARIES

Henley's famous contemporaries include:

Tennessee Williams (1911–1983): The South's most famous playwright, Williams is probably best known for his play *A Streetcar Named Desire* (1947), which later became a movie starring Marlon Brando.

Jimmy Carter (1924–): The former governor of Georgia who was U.S. president from 1977–1981.

Jonathan Demme (1944–). Best known for his film adaptation *Silence of the Lambs* (1991), this director worked with Henley in the 1980s.

David Byrne (1952–). Though most known for fronting the rock band Talking Heads, Byrne has since worked on many musical and visual projects and collaborations.

Anna Deavere Smith (1950–). Smith is an award-winning playwright known for her "documentary theater" style in such plays as *Fires in the Mirror* (1993).

The dry, honest comedy that was created in the play survived the transition to the screen, and, as a result, *Crimes of the Heart* was one of the most acclaimed films of the year, earning Henley an Oscar nomination for best screenplay adaptation.

... And Back to the Stage   After working for a while on films, Henley returned to playwriting; her most recent play is *Ridiculous Fraud* (2006). "It is not often that a girl from Jackson, Mississippi, can accomplish so much in what might be called a 'big city' world of film and theatre," declares Lucia Tarbox in a *Dictionary of Literary Biography Yearbook: 1986* article on the playwright. "However, Beth Henley has managed to succeed by bringing her southern small-town past with her. [Though she's known both financial success and failure], she does not allow the negative to overcome that which is positive." Quoting Henley, Tarbox concludes with the observation, "Something I'm sure has to do with the South's defeat in the Civil War, which is that you should never take yourself too seriously. You may be beaten and defeated, but your spirit cannot be conquered."

Works in Literary Context

Strong and Strange Women   Henley's plays focus on Southern women in settings where they often seek the support of other female characters. Male characters may be used to advance the plot but are generally not central to the story. In *Crimes of the Heart*, for example, three adult sisters, each with her own emotional scars, struggle with longstanding sibling conflicts while they react to a

COMMON HUMAN EXPERIENCE

In her plays, Henley has managed to write effective dialogue that reflects her Southern roots. Here are some other works that succeed thanks to their flavorful Southern dialects.

> "A Rose for Emily" (1930), a short story by William Faulkner. Miss Emily Grierson's death shakes up the world she lives in and is recounted by a typically nosy member of her small town.
>
> *A Streetcar Named Desire* (1947), a play by Tennessee Williams. Blanche DuBois represents the typical alcoholic old Southern belle, and her staged arguments with her brother in law, Stanley Kowalski, are the stuff of literary legend.
>
> *A Good Man is Hard to Find* (1955), a short story collection by Flannery O'Connor. O'Connor's colorful characters are frequently horrible and hypocritical, thanks to their reluctance to let go of their stereotypically Southern biases and prejudices.
>
> *Fried Green Tomatoes at the Whistle Stop Cafe* (1987), a novel by Fannie Flagg. Set in a diner in Alabama, this novel features a colorful cast of Southern women.

tragedy involving the youngest, who has murdered her husband. Despite the emotional gravity of the subject matter, the play generates near-constant laughter. Bizarre events and ideas establish a sort of black humor; for example, the women's mother had committed suicide some years ago, hanging not only herself but also the family cat. *The Miss Firecracker Contest* is another example of Henley's juxtaposition of pathos and comic absurdity. In this play, a young woman tries to win respect and success by entering a small-town beauty contest, showing her talent in a tap-dancing and baton-twirling rendition of "The Star Spangled Banner."

Dealing with Death Death, disaster, and freakish accidents play a major role in all of Henley's plays. However, Henley's treatment of this recurring motif is often humorous. Most of her southern characters accept such events matter-of-factly, so that when Babe shoots her husband in *Crimes of the Heart*, or when Bess is kidnapped by the Indians in *Abundance*, or when orphan Carnelle in *The Miss Firecracker Contest* speaks nonchalantly about people dying—"It seems like people've been dying practically all my life, in one way or another"—it is never maudlin.

Works in Critical Context

As Richard Schickel wrote in a *Time* review:

> [Henley's territory] is really a country of the mind: one of Tennessee Williams' provinces that has surrendered to a Chekhovian raiding party, perhaps. Her strength is a wild anecdotal inventiveness, but her

people, lost in the ramshackle dreams and tumbledown ambitions with which she invests them, often seem to be metaphors waywardly adrift. They are blown this way and that by the gales of laughter they provoke, and they frequently fail to find a solid connection with clear and generally relevant meaning.

Crimes of the Heart Despite the prestigious awards it received, Henley's *Crimes of the Heart* drew mixed reviews from critics. Some found it profound and genuinely funny, while others felt that the author generated laughter by ridiculing the very characters she had created. Some critics have also complained that too much action takes place offstage and that the characters and events are simply not credible. Nevertheless, even reviewers who are critical of Henley's play tend to find in it a redeeming quality. As Walter Kerr wrote in *The New York Times*, "*Crimes of the Heart* is clearly the work of a gifted writer. And, unstable as I feel it to be, it does mean to arrive at an original blend of folkways, secret despairs, sudden fun."

However, *New Leader* reviewer Leo Sauvage states, "I find nothing enthralling in spending an evening with three badly adjusted, if not mentally retarded sisters, who are given free rein to exhibit their individual eccentricities." And Michael Feingold of the *Village Voice* is openly critical both of the dramatic work and of its setting:

> Perhaps the play supplies a kind of sordid nostalgia for Southerners who, behind the facade of their new double-knit suits and non-union factories, like to think they are still pea-pickin', baccy-chewin', inbreedin', illiterate cretins at heart—Snopeses who have been taught, painstakingly, to sign their names and clip coupons. Or perhaps they still are exactly that, and the South is in desperate need of either cultural mercy missions from New York, or fire and brimstone from Heaven.

Responses to Literature

1. How does the use of a southern dialect add to the humor in Henley's plays?

2. How have the sisters' upbringing in *Crimes of the Heart* affected their present lives?

3. Do you agree that Henley stereotypes Southerners too much? Explain, possibly by contrasting her characters in *Crimes of the Heart* with those of Tennesee Williams's *Streetcar Named Desire*.

4. Read *Crimes of the Heart* and then watch the film version, for which Henley wrote the screenplay. Are the sisters in the film what you expected from reading the play? In what ways, if any, are the characters in the film different from those in the play?

BIBLIOGRAPHY

Books

"Beth Henley (1952–)." *Contemporary Literary Criticism*, Vol, 23. Edited by Sharon R. Gunton and Jean C. Stine. Detroit: Gale, 1983, pp. 214–218.

Periodicals

Brustein, Robert. Review of *Abundance. New Republic* (December 17, 1990): 28.

Ebert, Roger. Review of *Miss Firecracker. Chicago Sun-Times* (April 28, 1989).

Helbig, Jack. Review of *Collected Plays, Volume I: 1980–1989* and *Collected Plays, Volume II: 1990–1999. Booklist* (June 1, 2000): 1836.

Kauffmann, Stanley. Review of *Crimes of the Heart. New Republic* (February 2, 1987): 26.

———. Review of *Nobody's Fool. New Republic* (December 15, 1986): 22.

———. Review of *True Stories. New Republic* (November 10, 1986): 26.

Kendt, Rob. Review of *Control Freaks. Back Stage* (August 6, 1993): 8.

Miller, Daryl H. Review of *Tight Pants. Los Angeles Times* (May 7, 2004).

Scholem, Benjamin. Review of *Impossible Marriage. Long Island Business News* (November 6, 1998): 38.

Travers, Peter. Review of *Crimes of the Heart* (movie). *People* (December 15, 1986): 12.

Weinert, Laura. Review of *Sisters of the Winter Madrigal. Back Stage West* (July 19, 2001): 12.

⚘ O. Henry

BORN: *1862, Greensboro, North Carolina*

DIED: *1910, New York, New York*

NATIONALITY: *American*

GENRE: *Fiction*

MAJOR WORKS:

Cabbages and Kings (1904)

"The Gift of the Magi" (1905)

The Four Million (1906)

"A Municipal Report" (1909)

Whirligigs (1910)

Overview

William Sydney Porter is best remembered as the prolific writer by the pen-name O. Henry, whose engaging, warm, and satisfying short stories earned him worldwide popularity. His works are documents of social and cultural as well as literary importance, a vivid record of his times that offers excellent resources for exploring both our urban and regional folklore.

Works in Biographical and Historical Context

A North Carolina Education Born in 1862, the second son of Dr. Algernon Sidney Porter and Mary Jane Virginia Swaim Porter, Porter spent the first twenty years of his life in Greensboro, North Carolina. His mother died

O. Henry *Henry, O. (William Sydney Porter), photograph. AP Images.*

in 1865, and with her death his father's world collapsed. Dr. Porter gave up his home, moved to his mother's house, and gradually abandoned his practice. The upbringing of his two sons was taken over by his mother and his sister Evelina. "Miss Lina" was a forceful disciplinarian who served not only as Porter's surrogate mother for the next seventeen years but also as the best teacher he ever had—her enthusiasm and discipline were the primary forces that aroused Porter's youthful passion for reading and his later desire to write.

Porter left home at age seventeen to work in his uncle's drugstore; he earned a state license as a practicing pharmacist in 1881. In these years he met people and stored up countless impressions of their personal oddities, mannerisms, gestures, and modes of speech that were later to be reflected, along with his expert use of professional terminology, in many of his stories.

Freedom and Flight In 1882 Porter left Greensboro and went to Texas, where he spent the next fifteen years, first on a cattle ranch near the Mexican border; then as a bookkeeper and drug clerk in Austin. Following his marriage to Athol Estes Roach in 1887, he worked as a draftsman in the Texas Land Office for four years. Athol was a young woman of wit and vivacity who encouraged him in his ambition to become a writer. She gave birth to their second child, Margaret, in 1889; their first child, a boy, died in infancy. Soon after Porter's job at the land office was discontinued in January 1891, he went to work as a bank teller.

While Porter worked as a teller he continued writing; and in March 1894 he bought a cheap printing press and the rights to a local paper, the *Iconoclast*. Porter renamed it *The Rolling Stone*, and, while holding down a full-time job, filled eight pages each week with humorous writings on persons and events of local interest. *The Rolling Stone* survived a year, but as Porter worked tirelessly to keep it rolling, it gradually dragged him deeper into debt. He borrowed heavily, but at some point during the year he also began taking funds from the bank with the hope that he could replace them later. When the shortages were discovered, Porter was ordered to appear before a grand jury on charges of embezzlement; these charges would not amount to much at the time. *The Rolling Stone* folded in 1895, and he moved to Houston to begin writing at the *Houston Post*.

In February 1896 the embezzlement case was reopened. Porter was arrested in Houston and despite the goodwill and support of friends in both Houston and Austin, he fled the country and sailed to Honduras, where he remained for the rest of the year. His experiences in that country, like his experiences elsewhere, are veiled in legend and myth, the most romantic versions of which are presented in his own stories. Nearly thirty of these stories, written later, appeared in various popular magazines, and about twenty of them, reworked and tied together loosely, were published in 1904 as his first book, *Cabbages and Kings*. As a record of what actually happened to Porter they are wholly unreliable; but one of their special artistic merits, shared by most of his other stories as well, is their high concentration of realistic detail, captured chiefly in descriptive and dialogue passages. The unhappy news that Athol was dying of tuberculosis obliged him to return in January 1897 and to face trial.

Imprisonment and the Birth of O. Henry
Athol passed away in July of 1897. In February of the next year, Porter was convicted of embezzlement and evading prosecution. He was given a term of five years, which his good behavior ultimately reduced to three. While there are various versions of how and when Porter took his famous pen name, "O. Henry" was born during Porter's prison term. Besides the fourteen stories written and published in periodicals during this period (beginning with "Georgia's Ruling" in 1900), many others published later grew out of anecdotes and yarns Porter heard from his fellow prisoners. He also wrote a great deal of Western-themed stories in prison, with settings in Texas and Latin America, but virtually all of them reflect the conventional images associated with the West. His daughter Margaret was never told her father was in prison, and after his release they were reunited in Pennsylvania.

The Chronicler of Four Million
After a brief time in Pittsburgh, during which he published nearly a dozen stories in popular magazines, Porter went to New York in the spring of 1902. Appropriately enough, Porter's fame—as O. Henry—is most widely associated with his tales of New York's "four million," roughly the population of the city in 1906, and shrewdly chosen as the title of his second collection of tales in response to Ward McAllister's claim in 1892 that "there are only about four hundred people in New York society." For Porter's assertion that four million New Yorkers were well worth noticing in print touched a democratic chord that appealed to people everywhere.

The range of Porter's experience, from the provincial limitations of boyhood in an embittered Reconstruction South to ultimate triumph in New York, seemed limitless as more and still more of O. Henry's stories appeared in print—113 of them in the weekly *New York Sunday World* alone between 1903 and 1905, and at least 25 longer ones published during the same period in monthly magazines such as *McClure's*.

New York challenged the adventurous author to record its true voice and to penetrate its mystery. O. Henry eagerly accepted the challenge and captured the essence of New York in story after story, and quintessentially in a pair of perennial favorites, "The Gift of the Magi" and "The Furnished Room," which represent the polar opposites of joy and sadness with which his imagination clothed the domestic life of average New Yorkers.

When *The Four Million* appeared in 1906, Porter's fame was assured; besides strong public acceptance, this collection of twenty-five stories also received some favorable notice from serious critics, who began comparing O. Henry to Guy de Maupassant and other eminent writers. Porter could be sure that further volumes of his stories would be noticed, and these, indeed, appeared fairly regularly during his remaining years and after his death.

A Sad Ending
Toward the end of 1907, though Porter's stories were in great demand, he was on the verge of a breakdown. Because his need for money was greater than ever following his marriage to Sara Lindsay Coleman, a childhood sweetheart, he drove himself remorselessly, but the income was still insufficient. The strains and tensions in his marriage deepened as his health and energies declined. By the summer of 1909 all attempts to maintain a normal family life were abandoned, and, his health shattered, Porter could no longer summon up enough energy in a week to finish a short story that, a few years before, he could have written in several hours. Virtually an invalid during the spring of 1910, he kept on trying to write until he collapsed on June 3. He was taken to the hospital, where he succumbed two days later to cirrhosis of the liver. Owing thousands of dollars advanced to him by his father-in-law and his publishers, he died a pauper.

Works in Literary Context

The Short Story
Porter almost single-handedly proved—to the benefit of writers who succeeded him—that the

short story was a credible and lucrative art form. He left an imposing volume of work and perhaps, after Edgar Allan Poe and Mark Twain, is the most widely read of any American short-story writer. The "O. Henry Story," as it came in time to be recognized and admired, owed much of its popular appeal to Porter's sophisticated updating of two types of short fiction: the boisterous tall tale of the Old Southwest frontier, and the more sentimental, romantic adventure story of the postwar local-color movement. The basic themes dramatized in all his later stories are fundamentally the same as those underlying the earlier ones. The four themes that recur most often have to do with pretense and reversal of fortune, discovery and initiation through adventure, the city as playground for the imagination, and the basic yearning of all humanity. A persistent rumor states that Franklin Roosevelt was moved to create more government services for the poor in the 1930s after reading O. Henry's stories. Of literature today, Jhumpa Lahiri's short stories show a sensitivity and an interconnectedness familiar to fans of O. Henry.

Foreign Influence Porter had a remarkable ear and eye for detail that served him well in his career, especially when it allowed him to capture details of his time spent in unusual locations. His stay in Honduras, though by no means a high point in his life, left him with stories about that steamy locale, which were collected into *Cabbages and Kings*. The central story, about dramatic goings-on in the fictional banana republic (a term he coined) of Anchuria, is recounted in the introduction and in seven of its eighteen chapters. Ancillary tales in the novel describe portray various grafts and schemes of American speculators, and satirize the military bravado of Anchuria.

Beyond the relevance of embezzlement and flight to Central America to Porter's personal life, Porter's stories fixed in the American consciousness the notion of Latin America as a land of allure and romance, unpredictable and volatile, revolutionary but full of opportunity. Finally, the novel marks a stage in the portrayals of the "ugly American" from Mark Twain to Joan Didion. The short-story author Ben Fountain, who traveled extensively to the destinations he features in his collection, "Brief Encounters with Che Guevara," carries O. Henry's tradition of first-hand fact-gathering.

Works in Critical Context

Perhaps the reputation of no other American writer has undergone a more rapid and drastic reversal than that of William Sydney Porter. Writing as O. Henry during the first decade of the twentieth century, Porter commanded a readership in the millions. Critics spoke of "the Yankee Maupassant," discussed Porter in the same breath with Gustave Flaubert, Rudyard Kipling, and Robert Louis Stevenson, and regarded him as "the master of the American short story." C. Alphonso Smith declared in 1916 that "O. Henry's work remains the most solid fact to be reckoned with in the history of twentieth-century American litera-

ture." "The time is coming," Canadian critic Stephen Butler Leacock wrote in the same year, "when the whole English-speaking world will recognize in him one of the great masters of modern literature."

Soon after Porter's death in 1910, however, this began to change. Critics of the 1920s satirized mercilessly the hundreds of would-be writers who emulated Porter's formulaic plot constructions. H. L. Mencken dismissed Porter as a cheap stage magician with a repertoire of four or five shopworn tricks. Robert Penn Warren wrote scathingly of Porter in 1943; others were indifferent, at best, to the sentimental characterizations, impostures, scene changing, and rhetorical constructs of Porter's tales. While he continues to attract biographers, critics have shown little interest in Porter's work for several decades.

For many, Porter captures the spirit and flavor of early-twentieth-century America as memorably as another "popular" artist, Norman Rockwell. The gap between public and critical opinion of Porter's work is tenuously, and ironically, bridged by one of America's most prestigious short-story awards, named in O. Henry's honor.

"The Gift of the Magi" "The Gift of the Magi," which appeared in *The Four Million*, has been one of Porter's most popular and enduring stories. The story is about an impoverished young married couple in New York who agree to give up what they most treasure in order to buy the other an expensive gift. Early critics recognized its qualities. Frederick Houk Law, writing in *The Independent*, commented, "Written in a free and easy

COMMON HUMAN EXPERIENCE

O. Henry's *The Four Million* encapsulates the myriad wonder and tragedy that constitutes New York and its citizens. Here are some other artists who have found no greater muse than the great Gotham:

Annie Hall (1977), a film directed by Woody Allen. This film focuses on the lives of several somewhat neurotic, intellectual New Yorkers who try to find love and happiness in the Big Apple.

Breakfast at Tiffany's (1958), a novel by Truman Capote. This classic (which inspired a popular 1961 film starring Audrey Hepburn) offers the story of the adventurous heroine Holly Golightly, a charming young woman on her own in New York.

Winter's Tale (1983), a novel by Mark Helprin. Helprin's fantastical, beautiful novel about a flying horse and an unlikely hero set against an evolving New York City.

Motherless Brooklyn (1999), a novel by Jonathan Lethem. Lethem sets this hard-boiled crime novel in his own native Brooklyn.

style that makes for originality and personality; quick, vivid and sympathetic; with an application that leaves the reader with a sense of gain, 'The Gift of the Magi,' told in common language, illustrates a unique and artistic type of the short story, founded partly on French models, but springing more truly from the virile life and thought of America." N. Bryllion Fagin, writing in 1923, called the story a "masterpiece." He pointed to the skill in Porter's telling of the tale: "it is the wizards' mechanics, his stunning invention—that's the thing! Della sells her hair and buys a fob for hubby's watch; while at the same time hubby sells his watch and buys her a comb. But you don't know all this until they get together for the presentation of the gifts, and then you gasp." Modern reviewers have also recognized the power of the story. Hazel Rochman, reviewing in *Booklist* a 1997 reprint of Porter's stories, described "The Gift of the Magi" as "one of the greatest Christmas stories of all time."

Responses to Literature

1. Porter's most famous story is "The Gift of the Magi," which features an optimistic and surprising ending, which is characteristic of much of his work. Read the story and have a discussion with other students about endings. What does it mean for a story's ending to be "satisfying"? What are some of your favorite endings in literature? Which have disappointed you, and why?

2. Porter's beloved *The Rolling Stone* (no relation to the modern music magazine) was eventually a major cause of his downfall and subsequent prison sentence. But, while it was in operation, he would fill eight pages a week with short stories, skits, and articles about local goings-on. In a group, write your own school's version of *The Rolling Stone*, and distribute it to your class.

3. The modern writer who works exclusively in short stories has a very difficult time publishing in America. Research the history of the short story in the United States and write a three-page paper explaining why you believe the publishing business is not more friendly to that particular form.

4. Though it was a humiliating time for him, Porter came into his own as a writer during his imprisonment. Research other writers who have spent time in jail (Oscar Wilde and Ezra Pound, for example) and write a paper about the effects of jail on artistic output.

5. Read several O. Henry short stories. Attempt to write a short story of your own in the style he made famous. The stock elements of Porter's stories include: (1) a brisk opening that pulls the reader into the action with a surefire hook; (2) a confiding narrator who, nonetheless, withholds crucial information until the last possible moment; (3) a pleasant and worldly wise tone comprised of chitchat, wit, satire, philosophy, and swank; (4) liberal use of a "humane renegade"; (5) a healthy dose of coincidence, usually with a *deus ex machina* reversal in which everything is rescued and set right again; and (6) a surprise ending.

BIBLIOGRAPHY

Books

Davis, Robert H., and Arthur B. Maurice. *The Caliph of Bagdad: Being Arabian Nights Flashes of the Life, Letters, and Work of O. Henry*. New York: Appleton, 1931.

Long, E. Hudson. *O. Henry: The Man and His Work*. Philadelphia: University of Pennsylvania Press, 1949.

Kramer, Dale. *The Heart of O. Henry*. New York: Rinehart, 1954.

Langford, Gerald. *Alias O. Henry: A Biography of William Sydney Porter*. New York: Macmillan, 1957.

Scofield, Martin. *The Cambridge Introduction to the American Short Story*. Cambridge: Cambridge University Press, 2006.

Periodicals

Fagin, N. Bryllion. "O' Henryism" in *Short Story-Writing; An Art or a Trade?* New York: Thomas Seltzer, 1923, pp. 29–47.

Law, Frederick Houk. "The Gift of the Magi," *The Independent*, (April 7, 1917): 76–81.

Rochman, Hazel. Review of *The Gift of the Magi and Other Stories. Booklist* Vol. 94, no. 4 (October 15, 1997): 397.

"Through the Shadows With O. Henry." *New York Times* (December 18, 1921).

Web Sites

O Henry Biography and Works. Retrieved December 10, 2008, from http://www.online-literature.com/o_henry/.

Bibliomania. Retrieved December 10, 2008, from http://www.bibliomania.com/0/5/221/frameset.html.

✳ Patrick Henry

BORN: *1736, Studley, Virginia*

DIED: *1799, Red Hill, Virginia*

NATIONALITY: *American*

GENRE: *Nonfiction*

MAJOR WORKS:

The "Parson's Cause" Speech (1763)

The Stamp Act Speech (1765)

The Bill of Rights (with additional authors) (1787)

Patrick Henry *AP Images*

Overview

Patrick Henry was a lawyer and statesman who used his rare ability for oratory to oppose English tyranny (real and imagined), to conduct a war for independence, and to proclaim and fight for the eternal and "unalienable" rights of humankind.

Works in Biographical and Historical Context

Education Through Experience As the second son of Colonel John and Sarah Henry, the future "Trumpet of the Revolution" was born into an assured position among the gentry of colonial Virginia. From his Scottish-born and educated father, Patrick Henry inherited independence of mind and spirit; from his aristocratic mother, he not only gained acceptance from the slave-owning, plantation-owning Virginia provincial aristocracy, but also seemed to have inherited an easygoing and pleasant disposition and demeanor.

During his formative years, there was little to indicate future greatness. His academic training was spotty and brief. Up to the age of ten, Patrick Henry attended a "common English school" where he learned to read and write. He also appeared to have acquired a basic knowledge of arithmetic. Thereafter he fell under the educational influence of his father from whom he acquired a limited knowledge of Latin, Greek, mathematics, and history (both modern and ancient). Unlike most of his compatriots, the young man did not acquire a mastery of the classics. Rather, his education, both formal and informal, was practical and pragmatic, designed to be a preparation for managing plantations in rural, western Virginia.

The decision to forgo college was dictated as much by a perceived need to learn a practical trade as it was that the family could not afford to send young Henry to the College of William and Mary, Harvard College, Yale College, or to England. Given his alleged "aversion to study," it seems fair to surmise that the fifteen-year-old son acquiesced in his father's decision to apprentice him out as a clerk in a nearby country store. During this year-long apprenticeship, he undoubtedly gained valuable knowledge regarding the real world away from a strict father and a well-connected, loving mother. In 1752, Colonel John Henry purchased the necessary goods to set up the young clerk and his older brother William in business for themselves. But the brothers' initial foray into the business world was a notable failure. They were both too generous in granting credit to untrustworthy friends and neighbors.

Endings and Beginnings In 1754, with few worldly possessions, Patrick Henry took a wife. Sixteen-year-old Sarah Shelton brought to this marriage respectability, three hundred acres of hard-scrabble farmland, and six black slaves. But Patrick Henry's career as a farmer lasted only a few years. In 1757, a fire destroyed his modest farm house and most of his tangible possessions, and the young couple was forced to move in with his wife's family. After a second storekeeping attempt ended in bankruptcy, the now destitute Henrys took up residence in his father-in-law's Hanover County tavern where Patrick earned his keep by working as a bartender.

In 1760, Henry took up the study of the law. Although seemingly ill-trained and ill-suited for a legal career, Henry would soon reveal those talents that would ensure success both at the bar and in the political arena of revolutionary Virginia. The 1760s were exciting years in which to be coming into manhood. The anti-British revolutionary movement in the thirteen mainland colonies provided ample opportunities for men of vision and ability to display their talents for legal advancement, political leadership, and, especially for Patrick Henry, effective oratory. Virginia in the 1760s was indeed the nursery of statesmen and distinguished barristers. George Washington, James Madison, James Monroe, and Thomas Jefferson all gained experience in the tumultuous political arena that was pre-revolutionary Virginia. In such eminent company, Patrick Henry would soon emerge as a leader both at the bar and in the House of Burgesses.

The Parson's Cause   It was the so-called "Parson's Cause" of 1763 that propelled Patrick Henry to legal and political prominence. This legal case resulted from a Virginia statute that regulated the salaries of Anglican ministers. By law, Anglican clerics were to be paid in tobacco. As a result of a crop-destroying drought in 1755, the colonial legislature commuted such pay into currency at the rate of two pence per pound of tobacco. Acting on petitions received from the Virginia clergy, the king and Privy Council in England disallowed or vetoed the Virginia act. After the act was repealed, several Virginian clergymen sued for back salary, because they had been paid less under the terms of the act. On December 1, 1763, Patrick Henry entered public life with an impassioned speech in which he argued convincingly that in disallowing a law passed by the Virginia legislature, the British Crown had broken the compact between the ruler and the ruled and had therefore forfeited "all rights to his subjects' obedience." Although the jury found in favor of the clergyman, they awarded him only one penny—a clear indication of the effectiveness of Henry's message.

The Stamp Act and Speaking Out   In 1765, during what is called the Stamp Act crisis, Henry gained additional fame as a champion of colonial rights. Lord George Grenville introduced the Stamp Act resolution in Parliament on February 6, 1765. A revenue-raising measure, it imposed taxes on a whole range of official and unofficial documents such as court papers and newspapers (including the advertisements contained therein). Elected to the House of Burgesses to fill a vacant seat, Henry introduced seven resolutions in opposition to the hated Stamp Act in late May. Although five of the resolutions were relatively moderate, two of the resolves claimed virtual legislative independence for the colony. Since contempo-

rary accounts of this oration, including a famous one written by Thomas Jefferson in 1814, differ significantly, it is not known with precision just what was said. However, what is known is that Henry's speech acted as a catalyst for colonial opposition to the Stamp Act and thrust him into a leadership role in the anti-British agitation of the late 1760s and early 1770s.

In part because of his speaking and persuasive skills, Patrick Henry was elected Virginia's first governor. His election appeared to represent a victory for the more radical faction. Under Henry's prodding, the Virginia legislature in 1774 appointed a seven-man delegation to attend the Continental Congress. Meeting in Philadelphia in September, this gathering represented the first successful attempt at colonial union. For the first time, Henry, overwhelmingly elected as a member of the Virginia delegation, would be working at the national level. Among the fifty-plus delegates would be many of the leaders of the revolutionary movement. As a radical, Patrick Henry would be joined by "a brace of Adamses" (John and Samuel) from Massachusetts, Christopher Gadsden from South Carolina, and fellow Virginian Richard Henry Lee. Henry and his radical allies were able to issue a call for yet another congress to meet in May of 1775 if American grievances had not been resolved.

It was in Virginia that Patrick Henry was to achieve the fame and successes now associated with his name. In March of 1775, as a member of the second session of the Virginia Convention, Henry gave his most famous speech, in which he concluded: "Give me liberty or give me death!" Everyone who heard his spirited defense of his three motions proposed to prepare the commonwealth for what he considered to be the inevitable armed conflict and who recorded their recollections all agreed that this oration was the most powerful, the most rousing, the most elegant ever heard among a learned gentry known for its forensic abilities. Interestingly, no copy of this well-known speech remains in existence.

While 1775 was full of opportunities for professional achievement, it was also fraught with personal conflicts. Henry's first marriage in 1754 to Sarah Shelton tragically ended that year when the mother of his first six children died insane. The exact nature of Sarah's malady is not known, but it is known that she was confined in a basement for her last few years, where she was cared for by a trusted female slave. Eventually, in 1778, the governor, then forty-two years old, married again, into the socially prominent Dandridge family. Dorothea Dandridge brought tranquility and respectability to the Henry household; she would ultimately be the mother of a family totaling eleven children.

The Bill of Rights   In 1787, long after the end of the American Revolution, Henry was a member of the Virginia convention considering ratification of the U.S. Constitution. He there led the anti-Federalist opposition to the Constitution because it created what he called a "consolidated government." Supported by such worthies as

Benjamin Harrison, George Mason, and James Monroe, Henry adopted the strategy of delay and attrition. The convention almost turned into a political battle between the flamboyant Patrick Henry for the anti-Federalists and the scholarly, self-effacing James Madison for the Federalists. Although the Constitution was finally ratified by a vote of 89 to 79, Henry and his followers (most notably George Mason) were responsible for securing assurances that a clear exposition of individual rights would be added after ratification. Thus, along with Mason (author of the Virginia Declaration of Rights) and Madison (who pushed the first ten amendments through the First Congress), Patrick Henry became one of the "fathers" of the Bill of Rights. All along, his opposition had been based primarily on the fact he deemed the lack of such a bill was dangerous to the liberties of the people. Although not a member of the First U.S. Congress, Henry greatly helped Madison's sponsorship of the first ten amendments.

The last few years of Henry's public career were an enigma. He openly opposed Secretary of the Treasury Alexander Hamilton's proposals for federal funding as being overly ambitious, nationalistic, and detrimental to his Virginia constituency. However, by the late 1790s, Henry had become a Federalist philosophically and a firm supporter of Federalist policies. His swing toward conservatism could have been either the natural tendency of politicians to become less radical in old age or the result of being openly courted by President Washington. In the space of a little over one year, the president offered the positions of secretary of state, envoy to Spain, and chief justice of the United States to the now retired former governor. In refusing these honors, Patrick claimed ill health and disinterest. As if to substantiate his high standing even in retirement, Henry was elected governor for the sixth time in 1796, but he refused to take office. In 1799, shortly before his own death, Washington was successful in persuading Henry to become a candidate for the state legislature. During this campaign, Patrick Henry in his last great speech forcefully denied a state's right to decide the constitutionality of national laws.

In a public career that spanned some twenty-five years, Henry exhibited extraordinary ability as an orator. But public service left Henry heavily in debt. Although he practiced law intermittently from 1760 to 1794, the first demand on his time was always his political career. In 1788, he resumed an active legal career prospering to such an extent that by his retirement in 1794, he had largely discharged his debts and built up a landed estate of some 22,000 acres. Interestingly, for the last few years of his life, this longtime champion of the downtrodden was among the largest landowners in all of Virginia.

Patrick Henry died on June 6, 1799, from what was probably stomach or intestinal cancer. His passing was greatly lamented and widely noted. In his obituary in the *Virginia Gazette*, Virginians bade goodbye with these simple, but heartfelt words: "Farewell, first-rate patriot, farewell!"

LITERARY AND HISTORICAL CONTEMPORARIES

Patrick Henry's famous contemporaries include:

Voltaire (1694–1778): French writer who contributed to the Enlightenment in Europe with his *Philosophical Dictionary* (1764), which heartily supported freedom of religion.

Benjamin Franklin (1706–1790): One of the most important Founding Fathers of the United States, Franklin was, along with Henry, partially responsible for the repeal of the Stamp Act.

George Washington (1732–1799): Leader of American forces during the Revolutionary War, first president of the United States, and an inspiration for Federalists.

John Adams (1735–1826): The second president of the United States and a major supporter of the Declaration of Independence.

Thomas Jefferson (1743–1826): The third president of the United States and the primary author of the Declaration of Independence.

Wolfgang Amadeus Mozart (1756–1791): Mozart was an Austrian composer whose musical compositions were viewed as both revolutionary and wildly popular.

Works in Literary Context

The Enlightenment The Enlightenment was an intellectual movement of the seventeenth and eighteenth centuries that began in Europe and spread to America in time for the Revolutionary War. Enlightenment ideas concerning God, reason, nature, and humankind were synthesized into a world view that gained wide assent and that instigated revolutionary developments in art, philosophy, and politics. Central to Enlightenment thought were the use and the celebration of reason, the power by which the individual understands the universe and improves the human condition. The goals of the rational individual were considered to be knowledge, freedom, and happiness.

The Power of the Colonial Press More than any other group in eighteenth-century America, printers were capable of having their opinions heard near and far. They controlled the volume and intensity of news coverage, and by working in conjunction with the Sons of Liberty, newspaper editors and pamphleteers instigated opposition to the Stamp Act and contributed to its repeal in 1766. Although the assembly endorsed only four of Henry's seven resolutions, local newspapers conveyed the impression it had passed all seven by printing Henry's proposals. Moreover, they reported Henry as making a fiery speech, including the statement, "In former times

COMMON HUMAN EXPERIENCE

Henry's Stamp Act speech and his contributions to the Bill of Rights were crucial in the formation of our country. Here are some other works that have contributed to revolution and change around the world.

The Magna Carta (1215). This document, written by a group of barons, declared that King John of England must, under penalty of law, grant certain rights to his subjects.

The Declaration of Independence (1776), the famous document written by Thomas Jefferson. The United States of America was in effect born with the promulgation of this declaration, which stated that the thirteen colonies were no longer part of Britain.

The Age of Reason (1793–94), a book by Thomas Paine. In this book, Paine argues against many Christian doctrines and promotes reliance on logic and reason instead of faith.

"I Have a Dream" (1963), a speech by Reverend Martin Luther King, Jr. With this seminal speech, given during the March on Washington, King defended the civil rights movement and became one of our nation's most respected speakers.

Tarquin and Julius had their Brutus, Charles had his Cromwell, and he did not doubt but some good American would stand up in favour of his Country."

Works in Critical Context

The Parson's Cause   Henry argued to the jury about natural rights and said that there was a conditional covenant between the King and his subjects. He told the jury that the 1758 act was a good law, enacted by the provincial assembly for a valid purpose. The compact between the king and the people, providing protection in exchange for obedience, did not allow such a law to be annulled. In fact, Henry said that the King, by annulling such an act "from being the Father of his people degenerated into a Tyrant, and forfeits all right to his subjects' Obedience . . . ." Henry went on to attack the clergy in general and Maury in particular in an inflammatory appeal to anticlerical prejudice. Clergymen were "rapacious harpies who would snatch from the hearth of their honest parishioner his last hoe-cake, from the widow and her orphan children their last milch cow, the last blanket, nay, the last blanket from the lying-in woman." Then tying together the two threads of his argument, he urged the jurors to "make such an example of the plaintiff, as might hereafter be a warning . . . not to dispute the validity of such laws, authenticated by the only authority which . . . would give force to laws for the government of the colony." Henry spoke for more than an hour. The jury retired and returned almost immediately with a verdict for the plaintiff of one penny; at that moment Henry became a leader in the struggle that led to the Revolution.

Responses to Literature

1. Patrick Henry is often regarded as an example of an Enlightenment thinker. Using the library or the Internet, research the philosophical movement known as the Enlightenment. What are its basic principles? Who was involved in the movement? Do you think the principles of the Enlightenment are alive and well today? Explain.

2. Henry was instrumental in getting the newly established United States government to acknowledge certain basic rights for its citizens. However, these rights were not granted to all citizens. Indeed, Henry—like many other Founding Fathers—kept slaves, and few supported a woman's right to vote. In your opinion, does this weaken the message of the Founding Fathers, or does it provide a goal that was simply beyond their reach within their lifetimes? Explain your position.

3. "Give me liberty or give me death" is an example of a rhetorical device called a chiasmus. Using the library or the Internet, look up this term. Why do you think this linguistic pattern is effective? Can you find other examples of this device?

4. Do you think Henry's lack of a classical education negatively affected his speeches? Why or why not?

BIBLIOGRAPHY

Books

Beeman, Richard R. *Patrick Henry: A Biography.* New York: McGraw-Hill, 1974.

Gipson, Lawrence Henry. *The Coming of the Revolution, 1763–1775.* New York: Harper, 1954.

Mayer, Henry. *A Son of Thunder.* New York: Franklin Watts, 1986.

Meade, Robert Douthat. *Patrick Henry: Patriot in the Making.* Philadelphia: Lippincott, 1957.

Tyler, Moses Coit. *Patrick Henry.* Boston: Houghton, 1887.

Wirt, William. *Sketches of the Life and Character of Patrick Henry.* Ithaca, N.Y.: Mack, Andrus, 1817.

✹ John Hersey

BORN: *1914, Tientsin, China*

DIED: *1993, Key West, Florida*

NATIONALITY: *American*

GENRE: *Fiction, nonfiction*

MAJOR WORKS:

A Bell for Adano (1944)

Hiroshima (1946)

The Wall (1950)

John Hersey   *Hersey, John, photograph. AP Images.*

Overview

John Hersey, the author of more than a dozen novels as well as many sketches, commentaries, articles, and essays, has a well-earned reputation as one of America's most important novelists of the post–World War II period, but it is his work as a journalist that is his most significant legacy to American literature of the second half of the twentieth century. In particular, his nonfiction account of the atomic bombing of Hiroshima in 1945, which awakened America to the human consequences of nuclear warfare, is significant both as a literary accomplishment and as a cultural event. *Hiroshima*, first published in August 1946 and reissued in 1985 with an update on the fates of its characters, is often cited as a seminal example of the nonfiction novel in America.

Works in Biographical and Historical Context

A Missionary Child   Born on June 17, 1914, to Presbyterian missionaries Roscoe and Grace Baird Hersey in Tientsin, China, John Richard Hersey lived there until 1924, when the family returned to the United States. He and his two brothers were educated in public and private schools, and Hersey graduated from Yale with a combined major in history, arts, and letters in 1936. Hersey then studied eighteenth-century literature at Cambridge

University in England until 1937, when he worked for a summer as secretary to author Sinclair Lewis. That same year, Hersey accepted a job at *Time*. Hersey married Frances Ann Cannon on April 27, 1940; the couple had four children, Martin, John, Ann, and Baird.

Life during Wartime   As a reporter during World War II for *Time* and *Life*, Hersey covered events in China, the South Pacific, the Mediterranean Theater, and Moscow. Hersey used his experiences in Italy as the basis for his novel *A Bell for Adano* (1944), which tells of an American officer who, during the Allied occupation of Italy and subsequent battle against its fascist government, secures a new bell for a small coastal town that had its seven-hundred-year-old bell melted down by fascists to make bullets. The book, published while World War II was still raging, won the Pulitzer Prize in 1945.

Hersey first encountered the Warsaw ghetto when he was working in Eastern Europe after the liberation. After Hitler and his Nazi troops had seized control of Warsaw during World War II, they forcibly relocated all the Jews in the city to a small, secure neighborhood called the Ghetto. Many Jews went willingly, believing it would be an inconvenient but ultimately safe haven where they would be kept alive. Once inside, Jews were walled off from the rest of the city and put under armed guard; they were given very little food, resulting in massive starvation. When the Nazis began clearing the Ghetto by transporting Jews to nearby concentration camps—where they faced almost certain death—a group of remaining Ghetto Jews decided to fight back against the Nazi guards. Their armed resistance was defeated within months, and afterward the Nazis destroyed the Ghetto completely.

Hersey visited Warsaw in 1945, where the leveled ghetto received little notice, then continued on to Rodogoszecz (a camp for Aryan Polish prisoners) and Lodz. The enormity of the slaughter became his subject for *The Wall* (1950): "I knew that…I would have to try, at least, to pass on to American readers some of the sorts of things my eyes had seen and my ears had heard," he stated in a 1989 lecture at Baltimore Hebrew University.

Between Hersey's awakening to the Holocaust in the winter of 1945 and the publication of *The Wall*, a deepened awareness of being a witness to history altered his consciousness as well as his reputation. On assignment in China and Japan in September 1945, Hersey interviewed people who had been damaged by the bombing of Hiroshima. Using Thornton Wilder's *The Bridge of San Luis Rey* (1927) as a model, the reporter reconstructed the stories of six people and allowed their points of view to make a strong statement. First published in *The New Yorker* on August 31, 1946, *Hiroshima* has been recognized as a literary breakthrough—a means of recording history while acknowledging the personal nature of testimony and chronicling.

Facts into Fiction   *The Black Book of Polish Jewry*, edited by Jacob Apenszlak, had been published in New York in

LITERARY AND HISTORICAL CONTEMPORARIES

Hersey's famous contemporaries include:

Henry Luce (1898–1967): Founder of *Time* and *Life* magazines, and one of the greatest American publishers.

Adlai Stevenson (1900–1965): Liberal Democrat and friend of Hersey's who ran for president against Dwight Eisenhower in the 1950s.

John Steinbeck (1902–1968): American novelist famous for his epic chronicle of the Great Depression, *The Grapes of Wrath* (1940).

Elie Wiesel (1928–): As a Holocaust survivor and writer, Wiesel is one of the most famous chroniclers of World War II and won the Nobel Peace Prize in 1986.

1943, and when he discovered it, Hersey read this source as he began to prepare for writing a novel about what he had learned in Europe in 1945. He cast about for a way to write about Auschwitz, but Warsaw haunted his imagination. He saw there the story he wanted to tell, because he thought the 1944 ghetto uprising there constituted an incredible moment in history.

Early in his work on *The Wall*, Hersey identified an important cache of documentary materials, all in Polish or Yiddish, archived in New York. A friend helped him locate translators through YIVO, the Yiddish Scientific Institute. As they made recordings of their oral translations, they paused to comment on materials, using various intonations and emphases based on their personal knowledge and emotion. Listening over and over to these transcriptions, Hersey immersed himself in the Warsaw Ghetto.

After a year and a half, Hersey began a draft of a novel that employed a universal, third-person point of view. He interspersed the narrative with comments by one of more than fifty characters he invented, a Judenrat (Jewish Council) official who evolved into the ghetto historian, Noach Levinson. With 1,276 longhand pages written by late 1948, Hersey decided his writing was not worthy of his subject. In order to continue, Hersey had to "invent a memory." His entries focus on three families: the Bersons, the Apts, and the Mazurs. This strategy allowed the presentation of religious themes, assimilation issues, and complex family loyalties and betrayals.

Suppressing The Wall *The Wall* enabled Americans and Germans to learn about the Warsaw Ghetto and the resistance movement. The novel was not, however, circulated in Poland. Its suppression there is similar to the case of *Hiroshima*, which was not known in Japan even though it alerted Americans and others to dangers of atomic war. The earliest responses to *The Wall* situate the work more in the realm of morality than in literary history. The category of Holocaust literature was not yet formulated when Hersey wrote the story. Yet, even as a growing number of critics began describing such artistic work, they tended to be silent about this account of the Warsaw ghetto and the uprising against the Nazis. Another strand of criticism endorses the idea that only survivors could begin to tell the horror, and the preemption of the experience by nonvictims, especially non-Jews, constitutes further persecution. Thus, many books about Holocaust literature pass over Hersey's name.

As a journalist and novelist, Hersey created a role as a political writer and witness to contemporary events. Beginning in 1948, Hersey held memberships in the Authors' League of America, PEN, and other writers' organizations, where he often took leadership positions that articulated the public responsibility of writers and the harmful effects of censorship. He worked in the presidential campaign of Adlai Stevenson, helping to shape the candidate's 1956 speech that advocated a nuclear test ban. He read from his nonfiction narrative *Hiroshima* at the White House Arts Festival on June 2, 1965, published an account of war protests at Yale in the spring of 1970, and took public advocacy positions about racism, education, and foreign policy. From 1965 until his retirement in 1984, he taught writing at Yale. In all, he produced fourteen novels, many short stories, and journalism that included commentary on the Detroit race riots, radical student movements, and public education. He continued other writing projects in retirement until his death from cancer on March 24, 1993.

Works in Literary Context

Relatable Realism Relying mainly on the fictional historian Levinson and other narrative voices, the novel *The Wall* uses techniques of literary and documentary realism to engage the reader. When writing *Hiroshima*, in addition to locating figures who adequately symbolized the reality of the atomic bomb blast, Hersey was faced with the task of translating Japanese culture into a vocabulary familiar to Western sensibilities. He does this by choosing as settings for the book institutions common to both Japanese and American cultures: churches, banks, a police station, a lower-middle-class home, hospitals, and doctors' offices. Whenever possible, Hersey describes Japanese life by using terms familiar to Americans: Hiroshima's outlying residential districts, for example, are referred to as "suburbs." The city of Hiroshima thereby assumes a quality of everyday life that American readers may associate with their own lives.

Political Accuracy In many of his books, Hersey records events chronologically. In *The President* (1975), he provides actual clock times to mark the occurrence of incidents, both large and small, meetings with visiting heads of state, a reception for the Cotton Queen, the entrance of staff members into the Oval Office, departures for luncheons and official events, even early morning exercise routines and dental appointments. As in all of his literary journalism, Hersey's concern is with the immediacy of human experience. Thus, readers learn not only when the president eats lunch each day but also what he has: a scoop of cottage cheese topped with A-1 Steak Sauce, followed by a small dish of butter pecan ice cream. While such details help to humanize the president, Hersey also reports on more significant events, including high-level discussions involving the military situation in Cambodia, agricultural price supports, and civil rights legislation. Discussions with presidential advisers, including Henry Kissinger, Donald Rumsfeld, and Brent Scowcroft, are transcribed, largely without comment or interpretation.

Works in Critical Context

"Hersey is an impressive figure in contemporary American letters," writes Nancy L. Huse in her study *The Survival Tales of John Hersey*. Huse finds in Hersey's work "a mind rebelling at the age's acceptance of nuclear weapons, the Holocaust, racism, and the annihilation of the individual in a technological society." This attitude "places Hersey as an intellectual contemporary of Bellow, Wright, Mailer and Agee," Huse argues. Jonathan Yardley of the *Washington Post Book World* finds that "Hersey's decency is both transparent and transcendent. He cares about matters that deserve to be cared about, and he writes about them with palpable passion."

The Wall   Hersey's novel *The Wall* still stands as one of the few books that has been able to relate in human terms the destruction of European Jews by the Nazis. However, he has been ignored by most literary scholars while others such as Leslie Fiedler have accused him of naively believing that problems such as racism have simple solutions. Hersey himself suggested a reason for his lack of critical attention: "Leaving the issue of quality, or lack of it, aside for the moment, one fundamental reason, I would guess, is that I have always written against the grain, both of literary fashion and of establishment values." In contrast to more avant-garde writers, Hersey dedicated himself to the goal of chronicling the events and issues of his time ranging from World War II itself, the atomic bomb, and the Holocaust to the dominant social issues of the postwar decades such as racism, overpopulation, education, the generation gap, the attack on democratic institutions, and, more generally, the malaise of modern life.

Hiroshima   Hersey's *Hiroshima* is a modern classic partly because it incorporates so well the techniques and style of the novel within a work of journalism. Thus, in this book Hersey anticipates what later critics and writers celebrated as the new mode of the nonfiction novel, a term Hersey himself disdains. When the work first appeared as the entire August 31, 1946, issue of the *New Yorker* magazine, its impact was instantaneous and unprecedented. Charles Poore of the *New York Times* noted that "Talking to people in that week, listening to the commentators on the air, reading the editorials and the columnists, you soon

---

COMMON HUMAN EXPERIENCE

Hersey is known for his clear, precise writing, which was largely influenced by his experience working for newspapers. Here are some other works that have a strong historical or political basis:

War and Peace (1865–1869), a novel by Leo Tolstoy. This work about Napoleon's invasion of Russia in the early 1800s is one of the most revered texts in Western literature, noted mainly for its historical accuracy and the use of real people as characters.

A Farewell to Arms (1929), a novel by Ernest Hemingway. Hemingway's efforts in World War I influence this story of Lieutenant Frederic Henry and his time on the Italian front.

The Grapes of Wrath (1940), a novel by John Steinbeck. This novel chronicles the plight of the Joad family as they lose their family farm and travel to California, like many Americans did during the Great Depression.

Night (1958), a memoir by Elie Wiesel. Though this book is a memoir of Wiesel's personal Holocaust experience, its stylistic, beautiful language reads like a novel.

---

realized what a profound impression the story had already made." When *Hiroshima* appeared in book form, Albert Einstein ordered one thousand copies of it, and Bernard Baruch ordered five hundred. Free copies were distributed by the Book-of-the-Month Club on the grounds that nothing else in print "could be of more importance at this moment to the human race."

Responses to Literature

1. What would you choose to write a historical novel about, if you could? Would you be as factual as Hersey, or would you rely more upon your imagination?

2. Find examples of how Hersey altered his depictions of Japanese culture to fit with American readers in *Hiroshima*.

3. Do you think, as some critics do about *The Wall*, that work about the Holocaust should be written only by its victims? Why or why not?

4. Find some examples in Hersey's works of his political views. What are they? How does he get his views across, when his writing is fairly objective? Do you think this diminishes the factual worth of his journalism?

BIBLIOGRAPHY

Books

Ezrahi, Sidra DeKoven. *By Words Alone: The Holocaust in Literature*. Chicago: University of Chicago Press, 1980, pp. 33–36.

Huse, Nancy Lyman. *John Hersey and James Agee: A Reference Guide.* Boston: G. K. Hall, 1978.
———. *The Survival Tales of John Hersey.* Troy, N.Y.: Whitston, 1983.
Kazin, Alfred. *Bright Book of Life: American Novelists and Storytellers from Hemingway to Mailer.* Boston: Little, Brown, 1971.
Sanders, David. *John Hersey Revisited.* Boston: Twayne, 1991.

Periodicals

Daiches, David. "Record and Testament." *Commentary* 9 (April 1950): 385–388.
Foley, Barbara. "Fact, Fiction, Fascism: Testimony and Mimesis in Holocaust Narratives." *Comparative Literature* 34 (1982): 330–360.
Sollers, Werner. "Holocaust and Hiroshima: American Ethnic Prose Writers Face the Extreme." *PMLA* 118, no. 1 (2003): 56–61.

⊛ Patricia Highsmith

BORN: *1921, Fort Worth, Texas*

DIED: *1995, Locarno, Switzerland*

NATIONALITY: *American*

GENRE: *Fiction*

MAJOR WORKS:
Strangers on a Train (1950)
The Talented Mr. Ripley (1955)
Ripley's Game (1974)

Overview

An American-born author who resided in Europe for most of her adult years, Highsmith is best known for her suspense novels, which challenge many of the conventions of the genre. She avoided gimmicks and formulaic plots, concentrating on developing the motivations behind criminal behavior rather than on apprehending the villain. The presence or absence of guilt for one's actions dominates Highsmith's fiction, and often the innocent characters suffer more than the guilty. Critics generally agree that Highsmith's subtle, restrained style emphasizes her premise that anyone is capable of murder.

Works in Biographical and Historical Context

Childhood Moves Highsmith was born Mary Patricia Plangman in Fort Worth, Texas, on January 19, 1921, the only child of Jay Bernard Plangman, a graphic artist, and Mary Coates Plangman, an illustrator and fashion designer. Patricia's parents divorced five months before her birth, and she was raised with her cousin Dan Coates by her maternal grandparents in Fort Worth. She did not meet her father until she was twelve years old, and even though she found

Patricia Highsmith   *Patricia Highsmith, 1990, photograph. Horst Tappe / Hulton Archive / Getty Images.*

him likable, they had nothing to say to each other. In 1925 Patricia's mother married Stanley Highsmith, an advertising illustrator, and the family moved to New York City two years later. Patricia Highsmith recalled in a 1979 interview with Noelle Loriot the trauma she suffered because of the move: "Something went to pieces in me when I left my grandmother. I completely withdrew into myself." Stanley Highsmith did not officially adopt his stepdaughter, but her mother registered her as Patricia Highsmith when she enrolled her in elementary school. Patricia later decided to keep the name as a tribute to this extremely patient and upright man.

New York Stories While she liked her stepfather, Highsmith did not love her mother and, as she revealed to Loriot, blamed the failure of her second marriage on her mother's quarrelsomeness and selfishness: "Why don't I love my mother? First, because she turned my childhood into a little hell. Second, because she herself never loved anyone, neither my father, my stepfather, nor me." Her feeling that she was unloved and unwanted was confirmed when her mother confessed that, while she was pregnant with Highsmith, she had unsuccessfully tried to induce abortion by drinking turpentine.

In an attempt to escape the frequent quarrels that she was forced to witness in the cramped two-room apartment in Greenwich Village, Highsmith immersed herself in the works of Fyodor Dostoyevsky, Charles Dickens, Henry James, Edgar Allan Poe, Robert Louis Stevenson, Hugh Walpole, and T. S. Eliot. She was also fascinated by Karl Menninger's *The Human Mind* (1930), a book including case studies of kleptomaniacs, pyromaniacs, and serial killers, because she realized that the man, woman, or child next door could be strange even while appearing normal and that anybody one met on the street could be a kleptomaniac, a sadist, or even a murderer.

Upon graduating from college in 1942, Highsmith moved into a room of her own on Sixtieth Street in Manhattan and eked out a living by composing text for comic strips such as *Superman* and *Batman*. She wrote short stories and immersed herself in the bohemian life of Greenwich Village, meeting Truman Capote, Paul and Jane Bowles, and Carson McCullers. In 1943 she spent five months in Taxco, Mexico, where she worked on an unfinished novel titled *The Click of the Shutting* and considered becoming a professional painter. The novel revolves around the relationship between two New York boys, prefiguring the pattern Highsmith later followed in many of her works.

Murder Most Interesting Highsmith's first novel, *Strangers on a Train* (1950), set the tone for her subsequent work. In this novel, Highsmith brings together two unhappy men who, although opposites in many ways, are drawn into a web of murder and betrayal. The financial success of her first two novels enabled Highsmith—who had visited England, France, and Italy briefly in 1949—to begin a European sojourn in 1952 that lasted more than two years. She traveled in the footsteps of her literary idol, Henry James, from London to Paris, Munich, Salzburg, Trieste, and Florence. In the southern Italian town of Positano she rented a house and, watching a young, possibly American man walk along the deserted beach one morning lost in thought, she was inspired to invent a story about a young American vagabond who is sent to Europe with the mission to convince another American to return to the States. After returning to the United States at the beginning of 1954, Highsmith moved into a cottage near Lenox, Massachusetts, where she began writing the first in a series of five adventures featuring her best-known creation, Tom Ripley.

Life and Death Abroad After Highsmith settled in Europe permanently in 1963, she only grudgingly promoted her books and avoided book signing tours and readings as much as possible. Even though she granted interviews, she ferociously protected her privacy and deliberately shocked her interviewers with such outrageous statements as her 1976 assertion to Peter Ruedi: "If I saw a kitten and a little human baby starving in the street, I would feed the kitten provided no one saw me." Otto Penzler, one of Highsmith's American publishers, attested to her abrasive personality in a quote for *Entertainment Weekly*: "She was a mean, cruel, hard, unlovable, unloving human being. I could never penetrate how any human being could be that relentlessly ugly. . . . But her books? Brilliant."

LITERARY AND HISTORICAL CONTEMPORARIES

Highsmith's famous contemporaries include:

Lyndon B. Johnson (1908–1973): Johnson, a Texan like Highsmith, was vice president of the United States from 1961 to 1963, under President John F. Kennedy. He became president when Kennedy was assassinated in 1963, and won the 1964 presidential election in a landslide. His administration was notable for its passage of the Civil Rights Act of 1964 and the Voting Rights Act of 1965, both landmarks in the struggle for civil rights in America. He was criticized for his escalation of U.S. military involvement in the Vietnam War.

Gertrude Stein (1874–1946): Stein was an American writer who, like Highsmith, lived abroad for much of her life and explored similar themes of homosexuality in her works.

Raymond Chandler (1888–1959): While Highsmith excelled in mystery novels where the sympathies lie with the killer, Chandler is famous for creating Philip Marlowe, a charming detective.

Arthur Koestler (1905–1983): A friend of Highsmith's who is most famous for his novel *Darkness at Noon* (1940) and his anti-Stalinist stance.

Truman Capote (1924–1984): Capote encouraged Highsmith to work on her first novel and was himself a famous New York writer and socialite.

In the last ten years of Highsmith's life her literary output dwindled considerably, and the writer isolated herself more and more. In 1982 she moved from France to Switzerland, first settling in Aurigeno and then in Tegna, where she withdrew into a house that she had built according to her own designs. The home resembled a bunker: situated at the foot of the Alps, it kept the world at bay. In 1990 Highsmith was honored by the French government when she was named Officer of the Order of Arts and Letters, and in 1991 she was nominated for the Nobel Prize in Literature. The same year she published *Ripley Under Water* (1991), the last novel of the cycle, in which Ripley is the victim of a meddlesome American couple.

Highsmith died in a Locarno hospital on February 4, 1995, of cancer, and her ashes were interred in Tegna on March 11. Her legacy lives on through her books and their movie adaptations, and critic Ed Siegel, writing in the *Boston Globe*, believes that changes in American society have contributed to the reassessment of Highsmith's importance: "In the wake of September 11, Highsmith's world is not only more like ours, where crime and punishment or cause and effect don't necessarily go hand in hand, she seems a more important writer than ever."

COMMON HUMAN EXPERIENCE

Highsmith is known for her grisly and cold portrayal of murders and murderers. Here are some other works that explore the different motives of the criminal mind:

The Big Sleep (1939), a novel by Raymond Chandler. This novel is the first to introduce Philip Marlowe, one of the most famous detectives in all of literature.

Psycho (1960), a film by Alfred Hitchcock. Norman Bates, a disturbed motel owner, is much more than he seems in this classic film noir thriller.

Silence of the Lambs (1988), a novel by Thomas Harris. This sequel to the serial-killer thriller *Red Dragon* (1981) features the memorable Dr. Hannibal "The Cannibal" Lecter as the unlikely ally of a fledgling FBI agent trying to stop a string of grisly murders.

The Executioner's Song (1980), a novel by Norman Mailer. This nonfiction novel, which won the Pulitzer Prize, offers a complex portrayal of convicted killer Garry Gilmore, the first person executed in the United States after the death penalty was reinstated by the Supreme Court in 1976.

Works in Literary Context

The Meeting *Strangers on a Train* established a pattern that recurs, with variations, in many of Highsmith's works. In her book *Plotting and Writing Suspense Fiction* (1966), Highsmith describes this motif: "The theme I have used over and over again in my novels is the relationship between two men, usually quite different in make-up, sometimes an obvious contrast in good and evil, sometimes merely ill-matched friends." Much of her writing is about this often symbiotic relationship that develops between two people (almost always men) who are at the same time fascinated and repelled by each other.

Guilt and Pleasures Highsmith's preoccupations with guilt and contrasting personalities surfaced as early as her very first novel. *Strangers on a Train* chronicles the relationship between Guy Haines, a successful young architect, and Charles Bruno, a charming but unstable man slightly younger than Haines. The two men first meet on a train journey when Bruno repeatedly tries to engage his traveling companion in conversation. They discuss troublesome relationships and speculate on striking a deal: Bruno will kill Haines's wife for him, and Haines in turn will kill Bruno's father. Since there is no connection between the victims and their killers, Bruno theorizes, the police will be at a loss to solve the murders. Haines dismisses the plan as mere fantasy, but Bruno takes their bargain seriously and proceeds to carry out his part. This type of cold-blooded killing recurs in the Ripley novels, where the title character is cool and calculating about his crimes.

Works in Critical Context

The art in Highsmith's work springs from her skillful fusion of plot, characterization, and style, with the crime story serving primarily "as a means of revealing and examining her own deepest interests and obsessions," according to a *Times Literary Supplement* reviewer. Highsmith's works therefore "dig down very deeply into the roots of personality," says Julian Symons in the *London Magazine*, exposing the dark side of people regarded by society as normal and good. Or, as Thomas Sutcliffe explains in the *Times Literary Supplement*, Highsmith wrote "not about what it feels like to be mad, but what it feels like to remain sane while committing the actions of a madman."

The Talented Mr. Ripley In Highsmith's best-known and arguably most accomplished novel, *The Talented Mr. Ripley*, the "criminal-hero," as she calls him in *Plotting and Writing Suspense Fiction*, receives no punishment for his misdeeds. A reviewer for the *New Yorker* called the novel "remarkably immoral" and its protagonist "one of the most repellent and fascinating characters." Craig Brown stated in the *Times Literary Supplement*: "it is a rare villain or psychopath whom the reader does not find himself willing toward freedom, a rare investigator or victim (sometimes the one becomes the other) whom the reader is unhappy to see dead."

Responses to Literature

1. Why do you think readers root for Ripley even though he is a killer? Is it because those around him seem even more morally corrupt? Explain your views in a short essay.

2. Stereotypically, murder novels are a male-dominated genre. Highsmith managed to be just as successful as most male authors. Is there any indication in her writing that she is a woman? Why do you think crime novels were primarily written by men? Do you think this is still true today?

3. Bruno and Haines from *Strangers on a Train* are often considered to be doppelgangers. Look up the term and decide whether or not you agree, then find other examples of doppelgangers in literature.

4. Highsmith was often described as antisocial and mean. Do you think a writer's personality and character is inevitably reflected in his or her writing? If so, how is Highsmith's personality revealed in her books?

BIBLIOGRAPHY

Books

Bronski, Michael. "Patricia Highsmith." In *The Gay and Lesbian Literary Companion*. Edited by Sharon Malinowski and Christa Brelin. Detroit: Visible Ink, 1995, pp. 253–258.

Brophy, Brigid. "Highsmith." In *Don't Never Forget: Collected Views and Reviews*. New York: Holt, Rinehart & Winston, 1967, pp. 149–155.

Cavigelli, Franz, Fritz Senn, and Anna von Planta, eds. *Patricia Highsmith: Leben und Werk*. Rev. and enlarged edition. Zurich, Switzerland: Diogenes, 1996.

Harrison, Russell. *Patricia Highsmith*. New York: Twayne, 1997.

Symons, Julian. *Mortal Consequences: A History—From the Detective Story to the Crime Novel*. New York: Harper & Row, 1972.

Wilson, Andrew. *Beautiful Shadow: A Life of Patricia Highsmith*. New York and London: Bloomsbury, 2003.

Periodicals

Tuss, Alex. "Masculine Identity and Success: A Critical Analysis of Patricia Highsmith's *The Talented Mr. Ripley* and Chuck Palahniuk's *Fight Club*." *Journal of Men's Studies* 12 (Winter 2004): 93–102.

✺ Tony Hillerman

BORN: *1925, Oklahoma*

NATIONALITY: *American*

GENRE: *Fiction*

MAJOR WORKS:
The Blessing Way (1970)
Dance Hall of the Dead (1973)
Coyote Waits (1990)

Overview

Tony Hillerman is primarily known for his mystery novels set in the Navajo country of the American Southwest. From *The Blessing Way* (1970) to *Sacred Clowns* (1993), a generation of readers has enjoyed getting to know Jim Chee and Joe Leaphorn, the protagonists of most of Hillerman's thirteen detective novels and stories. Educated at universities but cognizant of Navajo customs,

Tony Hillerman   *Hillerman, Tony, photograph. AP Images.*

the two protagonists show sharp contrasts between the majority and minority cultures of the Southwest. Constantly mediating between Native American groups and numerous white law enforcement agencies, Leaphorn and Chee solve mysteries through a judicious blend of logic and nature-oriented metaphysics.

Works in Biographical and Historical Context

An Education Among Native Americans Anthony Grove Hillerman was born in Sacred Heart, Oklahoma, on May 27, 1925, the youngest child of August Alfred and Lucy Grove Hillerman. His father taught at a one-room school in rural Texas and then was a farmer, cowboy, farrier, and storekeeper. His mother was a homemaker. Between 1930 and 1938, Tony, his brother Barney, and sister Mary Margaret were among a handful of white children attending St. Mary's Academy, a boarding school for Native Americans in Sacred Heart. In *Seldom Disappointed: A Memoir* (2001), Hillerman says of his childhood: "Everybody was poor and when you're a kid you don't know you're deprived unless you see someone who isn't." He grew up with children of the Potawatomi and Seminole tribes as playmates and said the experience permitted him to feel comfortable among Native Americans.

A Soldier's Struggle and Return Beginning in 1939, Hillerman attended Konawa (Oklahoma) High School, graduating in 1942. He spent one semester at Oklahoma Agricultural & Mechanical College in 1942, working as a dishwasher and ditch digger to pay tuition and expenses. In 1943, his mother, whom he credits with teaching him to seek adventure and never to whine or be afraid, consented to his enlisting in the army to serve in World War II. He went to France in 1944 as a mortar gunner in the 410th Infantry Regiment, seeing combat in the Ardennes during the Battle of the Bulge and receiving a Silver Star and a Bronze Star with Oak Leaf Cluster. In 1945, he stepped on a landmine and was temporarily blinded, and suffered broken legs and severe burns. He received the Purple Heart.

After five months of hospitalization in France, Hillerman was returned to the United States. While still on convalescent leave from the army in 1945, he took a job transporting oil-field equipment. On one trip to the Navajo Reservation, he observed an Enemy Way curing ceremony for Navajos who had served in the marines. The purpose of the ceremony was to cure them of the evil influences they had encountered in seeing death in the war and to restore them to harmony with the Navajo people. It sparked his interest in learning more about the tribe.

In 1946, Hillerman enrolled at the University of Oklahoma under the G.I. Bill, majoring in journalism. While there, he met Marie Unzner, a fellow student, from Shawnee, Oklahoma. The couple married in 1948, the year Hillerman graduated with a B.A. degree, and have raised six children, five of whom were adopted.

Finding a Character Hillerman had long wanted to write fiction, and in the late 1960s, despite the pressures of supporting a large family, he was encouraged to do so by his wife. He began working on a novel. Hillerman enjoyed mystery fiction and had been impressed by Arthur W. Upfield, who created a part-Aborigine Australian police detective who often solves cases in his country's outback, using his knowledge of native culture and his ability to track and interpret physical clues. Hillerman decided to set his mysteries among the Navajos, whose reservation covers more than sixteen million acres in the "four corners" area where New Mexico, Arizona, Utah, and Colorado abut.

Hillerman introduced Joe Leaphorn, a lieutenant in the Navajo Tribal Police, in his first novel, *The Blessing Way* (1970). In the initial draft of this book, a white anthropology professor, Bergen McKee, plays a larger role than Leaphorn. In his memoir, Hillerman recalls that his agent, Ann Elmo, recommended that he "Get rid of the Indian stuff." The editor at Harper and Row, Joan Kahn, to whom Hillerman then submitted the manuscript directly, liked it and advised him to increase the amount of the book devoted to Leaphorn and Navajo culture.

Hillerman returned to the Navajo Reservation and Joe Leaphorn with *Dance Hall of the Dead* (1973), a novel in which he also explores the culture of the Zuni tribe. Hillerman earned his third straight Edgar nomination from the Mystery Writers of America for this book, and this time won the prize for best novel. H. R. F. Keating, critic and mystery writer, included *Dance Hall of the Dead* in *Crime and Mystery: The 100 Best Books* (1987).

Five years passed before Hillerman's next mystery appeared, but during the interim, he published much nonfiction. *The Great Taos Bank Robbery and Other Indian Country Affairs* (1973) is a collection of essays Hillerman wrote regarding the various cultures of New Mexico. The title essay about Taos and its clumsy criminals is regarded as Hillerman's funniest writing.

Hollywood Visions Hillerman's experience with Hollywood became legendary when in 1990 he agreed with Robert Redford to make a movie of his novel *The Dark Wind*. Their original discussion has become part of Hillerman lore, as he refused Redford's offer of sending a private airplane to Albuquerque to bring him to Redford's retreat in the Utah mountains because the invitation clashed with Hillerman's weekly poker game. The two men did eventually meet and toured the reservation together, but the movie, made in 1991, was a disappointment. Additional filmed adaptations have been made for public television, including *Skinwalkers* (2002) and *Coyote Waits* (2003).

In addition to regularly producing novels that are bestsellers, Tony Hillerman has become arguably the most interviewed and written-about mystery writer in America since 1970. Part of the reason may be that his books explore social problems through their depiction of a native culture previously unrepresented in crime fiction. It is no wonder that Hillerman has won awards for best western as well as best mystery: readers emerge from his tales with a deep sense of the character of the Southwest and of the convergence of landscape, history, and cultures that shape the detective plots, characters, and themes of his mysteries.

Works in Literary Context

Cross-Cultural Contemporary Issues Hillerman's journalistic background informs all of his writing; critics have widely noted how Hillerman's detective plots resonate with contemporary events and issues. In an interview with Ernie Bulow published in *Words, Weather, and Wolfmen* (1989), Hillerman comments:

> It's very important to me that the stories seem realistic. They seem [to be] about people who could really be people and things that could really happen. I'm writing about the reality, and frequently the headlines happen after the book is started, or long finished.

The reality to which Hillerman addresses himself is often the Native American cultures of the Southwest. From his plots, which often center on Native American tradition, legends, and rituals, to his characterizations of Navajo detectives Jim Chee and Joe Leaphorn, who struggle to reconcile their Navajo heritage with their Anglo education and U. S. government jobs, Hillerman's fiction is valuable for its portrayal of true cross-cultural perspectives. Many readers have compared Hillerman's mysteries to ethnographies, as they provide a fictional window into the cultural and political issues of contemporary Navajo life.

Writing the Land Critics praise Hillerman's infusion of Southwestern landscapes into his fiction and nonfiction writing. Essays such as *New Mexico, Rio Grande*, and the pictorial essay *Indian Country: America's Sacred Land* incorporate a sense of place and regional identity directly, but Hillerman's detective fiction also depends on a deep knowledge of Southwestern landscapes. "For some reason when I'm writing it's essential for me to have in my mind a memory of the landscape, the place where that chapter's action is to take place," he told Bulow. Like the Southwest wind, Hillerman's fiction sweeps across the vastness, rich textures and colors, and desolate beauty of the Southwest landscape, giving his stories and characters a rich sense of place and history linked with the region.

Works in Critical Context

Reviews of Hillerman's work continues to be favorable. Most reviewers esteem Hillerman's novels less for their conventional detective plots than for their illumination of American Indian cultures. Robin W. Winks observed:

> [Hillerman] has developed his own niche in mystery and detective fiction . . . by turning the mystery and its solution upon the intricate social and religious life of the Indians of the American Southwest. These books could exist nowhere else, they are authentic, and the resolutions grow out of the character of an entire people.

LITERARY AND HISTORICAL CONTEMPORARIES

Tony Hillerman's famous contemporaries include:

Georgia O'Keeffe (1887–1986): O'Keeffe is known for her paintings of the New Mexico landscape and also for the creative life she led on her ranch in Taos.

Raymond Chandler (1888–1959): Chandler's famous fictional detective, Philip Marlowe, appeared in classic mystery novels such as *The Big Sleep* (1939) and *The Long Goodbye* (1953).

Bill Richardson (1947–): This governor of New Mexico since 2003 is known for his progressive energy policies.

Carl Hiaasen (1953–): This novelist sets his mysteries in the state of Florida, where his characters usually champion the preservation of the landscape and the fight against corporate greed.

The Blessing Way Critics differed on how suspenseful *The Blessing Way* was, with A. L. Rosenzweig writing in *Book World* that Hillerman was " . . . weak on twanging the nerves," while Sergeant Cuff in the *Saturday Review* opined, "Here's suspense enough for anyone." Reviewers generally agreed that Hillerman's writing about Navajo culture had added a dimension to the mystery, causing W. H. Farrington in *Library Journal* to conclude, "Here we have that rarity: a mystery with literary value, one you can recommend to people who don't like mysteries."

Despite favorable reviews and a nomination for the Edgar Award from the Mystery Writers of America, *The Blessing Way* did not entirely satisfy Hillerman. Twenty years later, in an interview with Ernie Bulow in *Talking Mysteries* (1991), Hillerman agreed with criticisms of this book for inaccuracies regarding the Navajos, saying, "a lot of it makes me flinch."

Sacred Clowns Reviewers had more reservations about *Sacred Clowns* than about most Hillerman books. In *The New York Times Book Review*, Verlyn Klinkenborg, calling this Hillerman's most "pallid" mystery, questioned his tendency to make whites guilty of murder as well as insensitive to Indians. Though feeling that the identification of the killer did not ring true, Barry Gardner in *Mostly Murder* praised the description of Leaphorn and Chee as characters: "Their lives and problems are very much part of the story, and each here is struggling with a personal relationship that troubles and confuses him." In the *Los Angeles Times Book Review*, Charles Champlin stated that *Sacred Clowns* "is neither the most suspenseful nor the most active of the Leaphorn series" but it is "one of the warmest and most pleasing." While *Chicago Tribune Books* reviewer Dick Adler called the book "as good

COMMON HUMAN EXPERIENCE

Hillerman uses many legends and myths from Native American cultures in his works. Here are some other works that rely heavily on colorful Native American customs and traditions.

Ceremony (1977), a novel by Leslie Marmon Silko. In this book, the hero, Tayo, returns from fighting in World War II only to meet with alcoholism and the deterioration of his reservation.

Green Grass, Running Water (1993), a novel by Thomas King. King's characters in this novel include the wily Coyote, a trickster figure of many Native American tales.

The Lone Ranger and Tonto Fistfight in Heaven (1993), a story collection by Sherman Alexie. This book, set on a reservation in the Northwest, was the basis for the movie *Smoke Signals*.

Smoke Signals (1998), a movie directed by Chris Eyre. Partly set on an Indian reservation, this film highlights the troubled bond between friends trying, in different ways, to identify with their culture.

as anything [Hillerman's] done," Donald McCraig asserted in *Washington Post Book World* "on the whole the novel is disappointing and sometimes irritating."

Responses to Literature

1. Why do you think Hillerman chooses the Native American culture to base his works on?

2. Why do you think Hillerman uses and reuses Joe Leaphorn as the main character in his novels? What are the advantages and disadvantages of a writer using a recurring character throughout several books?

3. Find two examples of how Hillerman incorporates Native American mythology into his contemporary mystery stories. Does he rely on supernatural events and explanations to resolve his mysteries?

4. Hillerman has often been compared to the Florida writer Carl Hiaasen. Why do you think this is, other than the fact that they both write mysteries?

BIBLIOGRAPHY

Books

Erisman, Fred. *Tony Hillerman. Western Writers Series*, no. 37. Boise, Idaho: Boise State University Press, 1989.

Greenberg, Martin, ed. *The Tony Hillerman Companion: A Comprehensive Guide to His Life and Work.* New York: HarperCollins, 1994.

Linford, Laurence D. *Tony Hillerman's Navajoland: Hideouts, Haunts and Havens in the Joe Leaphorn and Jim Chee Mysteries.* Salt Lake City, Utah: University of Utah Press, 2001.

Sobol, John. *Tony Hillerman: A Public Life.* Toronto, Ontario: ECW Press, 1994.

Periodicals

Ames, Katrine. "In the Heart of Navajo Country." *Newsweek* 97 (June 19, 1981): 60–61.

Bulow, Ernie. *Words, Weather and Wolfmen: Conversations with Tony Hillerman.* Gallup, N. Mex.: Southwestern, 1989.

Gaugenmaier, Judith Tabor. "The Mysteries of Tony Hillerman." *American West* 26 (December 1989): 46–47, 56–58.

Parfit, Michael. "Weaving Mysteries That Tell of Life among the Navajos." *Smithsonian* 21 (December 1990): 92–96, 98, 100, 102, 104–105.

Strenski, Ellen and Robley Evans. "Ritual and Murder in Tony Hillerman's Indian Detective Novels." *Western American Literature* 16 (November 1981): 205–216.

Holt, Patricia. "PW Interviews Tony Hillerman." *Publishers Weekly* (October 24, 1980): 6–7.

✹ Rolando Hinojosa-Smith

BORN: *1929, Mercedes, Texas*

NATIONALITY: *American*

GENRE: *Fiction*

MAJOR WORKS:
Sketches of the Valley and Other Works (1973)
Klail City: A Novel (1976)
Korean Love Songs (1980)

Overview

Rolando Hinojosa-Smith intends each of his works, regardless of genre, to form a part of a lifelong novel that he calls *Klail City Death Trip*. He has created the fictional world of Klail City, Belken County, Texas—located somewhere in the lower Rio Grande Valley and filled with memorable characters whose ordinary lives take on tragicomic proportions as they go about their daily tasks and deal with conflicts arising out of generations of racial strife and cultural misunderstanding.

Works in Biographical and Historical Context

A Childhood in Mercedes Born in Mercedes, Texas, Hinojosa-Smith is the son of Manuel Guzman Hinojosa, a Mexican American, and Carrie Effie Smith, an Anglo-American. His paternal grandparents were born in the United States; their ancestors arrived in the Lower Rio Grande Valley in 1749 as part of the expedition of José

Rolando Hinojosa-Smith   *The University of Texas at Austin*

Escandón when the area was part of Nuevo Santander, Spain's northern frontier.

The youngest of his family, Hinojosa-Smith had a peaceful childhood and adolescence in Mercedes. He first attended private schools taught by Mexican exiles and funded by the town's Spanish-speaking parents. This schooling reinforced his Mexican cultural legacy. For example, in these schools the day began with the singing of the "Himno Nacional," the Mexican national anthem. Then, at age six, Hinojosa-Smith began attending public schools where the vast majority of the children were Mexican-Americans, but where the teachers were exclusively Anglo. He did not come to know Anglo children until junior high school, where adolescents from all neighborhoods came together.

The years he spent living in the Rio Grande Valley form the substance of most of Hinojosa-Smith's later works. He heard the old people telling stories about their early lives, the difficulties of survival, the conflicts and tension between Hispanics and Anglos, and their joys and disappointments. In an essay reprinted in *The Rolando Hinojosa Reader, Essays Historical and Critical* (1985), he observes that the Valley was a place characterized by

> the sharing of names, of places, of a common history, and of belonging to the place; one attended funerals, was taken to cemeteries, and one saw names that

corresponded to one's own or to one's friends and neighbors, and relatives.

Early Career   After graduating from high school in 1946, Hinojosa-Smith left the valley, but he returned there hundreds of times in the ensuing years. He joined the army at seventeen and served two years, spent a short time attending the University of Texas, and was reactivated in the military in 1950 when the Korean conflict erupted. Besides serving in Korea—an experience about which he is reluctant to talk—he was stationed at Fort Eustis, Virginia, where he edited a camp publication. Sent to the Caribbean, he became a radio announcer and the editor of the Caribbean Army Defense Command newspaper, which enjoyed wide distribution throughout the region. He graduated from the University of Texas in 1954 with a degree in Spanish, having been a student employee in the reserve section of the university library. This work provided him the opportunity to read widely and avidly.

After graduation, Hinojosa-Smith taught government, Spanish, history, Latin, and typing for a short time at Brownsville High School, located at the southern tip of the Rio Grande Valley. He soon quit to earn more money as a common laborer in a chemical-processing plant. During this period (1954–1958), he wrote little but continued to read voraciously, especially the works of Russian novelists and Spanish literature. In 1959 he went to work for a clothing manufacturer in Brownsville, then spent two more years as a high-school teacher. He earned his Ph.D. at the University of Illinois in 1969.

In 1970, while serving as chairman of the modern language department at Texas A & M University in Kingsville, Texas, Hinojosa-Smith began to write *Sketches of the Valley and Other Works* (1973). In 1971 he began a close friendship with Tomás Rivera, the highly regarded Chicano writer, academic, and university administrator. Rivera sent parts of a manuscript Hinojosa-Smith was working on to Quinto Sol Publications, who printed excerpts from it in *El Grito*, an important early Chicano journal of the humanities and the social sciences, marking the beginning of Hinojosa-Smith's success as a published writer.

Awards   In 1976 Hinojosa-Smith was promoted to vice-president for academic affairs at Texas A & M University and received the prestigious Premio Casa de las Américas for his second novel, *Klail City: A Novel* (1976; first English publication 1987). Hinojosa-Smith said in a 1986 interview that he wrote *Klail City* in order to keep alive the memory of his youth in light of a new and changing world that removes him further and further from his past.

In 1976 Hinojosa-Smith resigned his administrative position at Texas A & M to accept an appointment as professor of English and chair of the program in Chicano

LITERARY AND HISTORICAL CONTEMPORARIES

Hinojosa-Smith's famous contemporaries include:

Tom Landry (1924–2000): Landry is a native of the Rio Grande Valley who later became famous as the head coach of the Dallas Cowboys, a team he led to twenty winning seasons in a row, including two Super Bowl victories.

Ruben Salazar (1928–1970): Salazar was a Mexican American journalist who was killed by police officers during a Vietnam War protest in East Los Angeles.

Oscar Zeta Acosta (1935–1974?): Author, attorney and Chicano activist, Acosta is known for his friendship with Hunter S. Thompson and for his mysterious disappearance in Mexico.

Tomás Rivera (1935–1984): Rivera was an author and close friend of Hinojosa-Smith, and was known for his novel *. . . and the earth did not swallow him* (1971).

Rudolfo Anaya (1937–): Anaya is a Mexican American author recognized for his insight into Chicano and Native American culture with books such as *Bless Me, Ultima* (1970).

studies at the University of Minnesota. He was responding in part to his wife's decision to enter law school. During the early part of his stay in Minnesota, he immersed himself in reading the great war novelists and poets such as Siegfried Sassoon, Evelyn Waugh, and Robert Graves in preparation for the drafting of *Korean Love Songs* (1980), a book of poems. Hinojosa-Smith left the University of Minnesota in 1981 to accept a position in the department of English at the University of Texas at Austin, where he is currently located. His work written after *Korean Love Songs* traces the changes that have occurred in the Rio Grande Valley since the 1950s. *Dear Rafe* (1981) received the Southwestern Conference on Latin American Studies prize for best writing in the humanities in 1982. He continues to write and work on the *Klail City* series, the most recent book of which is *We Happy Few* (2006).

Although Hinojosa-Smith is among the best-known and most celebrated Chicano writers in the United States, he is much better known in Europe and Latin America than in his own country. His *Klail City Death Trip* series presents a vast panorama of Chicano and Anglo life in South Texas, depicted with sensitivity and skill.

Works in Literary Context

The Sketch Technique   Hinojosa-Smith's first book, *Sketches of the Valley and Other Works*, does not fit easily within the traditional concept of a novel because it lacks a plot. There is no denouement, nor does the work provide a sense of completion or resolution. It is, rather, a series of *estampas* (sketches) that forms a rich tapestry of the Chicano community in and around the fictional town of Klail City—a locale clearly meant to represent the lower Rio Grande Valley, where the author grew up. Each sketch forms an integral part of the complex of lives, joys, struggles, and tragedies of the community. The author warns readers at the outset of the work that the sketches are individual strands of hair matted together with the sweat and dirt of generations of human toil. To separate them would interrupt the flow of vitality and spontaneity that surges through the work. *Sketches* is characterized by a wide range in tone, from terse, direct presentation to rich and subtle folk humor. The voice in the work alternates between omniscient author and a first-person narrator. The first sketch begins at an indefinite point in time and place with the marriage of Roque Malacara and Tere Tapia; in every sketch, a new character is added or a different facet of one already presented is revealed. Over twenty-five characters appear in the work's relatively few pages.

Blurring Characters   The few central characters in *Klail City* give the work its continuity, but they possess little of the stuff of protagonists. They are not literary heroes or even antiheroes; on the contrary, Hinojosa-Smith makes an effort to convince readers how plain his characters are, by noting that "these people go to the bathroom, sneeze, wipe their noses, raise their families, know how to die without a cent, to give in a little with difficulty and [like green wood] to resist giving up." Hinojosa-Smith intentionally obscures relationships between characters, does not identify the narrator until late in the work, and blurs characterization in order to create an overall impression of the collective nature of the community of Klail City. Hinojosa-Smith's intent seems to be to place the focus on the shared traditions, values, language, and history.

Works in Critical Context

Sketches of the Valley   *Sketches of the Valley* was generally well received upon its publication in 1973. The Quinto Sol prize signaled to readers that the novel merited serious consideration. Teresinha Alves Pereira, in *Revista Chicano-Riqueña*, comments that the novel's movement, themes, and structure indicated that the writer had learned well from his literary forerunners. She also notes that the black humor that abounds throughout goes far in providing release for the reader from the hard reality the characters suffer at the hands of both Hispanics and Anglos. Salvador Rodríguez del Pino, in his book *The Chicano Novel in Spanish: Five Socially Committed Writers* (1982), praises Hinojosa-Smith for having gone beyond regionalism. José David Saldívar, in a critical introduction to Hinojosa-Smith's *Klail City Death Trip for The Rolando Hinojosa Reader* (1985), considers it the important first work in a "sensitive and skillful literary metahistory of the Rio Grande Valley, one of the most important dialogical productions of narrative in the Southwest today." Luis María Brox, however, in his review essay for *Mester*, is of the opinion that *Sketches* is flawed by the author's choice, especially in the first part of the book, of the *costumbrista* form—that is, the superficial description of typical characters mouthing typical language. He saw this choice as unnecessarily limiting because it depicted a static and closed society in which change and response to exterior influences were not possible. The book's nontraditional form created a dilemma for some critics who seemed confused about how to classify the work. This identification was to carry over to Hinojosa-Smith's other works as well, an unfortunate development that affected critical appreciation of his subsequent publications.

Klail City Most reviewers and critics have responded favorably to *Klail City*. Marvin Lewis, for example, in his review appearing in *Revista Chicano-Riqueña*, concludes: "In this work Hinojosa sets high literary standards.... [T]he author has established himself as an international writer of the first order and has helped to elevate Chicano fiction ... to its rightful place among world literatures." But Yolanda Guerrero's comments in *La Palabra* are representative of some of the negative criticism the novel received. Guerrero states that his treatment of Chicano life is superficial and misleading, in that it does not sufficiently highlight the conflictive nature of Chicano-Anglo relations and the contradictions inherent in Chicano culture itself.

Responses to Literature

1. What effect does Hinojosa-Smith's use of so many different voices in *Sketches of the Valley* have on the reader? What point do you think the author is trying to make with this style, and do you think it works? Why or why not?

2. In his poetry collection *Korean Love Songs*, what is the author's message about war? Provide examples from the text to support your view.

3. Hinojosa-Smith has chosen to link most of his works into what he calls the "Klail City Death-Trip Series." What do you think are the advantages of linking so many works in such a way? What are some possible disadvantages, from a reader's perspective?

4. South Texas is important to Hinojosa-Smith primarily because he grew up there. Find another author who writes primarily about the region in which he grew up. How are the messages and themes of the two authors the same? How are they different?

COMMON HUMAN EXPERIENCE

Hinojosa-Smith is known for his skillful portrayal of the sense of community in his fictional Belken County. By focusing on the town rather than specific people, he creates a world of his own, which the reader is invited to enter and explore. Here are some other works that show readers whole new worlds.

The Great Gatsby (1925), a novel by F. Scott Fitzgerald. Narrator Nick Carraway moves to wealthy West Egg, and befriends his rich and mysterious neighbor in this classic tale of the lost American dream.

The Sound and the Fury (1929), a novel by William Faulkner. Set in the imaginary Yoknapatawpha County, this novel tells the story of the Compson family's decline, through various Southern voices.

The Chronicles of Narnia (1949–1954), a series of fantasy novels by C. S. Lewis. Four English children walk through a wardrobe and enter the magical world of Narnia.

The Lord of the Rings (1954–55), by J. R. R. Tolkien. In this three-volume series, Middle-earth must be delivered from the evil Lord Sauron with the help of Frodo Baggins, a simple Hobbit from the Shire.

BIBLIOGRAPHY

Books

Lee, Joyce Glover. *Rolando Hinojosa and the American Dream*. Denton, Tex.: University of North Texas Press, 1997.

del Pino, Salvador Rodríguez. *La novela chicana escrita en español: cinco autores comprometidos*. Ypsilanti, Mich.: Bilingual/Editorial Bilingüe, 1982, pp. 117–137.

Saldívar, José David, ed. *The Rolando Hinojosa Reader: Essays Historical and Critical*. Houston, Tex.: Arte Publico, 1985.

Periodicals

Brox, Luis María. "Los límites del costumbrismo en Estampas del valle y otras obras." *Mester* 5 (April 1974): 101–104.

Guerrero, Yolanda. "Literatura y sociedad: Análisis de Generaciones y semblanzas." *La Palabra* 1 (Fall 1979): 21–30.

Houston, Robert. Review of *Dear Rafe*. *New York Times Book Review* (August 18, 1985): 9.

Pereira, Teresinha Alves. "Estampas del valle y otras obras." *Revista Chicano-Riqueña* 3 (Winter 1975): 57–58.

✳ S. E. Hinton

BORN: *1950, Tulsa, Oklahoma*

NATIONALITY: *American*

GENRE: *Fiction*

MAJOR WORKS:
The Outsiders (1967)
That Was Then, This is Now (1971)
Rumble Fish (1975)
Tex (1979)

Overview

Novelist Susan Eloise Hinton is credited with revolutionizing the young-adult genre by creating realistic characters, settings, and dialogue that are representative of teenage life in America. Her classic novel *The Outsiders* (published in 1967 when she was seventeen years old) was the first in her short but impressive list of books to feature troubled but sensitive male adolescents as main characters. Hinton's subjects include social-class rivalry, poverty, alcoholism, drug addiction, and teenage cruelty.

Works in Biographical and Historical Context

Growing up in a City on the Plains S. E. Hinton was born and raised in Tulsa, Oklahoma, the setting of most of her novels. She was an avid reader as a child and soon began writing stories about cowboys, horses, and other topics of interest to her. As a teenager, Hinton enjoyed reading but often found her options limited: "A lot of adult literature was older than I was ready for. The kids' books were all Mary-Jane-Goes-to-the-Prom junk. I wrote *The Outsiders* so I'd have something to read." While a student at Will Rogers High School, she began writing *The Outsiders* and saw the novel evolve through four drafts before submitting it to Curtis Brown literary agent Marilyn Marlow. A publication contract with Viking arrived during her high school graduation ceremony. Loosely based on her own experiences and those of friends and acquaintances, the book is about the ongoing rivalry and conflict that leads to a deadly confrontation between two gangs—the lower-class "greasers" and their upper-middle-class counterparts, the "socs" (short for "socials"). *The Outsiders* was an instant hit among teenagers and sold more than four million copies in the United States.

Steady Success With the money she earned from *The Outsiders*, Hinton attended the University of Tulsa and earned a degree in education in 1970. She met her future husband, David Inhofe, while in school, and it was he who encouraged her to write her second novel, *That Was Then, This Is Now*, published in 1971. Hinton considered

her second novel superior to the first. Hinton continued her pattern of producing a novel every four years with the publication of *Rumble Fish* in 1975 and *Tex* in 1979. The former work centers on a delinquent youth struggling to gain a tough reputation, and the latter (set in California) on two teenage brothers left in each other's care by their traveling father.

In 1988 Hinton's fifth novel, *Taming the Star Runner*, was published. During the nearly ten-year interim between the publication of *Tex* and *Taming the Star Runner*, Hinton started a family and worked as a consultant on the film adaptations of her novels. Involved in the casting, scriptwriting, directing, and even acting, Hinton found the experience pleasurable, but she still preferred writing to consulting. Through her popular novels and their equally popular film adaptations, Hinton has developed a reputation as a perceptive writer of young-adult fiction. In 1988, she was honored with the first American Library Association/School Library Journal Author Achievement award for her body of work.

Current Ventures and Film Career In the 1990s, Hinton wrote the text for two children's picture books, *Big David, Little David* (1995) and *The Puppy Sister* (1995). The books for the most part have been well reviewed. "I don't think I have a masterpiece in me, but I do know I'm writing well in the area I choose to write in," Hinton explained to Dave Smith of the *Los Angeles Times*. "I understand kids and I really like them. And I have a very good memory. I remember exactly what it was like to be a teenager that nobody listened to or paid attention to or wanted around."

Works in Literary Context

The Sensitive Male Writing from the male perspective, Hinton has a unique understanding of her subjects that allows her to create believable characters. Ponyboy Curtis, the fourteen-year-old narrator in *The Outsiders*, has warranted comparison to J. D. Salinger's Holden Caulfield of *The Catcher in the Rye*. Hinton's books are usually narrated by macho, poor, and "cool" teenage boys who are also vulnerable and occasionally cry. They are often orphans, as in *The Outsiders*, or have been abandoned by their parents, as in *Tex*. Despite the fact that Hinton's protagonists often skip school and get into trouble with their teachers, they frequently enjoy reading, and three of them—Ponyboy Curtis, Tex McCormick, and Travis Harris—are presented as potential poets or writers. Indeed, Hinton's characters make frequent allusions to their favorite books which include works as diverse as *Great Expectations* (1861), *Gone with the Wind* (1936), *Smoky the Cow Horse* (1926), and the poems of Robert Frost.

Social Outcasts Hinton has produced five novels about "greasers," "hoods," and abandoned teenagers.

Her characters are frequently larger than life, almost mythic, and are social outcasts, such as Dallas Winston of *The Outsiders* and Motorcycle Boy of *Rumble Fish*. Hinton's novels suggest how young adults are frequently shaped by their environment and are concerned with their struggles, only sometimes successful, to leave the past behind and face the future. Hinton has the great ability to create authentic characters who sound like real young adults and their journeys towards adulthood will likely remain popular with future readers, whether "Socs" or "greasers."

Works in Critical Context

Some critics, like Michael Malone of *The Nation*, have chastised Hinton for "mythologizing the tragic beauty of violent youth" and "avoiding the problem of parental authority and conflict" by placing her characters outside of their families. She has also been criticized for creating similar plots in consecutive books. But librarians cite Hinton as one of the most popular authors among "reluctant readers" in the junior-high age group, as well as among teachers, who regularly use her novels as assigned reading. "Teen-agers should not be written down to," Hinton said in the *New York Times Book Review*. "Anyone can tell when his intelligence is being underestimated. Those who are not ready for adult novels can easily have their love of reading killed by the inane junk lining the teen-age shelf in the library."

The Outsiders   *The Outsiders* is Hinton's most popular novel. Thomas Fleming writes in the *New York Times Book Review*, "[Hinton] has produced a book alive with the fresh dialogue of her contemporaries, and has wound around it a story that captures, in vivid patches at least, a rather unnerving slice of teen-age America." *Saturday Review* critic Zena Sutherland similarly observes that *The Outsiders* is "written with distinctive style by a teen-ager who is sensitive, honest, and observant." A *Times Literary Supplement* reviewer, however, notes that "the plot creaks and the ending is wholly factitious," and remarks that the language "is both arresting and tiring to read in its repetitiousness." While also faulting the author for unlikely plot twists and occasional overwriting, Lillian N. Gerhardt comments in *School Library Journal* that Hinton is a writer "seeing and saying more with greater storytelling ability than many an older hand."

Tex   In *Tex*, Hinton "has taken a larger canvas on which to group more varied characters," asserts Margery Fisher of *Growing Point*. But *New York Times Book Review* contributor Paxton Davis believes that the number of unusual events occurring in the story strains credulity: "Even by the standards of today's fiction, S. E. Hinton's vision of contemporary teen-age life is riper than warrants belief.... [*Tex* is] busier and more melodramatic

LITERARY AND HISTORICAL CONTEMPORARIES

S. E. Hinton's famous contemporaries include:

J. D. Salinger (1919–): This author is best known for his novel *The Catcher in the Rye* (1951), considered by many to be the quintessential teenage novel.
Judy Blume (1938–): Along with Hinton, Blume is known for her young-adult novels of the 1970s and 80s, such as *Are You There God? It's Me, Margaret.* (1970) and *Then Again Maybe I Won't* (1971).
Francis Ford Coppola (1939–): This director made *The Outsiders* in 1982 but is best known for his *Godfather* series.
Matt Dillon (1964–): This actor played Dallas Winston in the movie *The Outsiders* (1983) and also starred in two other Hinton film adaptations, *Tex* (1982) and *Rumble Fish* (1983).
Stanley "Tookie" Williams (1953–2005): Williams, along with Raymond Washington, founded the notoriously violent Los Angeles street gang called the Crips in 1971. He was convicted of multiple murders and robbery in 1981, and was sentenced to death. He was executed in 2005.

COMMON HUMAN EXPERIENCE

S.E. Hinton's novels are mostly focused on the teenage years, a difficult transitional time for her characters but a period of life many American adults wax nostalgic about. Here are some other works that focus on the growing pains of teenagers.

The Catcher in the Rye (1951), a novel by J. D. Salinger. The charming but troubled hero of this novel, Holden Caulfield, is one of the most famous teenagers in literary history.
Sixteen Candles (1984), a film written and directed by John Hughes. Molly Ringwald stars as awkward teenager Samantha Baker, whose sixteenth birthday goes unnoticed by her preoccupied family.
Beverly Hills 90210 (1990–2000), a television series created by Darren Star and Aaron Spelling. This series captivated American audiences in the 1990s by depicting a group of (mostly) wealthy friends in southern California.
King Dork (2006), a novel by Frank Portman. In this book, the main character is a troubled teenage boy trying to investigate his father's death by reading through his books, namely *The Catcher in the Rye*.

than the real life it purports to show." Lance Salway agrees that *Tex* is very theatrical, but comments in *Signal* that "a writer as good as Hinton can carry it off effortlessly; one believes implicitly in the characters and cares what happens to them." "In this new book," Fisher concludes, "Susan Hinton has achieved that illusion of reality which any fiction writer aspires to and which few ever completely achieve."

Responses to Literature

1. Do you think Hinton's work remains relevant today? How have teenagers changed since she wrote *The Outsiders*? What things have remained the same?

2. Watch the film adaptation of *The Outsiders*. Are the characters as you pictured them? What differences are there between the movie and the book?

3. *The Outsiders* documents a conflict between rival social groups. Write an essay describing the social groups you see in your school or community. Are there conflicts between the groups?

4. Why might the protagonists of Hinton's novels be so interested in reading? Why do you think they are interested in Robert Frost in particular?

BIBLIOGRAPHY

Books

Authors and Artists for Young Adults, Vol. 2. Detroit: Gale, 1989, pp. 65–76.

Collier, Laurie and Joyce Nakamura. *Major Authors and Illustrators for Children and Young Adults*. Detroit: Gale Research Inc., 1993, pp. 1117–1120.

Daly, Jay. *Presenting S. E. Hinton*. Boston: Twayne, 1987.

"S. E. Hinton." In *Twentieth-Century Young Adult Writers*, 1st ed. Ed. Laura Standley Berger. Detroit: St. James Press, 1994.

Periodicals

Hinton, Susan. "Teen Agers Are for Real." *New York Times Book Review* (August 27, 1967).

Jacobs, William Jay. "Reaching the Unreached." *The Record* Volume 69, No. 2 (November 1967): 201–202.

Lempke, Susan Dove. Review of *Big David, Little David. Bulletin of the Center for Children's Books* (February 1995): 200.

Malone, Michael. "Tough Puppies." *Nation* (March 8, 1986): 276.

McCoy, Jody. Review of *Big David, Little David. School Library Journal* (April 1995): 102.

Rodell, Susanna. Review of *The Puppy Sister. New York Times Book Review* (November 19, 1995): 37.

Smith, Dave. "Hinton, What Boys Are Made Of." *Los Angeles Times* (July 15, 1982).

Wallace, Carol. "In Praise of Teenage Outcasts." *Daily News* (September 26, 1982).

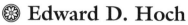

Edward D. Hoch

BORN: *1930, Rochester, New York*

DIED: *2008, Rochester, New York*

NATIONALITY: *American*

GENRE: *Fiction*

MAJOR WORKS:

The Judges of Hades and Other Simon Ark Stories (1971)

Leopold's Way (1985)

The Velvet Touch (2000)

Overview

Edward D. Hoch was the most prolific of modern writers of mystery short stories, with more than nine hundred stories published by 2004. He almost single-handedly maintained the "fair play" tradition of the Golden Age of the mystery, between World Wars I and II, in which the clues the main characters use to solve crimes are presented to readers in such a way that they, too, can "work the case." His sleuths solve such seemingly impossible crimes as disappearances under unusual circumstances and murders

Edward D. Hoch   *Matthew Peyton / Getty Images*

in locked rooms. From May 1973 until his death, Hoch published a story in almost every issue of what is generally considered the leading periodical of this genre, *Ellery Queen's Mystery Magazine*. Of the many books he produced, only five are novels; the rest short-story collections.

Works in Biographical and Historical Context

Mystery Fan First, Writer Second Edward Dentinger Hoch was born in Rochester, New York, on February 22, 1930, the son of Earl G. and Alice Dentinger Hoch. His father was vice president of a bank; his mother was a homemaker. After attending Sacred Heart School and Aquinas Institute High School, he went to the University of Rochester, but left after just two years, in 1949. While attending high school and college, he wrote and submitted short stories, though none were accepted for publication. He became interested in detective fiction when he first listened to *The Adventures of Ellery Queen* on radio in 1939. He also cites Queen's *The Chinese Orange Mystery* (1934), which was reprinted in paperback that year, as a major influence on his life. In 1949 Hoch joined Mystery Writers of America (MWA) as an unpublished, affiliate member. He attended MWA meetings in New York, especially from 1950 to 1952, when he was in the army, serving as a military policeman at Fort Jay, on Governor's Island. After being discharged, he worked for the publisher Pocket Books in a noneditorial capacity. In late 1953, he returned to Rochester. There, in January 1954, he took a job writing for an advertising agency. Three years later he married Patricia McMahon, with whom he lived in the Charlotte neighborhood of Rochester until his death in 2008.

Hoch wrote stories in his spare time while working in advertising. "Village of the Dead" was the first of his stories to be accepted for publication, and it appeared in the December 1955 issue of *Famous Detective Stories*, one of the last of the pulp magazines. In this story, Hoch introduced Simon Ark, an eccentric detective who travels the world seeking to eradicate the devil and other manifestations of evil. Hoch's stories soon were published widely in the "pulps" and then the digest-sized magazines that replaced them. Among these long-defunct magazines were *Crack Detective and Mystery Stories, Keyhole Detective Stories, Tightrope Detective Magazine*, and *Two-Fisted Detective Stories*.

Beginning early in his career, Hoch often employed pseudonyms—also known as "pen names"—because he found that editors were reluctant to have more than one story by an author in a single issue of a magazine. In March 1956, using his middle name, he published the first of twenty-three stories he would produce over the next twenty years as "Stephen Dentinger." He also published three stories, in 1956–1957, as "Irwin Booth."

Later, as "Pat McMahon" (his wife's maiden name), he wrote four stories, published 1962–1966.

Serial Detectives While Hoch's pseudonyms were plentiful, Hoch serial characters were even more so. Simon Ark, Ben Snow, Captain Leopold, Nick Velvet, and Dr. Sam Hawthorne are among his most popular, and he used them often. A 1980s series character, Sir Gideon Parrot, was featured in five parodies of "Golden Age" mysteries. Parrot was based on Agatha Christie's Hercule Poirot (he says he pronounces his name the French way), and the impossible crimes he solves are based on Christie's cases, which take place at dinner parties or among people stranded on remote islands. In one instance, "The Flying Fiend" (1982), several people are found with their throats cut on the beach, but the sand leading up to the bodies is unmarked. Yet another short-lived 1980s detective was Libby Knowles, a private detective who works as a bodyguard.

The height of popularity of spy fiction occurred during the mid-1960s, largely because of Ian Fleming's James Bond series and the best-selling John Le Carré novel, *The Spy Who Came in from the Cold* (1965). A new character created by Hoch, first appearing in "The Spy Who Did Nothing" (1965), combined elements of both Le Carré and Fleming. Hoch's main character has a four-letter name similar to Bond—Rand—and the story titles always begin with the phrase "The Spy Who…" However, the series focused less on sensational aspects of espionage—Rand is a cryptologist for Britain's Department of Concealed Communications—and displayed

COMMON HUMAN EXPERIENCE

Though Hoch experimented with genres such as the Western and science fiction, he is best known for his mysteries. His detectives specialized in solving crimes that were seemingly impossible and situations that looked preposterous. Here are some other works where an apparently complicated crime is neatly solved.

> *And Then There Were None* (1939), a novel by Agatha Christie. A dinner party on a remote island goes horribly awry in this tale of murder and vigilante justice.
> *Farewell, My Lovely* (1940), a novel by Raymond Chandler. Philip Marlowe intends to go after a jade necklace, but, as usual, gets more than he bargained for in this novel of mistaken identities.
> *Rear Window* (1954), a film by Alfred Hitchcock. In this movie, an injured photographer spends the summer spying on his neighbor—and becomes a witness to murder.

little of the cynicism and angst typical of Le Carré. Despite this, Rand appears in eighty-two stories.

Side Projects In May 1965 the first of Hoch's stories to be adapted for television, "Winter Run," appeared on the last broadcast of *The Alfred Hitchcock Hour* under the title "Off Season." Three of Hoch's stories were televised on *McMillan and Wife*, a series starring Rock Hudson as Police Commissioner McMillan and Susan Saint James as his wife, Sally. Hoch's work has also appeared on the television anthology series *Night Gallery* and *Tales of the Unexpected*, though he did not work on any of the scripts.

Hoch often contributed to *The Mystery Writers' Annual*, published by MWA each year for the Edgar awards banquet. Until his death, he was active in MWA affairs, and regularly traveled from Rochester to New York City for its meetings. From 1982 through 1983 he served as president of MWA, the organization he first joined as a teenager. In 2001, he was awarded the title of Grand Master by the MWA.

Works in Literary Context

Religion Religion is an important part of Hoch's early work, especially the Simon Ark series. In "Sword for a Sinner" (1959), which appeared in *The Saint Mystery Magazine*, Ark implies that he may have been a Coptic priest two thousand years ago: "In Egypt, long ago, I practiced in the Coptic rite." Ark speaks of himself as having lived in the first century after Christ and having been "doomed to walk the earth forever." In 1964,

Hoch introduced amateur sleuth Father David Noone, a Roman Catholic parish priest at Holy Trinity Church, who shares Hoch's religious affiliation. The priest-sleuth has appeared in seven stories, but no collection of Noone stories has been published. *The Night People and Other Stories* (2001) is composed of twenty non-series stories published between 1957 and 1979. "Ring the Bell Softly" shows Hoch's interest in religion and evil, already evident in his Simon Ark stories and the anthology of Catholic stories he edited. A mysterious stranger named Chance visits a priest in a valley from which almost everyone else has moved.

The Displaced Western In the September 1961 issue of *The Saint Mystery Magazine*, Hoch introduced one of his most popular characters, Ben Snow, in "The Valley of Arrows." Most of Snow's adventures take place during the last two decades of the nineteenth century or the first decade of the twentieth. He is a reluctant gunfighter because there are persistent rumors that he is really the outlaw Billy the Kid, and he is often forced to solve the murders of which he, as a supposed criminal, is suspected. "The Valley of Arrows" is more Western thriller than detective story, with Snow at a fort that is besieged by Navajo Indians near the Arizona–New Mexico border. Snow's adventures take him to most of the western states and Canada, but he also pursues killers at the Buffalo Pan-American Exposition when President McKinley is assassinated in "The Man in the Alley" (1962), and in North Carolina during the Wright Brothers' first flight in "Brothers on the Beach" (1984). Snow evolves into a detective who can solve seemingly impossible crimes, as in "The San Agustin Miracle" (2001), in which he solves the murder of someone who vanishes from a hot-air balloon that is being closely watched by a crowd.

Works in Critical Context

Hoch was one of the most recognized and honored of mystery short-story writers partly because of his prodigious output and longevity. In writing of Hoch's receiving MWA's Grand Master Award, Janet Hutchings, editor of *Ellery Queen's Mystery Magazine*, pointed out:

> Ed Hoch could not have maintained his unbroken streak of publication in *EQMM*, or held his place of esteem with readers and other writers had he failed to provide, with each tale, the brilliant plotting, the sleight of hand, and the full cast of characters that are his trademarks. The almost legendary nature of his achievement derives from the merging of quantity with quality.

"The Oblong Room" "The Oblong Room" (1967), a Captain Leopold story first published in *The Saint Magazine*, won the coveted Edgar Award as the best mystery short story of the year. It was later collected in *Leopold's Way* (1985). A university student, the only suspect, is found standing over the body of a murder victim, and he has been there for twenty-two hours. Though Leopold appears, this story is more a mystery of abnormal psychology than of physical clues, with the key question being why the killer did not attempt to escape. In selecting it for his anthology of the best stories of 1967, Anthony Boucher praised its "deceptively simple plot...patient detection, strong creation of mood...and a final breath-taking shock of illumination." One of Hoch's most popular stories, it has been reprinted at least thirteen times in various publications.

Responses to Literature

1. Hoch is known for the fact that he has written so many mystery stories. Some critics view such a large output as a sign that the writer is interested in making money instead of creating lasting literature. Do you think there is necessarily a conflict between creating art and creating popular fiction as a way to make a living? What kinds of conflicts might a writer experience when aiming to satisfy both of these goals?

2. Why do you think Hoch often sticks to characters he has already introduced, rather than inventing new ones? What are some of the advantages and disadvantages of this strategy?

3. Which of Hoch's serial detectives do you find most believable? Does it matter whether a fictional detective is believable or not, or is the crime itself more important?

4. Although it can be argued that he ranks alongside such detective-fiction writers as Agatha Christie and Raymond Chandler, Hoch is hardly known to mainstream readers. Why do you think he is not more well-known, despite his prolific output?

BIBLIOGRAPHY

Books

Hutchings, Janet. "Edward D. Hoch: Grand Master." *Edgar Allan Poe Awards: Millennium Edition.* New York: MWA, 2001.

Lachman, Marvin S. "Edward D. Hoch: A Brief Biography." *Bouchercon .22 Souvenir Program Book.* Pasadena, Calif.: Bouchercon .22, n.d.

———. "Edward D. Hoch: An Appreciation." *Bouchercon 2001: A Capital Mystery.* Washington, D.C.: Bouchercon, 2001.

———. "Introduction." *Edward D. Hoch Bibliography,* 11th ed. Downey, Calif.: Moffatt House, 2001.

Moffatt, June M. and Francis M. Nevins, Jr. *Edward D. Hoch Bibliography (1955–2004),* 13th ed. Downey, Calif.: Moffatt House, 2004.

Periodicals

Hare, Mark. "Hoch Writes a Life of Mystery." *Rochester Democrat and Chronicle* (March 4, 2001): 1, 8–9.

Kovaleski, John. "Shortcut to Murder." *Armchair Detective* 23 (Spring 1990): 152–169.

Lewis, Steve. "An Interview with Edward Hoch." *Mystery* 45 (August 2004): 37–40.

Skillman, Brad. "Edward Hoch: Master in His Own Write." *Drood Review* 11 (October 1991): 4–5.

West, J. Alec. "An Interview with Ed Hoch." *Murderous Intent Mystery Magazine* 3 (Spring 1997): 14–16.

✸ Linda Hogan

BORN: *1947, Denver, Colorado*

NATIONALITY: *American*

GENRE: *Fiction, poetry*

MAJOR WORKS:

Eclipse (1983)

Savings (1988)

Book of Medicines (1993)

Overview

As a writer of Chickasaw heritage, Linda Hogan centers herself and, consequently, her readers on what nature has to teach human beings and on the regenerative female forces that shape the world. The Chickasaw were matrilineal, which means the family line is passed down through the mother; other tribes, though recognizing men as their leaders, revered their women as the creative

Linda Hogan © *Christopher Felver / Corbis*

LITERARY AND HISTORICAL CONTEMPORARIES

Hogan's famous contemporaries include:

Martin Luther King, Jr. (1929–1968): King's contributions to the civil rights movement helped Native Americans realize and fight for their own rights.

Dennis Banks (1932–): Banks is co-founder of the American Indian Movement (AIM), an organization begun in 1968 to protect the rights of Native Americans.

N. Scott Momaday (1934–): Momaday is an author whose novel *House Made of Dawn* (1968) began the Native American movement in literature and won a Pulitzer Prize in 1969.

Leslie Marmon Silko (1948–): Silko's 1977 novel *Ceremony* alerted readers to the plight of Tayo, a Vietnam veteran, and by extension to the plights of many Pueblos and other Indians.

Sherman Alexie (1966–): Primarily a short story writer, Alexie also wrote *Smoke Signals* (1998), one of the first popular films about and starring Native Americans.

life force of the universe. Domination by Christian Europeans, Hogan maintains, has altered the traditional tribal balance between male and female power in American Indian life. In her works Hogan seeks to restore that balance and to offer ancient wisdom about nature in mythological yet contemporary terms.

Works in Biographical and Historical Context

Working, Class Born in Denver on July 17, 1947, to Charles Henderson, a Chickasaw, and Cleona Bower Henderson, Hogan was raised in various locations as her father was transferred from post to post by the U.S. Army. But, she has always regarded Oklahoma, where her father's family lives, as her home. In her autobiographical essay "The Two Lives" (1987), she writes of her mother's ancestors, who settled in the Nebraska Territory. Drawing on a journal she inherited, Hogan describes the settlers' desperation after crop failures and grasshopper plagues, which was compounded by the government's policy of killing the buffalo that both Indians and non-Indians needed for survival. At the same time, Native Americans were being forced off their lands, removed to new places, crowded together, and sometimes killed outright. As Hogan notes, "It was a continuing time of great and common acts of cruelty and violence."

In her recitation of her job history in "The Two Lives," one can readily see why Hogan feels loyalty toward the working poor: "I worked at many…low-paying jobs,

in nursing homes, in dental offices, and filing for a collection agency." She obtained her undergraduate degree as a commuter student at the University of Colorado at Colorado Springs and other schools, only to find much of the educational experience lacking in relevance to her own life. Nonetheless, she became aware of working-class writers whose stories run parallel to those of her family and the family of her former husband, Pat Hogan.

Hogan received her M.A. in English and creative writing from the University of Colorado at Boulder in 1978. She taught at several universities in Colorado and Minnesota between 1977 and 1989; since 1989 she has taught in the American Indian Studies Program and the English department at the University of Colorado at Boulder. In addition, she gives lectures, readings, and workshops at other universities and in Native American communities and for Native American organizations. As a poet, fiction writer, essayist, and playwright Hogan has been committed to environmental preservation; she has worked as a volunteer in wildlife rehabilitation clinics in Minnesota and in Colorado.

Family and Fiction Hogan adopted two daughters of Oglala Lakota heritage, Sandra Dawn Protector and Tanya Thunder Horse, in 1979. Many of the poems in her collection *Eclipse* (1983) portray a mother's sense of helplessness in shielding her children from such destructive forces as war and nuclear waste.

In addition to poetry, Hogan also writes short stories and novels. In a 1988 interview Bo Schöler asked Hogan how she perceived the distinctions among "fact, history, fiction and truth." "Fiction may be a dance along the razor's edge of paradox," she replied. Fiction at its best functions much as myth does, as a spotlight on greater truths than who did what, where, and why, according to Hogan. First published in the *Missouri Review* in 1989 and selected for inclusion in *The Best American Short Stories* the same year, "Aunt Moon's Young Man" is narrated by a Chickasaw girl. Hogan captures the sensibility of budding womanhood in her young protagonist's struggles to understand sex and family; through conversations and interactions between the protagonist and her mother, Hogan delicately presents the mother's valiant efforts at parenting, in spite of her feelings of dissatisfaction. Throughout, the reader sees the little things people do—for better or for worse—to make themselves feel important and useful.

As the bearers of life, women have, says Hogan, a special responsibility in taking care of life. Her poetry collection *Book of Medicines* (1993) lays out a plan in which a new vision of the world takes shape; in Hogan's poem, God resides not above, but within nature. Biblical events from the Creation to the Fall from Grace to the Redemption are reinterpreted. "The History of Red" presents a vision of the first humans' harmony with animals and the rest of creation; the sections that follow, "Hunger" and "The Book of Medicines," represent the Fall and the Redemption, respectively.

Recent Projects Two books appeared late in 1995. *Dwellings: A Spiritual History of the Living World* gathers seventeen essays that express Hogan's belief in the interconnectedness of all life forms. In the preface she says that she writes "out of respect for the natural world, recognizing that humankind is not separate from nature." In the novel *Solar Storms*, seventeen-year-old Angela Jensen leaves her foster home in Oklahoma and travels to a rural village in Minnesota called Adam's Rib. There she meets her great-grandmother, her great-great-grandmother, and Bush, the woman who cared for her when she was a baby. Together, they journey in canoes searching for the great-great-grandmother's birthplace, which will be destroyed by a proposed hydroelectric dam. Both *Dwellings* and *Solar Storms* continue Hogan's celebration of the natural world and her powerful critique of those who scar that world. In 2008 she published another novel, *People of the Whale*, and a book of poems, *Rounding the Human Corners*.

Works in Literary Context

Spirituality In *Savings* (1988) there is an awareness that spiritual consciousness and material political action may stand in complementary relation to one another. The interconnectedness, not only of spiritual and material but of inner and outer worlds, is evidenced, not only in the title, but also in the two-part structure of *Savings*.

Mean Spirit (1990) is a novel about survival—of the spirit and of the land. It is significant that Michael Horse, when he loses his powers of divination, retreats to Sorrow Cave to rejuvenate himself and record the history of his people during the troubled times depicted in the novel. He tells a friend that he is writing a new book of the Bible. He does not want to rewrite or throw out the White man's Bible; he simply wants to add to it, to include the Indian way along with the Ten Commandments.

Native Rights In her novel *Mean Spirit*, Hogan takes the reader on a journey to the heart of America, showing it not as a land of opportunity but as a land of the American Dream gone dreadfully and shamefully wrong. The novel is set in northeastern Oklahoma in the 1920s, during the Osage oil boom—known among the Indians as the Osage Reign of Terror or "the great frenzy"—and follows the Graycloud and Blanket families through a time when whites were exploiting, oppressing, and killing Native Americans to obtain the tribe's oil wealth. Since the income from oil was divided equally among all enrolled Osage tribe members, marrying an Osage woman could make a non-Indian man rich, particularly if the couple had children. Hogan quotes from an actual letter written by a young white man, C. J. Plimer of Joplin, Missouri, to the Indian agent in Pawhuska, Oklahoma, on October 16, 1907; in the novel the writer is unnamed and the agent is in the fictional town of Watona, Oklahoma. The writer says that he is seeking an Osage wife, "not a full blood, but . . . one as near white

---

COMMON HUMAN EXPERIENCE

Hogan champions many causes in her works—women's issues, native rights, animal rights, and the environment. Of these, she seems particularly interested in nature and protecting resources and land. Here are some other works that celebrate the environment and attempt to spark efforts to preserve nature.

Walden (1854), a book by Henry David Thoreau. Thoreau documents his time spent in a cabin near Walden Pond in Massachusetts, on his friend Ralph Waldo Emerson's beautiful land.

Silent Spring (1962), a nonfiction work by Rachel Carson. This book was effective in bringing to attention the dangers of pesticides, most notably DDT.

Pilgrim at Tinker Creek (1974), an essay collection by Annie Dillard. Dillard's book of essays about her time reflecting on nature in the Blue Ridge Mountains was awarded the Pulitzer Prize in 1975.

Turtle Island (1974), a book of poetry by Gary Snyder. This book of poems, named after what natives called America, won the Pulitzer Prize in 1975.

The Monkey Wrench Gang (1975), a novel by Edward Abbey. This book promotes saving the environment by wreaking havoc and minor destruction on corporate facilities and polluting plants.

---

as possible." In exchange for helping him find a woman, the man offers to pay a fee: "for every Five Thousand Dollars she is worth I will give you Twenty-Five Dollars." Such blatantly materialistic grasping went hand-in-hand with spiritual intrusion on the part of the government, in its assimilation policies and its encouragement of missionaries among the Indians.

Works in Critical Context

Eclipse In *Eclipse* (1983), Hogan retains the perspective established in *Calling Myself Home* (1978) and based in her Chickasaw heritage and her faith in female strength. *Eclipse* also includes poems that attempt to reconnect readers with the natural world, honoring each of the four winds, the sky father, and the mother earth. "Hogan crafts phrases of common speech and weaves the lines in natural idioms," notes Kenneth Lincoln in the book's foreword. "The verses carry the muted voices of talk before sleep, quieting the world, awaiting the peace of home. . . . Her poems offer a careful voicing of common things not yet understood, necessary to survival."

The Book of Medicines With her 1993 poetry collection *The Book of Medicines*, Hogan invokes the therapeutic power of rhyme to treat the psychic damage inflicted by human conquest over nature and other people. Drawing on Native American folklore, ritual, and female spirituality, Hogan's incantations address profound manifestations of illness, grief, and the failure of science in the modern world. Robyn Selman describes Hogan's work as "ecopoetry" in her essay in the *Voice Literary Supplement*, particularly as the poems in this volume "take as their subject the very elements of life—fire, air, earth, and water—set into motion with bears, fishes, and humans." Carl L. Bankston notes in the *Bloomsbury Review*, "Hogan's fine sense of rhythm weaves through images of nature and of humankind's uneasy place in nature." As Robert L. Berner concludes in *World Literature Today*, "*The Book of Medicines* is a significant step, indeed a giant stride, in the development of a major American poet."

Responses to Literature

1. Do you think Hogan's focus on the environment detracts from her poetry or adds to it? In what way?

2. What are some of the different meanings of the word "savings" in Hogan's book by the same title?

3. Research the Osage Reign of Terror that came with the oil boom in Oklahoma. Based on your findings, does *Mean Spirit* accurately represent historical events?

4. Michael Horse in *Mean Spirit* can be compared to Tayo in Leslie Marmon Silko's *Ceremony*. Read both works and compare the two characters. How are their quests similar? How are they different?

BIBLIOGRAPHY

Books

Coltelli, Laura. "Linda Hogan," in her *Winged Words: American Indian Writers Speak*. Lincoln, Nebr.: University of Nebraska Press, 1990, pp. 71–86.

Smith, Patricia Clark. "Linda Hogan," in *This is about Vision: Interviews with Southwestern Writers*, edited by William Balassi, John F. Crawford, and Annie O. Eysturoy. Albuquerque, N.M.: University of New Mexico Press, 1990, pp. 141–155.

"To Take Care of a Life," in *Survival This Way: Interviews with American Indian Poets*, edited by Joseph Bruchac. Tucson, Ariz.: University of Arizona Press, 1987, pp. 119–133.

Wilson, Terry P. *The Underground Reservation: Osage Oil*. Lincoln, Nebr.: University of Nebraska Press, 1985.

Periodicals

Bankston, Carl L. III. A review of *The Book of Medicines*. *The Bloomsbury Review*, Vol. 13, No. 6 (November–December 1993): 10.

Bell, Betty Louise, ed. Special issue on Hogan. *Studies in American Indian Literature* 6 (Fall 1994).

Hurley, Joanna T. "A Dark Vision of Hope." *The Bloomsbury Review*, Vol. 11, No. 1 (January–February 1991): 1.

Schöler, Bo. "A Heart Made out of Crickets: An Interview with Linda Hogan." *Journal of Ethnic Studies* 16 (Spring 1988): 107–117.

St. Clair, Janet. "Uneasy Ethnocentrism: Recent Works of Allen, Silko, and Hogan." *Studies in American Indian Literature* 6 (Spring 1994): 83–98.

Oliver Wendell Holmes

BORN: *1809, Cambridge, Massachusetts*

DIED: *1894, Boston, Massachusetts*

NATIONALITY: *American*

GENRE: *Fiction, poetry, nonfiction*

MAJOR WORKS:

"Old Ironsides" (1830)

The Autocrat of the Breakfast Table (1858)

Elsie Venner: A Romance of Destiny (1861)

Overview

During his long career, Oliver Wendell Holmes wrote in a variety of genres and attained considerable popularity among his nineteenth-century contemporaries. Though interest in his work has declined, he is still remembered for four significant works, three of them literary, the

Oliver Wendell Holmes   *The Library of Congress.*

fourth scientific. Two of them—his poem "Old Ironsides" (1830) and his medical investigation of puerperal fever (1843)—appeared early in his career. The other two—his collection of essays *The Autocrat of the Breakfast-Table* (1858) and his novel *Elsie Venner: A Romance of Destiny* (1861)—were published in mid-career, just as Holmes entered his most productive period. Taken together, the four works represent Holmes's versatility and his dedication to writing.

Works in Biographical and Historical Context

The fourth of five children and a descendant of the noted seventeenth-century poet Anne Bradstreet, Oliver Wendell Holmes was born to Abiel Holmes and his second wife, Sarah, on August 29, 1809, in Cambridge, Massachusetts. His father was a graduate of Yale and a moderate Congregationalist minister, while his mother was part of what eventually would be the Unitarian Church. His father was probably the parent who fostered Holmes's interest in books and authorship.

A Childhood Full of Classics Abiel Holmes possessed an impressive library that included some British classics among its mostly religious texts. He did not encourage an interest in fiction, however; for novels Holmes had to turn to his brother, who borrowed them from the library at Harvard. Holmes began his formal education with Dame Prentiss at her Dame School, continued it at William Biglow's school, and then entered the private Port School, which his father had helped found. Here, Holmes first met Richard Henry Dana Jr. and Margaret Fuller. To prepare him for college, Abiel then sent his son to the Phillips Academy in Andover, Massachusetts. A year later, in 1825, Holmes entered Harvard, and after his 1829 graduation, he began to study law, eventually abandoning it in favor of medicine.

Possibly Holmes published some of his work prior to his 1829 graduation, but his earliest known pieces appeared in *The Collegian*, a monthly magazine begun by his college friends. The first copy was published in February 1830 and featured three of Holmes's poems. He contributed to every issue until the periodical ceased production later that year. Occasionally, the newspapers picked up his poems and gave them a wider circulation. Before the end of 1830 Holmes had already produced fifty poems, and in 1831 he wrote one of his most popular ones, "The Last Leaf." The poem depicts Major Thomas Melvill—Herman Melville's grandfather—as the last of his generation, an anachronism in contemporary Boston. The poem was one of his finest achievements and eventually gained the approval of both Edgar Allan Poe and Abraham Lincoln.

Overnight Sensation None of Holmes's early poems, however, produced the sensation that "Old Ironsides" did in late 1830. On September 14, 1830, the *Boston Daily Advertiser* printed a brief notice stating that the warship USS *Constitution* was to be dismantled and used as scrap. Outraged that the United States would allow one of the most prized and famous vessels in the short history of the country to meet with such an end, Holmes wrote his poetic response and submitted it to the *Advertiser*, which printed it on September 16. Soon, the poem appeared across the country in newspapers and on broadsides, stirring up enough public outcry to ensure the preservation of the ship for future generations. While Holmes had not used his full name (he was in the habit of publishing anonymously or with his initials), "Old Ironsides" significantly shaped his career. For the next sixty-four years Holmes continued to produce occasional poems, many of them linked to specific gatherings, such as college commencements and professional meetings.

Shortly, an essay by Holmes appeared in the November 1831 issue of the *New England Magazine*, and a second appeared in February 1832. Both featured a small group of characters gathered around a boardinghouse table (Holmes was living in a boardinghouse at the time), talking among themselves. Though he wrote no more than two of these essays in the 1830s, twenty-five years later they evolved into his popular series, *The Autocrat of the Breakfast Table* (1858).

Back to Medicine By 1833 Holmes had advanced his medical education as far as he could in the United States. Many American doctors of the period spent at least some time training in Europe, so on March 10, 1833, he sailed for England. Stopping there long enough to visit Stonehenge, Salisbury Cathedral, and the estate of the Earl of Pembroke, he then traveled on to Paris on May 4. There, he studied under the pathologist Charles Pierre Alexandre Louis. Medical studies in the French capital were highly respected in the 1830s, and Holmes learned the scientific method, worked with the microscope, and gained an appreciation for the value of observation and experience. He stayed on in Europe for two years, studying and traveling, and in December 1835 he returned to New York City.

Holmes largely ignored writing and focused on medicine for several years. In 1847 he accepted the position of Dean of the Medical School at Harvard, a position he held for six years, and delivered the opening address of the year for the Medical School. Though Holmes dedicated much of his time to producing literary pieces in *The Atlantic Monthly*, he did not abandon medicine. He published *Currents and Counter-Currents in Medical Science* (1861), a collection of his best medical essays. In this volume appeared his now classic essay on puerperal fever and his attacks on the use of "cures" and "remedies" to treat illness. Holmes was disgusted by quacks peddling cures that really only treated the symptoms of illness or had no beneficial effect at all. He believed that such drugs were merely a placebo to relieve the pain and suffering of patients, and he severely criticized those who claimed otherwise.

LITERARY AND HISTORICAL CONTEMPORARIES

Holmes's famous contemporaries include:

Ralph Waldo Emerson (1803–1882): Emerson was a friend of Holmes and major figure in the Transcendentalist movement.

Nathaniel Hawthorne (1804–1864): Hawthorne's classic novel, *The Scarlet Letter* (1850), deals with issues of adultery and guilt.

Abraham Lincoln (1809–1865): The sixteenth president of the United States, Lincoln led the country through the American Civil War and the abolishment of slavery.

Margaret Fuller (1810–1850): Fuller was a women's rights activist who wrote *Woman in the Nineteenth Century* (1845).

Herman Melville (1819–1991): The author of *Moby-Dick* (1951) and a friend of Holmes.

The Last Leaf The 1870s were a sad time for Holmes personally, because he suffered the loss of his sister and his son-in-law as well as several close friends and colleagues. Despite his personal difficulties and his hiatus from writing literature, major literary figures of both the pre- and post-war generations turned out on December 3, 1879, to celebrate his seventieth birthday. William Dean Howells organized the breakfast, and many of the guests delivered presentations. John Greenleaf Whittier, Annie Fields, Julia Ward Howe, and Julia Dorr all contributed poems. Mark Twain found a receptive audience for his speech as well.

In November 1893 Holmes made his last public appearance. His literary career had slowed considerably; he produced only a few poems and introductions in the 1890s. A long illness plagued him in the spring of 1894. On October 10, 1894, he was sitting with his son when he simply stopped breathing. He was, like the old man in his famous poem "The Last Leaf," the last of his literary generation to die, "the last leaf" to fall.

Works in Literary Context

Holmes was a student, a researcher, a lecturer, a physician, a teacher, and a poet. He was acknowledged as a wit and a brilliant conversationalist in a circle that included James Russell Lowell, Ralph Waldo Emerson, and Henry Wadsworth Longfellow. While literary history is replete with examples of writers who were physicians—including François Rabelais, W. Somerset Maugham, and William Carlos Williams—few expended as much energy in the practice and profession of medicine as Holmes did. Indeed, it has often been argued that medicine was Holm-

es's vocation and literature his avocation. His commemorative tablet at King's Chapel, Boston, reads "Teacher of Anatomy, Essayist, and Poet"—in that order.

Determinism During the 1870s Holmes produced two essays that summarized his positions on determinism, freedom, and responsibility. "Mechanism in Thought and Morals" was delivered as a lecture in June 1870 before the Phi Beta Kappa Society of Harvard University. Holmes began with a description of thought as a mechanical function of the brain. According to Holmes, people control their thinking no more than they control their breathing. Additionally, one's thoughts are activated or propelled by one's unconscious—an idea that was current in Holmes's time and that he used to underpin his argument that people's thinking is mechanical and automatic. Yet, the condition of the moral world according to Holmes is that every act depends upon choice, upon a personal and individual act of the will. How does one reconcile the mechanistic nature of one's being with the freedom of the will that is a prerequisite for a moral order? Holmes turned to this issue in "Crime and Automatism," a review of a study by a French criminologist that he wrote for the *Atlantic Monthly* in April 1875. He believed that human will was not free. In the case of criminals it was frequently governed by organic conditions, such as insanity, and environmental conditions, such as child abuse. Individuals who suffered these conditions could not be held legally or morally accountable for their behavior. Holmes asserted that criminals were damaged physically and emotionally. His position augmented a general shift in society's attitude toward criminals and the insane from a moral model (that they were evil) to a medical model (that they were diseased and needed treatment).

Patriotism Holmes's poem "Old Ironsides" is a good example of how the author infused much of his work with patriotic themes. In the poem, Holmes offers emotional reminiscence of the ship's past glory, of her deck "red with heroes' blood." Although the poem's patriotic tone might seem a bit maudlin, it still provides a good example of poetry's ability to sway public sentiment: the *Constitution* was saved in 1830 and is today docked just north of Boston, making it the U.S. Navy's oldest commissioned vessel.

Works in Critical Context

By the early part of the twentieth century, literary criticism of Holmes had established common themes. If he no longer enjoyed the popular audience that his works had commanded during his lifetime, he nevertheless appeared regularly in literary histories. He was admired for his liberal spirit, for his common sense and practical philosophy, for his rationalism, and, above all, for his impeccable style in the breakfast-table books. But, a number of negative evaluations of Holmes's work were published in the 1920s. He was seen as social conservative who failed to appreciate the economic and social changes of his own time. One critic chided him for his reticence about sex, and he was dismissed as a minor figure in New England's literary history.

"Old Ironsides" Holmes's most famous poem was first published in book form in his collection *Poems* (1836). "He knows how to be sentimental without silliness, and vigorous without violence," an anonymous reviewer commented in *The Yale Literary Magazine* in 1837. The reviewer noted that Holmes avoids the "sin" of clever writers: "a disposition to run as near to mawkishness as possible without falling into it." On the contrary, the reviewer gently accused Holmes of failing to exploit the more serious side of his vision. If anything, the reviewer suggested, "there is too little sentimentality; and we could wish he had allowed himself more latitude where he shows himself most capable." Another anonymous critic, writing in an 1837 volume of *The North American Review*, remarked upon the "easy and natural flow" of Holmes's lyrics.

Elsie Venner: A Romance of Destiny Holmes's first novel, *Elsie Venner: A Romance of Destiny*, includes a mysterious heroine, a marriage plot, and a touch of darkness. Still, Holmes showed great creativity in developing his story by writing what he knew—medicine and issues of religion in science. Although twentieth-century readers would later criticize Holmes for being too politely Victorian about matters of sex, the content shocked and outraged some of his conservative contemporaries. Religious conservatives in particular singled out *Elsie Venner*, and the *Northwest Christian Advocate of Chicago* chose to run an attack on the novel each time a new installment appeared in *The Atlantic Monthly*. The story apparently placed too much emphasis on Elsie's physicality for some people, while Holmes's remarks on religion infuriated others. Nevertheless, the work was popular with many readers, and in 1861 Ticknor and Fields brought out *Elsie Venner* in book form. Several subsequent editions have appeared, including a centennial edition, and it has become the best known of Holmes's novels.

Responses to Literature

1. *Elsie Venner* seeks to explain "hysteria," while Holmes's article on puerperal fever (an infection contracted by mothers during childbirth) helped lessen the spread of this potentially deadly women's disease. Compare Holmes's progressive attitudes towards women's health to those of his contemporaries, particularly of Charlotte Perkins Gilman in her story, "The Yellow Wallpaper" (1892).

2. Research determinism and explain how it applies to Holmes's medical writing.

3. The publication of "Old Ironsides" resulted in the USS *Constitution* being preserved. Can you find

---

COMMON HUMAN EXPERIENCE

Though Holmes is most known for his writing and lecturing, his primary passions were always medicine and science. Here are some other works that highlight the role of science and scientific evidence:

The Foundation Trilogy (1951–1988), a series of novels by Isaac Asimov. Statistical analysis is applied to large-scale human behavior in this lengthy series by one of science fiction's most famous authors.

The Panda's Thumb (1980), an essay collection by Stephen Jay Gould. Gould's book is full of entertaining, accessible essays about evolution and the wonders of science.

Hyperspace (1994), a nonfiction book by Michio Kaku. In this work, the renowned physicist Kaku attempts to describe the forces of the universe through engaging stories and anecdotes.

Ship Fever (1996), a short story collection by Andrea Barrett. Such noted scientists as Carl Linnaeus and Gregor Mendel are fictionalized in this collection.

---

other instances where a single work of literature swayed public opinion in a significant way?

4. Why do you think Holmes despised unconventional medical treatments? Study his *Homeopathy and Its Kindred Delusions* (1842) and determine what he would think of today's alternative medicine practices.

BIBLIOGRAPHY

Books

Brown, E. E. *Life of Oliver Wendell Holmes*. Akron, Ohio: Saalfield, 1903.

Currier, Thomas Franklin and Eleanor M. Tilton. *A Bibliography of Oliver Wendell Holmes*. New York: New York University Press, 1953.

Howe, M. A. DeWolfe. *Holmes of the Breakfast-Table*. New York: Oxford University Press, 1939.

Hoyt, Edwin P. *The Improper Bostonian: Dr. Oliver Wendell Holmes*. New York: William Morrow, 1979.

Kennedy, William Sloane. *Oliver Wendell Holmes: Poet, Litterateur, Scientist*. Boston: S. E. Cassino, 1883.

Menikoff, Barry. "Oliver Wendell Holmes," in *Fifteen American Authors Before 1900*, edited by Robert A. Rees and Earl N. Harbert. Madison, Wis.: University of Wisconsin Press, 1971; revised edition, 1984.

Morse, John T., Jr. *Life and Letters of Oliver Wendell Holmes*, 2 volumes. Boston: Houghton Mifflin, 1896.

Oberndorf, Clarence P. *The Psychiatric Novels of Oliver Wendell Holmes.* New York: Columbia University Press, 1943.

Small, Miriam Rossiter. *Oliver Wendell Holmes.* New York: Twayne, 1962.

Tilton, Eleanor M. *Amiable Autocrat: A Biography of Oliver Wendell Holmes.* New York: Shuman, 1947.

✸ Garrett Hongo

BORN: *1951, Volcano, Hawaii*

NATIONALITY: *American*

GENRE: *Poetry, nonfiction*

MAJOR WORKS:

The River of Heaven (1988)

Volcano (1995)

Overview

A *yonsei* (fourth-generation Japanese American) who was born in Hawaii and claims it as his emotional home, Garrett Kaoru Hongo is not only an important voice in post–World War II Asian American literature but also a celebrated mainstream American poet. Hongo's poetry collection *The River of Heaven* (1988) was a finalist for the Pulitzer Prize in 1989.

Garrett Hongo   *Courtesy of the author*

Works in Biographical and Historical Context

American with Japanese Roots   Garrett Kaoru Hongo was born May 30, 1951, in an area known as 29 Miles Volcano Highway, in Volcano, Hawaii. His parents, both of Japanese ancestry, are Albert Kazuyoshi Hongo, an electrical technician, and Louise Tomiko Kubota Hongo, a personnel analyst. Because of Hongo's emphasis on the importance of family, his parents play important roles in his collection *Yellow Light* (1982). The Hongo family moved to Oahu (the setting for Hongo's prosaic *Volcano*, 1995) when the poet was eight months old, and relocated to Los Angeles when he was six, finally settling in Gardena, California.

Though born after the war, Hongo's poetry is affected by the fact that during World War II (1939–45), the United States government unjustly removed over 120,000 Japanese Americans from their homes and sent them to internment camps throughout the western United States. The shared anguish of the experience of internment—and the shattered illusion that Asian Americans were as "American" as their European peers—resulted in an eloquent outpouring of literary works, and Hongo's poetry refers often to the resultant identity crisis many Asian Americans faced.

A Change of Scene   In Gardena, Hongo attended a high school that had a racial makeup of approximately one thousand Caucasian students, one thousand African American students, and one thousand Japanese American students, a mixture that introduced the poet to the problems and advantages associated with race and ethnicity that inform both *Yellow Light* and *The River of Heaven*. After he graduated, he attended Pomona College and the University of California at Irvine, where he earned a B.A. in English in 1973. That year Hongo met Wakako Yamauchi, a former internee at the Poston Relocation Center in Arizona during World War II, who published poetic reminiscences about Japanese American farm life. She became his mentor, encouraging him to explore his ancestral roots in his poetry.

In 1973–1974 Hongo was awarded a Thomas J. Watson Fellowship to spend a year studying and writing in Japan. Immediately after his year in Japan, Hongo entered the University of Michigan as a graduate student in Japanese language and literature. Although he left after a year of studies, during that time he won the university's Hopwood Poetry Prize for 1975. He abandoned his graduate studies in order to move to Seattle because of his identification with the West Coast (which is the backdrop for his co-authored *The Buddha Bandits Down Highway 99*, 1978) and its Asian American literati, namely Frank Chin and Lawson Inada.

Professional and Cultural Identity   In Seattle he worked as poet in residence for the Seattle Arts Commission and was the founder and director of the Asian Exclusion Act, a local theater group. In his ongoing efforts to support the cause of Asian American authors, he staged various plays at the Theater of the Ethnic Cultural Center at the University of Washington, including a portion of his own *Nisei Bar & Grill* (1977), an incomplete work, and Chin's *The Year of the Dragon* (1974), which he chose for its symbolic value. Hongo has taught at the University of Washington; the University of California at Irvine, where he earned an M.F.A. in creative writing in 1980; the University of Missouri, where he was poetry editor of the *Missouri Review* from 1984 to 1988; and the University of Oregon, where he was director of the creative writing program from 1989 to 1993. In 1982 he married Cynthia Anne Thiessen, a violinist and musicologist, and they have two sons, Alexander, born in 1984, and Hudson, born in 1987. Hongo and his wife separated in 1995 and divorced in 2000.

In 1996, Hongo published *Volcano*, a memoir of his early childhood spent in Hawaii and an attempt to reconnect spiritually with the place where he was born. Although he has published no full-length works since that time, Hongo continues to teach creative writing at the University of Oregon at Eugene.

Works in Literary Context

Connection with the Land Hongo's emphasis on finding or establishing a community of Asian American writers is reflected in the fact that his first publication was a communal effort. Along with Inada and Alan Chong Lau, he published his first collection of poetry in 1978 in a book titled *The Buddha Bandits Down Highway 99*. In this text, Highway 99, which connects many cities in its winding path along the West Coast, represents the geographical connectedness of poetry to the land, a theme that Hongo has revisited throughout his career. One of the poems here, "A Porphyry of Nature," includes a catalogue of nature: "the ancient tidepools of the Pleistocene era . . . / California oak and acorn / scrubgrass, rivermist,/ and lupine in the foothills . . . /gathering of sand, rock, gypsum, clay,/ limestone, water and tar." The theme of connection with the land is also shown in his memoir *Volcano*, which places heavy emphasis on the natural environment into which Hongo was born.

A Melting Pot of Words Hongo is postmodern in his poetic techniques, which feature the appropriation and sampling of popular melodies and lyrics, real conversations, others' diary entries, diverse histories, and personal postcards. Yet, according to Laurie Filipelli, he lists as his influences the Romantic poets, American poet Walt Whitman, fourteenth-century Shinto priest Yoshida Kenko, and American blues singer and guitarist Robert Johnson. Hongo is considered at his best when his poetry relates stories, whether confessional or in the form of dramatic monologue, and his lines are often narrative. He is comfortable creating narratives by piecing together fact and conjecture, things gleaned from family anecdotes, written and oral histories, diaries and letters, and his grandfather Kubota's "talk stories," informal accounts of Japanese, Chinese, Native Hawaiian, and American Blues lore. For

example, according to one of Hongo's notes in the text, the dramatic monologue "Pinoy at the Coming World," from *The River of Heaven*, is derived from Filipino American lore, while "Stepchild" from *Yellow Light* is informed by Hongo's retelling of painful and usually ignored aspects of Japanese American history, such as the World War II internment camps, the exploitation of immigrant laborers, and the aftermath of these events.

Works in Critical Context

Unlike that of many of his contemporaries, Garrett Hongo's poetry is not confrontational. Yet, his subtle style brings to the forefront the issue of discrimination against Japanese Americans and other ethnic groups. According to Barbara Drake, Hongo "speaks for an idealistic generation intent on learning, understanding, and possibly correcting the mistakes of recent history." Hence, Hongo has devoted his life not only to publishing his own poems, but also helping other Asian American writers get published.

The River of Heaven Gayle K. Sato notes that *The River of Heaven* is a "recuperative project . . . where the act of writing is inseparable from a longing for 'ancestral help.'" According to Sato, the first section of *The River of Heaven* is prefaced with a line from Li Po because Hongo associates cultural recuperation and nostalgia with the eighth-century Chinese poet. Yet the poems that conclude the first section invoke many old Hawaiian ghosts, either in the form of ancestors who are given voice in dramatic monologues, or in wistful remembrances of boyhood events in the Hawaiian landscape, the "unreal dwelling" of *Volcano*.

COMMON HUMAN EXPERIENCE

Perhaps because of his mixed culture and his constant moving around as a child, Hongo is preoccupied with finding a sense of belonging. Here are some other works that deal with the process of finding one's place in the world, often via seemingly aimless wandering.

The Dharma Bums (1958), a novel by Jack Kerouac. Here a pair of disenchanted Beat Generation writers travel the country to find a place that offers solace, and, with the help of some Buddhist philosophy, eventually settle on the Pacific Northwest.

Ceremony (1977), a memoir by Leslie Marmon Silko. In this novel, Tayo returns from the Vietnam War to find his Laguna Pueblo reservation altered, and must find a place for himself with the help of a shaman.

Tender Mercies (1983), a film by Bruce Beresford. Robert Duvall plays an aimless, alcoholic country songwriter who connects with a young widow and her son in a small Texas town.

The Motorcycle Diaries (1996), a memoir by Che Guevara. This book is a posthumous account of Che Guevara's journey across South America, where he became inspired by the people he met and went on to become a revolutionary.

Volcano Although *The River of Heaven* won acclaim for Hongo, he felt he needed to supplement its vision in his next work, *Volcano*. As he stated in an interview with Sharon E. Colley, "I was kind of holding back in *The River of Heaven*. And I really felt there was just so much more to say. So those stories I needed to revisit and tell more fully." He went on to explain that in *Volcano* he attempted to "develop a language that would be fitting and include the natural figures of the landscape." The form of the book is that of the zuihitsu, the "poetic essay" developed in fourteenth-century Japan that is similar to the personal essays of Henry David Thoreau and Ralph Waldo Emerson. Chapters loosely alternate between discussions of the volcano and the physical landscape and insights about life, a technique that Hongo claims is modeled after Herman Melville's *Moby-Dick* (1851). In *The Southern Review*, reviewer Mark Jarman calls *Volcano* "a remarkable, profound, and haunting book" and "certainly one the reader will not soon forget."

Responses to Literature

1. Why do you think Hongo abandoned traditional poetic techniques to write the more essay-like *Volcano*?

2. Why do you think writings related to the search for identity are more common among writers who belong to a cultural, ethnic, or philosophical group that is different from mainstream society? Does this mean such themes are not entirely universal?

3. Compare Hongo's personal history to that of Li-Young Lee's. Does their poetry reflect their different experiences of settling into mainland America?

4. For many people, Hawaii seems like paradise. Do you think Hongo feels this way about his native state? Why or why not? Find examples in his work that indicate his attitude toward Hawaii.

BIBLIOGRAPHY

Books

Filipelli, Laurie. *Garrett Hongo*. Boise, Idaho: Boise State University Press, 1997.

Fonseca, Anthony J. *Dictionary of Literary Biography, Volume 312: Asian American Writers*. A Bruccoli Clark Layman Book. Edited by Deborah L. Madsen, University of Geneva. Detroit: Gale, 2005, pp. 117–122.

Lee, A. Robert. "Ethnicities: The American Self-Tellings of Leslie Marmon Silko, Richard Rodriguez, Darryl Pinckney, and Garrett Hongo." *Writing Lives: American Biography and Autobiography*, edited by Hans Bak and Hans Krabbendam. Amsterdam: Vrije Universiteit University Press, 1998, pp. 122–135.

Ling, Amy, ed. *Yellow Light: The Flowering of Asian American Arts*. Philadelphia, Pa.: Temple University Press, 1999, pp. 103–110.

Moyers, Bill. "Garrett Hongo." *The Language of Life: A Festival of Poets*. New York: Doubleday, 1995.

Periodicals

Colley, Sharon E. "An Interview with Garrett Hongo." *Forkroads: A Journal of Ethnic American Literature* 4 (Summer 1996): 47–63.

Jarman, Mark. "The Volcano Inside." *Southern Review* (April 1996): 337–343.

Nishimoto, Warren. "Interview with Writer Garrett Hongo, Oral History and Literature." *Oral History Recorder* (Summer 1986): 2–4.

Sato, Gayle K. "Cultural Recuperation in Garrett Hongo's *The River of Heaven*." *Studies in American Literature* 37 (February 2001): 57–74.

Slowik, Mary. "Beyond Lot's Wife: The Immigration Poems of Marilyn Chin, Garrett Hongo, Li-Young Lee, and David Mura." *MELUS* 25, nos. 3–4 (Fall/Winter 2000): 221–242.

✲ Frank Horne

BORN: *1899, Brooklyn, New York*

DIED: *1974, New York, New York*

NATIONALITY: *American*

GENRE: *Poetry, fiction*

MAJOR WORKS:

Haverstraw (1963)

Overview

Frank Horne was a significant voice of the Harlem Renaissance, whose reputation rests primarily upon a group of award-winning poems he published in the *Crisis* in 1925. His success during this period links him to New Negro Renaissance poets, but his poems are generally more personal and traditional in concern than many of those of the other young writers of the 1920s. A northerner who went against the pattern of migration by going to live in the South, Horne wrote poetry early in his life before becoming a physician and an administrator with the United States Housing Authority in Washington, D.C., and later in New York.

Works in Biographical and Historical Context

A Doctor and a Poet Horne was born in Brooklyn, New York, and grew up in that area. He attended undergraduate program at the City College of New York, where he received his bachelor's degree in 1921. He was an outstanding track star at City College, and he gained experience that would serve him well during his teaching career in the late 1920s. He earned a master's degree from the University of Southern California and a Doctor of Optometry degree from Northern Illinois College of Ophthalmology and Otology in 1923. While he was able to practice ophthalmology in Chicago and New York for a few years, his medical profession was cut short by what he called a "mean illness," which forced him to seek a warmer climate. Although information about Horne's life is incomplete, it may be assumed that the illness resulted in some loss of the use of his legs. Many of his later poems use images of failing to walk, of the legs being strapped into cumbersome contraptions, and of the pain associated with "reluctant" legs.

Though he developed an early interest in writing, Horne acknowledged that Charles S. Johnson, editor of *Opportunity*, and Gwendolyn Bennett, a poet, urged him to publish his work. His first prose was published while he was still working as an ophthalmologist; "Black Verse," a review of *Anthology of Verse by American Negroes*, edited by Newman Ivey White and Walter Clinton Jackson, appeared in the November 1924 issue of *Opportunity*. Horne praised the editors for their effort to mark the achievements of African-American poets but criticized them for their stereotypical expectations of poetry purely of a racial bent. He singled out the inclusion of work by Countee Cullen for special praise and encouraged other young poets to sound distinct notes in their creativity.

Although Horne wanted to write good prose, he was more successful as a poet. He reached his height of success in 1925, when he received second prize in the poetry category in the Amy Spingarn Contest in Literature and Art sponsored by the magazine *Crisis*. He submitted his winning entry, "Letters Found near a Suicide," under the pseudonym of Xavier I; the poems were pub-

lished in the November 1925 issue of the journal. There were eleven "letters" in the prize-winning version of the poem; by 1930 Horne had added an additional seven poems to "Letters," all of which would be published as the first section of *Haverstraw*, his collection brought out by Breman in 1963.

A Change of Climate In 1927 illness forced Horne to move from New York to Georgia, where he began a teaching and administrative career at Fort Valley High and Industrial School (later Fort Valley State College). Although he was light-skinned enough to pass for white, he did not choose to do so. He was especially sensitive to the changes in accommodation and treatment as he journeyed into the South. In "I Am Initiated into the Negro Race," published in *Opportunity* in 1928, he described the transition from privilege and comfort to the deprivation of these luxuries, and he connected them to actual travel from points north to those in the South. His initial negative impressions, however, did not prevent him from doing useful work or from supporting the industrial school concept.

He continued his creative efforts in 1928 by publishing "Harlem," a poem, and "The Man Who Wanted to be Red," a short story, in the *Crisis*. "Harlem" most approximates the work of other young writers of the period, especially Langston Hughes. Horne uses the background of a saxophonist's performance to conjure up images of what Harlem means. In its experimental form and its attempt to imitate jazz rhythms, it is reminiscent of many of the folk-based poems Hughes wrote.

As trainer of the track team at Fort Valley High, Horne led his runners to several championships in the late 1920s and early 1930s. In "Running Fools: Athletics in a Colored School," published in the *Crisis* in 1930, he discusses the exploits of some of his famous stars both male and female, and introduces the larger world to life in an industrial school. He extends this introduction in "The Industrial School of the South," the two-part series published in *Opportunity* in 1935. In it, it becomes clear that he shared the philosophy of training espoused by Booker T. Washington at Tuskegee and was greatly inspired by his example.

Eventual Recognition During the nine years he worked at Fort Valley High and Industrial School, Horne moved from teaching to serving as dean and acting president. He also occasionally completed prose pieces for journals. In 1930 he wrote an essay for *Crisis* in which Henry A. Hunt, the former principal of Fort Valley High and Industrial School, was recognized for receiving the Spingarn medal. In 1936 he moved out of education and into work with various housing agencies. By 1940 he was acting special assistant to the administrator of the U.S. Housing Authority, and he had turned his attention to writing about problems connected with public housing; his article "Providing New Housing for Negroes" appeared in the October 1940 issue of *Opportunity*. His life of public service eclipsed his poetry writing, and it was not until 1963, when the Englishman Paul Breman brought out

Haverstraw, a collection of his poems, that Horne's poetry became readily accessible to a larger audience.

After the publication of *Haverstraw*, Horne published poems occasionally in the *Crisis. Haverstraw* and Horne's sporadically published poems are a testament to the fact that, in spite of the pressures of illness and public service, he cared enough about creativity to leave a monument for posterity. When he died in 1974, he was far from being a famous poet, but those who had consistently anthologized his work over the years recognized that his poems were worthy of continued reading and discussion.

Works in Literary Context

Death as a Theme "Letters Found near a Suicide" is characteristic of the variety of somber issues Horne treats. He describes a man's preparation for death, in which the subject writes several short poems to individuals who have had significant roles in his life. "To All of You," the first letter in the series, sets the stage for the poetic flirting with suicide; the subject is curious about "the bosom of this deep, dark pool / Of oblivion" and is destined to explore "those far shores / That knew me not." "To Mother," the third letter in the series, bemoans the fact that living is a painful existence beyond man's control. The speaker wonders how anybody—particularly his mother, whom he has caused much agony—can care, but he knows the power of a black mother's love. If he dies she will grieve and want him back, because to her, suicide is not the answer.

Lessons on Race "The Man Who Wanted to be Red" is called "a fairy tale for children of the earth." The story is an allegory of the slave trade and the animosity between blacks and whites in the United States. Horne depicts the "Reds," a predatory race who enslave the "Greens," bringing them to the Kingdom of Ur to work for them. Eventually, some of the Red men notice the beautiful Green women and have children by them. These children become the "Whites," a degraded outcast group. Juda, the protagonist of the story, is a "White." From experiments initially begun by his Red father, he perfects a technique for turning Greens into Reds. He abandons his plan, however, when he witnesses a group of Reds abusing a Green; he does not want the people with whom he identifies through his mother to turn into such brutes. As a story for children, the piece is engaging; its fanciful use of skin colors shows how absurd racial prejudices can be.

In "Nigger, A Chant for Children," Horne teaches history by listing names of such famous black people as Hannibal, Othello, and Crispus Attucks. He feels that the world should know these "Niggers," and black children should not be hurt by name-calling but should be proud of the great members of their own race. The use of "nigger" in the title is a deliberate effort to transcend the negative connotations of that word. It is also a declamation against injustice. In this seven-stanza poem, Horne repeats "nigger" for dramatic emphasis and creates ironic contrasts through the juxtaposition of children's songs and the shouts of the bigot. Despite persecution and prejudice, he was able to say to African-American children that blacks have a great deal to be proud of, and that no race-baiting epithets should cause them to lose sight of that fact.

Works in Critical Context

James Weldon Johnson, in his introduction to Horne in *The Book of American Negro Poetry*, noted that Horne "is in every sense modern." Johnson adds, "He is ironical and skeptical, and his philosophy is often gathered up into a keen thrust. He possesses the authentic gift of poetry." Although Horne's poetry was more traditional than that of many other young blacks of his generation, "Harlem" utilized jazz rhythms and experimental forms that were more typical of the day. Many of Horne's poems were reprinted in anthologies and two were translated for inclusion in a 1929 German anthology.

"Nigger: A Chant for Children"

Critic Ronald Primeau divided Horne's poems into three types. Some poems described a quest, such as athletics or planning a suicide. Other poems honored black heritage, including "Nigger, A Chant for Children:" "Little Black boy / Chased down the street—/ 'Nigger, nigger never die / Black face an' shiny eye, / Nigger . . . nigger . . . nigger.'" Subsequent stanzas praised black heroes. The final stanza is identical to the first except that the little black boy is no longer chased. The third category of Horne's poetry relied on Christian images to connect black religion and spirituality with black militancy, as in the often reprinted "Kid Stuff (December, 1942)."

Responses to Literature

1. Horne often referred to feet and running in his poems. What other symbols can you find in his work?

2. Research the Harlem Renaissance and explain why Harlem was the perfect place for such an artistic movement to occur.

3. Horne worked in education; how is this aspect of his career obvious in his poem "Nigger"?

4. Horne is often compared to Countee Cullen and Langston Hughes. Other than writing about race, what do these three poets have in common? Compare their styles and provide specific examples from each poet to support your statements.

BIBLIOGRAPHY

Books

Brown, Sterling. *Negro Poetry and Drama*. Washington, D.C.: Associates in Negro Folk Education, 1937.

Chapman, Abraham, ed. *Black Voices*. New York: St. Martin's Press, 1968, pp. 401–403.

"Frank S. Horne." *Contemporary Black Biography*. Vol. 44. Detroit: Gale, 2004.

Johnson, James Weldon, *The Book of American Negro Poetry*. Fort Washington, Pa.: Harvest Books, 1969.

Kerlin, Robert T. "The New Forms of Poetry: Frank Horne," in *Negro Poets and Their Poems*, rev. ed. New York: Associated Publisher, 1947, pp. 206–208.

Primeau, Ronald. "Frank Horne and the Second Echelon Poets of the Harlem Renaissance," in *The Harlem Renaissance Remembered*, ed. Arna Bontemps. New York: Dodd, Mead, 1972, pp. 247–267.

Witalec, Janet, ed. *Harlem Renaissance: A Gale Critical Companion*, Vol. 2. Detroit: Gale, 2003, pp. 587–594.

✿ Khaled Hosseini

BORN: *1965, Kabul, Afghanistan*

NATIONALITY: *American*

GENRE: *Fiction*

MAJOR WORKS:
The Kite Runner (2003)
A Thousand Splendid Suns (2007)

Khaled Hosseini   *Hosseini, Khaled, photograph. Matthew Simmons / WireImage / Getty Images.*

Overview

Khaled Hosseini's fiction is inspired by his memories of growing up in pre-Soviet-controlled Afghanistan and Iran, and of the people who influenced him as a child. His debut novel, *The Kite Runner*, introduces readers to life in the pre-Soviet Afghanistan of the author's childhood and honors his memories of the servant Hossein Khan, a member of the Hazara people who worked in the Hosseini household during their years in Tehran and taught the young Hosseini to read and write. Hosseini's second novel, *A Thousand Splendid Suns*, follows thirty years of tumultuous Afghan history, a history torn by civil war, the rise of the Taliban. It also describes the lives of two women who work to sustain their families, friendships, and hope for the future despite challenging circumstances. As Barbara Hoffert noted in a *Library Journal* review, *A Thousand Splendid Suns* "proves that one can write a successful follow-up after debuting with a phenomenal best seller."

Works in Biographical and Historical Context

Exiled by Turmoil Khaled Hosseini was born in Kabul, Afghanistan, in 1965, the son of a diplomat father and teacher mother. When the Afghan Foreign Ministry assigned Hosseini's father to Iran in 1970, his family accompanied him and lived in Tehran until 1973. That year, Afghan king Zahir Shah was overthrown in a bloodless coup, leaving the government unstable and the country vulnerable. In 1976, the family moved to Paris, again on diplomatic assignment. They were still living there in 1980 when the Afghan government fell in a bloody communist coup and Soviet troops took control of Afghanistan.

The Hosseinis were granted political asylum in the United States and moved to San Jose, California. Arriving in their new country with nothing, the Hosseini family relied on welfare before their financial condition improved. Fifteen years old at the time of his arrival in the United States, Hosseini eventually trained as a physician. Writing remained his main love, however, and he worked on *The Kite Runner*, his first novel, when he was not working as a medical internist at a Los Angeles hospital. In 2003, *The Kite Runner*, was published and quickly became an international bestseller in forty-eight countries. It sold 1.25 million copies in paperback, largely due to word of mouth and its inclusion in innumerable book-group reading lists at a time when sales of fiction were reportedly low. Four years later, the film adaptation of the novel was nominated for an Academy Award.

Spanning four decades, *The Kite Runner* is narrated by Amir, a writer living in California. Amir begins his story with his affluent childhood in Kabul, where the quiet, motherless boy yearns for attention from his busy father, Baba, and finds a friend in Hassan, the son of his father's servant. Eventually, Amir and Hassan are separated—emotionally, by a traumatic attack against

Hassan, and geographically, when Amir's father is relocated. Amir flees Afghanistan during the Soviet occupation, settling in the Bay Area of California and eventually becoming a successful writer. Though the story is fiction, it is clearly shaped by Hosseini's childhood memories of Kabul and the relationships he developed when young.

A Return to the Homeland A trip to Kabul in 2003, the year *The Kite Runner* was published, provided Hosseini with the inspiration for his second novel. As he explained to Louise Ermelino in *Publishers Weekly*, he witnessed Afghan women "walking down the street, wearing burqa, with five or six children, begging." Talking to these women, Hosseini heard stories that both shocked and saddened him: "One woman told me she was the wife of a policeman who hadn't been paid in six months. The family was starving, so she sent her children out to beg." These stories were the germ, the starting point, for Hosseini's next novel.

In 2006 Hosseini, himself a former Afghan refugee, was named a goodwill envoy to the Office of the United Nations High Commissioner for Refugees (UNHCR). This humanitarian organization, the winner of the Nobel Peace Prize, provides shelter, protection, emergency food, medical care, and other necessities to those who have been forced to abandon their homes due to violence, persecution, or war. The U.S. office of the organization recognized *The Kite Runner*'s impact by naming Hosseini the 2006 Humanitarian of the Year. Hosseini returned to Afghanistan as a UNHCR envoy in September of 2007, just four months after his second novel, *A Thousand Splendid Suns*, was published. Taking its title from a seventeenth-century poem by Saib-e-Tabrizi, which praises the cultured and ancient city of Kabul, the novel chronicles forty-five years of Afghan history, including the country's occupation by Soviet forces and the subsequent fundamentalist Islamic rule of the Taliban. Hosseini uses the relationship between two very different women, wives to the same brutal man, to shine a light on the plight of contemporary Afghan women and makes them the focus of the novel's heartbreaking story. *A Thousand Splendid Suns* was favorably compared to *The Kite Runner* and matched the first novel's critical and popular success. *Booklist* gave the novel a starred review and said, "Readers who lost themselves in *The Kite Runner* will not want to miss this unforgettable follow-up."

Works in Literary Context

Hosseini's two novels *The Kite Runner* and *A Thousand Splendid Suns* have garnered widespread popular and critical praise. Noted for their style as well as their subject matter, Hosseini's novels inspired readers to become interested in the people of Afghanistan in a way no other works of contemporary fiction or nonfiction were able to do in the first decade of the twenty-first century. To keep his wartime stories from being too depressing, Hosseini relies on elements of melodrama to balance the mood. Known for his simple prose style, the author writes stories that resonate with audiences from many cultural, ethnic, and economic backgrounds.

Hope in Wartime   In *A Thousand Splendid Suns*, two victimized but courageous female characters are forced to endure unspeakable daily suffering at home and in public. With the rise of the Taliban, their difficult lives become even more challenging, yet they find ways to endure. Hosseini provides detailed glimpses of normalcy and everyday living that remind the reader that this novel is as much about life as it is about war. Amidst the cruelty and death, the characters find ways to ease their suffering.

Melodrama   Defined as the predominance of plot and physical action over characterization, melodrama usually carries negative connotations. Critics, though, have found that Hosseini's melodramatic flourishes work in his favor in both his novels, perhaps due to the novels' weighty subject matter. In *The Kite Runner*, melodramatic touches include such stereotypical story lines as the father who wants his son to be a doctor instead of a writer, and who wants his son to fight back instead of cowering. A despicable villain and a saintly sidekick are two of the more stereotypical characters found in melodrama. The last two appear in *A Thousand Splendid Suns*, this time as a brutal husband and his young, beautiful bride, respectively. Critics have faulted Hosseini for his one-dimensional characters, yet note that the melodrama usually gives way to intimate renderings of everyday Afghani life.

Works in Critical Context

Hosseini's two novels have received widespread critical and popular success. Employing a largely melodramatic style to tell heartbreaking stories set against the backdrop of war, Hosseini is known for his deft portrayal of the complexities of human nature. His reliance on simple prose lends his stories a graceful power that has become something of a trademark.

The Kite Runner   "Rather than settle for a coming-of-age or travails-of-immigrants story, Hosseini has folded them both into this searing spectacle of hard-won personal salvation," wrote a *Kirkus Reviews* critic in a review of *The Kite Runner*. This reviewer added that the novel also serves up "a rich slice of Afghan culture." Edward Hower wrote in the *New York Times Book Review* that the author's "depiction of prerevolutionary Afghanistan is rich in warmth and humor but also tense with the friction between the nation's different ethnic groups." "The novel's canvas turns dark when Hosseini describes the suffering of his country under the tyranny of the Taliban," Hower continued, noting that "the final third of the book is full of haunting images." *School Library Journal* reviewer Penny Stevens called *The Kite*

LITERARY AND HISTORICAL CONTEMPORARIES

Khaled Hosseini's famous contemporaries include:

Dai Sijie (1954–): Chinese-born French author of *Balzac and the Little Chinese Seamstress*, a semi-autobiographical novel about the author's experience during the Chinese cultural revolution in the late 1960s and early 1970s.

Dmitri A. Medvedev (1965–): This Russian president came to power in 2008 after his predecessor Vladimir Putin stepped down from the presidency.

Hamid Karzai (1957–): President of Afghanistan since 2004, Karzai was active in the Afghans efforts to drive out the Soviet occupation force in Afghanistan during the 1980s.

Azar Nafisi (1955–): Iranian professor and writer who wrote the award-winning bestseller *Reading Lolita in Tehran: A Memoir in Books* (2003).

Runner a "beautifully written first novel," and a *Publishers Weekly* contributor dubbed the book "stunning. It is rare that a book is at once so timely and of such high literary quality."

A Thousand Splendid Suns   Described by a *Publishers Weekly* contributor as "another searing epic of Afghanistan in turmoil," *A Thousand Splendid Suns* brings to life the brutal treatment endured by women in the repressive patriarchy promoted by Taliban culture, while also presenting what the *Publishers Weekly* contributor dubbed a "lyrical evocation of the lives and enduring hopes of [his]...resilient characters." "Unimaginably tragic, Hosseini's magnificent second novel is a sad and beautiful testament to both Afghani suffering and strength," concluded *Booklist* contributor Kristine Huntley, and a *Kirkus Reviews* writer noted that *A Thousand Splendid Suns* "is never depressing." Praising Hosseini's prose as "simple and unadorned," Barbara Hoffert, in her *Library Journal* review, observed that the author "deftly sketches the history of his native land," creating a "heartbreaking" and "highly recommended" tale.

Responses to Literature

1. In *The Kite Runner*, the United States serves as a place for Amir to rehash his memories and for Baba to mourn his. Hosseini writes that in the United States there are "homes that made Baba's house in Wazir Akbar Khan look like a servant's hut." Do you detect any irony in this statement? If so, how does irony present itself in the novel?

COMMON HUMAN EXPERIENCE

A recurring theme running through Hosseini's books is the plight of women in contemporary Afghanistan. Here are some other works that shine a light on Afghani women living under fundamentalist Islam.

> *Torn Between Two Cultures* (2004), an autobiography by Maryam Qudrat Aseel. The author describes her life as an Afghan-American born to first generation Afghan immigrants. Aseel wrote her autobiography as an attempt to bridge the gap of understanding between the Islamic world and the West.
>
> *Kabul Beauty School: An American Woman Goes Behind the Veil* (2007), a memoir by Deborah Rodriguez. This work describes the author's attempts at establishing a modern beauty school in the war-torn nation of Afghanistan and offers a rare glimpse of the daily lives of Afghan women.
>
> *The Bookseller of Kabul* (2003), a work of nonfiction by Norwegian journalist Asne Seierstad. This international bestseller describes a nation recovering from war, mired in poverty and misogyny. The book's sometimes shocking stories give readers a brutal view of life under fundamentalist Islam.

2. Khaled Hosseini provides a vivid portrait of Afghanistan, both the privileged world of Amir's childhood and the stricken country under the Taliban. Do his descriptions differ from the ideas you may already have had about Afghanistan? How so? Write a brief essay outlining the differences in Hosseini's portrayal and what you previously imagined.

3. Using library resources and the Internet, research the Soviet invasion of Afghanistan. What significant events led to the invasion? Where did the majority of fighting take place? What caused the Soviets to eventually withdraw? How did the invasion impact Afghan life? Use your findings to write an essay that explores the invasion and its place in Afghanistan's history.

4. Imagine what it was like for Afghan women to have to adjust to the laws enforced by the Taliban. What do you think it was like for women who were used to working to quit their jobs and stay inside every day? How would you feel if you could not go out in public without a male relative escort? Write a paper that details your thoughts and feelings about these repressive laws and how you might react to them.

5. After September 11, 2001, Muslims received widespread negative attention in the U.S. What can be done to replace the negative stereotypes that have become common since the terrorist attacks on the Pentagon and World Trade Center? List your findings in a paper and provide at least three reasonable methods to end the negative stereotyping of Muslims.

BIBLIOGRAPHY

Periodicals

Huntley, Kristine. Review of *The Kite Runner*. *Booklist* (July 2003): 1864.

Review of *The Kite Runner*. *Kirkus Reviews* (May 1, 2003): 630.

Hoffert, Barbara. Review of *A Thousand Splendid Suns*. *Library Journal* (March 14, 2007): 58.

Hower, Edward. Review of *The Kite Runner*. *New York Times Book Review* (August 3, 2003): 4.

Ermelino, Louisa. Interview with Khaled Hosseini. *Publishers Weekly* (March 19, 2007): 34.

O'Brien, James. Review of *The Kite Runner*. *Times Literary Supplement* (October 10, 2003): 25.

Web sites

The 2008 Time 100: Khaled Hosseini. Retrieved September 27, 2008, from http://www.time.com/time/specials/2007/article/0,28804,1733748_1733752_1735971,00.html.

O'Rourke, Meghan. *Do I Really Have to Read The Kite Runner?* Retrieved September 27, 2008, from http://www.slate.com/id/2123280/.

Khaled Hosseini Online. *A Thousand Splendid Suns* Retrieved September 27, 2008, from http://www.khaledhosseini.com/index2.htm.

✸ Jeanne Wakatsuki Houston

BORN: *1934, Inglewood, California*

NATIONALITY: *Japanese American*

GENRE: *Memoir, fiction*

MAJOR WORKS:
Farewell to Manzanar: A True Story of Japanese–American Experience During and After the World War II Internment (1973)
Don't Cry, It's Only Thunder (1984)
The Legend of Fire Horse Woman (2003)

Overview

According to a *Los Angeles Times* reporter, the publication of the memoir *Farewell to Manzanar: A True Story of Japanese–American Experience during and after the World War II Internment* (1973) made Jeanne Wakatsuki Houston "quite unintentionally, a voice for a heretofore silent segment of society." The book, which Houston wrote with her husband, James D. Houston, describes her family's experience as residents of an internment camp in Nevada where Japanese Americans were forced to live during World War II. The book, which has sold more than a million copies since it was first published in 1973, was also made into a film for television. Copies of the film were distributed to every public school and library in California in 2001 as part of a curriculum focusing on history and civil rights. Houston has been honored with many awards and prizes, including the 1979 Woman of Achievement Award from the National Women's Political Caucus and a 1976 Humanitas Prize for her television adaptation of *Farewell to Manzanar*.

Works in Biographical and Historical Context

Executive Order 9066   After declaring war on Japan, in an atmosphere of World War II hysteria, President Roosevelt authorized the internment of tens of thousands of American citizens of Japanese ancestry and resident aliens from Japan. Roosevelt's Executive Order 9066, dated February 19, 1942, authorized the evacuation of these citizens to hastily organized assembly centers governed by the military in Arizona, California, Oregon, and Washington state. The rationale behind the order was that Japanese immigrants—most of whom were not United States citizens, simply because the government at the time refused to allow Asian immigrants to obtain citizenship—would be likely to spy on American military activities and report back to their native country. In addition to Japanese immigrants, however, the government also forcibly detained many children of immigrants who, because they were born on United States soil, were fully American citizens in the eyes of the law. The same executive order, as well as other wartime orders and restrictions, was also applied to smaller numbers of residents of the United States who were of Italian or German descent. While these individuals suffered grievous civil liberties violations, the wartime actions applied to Japanese Americans were worse and more sweeping, uprooting entire communities and targeting citizens as well as resident aliens.

Early Years   Jeanne Wakatsuki Houston was born on September 26, 1934, in Inglewood, California, to George Ko Wakatsuki, a fisher and farmer, and Riku Sugai Wakatsuki, a homemaker. She was seven years old when she and her family of first- and second-generation Japanese Americans were forcibly removed to an internment camp near the Sierra Nevada Mountains. The Manzanar Relocation Center, located in the desert of southeastern California, was home to the Wakatsuki family for the next three years.

After the war, the Wakatsukis settled in San Jose, California, where Mr. Wakatsuki took up berry farming and Jeanne attended San Jose State University. She received a degree in journalism from the university in 1956 and married her classmate and fellow writer John D.

Houston a year later. His tour in the United States Air Force took them to England, and eventually to France, where Houston studied French civilization at the prestigious Paris University, the Sorbonne.

Writing Her Life   Silenced by guilt, Houston was thirty-seven years old before she felt comfortable expressing her feelings about the internment. As she later explained to the *Los Angeles Times*, her experiences made her feel "sullied, like when you are a rape victim. . . . You feel you must have done something. You feel you are part of the act." *Farewell to Manzanar* was among the first works of literature to publicize the story of Japanese American internment. According to *Los Angeles Times* contributor Ajay Singh, almost twenty-five years after its original publication, the book remains an "accessible and unsentimental work" that "sheds light on a subject that had been largely ignored in popular histories." The U.S. government formally apologized for interning 120,000 Japanese Americans during wartime in 1998.

Houston further explored the difficulties of post–World War II Asian Americans in *Beyond Manzanar: Views of Asian-American Womanhood* (1985). Using a combination of short fiction and essays, she describes the problems she and other women have found in trying to assimilate with American culture while maintaining the traditions of their Japanese upbringing. *Los Angeles Times Book Review* contributor Jonathan Kirsch described the book as a worthwhile endeavor. Kirsch wrote, "Houston writes poignantly of the chasms of myth and expectation

COMMON HUMAN EXPERIENCE

A recurring theme running through Houston's work is the Japanese-American experience of life in the internment camps during World War II. Here are some other works that explore the same theme:

Unfinished Business (1984), a film directed by Steven Okazaki. This Oscar-nominated documentary was one of the first to confront the relocation of Japanese Americans to internment camps during World War II.

Come See the Paradise (1990), a film directed by Alan Parker. This film, set in the late 1930s, focuses on the illegal mixed marriage of a white union activist and a Japanese-American woman and what happens when she is taken to an internment camp.

Snow Falling on Cedars (1995), a novel written by David Guterson. Set on an island north of Puget Sound in the 1950s, *Snow Falling on Cedars* deals with lingering memories of World War II, internment camps, racism, and a murder trial in which a Japanese-American fisherman is suspected.

American Pastime (2007), a film directed by Desmond Nakano. This fictional account of life in Utah's Topaz War Relocation Center focuses on baseball, a major diversion for Japanese-American prisoners.

that must be spanned when a Japanese-American woman marries 'a blond Samurai.'"

Fictionalizing the Past   Houston has published other books, including *The Legend of Fire Horse Woman* (2003). Although a novel, the book covers the same ground as *Farewell to Manzanar*. Its focus is three generations of women living in a United States detention camp during World War II. In her interview with *Notable Asian-American Authors*, Houston discussed how hard it was to fictionalize the experience. The first draft ended the book "just before World War II. I couldn't write any fictionalized accounts of the war, specifically about the camps. In the past, I could only write from my own memories, from the family's history."

Despite Houston's initial difficulties, much of the novel centers around Manzanar. Sayo, Hana, and Terri represent three generations of Japanese-American women imprisoned at the internment camp. Even though the camp strips power from all those interned within it, each woman finds something of herself during the experience. In an interview with *Publishers Weekly* contributor Suzanne Mantell, Houston said: "I wanted to write a book women would read and enjoy and identify but by the end would have learned something. I still believe in stories."

According to *Los Angeles Times* contributor Ajay Sing, Houston considers *Farewell to Manzanar* "not a sermon on political injustice nor an essay on the Constitution. It allows readers to enter the experience on the level of empathy." Yet Houston's message is nevertheless clear. According to Sara Toth of the *St. Louis Dispatch*, Houston explained to a group of students, "For me to stand up here today and talk about injustice is freedom. We as Americans cannot forget the injustices of history."

Works in Literary Context

Houston is widely recognized as the first writer to expose what life was like for Japanese Americans held in internment camps during World War II. She deals with this theme in all three of her major works, covering it in both fictional and nonfictional forms.

Memoir   A memoir is a book of autobiographical writing, usually shorter than a comprehensive autobiography. The memoir often tries to capture certain highlights or meaningful moments in one's past, including a contemplation of the meaning of that event at the time of the writing of the memoir. The memoir is usually more emotional and concerned with capturing particular scenes, or a series of events, as opposed to documenting every fact of a person's life. *Farewell to Manzanar* meets all of the above criteria. Houston chooses to focus primarily on her and her family's experience as prisoners in Manzanar; she elicits an emotional response with her story; and she contemplates the meaning of that experience and how it shaped her as a person, a woman, and a writer.

Japanese American Experience   Japanese citizens who began migrating to the United States in the late 1800s were typically met with hostility. Anti-Asian hostility led to segregation, brutality, and unjust treatment that eventually led to the passage of the Immigration Act of 1924, which halted Japanese immigration completely. Yet it is the internment of Japanese Americans during World War II that has become the defining element of the Japanese American experience. In a *San Francisco Chronicle* interview with Annie Nakao, Houston admitted that fictionalizing the internment experience was very difficult. She said, "It's like a sacred cow, the landmark communal experience of Japanese Americans." This communal experience so traumatized the majority of Japanese Americans aged forty-five and over, it serves as something of a starting point in discussions about the Japanese American experience.

Works in Critical Context

Houston's writing is marked by honesty, which lends her autobiographical works, which could tend to be angry or depressing, emotional authenticity. Her books about the World War II Japanese-American internment camps, and her experience as a prisoner in one, continue to inform, educate, and inspire generations interested in American history.

Farewell to Manzanar   *Farewell to Manzanar* describes the indignities of the camp experience and the harmful effects it had on Houston's family, particularly her father. As a *New Yorker* critic observed, Ko Wakatsuki "was too old to bend with the humiliations of the camp.... His story is at the heart of this book, and his daughter tells it with great dignity." As Dorothy Rabinowitz wrote in the *Saturday Review*: "Houston and her husband have recorded a tale of many complexities in a straightforward manner, a tale remarkably lacking in either self-pity or solemnity." A *New York Times Book Review* critic concluded that *Farewell to Manzanar* is "a dramatic, telling account of one of the most reprehensible events in the history of America's treatment of its minorities."

Responses to Literature

1. In *Farewell to Manzanar*, when Jeanne returns from the camp, she finds that the hatred she faces is very different from the "dark cloud" she imagined. What are the different forms of hatred depicted in the book, and how do they manifest themselves?

2. What role do non-Japanese characters play in *Farewell to Manzanar*?

3. In *Farewell to Manzanar*, the author never seems bitter about her experience in the internment camp and never specifically condemns the relocation policy. Write a brief essay explaining why you think she chooses not to pass judgment.

4. In *Farewell to Manzanar*, why does Houston develop Papa as a tragic figure? Write a brief essay about why he is so central to her story.

5. Using the library or Internet sources, research Executive Order 9066. What other groups besides Japanese Americans were affected by it? How have Americans viewed the order, both during World War II and in retrospect? Write a brief essay about your findings.

BIBLIOGRAPHY

Periodicals

Review of *Farewell of Manzanar*. *Book Report* (January 1994): 25.

Review of *Don't Cry, It's Only Thunder*. *Library Journal* (March 1, 1984): 484.

Kirsch, Jonathan. Review of *Beyond Manzanar: Views of Asian-American Womanhood*. *Los Angeles Times* (November 15, 1984).

Singh, Ajay. "The Lessons of History." *Los Angeles Times* (November 6, 2001): E1.

Review of *Farewell to Manzanar*. *New Yorker* (November 5, 1973).

Review of *Farewell to Manzanar*. *New York Times Book Review* (January 13, 1974).

Mantell, Suzanne. Review of *The Legend of Fire Horse Woman*. *Publishers Weekly* (August 11, 2003): 138.

Toth, Sara. "Students Revel in Visit with Author of Readmore Novel, Farewell to Manzanar." *St. Louis Post-Dispatch* (April 15, 2002): 3.

Shuman, Barbara Langsam. "The Truths of 'Manzanar' Turn into Lyrical Fiction." *St. Louis Post-Dispatch* (November 16, 2003): C12.

Nakao, Annie. "'Farewell to Manzanar' Author Returns to Internment Days in First Novel." *San Francisco Chronicle* (December 14, 2003): E1.

Web sites

History Matters Web site. *Executive Order 9066: The President Authorizes Japanese Relocation*. Retrieved September 30, 2008, from http://historymatters.gmu.edu/d/5154.

Japanese-American Internment Camps. Retrieved September 30, 2008, from http://www.umass.edu/history/institute_dir/internment.html.

✸ Langston Hughes

BORN: *1902, Joplin, Missouri*

DIED: *1967, Harlem, New York*

NATIONALITY: *American*

GENRE: *Poetry, fiction, drama*

MAJOR WORKS:
"The Negro Speaks of Rivers" (1921)
The Weary Blues (1926)
Montage of a Dream Deferred (1951)

Overview

An influential figure of the Harlem Renaissance, a period during the 1920s of unprecedented artistic and intellectual achievement among black Americans, Hughes devoted his versatile and prolific career to portraying the urban experience of working-class blacks. Called "the Poet Laureate of Harlem" by Carl Van Vechten, Hughes integrated the rhythm and mood of jazz and blues music into his work, and used colloquial language to reflect black American culture. Hughes's gentle humor and wry irony often belie the magnitude of his themes. Having been a victim of poverty and discrimination, Hughes wrote about being seduced by the American Dream of freedom and equality only to be denied its realization. Speaking of Hughes's wide range of works, Theodore R. Hudson stated: "Dipping his pen in ink, not acid, [Hughes's] method was to expose rather than excoriate, to reveal rather than revile."

Works in Biographical and Historical Context

Harlem Renaissance   Several factors led to the emergence of the Harlem Renaissance, the African American artistic movement of the 1920s and early 1930s. Prior to

Langston Hughes   *Hughes, Langston, 1943, photo by Gordon Parks. The Library of Congress.*

the Renaissance, thousands of blacks migrated from southern states to the Northern industrial cities due to increased employment opportunities brought about by World War I. The black middle class was also growing and more and better educational opportunities were becoming available to blacks. Another important factor was that a new radicalism among blacks was emerging at this time. The black magazines that were being published—including *The Crisis*, published by the NAACP and edited by W. E. B. Du Bois—helped spur a "new consciousness" about racial identity. Finally, Marcus Garvey, founder of the Universal Negro Improvement Association, began spreading radical ideas of an independent black economy and racial purity. Hughes contributed works of poetry, fiction, and drama that gave literary expression to these themes of racial pride, a desire for social and political equality, and an interest in the twentieth-century African American experience. The Renaissance was so named for the diversity of artistic forms, including painting, music, and theater, that characterized the movement. Hughes's contribution is significant because of the range of artistic forms he experimented with, as well as the quality of his body of work.

Early Years Langston Hughes was born in Joplin, Missouri, to James Nathaniel and Carrie Mercer Langston Hughes, who separated shortly after the boy's birth. His father left the United States for Cuba and later settled

in Mexico, where he lived the remainder of his life as a prosperous attorney and landowner. In contrast, Hughes's mother lived a transitory life, often leaving him in the care of his maternal grandmother while searching for a job. In 1920, Hughes decided to travel to Mexico for the summer, a decision his mother greeted angrily. The misery of his parting from her not only persisted but generated some of his early published work. "I felt pretty bad when I got on the train," he wrote about this episode. "I felt bad for the next three or four years, to tell the truth, and those were the years when I wrote most of my poetry." On the way to Mexico, as the train crossed the Mississippi River to St. Louis, he jotted down on the back of an envelope one of his best known poems, "The Negro Speaks of Rivers." Through the images of water and pyramid, the verse suggests the endurance of human spirituality from ancient Egypt to the nineteenth and twentieth centuries.

Hughes enrolled at Columbia University in New York City in 1921, favoring classes in English literature. Subjected to teachers he found boring as well as to bigotry on campus—he was assigned the worst dormitory room because of his color—Hughes often missed classes in order to attend shows, lectures, and readings sponsored by the American Socialist Society. Following his freshman year, Hughes dropped out of college and worked at a series of odd jobs while supporting his mother, who had recently moved to Harlem. In 1923, he signed on as a cabin boy on a merchant freighter en route to West Africa. His first sight of Africa was an emotional experience that he would refer to again and again: "My Africa," he wrote in "The Big Sea" (1940), "Motherland of the Negro peoples! And me a Negro! Africa! The real thing." At the same time, though he did not feel its force until later in life, Africa provided the young Hughes with a sharp object lesson in white colonialism and black subjugation; it was an Africa of "white men with guns in their belts" which taught him that "civilization" survives only through exploitation. It was also, ironically, an Africa which rejected him as a black: in spite of his protestations, Africans insisted he was white.

The Busboy Poet Hughes spent the majority of the following year overseas. After resigning his position on the S. S. McKeesport in the Netherlands, he lived in virtual poverty in France and Italy. Returning to the United States in 1925, he resettled with his mother and half brother in Washington, D.C. He continued writing poetry while working menial jobs, experimenting with language, form, and rhythms reminiscent of the blues and jazz compositions he had heard in Paris nightclubs. In May and August of 1925, Hughes's verse garnered him literary prizes from both *Opportunity* magazine and *The Crisis*. In December, Hughes, then a busboy at a Washington, D.C., hotel, attracted the attention of poet Vachel Lindsay by placing three of his poems on Lindsay's dinner table. Later that evening, Lindsay read Hughes's poems to an audience and announced his discovery of a "Negro busboy poet." The next day, reporters and photographers eagerly greeted Hughes at work to hear more of his compositions.

Shortly thereafter, with the help of critic and art patron Carl Van Vechten, Hughes published his first book, *The Weary Blues* (1926), a collection of poems that reflect the frenzied atmosphere of Harlem nightlife. Hughes also included several pieces about his travels in Africa, as well as "The Negro Speaks of Rivers," a much-anthologized poem Hughes wrote during his second visit to Mexico in 1920. *The Weary Blues* received mixed reviews, with some critics questioning the motives and appropriateness of using blues and jazz verse to describe Harlem life.

In the spring of 1927, Hughes published his second collection of verse, *Fine Clothes to the Jew* (1927). During the late 1920s, Hughes met Mrs. R. Osgood Mason, an elderly white widow whom he called "Godmother" and who served as both his literary patron and friend. Strongly committed to developing the talents of young black artists, Mason supported Hughes while he wrote his first novel, *Not Without Laughter* (1930). Following this book's publication, however, Hughes and Mason suffered a dramatic and bitter break in their relationship. Hughes later reconstructed these events in his short story "The Blues I'm Playing."

Legacy as a Poet   Despite his success in a variety of genres, Hughes considered himself primarily a poet. In the late 1930s, after producing numerous plays and short stories, he returned to writing poetry. These later collections of verse, however, show an increasingly bleak view of black America. In *Montage of a Dream Deferred* (1951) Hughes contrasted the drastically deteriorated state of Harlem in the 1950s to the Harlem he had known in the 1920s. *Ask Your Mama: 12 Moods for Jazz* (1961) consists of twelve poems that comment on the political turbulence of the early 1960s. Hughes's final collection of verse, *The Panther and the Lash: Poems of Our Times*, was published posthumously in 1967.

Works in Literary Context

During the forty-six years between 1921 and 1967, Hughes became well known and loved. Even before he helped to open the doors of the major periodicals and publishing houses to young black writers, he worked to free American literature from the plantation tradition, infusing his technically accomplished writings with self-assurance and racial pride and earning acclaim for his innovations in literary blues and jazz.

Jazz Poetry   Hughes is perhaps most famous for the way in which his poetry is informed by jazz music. The genre is characterized by the poet responding to and writing about jazz, or using the musical sounds and structures of jazz as the basis for poetic forms. Like the music it reflects, jazz poetry encompasses a variety of

---

LITERARY AND HISTORICAL CONTEMPORARIES

Langston Hughes's famous contemporaries include:

Zora Neale Hurston (1891–1960): This American author and Harlem Renaissance figure is most famous for her 1937 novel, *Their Eyes Were Watching God.*

Ansel Adams (1902–1984): This American landscape photographer and environmentalist worked to preserve wilderness and park areas across the country, most notably in the western United States.

Max Ophuls (1902–1957): This German film director is known for his obsession with detail, elaborate camera movements, and his 1948 film *Letter From an Unknown Woman.*

Norma Shearer (1902–1983): This Canadian-American actress is best known for her Academy Award–winning performance in *The Divorcee.*

Strom Thurmond (1902–2003): This American politician, known for his early segregationist campaigns, was the longest-serving senator in United States history.

---

forms, sounds, and rhythms. Beginning with the birth of blues and jazz at the beginning of the twentieth century, jazz poetry can be seen as a constant running through the Harlem Renaissance, the Beat Generation, and the Black Arts Movement. It is still quite vibrant today. From early blues to experimental music, jazz poets use their love of the genre to inspire their poetry. One of the best examples of Hughes's use of music to inform his poetry can be found in "The Weary Blues," one of his most well known poems. The poem is about a piano player in Harlem, and it captures the flavor of the night life, people, and folk forms that became characteristic of the experimental writing of the Renaissance.

Racial and Cultural Pride   Influenced by Alain Locke's 1925 anthology *The New Negro*, Hughes responded by reinterpreting the black experience to promote a positive identity for the African American and to subvert white stereotypes of "Negroes." He also experimented in order to embrace those the black elite would rather obscure. The criticism each Hughes production brought from one group or another, even within the African American population, shows the difficulty of writing for the stage during this era. African Americans could not agree on what an authentic black production should be, and because of racism prevalent in American culture, they were especially sensitive to what audiences made of black representations. This critical judgment from all sides did not diminish Hughes's efforts to portray the African American spirit and culture in various ways. Many of Hughes's dramas

COMMON HUMAN EXPERIENCE

The rhythm and mood of jazz music is found throughout Hughes's body of work. Here are some other works of literature in which jazz plays an integral role.

On The Road (1957), a novel by Jack Kerouac. This largely autobiographical work was inspired by the jazz, poetry, and drug experiences of the author and his friends on their many road trips across postwar America.

The Horn (1958), a novel by John Clellon Holmes. This work by one of Jack Kerouac's contemporaries focuses on the last twenty-four hours of the life of tenor saxophonist Edgar Pool, a legendary forerunner of bop music. This classic novel reflects the history of jazz as it reconstructs Pool's career through the memories of friends and lovers.

Jazz (1992), a novel by Toni Morrison. This Nobel Prize–winning historical novel takes place in Harlem during the 1920s and deliberately mirrors the music of its title. Morrison employs the call and response of jazz music in the novel and allows her characters to improvise solo compositions that come together to create a cohesive whole.

remain unproduced—and unpublished in some cases. Increasing critical recognition of his contributions may, however, lead to production and publication of some of these works.

Works in Critical Context

Hughes encountered mixed reactions to his work throughout his career. Black intellectuals often denounced him for portraying unsophisticated aspects of lower-class life, claiming that this furthered the unfavorable image of his race. Toward the end of his life, as the struggle for American civil rights became increasingly widespread, Hughes was also faulted by militants for failing to address controversial issues. Nevertheless, Hughes's reputation with readers has remained consistently strong, chiefly due to his poetry and short stories.

The Weary Blues Critical response to *The Weary Blues* was mixed. Reviews in the *New York Times*, *Washington Post*, *Boston Transcript*, *New Orleans Picayune*, *New Republic*, and elsewhere were positive; the only negative review in a white publication was in the *Times Literary Supplement*, in which the reviewer called him a "cabaret poet." Reviewing the book in the February 1926 issue of *Opportunity*, however, Countee Cullen found some of the poems "scornful in subject matter, in photography and rhythmical treatment of whatever obstructions time and tradition...placed

before him" and called Hughes one of those "racial artists instead of artists pure and simple." Jessie Fauset, writing in the *Crisis*, praised Hughes's liberation from established literary forms. No other poet, she said, would ever write "as tenderly, understandingly, and humorously about life in Harlem." Admiring the book for its cleanness and simplicity, Alain Locke viewed Hughes, in *Palms*, as the spokesman for the black masses.

Responses to Literature

1. Langston Hughes explained that the purpose of his writing was "to explain and illuminate the Negro condition in America." How does his early poetry illustrate his attempt?

2. Discuss what Hughes's poetry tells a reader about his theory of poetry. What poetic elements are most important to him, and what elements seem to be less important?

3. How does Hughes's poetry reflect the African American musical forms of jazz and blues? What are the characteristics shared by his poetry and these musical forms? Find at least three examples from his work that exhibit these characteristics.

4. In poems like "Mother to Son," "Madam and Her Madam," and "Madam's Calling Card," Hughes reveals an exploration of the experience of women. Analyze how Hughes treats the female experience in relation to the African American experience.

5. Hughes's poetry is not considered modern, even though his themes, use of imagery, and style can all be called modern. Identify specific elements that reveal Hughes's modernism and write about them in an essay.

BIBLIOGRAPHY

Books

Bardsdale, Richard K. *Langston Hughes: The Poet and His Critics*. Chicago: American Library Association, 1977.
———. "Langston Hughes: His Times and His Humanistic Techniques." *Black American Literature and Humanism*, edited by R. Baxter Miller. Lexington, Ky.: University Press of Kentucky, 1981, pp. 11–26.
Berry, Faith. *Langston Hughes: Before and Beyond Harlem*. Westport, Conn.: Lawrence Hill, 1983.
Dickinson, Donald C. *A Bio-Bibliography of Langston Hughes, 1902–1967*. Hamden, Conn.: Shoe String Press, 1967.
Holman, C. Hugh and William Harmon. *A Handbook to Literature*. New York: Macmillan, 1986.
Huggins, Nathan. *Harlem Renaissance*. New York: Oxford University Press, 1971.
Miller, R. Baxter. *Langston Hughes and Gwendolyn Brooks: A Reference Guide*. Boston: G.K. Hall, 1978.

Periodicals

Brown, Lloyd W. "The Portrait of the Artist as a Black American in the Poetry of Langston Hughes." *Studies in Black Literature* 5 (Winter 1974): 24–27.

Davis, Arthur P. "Langston Hughes: Cool Poet." *CLA Journal* 11 (June 1968): 280–296.

Web sites

Reuben, Paul P. *PAL: Perspectives in American Literature - A Research and Reference Guide - An Ongoing Project.* Retrieved September 25, 2008, from http://www. csustan.edu/english/reuben/pal/chap9/Hughes. html. Last updated February 2, 2008.

⊛ Charlayne Hunter-Gault

BORN: *1942, Due West, South Carolina*

NATIONALITY: *American*

GENRE: *Journalism, memoir, nonfiction*

MAJOR WORKS:

In My Place (1992)

New News Out of Africa: Uncovering Africa's Renaissance (2006)

Overview

Charlayne Hunter-Gault is a broadcast journalist who has served as an investigative correspondent and anchorwoman on television and radio. Best known for her twenty-year tenure with Public Broadcasting System (PBS)'s *MacNeil/Lehrer NewsHour*, Hunter-Gault has covered breaking events in the United States, the Middle East, Europe, and Africa, and she has interviewed numerous important international figures, such as former South Africa president Nelson Mandela. In 1999 Hunter-Gault became South African bureau chief for the Cable News Network (CNN). From that base, she has traveled widely in Africa to report on news events and political trends. Honored with Emmy Awards and George Foster Peabody awards for her work in television journalism, Hunter-Gault is one of the best known African-American women broadcasters at work today.

Works in Biographical and Historical Context

Charlayne Hunter-Gault was born on February 27, 1942, in Due West, South Carolina, to Charles S. Hunter, Jr., a minister and chaplain, and Althea Hunter. A gifted student, Hunter-Gault decided in high school she was going to be a journalist and applied to a number of colleges. Although she was accepted at Wayne State University in Detroit, Hunter-Gault was "encouraged by local civil rights leaders to apply . . . to the University of Georgia," according to a *Kirkus Reviews* contributor. As a result, in

Charlayne Hunter-Gault *Hunter-Gault, Charlayne, photograph. AP Images.*

1961 she and Hamilton Holmes became the first two black students at the University of Georgia.

She recalled what it was like to be on the front lines of desegregation in her memoir, *In My Place* (1992). The author begins with a pleasant account of her childhood in the Deep South (and, for a brief period, Alaska), describing school and church activities. The same *Kirkus* reviewer commented that Hunter-Gault's account of facing racial prejudice there is "remarkably generous." Indeed, Hunter-Gault told *Publishers Weekly* that "the people who attacked me didn't know me." The author added: "They stood outside my dormitory and threw rocks, but it was the idea, not the person they were against." *In My Place* concludes with Hunter-Gault's graduation from college and presents her "stirring" 1988 University of Georgia commencement speech "as a sort of epilog," commented Gwen Gregory in *Library Journal*. A contributor to *Publishers Weekly* considered the work a "warmhearted, well-observed memoir" and believed "that Hunter-Gault could write a rich sequel."

She went to work at the *New Yorker* and the *New York Times* in the 1960s, covering the civil rights movement and urban race riots. She joined the *MacNeil/Lehrer Report* in 1978 as a national correspondent and anchorwoman and

LITERARY AND HISTORICAL CONTEMPORARIES

Hunter-Gault's famous contemporaries include:

Muhammad Ali (1942–): This American boxer won six Kentucky Golden Glove titles, two National Golden Gloves, two Amateur Athletic Union championships, a Gold Medal in the light heavyweight division at the 1960 Rome Olympic games, and three world professional heavyweight championships.

Michael Crichton (1942–2008): This American novelist and film director is most widely known for writing *The Great Train Robbery* (1975) and *Jurassic Park* (1990).

Aretha Franklin (1942–): This American singer was inducted into the Rock and Roll Hall of Fame in 1987 and has won over twenty Grammy awards, including the Grammy Legend Award, the National Medal of Arts, the Kennedy Center Honor, and the Presidential Medal of Freedom.

Dith Pran (1942–2008): This Cambodian journalist and genocide survivor was the subject of the Academy Award-winning film *The Killing Fields*.

Muammar Qaddafi (1942–): This Libyan dictator took power in a 1969 military coup.

stayed with the PBS nightly newscast for nearly twenty years. When her duties allowed, she also served as a reporter for numerous PBS specials on human rights and on breaking political stories such as the Gulf War and the civil war in Yugoslavia. Her move to Africa in 1997 was undertaken on both a professional and personal front, as her husband, Ronald T. Gault, whom she married in 1973, had a position with a banking firm in Johannesburg, South Africa.

Reporting first for National Public Radio, and more recently for CNN, Hunter-Gault has helped to cast African news reporting in a more optimistic light. Her dispatches from South Africa reveal a continent full of nations that are industrializing, improving the lot of their citizens, and making important strides in the areas of human rights and desegregation. As she noted in *Essence*: "There are dynamics here [in Africa] that seem to be delivering something new not only for the continent but also for the world in the coming century."

The journalist told Frazier Moore in the *Detroit News*:

I like to think of myself as a journalist who is (a) a woman, (b) black, and (c) out of a particular historical experience, and all of the above have had an impact on my values and perspective. It's not the sort of baggage you carry from a lifetime of experience, not in the sense of a yoke or a millstone, but in the Louis Vuitton sense of baggage.

After making her home in South Africa for several years and serving as a correspondent there for both CNN and National Public Radio, Hunter-Gault wrote *New News out of Africa: Uncovering Africa's Renaissance* (2006). "The book grew out of three...lectures that I gave at Harvard University," Hunter-Gault told Jason Zasky in an interview for *Failure Magazine Online*. She found that American students had a distorted notion of Africa: "The [audience] questions revolved around what I call the four D's of the African apocalypse—death, disease, disaster and despair.... I tried to focus on things I thought were important for Americans to know about Africa."

In *New News out of Africa* Hunter-Gault writes about various positive or improving aspects of life on the continent of Africa, including the progressive democracy in South Africa. She also sheds light on a changing Africa through the prism of her own experiences growing up during the civil rights movement in the United States. Writing in *African Business*, a contributor noted that

Hunter-Gault argues that America's knowledge of the continent is hugely distorted by the dictum 'if it bleeds, it leads'—in other words, only Africa's conflicts and disasters make the news. Hunter-Gault illustrates how pervasive this editorial policy is by telling us that just three years after the democratic dispensation that saw a relatively peaceful transition to majority rule in South Africa, three U.S. broadcasters quit the country, leaving only CNN with a local bureau.

Works in Literary Context

Hunter-Gault's experience as a television and print reporter and journalist primed her to be an authoritative author. That she chose the memoir genre as her first foray into authorship makes perfect sense. Her personal narrative is filled with interesting events as well as emotional and comtemplative moments. Returning to a journalistic style of writing for her second book also seems natural, as her subject matter, the African Renaissance of the twenty-first century, requires the kind of direct, clear-eyed style Hunter-Gault has perfected over the years.

Memoir A memoir is a book of autobiographical writing, usually shorter than a comprehensive autobiography. The memoir often tries to capture certain highlights or meaningful moments in one's past, including a contemplation of the meaning of that event at the time of the writing of the memoir. The memoir is usually more emotional and concerned with capturing particular scenes, or a series of events, as opposed to documenting every fact of a person's life. *In My Place* focuses on Hunter-Gault's loving and supportive upbringing, her experience as being one of only two black students at the University of Georgia during the civil rights era, and ends with her commencement speech at the same university.

Journalism   Journalism is the collecting, writing, editing, and presenting of news or news articles in newspapers and magazines and in radio and television broadcasts. It also includes matter written for publication in a newspaper or magazine or for broadcast. Journalistic writing is marked by its direct presentation of facts with little attempt at analysis or interpretation. Hunter-Gault's second book, *New News Out of Africa: Uncovering Africa's Renaissance*, makes use of the author's experience reporting the news for print and television by implementing its writing style.

Works in Critical Context

Hunter-Gault's two books are very different, yet both have been warmly received by readers and critics alike. Using her experience growing up in the South during the civil rights era for *In My Place*, and her firsthand observations of African progress for *New News Out of Africa: Uncovering Africa's Renaissance*, shows the author's ability to transform personal experiences into acclaimed literature.

In My Place   A *Publishers Weekly* contributor calls the book a "warmhearted, well-observed memoir," noting however that the book dwells "a bit too much on her family history and descriptions of the southern towns where she grew up." The reviewer also suggests that "Hunter-Gault could write a rich sequel." Jackie Gropman for the *School Library Journal* writes, "It is . . . a compelling documentation of the ugly turmoil of the times. An inspiring historical journey."

New News Out of Africa: Uncovering Africa's Renaissance   Reviewers also praised *New News Out of Africa* upon its publication in 2006. Robtel Neajai Pailey on the *News America Media* Web site writes, "With more than 40 years of experience in the industry, Hunter-Gault has painted a poignantly complex picture of Africa in her latest book." Todd Steven Burroughs, writing in *Black Issues Book Review*, states that Hunter-Gault "takes the reader deep into the post-apartheid era, warts and all." In his review for the *Library Journal*, James Thorsen calls the book "a well-researched, fact-filled account of recent positive changes in Africa."

Responses to Literature

1. How do you think Hunter-Gault's career as a journalist prepared her for being a memoirist? What skills are required in both endeavors?

2. Hunter-Gault was a pioneer of the civil rights movement. Being one of the first two black students to attend the University of Georgia put her on the forefront of desegregation. Using Internet resources or the library, research desegregation during the civil rights movement and write a brief history of the subject. Be sure and include other pioneers of desegregation.

3. In *In My Place*, Hunter-Gault downplays her heroism as a leader of desegregation in the South. Why

---

COMMON HUMAN EXPERIENCE

A prominent theme running through Hunter-Gault's memoir *In My Place* is the African-American experience during the civil rights era. Here are some other works that share this theme:

Freedom Riders: 1961 and the Struggle for Racial Justice (Pivotal Moments in American History) (2006), a book by Raymond Arsenault. Based on interviews with over two hundred Freedom Riders, as well as personal papers and F.B.I. files, this is an authoritative and compelling story of how a group of idealistic, ingenious, and courageous Americans helped change history in the twentieth century.

Parting the Waters: America in the King Years 1954–63 (1989), a book by Taylor Branch. The first in a trilogy about the history of the civil rights movement, this Pulitzer Prize-winning biography of Martin Luther King Jr. is a portrait of an era.

Eyes on the Prize: America's Civil Rights Years, 1954–1965 (1988), a book by Juan Williams. Based on a PBS television series, this book details the struggles of the civil rights movement using brief asides provided by movement participants.

Voices of Freedom: An Oral History of the Civil Rights Movement from the 1950s Through the 1980s (1991), a book by Henry Hampton. This oral history of the civil rights movement gives voice to ordinary people involved in the struggle as well as well-known activists and public officials.

---

do you think she does this? What purpose does it serve, if any?

4. Using the library and Internet resources, research the American civil rights movement. Why do you think it gained momentum in the 1950s and 1960s? Why did it lose momentum in the late 1960s and 1970s? Write a brief essay about your findings.

5. As Hunter-Gault proves in *New News Out of Africa: Uncovering Africa's Renaissance*, very often it is only Africa's conflicts and disasters make news in the United States. Write a brief essay explaining why you think this happens, or refuting Hunter-Gault's assertion.

BIBLIOGRAPHY

Periodicals

Bond, Julian. Review of *In My Place*. *Teachers College Record* 95, no.1 (Fall 1993): 127–131.

Brush, Silla and Eric Wills. "Sense & Censorship." *The Chronicle of Higher Education* 51, no.31 (April 8, 2005).

Gregory, Gwen. Review of *In My Place. Library Journal* 117, no.17 (Oct 15, 1992): 74.

Harris, Nora. "Restoring Hope: Conversations on the Future of Black America." *Library Journal* 122, no.17 (Oct 15, 1997): 80.

Malveaux, Julianne. "Reparations and Affirmative Action: What You Owe Me." *Black Issues in Higher Education* 18, no.16 (Sept 27, 2001): 47.

Ndangam, Lilian. Review of *New News out of Africa: Uncovering Africa's Renaissance. Media, Culture & Society* 30, no.3 (May 2008): 432–434.

Thorsen, James. Review of *New News Out of Africa: Uncovering Africa's Renaissance. Library Journal* 131, no.11 (June 15, 2006): 87.

"University of Georgia Marks 40th Anniversary Of Desegregation." *Black Issues in Higher Education*17, no.23 (Jan 4, 2001): 10.

"University of Georgia unveils exhibit honoring Charlayne Hunter-Gault." *Black Issues in Higher Education* 21, no.26 (Feb 10, 2005): 14.

✸ Zora Neale Hurston

BORN: *1901, Eatonville, Florida*

DIED: *1960, Fort Pierce, Florida*

NATIONALITY: *American*

GENRE: *Fiction, autobiography*

MAJOR WORKS:

Mules and Men (1935)

Their Eyes Were Watching God (1937)

Overview

Zora Neale Hurston was the most published black female author in her time and arguably the most important collector of African-American folklore ever. She achieved moderate success during the Harlem Renaissance as a short story writer, although her stories deserve attention beyond the concerns of black or feminist literature because of their local color and strong characterization. She has been described by her biographer, Robert E. Hemenway, as

Zora Neale Hurston   Hurston, Zora Neale, at the New York Times book fair, photograph. The Library of Congress.

"flamboyant and yet vulnerable, self-centered and yet kind, a Republican conservative and yet an early black nationalist." Her stories reflect this complexity.

Works in Biographical and Historical Context

Facts Mixed with Fiction No record of Hurston's birth exists, but, as she wrote in her autobiography, *Dust Tracks on a Road* (1942), she "heard tell" she was born on January 7, 1903, in Eatonville, Florida, one of eight children. Hurston used 1903 most often but variously gave the year as 1900, 1901, and 1902. Hurston scholars Hemenway and Alice Walker use 1901. Modern attempts to establish an accurate record of her birth point toward an earlier birth year and a different location (Alabama), though it is unknown if Hurston's various accounts were deliberate fiction or errors. According to her own account, Hurston's parents, Lucy Ann Potts, a country schoolteacher, and John Hurston, a carpenter and Baptist preacher, met and married in Alabama, then moved to Eatonville three years before Hurston's birth.

At fourteen, Hurston left Eatonville, working as a maid for whites, but she refused to act humble or to tolerate sexual advances from male employers. Consequently, she never stayed at one job long. Hired as a wardrobe girl with a Gilbert and Sullivan repertory theater company, she traveled around the South for eighteen months, always reading in hopes of completing her education. Later she enrolled in a Baltimore high school, Morgan Academy (now Morgan State University), while working as a live-in maid. In 1918, she entered Howard University, paying for her expenses by working as a barbershop manicurist and as a maid for prominent blacks.

Launching Her Literary Career Hurston's literary career began at Howard. She joined the literary society (sponsored by Alain Locke), which published her first story, "John Redding Goes to Sea," in the club's literary magazine, *Stylus*, in May 1921. In January 1926, it was republished in *Opportunity: A Journal of Negro Life*, a new magazine for beginning black writers. In May 1925, Hurston won second prize in an *Opportunity*-sponsored contest for her short story "Spunk," and at the awards banquet met several influential people who furthered her career. One important person who befriended Hurston was Annie Nathan Meyer, a novelist and a founder of Barnard College, who arranged for Hurston to attend Barnard on scholarship. She entered in the fall of 1925 as its first black student.

"Black Death," a companion piece to "Spunk," was never published in its original short story form, even though it won an honorable mention in the prestigious 1925 *Opportunity* contest and was considered for inclusion in the groundbreaking anthology *The New Negro* (1925). The story was rewritten as an article about Eatonville hoodoo men entitled "Hoodoo in America"

LITERARY AND HISTORICAL CONTEMPORARIES

Hurston's famous contemporaries include:

Stella Adler (1901–1992): This American actress went on to become a famous acting teacher. The Stella Adler Studio of Acting taught such notable actors as Robert De Niro, Martin Sheen, and Warren Beatty.

Louis Armstrong (1901–1971): This American trumpeter had a significant influence on the development of jazz and was the leading musician to emerge during its formative years.

Marlene Dietrich (1901–1992): This German actress is famous for her roles in the movies *The Blue Angel* (1930), *Blonde Venus* (1932), and *A Foreign Affair* (1948).

Margaret Mead (1901–1978): This American anthropologist and activist is famous for her studies on native Polynesian behavior.

Linus Pauling (1901–1994): This Nobel Prize-winning American chemist, peace activist, and author ranks among one of the most important scientists in any field of the twentieth century.

---

and published in the October–December 1931 issue of *Journal of American Folklore*, the nation's most respected folklore journal. Undoubtedly, Hurston mixed folklore reports and fiction in both versions, having become skillful at blending the folklore of many generations with her imaginative storytelling.

Becoming a Folklorist "Eatonville Anthology" was published in three installments in the *Messenger*. This series of fourteen brief sketches, some only two paragraphs long, illustrates her artistic use of cultural experiences, fusing folklore studies with fiction. These self-contained tales include glimpses of a woman beggar, an incorrigible dog, a backwoods farmer, the village's greatest liar, and a cheating husband. They become an appropriate transition to mark the end of her short stories of the 1920s and the beginning of her work as folklorist. An English major at Howard, she took anthropology courses at Barnard and, on the merit of an excellent paper, came to the attention of anthropologist Franz Boas. She worked as his apprentice after graduating with a BA degree in 1928, accepting a fellowship he arranged for her so she could record "the songs, customs, tales, superstitions, lies, jokes, dances, and games of Afro-American folklore" in the South.

Hurston had done considerable work collecting folklore and historical material in the four years after she graduated from college. It appears as though Hurston was at the crossroads with dual careers as a writer and folklorist/anthropologist. She was unsuccessful in her attempt to enter Columbia University to study for a PhD in 1934, at which point she published her first novel, *Jonah's Gourd Vine*, and, a year later, her first collection of folklore, *Mules and Men*. Hence, her fiction allowed her to affirm more forcefully the rich humanistic values of black life as opposed to the scientific objectivity of her anthropological studies. Collecting folklore gave her a new perspective as a storyteller of black culture; thus, studying anthropology both analytically and emotionally enriched her literary career.

Writing Her Best Fiction   Seven years after the publication of the "Eatonville Anthology" sketches, Hurston returned to her Eatonville remembrances in "The Gilded Six-Bits," originally published in *Story Magazine* and later her most frequently anthologized story. In the 1930s, Hurston produced the novel *Their Eyes Were Watching God* (1937), written in Haiti in seven weeks, and considered to be her best work. Her autobiography, *Dust Tracks on a Road* (1942), her most successful publication, gave a partially accurate, partially fictionalized account of her life. In the following years, she made many attempts to receive funding for folklore research trips to Central America. Finally, an advance on a new novel allowed her to travel in 1947 to British Honduras, where she completed *Seraph on the Suwanee* (1948), her last book. In 1959, she suffered a stroke, leaving her unable to care for herself adequately. Wracked with pain, she continued to labor at a three-hundred-page manuscript about Herod the Great. Against her will, she entered the St. Lucie County Welfare Home in October 1959. She died of hypertensive heart disease on January 28, 1960.

Works in Literary Context

Hurston was devoted to her career as a folklorist and used the stories she collected to enliven and inspire her writing. Blending folk tales and fiction became a trademark of the famous author and a style that is now synonymous with her name. In works such as "The Fire and the Cloud" (1934) and *Hoodoo in America* (1931), Hurston's perspective as a storyteller of black culture really shines. As a leader of the Harlem Renaissance, she received some critical attention for her promotion of African-American folklore, dance, and language. She continues to be one of the movement's most famous members.

Folklore   Folklore refers to the traditional beliefs, myths, tales, and practices of a people that have been spread in an informal manner—usually orally, although in modern times the Internet has become a pivotal source for folklore. Folklore may also be used to define the comparative study of folk knowledge and culture. First coined by William J. Thomas in 1846, "folklore" was conceived as a simple term to replace various phrases common at the time which described the same concept. Folklore, then, replaced such awkward descriptions as "the lore of the people," "popular antiquities," and "the manners, customs, observances, superstitions, ballads, proverbs, etc., of the olden times."

Harlem Renaissance   The Harlem Renaissance was an artistic and cultural revolution that took place in Harlem, New York, between the World Wars. Instead of using more direct political means, African-American artists and writers used culture to promote civil rights and equality. As a result, jazz and African-American paintings and books were absorbed into mainstream culture. Hurston was closely associated with the movement and has influenced such writers as Ralph Ellison, Toni Morrison, and Alice Walker. Hurston's four novels and two books of folklore resulted from extensive anthropological research and have proven invaluable sources on the oral cultures of African America. Through her writings, Robert Hemenway wrote in *The Harlem Renaissance Remembered*, Hurston "helped to remind the Renaissance—especially its more bourgeois members—of the richness in the racial heritage."

Works in Critical Context

Hurston's work of folklore, *Mules and Men*, focuses on her excursions to the South and is regarded as the best and most important book of its kind. Its pages are filled with what many consider the integral ingredients of America's black culture: stories, or "big old lies," songs, superstitions, and even "formulae of Hoodoo Doctors." Hurston's masterpiece and the book she is most identified with is her novel *Their Eyes Were Watching God*, the jewel that Hurston cut from her Eatonville experience. It is the story of a young black woman, Janie, following her through three very different relationships and her transformation into a self-sufficient, whole human being. In the novel, Janie learns that there are "two things everybody's got tuh do fuh theyselves. They got tuh go tuh God, and they got tuh find about livin' fuh theyselves."

Mules and Men In his *New York Times Book Review* from November 10, 1935, H. I. Brock wrote of *Mules and Men*, "The book is packed with tall tales rich with flavor and alive with characteristic turns of speech." Other critics found similar value in the book. Henry Lee Moon wrote in his December 11, 1935 *New Republic* review,

> *Mules and Men* is more than a collection of folklore. Miss Hurston records things as they were told to her, in an intimate and good style; and the intimacy she established with her subjects, she reproduces on the printed page, enabling the reader to feel himself a part of that circle.

Their Eyes Were Watching God Hurston's best known novel was given rave reviews at its time of publication. In her 1937 review for the *New York Times Book Review*, Lucille Tompkins wrote, "This is Zora Hurston's third novel, again about her own people—and it is beautiful. . . . Indeed, from first to last this is a well nigh perfect story." That same year, Sheila Hibben praised the novel in the *New York Herald Tribune Weekly Book Review*. She wrote that "Miss Hurston can write of [Negroes] with simple tenderness, so that her story is filled with the ache of her own people," and calls Hurston "an author who writes with her head as well as with her heart."

Responses to Literature

1. Using the Internet and library resources, research the Harlem Renaissance. Who were some of Hurston's contemporaries in that movement? How many were women? How did those women contribute to the movement? Write a brief essay describing your findings.

2. Harlem Renaissance artists and scholars—the Negro literati, they were called—promoted a refined, educated, and literate image of African Americans, which they referred to as the "New Negro." Hurston, however, was sometimes seen as working against the progress of the movement's leaders with her interest in black folklore, dance, and language. Why do you think this is?

3. *Their Eyes Were Watching God* is concerned with issues of speech and how it is both a means of liberation and an element of control. Why do you think Janie remains silent during key moments in her life? Discuss the role silence plays in the book and how that role changes throughout the novel.

4. Discuss how Hurston's background as an anthropologist and folklorist impacted her fiction. Be sure and review her education and the difficulties she faced choosing between pursuing folklore or cultivating her writing.

BIBLIOGRAPHY

Books

Hemenway, Robert E. *Zora Neale Hurston: A Literary Biography.* Urbana: University of Illinois Press, 1977.
———. "Zora Neale Hurston and the Eatonville Anthropology." *The Harlem Renaissance Remembered*, edited by Arna Bontemps. New York: Dodd, Mead, 1972.
Barksdale, Richard and Keneth Kinnamon. *Black Writers of America: A Comprehensive Anthology.* New York: Macmillan, 1972.
Bloom, Harold, ed. *Zora Neale Hurston.* New York: Chelsea House, 1986.
Bone, Robert. *Down Home: A History of Afro-American Short Fiction From Its Beginnings to the End of the Harlem Renaissance.* New York: Putnam's, 1975.
Davis, Arthur P. *From the Dark Tower: Afro-American Writers, 1900–1960.* Washington, D.C.: Howard University Press, 1974.
Holloway, Karla F. *The Character of the Word: The Texts of Zora Neale Hurston.* New York: Greenwood Press, 1987.
Howard, Lillie P. *Alice Walker and Zora Neale Hurston.* Westport, Conn.: Greenwood Press, 1993.

Web sites

The Zora Neale Hurston Digital Archive. "Contemporary Reviews." Retrieved October 2, 2008, from http://www.zoranealehurston.ucf.edu/contemporaryreviews.php.
American Folklore. "Folklore Definitions: What is Folklore?" Retrieved October 2, 2008, from http://www.americanfolklore.net/what-is-folklore.html.

David Henry Hwang

BORN: *1957, San Gabriel, California*

NATIONALITY: *American*

GENRE: *Drama*

MAJOR WORKS:
M. Butterfly (1988)
Golden Child (1996)
Flower Drum Song (2001)

Overview

In 1988, playwright David Henry Hwang became the leading theatrical voice of the Asian American community and one of the leading Asian American voices in the United States. Hwang previously had modest success with several Off-Broadway productions, but his *M. Butterfly* (1988), the first Asian American play to be performed on Broadway and win a Tony Award for best play, brought him national renown. His body of work since 1988 includes plays, opera librettos, books for musicals, and motion picture and television screenplays.

David Henry Hwang *Hwang, David Henry, 1988, photograph. AP Images.*

Works in Biographical and Historical Context

A Self-Made Education in Theater Hwang was born on August 11, 1957, in San Gabriel, California, a suburb of Los Angeles. Hwang enrolled at Stanford University in 1975 with the intention of studying law. As a freshman, Hwang saw Thornton Wilder's *The Matchmaker* (1954) at the American Conservatory Theatre in San Francisco. He told Jackson R. Bryer, "I thought, 'I think I can do that,' so I started trying to write." He showed his early attempts to a Stanford professor, the novelist John L'Heureux, who described them as "horrible." This criticism led Hwang to begin a process that he still continues: when he does not know enough about a topic, he educates himself on it. "So I spent the next two or three years trying to read as many plays and see as many plays as I could," he told Bryer. "I'd go up to San Francisco to the Magic and see all the Sam Shepard premieres that were going on at the time." Among the playwrights whose works he read were Tom Stoppard, John Osborne, Harold Pinter, Anton Chekhov, Peter Shaffer, and Ntozake Shange. He also changed his major to English.

In the summer of 1977, Hwang interned at East/West Players, performing odd jobs around the theater. The next summer, he attended the Padua Hills Playwrights Festival, where Shepard and Maria Irene Fornes taught him about incorporating ritual into drama. While Hwang has called Fornes the best playwriting teacher in the world, Shepard's influence is more apparent in his early plays. Maxine Hong Kingston was another early influence. Hwang read her play *The Woman Warrior: Memoirs of a Girlhood Among Ghosts* (1976) at Stanford. He told Lyons that while Shepard and Fornes provided the structure for his plays, Kingston's was the first "that made me feel that I could find my own voice. As an Asian-American, she was the first author who spoke in a voice that seemed special, directly related to me."

East Versus West Shortly after the festival, Hwang began writing his first play, *FOB* (1979). *FOB*—the title refers to Chinese immigrants who are "fresh off the boat"—is based on a double date Hwang went on with his cousin. As he attempted to transcribe the evening into a play, two legendary characters continually materialized in his mind: Fa Mu Lan, who poses as a man and takes her father's place in the military in Kingston's play, and Gwan Gung, the god of fighters and writers in Frank Chin's play *Gee, Pop!* (1974). Blending the double date and the two mythic figures, Hwang discovered a thematic technique that has served him throughout his career: the juxtaposition of two contrasting and seemingly ill-fitting concepts, usually one Eastern and one Western. One year after Hwang graduated from Stanford in 1979, *FOB* received an Obie Award as best Off-Broadway play. The play also received the Drama-Logue Playwriting Award and the U.S.-Asia Institute Award. Kingston writes in her preface to *FOB and Other Plays*: "To have a fellow writer who works an ocean and a continent away meet me at an intersection reassures me that there is a place called Chinese America and that I am seeing it with an authentic vision."

Hwang taught writing for a year at Menlo-Atherton High School in Menlo Park, near Stanford. In 1980, he enrolled in the Yale University School of Drama, where he began writing *The Dance and the Railroad* (1981). He left Yale in 1981, because the last two years of the program involved workshop productions of the students' plays; by that time Hwang was already having his plays produced Off-Broadway.

Spy and Butterfly Hwang first encountered the material for his next play, *M. Butterfly* (1988), during a dinner conversation in which a friend related a story in *The New York Times* about a French diplomat, Bernard Bouriscot, who had had a twenty-year-long romantic relationship with Shi Peipu, a Beijing Opera performer and Chinese government spy, without realizing that Shi was actually a man. Their affair, and Shi Peipu's spying and true sex, were discovered after the couple returned to France. Bouriscot was sentenced to six years in prison, and Shi was expelled from the country. The international incident provided Wang with the chance to address issues of imperialism, racism, and sexism through one unbelievable love affair. To augment his thematic interests, Hwang added the iconography of the title character of Giacomo Puccini's tragic opera *Madame Butterfly* (1904), about a Japanese woman who sacrifices herself for her caddish American husband. Using the story and music of *Madame Butterfly* as a counterpoint to the stage action, Hwang transforms the relationship between his two lovers from a quirky news article to an indicting subversion of stereotypical expectations between East and West.

With *M. Butterfly*, Hwang evolved from a respected Off-Broadway dramatist to one of the top playwrights in the country, as well as the first Asian American to have a play produced on Broadway. The play received seven Tony nominations, winning the award for best play; John Dexter won for best director, and B. D. Wong, who played Song, was named best featured actor. The play received Drama Desk Awards in the same categories. *M. Butterfly* was also nominated for a Pulitzer Prize.

Subverting Stereotypes A constant component of Hwang's work has been the tweaking, reinvigorating, or subverting of myths and stories, whether Eastern as in *The Dance and the Railroad*, or Western as in *M. Butterfly*. His twenty years of experience in such undertakings prepared him for one of his most difficult tasks, updating the 1958 Richard Rodgers and Oscar Hammerstein II musical *Flower Drum Song*, based on the 1957 novel by C. Y. Lee. The musical premiered in Los Angeles and was a box office success. It then moved to Broadway, where the reviews were, for the most part, strong.

David Henry Hwang has amassed a body of work that is impressive, unpredictable, diverse, and controversial in terms of scope, depth, and versatility. Clearly, one of the impacts of his career has been his success in subverting Asian American stereotypes in American culture. Perhaps the most telling stereotype he has destroyed is the one mentioned by Williamson B. C. Chang in analyzing *M. Butterfly*: with his success, longevity, and versatility, Hwang is most certainly not an "invisible" Asian male.

Works in Literary Context

At the heart of Hwang's works is his struggle to confront and conquer a stigma that Asian Americans face in the United States. In his introduction to *FOB and Other Plays* (1990) he writes, "One of the particular burdens of my minority is that we are never completely accepted as Americans; we are perpetual foreigners." That nagging feeling of not being accepted has inspired him to challenge what he considers the shallow American concept of identity and to subvert the stereotypes that accompany ethnicity, gender, and religion. Looking back on his career in an October 13, 2002 article in *The New York Times*, he writes,

> As a playwright, I find that much of my work has involved a search for authenticity; if I could discover more truthful images to replace the stereotypical ones of my youth, perhaps I could also begin to understand my own identity.

The East/West Conflict Hwang has explored the social and cultural conflict between the East and the West

in many of his plays. Often, his work is criticized for relying too heavily on Asian stereotypes. To critics who found the characters in *M. Butterfly* too pat, Hwang declared that debate over his plays was useful, answering, "It allows Asian-American audiences to define themselves in relation to a particular artist by either rejecting or accepting that person's vision." When given the opportunity to update the Rodgers and Hammerstein musical *Flower Drum Song*, Hwang was particularly interested in using an all-Asian cast and to present a romance between an Asian man and woman—an image absent from popular American culture and one he rarely examined in his own work. He reincorporates Rodgers and Hammerstein's songs into the story but also juxtaposes the Western songwriters' work with Chinese opera. Like his other plays, *Flower Drum Song* addresses issues of identity, assimilation, and the Asian American experience.

Works in Critical Context

Widely recognized as the leading theatrical voice of the Asian American community, Hwang has received his share of rave reviews and awards. *M. Butterfly*, his best known work, has garnered a variety of responses, including divided reactions from the academic community. *Golden Child*, despite largely positive reviews, also had its share of detractors.

M. Butterfly After its debut in 1988, *M. Butterfly* received three Tony Awards. Academics, though, took issue with some of the play's themes. While Suzanne Kehde notes that Hwang gives the female characters in the play sexually, intellectually, and politically dominant roles, other scholars claim that *M. Butterfly* merely reinforces Asian stereotypes. Williamson B. C. Chang states that the play "was written for

COMMON HUMAN EXPERIENCE

A recurring theme running through Hwang's work is the idea of identity and how religion, gender, and ethnicity affect it. Here are some other works that explore the same theme:

Identity (1998), a short novel by Milan Kundera. In this story, two lovers come to realize that what they know about one another is predicated on projection and what they know about themselves is based on the perceptions of strangers.

The Namesake (2003), a novel by Jhumpa Lahiri. This story of a second-generation immigrant of Indian parentage features Gogol Ganguli, an outwardly successful American who cannot quite find his place in the world.

Lucy (1990), a novel by Jamaica Kincaid. Lucy, a West Indian girl who comes to the United States and becomes a nanny for a wealthy white couple, faces both gender and ethnic identity issues.

white men and Asian women . . . . As has become the standard framework for dramas about East meets West, Asian males are again simply not there, they are invisible." He continues,

Asians, particularly Asian women, are portrayed as cunning, shrewd, manipulative, and deceptive. Westerners are trusting, idealistic, misinformed, and generous, but simply short-sighted in their dealings with the East.

Golden Child Hwang's *Golden Child*, commissioned by South Coast Repertory, opened Off-Broadway in 1996. Ben Brantley, in his *New York Times* review, called the play an "earnest, sweet-tempered work by a dramatist who is teaching himself to look back not in anger but in forgiveness"; but, Brantley continued, though "likable, educational and, at times, very poignant . . . it's never able to generate much urgency." One of the reasons for this absence of urgency, according to Brantley, is that "there's little sense of the emotional link between the generations." Nevertheless, *Golden Child* received a 1997 Obie Award as best play. A revised version of *Golden Child* opened on Broadway in 1998. Matt Wolf noted in his *Daily Variety* review that the play still had the same problems Brantley had identified two years earlier: the play never fully came to life, and never met its obligation to be a dramatic piece of work onstage. Nevertheless, the Broadway version received three Tony nominations, including one for Best Play.

Responses to Literature

1. How does Hwang blend Puccini's *Madame Butterfly* into his play, *M. Butterfly*? How do the two works differ in their depiction of Asian characters?

2. In what ways does *M. Butterfly* allow Hwang to explore the relationship of the West to the East?

3. Using the Internet and library resources, trace the influence of traditional Asian theater in *M. Butterfly*. What traditional forms does Hwang utilize? How does he adapt them to his work?

4. Read Maxine Hong Kingston's *The Woman Warrior: Memoirs of a Girlhood Among Ghosts* (1976), the play that made Hwang feel he could find his own voice. Why do you think this play had such an effect on him? Write a brief essay about your findings.

5. Why do you think Hwang found such a kindred spirit in Sam Shepard, whose work he was inspired by? Write a brief essay defining the two playwrights' similarities and differences. Be sure to include particular plays that Hwang found especially influential.

BIBLIOGRAPHY

Books

Bryer, Jackson R. "David Henry Hwang," in his *The Playwright's Art: Conversations with Contemporary American Dramatists*. New Brunswick, N.J.: Rutgers University Press, 1995, pp. 123–146.

Cooperman, Robert. "Across the Boundaries of Cultural Identity: An Interview with David Henry Hwang." *Staging Difference: Cultural Pluralism in American Theatre and Drama*, edited by Marc Maufort. New York: Peter Lang, 1995, pp. 365–373.

DiGaetani, John Louis. "David Henry Hwang," in his *A Search for a Postmodern Theater: Interviews with Contemporary Playwrights*. New York: Greenwood Press, 1991, pp. 161–174.

Moss-Coane, Marty and John Timpane. "David Henry Hwang." *Speaking on Stage: Interviews with Contemporary American Playwrights*, edited by Philip C. Kolin and Colby H. Kullman. Tuscaloosa, Ala.: University of Alabama Press, 1996, pp. 277–290.

Revilla, Linda A. and others, ed. "A Conversation with David Henry Hwang." *Bearing Dreams, Shaping Visions: Asian Pacific American Perspectives*. Pullman, Wash.: Washington State University Press, 1993, pp. 185–191.

Savran, David. "David Henry Hwang," in his *In Their Own Words: Contemporary American Playwrights*. New York: Theatre Communications Group, 1988, pp. 117–131.

Periodicals

Berson, Misha. "The Demon in David Henry Hwang." *American Theatre* 15 (April 1998): 14–18, 50–52.

Lyons, Bonnie. "'Making His Muscles Work for Himself': An Interview with David Henry Hwang." *Literary Review* 42 (Winter 1999): 230–244.

Marx, Robert. "Hwang's World." *Opera News* 57 (October 1992): 14–17.

Web sites

Steven Barclay Agency Web site. *David Henry Hwang*. Retrieved October 3, 2008, from http://www.barclayagency.com/hwang.html.

I-K

David Ignatow

BORN: *1914, East Hampton, New York*

DIED: *1997, East Hampton, New York*

NATIONALITY: *American*

GENRE: *Poetry, memoir*

MAJOR WORKS:

The Gentle Weight Lifter (1955)

Say Pardon (1961)

Rescue the Dead (1968)

Tread the Dark (1978)

Living is What I Wanted: Last Poems (1999)

Overview

David Ignatow is a poet known for turning autobiography into art and examining the self's relationship with the environment. He offers both the enlightening spectacle of a man who has paid for his accommodation with life and a body of poetry combining deep-felt emotion, intellectual penetration, and a considerable technical facility. In addition to creating his own poetry, Ignatow worked as a poetry editor for *American Poetry Review* and *The Nation*.

Works in Biographical and Historical Context

The Great Depression The Great Depression was a severe economic slump that affected North America, Europe, and other industrialized nations around the world from 1929 to 1939. This long global downturn was the worst financial disaster ever experienced by the Western world. The economic distress led to the election of Democrat Franklin D. Roosevelt in 1932. Roosevelt put into place a number of interventions designed to stabilize the American economy, including using increased government regulation and sweeping public works projects to stimulate a recovery. His Works Progress Administration, established in 1935, offered work to the unemployed on an unprece-

dented scale. Despite his efforts, economic stagnation and widespread unemployment continued. It was not until the outbreak of World War II that the American economy started to improve. It was during the Great Depression that Ignatow came to maturity and formed the basic ideas that would appear in his later writing.

Finding Himself David Ignatow was born in Brooklyn on February 7, 1914, and spent most of his life in the New York City area. As a child, his parents openly discussed their anxieties about the family business. This made a lasting impression on Ignatow. As an adult, he recognized that he valued personal freedom above material success, and so opted not to join the family business after graduating from high school. Instead, he left home and took jobs that allowed him time and leisure enough to write poetry. Many of his later works would rail against materialism and other trappings of the modern world.

Early in his career he worked in a butcher shop. He also helped out in a bindery in Brooklyn, New York, which he later owned and managed. During the Great Depression in the 1930s, he sought employment with the Works Progress Administration (WPA) as a journalist. His father helped him with the funding to produce his first book, *Poems*, in 1948. Although the volume was well received, he had to continue working various jobs and find time in between to pursue writing. These jobs included work as a messenger, hospital admitting clerk, vegetable market night clerk, and paper salesman. Other books followed, such as *The Gentle Weight Lifter* (1955) and *Say Pardon* (1961).

Finding His Voice *The Gentle Weight Lifter* resembles *Poems*. Personal, familial concerns are largely absent; the attack on the System is still present, although more sharply focused, as in the succeeding volume on business. For example, Ignatow adopts the role of the enraged executive to striking effect in "I Want": "I'll tell him I want to be paid immediately. / I'll sue him, I'll tear down his place, / I'll throw a fit." On balance, however, this volume is quite different from *Poems*. Instead of actual social abuses, *The Gentle Weight Lifter* centers on

David Ignatow   *Ignatow, David, photograph. Reproduced by permission by the Estate of David Ignatow.*

reviews the agonies presented in his earlier poetry. The first of the book's six sections treats the subject of parents and children.

Ignatow's later volumes, *Facing the Tree* (1975) and *Tread the Dark* (1978), explore the self's complex relationship with nature. Humanity is both part of nature and not a part: to sense one's kinship with nature is comforting (but may be lethal); to perceive one's difference from nature may increase his sense of self (but is lonely). On one hand, both books feature the consoling, Whitmanesque idea that since humans are part of the natural pattern of cyclic renewal, they never perish entirely. The second section of *Tread the Dark* can be seen as a celebration of suicide. The volume concludes with a section of poems about poetry, a subject Ignatow has addressed occasionally in his previous work.

Defying Labels   Ignatow's work defies ready categorizing, and he has, in various pronouncements, rejected association with many of the prominent literary movements of his time. He disclaims identification with the proletarians of the 1930s, with the New Critical poets of the 1940s and 1950s, and with the confessional poets of the 1960s as well, although his agonized poems on personal relationships often seem confessional. Instead, he points to William Carlos Williams, another free verse poet, whose use of the American vernacular has clearly influenced Ignatow's style, often termed "plain," "prose-like," and "unrhetorical" by his critics.

Ignatow has written poetry on all aspects of both his personal and social/political experiences, and while the relative emphasis on these two categories varies from book to book, a dual focus has remained broadly typical in his career. Ignatow's social poetry manifests a certain topicality: in the 1930s, he wrote poems about the Depression, in the 1940s, about World War II, in the 1960s, about Vietnam. More generally, the early work tends to concentrate upon the evils of business, while the later presents a more surreal vision of social violence and insanity. Ignatow's double focus on social and personal matters is evident in his earliest work. His 1930s poetry collected in *Poems 1934–1969* (1970) plays the topic of the Depression against unabashedly romantic views of sexual love. The poems of the 1940s treat the war and also the marital state, in which sexual excitement has given way to a dull domesticity.

Literary Accomplishments   Ignatow's literary career consisted of a range of jobs. He edited *American Poetry Review*, *Chelsea Magazine*, *Analytic*, and *Beloit Poetry Journal*, and held the post of poetry editor for *The Nation*. The many schools and universities he taught at include Vassar College, the University of Kentucky, Columbia, and New York University. After serving as president of the Poetry Society of America from 1980 to 1984, he was poet-in-residence at the Walt Whitman Birthplace Association in 1987. Ignatow was the recipient of many

the inner sense of alienation such abuses create. The general effect of *The Gentle Weight Lifter* is one of distance and impersonality, certainly not one of glossing over reality. Ignatow never wanders so far again, however, from the contemporary scene, and in the later volumes his parable poems are set in the present.

The parable technique dominates Ignatow's social poetry in the early 1960s. A parable is a tale meant to convey a message or lesson to the reader. While *Say Pardon* contains several straightforward business poems and *Figures of the Human* (1964) includes some equally straightforward pieces on the evils of money, Ignatow directs his creative rage toward the broader subject of violence and social dissolution in the America of the Vietnam era. He employs a style with a distinctly surreal quality ("we're a kind of surrealist nation," Ignatow has stated).

Ignatow's next book is widely considered his finest. More ambitious in style and thematic scope than *Figures of the Human*, *Rescue the Dead* (1968) makes obvious the essentially Romantic orientation of the poet. The collection depicts the achievement of a personal redemption, but before doing so Ignatow brings all to mind and awards, including two Guggenheim fellowships, the John Steinbeck Award, and a Bollingen Prize.

Works in Literary Context

When asked to name his influences, Ignatow replied, "The modern poet most influential in my work was William Carlos Williams. Earlier influences were the Bible, Walt Whitman, Baudelaire, Rimbaud, Hart Crane." In Williams, as in the works of Peruvian surrealist Cesar Vallejo, Ignatow most appreciated "the language of hard living; the universal language," which is perceived "in the lines of the poets where you can feel the mind running like an electrical current through the muscles," he told *Paris Review* contributor Gerard Malanga. To do this, Ignatow employed a meditative, vernacular free verse to address social as well as personal issues.

Free Verse Free verse poetry relies on the irregular rhythmic cadence of recurring phrases, words, and sounds rather than the conventional use of a set number of stressed and unstressed syllables per line. Free verse may or may not use rhyme. When it is used, it is with great freedom. Unlike conventional verse whose unit is measured by the foot or the line, free verse units are larger, sometimes running as long as a paragraph. Free verse was widely used by twentieth century poets. T. S. Eliot, Ezra Pound, Wallace Stevens, and William Carlos Williams all employed free verse in their poems. As indicated by this list, free verse allows a great variety of subject matter and tone as well as modification of language. In an interview published in *Boundary 2*, Ignatow said of his method that he "must try to structure the poem without losing the unstructured, random, elemental quality of things as they happen."

Realism William Dean Howells, one of realism's greatest advocates, defined realism as "the truthful treatment of material." Realists, then, are believers in pragmatism. The truth they seek to find and express is a pluralistic, or diverse, truth. They believe in democracy and the subjects they choose to describe are common, average, and everyday. Realism's chief subject matter is the surface details and minor catastrophes of middle-class society. Realists are broadly optimistic and their tone runs from comic and satirical to grim or somber.

Works in Critical Context

Direct statement and clarity were two of Ignatow's primary objectives in crafting a poem. Fidelity to the details and issues of daily life in Ignatow's poetry won him a reputation for being highly autobiographical. The poet Robert Bly said of Ignatow, "In form, David Ignatow is a master of the natural or non-academic style pioneered by Whitman and William Carlos Williams. In content, he is a master also, this time of the harsh perception, the self-judgment reluctantly made." Bly also remarked, "I find him a great poet and a friend of the soul." Ralph J. Mills

observed in *Cry of the Human: Essays on Contemporary American Poetry* that Ignatow

> has placed himself in the tradition of those genuine poets who have, in independent ways, struggled to create a living American poetry from the immediacies of existence in this country, from the tragedies and potentialities of its legacy, and from the abundant music and vitality of its language.

Mills also asserted, "Authenticity speaks to us from every line of Ignatow's poetry, reaching into our lives with the force and deliberation of the seemingly unassuming art which he has subtly and skillfully shaped."

Living is What I Wanted: Last Poems David Ignatow was, in writer Gerald Stern's words, the "gatekeeper between life and death." Nowhere is that more apparent than in *Living is What I Wanted: Last Poems*, the poet's twentieth and final collection. Vibrant with what Harvey Shapiro called "the life of struggle," the poems address the imminence of death honestly and boldly, acknowledging its necessity and its mystery. Ray Olson of *Booklist* noted that in this collection, Ignatow "look[s] back on, over, and squarely at life." Olson went on to praise the book for its "simply wise and elegant pieces."

Responses to Literature

1. Why do you think Ignatow chose to write in free verse? Write a brief essay explaining your answer and be sure to include examples of his poetry to support your findings.

2. How does Ignatow's poetry resemble the work of Walt Whitman or William Carlos Williams? Use

COMMON HUMAN EXPERIENCE

A recurring theme running through Ignatow's later works is humanity's complex relationship with nature. Here are some other works that share this theme:

Leaves of Grass (1855), a poetry collection by Walt Whitman. In this famous volume, Whitman celebrates nature, man, America, and sexual love in long rhythmical lines that create a natural, organic poetic structure.
Walden (1854), a nonfiction book by Henry David Thoreau. The author, an American naturalist and transcendentalist, wrote *Walden* after living in relative solitude along the shores of Walden Pond near Concord, Massachusetts. A recounting of his time there, the book explores the idea of nature as a model for a just society.
Fallingwater, a house designed in 1935 by Frank Lloyd Wright. This rural southwestern Pennsylvania house, built over a waterfall in the Laurel Highlands of the Allegheny Mountains, is widely regarded as Wright's finest work. The house, now a historic landmark, represents the best of Wright's organic architecture both for its dynamic quality and for its integration with its natural surroundings.

examples from these poets' body of work to support your answer.

3. Ignatow wrote about both personal and social topics. Using the Internet and library resources, familiarize yourself with Ignatow's poetry from a range of decades. What social topics does he cover in different time periods? How do these social topics affect his personal life, at least the part of his life revealed in his poetry? Use examples to support your findings.

4. Why do you think Ignatow chose to use such plain, straightforward language in his poetry? How does it affect his subject matter? How does it affect the reader's understanding of his poetry?

5. Ignatow is considered a realist poet. Using the Internet and library resources, research other realist poets. Who are they? What is their subject matter? What or who do they name as influences?

BIBLIOGRAPHY

Books

Holman, C. Hugh and William Harmon. *A Handbook to Literature*. New York: Macmillan, 1986.
Ignatow, David. *The Notebooks of David Ignatow*, edited by Ralph J. Mills. Ohio: Swallow Press, 1974.
Ignatow, Selected Poems, edited by Robert Bly. Connecticut: Wesleyan University Press, 1975.
Ignatow, Open between Us, edited by Ralph J. Mills. Michigan: University of Michigan Press, 1980.
Ignatow, The One in the Many: A Poet's Memoirs. Connecticut: Wesleyan University Press, 1988.
Mills, Ralph, J., Jr. *Cry of the Human: Essays on Contemporary American Poetry.* Illinois: University of Illinois Press, 1975.

Web sites

Poetry Foundation Online. *David Ignatow (1914–1997).* Retrieved October 8, 2008, from http://www.poetryfoundation.org/archive/poet.html?id=3396.
Web Del Sol. *David Ignatow* Retrieved October 8, 2008, from http://www.webdelsol.com/ignatow/.
Boa Editions, Ltd. *Living Is What I Wanted: Last Poems by David Ignatow.* Retrieved October 8, 2008, from http://boaeditions.org/bookstore/details.php?prodId=102&category=0&secondary=&keywords=.
Poets Org. *David Ignatow.* Retrieved October 8, 2008, from http://www.poets.org/poet.php/prmPID/777.
Upne. *Shadowing the Ground.* Retrieved October 8, 2008, from http://www.upne.com/0-8195-2195-7.html.

⊛ Lawson Fusao Inada

BORN: *1938, Fresno, California*

NATIONALITY: *American*

GENRE: *Poetry*

MAJOR WORKS:
Before the War: Poems As They Happen (1971)
Legends from Camp (1993)
Drawing the Line (1997)

Overview

Lawson Fusao Inada is a Japanese-American poet and editor. In addition to creating several adaptations of Mother Goose rhymes, he has written extensively about his experiences in a Japanese internment camp during World War II. Inada spent a significant part of his childhood as a prisoner and was one of the youngest Japanese Americans in the camps. The poet has been recognized by the president of the United States and was a guest at the White House as part of "A Salute to Poetry and American Poets." He is the recipient of the American Book Award and the Pushcart Prize for poetry.

Works in Biographical and Historical Context

Executive Order 9066 After declaring war on Japan, in an atmosphere of World War II hysteria, President Roosevelt authorized the internment of tens of thousands of American citizens of Japanese ancestry and resident aliens from Japan. Roosevelt's Executive Order 9066,

Lawson Fusao Inada   *Inada, Lawson Fusao, photograph by Paul Schraub. Reproduced by permission of Lawson Fusao Inada.*

dated February 19, 1942, authorized the transport of these citizens to hastily organized assembly centers governed by the military in California, Arizona, Washington State, and Oregon. The rationale behind the order was that Japanese immigrants—most of whom were not United States citizens simply because the government at the time refused to allow Asian immigrants to obtain citizenship—would be likely to spy on American military activities and report back to their native country. In addition to Japanese immigrants, however, the government also forcibly detained many children of immigrants who, because they were born on United States soil, were fully American citizens in the eyes of the law. Although it is not well known, the same executive order, as well as other wartime orders and restrictions, was also applied to smaller numbers of residents of the United States who were of Italian or German descent. While these individuals suffered grievous civil liberties violations, the wartime measures applied to Japanese Americans were worse and more sweeping, targeting citizens as well as resident aliens and uprooting entire communities.

Becoming a Jazz Poet   Lawson is a *sansei*—an American-born grandchild of Japanese immigrants to America. He

was born in Fresno, California, in 1938. In May 1942, his family joined over a hundred thousand other Japanese Americans in war relocation camps where they were confined for the duration of World War II. After the war, Lawson played bass and followed the jazz of Miles Davis, John Coltrane, and Billie Holiday. He also attended Fresno State, where he began his studies with Pulitzer Prize–winning poet Phil Levine, who introduced him to writing.

Inada's first volume of poetry, *Before the War: Poems As They Happen* (1971), was published by William Morrow. This made the poet the first Asian American to have a collection of poems published by a major New York publishing house. In this work, the writer reflects on his feelings of dispossession and traces themes from his childhood before and after his imprisonment. The poems have been applauded for the way they connect personal and social history, along with images of family, and for their tough, unsentimental language.

Legends from Camp   In 1993 Inada published *Legends from Camp*, a collection of poems that reflect on life in the World War II internment camps. With his firsthand experience, Inada "carries a reader into a child's world behind barbed wire," as R. C. Doyle explains in *Choice*. The collection was well received and earned Inada an American Book Award in 1994.

Divided into five sections, *Legends from Camp* begins with Inada's time in the internment camp, then moves to "Fresno," "Jazz," "Oregon," and "Performance." As Andrew J. Dephtereos writes in a review for *American Book Review*, the collection creates "a decidedly personal history of Inada, told in chapters that represent significant stages in his persona's life." Inada's poems embody his conviction that poetry must be accessible to all readers, not just to those who are most knowledgeable about the genre. "Poetry happens—whenever, wherever it wants," Inada asserts in the preface to *Legends from Camp*, "and the poet simply has to be ready to follow through on the occasion."

The Writing Life   Since the publication of *Legends from Camp*, Inada has continued writing poetry and teaching. An emeritus professor of writing at Southern Oregon University in Ashland, Inada has written several other poetry collections and served as editor of three important volumes, including the acclaimed *Only What We Could Carry: The Japanese-American Internment Experience* (2000). In addition to these individual publications, Inada has written critical introductions to a number of works, including John Okada's *No-No Boy* (1957), and his work has appeared in *The Best American Poetry*. Inada is also a contributing editor for the *Northwest Review* and was the narrator for the PBS specials "Children of the Camps" and "Conscience and the Constitution."

Accolades   Inada's work has been the subject of a documentary titled "What It Means to Be Free: A Video

LITERARY AND HISTORICAL CONTEMPORARIES

Lawson Fusao Inada's famous contemporaries include:

Kofi Annan (1938–): This Nobel Peace Prize–winning Ghanaian government agent has been secretary general of the United Nations since 1997.

Nobuyoshi Araki (1940–): This Japanese photographer has been called one of the most prolific Japanese artists of all time.

Taro Aso (1940–): This Japanese government official served as Japanese foreign minister from 2005 to 2007.

Raymond Carver (1938–1988): This American short story writer and poet helped revitalize the short story genre in the 1980s.

Bruce Lee (1940–1973): This American-born, Hong Kong-raised actor and karate master is best known for his film *Enter the Dragon* (1973).

COMMON HUMAN EXPERIENCE

A recurring theme running through Inada's work is his experience as a prisoner in a Japanese internment camp during World War II. Here are some other works that share this focus:

Impounded: Dorothea Lange and the Censored Images of Japanese American Internment (2006), a book of photographs by Dorothea Lange. Lange, who is best known for her photographs of Depression-era migrant farmers, was hired by America's War Relocation Authority in 1942 to photograph the internments of Japanese Americans. She was told not to show barbed wire, watchtowers, or armed soldiers, but the content of most of what she shot—barbed wire or not—was so stirring that most of her photographs were suppressed.

Desert Exile: The Uprooting of a Japanese-American Family (1984), a memoir by Yoshiko Uchida. Like most of Inada's work, this autobiographical narrative focuses on the author's family's experiences in a Japanese internment camp during World War II.

Seventeen Syllables and Other Stories (1989), a collection of short stories by Hisaye Yamamoto. As the daughter of Japanese immigrants, Yamamoto's perspective on the American experience is unique. These stories about the daily lives of Japanese-American women include internment camp tales as well as glimpses into the Japanese experience in America.

about Poetry and Japanese-American Internment," and an award-winning animated film adaptation of *Legends from Camp* made in collaboration with his son, artist Miles Inada. In 2004 he was one of only 185 artists, scholars and scientists chosen from a nationwide pool of applicants to receive a Guggenheim Fellowship. In 2006 Inada was named Oregon's poet laureate.

Works in Literary Context

Much of Inada's poetry is referred to as "jazz poetics," and he admits to being strongly influenced by jazz music and musicians. As Juliana Chang observed in her *Modern American Poetry* essay "Time, Jazz, and the Racial Subject: Lawson Inada's Jazz Poetics," "His jazz poetics of repetition and improvisation enable re-stagings and re-workings of a troubled past." Chang also added that while Inada is not the first Asian-American poet to use jazz characteristics in his poetry, his poetry "stands out in its consistency and depth of engagement with jazz."

Jazz Poetry Jazz poetry is simply poetry informed by jazz music—that is, poetry in which the poet responds to and writes about jazz or uses the same compositional structures as the music. Jazz poetry, like the music it reflects, encompasses a variety of forms, rhythms, and sounds. Beginning with the birth of blues and jazz at the beginning of the twentieth century, jazz poetry can be seen as a constant running through the Harlem Renaissance, the Beat Generation, and the Black Arts Movement—and it is still quite vibrant today. From early blues to free jazz to experimental music, jazz poets use their appreciation for the music to inspire their poetry.

Not only the music but jazz singers and musicians make frequent appearances in jazz poetry: Louis Armstrong, Miles Davis, Billie Holiday, Thelonious Monk, and Charlie Parker are just some of the primary muses for jazz poetry. Reviewing *Legends from Camp* for *Amerasia Journal*, Lonny Kaneko explains that Inada creates work "built for the listener's ear, aware, like jazz, of the need to capture in sound the spirit of his theme, of letting it build and reverberate in repeated phrases, little riffs and refrains that play through the poems." In doing so, Inada not only pays homage to an art form he reveres, he makes his poetry accessible to a range of readers, not just those familiar with the genre.

Works in Critical Context

Inada has been called the "father of Asian-American literature" and a "poet-musician in the tradition of Walt Whitman." The recipient of many awards and honors, Inada writes poetry that resonates with emotion, personal reflection, and lyricism. Hewing to the notion that poetry should be accessible to all, his language is often plain, which allows his stories to be easily digested. Despite his sometimes solemn subject matter, his poetry is known for having an uplifting, joyful quality.

Legends from Camp While a critic for *Publishers Weekly* finds Inada's work to be "unsophisticated in tone, technique and conceptual structure," Jessica Grim of the *Library Journal* judges the book to be "playful, full of life, and easy to understand, even when the subject is somber." R. C. Doyle comments that the powerful "Camp" section "will add a fresh dimension to a growing body of literature that remembers, humanizes, and shares the Japanese-American internment experience for new generations."

Drawing the Line In 1997 Inada published *Drawing the Line*, a tribute to his ancestors who survived the camps. The title is taken from a story about Yosh Kuromiya, the collection's main character, who created a line drawing of a nearby mountain in an attempt to use art as an escape from the daily indignities and labor of the camp. Rapee Malinee Thongthiraj, a critic for *Amerasia Journal*, notes that in these poems Inada seems to be "facing the memories of his personal and collective past, [creating] his own strategy of survival and resistance by re-envisioning American history and producing poetry that can move and stimulate us all." Thongthiraj also comments that these poems force the reader to "capture the emotions deep within ourselves." *Booklist* contributor Patricia Monaghan writes, "Despite its often somber subjects...this is a joy-filled book. This joy arises in part from Inada's irrepressible wit—a sort of slanting regard for the world that shows its peculiarity and loveliness at once."

Responses to Literature

1. Using the library or Internet sources, research Executive Order 9066. What other groups besides Japanese Americans were affected by it? How have Americans viewed the order, both during World War II and in retrospect? Write a brief essay about your findings.

2. Inada is known for writing jazz poetry. Using the library or Internet sources, research this term. What other poets write in this genre? Who is responsible for its birth? What are some famous jazz poems? Write a brief essay about your findings.

3. It is important to Inada that his poetry be accessible to all, even to readers who are unfamiliar with poetry and may not feel that they understand it. Why do you think this is important to the author? How does he make his poetry more accessible?

4. Inada includes his family in much of his work. How do his poems differ from traditional autobiography?

BIBLIOGRAPHY

Books

Baker, Houston A., ed. *Three American Literatures: Essays in Chicano, Native American, and Asian-American Literature for Teachers of American Literature*. New York: Modern Language Association of America, 1972, pp. 197–228.

Chow, Balance. "Asian-American Poetry." In *Critical Survey of Poetry: English Language Series, Vol. 2, revised edition*. Edited by Frank N. Magill. Pasadena, Calif.: Salem Press, 1983, pp. 3913–3919.

Periodicals

Review of *Before the War. Kirkus Reviews* (November 15, 1970): 1275.

Web sites

The Academy of American Poets Web site. *A Brief Guide to Jazz Poetry*. Retrieved October 13, 2008, from http://www.poets.org/viewmedia.php/prmMID/5660.

Oregon Poet Laureate official Web site. *Biography for Lawson Inada*. Retrieved October 13, 2008, from http://www.oregonpoetlaureate.org/lawson-inada.html.

Pacific University Asian Studies Web site. *Memoirs of Lawson Fusao Inada*. Retrieved October 13, 2008, from http://mcel.pacificu.edu/as/students/jintern/interview.html.

⚜ John Irving

BORN: *1942, Exeter, New Hampshire*

NATIONALITY: *American*

GENRE: *Fiction*

MAJOR WORKS:
The World According to Garp (1978)
The Hotel New Hampshire (1981)
The Cider House Rules (1985)
A Prayer for Owen Meany (1989)

Overview

John Irving enjoys a rare and prominent place among contemporary American writers, not only for having published a string of bestsellers, but also for having received accolades from critics in the popular and academic press alike. His status has been assured since the dizzying success of *The World According to Garp* in 1978. In addition to selling more than three million copies, *The World According to Garp* established Irving as an American cultural icon—a phenomenon that R. Z. Sheppard subsequently referred to in *Time* magazine as "Garpomania" in the early 1980s. Since the publication of *The World According to Garp*, Irving's novels have been adapted into four motion pictures, including *The Cider House Rules* (1999), for which Irving received an Oscar for best screenplay in 2000. These and other works have secured Irving's stature as one of America's most significant men of letters.

Works in Biographical and Historical Context

Writing and Wrestling John Irving was born in Exeter, New Hampshire, on March 2, 1942. His birth

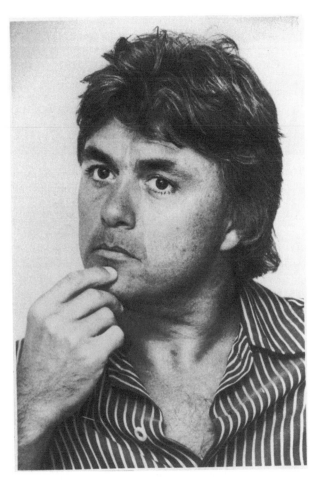

John Irving   *Irving, John, photograph. AP Images.*

name was John Wallace Blunt, Jr., in honor of his biological father, a World War II flyer who was shot down over Burma. Irving's later fiction would repeatedly address the theme of a missing parent, particularly an absent father. Irving's mother, Frances Winslow Irving, legally changed his name to John Winslow Irving when he was six years old after he had been adopted by her second husband, Colin F. N. Irving. Because his stepfather taught in the history department at Phillips Exeter Academy, Irving was granted admission, but his struggles as both an outsider (he was one of the few students at the academy who, like the other faculty children, was actually from Exeter) and as a foundering student who was later diagnosed as dyslexic, became the backdrop for his journey as a writer. At Exeter, under the tutelage of his wrestling coach and his writing teacher, Irving began to cultivate his two lifelong passions: wrestling and writing. Most of his later novels are set in his childhood home of New England, and several—including *A Prayer for Owen Meany* (1989) and *A Widow for One Year* (1998)—depict Phillips Exeter Academy specifically.

After his first year of wrestling at the University of Pittsburgh—a source of athletic disappointment—Irving

decided to travel to Vienna to study abroad. He told Greil Marcus in a 1979 *Rolling Stone* interview that Vienna "was so new and strange—or so old, as it turns out, and strange—that it forced me to pay attention to every aspect of it." Irving's insight into the concept of difference—initially triggered by the stark contrasts between Vienna and the familiar New England landscape of his youth—serves as the basis for his penchant for detail. His recognition that the nuance of detail is what represents the singularity of a setting or character complements his devotion to the novelistic forms of Charles Dickens, another master of such techniques. Irving's work poses the aesthetic question of range, asking how a story may be told truthfully if the reader does not receive as full and descriptive a picture as possible.

The University of Iowa Writer's Workshop

In 1965, after returning from Vienna, Irving received his B.A., cum laude, from the University of New Hampshire. In the same year, he published his first story, "A Winter Branch," in *Redbook* and traveled west to the University of Iowa Writers's Workshop, where he studied with Vance Bourjaily and Kurt Vonnegut. Irving developed a friendship with Vonnegut, and Vonnegut's own sense of discomfort with mainstream America, and the literary establishment served as an example and encouragement to Irving. In fact, as a defender of Vonnegut's work in "Kurt Vonnegut and His Critics," published in *The New Republic* in 1979, Irving creates his own manifesto for writing. In the article, he damns the contemporary novels that seem obscure and philosophically obtuse, arguing against "the assumption that what is easy to read has been easy to write." Naming Thomas Pynchon in particular, Irving suggests that such writers have not "struggled hard enough" to make their work "more readable."

Professor Irving

Although Irving's career is marked by a radical separation from both mainstream academic and popular fiction, his early writing life mirrors that of many contemporary American authors. With the rise of creative writing programs and M.F.A. workshops, the vast majority of writers in the latter half of the twentieth century found themselves aligned in some fashion with the academy, often as writers in residence or tenured faculty members. Upon receiving an M.F.A. from the University of Iowa in 1967, Irving entered the academic world as a professor at the now defunct Windham College in Putney, Vermont. Putney was Irving's primary residence until his 1981 divorce from his first wife, painter Shyla Leary, whom he had married in 1964. Between 1967 and 1978, however, Irving traveled to various colleges and universities, hoping to find time to write while supporting his young and growing family. In 1969 Irving, his wife, and his first son, Colin, journeyed to Vienna so that Irving might work on the screenplay of his first novel, *Setting Free the Bears* (1968); Irving's second son, Brendan, was born in Vienna. Upon his return to the United States, Irving taught at the Iowa

Writers's Workshop for three years, at Mount Holyoke College in South Hadley, Massachusetts, for two years, and at Brandeis University in Waltham, Massachusetts, for another year. The only exception to his teaching schedule during this eleven-year period came as the result of a grant from the Rockefeller Foundation in 1972 and later a Guggenheim Fellowship in 1976.

Becoming a Full-Time Novelist Although such a rigorous course load did not hamper Irving's productivity—he wrote and published four novels over eleven years—it did wear upon him. The success of *The World According to Garp* made it possible for Irving to forego a dual career as a teacher and a novelist. But his dedication to the sport of wrestling did not waver, and despite having no financial need to do so, he continued to coach wrestling until 1989. In 1987, he married literary agent Janet Turnbull, with whom he had a third son, Everett.

What the Future Holds In his novels Irving has crafted a peculiar form of postmodernism in which he fashions immense Dickensian narratives that explore various aspects of postwar Americana—from the politics of sex and love to the often corrosive intersections between violence and the family in contemporary life. From his first novel, *Setting Free the Bears*, many of the motifs that characterize Irving's fictions—including his penchant for magical bears, moments of devastating violence, the netherworld of Vienna, and earthy doses of sexuality—exist, albeit in relatively primitive forms. Irving's most recent novel, *Until I Find You* (2005), continues to expand upon his exploration of his personal experiences; in it, he addresses for the first time through his fiction his early experiences as a victim of sexual abuse, as well as his first experiences meeting the family of his biological father.

Works in Literary Context

Although he is not a prolific novelist, Irving remains highly popular with the reading public, as well as with moviegoers through his increasing activity as a screenwriter. Afforded the opportunity due to his stature within American letters, he regularly and publicly debates the nature and worth of novelists and their works. Long a proponent of character and plot driven fiction, Irving has been compared to such luminaries as Charles Dickens and Henry James, both of whom had a similar preoccupation with the moral choices and failings of their characters.

Family and Morality Though a contemporary novelist, Irving's concerns are traditional, a characteristic some critics have cited as distinguishing Irving's work from that of other contemporary fiction writers. Indeed, Irving's values are reflected in *The World According to Garp*, a work he described in *Washington Post Book World* as "an artfully disguised soap opera." "The difference is that I write well," Irving added, "that I construct a book with the art of construction in mind. . . . I mean to make

LITERARY AND HISTORICAL CONTEMPORARIES

John Irving's famous contemporaries include:

Isabel Allende (1942–): This Chilean novelist, journalist, and playwright is best known for her 1982 novel, *The House of the Spirits*.

Mohamed el-Baradei (1942–): This Egyptian government agent won the 2005 Nobel Peace Prize and serves as Chairman of the International Atomic Energy Agency.

John Cale (1942–): This Welsh musician and music producer was a multi-instrumentalist for The Velvet Underground, an influential New York rock band, from 1965 to 1968.

Harrison Ford (1942–): This American actor is best known for playing the role of Han Solo in the first three *Star Wars* movies (1977, 1980, and 1983) and the title character of the *Indiana Jones* series beginning in 1981.

Thabo Mbeki (1942–): This South African government official has been President of South Africa since 1999.

you laugh, to make you cry; those are soap opera intentions, all the way." A lengthy family saga, the novel focuses on nurse Jenny Fields, her illegitimate son, novelist T. S. Garp, and Garp's wife and two sons. *The World According to Garp* explicitly explores the violent side of contemporary life. Episodes involving rape, assassination, mutilation, and suicide abound, but these horrific scenes are always infused with comedy.

Despite its fairytale-like qualities, Irving's *The Hotel New Hampshire* (1981) also explores adult issues like incest, terrorism, suicide, freakish deaths, and gang rape, all infused with the novelist's trademark macabre humor. A family saga in the tradition of *The World According to Garp*, *The Hotel New Hampshire* spans nearly four generations of the troubled Berry family.

Works in Critical Context

John Irving is praised as a gifted storyteller with a fertile imagination and a penchant for meshing the comic and the tragic. Caroline Moore wrote in *Spectator* magazine, "the greatest popular artists—from Dickens to Chaplin—are circus lovers and showmen, with an unabashed streak of sentimentality and sensationalism. . . . Irving at his best, combining the grotesque, tragic and warmhearted, has something of their quality."

The World According to Garp Irving could scarcely have begun to imagine the remarkable popular and critical response to *The World According to Garp*, which became an international phenomenon. Directed by George Roy Hill, scripted by Steve Tesich, and starring Robin Williams, the 1982 motion picture adaptation of the novel enjoyed rave reviews as well. The critical response to the new direction in

COMMON HUMAN EXPERIENCE

A recurring theme running through Irving's work is his reliance on realism, even when his novels are filled with weird characters and strange events. Here are some other works that share this theme:

Infinite Jest: A Novel (1995), by David Foster Wallace. Set in the near future, this sprawling novel is loaded with zany political satire, cerebral humor, and a cast of hundreds.

Bluebeard (1997), a novel by Kurt Vonnegut. Written by Irving's writing teacher at the University of Iowa, this novel features genocide, the surrealist quality of the modern world, and a less-than-heroic main character.

Skinny Legs and All (1990), a novel by Tom Robbins. The author mixes philosophy and satire in this politically-charged tale about the Middle East, religious fanaticism, and art.

Irving's postmodern approach to narrative was overwhelmingly positive. In his analysis of the novel in *The New York Times Book Review*, Christopher Lehmann-Haupt observed in 1978 that "*The World According to Garp*, for all its realism, is not a realistic novel.... However you see it, between the imagined event and mundane reality that inspired its invention, there is room for laughter."

Literary critics continue to characterize *The World According to Garp* as the signal moment in Irving's evolution as a writer. Josie P. Campbell, for example, praises the novel in her 1998 study for the "richness of its many layers, the extraordinary flexibility and grace of its prose, and the fulfillment of Garp's—and Irving's—criteria for good fiction; the novel makes the reader wonder what will happen next..."

A Prayer for Owen Meany   In many ways Irving's seventh novel, *A Prayer for Owen Meany* (1989), has emerged as his most popular narrative. Despite a mixed critical response, the novel continues to enjoy a tremendous following among Irving's substantial readership. In his 1989 *New York Times Book Review* analysis of the novel, Alfred Kazin challenged the serious pretensions of *A Prayer for Owen Meany*: "The book is as cunningly contrived as the most skillful mystery story—that is the best of it. But there is absolutely no irony." Yet, other critics praise the deliberate lack of irony and deceptively simple structural design. In her critique of the novel, Debra Shostak praises Irving's intentionally "earnest" narration of Owen's act of self-sacrifice. Owen's miracle, she writes, "is an ambiguous discovery" for Johnny, and she states, "His recovery of origin does not grant him the power in the worlds of matter or spirit that we have come to expect from the conventions of such a narrative quest."

Responses to Literature

1. John Irving has been praised for his timely sensitivity to women in *The World According to Garp*. What made his sensitivity timely? What about the characters and the events in the novel reveal authorial sensitivity?

2. Using the Internet and library resources, research the wildly positive response given to *The World According to Garp* upon its publication in 1978. Why did the reading public react so powerfully to the book? Give examples of your finding in a brief essay.

3. How does American history impact the storyline in *A Prayer for Owen Meany*? Use the Internet and library sources as well as the novel to back up your answer.

4. How does Irving use symbolism in *A Prayer for Owen Meany*? Taking one of the book's important symbols (armlessness, doubles, American history, Owen himself, etc.), describe the author's development of a symbolic theme, and discuss the specific meanings with which your symbol is invested in the story.

5. John Irving often writes about extended families. In what ways do his own personal experiences affect his depictions of family?

BIBLIOGRAPHY

Books

Holman, C. Hugh and William Harmon. *A Handbook to Literature*. New York: Macmillan, 1986.

Neubauer, Alexander. "John Irving." *Conversations on Writing Fiction: Interviews with Thirteen Distinguished Teachers of Fiction Writing in America*. New York: HarperPerennial, 1994, pp. 141–152.

Periodicals

Bernstein, Richard. "John Irving: Nineteenth-Century Novelist for These Times." *New York Times* (April 25, 1989): C13, C17.

Interview with John Irving. *New York* (August 17, 1981): 29–32.

Kakutani, Michiko. "Randomness, Luck, and Fate, but Whew, No Bears." *New York Times* (May 1, 1998): 51.

Lehmann-Haupt, Christopher. Review of *The Cider House Rules*. *New York Times* (May 20, 1985).

Marcus, Greil. "John Irving: The World of The World According to Garp." *Rolling Stone* (December 13, 1979): 68–75.

Moore, Caroline. Review of *The Fourth Hand*. *Spectator* (July 21, 2001): 36.

Robinson, Phyllis. "A Talk with John Irving." *Book-of-the-Month Club News* (April 1989): 3.

Shostak, Debra. "The Family Romances of John Irving." *Essays in Literature* 21 (1994): 129–145.

———. "Plot as Repetition: John Irving's Narrative Experiments." *Critique* 37 (1995): 51–70.

⊛ Washington Irving

BORN: *1783, New York, New York*

DIED: *1859, Tarrytown, New York*

NATIONALITY: *American*

GENRE: *Fiction, nonfiction*

MAJOR WORKS:

"Rip Van Winkle" (1819)

"The Legend of Sleepy Hollow" (1820)

The Conquest of Granada (1829)

The Alhambra (1832)

Overview

Washington Irving was America's first successful professional man of letters, a gifted teller of tales, a romantic historian, and an influential prose stylist. With *The Sketch Book of Geoffrey Crayon* (1819–1820) he achieved both critical and financial success on both sides of the Atlantic, an exceptional feat considering the infancy of American publishing at the time. Never a major writer, he still

Washington Irving   *Mansell / Time Lfe Pictures / Getty Images*

remains significant for his best pieces and for landmark gains as a pioneering professional.

Works in Biographical and Historical Context

Becoming a Writer Irving was born and raised in New York City, the youngest of eleven children of a prosperous merchant family. A dreamy and ineffectual student, he apprenticed himself in a law office rather than follow his elder brothers to nearby Columbia College. In his free time, he read avidly and wandered when he could in the misty, rolling Hudson River Valley, an area steeped in local folklore and legend that would serve as an inspiration for his later writings.

As a nineteen-year-old, Irving began contributing satirical letters under the pseudonym Jonathan Oldstyle to a newspaper owned by his brother Peter. His first book, *Salmagundi; or, The Whim-Whams and Opinions of Launcelot Langstaff, Esq., and Others* (1807–1808), was a collaboration with another brother, William, and their friend James Kirke Paulding. This highly popular collection of short pieces poked fun at the political, social, and cultural life of the city. Irving enjoyed a second success in 1809 with *A History of New York, from the Beginning of the World to the End of the Dutch Dynasty*, a comical, deliberately inaccurate account of New York's Dutch colonization narrated by the fictitious Diedrich Knickerbocker, a fusty, colorful Dutch American.

His carefree social life and literary successes were overshadowed at this time, however, by the death of his fiancée, Matilda Hoffmann, and for the next several years he floundered, wavering between a legal, mercantile, and editorial career. In 1815, he moved to England to work in the failing Liverpool branch of the family import-export business. Within three years the company was bankrupt, and, finding himself at age thirty-five without means of support, Irving decided that he would earn his living by writing. He began recording the impressions, thoughts, and descriptions which, polished and repolished in his meticulous manner, became the pieces that make up *The Sketch Book*. The volume was brought out under the pseudonym of Geoffrey Crayon, who was purportedly a good-natured American roaming Britain on his first trip abroad.

The Sketch Book *The Sketch Book* comprises some thirty parts: about half English sketches, four general travel reminiscences, six literary essays, two descriptions of the American Indian, three essentially unclassifiable pieces, and three short stories: "Rip Van Winkle," "The Legend of Sleepy Hollow," and "The Spectre Bridegroom." Although only the last-named tale is set in Germany, all three stories draw upon the legends of that country. The book was published almost concurrently in the United States and England in order to escape the piracy to which literary works were vulnerable before international copyright laws, a shrewd

LITERARY AND HISTORICAL CONTEMPORARIES

Washington Irving's famous contemporaries include:

James Biddle (1783–1848): This American commodore attempted to open trade relations with Japan in 1846.

Simon Bolivar (1783–1830): This Venezuelan leader is credited with contributing to the independence of present-day Venezuela, Colombia, Ecuador, Peru, Panama, and Bolivia.

Christoffer Wilhelm Eckersberg (1783–1853): This Danish painter laid the foundation for the Golden Age of Danish Painting and is known as the father of Danish painting.

Samuel John Mills (1783–1818): This American missionary organized the American Bible Society and helped found the American Colonization Society in 1817.

Jane Taylor (1783–1824): This English poet and novelist is best known for writing the words to the song "Twinkle, Twinkle, Little Star" in 1806 at the age of twenty-three.

move that many subsequent authors copied. The miscellaneous nature of *The Sketch Book* was an innovation that appealed to a broad range of readers; the work received a great deal of attention and sold briskly, and Irving found himself America's first international literary celebrity. In addition, the book's considerable profits allowed Irving to devote himself full-time to writing.

Travel as Inspiration Remaining abroad for more than a decade after the appearance of *The Sketch Book*, Irving wrote steadily, capitalizing on his international success with two subsequent collections of tales and sketches that also appeared under the name Geoffrey Crayon. *Bracebridge Hall; or, the Humorists: A Medley* (1822) centers loosely around a fictitious English clan that Irving had introduced in several of the *Sketch Book* pieces. *Bracebridge Hall* further describes their manners, customs, and habits, and interjects several unrelated short stories, including "The Student from Salamanca" and "The Stout Gentleman." *Tales of a Traveller* (1824) consists entirely of short stories arranged in four categories: European stories, tales of London literary life, accounts of Italian bandits, and narrations by Irving's alter-ego, Diedrich Knickerbocker. The most enduring of these, according to many critics, are "The German Student," which some consider a significant early example of supernatural fiction, and "The Devil and Tom Walker," a Yankee tale that like "Rip Van Winkle" draws upon myth and legend for characters and incident. After 1824, Irving increasingly turned his attention from fiction and descriptive writing toward history and biography. He lived for several years in Spain, serving as a diplomatic attaché to the American legation while writing

a life of Christopher Columbus and a history of Granada. During this period he also began gathering material for *The Alhambra* (1832), a vibrantly romantic collection of sketches and tales centered around the Moorish palace in Granada.

Final Years Irving served as secretary to the American embassy in London from 1829 until 1832, when he returned to the United States. After receiving warm accolades from the literary and academic communities, he set out on a tour of the rugged western part of the country, which took him as far as Oklahoma. The expedition resulted in three books about the region, notably *A Tour on the Prairies* (1835), which provided Easterners with their first description of life out west by a well-known author. Irving eventually settled near Tarrytown, New York, in a small estate on the Hudson River, which he named Sunnyside. Apart from four years in Madrid and Barcelona, which he spent as President John Tyler's minister to Spain, Irving lived there for the rest of his life. Among the notable works of his later years is an extensive biography of George Washington, which Irving worked on determinedly, despite ill health, from the early 1850s until a few months before his death in 1859.

Irving's Legacy Today, many critics concur with Fred Lewis Pattee's assertion that the "American short story began in 1819 with Washington Irving." Commentators agree, moreover, that in "Rip Van Winkle" and "The Legend of Sleepy Hollow," Irving established an artistic standard and model for subsequent generations of American short story writers. As George Snell wrote: "It is quite possible to say that Irving unconsciously shaped a principal current in American fiction, whatever may be the relative unimportance of his own work." In their continuing attention to the best of Irving's short fiction, critics affirm that while much of Irving's significance belongs properly to literary history, such stories as "Rip Van Winkle" and "The Legend of Sleepy Hollow" belong to literary art.

Works in Literary Context

Irving's early writings were primarily satirical essays. The essay form suited Irving well, allowing him to publish his impressions of American and European customs without the restrictions of a novel's controlling narrative line. *The Sketch Book* also contained several stories whose origins, although based on native history, can be found in legend and myth. In this way, Irving fused his own Hudson River Valley experiences with Old World storytelling traditions. The mix, skillfully handled, resulted in characters and themes that had both local and universal appeal and meaning.

Satire Satire is a literary device that blends a critical attitude with humor and wit for the purpose of improving human institutions. A satirist often appears to support an opinion that is opposite of his or her true feelings as a way of exposing the shortcomings of the "supported" opinion. Satire can be found in the literature of Greece and Rome, through the Middle Ages, and on to eighteenth-century England. At that time, writers such as Dryden, Swift, Addison, Steele, and Pope wrote poetry, essays, drama, and criticism that made liberal use of the genre. Early American satire, such as Irving's, naturally followed English satire in style. In modern literature, satire is usually found in fictional narratives, particularly the novel. Mark Twain, Edith Wharton, Jane Austen, Aldous Huxley, Joseph Heller, and Thomas Pynchon have all used extended fictional narratives as vehicles for their satiric treatment of humans and their institutions.

Works in Critical Context

Irving's body of work, especially his best known *Sketch Book*, has been praised for its style as well as its content. He borrowed the elegant prose of writers such as Joseph Addison and Oliver Goldsmith—their lightly humorous and lyrical essays were highly influential—and injected his tales with innovation. In doing so, he captured a wider, broader range of readers and secured for himself international literary celebrity that continues nearly two hundred years after being published.

The Sketch Book   The Sketch Book prompted the first widespread critical response to Irving's writings. Reviewers in the United States were generally delighted with the work of their native son, and even English critics, normally hostile in that era to American authors, accorded the book generally favorable—if somewhat condescending—notice. Among the pieces singled out for praise in the early reviews were most frequently the three short stories, particularly "Rip Van Winkle." Critics found Irving's style pleasingly elegant, fine, and humorous, although some, including Richard Henry Dana, perceived a lack of intellectual content beneath the decorative surface. Dana also observed that in adopting the authorial persona of Geoffrey Crayon—with his prose style modeled after the eighteenth-century essayists—Irving lost the robustness, high color, and comic vigor of his previous incarnations as Jonathan Oldstyle, Launcelot Langstaff, and Diedrich Knickerbocker, an observation that was echoed by later critics. Subsequent "Crayon" works, such as *Bracebridge Hall, Tales of a Traveller*, and *The Alhambra*, while generally valued for their prose style, tended to prompt such complaints as that by the Irish author Maria Edgeworth that "the workmanship surpasses the work."

Beginning in the 1950s, however, critics began to explore technical and thematic innovations in Irving's short stories. These include the integration of folklore, myth, and fable into narrative fiction; setting and landscape as a reflection of theme and mood; the expression of the supernatural and use of Gothic elements in some stories; and the tension between imagination and creativity versus materialism and productivity in nineteenth-century America. Many critics read Rip's twenty–year sleep as a rejection of the capitalistic values of his society—ferociously personi-

---

COMMON HUMAN EXPERIENCE

A common theme running through Irving's work is that of political, cultural, and social reflection—sometimes rendered satirically. Here are some other works that reflect the author's impressions of contemporary events.

The Spectator (1709–1711), magazine co-founded by Joseph Addison. This British daily was read by the important people of the day, which made it quite influential. The essays found in its pages, most written by Addison and *Spectator* co-founder Richard Steele, concerned themselves with good and bad manners, life in the town and in the country, as well as literary and philosophical questions.

"The Traveller" (1764), a poem by Oliver Goldsmith. This panoramic tour through Switzerland, Italy, and France expresses the conventional ideas of Goldsmith's age, including the vanity of human wishes and sadness in the search for happiness.

"Tale of a Tub" (1704), a prose parody by Jonathan Swift. This tale is a satire of religious excess, written when politics and religion were still closely linked in England.

The Colbert Report (2005–), a nightly talk show created by Stephen Colbert, Ben Karlin, and Jon Stewart. In this satire of political pundit talk-shows, Colbert portrays an ultra-conservative, egocentric host whose endorsements of various political policies invariably reveal their weaknesses.

---

fied by the shrewish Dame Van Winkle—and an embracing of the world of the imagination. Ichabod Crane, too, has been viewed by such critics as Robert Bone as representing the outcast artist-intellectual in American society, although he has also been considered, conversely, as a caricature of the acquisitive, scheming Yankee Puritan, a type that Irving lampooned regularly in his early satirical writings.

Responses to Literature

1. Conduct a group discussion that addresses the idea of the American dream in "Rip Van Winkle." Can you think of various versions of the American dream as they relate to the story? Be sure and provide examples that support your ideas.

2. "Rip Van Winkle" casts the American woman as a cultural villain. Conduct a group discussion about the character of Dame Van Winkle. How would you analyze her character? What is the significance of her death?

3. Although Irving is known for his fiction, his *Sketch Book* reveals his talent for writing essays. Read the

Sketch Book and write a brief essay describing the various literary genres used by Irving in the book.

4. It has been said that the short story began with Irving's "Rip Van Winkle" and "The Legend of Sleepy Hollow." Do you agree? Why or why not? Using the Internet and library resources, trace the history of the short story and write a brief essay about it. Be sure to include information about Irving and his contribution to this literary form.

5. Satire has been a popular literary form since Greek and Roman times. What are some of literary history's most famous satires? Why do you think they remain powerful today?

BIBLIOGRAPHY

Books

Bleiler, E. F., ed. *Supernatural Fiction Writers: Fantasy and Horror 2: A. E. Coppard to Roger Zelazny.* New York: Scribners, 1985.

Bowden, Mary Weatherspoon. *Washington Irving.* Boston: Twayne, 1981.

Concise Dictionary of American Literary Biography: Colonization to the American Renaissance, 1640–1865. Detroit: Gale, 1988.

Harbert, Earl N. and Robert A. Rees, eds. *Fifteen American Authors Before 1900: Bibliographic Essays on Research and Criticism.* Madison, Wis.: University of Wisconsin Press, 1984.

Hedges, William L. *Washington Irving: An American Study, 1802–1832.* Baltimore, Md.: Johns Hopkins Press, 1965.

Holman, C. Hugh and William Harmon. *A Handbook to Literature.* New York: Macmillan, 1986.

Leary, Lewis. *Washington Irving.* Minneapolis, Minn.: University of Minnesota Press, 1963.

Myers, Andrew B., ed. *A Century of Commentary on the Works of Washington Irving, 1860–1874.* Tarrytown, N.Y.: Sleepy Hollow Restorations, 1976.

✸ Helen Hunt Jackson

BORN: *1830, Amherst, Massachusetts*

DIED: *1885, San Francisco, California*

NATIONALITY: *American*

GENRE: *Fiction, nonfiction*

MAJOR WORKS:

A Century of Dishonor: A Sketch of the United States Government's Dealings with Some of the Indian Tribes (1881)

Ramona: A Story (1884)

Overview

One of the most prolific women writers of her time, Helen Hunt Jackson hoped to be remembered mainly for *A*

Helen Hunt Jackson   Jackson, Helen, photograph. The Library of Congress.

Century of Dishonor: A Sketch of the United States Government's Dealings with Some of the Indian Tribes (1881) and *Ramona: A Story* (1884). Before Jackson's death, more than fifteen thousand copies were sold of *Ramona*, the novel she hoped would arouse public outrage at the plight of Native Americans in the California missions, just as Harriet Beecher Stowe's *Uncle Tom's Cabin* (1852) had called attention to the plight of African Americans. While the success of the novel in fulfilling that objective is still debated, the story and its leading characters have continued to attract audiences for more than one hundred years. Since its first publication, *Ramona* has been reprinted more than three hundred times; the story has been represented in many pageants and plays for stage, motion pictures, and television; and its main characters and settings have been blended into the legendary past of southern California.

Works in Biographical and Historical Context

Personal Tragedy Leads to Successful Career Helen Maria Fiske Hunt Jackson was born on October 14, 1830, in Amherst, Massachusetts. She married Edward Bisell Hunt, a lieutenant and eventually a major in the United States Army Corps of Engineers. The Hunts' first child, born a year after their marriage, died in infancy of a brain tumor. After serving in several important Civil War battles, Major Hunt died in 1863. Two years later their second son died of diphtheria. Devastated and alone while recovering from these losses, Helen Hunt began to write. It was 1865, the end of the Civil War and the beginning of the Gilded Age. Industrialization was transforming American culture, and women writing about children, home, and family values were reaching vast audiences in newspapers and magazines.

The favorable response to her first published poems about the loss of her son surprised Hunt, for she had never considered becoming a writer. Encouraged by that response, she published several more poems and a travel sketch on Bethlehem, New Hampshire, during the next six months. In 1866 she moved back to Newport, Rhode Island, where she became reacquainted with Thomas Wentworth Higginson, a resident at the same boardinghouse, and met other well-known figures in the circle of artists who summered in Newport. Higginson, who had become an important editor, became Hunt's literary mentor and personal editor for the rest of her life. During the next ten years she published hundreds of poems, travel articles, editorials, book reviews, and short stories in magazines and newspapers. In the fashion of the day she maintained anonymity by signing her work as Marah, Rip Van Winkle, Saxe Holm, and, most frequently, H. H.

Jackson Heads West   In May 1872 Hunt made her first trip to the West. Hunt's collected sketches of Europe enabled her to negotiate a contract with the *New York Independent* for a series on the West to subsidize her journey. In writing her Western sketches for the *New York Independent* and *Scribner's Monthly Magazine* she joined a popular new industry for authors.

Hunt's next trip west was to Colorado in 1873. While boarding at the Colorado Springs Hotel, Hunt became acquainted with another resident—William Sharpless Jackson, a Colorado banker and Quaker from Pennsylvania. In less than a year Jackson proposed marriage; although Helen declined his proposal for several months, they were married in October 1875. Three years later, Jackson published a novel for children, *Nelly's Silver Mine: A Story of Colorado Life, and Bits of Travel at Home* (1878). A reviewer in the *Atlantic Monthly* regarded the novel highly for introducing young readers to realistic and respectable Colorado characters who were notably absent in much popular fiction about frontier Western life. *Nelly's Silver Mine* became a staple in children's literature and was reprinted at least a dozen times through the 1930s.

A Life Change   In late October 1879, Jackson attended a lecture by Standing Bear, a Ponca chief whose address became an event that changed the course of her life and writing. Standing Bear was on an organized tour of the East to call attention to the plight of the Poncas, an agricultural Plains tribe that the U.S. government had mistakenly moved from the Dakota homelands of the tribe to a section of the Sioux Reservation and then farther south onto barren land that was depressingly uninhabitable. Within weeks of meeting Standing Bear, Jackson began to research and write about the Indian cause. After writing about the Poncas in the *New York Independent*, she wrote articles for the *New York Times* and the *New York Daily Tribune* to publicize her findings. Early that winter she decided that she would incorporate this material into a larger study, *A Century of Dishonor: A Sketch of the United States Government's Dealings with Some of the Indian Tribes* (1881). Jackson was proud of her work. She considered it one of her finest accomplishments, but the book did not sell well. Critics blamed the lackluster response on the fact that the book was written quickly and edited poorly. Despite poor popular and critical response, *A Century of Dishonor* did succeed in bringing the U.S. government's flawed Indian policy and the unfair and cruel treatment of North American Indians by expansionist Americans to public consciousness.

In September 1881 Richard Watson Gilder commissioned Jackson to write several articles on the California mission Indians for *Century Magazine*. Jackson's research on the Poncas and the California mission Indians prepared her to write *Ramona: A Story* (1884), the work for which she is best remembered. The novel was serialized in the *Christian Union* in May 1884 and published in book form by Roberts Brothers in November. Her Native American characters are just as imaginary as those of James Fenimore Cooper, but by refusing to confirm cultural stereotypes in her depictions of her characters and describing communities of Indians who were hard-working, law-abiding citizens, Jackson stirred popular sympathy for them as victims during the century of dishonor that she had attacked in her nonfictional reports.

A Final Novel   During this period she worked on her last novel, *Zeph: A Posthumous Story* (1885), which, like *Nelly's Silver Mine*, is set in the mining country of Colorado. She sent *Zeph* to her publisher a week before she died. The novel was included in a series of works written by American authors and published in Edinburgh, a series including fiction by William Dean Howells, Oliver Wendell Holmes, Mary E. Wilkins, and Joel Chandler Harris. With her husband by her side, Jackson died of stomach cancer in San Francisco on August 12, 1885.

Works in Literary Context

Hunt showed a knack for travel writing in her early articles on New England, and her European travel sketches were widely praised for their vivid descriptions that avoided the musty flavor of a guidebook. In writing her Western sketches for the *New York Independent* and *Scribner's Monthly Magazine* she joined a popular new industry for authors. During the early 1870s *Scribner's*, for example, was running lead articles on the West and the South in nearly every issue and began to replace its serials from English writers with articles, poetry, and

LITERARY AND HISTORICAL CONTEMPORARIES

Jackson's famous contemporaries include:

Emily Dickinson (1830–1886): This prolific and reclusive American poet wrote primarily about death and immortality. Fewer than a dozen of her nearly eighteen hundred poems were published in her lifetime.

Harriet Lane (1830–1903): Lane was President James Buchanan's niece and, due to Buchanan's unmarried status, served as the acting First Lady during his presidency.

Belva Lockwood (1830–1917): This American suffragist, attorney, politician, educator, and author supported the movement for world peace and temperance.

Camille Pissarro (1830–1903): This French impressionist painter re-created the teeming life of the streets, bridges, and boulevards of Paris.

Christina Rossetti (1830–1894): This British poet was the sister of painter Dante Gabriel Rossetti. She is considered one of the foremost poets of her time.

fiction by Hunt, Bret Harte, Joaquin Miller, and John Muir. Each of these writers shared a tendency toward naturalism.

Naturalism   In the late nineteenth and early twentieth centuries in France, America, and England, the literary movement known as naturalism came into being. Naturalism as a style of writing is used to describe any form of extreme realism as well as writing that demonstrates a deep interest in nature. It draws its name from its basic assumption that everything that is real exists in nature. The works produced in this movement tend to portray humans either engaged in a struggle for survival or as victims of environmental forces and the products of social and economic factors beyond their control or full understanding.

Native Americans in American Literature   The portrayal of Native Americans by white writers of American literature underwent considerable evolution between the seventeenth and nineteenth centuries. In the earliest works of American literature, specifically the nonfiction accounts written by the Puritan settlers of New England, the Native Americans are virtually equated with the then-untamed wilderness as something threatening and frightening—and, indeed, the white settlers had good reason to fear the Native Americans, who sought actively to repel the foreigners. Native American warriors frequently raided European settlements in the seventeenth century, killing or taking captive the inhabitants. The Europeans responded in kind, and the ferocity of their actions was sufficient to spark at least occasional pity from the contemporary chroniclers. William Bradford remarked in his *His-*

tory of Plymouth Plantation (1650) on the horror of watching as a Native American village was destroyed and its inhabitants burned alive. But despite his pity, Bradford counted the "victory" a "sweet sacrifice." Cotton Mather, an influential Puritan minister, added his support to the idea that Native Americans were a barbaric, even demonic, force to be conquered in the name of Christianity in such works as *Magnalia Christi Americana* (1702).

Throughout the seventeenth, eighteenth, and even into the nineteenth century, American settlers moving west clashed with Native Americans. During this time, a type of literature known as the captivity narrative—firsthand accounts of abduction and captivity of white settlers by Native Americans—was extremely popular. Such accounts as Mary Rowlandson's *A Narrative of the Captivity and Restoration of Mrs. Mary Rowlandson* (1682) (a best seller and one of the first of the genre) found an eager audience, and the pictures of the suffering of the mostly white female captives at the hands of the Native Americans continued to reinforce in the mind of the public the image of the Native American as a bloodthirsty savage.

By the time Helen Hunt Jackson wrote *Ramona*, white America's struggle with the Native Americans was nearly over. The Battle of Wounded Knee in 1890, between the United States army and Sioux factions, is generally considered the last battle of the so-called Indian Wars. By Hunt's time, the Native Americans had become less of a threat in popular perception and more of a social issue, and readers were ready to accept sympathetic portraits of Native American characters.

Works in Critical Context

Author of more than twenty books and hundreds of articles, Helen Hunt Jackson is remembered for the two books she considered her most significant contributions. Before her death she stated, "*A Century of Dishonor* and *Ramona* are the only things I have done for which I am glad now." For historians, *A Century of Dishonor* and *Ramona* remain important artifacts of late-nineteenth-century Indian reform, but the question remains how influential they were in shaping government policy.

A Century of Dishonor   Although Jackson viewed the book as the best work she had done, *A Century of Dishonor* suffers from hurried writing and poor editing. Never a best seller, the book nonetheless attracted attention from humanitarian reformers and many others who for the first time read of the horrible living conditions of Indians. In April 1881 Francis Parkman wrote to Jackson that her book was "an honest and valuable record of a scandalous and shameful page in the history of the American people—for the blame lies with them in the last resort." At her own expense Jackson sent every member of Congress a copy of her book, the cover embossed with the words of Benjamin Franklin: "Look upon your hands! They are stained with the blood of your relations."

Ramona: A Story The immediate success of *Ramona: A Story* was followed by its steady popularity for more than one hundred years. By 1940 six hundred thousand copies of it had been sold. Most contemporary critics praised the work highly and often cited it as the best work Jackson had done, although she was disappointed that some were more impressed by the novel's tragic love story than by the depictions of the suffering of the Indians. Other critics valued the literary merit of the novel more than its message. A reviewer in the *Atlantic Monthly*, however, noted that the narrative worked extremely well because although readers became indignant about the plight of the Indians, they never lost interest in the unfolding story. A year after Jackson's death, Albion W. Tourge, in reviewing *Ramona* for the *American Scholar*, wrote that it was the best novel yet produced by an American woman.

While twentieth-century assessments have had to acknowledge changes in literary taste, several have recognized the merit of Jackson's achievement. Howard Mumford Jones, in a review for the *Boston Evening Transcript* in 1939, argued that *Ramona* has the strength of Longfellow's *Evangeline* (1847) in depicting the spectacle of human suffering. Allan Nevins lauds the eloquence, vitality, and fiery truth of *Ramona*, which he calls a tour de force in its field.

Responses to Literature

1. What elements and/or characteristics of Jackson's *Ramona: A Story* make it an enduring classic? Are these elements/characteristics the same as those that made the novel so appealing when it was first published? Why or why not? Be specific in your answer.

2. Using the Internet and library resources, research the history of the Poncas and their treatment by the American government. Has the situation among the Poncas improved since Jackson wrote *A Century of Dishonor*? Do you feel the book made any impact on government policy toward Native Americans?

3. The Western sketches Jackson wrote for the *New York Independent* and *Scribner's Monthly Magazine* beginning in 1872 helped her join a popular new industry for authors. Using the Internet and library resources, research this new industry of travel writing. Who were Jackson's contemporaries? What drove the success of this niche literary industry?

4. Jackson and Emily Dickinson were close friends. Compare and contrast their poetry. How does their literary output compare to their respective legacies? Be specific in your answer.

5. Jackson suffered a great deal of personal tragedy. How did the tragic events of her life influence her writing career?

COMMON HUMAN EXPERIENCE

A recurring theme running through Jackson's work is her love for the land and culture of the West—especially California. Here are some other works that share this theme:

The Pastures of Heaven (1932), a book by John Steinbeck. These twelve interlinking stories feature a valley in Monterey, California, and the lives of the people that relocate there. One of Steinbeck's least-known works, *The Pastures of Heaven* paints a portrait of California as it emerged from its infancy.

The Mountains of California (1894), a book by John Muir. In this, Muir's first and best-selling book, the author provides sketches of the beauty, wildness, and grandeur of the Sierra Nevada Range region at the end of the nineteenth century.

The Land of Little Rain (1903), a book by Mary Austin. Considered Austin's masterpiece, *The Land of Little Rain* is a classic in the field of nature writing. The book focuses on the desert regions of southeast and east-central California and the people—particularly Euro-Americans, Hispanic-Americans, and Native Americans—that make up the communities of that region.

BIBLIOGRAPHY

Books

Banning, Evelyn I. *Helen Hunt Jackson*. New York: Vanguard, 1973.

Higginson, Thomas Wentworth. "Helen Jackson ('H. H.')." *Contemporaries*. Boston and New York: Houghton Mifflin, 1899, pp. 142–167.

Odell, Ruth. *Helen Hunt Jackson*. New York: Appleton-Century, 1939.

Rolle, Andrew F. "Introduction to Jackson's A Century of Dishonor." New York: Harper & Row, 1965, pp. vii–xxii.

Periodicals

Byers, John R., Jr. "Helen Hunt Jackson (1830–1885)." *American Literary Realism, 1870–1910* 2 (Summer 1969): 143–148.

Dobie, J. Frank. "Helen Hunt Jackson and Ramona." *Southwest Review* 44 (Spring 1959): 93–98.

Hamblen, A. A. "Ramona: A Story of Passion." *Western Review* 8, no. 1 (1971): 21–25.

Kime, Wayne R. "Helen Hunt Jackson." *American Literary Realism, 1870–1910* 8 (Autumn 1975): 291–292.

McWilliams, Carey. "Southern California: Ersatz Mythology." *Common Ground* 6 (Winter 1946): 29–38.

Nevins, Allan. "Helen Hunt Jackson: Sentimentalist vs. Realist." *American Scholar* 10 (Summer 1941): 269–285.

Pound, Louise. "Biographical Accuracy and 'H. H.'" *American Literature* 2 (January 1931): 418–421.

Shinn, M. W. "The Verse and Prose of 'H. H.'" *Overland Monthly*, second series, 6 (September 1885): 315–323.

✸ Shirley Jackson

BORN: *1916, San Francisco, California*

DIED: *1965, Bennington, Vermont*

NATIONALITY: *American*

GENRE: *Fiction*

MAJOR WORKS:

"The Lottery" (1948)

The Haunting of Hill House (1959)

We Have Always Lived in the Castle (1962)

Overview

Shirley Jackson wrote several best-selling novels, but she is usually identified with "The Lottery," a classic short story that established her literary reputation as an author of gothic horror fiction. This frequently anthologized tale of victimization exemplifies the central themes of Jackson's fiction, which include ordinary yet grotesque realities as prejudice, psychological malaise, loneliness, and cruelty. In works that often contain elements of conventional gothic horror, Jackson chronicles the universal evil underlying human nature.

Works in Biographical and Historical Context

Private Life Jackson was born in San Francisco on December 14, 1916, to Leslie Hardie Jackson and Geraldine Bugbee Jackson. She started writing poetry and keeping a journal at an early age. In 1934, the Jacksons moved to Rochester, New York, where Jackson enrolled in the University of Rochester. She withdrew after two years to spend a year pursuing her career as a writer, but she later returned to school and attended Syracuse University for two years (from 1938 to 1940). During this time she published several pieces of fiction and nonfiction in campus magazines. At Syracuse she met Stanley Edgar Hyman, whom she married in 1940; together they founded one of the campus magazines, *The Spectre.*

After graduation and marriage, Jackson moved to New York City. Her first national publication came in 1941 when *The New Republic* printed "My Life with R. H. Macy," a short story based on her experiences working at Macy's Department Store. She continued to publish short stories regularly over the next few years and also gave birth to a son, Laurence, and a daughter, Joanne.

Shirley Jackson   *Jackson, Shirley, photograph. AP Images.*

Ensuring Her Reputation In 1945 Jackson and her family left New York City for Bennington, Vermont, where Hyman had a teaching position. She published more short stories, including "The Lottery" in 1948. That same year, Jackson's first novel, *The Road through the Wall* (1948), was published, followed a year later by a collection of short stories, *The Lottery, or, The Adventures of James Harris* (1949). Two more children were born: Sarah in 1948 and Barry in 1951.

The Road Through the Wall is Jackson's only novel set in suburban California, in a neighborhood much like the one in which she grew up. It features several households on the same block and the rather spiteful interactions between the individuals and families that live there. The characters' lives reflect a certain moral bankruptcy, which is passed from parents to children. The novel was received with moderate acclaim and demonstrated that Jackson could sustain reader interest in the novel form. On June 28 of that year the *New Yorker* printed "The Lottery." The story occasioned so much public outcry that Jackson's reputation—and notoriety—were assured from then on.

The Lottery, or, The Adventures of James Harris was the only one of Jackson's short-story collections to be published during her lifetime. The title story, "The Lottery," is, in short, her masterpiece, and it has garnered a considerable amount of attention. As soon as it was published, literally hundreds of letters deluged the offices of *The New Yorker*, more than any other story had generated before. The letters were overwhelmingly negative, expressing, as Jackson said in "Biography of a Story," published in *Come Along With Me* (1968), "bewilderment, speculation and plain old-fashioned abuse." Jackson also noted tellingly, "People at first were not so much concerned with what the story meant; what they wanted to know was where these lotteries were held, and whether they could go there and watch."

The plot is deceptively simple: all the action takes place on a sunny afternoon in an average little American town. Tessie Hutchinson arrives late for the annual town lottery, which at first appears to be a rather festive event. The true horror of the rite is gradually exposed through the villagers' nervousness and reluctance until, in the end, Tessie, terrified and desperately defiant, stands revealed as the lottery winner and is summarily stoned to death by the populace.

Addressing Mental Pathology   In her second novel, *Hangsaman* (1951), Jackson writes about a young woman who is perilously close to psychological disintegration. Interpretations of the book vary, depending upon whether the reader accepts the main character's companion as real or imagined. Because of this ambiguity, the book received mixed reviews. Whatever Jackson intended in *Hangsaman*, she clearly set out to fictionalize a dissociated personality in *The Bird's Nest* (1954). This book was the fruit of Jackson's extensive study of mental illness, and the multiple personality of her character, Elizabeth-Beth-Betsy-Bess, is based on an actual case history she turned up in the course of her research.

Metro-Goldwyn-Mayer purchased film rights and eventually made a movie of *The Bird's Nest*. The film was released in 1957 under the title *Lizzie*. Jackson's fame received another boost when MGM purchased film rights to a novel published in 1959, *The Haunting of Hill House*. The movie, *The Haunting*, was released in 1963. In this book, the themes of isolation, loneliness, and emotional deterioration are explored through the character of a young unmarried woman named Eleanor.

Jackson returns to the theme of psychological pathology in her last completed novel, *We Have Always Lived in the Castle* (1962). Writing in the first person, a technique she otherwise rarely employed, Jackson develops the central character of Mary Katherine Blackwood (Merricat), a sociopathic girl who, at the age of twelve, poisoned four members of her family, including her mother and father, with arsenic. The exploration of the mind of this bizarre and oddly pathetic character is considered by many to be Jackson's finest fictional achievement. Certainly the novel is more consistently successful than any of her previous works, sustaining a tone that can only be

described as eerily poetic. Almost universally recognized as her finest novel, it was nominated for the National Book Award. It became a bestseller and was adapted for a Broadway production. The play had a short run at the Ethel Barrymore Theatre in 1966.

Final Years   Not all of Jackson's stories were explorations of evil, however; she wrote several stories she termed "pot-boilers," which were essentially slightly fictionalized versions of her domestic life. (She often did not even bother to change the names of her family members.) Centering on family squabbles, they were published regularly in women's magazines, such as *Good Housekeeping* and *Woman's Home Companion*. Jackson herself did not put much value on these stories, distinguishing them from her serious fiction. She claimed in a letter to her parents that she wrote these stories "simply for money." Many of these stories were later collected into the books *Life Among the Savages* (1953) and *Raising Demons* (1957).

Jackson died suddenly of heart failure in 1965. She had been active during her last years, delivering lectures at colleges and writers' conferences; three of the lectures are included in the same volume with the novel she was working on at the time of her death, *Come Along With Me* (1968). Jackson's next collection of unpublished short fiction, *Just An Ordinary Day*, did not appear until 1997, when previously unpublished and uncollected stories were interwoven and edited by her children, Laurence Jackson Hyman and Sarah Hyman Stewart. The stories cover the same themes as those in her other collections, running the gamut from humorous domestic pieces to tales of twisted psyches and supernatural horror.

COMMON HUMAN EXPERIENCE

A recurring theme running through Jackson's work is the savagery that exists beneath "civilized" society. Here are some other works that share this theme:

> *Lord of the Flies* (1954), a novel by William Golding. This novel has been called many things, including a parable, a myth, an allegory, and a morality tale, but at its heart *Lord of the Flies* is a novel about human nature and the good of the individual versus the common good. The story involves a group of British school boys left to govern themselves when trapped on an otherwise deserted island.
>
> *The Ballad of the Sad Café* (1951), a novella by Carson McCullers. Set in a desolate small town and peopled with grotesque characters, McCullers' tale is one of unrequited love. A triangle of desire exists between Miss Amelia, Cousin Lymon, a strutting hunchback that arrives out of nowhere, and Miss Amelia's rejected husband, Marvin Macy. Violence lurks everywhere in the story, which foreshadows a tragic ending.
>
> *Kind Hearts and Coronets* (1949), a film directed by Robert Hamer. This British black comedy, starring Alec Guinness and Dennis Price, is about one man's plot to kill eight members of an aristocratic family in order to achieve the title of duke for himself.

Works in Literary Context

In Jackson's body of work, humankind is more evil than good, profoundly misguided and seemingly incapable of enlightenment. Lacking either the capacity to reason or the strength to act upon moral convictions, individuals are dictated by habit and convention. They often behave with callous disregard of those around them. Yet, even in the novels and stories that deal almost exclusively with the private worlds of individuals, the isolation of these lonely figures is intensified by the sense that the world surrounding them is cruel and peopled with weak or malignant characters. Emotional warmth and closeness are rare in Jackson's fictional universe; there is little to sustain a healthy personality. Thus, it can be said that Jackson's body of work is representative of both gothic and dystopian literature, or literature that features a world that is problem-filled and bleak.

Gothic Literature Gothic literature is generally marked by elements of magic, mystery, and horror. Horace Walpole's *Castle of Otranto* (1764) was the originator of the form, with its medieval castle, trap doors, dark stairways, and mysterious rooms. Contemporary gothic literature usually features a medieval atmosphere of brooding and unknown terror. The combination of realism and horror is also indicative of gothic literature. In Jackson's body of work, psychological dissections of the darkness in human souls—the fear, loneliness, and hatred of the other that both cause and are the result of human evil—serve as the basis for her particular gothic style. In addition, the titular mansion of *The Haunting of Hill House* is much like the menacing structures found in classic works of gothic fiction, as are its paranormal occurrences.

Dystopian Literature The term "dystopia" refers to a future world in which contemporary problems have expanded to intensely unpleasant ends. Jackson's "The Lottery" is a perfect example of a dystopia. The story is about the reenactment in contemporary society of an ancient scapegoat ritual. The juxtaposition of the savage and the modern works to unsettle the reader and lays the foundation for its dystopic ending. A public stoning performed in the town square of an otherwise peaceful community communicates a powerful shock to the reader, an effect heightened by Jackson's unemotional narrative style. A modern fable, "The Lottery" reveals men and women to be timid, conformist, callous, and cruel. For example, while there is some resistance to the lottery, it is only voiced indirectly and never acted upon. Even Tessie, who perhaps displays an unspoken resistance to the lottery by showing up late, only protests when her family is chosen.

Works in Critical Context

With her frequent appearances in story anthologies, Jackson has never been far from the minds of scholars. Her short story "The Lottery" has been interpreted in several ways. Its symbolism, for instance, has been carefully scrutinized for its religious meanings. The story has been read as an attack on a capitalistic society, or as a feminist assault on an inherently patriarchal system. One of the wonders of the story is that it can sustain so many interpretations and still retain, decades after its original publication, the power to shock, enlighten, and entertain. Jackson's novel *We Have Always Lived in the Castle* was praised especially for its imaginative treatment of its narrator and main character, Merricat, who is far removed from a textbook sociopath and made into a believable, even sympathetic, character.

"The Lottery" In her *Library Journal* review of "The Lottery," Erica Bauermeister writes, "(the story is) a memorable and terrifying masterpiece, fueled by a tension that creeps up on you slowly without any clear indication of why." Other critics cite Jackson's ability to tap into readers' most basic fears. James Hilton of the *Herald Tribune* writes that "The Lottery" and other stories "remind one of the elemental terrors of childhood." A *Newsweek* contributor wrote of the collection: "In her art, as in her life, Shirley Jackson was an absolute original. She listened to her own voice, kept her own counsel, isolated herself from all intellectual and literary currents. . . . She was unique."

We Have Always Lived in the Castle   Jackson's last published novel before her death, was received warmly by critics and readers alike. An unnamed reviewer for the *New York Times Book Review* writes that the book is "A marvelous elucidation of life...a story full of craft and full of mystery." A reviewer for the *New York Times* calls the book "A witch's brew of eerie power and startling novelty."

Responses to Literature

1. Much has been written about the symbolism found in Jackson's story "The Lottery." Using the Internet and library resources, research the many symbolic meanings critics have attached to the story and write a brief essay about your findings.

2. "The Lottery" was published in 1948. What major cultural changes or historical events happened at about this time? Do you think Jackson was commenting on these events in some way? What do you think she is trying to say about human nature?

3. Why do you think "The Lottery" received the volume and intensity of feedback it did when first published by the *New Yorker* in 1948? Do you think it would invite the same kind of response today?

4. Jackson's novel *The Haunting* has been adapted for film twice, first in 1963 and then again in 1999. Compare the original novel to either film adaptation. Does the film convey the same moods and themes as the novel? How are the two works different?

BIBLIOGRAPHY

Books

Friedman, Lenemaja. *Shirley Jackson*. Boston: Twayne, 1975.

Hall, Joan Wylie. *Shirley Jackson: A Study of the Short Fiction*. New York: Twayne, 1993.

Periodicals

Allen, Barbara. "A Folkloristic Look at Shirley Jackson's 'The Lottery.'" *Tennessee Folklore Society Bulletin* 46 (December 1980): 119–124.

Kosenko, Peter. "A Marxist/Feminist Reading of Shirley Jackson's 'The Lottery.'" *New Orleans Review* 12 (Spring 1985): 27–32.

Nebeker, Helen E. "'The Lottery': Symbolic Tour de Force." *American Literature* 46 (March 1974): 100–107.

Oehlschlaeger, Fritz. "The Stoning of Mistress Hutchinson: Meaning and Context in 'The Lottery.'" *Essays in Literature* 15 (Fall 1988): 259–265.

Parks, John G. "The Possibility of Evil: A Key to Shirley Jackson's Fiction." *Studies in Short Fiction* 15 (Summer 1978): 320–323.

✸ Harriet Jacobs

BORN: *1813, Edenton, North Carolina*

DIED: *1897, Washington, D.C.*

NATIONALITY: *American*

GENRE: *Autobiography*

MAJOR WORKS:

Incidents in the Life of a Slave Girl, Written By Herself (1861)

Overview

Harriet Jacobs published her autobiography, *Incidents in the Life of a Slave Girl, Written By Herself* (1861) under the pseudonym Linda Brent. Unlike ordinary slave narratives that tell the story of a male slave's journey to freedom, Jacobs's slave narrative focuses on her unflagging devotion to her family. As a female fugitive slave, Jacobs loved her family so much that she chose to live for years in a crawl space where she could keep an eye on her children, rather than escape to her own liberty. Jacobs's memoir is regarded as a prime example of the slave-narrative tradition, though for a time the book was critically neglected.

Biographical and Historical Context

Child Slave, Young Dream of Freedom   In 1813, Harriet Jacobs was born a slave in Edenton, North Carolina, to Delilah Horniblow and Daniel Jacobs, two slaves owned by different masters. Jacobs did not learn about her slave status until she was six years old; when her mother died, Jacobs went to live with, and help, her mother's mistress, Margaret Horniblow. Mistress Horniblow taught Jacobs how to read and write, and, though technically a household slave, Jacobs was allowed the freedom of a child. Jacobs dreamed of freedom, but when she was almost twelve, her mistress died and Jacobs was bequeathed to the mistress's five-year-old niece, Mary Matilda Norcom. Jacobs's position with the Norcoms began a lifetime of much mental and physical anguish, a story she would one day chronicle.

Obsession and the Hope of Escape   At the Norcom house, Jacobs suffered emotional and sexual abuse at the hands of Mary Matilda's father, Dr. Norcom. Norcom's attraction grew into an obsession, and he began to relentlessly pursue her. She longed to escape, and had a moment of inspiration and hope in 1828 when her uncle Benjamin tried to escape to the North. But he did not succeed and was thrown in jail, where he was sorely mistreated for weeks. Once free from jail, he ran away again to Baltimore. From Benjamin's experience, Jacobs realized that enduring the pain and suffering of slavery was, in the end, the price of freedom.

Eventually the sexual and mental attentions of Dr. Norcom's advances became too much for Jacobs to bear. When Norcom's wife began to suspect the interaction

LITERARY AND HISTORICAL CONTEMPORARIES

Jacobs's famous contemporaries include:

Frederick Douglass (1818–1895): A former slave, Douglass became a famous editor, orator, abolitionist, author, and reformer, and in 1872, was a candidate for vice president.

Amy Post (1802–1872): A Quaker, Post was active in promoting abolition, women's rights causes, and reform.

Harriet Beecher Stowe (1811–1896): An American author and abolitionist, Beecher Stowe is known for her novel *Uncle Tom's Cabin* (1852).

Harriet Tubman (1820–1913): A former slave turned abolitionist, Tubman helped slaves reach freedom through the Underground Railroad.

between her husband and Jacobs, Jacobs came up with a plan. She had once asked Norcom if she could marry a free black man, and Norcom had refused her request. At this point, however, Jacobs figured that having an affair with Samuel Treadwell Sawyer, an unmarried white lawyer, would provoke Norcom's anger and would motivate him into selling both her and her children. Soon, Jacobs became pregnant by Sawyer and was allowed to live with her grandmother, but Norcom did not sell her, much to Jacobs's chagrin. Instead, enraged and jealous over her relationship with Sawyer, Norcom transferred Jacobs from housework to hard labor in the fields of his plantation. Jacobs, afraid that Norcom would assign her children to the fields as well, made up her mind to run away. This decision began a life of hiding with the help of friends and acquaintances, yet despite longing for freedom, Jacobs did not want to go far. She did not want to leave her children behind.

Nine Feet Long and Seven Feet Wide   After running away, since she knew he would try to hunt her down, Jacobs managed to seed rumors that she was in the North. But, Norcom was relentless. Jacobs, concerned that the friends who concealed her would become involved in her plight, chose a final place to hide: a small crawl space high in her grandmother's porch. This space measured only "nine feet long and seven feet wide," and only three feet high at one end. Jacobs shared the space with rodents and insects and did not have much fresh air or light. She had some comfort: her children had been purchased by their father, Sawyer, and lived with her grandmother. For seven years, Jacobs watched her children grow, "under the same roof."

Freedom and Writing   In 1842, after long imagining the day when she would eventually escape, Jacobs saw her chance for freedom. Since her children now lived and worked in the North, she decided, with the kindness and aid of friends, to head for New York City. After boarding a ship under a friend's assumed identity, she made her way North, where she found her children, a job, and new interests. She joined a group of anti-slavery feminists that included Amy Post, a Quaker abolitionist, or anti-slavery activist, who also advocated women's rights. Post, along with Jacobs's employer Mary Willis (whom Jacobs worked for as a baby nurse), encouraged Jacobs's love of writing, and Jacobs penned newspaper and journal essays about slavery. In 1852, Willis would buy Jacobs's freedom and, in that same year, Jacobs began writing her memoir.

After bad luck with publishing houses, Jacobs decided to publish the book herself and purchased the plates to print the manuscript. The book came out in 1861, prefaced by Lydia Maria Child, an abolitionist writer and editor. Through the years of the American Civil War—in which the issue of slavery was of paramount importance to many—Jacobs helped rebuild lives for fugitives, contrabands, and freedmen. After the war, she and her daughter traveled to North and South Carolina to develop relief societies in hopes of helping to reconstruct the defeated South. To raise money and support for the cause, she would travel all the way to London with her message. In 1897, just before her death, she helped inaugurate the National Association of Colored Women in Washington, D.C.

Works in Literary Context

Jacobs's *Incidents in the Life of a Slave Girl* is considered a slave narrative, a genre that chronicled the personal agency and emancipation of slaves before, during, and after the Civil War. The slave narrative followed the narrator's journey from slavery to freedom and detailed horrifying circumstances and tragic events, all the while evoking a theme of triumph over adversity. These narratives influenced many canonical twentieth-century works, including Richard Wright's *Black Boy* (1945).

The Rhetoric of the Slave Narrative   Usually, slave narratives relied on the rhetoric of abolition to connect with their readers, for the most part, those who already opposed slavery. This rhetoric frequently used Biblical allusion to appeal to Christian morality and would be rich in details that would incite the reader's compassion and sympathy. In style and tone, the slave narrative might resemble a sermon or, in contrast, a humble tale delivered with shame or apology. For example, in her autobiographical narrative, Jacobs begins by excusing the material to follow: "The remembrance [of this period in my unhappy life] fills me with sorrow and shame. It pains me to tell you of it."

Jacobs and Truth   Former slave Sojourner Truth, like Jacobs, used first-person rhetoric to support her opinions and persuade her audience, but Truth employed a sermon-like repetition to drum up audience sympathy, as this excerpt from her speech "Ain't I a Woman," given in 1851 at a women's rights convention, shows:

> I have ploughed and planted, and gathered into barns, and no man could head me! And ain't I a woman? I could work as much and eat as much as a man—when I could get it—and bear the lash as well! And ain't I a woman?

Though her work is stylistically different than Jacobs's, Truth also argues for the rights of women, particularly black women with histories like her own. Both Truth and Jacobs brought their personal experiences to the fore in order to inspire other women and to given voice to those who could not be heard.

Works in Critical Context

For years, *Incidents in the Life of a Slave Girl* was dismissed or neglected by scholars and critics who challenged its authenticity. In 1981, however, Jean Fagan Yellin used a collection of Jacobs's letters to directly address any questions about her authorship or experience. Since then, critics have examined the autobiography through various critical perspectives.

Incidents in the Life of a Slave Girl On January 21, 1861, William C. Nell wrote a letter to an abolitionist newspaper called *The Liberator*. Nell, a black abolitionist journalist, had introduced Jacobs to editor Lydia Maria Child, the woman who would help Jacobs publish her book. Nell tells the readers that they will enjoy the book's authentic and morally upstanding message and delivery:

> [This book] presents features more attractive than many of its predecessors purporting to be histories of slave life in America, because, in contrast with their mingling of fiction with fact, this record of complicated experience in the life of a young woman, a doomed victim to America's peculiar institution...surely need[s] not the charms that any pen of fiction, however gifted and graceful, could lend....[From it] all, especially mothers and daughters, may learn yet more of the barbarism of American slavery and the character of its victims.

Many abolitionist newspapers praised Jacobs's narrative. A reviewer in the *Anti-Slavery Bugle* wrote on February 9, 1861: "We have read this unpretending work with much pleasure....The style is simple and attractive—you feel less as though you were reading a book, than talking with the woman herself." In the same vein, on April 13, 1861, a reviewer for the *Weekly Anglo-African* wrote:

> In such volumes as this, the true romance of American life and history is to be found. Patient suffering, heroic daring, untiring zeal, perseverance seemingly unparalleled, and growth from surroundings of degradation and ignorance to education, refinement, and power: all find in these modest pages their simple, yet affecting narrative.

COMMON HUMAN EXPERIENCE

In *Incidents in the Life of a Slave Girl*, Jacobs used her own personal experiences to illuminate the lives of black female slaves. Other books that spoke for these oft-silenced women include:

Ain't I a Woman, a speech given in 1851 by Sojourner Truth. Truth gave this extemporaneous speech at a women's convention in Ohio and charged that black women deserved the same rights as white women and men. Different transcripts of the speech survive.

The History of Mary Prince, a West Indian Slave (1831), a slave narrative edited by Thomas Pringle. Prince's story was recorded by a friend of Pringle's family and was written out fully in Prince's natural speech.

The Narrative of Bethany Veney, A Slave Woman (1889), a slave narrative edited by Rev. Bishop Mallaleiu, Rev. V.A. Cooper, and Rev. Erastus Spaulding. The "plain and unvarnished tale" of female slave Bethany Veney.

Memories of Childhood's Slavery Days (1909), a collection of essays, verse, and personal observations by Annie L. Burton. This unique slave narrative includes reminiscences, poetry, and a short biographical account of Abraham Lincoln.

Responses to Literature

1. In the last chapter of *Incidents in the Life of a Slave Girl*, Jacobs lingers on the moment when she obtains her hard-won freedom. With a group of your classmates, discuss how "free" you think she was at that time. Then, discuss the way Jacobs defines freedom in comparison to the way we define freedom today. What does freedom mean to you?

2. With her memoir, Jacobs uses many conventions of sentimental fiction. Using resources at the library or on the Internet, research the conventions of sentimental fiction. Do you think Jacobs is a sentimental heroine? Do you think the plot of her narrative fits the sentimental mold? Can you think of other stories that have sentimental characteristics? Be ready to discuss your findings and thoughts with the class.

3. Harriet Jacobs's grandmother inspires Jacobs to triumph over adversity. Write an essay about how women throughout Jacobs's narrative influence her life. How does Jacobs view motherhood and the role of women in society?

4. With your classmates, discuss how the rhetoric of Jacobs's narrative might have appealed to "women of the North." Does she address these women directly anywhere in the text? What type of "voice" does Jacobs use to generate their sympathy?

BIBLIOGRAPHY

Books

Baym, Nina. *Woman's Fiction: A Guide to Novels by and about Women in America, 1820–1870*. Ithaca, N.Y.: Cornell University Press, 1978.

Braxton, Joanne M. and Sharon Zuber. "Silences in Harriet 'Linda Brent' Jacobs's Incidents in the Life of a Slave Girl." *Listening to Silences: New Essays in Feminist Criticism*. Edited by Elaine Hedges and Shelley Fisher Fishkin. New York: Oxford University Press, 1994, pp. 146–155.

Carby, Hazel V. *Reconstructing Womanhood: The Emergence of the Afro-American Woman Novelist*. New York: Oxford University Press, 1987.

Ernest, John. *Resistance and Reformation in Nineteenth-Century African-American Literature: Brown, Wilson, Jacobs, Delany, Douglass, and Harper*. Jackson, Miss.: University Press of Mississippi, 1995.

Foster, Frances Smith. "Harriet Jacobs's Incidents and the 'Careless Daughters' (and Sons) Who Read It." *The (Other) American Traditions: Nineteenth-Century Women Writers*. Edited by Joyce W. Warren. New Brunswick, N.J.: Rutgers University Press, 1993, pp. 92–107.

————. *Written by Herself: Literary Production by African American Women, 1746–1892*. Bloomington, Ind.: Indiana University Press, 1993, pp. 95–116.

Gwin, Minrose C. "Green-eyed Monsters of the Slavocracy: Jealous Mistresses in Two Slave Narratives." *Conjuring: Black Women, Fiction, and Literary Tradition*. Edited by Marjorie Pryse and Hortense J. Spillers. Bloomington, Ind.: Indiana University Press, 1985, pp. 39–52.

Humphreys, Debra. "Power and Resistance in Harriet Jacobs's Incidents in the Life of a Slave Girl." *Anxious Power: Reading, Writing and Ambivalence in Narrative by Women*. Edited by Carol J. Singley and Susan Elizabeth Sweeney. Albany, N.Y.: State University of New York, 1993, pp. 143–155.

Nudelman, Franny. "Harriet Jacobs and the Sentimental Politics of Female Suffering." *ELH* 59 (1992): 939–964.

Yellin, Jean Fagan. "Jacobs, Harriet Ann (1813–1897)." *Black Women in America: An Historical Encyclopedia*. Edited by Darlene Clark Hine. New York: Carlson, 1993, pp. 627–628.

Periodicals

Braxton, Joanne M. "Harriet Jacobs' Incidents in the Life of a Slave Girl: The Redefinition of the Slave Narrative Genre." *Massachusetts Review* 27 (1986): 379–387.

Yellin, Jean Fagan. "Legacy Profile: Harriet Ann Jacobs." *Legacy* 5, no. 2 (1988): 55–61.

Web sites

Campbell, Donna M., Washington State University Online. "The Slave Narrative." Retrieved October 19, 2008, from http://www.wsu.edu/~campbelld/amlit/slave.htm. Last updated May 21, 2007.

University of North Carolina, Chapel Hill Online. "Documenting the American South: Harriet Jacobs's 'Life Among the Contrabands.' from *The Liberator*, 5 September 1862." Retrieved October 19, 2008, from http://docsouth.unc.edu/fpn/jacobs/support5.html. Last updated October 19, 2008.

John Jakes

BORN: *1932, Chicago, Illinois*

NATIONALITY: *American*

GENRE: *Fiction*

MAJOR WORKS:

The Seekers (1975)

North and South (1982)

Overview

Known for his historical family sagas, John Jakes has been nicknamed "the people's author." His most popular works include a series of books known together as "The Kent Family Chronicles" (1974–1980), as well as the *North and South* trilogy (1982–1987). The 1985 *North and South* miniseries developed for television was among the ten highest Nielsen-rated miniseries at the time. While Jakes's mainstream success has drawn some negative criticism, many critics do acknowledge his power in dealing with important issues in America's flawed history, such as slavery, the usurpation of Indian lands, and government corruption.

Works in Biographical and Historical Context

An Only Child, An Education in Writing As an only child, Jakes was heavily influenced by his parents' cultural interests, which included reading, watching films, and going to plays. Jakes wanted to become an actor, but began professionally writing as a freshman at Northwestern University when he sold his first science-fiction story. In his sophomore year, Jakes transferred to DePauw University and began seriously pursuing a writing career while carrying a full academic load. In 1951, he married his former zoology lab instructor Rachel Ann Payne and, two years later, graduated from the creative-writing program. Jakes continued his studies in American literature at Ohio State University, eventually earning an MA. To support his wife and four children, Jakes wrote marketing material for a pharmaceutical company and several advertising agencies. At night after work, he wrote short stories and eventually became prolific in that genre, publishing over two hundred pieces of short fiction, many of which crossed genres such as science fiction, western, and fantasy. He also wrote nearly eighty paperback novels under pseudonyms such as Alan Payne, Rachel Ann Payne, and Jay Scotland.

Bottoming Out and Breaking Out Jakes's short stories and pulp fiction generated very little acclaim and very little income. In 1973, after taking a job adapting the last film of the "Planet of the Apes" series into a novel, Jakes felt as though he had hit rock-bottom in his writing career. At this point, Jakes doubted his skills and his future as a writer, but friend and fellow writer Don Moffit urged Jakes on and gave him an opportunity that would change his attitude. Moffit had been asked by Lyle Kenyon Engel, a packager in the paperback trade industry, to write a series of historical novels that would span generations to chronicle the lives of the Kent family and take place during the first hundred years of America. Moffit, unable to do the job himself, convinced Engel to hire Jakes. Although Engel contracted Jakes to write five books, the series was so successful that Engel asked Jakes for three more. Eight titles in all were published, starting with *The Bastard* (1974) and ending with *The Americans* (1980). Engel wanted Jakes to continue the profitable series, but Jakes was ready to move on to new projects, new sagas.

North and South Not long after, Jakes made a deal with Harcourt Brace to write a trilogy of hardcover novels about the Civil War. The successful *North and South* trilogy includes the titles *North and South* (1982), *Love and War* (1984), and *Heaven and Hell* (1988). This series would become part of American television history when the first book was made into a popular miniseries in 1985 starring Patrick Swayze.

California Gold and a Return to Family Sagas
His next novel, *California Gold* (1989) was Jakes's first novel not connected with a family saga or book series, yet still had a historical slant. But Jakes returned to the saga format with *Homeland* (1993), a story about a family of German immigrants set in nineteenth-century America. Around the time of publication for *Homeland*, many Americans felt the United States was falling in its global reputation and power. Because of this national attitude, Jakes wanted to write about a time when America was vast, limitless, free, and full of promise. In 2002, after another break with the saga genre, Jakes published *Charleston*, a novel that follows six generations of the Bell family, beginning with the American Revolution and moving through to post–Civil War Reconstruction. The novel is a single volume divided into three books: "City at War, 1779–1793," "City on Fire, 1822–1842," and "City of Ashes, 1863–1866." This novel was Jakes's sixteenth consecutive *New York Times* bestseller.

Honors and Recent Works John Jakes has continued his active writing career over the last decade, working

as usual in a variety of genres. Currently, he is collaborating with two writers of Broadway plays to adapt *North and South* into a musical.

Works in Literary Context

Although Jakes has written books across various genres, including science fiction, mystery, and westerns, he is best known for his work with the American family saga. Rory Quirk for the *The Washington Post* praises Jakes for constructing throughout his work "a graphic, fast-paced amalgam of good, evil, love, lust, war, violence and Americana."

Historical Inspiration Jakes conducted a vast amount of research for his historical novels and populated his work with both "real" and created characters. Stephen Crane, a nineteenth-century journalist and novelist, for example, appears both in Jakes's early *Great War Correspondents* (1968) and also in *Homeland*, covering the Spanish-American War. Susanna Dickinson, a survivor of the Alamo, served as the title figure of a children's book by Jakes in 1986, but also appeared in *The Furies* (1976). In *The Bastard* (1974), Jakes incorporates Paul Revere, John Hancock, and Samuel Adams into the story of fictional American immigrant Phillipe Charboneau as he and other American patriots try to build a new nation. The novel *American Dreams* (1998) includes the real-life figures Charlie Chaplin and Thomas Edison.

The Mythology and History of War Many of Jakes's novels, particularly the *North and South* trilogy, focus on America at war. The books, though works of fiction,

COMMON HUMAN EXPERIENCE

Jakes is known for his sweeping historical sagas. Other famous sagas include:

Gone with the Wind (1936), a novel by Margaret Mitchell. This famous novel, which includes iconic characters like Scarlett O'Hara, is set during the American Civil War and the Reconstruction period.

The Thorn Birds (1977), a novel by Colleen McCullough. The novel is set on a fictional sheep farm in the Australian outback and spans five decades in the lives of the Cleary family.

Shogun (1975), a novel by James Clavell. Set in 1600, this novel follows the experiences of an English sailor in feudal Japan.

Roots (1976), a novel by Alex Haley. This novel was inspired by Haley's own family history of slaves brought to America from Africa.

One Hundred Years of Solitude (1967), a novel by Gabriel García Márquez. This novel covers more than a century of a family's history in a fictional town called Macondo.

depict actual events of the Mexican War, the Civil War, and the Plains Indian wars. Yet, in the epilogue to *Love and War*, the last book in the series, Jakes writes, "As a people we all tend to be myth makers as the generations pass. . . . We mythologize not only individuals (such as Abraham Lincoln and Robert E. Lee) but also the war itself." Jakes goes on to write that we as human beings tend "to prefer the glamorous to the gory," and subsequently "put a patina on the war. To render it romantic." Jakes is known for his optimistic, even mythic, portrayal of American history, yet at the same time, his attention to realistic and accurate detail does not neglect gritty undertones of racism, violence, corruption, and betrayal. This balance is noticed by Nick Salvatore and Ann Sullivan of the *Radical History Review*, who argue that "the themes Jakes presents constitute an important and influential source of public history in modern American culture."

Works in Critical Context

With his epic family sagas, Jakes became a regular fixture on the bestseller lists, and television adaptations of his works only solidified his popularity in mainstream culture. It is perhaps surprising that an author of such popular genre novels has earned a great deal of praise from reviewers and critics as well. In particular, Jakes is credited with his skill at exhaustive research and his eye for historical detail.

The Civil War: North and South and On Secret Service
Jakes has been lauded for his recreation of America during the Civil War. Rory Quirk of the *Washington Post* states

that although the historical facts are familiar, "Jakes manages to resift the historical information, meld it with his fictional characters and produce an informative and nicely crafted narrative." *On Secret Service* (2000) also deals with the popular subject, chronicling the development of the U.S. Secret Service and its role following the assassination of President Abraham Lincoln. Like Quirk, *Booklist* reviewer Brad Hooper praises Jakes perspective on history and calls Jakes's Washington "brimming with as much espionage as a European capital during one of that continent's frequent internecine struggles." Kelly Milner Halls of *Book* praises Jakes's historical research as "impeccable." *Publishers Weekly* describes Jakes as "the foremost historical novelist of [the Civil War]."

Homeland and American Dreams
Critics praised Jakes's keen historical texture in the novel *Homeland* and its sequel *American Dreams*. Writing in the *New York Times Book Review*, Frank Wilson categorizes Jakes as "a master of the ancient art of storytelling." *Washington Post Book World* reviewer Bruce Cook notes that "Jakes researches exhaustively. He writes acceptably. He is a master of an old-fashioned sort of novel that readers still enjoy." Eric Robbins of *Booklist* writes that the novel provides "a popular vehicle for readers who want tasty vignettes of the past."

Responses to Literature

1. John Jakes is known for his family sagas that span many generations. Choose one of Jakes's novels and make a poster that presents a "family tree" of the main characters in the book. Make sure you clearly denote the relationships between each person and differentiate one generation from another.

2. Watch the first installment of the television miniseries *North and South* and read the novel. Write an essay in which you compare and contrast the adaptation. Think about how characterization, plot, and setting translate from page to screen.

3. Choose a historical figure from Jakes's *Homeland* and research that figure on the Internet or in your library. Write a report in which you provide a factual description of the historical figure, as well as a brief discussion about the accuracy of Jakes's depiction of that figure.

4. Jakes has said that we as a society tend to glamorize or romanticize war. Using examples from one of Jakes's novels, write an essay in which you agree or disagree with his statement.

BIBLIOGRAPHY

Books

Hawkins, Robert. *The Kent Family Chronicles Encyclopedia.* New York: Bantam, 1979.

Jones, Mary Ellen. *John Jakes: A Critical Companion.* Westport, Conn.: Greenwood Press, 1996.

Periodicals

Cook, Bruce. Review of *Homeland*. *Washington Post Book World* (July 18, 1983): 64–80.

Halls, Kelly Milner. Review of *On Secret Service*. *Book* (July–August 2000): 64–80.

Quirk, Rory. Review of *Love and War*. *Washington Post*. November 3, 1984: 2. 64–80.

Review of *American Dreams*. *Publishers Weekly* (May 25, 1998): 64.

Review of *On Secret Service*. *Publishers Weekly* (April 17, 2000): 49.

Salvatore, Nick and Ann Sullivan. "From Bastard to American: The Legitimization of a Fictional Family." *Radical History Review* 26 (1982): 140–150.

Wilson, Frank. Review of *Homeland*. *New York Times Book Review* (August 22, 1993): 14.

Web sites

John Jakes Home Page. Retrieved October 4, 2008, from http://www.johnjakes.com/.

✸ Henry James

BORN: *1843, New York, New York*

DIED: *1916, London, England*

NATIONALITY: *American*

GENRE: *Fiction*

MAJOR WORKS:
Daisy Miller (1878)
Portrait of a Lady (1881)
The Turn of the Screw (1898)
The Wings of the Dove (1902)

Henry James   *James, Henry, photograph. The Library of Congress.*

Overview

Victorian Henry James is known for his novel writing, though he experimented prolifically across genres. Though a nineteenth-century cosmopolitan viewpoint is common to many of his books, James straddled the stylistic line between the extremes of romanticism, with its emphasis on spirituality, and naturalism, with its focus on external, deterministic forces. James is also known for the well-developed women characters found throughout his work, as well as for the running theme of New World innocence in conflict with Old World experience, knowledge, and corruption.

Works in Biographical and Historical Context

World Traveler, Voracious Reader   Henry James was born in New York City, and was the second of five children. The son of an anti-Calvinist minister, James was raised to think of himself as a citizen of the world. In 1844, supported by a huge inheritance left by own his

wealthy father, Henry James Sr. moved his family to London to be near Thomas Carlyle and other distinguished thinkers. In 1845, the family returned to New York, but Henry traveled abroad throughout his youth. These trips would inspire his future work. James became a voracious reader proficient in French and French literature. Friends from his parents' social circles helped develop his early literary interests.

As a young man, James attended the Law School at Harvard so he could have access to the library and to lectures from such esteemed authors as James Russell Lowell, an American poet of the Romantic school. While at Harvard, James socialized in literary circles and became friends with social critic and activist Charles Eliot Norton and the future Supreme Court Justice Oliver Wendell Holmes Jr. James attended Harvard while the Civil War raged. His military service was precluded by a severe (if never fully disclosed) injury he had previously sustained while putting out a stables fire, During his time at Harvard, James began publishing short stories and reviews.

The Grand European Tour and Travel Writings
In 1869, James, financed by his family, traveled across Europe. His parents wanted him to study philosophy and languages in Germany (to add to his fluency in French and Italian), but James wandered through France, Switzerland,

and finally Italy, a country with which he became smitten. Several of his future works would feature Italy as a setting.

James returned to the United States in 1870 and wrote his first novel, *Watch and Ward*, which was serialized in *The Atlantic Monthly* in August–December of 1871 and published in book form in 1878. In 1870, James also published his first travel writings, not about his visit to Europe but sketches of New York, New England, and Quebec, in *The Nation*. Some critics compare the thematic exploration of past and present, and Old World and New in these essays to the themes in James's larger works.

Career in Europe In 1872, James played European tour guide for his sister, Alice, during her visit. On the trip, James drafted his first European travel essays as he visited several American expatriate communities and saw various sights in England, France, and Switzerland. The "sketches" of these travels ran in *The Nation* in 1872 and 1873. In these pieces, James created what critics would later call his "spirit of place." James called himself the "sentimental tourist."

Alice returned to the United States, but Henry remained abroad to build a professional career as an author. He traveled and wrote steadily for the next two years, publishing several short stories and finishing most of his second novel, *Roderick Hudson* (1875). James finally left Europe for America in 1874 and started his American writing career. He produced more than a dozen travel pieces for American magazines, including *The Atlantic Monthly* and *The Independent*. These writings helped support him financially and grew an audience for his fiction. *Transatlantic Sketches*, his first collection of travel pieces, was published in April 1875.

Travel, Biography, Novels, and More James went back to Europe later in 1875, after persuading the *New York Tribune* to hire him as their Paris correspondent on politics and culture. The job allowed him the time to work on his novel, *The American* (1877), first published as a serial in *The Atlantic*. During the late 1870s, James wrote in various genres ranging from travel essays to reviews. Some of these articles, as well as some early work, were published in *French Poets and Novelists* (1878). James wrote a critical biography called *Hawthorne* (1879), about the author Nathaniel Hawthorne, for an English Men of Letters series. At this time, James also published some of his most successful shorter fiction, including the novella *Daisy Miller* (1878), in addition to four novels, most notably *The Portrait of a Lady* (1881). Both works focus on American women traveling in Europe, and the conflicts that occur between them, traditional Europeans, and other American expatriates living there. In this way, James reflected his own experiences both as an American expatriate and as an observer of European culture. James developed a rather famous collection of friends and acquaintances, including the writers George Eliot, Robert Browning, Anthony Trollope, and Ivan Turgenev, his closest friend abroad.

In the 1880s, James suffered a tremendous loss when his parents both died within a short period of time. After a brief return to the United States, James headed back to Europe, where his writing career continued to prosper. He wrote, among many other things, a manifesto of literary realism called *The Art of Fiction* (1884), which was inspired by a lecture from critic and novelist Walter Besant, who said that novels should have moral purpose. James argued that fiction, like the best history and painting, should offer a direct impression of real life. At the same time, he believed a writer should run with his imagination, which "takes to itself the faintest hints of life [and] converts the very pulses of the air into revelations."

Serial Success and Failed Playwriting At the end of the 1880s came the American serialization of two of his longest novels, *The Bostonians* (1885–1886) and *The Princess Casamassima* (1885–1886), as well as the serialization of *The Tragic Muse* (1889–1890). When *The Tragic Muse* did not do as well as he hoped, James decided to try his hand at another genre: playwriting. With the help of an actor named Edward Compton, he turned his novel *The American* into a play. The drama starred Compton in the leading role, with James's young American friend and famous actress Elizabeth Robins as his leading lady, and included a happy ending. The play was not well received, yet James was not deterred. By 1892, he had written four new plays, the majority of which of which were failures when produced.

In Lamb House In his later years, James moved to Rye, a coastal town southeast of London, and bought Lamb House, an eighteenth-century mansion where he would live the rest of his life. He lavishly entertained there and created some of his finest literary works in his garden-house studio. Much of the fiction James wrote during this time was technically innovative and included the works *What Maisie Knew* (1897) and *The Turn of the Screw* (1898). His final writings were dictated to a typist, not only because of weakness in his right wrist, but also because he could no longer manage the volume of his personal correspondence. During this period, he wrote a trilogy that began with *The Wings of the Dove* (1902). After a visit back to the United States, he wrote *The American Scene* (1907), which some critics call James's most penetrating travel book and one of the best of the travel genre. In 1916, James died after complications from two strokes.

Works in Literary Context

Morton Dauwen Zabel, in the introduction to *The Art of Travel* (1958), his anthology of James's travel essays, proclaims that "Travel [for James] is not a marginal matter of romantic atmosphere," but rather a "conflict of culture he saw as basic to his century." At the same time, James considered himself a "sentimental tourist." In either case, James's work, no matter the genre, is textured with a richness of place and an appreciation of Old World history over New World progress and restoration.

Europe Versus America Throughout his novels, James often comments on the contrast between America and its European counterparts and creates wide-eyed American characters who view Europe through rose-colored glasses. For example, in *A Passionate Pilgrim* (1871), James uses the opposition to create the work's central conflict: the protagonist, an ailing American who has idolized England and English life, is too frail to achieve his dream of owning an English estate. This ironic idealization and reevaluation of cultures also comprises the main theme of *The American* (1877). The novel follows the American Christopher Newman, a kind but uncouth businessman on his first visit to Europe. Newman becomes aware of the European Continent's classic beauty as well as its seamy side. Years later, in *The Portrait of a Lady* (1881), a novel set mostly in Europe, James tells the story of a young American woman who inherits a great sum of money and is duped by two American expatriates.

James was inspired to write *The American* by Alexandre Dumas, fils' *L'Etrangere* (*The Female Stranger*, 1876), a play that portrayed Americans as crude, brash, and untrustworthy. James's protagonist Newman offers an honesty and positive attitude that depicts Americans in a more positive light. The book also borrows conventions from the popular melodrama genre, particularly elements such as the dark secret, the duel, and the convent.

Works in Critical Context

James has been classified as "the first of the great psychological realists of our time" and the "creator of the cosmopolitan novel." Though his work experienced a period of decline at the turn of the twentieth century, famous writer-critics like T. S. Eliot and Ezra Pound pulled attention back to his vast, varied, and successful career in the 1940s.

Robert Gale of the University of Pittsburgh summed up contemporary critical perception of both James and his now canonical body of work:

> James's work is stylistically complicated, demanding much of the reader. He is verbally subtle and delicately comic. His use of the restricted point of view, especially in his later, more realistic work, makes his plots hard to follow but exciting because the reader shares the same delusions, limited perceptions, and dawning awarenesses as the character through whose consciousness the story is filtered. James's imagery adds a poetic dimension to his prose, and individual similes and metaphors cluster into patterns which elucidate human conduct. James's plots are precise and usually quite simple. His purpose is not to tell a story so much as it is to show the interaction between character and character and between character and setting, which is often presented pictorially and usually has symbolic import.

LITERARY AND HISTORICAL CONTEMPORARIES

Henry James's famous contemporaries include:

Paul Verlaine (1844–1896): Verlaine, a French poet, is known as one of the founders of the Symbolist movement.

Gerard Manley Hopkins (1844–1889): Hopkins was an experimental poet whose work resisted the traditional poetic meter of the period.

Edith Wharton (1862–1937): An American novelist and short story writer, Wharton is known for her novel *The House of Mirth* (1905).

Gustav Flaubert (1821–1880): Flaubert is known for his novels, most famously his first, *Madame Bovary* (1857).

Ivan Turgenev (1818–1883): A Russian novelist and playwright, Turgenev is known for his novel *Fathers and Sons* (1862).

Turn of the Screw *The Turn of the Screw* has been lauded as a work of literary artistry and originality. When the novella was published in 1898, *The New York Times Saturday Review of Books and Art* called the work "a deliberate, powerful, and horribly successful study of the magic of evil, of the subtle influence over human hearts and minds of the sin with which this world is accursed." The anonymous reviewer saw the story as "one of the most moving and . . . most remarkable works of fiction published in many years." A reviewer in *Literature* states that the novella is "so astonishing a piece of art that it cannot be described." A reviewer for *The New York Tribune* suggests the book "crystallizes an original and fascinating idea in absolutely appropriate form." James himself, in his preface to the novella included in the New York Edition, classifies the work as "a piece of ingenuity pure and simple, of cold artistic calculation, an amusette to catch those not easily caught . . . the jaded, the disillusioned, the fastidious."

Responses to Literature

1. Choose one of James's novels and write an essay that describes how he illustrates the relationship between the United States and Europe. Use specific examples from the text to support your main points.

2. Using the Internet or resources in your library, research realism as a literary movement. Choose one of James's novels and write an essay discussing how that particular book can be classified as realism. Use examples from the text to support your argument.

3. Research the term *melodrama* . Some critics suggest that James uses melodrama in his construction of *The*

COMMON HUMAN EXPERIENCE

James is known for his realism, especially with regard to personal relationships. Other books with this attention to realism include:

Middlemarch (1874), a novel by George Eliot. Eliot's seventh novel was first published as a serial in 1871–1872 and is set in the fictional town of Middlemarch.

Madame Bovary (1857), a novel by Gustave Flaubert. This tale of a woman who attempts to break free from her limited social status was considered obscene and grotesque when it was first published, though it is now regarded as one of the greatest novels ever written.

Vanity Fair (1847), a novel by William Makepeace Thackeray. This novel is about human pretensions, betrayals, lies, and the upward climb for social class.

Tess of the D'Urbervilles (1891), a novel by Thomas Hardy. This novel follows the tragic incidents that occur in the life of heroine Tess.

Adventures of Huckleberry Finn (1884), a novel by Mark Twain. This classic American novel is a satirical story of boyhood in the mid-nineteenth century.

American. Based on your research, do you think the work qualifies as melodrama? Why or why not?

4. James spent much of his career writing in the travel genre. Read a few of his travel sketches, and then, find a few contemporary travel articles on the same destinations. Compare and contrast, in an essay, the rhetoric of James's sketches with those you selected. What seems to be James's main intention? What are the intentions of the other authors? What is the tone of each piece? Do the authors use different techniques to convey a sense of place? Are their intended audiences different? If so, how?

BIBLIOGRAPHY

Books

Albers, Christina A. *A Reader's Guide to the Short Stories of Henry James*. New York: G. K. Hall, 1997.

Anderson, Charles R. *Person, Place, and Thing in Henry James's Novels*. Durham, N.C.: Duke University Press, 1977.

Edel, Leon. *Henry James*. Minneapolis, Minn.: University of Minnesota Press, 1960.

Fogel, Daniel Mark. *Henry James and the Structure of the Romantic Imagination*. Baton Rouge, La.: Louisiana State University Press, 1981.

Gale, Robert L. *The Caught Image: Figurative Language in the Fiction of Henry James*. Chapel Hill, N.C.: University of North Carolina Press, 1964.

Hardy, Barbara. *Henry James: The Later Writing*. Plymouth, England: Northcote House, 1996.

Haviland, Beverly. *Henry James's Last Romance: Making Sense of the Past*. New York: Cambridge University Press, 1997.

Nowell-Smith, Simon. *The Legend of the Master: Henry James*. Oxford: Oxford University Press, 1985.

Zabel, Morton Dauwen, ed. *The Art of Travel: Scenes and Journeys in America, France, and Italy from the Travel Writings of Henry James*. New York: Doubleday and Company, 1958.

Web sites

Parkinson, Edward J. *The Turn of the Screw: A History of its Critical Interpretations 1898–1979*. Retrieved October 4, 2008, from http://www.turnofthe screw.com/ch2.htm.

✱ Randall Jarrell

BORN: *1914, Nashville, Tennessee*

DIED: *1965, Greensboro, North Carolina*

NATIONALITY: *American*

GENRE: *Fiction, nonfiction, poetry*

MAJOR WORKS:
"The Death of the Ball Turret Gunner" (1945)
Pictures from an Institution (1954)
The Bat-Poet (1964)
The Animal Family (1965)

Overview

Though respected as a literary critic, Randall Jarrell was also widely known as a poet and novelist. His reputation in these genres grew after World War II, and he had published seven volumes of poetry, two books of criticism, and a novel by the time he started a new career writing children's literature in 1962. At that time, three years before his death, Jarrell's work, especially books like *The Bat-Poet* (1964), became popular with an entirely new audience.

Works in Biographical and Historical Context

Childhood Motifs The first of two sons born to Owen and Anna Campbell Jarrell, Randall was from a young age greatly affected by his family's loss of an infant daughter, who died before he was born. The motif of the lost sibling appears throughout Jarrell's work, including the poems "Orestes at Tauris" (1948) and "The Black Swan" (1946). His mother Anna, who was from a wealthy Nashville family, also influenced his work. Jarrell captures her frequent fainting spells in the poem "Hope" (1961). From 1915 to 1925 the family lived in California, mostly in Long Beach, but then Anna separated from her husband and took her sons back to Nashville. In 1926,

Randall Jarrell   *Jarrell, Randall, photograph. Mary von S. Jarrell for The Literary Estate of Randall Jarrell. Reproduced by permission.*

Randall returned to California for a long visit with his paternal grandparents. He did not want to leave, but they forced him to go back to Nashville. Jarrell, young and upset, never communicated with or saw them again. The guilt that resulted ate at Jarrell all his life, but he could not directly write about it until 1962, when he based the couple called Mama and Pop in the poem "The Lost World" (1966) on his grandparents.

Education and Famous Friends As a young man, Jarrell helped to support his divorced mother by delivering newspapers and doing odd jobs, but he also found time to participate in writing, music, and dramatics at school. After high school, his uncle wanted him to work at the family candy business, but Jarrell was not interested. Instead, his uncle sent him to Vanderbilt University in Nashville, where Jarrell earned a BA degree in 1936 and an MA in 1939. During that time, Jarrell edited an undergraduate humor magazine, the *Masquerader*. From 1938 to 1939, Jarrell moved into college housing with future poet Robert Lowell and future short-story writer Peter Taylor. Taylor and Lowell became Jarrell's lifelong friends.

While at Vanderbilt, Jarrell dated Amy Breyer, a medical student several years older than he. The relationship was tumultuous because Breyer did not think she could live up to Jarrell's intellectual and emotional expectations. Eventually, she broke up with him and married a young surgeon from Boston. Jarrell recorded his pain in various poems, including "The Christmas Roses," "The Bad Music," and "Che Faro Senza Euridice?"

Teaching and Marriage In 1939, while Jarrell was a professor at the University of Texas at Austin, he met his first wife, Mackie Langham, who had just received her MA from that university. They were married in June 1940, the same year his collection of twenty poems,

called "The Rage for the Lost Penny," appeared in *Five Young American Poets* alongside work by John Berryman, W. R. Moses, Mary Barnard, and George Marion O'Donnell. Jarrell's first independent volume, *Blood for a Stranger* (1942), included the poems from "The Rage for the Lost Penny" plus two dozen others.

In the Army In 1942, Jarrell enlisted in the U.S. Army Air Force. Though assigned to aviation training at Sheppard Field in Wichita Falls, Texas, he "washed out" as a pilot and was sent to Chanute Field in Illinois to train as a flight instructor as well as a celestial-navigation instructor. While in the Army, he wrote his wife many letters that would later become fodder for such poems as "Lines," "The Soldier," and "Soldier, T.P." His other training experiences inspired his writing as well. For example, a mailroom stint grew into the poem "Mail Call," while hospitalization for an illness prompted "The Sick Nought."

Little Friend, Little Friend As Jarrell taught flight navigation from 1943 until his discharge from the Army in 1946, he finished the collection *Little Friend, Little Friend* (1945), as well as several poems that he would include in *Losses* (1948). Both books used war as a theme, but Jarrell also embodied "the particular part of the dead," who try to find meaning in their deaths. *Little Friend, Little Friend* includes one of Jarrell's most famous poems, "The Death of the Ball Turret Gunner."

Editor, Teacher, Prose Writer Because of the critical acclaim garnered from *Little Friend, Little Friend*, Jarrell received his first Guggenheim Fellowship just after his Army discharge in 1946. At this time, he was writing the "Verse Chronicle," a reviewing column for *The Nation*, but he ended up taking the job of interim literary editor for a year while the actual editor, Margaret Marshall, took a sabbatical. Jarrell also taught part-time at Sarah Lawrence College in Bronxville, New York, where he collected material for his prose fiction work, *Pictures from an Institution* (1954). Many of his friends and acquaintances served as models for the characters in the novel. These real-life models included college president Henry Taylor, his wife, and the famous political theorist Hannah Arendt. Sarah Lawrence, its campus, students, and progressive educational philosophy also influenced the book.

Greensboro, Salzburg, and Colorado In the fall of 1947, Jarrell went to Woman's College of the University of North Carolina, later renamed the University of North Carolina at Greensboro, as an associate professor. This move was encouraged by his friend Peter Taylor, who was already teaching there. The next year, Jarrell published *Losses* (1948), a book with themes related to World War II and its aftermath. Around this time, Jarrell's relationship with his wife became rocky, prompting him to teach at the Salzburg Seminar in American Civilization, in Austria. Here, he met a woman named Elisabeth Eisler who inspired several poems, including "Hohensalzburg:

LITERARY AND HISTORICAL CONTEMPORARIES

Jarrell's famous contemporaries include:

John Berryman (1914–1972): Berryman, a friend of Jarrell's, is considered one of the founders of the Confessional school of poetry, a movement that focuses on revealing intimate details about the poet's life.

Robert Lowell (1917–1977): An American poet, Lowell wrote works that leaned toward confession, engaged with history, and investigated the self.

Dylan Thomas (1914–1953): Though known for his poetry, Thomas, a Welshman, also wrote short stories and film/radio scripts that he often performed himself.

William Jay Smith (1918–): Smith, an American poet, was appointed Poetry Consultant to the Library of Congress, a position now called the Poet Laureate Consultant in Poetry, from 1968 to 1970.

Howard Nemerov (1920–1991): This American poet won the National Book Award, Pulitzer Prize, and Bollingen Prize for his book *The Collected Poems of Howard Nemerov* (1977).

COMMON HUMAN EXPERIENCE

Jarrell is known as a World War II poet because of the work inspired by his war experiences. Other books that emerged from memoirs of war include:

Memoirs of an Infantry Officer (1930), a novel by Siegfried Sassoon. The novel offers a fictionalized account of Sassoon's experiences during and after World War I.

Across the River and into the Trees (1950), a novel by Ernest Hemingway. This novel is set in post–World War II Venice, Italy.

MASH: A Novel About Three Army Doctors (1968), a novel by Richard Hooker. This novel about a fictional U.S. Mobile Army Surgical Hospital in Korea during the Korean War was adapted into a film as well as a successful television series.

Sophie's Choice (1979), a novel by William Styron. This bestseller is about a young American writer who gets involved with a Jewish man and his beautiful lover, a Polish survivor of the Nazi concentration camps.

Verses of a V.A.D. (1919), a poetry collection by Vera Brittain. This volume was written while Brittain was a Voluntary Aid Detachment nurse during World War I.

Variations on a Theme of Romantic Character," "A Game at Salzburg," and "An English Garden in Austria."

Colorado, Mary von Schrader, and the Library of Congress In the summer of 1951 Jarrell taught at the University of Colorado School for Writers and also legally separated from his wife. Jarrell then met aspiring novelist Mary von Schrader, with whom he began a relationship. Jarrell frequently wrote to her after he left Colorado to teach creative writing and lecture in criticism at Princeton. In 1952, after his divorce from his first wife was granted, Jarrell married van Schrader. In 1956, Jarrell received a two-year appointment as Poetry Consultant at the Library of Congress. Two of his later poems, "The Woman at the Washington Zoo" and "Jerome," came from this experience.

A New Career in Children's Literature and His Untimely Death After a successful career in poetry and criticism, Jarrell branched out into children's literature. His book *The Animal Family* (1965) was illustrated by well-known illustrator Maurice Sendak and was named a Newbery Honor book. While Jarrell was working on that project, he suffered from depression and intestinal problems and was eventually admitted to a hospital in Chapel Hill, North Carolina, as a manic-depressive. That April, still in the hospital, he attempted suicide by cutting his left wrist and arm, but by July he had returned home to Greensboro. In October, while walking along a country road a mile from the hospital, he was hit by a car and killed. Evidence from the scene led investigators to pronounce his death accidental.

Works in Literary Context

Critics have noted that Jarrell wrote with a clear, straightforward style and in vivid detail. Jarrell is often compared to English poet W. H. Auden, who was known for his technical prowess in form, his contemporary and personal subjects, and his use of the vernacular.

War Poetry Robert Lowell, a close friend of Jarrell's, wrote that, in his war poetry, Jarrell drew from firsthand experiences in the Army and knew the subjects of his poems well, which allowed him to "peculiarly sympathize" with the men. Lowell also noted that because of Jarrell's personal closeness, the "portraits of his pilots have been downgraded sometimes as unheroic, naive, and even sentimental." Jarrell's poem "The Death of the Ball Turret Gunner" exemplifies his work on this subject. The poem is deceptive in its five lines; Jarrell uses unexpectedly raw imagery to depict the gunner as a tender, unborn fetus, showing the vulnerability of men socially and culturally revered as impenetrable warriors. The gunner realizes that he is no soldier but rather a victim of something larger and more powerful than he is. He is an "assembly line product," as Richard Fein notes, important in his "public usefulness." He, like other soldiers in Jarrell's war poems, loses his individual identity and is consumed by the "State," an institution that is the harbinger of his death.

Works in Critical Context

In an essay on Jarrell, Helen Hagenbüchle summarizes reviews of Jarrell's oeuvre when she writes that "much of Jarrell's poetry springs from the conflict between intellect and imagination. His remarkable genius for articulate form is felt to be struggling with the desire to yield to an upsurge of unconscious images and dreams." However, Jarrell's work did not earn praise from everyone, particularly his writings that touched thematically on war. Some critics suggested that Jarrell's imagery and observation lost impact in his attempt to promote a self-indulgent political message. But, Jarrell was inspired by his personal experiences while in the army during World War II and felt a general hopelessness about the conformity demanded by the institutions of modern society.

"The Death of the Ball Turret Gunner" (1945) Richard Fein called "The Death of the Ball Turret Gunner" "the center of Jarrell's concerns and art." John Crowe Ransom echoes the sentiment in *The Southern Review*: "How fast it sticks in the reader's memory, if he will read [the poem] twice. This poem is quite worth any half dozen of the many others which Randall wrote about the Air Force in World War II." Critic Ted Humphrey suggests the poem "details in unsparing clarity the nature of modern warfare as waged with behemoth airplanes, anthropomorphized as beasts with bellies and wombs." Though some critics disliked Jarrell's less-than-patriotic take on the war, "The Death of the Ball Turret Gunner" is one of his best-known poems, often recognized for its "grisly determinism," in the words of Frances Ferguson, writing for the *Georgia Review* in 1974. The poem was also frequently placed in the category of postmodern elegy. Because of its dark irony, scholar Charlotte Beck suggested that "the poem caught the imagination of many readers who might not otherwise know of Randall Jarrell," but she was careful to note that "it is far from his best poem."

"Mail Call" (1945) Vernon Scannell classifed the war poem "Mail Call" as another example of a work in which Jarrell demonstrates man becoming reduced to infant, "animal or instrument by the calculated process of military training and by the uniformed civilian's enforced acceptance of the murderer's role, the cruel larceny of all sense of personal identity." Jonathan Galassi in *Poetry Nation* remarks that Jarrell's "grisly irony reminds one of [W. H.] Auden . . . but there is a horrible closeness to the event which Auden would not have ventured. . . . His ubiquitous generalizations earn their significance from gorgeously terrible descriptions of carnage and fear."

Responses to Literature

1. One of the main themes in Jarrell's poetic work is war. Using the Internet or resources from your library, find a poem about war that was published in the last twenty years. Then, compare one of Jarrell's war poems to the one you found. Write an essay discussing similarities and differences in tone, imagery, and theme.

2. In a short essay, compare and contrast the style of one of Jarrell's children's books with a selection of his poetry. How does the language, imagery, or tone differ based on his audience?

3. Jarrell's *The Bat-Poet* has been described as a parable about the poet's relationship with his audience. Analyze the tale in a short essay and discuss this interpretation. Do you agree? Why or why not?

4. Robert Weisberg in the *New York Times Book Review* wrote that Jarrell's "most famous piece of writing is a stark five-line lyric ('The Death of the Ball Turret Gunner'), the ultimate poem of war." Write a short essay explaining why this brief poem could be given that impressive assessment.

BIBLIOGRAPHY

Books

Beck, Charlotte. *Worlds and Lives: The Poetry of Randall Jarrell*. New York: Associated Faculty Press, 1983.

Ferguson, Suzanne. *Critical Essays on Randall Jarrell*. Boston: Hall, 1983.

Humphrey, Ted. "Randall Jarrell, (1914–1965)." *Poetry for Students*. Detroit: Gale Group, 1997.

Lowell, Robert, Peter Taylor, and Robert Penn Warren. *Randall Jarrell, 1914–1965*. New York: Farrar, Straus & Giroux, 1967.

Scannell, Vernon. *Not Without Glory: Poets of the Second World War*. Woburn, Mass.: Woburn Press Ltd., 1976.

Periodicals

Hardwick, Elizabeth. Review of *The Bat-Poet*. *New York Times* (May 3, 1964).

Updike, John. "Randall Jarrell Writing Stories for Children." *New York Times* (November 16, 1976).

Web sites

"Randall Jarrell." *Poets.org*. Retrieved October 23, 2008, from http://www.poets.org/poet.php/prmPID/9.

"Randall Jarrell, 1914–1965." *Modern American Poetry*. Retrieved October 23, 2008, from http://www.english.uiuc.edu/maps/poets/g_l/jarrell/jarrell.htm.

✸ Robinson Jeffers

BORN: *1887, Pittsburgh, Pennsylvania*

DIED: *1962, Carmel, California*

NATIONALITY: *American*

GENRE: *Poetry, drama*

MAJOR WORKS:

Roan Stallion, Tamar, and Other Poems (1925)

Descent to the Dead, Poems Written in Ireland and Great Britain (1931)

Thurso's Landing (1932)

Robinson Jeffers   *Jeffers, Robinson, photograph. The Library of Congress.*

Overview

Robinson Jeffers did not launch his poetic career until he was in his thirties, but he ultimately became known both as a "poet of place" and as a "scientific poet." Stylistically, Jeffers composed long, straightforward narratives and combined scientific theory, an ecologist's observations, and knowledge of the classical canon with a directness that offered a fresh and controversial vision of the world, often through the landscape of California.

Biographical and Historical Context

A Boarding-School Education   Jeffers was born John Robinson to Annie Tuttle and William Hamilton Jeffers. His father, a professor of Old Testament literature at Western Theological Seminary in Allegheny, Pennsylvania, was a strict disciplinarian and had high standards for his son. To motivate his son, he used corporal punishment to encourage good study habits and forced him to run timed sprints for exercise. At eleven years old, Jeffers was sent to boarding school in Switzerland, and, over the course of his education, attended four different schools: in Vevey, Lausanne, Geneva, and Zurich. Jeffers's intense education influenced his later poetry, which draws heavily on classical Greek drama, the Bible, science, medicine, and nature.

College, California, and Love   In 1902, after his stint at boarding schools abroad, fifteen-year-old Jeffers graduated from the University of Western Pennsylvania. In 1903, he attended Occidental College in Los Angeles when his family moved to Pasadena, California. This move was a catalyst for the creative direction his life would take. California, to Jeffers, felt like a physical, social, and spiritual home. The state stimulated Jeffers's imagination and finally, after many years of moving around, allowed him to put down roots and identify with a particular place. Jeffers enjoyed hiking and camping in the Los Angeles mountains, and, in his poetry, Jeffers employed rich detail of land, water, and sky from a life spent close to nature. He also moved increasingly toward a view of nature as being superior to any works of humankind, and even toward the idea that humans in general were neither worthy nor fully capable of appreciating the beauty of nature.

Jeffers graduated from Occidental College in 1905 and took graduate courses in German literature at the University of Southern California where he met his future wife, Una. At the time, Una Call Kuster was married to a young attorney. Two years older than Jeffers, she took an interest in both his poetry and him. Their romance became a great influence on his later poetry, despite the fact that the families of both Jeffers and Una tried to stop the scandalous relationship. In the introduction to his *Selected Poetry* (1938), he writes that, although Una never saw any of his poems until they were finished, "by her presence and conversation she has co-authored every one of them."

Forestry and First Works   Jeffers and his family moved to Seattle in 1910, so that Jeffers could enroll in the forestry program at the University of Washington. Jeffers left the program, however, after discovering the course of study focused on timber harvests rather than an ecological study of forests. Still, he ultimately finished his forestry studies in the spring of 1913 and married Una in the fall. Their marriage was fodder for gossip, splashed across the front page of the *Los Angeles Times*, but the couple did not care. They moved to the coastal town of Carmel where Jeffers concentrated on writing poetry.

Before marrying Una, Jeffers, with a small inheritance from a relative, published a small volume of his poetry called *Flagons and Apples* (1912). In 1916, he submitted the collection *Californians* to Macmillan, and it was published late that year. Though the book did not receive much critical attention, Oscar Firkins of *The Nation* noted that Jeffers reminded him of the poet-philosopher Ralph Waldo Emerson.

Because Jeffers realized that the unique *Tamar and Other Poems* (1922) might be controversial, he published the volume himself. After a pair of well-known editors got hold of the collection, the volume became a critical success, went through several editions, and was translated in foreign languages. After this collection, Jeffers came out with *The Women at Point Sur* (1927), a volume that garnered mixed reviews. The narrative focuses on Barclay, a minister experiencing a crisis of religious faith following World War I. Jeffers's reputation remained solid, and he published *Cawdor and Other Poems* (1928) and *Dear Judas and Other Poems* (1929).

Ireland and Writing in the 1930s After *Dear Judas*, Jeffers and his wife went to Europe and lived in a cottage in the Irish countryside near Una's relatives for almost a year. Jeffers began to see Ireland as his native home. This outlook resulted in a series of poems called *Descent to the Dead, Poems Written in Ireland and Great Britain* (1931) and the collection *Thurso's Landing and Other Poems* (1932). Jeffers also wrote *Give Your Heart to the Hawks and Other Poems* (1933), *Solstice and Other Poems* (1935), and *Such Counsels You Gave to Me and Other Poems* (1937).

World War II In 1941, Jeffers, with his wife, went on a reading tour of the American East Coast. At every university, Jeffers was received by huge audiences. As World War II raged on, Jeffers wrote political poems, accusing the government of lying to its people. These poems were not published during the war but were printed in the 1948 collection *The Double Axe and Other Poems*. Random House published a disclaimer with the volume, disavowing the political content.

Rising on Broadway, Losing Love In 1947, Jeffers adapted Euripides's play *Medea* at the request of actress Judith Anderson. With the famous actress playing the title role, Jeffers's adaptation opened on Broadway to rave reviews. He also adapted poetic narratives, including his "Dear Judas," for the stage. As Jeffers's popularity as a poet declined, his reputation as a playwright rose correspondingly. In 1950, after he and Una went to Europe and returned to the States, Una died. Jeffers dedicated his last volume of poetry, *Hungerfield and Other Poems* (1954), to her. Between 1954 and 1962, Jeffers lived in the home they had shared, editing poems despite his declining health and near blindness. On January 20, 1962, Jeffers passed away in the bed he had memorialized in his poem "The Bed by the Window."

Works in Literary Context

Thematically, Jeffers tends to present the same ideas throughout his work: the notion of an organic universe, the intersection of science and spirituality, man's relationship to God, the definition and existence of God, the indifference of the universe to man, and the moral obligations of humanity.

The Poet, Nature, and Human History Jeffers's interest in the individual's spiritual and physical connection to nature and the world at large resembles the Romantic style of poets like Ralph Waldo Emerson and Walt Whitman. For Jeffers, human history was insignificant compared to the infinitely larger and more important cyclical narrative of the history of the earth and cosmos. Stuart

Noble-Goodman wrote, "Living apart from nature, man is like a severed hand, useless and repellent. Jeffers insisted that man live within the world of phenomena, of rocks and hawks and sky—an existence that does not really require a higher consciousness."

Contrarian Views Jeffers was often known for having views that went against the mainstream. In many of his works about nature, he suggests that humans are too caught up in modern existence to grasp the divine qualities of the natural world. In *The Double Axe and Other Poems*, he so staunchly opposes American participation in World War II that many considered him anti-American. In *Dear Judas and Other Poems*, Jeffers stirs controversy by making the Biblical figure Judas a hero. In the poem, the ghosts of Judas, Jesus, and the Virgin Mary comment on what happened before and after the crucifixion, offering their hindsight and firsthand points of view. Through their comments, Judas becomes human, even admirable in his actions. Jeffers portrays him as a man who predicts that any attempt to rebel against the occupying Romans would worsen the social and political situation, and who therefore tries to prevent rebellion by having its most probable leader put to death.

Works in Critical Context

At his most popular in the 1920s and 1930s, Jeffers wrote in the voice of a sturdy outdoorsman living alone in the American wild. During his rise, he was featured on the cover of *Time Magazine*, one of the few poets to be showcased. He was also invited to read his work at the

COMMON HUMAN EXPERIENCE

Jeffers is known as a "poet of place" because his work was inspired by the relationship between humanity and the environment. Other books inspired by this profound identification with nature include:

Lyrical Ballads (1798), a poetry collection by William Wordsworth. The theme of this collection is man's return to what the poet perceived as the original state of nature.

Nature (1836), an essay by Ralph Waldo Emerson. Emerson theorizes that nature is an all-encompassing entity with which humans can connect on a spiritual level. The essay is one of the foundational texts of the Transcendentalist movement.

Six Sections from Mountains and Rivers with No End (1965), a poetry collection by Gary Snyder. For this collection, Snyder called on his varied employment experiences (which included those of logger, fire lookout, and carpenter) and perspectives on the environment.

Field Guide (1973), a poetry collection by Robert Hass. This collection was inspired by Hass's native California countryside and his background in Slavic studies.

The Measure of a Mountain (1998), a memoir/"natural history" by Bruce Barcott. Barcott details his trek to the top of Mount Rainier with both historical and scientific observations, as he struggles to understand the mountain and its effects on the surrounding land and people.

but when Jeffers submitted a few poems to an anthology, he sent the editors copies of the book. Impressed, the editors sent copies to Babette Deutsch and Mark Van Doren, influential poetry critics of the day. Reviews then appeared in the *New York Herald Tribune* and *The Nation*. Jeffers's originality began to generate critical debate that only intensified as his career continued.

Responses to Literature

1. Critics often suggest Jeffers echoes the themes found in Ralph Waldo Emerson's work. Choose a trio of poems from Jeffers's canon and write an essay in which you show how the work reflects Emerson's philosophic outlook.

2. Jeffers's work is often described as controversial. Read his collection *Dear Judas and Other Poems*, then write an essay in which you discuss how the collection might be viewed that way. Use examples from the text to support your ideas.

3. Frederic Carpenter wrote that "The Women at Point Sur" is "the most violent and unrelieved of all the long poems." With a group of your classmates, discuss why the poem might be described that way. Then take the opposite approach and argue against this view.

4. Jeffers is sometimes known as a "poet of place." Write a ten-line poem that evokes a place of your choosing. Use Jeffers's work as an example. You can imitate his form or voice, or create a form or voice of your own.

BIBLIOGRAPHY

Books

Coffin, Arthur B. *Robinson Jeffers: Poet of Inhumanism.* Madison, Wis.: University of Wisconsin Press, 1971.

Gelpi, Albert. *The Wild God of the World: An Anthology of Robinson Jeffers.* Stanford, Calif.: Stanford University Press, 2003.

Karman, James. *Robinson Jeffers: Poet of California.* Rev. ed. Brownsville, Ore.: Story Line Press, 1995.

Jeffers, Robinson. *The Beginning & the End: And Other Poems.* New York: Random House, 1963.

Noble-Goodman, Stuart. *Dictionary of Literary Biography, Volume 342: Twentieth Century American Nature Poets.* A Bruccoli Layman Book. Edited by J. Scott Bryson and Roger Thompson. Detroit: Gale Group, 2008, pp. 191–203.

Steinman, Lisa M. *Made in America: Science, Technology, and American Modernist Poets.* New Haven, Conn.: Yale University Press, 1987.

Winters, Yvor. *In Defense of Reason.* Denver: Swallow Press, 1937.

Library of Congress and, after his death, he was honored by having his image put on a U.S. postage stamp. Jeffers's career did sink when he vocally opposed United States involvement in World War II. The collection *The Double Axe and Other Poems* (1948) strongly criticized U.S. foreign policy. At the same time, Jeffers's work has greatly influenced such contemporary poets as William Everson, Gary Snyder, and Mark Jarman.

The Women at Point Sur *The Women at Point Sur* (1927) received mixed reviews. The title poem was described by Frederic Carpenter as "the most violent and unrelieved of all the long poems." Even those who championed Jeffers's early work found fault with the collection. These critics included Yvor Winters, who, in *Poetry*, calls Jeffers's writing "pretentious trash" filled with "hysteria." However, some critics did recognize that Jeffers was employing incest and murder to heighten drama and as motifs for the unhealthy ways in which humans are attracted to each other.

Tamar and Other Poems *Tamar and Other Poems* (1922) was different than Jeffers's previous work. The book, published privately, hardly received critical notice,

Periodicals

Carpenter, Frederic I. "The Inhumanism of Robinson Jeffers." *Western American Literature* 16:1 (1981): 19–25.

Winters, Yvor. Review of *The Women at Point Sur. Poetry* 35 (February 1930): 279–286.

✸ Thomas Jefferson

BORN: *1743, Shadwell (now Albemarle County), Virginia*

DIED: *1826, Charlottesville, Virginia*

NATIONALITY: *American*

GENRE: *Nonfiction*

MAJOR WORKS:

A Summary View of the Rights of British America (1774)

The Declaration of Independence (1776)

Act for Establishing Religious Freedom (1779)

Notes on the State of Virginia (1785)

Overview

Thomas Jefferson was the penman of the American Revolution. The author of *The Declaration of Independence* and third president of the United States did more than any other single person to create the characteristic language of the new American experiment in representative democracy. He gave clear, definitive articulation to the concept of natural (as distinguished from civil) rights, to the ideas of both civil and religious liberty, to the concept of minimal government, and to the preference for a rural agricultural citizenry over urban industrialism. Perceiving the need for an educated citizenry if democracy were to work, he advocated an aristocracy of virtue and talent over the "tinsel aristocracy" of inherited wealth and privilege. Jefferson was also an early advocate for the development of a specifically American English. He was a major spokesman in the eighteenth-century revival of the Greek and Roman ethical thought of the Stoic and Epicurean schools, making the ideas and language of those schools a part of subsequent American values and language. Important as an early writer against a state-established church, he was also a key figure in the revolt against Calvinism that took place in the late eighteenth and early nineteenth centuries, replacing the dogmas of damnation and predestination with an enlightenment faith in human nature and progress through education and free will.

Works in Biographical and Historical Context

Education through Experience Jefferson's early years were spent at Tuckahoe on the James River, not far from Richmond, Virginia. His father, Peter Jefferson, was a self-

Thomas Jefferson   *Jefferson, Thomas, photograph. The Library of Congress.*

made man. Jefferson's mother, Jane Randolph, came from an influential Virginia family. From the age of nine, Jefferson attended parish schools. His admiration for the classics, especially for the tradition of Greek and Roman ethical thought, dates from this early schooling. In March 1760, at the age of sixteen, he entered the College of William and Mary at Williamsburg. Upon his arrival, Jefferson studied under Dr. William Small, a professor of natural philosophy and rhetoric. It was Small, said Jefferson, who "probably fixed the destinies of my life." Small introduced Jefferson to Governor Francis Fauquier and George Wythe, a renowned instructor of law. In 1762, the nineteen-year-old Jefferson began the study of law with Wythe. His education was therefore entirely American and entirely local. He was twenty-three before he ever made a trip out of Virginia. At twenty-four, Jefferson was admitted to the bar; at twenty-five (in 1768) he was elected to the Virginia Assembly. In the same year he began work on what would be his lifelong home, Monticello.

Drafts the Declaration of Independence Jefferson made his first substantial contribution to political literature in 1774 with *A Summary View of the Rights of British America*. Jefferson wrote this twenty-three-page pamphlet in response to the English closure of the port of Boston in retaliation for the Boston Tea Party. Dumas Malone says Jefferson's pamphlet "gained wider currency than any other writing of his that was published during the Revolution except the *Declaration*." It is a major articulation of the idea of natural rights, that is, that people have certain rights simply by virtue of being people, rights prior and superior to any rights created by civil law. This impassioned and forcefully written philosophical preliminary to the more celebrated *Declaration of Independence* also contains Jefferson's legal argument for denying the authority of the English Parliament over the colonies.

Elected in 1775 to the Continental Congress, Jefferson, now thirty-two, arrived in Philadelphia with what John Adams called "a reputation for literature, science and a happy talent of composition." Returning to the second session in 1776, he was appointed to a five-man committee charged with drawing up a formal declaration of independence from Great Britain. Jefferson alone was asked to prepare the first draft. This version underwent heated debate; some changes were made, but the resulting document, passed by Congress July 4, 1776, was almost entirely the work of Jefferson. The ideas in it owe much to others, but Jefferson was not striving for originality. *The Declaration of Independence* was intended to give plain, emphatic, and above all persuasive expression to a group of generally held ideas about the natural rights belonging to all human beings, the revocable contract that underlies all government, and the right of the people to revolution whenever government becomes destructive of the ends for which it is instituted, namely the individual person's right to "life, liberty, and the pursuit of happiness." The cadences of this document—"We hold these truths to be self-evident: that all men are created equal"—became the fundamental expression of the ideals and values underlying the American democratic experiment. Jefferson's lasting achievement in the *Declaration of Independence* was summed up by Abraham Lincoln, who described Jefferson as "the man who, in the concrete pressure of a struggle for national independence by a single people, had the coolness, forecast, and capacity to introduce into a merely revolutionary document an abstract truth, applicable to all men and all times."

Elected Governor of Virginia

In 1779 Jefferson, then thirty-six, was elected governor of Virginia. As a war governor for the next three years, he was adequate if not brilliant. During his first year in that office, he ratified the Act for Establishing Religious Freedom. Though intended originally only for Virginia and not passed there until 1786, Jefferson himself believed the act was one of the central achievements of his career, for it codified the novel American experiment in separating church and state. Based, like the declaration of 1776, on the assumption that people have natural rights, the religious freedom act appeals beyond all institutions, sacred and secular, to recognize the individual conscience as the last, highest court of appeal. In preferring individual conscience to civil or religious authority, Jefferson marks the turn away from the America of Jonathan Edwards (a theologian noted for his severity) toward that of Emerson, Thoreau, and William James.

Toward the close of his busy, war-beset term as governor, Jefferson assembled his *Notes on the State of Virginia*, his only original full-length book. With little formal unity, *Notes on the State of Virginia* has nevertheless a profound thematic center in Jefferson's love for his native Virginia. The book is important for its scientific presentation and its expression of Enlightenment ideals. By far its least fortunate portion is Jefferson's account of blacks as inferior to whites, even though he also argued for emancipation of slaves.

On September 6, 1782, when Jefferson was thirty-nine, his wife Martha died, leaving him with three daughters, including an infant who had been born the previous May and would die in September 1784. The loss affected Jefferson deeply and it was only made worse in that it coincided with the intensification of the war with England and the end of his troubled governorship.

Parisian Interlude

In 1784 Jefferson drew up a "Report of Government for the Western Territories," outlining conditions for the creation of new states. Growing out of Virginia's effort to find an acceptable way to cede its territory west of the Ohio, Jefferson's anti-imperialist draft provided that all new states were to be politically equal to the original thirteen, that any person with a hereditary title must forfeit it before becoming a citizen, that any new state must remain part of the union "forever," and that there would be no slavery in any new state after 1800. Congress deleted the last two provisions of this farsighted report, which, had it been passed in its original form, might have prevented the Civil War.

In 1787, Jefferson was named one of the American Commissioners in Paris, appointed to look after American business interests in Europe. The next year, he was appointed to succeed Benjamin Franklin as American Minister to France. Jefferson spent four years in Paris. France was edging toward revolution; it was an immensely exciting time. Despite persistent shortages of funds, he loved Paris and reveled in its life.

Years in Office

In 1789, as the French Revolution was beginning and George Washington was elected first president of the United States, the forty-six-year-old Jefferson returned to America, where he was appointed Secretary of State, a post he would occupy till 1793. Now began the twenty-year period of Jefferson's almost complete immersion in politics. After a short hiatus at Monticello, he was Vice President from 1797 to 1801, and from 1801 to 1809 he served two terms as President. His administration was noted for the Louisiana Purchase (1803), for the war against the Algerian pirates (1801–1805), American expansion westward, and the prohibition of the importation of slaves (1806). Despite the manifold responsibilities of office, Jefferson maintained his many intellectual and artistic interests. At some point between 1791 and 1802 he translated the first twenty chapters of Constantine Volney's celebrated *Ruins; or Meditations on the Revolution of Empires* (1791). This minor masterpiece of romantic skepticism is a full-scale attack on institutionalized religion; it surveys the major ones, noting the claim of each to possess the only truth. Jefferson's conclusion was that it was better to believe nothing than to believe what was not true.

Jefferson and Adams   In 1809, aged sixty-six, Jefferson reached the end of his second term as President and retired to Monticello. Here he soon resumed his friendship with John Adams, with whom he had differed on political issues, and their lengthy, wide-ranging correspondence is one of the great achievements of American letters. They discussed a vast array of subjects with verve, wit, and learning. In some ways the letter was Jefferson's ideal literary form.

Religion and ethics continued to interest him, and Adams's own eager and informed curiosity about such matters was a fresh encouragement. In 1813 Jefferson wrote to Adams, comparing the ethics of the Old Testament with those of the New, concluding that we need to remove from the New Testament everything except "the very words only of Jesus," leaving out all the miracles and interpretations. The demythologized result would be, he thought, "the most sublime and benevolent code of morals which has ever been offered to man." Thus was conceived the celebrated "Jefferson Bible" (usually known as *The Life and Morals of Jesus of Nazareth*, first published in 1904).

But it was education even more than religion that was, in James Bryant Conant's words, "Jefferson's main pre-occupation in the last ten years of his life." In 1817 one of Jefferson's longest-cherished ideas became a reality with the founding of the University of Virginia. Jefferson himself wrote the report setting forth its aim and curricula the following year.

For all the clarity of his thought, Jefferson remains a paradoxical figure. He gave us the idea of the West, yet he never went west himself. He distrusted cities, but loved Paris, and he habitually linked agricultural life with virtue, but overlooked the fact that in the American South, slaves did the labor that made such a life possible. He is one of the great modern spokesmen for individual liberty, yet he held many slaves. He was an aristocrat, yet an egalitarian and a democrat. But in the end, Jefferson correctly estimated his own major contributions. The driving forces of his life had been his belief in freedom from political and religious tyranny and the absolute necessity of education for a people who wished to be free. On his grave marker, therefore, he wanted the following "and not a word more" engraved: "Here lies Thomas Jefferson, Author of the Declaration of American Independence, of the Statute of Virginia for Religious Freedom and Father of the University of Virginia." He died on July 4, 1826, on the same day

LITERARY AND HISTORICAL CONTEMPORARIES

Thomas Jefferson's famous contemporaries include:

Voltaire (1694–1778): The French writer who contributed to the Enlightenment in Europe with his *Philosophical Dictionary* (1764), which heartily supported freedom of religion.

Benjamin Franklin (1706–1790): One of the most important Founding Fathers of the United States, Franklin was, along with Patrick Henry, partially responsible for the repeal of the Stamp Act.

George Washington (1732–1799): The commander of American forces during the Revolutionary War, the first President of the United States, and an inspiration for Federalists.

John Adams (1735–1826): The first Vice President and second President of the United States. Adams was a major supporter of the *Declaration of Independence*.

William Blake (1757–1827): This British poet and painter was a forerunner of the Romantic movement; among his famous illuminated books is *America: A Prophecy* (1793).

Wolfgang Amadeus Mozart (1756–1791): Mozart was a preeminent Austrian composer whose musical compositions were among the greatest of the Classical (pre-Romantic) school.

as John Adams—the fiftieth anniversary of the signing of the *Declaration of Independence*.

Works in Literary Context

From a literary standpoint, Jefferson's style and themes are rooted in classical tradition. From about 1764 to about 1772, Jefferson compiled a notebook, published only in 1928 as *The Literary Bible of Thomas Jefferson*. Filled with his favorite quotations from Greek, Latin, and English writers, this notebook reveals the early Jefferson already absorbed by ideas, particularly ethical ideas, in literature. He clearly valued Homer, Cicero, and others for what they could teach him about how to live. From *The Literary Bible* it is clear that Jefferson was far more strongly impressed by Greek and Roman ethical thought than by Christianity.

The Enlightenment   The Enlightenment was an intellectual movement of the seventeenth and eighteenth centuries that began in Europe and spread to America in time for the Revolutionary War. Enlightenment ideas concerning God, reason, nature, and humankind were synthesized into a world view that gained wide assent and that instigated revolutionary developments in art, philosophy, and politics. Central to Enlightenment thought were the use

COMMON HUMAN EXPERIENCE

Here are some other works that have contributed to revolution and change around the world.

The Magna Carta (1215). This document, written by a group of barons, declared that King John of England must, under penalty of law, grant certain rights to his subjects.

Articles of the Confederation (1777). A governing document of historic proportions in which the original thirteen colonies first declare sovereignty from English rule. The Articles of Confederation predates the U.S. Constitution.

The Age of Reason (1793–94), a pamphlet by Thomas Paine. In this treatise on politics, religion, and society, Paine argues against many Christian doctrines and promotes reliance on logic and reason instead of faith.

"I Have a Dream" (1963), a speech by Reverend Martin Luther King, Jr. With this seminal speech, delivered at the Lincoln Memorial in Washington, King upheld the vision of the civil rights movement and became one of our nation's most respected speakers.

and the celebration of reason, the power by which the individual understands the universe and improves the human condition. Thomas Jefferson embraced reason to challenge ignorance, as we see in many of his notes and reports that were disseminated to the public. The goals of the rational individual were considered to be knowledge, freedom, and happiness. Such an ideology is the foundation of Thomas Jefferson's revolutionary works, specifically the *Declaration of Independence*, which was crucial to the formation of the United States.

Works in Critical Context

Jefferson is best known as a revered statesman whose belief in natural rights, equality, individual liberties, and self-government found its fullest expression in the *Declaration of Independence*. As the *Declaration* demonstrates, Jefferson was also a skilled writer noted for his simple yet elegant prose. Through the clear and persuasive articulation of the revolutionary political philosophy of an emerging nation, Jefferson profoundly influenced the direction of American politics, inspiring generations of Americans.

The Declaration of Independence Although debate continues to this day over the exact circumstances of its composition, most historians agree that Jefferson wrote the original draft of the *Declaration of Independence* during June 1776; that he then submitted it to two committee members, Adams and Benjamin Franklin; and that

they suggested minor changes before sending it to Congress. The delegates debated its text line by line for two and a half days and adopted it on July 4, 1776. Despite changes made by members of Congress, Jefferson is generally credited with authorship of the *Declaration*.

In addition to its significance as a political manifesto, the *Declaration* is an important literary text, and Jefferson employed various structural and stylistic elements to enhance his political message. The *Declaration* consists of four parts: the opening paragraph, which introduces the purpose of the document; the second paragraph, the best-known segment, which outlines the political philosophy of the American Revolution; the third part, which lists twenty-eight grievances against King George III and enumerates the specific causes for rebellion; and the closing paragraph, which declares independence from Great Britain. The *Declaration* is said to possess a high degree of structural unity, for all of its parts contribute to a single idea: that the colonists were not rebelling against an established authority, but were instead maintaining their rights against a usurping king. Among other literary devices, Jefferson used sharply contrasting styles to further his purpose. The opening and closing paragraphs are marked by a cadenced, majestic style depicting the colonists as passively and submissively awaiting their fate, while the grievances are characterized by a crisp, incisive style describing the king as an aggressive force over the colonists. Many critics have recognized the influence of the Enlightenment writers on Jefferson's prose, praising its clarity, subtlety, persuasiveness, eloquence, and above all, its distinctiveness. Thus, Jefferson is revered for creating the foremost literary work of the American Revolution and the single most important political document in American history.

Responses to Literature

1. Thomas Jefferson is often regarded as an example of an Enlightenment thinker. Using the library or the Internet, research the philosophical movement known as the Enlightenment. What are its basic principles? Who was involved in the movement? Do you think the principles of the Enlightenment are alive and well today? Explain.

2. Jefferson was instrumental in getting the newly established United States government to acknowledge certain basic rights for its citizens. However, these rights were not granted to all citizens. Indeed, Jefferson—like many other Founding Fathers—kept slaves, and few supported a woman's right to vote. In your opinion, does this weaken the message of the Founding Fathers, or does it provide a goal that was simply beyond their reach within their lifetimes? Explain your position.

3. Using the library or the Internet, look up the *Declaration of Independence*. Review lines from the *Declaration*. Next look up and review other writings by Jefferson as well as Benjamin Franklin, George

Washington, and Patrick Henry. Do their writing styles have much in common? Identify the topics they chose to address, the language patterns they used. How did the public identify with these writings? Explain.

4. Do you think Jefferson's European visits influenced his thinking, writing, and leadership? Do you think Jefferson influenced European thinking? Why or why not?

BIBLIOGRAPHY

Books

Bernstein, R.B. *Thomas Jefferson*. New York: Oxford University Press, 2003.

Ellis, Joseph. *American Sphinx: The Character of Thomas Jefferson*. New York: Alfred A. Knopf, 1997.

Ferris, Jeri. *Thomas Jefferson: Father of Liberty*. Minneapolis: Carolrhoda Books, 1998.

Hitchens, Christopher. *Thomas Jefferson: Author of America*. New York: HarperCollins, 2005.

Maier, Pauline. *American Scripture: Making the Declaration of Independence*. New York: Alfred A. Knopf, 1997.

Peterson, Merrill. *The Jefferson Image in the American Mind*. New York: Oxford University Press, 1988.

Vidal, Gore. *Inventing a Nation: Washington, Adams, Jefferson*. New Haven, Conn.: Yale University Press, 2004.

Periodicals

Jewett, Thomas O. "Thomas Jefferson: Father of Invention." *Early American Review* (Winter 2000).

✺ Gish Jen

BORN: *1955, Long Island, New York*

NATIONALITY: *American*

GENRE: *Fiction*

MAJOR WORKS:

Typical American (1991)

Mona in the Promised Land (1996)

Who's Irish? (1999)

The Love Wife (2004)

Overview

Although Gish Jen writes short stories and novels that offer an Asian-American perspective on life in the U.S., she differs in tone, approach, and style from such other Asian-American authors as Maxine Hong Kingston and Amy Tan. Jen is often praised for illuminating the humor in otherwise serious, even tragic situations. Critics also single Jen out for her three-dimensional, non-stereotypical depictions of Asian-American life.

Gish Jen   *Gish, Jen, photograph. © Jerry Bauer. Reproduced by permission.*

Works in Biographical and Historical Context

A Childhood Love of Stories   Jen was born Lillian Jen in 1955 in Long Island, New York, to Chinese immigrants from Shanghai. She grew up in the New York City suburbs of Yonkers and Scarsdale, where not many Asian-American families lived. When Jen was small, her reading was limited to the selections in a small school library, but in Scarsdale, Jen discovered a public library with plentiful resources. She devoured books ranging from Walter Farley's *The Island Stallion* (1948) to Albert Camus's *The Stranger* (1943). Her love of stories inspired her to begin writing poetry in junior high, and in high school she became editor of the literary magazine, at about the time she took the nickname Gish, after the silent film actress Lillian Gish.

From Med School to the Iowa Writers' Workshop But Jen's interest in writing could not compete with familial duty and parental expectations for her personal success. Her parents pushed their five children to achieve: her three brothers would become successful businessmen, and her sister would become a doctor. Jen attended Harvard University, but her plans for medical school veered off course when she took a prosody course taught

LITERARY AND HISTORICAL CONTEMPORARIES

Gish Jen's famous contemporaries include:

John Updike (1932–2009): An American Pulitzer Prize-winning novelist, poet, short story writer, and critic, Updike is known for his "Rabbit" series of novels and his focus on middle-class life in an American small town.

Amy Tan (1952–): Tan is a Chinese-American writer known for her widely successful novel *The Joy Luck Club* (1989).

Louis Chu (1915–1970): A Chinese-American author, Chu is known for his single novel, *Eat a Bowl of Tea* (1961), about life in 1940s Chinatown.

Gary Soto (1952–): A Mexican-American poet and author, Soto won an American Book Award for his memoir *Living Up the Street* (1985).

Jessica Hagedorn (1949–): Hagedorn is a Filipino-American author whose novel *Dogeaters* (1990) won an American Book Award and a National Book Award and was adapted into a play.

Meena Alexander (1951–): An Indian-born writer across numerous genres, Alexander's works include poetry, literary memoirs, and works of literary criticism.

Lisa See (1955–): See is an author whose Chinese heritage influenced a prolific career of Chinese-themed novels, including *Peony in Love* (2008), and has garnered her many cultural honors like the 2003 History Makers Award from the Chinese American Museum in Los Angeles.

by poet and journalist Robert Fitzgerald, who inspired her with his weekly assignment of writing verse. Jen eventually graduated with a BA in English literature in 1977 and then accepted a job in the nonfiction department of Doubleday Publishing. Though she enrolled in Stanford University business school in 1979, she could not abandon her passion for fiction writing and dropped out of the program in her second year, much to the dismay of her parents. Uncertain of her direction, she looked toward her Chinese roots and decided to take a temporary job in China as an English-language instructor at a coal-mining institute. This trip inspired much of her first novel *Typical American* (1991). When she returned to the United States, she was accepted to the Iowa Writers' Workshop at the University of Iowa. She earned an MFA in creative writing in 1983 and was a recipient of a National Endowment for the Arts fellowship in 1988.

First Novel Jen married David O'Connor, a graduate of Harvard and Stanford Business School. When O'Connor took a job with Apple Computer, Inc., she moved with him to the Silicon Valley of California. In 1985, the couple relocated again to Cambridge, Massachusetts, where Jen was awarded a fellowship at Radcliffe University's Bunting Institute. The fellowship was one of several grants, including those from the Guggenheim Foundation and the National Endowment for the Arts, that Jen received to support her craft. With the fellowship at the Bunting Institute, Jen began writing *Typical American* (1991). The novel was named "Notable Book of the Year" by *The New York Times* and was a finalist for the 1991 National Book Critics Circle Award.

A Continuing Success with Novels In 1996, Jen published her second novel, *Mona in the Promised Land*, which was also named one of the "Notable Books of the Year" by *The New York Times*. A few years later, Jen's *Who's Irish?* (1999), a collection of eight short stories—most of which were published previously—won the Lannan Award for Fiction. Jen was also honored for this collection in 2003, with the Strauss "Living" Award from the American Academy for Arts and Letters.

Jen's most recent novel, *The Love Wife*, appeared in 2004. Jen currently resides in Cambridge, Massachusetts, with her husband, her son Luke, and her daughter Paloma.

Works in Literary Context

Throughout Jen's work runs the theme of travel, as filtered through the Asian-American culture and its history of migration and displacement. Jen's fiction redefines travel to encompass different modes of transport, different means of mobility, and different markers of home.

The Theme of Home and Family In Jen's work, home is defined by family; the idea of families moving from one country to the next, distancing themselves from their native nation, does not generate conflict. Instead, a person who moves away from his family creates the fictional tension. Jen frequently illustrates the theme of the home's disintegration by having certain characters leave their families—literally and figuratively—and by illustrating how this move from the family center creates an imbalance in the family structure and even cracks cultural foundations. The novel *Mona in the Promised Land*, for example, focuses on Chinese American teenager Mona, who denies her Chinese identity by becoming assimilated into the Jewish culture of the upscale New York suburb where her family relocates. The conflict in Jen's short story "Duncan in China" derives from a Chinese immigrant matriarch who is ousted from her daughter's home and must deal with the harsh consequences.

A Balance of Humor and Gravity Jen's work is often characterized as exposing the lighthearted elements in otherwise grave situations. The title story of the collection *Who's Irish?* draws humor from the narrator's Irish-American son-in-law, whose quips about the "hyphenated American identity" allow for levity with what could be cause for serious cultural conflict. In "House House Home," unconventional art professor Sven Anderson encourages his wife, aspiring Chinese-American painter Pammi, to worship at the altar of Art, and to rebel against all things domestic. In "Birthmates," Art Woo, a middle-aged computer salesman attending a trade conference, mistakenly books himself a room in a welfare hotel, with a wooden plaque above the checkout desk claiming "Fewest Customer Injuries, 1972–1973." One *Entertainment Weekly* reviewer praised Jen for shading "the Chinese-American experience with tart realism and sometimes guffaw-inducing humor."

Works in Critical Context

Jen's work is regarded alongside the writing of prominent Asian-American writers of the late twentieth century, most notably Maxine Hong Kingston and Amy Tan. Critics praise Jen's unique and complex depiction of the immigrant experience. Many critics, including Yuko Matsukawa, believe Jen "brilliantly challenges readers to reexamine their definitions of home, family, the American dream, and, of course, what it is to be a 'typical American.'" Scholar Zhou Xiaojing suggests that Jen departs from previous Chinese American fiction in location and literary strategies and depicts immigrant characters as individuals rather than "as ethnic cultural signs." Other reviewers of her novel *Mona in the Promised Land* also recognize Jen's exploration of individual identity in multicultural America. However, some of Jen's readers have criticized her for weak characterization.

Mona in the Promised Land   Jen received wide praise for *Mona in the Promised Land*. For example, Marina Heung suggested that Jen shattered "accepted notions of identity boundaries" and proposed that "identities are willfully chosen, not made." In the *Los Angeles Times Book Review*, Richard Eder praised Jen's treatment of identity: "It is a kind of joyful irony that, among other things, makes *Mona* a kind of shining example of a multicultural message delivered with the wit and bite of art."

Who's Irish?   The collection *Who's Irish?* also garnered much praise from the press. Jean Thompson in the *New York Times Book Review* seems to sum up the general opinion:

> Jen's gift is for comedy that resonates, and sadnesses that arise with perfect timing from absurdities. Her subject matter is so appealing, it almost obscures the power and suppleness of her language. *Who's Irish?*, at its considerable best, finds words for all the high and low notes of the raucous American anthem.

Responses to Literature

1. Critics often remark on Jen's fresh perspective on Asian-American culture, particularly her use of

---

COMMON HUMAN EXPERIENCE

Who's Irish? addresses the clash and interaction of Asian and American cultures, a theme present in much of Jen's work. Other works based on this same theme include:

> *The Joy Luck Club* (1989), a novel by Amy Tan. The novel focuses on a group of women who gather to eat and play mahjong. The plot, structured in vignettes, revolves around each woman's experiences before and after they arrived in America.
>
> *Dogeaters* (1990), a novel by Jessica Hagedorn. *Dogeaters* addresses social, political and cultural issues present in the Philippines during the 1950s, as seen through the eyes of a variety of interrelated characters.
>
> *Native Speaker* (1995), a novel by Chang-Rae Lee. In the novel, Henry Park is confronted with conflict as he tries to become assimilated into American society and be recognized as a "native speaker."
>
> *The Woman Warrior: Memoirs of a Girlhood Among Ghosts* (1975), a nonfiction book by Maxine Hong Kingston. This memoir uses many elements of fiction to explore Kingston's experience as a Chinese-American woman.
>
> *Home to Stay* (1990), an anthology edited by Sylvia Watanabe and Carol Bruchac. These short stories, mostly written by new and established Asian-American women writers, address the ways in which characters must cope with being different in America.

---

humor. Choose a short story in the collection *Who's Irish?* and write an essay in which you discuss how Jen uses humor to defuse cultural conflicts or tension.

2. Critic Marina Heung has suggested that Jen shattered "accepted notions of identity boundaries" and proposed that "identities are willfully chosen, not made." Choose a short story in the collection *Who's Irish?* and, with a group of your classmates, discuss how Heung's idea is reflected in that story.

3. Jen explores individual identity in both multicultural American society and the family. Interview a classmate, friend, or family member about their "American experience." Ask them questions about how their heritage has shaped their personal character, and how they see themselves with regard to an "American" identity.

4. A popular theme in Jen's work is displacement. In a short essay, discuss how this theme manifests itself in the novel *Mona in the Promised Land*, both literally and figuratively.

BIBLIOGRAPHY

Books

Lee, Rachel. *The Americas of Asian–American Literature: Gendered Fictions of Nation and Transnation.* Princeton, N.J.: Princeton University Press, 1999.

The Immigrant Experience in North American Literature: Carving Out a Niche. Edited by Katherine B. Payant and Toby Rose. Westport, Conn.: Greenwood Press, 1999.

Periodicals

Eder, Richard. "A WASP-Free America." *Los Angeles Times Book Review* (May 26, 1996): 2.

Lee, Rachel. "Who's Chinese?" *Women's Review of Books* 19:5 (February 2002): 13–14.

Lin, Erika T. "Mona on the Phone: The Performative Body and Racial Identity in *Mona in the Promised Land.*" *MELUS* 28:2 (Summer 2003): 47–57.

Matsukawa, Yuko. "MELUS Interview: Gish Jen." *MELUS* 18:4 (Winter 1993): 111–120.

Miner, Valerie. "Asian-American Pancake." *Nation* 262: 24 (June 17, 1996): 35–36.

Snell, Marilyn. "Gish Jen: The Intimate Outsider." *New Perspectives Quarterly* 8:3 (1991): 56–60.

Thompson, Jean. Review of "*Who's Irish?.*" *New York Times.* (July 27, 1999): 13.

Zierler, Wendy. "Laughter with a Twist." *Far Eastern Economic Review* 163:5 (February 2000): 36–37.

Sarah Orne Jewett

BORN: *1849, South Berwick, Maine*

DIED: *1909, South Berwick, Maine*

NATIONALITY: *American*

GENRE: *Fiction*

MAJOR WORKS:

Deephaven (1877)

A White Heron and Other Stories (1886)

The Country of the Pointed Firs (1896)

Overview

Sarah Orne Jewett is often classified as a writer of New England fiction as part of what was known as the "local color movement" during the last half of the nineteenth century. Jewett, like other writers of this movement, stayed true to a particular setting, making sure to capture the flavor of a local history, speech, and culture. Jewett focused on the rural past of her native Maine and faithfully depicted the characters, culture, and flavor of that area. Jewett wrote across genres, publishing several novels, short stories, verses, and one book of nonfiction, but is best known for her sketches about provincial life in New England during the 1800s.

Sarah Orne Jewett   *Jewett, Sarah, photograph. Source unknown*

Biographical and Historical Context

Family, Education Jewett, the second of three daughters, was born on September 3, 1849, in South Berwick, Maine, to Caroline F. Perry and Dr. Theodore H. Jewett. Her childhood was spent with a large extended family in her paternal grandfather's home, where she cultivated diverse reading interests in discovering authors like Henry Fielding, Jane Austen, and Harriet Beecher Stowe.

Jewett's formal education was inconsistent as a result of her rheumatism, a type of arthritis or soreness of the joints. Since her father, a doctor, prescribed being outdoors for the serious illness, she freely explored her surroundings and even accompanied her father on house calls. Along the way, he taught her about nature and literature, and Jewett learned the intimate ways of local community, to be reflected in her future creative work.

Writing and Pseudonyms Born into a financially comfortable family, Jewett began to write at her leisure, and by 1867, was ready to submit short stories to magazines under the pseudonyms A. D. Eliot, Alice Eliot, and Sarah C. Sweet. During the next few years, she published several pieces on the "local color" of villages in coastal

Maine in the *Atlantic Monthly*. William Dean Howells, an editor of the periodical as well as a novelist, encouraged Jewett to revise the stories and publish them in a single volume. To frame the different sketches, she created two fictional narrators—Helen Denis and her friend Kate Lancaster, two Bostonians spending the summer in a Maine fishing village. The work became the episodic novel *Deephaven* (1877).

Literary Circle and Friendship   After the publication of *Deephaven*, Jewett participated in a literary circle fostered by *Atlantic* publisher James T. Fields and his wife, socialite and biographer Annie Fields, a close friend of Jewett's since childhood. When James died in 1881, Annie deepened her relationship with Jewett and leaned on her for comfort and companionship. The two women toured Europe and socialized with notable writers, including English poets Christina Rossetti and Alfred Tennyson. When they returned to Boston, Jewett would live with Annie for six months of every year after 1882. Together, they held literary salons and invited the likes of novelist and short story writer Henry James, "fireside poet" and physician Oliver Wendell Holmes, and novelist Harriet Beecher Stowe. Jewett and Annie's close relationship was characterized as a "Boston marriage," the common nickname for close relationships between financially independent, intellectual, progressive women during that time. Many scholars debate whether Annie and Jewett's relationship should be classified as lesbian. Jewett biographer Paula Blanchard argues: "Sarah Orne Jewett's love for other women was as passionate and absorbing as any heterosexual man's, but from all available evidence, it never led to direct sexual expression."

Short Story Collections and A Country Doctor   Jewett published the collections *Old Friends and New* (1879), *Country By-Ways* (1881), and *The Mate of Daylight, and Friends Ashore* (1884), a book dedicated to Annie. Jewett wrote about the intense connection to her friend, a heart-felt "understanding" that was "like a flame on the altar to friendship."

In 1884, Jewett published a novel, *A Country Doctor*. This semi-autobiographical novel focuses on orphan Nan Price as she accompanies her guardian, Dr. Leslie, on his country rounds and ultimately grows to become a young woman inspired to pursue a career in medicine. *A Country Doctor* received praise for its characterization and setting, but negative press for its dull and unrealistic romance between Nan and suitor George.

A White Heron and Other Works   Critics praise Jewett's *A White Heron and Other Stories* (1886) as an example of her strongest fiction. After the successful collection, Jewett switched genres and published *The Story of the Normans* (1887), a historical volume in the "Story of the Nations" series published by G. P. Putnam's. Critics consider the work one of Jewett's worst, as Jewett combines history, legend, and anecdote with the personal

---

LITERARY AND HISTORICAL CONTEMPORARIES

Jewett's famous contemporaries include:

Willa Cather (1873–1947): Cather was an American author known for depicting the frontier in novels like *O Pioneers!* (1913).

Henry James (1843–1916): An American-born British author, James was known for the realism in his novels, which include *The Portrait of a Lady* (1881) and *Daisy Miller* (1879).

Harriet Beecher Stowe (1811–1896): Stowe was an American author and abolitionist most famous for her novel *Uncle Tom's Cabin* (1852).

Rudyard Kipling (1865–1936): Kipling was an English novelist and poet commonly noted for his novels *The Jungle Book* (1894) and *Kim* (1901).

Sinclair Lewis (1885–1951): A novelist, short story writer, and playwright, Lewis was the first American awarded a Nobel Prize in Literature.

---

theory that the Norman race was superior to other races. Jewett returned to fiction with the short story collection *The King of Folly Island and Other People* (1888).

The 1890s   In the 1890s, the prolific Jewett published four more collections of short stories, a children's book, and her most famous novel, *The Country of the Pointed Firs* (1896), which was serialized before its print in book form. Jewett and Annie traveled to Florida, the Caribbean, and Chicago, where they attended the Columbian Exposition, and sailed twice to Europe where they socialized with Rudyard Kipling and Henry James, among other literary figures. In 1889, friend Alice Longfellow suggested Jewett holiday in the Boothbay Harbor region of Maine, and from then on, Jewett frequented the area. In September 1895, she and Annie rented a small guest house, the Anchorage, in Martinsville for a month of reading, rest, and long walks. The geography—the rocky coast, the view of offshore islands, the fir trees of the St. George Peninsula—seems to have inspired the creation of Dunnet Landing, the village in *The Country of the Pointed Firs*.

Her Last Fiction   Jewett's last volume of short fiction, *The Queen's Twin and Other Stories*, published in 1899, included two more Dunnet Landing sketches that were later incorporated into most editions of *The Country of the Pointed Firs*. In 1901, Jewett was the first woman presented an honorary doctorate by Bowdoin College, her father's alma mater. Also in 1901, Jewett published her last novel, a historical romance set in the American Revolution about her hometown of Berwick, called *The Tory Lover*. On her fifty-third birthday, she was thrown from a

COMMON HUMAN EXPERIENCE

Jewett's short stories and novels evoke a rich sense of place and local character. Other books that echo this same style of realism are:

Middlemarch (1874), a novel by George Eliot. Set in the fictitious English Midlands town of Middlemarch during the period 1830–1832, the novel follows multiple plot lines involving a large cast of characters.

Bayou Folk (1894), a short story collection by Kate Chopin. Chopin gathers vignettes of nineteenth-century citizens of New Orleans and Natchitoches Parish, Louisiana, into a larger narrative of Southern custom.

O Pioneers! (1913), a novel by Willa Cather. This novel focuses on the Bergson family, Swedish immigrants who live in a rural area near fictional Hanover, Nebraska, at the turn of the twentieth century.

House of Mirth (1905), a collection by Edith Wharton. This novel of manners details the life in high society New York as Lily Bart attempts to secure a husband.

carriage and sustained serious head and spinal injuries. Jewett never fully recovered. In 1904, "A Spring Sunday" was her last story published. Jewett still wrote letters to friends and established a new pen pal in author Willa Cather. Jewett had a stroke in March 1909, and on June 24 of that year, died at home of a cerebral hemorrhage. She was buried with her parents and sisters in South Berwick.

Works in Literary Context

Jewett strove to depict the truth through authentic characterization and realism, a result of reading famous contemporary authors George Eliot, known for her realism, and Harriet Beecher Stowe, known for her sentimentalism. Jewett was also influenced by French realist Gustave Flaubert, who emphasized the ordinary. She pinned two quotations from him over her desk: "Write ordinary life as if writing history," and "The writer's job is to make one dream."

Depictions of Maine Like much of Jewett's body of work, *The Country of the Pointed Firs* is built on themes of nostalgia, community, family, and friendship. She looks to a village of Maine seamen and their families and uses a narrator, Mrs. Todd, to provide personal and specific description of the rural Dunnet Landing. The novel's narrative holds together through the narrator's encounters with various townspeople who tell her long stories from their past. The novel uses the idea of storytelling to demonstrate how individuals connect to their larger community through their sense of common experience. Mrs. Todd becomes the keeper of the town history as she encounters each person and collects their stories.

Nature in "A White Heron" (1886) In the short story "A White Heron," the female protagonist, Sylvia, has a close relationship with nature, as she lives with her grandmother in a pastoral setting. In keeping silent about the heron's nest when a hunter offers her money for information about finding the bird, Sylvia values the natural world over her own human community, particularly since she sacrifices the means to help her grandmother save the aging farm. In "A White Heron," as throughout much of her work, Jewett addresses the questions that surround a woman's relationship to herself, a woman's relationship to humanity at large, and a woman's relationship to the natural world.

Works in Critical Context

Jewett's critical contemporaries praised her for the sense of regionalism or "local color" in her work. Today, criticism of Jewett's work is much more multi-faceted. Many modern-day critics mark her canon as a nostalgic archive of American history. Other critics see a timely environmental message in Jewett's rich detail of the Maine coast, while still others focus on the characterization of independent women and analyze the proto-feminist/lesbian aspects of her work.

A Very Charming Characterization Jewett was known for the details of her fictional worlds, most specifically in the way she depicted her characters. Eleanor M. Smith in the *New England Quarterly* writes that Jewett's work "was centered in the misunderstood people of her countryside." Martha H. Shackford of *Sewanee Review* elaborates on the idea, suggesting Jewett's stories are "always stories of character." Shackford goes on to say that "[p]lots hardly exist in [Jewett's] work; she had little interest in creating suspense or in weaving threads of varied interests." Author Willa Cather remarked that Jewett "had with her own stories and her own characters a very charming relation; spirited, gay, tactful, noble in its essence and a little arch in its expression."

Deephaven Though Jewett's contemporaries, Willa Cather and William Dean Howells, praised Jewett's first book, many critics did not think the episodic novel was very successful. Some reviewers argued that the two female narrators failed to unite the novel's "episodes" in a coherent plot. But Patti Capel Swartz argues for a more complex reading and proposes in *Gay and Lesbian Literature* that *Deephaven* contains meaning for lesbian readers: "The relationship of Kate and Helen in Jewett's *Deephaven*, particularly the scene where they dance in the moonlight, has touched deeply the hearts of lesbian readers attempting to find themselves in literature." One popular analysis of the novel, as with other Jewett works, has, in fact, been a lesbian interpretation, as exemplified by Judith Fetterley's "Reading *Deephaven* as a Lesbian

Text." However, Margaret Roman, in *Reconstructing Gender,* suggests that the relationship between the female narrators in the novel illuminate the development—and stagnation—of a young woman's identity and her search to break free from the conventional gender roles to which she is assigned.

Responses to Literature

1. In the short story "A White Heron," how does Jewett appear to see the connection between nature and society? How does Sylvia's choice to keep the secret of the heron's nest relate to this?

2. With a partner, research the term "local color fiction" and devise a presentation for the class. Make sure to define its characteristics and discuss one or two other authors who could be considered "local color" artists.

3. With Jewett's detailed sense of place in mind, write a short essay about a particular place that is important to you. Describe what makes it special, using sensory details and descriptions of local characters.

4. In *The Country of the Pointed Firs,* Jewett writes, "Such is the hidden fire of enthusiasm in the New England nature that, once given an outlet, it shines forth with almost volcanic light and heat." Write an essay in which you discuss how this quotation seems to exemplify the essence of the novel's setting. Use examples from the text to support your ideas.

BIBLIOGRAPHY

Books

Roman, Margaret. *Sarah Orne Jewett: Reconstructing Gender.* Birmingham, Ala.: University of Alabama Press, 1992.

Cather, Willa. *Not Under Forty.* New York: Knopf, 1936, p. 84.

The Country of the Pointed Firs: Novels for Students. Ed. David Galens. Detroit: Gale, 2002, pp. 21–38.

Feminism in Literature: A Gale Critical Companion. Eds. Jessica Bomarito and Jeffrey Hunter. Vol. 3. Detroit: Gale, 2005, pp. 251–261.

Sarah Orne Jewett (1849–1909), Modern American Literature. Eds. Joann Cerito and Laurie DiMauro. Vol. 2. Detroit: St. James Press, 1995, pp. 101–103.

Women in World History: A Biographical Encyclopedia. Eds. Anne Commire and Deborah Klezmer. Vol 8. Detroit: Yorkin Publications, 2002, pp. 145–149.

Periodicals

Shackford, Martha H. "Sarah Orne Jewett: General Commentary." *Sewanee Review* (January 1922): 23.

Smith, Eleanor M. *New England Quarterly* (December 1956): 474–475.

Ha Jin

BORN: *1956, Jinzhou, China*

NATIONALITY: *American*

GENRE: *Fiction*

MAJOR WORKS:

Ocean of Words (1996)

Under the Red Flag (1997)

Waiting (1999)

War Trash (2004)

A Free Life (2007)

Overview

Few writers have appeared on the American literary scene to such sudden acclaim as the Chinese émigré Ha Jin, the pen name of Xuefei Jin. His spare prose style in narrating the lives of ordinary individuals trapped in political and moral ambiguities has led to comparisons with Nikolai Gogol and Anton Chekhov. Indeed, he explores a world

Ha Jin *Rogan Coles / Getty Images*

as unfamiliar to most of his readers as Tsarist Russia: the Maoist Chinese culture of his youth.

Works in Biographical and Historical Context

A Revolutionary Youth   Ha Jin was born on February 21, 1956, in the city of Jinzhou in Liaoning province, to Danlin Jin, an officer in the People's Liberation Army, and Yuanfen (Zhao) Jin. The arrival of the Cultural Revolution in 1966 ended Jin's formal education, because schools were closed. Jin witnessed the rise of the cult of Mao and even joined a youth auxiliary of the Red Guards, but he also experienced the cruelty and hysteria of attacks on those accused of counterrevolutionary thinking when his family was publicly criticized and harassed because his maternal grandfather had once been a landholder.

Amid rising tensions between the People's Republic of China and the Soviet Union, he lied about his age and enlisted in the People's Liberation Army (he was thirteen). His army service lasted five and a half years, one of which he spent on a frigid outpost on the border of China and Soviet Russia. He eventually developed an affinity for Russian literature that remains a strong influence on his work today. Jin left the army when he was nineteen and became a telegraph operator in a remote city in northern China. He spent three years there, learning English from a radio program and reading literature. Jin enrolled as an English major at Heilongjiang University, from which he graduated with a bachelor's degree in 1981. He then studied American literature at Shangdon University, and he familiarized himself with his new favorites, William Faulkner and Saul Bellow.

Devotion to English   In Shandong, he met Lisha Bian, a mathematics teacher; they married in 1982 and have one son, Wen. Jin completed his master's degree in 1984, and leaving his young wife and son behind in China, he arrived in the United States in 1985 to pursue a PhD in English at Brandeis University in Boston—Jhumpa Lahiri was a classmate—with the expectation that he would return to China as a teacher or translator. Although the Chinese government initially kept his family behind, his wife was allowed to join him in 1987, and, surprisingly, his young son was granted an exit visa just a few weeks after the 1989 massacre of students and protesters at Tiananmen Square. The repression of China's pro-democracy movement was a turning point for Jin. He was convinced he would not be able to write honestly in China. Accordingly, he began to think of himself as a permanent exile, and this new identity profoundly changed the direction of his career.

While finishing his doctoral research on modernist poetry, Jin worked as a busboy, housecleaner, and night watchman to help support his family. He also enrolled in creative-writing courses at Boston University and made the decision to write and speak exclusively in English. He likened the process to changing his blood. All of his published literary works (with the exception of dialogue) have been painstakingly conceived and composed in Eng-

lish. Nonetheless, they bear strong signature traces of the Chinese worldview and its metaphorical structures.

When *The Paris Review* accepted his first poem, he chose the pseudonym Ha because Xuefei was so difficult for English-speaking readers to pronounce. Jin's first book of poetry, *Between Silences*, was published in 1990 and his PhD dissertation on modernist poetry—the works of Ezra Pound, William Butler Yeats, T. S. Eliot, and W. H. Auden—and its relationship to Chinese literature and culture was finished at Brandeis in 1992. It was also in 1992 that he read what for him was a life-changing work: Trinidadian-Indian novelist V. S. Naipul's *A Bend in the River* (1979). That book convinced Jin that he was not solely responsible for speaking for downtrodden Chinese—his first responsibility was to write well. He took this lesson with him when he began teaching creative writing and literature at Emory University in 1993.

Continued Success as Novelist and Poet   His first book of poetry was followed by *Facing Shadows* in 1996. That same year, Jin also published *Ocean of Words*, a highly acclaimed collection of short stories based on his experiences in the Chinese army. In 1997, another collection, *Under the Red Flag* was published, followed by his first novel, *In the Pond*, and his next and most celebrated—*Waiting*.

Although the liberalizing of China is hinted at in *The Bridegroom* (2000), another collection of short stories, its focus is on the frustration and repression of ordinary citizens. Jin's third collection of poetry, *Wreckage*, appeared in 2001. Frank Allen wrote in *Library Journal* that the subjects of many of the poems are "both stunning and horrific" and that the volume "bears witness to a sad, troubled bond with his [Jin's] homeland." In 2002 Jin published his next novel, *The Crazed*. It is set against the background of the Tiananmen Square massacre and tells the story of Jian Wan, a Chinese graduate student who becomes a caregiver to his literature professor and future father-in-law, who has suffered a stroke.

His next novel, the antiwar *War Trash*, marked a departure for Jin—it was his first novel not set in China. *War Trash* tells the story of a Chinese prisoner of war held by American forces during the Korean War who commences his memoir—the story of his time imprisoned, and of the tattoo he wears across his belly. He writes the story for his two American grandchildren. *War Trash* won the PEN/Faulkner award and further solidified Jin's reputation as a writer of uncommon power and skill.

Jin has continued to focus on all three literary modes—poems, short stories, and novels—in which he has had previous success. In 2001 he left his teaching position at Emory and after a short sabbatical began teaching at Boston University in 2002, thereby continuing his career at the place where he first took courses in creative writing. It is where he made the decision to write solely in English, to resist the silence imposed in China, and to become an important new voice in American literature. He mostly avoids public appearances and requests for him to assume a more public or political role as a Chinese expatriate. His latest novel, *A Free Life*, is set in America.

Works in Literary Context

The Short Story Ha Jin makes his short stories do as much emotional and intellectual thought-provocation as novels ten times as long accomplish. Not one to shy away from violence, heartbreaking honesty, and the displaying of his former countrymen in very unflattering light, he nonetheless ensures that his stories are often hopeful and humane. As in his poetry, spare prose and minimal embellishment are his hallmarks, as is a unique and quiet humor. Jhumpa Lahiri, author of the Pulitzer Prize–winning *Interpreter of Maladies* (1999), is an apt comparison.

Expatriate Literature Jin has mentioned that the work of other great immigrant writers—Vladimir Nabokov among them—helped him get into a place where he could write the nearly autobiographical *A Free Life*, his first book set in the United States. Unlike Aleksandr Solzhenitsyn, (author of *The Gulag Archipelago*, 1973–78) another exile from a communist country who wrote about his personal experiences, Ha Jin left China of his own accord, and has even had a novel translated and published since he left. Jin has bristled at being labeled a dissident, yet his work bears the hallmark of criticism spiked with longing. This mood is also felt in the work of Khaled Hosseini, the Afghan-American author of the extraordinary novel *The Kite Runner* (2003), and in the characters of Nell Freudenberger's novel *The Dissident* (2006), which tells the story of an identity-challenged Chinese artist's time in America. The book is influenced by the lives of many artists and activists like Ha Jin, though Freudenberger herself is an American.

Works in Critical Context

Critics regard Ha Jin as one of the best Asian contemporary writers who writes in English. His writings are described as ponderous, yet light and easy to read. He is not only a celebrated novelist and short story writer, but a renowned poet as well. According to Roger Gilbert of the *Hungry Mind Review*, Ha Jin's first collection of poetry, *Between Silences*, "brings a great empathy and compassion to his depiction of the fallible men and women whose acts and attitudes together make up history." *Midwest Book Review* further dubbed Jin as "one of the most talented poets writing today." Ha Jin's short fictions are also commended by critics for their "luminous prose." *Publishers Weekly*, in a review of *Ocean of Words*, stated that "Jin's characters make hard choices that will move not just readers interested in China or the army life, but any reader vulnerable to good writing and simple human drama." His first novel, *In the Pond*, was highly received by the literary community as well. Critics commend this novel for its vivid descriptions that complement its humor. According to the *New York Times Book Review*, "though art and politics figure in the action,

In the Pond is first and foremost a comedy—naughty, lusty, and raucously entertaining. Ha Jin's language echoes working-class Chinese at its rough, bawdy best."

Under the Red Flag *Under the Red Flag*, Jin's second collection of short stories, is set in the fictional village of Dismount Fort in China. The book focuses on the traditional harshness of life in a poor, rural town as well as on the disruptive social changes that came with the Cultural Revolution of the 1960s. Katherine Riegel noted in *Crab Orchard Review* that Jin "does not idealize the old ways, and the Red Guards are not always the most vicious enemy." Rather, it is the "cultural splintering" brought about by the frustration of the inhabitants of Dismount Fort combined with the implementation of cold and destructive political theories about modernization and progress that contribute to what she describes as "a sense of hollowness inside these characters as if each one were lost in a lost country." Jin's genius, according to Fatima Wu in a *World Literature Today* review, is rooted in his genuine sympathy for the ordinary people whom he chooses as protagonists. Wu wrote that "Ha Jin is a satirist, but at his best he is a writer of compassion, warmth, and love."

COMMON HUMAN EXPERIENCE

Ha Jin's masterful command of written English is an extraordinary accomplishment. Here is a list of works by other celebrated authors who spoke at least one other language before learning English, yet have seamlessly written in—or translated their own work into—English.

Heart of Darkness (1899), a novella by Joseph Conrad. Conrad was Polish, and did not learn English until he was twenty years old. *Heart of Darkness*, a tale of madness and exploitation in the Belgian Congo, is one of the finest works of fiction written in English.

The Prophet (1923), a philosophical work by Khalil Gibran. Lebanese-American Gibran wrote his earliest work in Arabic, but wrote his masterpiece, *The Prophet*, in English.

Lolita (1955), a novel by Vladimir Nabokov. This novel by Russian-born Nabokov employs a great deal of distinctive wordplay and a wholly original style to tell the story of a pedophile and the object of his affections.

Waiting *Waiting*, a bittersweet love story, explores themes of entrapment, powerlessness, and self-delusion; it dramatizes the stifling consequences of both the traditional Chinese value of filial piety and more modern notions of Maoist purity. The novel covers more than two decades, from the early 1960s to the mid-1980s, and includes scenes in both a tradition-bound rural village and a modern city. *Waiting* won the PEN/Faulkner award and National Book Award, one of only three to be given to a writer whose first language is not English. He was also granted a Guggenheim fellowship following its publication. Writing in the *New York Times*, author and critic Francine Prose opined, "Ha Jin observes everything about army and civilian life, yet he tells the reader only—and precisely—as much as is needed to make his deceptively simple fiction resonate on many levels: the personal, the historical, the political." In the Summer of 2000, the critic for *World Literature* wrote about *Waiting*'s protagonist's conundrum: "an absurd impasse of the sort the author excels at creating, quintessentially Maoist but also universally human."

Responses to Literature

1. Read the poem "The Dead Soldier's Talk," which is based on the famous true story of a young soldier who drowned in a river while trying to save a plaster statue of Mao Zedong, the Chinese Communist leader. Discuss Jin's treatment of the young man in his poem, keeping in mind that the real-life inspiration was revered in Communist China.

2. Read the novel *Waiting*. Write a short paper speculating on the future of the characters, focusing on Lin. What about his past decisions support your prediction? Do you sympathize with this man and his circumstances?

3. Ha Jin falsified his age, then enlisted in the Chinese army when he was thirteen years old. Research the history of juvenile conscription in this country and elsewhere, and have a discussion about it with other students. What governments still condone or support child soldiers? Do you think an underage individual has the maturity to decide that he wants to volunteer for the military?

4. Read the poem "A Child's Nature", which describes the arrival of Jin's son in San Francisco. Jin is dismayed that the Chinese media, along with his own family, had taught the boy that the students in Tiananmen Square were hooligans who deserved to be killed.

5. Ha Jin has invited comparisons to many Russian writers, including Anton Chekhov. Read Chekhov's short story "The Lady with the Pet Dog" (1899; first English translation, 1903) and write a paper comparing it to *Waiting*. What do these stories teach you about the time and place in which they were set? What, stylistically, did Jin adopt from Chekhov?

BIBLIOGRAPHY

Periodicals

Garner, Dwight. "'Somehow I Couldn't Stop': An Interview with Ha Jin." *New York Times* (October 10, 2004).

Garner, Dwight. "Ha Jin's Cultural Revolution." *New York Times* (February 6, 2000).

Kirn, Walter. "Pleased to Be Here." *New York Times* (November 25, 2007).

Phillips, Caryl. "Exile on Main Street." *New Republic* (December 24, 2008).

Solomon, Deborah. "Questions for Ha Jin." *New York Times* (April 10, 2005).

Web Sites

The National Book Award. Retrieved December 12, 2008, from http://www.nationalbook.org/nba2006_fict_powers.html.

⊛ James Weldon Johnson

BORN: *1871, Jacksonville, Florida*

DIED: *1938, Wiscasset, Maine*

NATIONALITY: *American*

GENRE: *Fiction, poetry*

MAJOR WORKS:
The Autobiography of an Ex-Colored Man (1912)

James Weldon Johnson   *Johnson, James Weldon, photograph. The Library of Congress.*

Fifty Years and Other Poems (1917)

God's Trombones (1927)

Black Manhattan (1930)

Along This Way (1933)

Overview

Equipped with restless intelligence and abundant energy, James Weldon Johnson crowded almost a dozen occupations into a busy lifetime, excelling in most of them. He was an educator, journalist, lawyer, songwriter, diplomat, novelist, poet, civil-rights crusader, anthologist, and professor. Through his belletristic writing and his anthologies he was both contributor to and preserver of the African-American literary tradition, linking the nineteenth century to the Harlem Renaissance.

Works in Biographical and Historical Context

A Sheltered Youth   James Weldon Johnson was born on June 17, 1871, in Jacksonville, Florida. His father, James Johnson, was a self-educated man who, as a waiter, achieved economic security and adopted middle-class values. In New York he met and courted Helen Louise Dillet,

a young woman of African-French-English ancestry. She, a native of Nassau who had grown up in New York, received a good education and had developed her musical talent. When Dillet returned with her mother to her native island in 1861, James Johnson followed her and secured a position in a large hotel. They were married in 1864 and for economic reasons then moved to Jacksonville, a rapidly expanding city and tourist center. Here were born James William (changed in 1913 to Weldon) Johnson and, two years later, John Rosamond Johnson.

Growing up in a middle-class home with books and a piano, Johnson was inculcated with strict notions of integrity by his father and with intellectual and artistic interests by his mother. The first black woman to become a public school teacher in Florida, Helen Johnson encouraged a love of learning; she taught piano and reading at home and also instructed her students in the classroom at Stanton School. A precocious child, James read Charles Dickens, Sir Walter Scott, John Bunyan, and Jacob and Wilhelm Grimm. Formal education at Stanton School extended only through the eighth grade, from which James graduated in 1887, but travel and friends had a broadening effect.

Discovering the World Outside   In 1884 he spent a summer in New York with his grandmother and her sister. He recalled feeling that he was born to be a New Yorker, and this cosmopolitan sense of self was reinforced by his friendships with Ricardo Rodriguez Ponce, a Cuban youth from whom he learned Spanish, Judson Douglass Wetmore, the near-white prototype for the protagonist of *The Autobiography of an Ex-Colored Man*; and, somewhat later, a cultured and widely traveled white physician named Dr. Thomas Osmond Summers, for whom he worked as an assistant and whose library of literary erotica and religious agnosticism expanded Johnson's interests in additional directions.

Johnson earned an associate's degree from Atlanta University in 1894—a place where he received an education in racial issues from which he had been somewhat sheltered in Jacksonville. Johnson spent two summers teaching in a black rural school. This proved to be an invaluable experience; he witnessed a mode of African-American life new to him. After his graduation he returned as the principal of Stanton, and added ninth- and tenth-grade courses. In the summer before his senior year he heard the aged Frederick Douglass speak and the young Paul Laurence Dunbar read from his poetry. With Dunbar, who was not yet famous, he quickly initiated a friendship and literary relationship that would continue for many years thereafter.

During his time as principal at Stanton, Johnson studied for a year and a half and became the first black individual to pass the Florida bar, though he did not enjoy working as a lawyer. Stanton was growing restless in Jacksonville, which was too small an arena to contain either his talents or his ambitions. Furthermore, racial restrictions were tightening as the new century began.

Poet and Songwriter When Johnson's brother John returned to Jacksonville in 1897, after having studied at the New England Conservatory of Music and completing a tour with a black variety show, the brothers wrote "Tolosa, or The Royal Document,"a comic opera in a Gilbert-and-Sullivan mode. A trip to New York in the summer of 1899 did not lead to the production of the work, but it did introduce them to some of the key figures of the musical stage, including Oscar Hammerstein and a number of celebrated black theatrical personalities.

The life of black bohemia in New York fascinated Johnson, yet he returned to Jacksonville, where he wrote one of his best dialect poems, the plaintive love lyric "Sence You Went Away," [sic] which was published in *Century* in 1900, the first time the author appeared in print in a national magazine. With his brother he then wrote "Lift Every Voice and Sing," which was to become known as the "Negro National Anthem." The brothers spent summers in New York, writing songs. The situation was made permanent in the fall of 1902, after a fire destroyed a large area of Jacksonville, including the Stanton School, and after an ugly and dangerous personal encounter with state militiamen brought in to keep order.

Johnson, his brother, and their new collaborator Bob Cole wrote a string of hits. The income these songs brought was welcome, and the life was glamorous, on Broadway and on tours across the United States and in Europe. however, Johnson had serious reservations about such ephemeral work as genuine artistic expression. Reading Walt Whitman's *Leaves of Grass* (1855) in 1900, he became aware of the limitations of what he had been writing, depending as it did on white stereotypes of black life. In his spare time, he began graduate study at Columbia University.

Diplomat and Novelist Johnson was appointed a United States Consul in Venezuela in 1906. Here he produced many poems and made progress on a novel. His next consular position, a slightly more desirable one in Nicaragua, kept him busier, and he found himself dealing with business affairs, political unrest, and then revolution. In 1910 he took a furlough to marry Grace Nail, the cultivated daughter of a prosperous New York tavern owner and real estate dealer, and he also found time to complete the novel *The Autobiography of an Ex-Colored Man*, the story of a light-skinned black man who finally crosses the color line and passes as white. It was published anonymously in 1912.

The Autobiography of an Ex-Colored Man is a novel, not an autobiography, but by issuing it anonymously Johnson hoped that it would be read as a true-life story, giving it greater authenticity and impact than a work perceived as mere fiction. Johnson could not pass as white and would not have wanted to. Nevertheless, the sources of the novel lie largely in Johnson's own experiences and friendships. Confused about his racial and sexual identities, the protagonist, like Ralph Ellison's *Invisible Man* (1952), lacks even a name, and this makes his grasp of who he is

even more tenuous. Despite a failure to resolve artistic and didactic aims, Johnson's novel is a significant achievement for its time, giving memorable expression to an important theme and preparing the way for the mature fictional art that was to come later in the century.

Politics and Advocacy Johnson resigned from the diplomatic service in September 1913, spent some time in Florida, and then returned to New York where he wrote editorials pressing for equal rights and racial cooperation. All the while, he was writing poetry and preparing the collection *Fifty Years and Other Poems*, which was published in 1917 and contained both standard English verse and dialect poetry.

From about the turn of the century Johnson had known Charles W. Anderson, an influential ally of Booker T. Washington, but he had also known W. E. B. Du Bois almost as long. Johnson accepted an offer to become field secretary, then later the director, of the National Association for the Advancement of Colored People, which had been organized in 1910 by whites and blacks to provide a more militant vehicle for racial protest than Washington offered. Johnson was to prove extremely effective in organizing local branches throughout the country, and he greatly expanded the membership of the organization. Emphasizing legal action, publicity, and political pressure, he coordinated the most effective movement against racism of its time.

Later Career Official duties occupied most of his time, but Johnson managed to compile three important anthologies in the 1920s: *The Book of American Negro Poetry* (1922), *The Book of American Negro Spirituals* (1922), and *The Second Book of American Negro Spirituals* (1926), all credited with increased respect for black creativity. It is ironic that Johnson, an avowed agnostic, contributed so significantly to increased respect for the soulful richness of black Christianity, most notably in *God's Trombones: Seven Negro Sermons in Verse* (1927). Eschewing regularities of meter, rhyme, or length of line, *God's Trombones* relies on speech rhythms—especially syncopation—and the Biblical narratives to give structure to the poems. The language of the collection is easy, colloquial, sinewy, yet capable of a vast range of emotion.

Johnson's writing of the 1930s is more retrospective and historical than creative. *Black Manhattan*, published in 1930, is a popular historical treatment of African-American life in New York. *Along This Way*, Johnson's autobiography, is less revealing of his private personality. The reserve and detachment characteristic of writers of his generation are always maintained. For instance, his wife is not mentioned a single time in the last hundred pages of the work. Even when he discusses religion or politics, he tends to move toward generalization rather than to probe psychological sources. For our sense of the private man then, we have to rely on the covert hints of his fiction and some of his poetry. The book ends with speculation on the future of blacks in America, and he advocates assimilation and education, rejecting separatism.

Johnson's life came to an abrupt end on June 26, 1938, when his automobile was struck by a train while he was traveling to his summer home in Maine. The accomplishments of his career, literary and otherwise, constitute a major and imperishable part of the history of African-American experience and expression in the early twentieth century.

Works in Literary Context

The Harlem Renaissance   Johnson was one of the leaders of the movement known as the Harlem Renaissance. Around the turn of the century, New York blacks migrated in substantial numbers to the uptown neighborhood of Harlem. In the 1920s and 1930s, a confluence of black individuals—writers, poets, musicians, artists and intellectuals—in Harlem found themselves at the center of a movement to both confront racism and create a distinct identity that would encompass the exciting works of art and literature their community was producing and the newfound sense of black identity that was rapidly developing. The movement produced such luminaries as Langston Hughes, and Johnson was one of its principal poets, anthologizers, and intellectual leaders. The poetry and literature of Johnson and his cohorts would influence generations of African-Americans, including the Pulitzer Prize–winning Gwendolyn Brooks, author of *Annie Allen* (1950), and United States Poet Laureate Robert Hayden.

Fictional Autobiography   Unusually, Johnson wrote two autobiographies—the first was fictional, written more as a political statement than an artistic gesture. The second was his own, magisterial version, which charted his personal story in tandem with the historical events occurring around him. Johnson's faux version is generally thought to be the more successful of the two, even as it has the tendency to flounder. But in *Autobiography of an Ex-Colored Man*, there seem to live more instances of genuine truth and humanity. Perhaps through his unnamed character, so similar in so many ways to himself, Johnson was able to express more of his soul than he felt it was possible in the nonfiction version. A frustrated narrator, struggling with his identity, and left nameless by his creator, is a tradition that is carried on by Ralph Waldo Ellison's groundbreaking novel *Invisible Man*, and, half a century later, in Colson Whitehead's *Apex Hides the Hurt* (2006).

Works in Critical Context

Johnson's novel *The Autobiography of an Ex-Colored Man* anticipated the work of later writers concerned with the nature of racial identity. While contemporaries considered Johnson's novel an accurate and revealing sociological document about the lives of black Americans, it is studied today as a complex work providing an ambiguous psychological study of its anonymous title character. As a poet, Johnson is best known for *God's Trombones*, a

LITERARY AND HISTORICAL CONTEMPORARIES

James Weldon Johnson's famous contemporaries include:

W. E. B. Du Bois (1868–1963): A pioneering civil-rights activist, author, and intellectual, Du Bois helped to found the National Association for the Advancement of Colored People (NAACP). Born in Massachusetts, he became a naturalized citizen of Ghana when he was ninety-five.

Ezra Pound (1885–1972): An American poet, critic, and editor. Pound was an expatriate, living in Europe for most of his professional life. His seminal work, the *Cantos* were written over four decades (1925–1969). Pound's legacy is marred by his support for fascism and by his anti-Semitic leanings.

Helen Keller (1880–1968): Keller, born deaf and blind, was the first individual with her disabilities to graduate from college. She was a writer and activist for women's suffrage and helped to found the American Civil Liberties Union (ACLU).

Charlie Chaplin (1889–1977): A legendary English filmmaker and actor, Chaplin was a major figure in early Hollywood, notable for his iconic performances in the silent films of his era.

Eleanor Roosevelt (1884–1962): The greatly admired wife of Franklin Delano Roosevelt, the thirty-second President of the United States. Eleanor Roosevelt was a civil-rights activist, feminist, intellectual, and delegate to the United Nations General Assembly.

collection of seven poems that captures the rhythmic and spiritual essence of traditional black sermons. In general, Johnson's efforts to preserve and win recognition for black cultural traditions drew praise from such prominent literary figures as H. L. Mencken and Mark Van Doren and contributed to the spirit of racial pride and self-confidence that marked the efflorescence of black music, art, and literature in the Harlem Renaissance.

God's Trombones   *God's Trombones*, Johnson's finest literary achievement, was inspired by sermons—he used them in the same way a composer might make use of a folk tale. Rather than conventional melancholy or plantation stereotypes, Johnson expresses the dignity and depth of the racial religious experience in its own idiom, but in a way that does indeed appeal finally to the universal hunger for spiritual consolation. Ranging from cosmic grandeur to fiery denunciation of sinners to the most tender solicitude for bereavement, the themes of *God's Trombones* receive expression that has the inevitability, resonance, and emotional authority of great art. Critics credited the poet with capturing the oratorical tricks and flourishes that a skilled

COMMON HUMAN EXPERIENCE

Johnson initially published *The Autobiography of an Ex-Colored Man* anonymously, in the hopes that it would make a greater impact if the public believed it was a true autobiography. Here are some other works published anonymously: some for whom the writer is now known, and others that remain enigmas of authorship.

Dream of the Red Chamber (1791), a novel by Cao Xuequin. Cao wrote the novel, considered a high point in classical Chinese literature, sometime in the mid-eighteenth century. It was published anonymously after his death.

Go Ask Alice (1971) a purported diary. This book, published as the diary of a girl who died of a drug overdose, contained details of her exploits with drugs and sex and is meant to be read as a cautionary tale. Copyright evidence, among other things, has led the general public to believe that the woman who claimed only to have edited the diary, a counselor named Beatrice Sparks, probably wrote it.

Primary Colors (1996), a novel by Joe Klein. This lightly fictionalized account of the rise of Bill and Hillary Clinton took Washington, D.C., by storm.

preacher would use to sway his congregation, including hyperbole, repetition, abrupt mood juxtapositions, an expert sense of timing, and the ability to translate biblical imagery into the colorful, concrete terms of everyday life. "The sensitive reader cannot fail to hear the rantings of the fire-and-brimstone preacher; the extremely sensitive reader may even hear the unwritten 'Amens' of the congregation," declared Eugenia W. Collier in a 1960 essay for *Phylon*. The book was favorably reviewed by such fellow luminaries of the Harlem Renaissance as Du Bois, White, Alain Locke, and Countee Cullen. Cullen wrote, "Johnson has blown the true spirit and the pentecostal trumpeting of the dark Joshuas of the race in *God's Trombones*, composed of seven sermon-poems and a prayer. The seven sermons are like the seven blasts blown by Joshua at Jericho." Cullen added, "There is a universality of appeal and appreciation in these poems that raises them, despite the fact that they are labeled 'Seven Negro Sermons in Verse'... far above a relegation to any particular group or people." White poets and critics such as Joseph Auslander, Arthur Guiterman, Harriet Monroe, and Harry Alan Potamkin also reviewed *God's Trombones* favorably.

Responses to Literature

1. Read Johnson's *Along This Way*, and then read *Narrative of the Life of Frederick Douglass* (1845). Write a paper in which you compare the books. Focusing on their merits as autobiographies and their historical heft. From which book did you gain the most insight into the individual author? Do you see a clear line of succession from Douglass to Johnson, with regard to their politics and aspirations for blacks in America?

2. Obtain recorded versions of any number of Johnson's songs. Play the music in class and have a discussion about it. What does it remind you of? Can you trace its influence to any popular music today? Does anything about it surprise you?

3. Write a research paper on the history and contemporary efforts of the NAACP, focusing on the tenure of Johnson at the helm of the organization.

4. Stage a Harlem Renaissance poetry reading for your class. Read selections from Johnson, Langston Hughes, Countee Cullen, Arna Bontemps, and any other poets from the era that you discover in your research.

5. In *Black Manhattan*, written in 1930 at the beginning of the Great Depression, Johnson chose to ignore the rapidly declining financial state of blacks (and practically everyone else) in favor of highlighting the creative output of the community. Because the book failed to meet the needs of the time, it received little attention. Write a short history of similar moments in literature, when works have suddenly been upstaged by massive cultural change and have had to wait for a later age to evaluate them objectively

BIBLIOGRAPHY

Books

Bone, Robert A. *The Negro Novel in America*. New Haven, Conn.: Yale University Press, 1958.

Fleming, Robert E. *James Weldon Johnson*. Boston: Twayne, 1987.

Levy, Eugene. *James Weldon Johnson: Black Leader, Black Voice*. Chicago: Chicago University Press, 1973.

Price, Kenneth M., and Lawrence J. Oliver. *Critical Essays on James Weldon Johnson*. Boston: G. K. Hall, 1997.

Tolbert-Rouchaleau, Jane. *James Weldon Johnson*. New York: Chelsea House, 1988.

Web sites

A Brief Guide to the Harlem Renaissance. Retrieved December 14, 2008, from http://www.poets.org/viewmedia.php/prmMID/5657.

James Weldon Johnson. Retrieved December 14, 2008, from http://www.poets.org/poet.php/prmPID/72.

Go Ask Alice. Retrieved December 14, 2008, from http://www.snopes.com/language/literary/askalice.asp.

Resources for the Study of Beowulf. Retrieved December 13, 2008, from http://greenehamlet.com/.

The Story of the Stone (The Dream of the Red Chamber).
Retrieved December 14, 2008, from http://
www.complete-review.com/reviews/orientalia/
tsots.htm.

James Weldon Johnson. Retrieved December 14, 2008,
from http://www.sc.edu/library/spcoll/amlit/
johnson/johnson.html.

■ LeRoi Jones
Sᴇᴇ *Amiri Baraka*

⊛ Barbara Jordan

BORN: *1936, Houston, Texas*

DIED: *1996, Austin, Texas*

NATIONALITY: *American*

GENRE: *Nonfiction*

MAJOR WORKS:

Barbara Jordan, A Self-Portrait with Shelby
Hearon (1979)

*Barbara Jordan: Speaking the Truth with Eloquent
Thunder*, edited by Max Sherman (2007)

Overview

With an unshakeable belief in honesty in life and government, Texas legislator Barbara Jordan worked tirelessly to
promote justice and democracy. Her skill as a stirring
orator resulted in legendary speeches, both on and off
the floor of the U.S. House of Representatives.

Works in Biographical and Historical Context

Born into a Hostile World   Barbara Charline Jordan
was born in Houston, Texas, at home, on February 21,
1936, to Benjamin Meredith and Arlyne Patten Jordan.
Her father, a Baptist minister, immediately took notice of
her dark skin—a trait that Jordan would not allow to
become her currency, even as the degree of darkness
was seen by many in her community, and beyond, as a
measure of personal worth. The lighter one's skin was,
the easier time one had at school, with family, and with
the law. Partly because of this, her father was very upset
when she announced, at age eleven, that she would no
longer take piano lessons. He was concerned that the only
employment available to her would be teaching music, but
she assured him she would find suitable employment in
another field.

Jordan attended school only with other black children.
She took it upon herself to study exceedingly hard and take
comfort and inspiration from such individuals as Frederick
Douglass, whom she quoted frequently. At Phyllis Wheatley High School, Jordan was a star debater and a member of

Barbara Jordan   *Jordan, Barbara, photograph. The Library of Congress.*

the honor society, and she graduated in 1952 in the top five
percent of her class. Her family did not have any money,
but because that was the case with every student in her
class, Jordan did not take much notice.

Education and Independence   As a youngster, Jordan was very close to her maternal grandfather, John Ed
Patten, who encouraged her to choose her company wisely
and who fostered her independent streak. After graduation,
she decided to study political science at the University of
Texas at Austin—but she became irreconcilably deterred
because the school was still racially segregated. Instead, she
matriculated at Texas Southern University, where once
again she excelled at debate. Her father Benjamin, still
disappointed in his daughter's refusal to learn the piano,
hedged his bet and took a night job to help her pay for
college. In 1956 she graduated magna cum laude with a

LITERARY AND HISTORICAL CONTEMPORARIES

Barbara Jordan's famous contemporaries include:

Molly Ivins (1944–2007): An outspoken, brutally funny Texas journalist, Molly Ivins was a friend of Barbara Jordan and, before her death from breast cancer, an outspoken critic of George W. Bush.

Toni Morrison (1931–): Nobel Prize–winning African-American novelist, Morrison is best known for *Beloved* (1987), which won the Pulitzer Prize in 1988. Morrison is a professor at Princeton University.

Ann Richards (1933–2006): A former Democratic governor of Texas, Ann Richards was a much-beloved liberal politician. She was defeated for reelection by George W. Bush in 1994, and she died from esophageal cancer in 2006.

Alice Munro (1931–): A much-lauded Canadian short story writer, Munro is considered by many to be her generation's Anton Chekhov.

Joe Biden (1942–): Biden, a longtime Delaware senator, was elected Vice President of the United States on a ticket with the first African-American President, Barack Obama.

double major in political science and history. Continuing her academic career, she graduated from Boston University Law School in 1959. She was the only woman, black or white, in her class of 128.

After law school, Jordan accepted a position teaching political science at Tuskegee Institute in Alabama, but after a year she returned to Texas to study for the bar. She began her law practice at her family's dining room table, and moved to an office near her family's home a bit later.

Jordan decided to try for public office not long after setting up her law practice. She ran for the Texas House of Representatives in 1962 and was defeated. She tried again in 1964, and lost again. However, in 1966, with the civil-rights movement changing public attitudes to matters of race, she was elected to a Texas Senate seat. She was the first and only black woman in the Texas State Senate. She was also the first black state senator to serve in that legislative body since the Reconstruction era (1865–77). After six years, she became the Speaker pro tem.

U.S. House of Representatives   Jordan was elected to the United States House of Representatives in 1972, as representative from the eighteenth congressional district in Houston. She was a consummate Southern politician and used her friendship with former U.S. president Lyndon Johnson to secure a position on the House Judiciary Committee. It was from this post, in 1974, that she delivered her affecting and astounding speech during the impeachment

hearings against President Richard M. Nixon; she did in fact vote to impeach. Her words spoke to an unwavering belief in the Constitution and her commitment to upholding the laws and virtues contained therein.

In her time as an elected official, Barbara Jordan sponsored and supported bills that protected poor, disadvantaged, and minority individuals. Notable among these are the Workman's Compensation Act and the Voting Rights Act of 1965. She was asked to deliver the keynote address at the Democratic National Convention in 1976, and had she not become ill, it is possible that Democratic presidential nominee Jimmy Carter would have selected her as his running mate.

Later Career   In 1978 Jordan became a public affairs professor at the Lyndon Baines Johnson School of Public Affairs at the University of Texas in Austin. Though technically no longer a public servant, Jordan continued to advocate causes close to her heart. She was a passionate, vocal opponent of controversial Supreme Court nominee Robert Bork in 1987. She also served on President Bill Clinton's committee on immigration reform, and she was awarded the Presidential Medal of Freedom in 1994.

Barbara Jordan had not been in good health for some time—she had been diagnosed with multiple sclerosis in the early 1970s—and she died in 1996 from complications due to pneumonia. Former presidents and first ladies, and politicians of all parties and stripes, mourned her passing.

Works in Literary Context

Political Oratory   The United States boasts an extraordinary number of moving and groundbreaking speeches by politicians—as befits a country with a complex and groundbreaking republic. From Daniel Webster to Abraham Lincoln, John F. Kennedy, and Barack Obama, the tradition of passionate oratory as a critical component of democracy is alive and well. Jordan belongs in this tradition. She showed that the power of honest words, delivered sincerely and with passion, have the undeniable ability to change hearts and minds. Jordan also belongs squarely in the tradition of African-American orators who have used their speechmaking skills in the cause of freedom and civil rights. This tradition includes such outstanding figures as W. E. B. Du Bois, Ida B. Wells-Barnett, Marian Edelman, Marcus Garvey, Martin Luther King, Jr., Jesse Jackson, Malcolm X, and Thurgood Marshall.

After Jordan's death, Barbara Boxer said this about her on January 22, 1996, in the U.S. Senate: "Throughout her life Barbara Jordan was a voice for common ground, for the ties that bind. Hers were powerful, healing, uplifting words that challenged and inspired women and minorities, indeed all Americans, to reach for something higher and to believe in themselves and their own ability to change the world and make it a better place."

Works in Critical Context

Because they were primarily oral addresses, Barbara Jordan's works do not have a solid base of criticism from which to cull a general opinion. However, her keynote address to the Democratic National Convention in 1976, in which she said that she hoped to build a "national community" in which everyone would be able to share in the American dream, was placed fifth in a list of the top one hundred speeches in America in the twentieth century. The list was compiled by researchers at the University of Wisconsin-Madison and Texas A & M University in 1999, and reflects the opinions of 137 leading scholars. That speech was placed below only speeches by Martin Luther King, Jr., John F. Kennedy, and two by Franklin Delano Roosevelt. Jordan's televised speech before the House Judiciary Committee during the Nixon impeachment hearings in 1974 was placed thirteenth on the same list. That speech too, made on July 25, 1974, made a huge impression at the time. "In a powerful, ringing voice, each word precisely articulated, she expressed the outrage of many Americans over the Watergate scandal and captured the turbulent emotions of a nation watching history unfold," the *Detroit Free Press* noted. The nation heard Jordan intone: "My faith in the Constitution is whole. It is complete. It is total. I am not going to sit here and be an idle spectator to the diminution, the subversion, the destruction of the Constitution." The Judiciary Committee approved three articles of impeachment; Nixon resigned on August 9, 1974. Democratic strategist Ann Lewis told *USA Today* that "when Barbara Jordan spoke those sorts of wonderful, rolling phrases, you knew they hadn't been written by some speechwriter. She was the voice of moral authority."

Jordan's speeches are almost uniformly described as stirring and deeply patriotic, but they were not until recently subjected to the critical rigor of published literature. The columnist Molly Ivins did once liken interviewing Jordan to grilling God—her words were always carefully chosen and there was evidentiary support for every statement she put forth. Bill Clinton called her "the most outspoken moral voice in the American political system." It is likely that Jordan's speeches will continue to live in the collective memory of the nation because many of them have been collected in *Barbara Jordan: Speaking the Truth with Eloquent Thunder*, published by the University of Texas Press in 2007. The book, which is edited by Jordan's friend and colleague of twenty-five years, Senator Max Sherman, also includes a DVD of many of her most memorable speeches.

Responses to Literature

1. Research and write a short paper on the Voting Rights Act of 1965. What provisions did it enact? How would our political and social landscape be different if this piece of legislation had not passed?

COMMON HUMAN EXPERIENCE

The circumstances of Barbara Jordan's birth—she was poor, black, and female in the segregated South—were not very auspicious, yet her intelligence, drive, and confidence propelled her to success. Here are some other works that describe public figures from humble beginnings who went on to enjoy uncommon success.

Oprah Winfrey: A Biography (2004), a biography by Helen S. Garson. It is hard to peg down a more awe-inspiring rags-to-riches story than that of Oprah Winfrey, media mogul. She was born to a poor, teenage single mother in Mississippi, was the victim of sexual abuse as a child, and famously and honestly battles obesity. Oprah, however, used her natural warmth and savvy business sense to create a fortune worth billions of dollars.

Autobiography of Andrew Carnegie (1920), by Andrew Carnegie. With his parents, Andrew Carnegie immigrated to the United States from Scotland. As a boy he worked twelve hours a day in a cotton mill, but he went on to become one of the nineteenth century's richest industrialists and also a leading philanthropist.

Evita: The Real Life of Eva Peron (1996), a biography by Nicholas Fraser and Marysa Navarro. Born poor in rural Argentina, Eva Perón became an actress and then, through her marriage to Colonel Juan Perón, first lady of Argentina from 1946 until her death in 1952 at the age of thirty-three. She became politically powerful, was popular with the masses, and is sometimes credited with gaining for Argentinian women the right to vote. Today, Perón is an almost legendary figure, a cultural icon in Argentina and elsewhere.

The Collected Autobiographies of Maya Angelou (2004), a series of six autobiographies by African-American poet Maya Angelou. This series, highly praised by reviewers, includes the story of the author's early, difficult years growing up in St. Louis, Missouri.

---

2. Barbara Jordan was an inveterate lover of the United States Constitution—she carried a copy in her purse. Peruse this document, pick one amendment or article, and write a paper about how that section came to be, how it has been interpreted in the past, and what controversies surround it in the present.

3. Barbara Jordan was involved in a two decade-long relationship with a female partner. She did not publicly reveal her sexual orientation, and it has been reported that after her first election losses, she was advised against ever doing so. Do you think she would receive the same advice if she were running today? Do you think it would be a relevant concern in your congressional district? Imagine that you are a

campaign adviser and write a paper, making an argument for either position.

4. Review the transcript of Barbara Jordan's 1976 Democratic Convention keynote speech. Compare it with other recent keynote addresses, notably Barack Obama's 2004 Democratic National Convention speech. With a group of students, discuss the content of these speeches. What do convention delegates, politicians, and television viewers want to hear from a speech like this? How well do you think these speeches will hold up over time?

5. Research the duties and responsibilities of the House Judiciary Committee and write a short paper detailing Barbara Jordan's contribution to it.

BIBLIOGRAPHY

Books

Bryant, Ira Babington. *Barbara Charline Jordan: From the Ghetto to the Capitol.* Houston, Tex.: D. Armstrong, 1977.

Jordan, Barbara, and Shelby Hearon. *Barbara Jordan: A Self-Portrait.* Garden City, N.Y.: Doubleday, 1979.

Rogers, Mary Beth. *Barbara Jordan: American Hero.* New York: Bantam Books, 1998.

Periodicals

"Barbara Jordan's Ideals." *New York Times* (January 19, 1996).

Verhovek, Sam. "At Funeral, Praise for Barbara Jordan" *New York Times* (January 21, 1996).

Web Sites

Boxer, Barbara. *Life of Barbara Jordan.* Retrieved December 16, 2008, from http://www.elf.net/bjordan/boxer.html.

Barbara Jordan. Retrieved December 14, 2008, from http://www.beejae.com/bjordan.htm.

Barbara Jordan: Speaking the Truth. Retrieved December 14, 2008, from http://books.google.com/books?id=684Qqf1CTL4C&dq=barbara+jordan&source=gbs_summary_s&cad=0.

◉ Chief Joseph

BORN: *1840, Wallowa Valley, Oregon*

DIED: *1904, Colville Reservation, Washington*

NATIONALITY: *American, Native American*

GENRE: *Nonfiction*

MAJOR WORKS:

Chief Joseph's Surrender Speech at Bears Paw Battle (1877)

"An Indian's Views of Indian Affairs" (1879)

Chief Joseph   *Chief Joseph, photograph. The Library of Congress.*

Overview

Chief Joseph, leader of a Nez Perce band that lived in the Wallowa River Valley of present-day Oregon, embodies Native American heroism. With his courage and wisdom, he offered his people hope for the future; with his intelligence and oratory skills, he impressed his white adversaries. Best remembered for his leadership during the Nez Perce War of 1877 and the eloquence of his surrender speech, Chief Joseph was also highly respected by numerous white Americans for his attempts to negotiate his people's return to the Wallowa Valley following their surrender.

Works in Biographical and Historical Context

White Encroachment By the time Chief Joseph was born in the Wallowa Valley in what is now Oregon, his people were well known to nineteenth-century white settlers in the Pacific Northwest. Although his given name was Hin-mah-too-yah-lat-kekt, or Thunder Rolling in the Mountains, he was widely known as Joseph, or Joseph the Younger, because his father, one of the first Nez Perce to convert to Christianity, had adopted the Christian name "Joseph." The Nez Perce had maintained peaceful relations with the settlers since their 1805 encounter with the Lewis and Clark expedition, and Joseph the Younger was educated in Christian mission schools.

As white settlement increased during the 1850s, the United States federal government pressured the Nez Perce to sign treaties relinquishing their territories in exchange for money and reservation land in western Idaho. However, following an 1863 gold rush into Nez Perce territory, the federal government took back almost six million acres of this land. Once a proponent of amiable dealings with the settlers, Joseph the Elder denounced the United States and refused to both move his tribe from the Wallowa Valley and sign the agreement that would officially recognize the new reservation's boundaries.

Like his father, whom he succeeded as chief in 1871, Chief Joseph and other Nez Perce chieftains questioned the validity of the U.S. government's treaties, arguing that the signers did not represent all of the Nez Perce people. For the next six years, Chief Joseph and his band passively resisted white encroachment until 1877, when even more whites began settling in the Wallowa Valley. The federal government gave the Nez Perce living in the region thirty days to relocate to western Idaho, threatening a cavalry attack to force Chief Joseph and his people onto the reservation.

Retreat and Surrender   Enraged and unwilling to submit to such intrusion, Nez Perce warriors mounted a series of attacks on the settlers. As the U.S. Army detached troops for retaliation, Chief Joseph and approximately eight hundred Nez Perce men, women, and children retreated from the Wallowa Valley and headed to Canada. Pursued by federal troops, the Nez Perce trekked across Idaho, Ohio, Montana, and Washington under the military leadership of Chief Joseph. During the march, which lasted several months, the Nez Perce engaged U.S. troops on at least thirteen occasions and either defeated them or fought them to a standstill.

After traveling more than fourteen hundred miles, Chief Joseph and his band were finally surrounded by federal forces in the Bear Paw Mountains of Montana, only thirty miles from the Canadian border. On October 5, 1877, Chief Joseph surrendered, giving his famous speech to an Army scout who then relayed the message to American commanders. Although the band of Native Americans under Chief Joseph surrendered, approximately two hundred other Nez Perce did manage to reach Canada.

Indian Affairs   Much to Chief Joseph's dismay, the terms under which he surrendered were not upheld. Instead of being allowed to return to a reservation in the Wallowa Valley, Chief Joseph and his people were relocated to reservations in Kansas and Oklahoma, where many of them became sick and died. He traveled to Washington, D.C., twice in 1879 to present his case to the federal government, and in its April 1879 issue, the *North American Review* published "An Indian's Views of Indian Affairs," an article written by Chief Joseph that gave an account of his people's dealings with the whites.

LITERARY AND HISTORICAL CONTEMPORARIES

Chief Joseph's famous contemporaries include:

George Armstrong Custer (1839–1876): U.S. Army General Custer is best remembered for his unsuccessful last stand against Lakota, Cheyenne, and Arapaho warriors at Little Big Horn.

William "Buffalo Bill" Cody (1846–1917): Once a scout for the U.S. Army, Buffalo Bill traveled the world with his Wild West show, an outdoor spectacle that used actual cowboys and real animals from the western United States.

Tsar Alexander III (1845–1894): In addition to persecuting Jews and others who were not members of the Russian Orthodox Church during his reign, Alexander forced national minorities to learn the Russian language and attend Russian schools.

Bret Harte (1836–1902): After moving from New York to California, Harte became a journalist whose local-color writing of the West became known throughout the United States and Europe.

Theodore Roosevelt (1858–1919): Before he was president of the United States, Roosevelt wrote a series of articles about western life based on the years he lived in the Dakota Badlands.

Looking Glass (c.1832–1877): Along with Chief Joseph, Looking Glass, who opposed going to war with the United States, directed the Nez Perce retreat toward Canada.

During his trips east, Chief Joseph gained the respect and support of many influential Americans who lobbied the federal government for the return of his people to the Pacific Northwest. In 1885, the Nez Perce were relocated to a reservation in Idaho. For the remainder of his life, Chief Joseph lived on various reservations in the Northwest and continued his efforts to negotiate his people's return to the Wallowa Valley. On September 21, 1904, Chief Joseph died alone in his lodge, still in exile from his homeland; his doctor reported that he died of a broken heart.

Works in Literary Context

Chief Joseph has proven to be an enduring symbol of the tragedy suffered by nineteenth-century Native Americans. Chief Joseph's popularity with the American public has been partly a result of the fact that his powerful speeches and writings carry strong echoes of a familiar theme: freedom. According to scholar David M. Buerge,

Sympathy for Joseph and the cause of his people has never flagged, . . . and his dramatic appeal has not lessened, and his poignant efforts to sustain his peoples' hopes continue to haunt the popular mind. He

COMMON HUMAN EXPERIENCE

Chief Joseph's appeals affected many white Americans because he was seeking basic human rights, much like those delineated in the Declaration of Independence. Listed below are works that share Chief Joseph's message in their exploration of equal rights for various races and nationalities:

"I Have a Dream" (1963), by Martin Luther King. Delivered on the steps of the Lincoln Memorial in Washington, D.C., on August 28, 1963, King's moving speech addressed civil rights and discrimination, earning him the Nobel Peace Prize in 1964.

Snow Falling on Cedars (1994), by David Guterson. Set in the Pacific Northwest during the time of Japanese internment in response to the bombing of Pearl Harbor, Guterson's novel is a love story between a white man and a woman of Japanese ancestry.

San Souci and Other Stories (1989), by Dionne Brand. The characters in this collection of short stories, set in the Caribbean and in Canada, face racism, sexism, and alienation in both cultures.

Big Bear (1998), a film directed by Gil Cardinal. An epic story of the Cree chief Big Bear, whose ancestral lands in Canada were being claimed by settlers, Cardinal's movie tells of the Native Americans' desperate struggle for justice and dignity.

remains an outstanding native leader and his appeal to both native and white audiences serves, as he had hoped it would, as a bridge of understanding between two races estranged and yet bound together by history.

Simply Complex Linguists often commend the simplicity and conciseness of Native American languages. Free from the English language's rules of rhetoric, Native Americans could eloquently express their feelings with a directness not commonly found in the orations of white men. Scholar Thomas H. Guthrie quotes John Hecke-welder in 1819: "The eloquence of the Indians is natural and simple; they speak what their feelings dictate ... and when they mean to persuade ... they take the shortest way to reach the heart." (In fact, Chief Joseph repeatedly referred to his heart and the hearts of others when addressing the whites.) Guthrie reasons that "a thought presented in one word is more vivid and stimulating to the imagination, more individual and picturesque, than when narrated in a number of words." As evidenced by the brevity of Chief Joseph's surrender speech, he surely understood the force of his succinct sentiment.

Pacifism The main message of Joseph's surrender speech, and a theme found also in "An Indian's Views

of Indian Affairs," is that of pacifism, or the rejection of violence as a means to solve problems. The most famous line of his surrender speech is its last: "From where the sun now stands, I will fight no more forever." In these words, Chief Joseph expresses his realization that the war against white settlers was not worth the cost paid by his people, and that other solutions must be found. In "An Indian's Views of Indian Affairs," Chief Joseph states that violence was never initiated by his people, and that the only thing he and his tribe members seek is fairness and the fulfillment of promises made by the United States government.

Works in Critical Context

As the public became increasingly aware of Chief Joseph's story, he emerged as a champion of freedom. Along with "An Indian's Views of Indian Affairs," every speech he presented and every interview he granted received favorable press. Whether or not they agreed with his position, audiences throughout the United States recognized that Chief Joseph's eloquent arguments came from an intelligent and penetrating mind.

Public Perceptions When Chief Joseph surrendered, the American press widely referred to him as the "Red Napoleon," an insult comparing the Nez Perce chief to Napoleon Bonaparte, the French Emperor (1804–1815) who was forced twice to surrender to opposing forces and eventually exiled to an island under British supervision. However, public perception of the Nez Perce leader changed markedly when Chief Joseph's surrender speech circulated in print, followed by "An Indian's Views of Indian Affairs." Even his harshest critics were impressed by the intensity of his writing. Indeed, writes Native American scholar Buerge,

The beauty and sadness of his surrender speech, his compelling argument on his peoples' behalf, and the sheer moral force of his presence won him admiration and even adulation among those disposed to be sympathetic toward his people. As a man of principle and courage defeated by a powerful and relentless foe, he became an attractive symbol to many.

Responses to Literature

1. Chief Joseph followed the Dreamer religion taught by Smohalla, a Native American prophet whose teachings emphasized traditional Native American values. Research the Dreamer beliefs. Why do you think this religion appealed to Chief Joseph?

2. Research what happened to the Nez Perce and other Native American nations after Franklin D. Roosevelt introduced the New Deal in the 1930s. How did this policy differ from the Dawes Act of 1887? How do you think Chief Joseph would have reacted to the Indian Reorganization Act of 1934? Write a letter to Chief Joseph in which you inform him of the

changes the United States government put into effect under the Indian Reorganization Act.

3. Why do you think Chief Joseph was not able to return his people to their homeland despite admiration, sympathy, and advocacy from many influential Americans? What could he have done differently to help his cause?

4. Create a timeline showing major events in Nez Perce history from the tribe's earliest existence to the present day. What makes these particular events important enough to be included in your timeline?

BIBLIOGRAPHY

Books

Brown, Mark H. *The Flight of the Nez Perce*. New York: G. P. Putnam's Sons, 1967.

Chalmers, Harvey. *The Last Stand of the Nez Perce: Destruction of a People*. Boston: Twayne Publishers, 1962.

Josephy, Alivin. *The Nez Perce Indians and the Opening of the Northwest*. New Haven, Conn.: Yale University Press, 1965.

McAuliffe, Bill. *Chief Joseph of the Nez Perce: A Photo-Illustrated Biography*. Mankato, Minn.: Bridgestone Books, 1998.

Shaughnessy, Diane, and Jack Carpenter. *Chief Joseph: Nez Perce Peacekeeper*. New York: Rosen Publishing Group's PowerKids Press, 1997.

Taylor, Marian W. *Chief Joseph: Nez Perce Leader*. New York: Chelsea, 1993.

Warren, Robert Penn. *Chief Joseph of the Nez Perce*. New York: Random House, 1983.

Yates, Diana. *Chief Joseph: Thunder Rolling Down from the Mountains*. Staten Island, N.Y.: Ward Hill Press, 1992.

Web sites

Buerge, David M. *Chief Seattle and Chief Joseph: From Indians to Icons*. Retrieved August 27, 2008, from http://content.lib.washington.edu/aipnw/buerge2.html.

Guthrie, Thomas H. *Good Words: Chief Joseph and the Production of Indian Speech(es), Texts, and Subjects*. Retrieved August 25, 2008, from http://ethnohistory.dukejournals.org/cgi/reprint/54/3/509.pdf.

✇ Sebastian Junger

BORN: *1962, Belmont, Massachusetts*

NATIONALITY: *American*

GENRE: *Nonfiction*

MAJOR WORKS:

The Perfect Storm (1997)

Sebastian Junger   *AP Images*

Overview

Best known as the author of *The Perfect Storm*, Sebastian Junger is a writer and journalist who shaped and popularized modern adventure nonfiction at the end of the twentieth century.

Works in Biographical and Historical Context

Education in the Extreme Sebastian Junger was born on January 17, 1962, in Belmont, Massachusetts. His father ran a consulting firm that specialized in applied physics, and his mother was an artist. Both parents encouraged Junger to explore his passions as a young adult. Junger received a Bachelor of Arts degree in cultural anthropology from Wesleyan University in 1984. The techniques and methods of cultural anthropology, which is the study of human society and culture, has been influential and useful throughout Junger's diverse writing and journalism career.

Despite his interest in the field, Junger was unclear about his career plans after graduation. Attracted to the

LITERARY AND HISTORICAL CONTEMPORARIES

Junger's famous contemporaries include:

Barry Lopez (1945–): Puschcart Prize winner Lopez is an influential American writer on natural history.

William Jefferson Clinton (1946–): President of the United States from 1993 to 2001, Clinton presided over many of the international events that Junger reported on for his essays.

Bill Bryson (1951–): Bryson is a critically acclaimed travel and nonfiction writer.

Jon Krakauer (1954–): A noted nonfiction and outdoor writer, Krakauer is best known for his account of real tragedy on Mount Everest, *Into Thin Air* (1998).

Yann Martel (1963–): Martel is a Canadian author whose breakthrough novel, *Life of Pi* (2001), concerns a boy adrift at sea with a tiger and several other animals.

Malcolm Gladwell (1963–): Gladwell is a British-born, Canadian nonfiction writer and journalist who is well known for his 2000 book *The Tipping Point: How Little Things Can Make a Big Difference*.

idea of a writing career and drawn to exploring extreme situations, Junger spent many years after graduation traveling and attempting to begin a career in freelance writing. After a number of years of unsuccessful attempts to support himself through writing, Junger took a job as a high-climber for tree removal companies, an extremely dangerous occupation. His experience inspired him to begin investigating and writing about dangerous occupations. He was recovering from a leg injury suffered from his climbing job in 1991 when he heard the news about the tragedy of a swordfishing boat that was lost at sea during one of the worst storms of the last century. This event inspired him to begin his groundbreaking nonfiction work *The Perfect Storm*.

Writing the Perfect Best Seller *The Perfect Storm* is the story of the *Andrea Gail*, a fishing boat that was sailing for her home port of Gloucester, Massachusetts, after a taking in a swordfishing haul on October 28, 1991. The trip coincided with what one meteorologist called a "perfect storm": the collision of two massive storm fronts with Hurricane Grace. The *Andrea Gail* encountered the storm near the coast of Nova Scotia when she was nearly halfway home, and tragedy struck: the ship and crew were lost at sea. In *The Perfect Storm*, Junger re-creates the final hours of the *Andrea Gail*'s journey based on interviews he conducted with survivors from other ships who encountered the storm, news footage, and meteorological data. In the book, Junger imagines the experience from the point of view of the *Andrea Gail* crew, and documents the experi-

ences of their families and friends in Gloucester. A nonfiction book, *The Perfect Storm* is nevertheless creatively imagined, and the combination of fact and rich storytelling made the book a critical and commercial success.

The Perfect Storm was also an exploration of the history and fishing industry of Gloucester and the lives of the *Andrea Gail* crew. Junger was particularly concerned with accurately portraying the lives of the crew and dramatizing their reasons for choosing such an extremely dangerous occupation. In doing so, Junger exposed to readers the many issues of the struggling fishing industry and towns that are dependent on fishing economies. In order to present an even-handed and compelling story, Junger conducted a tremendous amount of research and spent time in the Gloucester community.

Making a Name in Nonfiction *The Perfect Storm* was immensely successful and was adapted into a feature film in 2000. Junger capitalized on the book's success by becoming a prolific writer of nonfiction essays for prestigious magazines and publications, including *Vanity Fair*, *Esquire*, *Outside*, and *Men's Journal*, as well as contributing to ABC News. The vast majority of his assignments and topics have involved extreme or dangerous situations: human rights injustices in Sierra Leone; war crimes in Kosovo; the war in Bosnia; and reporting from the frontlines of wildfires in the United States. In 2000 Junger won a prestigious National Magazine Award for his essay "The Forensics of War," published in *Esquire* magazine. In 2001 Junger republished many of his best essays in the collection *Fire*, which was a commercial success despite mixed reviews from critics. In 2006 Junger focused his journalism on a murder in his home town, unsolved for forty years, in the nonfiction crime drama *A Death in Belmont*. Junger has continued to write and publish nonfiction for magazines and other publications.

Works in Literary Context

Investigative Journalism Regardless of subject matter, Junger's works are all based on his in-depth, investigative reporting. This type of reporting is characterized by a detailed and lengthy study of a particular topic of interest, and contrasts sharply with daily or weekly news reporting. For both of his book-length works, *The Perfect Storm* and *A Death in Belmont*, Junger utilized investigative reporting techniques. For the essays in *Fire*, Junger turned his investigative reporting to extreme topics: a profile and interview with the Afghan North Alliance leader Ahmad Shah Massoud; the hazards of fighting wildfires in North America; the Sierra Leone diamond trade; and genocidal conditions in Kosovo.

Adventure Writing Junger's works are also influenced by the American tradition of adventure writing, a literary genre that crosses over both fiction and nonfiction. *The Perfect Storm*, while a nonfiction re-creation of real events, was stylistically influenced by adventure writing, which is characterized by richly drawn characters who embark on challenging journeys and are often pitted against nature. While Jack London remains the most well-known American adventure writer, Junger is among a new wave of adventure writers that also includes noted nonfiction writer Jon Krakauer.

Works in Critical Context

Junger is widely regarded as both an accomplished researcher and journalist and a dynamic storyteller.

The Perfect Storm A tremendous commercial success, *The Perfect Storm* was also widely praised by critics. Calling Junger's depiction of the events "terrifyingly, awesomely real," Richard Ellis concludes that the book is a "wild ride that brilliantly captures the awesome power of the raging sea and the often futile attempts of humans to withstand it." Christopher Lehmann-Haupt praises Junger for his outstanding research and evocative use of detail, writing, "Perhaps most compelling of all, he explains in concrete detail why hurricanes blow, how waves rise, what happens to boats in a storm and the way human beings drown." Critic Anthony Bailey further comments on how Junger's investigative journalism contributed to an authentic, dynamic reading experience:

> Sebastian Junger declares that his own confrontation with the storm was limited to standing on the backshore of Gloucester, watching 30-foot swells approach Cape Ann. But he clearly went on to experience it through the words of the storm's survivors and those connected with the *Andrea Gail*. Interviewing them must have been a difficult, even intrusive job, but the result is thrilling—a boat ride into and (for us) out of a watery hell.

Responses to Literature

1. Rather than simply fictionalizing events in *The Perfect Storm*, for which he had no firsthand sources, Junger drew upon accounts of people who had been in similar situations to dramatize the events. What impact does this approach have upon the story? How would the book have been different if Junger had fictionalized those events?

2. Describe Junger's role and voice in *The Perfect Storm*. What type of character is he in the book?

3. Compare *The Perfect Storm* to other well-known adventure stories such as Jon Krakauer's *Into the Wild*, in terms of narrative technique, themes, and the questions and ideas they raise.

BIBLIOGRAPHY

Periodicals

Bailey, Anthony. "The Tempest." *New York Times Book Review* (June 22, 1997): 8.

COMMON HUMAN EXPERIENCE

Central to many of Junger's works is an exploration of how humans struggle against nature and what that conflict reveals about humanity. Here are some other works that explore the conflict of human against nature:

"To Build a Fire" (1908), a short story by Jack London. This popular short story is the tale of a man and his dog facing hardship on the Yukon trail.

The Old Man and the Sea (1951), a novella by Ernest Hemingway. One of the most acclaimed works of American fiction, *The Old Man and the Sea* is the story of an old man who struggles with a giant marlin.

Alive: The Story of the Andes Survivors (1974), a book by Piers Paul Read. This popular book documenting the real-life survival story of a group of people who crashed in the Andes mountains was adapted to film in 1993.

Hatchet (1974), a children's novel by Gary Paulsen. Paulsen's Newberry award–winning book tells the story of a young man who struggles to survive in the wilderness.

Into the Wild (1996), a book by Jon Krakauer. Krakauer's gripping novel, which was adapted into a film of the same title in 2007, is a true story about a young man's tragic journey into the Alaskan wilderness.

Ellis, Richard. "Sturm and Drang." *Los Angeles Times Book Review* (May 25, 1997): 8–9.

Lehmann-Haupt, Christopher. "The Shipwreck Story No One Survived to Tell." *New York Times* (June 5, 1997): C20.

Web sites

Fabrikant, Geraldine. "Talking Money with Sebastian Junger; From *The Perfect Storm*, A Passage to Financial Freedom." *New York Times* (December 3, 2000). Retrieved November 28, 2008, from http://query.nytimes.com/gst/fullpage.html?res=9C03E2D6113DF930A35751C1A9669C8B63&sec=&spon=&pagewanted=1.

Kakutani, Michio. "Books of the Times; From Fighting the Taliban to Battling Blazes in Idaho." *New York Times* (October 17, 2001). Retrieved November 28, 2008, from http://query.nytimes.com/gst/fullpage.html?res=9B03EEDF163EF934A25753C1A9679C8B63.

Shnayerson, Michael. *After the Storm: Sebastian Junger Interview*. Accessed November 28, 2008, from http://www.nationalgeographic.com/afterthestorm.

⊛ Donald Justice

BORN: *1925, Miami, Florida*

DIED: *2004, Iowa City, Iowa*

NATIONALITY: *American*

GENRE: *Poetry, fiction, essays*

MAJOR WORKS:

The Summer Anniversaries (1960)

Departures (1973)

Selected Poems (1979)

The Sunset Maker (1987)

New and Selected Poems (1995)

Overview

Often regarded as an "experimental poet," Donald Justice is known for versatility and craftsmanship. He was awarded the Pulitzer Prize in Poetry for his collection *Selected Poems* (1979).

Works in Biographical and Historical Context

Torn between Musical Composition and Writing

Born in Miami, Justice was raised in the American South and never even traveled far enough from home to see snow until he was almost an adult. As he grew up, Justice maintained an interest in piano, clarinet, and musical composition. Of these, composition was his greatest passion. At the age of eighteen, he felt torn between music and writing. After considering the matter seriously one summer, Justice, believing he could express more with writing, decided to leave musical composition behind him.

Iowa and Pulitzer

After receiving degrees from the Universities of Miami and North Carolina and studying with Yvors Winters at Stanford University, Justice entered the University of Iowa Writers Workshop, the program with which he is most often associated. Working with poets such as John Berryman and Robert Lowell, Justice received his PhD in 1954. He later taught at the university for two separate periods totaling twenty years.

Justice published his first volume of verse, *The Summer Anniversaries*, in 1960; its meticulously crafted poems garnered him a Lamont Poetry Selection from the Academy of American Poets. Justice first investigated themes of loss, memory, and the acceptance of change in *The Summer Anniversaries*, which contained several painful recollections of his childhood. The collection also displayed his facility with poetic forms, and demonstrated his ability to make the structure of a poem just as expressive as its language.

Night Light (1967) also explored issues of decay—this time from an adult perspective—while *Departures* (1973) introduced several experimental forms, including variations or "mistranslations" taken from poems written in other languages and poems created by shuffling and dealing word cards at random. Many of the verses reflect the author's continuing fascination with the possibilities of language and the idea that poetry can overcome loss by preserving memory. *Selected Poems* (1979), culled from his previous collections and including previously unpublished work, demonstrates all of Justice's talents in one volume; critic Dana Gioia noted that it "reads almost like an anthology of the possibilities of contemporary poetry." It is for this work that Justice was awarded the 1979 Pulitzer Prize in Poetry.

Bringing Back the Music

It is perhaps not surprising that loss as a theme is prevalent in *Selected Poems*. By the time the work was published in 1979, Justice's generation had lived through the Great Depression, World War II, the Korean War, and the Vietnam War—leaving many with unprocessed experiences of grief and suffering. Still, what little autobiographical reference there is to be found in Justice's work must be gleaned despite the poet's refusal to let his personality dominate his later writings. However, there is one work in which Justice clearly relied upon the inspirations that shaped him when he was young. Piano lessons Justice enjoyed as a child provide the central motif of *The Sunset Maker: Poems/Stories/A Memoir* (1987), which seems like a "complex piece of music" dedicated to the working out of a single theme, "the pain and beauty of memory and loss," as Frances Ruhlen McConnel of the *Los Angeles Times* notes.

Justice retired from teaching in 1992, but continued to publish his own poems and edit collections of poetry by others. *A Donald Justice Reader: Selected Poetry and Prose* (1991) gathers into one volume seventy-three poems and six prose pieces: three essays, two stories, and a memoir of Justice's Miami childhood. *New and Selected Poems*, published four years later in 1995, offers another collection of Justice's poems.

Justic served as chancellor of the Academy of American Poets from 1997 to 2003. After a distinguished career of letters, Donald Justice died in Iowa City on August 6, 2004, a few weeks after suffering a stroke.

Works in Literary Context

Known for his simple, controlled language and mastery of poetic forms, Justice deals with themes of loss, memory, and identity in his work. Although his literary output has been relatively modest, he is considered by many to be one of America's most prominent poets, and his versatility and virtuosity has led him to be referred to as a "poet's poet." Commenting on the creative sources for his work, Justice says that "one of the motives for writing is surely to recover and hold what would otherwise be lost totally—memory or experience. Put very simply, so that one might not wholly die."

Nostalgia Without Sentimentality

Despite the often introspective tone of Justice's work—mirrors are a frequent image in his poems—Justice displays a humble, self-effacing approach in his writing. Using the perspective of time and the manipulation of poetic form to distance himself from his subjects, Justice involves the reader more deeply in the poem. Some critics have observed that his emphasis on poetic structure can create overly rigid poems, and that his understated language makes for a sense of passivity. Others, however, have noted that the poet's expert grasp of form—especially since the experimental poems of *Departures*—allows him to go beyond the limitations of structure and fully explore the potential of poetry; Justice never exhibits form for form's sake. His poems have earned such epithets as "flawless," "stunning," and "fascinating." According to Richard Howard, Justice is nostalgic without being sentimental, and has created "some of the most assured, elegant and heartbreaking . . . verse in our literature so far."

Works in Critical Context

While *The Summer Anniversaries* established Justice's reputation as a talented writer, it was not until *Selected Poems* was awarded the Pulitzer Prize in 1979 that his work became known outside literary circles.

The Summer Anniversaries The Summer Anniversaries established Justice's reputation for craftsmanship. The book, relates Greg Simon in the *American Poetry Review*, "consists of flawless poems, moving as inexorably as glaciers toward beautiful comprehension and immersion in reality." Writing in the *Washington Post Book World*, Doug Lang suggests, "Justice's concern for form is really a concern with experience" that seeks to be conveyed in "an appropriate arrangement of words." In his essay on Justice in *Contemporary American Poetry*, A. J. Poulin calls Justice "a master of what might be called sparse elegance. . . . [His] poems are moving because of his consummate linguistic, tonal, and formal exactitude." But less attention to form may have improved the poems in this first book, some readers suggest; *New York Times Book Review* contributor Charles Molesworth explains, "What some might see as proper formality might strike others as unnecessary stiffness."

Since his death in 2004, some critics and scholars have attempted to define Justice's place in the literary canon. For example, critic and former student Tad Richards argues that "Donald Justice is likely to be remembered as a poet who gave his age a quiet but compelling insight into loss and distance, and who set a standard for craftsmanship, attention to detail, and subtleties of rhythm."

Responses to Literature

1. Discuss the meaning of a frequently occurring image—the mirror, for example—that appears in Justice's poetry.
2. In what ways is Donald Justice an experimental poet? How does he vary the traditional forms of poetry in his work?

LITERARY AND HISTORICAL CONTEMPORARIES

Donald Justice's famous contemporaries include:

Jan Wolkers (1925–2007): Dutch author and artist who wrote the novel *Turks Fruit* (1969)—later adapted to an Academy Award-nominated film directed by Paul Verhoeven.

Gerald Durrell (1925–1995): British author, animal collector, and conservationist who founded the Durrell Wildlife Conservation Trust.

Flannery O'Connor (1925–1964): American author of Southern Gothic novels and short-story collections including *Wise Blood* (1952) and *The Violent Bear it Away* (1960).

Edward Gorey (1925–2000): American author and illustrator who is most famous for his macabre book *The Gashlycrumb Tinies, or, After the Outing* (1963)—which describes the deaths of twenty-six children—one for each letter of the alphabet.

Gore Vidal (1925–): American author and politician who stirred up significant controversy by publishing *The City and the Pillar* (1948), one of the first gay novels to emerge after World War II.

COMMON HUMAN EXPERIENCE

Much of Justice's work deals with the pain of loss. Other works that explore this theme include:

A Grief Observed (1961), a poetry collection by C. S. Lewis. Written after his wife, Joy Gresham, died of cancer, this work reflects upon the experience losing a loved one.

A Heartbreaking Work of Staggering Genius (2000), a memoir by Dave Eggers. This work details the narrator's experiences of loss after the death of both of his parents.

Grief (2006), a novel by Andrew Holleran. Winner of the 2007 Stonewall Book Award, this work follows a man's experiences dealing with the death of his mother.

3. Some critics argue that, in spite of the sadness that pervades much of his poetry, happiness is part of Donald Justice's aesthetic. To what extent to you agree with this assessment of his work? Can you find examples in his work to support this?

4. In *The Sunset Maker*, how does Justice reference music on a thematic level? How does he incorporate musical elements into his writing style?

BIBLIOGRAPHY

Books

Gioia, Dana and William Logan, eds. *Certain Solitudes: On the Poetry of Donald Justice.* Fayetteville, Ark.: University of Arkansas Press, 1998.

Hoy, Philip. *Donald Justice in Conversation with Philip Hoy.* London: Between the Lines, 2001.

Richards, Tad. "Donald Justice." *Greenwood Encyclopedia of American Poets and Poetry.* Westport, Conn.: Greenwood Press, 2005.

Periodicals

Harrison, J. "For Donald Justice." *Southwest Review* 92, no. 3 (2007): 446.

Hudgins, A. "Homage: Donald Justice." *Southern Review* 38, Part 3 (2002): 654–661.

Orr, D. "Collected Poems. By Donald Justice." *New York Times Book Review* 109, Part 35 (August 29, 2004): 16.

Web sites

Jarman, Mark. *Happiness: The Aesthetics of Donald Justice.* Retrieved September 25, 2008, from http://www.blackbird.vcu.edu/v1n2/nonfiction/jarman_m/justice.htm.

✸ Mary Karr

BORN: *1955, Groves, Texas*

NATIONALITY: *American*

GENRE: *Nonfiction, poetry*

MAJOR WORKS:

Abacus (1987)

The Devil's Tour (1993)

The Liars' Club (1995)

Viper Rum (1998)

Cherry (2000)

Overview

Poet and nonfiction author Mary Karr is widely known for her 1995 best-seller *The Liars' Club: A Memoir.* She has been praised for her savvy storytelling, lyrical prose, sensual detail, emotional honesty, humor, and ability to capture the colloquial speech of small-town East Texas.

Works in Biographical and Historical Context

Small Town Childhood Karr was born on January 16, 1955, in Groves, a small town in East Texas known

Mary Karr   *Karr, Mary, photograph.* © Ralf-Finn Hestoft / Corbis.

for its oil refineries and chemical plants. She later wrote about the town, calling it by the fictional name of Leechfield, in her memoirs. Her writing evokes the social and cultural milieu of the working-class town. Karr's father worked in an oil refinery and her mother was an amateur artist and business owner. Karr's sister, older than her by two years, is a key figure in her memoirs.

Karr developed an early interest in literature that she credits with changing her life. As she once told *BookPage* interviewer Ellen Kanner, "I'm invigorated by language. Poetry saved my life. Really transformed me, really saved me." Upon graduating from high school, she traveled with a group of friends to Los Angeles, where she immersed herself in the lifestyle of the California hippie and surfer counter-cultures. Later that year, she enrolled in Macalester College in Saint Paul, Minnesota, but left school after two years to travel. She has explained her wanderlust as the result of having multiple interests that made it difficult to conform to just one lifestyle: "I felt like I was strapping things onto myself," she once said. "One day I would want to be a hippie and then a surfer, then Emily Dickinson. You change a million times."

A Writer with a Conscience Karr became politically involved in the antiapartheid movement that began in 1956. Activists opposed the racial segregation of blacks in South Africa, and the movement culminated in the end of apartheid in that country in 1994. During this time, she met African-American poet Ethridge Knight, who became an important influence on the development of her poetry.

Karr eventually entered graduate school to study creative writing, and earned an MFA from Goddard College.

Among her mentors at Goddard was Tobias Wolff, whose memoir *This Boy's Life* (1989) served as a major influence on Karr's own writing. She also studied with noted poets Robert Bly and Robert Hass. Karr graduated from Goddard in 1979 and published her first poem that same year in *Mother Jones* magazine. She moved to Boston in 1980, where she held various jobs in the computer and telecommunications industries while she continued to write and publish poetry.

In 1983, she married poet Michael Milburn, with whom she had a son, but the couple divorced in 1991. In 1987, Karr published her first volume of poetry, *Abacus*, and her second, *The Devil's Tour*, in 1993. Karr won the Pushcart prize for both her poetry and essays.

Best-Selling Author and Professor It was in 1995 that Karr became a literary sensation with the publication of her memoir, *The Liars' Club*. The book remained on the *New York Times* best-seller list for over a year and won Karr the 1996 PEN Martha Albrand Award for first nonfiction. *The Liars' Club*, takes place in a small industrial East Texas town during the mid-1960s when Karr was eight years old. It conveys a strong sense of place and evokes the powerful emotional climate of a family circle characterized by alcoholism, mental illness, and strong passions. Critics applauded Karr's use of narrative voice, inflected with the colloquial speck of East Texas and the unique perspective of a precocious young girl. In the literary world, *The Liars' Club* inspired an explosion of memoirs to be written in the confessional mode. Karr's next work, *Cherry: A Memoir* (2000), is a sequel to *The Liars' Club*, and portrays Karr's adolescent years of intellectual and sexual awakening.

Karr has worked as an assistant professor at several academic institutions, including Tufts University, Emerson College, Harvard University, and Sarah Lawrence College. She currently teaches in the department of English at Syracuse University in Syracuse, New York.

Works in Literary Context

Memoir Writing as Confessional Literature In confessional literature, writers convey intimate details about their real lives and experiences. Mary Karr, whose body of work falls largely in this area, wrestles with the idea that for everyone who has ever told a story or recalled a personal memory, personal perspective makes it impossibile to ever convey truth objectively. Nevertheless, Karr strives to convey the truth of her experiences through memoir writing and poetry.

Karr has explained to interviewer Ellen Kanner that "with memoir, there's an intimacy, a sense of emotional engagement." Karr strives to impart both intimacy and emotional engagement in both of her memoirs *The Liars' Club* and *Cherry*. In each of these works, Karr explores themes of truth, lies, memory, confession, and storytelling.

LITERARY AND HISTORICAL CONTEMPORARIES

Karr's famous contemporaries include:

Robert Bly (1926–): One of America's most influential poets. Considered a champion of the nonacademic poetry of nature, the visionary, and the irrational, Bly's subjects include the surreal interactions of the natural world and the human mind.

Robert Hass (1941–): An American translator, critic, and poet. Haas is primarily recognized for his musical, descriptive, and meditative poetry.

Nelson Mandela (1914–): A leader of the movement against legalized racial segregation in South Africa. Mandela became the first president of South Africa to be elected in a democratic election after the fall of apartheid in 1994.

Philip Roth (1933–): A dominant voice in Jewish American literature, Roth's novels and collections of short stories have attracted a range of critical commentary for their intimate and raw depictions of life.

Tobias Wolff (1945–): An American author widely considered a master storyteller. His memoir *This Boy's Life* served as a significant influence on Karr's work.

Both books are set in the fictional town of Leechfield, Texas, which is based on Karr's home town.

The Liars' Club takes place from 1961 to 1963, when Karr was seven and eight years old. The novel's title refers to the local American Legion pool room and bar, as well as the back room of the bait shop, where Karr's father and other local men socialized in their free time. In the book, Karr recounts the traumatic events she experienced in the context of her dysfunctional family life. For example, Karr's mother, an alcoholic and mentally unstable woman whose artistic and intellectual interests were stifled by small-town life, once burned all of the family's possessions and called the local police station to report that she had killed her two daughters, a claim that turned out to be untrue. Against this chaotic emotional backdrop, Karr reports being raped by a neighborhood boy at the age of seven and sexually assaulted by an adult male babysitter at the age of eight.

Cherry follows Karr's adolescent years. It has been referred to as Karr's coming-of-age story, in which she describes how she developed a sense of individuality distinct from her turbulent family. In *Cherry*, Karr shares with raw abandon her early experiences of sexual awakening. At the same time, however, the book is also an account of her intellectual awakening and development as a budding writer. The first half of *Cherry* is narrated by Karr in the first-person voice. The second half of the novel switches to

COMMON HUMAN EXPERIENCE

Mary Karr's writings convey intimate details about her adolescent life in East Texas. Other works that reveal an author's experiences through real or fictitious characters include:

Confessions (c. 397), an autobiography by St. Augustine of Hippo. Considered one of the earliest examples of confessional literature, St. Augustine writes about the immoral behavior of his youth and later conversion to Christianity.
The Kiss (1997), a memoir by Kathryn Harrison. Harrison describes the disturbing relationship that developed between her young mother, her father, and herself.
This Boy's Life: A Memoir (1989), a memoir by Tobias Wolff. Wolff portrays himself as a young man who deals with the powerful impetus to establish a masculine identity and questions the familial and social limits conditioning that development.

a second-person voice. This switch suggests that in conveying her own personal experiences as a teenager in the late 1960s and early 1970s, Karr was speaking broadly to an entire generation of adolescent girls.

Poetry as Confessional Literature Like her memoirs, Karr's poetry has been described as confessional due to the frank revelations of self doubt and dysfunctional family that are a common subject of her work. The settings of her poems are primarily of the same working-class East Texas milieu that is treated more extensively in her memoirs, and a number of the characters and incidents introduced in her poetry are revisited in her memoirs. Karr's poetry is characterized by brevity, clarity, meticulous detail, and careful attention to metrical form. She has developed a personal style of using the three-line stanza in many of her poems.

The poems in her collection *Abacus* are introspective reflections on personal relationships, love, friendship, and self-questioning. *The Devil's Tour* grapples with broader struggles of human existence and consciousness, exploring themes of death, mortality, evolution, and existential angst, as well as parenting and family relationships. The recurring motif of skull imagery in *The Devil's Tour* invokes the themes of mortality and introspection. The poems in *Viper Rum* continue to explore these themes, and include reflections on Karr's personal life, her relationship with her parents, her struggle with alcoholism, and an awakening to religious sentiment.

Works in Critical Context

Karr had already risen as a celebrated and award-winning poet by the time *The Liars' Club* earned her even more acclaim in the literary community.

The Liars' Club *The Liars' Club* is undoubtedly Karr's most highly regarded work. Reviewers comment that themes of sexual abuse and dysfunctional family in this book are handled by Karr without the bitterness, self-pity, melodrama, or sentimentality that characterizes many other confessional memoirs. Writer Scott Donaldson commends Karr in that she "neither shies away from the truth nor erects signposts to guide her readers' reactions. . . . Instead, she lets her story speak for itself." She has been praised for her frank yet nonjudgmental portrayal of her father and mother, which effectively expresses both the love and the pain associated with each parent. Reviewers admire her use of narrative voice in the book, which convincingly portrays the perspective of a young girl.

Some critics, including Gaby Wood of the *London Review of Books*, have questioned the authenticity of the memories collected in works like *The Liars' Club*. He writes: "[T]he story is one of incredible torment, told by the injured party. It is remembered as Karr saw it when she was eight . . . here the 'lies' are tricks of memory." But even as some are suspicious of the nature of memories conveyed in autobiographical memoirs, readers continue to admire *The Liars' Club* for being skillfully written, powerfully expressive, and entertaining to read. Reviewer Cyra McFadden comments on Karr's skillful use of language and praises the author for her multifaceted writing efforts: "The Language of *The Liars' Club* crackles with energy and wit. Then Karr's tone will shift abruptly again; when called for, she can be tender."

Viper Rum Although not as many people have read Karr's poetry as her memoirs, her collections of verse have been highly regarded by critics. Her use of language is consistently praised, especially her use of formal meter, which captures the rhythms of everyday speech. Her evocative imagery and meticulous attention to detail are also frequently credited with making her poetry enjoyable to read. As with her memoirs, critics have applauded Karr's ability to express strong emotions and describe poignant situations without lapsing into melodrama or sentimentality. As Barbara Jordan of the *Chicago Review* writes, "Karr is a poet who refuses to flinch, even if the landscape of memory and experience resembles a particularly gruesome . . . canvas."

Karr reprinted her Pushcart Award–winning essay "Against Decoration" in *Viper Rum*. In this piece, Karr decries how overemphasizing form in poetry often trumps the true meaning and emotion behind the words. Writer Judith Kitchen commends Karr for her faithfulness to clarity of meaning over form. "Karr has made her case for the emotive voice, for the poetry of feeling," says Kitchen. "She has not shunned form [but] found a form in which she can explore the qualities of language . . . that will lead toward clarity."

Responses to Literature

1. In her essay, "Against Decoration," Karr expresses support for meaning over poetic style. Read William Butler Yeats's poem "Easter 1916." In your opinion,

how, if at all, does the form in this poem enhance the meaning Yeats is trying to convey? Do you agree with Karr's assertions in her essay?

2. Explore the theme of memories and truth in *The Liars' Club*. In your opinion, is Karr a reliable narrator as she retells the events of her past? Is there reason to doubt the authenticity of these memories? Support your answer using evidence from the text.

3. Memoirs like *The Liars' Club* have become increasingly popular with readers. Why do you think this form of storytelling appeals to so many people? What advantages do you think the memoir offers both readers and writers? What are the disadvantages?

BIBLIOGRAPHY

Periodicals

Donaldson, Scott. "Mary Karr Recounts her Tough East Texas Childhood." *Chicago Tribune Books*, (July 23, 1995): p. 3.

Jordan, Barbara. "Review of *Viper Rum*, by Mary Karr." *Chicago Review* 44, nos. 3–4 (1998): p. 213–217.

Kitchen, Judith. "Against." *Georgia Review* 52, no. 4 (1998): p. 755–772.

McFadden, Cyra. "There's No Lie as Big as the Truth." *Los Angeles Times Book Review* (July 16, 1995): p. 1, 12.

Witalec, Janet, ed. "Mary Karr (1955–)." *Contemporary Literary Criticism*. Vol. 188. Detroit: Thomson Gale, 2004. p. 1-67.

Wood, Gaby. "What Did It Matter Who I was?" *London Review of Books* (October 19, 1995): p. 39.

Web sites

Garner, Dwight. *A Scrappy Little Beast*. Retrieved December 4, 2008, from http://www.salon.com/may97/karr970521.html.

Gerrard, Nicci. *Sex, drugs and poetry*. Retrieved December 4, 2008, from http://www.guardian.co.uk/books/2001/jun/24/biography.features1.

Kanner, Ellen. *Mary Karr: Remembering the Agonies and Ecstasies of Adolescence*. Retrieved December 3, 2008 from http://www.bookpage.com/0010bp/mary_karr.html. Last updated in 2000.

Robinson, Harriet Hanson. *Dostoevsky and Existentialism*. Retrieved October 31, 2007, from http://fyodordostoevsky.com. Last updated on May 17, 2007.

✿ Garrison Keillor

BORN: *1942, Anoka, Minnesota*

NATIONALITY: *American*

GENRE: *Fiction, nonfiction*

MAJOR WORKS:
Lake Wobegon Days (1985)

Garrison Keillor   Keillor, Garrison, 1987, photograph. AP Images.

Overview

Garrison Keillor is best known for his highly popular and critically acclaimed novel *Lake Wobegon Days* (1985), his humorous stories and essays (most of which first appeared in the *New Yorker*), and for his role as the creator and host of the weekly public radio program "A Prairie Home Companion."

Works in Biographical and Historical Context

Growing up in Minnesota   Gary Edward Keillor was born on August 7, 1942, in Anoka, Minnesota, the third of six children of John Philip, a railway mail clerk and carpenter, and Grace Ruth Denham Keillor. Always a shy person, Keillor was an avaricious reader who was so obsessed with books that his mother frequently had to force him outside to play. Because of his withdrawn nature, his sharp sense of humor was essentially unknown to his classmates until he delivered a satire in front of his class about what the principal kept in his office records. Later, he submitted articles to his school paper under the name Garrison Edwards and began submitting his articles to the *New Yorker*. He attended college and graduate school at the University of

LITERARY AND HISTORICAL CONTEMPORARIES

Keillor's famous contemporaries include:

Michael Crichton (1942–2008): American author best known for his science fiction and techno-thriller novels, such as *Jurassic Park* (1990), Crichton was also a successful television and film producer and one of the creators of the hit TV drama *ER*.

Isabel Allende (1942–): Chilean American author of popular novels that employ magic realism, including *The House of Spirits* (1982) and *City of Beasts* (2002).

John Irving (1942–): American author and award-winning screenwriter whose script *The Cider House Rules* (1999) won an Academy Award for Best Adapted Screenplay in 2000.

Anne Tyler (1941–): American author of award-winning novels including *Breathing Lessons* (1988), which was awarded the Pulitzer Prize for Fiction in 1989, *The Accidental Tourist* (1985), and *Dinner at the Homesick Restaurant* (1982).

Peter Carey (1943–): Australian author who has won the Booker Prize for fiction twice, once for *Oscar and Lucinda* (1988) and once for *True History of the Kelly Gang* (2000).

Minnesota, where he continued to pursue his love for writing by working for the *Ivory Tower*, the student literary magazine. It was at this time that he began to get involved with radio, staff announcing for KUOM, the University of Minnesota station.

"A Prairie Home Companion" After graduating, Keillor applied for jobs at New York-based magazines but was repeatedly turned down. He decided, then, to return to radio announcing; it was while working for KSJN in St. Paul, Minnesota, where he was to remain until 1987, that he first invented the mythical town of Lake Wobegon. Capitalizing on his childhood memories of life in a religious, small town in the Midwest, Keillor added characters and formed stories about this little burg, which later became the main feature of his popular program, "A Prairie Home Companion." The idea for the radio show, which ran from 1974 to 1987 on Minnesota Public Radio and National Public Radio, was sparked by Keillor's fondness for the "Grand Ole Opry" broadcasts of the 1930s and 1940s.

His program was a combination of music and storytelling broadcasted from the World Theater in St. Paul. For music, Keillor supplied his audiences with folk, bluegrass, gospel, choral, yodeling, and other traditional forms. The storytelling part of the show was provided by Keillor, who had to overcome his stage fright in order to perform. He disguised his fear well, treating his listeners week after week to the latest news from Lake Wobegon, "where all the women are strong, all the men are good looking, and all the children are above average," as he always concluded. The program was also punctuated by commercials for such renowned Lake Wobegonian establishments as Ralph's Pretty Good Grocery and the Chatterbox Cafe, as well as products like Powdermilk Biscuits, which are "made from whole wheat raised by Norwegian bachelor farmers in the rich bottomlands of the Wobegon Valley, so you know they're not only good, they're also pure mostly."

Although the "Prairie Home Companion" attracted an audience sometimes estimated at four million people and won the Peabody award in 1980, Keillor eventually decided to leave the show and move to Denmark to marry his former classmate Ulla Skaerved. He remained there only three months, however, before moving back to the United States and taking up residence in New York City. There, he continued to write articles for the *New Yorker* and *Atlantic Monthly* and also wrote several books relating tales about his now-familiar Lake Wobegon residents. After a two-year absence from radio, Keillor decided to return to the U.S. airwaves with a program similar in format to "A Prairie Home Companion," *Garrison Keillor's American Radio Company of the Air*. In 1993 the show returned to the World Theater in St. Paul, Minnesota, and changed its name back to "A Prairie Home Companion."

Career as a Fiction Writer In addition to writing articles and radio scripts, Keillor has authored books for both adults and children. After publishing the highly successful novel *Lake Wobegon Days* (1985), he continued the Lake Wobegon series with two story collections, *Leaving Home* (1987) and *We Are Still Married: Stories and Letters* (1989), which first appeared on the *New York Times* bestseller list on April 16, 1989, and remained on the list for more than seven weeks. Keillor returned to the world of novel writing with the release of *WLT: A Radio Romance* (1991). The book is about Ray and Roy Soderbjerg, two brothers who establish a radio station during the glory days of radio in 1926. They bumble through their new enterprise, booking acts small and smaller as they explore the frontier of radio broadcasting. Keillor's next work was a book of short stories and vignettes called *The Book of Guys* (1993). A comic spin-off of the work of Robert Bly, the poet who wrote best-selling works about male bonding in the wilderness, *The Book of Guys* tracks the struggles of manhood as experienced by such diverse protagonists as Dionysus and Buddy the Leper.

Keillor's two books for children, *Cat, You Better Come Home* (1995) and *The Old Man Who Loved Cheese* (1999), feature Keillor's trademark sense of the absurd. In *Cat, You Better Come Home*, Keillor fictionalizes the life of a feline who wants more than she gets in her own house, so she runs away to a life of show business, only to return broken down to the man who loves her. *The Old Man Who Loved Cheese* features Wallace P. Flynn, a man whose love for the dairy product causes him to lose his wife and his family. However, after he realizes that the joys of human companionship are much more satisfying than his favorite food, he gives it up and his life is restored.

Keillor returned to the Lake Wobegon series with *Wobegon Boy* (1997), a tale of a young man who escapes his town of Lake Wobegon to go to upstate New York and experiences a series of amusing events. Since *Wobegon Boy*, Keillor has added three books to the Lake Wobegon series: *Lake Wobegon Summer 1956* (2001), *Pontoon: A Novel of Lake Wobegon* (2007), and *Liberty: A Novel of Lake Wobegon* (2008).

Works in Literary Context

Drawing from his childhood memories of growing up in a small town, Keillor's work paints a humorous but endearing portrait of life in the Midwestern United States.

Satire of the Midwest *Lake Wobegon Days* evolved from "News from Lake Wobegon," a segment of "A Prairie Home Companion," which Keillor always introduces with the words "It's been a quiet week in Lake Wobegon, my hometown." Like the town depicted in Keillor's radio monologues, *Lake Wobegon Days* is inhabited by a variety of characters, including Mayor Clint Bunsen and Father Emil of the Church of Our Lady of Perpetual Responsibility, who are described in a fond yet frequently sarcastic tone. The book is presided over by a persona who sometimes rebels against the strict conventions of the predominantly Scandinavian Lutheran Wobegonians but retains an affectionate respect for them. Many critics place Keillor's satire and droll observations in the tradition of such prominent American humorists as Mark Twain, Robert Benchley, and particularly James Thurber, whose works, like *Lake Wobegon Days*, provide a humorous yet incisive portrait of Midwestern American life.

Works in Critical Context

Following its debut in 1974, "A Prairie Home Companion" gradually attracted a small but devoted local audience, and in 1980 it was syndicated nationwide. The program received the George Foster Peabody Award for Broadcasting in 1981. With the publication of *Lake Wobegon Days*, Keillor's reputation as a first-rate storyteller and humorist became firmly established.

"A Prairie Home Companion" Keillor's audience originally came from his live radio performances. Roy Blount Jr., writing in the *New York Times Book Review* about "A Prairie Home Companion," states that it was *"impossible* to describe. Everyone I have met who has heard it has either been dumbfounded by it, or addicted to it, or both." "The same is true of Keillor's prose," Blount continues, referring to a series of pieces written for the *New*

COMMON HUMAN EXPERIENCE

Keillor's written work and radio show both concern the lives of ordinary people living in the Midwestern United States. Other works that focus on life in the Midwest include the following:

Main Street (1920), a novel by Sinclair Lewis. Set in the fictional Gopher Prairie, Minnesota, and a best seller of its time, this story offers a satirical presentation of small-town life in the Midwest.

My Life and Hard Times (1933), an autobiography by James Thurber. In this work the author describes his life in Columbus, Ohio, the location that inspired many of his popular short stories.

Winesburg, Ohio (1919), a short story collection by Sherwood Anderson. This group of related short stories centers on the life of George Willard and other inhabitants of Winesburg who tell him about their loneliness and frustrations.

Yorker and collected in *Happy to Be Here: Stories and Comic Pieces* (1982).

Lake Wobegon Days In 1985 the publication of *Lake Wobegon Days* brought Keillor's small town to national prominence. Beginning with the first explorations of the French traders in the eighteenth century, Keillor goes on to describe the town's history up to the present day. But Lake Wobegon is, according to Mary T. Schmich in the *Chicago Tribune*, "a town that lies not on any map but somewhere along the border of his imagination and his memory." Lake Wobegon, in Keillor's stories, becomes a sort of American Everytown, "the ideal American place to come from," writes Peter A. Scholl. He continues:

> One of the attributes of home in Keillor's work is evanescence.... Dozens of his stories concern flight from Lake Wobegon, and the title of his radio show gains ironic force with the realization that it was adapted from the Prairie Home Lutheran cemetery in Moorhead, Minnesota; we are permanently at home only when we are gone.

Responses to Literature

1. How does Keillor's fiction compare with his radio show? Identify key similarities and differences in the content of each, citing examples to support your opinions.

2. Does Lake Wobegon seem realistic as a small town in the Midwest? In what ways does Keillor use fantastic, mythical, or absurd elements to create a larger-than-life portrait of the town?

3. In a 1985 review of *Lake Wobegon Days*, author Veronica Geng described the work as "a genuine work of American history." Do you agree? Support your opinion with examples from the book.

4. Why do you think Keillor's portrayal of small-town America has been so successful in an increasingly urban society?

BIBLIOGRAPHY

Books

Fedo, Michael W. *The Man from Lake Wobegon.* New York: St. Martin's Press, 1987.

Lee, Judith Tayoss. *Garrison Keillor: A Voice of America.* Jackson: University Press of Mississippi, 1991.

Scholl, Peter A. *Garrison Keillor.* New York: Twayne Publishers, 1993.

Web sites

A Prairie Home Companion with Garrison Keillor. Retrieved October 25, 2008, from http://prairiehome.publicradio.org. Last updated on October 25, 2008.

✸ Helen Keller

BORN: *1880, Tuscumbia, Alabama*

DIED: *1968, Westport, Connecticut*

NATIONALITY: *American*

GENRE: *Nonfiction*

MAJOR WORKS:
The Story of My Life (1903)
The World I Live In (1908)

Overview

Author and activist Helen Keller was America's most famous deaf and blind citizen, and the first to graduate from college. Her 1903 autobiography *The Story of My Life* and her lifelong work advocating on behalf of people with disabilities earned her the gratitude and admiration of people around the world.

Works in Biographical and Historical Context

Debilitated by Illness at Nineteen Months Helen Adams Keller was born on June 27, 1880, in Tuscumbia, a small town on the Tennessee River in northwest Alabama. Her father, Arthur Henley Keller, was editor of a weekly local newspaper, the *North Alabamian*, and had been a captain in the Confederate Army. Kate Adams Keller, Helen's mother, was from a socially prominent Memphis family. Helen Keller was born with normal faculties of sight and hearing. At nineteen months she developed an illness—believed at the time to be scarlet fever, although it may have been meningitis—which,

Helen Keller   *Keller, Helen, photograph. The Library of Congress.*

having run its course, left her completely blind and deaf. Keller was a terror in the household, as no one, least of all Captain Keller, had the heart to discipline her and she ran more or less wild.

An Inseparable Companion In 1886, the Kellers visited a distinguished eye doctor in Baltimore who advised them to consult with scientist and inventor Alexander Graham Bell, who had devoted considerable time to exploring education options for the deaf. He later became one of Keller's closest friends and mentors. Bell referred the family to Michael Anagnos, director of the Perkins Institute for the Blind. The following year, Anagnos sent Anne Sullivan to Tuscumbia. Sullivan became Keller's teacher. The two became inseparable companions and intimate friends until Sullivan's death in 1936. The daughter of illiterate Irish immigrants, she had been orphaned at age ten and had herself spent time at the Perkins Institute until an operation partially restored her vision.

Emergence from Darkness at Age Seven At age seven, Keller began to emerge from her severely limited world. She learned the manual alphabet, a system of sign language also expressed into the palm, and she became adept at reading lips. She also learned to speak, though imperfectly. Much of the time she was forced to have books read to her by having them spelled into her hand by someone familiar with the manual alphabet. This indispensable labor on the part of her friends and Sullivan, who for many years received no salary from the heavily indebted Captain Keller, left Keller with a deep understanding of sacrifice. "My education," she writes in *Midstream: My Later Life* (1929), "was accomplished in the tragedy of my teacher's life."

Reputation Fueled by Stories of Genius Keller's acquisition of language was described in the first of her nine autobiographical books, *The Story of My Life* (1903), in nearly miraculous terms. In *Midstream* she amends this unrealistic representation of the daily, painstaking labor required of teacher and pupil. Keller and "Teacher," as she referred to Sullivan, soon began to spend their winters in Boston, where they could utilize the resources of the Perkins Institute. By age ten, Keller was a public figure in her own right, as Americans and people around the world were fascinated by reports of her education. Sullivan's role in her development was acknowledged to Keller's satisfaction in 1931, when Temple University awarded Sullivan an honorary doctorate.

Keller's reputation as a phenomenon continued to grow, fueled in part by highly sensational stories of her genius and the telepathy by which she supposedly communicated with her teacher. Much of Keller's teen years was spent in New York City attending a new school for the deaf, riding horses in Central Park, and making the acquaintance of many influential and well-connected persons, including author Mark Twain, who became her defender against critics and those who doubted her cognitive abilities.

Preparing for Radcliffe Keller attended the Cambridge School for Young Ladies to prepare for Radcliffe College, and while in Boston, received instruction from the Episcopal bishop Phillips Brooks, who impressed upon her his view of religion as universal love, a perspective that left a deep imprint on Keller's religious and political convictions. Another important early mentor was John Hitz, Bell's secretary, who introduced her to the work of Emanuel Swedenborg, the eighteenth-century theologian. Keller's long meditation on Swedenborg influenced her in profound ways.

In 1896, Captain Keller died, heavily in debt, and Keller was forced to rely increasingly on affluent patrons, such as Andrew Carnegie, for support. In 1900, Keller entered Radcliffe as a regular student, where she studied languages, history, and literature, graduating cum laude in 1904. Keller was the first deaf-blind person to attend college, and her difficulties at Radcliffe were considerable. All of the lectures and most of the reading had to be spelled into Keller's hand by Sullivan. Sullivan's already weak eyesight was increasingly strained by the Radcliffe experience, and Keller's health was regularly in danger of breaking down. One lasting consequence of this struggle was their introduction to a Harvard instructor, John Macy, who learned the manual alphabet and began to assist Keller with her reading.

While at Radcliffe, Keller was encouraged by an instructor to publish her themes, which were first serialized in *Ladies' Home Journal*, then expanded into book form as *The Story of My Life*. Keller's first attempt at authorship sold well, further strengthening her standing as a public person who could command an audience. *The Story of My Life*—edited by Macy, who provides a substantial introduction—includes an account of Keller's life through her sophomore year at Radcliffe. In later years she expressed conflicting attitudes toward the Radcliffe experience.

Graduation and Life in Wrentham Keller left Radcliffe with her degree in 1904, and she and Sullivan purchased a home in Wrentham, Massachusetts, with the help of a wealthy benefactor, J. P. Spaulding. They lived in Wrentham until 1916, when finances forced them to sell and relocate to a more modest home in Forest Hills, New York. At Wrentham, Keller had leisure to begin her study of the conditions of the blind, and her notoriety made her an obvious spokesperson for the handicapped. In 1905, Sullivan married Macy, who was already a significant member of their household, periodically relieving Sullivan from the exhausting work of reading to her pupil, and an important intellectual and literary influence on Keller. At Wrentham, Keller engaged in the only serious romance of her life, with the socialist editor Peter Fagan. Fearing to lose control over their charge, however, Sullivan and Kate Keller managed to stop the planned elopement, and the remainder of Keller's life was by default thrown into her activism and public service.

The World I Live In (1908) is Keller's answer to the critics who suggested she wrote about things she had not seen and used a language of reference inappropriate and misleading for a deaf and blind person. Perhaps the most personal of her highly personal books, *The World I Live In* is a compelling attempt to re-create the daily reality of the deaf-blind, with special attention given to her ability to distinguish between objects by her sense of feel, sounds (and thus events) by their vibrations, and personalities by the clasp of a hand or the tread of a foot.

Joining the Socialist Party From 1909, when Keller joined the Socialist Party, through the early 1920s, was her most intense period of activity as a socialist, after which she primarily worked as a spokesperson and fund-raiser for the American Foundation for the Blind. Keller was a radical and friend of prominent radicals such as Emma Goldman and John Reed, an outspoken party member, and a frequent contributor to the *New York Call*, the leading socialist daily. The FBI maintained a permanent file on her activities. Keller concurred with the revolutionary tenor of the labor movement, in particular the Industrial Workers of the World (IWW), and wrote vigorously in defense of their legal rights. With the exception of her opposition to Adolf Hitler during World War II, Keller was a lifelong pacifist and a courageous critic of war.

"The Modern Woman," published in three installments in the *Metropolitan Magazine* in 1912 (eight years

LITERARY AND HISTORICAL CONTEMPORARIES

Helen Keller's famous contemporaries include:

Seán O'Casey (1880–1964): Irish author and socialist playwright who is best known for his sensitive treatment of women in his dramatic works and his influence on J. M. Synge and Samuel Beckett.

Virginia Woolf (1882–1941): English author known for her stream-of-consciousness technique and the feminist work *A Room of One's Own* (1928).

James Joyce (1882–1941): Irish author best known for his novels *Ulysses* (1922) and *Finnegans Wake* (1939).

Adolf Hitler (1889–1945): Leader of the Nazi Party, Hitler was an Austrian-born German political leader who is best known for precipitating World War II and the genocide of approximately six million Jews during the Holocaust.

Ezra Pound (1885–1972): American poet, critic, intellectual, and major figure of the Modernist movement of the twentieth century.

before women were granted the right to vote with the Nineteen Amendment to the Constitution) and collected in *Out of the Dark: Essays, Letters, and Addresses on Physical and Social Vision* (1913), is Keller's masterpiece of social criticism.

Public Speaking Career and Profound Loss Tapping into public curiosity about her condition, Keller began her career of public speaking in 1913, initially as a means of financial support. Following World War I, many suffered a loss of optimism and tastes in literature changed. In an attempt to relieve their ongoing financial difficulties, Keller agreed to appear in a movie version of her life, released as *Deliverance* in 1919. In 1920, Keller assisted Roger Baldwin with the founding of the American Civil Liberties Union. As a last resort to ease their financial difficulties, Keller and her teacher went on the vaudeville circuit from 1920 to 1924, sharing billing with other human "oddities."

The death of Sullivan in 1936 was a severe blow to Keller. In 1939, having sold their home in Forest Hills, Keller and Polly Thompson—who had been hired to help Keller when Sullivan's health declined—moved into a home in Westport, Connecticut, known as Arcan Ridge, built for them by a benefactor, where Keller spent the remainder of her life when not pursuing her considerable travels in the United States and abroad. In 1946, while Keller was traveling in Europe on behalf of the American Foundation for the Overseas Blind, her home at Arcan Ridge burned. Although funds were quietly raised to rebuild, the fire destroyed Keller's possessions accumulated

over a lifetime; countless papers and documents, including valuable correspondence; and the better portion of her original manuscript of her book on Sullivan.

Keller suffered a stroke in 1961 and passed the remainder of her life as an invalid at her home in Connecticut. In 1964, President Lyndon Johnson awarded her the Presidential Medal of Freedom. She died on June 1, 1968. Family members disregarded her request for a Swedenborgian service, and a Presbyterian minister presided at the funeral in Westport. Following her cremation, a large nondenominational memorial service, led by U.S. chief justice Earl Warren, was held in Washington, and Keller's ashes were interred in the columbarium of the Chapel of St. Joseph of Arimathea at the National Cathedral.

Works in Literary Context

Keller's writing was influenced by the work of Emanuel Swedenborg, H. G. Wells, and her lifelong teacher and companion, Anne Sullivan, among others. Sullivan taught Keller to use language as if she were a sighted person, so that in her early books in particular, she writes about visual and auditory features of the external world that she could not herself witness. This "verbalism," as it was called, provoked strong criticism of Keller's published work over the course of her career.

Social Blindness Throughout her published work, Keller makes effective rhetorical use of the connections between her personal experience and her social vision. Given her unusual situation, she had to rely exclusively on her hands as point of access to the world. In "The Hand of the World" (1912), she juxtaposes her hand of knowledge with the hand of labor that was kept in chains by industrial oppression. Keller made a similar connection using the metaphor of blindness to compare her physical condition with the negligence and the dangerous indifference of big industry, which she characterized as a form of social blindness.

Women's Rights Keller frequently turned her attention to issues particular to women, first speaking at a women's suffrage march in 1913. Women's suffrage was a key component to Keller's social vision, as she believed that public policies pertaining to the family, the production of food, the role of children in labor, and national policies of war required women's voices for the collective good of the nation. Keller spoke out against the legal harassment of birth-control advocates, arguing that industrial capitalism encouraged high birth rates in order to exploit child labor, and that consequently it was in the interest of the race to "hold back the power of propagation."

Keller is credited with bringing attention to the needs of people with disabilities, fighting for women's suffrage, and advancing the socialist agenda. She continues to inspire readers through her writings, many of which are still in print. The numerous depictions of Keller and her teacher Anne Sullivan—adapted for both theater and film—continue to bring Keller's story to audiences worldwide. Perhaps the most famous of these was *The Miracle Worker*, by Willliam Gibson, first a Broadway play in 1959 and then an Academy Award–winning film in 1962.

Works in Critical Context

Just when Keller was starting to draw public attention as a child prodigy, she was accused of plagiarism, prompting critics to denounce her as a fraud. The matter was resolved when it was revealed that the story she had published was one she had forgotten she had been read. Helen Keller was a celebrity long before her works were widely read, so when she published an autobiography, it was immediately read by many. Inspired by the content of her autobiography, *The Story of My Life*, many critics praised the work and Keller's perseverance. She was only twenty-two years old when the work came to print. The book's editor, John Albert Macy, writes, "What is remarkable in her career is already accomplished, and whatever she may do in the future will be but a relatively slight addition to the success which distinguishes her now." And he was correct in his assessment. Even her debut on the vaudeville circuit was a success. A review published in the *New York Times* reads, "Helen Keller has conquered again, and the Monday afternoon audience at the Palace, one of the most critical and cynical in the world, was hers." Keller's social views provoked considerable resistance—Andrew Carnegie said that she needed a spanking—from an admiring public that saw in her a cathartic mixture of vulnerable womanhood and Victorian purity. Of her lifetime accomplishments, Alden Whitman, writing for the *New York Times*, states that "she became an artful and subtle writer; she led a vigorous life; she developed into a crusading humanitarian who espoused Socialism; and she energized movements that revolutionized help for the blind and the deaf."

Responses to Literature

1. How does Keller use hands as a symbol of her political and social philosophies? Why do you think she chose that particular symbol?

2. Discuss the relationship between Helen Keller and her teacher Anne Sullivan. In your opinion, did Anne Sullivan's background have an effect on the development of Keller's political and social philosophies? Do you think Sullivan deserves credit as a collaborator on Keller's works? Why or why not?

3. Do you get the impression from her work that Keller was a feminist? Why or why not? Provide examples from her work to support your opinion.

4. Use your library or the Internet to research modern laws related to disabled persons. Explain the impact Helen Keller had on the rights of the disabled.

COMMON HUMAN EXPERIENCE

Helen Keller emphasized the oppressive power of big industry in both her writing and public speeches. Other works that explore similar socialist themes include the following:

The Communist Manifesto (1848), a political manuscript by Karl Marx and Friedrich Engels. This influential work calls workers to overthrow the bourgeois and calls for the establishment of a classless society without private property.
The New Worlds of Old (1908), a nonfiction book by H. G. Wells. This work provides an account of the author's experience with the socialist movement in England and America.
God and the State (1882), a political manuscript by Mikhail Bakunin. This work forwards the theory of collectivist anarchism, in which all societal property is shared not equally but based on the length of an individual's productive output.

BIBLIOGRAPHY

Books

Braddy, Nella. *Anne Sullivan Macy: The Story behind Helen Keller*. Garden City, N.Y.: Doubleday, Doran, 1933.

Brooks, Van Wyck. *Helen Keller: Sketch for a Portrait*. New York: Dutton, 1956.

Lash, Joseph P. *Helen and Teacher: The Story of Helen Keller and Anne Sullivan Macy*. New York: Delacorte, 1980.

Golden, Kristen and Barbara Findlen, eds. *Remarkable Women of the Twentieth Century: 100 Portraits of Achievement*. New York: Friedman/Fairfax, 1998.

Hermann, Dorothy. *Helen Keller: A Life*. New York: Knopf, 1998.

Shnookal, Deborah. *Helen Keller*. Melbourne: Ocean Press / London: Global Press, 2002.

Longmore, Paul K. and Lauri Umansky, eds. *The New Disability History: American Perspectives*. New York and London: New York University Press, 2001.

Miller, John and Anjelica Huston, eds. *Legends: Women Who Have Changed the World: Through the Eyes of Great Women Writers*. Novato, Calif.: New World, 2001.

Nielsen, Kim E. *The Radical Lives of Helen Keller*. New York: New York University Press, 2004.

Periodicals

Giffin, Frederick C. "The Radical Vision of Helen Keller." *International Social Science Review* 4 (1984): 27–32.

Wolf, Kathi. "Helen Keller, Radical: What They Never Taught You about an American Heroine." *Utne Reader* 76 (July/August 1996): 16.

⚜ John F. Kennedy

BORN: *1917, Brookline, Massachusetts*

DIED: *1963, Dallas, Texas*

NATIONALITY: *American*

GENRE: *Nonfiction*

MAJOR WORKS:

Why England Slept (1940)
Profiles in Courage (1955)
A Nation of Immigrants (1959)
To Turn the Tide (1962)

Overview

The thirty-fifth President of the United States as well as the first Roman Catholic and youngest man to hold that office, Kennedy was a consummate politician whose eloquent vision for the nation and his assassination in 1963 make him one of the most intriguing figures in American history.

Works in Biographical and Historical Context

Irish-Catholic Immigrants with High Ambition
John F. Kennedy's Irish-Catholic ancestors fled famine in

John F. Kennedy   *Kennedy, John F., photograph. The Library of Congress.*

Ireland during the nineteenth century, and hoped to find a better way of life in the United States. After leaving Dunganstown in 1849, Kennedy's great-grandfather, Patrick Kennedy, arrived in Boston, Massachusetts. His son, Patrick J. Kennedy Jr. found success in the arenas of banking and Boston politics after owning three saloons in the city. His son, Kennedy's father, Joseph Patrick Kennedy, went on to gain admission to Harvard College, thereby breaking through social barriers that favored Boston's Protestant elite. Joseph later married Rose Elizabeth Fitzgerald, Kennedy's mother.

Joseph Kennedy established a reputation for using ruthless business practices in banking, real estate, stock market speculation, motion pictures, and liquor imports—all of which brought him immense wealth. After making contributions to the 1932 presidential campaign of Franklin D. Roosevelt, Joseph Kennedy was appointed to several government positions: chairman of the Securities Exchange Commission (1934–36), chairman of the Maritime Commission (1937), and ambassador to Great Britain (1937–40). However, he retreated from the public eye abruptly after expressing the belief that Nazi leader Adolf Hitler could not be defeated. By this act he alienated himself from Roosevelt and inadvertantly checked the momentum of his political career.

A Childhood of Competition and Illness   The second of nine highly competitive children, John F. Kennedy was born on May 29, 1917, in Brookline, Massachusetts. Of his siblings, Joe Jr., the eldest, was their father's favorite and he prided himself on being a role model for the rest of the children. Throughout his youth, John Kennedy was frequently ill with complications from what was later diagnosed to be Addison's disease, a failure of the adrenal glands. In fact, his condition was so serious that last rites were administered by a Catholic priest on four separate occasions. His image-conscious father hid Kennedy's low energy, chronic pain, impaired immune functioning, and exceptionally high fevers from public view as much as possible; he feared that a weak image would damage Kennedy's image as a future leader. To explain Kennedy's condition, his father offered stories about injuries from athletics and war. Extending upon his efforts to shape the image of each of his children, Joseph Kennedy took care to educate them in international affairs and politics, impressing upon them the legacy of the family's success.

When Kennedy was ten, the family moved to an estate outside of New York City, in Bronxville. Apart from a two-year stay in London, England, the Kennedys stayed in New York until 1941, when they began to split their time between seasonal homes in Hyannis Port, Massachusetts; Florida; the French Riviera; and various apartments in New York City. Kennedy eventually came to manage his disease with regular injections of steroids, which altered his physical appearance, causing inflammation of his face and a discoloration of his skin.

Harvard Education   Kennedy was educated at Choate, an Episcopal preparatory school located in Connecticut. His higher education, however, was delayed due to illness. Later, from 1936 until 1940, he attended Harvard University, where he majored in history. During that time, he took leave to act as a personal secretary for his father, who was traveling through Europe as the U.S. ambassador to Great Britain. In 1940, Kennedy was awarded an honors degree for his thesis, which analyzed England's slow response to German rearmament. The next year, Kennedy made his debut in the literary world by republishing this thesis under the title *Why England Slept*. The work quickly became a best-seller.

Romantic Life   During his youth, Kennedy developed a reputation as a ladies' man. Shortly after his election to the U.S. Senate in January 1953, he began dating Jacqueline (Jackie) Bouvier, who was thirteen years his junior. Born to a wealthy family in Southampton, New York, Jacqueline was working as a reporter for a Washington newspaper. She challenged and stimulated Kennedy with her sharp wit and vibrant spirit. That September, they married in Newport, Rhode Island, in an event labeled the social event of the year.

Marital Trouble   Although the Kennedys maintained an apartment in Boston, most of their time was spent living in the Georgetown neighborhood of Washington, D.C. They spent their weekends at a country house near Middleburg, Virginia, where Jacqueline rode horses. Despite outward appearances, the Kennedys' marriage was deeply troubled. Kennedy's infidelities, Jacqueline's dislike of politics, and tension between the two families all contributed to the strain on the bond between the couple, which appeared dire at several points during their marriage. Things were made even worse in 1956 when Jacqueline's first child was stillborn and John was away in Europe, partying. Two healthy children followed: Caroline Bouvier Kennedy in 1957 and John Fitzgerald Kennedy Jr. in 1960. A fourth child, Patrick Bouvier Kennedy, was born August 7, 1963, but died two days later.

Service in the Navy during World War II   In September of 1941, not long before the United States entered World War II (1939–45), John Kennedy enlisted into the U.S. Navy, following in the footsteps of his older brother Joe, Jr. After being accused and then cleared of being a Nazi spy, in part due to his romantic involvement with an F.B.I. employee, he was sent to the Pacific theater of war with a patrol torpedo (PT boat) squadron. While stationed in the Solomon Islands, a boat under his command was destroyed by a Japanese destroyer, leading some people to question his abilities as a commander. However, he was commended for his heroism in rescuing his injured crew. He was later awarded the Navy and Marine Corps Medal and the Purple Heart, and proclaimed a hero by the *New York Times*. A recurring back problem forced him to return home not long after the incident.

LITERARY AND HISTORICAL CONTEMPORARIES

John F. Kennedy's famous contemporaries include:

Pablo Casals (1876–1973): Casals was a renowned cellist who expressed his admiration for President Kennedy. Kennedy invited him to perform in a chamber concert at the White House on November 13, 1961.

Robert Lowell (1917–1977): Widely considered the most influential American poet of the mid-twentieth century, Lowell is acclaimed for his mastery of diverse forms, intense expression of personal concerns, and candid commentary on social and moral issues.

Albert Camus (1917–1960): Camus was an Algerian-born French author. He was the first African to be awarded the Nobel Peace Prize in Literature in 1957.

Ella Fitzgerald (1917–1996): Fitzgerald was a highly influential jazz legend known for her exceptional vocal range and her ability to scat (to improvise using invented nonsense words).

William S. Burroughs (1914–1997): An American author and painter associated with the Beat Generation, Burroughs is most famous for his novel *Naked Lunch* (1959).

Durong Van Minh (1916–2001): Military advisor to Ngo Dinh Diem, Durong Van Minh was President of South Vietnam for three months after Ngo Dinh Diem was assassinated in 1963.

Return to Political Career   In 1946, Kennedy won election to the U.S. Congress from Massachusetts' 11th District, and then served as a representative for parts of Boston and Cambridge. In 1952, Kennedy challenged Henry Cabot Lodge Jr. for the U.S. Senate from Massachusetts and won by a narrow margin. He was easily reelected in 1958.

Best-seller Establishes Intellectual Reputation   Throughout the 1950s Kennedy amassed a reputation based largely on his charisma, good looks, and family name. However, in 1955, he published a best-selling book, *Profiles in Courage*, which marked Kennedy as an intellectual in politics and poised him for the presidency. The book consists of biographical sketches of political leaders who had risked everything, displaying exceptional courage, for their convictions. With the help of his father's connections and active efforts lobbying influential friends, the book won the 1956 Pulitzer Prize. Kennedy accepted the prize despite indications that the book had been coauthored by his speechwriter Theodore Sorensen, thereby arousing suspicions about Kennedy's integrity and reputation. Those suspicions were never resolved during Kennedy's lifetime and extended into the historical assessments

COMMON HUMAN EXPERIENCE

In *Profiles in Courage*, Kennedy writes about the troubled relationship between politics and values. Other works that explore this theme include:

The Republic (c. 380 B.C.E.), a philosophical text by Plato. In this highly influential work, Plato defines justice and "the good life" with regard to how values tend to serve the interests of the ruler.

Mr. Smith Goes to Washington (1939), a film directed by Frank Capra. While serving in the U.S. Senate, Jefferson Smith (played by James Stewart) is betrayed by his colleagues, wrongly accused of abusing his power, and must persevere in the face of immense pressure to defend his innocence.

All the King's Men (1946), a novel by Robert Penn Warren. This work tells the story of political morality and its corruptions as they surface in the rise and fall of a potential dictator.

of his legacy. Kennedy published a third book, *A Nation of Immigrants*, in 1959. It surveys the history of immigration to the United States and makes suggestions for future policy.

Presidency Kennedy won the 1960 presidential election against Richard Nixon by an extremely narrow margin. During his brief term as president, Kennedy narrowly averted nuclear war during the Cuban missile crisis in 1962 and worked for détente with the Soviet Union. In an effort to contain communism, he expanded the U.S. military and committed to aiding the government of South Vietnam. In the domestic arena, Kennedy established the Peace Corps and mandated a manned mission to the Moon by 1970. He also enforced laws to integrate American society and uphold the civil rights of African-Americans, which later led to passage of the Civil Rights Act in 1964.

Assassination and Aftermath On November 22, 1963, while riding in a motorcade through Dallas, Texas, Kennedy was assassinated by rifle fire. Vice President Lyndon B. Johnson was sworn in as President of the United States that same day. The news of Kennedy's death spread throughout the United States, profoundly shocking everyone. Two days later, on November 24, Kennedy's suspected assassin, Lee Harvey Oswald, a disgruntled leftist who had defected to the Soviet Union and then returned, was himself shot to death by Jack Ruby, a Dallas nightclub operator. An enormous emotional reaction reverberated for decades after these events and contributed to the plethora of conspiracy theories about Kennedy's death, many of which are still debated by scholars today.

Works in Literary Context

In speeches, books, and essays, Kennedy challenged complacent attitudes on a number of disturbing issues facing the country and urged active citizenship among Americans, inspiring hope for peace and prosperity in a nuclear age mired in cold war. His work was heavily influenced by contributions from and collaborations with his speechwriter Theodore Sorsensen.

Political Rhetoric In *Profiles in Courage*, Kennedy makes a case for courage as one of the most important human virtues by presenting nine individuals who exhibited the trait during their political career. In it, he persuades readers by commenting on the flaws of each person as well as their more admirable qualities, thus creating hope for honesty in the political arena. Kennedy continued to generate hopeful expectations upon his entry into the presidency, proclaiming: "Let the word go forth from this time and place, to friend and foe alike, that the torch has been passed to a new generation of Americans." Perhaps most memorably, Kennedy exhorted Americans to action with this memorable directive: "And so, my fellow Americans: ask not what your country can do for you—ask what you can do for your country."

Influence and Legacy During his lifetime, Kennedy captured the imagination of the public, who largely considered him a dynamic leader during difficult times. He is among the most-discussed presidents in the history of the United States, who continues to be the subject of a wide body of historical scholarship. He is remembered for his somewhat ironic personality, hesitant contribution to the civil-rights movement, leadership during the cold war, and tragic early death.

Works in Critical Context

Concerning Kennedy's presidency, critics have marked an abrupt change of style from past administrations, and some have noted Kennedy's use of the relatively new medium of television to imprint his distinct style. Some have doubted the sincerity of his rhetoric, citing the illusory nature of his language in relation to his actual achievements in both foreign and domestic policy. Yet many others have seen wit, intelligence, and linguistic simplicity in his thought that often articulate the concerns of cultural diversity and appeal for unity of purpose.

Three of Kennedy's four books remain in print today. *Why England Slept* may now be of only historical interest, as the product of Kennedy's undergraduate years. However, Kennedy's observations about immigration in *A Nation of Immigrants* continue to be valued as the issue remains a vexed one in the twenty-first century. The book appears in a modern edition, with an introduction by Kennedy's brother, Senator Edward M. Kennedy, and a foreword by the national director of the Anti-Defamation League. However, it is *Profiles in Courage* that remains Kennedy's most notable and lasting literary achievement.

Profiles in Courage Upon its publication, *Profiles in Courage* became an immediate best-seller, receiving praise from scholars and critics across the United States. In her book *The Fitzgeralds and the Kennedys* (1991), Doris Kearns Goodwin explains that *Profiles in Courage* was "written in clear, dramatic language" such that it "found a responsive chord with the 'silent generation'—the generation that had seemingly opted for conformity and success." Indeed, Cabell Phillips of the *New York Times* found that the book was "the sort to restore respect for a venerable and much abused profession." However, the question of authorship of *Profiles in Courage* remains subject to lively debate. As John A. Barnes explains in his biography *John F. Kennedy on Leadership* (2005), "While biographers such as Herbert Pamet have concluded that Kennedy did little or no work on *Profiles in Courage*, new research, especially by author Thurston Clark has revealed otherwise." However, in his autobiography, *Counselor: A Life at the Edge of History* (2008), Kennedy's speechwriter Theodore C. Sorensen writes that he "did a first draft of most of the chapters."

Responses to Literature

1. Consider Kennedy's definition of immigrants in *A Nation of Immigrants*. Do you agree that "every American who has ever lived, with the exception of [Native Americans], was either an immigrant himself or a descendent of immigrants?" If not, how would you define immigrants?

2. Does Kennedy succeed in persuading you as a reader of the need to reform the 1952 Immigration and Nationality Act in *A Nation of Immigrants*? What rhetorical techniques does he use and to what extent are they effective?

3. How does Kennedy define courage in *Profiles in Courage*? Can you identify someone in politics today who has exhibited this type of courage? To what extent is Kennedy's book relevant today?

4. Did your reading of Kennedy's writing influence your opinion of him? *Profiles in Courage* has a reputation for being a highly influential book. Do you think reading it has influenced your beliefs or attitudes toward the world?

BIBLIOGRAPHY

Books

Bernstein, Irving. *Promises Kept*. New York: Oxford University Press, 1991.

Bishop, Jim. *A Day in the Life of President Kennedy*. New York: Random House, 1964.

Brogan, Hugh. *Kennedy*. New York: Longman, 1996.

Brown, Thomas. *JFK: History of an Image*. Bloomington, Ind.: Indiana University Press, 1988.

Dallek, Robert. *An Unfinished Life: John F. Kennedy, 1917–1963*. Boston: Little, Brown, 2003.

Goodwin, Richard N. *Remembering America: A Voice from the Sixties*. Boston: Little Brown, 1988.

Hoare, Stephen. *The Assassination of John F. Kennedy*. Takoma Park, Md.: Dryad Press, 1988.

Hunt, Conover. *JFK for a New Generation*. Dallas, Tex.: Southern Methodist University Press, 1996.

Levine, I. E. *John Kennedy: Young Man in the White House*. Bellmore, N.Y.: Marshall Cavendish, 1991.

Lowe, Jacques. *Camelot: The Kennedy Years*. Kansas City, Mo.: Andrews and McMeel, 1996.

Mayer, Robert. *JFK*. New York: Dutton, 1989.

Pietrusza, David. *John F. Kennedy*. San Diego.: Lucent Books, 1997.

Randall, Marta. *John F. Kennedy*. New York: Chelsea House, 1988.

Reeves, Richard. *President Kennedy: Profile in Power*. New York: Simon & Schuster, 1993.

Schwab, Peter, and J. Lee Shneidman. *John F. Kennedy*. Boston: Twayne, 1974.

✹ Robert F. Kennedy

BORN: *1925, Brookline, Massachusetts*

DIED: *1968, Los Angeles, California*

NATIONALITY: *American*

GENRE: *Nonfiction*

MAJOR WORKS:

Speech Given on the Death of Martin Luther King, Jr. (1968)

Thirteen Days: A Memoir of the Cuban Missile Crisis (1969)

Overview

During the 1960s, Robert F. Kennedy distinguished himself as a politician who advocated for good housing for the poor, an end to hunger, for high-quality education, and equal rights for all Americans. However, the dream that Robert F. Kennedy might become the next president of the United States was shattered in 1968 when, like his brother John, Robert was assassinated. Although Bobby Kennedy's life came to a tragic early end, he left behind an enduring legacy as both a social reformer and a writer. His book, *Thirteen Days: A Memoir of the Cuban Missile Crisis* (1969), and the much-anthologized speech he composed in memorial of Martin Luther King, Jr., are classics of their respective forms.

Works in Biographical and Historical Context

Born into an Extraordinary Family Robert Francis Kennedy was born into the large Kennedy family on November 20, 1925. His parents, Joseph and Rose, already had six children, and after Bobby was born, they would have two more. The Kennedys were a wealthy Irish

Robert F. Kennedy   *Kennedy, Robert F., photograph. The Library of Congress.*

Catholic family living in Brookline, Massachusetts. Politics surged in the blood of the Kennedy children, perhaps a vestige of Rose's father, who had been mayor of Boston. At the age of four, the family relocated to New York where Kennedy attended school in Bronxville. He was not an extraordinary student, although he did display the true love of reading that his parents had instilled in him. Joseph and Rose raised their children according to a strict code of values. They emphasized hard work and dedication, and Kennedy absorbed these values eagerly.

The Kennedys relocated to Great Britain in 1936, after President Franklin Delano Roosevelt elected Joseph to be an ambassador in England. The Kennedys were given the royal treatment during their time in England, but returned to the States when World War II broke out in 1939. Back in America, despite mediocre grades, Kennedy managed to gain attendance to Harvard University in 1944, where he made more of a name for himself as a football player than as someone who excelled at academics. Kennedy's life would continue to be affected by World War II. During the conflict, his brother, Joe, Jr., was killed while serving in the Air Force. Joe's death kept

Robert from having to enter battle during his own stint in the Navy, but the tragic event set a precedent of early deaths that would haunt the Kennedy family for years to come.

After his time in the military, Kennedy returned to school, first completing his studies at Harvard; then attending the University of Virginia Law School. While there, his sister Jean introduced him to her roommate, a young woman who had quite a lot in common with Kennedy. Both he and Ethel Skakel were from Catholic families, came from great wealth, and had tremendous ability in sports. Kennedy and Ethel fell in love.

Mounting a Career in Politics   In 1946, Robert Kennedy took his first steps into the arena of politics. His older brother, John, was running for congress in Massachusetts, and Robert was enlisted to manage the campaign. Kennedy's next political move was a controversial one as he worked as a legal assistant to Senator Joseph McCarthy, who was mounting his infamous hunt for communists in the United States. The Kennedy family were all strong McCarthy supporters and anti-communists, despite the fact that McCarthy's efforts were eventually regarded as little more than a self-serving witch hunt. During that time, Kennedy made a decidedly less controversial move when he wed Ethel in 1950.

In 1952, Kennedy continued helping his brother John's political career when he worked as campaign manager for the elder Kennedy's run for the Senate. Eight years later, he managed John's successful presidential campaign. Once in office, John offered his brother a position in his cabinet as attorney general. Although Kennedy was reluctant to accept the job—fearing that some would regard it as mere nepotism—he eventually took the position.

Throughout John F. Kennedy's presidency, Robert Kennedy worked as a close advisor to his brother, who had quite a lot to handle during the socially and politically volatile decade that was just beginning. The early 1960s were marked by civil rights demonstrations that often exploded into violence. The Kennedys worked to keep such violence from escalating, and became strong supporters of the civil rights movement, which sought to win equal rights for black Americans. In October of 1962, the Kennedys faced one of the greatest challenges any politician would ever face, when the communist Soviet Union moved nuclear-armed missiles into Cuba, just ninety miles from Florida, and pointed them at the United States. The thirteen-day period, during which the Kennedys raced to defuse this potentially disastrous situation, came to be known as the Cuban Missile Crisis. The Kennedys hoped to avoid going to war, but refused to accept a missile threat at such proximity. Robert Kennedy suggested a naval quarantine approach, and the Soviets eventually began to retreat.

Kennedy chronicled the terrifying events of the Cuban Missile Crisis in his book, *Thirteen Days: A Memoir of the Cuban Missile Crisis.* In his book, Kennedy provides an enthralling account of the face-off between the U.S. and the Soviet Union that could have resulted in nuclear war. His writing is clear and direct as he details the events with an insider's perspective. Despite the simplicity of his prose, the sheer tension of the situation makes the book a decidedly dramatic read. The book became a bestseller when it was published in 1969.

The Tragic Deaths of Family and Friends Tragedy may have been averted when Robert Kennedy helped resolve the Cuban Missile Crisis, but it reared its head again on a fateful day in November 1963. During a motorcade trip through Dealey Plaza in Dallas, Texas, John F. Kennedy was assassinated by Lee Harvey Oswald. Whether or not Oswald had accomplices has been a matter of debate ever since that day. Robert Kennedy was stunned by the second untimely death of one of his brothers. Perhaps no one else in the family was as close to John as was Robert.

Following John F. Kennedy's death, Robert Kennedy continued to serve as attorney general under Lyndon B. Johnson until 1964, when he decided to run for the Senate in New York. Upon winning the race, Robert was not the only senator in the Kennedy family; his brother, Edward "Ted" Kennedy, was a senator in Massachusetts, continuing the family's role in politics. His commitment to civil rights and to fighting poverty endeared him to many Americans. In spite of his wealthy background, Kennedy was empathetic to the trials of America's poor. His tours through impoverished communities throughout the nation made him aware that many others were not as lucky as he.

Robert Kennedy, and the nation as a whole, suffered a horrible blow on April 4, 1968 when Martin Luther King, Jr., was assassinated. The death of the man who had done so much to forward the civil rights movement inspired Kennedy to compose another significant piece of literary significance. Like *Thirteen Days: A Memoir of the Cuban Missile Crisis*, the speech Kennedy delivered on the day of King's death is a direct, clearly phrased meditation on a moment that would live in infamy. He began simply, speaking to the American people with the intimacy of a friend: "I have bad news for you, for all of our fellow citizens, and people who love peace all over the world, and that is that Martin Luther King was shot and killed tonight." Kennedy goes on to praise a man who "dedicated his life to love and to justice for his fellow human beings, and died for that effort." Kennedy also conjures an image of racial unity when he says, "But the vast majority of white people and the vast majority of black people in this country want to live together, want to improve the quality of our life, and want justice for all human beings who abide in our land" and ends with the eloquent plea to "tame the savageness of man and make gentle the life of this world." The speech would be regarded as a classic of oration and appear in numerous anthologies over the years.

A Tragic End to a Promising Career Kennedy boldly chose not to support President Johnson's increasing mili-

LITERARY AND HISTORICAL CONTEMPORARIES

Kennedy's famous contemporaries include:

Kenneth Keating (1900–1975): Keating had a nearly thirty-year political career in the United States, first serving in Congress, then as a senator from New York. In 1964, Robert F. Kennedy defeated Keating and succeeded him as senator from New York the following January. Keating later served as Ambassador to India and Israel.

Joseph McCarthy (1908–1957): McCarthy became well-known outside of Wisconsin (where he served as a senator) when he embarked on a public hunt for communists in the United States during the 1950s. Robert F. Kennedy worked with the senator as his legal assistant and made McCarthy the godfather of his daughter, Kathleen.

Lyndon B. Johnson (1908–1973): Johnson served as Vice President under John F. Kennedy before he succeeded Kennedy after his assassination in 1963. Johnson was elected president in 1964, and established a program he called the "Great Society" that consisted of progressive changes in civil rights laws, health-care programs, and the situation of the nation's poor. Conversely, Johnson was also responsible for escalating the war in Vietnam.

Richard M. Nixon (1913–1994): Nixon was the thirty-seventh President of the United States, as well as former Vice President under Dwight D. Eisenhower. Nixon's presidency ended in embarrassment when he resigned following the infamous Watergate Scandal in which he authorized a burglary of the Democratic Party headquarters at the Watergate Hotel in Washington D.C. Nixon was elected president in 1968, the year that Robert Kennedy ran on the Democratic ticket.

Norman Mailer (1923–2007): Mailer was an American novelist and "New Journalist" who ran unsuccessfully for mayor of New York in 1969.

Gore Vidal (1925–): Vidal is an American-born novelist, playwright, and essayist, and a relative by marriage to Jacqueline Kennedy Onassis, John F. Kennedy's widow.

Fidel Castro (1926–): Castro was prime minister of Cuba for seventeen years before becoming president of the country in December of 1976, a position he held until February of 2008. The revolutionary, communist leader urged the Soviet Union to attack the U.S. during the Cuban missile crisis.

tary campaign in communist Vietnam. Kennedy called for an end to the Vietnam War through peaceful negotiations. Johnson, however, called on his military to mount bombing campaigns in the Asian country, formerly colonized by the French. Many politicians and Americans denounced

COMMON HUMAN EXPERIENCE

In his book, *Thirteen Days: A Memoir of the Cuban Missile Crisis*, Robert F. Kennedy gives a harrowing account of two weeks in which the United States came dangerously close to nuclear war with the Soviet Union. Other works about nuclear war include:

On the Beach (1957), a novel by Nevil Shute. Set in the near future of 1963, following the fictional nuclear conflict of World War III, *On the Beach* is a chilling tale of the devastation the Northern Hemisphere has experienced as a result of chemical pollution. Since the Southern Hemisphere is the only area of Earth with habitable land, the planet's survivors begin to migrate, even though the South will soon be contaminated as well.

Red Alert (1958), a novel by Peter George. George's tense, terrifying novel describes the mistaken initiation of a nuclear attack from the U.S. upon the Soviet Union. The military must scramble to diffuse the situation before all-out nuclear war is ignited.

Dr. Strangelove or: How I Learned to Stop Worrying and Love the Bomb (1964), a film by Stanley Kubrick. Originally conceived as a faithful adaptation of Peter George's novel, *Red Alert*, film director Stanley Kubrick decided that the events in the novel were simply too absurd to handle seriously, so he decided, instead, to make his film a black comedy. With its ridiculously named characters like Major "King" Kong and its "laugh in the face of doom" humor, *Dr. Strangelove* is widely considered to be one of the most brilliant American comedies ever produced.

The Fate of the Earth, a nonfiction work by Jonathan Schell. Journalist Schell's measured, but devastating, description of the likely effects of a nuclear war—and his criticism of military policies that threaten to initiate one—helped educate the American public and build the anti-nuclear movement in the early 1980s.

The Day After (1983), a television movie by Nicholas Meyer. The chilling movie, *The Day After*, follows a select cast of American citizens as they deal with the aftereffects of a nuclear war between the United States and the Soviet Union. The film shows them dealing with their devastated environment and radiation sickness. The film was highly controversial and sparked much public debate about nuclear proliferation.

Kennedy for his anti-war sentiments, but many—particularly the increasingly politically-aware younger generation—supported him as a new brand of politician. On March 31, 1968, Kennedy announced that he intended to run for president.

Kennedy's campaign was an impressive one. In the California primaries, he defeated Senator Eugene McCar-

thy, who had been shaping up as the only other viable candidate for the party's nomination. On June 4, 1968, Kennedy gave an address to his supporters at the Ambassador Hotel in Los Angeles. While the candidate was passing through the hotel's kitchen, a young Palestinian man named Sirhan Sirhan assassinated Robert Kennedy.

Works in Literary Context

Political Memoir In the second half of the twentieth century, politicians often composed their memoirs as a means to preserve their political legacy in their own words, apologize for some wrongdoing, or "set the record straight" on some controversial issue. One of the first examples of the political memoir arrived in 1947 when former Secretary of State James F. Byrnes published *Speaking Frankly*, an account of his time in office. The political memoir would not become a prominent genre until the 1960s, when CIA director Allen W. Dulles, Secretary of State Dean Acheson, Secretary of Defense Robert McNamara, and Senator Robert F. Kennedy published their memoirs. Today, the political memoir is a major genre, responsible for bestselling books by former president Bill Clinton, his wife Senator Hillary Clinton, and President Barack Obama.

Eulogy A eulogy is a speech written in praise of a person, often composed after that person has died. The word is a derivation of the Greek words for "you" and "word." Although eulogies are often given during funeral services, certain religions—such as Catholicism—generally do not include them. Eulogies in praise of public figures have occasionally achieved a degree of literary fame outside their original contexts. The eulogy that Robert F. Kennedy gave in honor of slain civil rights leader, Martin Luther King, Jr., is one of the most famous eulogies and has often been anthologized in literary collections. Other famous eulogies include actor Ossie Davis's eulogy of human rights activist Malcolm X and comedian John Cleese's eulogy for friend and partner in comedy Graham Chapman.

Works in Critical Context

Thirteen Days: A Memoir of the Cuban Missile Crisis Robert F. Kennedy's posthumously published memoir has received its share of praise. A review in *The New York Times Book Review* by David Schoenbrun declared, "As a principal figure in resolving the crisis Robert Kennedy brings to it extraordinary authority, with his own insights, perspectives and very important revelations of the decision-making process at the highest level, on the brink of nuclear holocaust.... Above all, perhaps his most valuable contribution is the way he recounts the events of what, superficially, seems to have been exclusively a military crisis, while constantly posing moral and philosophical problems." However, the book has also been called into question by critics who debate its accuracy regarding the events of the Cuban Missile Crisis. In 2008, diplomat

Richard Holbrooke wrote in *The New York Times*: "In 'Thirteen Days'...Bobby Kennedy carefully edited his account of [the negotiations] to remove any hint of a deal on Turkey. But almost from the beginning, many people suspected the truth, and looking back on it today, it may seem surprising to see how hard the Kennedys sought to conceal it."

Responses to Literature

1. The famous speech that Robert F. Kennedy gave on the day Martin Luther King, Jr., was assassinated is notable for both its quality and for the fact that King, himself, was also a fine speech maker. Read Kennedy's speech, then read King's famous "I Have a Dream" speech. What are the differences in their respective styles? What are the similarities?

2. Robert F. Kennedy uses a quote from the Greek poet Aeschylus in his speech about Martin Luther King, Jr. Why do you think Kennedy chose to include this quote in his speech? How does it affect the speech?

3. Robert F. Kennedy's book, *Thirteen Days: A Memoir of the Cuban Missile Crisis*, is unique for both the events it describes and the way it is written. Read the book and explain how his style of writing affects the story he tells. Does his style enhance the story or detract from it? Support your response with specific details from the book.

BIBLIOGRAPHY

Books

Clarke, Thurston. *The Last Campaign: Robert F. Kennedy and 82 Days That Inspired America*. New York: Henry Holt and Co., 2008.

Eppridge, Bill. *A Time it Was: Bobby Kennedy in the Sixties*. New York: Abrams, 2008.

Halberstam, David. *The Unfinished Odyssey of Robert Kennedy*. New York: Random House, 1969.

Newfield, Jack. *Robert Kennedy: A Memoir*. New York: Dutton, 1969.

Schlesinger, Arthur M., Jr. *Robert Kennedy and His Times*. New York: Mariner Books, 2002.

Thomas, Evan. *Robert Kennedy: His Life*. New York: Simon & Schuster, 2002.

Periodicals

Holbrooke, Richard. "Real W.M.D.'s." *The New York Times* (June 22, 2008).

Web Sites

Death of Martin Luther King Speech by Robert F. Kennedy: April 4th 1968. Accessed December 9, 2008, from http://www.famousquotes.me.uk/speeches/John_F_Kennedy/8.htm.

Robert F. Kennedy Memorial.com. *Robert F. Kennedy Memorial*. Accessed December 9, 2008, from http://www.rfkmemorial.org.

❀ William Kennedy

BORN: *1928, Albany, New York*

NATIONALITY: *American*

GENRE: *Fiction*

MAJOR WORKS:
Ironweed (1983)

Overview

After struggling in obscurity, Kennedy has become a major voice in contemporary American letters. An author of regionalist literature whose works examine universal themes, Kennedy is best known for his novel *Ironweed* (1983), which won both the 1983 National Book Critics Circle Award for fiction and the Pulitzer Prize for Fiction.

William Kennedy   *Kennedy, William, photograph. AP Images.*

LITERARY AND HISTORICAL CONTEMPORARIES

Kennedy's famous contemporaries include:

Martin Luther King Jr. (1929–1968): an American minister and orator who is recognized as the driving force of the civil rights movement in the United States during the 1960s.

Kurt Vonnegut (1922–2007): Best known as the author of *Slaughterhouse-Five* (1969), Vonnegut is acknowledged as a major voice in American literature and applauded for his satirical depictions of modern society.

Daniel Keyes (1927–): American author best known for his novel *Flowers for Algernon* (1966), a poignant story of a mentally handicapped man who temporarily acquires extraordinary intelligence.

Allen Ginsberg (1926–1997): American author most famous for his poem "Howl" (1956), which is considered to be a seminal work of the Beat Generation.

Jack Kerouac (1922–1969): American author best known as the key figure of the artistic and cultural phenomenon of the 1950s known as the Beat Movement; his best-known novel, *On the Road* (1957), depicts the counterculture lifestyle of the Beats.

Works in Biographical and Historical Context

Irish Catholic Roots   Kennedy was born in Albany, New York, on January 16, 1928, to William Joseph and Mary Elizabeth McDonald Kennedy, whose Irish ancestors had settled in North Albany several generations before. Kennedy was reared in North Albany, a predominantly Irish Catholic neighborhood, often called the North End or Limerick. He attended Public School 20, was an altar boy at Sacred Heart Church, and even aspired to the priesthood. In his nonfiction work *O Albany!* (1983), however, he emphasizes that his religious aspirations lasted until about the seventh grade, when he began drawing cartoons, printing his own newspaper, and was "fixated on the world of print."

Discovering Roots by Way of Puerto Rico   Having developed a love for journalism, Kennedy worked on his high school newspaper at Christian Brothers Academy, became executive editor for the Siena College newspaper, and worked for the *Post Star* in Glens Falls, New York, as sports editor and columnist. After he was drafted into the army in 1950, Kennedy became a journalist for the Fourth Division's newspaper in Europe, which was still recovering from World War II. After his discharge in 1952, he worked for newspapers in both Albany and Puerto Rico, eventually moving into editorial positions.

Kennedy married Ana Daisy (Dana) Segarra while in Puerto Rico. He also enrolled in Saul Bellow's creative writing class at the University of Puerto Rico at Río Piedras. In 1983, Kennedy told Joseph Barbato that Bellow was "very, very encouraging" and confirmed Kennedy's belief that "I had something to say."

Kennedy had eagerly left Albany in search of his muse and thought Puerto Rico would be the catalyst. Indeed it was, but with an ironic twist. After trying to write stories about Puerto Rico—but failing because he felt like a tourist and could not write convincingly about the island and its people—he finally discovered his literary turf when he began poring over picture histories of Albany from 1842, 1867, and 1899.

When he returned to Albany in 1963 to care for his ailing father, Kennedy wrote a series of articles about Albany that served as the genesis for *O Albany!* Although nominated for a Pulitzer Prize for some of his Albany articles, Kennedy realized that his hometown provided the natural setting and material for his fiction and abandoned his journalistic career. In his first novel, *The Ink Truck* (1969), Kennedy introduces the city of Albany from the perspective of a mentally unstable syndicated columnist whose unsuccessful efforts to disable a newspaper firm culminate in a desperate attempt to drain an ink truck of its cargo. The book initially received mixed reviews.

Persistence Pays Off   In the 1970s, Kennedy initiated a trilogy of novels set in Albany during the Great Depression that interweaves related characters and events in the manner of William Faulkner's works about the fictional region of Yoknapatawpha County. Although Kennedy garnered several positive reviews for *Legs* (1975) and *Billy Phelan's Greatest Game* (1978), the first two volumes of his triad, both books failed commercially. When *Ironweed* (1983) was rejected by thirteen publishers—including Viking, its eventual publisher—Kennedy's future seemed even bleaker, until Saul Bellow admonished Viking for not publishing *Ironweed* and even prophesied that this novel would be both a commercial and a literary success. Not only was *Ironweed* a financial boon for Viking, but it also won both the 1983 National Book Critics Circle Award for fiction and the Pulitzer Prize for Fiction. Kennedy's earlier novels were republished in 1983.

Other Literary Efforts Prove Successful   In addition to his fictional Albany cycle, Kennedy published *O Albany!*, which combines a nostalgic memoir of his youth in Albany with a nonfiction examination of the city's neighborhoods, ethnic history, and Irish American political dominance under Mayor Dan O'Connell. On his fifty-fifth birthday he received a $264,000 grant from the John D. and Catherine T. MacArthur Foundation; he used part of that money to establish the Writers Institute in Albany. He coauthored the screenplay for *The Cotton Club* (1984) with Francis Ford Coppola, and the film version of *Ironweed* premiered in Albany in 1987. In his novel *Quinn's Book* (1988), Kennedy examines the history of Albany from the perspective of a young orphan who witnessed the progress of the Underground

Railroad, the chaos of the Civil War, and the New York City draft riots of 1864.

In 1993 Kennedy was elected to the American Academy of Arts and Letters. That year he also completed a three-act play, *The Angels and the Sparrows*, taken from his novel *Very Old Bones* (1992). Kennedy and his only son, Brendan, have collaborated on two children's books, *Charlie Malarkey and the Belly-Button Machine* (1986) and *Charlie Malarkey and the Singing Moose* (1994).

Kennedy published two more works of fiction set in Albany, *The Flaming Corsage* (1996) and *Roscoe* (2002). He continues to submit book reviews and articles to literary journals, including *Harper's* and the *New York Times Book Review*.

Works in Literary Context

Drawing on his extensive knowledge of the history, idiom, and people of his hometown of Albany, New York, Kennedy depicts the outcasts, vagabonds, derelicts, and gangsters that he encountered in his childhood and, later, as a journalist. Kennedy often embellishes the stark realism of his settings with surrealistic events and imagery, prompting many critics to link his approach with magic realism, a technique in which fantastic events are presented within the scope of rational experience. Kennedy's focus on such concerns of the typical Irish Catholic novel as sin, suffering, and redemption has prompted critics to compare his works to those of novelist James T. Farrell.

Blending History with Lyrical Fantasy With *Ironweed*, Kennedy garnered acclaim for his command of historicity and setting and his use of varied prose styles. Written in an ironic, elegiac mode, this novel compassionately yet unsentimentally relates the story of Billy Phelan's alcoholic vagrant father, Francis, a haunted but resilient man who returns to Albany after having accidentally dropped and killed his thirteen-day-old son twenty-two years earlier. Using language and imagery suggestive of classical myth, as well as allusions to James Joyce's epic novel *Ulysses* (1922) and Dante Alighieri's *Purgatory* (1308–1321), Kennedy shifts from past to present and from brutal realism to lyrical fantasy as Francis confronts the ghosts of friends and family members. Like *Ulysses*, Francis visits the spiritual underworld and feels compelled by a sense of fate to face mortal dangers and the vengeful furies of his past in hopes of atoning for his guilt and shame.

The Criminal Perspective In *Legs*, Kennedy uses multiple viewpoints and a mix of styles to examine the gruesome facts and legends surrounding the life of Jack "Legs" Diamond, an actual Albany gangster. In his six years of research, Kennedy discovered so many conflicting facts and myths that the novel finally emerged as a study of American responses to criminality. Although some reviewers objected to Kennedy's unsentimental acceptance of American crime and violence, others commended his suspenseful narrative control. *Billy Phelan's Greatest Game* is based on the actual 1933 kidnapping of the nephew of former Albany mayor Dan O'Connell. This

COMMON HUMAN EXPERIENCE

Kennedy's novels are often framed by the cycle of sin, suffering, and redemption. Other works that share this frame include the following:

The Divine Comedy (1308–1321), an epic poem by Dante Alighieri. One of the most famous works of Italian literature, this poem tells of Dante's journey through three realms of the dead—Hell, Purgatory, and Paradise.

Crime and Punishment (1866), a novel by Fyodor Dostoyevsky. This book tells the story of Raskolnikov, who murders a pawnbroker and steals her money, suffers deeply, turns himself in, and awaits redemption in exile.

The Catcher in the Rye (1951), a novel by J. D. Salinger. This story of troubled young man Holden Caulfield's coming of age is read by some to parallel Christ's tale of sin, suffering, and redemption.

work centers on a gambler and hustler who must decide between preserving his street image and satisfying the demands of Albany's political figures by informing on the kidnappers.

Works in Critical Context

Kennedy's early novels did not receive much critical attention when they first appeared. He was known primarily as a respected and versatile journalist. *Columbia Journalism Review* writer Michael Robertson cites former editor William J. Dorvillier's comment that Kennedy was "one of the best complete journalists—as reporter, editor, whatever—that I've known in sixty years in the business." But, when Kennedy's 1983 novel *Ironwood* won the Pulitzer Prize, his fiction was given new life: three early novels were reissued and became best sellers.

Ironweed Kennedy believes that *Ironweed* is the best of his first four novels, and critics agree. In his *New Republic* review of the book, William H. Pritchard claims that *Ironweed* is the best of Kennedy's novels and "should bring this original and invigorating novelist to the attention of many new readers, especially since it is written in a language that is vital throughout." In a review for *Time*, Paul Gray praises the novel's characterizations and plot, mentions that *Legs* and *Billy Phelan's Greatest Game* are being republished, and then states: "Those who wish to watch a geography of the imagination take shape should read all three and then pray for more." Some critics even speculated about the impact *Ironweed*'s success would have on Kennedy's career. For example, in his review for *Newsweek*, Peter S. Prescott writes:

> William Kennedy has written good fiction before, which has largely gone unnoticed. This novel... should place him among the best of our current

American novelists. In its refusal to sentimentality, its freshness of language and the originality with which its author approaches scenes well worn before his arrival, *Ironweed* has a sense of permanence about it.

Responses to Literature

1. Describe your reaction to Kennedy's use of talking ghosts in *Ironweed*. Why do you think Kennedy chose to use this technique? Do you think it is effective?

2. How are the events that take place at night different from those that take place during the day in *Ironweed*?

3. In *Ironweed* Francis labels himself a bum. How does he compare to your conception of "bums"? What generalizations can you make about the author's feelings about the homeless in Albany?

4. What significance do cats have for Jack in the novel *Legs*?

BIBLIOGRAPHY

Books

Edinger, Claudio. *The Making of Ironweed*. New York: Penguin, 1988.

Reilly, Edward C. *William Kennedy*. Boston: Twayne, 1991.

Van Dover, J. K. *Understanding William Kennedy*. Columbia: University of South Carolina Press, 1991.

Periodicals

Agrest, Susan. "Tough Guy with a Golden Touch." *Hudson Valley Magazine* (July 1987): 42–49, 72.

Allen, Douglas R., and Mona Simpson. "The Art of Fiction CXI—William Kennedy." *Paris Review* 31 (Fall 1989): 35—59.

Beuttler, Bill. "O Albany." *American Way* 26 (January 1, 1993): 60–66, 85–87.

Black, David. "The Fusion of the Past and Present in William Kennedy's *Ironweed*." *Critique* 27 (Spring 1986): 177–184.

Bonnetti, Kay. "William Kennedy: An Interview." *Missouri Review* 8, no. 2 (1985): 71–86.

Clarke, Peter P. "Classical Myth in William Kennedy's *Ironweed*." *Critique* 27 (Spring 1986): 167–176.

Croyden, Margaret. "The Sudden Fame of William Kennedy." *New York Times Magazine* (August 26, 1984): 33, 43, 52–53, 57, 59, 64, 68, 70, 73.

Reilly, Edward C. "A William Kennedy Bibliography." *Bulletin of Bibliography* 48 (June 1991): 61–74.

———. "Dante's *Purgatorio* and Kennedy's *Ironweed*: Journeys to Redemption." *Notes on Contemporary Literature* 17 (May 1987): 5–8.

———. "William Kennedy's Albany Trilogy: Cutting Through the Sludge." *Publications of the Arkansas Philosophical Association* 12 (Spring 1986): 43–55.

Smith, Tom. "Very Bountiful Bones: An Interview with William Kennedy." *Weber Studies* 10 (Winter 1993): 21–44.

Tierce, William. "William Kennedy's Odyssey: The Travels of Francis Phelan." *Classical and Modern Literature* 8 (Spring 1988): 247–263.

Whittaker, Stephen. "The Lawyer as Narrator in William Kennedy's *Legs*." *Legal Studies Forum* 9, no. 2 (1985): 157–164.

Williams, Don. "William Kennedy: An Interview by Don Williams." *Poets & Writers* 22 (March/April 1994): 42–49.

Web sites

William Kennedy. Retrieved October 19, 2008, from http://albany.edu/writers-inst/wjkennedybio.html.

❁ Jane Kenyon

BORN: *1947, Ann Arbor, Michigan*

DIED: *1995, Wilmot, New Hampshire*

NATIONALITY: *American*

GENRE: *Poetry*

MAJOR WORKS:
From Room to Room (1978)
The Boat of Quiet Hours (1986)
Let Evening Come (1990)
Constance: Poems (1993)

Jane Kenyon *Bloodaxe / Writer Pictures*

Overview

Jane Kenyon epitomized many poets of the 1970s and 1980s: she was a feminist of sorts and an academic brought up through the ranks of little-magazine publication, who then won contracts with the independent presses. Her residence in New Hampshire and her marriage to well-known poet and editor Donald Hall were major influences on her work.

Works in Biographical and Historical Context

Marriages Real and Poetic   Born in Ann Arbor, Michigan, on May 23, 1947, Kenyon grew up in the Midwest. She attended the University of Michigan and earned her BA in 1970 and her MA in 1972. It was during her time at the University of Michigan that Kenyon met the well-known poet Donald Hall. She married him on April 17, 1972.

Her first book, *From Room to Room* (1978), is the poetic diary of a honeymoon, in which a young wife explores the spaces between her husband and herself, and her new and former homes. Several poems concern short spates of the husband's absence; "The First Eight Days of the Beard" explores the gender gap; and a furtive poem, "Cleaning the Closet," shows the wife finding a dusty suit her husband has not worn since his father's funeral. Turning to see her husband watching, she "fumble[s] to put the suit / back where it was." This last line of the poem tells the story of the book. There is no "back where it was" for either husband or wife.

The overlay of the new on the old continues as the main character progresses through her first anniversary, chronicled in "Year Day," revamping room after room of her new home. As she does so, she encounters the emblems, both universal and personal, of her female lineage, a grandmother's tablecloth here, an heirloom thimble there. Kenyon's young wife is alert to these emblems, perceiving them with a new feminist consciousness. So it is that, when she finds one of her gray hairs floating in the mop water, she feels akin to those who have scrubbed the floor before her, feels her life "added to theirs."

The Second Wave Feminist Movement   *From Room to Room* appeared during the Second Wave feminist movement, which began during the Civil Rights Movement of the 1960s. In contrast to the First Wave, which was focused primarily on women's suffrage, the Second Wave aimed to elevate the status of women at all levels of society. In particular, some women fought to escape their roles as wives and homemakers. Others reacted strongly against these efforts, advocating a return to the Victorian model of The Feminine Idea—a back-to-quilting approach to feminism. This coincided with the defeat of the Equal Rights Amendment to the U.S. Constitution, which would have guaranteed equal rights to all, regardless of gender.

Joining the Tradition of New England Poetry   In *From Room to Room* Kenyon asserts her connection to the New England poetic tradition less in her fairly standard rendering of that region than in her vocal style. Critics of this book hailed its simplicity but also mentioned Kenyon's thematic complexities and her masterful craftsmanship.

Kenyon closes *From Room to Room* with translations of six of Anna Akhmatova's poems. Clearly the two poets share concerns—for example, desire as reflected in the natural world—as well as musicality and economical imagery. Kenyon's follow-up to her first book was *Twenty Poems of Anna Akhmatova* (1985), which appears to be Kenyon's contribution to a feminist revision of the literary canon as well as a set of exercises in the economical poetic style Kenyon prefers.

Increased Poetic Flexibility   In *The Boat of Quiet Hours* (1986), Kenyon continues to employ a clear narrative framework for the poems, though a more flexible one than that of *From Room to Room*. The themes of her first book persist as well though this collection shows Kenyon's range, her keen alertness to the concrete world, and her ability also to render the abstract.

Going On in the Face of Life's Hardships   In 1989, Kenyon learned that her husband was suffering from colon cancer. The title of Kenyon's *Let Evening Come*

COMMON HUMAN EXPERIENCE

Kenyon's battle with depression appears often in her poetry. Other works that explore struggles against depression include the following:

The Bell Jar (1963), a novel by Sylvia Plath. This story captures one woman's experiences with mental illness.
Darkness Visible: A Memoir of Madness (1989), a memoir by William Styron. This short work chronicles the author's struggle with depression.
Prozac Nation: Young and Depressed in America (1994), an autobiography by Elizabeth Wurtzel. This national best-seller tells the story of the author's struggle with major depression during her years as young writer.

(1990) is perhaps a response to this fact, formatted to the chores and routines of the same contemplative but disciplined speaker as her previous work—one who, upon hearing news of a loved one's recurring cancer, retains the capacity to "snap the blue leash onto the D-ring / of the dog's collar," to attend to "that part of life / [which] is intact." Dog-walking is recurrent in this collection of close to sixty poems, a repetition that may bring accusations of mundanity and manipulativeness. However, that Kenyon dares use this simple image of coping, of the mind strolling with itself as it waits for what the speaker dreads, is somehow affirming.

Evoking John Keats The poet John Keats, alluded to in *The Boat of Quiet Hours*, is a character in Kenyon's 1990 collection, who is evoked, in the speaker's reconstruction of his last days, in various guises. Kenyon's reference to Keats is refreshing because it clarifies her awareness that she is subject, as was he, to the criticism that she is a poet's poet. She baits this criticism in her poems by making the speaker register alarm at or resistance to public places, events, the uneducated, and the unwashed, opting for the privileged retreat to "the sound of pages turning, and coals shifting."

A Battle with Leukemia Her husband's treatment for colon cancer proved effective, and in 1993, a Emmy award-winning documentary about Kenyon's life with Donald Hall, entitled *A Life Together*, was released. Ironically, the following year Kenyon herself was diagnosed with leukemia. She died in April of 1995. During the last year of her life she had been working on *Otherwise: New and Selected Poems*, which was published in 1996. In 1999, a collection of Kenyon's essays, interviews, Akhmatova translations, and newspaper columns were published as *A Hundred White Daffodils*. Graywolf Press published a compilation of her poetry in *Collected Works* (2005).

Works in Literary Context

Kenyon is frequently compared to Robert Frost and Emily Dickinson, though such comparisons should be viewed as more evocative than exact. Her work is often discussed in the context of Donald Hall's. Kenyon's writing was influenced by her close interpersonal relationships and a variety of poets, including Anna Akhmatova, whose work she translated from Russian into English.

Quiet Violence Kenyon's writing contains much of what has been called "quiet violence." Kenyon's violence is leashed, and is thus more alarming. In "The Socks" one finds the wife folding her husband's socks into "tight dark fists," for example. The anger expressed is a woman's, more specifically a twentieth-century woman's, insofar as it expresses the conflict of one who has been trained to desire security but who is also very aware of its costs, the sacrificing of individuality and sensitivity. Clearer examples of this anger might be found in a poem in which a wife inures herself to the fact that she has crushed a pet cat beneath the wheels of her car. Her response is to focus on what color to repaint the house. In another poem she uses the vacuum cleaner's drone to block the noise of a man's felling of the eighty-year-old oak, the branches of which menace the house.

Kenyon's work is often discussed in the context of her early death from leukemia and her struggle with depression. She is known for her simple but emotionally powerful writing.

Works in Critical Context

Reviews of Kenyon's work were largely positive when it was first published; critics found her poetry accessible and emotionally salient. As her career progressed, however, she was sometimes criticized for not experimenting with other writing styles. But she was also praised for the consistent high quality of her work.

The Boat of Quiet Hours The reviewers of *The Boat of Quiet Hours* were virtually unanimous that, within her selected boundaries, Kenyon is formidable. But she was criticized for failing to flirt with excess, as if, having walked a tightrope above a host of similar poetry, she should also be required to attempt a somersault or two. That said, *The Boat of Quiet Hours* is more concerned with literary tradition than *From Room to Room*. Allusions—to John Keats's *Endymion* (1818), William Shakespeare's *Hamlet*, the Bible, and the plays of Anton Chekhov—abound. And one anonymous critic for the *Women's Review of Books* observed that the persona of these poems has clearly become a New Englander as evidenced, for example, by the lines "How long winter has lasted—like a Mahler / symphony, or an hour in the dentist's chair." According to reviewer Marianne Boruch in *American Poetry Review*, the poems in *The Boat of Quiet Hours* read "like entries in a day book, patient commentary on things worth gathering."

Responses to Literature

1. Kenyon grew up in a house filled with music. After reading her poems out loud, do you consider her poetry to be lyrical?

2. In what ways do you think Kenyon's recurring themes of "quiet violence" relate to the feminist movement and the struggle for women's rights? Provide examples from her work to support your opinion.

3. In her poem "Having it Out with Melancholy," how does Kenyon connect faith to her experiences of depression?

4. Most critics agree that Kenyon's writing is accessible. Discuss the literary techniques Kenyon uses to connect with readers. How does her work differ from other poets whose work you also find accessible?

BIBLIOGRAPHY

Books

Hall, Donald. *The Best Day the Worst Day: Life with Jane Kenyon*. Boston: Houghton Mifflin, 2005.
Timmerman, John H. *Jane Kenyon: A Literary Life*. Grand Rapids, Mich.: Eerdmans, 2002.

Periodicals

Garrison, D. "The Poetry of Jane Kenyon." *The New Yorker* (September 9, 1996): 90.
Ignatow, David. "For Jane Kenyon." *Poetry* 168, no. 5 (1996): 276.
Mattison, Alice. "Let It Grow in the Dark Like a Mushroom: Writing with Jane Kenyon." *Michigan Quarterly Review* 39 (2000), 121–37.

⊗ Jack Kerouac

BORN: *1922, Lowell, Massachusetts*

DIED: *1969, St. Petersburg, Florida*

NATIONALITY: *American*

GENRE: *Fiction, poetry, essay, nonfiction*

MAJOR WORKS:
On the Road (1957)
The Dharma Bums (1958)

Overview

Kerouac is best known as a key figure of the artistic and cultural phenomenon of the 1950s known as the Beat Movement. Kerouac's best known novel, *On the Road* (1957), depicts the counter-culture lifestyle of the Beats, which was marked by manic travel and experimentation with sex and drugs. While *On the Road* stunned the public and the literary establishment when it was first published, its continuing popularity and the proximity of Kerouac's philosophy to that of such honored Amer-

Jack Kerouac   *Kerouac, Jack, photograph. © Jerry Bauer. Reproduced by permission.*

ican writers as Walt Whitman and Henry David Thoreau have garnered Kerouac a place in the canon of American authors.

Works in Biographical and Historical Context

A Troubled Life   Born in a French-Canadian community in Lowell, Massachusetts, Kerouac was raised a Catholic and educated in parochial schools. He was a highly imaginative child who created an imaginary world of racing stables and sports teams, and who then wrote his own newspapers to report their performances. An outstanding athlete, Kerouac received a football scholarship to Columbia University but withdrew from school during the fall of his sophomore year. He was beginning to feel deeply troubled by the great shift in morals brought about by World War II. Kerouac joined the Navy in 1943 and was released after six months for psychological reasons. He worked the remainder of World War II as a merchant seaman and associated with the bohemian crowd around the Columbia campus that included Allen Ginsberg and William Burroughs. The publication of *On the Road* brought Kerouac sudden notoriety, and eight of his books were produced during the next few years, as publishers rushed to capitalize on his popularity. Kerouac's natural

LITERARY AND HISTORICAL CONTEMPORARIES

Kerouac's famous contemporaries include:

Allen Ginsberg (1926–1997): The American author most famous for his poem "Howl" (1956), which is considered a seminal work of the Beat Generation.

Neal Cassady (1926–1968): An American poet of the Beat Generation who exerted a large influence on Jack Kerouac. The character of Dean in *On the Road* is based on Cassady.

John F. Kennedy (1917–1963): The thirty-fifth president of the United States, who served from 1961 until his assassination in 1963. His brief period of leadership has been idealized by many Americans and is sometimes referred to as "Camelot."

Martin Luther King, Jr. (1929–1968): A highly influential leader of the Civil Rights Movement during the 1960s who worked to end racial inequality in the United States.

William S. Burroughs (1914–1997): American author who wrote *Naked Lunch* (1959), a novel whose title was chosen by Jack Kerouac.

shyness, however, kept him from enjoying his fame. Hhe was known to arrive at interviews intoxicated and failed in his sporadic attempts to withdraw from society to concentrate on writing. A sincere patriot and Catholic, Kerouac became increasingly bewildered by and alienated from his bohemian fans in the 1960s. He returned to the place of his birth in 1966 and moved with his mother to St. Petersburg, Florida, in 1968. He died from complications due to alcoholism in St. Petersburg in 1969 and was buried in Lowell.

The Beat Movement The Beat Movement, which took its name from Kerouac's abbreviation of "beatific," began in Greenwich Village and San Francisco as a reaction against the conservatism in America during the Cold War era. Many of Kerouac's friends in the Beat Movement served as the basis for the characters in his novels. Novelist William Burroughs and poet Allen Ginsberg are portrayed in *On the Road* as Old Bull Lee and Carlo Marx. Beat poet Gary Snyder was the inspiration for Japhy Ryder, the main character in one of Kerouac's better-known novels, *The Dharma Bums* (1958). Undoubtedly the single most influential personality in Kerouac's circle of friends, and the main character in both *On the Road* and *Visions of Cody* (published posthumously in 1972), was Neal Cassady. Kerouac saw the energetic, charismatic Cassady as the quintessential Beat figure and the last of a vanishing breed of American romantic heroes. Kerouac also cited Cassady's stream-of-consciousness writing style, exemplified in his

voluminous letters, as having inspired his own "spontaneous prose" technique.

Autobiographical Narration Kerouac considered his novels a series of interconnected autobiographical narratives in the manner of Marcel Proust's *Remembrance of Things Past* (1922–1931). The novels that make up "The Legend of Duluoz," as Kerouac called the totality of his works, include *Visions of Gerard* (1963), which pictures Kerouac's childhood as overshadowed by the death of his beloved brother Gerard at age nine; *Doctor Sax: Faust Part Three* (1959), a surrealistic depiction of Kerouac's boyhood memories and dreams; *Maggie Cassidy* (1959), which recounts Kerouac's first love; and *Vanity of Duluoz: An Adventurous Education 1935–46* (1968), which chronicles Kerouac's years of playing football at prep school and Columbia. In *On the Road*, Kerouac wrote about the late 1940s, focusing on the years of traveling and socializing with Neal Cassady, Allen Ginsberg, and William Burroughs. *Visions of Cody* (1972), viewed by many critics as a late revision of *On the Road*, retells the story in spontaneous prose. Kerouac wrote about his love affair in 1953 with an African American woman in *The Subterraneans* (1958), and his adventures on the West Coast learning about Buddhism from the poet Gary Snyder are chronicled in *The Dharma Bums* (1959). *Desolation Angels* (1965) covers the years just prior to publication of *On the Road*, while *Big Sur* (1962) displays the bitterness and despair Kerouac experienced in the early 1960s and his descent into alcoholism. Together these novels portray the birth, education, and eventual disillusionment of an American idealist.

Works in Literary Context

On the Road is considered, along with Allen Ginsberg's poem "Howl" (1956) and William S. Burroughs's novel *Naked Lunch* (1959), to be one of the seminal texts of the Beat Generation. Kerouac's work was influenced artists including Thomas Wolfe, Fyodor Dostoyevsky, Marcel Proust, Jack London, and James Joyce, among others.

Searching for Belief *On the Road* is considered the quintessential statement of the 1950s literary movement known as the Beat Generation. *On the Road* describes the growing friendship of two men, Sal Paradise and Dean Moriarty, and their crisscrossing journeys over the American continent. On a deeper level, it was the story of the narrator's search for religious truth and for values more profound than those embraced by most of mid-twentieth-century America. In both form and subject *On the Road* was completely unlike the serious fiction that dominated the era. Accordingly, it was ridiculed by Kerouac's contemporaries in the literary establishment, who viewed it as "an insane parody of the mobility of automotive America," according to Dennis McNally in *Desolate Angel: Jack Kerouac, the Beat Generation, and America*. *On the Road* spoke to many readers, however; it expressed their own unarticulated dissatisfaction with the repressive climate of the United States after World War II.

There have been critical attempts to compare *On the Road* thematically with such American classics as *The Great Gatsby* (1925). Because of his flamboyant and tragic life and career, Kerouac has been the subject of several recent critical biographies. Past speculation on whether Kerouac would merit a permanent place in contemporary American fiction has ended. He is now widely recognized, if begrudgingly by some, as an important contributor to American literature. His writing has influenced many artists, including Thomas Pynchon, Tom Robbins, Ken Kesey, Hunter S. Thompson, Jim Morrison, John Lennon, Bob Dylan, Tom Waits, Jerry Garcia, and Ben Gibbard.

Works in Critical Context

On the Road A barely fictionalized portrait of the late 1940s when Kerouac and his friends traveled back and forth across the United States, *On the Road* was not universally perceived as literature upon publication. His narrative convinced some critics that *On the Road* signaled the moral demise of Kerouac's generation. The *New Yorker* labeled Dean Moriarty a "wild and incomprehensible ex-convict." Gilbert Millstein, representing the opposing view, decreed in the *New York Times* that the publication of *On the Road* was a "historic occasion" and the immoderate lifestyle of the Beats was a "search for belief." Critics who shared this attitude focused on the spiritual quest theme of *On the Road* which, along with its picaresque narrative, made this novel a descendant of American road literature, represented by such works as Mark Twain's *Adventures of Huckleberry Finn* (1884). Although *On the Road* was said to inspire the peripatetic Hippie generation of the 1960s, later critics paid greater attention to Sal's disillusionment with the road at the conclusion of the novel. Some now view *On the Road* as depicting the conflict within Sal between the contemplative life of a writer and spiritually oriented person and the gregarious, adventurous life on the road.

Much of the sensationalism and subjectivity that marked early Kerouac criticism has been replaced by traditional, scholarly critical effort. Some recent critical studies show considerable interest in Kerouac's "spontaneous prose" method and view it as an extension of the "stream of consciousness" technique utilized by James Joyce.

Responses to Literature

1. Why does Sal see Dean as a hero in *On the Road*?
2. Discuss the role of women in *On the Road*. Are they depicted in realistic terms? Does Kerouac seem to promote a feminist view of women, or a more traditional view?
3. How does Sal's view of the American West change throughout *On the Road*?
4. Research the way in which *On the Road* was written. Would you consider the work "spontaneous," as it

---

COMMON HUMAN EXPERIENCE

The friendship between Sal and the people he meets during his travels are an integral part of *On the Road*. Other works that explore the theme of friendship include the following:

The Epic of Gilgamesh (c. 2150 B.C.E.), an epic poem. This work explores the friendship between a mythological king, Gilgamesh, and his friend, Enkidu.

Nicomachean Ethics, Books 8 and 9 (c. 350 B.C.E.), two nonfiction works by Aristotle. Part of a set of ten, these two books discuss three types of friendships: those of utility, those of pleasure, and those of "good."

Friendship: An Exposé (2007), a nonfiction book by Joseph Epstein. This work explores the complexities and changing nature of friendship.

---

has often been called? How does the structure and narrative style of *On the Road* impact your reading of the text?

BIBLIOGRAPHY

Books

Amburn, Ellis. *Subterranean Kerouac: The Hidden Life of Jack Kerouac*. New York: St. Martin's Press, 1998.

Charters, Ann. *Kerouac, A Biography*. San Francisco: Straight Arrow, 1973.

Clark, Tom. *Jack Kerouac*. San Diego, Calif.: Harcourt Brace Jovanovich, 1984.

Cook, Bruce. *The Beat Generation*. New York: Scribners, 1971.

Donaldson, Scott, ed. *On the Road: Text and Criticism*. New York: Viking, 1979.

Feied, Frederick. *No Pie in the Sky, The Hobo as American Culture Hero in the Works of Jack London, John Dos Passos, and Jack Kerouac*. New York: Citadel, 1964.

Fiedler, Leslie. *Waiting for the End*. New York: Stein & Day, 1964.

French, Warren. *Jack Kerouac*. Boston: Twayne, 1986.

Gifford, Barry and Lawrence Lee. *Jack's Book: An Oral Biography of Jack Kerouac*. New York: St. Martin's, 1978.

Hipkiss, Robert A. *Jack Kerouac, Prophet of the New Romanticism*. Lawrence, Kans.: University of Kansas Press, 1977.

Holmes, John Clellon. *Nothing More to Declare*. New York: Dutton, 1967.

Hunt, Tim. *Kerouac's Crooked Road: Development of a Fiction*. Hamden, Conn.: Archon, 1981.

Jarvis, Charles E. *Visions of Kerouac*. Lowell, Mass.: Ithaca Press, 1973.

McNally, Dennis. *Desolate Angel: Jack Kerouac, the Beat Generation, and America.* New York: McGraw-Hill, 1979.

Nicosia, Gerald. *Memory Babe: A Critical Biography of Jack Kerouac.* New York: Grove, 1983.

Parkinson, Thomas, ed. *A Casebook on the Beat.* New York: Crowell, 1961.

Tanner, Tony. *City of Words.* New York: Harper & Row, 1971.

Tytell, John. *Naked Angels: The Lives and Literature of the Beat Generation.* New York: McGraw-Hill, 1976.

Weinreich, Regina. *The Spontaneous Poetics of Jack Kerouac.* Carbondale, Ill.: Southern Illinois University Press, 1987.

⬤ Ken Kesey

BORN: *1935, La Junta, Colorado*

DIED: *2001, Eugene, Oregon*

NATIONALITY: *American*

GENRE: *Fiction, essays, nonfiction*

MAJOR WORKS:

One Flew Over the Cuckoo's Nest (1962)

Sometimes a Great Notion (1964)

Overview

A transitional figure linking the Beat generation of the 1950s with the counterculture movement of the 1960s, Kesey is best known for his first novel, *One Flew Over the Cuckoo's Nest* (1962).

Works in Biographical and Historical Context

Early Years in the Country Ken Elton Kesey was born in La Junta, Colorado, on September 17, 1935, to dairy farmers Fred A. and Geneva Smith Kesey. As a boy, Kesey learned to do farm chores, to appreciate country ways and rural values, and to feed his imagination on comic books and the adventure stories of Edgar Rice Burroughs and Zane Grey, after whom he would name his own first son. After a stint in the navy during World War II, Fred Kesey moved his family to Springfield, Oregon. There Ken and his younger brother, Joe (known as Chuck), fished in the clear streams and hunted in the lush forests of the Willamette Valley and the Cascade Mountains. At Springfield High School, Kesey boxed, wrestled, played guard on the football team, and was voted "most likely to succeed" by his graduating class. At the University of Oregon in Eugene, he was a speech and drama major, an Olympic-class wrestler, an actor, an aspiring playwright, and a popular member of Beta Theta Pi fraternity. In his junior year, Kesey married Faye Haxby, his high-school sweetheart. He graduated in 1957 with a bachelor's degree in speech

Ken Kesey   *Kesey, Ken, 1990, photograph. AP Images.*

and communications. James B. Hall, a professor of creative writing, was a mentor for Kesey at Oregon.

After graduation, Kesey worked for a year, played some bit parts in Hollywood films, and completed his first novel, *End of Autumn*, an unpublished story about college athletics. He entered the graduate writing program at Stanford University on a Woodrow Wilson fellowship for the academic year 1958–1959, studying under Malcolm Cowley, Wallace Stegner, Richard Scowcroft, and Frank O'Connor. Kesey's friends and fellow writing students during his time at Stanford included Wendell Berry, Larry McMurtry, Ernest J. Gaines, Tillie Olsen, and Peter Beagle. Kesey's house on Perry Lane in the town of Stanford became a gathering place for this extraordinary group of young writers.

In 1959, at the suggestion of Vik Lovell, a psychology graduate student, Kesey volunteered for government drug experiments with LSD and other hallucinogenic substances. In the summer of 1960, Kesey completed a novel called *Zoo*, also unpublished, about bohemian life in San Francisco's North Beach community. In 1961, he took a night job as a psychiatric aide in the Veterans Administration hospital at Menlo Park, California. His experiences with drugs and mental patients helped to prepare Kesey for the writing of *One Flew Over the Cuckoo's Nest*, the novel that quickly established him as a strong new voice in American fiction. The narrator is a patient in a mental ward, a half-breed Columbia Gorge Indian called Chief "Broom" Bromden, who feigns deafness and dumbness to avoid human interaction and withdraws into a cerebral fog when life in the ward becomes too painful.

Popular response to *One Flew Over the Cuckoo's Nest* was mainly positive, because many felt that the book illustrated in compelling detail the sources of social tension in America that led to the activism of the 1960s. The previous decade had been marked by a national fear of communism, expressed in the "McCarthy Era," a period in which many people who were viewed as outsiders, or potential communists, were treated with hostility and even brought before Congress in a series of infamous hearings presided over by Senator Joseph McCarthy. By the end of the 1950s young people, like the leaders of the Beat Generation, began to take a stand against the status quo and started what is now known as the counterculture movement. It was also during this time that a shift in attitude towards the mentally ill took place, and drug therapy began to replace electroshock therapy and psychosurgery.

Following publication of the book, Kesey moved to Florence on the Oregon coast to continue research for his next novel, *Sometimes a Great Notion* (1964), a story of the logging industry in the Pacific Northwest. There he rode with the local loggers to and from the woods in the crew trucks, called "crummies," and socialized with the townspeople and loggers in the local bars, learning the lore and the lingo he needed for his book. After four months, Kesey returned briefly to Perry Lane and then, when Perry Lane was bought by a developer, to La Honda, California, where he completed his logging novel in 1963 and established a base of operations for the friends and rock-music enthusiasts who became the Merry Pranksters.

Communal Living, Social Engineering, and Drug Use

After moving to La Honda, Kesey bought a 1939 International Harvester school bus, which he and the other Merry Pranksters used to make a cross-country trip coinciding with the publication of *Sometimes a Great Notion*. The revelers recorded the trip on forty hours of film called simply "The Movie." The movie was often the centerpiece of Prankster presentations known as "acid tests," communal high jinks with LSD that fueled the hippie movement in America. Kesey continued to experiment with communal living and drugs. The drug use entangled him in two arrests on possession charges, extended court proceedings, and, ultimately, a five-month jail term. He was released in November 1967.

A Shift towards Stability

After the hectic period following the release of *Sometimes a Great Notion* and culminating in his jail term, Kesey moved with his family to his brother's farm in Pleasant Hill, Oregon, eventually buying his own farm there. From March to June 1969 Kesey took his family to live in London, where he worked with the Beatles' Apple Records in an unsuccessful project to record authors reading from their own works. Upon his return to the farm at Pleasant Hill he refused to join the Pranksters on their trip to the Woodstock rock festival in August. They went without him, but when they returned they found a sign Kesey had erected in his driveway, stating simply and irrevocably, "No." This sign marked both the disbanding of the Pranksters and the beginning of a period of relative stability in Kesey's life.

For the twenty years between 1969 and 1989, Kesey was erratically productive, but more interested in film, autobiography, little-magazine publication, and environmental activism than in conventional fiction. The movie

version of *One Flew Over the Cuckoo's Nest* was released in late 1975. Although it was a popular success and won five Academy Awards, Kesey—who was hired and then fired as screenwriter—refused at first to see the film and sued for breach of contract, collecting a small out-of-court settlement.

Tragedy Strikes

The next few years were often difficult ones for Kesey, both professionally and personally. Tragedy struck in 1984 when his younger son, Jed, a wrestler like his father, was killed in a highway accident while on a University of Oregon wrestling-team trip. The death hit Kesey very hard. As a hedge against a similar future disaster, Kesey donated a large new traveling van to the University of Oregon wrestling team. In August of 1986, Viking published Kesey's *Demon Box*, consisting mostly of previously published material. The dedication is "To Jed / across the river / riding point."

A Bold Experiment Lures Kesey Back to Writing

In 1989–1990, over the course of three academic terms, Kesey and thirteen graduate students in the creative writing program at the University of Oregon wrote, rewrote, and presented a completed novel to Viking Penguin. The work was published as *Caverns*, by O. U. Levon (an anagram for "U. O. novel"). Set in 1934, the novel follows convicted murderer Dr. Charles Loach as he leads an expedition of colorful characters in search of important archaeological caves in the badlands of the West. A bizarre and interesting tale, the novel is mainly significant as a bold pedagogical experiment. More important, it also drew Kesey back to the writing of fiction.

Kesey wrote two novels during the 1990s. In *Sailor Song* (1992), his first novel since *Sometimes a Great*

Notion, Kesey explored a time in the twenty-first century when human misuse of the environment produces predictable results. His next novel, *Last Go Round* (1994), is a tribute to the roundup and the cowboy tradition it represents, especially as embodied by the historical figures of George Fletcher, a famous black bronco rider; Jackson Sundown, a Nez Perce Indian and rodeo champion; and Jonathan E. Lee Spain, a seventeen-year-old cowboy from Tennessee.

The Merry Pranksters Reunite In 1994, Kesey and other members of the Merry Pranksters reunited to tour the country once more, this time performing a musical written by Kesey about the millennium entitled *Twister: A Ritual Reality.*

Kesey spent the end of his life with Faye, his devoted wife for more than forty years, living close to the livestock and the land on their seventy-five acre farm in Pleasant Hill, about an hour's drive from Eugene, Oregon. Over the course of their marriage they raised children: sons Zane and Jed, daughter Shannon, and Kesey's daughter out of wedlock, Sunshine. In 1997, Kesey suffered a stroke. He died on November 10, 2001, after undergoing surgery to remove a tumor on his liver. He was sixty-six years old.

Works in Literary Context

Most of Kesey's fiction focuses on alienated and non-conformist individuals who attempt, through love, hope, rebellion, and humor, to overcome their limitations and to retain their sanity and self-respect. Kesey was influenced by many authors including Ernest Hemingway, Jack Kerouac, William Faulkner, and Friedrich Nietzsche, among others.

Dehumanization in Modern Society *One Flew Over the Cuckoo's Nest* examines the disturbing effects of dehumanization in modern society. The novel's message is that people have become things. Society, the Combine, has become an intimidating force for consumerism and conformity. The Combine and Big Nurse are presented as the enemies in the novel, but they are only symptoms of the malady, not the cause of it. The real enemy, Kesey shows, is the failure of self-reliance growing out of fear. McMurphy discovers that most of the men in the ward are there voluntarily; in succumbing to the pressure of powerful institutional forces the inmates have given permission for their own victimization. Confronted by the complexity of the world and their own incapacities, they have consigned themselves to passive and inglorious escape. Fearing disorder, Big Nurse has devoted her life to control for its own sake, becoming a servant of the system and a tyrant over the men in the cuckoo's nest, both a victim and a victimizer.

Redemption The most prominent theme in Kesey's fiction is the idea of human redemption as seen in the hero from the traditional American Western. In Kesey's arrangement of forces around this figure, it is always clear what the author is for and against. He is against determinism, whether in the form of historical pattern, natural or environmental circumstance, or social pressure. He is against technology, especially the kind that leads to dehumanization, displacement, and despoliation. He is against the heedless depletion of natural resources. He is against oppression and mindless conformity. He is for freedom, dignity, friendship, love, sex, laughter, music, clean air, pure water, fair play, and good stories. Again and again in Kesey's work this character stands tall to validate the concept of redemptive heroism, to demonstrate that what is best in the human spirit can, if properly nourished, overcome what is worst.

Ken Kesey and his work have influenced writers such as Lester Bangs, Hunter S. Thompson, and Chuck Palahniuk, and songwriters such as Jerry Garcia and Paul McCartney.

Works in Critical Context

Ken Kesey's reputation as a writer depends mainly on his first two novels, *One Flew Over the Cuckoo's Nest* and *Sometimes a Great Notion*, both of which are significant imaginative and artistic achievements. In contrast to his work that followed, these novels were well received and continue to generate scholarly attention.

One Flew Over the Cuckoo's Nest Reviews of *One Flew Over the Cuckoo's Nest* were largely positive and enthusiastic, but some were mixed, and a few were negative. Rose Geld observes in the *New York Herald Tribune Book Review* that "undoubtedly there will be controversy over some material in Ken Kesey's novel but there can be none about his talent." A reviewer for *Time* admired Kesey's power and humor, characterizing his book as "a strong, warm story about the nature of human good and evil, despite the macabre setting." W. J. Smith, writing in *Commonweal*, calls Kesey "a rough diamond" but chides him for vitiating the "real horror and significance" in the book by "some quite misplaced slapstick." A reviewer for *The New Yorker* dismissed the book as "an almost novel, made up largely of symbols and a rapid shuffle of black-and-white vignettes."

Responses to Literature

1. What does it mean to be "insane"? How does Kesey raise this question in *One Flew Over the Cuckoo's Nest*?

2. Discuss Kesey's treatment of race and gender in *One Flew Over the Cuckoo's Nest*. Do you find evidence to support accusations made by some critics that Kesey is "blatantly racist" and "a misogynist"?

3. Discuss the use of Christian imagery in *One Flew Over the Cuckoo's Nest*. To what extent is Mac a Christ-like figure?

4. What role does laughter play in *One Flew Over the Cuckoo's Nest*?

BIBLIOGRAPHY

Books

Carnes, Bruce. *Ken Kesey*. Boise, Idaho: Boise State University Press, 1974.

Leeds, Barry H. *Ken Kesey*. New York: Unger, 1981.

Perry, Paul. *On the Bus: The Complete Guide to the Legendary Trip of Ken Kesey and the Merry Pranksters and the Birth of the Counterculture*. New York: Thunder's Mouth Press, 1990.

Porter, M. Gilbert. *The Art of Grit: Ken Kesey's Fiction*. Columbia, Mo.: University of Missouri Press, 1982.

———. *One Flew Over the Cuckoo's Nest: Rising to Heroism*. Boston: Twayne, 1989.

Tanner, Stephen L. *Ken Kesey*. Boston: Twayne, 1983.

———. "The Western American Context of *One Flew Over the Cuckoo's Nest*." *Biographies of Books*, edited by James Barbour and Tom Quirk. Columbia, Mo.: University of Missouri Press, 1996, pp. 291–320.

Wolf, Tom. *The Electric Kool-Aid Acid Test*. New York: Bantam Books, 1968.

✳ Daniel Keyes

BORN: *1927, Brooklyn, New York*

NATIONALITY: *American*

GENRE: *Fiction, nonfiction*

MAJOR WORKS:
Flowers for Algernon (1959; 1966)
The Minds of Billy Milligan (1981)

Daniel Keyes *Beth Gwinn / Writer Pictures*

Overview

Keyes is best known for his short story and novel *Flowers for Algernon* (1959; 1966), a poignant story of a mentally handicapped man who temporarily acquires extraordinary intelligence. Composed of the journal entries written by the protagonist, Charlie Gordon, the novel reveals the aftermath of his undergoing a neurosurgical procedure that previously had been tried only on a laboratory mouse named Algernon. Although *Flowers for Algernon* is generally classified as a work of science fiction, it addresses several themes considered atypical for the genre, such as discrimination, love, and self-esteem.

Works in Biographical and Historical Context

The Creation of Charlie Gordon   Born in Brooklyn, New York, Keyes was educated at Brooklyn College. At the age of seventeen, Keyes enlisted with the U.S. Maritime Service, working as a ship's purser. While working as a high school English teacher, Keyes wrote the short story "Flowers for Algernon" and published it in *The Magazine of Fantasy and Science Fiction* in 1959. He was inspired, in particular, while teaching a group of special needs students, and being approached by one student who expressed a desire to get smart and transfer to a "normal" class. Encouraged by a Hugo Award the same year and the successful adaptation of the story for the CBS television network in 1961, he expanded it into a novel.

Flowers for Algernon begins with the misspelled and simplistic prose of Charlie Gordon, who works as a janitor. Through these notes, the reader learns that an operation, developed by Professor Nemur and Dr. Strauss, has enabled a lab mouse named Algernon to run through its maze with surprising alacrity, and the doctors are eager to see whether it will have a comparable effect on human beings. Charlie is the test subject for the human operation.

LITERARY AND HISTORICAL CONTEMPORARIES

Keyes's famous contemporaries include:

Edward Albee (1928–): American author who wrote the award-winning play *Who's Afraid of Virginia Woolf?* (1962).

Maya Angelou (1928–): American author associated with the Civil Rights Movement; she is most known for her autobiographies including *I Know Why the Caged Bird Sings* (1969).

Flannery O'Connor (1925–1965): American author of Southern Gothic works including *A Good Man is Hard to Find and Other Stories* (1955) and *The Violent Bear It Away* (1960).

Philip K. Dick (1928–1982): American science fiction author whose work explores the delicate balance between illusion and reality.

John Knowles (1926–1997): American author best known for his first novel, *A Separate Peace* (1959); set in the World War II era, the work has been consistently popular with young adults since its publication.

Gradually, Charlie becomes aware of his predicament, and his writings increase in sophistication; he ponders the ethics of the operation, the behavior of his old and new friends, his own identity, and the emotional needs that have surfaced as a result of his intellectual skills. Further, he discovers a critical flaw in the doctors' calculations and witnesses Algernon's regression, shown in the animal's decreased ability to navigate the maze. It becomes apparent that Charlie will suffer the same end. *Flowers for Algernon* became a bestselling novel, and the film adaptation, *Charly* (1968), achieved popular and critical success, with Cliff Robertson winning an Academy Award for his performance in the title role.

The Civil Rights Movement of the 1960s   Charlie Gordon suffers discrimination because of his intelligence, both when it is significantly below average and when it is significantly above average. The people around him fail to recognize his humanity, causing him significant harm. Published during the Civil Rights Movement of the 1960s, a time when many people—African Americans and women, for example—were fighting to have their humanity recognized and respected, *Flowers for Algernon* joined the chorus of voices calling for the equal treatment of minorities. In 1964, the Civil Rights Bill was passed, outlawing discrimination on the basis of race. Subsequently, in 1966—the same year *Flowers for Algernon* was published as a novel—The National Organization for Women was founded. In 1968, the Declaration of the General and Specific Rights of the Mentally Retarded

was passed; the word "retardation" was replaced with "developmental disability" in the 1970s.

Psychology and the Ethics of Scientific Inquiry
In addition to the discrimination he faced as an adult, Charlie Gordon also suffered abuse as a child. Framing his problems in this context was compatible with attitudes towards psychology during the 1950s and 1960s which emphasized a Freudian reading of human motivation. Sigmund Freud, the founder of psychoanalysis, placed a heavy emphasis on unresolved issues from childhood in his explanations of people's problems.

The scientific experiment conducted on Charlie Gordon and Algernon, the mouse, raises questions about the human impact of unchecked scientific inquiry. The structural dynamics of the scientific community in the novel directly reflect a shift in the federal government's attitude toward science that occurred after World War II. After the United States used the atomic bomb in World War II, the 1950s and 1960s saw an incredible surge in funding for scientific research, including projects that aimed to better understand the world in general.

Exploring the Complexities of the Human Mind
While working as an English professor at Ohio University, Keyes continued to write fiction and nonfiction, exploring, in his own words, "the complexities of the human mind." While his later works did not achieve the phenomenal success of *Flowers for Algernon*, he received critical attention for his later works including *The Touch* (1968), a novel about human tragedy; *The Fifth Sally* (1980), a novel about a woman with four personalities; *The Minds of Billy Milligan* (1981), a nonfiction account of a rapist who was acquitted after it was discovered he had twenty-four personalities; and *Unveiling Claudia: A True Story of Serial Murder* (1986), detailing the police investigation into Claudia Elaine Yasko, who falsely confessed to committing three murders.

Popularity in Japan   After retiring from teaching at Ohio University, Keyes moved to Boca Raton, Florida. He continues to write and his most recent works—*Daniel Keyes Collected Stories* (1993), *The Daniel Keyes Reader* (1994), and *The Milligan Wars* (1993), the sequel to *The Minds of Billy Milligan*—have achieved immense popularity in Japan. In 2000, Keyes published a memoir, *Algernon, Charlie, and I: A Writer's Journey*.

Works in Literary Context

In *Algernon, Charlie, and I: A Writer's Journey*, Keyes offers readers the story behind himself as a writer and his most famous work, *Flowers for Algernon*, emphasizing the role his childhood experiences played in inspiring the work.

The Mysteries of the Human Mind   In addition to exploring the psychology of intelligence in *Flowers for Algernon*, Keyes is also the author of several works focusing on the human psyche. Two of his works, *The Fifth*

Sally and *The Minds of Billy Milligan*, deal with the subject of multiple personalities and are dramatic recreations of factual cases. The title character of *The Fifth Sally* is Sally Porter, a woman who harbors four personalities that embody her emotional states: Nola, an intellectual artist; Derry, a free-spirited tomboy; Bella, a promiscuous woman; and Jinx, a murderous personality. The novel examines the efforts of Sally and her doctor to fuse the four beings into one complete person. *The Minds of Billy Milligan* is based on the case of Billy Milligan, who was arrested on rape charges in Ohio in 1977, and who later became the first person in U.S. history to be acquitted of a major felony by reason of a multiple personality disorder. At the time of his arrest, Billy Milligan was found to possess no fewer than twenty-four personalities—three of them female—with ages ranging from three to twenty-four years old. As in his two previous works, Keyes unravels the bizarre incidents in a mentally ill person's life in *Unveiling Claudia: A True Story of a Serial Murder*. Claudia Elaine Yasko, having known both the victims and the murderers in three Ohio killings in the late 1970s, fantasized herself as the murderer. She confessed to the homicides in 1978 but the charges were dropped once the real killers were accidentally discovered.

Works in Critical Context

From the moment *Flowers for Algernon* was published as a short story, it was a success, earning Keyes the prestigious Hugo Award for science fiction. Its expansion into a serially published novel only increased the story's popularity, and the full-length work earned Keyes a Nebula Award from the Science Fiction and Fantasy Writers of America in 1966. In addition to being widely anthologized and translated internationally, the work was adapted for a motion picture which, itself, was quite successful. Having established himself as a talented author, Keyes drew critical attention when he published his later works. However, none proved as successful or widely read as his first.

Flowers for Algernon   Writing for *Punch*, literature critic B. A. Young offers a brief but enthusiastic review of *Flowers for Algernon*, assuring readers that the work is compelling and accessible: "There's a touch of science-fiction about *Flowers for Algernon*, but not enough to nauseate and unman readers not at home with this genre.... Charlie's mental vagaries are hardly subtle, but I found them continually interesting." A reviewer for the *Times Literary Supplement* judged: "Charlie's hopeless knowledge that he is destined to end in a home for the feeble-minded...is painful, and Mr. Keyes has the technical equipment to prevent us from shrugging off the pain."

The Minds of Billy Milligan   According to Robert Coles in the *New York Times Book Review*, "Keyes makes quite evident in *The Minds of Billy Milligan*, [that] historical tensions within the [medical] profession have yet to be resolved, and have, in fact, been given new expression in this instance." Coles ultimately commends Keyes for tell-

---

COMMON HUMAN EXPERIENCE

Keyes explores the lives of people who have an unresolved history of abuse which informs their psychopathology. Other works that deal with the impact of childhood abuse include the following:

Lolita (1955), a novel by Vladimir Nabokov. This work, which tells the story of one emotionally stunted man's obsession with a twelve-year old girl, was the subject of much controversy upon publication in England and France.

I Never Promised You a Rose Garden (1964), a novel by Joanne Greenberg. To deal with her experience of reality as cruel, Deborah Blau retreats into a fantasy world and remains disconnected from reality until she comes under the care of an understanding doctor.

Oryx and Crake (2003), a novel by Margaret Atwood. This work extrapolates the dangerous aspects of a commercial society and creates a world where dehumanization is normalized and the exploitation of children is rampant.

---

ing "this complicated story well. It reads like a play: Billy's 'personalities' come onstage, leave to be replaced by others and then reappear." Peter Gorner finds this distracting; in a *Chicago Tribune* review of the book, he states that the author "interviews everybody, reconstructs, flashes back, and confuses the story in a chatty, conversational style. The alter egos seem to dance before our eyes like a stroboscope." However, in the opinion of David Johnston in the *Los Angeles Times*, "Keyes, on balance, carries it off quite well. While it shortchanges the reader by limiting explanation of motives almost exclusively to Milligan's personalities, [*The Minds of Billy Milligan*] is nonetheless a fascinating work." Finally, *Washington Post Book World* reviewer Joseph McLellan points out that "The challenge of first unearthing this story...and then telling it intelligibly was a daunting one. He has carried it off brilliantly..."

Responses to Literature

1. Discuss the ethical concerns (scientific and social) raised in *Flowers for Algernon* and your emotional reaction to them.

2. Discuss the nature of Charlie's romantic relationship with Fay. What role does she play in his life? Why is she included in *Flowers for Algernon*?

3. Explain the significance of memory in *Flowers for Algernon*. To what extent is Charlie Gordon a

different person at the end of the novel than he was before the experiment with Algernon?

4. Explain the perspectives on science, intelligence, and Charlie that are held by Professor Nemur and Dr. Strauss. To what extent do they differ?

BIBLIOGRAPHY

Books

Devoe, Thelma. *Flowers for Algernon: Daniel Keyes.* Littleton, Mass.: Sundance, 1987.

Scholes, Robert. *Structural Fabulation.* Notre Dame, Ind.: University of Notre Dame Press, 1975.

Small, Robert, Jr. "*Flowers for Algernon* by Daniel Keyes." *Censored Books: Critical Viewpoints*, edited by Nicholas J. Karolides, Lee Burress, and John M. Kean. Metuchen, N.J.: Scarecrow, 1993, pp. 249–255.

Web sites

Keyes, Daniel. *The Daniel Keyes Homepage.* Retrieved September 25, 2008, from http://www.danielkeyesauthor.com/. Last updated December 2006.

✿ Sue Monk Kidd

BORN: *1948, Sylvester, Georgia*

NATIONALITY: *American*

GENRE: *Fiction, nonfiction*

MAJOR WORKS:
The Secret Life of Bees (2001)
The Mermaid Chair (2005)

Overview

Best known for two popular novels, *The Secret Life of Bees* (2001) and *The Mermaid Chair* (2005), Kidd writes about women dealing with secrets from their past as they undertake journeys of self-discovery. Drawing on her own background growing up in the South and her quest for understanding, the author explores relationships between women, especially between mothers and daughters, and the effects of the loss of a parent at an early age. In addition, religious and spiritual concerns underscore the stories. Early in her career, Kidd was the author of inspirational nonfiction works presenting her reflections on many of these ideas from a personal point of view. Critics have praised the language, dialogue, and form of Kidd's books.

Works in Biographical and Historical Context

Kidd was born in 1948 in Sylvester, Georgia. Inspired by listening to her father's stories, she spent much of her childhood writing, but she stopped the practice at the

Sue Monk Kidd   *Kidd, Sue Monk, photograph. AP Images.*

age of sixteen when she focused on her future career. After earning her BS degree in nursing from Texas Christian University in 1970, Kidd worked as a nurse at St. Joseph's Hospital in Fort Worth, Texas, and was later an instructor in nursing at the Medical College of Georgia.

Inspiration In the early 1970s, Kidd became interested in spirituality, psychology, and mythology and began writing again, but focused on personal nonfiction. She published freelance articles and essays about her experiences and spiritual journey, and eventually became a contributing editor for *Guideposts* magazine. Kidd also published books on similar subjects. When Kidd was in her forties, her nonfiction writing took on a new direction by becoming more oriented towards feminist religious studies, as she moved away from fundamentalist Christianity. Because she retained a deep desire to pen stories as well, she attended courses and conferences in writing fiction and began writing her first novel, *The Secret Life of Bees*, in 1997.

Personal quests are a theme of her spiritually informed nonfiction, which includes *God's Joyful Surprise* (1988) and *When the Heart Waits* (1990). *The Dance of the Dissident Daughter* (1996) looks at Kidd's move away from her Southern Baptist background and fundamentalist Christianity.

Awards *The Secret Life of Bees* became a runaway best-seller, producing more than 3.5 million copies and appearing in twenty languages. Kidd had already received such literary honors as the Isak Dinesen Creative Non-fiction Award in 1994. She also won many awards for *The Secret Life of Bees*, including the Book of the Year Award from the Southeast Booksellers Association, Literature to Life Award from the American Place Theatre, and the Book of the Year Award (paperback) from Book Sense.

Her short stories have been published in *Best American Short Stories*, and her articles have appeared in periodicals including *Reader's Digest* and *Anima*. In 2008, *The Secret Life of Bees* was made into a movie starring Queen Latifah and Dakota Fanning.

Works in Literary Context

Kidd's novels take place in the Southern U.S. and center on the relationships—often difficult and fraught with conflicting interests, as well as haunted by past mistakes and misfortunes—that occur there. Kidd's two novels focus on women who dissociate themselves from problematic relationships with men, go on a journey of self-discovery, and learn about themselves and secrets from the pasts of their loved ones. Psychological and spiritual concerns are also important. In *The Secret Life of Bees*, based on a short story she had written earlier, the author also touches on racism and race relations. Kidd names two books she read as a youth that influenced her world-view and writing career: *Walden* (1854) by Henry David Thoreau, and *The Awakening* (1899) by Kate Chopin.

Coming of Age Set in the mid-1960s, *The Secret Life of Bees* focuses on the story of teenage narrator Lily Owen, who is being raised by her cruel father, T. Ray, and Rosaleen, the family's African-American servant. Influenced by Kidd's memories of the civil-rights era, the author depicts Rosaleen being arrested for standing up to intimidation while registering to vote. Lily rescues Rosaleen and the pair flee to Tiburon, South Carolina, a location inscribed on her deceased mother's cross. The escape allows the two characters the freedom to find themselves. Kidd also emphasizes the strong female relationships at Tiburon's Black Madonna Honey apiary, where Lily and Rosaleen find refuge. There, Lily learns the truth about her mother's tragic death while finding a mother figure among the three African-American sisters who run the shop. In addition, Kidd emphasizes the concept of the Black Madonna as a metaphor for a larger, spiritual mother. The bees and their work are also a metaphor for life.

Spirituality In her second novel, *The Mermaid Chair*, Kidd explores another woman in crisis, but here the focus is on midlife concerns. Like Lily, Jessie Sullivan must leave home to find herself and a home with meaning. Jessie must also deal with a problematic parent—her devout mother is cutting off her fingers in what might be a fit of religious mania—and a deceased one—her father died more than three decades earlier. Jessie's journey involves leaving her

---

LITERARY AND HISTORICAL CONTEMPORARIES

Sue Monk Kidd's famous contemporaries include:

Flannery O'Connor (1925–1964): Known mostly for her well-plotted short stories, O'Connor was also a devout Christian and concerned with issues of salvation.

Fannie Flagg (1944–): The American author who turned to writing after a career as an actress and television personality; author of *Fried Green Tomatoes at the Whistle Stop Cafe* (1987).

Anne Tyler (1941–): Tyler is an American novelist who won the 1989 Pulitzer Prize for *Breathing Lessons* (1988).

Dorothy Allison (1949–): An American author whose first novel *Bastard Out of Carolina* (1992) presented a fresh and disturbing depiction of poverty in the American South.

Marianne Williamson (1952–): The American spiritual writer whose book *A Return to Love* (1992) interprets the self-help phenomenon known as A Course in Miracles.

Bill Clinton (1946–): This Southern politician was Governor of Arkansas before winning the 1992 presidential election: President of the United States, 1993–2001.

---

overbearing husband to return to her childhood home in Egret Island, South Carolina, and care for her mother. Jessie's quest to connect with her mother is as difficult as Lily's, but she is able to learn secrets of the past, including why her mother is still upset by her husband's long-ago death. The self-discovery is also personal as Jessie redis-covers aspects of herself, including her lost artistic vision and personal passion. She falls in love with a monk, Brother Thomas, who is about to take his final vows and has his own crisis of faith. Though this relationship does not work out and she returns to her husband, Jessie is freed from her past guilt about her father and has learned much about herself. The titular chair is a metaphor, a symbol of the depths to which one must look to solve spiritual problems.

Works in Critical Context

Kidd's two novels were generally well-received. Lauded as a solid debut effort, *The Secret Life of Bees* was praised especially for the portrayal of the female characters, who were seen as realistic, full, and deep. Kidd's depiction of Lily was especially singled out as an accurate depiction of a moody teen who evolves over the course of her journey. Critics also noted Kidd's subtle plotting, ability to balance issues with humor, rhythmic dialogue, and knowledge of the time and place in which the novel is set. While a few

COMMON HUMAN EXPERIENCE

Kidd's most popular novel, *The Secret Life of Bees*, is a coming-of-age story centered around a young girl, Lily, and her quest to find herself and her roots amidst troubling circumstances. Here are some other works that deal with the quests of children who are transitioning to adulthood.

To Kill a Mockingbird (1960), a novel by Harper Lee. The ten-year-old protagonist of this classic Southern novel witnesses hard truths about racism and injustice.

The Adventures of Tom Sawyer (1876), a novel by Mark Twain. The title character and his best friend, Huckleberry Finn, go rafting down the Mississippi River in this novel about friendship and mischief.

My Life as a Dog (1985), a film directed by Lasse Hallström. A young boy is sent by his mother to live with his relatives in rural Sweden.

The Tin Drum, (1959) a novel by Günter Grass. In this classic novel, the protagonist refuses to grow up, and thus remains child-sized throughout his life.

Black Swan Green (2006), a novel by David Mitchell. Thirteen-year-old Jason Taylor struggles with his parents' divorce and with bullies in Worcestershire, England.

critics found the plot of *The Secret Life of Bees* predictable and the story too tidy, *The Mermaid Chair* received even more mixed reviews. Kidd was again praised for her beautiful writing ability and use of language, vivid descriptions of life in the South and emotionally rich, sharp, writing. A number of commentators, however, found the book overly sentimental, generic, and saccharine. Kidd's nonfiction is generally praised for its form and content.

The Secret Life of Bees A writer for *Publishers Weekly* noted that the book "features a hive's worth of appealing female characters, an offbeat plot and a lovely style." In what he called a "sweeping debut novel" in his *Library Journal* review, David A. Berona pointed out that "the stunning metaphors and realistic characters are so poignant that they will bring tears to your eyes." Beth Kephart, reviewing the book for *Book* magazine, observed: "Goodness—what it is, what it looks like, who bestows it—is the frame within which this book is masterfully hung, the organizing principle behind this intimate, unpretentious, and unsentimental work."

The Mermaid Chair Kidd's follow-up to her successful first novel tells the story of Jessie Sullivan, a middle-aged housewife and part-time artist who is drawn back to her childhood home after receiving some disturbing news about her estranged mother. The secrets of the past collide with the uncertainties of the present in what a

writer for *Publishers Weekly* described as an "emotionally rich novel, full of sultry, magical descriptions of life in the South." In her review for *Entertainment Weekly*, Jennifer Reese panned this effort by Kidd as "a goopy follow up" to her best selling debut. Conversely, while reviewing Kidd's novel for *Time*, Lev Grossman pointed out that the author's "writing is so smart and sharp, she gives new life to old midlife crises, and she draws connections from the feminine to the divine to the erotic that a lesser writer wouldn't see, and might not have the guts to follow."

Responses to Literature

1. Why does Kidd choose bees as a metaphor in her first novel?

2. How does Kidd seem to feel about the South? Explain, perhaps using the main character Lily from *The Secret Life of Bees* as a focal point.

3. Compare Kidd's first novel to the film version of it. Do the actors portray the characters as you expected they would? How do the characterizations embody, or change, the tone of Kidd's story?

4. Kidd is indebted to other Southern writers before her. What writers may have influenced the character of Lily in *The Secret Life of Bees*? How do you detect these influences?

BIBLIOGRAPHY

Periodicals

Berona, David A. Review of *The Secret Life of Bees*. *Library Journal* (December 2001): 173.

Dyer, Lucinda. "Sue Monk Kidd: *The Secret Life of Bees*." *Publishers Weekly* (August 6, 2001): 49.

Grossman, Lev. "Sex and the Sacred: A Bittersweet Novel of Midlife Crisis and Forbidden Love from the Author of *The Secret Life of Bees*." *Time* (April 4, 2005): 69.

Huntley, Kristine. Review of *The Secret Life of Bees*. *Booklist* (December 1, 2001).

Kennedy, Dana. Review of *The Mermaid Chair*. *New York Times Book Review* (March 31, 2002): 24.

Kephart, Beth. "Sweet as Honey." *Book* (January-February, 2002).

Reese, Jennifer. Review of *The Mermaid Chair*. *Entertainment Weekly* (April 1, 2005): 75.

Reynolds, Susan Salter. Review of *The Secret Life of Bees*. *Los Angeles Times* (March 24, 2002): R15.

Rifkind, Donna. Review of *The Mermaid Chair*. *Book World* (April 10, 2005): 6.

Web sites

Sue Monk Kidd Home Page. Retrieved December 1, 2008 from http://www.suemonkkidd.com. Last updated August 12, 2005.

❀ Jamaica Kincaid

BORN: *1949, Antigua*

NATIONALITY: *American*

GENRE: *Fiction, nonfiction*

MAJOR WORKS:
Annie John (1985)
A Small Place (1988)
The Autobiography of My Mother (1996)

Overview

A native author of the West Indies, Kincaid is known for her personal style and honesty that characterizes both her fiction and nonfiction writing.

Works in Biographical and Historical Context

Childhood in Colonial Antigua Jamaica Kincaid was born Elaine Potter Richardson on May 25, 1949, on the tiny island of Antigua in the West Indies, daughter of Annie Richardson and a father she did not know. She was raised by her mother and her stepfather, a carpenter. When she was nine, the first of her three brothers was

Jamaica Kincaid   *Kincaid, Jamaica, photograph.© Jerry Bauer. Reproduced by permission.*

born, and Kincaid felt expelled from the "paradise" of her mother's love, as she recounts in her first novel, *Annie John* (1985). At about the same time, she became aware of the islanders' subservience to the British, a status she questioned but that others seemed to accept. Antigua had been colonized by the British in 1632 and remained under colonial rule until 1981 when it gained its independence. Kincaid left Antigua in 1966, coinciding with a transfer of ruling power to the French, a change that was reversed only a year later.

Though exceptionally bright, she began to be considered a problem in school; as punishment, she was forced to memorize long passages of John Milton's *Paradise Lost* (1667), a work she later credited with first suggesting the subversive idea that one may rebel against even overwhelming power. Although Kincaid later saw that the colonial education constituted an "erasure" of her own identity, which was replaced by a love of all things British, her childhood love of English literature was intense, and she became a voracious reader. This fascination with books annoyed her mother, Kincaid recounts in *My Brother* (1997), and when she neglected babysitting duties to read, her mother doused all of her books with kerosene and set them on fire.

Move to New York When family finances worsened, Kincaid was sent to the United States to work as a nanny and send money home. The year was 1966 and tensions in the United States were high, as President Lyndon B. Johnson increased the country's involvement in the Vietnam War. Protests against the war continued, contributing to the countercultural movement of the 1960s, a reaction against social norms including race relations, gender inequality, and sexual mores. During this time, Kincaid became interested in photography and took courses at the New School for Social Research. She attended Franconia College in New Hampshire for a time but returned to New York to find her first job in publishing at a magazine called *Art Direction*, only to be fired, as she recalled in a 1988 interview with Selwyn R. Cudjoe, for an article she wrote on black American advertising. Kincaid applied for jobs at *Mademoiselle* and *Glamour* but was hindered by her inability to type. Then, a story idea submitted to the magazine *Ingenue*—a proposal to ask Gloria Steinem what she was like when she was seventeen—was accepted. The article was a success and turned into a series.

Becoming Jamaica Kincaid Around 1973, Elaine Potter Richardson became Jamaica Kincaid, a change she has described as a way of shucking family disapproval of her writing and gaining a sort of anonymity. The choice of name was not particularly political, she has said, just something she thought up, sitting around with friends. The name change was not Kincaid's only act of liberation. She cut her hair short, dyed it blond, and wore outlandish clothing, apparently removing herself as far as possible from the proper, faux-English schoolgirl in her gray linen uniform.

LITERARY AND HISTORICAL CONTEMPORARIES

Kincaid's famous contemporaries include:

Salman Rushdie (1947–): Rushdie is the Indian British author of *Midnight's Children* (1981), which was awarded the prestigious Booker Prize, and *The Satanic Verses* (1988).

Amy Tan (1952–): Tan is a Chinese American author who is most famous for her novel *The Joy Luck Club* (1989), about the experiences of Chinese American immigrants.

Yusef Komunyakaa (1947–): American author whose poetry collection *Neon Vernacular* was awarded the Pulitzer Prize for Poetry (1994).

Alice Walker (1944–): American author most famous for her Pulitzer Prize–winning novel *The Color Purple* (1982), which concerns the hardships endured by African American women during the 1930s.

Isabel Allende (1942–): Chilean American author of popular novels that employ magic realism, including *The House of Spirits* (1982) and *City of Beasts* (2002).

Kincaid's first journalistic successes produced others, and a chance acquaintance with *New Yorker* writer George W. S. Trow resulted in lunch with William Shawn, editor of the *New Yorker*, and an assignment to write her first *Talk of the Town* piece for the magazine: an account of the annual West Indian parade in Brooklyn. The piece was the first of eighty *Talk of the Town* pieces spanning a decade—most of which were written within an autobiographical framework.

In 1978 Kincaid, under the influence of the Elizabeth Bishop poem "In the Waiting Room," wrote "Girl" in a single afternoon. The one-sentence story was published in the *New Yorker*, filling one magazine page. Later widely anthologized, "Girl" became Kincaid's first story in her collection *At the Bottom of the River* (1983).

French Influence Kincaid came to believe that a directional narrative was almost never an attempt to tell a true story but was almost always a way of creating self-serving lies. But, two things changed Kincaid's thinking about writing. One was a French movie, *La Jeteé* (1962), made up of black-and-white still photographs, and the other was the work of the experimental French writer Alain Robbe-Grillet. Both works showed Kincaid that there was a way to write without recourse to a storytelling mode she had come to see as archaic and dishonest. In her earliest work, as in the nonnarrative scenes of Robbe-Grillet, both writer and reader are freed of the need to make conventionally coherent arrangements of experience and reality and are invited instead to follow a chain of subliminal connections to find psychological, if not rational, sense.

From Servitude to Literary Stardom By 1983, seventeen years after leaving Antigua to work as a servant, Jamaica Kincaid was a literary star. Her first book, *At the Bottom of the River*, a collection of the *New Yorker* stories, won the Morton Dauwen Zabel Award of the American Academy and Institute of Arts and Letters, was nominated for the PEN/Faulkner Award, and was widely reviewed by critics who were often adulatory and always respectful, even when puzzled by the surreal nature of the book. In the ten dreamlike stories speakers are unidentified, identities merge, and fantasy and reality are inseparable. Taken together, the pieces trace a journey of mourning over the loss of a childhood paradise of perfect love and harmony in which time stands still and in which betrayal—including the great betrayal of death—is unknown.

At the Bottom of the River was followed in 1985 by the more accessible *Annie John*, also originally published as a series of short stories in the *New Yorker*. The book was one of three finalists for the 1985 international Ritz Paris Hemingway Award, and this time the reviews were almost universally positive. In this novel Kincaid covers similar emotional ground as in *At the Bottom of the River*, but in a less surrealistic, more autobiographical form.

Anger at Racial Domination Kincaid was bothered, she said, when people called her work "charming." This anger was expressed directly for the first time in the long essay *A Small Place* (1988). In this work, the writer addresses the reader, whom she assumes to be a relatively privileged *New Yorker* subscriber. An unrelenting attack takes up the first quarter of the eighty-one-page essay. Kincaid shows the white tourist as repeating the pattern of racial and cultural domination begun by slaveholding European colonists. The tourists, she concedes, like the Europeans who colonized the West Indies, would probably be good people if they had stayed home.

Despite the considerable disagreement and anger provoked by *A Small Place*, the *New Yorker* continued to publish Kincaid's fiction, and in 1990 five of these stories were collected and published as the novel *Lucy*. While *Lucy*, whose title character is named for John Milton's great rebel Lucifer, contains little of the overt political anger of *A Small Place*, it is still a work obsessed by the question of how domination hinders the formation of authentic identity. The stories take up where *Annie John* left off, showing the further progress of a West Indian girl who leaves her mesmerizing mother and her Caribbean home, going out to make her way in a new world and becoming the nanny to a beautiful and wealthy white family that seems to present a portrait of perfection until the young girl discovers a turmoil that will soon break the family apart.

With her next work of fiction, *The Autobiography of My Mother* (1996), Kincaid continues to explore her sense that the instinct to dominate others, as enacted by the colonial powers in the West Indies, is born in a vain emptiness that sends people out in the world on a mission of conquest and control.

Losing Her Brother to AIDS   In 1997 Kincaid published *My Brother*, the nonfiction account of the death of her half brother, Devon Drew, of AIDS. The third child of Kincaid's mother and stepfather, Drew was three when Kincaid left Antigua for the United States. She tells of returning to Antigua when she learns of her brother's illness and finding him in a decrepit hospital room. The hospital and the local attitude toward AIDS generally—there is no real effort to treat the disease, no funds for the expensive drugs, and no support from her brother's friends, who do not visit him in the hospital—seem to represent her home in microcosm as a place that is broken and where there is no attempt at repair. Kincaid closes the book in mourning not for her brother but for William Shawn, her former father-in-law and editor of the *New Yorker*, who died in 1992.

In 2002 Kincaid published *Mr. Potter*, a lyrical prose poem about a narrator whose father abandons her before she is born. In 2008 Kincaid was awarded an honorary doctorate degree from Wesleyan University. She currently teaches creative writing at Bennington College and Harvard University.

Works in Literary Context

In her work, Kincaid employs a highly poetic literary style celebrated for its rhythms, imagery, characterization, and elliptic narration. Her writing was heavily influenced by her experiences growing up poor in Antigua and immigrating to the United States, in addition to the relationships she forged with people in the literary community throughout her career. Kincaid's work has been compared to that of Toni Morrison and Wole Soyinka.

Colonialism and Race   A recurring theme in Kincaid's work is how colonialism—the occupation of a region by members of an outside culture, and the subsequent attempt to "civilize" the conquered—affects the native population, whose traditional beliefs and cultural touchstones are typically devalued. This issue is at the forefront of *Annie John*. While the traditional coming-of-age story traces the often painful journey from youth to maturity, in Annie's world, as defined both by the all-powerful mother and the colonial education system, there seems to be no viable maturity. For in her mother's kingdom—and by reflection in colonial Antigua—the coming-of-age black girl is expected to have only one preoccupation: to imitate as much as possible the white English girl, whom she can never become and against whom she will always be deemed inferior.

Love for the Betrayer   Whether she is writing about the loss of a mother's love, the cruelty of the colonial environment, her brother's death from AIDS, or the plants in her garden, Kincaid holds in solution a sense of endless loss and betrayal that is complicated by a love for the

---

COMMON HUMAN EXPERIENCE

In her nonfiction book *My Brother*, Kincaid gives her account of losing her half brother to AIDS. Other works that engage with this theme include the following:

As Is (1985), a play by William M. Hoffman. One of the first artistic works about AIDS to appear in the United States, this play combines a story about a lover and his partner with stories of other affected individuals.

Love Alone (1988), a poetry collection by Paul Monette. Written immediately following the death of his life partner, Roger Horwitz, this collection charts Monette's journey through loss and suffering caused by AIDS.

Hospital Time (1997), a memoir by Amy Hoffman. This work details the struggle against AIDS from a caregiving perspective as Hoffman tells of her experiences acting as primary caregiver for her friend Mike Reigle, a prisoner rights activist.

---

betrayer. This love, once implanted in the trusting young heart, can never truly die, despite what one may later learn. In inhabiting this space, Kincaid has made herself a rare, one-woman monument, not only to the legacy of European conquest and domination of the world's places and peoples but also to the immense paradox of that legacy.

Works in Critical Context

While her work has always been critically acclaimed—her nonfiction book *My Brother* was nominated for the National Book Award—Kincaid has at the same time, through her outspoken opinions on topics such as colonialism, managed to invite controversy with people on all points of the political spectrum.

A Small Place   Reviewing the essay *A Small Place*, Adewale Maja-Pearce in the *New Statesman and Society* excoriates Kincaid's "inexplicable" descent into a "sniveling attack on the sins of the nasty—and long-departed colonial power" that had dominated her West Indian home of Antigua. William Shawn, former editor of the *New Yorker*, liked the piece, but it was rejected as too angry by Robert Gottlieb, the editor who replaced Shawn. It was published in book form by Farrar, Straus and Giroux in 1988, and certainly no one found it "charming" as Kincaid was previously labeled by some. Nor did reviewers miss the anger. Salman Rushdie describes it in a *Wall Street Journal* review as "a jeremiad of great clarity and a force that one might call torrential were the language not so finely controlled." Many reviewers, such as Michiko Kakutani of the *New York Times*, did not find the anger at "Europeans and North Americans who routinely patronized and humiliated the Antiguans" misplaced, but Alison Friesinger deems the book "distorted" by Kincaid's anger in her review for the *New York Times Book Review*.

Responses to Literature

1. In *The Autobiography of My Mother*, Xuela experiences herself as incapable of loving until she meets Roland. What is it about Roland that allows Xuela to love? In your explanation, include specific details from the text.

2. What is the significance of Annie's education in *Annie John*? What kind of worldview does it reinforce? How does this type of education compare with your own?

3. Discuss your emotional reaction to *A Small Place*. Do you agree with Kincaid's views on white tourists in the West Indies? Why or why not?

4. Read Kincaid's nonfiction work *My Brother*. How do the attitudes toward AIDS compare with those in your community?

BIBLIOGRAPHY

Books

Birbalsingh, Frank. *Jamaica Kincaid: From Antigua to America*. New York: St. Martin's Press, 1996.

Bloom, Harold, ed. *Jamaica Kincaid*. Philadelphia, Pa.: Chelsea House, 1998.

Ferguson, Moira. *Jamaica Kincaid: Where the Land Meets the Body*. Charlottesville: University of Virginia, 1994.

Mistron, Deborah. *Understanding Jamaica Kincaid's Annie John*. Westport, Conn.: Greenwood Press, 1999.

Paravisini-Gebert, Lizabeth. *Jamaica Kincaid: A Critical Companion*. Westport, Conn.: Greenwood Press, 1999.

Simmons, Diane. *Jamaica Kincaid*. New York: Twayne, 1994.

✳ Martin Luther King Jr.

BORN: *1929, Atlanta, Georgia*

DIED: *1968, Memphis, Tennessee*

NATIONALITY: *American*

GENRE: *Essay, speech*

MAJOR WORKS:

Letter from Birmingham City Jail (1963)

"I Have a Dream" (1963)

Overview

Martin Luther King Jr. is recognized as the driving force of the civil rights movement in the United States during the 1960s. An eloquent orator, he delivered at the height of his fame an average of 450 speeches a year throughout the country, calling for racial equality.

Martin Luther King, Jr.   *King, Dr. Martin Luther, Jr., photograph.* The Library of Congress.

Works in Biographical and Historical Context

Growing up in the Jim-Crow South   King was a gifted and precocious child. He was born in Atlanta, Georgia, and grew up listening to his father, the Reverend Martin Luther King, Sr., preach at the Ebenezer Baptist Church. Young King took an interest in the power of words. King's parents and grandmother encouraged young Martin's public speaking, and he often sang and recited biblical passages for church audiences.

King's childhood was far from idyllic, however. Growing up in the Jim Crow South, one of the first phrases King learned to read was "Whites Only." Jim Crow laws, which were enforced primarily in southern states, ensured racial segregation in public places like schools, transportation, and restrooms. Encounters with overt racism frustrated and embittered the young King. Despite the discouraging aspects of his youth in Atlanta, he was a motivated and successful student, and he enrolled at Morehouse College at the age of fifteen.

From Agnosticism to Ministry In 1948, King enrolled at Crozer Theological Seminary in Pennsylvania, one of six black students in the predominantly white school. King was an excellent student, graduating at the top of his class in 1951. At Crozer, he formed strong friendships with a number of white students; for the first time in his life, King realized that whites could be his allies. Most importantly, however, at the seminary he was exposed to the works of two men who would shape him as a minister and as a civil rights leader: Walter Rauschenbusch, a theologian and social activist, and Mahatma Gandhi, leader of the India independence movement (India gained independence from British rule in 1947).

King Organizes Bus Boycott in Montgomery In the fall of 1951, King enrolled at Boston University to pursue a doctorate in theology. Two years later, he married Coretta Scott, a student at Boston's New England Conservatory of Music. In 1955, King organized a bus boycott in Montgomery, Alabama, to protest the arrest of Rosa Parks, an African American woman who had refused to give up her seat to a white person on a public bus. The boycott lasted more than a year. Despite receiving numerous threatening phone calls, being arrested, and having his home fire-bombed, King and the boycott prevailed. The U.S. Supreme Court eventually declared Montgomery's bus segregation laws illegal, and, in December 1956, King rode on Montgomery's first integrated bus.

King soon became president of the Southern Christian Leadership Conference (SCLC) with the goal of boosting black voter registration and ending segregation in the South. In 1959, King and his wife spent a month in India, visiting the sites of Gandhi's struggle against the British and meeting people who had known the Indian leader. He returned home inspired by Gandhi's enormous achievements. King resigned as pastor of Dexter Avenue Baptist Church in Montgomery so he could devote more of his time to the civil rights effort.

Protests in Birmingham Near the end of 1962, he decided to focus his energies on the desegregation of Birmingham, Alabama. Birmingham, the state's largest populated city, was at that time what King called in his book *Why We Can't Wait* (1964) "the most segregated city in America," which was precisely why he had chosen it as his target. In this work, King detailed the advance planning that went into the Birmingham campaign. Most important was the training in nonviolent techniques given to those who volunteered to participate in the demonstrations.

One of the unusual and most effective aspects of the Birmingham campaign was King's decision to use children in the demonstrations. When the protests came to a head on May 3, 1963, it was after the arrests of nearly 1,000 young people the previous day. As another wave of protestors, mostly children and teenagers, took to the streets, they were suddenly hit with jets of water from

high-powered fire hoses. Police dogs were also released on the demonstrators. The photographs circulated by the media of children being attacked brought cries of outrage from throughout the country and the world. President Kennedy sent a Justice Department representative to Birmingham to work for a peaceful solution to the problem. Within a week negotiators produced an agreement that met King's major demands, including desegregation of lunch counters, restrooms, fitting rooms, and drinking fountains in the city and hiring of blacks in positions previously closed to them.

Although the Birmingham campaign ended in triumph for King, at the outset he was criticized for his efforts. Imprisoned at the beginning of the protest for disobeying a court injunction forbidding him to lead any demonstrations in Birmingham, King spent some of his time in jail composing an open letter to his critics, the celebrated *Letter from Birmingham City Jail* (1963).

King Tells the Nation about His Dream of Racial Equality Another important event of 1963 was a massive march on Washington, D.C., which King planned together with leaders of other civil rights organizations. An estimated 250,000 people were on hand to hear King and other dignitaries speak at the march's end point, the Lincoln Memorial. While King's biographers have noted that the young minister struggled all night writing words to inspire the marchers, he subsequently deviated from his prepared text and gave the most eloquent and powerful speech of his career, the speech known as "I Have a Dream" (1963).

On January 3, 1964, King was proclaimed "Man of the Year" by *Time* magazine, the first black to be so honored. Later that year he received the Nobel Peace Prize, becoming the twelfth American, the third black, and the youngest—he was thirty-five—person ever to receive the award. He donated the $54,600 prize to the S.C.L.C. and other civil rights groups.

"Bloody Sunday" and the Voting Rights Act After facing months of intimidation and threats from white officials during their voter registration efforts in Alabama, civil rights activists organized a nonviolent protest march from Selma to Montgomery (the state capital) to draw attention to the disenfranchisement of black voters. About 600 marchers set out on March 7, 1965, and only made it a few blocks, to the Edmund Pettus Bridge, before they were attacked by state troopers and sheriff's deputies wielding tear gas and billy clubs. King led a second march two days later, which did not make it to Montgomery, and a third march, this one with court sanction, on March 21. King and some 25,000 supporters marched into Montgomery on March 25. Within a few days, President Lyndon Johnson made a televised appearance before a joint session of Congress in which he demanded passage of a voting rights bill. Later that year President Johnson signed the 1965 Voting Rights Act into law, with King and other civil rights leaders looking on.

LITERARY AND HISTORICAL CONTEMPORARIES

King's famous contemporaries include:

Malcolm X (1925–1965): A dynamic and influential twentieth-century African-American leader, who rose to prominence in the mid-1950s as the outspoken national minister of the Nation of Islam under Elijah Muhammad; he opposed the mainstream civil rights movement, publicly calling for black separatism and rejecting non-violence and integration as effective means of combating racism.

John F. Kennedy (1917–1963): The thirty-fifth President of the United States who served from 1961 until his assassination in 1963; the details of the assassination are the subject of on-going debates and conspiracy theories.

Betty Friedan (1921–2006): American author and gender equality activist most famous for fueling the Women's Rights Movement with her book *The Feminine Mystique* (1963).

Maya Angelou (1928–): Hailed as one of the great voices of contemporary African-American literature, Angelou is best known for *I Know Why the Caged Bird Sings* (1970), the first of her series of five autobiographical novels.

Kurt Vonnegut (1922–2007): Best known as the author of *Slaughterhouse-Five; or, The Children's Crusade: A Duty-Dance with Death* (1969), Vonnegut is acknowledged as a major voice in American literature and applauded for his pungent satirical depictions of modern society.

Discord Within the Civil Rights Movement By this time King was ready to embark on his next project: moving his nonviolent campaign to the black ghettoes of the North. Chicago was chosen as the first target, but the campaign did not go the way King had planned. Rioting broke out in the city just two days after King initiated his program. Discord was beginning to be felt within the civil rights movement as well. While King insisted on a non-violent approach to social change, other black leaders, including Malcolm X, believed that more aggressive, even violent, efforts were necessary to challenge the white power structure in the United States. Instead of non-violent protest like those in Montgomery, Birmingham, and Selma, riots broke out in Boston, Detroit, Milwaukee, and more than thirty other U.S. cities, as African Americans grew increasingly enraged at the failures of the local and federal governments to protect and uphold their rights. King also frustrated some followers by broadening his focus to include protests against the Vietnam War. Many of his followers were worried King would alienate

President Johnson by speaking out against the war. On April 4, 1967, King gave a speech titled "Beyond Vietnam" at New York City's Riverside Church in which he sharply criticized American military actions in Vietnam. The speech provoked outrage in the press and among white ministers, and King's broad popularity diminished somewhat.

Assassination by James Earl Ray? A year to the day after his Vietnam speech—on April 4, 1968—King was assassinated while standing on the balcony of the Lorraine Motel in Memphis, Tennessee. James Earl Ray, a white man whom King had never met, was later convicted of the crime. Ray, who died in prison in 1998, had confessed, but later recanted.

Since his death, King has been hailed around the world as a human rights icon. His legacy of nonviolent resistance to oppression and leadership during the Civil Rights Movement in the United States continue to inspire people still struggling to achieve equality. On November 2, 1983, President Ronald Reagan signed a bill creating a national holiday to honor King, Martin Luther King, Jr. It is now observed on the third Monday each January.

Works in Literary Context

Martin Luther King, Jr. passionately embraced nonviolence as a method for social reform and encouraged others to fight social injustice, not with anger or hate but with Christian love. He was influenced by a number of famous leaders including Jesus, Abraham Lincoln, Theodor Herzl, Mahatma Gandhi, Benjamin Mays, Rosa Parks, Bayard Rustin, Henry David Thoreau, Howard Thurman, Leo Tolstoy, and Walter Rauschenbusch.

Civil Disobedience King's oratory and writing were influenced by Gandhi's philosophy of nonviolence. Gandhi advocated *satyagraha*, which he translated as "the vindication of truth not by infliction of suffering on the opponent but on one's self." Furthermore, he encouraged his followers to denounce violence and to repay evil with good. King exhorted his followers to do the same. For example, in *Letter from Birmingham City Jail* King argues that if a law is unjust, civil disobedience—a nonviolent opposition to law or authority—is justified.

Sermons & Biblical Imagery Prior to his most famous written and spoken work, King established a reputation for moving crowds as a minister. With a commanding voice and message of hope, King combined emotionally-laden words with repetition and metaphor to reach his audience. He continued using this powerful rhetorical style when he began speaking to larger audiences outside of the church setting. By invoking frequent references to Christian doctrine and the U. S. Constitution, he grounded his call for freedom in a history familiar to his listeners, thus making his dream accessible to people of diverse backgrounds. *Letter from Birmingham City Jail* and "I Have a Dream" two of his most famous works, embody these techniques and have come to symbolize the civil rights struggle. Filled with biblical imagery and resounding emotion, they cry out for justice, equality, and freedom.

King has inspired many people with his work during the Civil Rights Movement including, but not limited to, Albert Lutuli, Jesse Jackson, and Al Sharpton.

Works in Critical Context

During his lifetime, King was a man of controversy, hated by whites who opposed racial equality and by militant blacks who considered his philosophy of nonviolence "self-deceiving." Eldridge Cleaver, for example, did not like King and instead supported Malcolm X, who called for "black liberation by any means necessary." The Nobel Prize gave King even wider recognition as a world leader. "Overnight," commented Flip Shulke and Penelope O. McPhee in *King Remembered*, (1986) "King became . . . a symbol of world peace. He knew that if the Nobel Prize was to mean anything, he must commit himself more than ever to attaining the goals of the black movement through peace."

The Controversy Continues Controversy about King was reignited during the late twentieth-century. Some works—particularly the Reverend Ralph Abernathy's *And the Walls Came Tumbling Down* (1991) and David J. Garrow's Pulitzer Prize-winning *Bearing the Cross: Martin Luther King, Jr. and the Southern Christian Leadership Conference* (1986)—allege that King had extramarital sexual relations. More recently, Clayborne Carson, engaged by Coretta Scott King to compile a collection of King's writings, announced that King may have plagiarized parts of his doctoral dissertation and other writings. These disclosures prompted scores of newspaper editorials and other responses arguing that the allegations had no bearing on King's contributions to the civil rights struggle. "[King's] achievement glows unchallenged through the present shadow," states a 1990 editorial in the *New York Times*. "Martin Luther King's courage was not copied; and there was no plagiarism in his power."

Responses to Literature

1. Who is the intended audience for King's "I Have a Dream" speech? Support your understanding with details from the speech.

2. King's "Dream" been realized in the United States? To what extent does inequality still exist?

3. What impact does King's use of anaphora have on you as you read or listen to his "I Have a Dream" speech. Are some uses more effective than others?

4. In *Letter from Birmingham City Jail* King differentiates between laws which are just and unjust. What rhetorical techniques does he use to justify civil disobedience? Do you find his argument compelling? To what extent is civil disobedience justified today?

COMMON HUMAN EXPERIENCE

King's most famous works, *Letter from Birmingham City Jail* and "I Have a Dream," are intended to persuade their audience of a moral imperative. Other works which are famous for employing this type of rhetoric include the following:

"Gettysburg Address" (1863), a speech by Abraham Lincoln. Delivered during the American Civil War, this address emphasized the importance of unifying the country according to the principle of equality stated in the United States Constitution; it is now one of the most famous speeches in United States history.

J'accuse (1893), an open letter by Émile Zola. Addressed to the President of France, Félix Faure, and published in a major newspaper, this letter accuses the French government of anti-Semitism and false imprisonment in the case of Alfred Dreyfus; its power sparked a major controversy and eventually led to his exoneration.

"Inaugural Address" (1961), a speech by John F. Kennedy. After barely defeating Vice President Richard Nixon in one of the closest Presidential elections in United States history, Kennedy exhorted U. S. citizens to "Ask not what your country can do for you; ask what you can do for your country."

BIBLIOGRAPHY

Books

Bennett, Lerone, Jr. *What Manner of Man*. Chicago: Johnson Publishing, 1964.

Bishop, Jim. *The Days of Martin Luther King, Jr.* New York: Putnam, 1971.

Bleinweiss, Robert M., editor. *Marching to Freedom: The Life of Martin Luther King, Jr.* Middletown, Conn.: American Education Publications, 1968.

Branch, Taylor. *Pillar of Fire: America in the King Years, 1963–65*. New York: Simon & Schuster, 1998.

Clarke, Thurston. *Ask Not: The Inauguration of John F. Kennedy and the Speech That Changed America*. New York: Henry Holt and Co., 2004.

Clayton, Edward T. *Martin Luther King, Jr.: The Peaceful Warrior*. Englewood Cliffs, N. J.: Prentice-Hall, 1968.

Davis, Lenwood G. *I Have a Dream: Life and Times of Martin Luther King, Jr.* Westport, Conn.: Negro Universities Press, 1969.

Daynes, Gary. *Making Villains, Making Heroes: Joseph R. McCarthy and Martin Luther King Jr. in American Memory*. New York: Garland Publishing, 1997.

Dyson, Michael Eric. *I May Not Get There with You*. New York: Freepress, 2001.

Fairclough, Adam. *Martin Luther King, Jr.* Athens: University of Georgia Press, 1995.

Franklin, V. P. *Martin Luther King, Jr.* New York: Park
  Lane Press, 1998.

King, Coretta Scott. *My Life with Martin Luther King,
  Jr.* New York: Holt, 1969.

Lewis, David L. *King: A Critical Biography.* New York:
  Praeger, 1970.

Lincoln, Eric C., editor. *Martin Luther King, Jr.: A
  Profile.* New York: Hill and Wang, 1984.

Lischer, Richard. *The Preacher King: Martin Luther
  King, Jr. and the Word that Moved American.*
  New York: Oxford University Press, 1995.

Miller, Keith D. *Voice of Deliverance: The Language of
  Martin Luther King, Jr. and Its Sources.* New York:
  Free Press, 1992.

Miller, William Robert. *Martin Luther King, Jr.: His Life,
  Martyrdom, and Meaning for the World.* New York:
  Weybright and Talley, 1968.

Moses, Greg. *Revolution of Conscience: Martin Luther
  King, Jr., and the Philosophy of Nonviolence.*
  New York: Gilford Press, 1997.

Oates, Stephen B. *Let the Trumpet Sound: The Life of Martin
  Luther King, Jr.* New York: Harper & Row, 1982.

Paulsen, Gary and Dan Theis. *The Man Who Climbed the
  Mountain: Martin Luther King.* Milwaukee:
  Raintree Editions, 1976.

Ray, James Earl. *Who Killed Martin Luther King?: The
  True Story by the Alleged Assassin.* Washington,
  D. C.: National Press Books, 1991.

Schulke, Flip and Penelope O. McPhee. *King
  Remembered,* with a foreword by Jesse Jackson.
  New York: Norton, 1986.

Schuman, Michael. *Martin Luther King, Jr.: Leader for
  Civil Rights.* Springfield, N. J.: Enslow, 1996.

Tucker, Deborah J. and Carrolyn A. Davis. *Unstoppable
  Man: A Bibliography.* Detroit: Wayne State
  University, 1994.

Witherspoon, William Roger. *Martin Luther King, Jr.: To the
  Mountaintop.* Garden City, N. Y.: Doubleday, 1985.

Web sites

The King Center. Retrieved October 12, 2008, from
  http://thekingcenter.com.

✺ Stephen King

BORN: *1947, Portland, Maine*

NATIONALITY: *American*

GENRE: *Fiction, drama*

MAJOR WORKS:

Carrie (1974)

The Stand (1978)

It (1986)

On Writing: A Memoir of the Craft (2000)

The *Dark Tower* Series (1982–2004)

Stephen King *King, Stephen, photograph. AP Images.*

Overview

Stephen King is a prolific and immensely popular author of
horror fiction who blends elements of the traditional
gothic tale with those of the modern psychological thriller,
detective, and science fiction genres.

Works in Biographical and Historical Context

Childhood in Maine Born in Portland, Maine, on
September 21, 1947, King is the second son of Donald
Edwin King, a master mariner in the U.S. Merchant
Marine, and Nellie Ruth Pillsbury King. His father abandoned the family when King was two, and King remembers nothing of him except for finding a box of his books
in 1959 or 1960, an experience he relates in his nonfiction work *Danse Macabre* (1981). King's mother was
highly influential, reading to him and later encouraging
him to submit his manuscripts to publishers. She died of
lung cancer in 1973.

King, his mother, and his older brother, David Victor, lived with relatives in many places: Durham, Maine;
Malden, Massachusetts; Chicago; West De Pere, Wisconsin; Stratford, Connecticut; and Fort Wayne, Indiana.
Nellie Ruth King kept the family together by working
at a succession of low-paying jobs. In 1958, the family
moved to Durham, Maine—later fictionalized in much of

King's work as Castle Rock, Maine—to care for her parents. King finished elementary school in a one-room building in Durham and attended high school in nearby Lisbon Falls. He gained his first experience as a professional writer while still in high school by covering high-school sports for the *Lisbon Enterprise*. He published his first story, "I Was a Teenage Grave Robber," (1965) in *Comics Review*, a fan magazine, and wrote his first novel-length manuscript, "The Aftermath," about life after an atomic-bomb explosion.

College Years King received a scholarship to the University of Maine at Orono. He majored in English and minored in speech, and wrote a column, "King's Garbage Truck," for the *Maine Campus*, the student newspaper. He also participated in student politics and the antiwar movement, which opposed United States involvement in Vietnam. During this period he also published the first fiction for which he was paid, "The Glass Floor" (1967), in *Startling Mystery Stories*. While still an undergraduate, King taught a seminar, "Popular Literature and Culture," after criticizing the English department's traditional approach to literature. He graduated in 1970 and, unable to find a teaching job, pumped gas and worked in a laundry. He later incorporated these experiences into his fiction.

Success with Carrie On January 2, 1971, King married Tabitha Jane Spruce, whom he had met in college. Prior to writing full-time, he worked as a teacher at Hampden Academy. During this time, King—with encouragement from Tabitha—completed the manuscript for *Carrie*, a story partially written in response to allegations that King could not write about women. The tale was also inspired by an odd girl with whom King went to school. He had originally thrown out his first few pages because he was convinced the story was not worth pursuing. The pages were salvaged by his wife, who persuaded him to continue. In 1973, the work was accepted for publication by Doubleday & Company. This allowed King to commit to writing full-time.

In 1976, when *Salem's Lot* (1975) was published in paperback and a paperback edition of *Carrie* was released in conjunction with Brian De Palma's film adaptation, King became a best-selling author. The two paperback editions of *Carrie* sold more than 3.5 million copies. In 1978, he was writer in residence and instructor at the University of Maine at Orono. Because of a course he taught there, and because Bill Thompson, who edited King's first five books at Doubleday, invited him to write about the horror genre, King produced *Danse Macabre* (1981), a nonfiction book that analyzes horror in literature, film, and other popular culture.

The Dark Tower Series: King's Magnum Opus After the release of *Carrie*, King went on to publish dozens of novels, short stories, comics, and nonfiction books during the following three decades. While many of these contain traditional elements of horror fiction,

King's writing frequently includes elements of science fiction, fantasy, and psychological insight. Among the most popular of these are the seven books of *The Dark Tower* (1982–2004) series that ties much of the thematic content from King's other novels together. Inspired by old western movies, Arthurian legend, and the work of authors including Robert Browning and J. R. R. Tolkien, these books concern the quest of the last surviving gunslinger, Roland Deschain, whose only goal is to find and reach the Tower. Many characters, places, and events from the series appear in other popular works by King, including *The Shining* (1977), *The Stand* (1978), *It* (1986), *Insomnia* (1994), and *Bag of Bones* (1998). King himself appears as a character in the series, tying the writer's real-life persona in the mythology of his fiction.

The Richard Bachman Novels In an effort to keep his name from being overpublished, and in response to the reluctance of the publishing community to release multiple works by the same author in a given year, King released several works under the pseudonym Richard Bachman. These novels include *Rage* (1977), *The Long Walk* (1979), *The Running Man* (1982), *Roadwork* (1981), *Thinner* (1984), *The Regulators* (1996), and *Blaze* (2007). King secretly used the Bachman name until 1984, the year his pseudonym was revealed to the reading world. The two Bachman novels published after that time were begun prior to 1984, but later rewritten or completed. Never one to back down from a good story, King has explained that these works were "discovered" among the personal effects of the "deceased" Bachman.

Commercial Success and Personal Pain The popularity of King's fiction brought him commercial success ranked among the "forty highest-grossing U.S. entertainers" according to *Forbes* magazine in 1996. In 1997, King left Viking Penguin, his publisher. In the most recent decade of his career, King has published more than two dozen books, including novels, short story collections, and nonfiction works.

On an afternoon in 1999, King was hit by a vehicle while he was walking down a road near his home in Maine. Despite a collapsed lung and multiple fractures to his leg and hip, King was able to make a full recovery and continue writing. Shortly after the accident, he wrote an eBook (available only on the Internet), *Riding the Bullet* (1999)—a ghost story that was adapted to film in 2004. Later that year, King finished his memoir *On Writing: A Memoir of the Craft* (2000) in which he discusses the role writing played in the process towards recovery after the accident. He writes, "Life isn't a support system for art. It's the other way around."

Literary Recognition In 2003, King was awarded The National Book Foundation's Medal for Distinguished Contribution to American Letters. Also in the early 2000s, King completed the final three installments of his popular *Dark Tower* series. The last one, titled *Dark Tower VII:*

LITERARY AND HISTORICAL CONTEMPORARIES

King's famous contemporaries include:

Tom Clancy (1947–): An American author of popular fiction about adventure and espionage, Clancy is best known for his Jack Ryan novels, which include *The Hunt for Red October* (1984) and *Patriot Games* (1987).

Michael Crichton (1942–2008): Crichton was an American author best known for his science fiction and techno-thriller novels, including *Jurassic Park* (1990).

Tim O'Brien (1946–): O'Brien is an American author most well-known for his fiction about the Vietnam War, which includes his collection of short stories *The Things They Carried* (1990).

Dean Koontz (1945–): Koontz is an American author best known for novels in which he combines the popular literary genres of science fiction, horror, suspense, and romance.

Rob Reiner (1947–): The American film director, author, and political activist Reiner was recognized by the Director's Guild of America for *Stand By Me* (1986), his adaptation of King's novella *The Body* (1982).

The Dark Tower, was released in 2004. That same year he cowrote a TV series, *Kingdom Hospital*, for ABC, which was inspired, in part, by a Danish series by Lars von Tier. Also in 2004, King released a pop-up version of *The Girl Who Loved Tom Gordon* (1999), a work that anticipates his nonfiction work *Faithful* (2005), a book co-written with Stewart O'Nan about the 2004 baseball season and the Red Sox. Tom Gordon, a Red Sox player, guides the lost protagonist in *The Girl Who Loved Tom Gordon* through her walkman. In October of 2006, King was awarded the Grand Master Award by Mystery Writers of America.

King and his wife Tabitha spend their winters in Florida and live the remainder of the year in Maine. King maintains an intense writing schedule, taking only three days off per year. His latest novel, *Duma Key* (2008), is set in Florida and is about a construction worker who suffers a terrible accident.

Works in Literary Context

King's fiction features colloquial language, clinical attention to physical detail and emotional states, realistic settings, and an emphasis on contemporary problems, including marital infidelity and peer-group acceptance, which lend credibility to the supernatural elements in his fiction. His stories often emphasize the presence of horror or evil in commonplace situations. Influenced by the naturalistic novels of writers such as Theodore Dreiser and Frank Norris, King confesses to Paul Janeczko in

English Journal that his personal outlook for the world's future is somewhat bleak. On the other hand, one of the things he finds most comforting in his own work is an element of optimism.

The Horror of the Commonplace King's writing frequently concerns to such subjects as growing up in the 1950s, life in small towns, the devastating impact of politics on ordinary human beings, technology in modern life, childhood (especially in *Carrie, Cujo* (1981), and *It*), and parenthood (especially in *The Shining, Cujo, Pet Sematary,* and *The Dark Half*, which was published in 1989.) Moreover, *Misery* and *The Dark Half* explore writing and the powerful relationships that writers have with their fans. Regardless of their subjects, King's novels display a strong moral bent, a sympathy for working people and residents of small towns, and a sensitivity to the often extreme cruelty of the ordinary world.

The Female Consciousness Although many of King's novels stem from his personal experiences, others examine the lives of young women growing up in the United States. This trend begins with his first novel, *Carrie*, and continues with *Dolores Claiborne* (1992). In between are *The Stand*, in which one major character is a pregnant adolescent; *Firestarter* (1980), whose main character is a girl with the mental ability to set fires; *Cujo*, whose heroine and her son are trapped in her broken-down Pinto by a rabid Saint Bernard; and *Gerald's Game* (1992), whose protagonist, handcuffed to the bedposts by her aging husband, must face her past as a sexually abused child and a future without her husband. Although many of King's earlier works are limited to a focus on women who are strong in their traditional maternal role, King seems to be moving to a full exploration of female consciousness and everything that lies behind women's public personas.

The Connection Between Psychology and the Paranormal King's interest in the paranormal is usually reflected in his protagonists, whose experiences and thoughts serve to reveal psychological complexities and abnormalities. *Carrie*, for example, concerns a socially outcast teenage girl whose emotional insecurities lead her to take violent revenge on taunting classmates by means of telekinetic powers. In *The Shining*, malevolent spirits in a remote resort hotel manipulate a recovering alcoholic caretaker into attempting to murder his wife and child. Similarly, a haunted car in *Christine* (1983) gains control of an alienated teenage boy. Other works in which paranormal events recur include *The Dead Zone* (1979) and *Firestarter*.

Works in Critical Context

Although the critical reception of his work has not necessarily matched its sweeping success with readers, colleagues and critics alike discern within it a substantial and enduring literary legitimacy. In *American Film*, for instance, Darrell Ewing and Dennis Meyers call King "the chronicler of contemporary America's dreams, desires, and fears." And fantasy writer Orson Scott Card, citing King's "brilliant" exploration of current American myths and legends, proclaims in a *Contemporary Authors* interview with Jean W. Ross: "If someone in the future wants to see what American life was like, what Americans cared about, what our stories were in the seventies and eighties, they'll read Stephen King." Moreover, says Card, in fifty years, King will be "regarded as the dominant literary figure of the time. A lot of us feel that way."

King is not yet a favorite with academics or literary critics, partly because they still regard him as "Bestsellasaurus Rex," as George W. Beahm notes in *The Stephen King Story* (1991), and partly because even his most tightly constructed works can be uneven. As he has admitted on many occasions, he recognizes terror and horror as finer emotions but even his best novels include occasional gratuitous violence and gore. However, he is gaining acceptance in the scholarly community: critical analyses of his works are regularly published by university presses, and the *MLA Bibliography* includes articles on King every year.

Carrie   Some reviewers of *Carrie* appreciated the horror of the title character's life and death, while others bemoaned the violence in the novel. The hardcover edition sold a modest thirteen thousand copies, but the paperback edition, published in April 1975, initially sold more than a million copies. "It was with *Carrie* that King established himself as the premier novelist of the supernatural, the dark, and the bizarre" according to Lois H. Gresh and Robert Weinburg in their recent book *The Science of Stephen King* (2007). In their revised edition of *The Complete Stephen King Universe* (2006), authors Stanley Wiater, Christopher Golden, and Hank Wagner note, "The book is also significant in that it would be the first of many novels in which a much-put-upon protagonist would be a strong, willful female—rather than traditionally male—character."

Responses to Literature

1. King wrote *Carrie* partly in response to the criticism that he could not write from a woman's perspective. Since then, he has penned many works from the point of view of a female protagonist. Analyze one of these books. How does King alter his style and subject matter—if at all—to project a feminine voice?

2. Some critics have challenged King's work on grounds that his writing lacks artistic merit. Discuss your opinions of what constitutes artistic merit in literature and evaluate King's work accordingly.

3. Stephen King has said that his aim is to provoke strong emotions, like fear, in his readers. What strategies does King employ to produce such strong emotions? To what extent are these tactics effective?

4. Some readers are put off by King's use of violence and gore. To what extent is there value to incorporating such elements in fiction?

COMMON HUMAN EXPERIENCE

Alienation in childhood is a theme that recurs throughout King's fiction. Other works that explore this theme include the following:

The Catcher in the Rye (1951), a novel by J. D. Salinger. After being expelled from high school, the lonely Holden Caulfield wanders about New York City, struggling to defend himself against the "phoniness" of the world around him.

The Secret Life of Bees (2002), a novel by Sue Monk Kidd. Set in South Carolina in 1964, this tale features Lily Owen, who, feeling unloved by her abusive father, strikes out on her own and gains a sense of identity and belonging with a family that makes honey.

Middlesex (2002), a novel by Jeffrey Eugenides. This story's protagonist, Cal, tells of the difficulties he faced growing up as a hermaphrodite, an individual born with both male and female sex organs.

BIBLIOGRAPHY

Books

Beahm, George. *The Stephen King Story.* Kansas City, Mo.: Andrews & McMeel, 1991.

Coddon, Karin S. *Readings of Stephen King.* San Diego: Greenhaven Press, 2004.

Davis, Jonathan P. *Stephen King's America.* Bowling Green, Ohio: Bowling Green State University Popular Press, 1994.

Herron, Don, ed. *Reign of Fear: Fiction and Film of Stephen King.* Lancaster, Pa.: Underwood-Miller, 1988.

Hoppenstand, Gary and Ray B. Browne, eds. *The Gothic World of Stephen King: Landscape of Nightmares.* Bowling Green, Ohio: Bowling Green State University Popular Press, 1987.

Keyishian, Amy and Marj. *Stephen King.* New York: Chelsea House, 1995.

Lloyd, Ann. *The Films of Stephen King.* New York: St. Martin's Press, 1993.

Magistrale, Tony. *Landscape of Fear: Stephen King's American Gothic.* Bowling Green, Ohio: Bowling Green State University Popular Press, 1988.

Matthew, Donald. *Stephen King.* London: Hambledon and London, 2002.

Murphy, Tim. *In the Darkest Night: A Student's Guide to Stephen King.* Mercer Island, Wash.: Starmont House, 1992.

Rolls, Albert. *Stephen King: A Biography.* Westport, Conn.: Greenwood Press, 2008.

Schweitzer, Darrell. *Discovering Stephen King.* Mercer
    Island, Wash.: Starmont House, 1985.

Spignesi, Stephen J. *The Shape Under the Sheet: The
    Complete Stephen King Encyclopedia.* Chicago:
    Popular Culture, Ink., 1991.

Underwood, Tim and Chuck Miller, eds. *Fear Itself: The
    Horror Fiction of Stephen King.* New York: Signet,
    1982.

———. *Kingdom of Fear: The World of Stephen King.*
    New York: NAL/Plume Trade Paperback, 1986.

Wiater, Stanley, Christopher Golden, and Hank Wagner.
    *The Complete Stephen King Universe: A Guide to the
    Worlds of Stephen King.* New York: Macmillan,
    2006.

Winter, Douglas E. *Stephen King: The Art of Darkness.*
    New York: Signet, 1986.

Zagorski, Edward J. *Teacher's Manual: Novels of Stephen
    King.* New York: New American Library, 1981.

✳ Barbara Kingsolver

BORN: *1955, Annapolis, Maryland*

NATIONALITY: *American*

GENRE: *Fiction, essay, nonfiction*

MAJOR WORKS:

The Bean Trees (1988)

High Tide in Tucson: Essays from Now or Never
    (1995)

The Poisonwood Bible (1998)

Animal, Vegetable, Miracle (2007)

Barbara Kingsolver   *Kingsolver, Barbara, photograph. AP Images.*

Overview

Barbara Kingsolver is a highly acclaimed contemporary author and social activist whose work often concentrates on feminist and environmentalist concerns. In 2000 she was awarded the highest honor for service through the arts, the National Humanities Medal.

Works in Biographical and Historical Context

Writing to Make Experience Real   Born on April 8, 1955, in Annapolis, Maryland, Kingsolver is the daughter of a county physician. Her youth was spent immersed in both the storytelling culture of Appalachia and the scientific culture of her father's profession. When she was in the second grade, she moved to Africa with her family, where her father worked for almost a year as a physician in the Congo. In Africa she began her lifelong habit of keeping a journal. "What I feel," Kingsolver told interviewer L. Elisabeth Beattie, "is that writing is the thing that makes my experience real to me." Wendell Roy and Virginia Lee Henry Kingsolver, her parents, instilled in Barbara and her siblings, Rob and Ann, a love for reading and a respect for the natural world.

Early Education and Travel Abroad   Although she was a prolific writer in her youth, Kingsolver told David King Dunaway that "it never crossed my mind that I'd be a writer when I grew up because I really didn't think of writing as a profession." She did, however, consider a career as a classical pianist, a result of a youth spent virtually without television and with parents who had wide-ranging musical tastes. Kingsolver went to DePauw University in Indiana on a music scholarship, but after realizing how scarce jobs were for pianists she switched her major to something more practical: biology.

During her junior year of college, Kingsolver left Indiana to live and work in Greece and France as an archaeologist's assistant. She returned to DePauw briefly, graduated magna cum laude in 1977, and then returned to France, where she lived until her work visa expired. During those and the following years she earned her living variously as a copy editor, typesetter, biological researcher, and translator.

Return to the United States   When Kingsolver returned to the United States, she settled in Tucson, Arizona. In 1981 she earned a master's degree in ecology and evolutionary biology from the University of Arizona.

She also became active in ecological and humanitarian causes, including the Sanctuary movement to assist Central American refugees. In her early twenties Kingsolver met Joseph Hoffmann, a chemist, to whom she was married from 1985 until 1992. Together they had one child, Camille. Kingsolver sought a PhD in evolutionary biology but left academia in favor of a scientific writing position with the Office of Arid Lands Studies at the University of Arizona. She later married Stephen Hopp, a professor of environmental sciences, with whom she had another daughter, Lily.

Freelancing Career   Getting paid to be a writer gave her the confidence to begin freelancing, at first for local newspapers and magazines and then for such national publications as the *Nation*, the *Progressive*, the *New York Times*, and *Smithsonian*. Through her writing Kingsolver was able to bring together her love of science and her love of the humanities. She continued her journal writing and produced "lots and lots" of poetry. In 1981, to her astonishment, she won a poetry contest sponsored by the University of Arizona and gave her first public reading. In 1983 *Virginia Quarterly Review* accepted her first "decent" fiction, a short story called "Rose-Johnny," which was later collected in *Homeland and Other Stories* (1989).

The Fruits of Insomnia   While pregnant with Camille, Kingsolver suffered from insomnia and as a result began writing a novel. She worked exclusively at night, in the closet of her tiny one-room cottage so she would not disturb her sleeping husband. Her doctor suggested she do something undesirable, such as scrubbing her bathroom tile, so as not to reward her sleeplessness—but instead she stayed awake crafting *The Bean Trees* (1988). Within twenty-four hours of delivering her daughter she had a book deal with Harper and Row.

Kingsolver's first novel was highly acclaimed. Like many stories in the Western American literary canon, *The Bean Trees* is a narrative of self-renewal brought about by a journey west. Self-named protagonist Taylor Greer leaves her Kentucky home in search of a new identity and an escape from what she sees as the inevitable future for a Pittman County girl: early pregnancy and marriage. Unlike the traditional Western hero, however, what Taylor finds is not independence but dependence, not self-determination but strength in community.

In her next book, *Holding the Line: Women in the Great Arizona Mine Strike of 1983* (1989), Kingsolver further characterizes the ways that women create and sustain community. As a stringer for several newspapers in the early 1980s, Kingsolver covered the devastating eighteen-month strikes in three southern Arizona Phelps Dodge mining communities. The book raises questions of economic decline, gender relationships, and corporate discrimination against Mexican Americans. Reviews of *Holding the Line* were mixed.

The same year that *Holding the Line* appeared, Kingsolver published her first collection of short stories, *Homeland and Other Stories* (1989). The central questions in *Homeland*, concerning how people are bound to each other and to place, anticipate Kingsolver's second novel, *Animal Dreams* (1990). *Animal Dreams* also grows out of Kingsolver's conviction that the personal is political and that her job as a writer of fiction is, simply put, to change the world. The characters in *Animal Dreams*, like those from Kingsolver's earlier fiction, are people who have been traditionally considered marginal in canonical literature. *Animal Dreams* is a complex postmodern story that explores the relationships among memory, truth, and experience. In it, Kingsolver relies on the power of stories to effect change. *Animal Dreams* won many accolades: the PEN/USA West Fiction Award, the Edward Abbey Award for Ecofiction, and the Arizona Library Association Book of the Year award.

Challenging the American Myth of Individuality Kingsolver's book of poetry, *Another America/Otra América* (1992) is a conversation between North America and South America. Many of the poems reflect ways in which the two continents view each other. Each of the poems in the volume is a story; each poem critiques a social ill to which Kingsolver is exposed, including homophobia, racism, colonialism, and sexism. The poetry in this volume revolves around a favorite theme of Kingsolver's: the American cultural myth of individuality.

While themes of conversation and conflict are evident in many of these poems, they are most fully developed in *Pigs in Heaven* (1993), the sequel to *The Bean Trees*. *Pigs in Heaven* is about the difficulty of single motherhood, the development of community consciousness, adoption, abuse, ethnic identity, and poverty. *Pigs in Heaven*, like *Animal Dreams* and *The Bean Trees*, was an ABBY nominee. Kingsolver's third novel also won the *Los Angeles Times* Fiction Prize and the Cowboy Hall of Fame Western Fiction Award.

Kingsolver's next book, a collection of twenty-five essays, is titled *High Tide in Tucson: Essays from Now or Never* (1995). She calls the essays "creative nonfiction" and likens her writing process in composing the essays to that of fiction. The essays are autobiographical and take as their subjects book tours; childhood; patriotism; life in the Canary Islands; her love of books; her critiques of such writers as Henry David Thoreau, Stephen Gould, and Charles Darwin; and her stint as keyboard player in the band Rock Bottom Remainders, which also featured novelists Stephen King and Amy Tan. As in her fiction and poetry, her background as social activist directly influences the essays. In its first four months the collection sold more than any of Kingsolver's previous books had during the initial months following their publication.

Establishment of the Bellwether Prize for Fiction In 1997 Kingsolver established the Bellwether Prize for Fiction, which recognizes literature of social change. By creating this award, Kingsolver hopes to give American trade publishers an incentive to publish and promote the

LITERARY AND HISTORICAL CONTEMPORARIES

Kingsolver's famous contemporaries include:

Madonna (1958–): An American singer, actress, and entertainer, Madonna is the best-selling female singer of the twentieth-century. She was inducted into the Rock and Roll Hall of Fame in March of 2008.

Amy Tan (1952–): Chinese American author who is most famous for her novel *The Joy Luck Club* (1989), about the experiences of Chinese American immigrants.

Chitra Divakaruni (1956–): A versatile Indian American author of fiction, poetry, children's stories, and nonfiction essays whose work brings to life the realities of living as an immigrant in America.

Oprah Winfrey (1954–): American television host of the internationally syndicated *Oprah Winfrey Show*, which has been awarded multiple Emmy Awards; Oprah is also a philanthropist, and her televised Book Club has helped shape the American best seller lists.

John Grisham (1955–): An immensely popular author of legal thrillers, Grisham is best known for his novel *The Firm* (1991), which centers around a recent Harvard Law School graduate who, after learning that his firm is heavily involved in organized crime, risks his life to help the FBI indict his associates and their Mob bosses.

kind of fiction she most admires—fiction that exposes injustice and explores issues of social responsibility.

Kingsolver's devotion to social justice through art continues in her novel *The Poisonwood Bible* (1998). In this book, zealous, uncompromising Baptist missionary Nathan Price takes his wife, Orleanna, and four daughters to the Belgian Congo in 1959, where they remain through the next three decades of stormy, violent African history. Orleanna and the four girls—teenaged Rachel, twins Leah and Adah, and five-year-old Ruth May—take turns narrating and responding to political developments in the Congo as well as the personal tragedies of the Price family. The book reflects Kingsolver's own experience living in the Congo for almost a year during the same time period as a child.

Kingsolver Awarded the National Humanities Medal

In 2000 she was awarded the highest honor for service through the arts, the National Humanities Medal. That same year, she published another novel, *Prodigal Summer*, and two years later, her second collection of essays, *Small Wonder* (2002). Kingsolver left the Southwest in 2004 and moved to a farm in southwestern Virginia, where she now lives with her family. Her most recent book, *Animal, Vegetable, Miracle* (2007) chronicles her family's food project, a year-long attempt to restrict their food consumption to local products.

Works in Literary Context

Kingsolver is a writer of fiction, poetry, and nonfiction, but as she told interviewer Donna Perry, if she had to categorize herself by genre, she would pick storytelling. Her work is deeply rooted in a sense of place, whether she is depicting rural Kentucky, the Belgian Congo, the arid Southwest, or her farm in Virginia. Kingsolver counts Southern writers such as Flannery O'Connor, Eudora Welty, and William Faulkner among her earliest literary influences. Other influences on her writing include her rural childhood, with its exposure to storytelling, community, and social responsibility; love and respect for the natural world; social activism; and scientific background.

Social Justice and Feminism

Barbara Kingsolver renews the Western literary landscape by debunking the myths of individuality and self-determination. Her heroines lead meaningful lives by relying on compromise and community. Kingsolver's work reflects the real West in which she lives—a West populated by people with different values, histories, and worldviews. Kingsolver's devotion to social justice and her commitment to activism shape her vision. As she writes in *High Tide in Tucson*, "Good art is political, whether it means to be or not, insofar as it provides the chance to understand points of view alien to our own." The points of view of single mothers, Guatemalan refugees, children, and even a hermit crab are among those Kingsolver presents to her readers. Kingsolver calls herself a feminist and writes "from a point of view that's unequivocally female." Kingsolver's female characters perform mundane yet heroic deeds: they feed children, support friends, and restore justice, all foundational acts that sustain community.

Kingsolver's literary contributions as feminist, social activist, environmentalist, and community advocate ensure her an important place in American letters. As a Western writer, she continues to revise the canon and set high standards for her Western American contemporaries.

Works in Critical Context

Kingsolver has enjoyed both critical acclaim and wide readership during her career as an author. While many regard her fiction as compelling, some reviewers have criticized her inattention to the male perspective, particularly in her nonfiction essays. Kingsolver has been awarded numerous accolades for her work, including the prestigious National Humanities Medal. She is admired and often praised for her commitment to social justice.

The Poisonwood Bible

The Poisonwood Bible garnered critical praise in advance of its fall release. A reviewer for *Publishers Weekly* stated that in this "risky but resoundingly successful novel" Kingsolver presents "a compelling family saga, a sobering picture of the horrors of fanatic fundamentalism and an insightful view of an exploited country crushed by the heel of colonialism and then ruthlessly manipulated by a bastion of democracy." A critic for *Kirkus*

Reviews praised the "consistently absorbing narrative" as well as Kingsolver's skillful blending of the personal and the political: "Kingsolver convinces us that her characters are, first and foremost, breathing, fallible human beings and only secondarily conduits for her book's vigorously expressed and argued social and political ideas." A national best seller, *The Poisonwood Bible* was chosen by the *New York Times* as one of the ten best books of 1998.

Responses to Literature

1. Like many of Kingsolver's novels, *Animal Dreams* explores the relationship between humans and the natural world. Discuss the role that creation stories, such as the Pueblo creation legend and the Garden of Eden story, play in shaping this relationship and other aspects of the human experience. Do the myths of different cultures illustrate their different perspectives on humanity's relationship with nature?

2. Discuss the context in which the title phrase, the poisonwood bible, comes into being. How does it relate to the main themes in *The Poisonwood Bible*?

3. What kinds of captivity are explored in *The Poisonwood Bible*? What are the causes and implications of each type of captivity?

4. Kingsolver often begins her essays with a story from her life before moving forward to make a more general argument. What are the advantages and disadvantages of this strategy? Are there places where her logic falters or that you disagree with her conclusions?

BIBLIOGRAPHY

Books

Beattie, L. Elisabeth. "Barbara Kingsolver." *Conversations with Kentucky Writers*. Edited by Elisabeth L. Beattie. Lexington: University of Kentucky Press, 1996, pp. 151–171.

Dunaway, David King. "Barbara Kingsolver." *Writing the Southwest*. Edited by David King Dunaway and Sara L. Spurgeon. New York: Penguin, 1995, pp. 93–107.

Perry, Donna. "Barbara Kingsolver." *Backtalk: Women Writers Speak Out*. Edited by Donna Perry. New Brunswick, N.J.: Rutgers University Press, 1993, pp. 145–168.

Periodicals

Bowdan, Janet. "Re-placing Ceremony: The Poetics of Barbara Kingsolver." *Southwestern American Literature* 20 (Spring 1995): 13–19.

Epstein, Robin. "Barbara Kingsolver." *Progressive Review* 60 (February 1996): 33–38.

Flemming, Bruce. "'Woolf Cubs': Current Fiction." *Antioch Review* 52 (Fall 1994): 548–565.

Pence, Amy. "An Interview with Barbara Kingsolver." *Poets and Writers* 21 (July 1993): 14–21.

Ryan, Maureen. "Barbara Kingsolver's Lowfat Fiction." *Journal of American Culture* 19 (Winter 1995): 77–82.

Web sites

Barbara Kingsolver. Retrieved October 9, 2008, from http://www.kingsolver.com.

> # COMMON HUMAN EXPERIENCE
>
> In her writing, Kingsolver frequently centers on the relationship between human beings and the natural world. Other works that explore this theme include the following:
>
> *Walden* (1854), a nonfiction book by Henry David Thoreau. In this work, Thoreau reflects upon his experiences during his two-year stay at a cabin near Walden Pond.
>
> "Mowing" (1915), a poem by Robert Frost. In this piece, a man in a field hears his scythe whispering to him.
>
> *Ox-Cart Man* (1979), a children's book written by Donald Hall and illustrated by Barbara Cooney. This adaptation of one of Hall's poems, which won a Caldecott Medal, depicts the simple but powerful connections between a farmer, his animals, and the land he works.
>
> *An Inconvenient Truth* (2006), a documentary directed by Davis Guggenheim. In this film, former vice president Al Gore links global warming to human activities by presenting scientific data and discussing the long-term implications of climate change.

Maxine Hong Kingston

BORN: *1940, Stockton, California*

NATIONALITY: *American*

GENRE: *Nonfiction, fiction*

MAJOR WORKS:

The Woman Warrior: Memoirs of a Girlhood among Ghosts (1976)

China Men (1980)

Tripmaster Monkey: His Fake Book (1989)

Overview

Maxine Hong Kingston is one of the most influential Asian American authors of the twentieth century. Her postmodernist amalgamation of oral histories, myths, family stories, and fictionalizations have become the yardstick against which Asian American writers are measured.

Maxine Hong Kingston   *Kingston, Maxine Hong, photograph. © Jerry Bauer. Reproduced by permission.*

Works in Biographical and Historical Context

The Daughter of Chinese Immigrants Maxine Hong Kingston was born on October 27, 1940, to Chinese immigrants living in Stockton, California. Her father, Tom Hong, had immigrated to the United States through Cuba, eventually co-founding a laundry service with three friends in New York City. Her mother, Chew Ling Yan (Brave Orchid), stayed behind in China until Tom could afford to send for her. In the interim she attended a Westernized medical school and became a physician and midwife. Hong's English name, Maxine, was inspired by a lucky gambler. Her Chinese name, Ting Ting, comes from a Chinese poem concerned with self-reliance. Her mother had two children in China, but they died overseas, leaving Kingston the eldest of six (American-born) children.

Finding Her Voice Kingston's education got off to a rocky start, for in kindergarten she refused to speak and covered all her drawings with ink from a heavy black marker. She flunked kindergarten, never finding the words to explain that the black lines over her drawings were black curtains reminiscent of those her parents used for privacy during World War II, a time when many Asian

Americans feared retribution and discrimination due to the Japanese attack on Pearl Harbor and alliance with Nazi Germany. However, she also attended Chinese school in the afternoons, and there she was able to find her voice and interact with other children. In time she learned the English language, and, by the time she began attending Sunset High School in Stockton, she had become an honor student and even won an award for her writing.

Protesting War Kingston received various scholarship offers and accepted one from the University of California, Berkeley, where she majored in English and wrote for the university newspaper. She graduated from Berkeley in 1962 with a BA in English, and that year married stage actor Earll Kingston, whom she had met during a production of Bertolt Brecht's *Galileo* (1943). Fellow Berkeley graduates, both were active in Vietnam War protests and in efforts to protect free speech. Kingston has remained active in antiwar movements: in March 2003 she was arrested, along with novelist Alice Walker, Nobel Peace laureate Jody Williams, singer Michelle Shocked, and comedian/actor Janeane Garofalo (all members of the organization Code Pink), for protesting the United States-led invasion of Iraq. The Kingstons' son, Joseph Lawrence Cheng Mei, was born in 1964.

Move to Hawaii In 1965, Kingston earned her teacher's certificate from Berkeley and began teaching English and mathematics at a high school in Hayward, California. However, the Kingstons soon became disturbed by the increasing violence of both police and protestors during the antiwar movement, as well as many of their Berkeley friends' drug addictions, so in 1967 they moved with their son Joseph to Oahu, Hawaii—a locale they thought would be immune to United States militarization. They lived there for nearly two decades, with Kingston teaching English as a second language at an exclusive school. In the meantime, she worked on the memoirs that eventually became *The Woman Warrior* and *China Men*, publishing excerpts during the 1970s in various magazines.

First Literary Success Ultimately, Kingston blindly chose three literary agents out of a telephone directory and sent them fifty polished pages of her manuscript of *The Woman Warrior*. One of those agents, John Schaffner, agreed to take on Kingston as a client and submitted her manuscript to Knopf, which agreed to publish *The Woman Warrior* under the category autobiographical nonfiction in order to make it more marketable. The book was reviewed by *New York Times* critic John Leonard, who was impressed with Kingston. He quickly informed other editors of Kingston; the result was that Kingston sold 40,000 copies of her first book-length work. *The Woman Warrior* was an overnight success.

Return to California Kingston returned to California with Earll in 1984 and took a position as senior lecturer in English at the University of California, Berkeley. While there, she published two limited edition texts, *Hawai'i One Summer* (1987) and *Through the Black Curtain* (1987), collections of previously published essays and sketches (although the latter included sections from her then-forthcoming novel, *Tripmaster Monkey: His Fake Book*). In *Hawai'i One Summer*, Kingston explains how being in Hawaii, where she was accepted as a local, nourished her artistically. She later fictionalized her Hawaii years via the characters Wittman Ah Sing and his wife Tana in the "Water" section of *The Fifth Book of Peace* (2003).

Considered by many to be her first actual novel, *Tripmaster Monkey: His Fake Book* (1989) is the story of a 1960s Berkeley graduate-turned-beatnik named Wittman Ah Sing. The gentle satire of the novel is hinted at in its title, *Tripmaster Monkey: His Fake Book*, which alludes to the "tripmaster" in an LSD or mushroom trip and the Monkey King of Chinese legend. While most reaction to *Tripmaster Monkey: His Fake Book* was favorable, some reviewers were disappointed because Kingston so drastically changed the direction of her prose. In fact, *Tripmaster Monkey: His Fake Book* was pegged by more than a few critics as an artistic failure.

Making More Time for Family Kingston's next publication was a chapbook co-authored with Luisa Valenzuela titled *Two Foreign Women*, in which she briefly discusses the writing of *Tripmaster Monkey: His Fake Book*. A decade later she finished her next book-length project, *To Be the Poet* (2002), a complete departure for her based on her William E. Massey Lectures at Harvard University in 2000. Here, Kingston decided to try her hand at a mixture of prose and poetry, noting that the "long book" (that is, *The Fifth Book of Peace*, which she was writing when *To Be the Poet* was published) takes away from her time with family.

Kingston continues to write and lives with her husband in Oakland, California.

Works in Literary Context

Kingston has often been called a "word warrior" because her prose confronts Chinese American sexism and American racism. But Kingston deals with these and other difficult issues not only in her literature, but outside of it as well. Whether she is fighting for equality or promoting pacifism, her tireless efforts to play the Monkey King (in one of his seventy-two incarnations) by subtly jabbing at "the system"—even while being received by dignitaries or given awards for her literature—show her devotion to having a real, positive impact on the world. Kingston's writing is primarily influenced by several things: her experience growing up in America as the daughter of first-generation Chinese immigrants; her mother's storytelling; and her education at Berkeley.

Translating Oral Tradition into Writing Kingston's belief that a life can be fictionalized in one continuous story, even if the story unfolds over four books written some thirty years apart, is certain to change the face of the

---

LITERARY AND HISTORICAL CONTEMPORARIES

Kingston's famous contemporaries include:

Luisa Valenzuela (1938–): Argentinean author of works which frequently employ magic realism; she has collaborated with Maxine Kingston.

Leslie Marmon Silko (1948–): Native American author who writes about the Laguna Pueblo tribe, her experiences living on the edge of Native American culture, and the impact of war on individuals.

Amy Tan (1952–): Chinese-American author who is most famous for her novel the *Joy Luck Club* (1989), about the experiences of Chinese American immigrants.

---

publishing industry. Her legacy to literary history also includes her experimentation with genres, combining fiction and mythology with nonfiction, mingling autobiography, biography, and history. In the process, Kingston has elevated the oral tradition—in the form of the talk story—so that it is equal with the written word in her works. She has poeticized the language spoken in her Stockton Cantonese community, a dialect called Say Yup, which has resulted in her distinctive sounds and rhythms. In essence, she has translated the oral tradition of a community into a written one. In fact, Kingston posits that community, or tribe, is what makes literature come alive, and her emphasis on community, comparable to authors such as Toni Morrison and Leslie Marmon Silko, has influenced those Asian American authors who have followed in her footsteps.

Kingston's thoughtful grappling with the issues of ethnicity and assimilation (from both the male and female points of view) has changed the way in which these problems are addressed by minority authors. Kingston's literary legacy has been enormous, as Tan, David Henry Hwang, Gish Jen, Fae Myenne Ng, Chitra Banerjee Divakaruni, Gus Lee, and Sigrid Nunez have been strongly influenced by her mythicizing of Chinese American history.

Works in Critical Context

Kingston first attracted critical attention when she published *The Woman Warrior*, which became an instant success. Her next work, *China Men*, received positive reviews for both its style and its political stance. While most reaction to *Tripmaster Monkey: His Fake Book* was favorable, some reviewers expressed disappointment in her change of style, some going so far as to label it an "artistic failure." Over the course of her career, Kingston has gained the respect of the literary community and is now credited with being an instrumental force in the battle for ethnic writers not to be judged as mouthpieces for their cultural heritages. Kingston also has helped to change the way Americans think about ethnicity, with her constant fight to change the English language to make it more inclusive.

The Woman Warrior Perhaps unsurprising given the complexity of *The Woman Warrior*, early reviews, though mostly positive, often reflected critics' and reviewers' confusion about, and wildly different reactions to, Kingston's narrative. For example, three articles from the late 1980s and early 1990s, Ya-Jie Zhang's "A Chinese Woman's Response to Maxine Hong Kingston's *The Woman Warrior*," Frank Chin's "The Most Popular Book in China," and Sau-ling Cynthia Wong's "Autobiography as Guided Chinatown Tour?" argue over the veracity and value of the myths and representations in *The Woman Warrior*. As Edward Iwata reported, Chin had concluded that Kingston was "the publisher's manipulation of another Pocahontas," insisting that Kingston's text offered "fake" myths and was informed by racist stereotypes. On the other hand, Zhang accepts the representative quality of Kingston's amalgamated characters, seeing her own upbringing reflected in the stories; she felt *The Woman Warrior* had captured the essence of growing up as a first-generation member of an ethnic minority. Meanwhile, Wong took on Chin and his "Chinatown Cowboys" who raided academic conferences attended by Kingston in order to challenge and ridicule her. Wong argues that the myths included in *The Woman Warrior* are not "fake," but rather remade and modernized so that they still have value.

According to critic Sami Ludwig, *The Woman Warrior* remained on the bestseller list for paperbacks until 1989 and by 1993 was still selling steadily, totaling some 450,000 copies. Since its publication in 1976, the book has gone through many editions and printings, and it has been translated into more than three dozen languages.

Time magazine named it one of the ten most important nonfiction works of the 1970s. And, as the Modern Language Association (MLA) points out, it is the most often taught text in universities, used in teaching a variety of disciplines, including education, sociology, psychology, anthropology, women's studies, Asian studies, American literature, and composition.

Responses to Literature

1. Discuss the use of humor in Kingston's *The Woman Warrior*.

2. According to Kingston, what does it mean to be "American-normal"? Do you agree with her?

3. How does the structure of *The Woman Warrior* impact your reading of the text?

4. Discuss the theme of silence in *The Woman Warrior*. How do women find their voice? How is a person's voice connected to their identity?

BIBLIOGRAPHY

Books

Chau, Patricia P. *Assimilating Asians: Gendered Strategies of Authorship in Asian America.* Durham, N.C.: Duke University Press, 2000.

Cheung, King-Kok. *Articulate Silences: Hisaye Yamamoto, Maxine Hong Kingston, Joy Kogawa.* Ithaca, N.Y.: Cornell University Press, 1993.

Chin, Frank. *Maxine Hong Kingston's The Woman Warrior: A Casebook.* New York: Oxford University Press, 1999.

Feng, Pin-Chia. *The Female Bildungsroman by Toni Morrison and Maxine Hong Kingston.* New York: Peter Lang, 1999.

Huntley, E. D. *Maxine Hong Kingston: A Critical Companion.* Westport, Conn.: Greenwood Press, 2001.

Ling, Amy. "Chinese American Women Writers: The Tradition Behind Maxine Hong Kingston." *Redefining American Literary History*, edited by A. LaVonne Brown Ruoff and Jerry W. Ward Jr. New York: Modern Language Association, 1990, pp. 219–236.

Simmons, Diane. *Maxine Hong Kingston.* New York: Twayne, 1999.

Skandera-Trombley, Laura E., ed. *Critical Essays on Maxine Hong Kingston.* New York: G. K. Hall, 1998.

❀ Galway Kinnell

BORN: *1927, Providence, Rhode Island*

NATIONALITY: *American*

GENRE: *Poetry*

MAJOR WORKS:

Selected Poems (1982)

A New Selected Poems (2000)

Galway Kinnell   *Kinnell, Galway, 2003, photograph. AP Images.*

Overview

Galway Kinnell is an award-winning poet whose work seeks to establish the significance of life through daily human experience. In 1983 Kinnell received both the American Book Award and the Pulitzer Prize for his *Selected Poems* (1982).

Works in Biographical and Historical Context

Early Show of Academic Promise   Born in Providence, Rhode Island, on February 1, 1927, Galway Kinnell was the youngest of four children. He attended public schools but showed such academic promise that during his senior year of high school he won a scholarship to a prestigious private school. He subsequently attended Princeton University, where he became acquainted with poet W. S. Merwin. After receiving his BA degree from Princeton in 1948, he attended the University of Rochester, where in 1949 he received his MA. Through the 1950s, he supervised the downtown campus of the University of Chicago, and then lived in France under a Fulbright scholarship, teaching at the University of Gre-

noble and translating. In the late 1950s, he lived on and off in the Lower East Side of New York City, alternately serving as visiting writer at several colleges, including Juniata College, Colorado State University, Reed College, University of California, Irvine, and the University of Iowa. Subsequently, he received another Fulbright, this time to Iran. His only novel, *Black Light* (1966), was based on his experience there.

Dickey and Bogan Praise First Poetry Collection
Kinnell's first published volume of poems, *What a Kingdom It Was* (1960), received favorable notice from both James Dickey and Louise Bogan. Not until the publication of *First Poems, 1946–1954* (1970) was his earlier poetry collected. These poems are found in the more widely available volume *The Avenue Bearing the Initial of Christ into the New World: Poems 1946–1964* (1974).

Relating Christianity and Nature   Compared to his early work, the poems in *What a Kingdom It Was* address the problem of the relationship between Christianity and nature much more directly. Overall, the book never loses sight of the relationship between poetry and nature. In "First Song" the poet describes how a boy learns "fine music" by listening to frogs and to a violin made of cornstalks. In the end the boy's song describes a happiness that emerges from the simultaneous presence of both sadness and joy. At the level of pure sound, poetry is part of nature itself. In "The Avenue Bearing the Initial of Christ into the New World," Kinnell presents the details of an urban landscape so that they are as transcendentally resonant as in the best of his poetry set entirely in nature.

Family Life and Activism in the 1960s   In 1961 Kinnell bought an old farm in rural Vermont and in 1965 he married Inez Delgado del Torres. The marriage lasted for twenty years. In 1966 a daughter, Maud Natasha, was born, and in 1968 a son, Finn Fergus, followed. Both children figure prominently in Kinnell's later poetry. Through the 1960s, Kinnell walked the path of the social activist, beginning with a 1963 trip to Louisiana to work with the Congress for Racial Equality. In the late 1960s, he was a prominent activist protesting against the Vietnam War.

In *Body Rags* (1968) Kinnell develops an extended metaphor that he had touched on in earlier work—the figure of life in relation to fire. This idea is developed in detail by Richard Howard in his essay on Kinnell in *Alone with America: Essays on the Art of Poetry in America since 1950* (1969). Kinnell's poem "The Last River" is widely acknowledged as a preeminent example of the poetry of social protest. In the context of the Vietnam War, in which firebombing by American airplanes was common, the trope is appropriate, especially in "Vapor Trail Reflected in Frog Pond," which resounds as preeminent among that category of antiwar nature poetry also written in the same period by Robert Bly. For Kinnell, as well as for Bly, the war in its essence was a war against Earth itself.

In *The Book of Nightmares* (1971) Kinnell reacts against the urban-technological domain by asserting that a "cruel but pure" poetic process serves in some sense to cleanse and perhaps to lead to a tentative kind of redemption. The speaker of the poem suffers the torture of simultaneously living in a nightmare and in day-to-day experience.

The Importance of Human Affection In 1975 the National Institute of Arts and Letters recognized Kinnell by awarding him its Medal of Merit. In 1978 he returned to France as a Fulbright scholar. He taught for part of the year in Australia at Macquarie University and part at the University of Hawaii, where he remained until 1982. In *Mortal Acts, Mortal Words* (1980), one finds on the surface what seems to be a shift away from the carefully structured and unified volume found in *The Book of Nightmares*. However, as John Unterecker has pointed out, *Mortal Acts, Mortal Words* is best read as having a musical structure with symmetries and repetitions that reinforce an overarching theme celebrating the importance of human affection. Such affections are always rooted in nature, in a geographical place wherein affections take on one or another kind of dimension.

Renewed Activism for the Antinuclear Movement In 1983 Kinnell received both the American Book Award and the Pulitzer Prize for his *Selected Poems* (1982), and in 1984 he received the prestigious MacArthur grant. This period was marked by his renewed activism, this time focused on the antinuclear movement. In *The Past* (1985), Kinnell reconciles with a deepening elegiac sense, as in "The Fundamental Project of Technology," in which he calls Time by both its names—past and future—simultaneously. While looking at uniformed children in Nagasaki, Kinnell takes from the past the awful event of the dropping of the atomic bomb and projects it into the future as silence. In the same year that *The Past* was published, Kinnell became the Samuel F. B. Morse Professor of Fine Arts at New York University. In 1987 he paid tribute to one of his most important influences, Walter Whitman, by publishing *The Essential Whitman*.

In *When One Has Lived a Long Time Alone* (1990), two erotically charged poems—"The Perch" and "Last Gods"—support Kinnell's concern with rooting human affection in geographical place. In 1990 Kinnell again paid tribute to a major literary influence by bringing out, in collaboration with Hannah Liebmann, a new translation of Rainer Maria Rilke's poetry.

Moral Questions Bound by Human Will In *Imperfect Thirst* (1994) Kinnell's poetic journey takes him deeper into the realm of domesticity. One of the most significant poems of nature in this volume is "Flies," more than one hundred and fifty lines long. In it Kinnell quotes fly-related poetic lore from Walt Whitman, Karl Shapiro, Miroslav Holub, Emily Dickinson, Christopher Smart, Antonio Machado, John Clare, James K. Baxter, William Blake, Martin Luther, Edward Taylor, and Federico Garcìa Lorca. This range of attitudes toward flies is bounded by human will, related to the essentially moral question of whether or not to kill flies. Within the boundaries of the poem, one can find, for example, Clare describing houseflies as members of the family, Blake pondering the oneness of man and fly, or Luther declaring war against flies. Kinnell refers to Clare as helping prepare the way for Charles Darwin. In this poem Kinnell's speaker internalizes the fly as keeping him awake at night, associating it with guilt or regret.

From 2001 until 2007, Kinnell served as a chancellor of the Academy of American Poets. During that time he published a new collection of poems, *Strong Is Your Hold* (2006). Now retired, Kinnell lives in Vermont.

Works in Literary Context

Throughout his career, Galway Kinnell has written poetry that investigates the complex and conflicted relationship between humanity and nature, spirituality, and issues of social justice. His work is influenced by the education he received while at Princeton, his travels abroad, the climate of the Vietnam War era, and authors including Walt Whitman, Edgar Allan Poe, and Emily Dickinson.

Humanity's Relationship with Nature In more than fifty years of active writing and publishing, Kinnell has consistently explored a range of alternative perspectives toward the natural world, including the shamanistic one he is particularly well known for portraying in "The Bear."

Kinnell's writing, as Richard J. Calhoun has described it, is postmodern and neoromantic, and, as Lee Zimmerman has explained in considerable detail, Kinnell's poetry manages to hold in conflict the polarities of humans' relationship to nature. Many poems empathetically participate in nature, and in this regard they sometimes arrive at terror. Alternatively, sometimes the poems portray nurturing, a sense of otherness, approaching the natural world as new and renewing.

As Robert Bly has suggested, Galway Kinnell's ability to recognize the eternal in nature at the same time that he represents essentially the "fallen" state of nature allows his poems to assert a transformative power. However, this way is never the easy path to grace. Kinnell's poems portray the inevitable struggle to live life fully; yet, they consistently show how poetry, in its drive to connect with readers, can bring meaning to the struggle.

Works in Critical Context

Kinnell's earliest poetry from the 1940s and 1950s went largely unnoticed until it was collected and republished in the 1970s. However, his first volume of poems, *What a Kingdom It Was* (1960), drew positive attention from reviewers including James Dickey and Louise Bogan. The antiwar poetry Kinnell produced during the 1970s resonated with readers and the antiwar sentiments of the decade. When Kinnell won the Pulitzer Prize for *Selected Poems*, his earlier work gained a larger audience and became subject to more critical attention.

Selected Poems *Selected Poems*, for which Kinnell won the Pulitzer Prize in 1983 and was co-winner of the American Book Award, is, to quote Morris Dickstein, "more than a good introduction to Galway Kinnell's work. It is a full scale dossier." The collection, published in 1982, contains works from every period in the poet's career. In his review of the book, Robert Hass concludes:

> Kinnell is widely read by the young who read poetry. If this were a different culture, he would simply be widely read.... The common reader—the one who reads at night or on the beach for pleasure and instruction and diversion—who wants to sample the poetry being written in [his] part of the 20th century could do very well beginning with Galway Kinnell's *Selected Poems.*

Kinnell is highly regarded by contemporary critics. For example, *New York Times Book Review* essayist Morris Dickstein calls Kinnell "one of the true master poets of his generation and a writer whose career exemplifies some of what is best in contemporary poetry." Similarly, Robert Langbaum observes in the *American Poetry Review* that Kinnell, "at a time when so many poets are content to be skillful and trivial, speaks with a big voice about the whole of life."

COMMON HUMAN EXPERIENCE

Throughout Kinnell's poetry, he engages with the relationship between humanity and nature. Other works that explore this theme include the following:

Leaves of Grass (1855), a poetry collection by Walt Whitman. With an emphasis on spirituality and the human body, Whitman explores the natural world.

Nature (1936), an essay and short book by Ralph Waldo Emerson. In this famous work, Emerson lays out the tenets of transcendentalism—a belief system that regards nature as divine.

Animal, Vegetable, Miracle (2007), a nonfiction book by Barbara Kingsolver. This work chronicles one family's food project, a year-long attempt to restrict their food consumption to local products.

Responses to Literature

1. In the poem "Another Night in Ruins," what does Kinnell conclude about creativity by the end of the poem? Do you agree with his perspective?

2. Based on your reading of Kinnell's poetry, how would you describe his view of the relationship between humanity and nature? Provide specific examples to support your opinion.

3. Some critics have praised Kinnell's ability to appeal to young readers. To what extent do you agree with this assessment of Kinnell's work? If you do agree, what is it about his work that you find compelling? If not, explain your views, citing examples from his work.

4. Read "When the Towers Fell" (2002), paying particular attention to the sections that are not written in English. Why do you think Kinnell decided to use more than one language in the poem? What effect does this have on your reading of the text?

BIBLIOGRAPHY

Books

Bly, Robert. "Galway Kinnell and the Old Farmer." In *On the Poetry of Galway Kinnell: The Wages of the Dying*. Edited by Howard Nelson. Ann Arbor: University of Michigan Press, 1988, pp. 178–184.

Bogan, Louise. "From 'Verse.'" In *On the Poetry of Galway Kinnell: The Wages of Dying*. Edited by Howard Nelson. Ann Arbor: University of Michigan Press, 1988, p. 67.

Calhoun, Richard J. *Galway Kinnell*. New York: Maxwell Macmillan International, 1992.

Dickey, James. "From 'Five First Books.'" In *On the Poetry of Galway Kinnell: The Wages of Dying*. Edited by Howard Nelson. Ann Arbor: University of Michigan Press, 1988, pp. 65–66.

Howard, Richard. "Galway Kinnell." In *Alone with America: Essays on the Art of Poetry in America since 1950*. New York: Atheneum, 1969, pp. 304–319.

Logan, John. "The Bear in the Poet in the Bear." In *On the Poetry of Galway Kinnell: The Wages of Dying*. Edited by Howard Nelson. Ann Arbor: University of Michigan Press, 1988, pp. 76–81.

Tuten, Nancy Lewis. *Critical Essays on Galway Kinnell*. New York: G. K. Hall, 1996.

Unterecker, John. "Of Father, Of Son: On 'Fergus Falling,' 'After Making Love We Hear Footsteps,' and 'Angling, a Day.'" In *On the Poetry of Galway Kinnell: The Wages of Dying*. Edited by Howard Nelson. Ann Arbor: University of Michigan Press, 1988, pp. 227–241.

Zimmerman, Lee. *Intricate and Simple Things: The Poetry of Galway Kinnell*. Urbana: University of Illinois Press, 1987.

❀ John Knowles

BORN: *1926, Fairmont, West Virginia*

DIED: *2001, Fort Lauderdale, Florida*

NATIONALITY: *American*

GENRE: *Fiction*

MAJOR WORKS:

A Separate Peace (1959)

John Knowles   *Knowles, John, 1972, photograph. AP Images.*

Overview

Knowles is best known for his first novel, *A Separate Peace* (1959). Set in the World War II era, the work has been consistently popular with young adults since its publication. Here, as in many of his other works, Knowles examines young heroes facing the tests of modern life and arriving at the painful realization that evil exists in society and in themselves—realizations that Knowles sees as major steps toward adulthood.

Works in Biographical and Historical Context

A Privileged Upbringing John Knowles was born in Fairmont, West Virginia, on September 26, 1926, to James Myron and Mary Beatrice Shea Knowles. He has an older brother and sister who are twins as well as a younger sister. Knowles left West Virginia at the age of fifteen to attend the Phillips Exeter Academy in New Hampshire during the World War II years, a setting and time period that would be significant as inspiration for his best-known work. After graduating in 1945, he enlisted in the U.S. Army Air Force Aviation Cadet Program, even-

tually qualifying as pilot. Following his discharge after eight months, Knowles attended Yale University, serving briefly as an assistant editor for the *Yale Alumni* magazine after graduating in 1949; he then worked from 1950 to 1952 as a reporter and occasional drama critic for the *Hartford Courant*. Knowles was a freelance writer from 1952 to 1956. After a year or so abroad, touring Italy and southern France and writing his first novel (which he decided not to publish, partly on the advice of his mentor Thornton Wilder), Knowles returned to the United States in 1955. He took up residence in the Hell's Kitchen section of New York City, where he shared an apartment with actor Bradford Dillman. He wrote occasional drama reviews while his first short stories (including "A Turn with the Sun" in 1953 and "Phineas" in 1956) were being published. During this period, he continued to benefit from Wilder's interest in his work and began to write *A Separate Peace*.

The idea for *A Separate Peace* grew out of his short story "Phineas," which appeared in *Cosmopolitan* in May 1956. It describes in rich, evocative language the idyllic lives of schoolboys during the first years of American involvement in World War II. During this time, patriotic sentiment in the United States was widespread, and while it was common for young men to feel anxious about going to war, avoiding the call to duty was extremely rare. Knowles draws from his experiences as an adolescent at Phillips Exeter Academy to create the narrator, Gene Forrester, and his friend, Phineas (Finny), who are both students at Devon, an Eastern seaboard private school much like Phillips Exeter. Though their bond is a strong one, it eventually suffers from competition. Gene, growing increasingly resentful of Phineas's popularity, finally causes him to suffer a crippling injury by pushing him from a tree. From this episode, Gene eventually accepts the necessity of exploring himself based upon his admission of guilt. Frequently compared critically to J. D. Salinger's *The Catcher in the Rye* (1951) and written despite Wilder's initial skepticism about the feasibility of the project, *A Separate Peace* is today one of the most widely read postwar American novels; by the time of its thirtieth anniversary, over seven million copies were in print. In 1960, it won the first William Faulkner Foundation Award for a notable first novel as well as the Rosenthal Award of the National Institute of Arts and Letters.

Success Makes Travel Abroad Possible After *Holiday* magazine published his article on Phillips Exeter Academy in late 1956, Knowles moved to Philadelphia in 1957 to assume the post of associate editor for *Holiday*. When it became clear soon after its American publication that *A Separate Peace* was to be highly successful, Knowles, then thirty-four, resigned his editorship in August 1960 to embark on a two-year tour of Europe and the Middle East. His 1964 travelogue, *Double Vision: American Thoughts Abroad*, recounts his sojourn.

Writer-In-Residence His second novel, *Morning in Antibes* (1962), was published while Knowles was still abroad. Established as a professional writer, Knowles returned from Europe and moved to New York City, where he lived throughout the 1960s while continuing to travel abroad for short periods. During these years, he served as a writer-in-residence, first at the University of North Carolina for the 1963–1964 session and then at Princeton in 1968–1969. His third novel, *Indian Summer*, which was dedicated to Thornton Wilder, was published in 1966, and a collection of short stories, *Phineas*, appeared in 1968. Two of his essays were published in the *New York Times*: "Where Does a Young Writer Find His Real Friends?" in 1962 and "The Writer-in-Residence" in 1965.

In 1970, the year his father died, Knowles took up permanent residence in Southampton, Long Island, where his neighbors in nearby villages have included Truman Capote, Winston Groom, Willie Morris, and Irwin Shaw. His fourth novel, *The Paragon*, appeared in 1971, and a motion picture version of *A Separate Peace* was released in 1972. *Peace Breaks Out*, designed to be a "companion piece" to *A Separate Peace*, was published in 1981, followed by *A Stolen Past* (which can be read as a companion piece to *The Paragon*) in 1983.

The novel *The Private Live of Axie Reed* was published in 1986. This book relates, as its tabloid-like title suggests, the private life of Alexandra Reed, an aging movie star who is at the end of her film career as she approaches her fiftieth

LITERARY AND HISTORICAL CONTEMPORARIES

Knowles's famous contemporaries include:

Daniel Keyes (1927–): American author best known for his short story and novel *Flowers for Algernon* (1959; 1966), a story about a mentally handicapped man who temporarily acquires extraordinary intelligence.

Harper Lee (1925–): American author who wrote the Pulitzer Prize-winning novel *To Kill a Mockingbird* (1960).

Flannery O'Connor (1925–1965): American author of Southern Gothic works, including *Wise Blood* (1952) and *A Good Man is Hard to Find and Other Stories* (1955).

J. D. Salinger (1919–): American author best known for his novel *The Catcher in the Rye* (1951).

Malcolm X (1925–1965): American activist and public speaker who fought for the rights of African Americans; he was assassinated while making a speech in New York.

birthday. The greatest crisis of her life occurs during the late summer of 1981, when she has an accident that causes a life-threatening injury. In 1995, Knowles published an autobiographical work *A Special Time, A Special Place*, in which he talks about the experiences he had growing up that formed the basis for *A Separate Peace*. John Knowles died in Fort Lauderdale, Florida, on November 29, 2001.

Works in Literary Context

Knowles's work was influenced by his own experiences coming of age at boarding school, serving in World War II, and living in American society that was forever changed by the impact of war.

Coming of Age through Love and Acceptance The setting and plot of *A Separate Peace* play upon a series of contrasts between negative and positive elements, the combination of which stresses the need to tolerate, understand, and integrate radically opposing perceptions and experiences. The school itself stands between two rivers, the Devon and the Naguamsett, one pure and fresh, the other ugly and dirty. As James Ellis concludes, the Devon symbolizes Eden, a place of joy and happiness, while the Naguamsett indicates a landscape destroyed by personal greed and callousness toward the environment. The winds of war, blowing just beyond the lives of the boys, and the battle between Gene and Phineas encapsulate Knowles's twin purposes—to explore the competing sides of an individual's personality and to imply, as some critics have noted, that the conflict of nations is an extension of self-conflict and of the antipathy one person feels toward another. These internal and external conflicts

COMMON HUMAN EXPERIENCE

The loss of innocence is an important concern of Knowles's fiction. Other works that explore this theme include the following:

Sold (2006), a novel by Patricia McCormick. After researching the plight of young female prostitutes in India, McCormick wrote this novel, told in a serious of almost poetic vignettes, about teenaged Lakshmi, a girl sold into sex slavery by her impoverished family.

Songs of Innocence and of Experience (1794), two poetry collections by William Blake. These works deal with the loss of innocence that human being inevitably endure upon their exposure to material concerns and sin.

The Things They Carried (1990), a collection of short stories by Tim O'Brien. These stories convey the experience of loss endured by American soldiers serving in the Vietnam War and the new view of life they have after confronting the reality of death.

result from fear, whether based on hatred, inadequacy, exposure, or rejection. This view of life as a battle between two opposing selves, persons, or camps—the solution being acceptance and love of others—is the most dominant theme of Knowles's fiction. It first appears in *A Separate Peace*, but it is never far from the center of later works.

A Balanced View of American Culture Throughout his fiction, Knowles shows a concern for middle- and upper-class Americans. He sees, and perhaps shares, their hunger for wealth, but he also knows their weaknesses and those of the American system. He exposes the effects of greed, obsessive social propriety, puritanical religion, and stifled emotions—qualities that lead to rivalry, suppression, and self-destruction. Yet, these forces can be countered, Knowles suggests, by letting go, by abandoning urban competition, by restoring the primacy of emotions, by allowing love to flourish, and by returning to nature.

Conflicting personality traits, genders, and ways of functioning infuse all of Knowles's work. These themes are reinforced in Knowles's nonfiction book, *Double Vision: American Thoughts Abroad*. In this travel account, Knowles regales the reader with his impressions of Arab spontaneity and Greek hospitality, while he also criticizes America's puritanical Protestant habits, repressed sexuality, tendency toward violence in its cities, and unfair distribution of jobs and wealth. Knowles's own personal apprehensions and fear about the strangeness of Arab culture, its "paralyzed battlefield," raises another concern, the American fear of other cultures. This fear of the unknown, the strangeness of other people, is, the author implies, deeply human, but especially character-

istic of Americans. Yet Knowles is not altogether negative about America and its ideals. He likes American directness and honesty, the great energy of its people, and the feeling of governmental stability. He is hopeful that America will, with time, create a civilization in harmony with nature, one that stresses tolerance and equal rights for blacks and women.

Works in Critical Context

Outside of commentaries on *A Separate Peace*, there has been little serious critical attention paid to Knowles's work. Critics of his work, both pro and con, generally concur in their assessment of Knowles as both a master craftsman and a serious student of that seemingly irreducible dualism he perceives at the heart of the American character.

A Separate Peace Referring to Knowles as "a master of characterization," literary scholar Anne Hiebert Alton praises *A Separate Peace* for "its structure, and particularly its treatment of time" and its "remarkable economy of language." Despite these attributes, Alton feels that *A Separate Peace* contains a few flaws: "Its detailed descriptions of setting are rarely well-integrated into the narrative. In addition, many of the minor characters (with the exception of Leper and Brinker) are poorly developed.... Furthermore, Knowles' symbolism falls short of its potential." Some recent critiques of *A Separate Peace* focus on the enduring nature of the work and its ability to attract young readers. For example, writing for *The New York Times Book Review*, Julian Moynahan argues that

> The continuing appeal of *A Separate Peace* has little to do with its wartime atmosphere, though that is well handled. Rather, the attraction is its central character, Phineas, the 16-year-old epitome of "schoolboy glamour" who is done to death over the course of a school year.

Responses to Literature

1. Is Gene a reliable narrator in *A Separate Peace*? In what ways might his description of events and other characters be biased?

2. What is your sense of the relationship between the characters Gene and Finny in *A Separate Peace*? How does it relate to the book's main themes?

3. What do you think the title phrase, a separate peace, means in the context of the book's focus on coming of age in the World War II era?.

4. Based on your reading of *A Separate Peace* and *Peace Breaks Out*, how would you describe the author's view of war? Provide specific examples from either work to support your analysis.

BIBLIOGRAPHY

Books

Bryant, Hallman Bell. *A Separate Peace: The War Within.* New York: Twayne, 1990.

Periodicals

Carragher, Bernard. "There Really Was a Super Suicide Society." *New York Times* (October 8, 1972) section 2, p. 2.

Ellis, James. "A Separate Peace: The Fall from Innocence." *English Journal* 53 (May 1964): 313–318.

Gardner, John. "More Smog from the Dark, Satanic Mills." *Southern Review* 5 (Winter 1969): 224–244.

Greiling, Franziska Lynne. "The Theme of Freedom in 'A Separate Peace.'" *English Journal* 56 (December 1967): 1269–1272.

Halio, Jay L. "John Knowles's Short Novels." *Studies in Short Fiction* 1 (Winter 1964): 107–112.

Henkel, Wayne J. "Pas de Feux." *Washington Post Book World* (June 23, 1974): 2.

MacDonald, James L. "The Novels of John Knowles." *Arizona Quarterly* 23 (Winter 1967): 335–342.

Slethang, Gordon E. "The Play of the Double in 'A Separate Peace.'" *Canadian Review of American Studies* 15 (1984): 259–270.

Veitch, Colin R. "The Devon School Fiction of John Knowles." *Arete: The Journal of Sport Literature* 3 (Spring 1986): 101–113.

Weber, Ronald. "Narrative Method in 'A Separate Peace.'" *Studies in Short Fiction* 3 (Fall 1965): 63–72.

Yusef Komunyakaa   *Komunyakaa, Yusef, photograph. AP Images.*

Yusef Komunyakaa

BORN: *1947, Bogalusa, Louisiana*

NATIONALITY: *American*

GENRE: *Poetry*

MAJOR WORKS:

Dedications and Other Darkhorses (1977)

Copacetic (1983)

Toys in a Field (1987)

Neon Vernacular (1993)

Overview

Yusef Komunyakaa began publishing his poetry during the turbulent 1960s and continued after serving in the Vietnam War. His poetry collection *Neon Vernacular* (1993) was awarded the Pulitzer Prize in Poetry in 1994.

Works in Biographical and Historical Context

From Louisiana to Vietnam   Born in Bogalusa, Louisiana, on April 29, 1947, Yusef Komunyakaa attended public school there, graduating from Central High School in 1965. Immediately thereafter he entered the U.S. Army, doing a tour in Vietnam, for which he earned the Bronze Star and during which he served as correspondent for and editor of the *Southern Cross*, a military paper. After returning to the United States, Komunyakaa entered the University of Colorado, where he earned his BA in 1975; he then attended Colorado State University and received his MA in 1979. He earned an MFA in creative writing at the University of California, Irvine, in 1980.

Teaching Career and Early Publication   Komunyakaa taught English at the Lake-front Campus of the University of New Orleans and for a brief period he taught poetry for grades three through six in the public schools of New Orleans. In 1985 Komunyakaa married Australian novelist Mandy Sayer and became a professor at Indiana University, where he taught until 1997. During the academic year 1989–1990 he held the Ruth Lilly Professorship, an endowed chair. In the fall of 1997, Komunyakaa accepted a professorship at Princeton University. His marriage to Sayer had ended during his tenure in Indiana.

LITERARY AND HISTORICAL CONTEMPORARIES

Komunyakaa's famous contemporaries include:

Rita Dove (1952–): Best known for *Thomas and Beulah* (1986), which received the Pulitzer Prize in Poetry, Dove is considered one of the leading poets of her generation; in addition to her many honors, Dove served as poet laureate of the United States from 1993 to 1995.

Salman Rushdie (1947–): An Indian British author of *Midnight's Children* (1981), which was awarded the Booker Prize, and *The Satanic Verses* (1988), which sparked controversy and protests in the Muslim world.

Jane Kenyon (1947–1995): An American poet who epitomizes many poets of the 1970s and 1980s: a feminist of sorts and an academic brought up through the ranks of little-magazine publication, followed by contracts with the independent presses.

Tim O'Brien (1946–): An American author most famous for his writing about the Vietnam War, including his collection of short stories, *The Things They Carried* (1990).

Annie Dillard (1945–): American essayist, poet, and fiction writer who is best known for her nonfiction narrative, *Pilgrim at Tinker Creek* (1974), which was awarded the 1975 Pulitzer Prize for General Nonfiction when she was twenty-nine.

Komunyakaa's early verse appeared in the periodicals *Black American Literature Forum*, the *Beloit Poetry Journal*, *Chameleon*, *Colorado Quarterly*, *Free Lance*, and *Poetry Now*. Some of his Vietnam verse has been collected in *Carrying the Darkness* (1985), an anthology edited by W. D. Ehrhart, and in *The Morrow Anthology of Younger American Poets* (1985), edited by Dave Smith and David Bottoms. In 1977 he published his first book, *Dedications and Other Darkhorses* and in 1979 his second, *Lost in the Bonewheel Factory*.

Jazz, Blues, and Contrasts Komunyakaa's next book-length collection, *Copacetic* (1983), presents jazz poems and blues poems in the manner of Langston Hughes and Amiri Baraka. The poems in *Copacetic* hearken back to his boyhood and early manhood. These poems examine folk ideas, beliefs, sayings, and songs, and the terminology of blues and jazz. He later published *February in Sydney* (1989), which was influenced by his experiences with jazz in Australia.

A Book of Contrasts *I Apologize for the Eyes in My Head* (1986) is a book of contrasts etched in verse. The mood changes from light and breezy to deeply sorrowful. From lost love in the city to loved ones and friends lost to the evils of slavery and Jim Crowism in the Deep South, Komunyakaa continued his fascination with ghosts reflected in life's looking glasses, with images of skeletons, and with other symbols of mortality and life's fragility. He experimented with longer poems, such as "Dreambook Bestiary" and "1984."

Vietnam Poetry *Toys in a Field* (1987) was his first work dedicated to Vietnam War poetry. It was well received and included on the American Library Association's "Best Books for Young Adults" list in 1988. His next volume, *Dien Cai Dau* (1988), also deals with his experiences in the Vietnam War. Its title, military slang for "crazy," suggests his reliance on surrealistic imagery to chronicle the Vietnam experience. These poems emphasize the mental warfare that the American soldiers waged along with their physical struggles. Each brief poem chronicles an aspect of Komunyakaa's wartime experience. He uses imagery from nature to describe the acts of war, which are superimposed on a bleak landscape.

Second Marriage Ends in Tragedy During the 1990s, Komunyakaa was involved in a new romantic relationship with fellow poet Reetika Vazirani, with whom he had a son, Jahan Vazirani Komunyakaa. During this time Komunyakaa published his most famous work, *Neon Vernacular*, which was awarded the Pulitzer Prize in Poetry. During his relationship with Vazirani, Komunyakaa published several other collections including *Thieves of Paradise* (1998), *Talking Dirty to the Gods* (2000), and *Pleasure Dome* (2001). Reekita and Jahan were found dead in 2003, Reekita having killed her son and then taken her own life. After this event, Komunyakaa attracted negative attention from critics who speculated about the events leading up to these deaths. In 2004 Komunyakaa published *Taboo: The Wishbone Trilogy, Part I*.

Other Prose In addition to his own poetry, Komunyakaa compiled and edited two jazz poetry anthologies with jazz saxophonist Sascha Feinstein. He has also published prose, including a co-translation of *Insomnia of Fire* (1995) by Nguyen Quang Thieu and a compilation of writings about blues, titled *Blues Notes: Essays, Interviews, and Commentaries* (2000).

Komunyakaa currently works as the Senior Distinguished Poet in the Graduate Writing Program at New York University.

Works in Literary Context

Komunyakaa is held in high regard for his Vietnam poetry, which many critics praise for its exceptional sensitivity and artistic merit. As a poet, he is careful to restrain the emotions and moods he creates, without overdoing ethnicity of any kind. In his Vietnam verse, he keeps before the world what it meant and still means to be American, black, and a soldier, and what the painful inequities of this combination add up to. His writing is influenced by other authors including William Carlos Williams, Amiri Baraka, Langston Hughes, Gwendolyn

Brooks, Melvin Tolson, Sterling Brown, Helen Johnson, Margaret Walker, Countee Cullen, and Claude McKay.

Resilience The headings of the six sequences of *Lost in the Bone Wheel Factory* (1979)—"Intermission," "Rituals and Rides," "Sideshows," "Testimonies," "Passions," and "Family Skeletons"—indicate the range of Komunyakaa's subject matter. In these sequences, as also seen in his subsequent volumes, he is absorbed in the pathos of the human experience, but he insists all the while that the reader accept and cope with hard reality, for only then can the beauty that lies within the human spirit come forth. The ability to see life's bareness and coldness is addressed in the first poem of the book, "Looking a Mad Dog Dead in the Eyes," a title that becomes a metaphor for life in the South of his youth, one of Komunyakaa's favorite and most fruitful themes.

Biblical Imagery In some of his poems Komunyakaa invokes biblical imagery, including crucifixion. The reader also discovers the root-and-vine imagery of the medieval mystic alongside Judeo-Christian metaphors, such as "Jacob and the Nocturnal Angel," a phrase in the poem "Following Floor Plans." Repeatedly stone and rock images surface, and the landscape of life is "granite-colored." A pretty woman's face becomes, again and again, a mirror reflecting humanity's nakedness, and the bones left by death's decay are not able to come to life again the way the biblical "dry bones of Ezekiel's vision will live." The human tongue is evil: like the Valley of Jehosophat, it is a sign and agent of sin, death, disease, the mortality that bespeaks God's judgment upon humanity's evil heart. Repeatedly, the reader sees a deformity of the skeleton, symbolizing the moral and physical grotesqueness of the poet's created world. In "Sitting in a Rocking Chair at the Window, Going Blind" Komunyakaa shapes the lines on the page to form the *s* curve of "a woman's dance . . . in a dark world." Beauty is tomorrow's "sack of bones," and no matter how much the dancer denies death and death's message, "what we deny comes full-swing around again," for "[e]verything isn't ha-ha in this valley."

Works in Critical Context

The critical reception of Komunyakaa's poetry has been largely positive. His Vietnam War poetry is widely anthologized, drawing praise for its complexity and emotional depth. Some critics celebrate his portrayal of the African American experience of Vietnam, while others note the breadth of his scope, applauding his engagement with the human condition and the hope he offers by conveying a belief in redemption.

Neon Vernacular Critics reacted positively to the publication of Komunyakaa's award-winning collection *Neon Vernacular*. Writing for the *Nation*, critic Marilyn Hacker praises the work: "*Neon Vernacular* includes some of the best Vietnam testimony, in verse or prose, that I've ever read." Similarly, Toi Derricotte, writing for

COMMON HUMAN EXPERIENCE

Komunyakaa is often praised for his poetry about the Vietnam War. Other written works that attempt to capture the experiences of the Vietnam War include the following:

Home Before Morning (1983), a memoir by Lynda Van Devanter. This book looks at the Vietnam War from the perspective of an army nurse during the year she spent working at the seventy-first Evacuation Hospital, near the Cambodian border.

Carrying the Darkness: Poetry of the Vietnam War (1985), a poetry anthology edited by W. D. Ehrhart. Containing the work of seventy-five poets, this collection conveys the depth of the emotions experienced by soldiers of the Vietnam War.

The Things They Carried (1990), a short story collection by Tim O'Brien. This work contains stories of the physical and emotional hardships endured by a platoon of soldiers during the Vietnam War.

the *Kenyon Review*, notes Komunyakaa's ability to engage readers with the depth and complexity of his work: "His voice, whether it embodies the specific experiences of a black man, a soldier in Vietnam, or a child in Bogalusa, Louisiana, is universal. It shows us in ever deeper ways what it is to be human." Offering a more general assessment, the *Harvard Review* calls *Neon Vernacular* "a vibrant look into another sense of memory and language, of history both personal and global." In *Parnassus Review* critic Michael Collins writes, "Komunyakaa's poetry conveys the pain and grace involved in maintaining not so much the middle ground *between* these two positions as the shifting ground of possibilities that lies under them both."

Responses to Literature

1. Analyze Komunyakaa's poem "Facing It" from his *Dien Cai Dau* collection. How does the structure of the poem relate to the speaker's experience of standing in front of the Vietnam War memorial?

2. Read and discuss Komunyakaa's poem "Ode to a Drum" from his *Thieves of Paradise* collection. What is the narrator communicating about the role of music in African American traditions?

3. Write an essay analyzing Komunyakaa's poem "Blackberries." What do the metaphors in the poem suggest about the boy's experiences in the world?

4. Compare Komunyakaa's poetry with that of his contemporaries. What distinguishing characteristics can you identify across his work?

BIBLIOGRAPHY

Books

Collins, Michael. *Yusef Komunyakaa.* Baltimore, Md.: Johns Hopkins University Press, 2005.

Ehrhart, W. D. *Carrying the Darkness: American Indochina: The Poetry of the Vietnam War.* New York: Avon Books, 1985.

Pettis, Joyce Owens. *African American Poets: Lives, Works, and Sources.* Westport, Conn.: Greenwood Press, 2002.

Salas, Angela. *Flashback through the Heart: The Poetry of Yusef Komunyakaa.* Selinsgrove, Pa.: Susquehanna University Press, 2004.

Periodicals

Bernard, A. "Talking Dirty to the Gods by Yusef Komunyakaa." *New York Times Book Review* 105, Part 50 (December 10, 2000): 36.

Collins, Michael. "Staying Human." *Parnassus* 18, no. 2, 19, no. 1 (1993): 134–135.

Kirsch, A. "Verse Averse: Talking Dirty to the Gods by Yusef Komunyakaa." *New Republic* no. 4493 (February 26, 2001): 38–41.

Leonard, Keith. "Yusef Komunyakaa's Blue: The Postmodern Music of the Neon Vernacular." *Callaloo* 28, no. 3 (2005): 825–849.

Pinson, Hermine. "Yusef Komunyakaa's New Blues." *Callaloo* 28, no. 3 (2005): 568–571.

Salas, Angela. "Race, Empathy, and Negative Capability: The Poetry of Yusef Komunyakaa." *College Literature* 30, no. 4 (2003): 32–53.

Stein, K. "Vietnam and the 'Voice Within': Public and Private History in Yusef Komunyakaa's Dien Cai Dau." *Massachusetts Review* 36, no. 4 (1996): 541–561.

✹ Dean Koontz

BORN: *1945, Everett, Pennsylvania*

NATIONALITY: *American*

GENRE: *Fiction*

MAJOR WORKS:

Whispers (1980)

Strangers (1986)

Overview

Dean Koontz is best known for novels in which he combines the popular literary genres of science fiction, horror, suspense, and romance. He is a prolific writer with more than seventy novels to his name in addition to nonfiction books, articles, and short stories. Throughout his career Koontz has built a large and supportive fan base while garnering little critical attention, except for the many

Dean Koontz   *Koontz, Dean, photograph. AP Images.*

book reviews published as each of his novels hits bookstore shelves.

Works in Biographical and Historical Context

A Nightmare Childhood Born in Everett, Pennsylvania, Koontz has described his childhood as "a nightmare" characterized chiefly by his father's violent behavior, alcoholism, and habitual unemployment. During Koontz's young life, he was plagued by his father's penchants for violent drunken rages and womanizing, a pattern of behavior that only worsened with age and was finally diagnosed as borderline schizophrenia, now more commonly called schizotypal personality disorder. According to biographer Katherine Ramsland, Koontz's villains often mirror Ray Koontz, exhibiting patterns commonly associated with schizotypal personality disorder.

With Koontz's troubled home life, he sought an escape in books, comic books, and movies. At the age of eight he began selling homemade books, which he wrote, illustrated, and fashioned himself. At twelve, Koontz entered a contest sponsored by a local newspaper in which he won $25.00 and a watch for his essay and thus began his writing career. Encouraged by a high school teacher to major in English at Shippensburg State College, Koontz won an *Atlantic Monthly* creative writing award in 1966. His professors were impressed; no one from his college had ever received any recognition from the contest.

Science-Fiction Days   While working as a high school English teacher, Koontz spent nights and weekends writing, getting several short stories published, followed by his first novel, a sci-fi tale called *Star Quest*, in 1967. Two more sci-fi novels followed, and in 1969, with Koontz's wife agreeing to support her husband for five years while he tried to make a go of writing full-time, Koontz quit teaching and embarked on a career as a writer. Over the next five years, Koontz would branch out from sci-fi to write in a variety of genres, for each of which he would adopt a pen name. For Gothic romance novels he wrote as Deanna Dwyer, while Owen West wrote horror novels and Leigh Nichols wrote suspense novels. All told, Koontz wrote under no fewer than a dozen pen names over the course of his career. In the process, Koontz built up a successful writing career, to the point where he became self-supporting and his wife was able to quit her job.

Though Koontz continued to use pseudonyms throughout the 1970s and into the late 1980s, by the mid-1970s he also began using his own name for what he deemed "cross-genre" pieces. The first of these was *Night Chills* (1976). According to Koontz's interview with Gorman, this new type of fiction was not well received by editors and publishers because it confused readers, and there was no single place for such volumes in bookstores. Publishing houses were convinced that non-genre-specific fiction could not last.

Cross-Genre Suspense   *The Vision*, published by Putnam in 1977, was originally promised to Random House. However, Random House did not like the new novel as written and wanted Koontz to rewrite it. Because he thought the novel could sell as it was, Koontz opted to pay back the advance he had received from Random House and gave the work to Putnam instead. The novel began as a horror novel but ended up as Koontz's second cross-genre novel, combining the classic suspense novel with the plain language normally associated with detective fiction.

Koontz would have two of his books adapted into movies in the 1970s, but *Whispers* (1980) is the dividing line between Koontz's early and later careers. Because it was the first novel published under Koontz's own name to reach best-seller status and was a prime example of Koontz's cross-genre style, it somewhat eased the criticism Koontz so often received from editors about writing this type of fiction. Koontz's fortunes continued to rise throughout the 1980s as his cross-genre suspense and horror novels vaulted him into the category of best-selling author.

Typical of Koontz's success is *Strangers* (1986), which he considers one of his best works along with *Whispers*. The novel was a departure from Koontz's normal fiction and therefore surprised many of the critics who thought they could predict his work. Putnam paid

---

LITERARY AND HISTORICAL CONTEMPORARIES

Koontz's famous contemporaries include:

Jimmy Carter (1924–): A senator from Georgia, Carter was elected thirty-ninth president of the United States in 1976. After his presidency, Carter became a noted humanitarian, winning the Nobel Peace Prize in 2002.

Umberto Eco (1932–): Italian philosopher, critic, and novelist, Eco is best known for his 1980 novel *The Name of the Rose*, a densely-layered medieval murder mystery that was made into a successful film in 1986.

Paul McCartney (1942–): A member of The Beatles, perhaps the best-known pop group of all time, McCartney continued to record and perform successfully after their breakup, both with his group Wings in the 1970s and as a solo act.

George Lucas (1944–): One of the new generation of independent Hollywood directors in the early 1970s, Lucas became an international celebrity with the debut of his *Star Wars* series in 1977.

Terry Pratchett (1948–): Popular and prolific British sci-fi and fantasy author Pratchett is best known for his long-running satirical fantasy *Discworld* series, begun in 1983.

Koontz $275,000 for *Strangers*, and the novel was chosen as a main selection for both the Literary Guild and Doubleday Book Club. Less than a month after its first printing, the novel was on *The New York Times* and *Publishers Weekly* best-seller lists. It was Koontz's first hardcover to be on any best-seller list.

Fighting the Pigeon Hole

After the success of *Strangers*, a new group called the Horror Writers of America was forming and convinced Koontz to become their first president. Though Koontz definitely did not want to be marked as a horror writer, he took the position; Koontz later regarded this move as one of the biggest mistakes of his career. The organization did not represent the solidarity of like-minded individuals as Koontz had originally hoped, but it was instead fraught with derision and politics.

Since that time, Koontz has continued to enjoy widespread popular success, publishing one best-seller after another. While continuing to write primarily in the cross-genre suspense format, he has also dabbled in children's books and even wrote a collection of fictional quotations that have been referenced in his previous works.

Works in Literary Context

Koontz's fictional characters are often pitted against unspeakable evil and insurmountable odds but nonetheless

COMMON HUMAN EXPERIENCE

Suspense-thrillers are among the most consistently best-selling books. Other works that, like Koontz, blend other genres with the suspense genre include:

> *Carrie* (1973), a novel by Stephen King. King's break-through book, this horror-thriller focuses on an outcast girl with psychic powers.
>
> *Foucault's Pendulum* (1988), a novel by Umberto Eco. This book has been called by some "the thinking man's *Da Vinci Code*" for its blend of conspiracy, secret histories, cover-ups, and paranoid suspense.
>
> *The Andromeda Strain* (1969), a novel by Michael Crichton. The first best-selling techno-thriller, this novel also established Crichton's career with its blend of alien menace and medical drama.
>
> *The Birds* (1963), a film directed by Alfred Hitchcock. A master of suspense, Hitchcock would occasionally dip into the realm of the inexplicably horrific, as in this film, which features wild birds suddenly becoming murderously intelligent.

emerge victorious. Concerning this optimism Koontz has said that he finds "the human species—and Western culture—to be primarily noble, honorable, and admirable." He actively rejects the misanthropy common to the horror genre and has explained that that is why he does not wish to be called a "horror author." "I am no Pollyanna," Koontz has said, "but I think we live in a time of marvels, not a time of disaster, and I believe we can solve every problem that confronts us if we keep our perspective and our freedom." He has further elaborated that he believes fiction exists to allow people to examine their lives, determine their best traits, and come up with ways in which they might improve their lot in the world.

Reason versus Emotion   Critics observe that the most prevalent theme in Koontz's work is the conflict between reason and emotion. Usually his characters learn to reconcile detached analysis with intuitive feeling, especially when dealing with technology. In *Phantoms*, for example, the protagonists initially turn to myth and religion when logic fails to explain the mass deaths in a resort town. That the characters in the novel finally use technology to defeat the "Ancient Enemy" indicates to commentators Koontz's fundamental faith in human resourcefulness. In *Darkfall* Koontz again presents religion and ritual as the foils of logic. For the protagonists to triumph they must believe in the potentially evil powers of voodoo and the ultimately superior powers of good. In *Watchers* Koontz explores the positive and negative potential of technology as represented by two genetically engineered beings: Ein-

stein, an endearing golden retriever with human intelligence who prevails over the Outsider, a monstrous superbeing capable of horrific deeds.

Works in Critical Context

Critics consider Koontz's work distinctive for its optimistic display of confidence in the ability of individuals to overcome extreme obstacles and hardships. Since moving from science fiction to cross-genre writing, Koontz has broadened his appeal and, according to critics, strengthened his storytelling. Bill Munster has suggested that Koontz's examination of "the tenuous nature of life and the tissue-thin barrier that separates us from sudden terror and tragedy" gives his work a resonance not often found in most popular fiction.

Whispers

Critical reaction to *Whispers* (1980) was mixed. A *Publishers Weekly* reviewer argues that readers will need "strong stomachs to tolerate the overheated scenes of rape and mayhem." The reviewer praises Koontz's portrait of Frye but finds the mystery too easy to solve because the author gives too many clues. *Library Journal* contributor Rex E. Klett sees Koontz edging "dangerously close to a ruinous occultism" with *Whispers*, but also finds the novel a smooth read. Denis Pitts, reviewing the novel in *Punch*, calls *Whispers* a "superior crime read." Pitts advises: "*Whispers* is not a book to be read by women of a nervous disposition living alone in a country house. Or men, come to think of it." Though biographer Ramsland praises the novel overall, she still finds some fault: "One flaw in this novel is the degree of explanation indulged in by characters who otherwise give no clue that they can be as sophisticated about complex psychological conditions as Hilary and Tony seem to be."

Responses to Literature

1. Critics are often suspicious of popular authors who produce a large volume of work. In your opinion, does quantity rule out quality? How do modern authors like Koontz or Stephen King compare with prolific authors such as Mark Twain or Charles Dickens, both of whom are now considered giants in the literary canon?

2. Koontz's fiction is characterized by a fundamentally optimistic outlook; Koontz has said that depressing fiction generally does not become classic literature. Can you think of any examples that might refute this claim? Do you think optimistic fiction is more likely to endure as literature? If so, why? If not, why not?

3. How does Koontz integrate supernatural elements into works such as *Darkfall*? Do you feel he is, as he claims, more than a horror writer, despite the use of supernatural elements? Why or why not?

4. How has Koontz's difficult relationship with his mentally unstable father been reflected in his fiction?

BIBLIOGRAPHY

Books

Costello, Matthew J. "Films, Television, and Dean Koontz." *The Dean Koontz Companion*, edited by Martin H. Greenberg, Ed Gorman, and Bill Munster. New York: Berkley, 1994, pp. 101–107.

Kotker, Joan G. *Dean Koontz: A Critical Companion.* Westport, Conn.: Greenwood Press, 1996.

Munster, Bill. *Discovering Dean Koontz: Essays on America's Bestselling Writer of Suspense and Horror Fiction.* San Bernardino, Calif.: Borgo Press, 1998.

———. *Sudden Fear: The Horror and Dark Suspense Fiction of Dean R. Koontz, Starmont Studies in Literary Criticism, no. 24.* Mercer Island, Wash.: Starmont House, 1988.

Ramsland, Katherine M. *Dean Koontz: A Writer's Biography.* New York: HarperPrism, 1997.

Silva, David B. "Keeping Pace with the Master." *The Dean Koontz Companion*, edited by Greenberg, Gorman, and Munster. New York: Berkley, 1994, pp. 57–73.

Periodicals

Alexander, Paul. "Dean Koontz." *Rolling Stone* 789 (June 25, 1998): 46–47+.

Collings, Michael. "Dean Koontz." *Mystery Scene* 45 (January–February 1994): 46–50.

Gillespie, Nick and Lisa Snell. "Contemplating Evil: D. Koontz." *Reason* 28 (November 1996): 44–49.

Gleick, Elizabeth. "Family Secrets: D. Koontz." *People Weekly* 42 (November 28, 1994): 141–142.

Springen, Karen. "The Cheery Titan of Terror: D. Koontz." *Newsweek* 117 (February 11, 1991): 62.

 # Ted Kooser

BORN: *1939, Ames, Iowa*

NATIONALITY: *American*

GENRE: *Poetry*

MAJOR WORKS:

Sure Signs: New and Selected Poems (1980)

The Blizzard Voices (1986)

Delights and Shadows (2004)

Overview

Ted Kooser is a Midwestern poet who did not gain national attention until relatively late in his career. Like Wallace Stevens, Kooser worked in the insurance business while writing his poetry. After retiring from his day job, Kooser began to gain increasing recognition, serving two terms as poet laureate of the United States and winning the Pulitzer Prize in 2005.

Ted Kooser   *Kooser, Theodore, photograph. AP Images.*

Works in Biographical and Historical Context

Poetry and the Insurance Business   Theodore J. Kooser, the son of Theodore B. Kooser and Vera Moser Kooser, grew up in Ames, Iowa, where he was born and where he attended college, earning a BS in English education from Iowa State University in 1962. He taught high school in Madrid, Iowa, for one year but then moved to Lincoln, Nebraska, where he has since lived. At first he did full-time graduate study in English at the University of Nebraska; however, when the department failed to renew his graduate appointment for his second year, he launched a successful career in insurance, meanwhile pursuing a master's degree part-time and earning it in 1968.

Kooser worked his way up to second vice president of marketing at the Lincoln Benefit Life Company where he simultaneously pursued his interest in poetry. Throughout his insurance career, Kooser maintained a regimen in which he would rise early and spend several hours writing. Unlike Wallace Stevens, who kept his careers in insurance and poetry completely separate, Kooser tried his poems out on his colleagues at the office and credited his daily association with them as helping "to keep the language of [his] poems from becoming literary." Mainly, though, he thinks his job in insurance was not particularly helpful in his literary career; still, as he once quipped, it prevented him from giving away good metaphors, as he did when teaching night classes. By giving readings from Berkeley to New York, publishing and editing two magazines—the *Salt Creek Reader* (1967–1975) and the *Blue Hotel* (1980–1981)—and continuing to operate Windflower Press, Kooser stayed involved in the literary world during his tenure with Lincoln Benefit. He also worked as an adjunct professor of writing at the University of Nebraska from 1970 to 1995.

LITERARY AND HISTORICAL CONTEMPORARIES

Kooser's famous contemporaries include:

Bernard Cornwell (1944–): English author of historical novels, most notably the Sharpe series, which follows the fortunes of its eponymous hero throughout the course of the Napoleonic Wars.

Peter Jackson (1961–): New Zealander film director, producer, and writer most famous for his filmed adaptations of the *Lord of the Rings* fantasy trilogy by J. R. R. Tolkien.

Pervez Musharraf (1943–): Coming to power as the president of Pakistan after a 1999 military coup, Musharraf catered the support of Western powers through his antiterrorist campaigns. A controversial figure, Musharraf was forced to resign the presidency in 2008, though he remained prime minister.

Ronald Reagan (1911–2004): Movie actor, governor of California, and fortieth president of the United States, Ronald Reagan is today considered a key figure in conservative politics and economics thanks to his policies implemented during his presidency.

Robert Bly (1926–): A poet and social activist, Bly most famously wrote *Iron John: A Book About Men* (1990), a cornerstone of the modern men's self-help movement.

Official Entry Blank (1969), Kooser's first book, unveils a novice experimenting with various forms, subjects, and voices. He tries rhymed quatrains, blank verse, sonnets, haiku, heroic couplets, and even found poems. Kooser's first nationally acclaimed collection of poetry, *Sure Signs: New and Selected Poems*, was published in 1980 and found the poet in full command of his form and voice. Thanks to Kooser's highly accessible approach, inspired by William Carlos Williams, he gained an instant and devoted following.

Poems on Postcards In 1999 Kooser retired from his insurance career. Around the same time, he developed cancer, which led him to stop writing poetry. During his convalescence, he began writing poetry again, taking his inspiration from early morning walks. He would send the results on postcards to his friend and noted poet Jim Harrison. In 2001 the collected poems were published as *Winter Morning Walks: One Hundred Postcards to Jim Harrison*. In 2004 Kooser's most acclaimed collection of poetry, his tenth, was published as *Delights & Shadows*. The book garnered Kooser the 2005 Pulitzer Prize for Poetry.

The same year *Delights & Shadows* was published, Kooser was named the thirteenth poet laureate of the United States, a post he held from 2004 to 2006. Kooser took his new post seriously, using it to advocate for poetry and encourage young, aspiring poets. To that end, Kooser published two nonfiction books full of advice for the beginning poet and wrote a regular column, "American Life in Poetry." Through all the increased notoriety, Kooser has maintained a residence on his Nebraska farm, writing and publishing his own poetry and teaching at the University of Nebraska–Lincoln.

Works in Literary Context

When discussing his biographical roots in the Midwest, Kooser fends off attempts by critics to lump Plains poets together simply because their work shares common literal images of setting, as he notes in this quote from *On Common Ground* (1983): "People have known for years that the best way to involve a reader in what he's reading is to introduce concrete imagery, and when you live in a place you draw your imagery from what's around you." Because his poems rely on vivid particular details of ordinary life and they are presented simply and clearly, some critics, such as Dana Gioia, have cited William Carlos Williams as a major influence.

Like many poets of the generation before him, Ted Kooser began his career writing poems in traditional forms but then switched to free verse, a mode that better suited his Midwestern voice. Through this change Kooser perfected a short, descriptive but strikingly metaphorical type of poem that undergirded all his books from 1971 to 1985. This style enables Kooser to explore the underlying mystery in ordinary rural subjects. Some critics have found his manner of writing distinctive but also limiting. One weakness of it is that, as Gilbert Allen has said, Kooser "writes essentially the same poem over and over again," or, more accurately, the same kind of poem.

Landscape as Metaphor What is most impressive and distinctive about Kooser's style, and what gives his work its poetic authenticity, is his own metaphorical imagination. In poem after poem, nearly all less than one page in both *Sure Signs* and other publications, Kooser first involves his readers through precise particulars and then transforms these images into insightful metaphors. Though Kooser is similar to Robert Bly in his use of Midwestern landscapes, Kooser's revelations, unlike Bly's, are rarely sublime. But his technique perfectly illustrates Robert Frost's idea that poetry essentially says one thing in terms of another. Just as Frost used New England for his metaphors, Kooser uses landscapes and portraits of the Plains states and their people as vehicles for expressing experiences and universal feelings, especially loss, decay, and loneliness.

This desolate image of emptiness recurs in different ways in memorable brief poems such as those in *Not Coming to Be Barked At* (1976). For instance, in "The Afterlife," Kooser presents a series of aptly chosen literal images that, juxtaposed, evoke the strange, vague atmosphere of a place where "a foreign-language newspaper" rolls "along the dock / in an icy wind," and "the horns of the tugs" turn "our great gray ship / back into the mist." Similarly "North of Alliance" is about the desolation of absence in a house so empty one finds "not even / a newspaper sodden with rain / under a broken window."

Works in Critical Context

The subjects and imagery of Kooser's poetry unmistakably bear the influence of his environment, the Great Plains, but Kooser insists he is not a regionalist writer. However, until the University of Pittsburgh Press published *Sure Signs* in 1980, Kooser had published four of his books with Nebraska presses and the others with a variety of other regional publishers. Hence, Kooser's audience remained narrow and primarily local. Furthermore, despite a favorable notice by William Cole in the November 2, 1974, issue of *Saturday Review*, Kooser continued to write without much critical notice beyond little Midwestern magazines, thus reinforcing the notion of his merely regional appeal. Then, with *Sure Signs*, critics in national publications began to recognize, as Peter Stitt said in the *Georgia Review*, that Kooser is "an authentic poet of the American people," a poet who wrests a universal resonance from regional subjects.

Sure Signs   *Sure Signs* impressed many critics with its consistency and unity. Peter Stitt concluded in the *Georgia Review* that "Kooser is a good poet... a clear and careful writer who deserves... attention." In more resounding terms, critic Dana Gioia announced that the "unified *oeuvre*" presented in *Sure Signs* demonstrates Kooser's status as "the master of the short colloquial imagistic poem.... Kooser [has] a genuine poetic style which accommodates the average reader" and exhibits "unexpected moments of illumination from the seemingly threadbare details of everyday life." However, in a *New York Times* review that Kooser calls "nasty" and "sneering," Charles Molesworth objected that Kooser's images, while sometimes "fresh and keen... can also be humdrum or clumsy." Molesworth also attacked the consistently brief length of Kooser's poems, which he said makes them risk quaintness. Gioia was also bothered by Kooser's narrow range of technique and his tendency to avoid the risks of failure associated with changing forms.

Responses to Literature

1. Take a look at Kooser's nonfiction advice book for poets, *The Poetry Home Repair Manual: Practical Advice for Beginning Poets* (2005). How well does he follow his own advice in his poetry? Can you see Kooser's advice present in the works of other well-known poets, such as Robert Frost?

2. Kooser has said, "If you can awaken inside the familiar and discover it strange, you need never leave home." Pick a poem in Kooser's *Delights & Shadows* collection that evokes this feeling in you, and then, in

COMMON HUMAN EXPERIENCE

Kooser is just one of several contemporary poets to explore clear imagery and plain language in poetry in the United States. Here are some other examples:

An Early Martyr and Other Poems (1935), a collection by William Carlos Williams. One of the foremost American modernist poets, Williams often mixed his somewhat radical left-wing politics with his verse, as in the oft-anthologized poem "The Yachts," contained in this collection.

Saving Daylight (2006), a book by Jim Harrison. Harrison, like Kooser, evokes the imagery of his native landscapes, which in Harrison's case encompass the wide open spaces of the American West.

The Road Not Taken (2002), a collection by Robert Frost. Perhaps America's best-known regional poet, Frost immortalized his beloved New England in such poems as "The Road Not Taken."

a group, have each person share why they chose their particular poem as representative of that idea.

3. What makes a poet regionalist? Can you find any regionalist poets in your own area? Try writing a poem of your own that discusses the imagery and landscape of your home region.

4. Kooser has said several times that he does not feel writers and poets require a difficult life in order to fuel their art. Do you agree with this? Can an artist create meaningful works if they have lead a comfortable, happy life? Find examples to support your opinion.

BIBLIOGRAPHY

Books

"Delights & Shadows." *Literary Newsmakers for Students*. Vol. 2. Detroit: Gale, 2006.

Gioia, Dana. "Explaining Ted Kooser." *On Common Ground: The Poetry of William Kloefkorn, Ted Kooser, Greg Kuzma, and Don Welch*. Edited by Mark Sanders and J. V. Brummels. Ord, Nebr.: Sandhills, 1983, pp. 83–99.

———. "Kooser, Ted." *Contemporary Poets*. Edited by Thomas Riggs. 7th ed. Detroit: St. James Press, 2001.

Hatcher, Arnold. "An Interview with Ted Kooser." *Voyages to the Inland Sea VI: Essays and Poems by Harley Elliott and Ted Kooser*. Edited by John Judson. La Crosse, Wis.: Center for Contemporary Poetry, 1976, pp. 37–50.

Sanders, Mark. "An Interview with Ted Kooser." *On Common Ground: The Poetry of William Kloefkorn,*

Ted Kooser, Greg Kuzma, and Don Welch. Edited by Mark Sanders and J. V. Brummels. Ord, Nebr.: Sandhills, 1983, pp. 99–105.

Periodicals

Allen, Gilbert. "Measuring the Mainstream—A Review Essay." *Southern Humanities Review* 17 (Spring 1983): 171–178.

Stitt, Peter. "The World at Hand." *Georgia Review* 34 (Fall 1980): 661–670.

Web sites

Apple Learning Interchange. "Ask Ted Kooser!" Retrieved October 4, 2008, from http://edcommunity.apple.com/ali/story.php?itemID=11179. Last updated on October 4, 2008.

✸ Jon Krakauer

BORN: *1954, Brookline, Massachusetts*

NATIONALITY: *American*

GENRE: *Nonfiction*

MAJOR WORKS:

Into the Wild (1996)

Into Thin Air (1997)

Under the Banner of Heaven: A Story of Violent Faith (2003)

John Krakauer *AP Wide World Photos*

Overview

Jon Krakauer is an American nonfiction writer, journalist, and mountaineer best known for his works about the outdoors and mountain climbing. His nonfiction works *Into the Wild*, *Into Thin Air*, and *Under the Banner of Heaven* have been best-sellers and received widespread critical attention. Aside from being nominated for a Pulitzer Prize, he has also been the recipient of the Academy Award in Literature from the American Academy of Arts and Letters and Book of the Year by *Time* magazine.

Works in Biographical and Historical Context

Childhood in the West Jon Krakauer was born in Brookline, Massachusetts in 1954 but grew up in Corvallis, Oregon, where his family moved when he was two years old. Though Krakauer himself was not raised as a Mormon, this community in Oregon had a large Mormon population, and Krakauer's experiences with members of the Church of Latter-Day Saints would inform his later work, *Under the Banner of Heaven*. In 2003 Krakauer wrote that "[Latter-Day] Saints were my childhood friends and playmates, my teachers, my athletic coaches. I envied what seemed to be the unfluctuating certainty of the faith professed so enthusiastically by my closest Mormon pals; but I was often baffled by it. I've sought to comprehend the formidable power of such belief ever since."

Mountaineering and Writing In addition to sustaining a large Mormon population, Corvallis, Oregon, is situated near a mountain range and served as a hub for mountain climbers and outdoor adventurers. Krakauer's father, an active alpinist, introduced his athletic child to the sport of mountain climbing when Krakauer was eight. Krakauer excelled at climbing, a sport that would later take him on the adventures to Alaska and Mount Everest that would inform his books *Into the Wild* and *Into Thin Air*. As a teenager Krakauer was also a competitive tennis player at Corvallis High School, where he graduated in 1972. He then enrolled at Hampshire College in Massachusetts and took up environmental science, which fostered his already pronounced love of nature and outdoor sport. While in college, Krakauer was part of a group of mountaineers who were the first to climb the Arrigetch Peaks in the Arctic National Park of Alaska. For this, he was invited by the *American Alpine Journal* to write about his experience. Krakauer received praise for his article, and began to contemplate a future career that would wed journalism to outdoor sport.

Experiences in Alaska Krakauer received his bachelor's degree in 1976, and in 1977 he spent three weeks alone in the wilderness of the Stikine Icecap region of Alaska. During this trip to Alaska he met former climber Linda Mariam Moore, whom he ultimately married, in 1980. In 1977 Krakauer published a popular magazine article about a climb he completed, alone, during which he charted a new route to the peak of Devil's Thumb in Alaska. After the publication of this article, Krakauer began receiving regular magazine assignments. Aside from writing, he worked as a commercial salmon fisherman and carpenter. In 1983, he abandoned these jobs to be able to write and climb full time. In 1990, Krakauer published his first book, *Eiger Dreams*, a collection of his magazine writing. In 1996, Krakauer utilized his extensive knowledge of the terrain of Alaska to publish *Into the Wild*, for which he researched and recreated the life of Christopher McCandless, a twenty-four-year-old who renounced all material possessions, hitchhiked to Alaska, and attempted to climb Devil's Peak. Determined to live off the land, McCandless carried with him only a shotgun, a bag of rice, and some books. Four months later, his body was found: he had starved to death. Near the body was a desperate note in which he begged to be saved. Krakauer used McCandless's journals and postcards, as well as interviews with those who knew him, to reconstruct the last two years of the boy's life. The book was an instant best-seller.

Climbing Mount Everest   In 1996, Krakauer joined fellow mountaineers and embarked on a guided ascent of Mount Everest, arguably his most famous climb. However, their descent from the mountain was hampered by a disastrous ice storm, which left four of his teammates dead. He relayed these experiences in an article for *Outside* magazine, for which he received a National Magazine Award. In 1997 he expanded the article into the book *Into Thin Air*. The book was a finalist for the Pulitzer Prize in General Nonfiction in 1998. In response to the events he recounted in *Into Thin Air*, Krakauer established the Everest '96 Memorial Fund, which provides humanitarian aid to the peoples of the Himalayan region through royalties from the book as a tribute to those who perished during the expedition. During this period Krakauer also published a *Smithsonian* article about Mt. Rainier, a prominent volcano in the state of Washington, which earned him a Walter Sullivan Award for Excellence in Science Journalism.

Examining Extremism in Religion   In 2003, Krakauer shifted away from outdoor adventure and published the book *Under the Banner of Heaven: A Story of Violent Faith*, which explored the history of the Mormon religion in America. While the book discussed the nineteenth-century roots of Mormonism with the revelations of prophet Joseph Smith, it also focused on twentieth-century Mormon fundamentalism. In particular, it focused on the 1984 murder of Brenda Lafferty by her fundamentalist brothers-in-law Ron and Dan Lafferty, and the kidnapping and subsequent brainwashing of fourteen-year-old Elizabeth Smart by Mormon polygamist Brian David Mitchell. Though receiving much critical praise, the book became an item of controversy and garnered much opprobrium by members of the Church of Latter-Day Saints. Krakauer's articles continue to appear in such

LITERARY AND HISTORICAL CONTEMPORARIES

Jon Krakauer's famous contemporaries include:

Carl Hiaasen (1953–): Hiaasen, a journalist and noted author of books for children, often weds mystery stories to environmental issues pertaining to his native Florida.

Lance Armstrong (1971–): Armstrong is an American cyclist who won the Tour de France a record-breaking seven times after surviving testicular cancer. In his best-selling book *It's Not About the Bike* (2000), Armstrong describes his battle with cancer and his ensuing career as a cyclist.

Rick Bass (1958–): Bass is an author, essayist, and polemicist who is one of America's leading writers of environmental literature. A petroleum geologist and ecological activist, Bass is recognized and revered for fusing art and activism to advance wilderness preservation and management.

Dan Lafferty (1948–): Mormon fundamentalist Dan Lafferty, along with his brother Ron, killed their sister-in-law Brenda Lafferty and her infant daughter in 1984. The brothers maintained that their killings were sanctioned by the will of God.

Bill Bryson (1951–): Humorist and travel writer Bryson is the author of the 1998 *A Walk in the Woods: Rediscovering America on the Appalachian Trail*, which documents his hike from Maine to Georgia.

Timothy Egan (1954–): Egan is an American novelist, journalist, and editorial writer best known for his nonfiction works on environmental and moral issues. Egan won the 2006 National Book Award for his book *The Worst Hard Time: The Untold Story of Those Who Survived the Great American Dust Bowl* (2005).

periodicals as *GEO, The Washington Post, National Geographic, Rolling Stone,* and *Architectural Digest*. He is currently an editor-at-large for *Outside* magazine. He lives in Seattle with his wife.

Works in Literary Context

Extremism   All three of Krakauer's major works revolve around the theme of extremism—albeit religious or environmental. In *Into the Wild*, Krakauer chose to chronicle the experiences of Christopher McCandless, a rich, university-educated twenty-four-year-old who decided to give away $25,000 in savings, renounce all material possessions, and seek spiritual transcendence in the wilderness. McChandless eventually succumbed to the harsh weather conditions of Alaska's mountains, for which he was woefully unprepared. Similarly, *Into Thin Air* acquaints readers with the travails of the extreme sport of mountain

COMMON HUMAN EXPERIENCE

Jon Krakauer's books *Into the Wild* and *Into Thin Air* document the experiences of individuals struggling to survive in harsh terrains and extreme climatic conditions. Other works which depict man's struggle against nature include:

When the Levees Broke (2006), a documentary film directed by Spike Lee. In this extensive documentary, director Spike Lee explores the lives affected by Hurricane Katrina in New Orleans.

The Worst Hard Time: The Untold Story of Those Who Survived the Great American Dust Bowl (2005), a nonfiction book by environmentalist writer and activist Timothy Egan. Drawing on interviews from survivors of the Dust Bowl that devastated the American Midwest during the Great Depression, Egan tells the stories of families who faced crop failure, starvation, and massive pilgrimages across the country in order to find work during the 1930s.

The Lost Explorer: Finding Mallory on Mount Everest (1999), a nonfiction book by Conrad Anker and David Roberts. This account recreates the 1999 expedition to find the body of famed British climber George Mallory, who perished on Everest in 1924. Though the body was well preserved due to the cold climate of the mountain, it remains unclear whether or not Mallory became the first man to reach the summit of Everest.

South: A Memoir of the Endurance *Voyage* (1931), a memoir by Ernest Shackleton. This memoir chronicles the extraordinary experiences of the 1914 British Imperial Trans-Antarctic Expedition. Shackleton's ship became embedded in ice, and he and his crew were stranded off Antarctica until 1917.

The Seven Pillars of Wisdom (1926), a memoir by by T. E. Lawrence. In this piece of autobiography, history, and cultural commentary, "Lawrence of Arabia" explains his exploits in the Middle East during the First World War, including a remarkable crossing of the Nefud Desert. The book was adapted into the Academy Award–winning movie *Lawrence of Arabia*, starring Peter O'Toole, in 1962.

"The Open Boat" (1897), a short story by Stephen Crane. Crane's story describes the experiences of four shipwrecked men who must struggle against the harshest forces of nature to survive.

climbing during the most dangerous season on the world's most difficult climb, Mount Everest. During 1996 fifteen climbers lost their lives trying to reach the summit of the mountain, an event Krakauer would partially blame on unpreparedness resulting from the commercialization of the climb. Nonetheless, the book gives an adventurous rendering of Krakauer's battles against

snow, ice, rock, cold, and starvation. In *Under the Banner of Heaven* Krakauer would shift his focus away from extremism relating to the elements, and would explore religious zealotry.

Fundamentalist Religion In *Under the Banner of Heaven*, Krakauer states that he began writing the book to answer the question, "How does a critical mind reconcile scientific and historical truth with religious doctrine? . . . I was fascinated by the paradoxes that reside at the intersection of doubt and faith, and I had a high regard for congenital skeptics . . . who somehow emerged from the fray with their beliefs intact." The result of Krakauer's investigation is a book that explores the faith, history, and politics of both the Church of Latter-Day Saints and their more fundamentalist Mormon counterparts. Utilizing exhaustive research and countless interviews, Krakauer traces the religion's roots in the teachings of evangelist Joseph Smith to its current state in all-Mormon communities in Utah and Arizona. Throughout the book—which focuses on the slaying of Brenda Lafferty and her infant daughter by her fundamentalist brothers-in-law in 1984—Krakauer points out how zealotry often leads to tyranny and violence. In addition, he pays particular attention to how the practice of polygamy can lead to the manipulation or abuse of women and children.

Works in Critical Context

Jon Krakauer has been praised by readers and reviewers for his ability to make nonfiction stories highly accessible and engaging, due to effective structure, narrative skill, and formidable descriptive powers. He is often praised for both the quality and the volume of his research.

Into the Wild *Into the Wild*, Jon Krakauer's first nonfiction work, was published in 1996 and became an instant success, spending more than two years on the *New York Times* best-seller list. It tells the tragic story of Christopher McCandless, a recent college graduate who was found dead in the wilderness of Alaska. The book was adapted into a 2007 motion picture directed by Sean Penn. *Into the Wild*, was described as "compelling and tragic, hard to put down," in the words of the *San Francisco Chronicle*. The *Los Angeles Times* was also impressed with the book, saying that the storyline was "engrossing, with a telling eye for detail," and praised Krakauer for capturing "the sad saga of a stubborn, idealistic young man." The *Washington Post* commended Krakauer for creating a narrative of "arresting force," and warned that "anyone who ever fancied wandering off to face nature on its own harsh terms should give [*Into the Wild*] a look."

Into Thin Air Krakauer's 1997 book, *Into Thin Air*, a firsthand account of his May 1996 Mount Everest tragedy, also spent time on top of the *New York Times* nonfiction best-seller list, and was given the Book of the Year award by *Time* magazine. In addition, it was called one of the Best Books of the Year by the *New York Times*

Book Review and was one of the finalists for the 1997 National Book Critics Award. In 1999 it won the Academy Award in Literature from the American Academy of Arts and Letters. *Into Thin Air* was praised for being "meticulously researched and deftly constructed," according to Alastair Scott, a *New York Times* reviewer. Scott also noted that the book's most interesting quality was Krakauer's depiction of the deadly storm, and commended Krakauer's "ability to recreate its effects with a lucid and terrifying intimacy." In another review, the *Wall Street Journal* simply called the book one of the best adventure works of all time.

Under the Banner of Heaven In 2003, Krakauer released another best-seller, *Under the Banner of Heaven: A Story of Violent Faith*, which investigates the story of Ron and Dan Lafferty, brothers of the Mormon fundamentalist faith who claim that they have the right to kill. The book attempts to uncover and raise questions about the nature of religious belief. *Under the Banner of Heaven*, however, received more mixed opinions than Krakauer's previous books. Many reviewers argued that the book offered a new perspective on the dark side of religion. John Freeman, in the *St. Louis-Dispatch*, noted that the book successfully exhibits "how extreme sects of the Mormon faith have persisted and continue to operate outside the oversight of the mainstream church and even the U.S. government." Rachel Collins of *Library Journal* said that the book was "a thoroughly engrossing and ultimately startling comment on all fundamentalist ideas." *Book Magazine* agreed by saying that *Under the Banner of Heaven* was a comprehensive study of "faith and violence in Mormonism," and that the book "reminds us of the power of the most pernicious form of evil—evil in the name of God." As expected, however, supporters of the Mormon faith objected to Krakauer's work, citing the inconsistencies in his account of the religion's history and criticizing him for putting the Mormons in a bad light. On June 26, just two weeks before the release of *Under the Banner of Heaven*, church spokesman Mike Otterson issued a statement charging that Krakauer was "promoting old stereotypes" and "tars every Mormon with the same brush."

Responses to Literature

1. In 2007, Jon Krakauer's *Into the Wild* was adapted into a film written and directed by Sean Pean, and starring Emile Hirsch. Watch the film and compare it to the text of Krakauer's book. Is the film's narration by McCandless's sister effective? What liberties does the film take with the content of the book? Do you find that the film is faithful to Krakauer's text, or does it moralize on the life of Christopher McCandless?

2. Upon its publication, Krakauer's *Under the Banner of Heaven* was heavily criticized by members of the Mormon community. Research the arguments these critics put forward against Krakauer's representation of the Church of Latter-Day Saints. Do you find that he presents facts in a biased manner? Pay particular attention to the role that issues of gender and polygamy play in the critical reaction to the book.

3. Throughout his works, Jon Krakauer develops the theme of extremism through the portrayal of harsh climactic conditions, such as in *Into Thin Air*, or in spiritual or religious beliefs, as in *Into the Wild* and *Under the Banner of Heaven*. What, in your opinion, is his view on the virtues and vices of extremism? When is extremist behavior beneficial, and when is it dangerous?

BIBLIOGRAPHY

Periodicals

Imbelli, Robert. Review of *Into Thin Air* and *Into the Wild*. *Commonweal* 125, no. 21 (December 4,1998): 23–4.

Freeman, John. "American Massacre and *Under the Banner of Heaven*." *St. Louis Post-Dispatch* (July 13, 2003): F10.

Lattin, Don. "Blood, Faith and Fanaticism." *San Francisco Chronicle* (July 13, 2003): M1.

Donahe, Deirdre. "Murder by Zealot Mormon Sect Sparks Deeper Look." *USA Today* (July 14, 2003): p. D1.

Wright, Robert. "Thou Shalt Kill." *New York Times Book Review* 108 (August 3, 2003): 7.

Harris, Mark. Review of *Into Thin Air*. *Entertainment Weekly*, no. 377 (May 2 1997): 50–1.

Scott, Alastair. Review of *Into Thin Air*. *New York Times Book Review* (May 18, 1997): G11.

Review of *Into Thin Air*. *Wall Street Journal* (May 29, 1997): A16.

Review of *Into the Wild*. *Los Angeles Times Book Review* (September 3, 1995): 9.

✸ Maxine Kumin

BORN: *1925, Philadelphia, Pennsylvania*

NATIONALITY: *American*

GENRE: *Fiction, poetry*

MAJOR WORKS:

Halfway (1961)

Up Country: Poems of New England (1972)

The Retrieval System (1978)

Overview

Maxine Kumin is best known for her poetry, which often portrays the simple workings of daily life on her New Hampshire farm. Animals, children, the seasons, and neighbors are recurring subjects.

Maxine Kumin   *Kumin, Maxine, 1973, photograph. AP Images.*

Works in Biographical and Historical Context

The Poetry of Maturity   Because her "well-made poems and stories are two ways of coming at the same immemorial preoccupations: aging and mortality," a contributor to *Nation* deems Kumin's work "the fiction and poetry of maturity." Her poems are also mature for another reason: Kumin did not begin to write and publish until mid-life, though she had shown an inclination to write poetry much earlier. During high school, she wrote "very bad late adolescent romantic poetry," she told an interviewer. And later, as a freshman at Radcliffe, Kumin presented a sheaf of poems to the instructor for his comments. Kumin told Joan Norris, "He had written on the front: 'Say it with flowers, but for God's sake don't try to write poems.' That just closed me off. I didn't try to write another poem for about six years." By that time she had become the wife of an engineer, the mother of three children, a resident of a Boston suburb, and "acutely miserable." When Kumin began writing again as a kind of therapy, she at last found encouragement in workshops at the Boston Center for Adult Education.

Anne Sexton   An outgrowth of the Boston workshops Kumin attended was Kumin's friendship with Anne Sexton. Both homemakers with children when they began their literary careers, they wrote four children's books

together, and in general contributed to each other's development. According to Linda Gray Sexton and Lois Ames, the editors of *Anne Sexton: A Self-Portrait in Letters* (1977), the two poets "often communicated daily, by letter if separated by oceans, otherwise by telephone. They supervised each other's poetry and prose, 'work-shopping' line by line for hours." Consequently, critics have tried to trace a strong mutual influence, but both poets have denied one.

Nonetheless, there were some significant exchanges. As Kumin relates in the chapter she contributed to *Anne Sexton: The Artist and Her Critics* (1978), Sexton had written several poems based on fairy tales that later became part of her Pulitzer Prize-winning book, *Transformations*. "I urged and bullied her to go on after the first few poems to think in terms of a whole book of them." Kumin also suggested the title. Sexton had reciprocated by suggesting the title for the book that was to become Kumin's Pulitzer Prize winner. "In that same conversation Annie was urging me to collect the 'pastoral' poems I'd written, and I said, 'but what would I call it?' and she said, 'Up Country, of course.'"

"It is the tie between Kumin and Sexton that fascinates many readers," Susan Ludvigson notes. The public's interest peaked when Sexton committed suicide in 1974. "There's a kind of sexual thrill that runs through the public every time a poet does himself in," Kumin said at the time, revealing her anger about the increased attention. "When a poet kills . . . herself, it confirms something very gratifying to the public view: that life is really tough, and these sensitive flowers can't take it." Kumin had little positive to say about those who regard Sexton's suicide as the "culmination of her work. What people don't understand is that writing about the topic, when you're depressed, or suicidal, is what keeps you alive."

Later Work   Kumin's prose collection *Women, Animals, and Vegetables* (1994) offers insight into the author's pastoral life on her farm in New Hampshire. In essays and short stories, she "describes the pleasures of raising and riding horses, of gardening and mushrooming, of learning how in the country 'things have a way of balancing out,'" explains Christopher Merrill in the *Los Angeles Times Book Review*. Anne Raver, writing in the *New York Times Book Review*, states that some of the material in the book pales in comparison to Kumin's poetry, which covers many of the same themes and issues "more brilliantly." She continues: "It is a Pulitzer Prize-winning poet's misfortune, perhaps, to be judged harshly by the standards she herself has set."

Throughout her latter-day poetry collections, which include *The Retrieval System* (1978), *Our Ground Time Here Will Be* (1982), *The Long Approach* (1985), and *Nurture* (1989), Kumin deepened her insight and increased her power as a poet, without substantially changing her style. Reviewing Kumin's multi-decade career, Philip Booth comments that the poet "has simply gotten better and better at what she has always been good at: a resonant language, an autobiographical immediacy, unsystematized intelligence, and radical compassion. One does not learn compassion without having suffered." Brad Crenshaw notes that "Americans traditionally have preferred their women poets to be depressed and victimized," but he claims that Kumin's "posture regarding despair" sets her apart from "the sweet innocents who have been driven to insane passions and flamboyant destructions." And Diane Wakoski writes in *Contemporary Women Poets*: "The one thing that is clear throughout [Kumin's] substantial body of work is that she believes survival is possible, if only through the proper use of the imagination to retrieve those things which are loved well enough."

Works in Literary Context

Kumin has been classified as a pastoral poet, a transcendentalist, and a confessional poet. She has been compared to Robert Lowell and Elizabeth Bishop as well as to Anne Sexton: Lowell for his sense of tradition, both in form and in his emphasis on family, religion, and New England; Bishop for her attention to precise, objective detail; and Sexton for her focus on the personal, the introspective. But it is the tie between Kumin and Sexton that fascinates many readers. Because the two women were close friends who regularly sought each other's advice about poems, critics have looked for and sometimes claimed to find mutual influence. Dabney Stuart says of one of Kumin's recent collections: "It's Anne Sexton . . . who presides over much of this book." In a 1974 interview in *Women's Studies*, however, each claimed she never tampered with the other's voice, and each offered, according to Sexton, "to think how to shape, how to make better, but not, how to make like me."

Confessional Poetry Kumin and Sexton do share a concern for the place of women in the world and for the intricate relationships between men and women. A few of Kumin's poems belong vaguely in the confessional category, which she says "is part of a long and honorable tradition in poetry: the voice of the *I*. I think we have that in every age to some degree or other." Like Sexton, Kumin began writing poetry as a kind of therapy, though she speaks of being "wretchedly discontented . . . and guilty about being discontented" rather than seriously distraught emotionally, as Sexton was. One of Sexton's greatest contributions, says Kumin, was that "she made it possible for women to write about the quality of womanhood in a way that just could not have been taken seriously twenty years ago." But despite a few common themes, Kumin's range is considerably broader than her friend's; and though Sexton wrote a good deal of formal verse, Kumin is more thoroughly committed to traditional poetic forms.

Transcendentalism "Transcendental" is another label sometimes applied to Kumin but in a modified sense; while Kumin's poetry may call up images of nineteenth-century philosopher Henry David Thoreau and "insist on man's

LITERARY AND HISTORICAL CONTEMPORARIES

Kumin's famous contemporaries include:

G. Gordon Liddy (1930–): Today a successful radio talk show host, Liddy became a household name in 1974 when he was convicted for masterminding break-ins at the Democratic campaign headquarters at the Watergate Hotel in 1972.

James A. Michener (1907–1997): An American author noted for his massive historical epics, often focusing on a specific nation or geographic area.

Anne Sexton (1928–1974): Considered the leading confessional poet of her time, Anne Sexton is equally known for her tragic suicide.

Muhammad Ali (1942–): Born Cassius Clay, Ali—a three-time World Heavyweight Boxing Champion—remains one of the most popular athletes of all time.

Dick Clark (1929–): Clark was a major figure in television and popular culture for a half-century, first making a name for himself as the long-time host of the influential televised dance show *American Bandstand*.

affinity with the natural world," Susan Ludvigson notes that it falls short of suggesting the "merging of the self with nature" that transcendentalism requires. Ludvigson suggests that "her unsentimental relationship with nature . . . allows Kumin to write poems . . . which chill us with her portrayal of man's capacity for brutality." Brad Crenshaw considers it "a major plus" that Kumin "is not much addicted to transcendental escapes." Rather, as he elaborates in a *Parnassus* review of *Our Ground Time Here Will Be Brief: New and Selected Poems* (1982), "Her poetry records how she stands up to the disasters of weather, disease, difficult births and lamentable deaths, and how she's confident she'll remain standing until the very end."

Regionalism and Nature Poetry Kumin is often referred to as a regional pastoral poet as her verse is deeply rooted to her native New England. Despite the necessity of traveling away from home to lecture at schools and universities around the United States, Kumin has retained close ties with her farmhouse in rural New Hampshire; in an interview with Joan Norris published in *Crazy Horse*, the poet disclosed that "Practically all of [my poems] have come out of this geography and this state of mind." Whereas critics debate Kumin's similarity to Thoreau, they unanimously recognize her similarity to Robert Frost. "I have been twitted with the epithet 'Roberta Frost,' which is not a bad thing to be," Kumin told interviewer Karla Hammond in the *Western Humanities Review*. The works of both poets show a close attention to the details of New England rural life. Attention to

COMMON HUMAN EXPERIENCE

Kumin's poetry is often called regionalist, a term used to describe poets who write more or less exclusively about their native countryside in an attempt to evoke the unique sights and experiences of their home. Like Kumin, most regionalists write about small town or rural experiences.

Flying At Night: Poems 1965–1985 (2005), a poetry collection by Ted Kooser. Kooser spent most of his life selling insurance, writing regional poetry about his beloved Midwest on the side. After years of publishing in regional journals, Kooser's poetry began to attract national attention, culminating in his two terms as America's Poet Laureate from 2004 to 2006.

New Hampshire (1923), a poetry collection by Robert Frost. Perhaps the prototypical regionalist, Frost won his first Pulitzer Prize for this volume of poems about his native New Hampshire.

Spoon River Anthology (1915), a book by Edgar Lee Masters. A collection of poems about a fictional small town based on Masters's home town, each of the over two hundred poems takes the form of a graveyard epitaph delivered by the deceased themselves.

nature provides Kumin with images well-suited to her themes of loss and survival. Philip Booth states that Kumin "lives in, and writes from, a world where constant (if partial) recovery of what's 'lost' is as sure as the procession of the equinoxes, or as familiar as mucking-out the horses' daily dung."

Loss   If there is one experience that Kumin confronts in all her works, it is loss. Accordingly, Kumin believes "very strongly that poetry is essentially elegiac in its nature, and that all poems are in one sense or another elegies [meditations on death]." As she explained to Hammond, "Love poems, particularly, are elegies because if we were not informed with a sense of dying we wouldn't be moved to write love poems."

Works in Critical Context

Even though the awards she has received for her work have included the prestigious Pulitzer Prize, Maxine Kumin has yet to be the subject of serious study by academics. Since the publication of *Halfway*, Kumin's verse has found much favor among critics. She is sometimes faulted for sentimentality and forced metaphors, among other things, but reviewers generally describe her work as impressive both technically and in its portrayal of emotions. Kumin has continued to demonstrate an increased awareness of the process of aging and death and the fleet-

ing nature of life. Critics have praised the intensity that this awareness has added to her work.

New York Times reviewer Michiko Kakutani finds her most like Galway Kinnell, since both are "concerned with human mortality, with the love shared between parents and their children, with the seasonal patterns of nature and the possibility of retrieving and preserving the past." In many ways, critics also point out, Kumin is not like other poets. "In a period when most contemporary poetry reflects a chaotic and meaningless universe, Kumin is one of a handful of poets who insist upon order," Susan Ludvigson elaborates in the *Dictionary of Literary Biography*. Whatever her link to other poets may be, Philip Booth maintains that "what is remarkable . . . is the extent to which poets like Maxine Kumin can survive and outdistance both their peers and themselves by increasingly trusting those elements of their work which are most strongly individual." For Kumin, as he notes in the *American Poetry Review*, these elements include "the dailiness of farm life and farm death."

Selected Poems   In 1997 Kumin published *Selected Poems 1960–1990*, a volume that presents thirty years' worth of her poetry. Extending from her first volume, *Halfway*, through 1989's *Nurture*, *Selected Poems* was praised by Judy Clarence in *Library Journal* for allowing the reader the opportunity to "move slowly, meanderingly, deliciously through the stages of Kumin's poetic life." Noting that the poet's "unsentimental affinity for animals has been her divining rod for locating and observing the natural world's seemingly inexhaustible beauty and mankind's terrifying willingness to destroy it," a *Publishers Weekly* reviewer praises the collection for illustrating this through Kumin's "plain style," "surprising imagery, . . . and recurring reflections." Praising Kumin's collection for its accessibility by the average reader, Richard Tillinghast comments in his review for the *New York Times Book Review*, "She has the versatility to build an orderly, measured structure in rhyme and meter, or to adopt the easier virtues of free verse for a more transient, informal effect." Furthermore, the critic maintains, Kumin's poems have purpose; they tell a story that carries the reader into the world Kumin creates and leads to a satisfying conclusion.

Responses to Literature

1. Compare a selection of poems by Anne Sexton to several by Kumin. In your opinion, how closely are they related, stylistically and thematically? How much influence do you think the two poets exerted over each other, based on the poetic evidence?

2. Research the history and writings of Henry David Thoreau. What were his philosophical beliefs? What was transcendentalism, and how did it impact the nineteenth-century psyche? Do you think Kumin's work qualifies as transcendentalism? Why or why not?

3. What appeal might Kumin's regional poetry have to readers who live in other parts of the world? Are the themes and subjects of her poems universal?

4. Do you agree with Kumin's assertion that all poetry, even love poetry, is a meditation on death and loss? Why or why not?

BIBLIOGRAPHY

Books

Grosholz, Emily. *Telling the Barn Swallow: Poets on the Poetry of Maxine Kumin*. Lebanon, N.H.: University Press of New England, 1997.

Periodicals

Burke, Herbert. Review of *Halfway*. *Library Journal* 86 (April 1, 1961): 1468.

Dickey, William. "Revelations and Homilies." *Poetry* 99 (November 1961): 124–129.

Ferrari, Margaret Burns. "House, Bridge, Fountain, Gate." *America* 134 (February 28, 1976): 165.

Gunn, Thom. "Imitations and Originals." *Yale Review* 51 (March 1962): 480–489.

Howes, Victor. "Book Briefings." *Christian Science Monitor* (February 28, 1973): 9.

———. "Maxine Kumin's Poems: 'Going Backwards in a Home Movie.'" *Christian Science Monitor* (July 10, 1975): 22.

Moore, Richard. "A Poet Who Needs His Poem." *Saturday Review* 48 (December 25, 1965): 29–31.

Nyren, Dorothy. Review of *The Nightmare Factory*. *Library Journal* 95 (June 1, 1970): 2163–2164.

Oates, Joyce Carol. Review of *Up Country*. *New York Times* (November 19, 1972): 7, 14.

Spector, R. D. "Betwixt Tradition and Innovation." *Saturday Review* (December 26, 1970): 24–25, 50–51.

Stuart, Dabney. Review of *House, Bridge, Fountain, Gate*. *Library Journal* 100 (May 15, 1975): 991.

✽ Tony Kushner

BORN: *1956, New York City*

NATIONALITY: *American*

GENRE: *Drama*

MAJOR WORKS:

A Bright Room Called Day (1987)

Angels in America: A Gay Fantasia on National Themes (1991)

Overview

Kushner is best known for his award-winning play *Angels in America*, which is unprecedented in its extensive treatment of homosexual themes and its use of gay characters to examine such traditional issues as culture,

Tony Kushner   *Kushner, Tony, photograph. AP Images.*

politics, and history. Kushner's themes encompass the gay experience from repression and hypocrisy through denial and self-loathing to the ultimate goals of self-acceptance and self-love.

Works in Biographical and Historical Context

Coming Out Kushner was born in New York City in 1956, but his parents, who were classical musicians, moved to Lake Charles, Louisiana, shortly after his birth. His parents encouraged Kushner and his siblings to explore literature and the arts; the children were given a dollar whenever they memorized a poem to recite. His mother was also an actress, and Kushner confided to Susan Cheever in the *New York Times* that "that's the major reason I went into the theater. I saw some of her performances when I was 4 or 5 years old and they were so powerful. I had vivid dreams afterwards." Kushner realized he was different from most other children in yet another significant way, however. "I have fairly clear memories of being gay since I was 6," the playwright told Richard Stayton in the *Los Angeles Times*. "I knew that I felt slightly different than most of the boys I was growing up with. By the time I was 11 there was no doubt. But I was completely in the closet."

LITERARY AND HISTORICAL CONTEMPORARIES

Kushner's famous contemporaries include:

Rodney King (1965–): In 1991 unemployed construction worker King was pulled over after a high-speed chase and subsequently beaten by four Los Angeles police department officers. The subsequent trial and acquittal of the officers sparked the 1992 Los Angeles riots.

Neil Simon (1927–): One of the most popular and influential American playwrights of the twentieth century, Simon is noted for his social comedies and commentaries on Jewish-American life, both on stage and screen.

Mike Tyson (1966–): Tyson won the heavyweight boxing championship at the age of twenty, becoming the youngest such champion in history.

Bret Easton Ellis (1964–): One of a group of young, hip authors in the 1980s nicknamed the "Literary Brat Pack," Ellis gained notoriety for his dystopian novels depicting graphic violence, drug use, and toxic relationships.

Tyler Perry (1969–): Louisiana-born Perry is a playwright, actor, and filmmaker most famous for his creation of Mabel "Madea" Simmons, an outspoken and argumentative matriarch of a Southern black family.

He continued to keep his sexuality a secret throughout his undergraduate years at Columbia University, during which time he underwent psychotherapy to try to become heterosexual, even though his therapist told him at the beginning of treatment that psychotherapy did not change people's sexual orientation. Kushner eventually accepted this and "came out"—that is, became open with family and friends about the fact that he was gay.

Early Efforts Kushner's early works include *Hydriotaphia* (1987), which, inspired by seventeenth-century essayist Sir Thomas Browne, was written in a style reminiscent of classical and traditional poetry; *The Illusion* (1988), adapted from Pierre Corneille's *L'illusion comique*; and *Widows* (1991), a collaboration with Ariel Dorfman based on that writer's novel of the same name. *A Bright Room Called Day* (1987), perhaps the best-known of his pre-*Angels* works, concerns a group of liberal-minded acquaintances in the Weimar Republic of Germany, just before the establishment of Adolf Hitler's Nazi regime. This main story is entwined, however, with the commentary of Zillah Katz, a contemporary young American woman, who draws parallels—sometimes extreme—between Hitler's regime and the administrations of U.S. presidents Ronald Reagan and George H. W. Bush.

When *A Bright Room Called Day* was performed in New York City in 1991, it received less than enthusiastic reviews. The play did, however, impress Oskar Eustis, then artistic director of the Eureka Theater in San Francisco, California, where the play was first produced. He commissioned Kushner to write a comic play for his theater; this was the play that would become *Angels in America*, though the Eureka would no longer exist by the time the entire play was ready for production.

A Gay Fantasia For Kushner, who had been disturbed by the "homophobic reaction" to Roy Cohn's AIDS-related death and had decided to write a play about that, Eustis's offer was oddly prescient. Says Eustis: "Tony took a deep breath and wrote about what was closest and scariest to him and that unleashed a complexity that is representative of our own lives."

A complex work, *Angels in America* was produced in two parts and includes over thirty characters. Though *Angels in America* is filled with many different characters, it is meant to be performed only by eight actors who each play several roles. In the first part, *Millennium Approaches*, the story focuses on two couples—two gay men named Louis and Prior dealing with Prior's AIDS, and Harper and Joe, a nominally straight couple—although the married Mormon man, Joe, is trying to suppress his secret homosexuality. Also central to the play is the figure of lawyer Roy Cohn, who is based on the real Cohn who helped Senator Joseph McCarthy persecute suspected communists during the 1950s. Cohn also persecuted gays, although he himself was a closet homosexual and died of complications related to AIDS.

Millennium Approaches takes its name from the sense of apocalypse the character Prior feels while dealing with his deadly disease. At the end, an angel descends dramatically to visit him, and he is declared a prophet, temporarily, at least, saved from death by AIDS. The second part, *Perestroika*, by contrast, is a somewhat quieter piece, getting its title from the Russian word ex-Soviet leader Mikhail Gorbachev used for his proposals for "restructuring" economic and social policies. In the second part of *Angels*, the glorious being that visited Prior at the end of the first part turns out to represent stasis, or death, and Prior decides to reject it. Cohn dies, but this does not prevent his ghost from reappearing later in the play—in the role of God's lawyer, no less. Lahr concluded that Kushner's work is "a victory . . . for the transforming power of the imagination to turn devastation into beauty."

In 1995 Kushner wrote and produced what he terms a "coda" to *Angels in America*, *Slavs! Thinking About the Longstanding Problems of Virtue and Happiness*, which Christopher Hawthorne of *Salon* magazine calls "a compact, quirky exploration of the collapse of the Soviet Union and the ruin, both philosophical and environmental, left in its wake." *Slavs!* resembles the *Angels in America* plays because, according to Kushner in an interview with Andrea Bernstein of *Mother Jones*, the play proceeds from the problem that if you do not know where you are heading, it is difficult to move or make choices.

Kushner—white, Jewish, gay, and coming of age in the South during the turbulent 1960s—developed both a healthy respect and skepticism for the idea of community, a conceit that would come to earmark his work as a dramatist. Says Kushner of the legitimacy of the idea of community, "It is a fundamental American question because that's what this country is—a community comprised of not only different [constituencies] but hostile ones and irreconcilably so."

For Kushner, the nation's gay and lesbian community is not only one with which he is intimately familiar, but it also serves as an exceptionally apt metaphor for his examination of America as a whole. "Because the demarcation line is sexual preference, the homosexual community is also a very disparate group of people of all races, cultures and political persuasions," says Kushner. "It is synthetic and artificial." Within these cobbled communities, Kushner ponders man's proclivity for both xenophobia and compassion.

Works in Literary Context

Kushner's plays generally focus on themes of change, transformation, and identity, often examined over long periods of time. These grand themes give his plays an epic scope, augmented by the overt politicism of *Angels in America* and *A Bright Room Called Day*.

Epic Theater   The term *epic* was originally used to describe the ancient Greek tradition of poems such as Homer's *Iliad* and *Odyssey*. These stories were distinguished by the scope of time they covered—often months, years, or even decades would pass in the course of a story—their wide-ranging, often far-flung locales, which could range from small bedrooms to huge battlefields, their large cast of characters and their complex, intertwining stories.

Several of Shakespeare's plays followed the epic tradition, and it was carried forward into the twentieth century by playwrights like Bertolt Brecht and Robert Schenkkan, whose *Kentucky Cycle* is a six-hour, nine-play saga covering two hundred years of history.

Angels in America is another such modern epic. Its locations range from living rooms and offices in New York City to the frozen continent of Antarctica and even the vaults of heaven. Its epic structure can be seen in the large cast of characters and how their various scenes overlap and interweave, often playing out at the same time on stage. This action creates the essential elements of an epic plot: juxtaposition and contrast. Epics, as opposed to climactic plots, do not move forward in a cause-and-effect fashion, where events in one scene directly impact those in the next. Rather, two seemingly unrelated scenes are often placed back-to-back, juxtaposing, or contrasting, characters or themes.

Political Theater   Brecht was a strong influence on Kushner, for Brecht's vision of Epic Theater, as he called it, was not simply about epic story structure but melding that ancient structure with overt political commentary.

COMMON HUMAN EXPERIENCE

Kushner was heavily influenced by Bertolt Brecht's Epic Theater, a movement started by the German playwright in the early twentieth century that aimed to combine epic story structure designed to elicit emotional response with overt political messages and deconstruction of common theatrical tropes. Here are some other examples of epic theater:

Mother Courage and Her Children (1939), a play by Bertolt Brecht. Possibly Brecht's finest play and one of the greatest antiwar plays ever written, this tale of the Thirty Years' War of the sixteenth century serves as a cautionary tale aimed at a Europe on the brink of plunging into world war.

Vinegar Tom (1976), a play by Caryl Churchill. A noted feminist playwright, Chruchill's early work was also strongly in the tradition of Epic Theater, as in this play about seventeenth-century witch trials that utilizes distinctly Brechtian storytelling techniques, such as the use of incongruent songs to break up the action.

Breathless (1960), a film directed by Jean-Luc Godard. One of the seminal examples of the so-called New Wave of French Cinema, Godard—who had studied under Brecht—made his first film a conscious attempt to bring the traditions of Epic Theater into a different medium.

What Brecht proposed, and what Kushner adopted, was a didactic approach—that is, the goal of the play is to educate and inform as much as to entertain. To this end, Brecht also used various devices to call attention to the artificiality of the play's format, a technique Kushner mirrored in *Angels in America*, which utilizes a minimum of scenery and often has scene changes occur in full view of the audience. Unlike Brecht, however, Kushner allows his political ideas to be subtly interwoven into the narrative, rather than explicitly stated.

Works in Critical Context

Kushner's early plays received scant and largely mixed reviews. It was not until *Angels in America* that he began receiving more widespread and positive critical attention.

Angels in America   Despite its grim subject matter and its open attacks on the administration of former president Ronald Reagan, *Angels in America* has proved quite popular with mainstream audiences from Broadway to Los Angeles and London. It has also won great acclaim from drama critics, garnering both the Pulitzer Prize for Drama and the Tony Award for best play in 1993.

Critical reaction to *Angels in America* has been overwhelmingly favorable. Commentators laud it as the proverbial "great American play," claiming it addresses such topics as the value and inevitability of change, the nature of self-interest and community, and the major political issues of the 1980s: gay rights, the end of the cold war, the place of religion in modern society, and the ideological struggle between conservatism and liberalism. Critics have also praised Kushner for avoiding the sentimentality that characterizes most dramas that deal with AIDS. As Don Shewey has stated, "*Angels in America* is a landmark not just among AIDS plays or gay dramas but in American theater, partly because Kushner has the audacity to equate gay concerns with the fate of this country."

Responses to Literature

1. With his minimal use of sets for *Angels in America*, how does Kushner convey time and place as critical components of the play? Provide examples from the play to illustrate.

2. Discuss one of the major themes, such as self-acceptance, running through all of Kushner's works and provide specific examples of how Kushner addresses the theme.

3. How does Kushner's early work differ from his later plays? Why do you think he shifted focus?

4. Kushner has cited as a major influence the German playwright Bertolt Brecht. Read a Brecht drama such as *Mother Courage*, then compare it to Kushner's work. How does Brecht's "epic" theater show its influence? How do both men approach such issues as plot, themes, and characterization?

BIBLIOGRAPHY

Books

"Angels in America." *Drama for Students.* Vol. 5. Edited by David Galens. Detroit: Thomson Gale, 1999.

Brask, Per, ed. *Essays on Kushner's Angels.* Winnipeg, Canada: Blizzard Publishing, 1995.

Geis, Deborah R., and Steven F. Kruger. *Approaching the Millennium: Essays on Angels in America.* Ann Arbor: University of Michigan Press, 1997.

Vorlicky, Robert, ed. *Tony Kushner in Conversation.* Ann Arbor: University of Michigan Press, 1997.

Periodicals

Blanchard, Bob. "Playwright of Pain and Hope." *Progressive* 58 (October 1994): 42–44.

Bottoms, Stephen J. "Re-staging Roy: Citizen Cohn and the Search for Xanadu." *Theatre Journal* 48 (1996): 157–184.

Cheever, Susan. "An Angel Sat Down at His Table." *New York Times*, September 13, 1992, section 2.

Glossary of Literary Terms

The glossary contains terms found in various entries throughout the *Gale Contextual Encyclopedia of American Literature*. This glossary includes terms for various literary components or techniques relevant to the work of the authors, terms for important artistic movements or groups discussed in relation to the authors, and terms for social, political, or philosophical ideas that profoundly impacted American literature. Definitions for more basic literary terms, such as "figurative language," have not been included.

ALLEGORY: A work in which the entire narrative serves as a symbol for something beyond the surface-level story.

ANACHRONISM: A thing or idea mentioned in a work of art that occurs outside its normal place in time. In William Shakespeare's play *Julius Caesar*, for example, the author mentions the striking of a clock to indicate time passing—even though no such clocks existed in ancient Rome, the time period in which the play is set.

ANTI-HERO: A main character in a literary work whose actions and ideals would not generally be regarded as heroic, though the character may still be portrayed sympathetically by the author. Holden Caulfield, the protagonist of J. D. Salinger's novel *The Catcher in the Rye* (1951), is an example of an anti-hero.

AVANT-GARDE: Meaning "advance guard" in French, a term used to describe artists or artistic works that are considered innovative or nontraditional.

BALLAD: A poetic work written in the form of a traditional song that commonly relates a folk tale, myth, or legend. Ballads are often written in four-line stanzas with alternating lines of eight and six syllables, in which the lines with six syllables contain end-rhyme.

BEAT GENERATION: A collective term for a group of writers who rose to prominence in the late 1940s and 1950s. Their work and their lifestyles were marked by defiance of legal and cultural authority, experimentation with drugs and unconventional sexual relationships, interest in Eastern religions, and an affinity for improvisational jazz music. Famous Beat writers include: Allen Ginsberg, Jack Kerouac, and William S. Burroughs.

BILDUNGSROMAN: Taken from a German term meaning "novel of formation," a novel that documents the maturation of the protagonist. The bildungsroman is also commonly known as a "coming of age" novel.

BLANK VERSE: A type of poetry which follows a set pattern of stressed and unstressed syllables in each line, but does not feature consistent rhyme. Poet Robert Frost wrote many of his poems in blank verse.

CAPTIVITY NARRATIVE: A first-hand, nonfiction account of the captivity of a white American settler by Native Americans.

COMEDY: In classical Greek drama, a play that ends happily for its major characters; many ancient comedies poked fun at political figures or cultural stereotypes, which inspired the laughter modern audiences now associate with the term.

CONFESSIONAL POETRY: Confessional poetry is a kind of poetry popularized in the 1950s and 1960s characterized by revelations of extremely intimate, often unflattering details of the poet's private life. Subjects often include sex and drug use. Major confessional poets include Sylvia Plath and Anne Sexton.

ENJAMBMENT: In poetry, the splitting of a continuous phrase or sentence into two or more lines. The result is that a single line may appear to express an incomplete thought, though the work as a whole is afforded a more complex rhythm and structure. Poet e. e. cummings made frequent use of enjambment.

EPIC: A literary work, originally a work in poetic form, that focuses on large-scale events and themes, and often takes place over a long period of time. *The Odyssey*, an ancient Greek epic by Homer, is one of the earliest examples. The term is now often applied to long works that cover a time span of many years, such as Margaret Mitchell's 1936 novel *Gone With the Wind*.

EPIGRAM: A short, clever statement—often in the form of a couplet—intended to impart humor and insight. Dorothy Parker was famous for her witty epigrams.

EPISTOLARY NOVEL: A novel in which the story is told through letters written by one or more characters. Samuel Richardson was an early practitioner of the epistolary novel, with works such as *Pamela* (1740) and *Clarissa* (1748). Alice Walker produced a more recent version with her 1982 novel *The Color Purple*.

EXISTENTIALISM: A philosophical movement that gained popularity in the first half of the twentieth century, thanks to literary works by Jean-Paul Sartre and Simone de Beauvoir, among others. Existentialism is characterized by the idea that life does not have a greater meaning or purpose beyond that which people choose to create for themselves. Many prominent African American writers have been labeled existentialist, including Ralph Ellison and Richard Wright.

EXPERIMENTAL NOVEL: A work which defies the traditional structure or subject matter of a novel, and emphasizes style or technique over content. Thomas Pynchon's 1973 novel *Gravity's Rainbow*, for example, is considered an experimental novel.

FABLE: A short tale whose purpose is to impart a message or lesson, usually featuring animals as characters. "The Tortoise and the Hare" is a well-known example of a fable. James Thurber and Joel Chandler Harris are known for their fables.

FARCE: A dramatic work characterized by characters being put into comedic situations that are unlikely or improbable, as in Thornton Wilder's *The Matchmaker* (1954).

FLASH FICTION: Short fiction, usually under one thousand words, that despite its length contains all the traditional elements of story such as a protagonist and conflict that is somehow resolved. O. Henry and Ray Bradbury are both authors of flash fiction.

FRAME NARRATIVE: A literary device in which the main story being told to the reader is presented as a story being told by one of the characters within the work, as in "The Celebrated Jumping Frog of Calaveras County," an 1865 short story by Mark Twain.

GONZO JOURNALISM: A subjective style of journalism in which events are described from the reporter's point of view. Gonzo journalism originated with Hunter S. Thompson.

GOTHIC FICTION: A literary sub-genre that emerged in the last half of the eighteenth century and was characterized by eerie atmosphere, melodrama, mystery, and romance.

IMAGISM: A poetic movement of the early twentieth century that emphasized direct expression through concise imagery and non-standard structure. Ezra Pound was instrumental in the development of the Imagist movement, and poet Amy Lowell was a leading practitioner.

IMPRESSIONISM: An artistic movement that emerged during the latter half of the nineteenth century, and focused on artistic impression over realistic representation. In literature, impressionism was characterized by a focus on the depiction of the interior, mental landscapes of characters, and was associated with other literary movements such as Symbolism.

IRONY: A literary device in which a character's perception of reality differs from actual reality, or in which a character's words do not express their true feelings. Sarcasm is a well-known form of irony. Dramatic irony occurs when an audience is given information that is not known by one or more characters in the play.

LIBRETTO: A text for the vocal portion of an opera or other musical work, often written in verse form. Composers frequently employ well-known writers to write libretti for their works, and writers such as Paul Laurence Dunbar, Langston Hughes, and Gertrude Stein sometimes worked as librettists.

LOST GENERATION: A term used to describe a loosely defined group of American writers who spent time in Europe—especially Paris—following World War I. These writers, including Ernest Hemingway, F. Scott Fitzgerald, and Sherwood Anderson, were notable for themes of disillusionment in their works.

MAGICAL REALISM: A literary style developed primarily in South America in which fantastic or supernatural elements are woven into otherwise realistic tales. Writers commonly associated with magic realism include Jorge Luis Borges, Alejo Carpentier, Gabriel García Márquez, and Carlos Fuentes; however, the work of some North American writers has been labeled magical realist, including Toni Morrison's 1987 novel *Beloved* and John Cheever's famous 1947 short story "The Enormous Radio."

MELODRAMA: A literary work which contains heightened or exaggerated emotions from the characters. The term originally applied to theatrical productions in which music (or melody) was used to accentuate the drama occurring on the stage.

MODERNISM: An artistic movement during the early twentieth century influenced by the rapid industrialization, scientific advancements, and devastating warfare of the time. Modernist writers were noted for their radical departure from traditional literary forms, with notable Modernist works including T. S. Eliot's poem "The Waste Land" (1922) and James Joyce's novel *Ulysses* (1922).

MUCKRAKERS: A term applied to journalists and fiction writers of the late nineteenth and early twentieth century whose work uncovered corruption in the government and big business. Authors Frank Norris and Upton Sinclair were both considered muckrakers.

NATURALISM: A literary movement of the late nineteenth century that focused on realistic portrayals of people and situations, and specifically dealt with the effects of heredity and environment on a character's personality and development. Stephen Crane is widely regarded as a Naturalist.

NEOCLASSICISM: A term describing art that sought inspiration in ancient Greek and Roman forms, with emphasis on rationalism and proportion. Phillis Wheatley is considered a neoclassical poet.

NEW JOURNALISM: A style of journalism popularized in the 1960s and 1970s in which the journalist employed such literary techniques as setting scenes, presenting subjects as fleshed out "characters," and offering details of setting and scene.

NIHILISM: A philosophical movement that first appeared in the nineteenth century and is characterized by the belief that life has no objective purpose, moral code, or value. Writers associated with nihilism include Ivan Turgenev, whose novel *Fathers and Sons* (1862) described the Russian Nihilist movement and popularized the concept. More recent fiction has also been labeled Nihilist, including Bret Easton Ellis's 1985 novel *Less Than Zero.*

PARABLE: A short tale meant to impart a message or lesson to the reader. Parables are similar to fables, but do not include supernatural or fantastic elements such as talking animals.

PARODY: A literary work designed to mock or criticize another, usually well-known literary work or genre. An early example is *Shamela* (1741), Henry Fielding's parody of the successful Samuel Richardson novel *Pamela* (1740). Wendy Wasserstein's *Sloth* (2006) is a recent example of a parody.

PASTORAL: Literature that depicts rural life, nature, and the people of a rural region in a highly idealized way. The *Eclogues* (c. 40 B.C.E.) by the ancient Roman poet Virgil are among the oldest examples of pastoral poetry. Some works by Willa Cather and Wallace Stegner contain pastoral elements.

PICARESQUE: A type of novel first developed in Spain that focuses on the adventures of a rogue, or clever anti-hero. Among many others, James Branch Cabell's 1919 novel *Jurgen* exhibits the key traits of the picaresque.

POSTMODERNISM: A post-World War II literary movement characterized by nonlinearity, or a nonstandard narrative timeline, as well as metafiction, in which the author shows awareness of the story as a work of fiction and may even appear as a character within it.

PSEUDONYM: An alternate name used by a writer, often to hide the writer's identity. For example, William Sydney Porter used the pen name O. Henry when writing his celebrated short stories.

PSYCHOLOGICAL FICTION: A type of fiction in which a great deal of attention is paid to the thoughts and feelings of the characters, as opposed to external action. Henry James was well known for his psychological fiction.

REALISM: An artistic movement characterized by a desire to portray characters and environments as objectively, or as close to reality, as possible. Realism relies heavily upon physical descriptions, and Gustave Flaubert's novel *Madame Bovary* (1856)—with its almost grotesque precision to detail—is considered a landmark work of realism. Prominent American realists include Mark Twain and Edith Wharton.

ROMAN À CLEF: A literary work containing fictionalized depictions of real people and events. The work may be autobiographical, as in Sylvia Plath's *The Bell Jar* (1963), or it may refer to thinly disguised versions of well-known people, as in Truman Capote's *Answered Prayers* (1987).

ROMANTICISM: An artistic and philosophical movement that developed throughout Europe in the late eighteenth and early nineteenth centuries, and was popular in the United States throughout the nineteenth century (thought it reached its peak near the middle of the century). Romantic literature is notable for its expression of powerful emotions and use of natural settings. The work of Walt Whitman, Ralph Waldo Emerson, and Harriet Beecher Stowe is considered Romantic.

SATIRE: A type of literature intended to attack a person, group, institution, or idea through parody or irony. Very often, the satirist exposes the shortcomings of its subject by ironically expressing a position in support or praise of the subject. Benjamin Franklin, Stephen Crane, and Dorothy Parker are a few of the many American writers known for their satires.

SERIAL PUBLICATION: The printing of consecutive portions of a novel or other lengthy work of literature in successive issues of a periodical. Some of Mark Twains's works were first printed through serial publication.

SOCIAL REALISM: An artistic movement of the nineteenth century defined by sympathetic yet realistic depictions of the working class and the poor conditions in which they lived. Upton Sinclair's 1906 novel *The Jungle* is an example of social realism.

SONNET (ELIZABETHAN): A poetic form typically consisting of fourteen ten-syllable lines and an alternating rhyme scheme. William Shakespeare is perhaps the most famous practitioner of English-language sonnets.

SOUTHERN GOTHIC FICTION: A type of Gothic fiction (see definition) in which grotesque, supernatural, melodramatic, and mysterious elements are deployed for the sake of exploring the culture of the American South. Prominent authors of Southern Gothic literature include Flannery O'Connor, William Faulkner, Carson McCullers, and Tennessee Williams.

STREAM OF CONSCIOUSNESS: A literary technique meant to emulate the flow of thought in a character's mind. This is sometimes expressed through disjointed or run-on sentences, repetitions of words or phrases, or tenuous associations between different subjects. Notable works that use the stream of consciousness technique include *The Sound and the Fury* (1929) by William Faulkner and *On the Road* (1957) by Jack Kerouac.

SURREALISM: An artistic movement of the early twentieth century noted for its embrace of the irrational. Surrealist literary works often contained jarring juxtapositions of unrelated things, seemingly random or nonsensical phrases, and dreamlike situations. William Burroughs is considered a surrealist.

TRAGEDY: In classical Greek drama, a play that focuses on themes such as love, fate and betrayal, and does not end happily for one or more of the main characters. The play *Antigone* (c. 442 B.C.E.) by Sophocles is a typical Greek tragedy. Eugene O'Neill wrote several famous tragedies that drew heavily on ancient Greek models.

TRANSCENDENTALISM: A philosophical movement that originated in New England in the first half of the nineteenth century, Transcendentalism prized individualism and forwarded the idea that each individual has the ability to achieve a transcendent spirituality by communing with nature and remaining true to his or her essential self.

VERNACULAR: The casual and natural speech of a group of people or culture. Mark Twain's 1884 novel *Adventures of Huckleberry Finn* makes masterful use of the American vernacular of the 1830s.

Index

B

B

C

C

D

F

G

H

H

I-J

K

M

N

O

Q-R

R

S

S

T

U-W

W

Y-Z

Nationality/Ethnicity Index